Encyclopedia of Demons
in World Religions
and Cultures

Encyclopedia of Demons in World Religions and Cultures

Theresa Bane

McFarland & Company, Inc., Publishers

Jefferson, North Carolina, and London

To Jim Butcher;
thank you for teaching me
so much about writing.

LIBRARY OF CONGRESS CATALOGUING-IN-PUBLICATION DATA

Bane, Theresa, 1969–
Encyclopedia of demons in world religions and cultures / Theresa Bane
p.   cm.
Includes bibliographical references (p.   ) and index.

ISBN 978-0-7864-6360-2

softcover : acid free paper ∞

1. Demonology—Encyclopedias.   2. Religions—
Encyclopedias.   I. Title.
BL480.B364 2012   133.4'203—dc23   2011049234

BRITISH LIBRARY CATALOGUING DATA ARE AVAILABLE

On the cover: (left to right, top row) Caravaggio's *Medusa*, 1597;
Devil illustration from the *Codex Gigas*, folio 270 recto, 13th century;
Mongolian ritual mask, 1971; (bottom row) woodcut of devil and woman
on horseback from the *Nuremberg Chronicle*, 1493; Japanese netsuke mask
of Hannya, 18th century; watercolor of Ravana from Sri Lanka, 1920

Manufactured in the United States of America

*McFarland & Company, Inc., Publishers
Box 611, Jefferson, North Carolina 28640
www.mcfarlandpub.com*

Table of Contents

Preface

As a writer, editor, and compiler of myths, it is my goal to contribute to the academic studies in the fields of anthropology, folklore, mythology, and religion. Being a professional vampirologist—a mythologist who specializes in cross-cultural vampire studies—I have come across a number of vampiric entities who were also described as being demonic in nature. According to their original mythologies, these infernal, vampiric demons were said to have been created in a hell-like dimension or were described as being agents of evil who worked directly against the best interests of humanity.

There are not so great a number of vampiric species that are demonic or demon-like in their nature or behavior, but the few that do exist and which were catalogued in my previous books did pique my interest. As is often the case, a little bit of research turned into a great deal of research, and a book of DEMONOLOGY began to write itself.

Demonology, the study of demons, has been in and out of vogue with mankind over the centuries. Its acceptability as a subject has varied depending on how threatening the changing, ruling religious powers deemed it. For example, King Solomon, the much famed last king of the united Kingdom of Israel, was a man of great influence, wealth, and wisdom; he is credited with having ordered and overseen the construction of the first temple in Jerusalem. This is covered in the pseudepigraphical work *The Testament of Solomon*, which describes quite clearly how the king was empowered by God to summon and bind numerous demons to work on the temple's construction. Obviously not only was it acceptable for a king to bind and utilize demons as a labor force, he had them working side by side with his human construction crews (Chapter Eighteen).

Solomon was not the only king who was concerned about and confronted by demons. Before King James the First acceded to the throne of England in 1603, he had written and published a book entitled *Daemonologie*. In it he speaks on the subject of witchcraft and the witches' relationship with the DEVIL. He discloses how these people, most often women, conspire to summon up the Devil and barter their souls for a pittance of power and ability. He mentions how they often become a demonic FAMILIAR, a companion gifted to someone by the Prince of Darkness, and how taking up the profession of witch-finding and hunting is both noble and necessary. As can be imagined, many witches were slain under his rule, even though the religion he embraced as his own clearly stated in the Epistle to the Romans (8:38–9) that neither sorcery nor witchcraft has the power to harm a Christian. This claim is based on the belief that when Christ died and was resurrected he simultaneously defeated all the forces of evil for all time. Nevertheless, in *Daemonologie*, James went on to very carefully and meticulously describe the fine line between a scientific scholar who studied the course of the stars, namely an astronomer, and an infernally aligned individual, an astrologer, who—empowered by demons (knowingly or not)—pretended through his ignorance to interpret their course across the night sky and explain how those movements relate to man and help predict a person's future. Throughout his life King James was obsessed with witches and their demonic familiars, believing they were constantly plotting to kill him.

As you can see with the study of demonology, timing is everything. It is fascinating that these two kings, separated by two thousand years of history, both list the names, abilities, and, in some cases, the physical attributes of the demons of which they spoke. They made, in essence, a very brief *demonolo-*

gia, a dissertation on demons. And they were not alone: many others before and since have done the same. Of special note are the French judge and DEMONOGRAPHER Pierre de Rosteguy de Lancre, who conducted the witch hunts of 1609 under the order of King Henry the Eighth; Pierre Leloyers, who authored *Discourse and Histories about Specters, Visions, and Apparitions, of Spirits, Angels, Demons, and Souls that appeared visibly to Men*; and Johann Wierus, a Dutch demonologist and physician, who in his moral publications was among the first to speak out against the persecution of witches. He is also the author of the influential works *De Praestigiis Daemonum et Incantationibus ac Venificiis* and *Pseudomonarchia Daemonum*.

It is not just in Christianity and Judaism that we find lists of demons and infernal servitors, but also Ashurism, Buddhism, Hinduism, Islam, Kemetic, Vodou, and Zoroastrianism. Demons appear in the mythologies and lore of virtually every ancient society, such as the ancient Africans, Assyrians, Chinese, Greek, Japanese, Mayans, Persians, Romans, and Scythians, to name just a few.

Throughout my research I have pulled together as many of the named demons as I could find from all of the various cultures and religions. Research was conducted not only among books written about the history of ancient peoples and their cultures, but among religious texts as well. I compiled all of the information found for each demon, be it an individual entity or a particular species, then carefully condensed it to its bare and relevant facts, and wrote it up as a succinct description or synopsis. The goal was to present to the reader a concise account for each of these prominent demons. Entries were purposely kept short and precise, as there were almost three thousand diabolical personalities to commit to paper.

There are a great number of books on the market that tell of individuals who claim to have been possessed by demons, as well as of people who admit to being able to drive infernal beings out of these afflicted souls. Personal beliefs in demonic possession, be it a spiritual or psychological condition, were not relevant to the writing of this reference book. The only concern was in naming those entities who are already considered relevant, especially those who played a part in the belief systems of the major religions. I did, however, consciously choose not to use any of the books that focused on the subject matter of demonic possession, especially those works written after what might be considered the New Age movement of the 1980s and after. This decision was based on the opinion that these cases and individuals have not yet proved to be either historically or mythologically relevant. Most of these may become the stuff of urban legends. Only time will tell.

There are a handful of books that proved very useful. Gustav Davidson's *A Dictionary of Angels Including the Fallen Angels* is a first-rate resource for anyone's personal library. As the title indicates, it lists the angels who were driven out of Heaven during the Fall as well as those from Enochian lore, the Watcher Angels (see WATCHERS), who exorcized what can only be described as free will (a blessing man alone is alleged to have) and chose to leave of their own accord when they opted to take a human woman as a wife. This book also contains an impressive bibliography and a useful appendix with samples of angelic scripts, demonic seals and pacts (see DIABOLICAL SIGNATURE), the various names of LILITH, the unholy sephiroth, and a list of fallen angels (see FALLEN ANGELS).

Francesso Maria Guazzo's *Compendium Maleficarum* and *Daemonologie* by King James the First of England do not name the most demons but are essential in understanding how demons and witches are aligned and work against mankind. Two other books that list and describe demons are Fred Gettings's *Dictionary of Demons* and Mack and Mack's *A Field Guide to Demons*.

References were chosen very selectively. Books like *The Satanic Bible* by Anton Szandor LaVey and the King James Bible had to be used sparingly because they are religious texts with content not only heavily flavored by opinion but also unverifiable by other sources. A favorite book on demons was written by Wade Baskin, but it is often overlooked because of its sensationalized title: *Satanism: A Guide to the Awesome Power of Satan.* I prefer this book because it contains short, brief descriptions and definitions with no hyperbole, opinion, fictional characters (such as the demons from the John Milton poem *Paradise Lost*), or erroneous entries. It is brilliant in that it is straightforward, simple, and concise in its nature.

As with my previous book, *The Encyclopedia of Vampire Mythology*, I document the sources from which information was taken, including page numbers (when given) so that it may be referenced by others. Also as before, I tried to use the oldest editions I could find by the most authoritative and reputable sources possible. Small caps are used to indicate to the reader words that may be cross-referenced as entries in the encyclopedia.

In the back of this book is a complete bibliography of all the works cited as well as a large and thorough index.

Some of the most knowledgeable people in the field of demonology have never been recognized for their contributions. It is fitting to acknowledge these scholars for their work in this field of study here: Heinrich Cornelius Agrippa von Nettesheim, Steven Ashe, Wade Baskin, Helena Petrovna Blavatsky, Augustin Calmet, Joseph Campbell, Richard Cavendish, Robert Henry Charles, Jacques-Albin-Simon Collin de Plancy, Rosemary Ellen Guiley, Heinrich Kramer, Manfred Lurker, Anthony Master, Samuel Liddell MacGregor Mathers, and Jacob Sprenger.

Deep appreciation also goes to those who assisted with this undertaking: my beta-reader, Gina Farago; my husband, T. Glenn Bane; and especially my linguistic contributors, Yair A. Goldberg and June K. Williams. Without this dedicated cadre of individuals, this book would not have been possible.

Introduction

Demons are amazing beings, simple in design and intent—to foster and promote evil in such a way as to undo the goodness of mankind and to cause the ruination if not outright destruction of all that is held to be pure and good. We should all have such clarity of purpose.

It does not matter where in the world you are, on what point in mankind's timeline you stand, what religion you believe in or practice (if any), your social or economic standing, or whether you are male or female—demons are promoters of immorality, sin, and vice. Historically, people understand and accept this about DEMONIALITY with little or no explanation required.

I have noticed that most stories of how the world was created involve some sort of benign, all powerful being having to overcome an entity of evil and malicious intent that is nearly as powerful. For the abstract idea of good to truly be appreciated, seen, and understood it must have something off which to reflect. It needs something to give it perspective and to personify all that we do not want or desire. If there is no struggle, there can be no triumphant victory to be thankful for or revel in.

Evil, be it an abstract idea or a maligned cosmic entity, often employs minions to do its bidding. Demons are those minions, and the most intriguing part of their nature is that we need not believe in their existence to feel the effect they have on our lives. The famed British occultist Dion Fortune (1890–1946) is quoted as having said on the matter that demons are "the personification of 'negative evil'...the firm substance that we must have to push against in order to walk and the DEVIL is the principle of resistance of inertia that enables Good to get a purchase."

Interestingly, demons were not always considered to be beings of pure and unchangeable evil. Once they were the fey of the woods, the free-willed DJINN of the deserts known on occasion to convert to Islam, and the ancestral or nature spirits that were respected if not worshipped to near god-head status. Fierce in their fighting ability and highly territorial, these beings could be summoned, and by conditional agreement or by magical bond were made to be guardians of sacred areas. Demons made excellent sentries, as they had excessively passionate dispositions, near limitless energy, a preference to work from concealment, and shape-shifting capability. You would be hard pressed to find an ancient culture that did not have some place through which travel was not only considered taboo but also protected by a semi-divine being with an overprotective temperament.

In ancient Greece, the word DAEMON referred to a spirit entity that may have been a force for either good or evil. During the spread of Christianity when the young church openly and aggressively condemned all things pagan, the intent of the word changed. No longer a neutral force that could be swayed one way or the other, demons, as they were now called, were considered to be beings of pure evil who were under the influence and control of the DEVIL himself. Even now when the word "demon" is used in our speech we instantly know something of the speaker's intent. To say "the devil made me do it" as an excuse for having been caught in some act of perceived wickedness almost seems to give the speaker the benefit of being somehow not wholly responsible. He is but mortal flesh and is by nature frail, he was tricked or pressured into it, he is not a bad person, simply weak-willed, and who among us has not at some point given in to more base desires? Shouldn't mercy be shown? Is that not how one would play the devil's advocate?

From mankind's earliest origins we have recognized the existence on some level of the supernatural world, and with our instinctual desire to understand we have placed beings who dwell in other realms as falling into either one of two categories: good or evil, divine or infernal, angels or demons. Truth be told, we need demons and the evil they represent. Without them there can be no moral to our stories, let alone a plot. If there is not an external or internal struggle to overcome, how can there be any progression?

There have always been demons in our folklore and mythologies, even when we called them by other names. *The Testament of Solomon* is one such example; it was purported to have been a firsthand account of the events of the king's court. Some scholars have claimed it was written as early as the first century C.E., while others date it to as late as the fifth century. Even at its earliest dating it was still published a thousand years after Solomon's rule, but this pseudepigraphal book may be the source from which the idea of a hierarchy germinated. According to the story, a vampiric demon by the name of Ornias harasses a young man, stealing both his blood and his wages. The boy's father beseeches the king for help in fighting the demon; he in turn seeks assistance from God. The archangel Michael is sent to earth and gives Solomon a signet ring and instructions on how to use it to bind and control demons. In chapter eighteen of *The Testament of Solomon* demons are summoned, one after another, after which they are forced to give their true names, reveal what they govern, and offer instructions on how to banish them. Nearly all of these demons are sent to work on the construction of the temple.

Introduced as a personality in the *Book of Job*, which dates back to 700 B.C.E., SATAN was portrayed as an instigator and accuser of man. In the second century apocryphal book *The Testaments of the Twelve Patriarchs*, the name Satan was already well known. Nevertheless, by the time *Twelve Patriarchs* was written, this same character had developed into the adversary of God, the arch-nemesis of humanity, and an entirely evil being.

However, it was not until Saint Paul laid out the hierarchy of the heavenly host in the fourth century A.D. that other scholars were empowered to lay out a similar hierarchy for one of the natural enemies of the angels—demons.

During the fifth century demons were believed to fall into five different categories. The first four were based on the elements of the natural world: air, earth, fire, and water; the last category was "the underground." In the eleventh century Michael Psellus, a Byzantine historian, monk, philosopher, politician and writer, added a sixth category to the classification of demons. Psellus characterized these demons as mere shades, likening them to ghosts. Saint Augustine, also a fourth century philosopher, believed that all ghosts were demons. Yet it was during the Middle Ages and the early Renaissance period that the classification and division of demons came into its own. This is no doubt related to revival in the interest of the magical and numerological arts as well as the witch craze sweeping across Europe at the time. To be a witch was a sin worthy of a gruesome death by burning or hanging, but to study demons so as to better understand the opposition of heaven was perfectly acceptable, providing of course you had no political ambitions or powerful enemies.

It was during this time that demons were named and departmentalized. They were not only assigned to have dominion over a very particular type of sin, but also assigned a planet and astrological sign to rule over, as well as a month, day of the week, and an hour of the day or night when they were particularly powerful and best summoned. Some were also assigned a rank, such as king, count, or master steward of the devil's winery. They were described in detail, down to the sound of their voices, the type of clothes they wore, or mounts they appeared on. Demons were often described as being hideously ugly or having breath so foul it could literally kill a man. This is because of Christianity's tendency to regard the body, the solid form, as corrupt and dirty; ugliness was equated with evil. Additionally, the personalities of these demons were also described on many occasions so that the summoner would know what to expect; hints and summoning tips were even given as to how best to trick the demons into doing your will without giving in to their evil. Many of the more powerfully ranked demons were also empowered with hordes of servitors to do their bidding, as they themselves were subject to their liege's command. Some ranked and named demons had only a few lesser spirits to act on their behest while others had servants in the hundreds of thousands. Always a few of the most important servitors were named but seldom if ever was any real or extensive information given about them.

When the Italian poet Dante Alighieri wrote his epic poem *The Divine Comedy*, it was meant to be an allegory for the journey of the soul on the path to God. He used the Roman poet Virgil as guide through what was the contemporary medieval view of Hell. On the course of this journey, Dante named and described many demons, some of which were pulled from accepted mythology and established hierarchies while others he created, loosely naming and basing them on powerful ruling families. So prevailing was this literary work that for centuries to come some of those fictional demons appeared in grimoires and serious demonographies.

Francis Barrett, an Englishman by birth and an occultist by profession, penned *The Magus*. Published at the height of the Age of Reason in 1801, it was considered to be one of the primary sources required to properly study ceremonial magic. Even today the book is in use by those who seriously practice magic. In it, Barrett gives nine different divisions of demons: The False Gods, who wish to be worshipped like a god; Spirits of Lies, who use divination and predictions to trick and deceive; Vessels of Iniquity, the inventors of all things evil, such as cards and dice; Revengers of Evil, who are ruled over by ASMODEUS; Deluders, the demons under the command of Prince SATAN who mimic and imitate miracles as well as work in conjunction with witches; Aerial Powers, who live in the air and cause lightning, thunder, and pestilence as it suits their prince, MERIRIM; FURIES, who are led by ABADDON and cause discord, devastation, and war; Accusers, demonic spirits led by Prince ASTAROTH; and the tempters, who reside in every man and are under the command of Prince MAMMON.

In this modern, enlightened age it is hard to believe we have not yet relinquished our belief in the supernatural. Television shows that claim to be in the pursuit of scientific fact-finding by capturing demonic forces and ghosts on film, by use of formalistic staged drama and over-hyped anticipation, have, in my opinion, done a great deal to convince rationally minded folks otherwise. Television alone is not to blame; a constant supply of books describes individual possessions and the hardships families must endure and overcome.

This book, at the other end of the spectrum, is an encyclopedic listing of various demons. I describe the demon without hype or hyperbole, what it looks like, who in the infernal hierarchy it is subjected to serve under, and how, if it is known, the demon operates. Readers may be surprised to discover that the vast number of demons herein described do not have the ability to possess a human. In modern times, possession and the rite of exorcism first truly came to light on a grand scale with the publication and commercial success of William Peter Blatty's *The Exorcist* (1971). Not so surprisingly, when the Catholic Church denounced the book and the claim that the story was based on actual, recent events, the popularity of *The Exorcist* only increased. In spite of the Church's dislike of the book, the message of *Exorcist* was spread: that demons are driven by evil instinct and only by the use of conscious reason, compassion, and love can they be defeated. Blatty went on to write the screenplay for the film, for which he won an Academy Award, the message spreading out and reaching an even wider audience.

Blatty's book is hardly a stand-alone example. Thousands of similar books have since been published. Some of them are more out-of-this-world in their claims than others, professing that the demon showed itself to be real in a number of fantastic ways, such as by demonstrating acts of levitation, causing both people and objects to float around the room or religious symbols and holy icons to burst into flame, and speaking through the mouths of their prey in long dead languages or sharing secrets only the victim could have known. As remarkable as all this may sound, it is even more remarkable that no one has ever managed to record such an event with either convincing still photography or video. These events never occur when a skeptic, non-believer, or open-minded third party is present. Nor are these types of people ever victimized by demons; it seems they would be rather easy prey when compared to the devoutly fortified religious individual who would be knowledgeable in how best to confront them. Yet the latter are exactly the sort of people that the infernal habitually afflict. Obviously this is an aspect of the nature of demons that I do not understand; neither have any of my colleagues addressed it, convincingly or otherwise, in their own works.

I am undecided as to my beliefs on cases of demonic possession. It may be possible but it may be equally improbable. The Old Testament Apocrypha refers to exorcisms only once, in the Book of Tobit, chapters six and seven. However, the real problem was not that Sarah was being possessed by a demon but rather that one was systematically killing off every man she ever married in an attempt to keep her available for itself. In the New Testament, Christ gave his apostles the gift of exorcism: "And when he had called unto him his twelve disciples, he gave them power against unclean spirits, to cast them out, and to heal all manner of sickness and all manner of disease" (Matthew 10:1). (It should be noted that demonic possession and disease were often linked.)

In the shadow of Alighieri, Barrett, Blatty, Fortune, and Milton as well as Baskin, Collin de Plancy, Gettings, Guazzo, King James the First of England, Leloyers, Mathers, Rosteguy de Lancre, and Wierus, I have collected and briefly described as many of the different demons I could find from a wide array of cultures and religions. If readers hope to learn here how to summon demons or how to perform an exorcism, they will be disappointed, but academics, researchers, and scholars alike will be pleased with what they find—a massive collection of demons, clearly defined and cataloged.

THE ENCYCLOPEDIA

Aamon

Variations: AMAIMON, AMAYMON, AMMON, Amon, AMOYMON

Aamon, Grand MARQUIS OF HELL, is the demon of life and reproduction. He is described both as having the head of a serpent and the body of a wolf (and vice versa) as well as having a raven's head with canine teeth set upon a man's body. According to Christian demonology, it is believed that he is most powerful during the day and has the ability to project flames from his mouth. Aamon is summoned for his knowledge of the past and his ability to predict the future. He also has the ability to reconcile friends who have become enemies as well as being able to secure the love of another to the one who summoned him. He is in direct service under the demon SATANACHIA. Aamon commands forty infernal legions and is one of the four personal ASSISTANTS OF ASHTAROTH (see ASHTAROTH). The seventh spirit mentioned in the *Goetia*, he is also a part of Christian demonology, as he is mentioned in *The Grimoire of Pope Honorius*. Oftentimes demonologists will associate him with both the Egyptian god Amun and the Carthaginian god Ba'al Hammon.

Sources: Baskin, *Dictionary of Satanism*, 9; Gettings, *Dictionary of Demons*, 21; Icon, *Demons*, 135; Maberry, *Cryptopedia*, 39; Masters, *Eros and Evil*, 176; Waite, *Unknown World 1894–1895*, 230; Wedeck, *Treasury of Witchcraft*, 96–7.

Aanalin

Variations: AMALIN

The *Sacred Magic of Abramelin the Mage* lists Aanalin as one of the fifty-three SERVITORS OF ASHTAROTH AND ASMODEUS (see ASMODEUS and ASHTAROTH) but calls him by the alias AMALIN. Aanalin, originally from Chaldaic demonology, is the demon of languidness.

Sources: Mathers, *Sacred Magic of Abramelin the Mage*, 119; Susej, *Demonic Bible*, 257.

Aariel

According to the *Theurgia Goetia*, Aariel is one of the sixteen SERVITORS OF ASYRIEL (see ASYRIEL) and commands twenty servitors. This diurnal chief duke is good-natured and willing to obey his summoner. In Hebrew, his name means "lion of God."

Sources: Davidson, *A Dictionary of Angels: Including the Fallen Angels*, 1; Peterson, *Lesser Key of Solomon*, 73.

Aatxe

Variations: Aatxegorri ("young red bull")

This demonic spirit from the Basque religion is described as looking like a young red bull but has the ability to shape-shift into human form. Aatxe, whose name translates to mean "young bull," has the ability to create storms and does so at night with the belief that people of quality and "goodness" will seek shelter indoors and that only the criminal element will venture forth in such weather. Then, in the darkness and further hidden by the weather, Aatxe will prey upon criminals and other socially undesirable people. Said to be a representation of the goddess Mari, or at the very least an enforcer of her will, he lives in a cave called Euskal Herria.

Sources: Eliade, *Encyclopedia of Religion*, 81; Illes, *Encyclopedia of Spirits*, 113; Lurker, *Dictionary of Gods and Goddesses, Devils and Demons*, 3; Rose, *Spirits, Fairies, Leprechauns, and Goblins*, 1; Sherman, *Storytelling*, 56.

Aax

According to Enochian lore, Aax is a CACODAEMON. His counterpart is the angel Axir (ENOCHIAN CACODAEMONS).

Sources: Chopra, *Academic Dictionary of Mythology*, 1; Kelley, *Complete Enochian Dictionary*, 71.

Abaasi, plural: abassy

Variations: Abassylar

In northeastern Russia, from the demonology of the Yakut people, comes a species of demon called abaasi, or abassy when more than one appears. In their native language of Sakha, *abaasi* means "black" and it is under the domain of the demon ULU TOJON ("Powerful Lord") who rules all nine clans of abassy.

HELIOPHOBIC DEVIL of destruction and disease, they are only seen at night. These beings are basically humanoid shaped but have only one eye and leg. Considered to be evil creatures, they prey on the souls of both animals and humans. Abassy are also known to cause madness and induce sexual manifestations in those who are about to receive their shamanistic powers. Their sacred animal is the raven.

Sources: Grimal, *Larousse World Mythology*, 434; Lanoue, *Poetics of Myth*, 413–14; Riordan, *Sun Maiden and the Crescent Moon*, 203; Universität Bonn, *Zentralasiatische Studien*, 110, 112, 121.

Abaddon

Variations: Abadon, 'Abadown, ABBADON, Abbadown, Apolloyon, the Destroying Angel, the King of the Grasshoppers, Prince of War, Sovereign of the Bottomless Pit

From the Hebrew word for "destruction," Abaddon ("the Destroyer") is one of the few demons mentioned by name in the Old Testament. In the King James commission of the Bible he is mentioned by name five times. Accredited by various sources to be the demon of anger, hate, vengeance, and war, Abaddon is said to command the sixth House of Hell and its demonic locust army, the very one that will torment the nonbelievers during the seventh, and final, trumpet blast of the Rapture. Perhaps this is why he is seen as both an angel of Hell and a destroying angel of God. The locusts themselves are demonic creatures, described as having a human face, the body of a winged warhorse, and the poisonous stinging tail of a scorpion.

Abaddon is described as a gigantic figure veiled in black and covered with whirling wheels. In his hands he holds a large wheel that is spinning. Some sources say he is snakelike in appearance and has a belly full of fire.

During medieval times it was common for scholars and demonologists to assign aspects to the more commonly known demons. It was said of Abaddon that he was particularly strong on Saturdays in January when Venus was visible; that his colors were blood red, brown, and green, and that the ruby and the sword were symbolic of him.

An advisor who inspires anarchy and chaos, he has been given the titles of Chief Demon of Locusts, Demonic Ruler of the Abyss, and the King of Demons.

Sources: Belanger, *Dictionary of Demons*, 16, 161; Bellamy, *Moons, Myths and Man*, 184–5; Chaplin, *Dictionary of the Occult and Paranormal*, 1; Davidson, *Dictionary of Angels*, 1–2; Gettings, *Dictionary of Demons*, 21; Icon, *Demons*, 135; Icon, *Hierarchy*, 199; Lewis, *Satanism Today*, 1; Van der Toorn, *Dictionary of Deities and Demons in the Bible*, 1, 6.

'Abaddown

Variations: ABADDON
'Abaddown, Hebrew for "the destruction of

Hades (or Shaul)," is said to be the demonic angel of the Bottomless Pit of Sheol. He stands there on constant and vigilant guard, ensuring that the demonic locust army, dragons, or any of the other creatures bound to the pit do not escape before their proper time.

Sources: Ayers, *Yahweh's Breath Bible*, 735; Cox, *Decoding the Lost Symbol*, 1–2; Gettings, *Dictionary of Demons*, 21.

Abadir

Variations: Ob, Ob-Adur, Orus, Oub
Possibly originally the Ophite serpent god Orus, Abadir is named as one of the sixteen SERVITORS OF ASMODEUS (see ASMODEUS). His name is taken from the Hebrew word meaning "scattered."

Sources: Bryant, *New System*, 201; Howey, *Encircled Serpent*, 31; Jennings, *Ophiolatreia*, 3; Mathers, *Sacred Magic of Abramelin the Mage*, 110; *Quarterly Oriental Magazine*, 29; Susej, *Demonic Bible*, 258.

Abagiron

The *Sacred Magic of Abramelin the Mage* lists Abagiron as one of the sixty-five SERVITORS OF KORE AND MAGOTH. His name is possibly a variant of a Greek word and if true would translate to mean "gathering together."

Sources: Mathers, *Sacred Magic of Abramelin the Mage*, 110; Susej, *Demonic Bible*, 258; Von Worms, *Book of Abramelin*, 250, 256.

Abahin

This demon likely takes its name from an ancient archaic Hebrew word meaning "terrible." Abahin is one of the fifty-three SERVITORS OF ASHTAROTH AND ASMODEUS (see ASMODEUS and ASTAROTH).

Sources: Mathers, *Sacred Magic of Abramelin the Mage*, 109; Susej, *Demonic Bible*, 257.

Abalam

Variations: Abali, Abalim, Labal
According to Christian demonology, Abalam is a king or prince of Hell and one of the two assistants of PAYMON (see PRINCES OF HELL, KINGS OF HELL). When summoned by a sacrificial offering, he will appear with the demonic King (or Prince) BEBALL.

Sources: Belanger, *Dictionary of Demons*, 14; Ford, *Luciferian Goetia*, 70; Icon, *Demons*, 135; Platts, *Dictionary of Urdu Classical Hindi and English*, 718; Scot, *Discoverie of Witchcraft*, 220.

Abaros

Variations: Abasdarhon, Arearos, ARMAROS, ARMERS, PHARMAROS
Fallen Angel Abaros is one of the WATCHERS

mentioned by name in the *Book of Enoch*. Said to have dominion over the fifth hour of the night, Abaros swore allegiance to SAMIAZA and went against God's will by not only teaching mankind how to both create and remove magical enchantments but also by taking a human female as his wife. The offspring of the union between these FALLEN ANGELS and the daughters of man were known as the NEPHILIM.

Sources: Budge, *Book of the Cave of Treasures*, 92, 93; Charlesworth, *Old Testament Pseudepigrapha*, 15; Davidson, *Dictionary of Angels*, 2; Laurence, *Foreign Quarterly Review*, Vol. 24, 370; Stuckenbruck, *Commentaries on Early Jewish Literature*, 278.

Abbadon

In early British paganism Abbadon was a demonic god of war. After battles when time permitted, a huge wooden structure would be erected in his honor and filled with captive enemy soldiers. It was then set ablaze, burning all inside alive so that their lives would be a suitable sacrifice to summon Abbadon and entice him to enter the fray in the next battle.

There is another demon by the name of Abbadon; he is also known as ABDON, the Angel of the Bottomless Pit, and Apollyon ("one that exterminates"). Abbadon ("The Destroyer") of Hebrew lore is mentioned in the Old Testament books of Job 28:22 and the Book of Revelation 9:11. He is said to be the leader of a swarm of demonic locusts that are described as having the face of a human, the body of a winged horse, and the tail of a scorpion. Abbadon is the demon of death and destruction; he inspires men to anarchy and to create chaos. He is variously described as an ARCHDEMON or Fallen Angel, and is himself said to be under the control of demon SAMMAEL. Insects are sacred to him (see also ABADDON). Abbadon VERRIER is named as the demon of knowledge, secrets, and sorcery. He is also listed as one of the FALLEN ANGELS.

Sources: Davidson, *Dictionary of Angels*, 1, 2; Guiley, *The Encyclopedia of Demons and Demonology*, 1; Icon, *Hierarchy*, 199; Van der Toorn, *Dictionary of Deities and Demons in the Bible*, 1, 2; Van Scott, *Encyclopedia of Hell*, 1, 71.

Abdiel

Abdiel is the demon of slaves and slavery. The name is Hebrew and translates to mean "servant (or slave) of God," "wanderer of God," or "destroyer of (or for) God," depending on its usage.

Sources: Chapone, *Lady's Pocket Library*, 51; Davidson, *Dictionary of Angels*, 4; Maberry, *Cryptopedia*, 41; Roberts, *Memoirs of the Life and Correspondence of Mrs. Hannah More*, Vol. 2, 47, 361.

Abdon

Mentioned in the Book of Job 28:22, Abdon ("destruction" or "servile") is considered to be a demon in Hebrew lore (see ABADDON); however, his name is also the name of a region in Gehenna, which is mentioned in the Book of Proverbs.

Sources: Belanger, *Dictionary of Demons*, 161; Von Nettesheim, *Three Books of Occult Philosophy*, 514.

Abduscias

Abduscias is a demon with a reputation for uprooting trees (see ACCARON).

Source: Guiley, *The Encyclopedia of Demons and Demonology*, 7, 246.

Abduxuel

According to Enochian lore, Abduxuel is the twelfth of the twenty-eight rulers of the lunar mansions.

Sources: Gettings, *Dictionary of Demons*, 21; McLean, *Treatise on Angel Magic*, 42.

Abere

Variations: Abele, Obere

From Melanesian folklore comes the singular demonic entity known as Abere ("Maiden"). Described as a beautiful young woman as well as a provocative seductress, she is a known cannibal that preys exclusively upon men. Abere will use her feminine guile to lure a man into the lake or swampy region she calls home. Once there, she strips naked and slides into the water, hiding just out of full sight in the mimia reeds; from her hidden position, she calls, enticing the man to follow. If her prey is foolish enough to do so, Abere will stealthily hunt him down, and, using her power over the reeds, will tangle and trap him there, after which she will drown him and consume his flesh. In addition to having control over the water reeds, she also commands several young and nearly as beautiful female companions.

Sources: Carlyon, *A Guide to the Gods*, 365; Herdt, *Ritualized Homosexuality in Melanesia*, 284–5; Riesenfeld, *Megalithic Culture of Melanesia*, 469–70; Rose, *Giants, Monsters, and Dragons*, 2; Turner, *Dictionary of Ancient Deities*, 7.

Abezethibou

Variations: Abez, Abasdarhon, Abezethibod, Abezithibod, Beelzeboul, BAALZEBUB, BEELZEBUB, Beelzebuth, Foe of Emmanuel, Lord of the Flies, Prince Prime Minister of Infernal Spirits; Ruler of Demons

Born the offspring of Beelzeboul (Beelzebub), Abezethibou is the demon of African spirits and the sin of pride; however, he is well known for his ability to lead people astray. A nocturnal, one-winged demon, he commands twelve servitors, although only eight of them are named (see SERVITORS OF ABEZETHIBOU), and is described in some texts as one of the FALLEN ANGELS, a GRIGORI, and a WATCHER. As the last of the Fallen Angels, he was imprisoned in the Red Sea. However, Abezethibou was also said to be the demon summoned up by Jambres and Jannes, the head sorcerers of the Egyptian court who did magical combat against Moses, and lost, in the book of Exodus (7:11, 22). He is most easily summoned in the month of July during the fifth hour of the night.

Sources: Conybeare, *Jewish Quarterly Review*, Vol. 11, 4; Guiley, *The Encyclopedia of Demons and Demonology*, 2; Pietersma, *Apocryphon of Jannes and Jambres*, 31, 193, 194; Webster, *Encyclopedia of Angels*, 3.

Abezi-Thibod

Variations: ABEZETHIBOU, Abezithibod, Angel of Egypt, Devil of the Red Sea, SAMAEL, the son of BEELZEBUB

Abezi-Thibod ("Father devoid of counsel") is one of two demonic spirits that rose up with the pillar from the depths of the Red Sea. He is known for his ability to harden the hearts of men, as he did to Pharaoh when Moses asked to free the Israelites. According to the Old Testament book of Exodus, as Moses led his people out of Egypt they saw a fierce, single winged being and were frightened "at the sight of the Angel of Egypt darting through the air as he flew to the assistance of the people under his tutelage." Abezi-Thibod once resided in Ameleouth, the first heaven, but he is now trapped in a cave under the Red Sea.

Sources: Conybeare, *Jewish Quarterly Review*, Vol. 11, 4; Belanger, *Dictionary of Demons*, 15; Central Conference of American Rabbis, *CCAR Journal*, Vol. 10, 23; Davidson, *Dictionary of Angels*, 4.

Abhiyoga

In Hindu and Buddhist mythology, Abhiyoga ("prosecution") is the demon of darkness and rain.

Sources: Bhāravi, *Kirātārjunīye*, 89; Davids, *Pali-English Dictionary*, 68; Mather, *Encyclopedic Dictionary of Cults, Sects, and World Religions*, n.p.

Abigar

Variations: ABIGOR, ELIGOR

The eighteenth century *Grimoire of Pope Honorius* tells us that Abigar is a grand duke and one of the eighteen named subordinate spirits. Unrivaled in combat, this non-corporeal demon has the ability to predict the future and possess any violent minded individual in order to share with him his expert military and tactical advice. The

counsel of Abigar is not without a price, for his presence in the human body is very taxing and causes severe side effects that are oftentimes long-lasting or even permanent.

Sources: Curry, *Dublin University Magazine*, Vol. 66, 521; de Givry, *Witchcraft, Magic and Alchemy*, 28; Shah, *Occultism*, 62; Wedeck, *Treasury of Witchcraft*, 96.

Abigor

Variations: ELIGOR, Eligos

Johann Wierus's book *Pseudomonarchia Daemonum* (*False Monarchy of Demons*, 1583) tells us that Abigor, a FALLEN ANGEL, is a duke of the Superior Order of demons and was also one of the seventy-two SPIRITS OF SOLOMON (see DUKES OF HELL). As one of the twelve SERVITORS OF ABEZETHIBOU, he commands sixty legions of devils. A demon of war, he appears before any who summon him as a handsome knight seated upon a winged horse, holding a lance, an ensign bearing his insignia, and a scepter. He will gladly tell the secrets of military victory to any prince who is willing to offer to him their soul in exchange. Unequaled in combat and a knowledgeable tactician, Abigor has all the knowledge of all wars ever waged in the past, present, and the future. He can teach military leaders how to be respected by their soldiers and how to gain the favor of lords and knights. If asked, he will tell the truth about the location of anything hidden.

Sources: Anderson, *Diary of Ancient Rites*, 208; Barnhart, *New Century Handbook of English Literature*, 4; Belanger, *Dictionary of Demons*, 117; De Laurence, *Lesser Key of Solomon, Goetia*, 27; Guiley, *The Encyclopedia of Demons and Demonology*, 2; Shah, *Occultism*, 64.

Abiron

Variations: Abeiron, Auberon, Oberon

According to a sixteenth-century French transcript of a witch trial that took place 1593, a male witch from Alest testified that he spoke with the DEVIL who gave his name as Abiron.

Sources: Murray, *Witch-cult in Western Europe*, 239; Oxford University Press, *The Periodical*, Vol. 8, Issue 113, 145; Rudwin, *Devil in Legend and Literature*, 28; Stephens, *Demon Lovers*, 223.

Abito

Abito ("Garment") is one of the many names of the demonic first wife of Adam, LILITH.

Sources: Ford, *Luciferian Witchcraft*, 451; University of Pennsylvania, *Museum Journal*, Vol. 3–4, 63.

Aborym

A devil commanding twenty-six legions, Aborym ("Regions Beyond") is a duke and is the demon of burning cities and castles. He has three heads, one of a cat, one of a man, and one of a snake.

Sources: France, *On Life and Letters*, 220; Rudwin, *Devil in Legend and Literature*, 28, 86.

Abracadabra

Variations: Abrakadabra, Abrasadabra

The word *abracadabra* was first recorded by the Roman physician Quintus Serenus Sammonicus in the second century A.D. in a Latin medical poem. Prior to this there is no written evidence that the word ever before existed. It is likely that it was a misinterpretation of some other word or phrase, and there are several likely candidates. *Abracadabra* is tied to demonology with the hypothesis that its origins lie in Hebrew. There the words *ha-brachah* ("the blessing") and *and dabra* ("pestilence") when used together may be a form of delimitative magic preformed when curing an illness that caused blindness believed to be sent by the female demon SHABRIRI. This Cabbalistic cure calls for her name to be written in an inverted cone.

A second possible origin of the word that also has medical roots comes from the ancient Chaldean phrase *abbada ke dabra*, which means "perish like the word." Again, the phrase would be written in an inverted cone and chanted as an incantation to cure an illness.

Not connected to any medical practice, *abracadabra* may have been a misinterpretation of the Aramaic phrase *avra kehdabra*, which means "I will create as I speak," a reference to how God created the universe. It may also have been a simple mistranslation of the Hebrew phrase *avar k'-davar*, which loosely translates as "it will be according to what is spoken." It is hard not to notice that *abracadabra* is similar to the Hebrew words *ab* ("father"), *ben* ("son"), and RUACH hacadosch *("holy spirit"). A final suggestion as to where the word may have come from lies with a Gnostic sect from Alexandria known as the Basilidians. There the demon ABRASAX was the name of their supreme deity.*

As an ancient medical word, *abracadabra* is a powerful invocation with mystical powers. To use it, when a person was sick they would wear an amulet around their neck that was made up of a piece of parchment inscribed with a triangular formula derived from the word. It was believed that when it was written out this way that it acted like a funnel and drove the sickness out of the body.

```
A B R A C A D A B R A
A B R A C A D A B R
A B R A C A D A B
A B R A C A D A
A B R A C A D
A B R A C A
A B R A C
A B R A
A B R
A B
A
```

Sources: Belanger, *Dictionary of Demons*, 15; Cavendish, *Man, Myth and Magic*, 16; Collin de Plancy, *Dictionary of Witchcraft*, 13; Houghton, *Word Histories and Mysteries*, 1; Prioreschi, Plinio. *Roman Medicine*, 508–9.

Abracax

Variations: ABRASAX, Abraxas

It is likely that Abracax was originally a Basilidean god that was later demonized. He appears in Greek magical papyri and in Gnostic texts, such as the *Gospel of the Egyptian*. The name Abracax has been found engraved on stones that were worn as magical amulets or charms and depict him as a short man with snakes for feet. After his demonization, he was associated with the dual nature of SATAN and the word *ABRACADABRA*.

Sources: Brewer, *Dictionary of Phrase and Fable*, 5; Cirlot, *Dictionary of Symbols*, 2; Collin de Plancy, *Dictionary of Witchcraft*, 13–4; Dunglison, *Medical Lexicon*, 21; Hyatt, *Book of Demons*, 72.

Abrasax

Variations: Abracad, Abraxas, the Lord of the 365 Virtues, the Supreme Being

Abrasax ("Supreme Being") was the title for the god worshipped by the second-century Gnostic Basilides of Alexandria. It is possible that he was a deity borrowed from Persian mythology where he had numerous descriptions such as looking like a cloud of light, a human torso with the head of a rooster and snakes for legs; a hydralike creature, a king with clawed dragonlike feet; a man with the crowned head of a king and snakes for feet; a man with the head of a lion and scorpions for feet; a white and red horse; and a wyvern with the head of a rooster, a protruding belly, and a knotted tail. Very often he is also depicted using a shield and a chariot whip.

As a demon he commands three hundred sixty-five different heavens and is the lord of three hundred sixty-five different virtues, one for each day of the year. He is the symbol of virtue, his holy number is three hundred sixty-five, and his holy symbol is that of the sun.

Abrasax was then known for his bad temper and struggles with his duality; however, in modern times he is best known for having his name engraved on gems and worn as an amulet of protection. These talismans are commonly called Abrasax stones.

According to one story of Abrasax that show his duality, in order to vindicate his power in the eyes of the Twelve Kingdoms, the creator god sent some of his angels to rain fire, sulphur, and asphalt upon the seed of Seth. However, the great eternal god sent his angels Abrasax, GAMALIEL, and Sablo in clouds of light to descend upon the seed of Seth, lift them out of the fire, and take them away to safety.

Sources: Collin de Plancy, *Dictionary of Witchcraft*, 13–4; Herzog, *New Schaff-Herzog Encyclopedia of Religious Knowledge*, 16–17; Hyatt, *Book of Demons*, 72; Knights of Columbus, *Catholic Encyclopedia*, 58; Mead, *Fragments of a Faith Forgotten*, 280–2.

Abrinael

Variations: Abrunael

According to Enochian lore Abrinael is one of the twenty-eight demonic rulers of the lunar mansions. He presides over the twenty-fourth mansion, Sadabatha, and is known to hinder the government (see ENOCHIAN RULERS OF THE LUNAR MANSIONS).

Sources: Barrett, *The Magus*, 57; Von Nettesheim, *Three Books of Occult Philosophy*, 875; Scheible, Sixth and Seventh Books of Moses, 75; Webster, *Encyclopedia of Angels*, 3.

Abro

Abro is one of the many secret names of the demonic first wife of Adam, LILITH.

Sources: Guiley, *Encyclopedia of Angels*, 216; Hanauer, *Folk-lore of the Holy Land*, 325

Abrulges

A nocturnal AERIAL DEVIL of Christian demonology who is mentioned in Trithemius's *Steganographia* (1506), Abrulges is one of the eleven SERVITORS OF PAMERSIEL (see PAMERSIEL). When he is summoned, it must be done from the second floor of a home or in a wide and open space, such as a field or a stadium. Demonologists would call upon him because of his usefulness in driving out other spirits from haunted places; however, they must be careful with what he says to them, as he is an expert liar. Abrulges has a reputation for telling secrets. He is arrogant and stubborn by nature and one of the DUKES OF HELL.

Sources: Belanger, *Dictionary of Demons*, 16; Peterson, *Lesser Key of Solomon*, 64; Rasula, *Imagining Language*, 130–1; Trithemius, *Steganographia*, 1.

Abussos

Variations: Aàbussov

Abussos's name is Greek for "immeasurable depth" or "without bounds." Literally is it understood to mean a bottomless pit. This demon's name was mentioned once in the King James Version of the Book of Revelation 19:20. His sacred number is twelve. Throughout the Bible this word is used in reference to the region of Hell to which Jesus banishes demons, as described in Luke 8:26–33.

Sources: Korban, *Anastasis Dunamis*, 117; Reiling, *Translator's Handbook on the Gospel of Luke*, 347; Watts, *Ancient Prophecies Unveiled*, 202.

Abutes

The *Sacred Magic of Abramelin the Mage* has Abutes ("bottomless, measureless") as one of the fifty-three SERVITORS OF ASHTAROTH AND ASMODEUS (see ASHTAROTH and ASMODEUS).

Sources: Belanger, *Dictionary of Demons*, 16; Forgotten Books, *Sacred Magic of Abramelin the Mage*, 112; Monier-Williams, *Sanskrit-English Dictionary*, 592.

Abzu

Variations: APSU, Apsû, Engur

In the Babylonian creation epic *Enuma Elish* (twelfth century B.C.E.), Abzu is a primal demonic creature made up of fresh water. He is the lover of fellow deity TIAMAT, a creature of salt water. Abzu is the demon of the semen, wisdom, and the Watery Abyss, a vast freshwater ocean beneath the earth that serves as the source of all lakes, rivers, springs, streams, and wells.

Sources: Black, *Gods, Demons, and Symbols of Ancient Mesopotamia*, 34, 57, 134; Bossieu, *Academy*, Issue 14, 13–14; Cunningham, *Deliver Me from Evil*, 11–2, 38; Sorensen, *Possession and Exorcism in the New Testament and Early Christianity*, 27–8.

Acaos

Acaos is one of the eighteen demons who possessed Sister Jeanne des Anges in Loudun, France, 1634. He was described as being a FALLEN ANGEL, formerly of the Order of Thrones. Interestingly, after her exorcism, Acaos was thereafter called upon during exorcisms and cases of collective possession for assistance in driving out other demonic spirits (see LOUDUN POSSESSION).

Sources: Aikin, *General Biography*, 493; Bayle, *Historical and Critical Dictionary*, 262; Dawes, *Pronunciation of the Greek Aspirates*, 41; Ramsay, *Westminster Guide to the Books of the Bible*, 349; Voltaire, *Works of M. de Voltaire*, 193.

Accaron

Variation: Acheron, Ekron

Accaron is a devil whose name translates to mean "a body or stump of a tree," "barrenness," "feebleness," and "weakness" (see also ABDUS-CIAS). In some translations of the Bible, Accaron is translated as the Palestinian homeland of BAALZEBUB (SATAN) while in others it is taken to mean a lesser, demonic servitor of BAALZEBUB (Satan).

Sources: Bullinger, *Decades of Henry Bullinger*, 357; France, *On Life and Letters*, 220; Jones, *Jones' Dictionary of Old Testament Proper Names*, 54; Rudwin, *Devil in Legend and Literature*, 28.

Acereba

Variations: Acerba

Theurgia Goetia, the second book of the *Lemegeton*, claims that Acereba, a nocturnal duke, is one of the fifteen SERVITORS OF BARMIEL (see BARMIEL and DUKES OF HELL).

Sources: Peterson, *Lesser Key of Solomon*, 70–1.

Achaniel

In the *Sacred Magic of Abramelin the Mage*, Achaniel ("Truth of God") is one of the fifteen SERVITORS OF PAYMON (see PAYMON). He is the demon of truth.

Sources: Belanger, *Dictionary of Demons*, 150; Mathers, *Sacred Magic of Abramelin the Mage*, 108.

Achas

Achas is one of the eighteen demons who possessed Sister Jeanne des Anges in Loudun, France, 1634. He was described as being a FALLEN ANGEL. After the exorcism, Achas was thereafter called upon during exorcisms and cases of collective possession for assistance in driving out other demonic spirits (see LOUDUN POSSESSION).

Sources: Aikin, *General Biography*, 493; Bayle, *Historical and Critical Dictionary*, 262; de Colange, *Standard Encyclopedia*, 14; Voltaire, *Works of M. de Voltaire*, 193.

Achot

As one of the twenty Duke SERVITORS OF SYMIEL (see SYMIEL), Achot is very amenable and quick to obey his summoner. He shares with the other diurnal SERVITORS OF SYMIEL seven hundred twenty servitors between them. In Hebrew his name translates to mean "of a relation," as in a sibling, spouse or lover.

Sources: Hoffman, *And God Said*, 163–4; Peterson, *Lesser Key of Solomon*, 88; Trithemius, *Steganographia*, 85.

Aciebel

Variations: ACIEL

Dr. Johannes Faustus, not to be confused with the printer Johann Fust, wrote a book in 1524 that he named *The Book of Dr. Faust*. In it he de-

scribed the demon Aciebel as being an aqueous demon who had the power to control all things upon and under the water. He also claimed that the sea demon had the ability to return lost items and raise up both ships and treasure that had been lost in lakes, oceans, and rivers. Faustus noted that the more sharply Aciebel is invoked, the faster the demon will fulfill his summoner's commands.

Sources: Butler, *Ritual Magic*, 177; Hall, *Secret Teachings of all Ages*, 297; Von Goethe, *Goethes Faust*, 259; Von Goethe, *Goethe's Letters to Zelter*, 377.

Aciel

Originally from Chaldean demonology, Aciel ("black sun," or "the Sun of the Night") is mentioned in both the *Testament of Solomon* and Heinrich Cornelius Agrippa Von Nettesheim's *De Occulta Philosophia* (1531). Ranked as one of the ELECTORS OF HELL and in service under Raphael ("healing one of God"), Aciel is an "ensnarer" and one of the seven planetary demons of Hell (Saturn). He appears as an attractive man but stands only about three feet tall. Aciel, who dwells in the bowels of the earth, must be invoked three times before he will appear, and will only do so in a magical circle prepared especially for him. He moves and acts as quick as human thought. Able to give riches to his summoner, Aciel will instantly bring forth items from a great distance. He has the power to affect the economy as well as the ability to cause earthquakes.

Sources: Chopra, *Academic Dictionary of Mythology*, 5; *Encyclopædia Britannica*, Vol. 1, 174; Von Goethe, *Goethes Faust*, 259; Von Goethe, *Goethe's Letters to Zelter*, 377.

Aclahayr

Apollonius of Tyana stated in his *Nuctemeron* (*Night Illuminated by Day*) that Aclahayr was one of the fourth of the seven DJINN of the Twelve Hours; their names are Eistibus, PHALGUS, PHARZUPH, SISLAU, Schiekron, and THAGRINUS. If he is to be summoned, it is best to do so on a Monday or Sunday. He is also the demon of gambling.

Sources: Gettings, *Dictionary of Demons*, 23; Lévi, *Transcendental Magic*, 418.

Acleror

Variations: Aclerorv, Acteras, Acterar

Acleror is one of the fifteen diurnal Duke SERVITORS OF BARMIEL (see BARMIEL) according to the *Theurgia Goetia*, the second book of the *Lemegeton* (see DUKES OF HELL).

Sources: Peterson, *Lesser Key of Solomon*, 70; Trithemius, *Steganographia*, 17.

Acuar

Acuar is one of the one hundred eleven SERVITORS OF AMAYMON, ARITON, ORIENS, AND PAYMON. His name in Hebrew translates to mean "a tiller of the earth."

Sources: Forgotten Books, *Sacred Magic of Abramerlin the Mage*, 121; Mathers, *Magia Della Cabala*, 140; Von Worms, *Book of Abramelin*, 255.

Ad Dajjal

Variations: Al-Masih Ad Dajjal ("The False Messiah"), ANTICHRIST, DAJJAL, Deggial, Meshiha Deghala

Eschatology is the study of the end of days, ends of time, or the end of the world, be it from a theological, philosophical, or metaphysical point of view. Ad Dajjal ("The Impostor") is a demon from Islamic eschatology who is believed to be the End-of-Days deceiver, otherwise known as the Antichrist.

It is believed that in the final days, Ad Dajjal will gather together all of those he has deceived and make them into an army that he will use to confront the Messiah, who will have an army of His own.

A large and bulky-looking man with a ruddy complexion and a thick head of hair, Ad Dajjal is blind in his right eye. Some sources say that the Arabic word for "infidel" (*kaafir*) will be written upon his forehead or between his eyes. Only a true Muslim will be able to see the writing. He will make himself known at *Yawm al-Qiyamah* ("The Day of Resurrection") while he is traveling between Syria and Iraq.

Ad Dajjal is described as being able to leap through the sky high enough to touch the clouds. He can fool others into thinking that he has the power to raise the dead and walk across the waters of the ocean. He rides upon a donkey that moves quickly over the land, but he is physically incapable of entering into Mecca and Medina.

To prevent attack from Ad Dajjal, one must repeat from memory the first ten verses of *Surat al Kahf* (*Chapter of the Cave*). These verses act like a verbal talisman against him.

Sources: Glassé, *New Encyclopedia of Islam*, 122; Kelley, *Methodist Review*, Vol. 83, 59; Le Strange, *Palestine Under the Moslems*, 411, 494.

Adad

Variations: ADDU, Anu's son, Hadad, Ishkur, Ramman ("the Thunderer"), Resheph, RIMMON, Teshub, the canal controller

From Assyrian, Babylonian, Hittite, and Mesopotamian demonology comes the demonic god of divination and storms, Adad. He is depicted as grasping lightning in his right hand and an axe in his left. Oftentimes he is shown standing near a bull or a lionlike dragon. His cult was widely spread throughout Asia Minor, Mesopotamia, Syria, and Palestine. Adad's sacred number is either six or sixty, sources vary; his sacred animal is the bull and his symbol is the lightning bolt. He is similar to the demon Rimmon.

Sources: Black, *Gods, Demons, and Symbols of Ancient Mesopotamia*, 76, 118, 75; Von Nettesheim, *Three Books of Occult Philosophy*, 514; Van de Toorn, *Dictionary of Demons in the Bible*, 909; Zenos, *Popular and Critical Bible Encyclopædia and Scriptural Dictionary*, 43.

Adar

Variations: ADRAMELECH

Adar ("Wing") is a demon from Chaldean lore born the son of the god, Bēl. It is also the name of the first month in the Chaldean calendar and is known as the 'dark month.'

Sources: Harper, *Biblical World*, Vol. 3, 109, 111; Hyatt, *Book of Demons*, 73; Lenormant, *Chaldean Magic*, 46, 118.

Addanc

Variations: Abac, Abhac, Adanc, Addane, Afanc ("beaver"), Avanc

British, Celtic, and Welsh mythology all tell of aqueous demons called addanc. Said to look like a beaver-, crocodile-, or dwarflike demon, it preys upon those who enter into the lake it lives in. Folklore tells us that it once lived in Llyn Barfog and/or in Llyn Llion Lake near Brynberian Bridge or in Llyn yr Afanc Lake. It can be lured out of the water by a maiden, and when this happens, the addanc is powerless. There are various stories regarding the addanc's destruction. Some tell how Hu Gadarn used oxen to drag it out of the water and slay it; other tales say it was lured out of the water where it fell asleep on her lap, was bound up in chains, and then either dragged off to Lake Cwm Ffynnon or slain by Peredur.

According to *Llyfr Coch Hergest* (*Red Book of Hergest*), written between 1382 and 1410, and *Llyfr Gwyn Rhydderch* (*White Book of Rhydderch*), written in 1350, the trashing of the addanc had once caused massive flooding, which drowned all the original inhabitants of Britain except for Dwyfan and Dwyfach, who went on to found a new race of Britons.

Sources: Gettings, *Dictionary of Demons*, 21; Lewis, *Gomer's Dictionary for Young People*, 141; McCoy, *Celtic Myth and Magick*, 252.

Addu

Variations: ADAD, Adapa, Marduk, Ramman

Addu is a storm demon in Babylonian demonology (see ADAD). It is possible that Addu was only an aspect ADAD and not an independent entity. Addu could have been an earlier forerunner of the god, Marduk, and was merged with him in later times.

Sources: Hastings, *Encyclopædia of Religion and Ethics*, 64; Mackenzie, *Myths of Babylonia and Assyria*, 143; Turner, *Dictionary of Ancient Deities*, 15.

Adi

According to Enochian lore, Adi is a CACO-DAEMON. His angelic counterpart is unknown (ENOCHIAN CACODAEMONS).

Sources: Chopra, *Academic Dictionary of Mythology*, 8; Laycock, *Complete Enochian Dictionary*, 73.

Adimiron

Variations: The Bloody

Adimiron is one of the twelve princes of the Qliphoth and is under the service of Uriens (see QLIPPOTHIC ORDERS OF DEMONS). He and the demons of his order look like a lion-lizard hybrid and swarms across the desolate places of the void leaving a "'rich brown juice' of annihilation in [his] wake." He lives in the tunnel of Uriens.

Sources: Ashe, *Qabalah*, 559; Guiley, *Encyclopedia of Magic and Alchemy*, 267; Mathers, *Sorcerer and His Apprentice*, 26.

Adirael

Variations: Adirion, Sannul

The *Book of Enoch* names Adirael ("Magnificence of God") as one of the FALLEN ANGELS who swore allegiance to SAMIAZA and rebelled against God. He lusted after and took a human wife against God's will, and went on to father the NEPHILIM. Other sources say that Adirael, a tall and powerful cherub, is one of the ANGELS OF PUNISHMENT, an Angel of Judgment who has dominion over Judgment Day, and one of the forty-nine SERVITORS OF BEELZEBUB (see BEELZEBUB).

Sources: Belanger, *Dictionary of Demons*, 18; Davidson, *Dictionary of Angels*, 7; Mathers, *Magia Della Cabala*, 136.

Adityas

Variations: The Twelve Sovereign Principles

Born the son of Kashyapa and Aditi, the mother of all gods, Adityas ("Progeny of Aditi") is one of a cadre of sun gods. Originally there were only seven of them, but later their ranks were expanded to twelve to correspond to the months of the year. Adityas falls under the domain of the Devas, a generic Hindu term for divine beings. He is represented as the spokes in the Wheel of Time and is symbolic for the laws that rule the human society and the universe.

Dwelling in the sky, these sovereign principles move about in pairs of even numbers and protect against diseases.

Sources: Kaegi, *Rigveda*, 58–61; Müller, *Rig-Veda-Sanhita*, 240–2; Wheeler, *History of India from the Earliest Ages*, 24.

Adjuchas

Apollonius of Tyana's *Nuctemeron* (*Night Illuminated by Day*) lists Adjuchas as a demon or DJINN. He has power over rocks and is one of the seven demons of the eleventh hour.

Sources: Davidson, *Dictionary of Angels*, 7; Gettings, *Dictionary of Demons*, 23; Lévi, *Transcendental Magic*, 422.

Adnachiel

Variations: Adernahael, Adnakhiel, Advachiel ("happiness of God")

Enochian lore and medieval demonology has Adnachiel as the demon of the constellation Sagittarius. He is most powerful during the month of November.

Sources: Camfield, *Theological Discourse of Angels*; Davidson, *Dictionary of Angels*, 7; Gettings, *Dictionary of Demons*, 23; Heywood, *Hierarchy of Angels*.

Adon

Adon ("lord" or "mighty") is one of the one hundred and eleven SERVITORS OF AMAYMON, ARITON, ORIENS, AND PAYMON (see AMAYMON, ARITON, ORIENS, and PAYMON) in Mather's translation of the *Sacred Magic of Abramelin the Mage*.

Sources: Belanger, *Dictionary of Demons*, 18; Mathers, *Book of the Sacred Magic of Abramelin the Mage*, 118; Von Worms, *Book of Abramelin*, 255.

Adonides

A duke or steward in service to MEPHISTOPHELES, Adonides ("garden" or "plant") is considered to be a lesser demon in the hierarchy of Hell. On occasion he is listed as being the husband of Venus, the goddess of adultery.

Sources: de Voragine, *Golden Legend*, 100; Melton, *Encyclopedia of Occultism and Parapsychology*, 315; Smedley, *Occult Sciences*, 176; Spence, *Encyclopedia of Occultism*, 153.

Adonis

Adonis is a devil from the demonology of the ancient Middle East.

Sources: Bienkowski, *Dictionary of the Ancient Near East*, 4; Conway, *Demonology and Devil-Lore*, Vol. 1, 79.

Adramaleck

Variations: Adramalek, Adramelec

Originally Adramaleck was a Samarian deity

and in Assyria where he was worshipped, children were sacrificed to him by being burned alive upon his altars. Considered to be an ARCHDEMON or devil, he is now said to be in the service of ASMODEUS. When summoned, he appears as a mule or peacock. Adramaleck holds many titles and positions in the hierarchy of Hell, such as Chancellor of Infernal Regions, Chancellor of the Grand Cross ORDER OF THE FLY, Commander of Hell, King of Fire, President of the Council, Prince of Fire, and the Superintendent of the Wardrobe.

Sources: Anthropological Society of Bombay, *Journal of the Anthropological Society of Bombay*, Vol. 15, 91; Chambers, *Book of Days*, 722; Guiley, *Encyclopedia of Demons and Demonology*, 3; Waite, *Literary World*, 170.

Adramelech

Variations: Adar-malik, Adramalek, Adrameleck, Adramelek, Adrammelech ("magnificence of the King"), the King of Fire

In Syria, Adramelech ("Wing King") was a Samarian sun god worshipped by the Sepharvites. Children were sacrificed to him. Later his name was demonized in Judeo-Christian tradition. He was placed in service under SAMMAEL, the angel of poison, and given a plethora of rank and titles such as Chancellor of Hell, Chancellor of the High Council, Evil Chief of Hod, Grand Chancellor of Hell, Grand Chancellor of the Infernal Empire, Minister of Beelzebub's Order of the Fly, President of the High Council, President of the Senate of the Demons, Superintendent of DEVIL's Wardrobe, Supervisor of SATAN's Wardrobe, and one of those who presides over the Devil's general council.

Adramelech is now described as being one of the FALLEN ANGELS, formerly of the Order of Archangels; so technically, he is an ARCHDEMON who has dominion over the hierarchy known as SAMAEL. He is also one of the ten evil sephiroths as well as the patron demon of hypocrisy. In art he is shown as having a human head and torso, but the body of a mule or sometimes of a peacock.

His personal adversaries are the angels Uriel and Raphael ("healing one of God"), not to be confused with the demon URIEL. Adramelech is the evil counterpart to one of the divine SEPHIROTHS, Hod. He has many similarities to the demon ADRAMALECK.

Sources: Ashley, *Complete Book of Devils and Demons*, 57; Chambers, *Book of Days*, 722; Chamchian, *History of Armenia*, 34; Collin de Plancy, *Dictionary of Witchcraft*, 15; Hyatt, *Book of Demons*, 50, 73; Patrich, *Sabaite Heritage in the Orthodox Church*, 166.

Adrastaeia

Adrastaeia is an AERIAL DEVIL who has the ability to fashion for himself a solid body out of the air. He flies through the air but keeps close to humans. Easily summoned by sorcerers, Adrastaeia is susceptible to the same passions that drive mankind. In addition to being able to take nearly any form he chooses, Adrastaeia causes natural disasters.

Source: Bhattacharji, *Fatalism in Ancient India*, 5.

Adriel

Variations: Hadraniel

According to both Enochian and Jewish lore, Adriel ("Flock of God") is one of the Angels of Death, along with Azrael ("help of God"), Bebriel, and Hemeh. He is also one of the twenty-eight demonic rulers of the lunar mansions; he has dominion over Alchil ("Crown of Scorpio"). Adriel is also said to assist sailors and strengthen buildings (see ENOCHIAN RULERS OF THE LUNAR MANSIONS).

Sources: Minchero, *Voice from the Jordan*, 66; Moura, *Mansions of the Moon for the Green Witch*, 44; Von Goethe, *Goethe's Letters to Zelter*, 378; Webster, *Encyclopedia of Angels*, 5, 124.

Adro

In the demonology of the Lugbara people who live along the West Nile River in Uganda, Adro is an evil earth spirit who starts grass fires and causes sickness in adolescent girls. He swims throughout the rivers of the world.

Sources: Beattie, *Spirit Mediumship and Society in Africa*, 225, 265; Ellwood, *Words of the World's Religions*, 52.

Aeglun

In Apollonius of Tyana's *Nuctemeron* (*Night Illuminated by Day*), Aeglun is said to be the demon or DJINN of lightning. He is one of the seven demons of the eleventh hour.

Sources: Davidson, *Dictionary of Angels*, 7; Gettings, *Dictionary of Demons*, 23; Lévi, *Transcendental Magic*, 422.

Aeriae Potestates

The aeriae potestates ("Aerial Powers") are from Enochian lore and of the sixth order of demons that fall under the dominion of MERIZIM. Considered to be a type of AERIAL DEVIL, they have under their command the four Angels of the Apocalypse. Aeriae potestates have the ability to cause storms at sea, and the thunder and lightning they create causes pestilence. They are furious by nature and constantly raging in the air.

Sources: Coleman, *Dictionary of Mythology*, 26; Gettings, *Dictionary of Demons*, 23; McLean, *Treatise on Angel Magic*, 70.

Aerial Devil

Variations: Sylphs

The Medieval theologian Friar Francesco Maria Guazzo described in his *Compendium Maleficarum* (1628) the nature of aerial devils. He defined them as being invisible servitors, spirits under the command of the Devil. In constant communication with Hell, they swarm invisibly through the spirit world and have been known to conspire with evil men. The enemy of all mankind, they use their powers to create natural disasters, shipwrecks, and violent storms. They also have the ability to create solid bodies for themselves from the very air, which they will use to grab up a victim and shake violently, all the while yelling out his sins, both real and imagined, for all to hear.

Immortal, invisible shape-shifters, they inspire man to question his faith, commit foolish actions, and create slander. Aerial devils are, however, susceptible to the passions of mankind and are easily invoked by sorcerers because even though they live in the spirit realm, they stay in the air around humans as much as they possibly can. This species of demon takes a special delight with the obscenities of the theater and the wild hyperbole of poets.

Sources: Conway, *Demonology and Devil-Lore*, Vol. 2, 210–11; Godwin, *Lives of the Necromancers*, 36–38; Guazzo, *Compendium Maleficarum*, 73; Kipfer, *Order of Things*, 255; Von Franz, *Alchemy*, 226.

Aeshma

Variations: Aesma, "fiend of the wounding spear"

There are records of Persian lore dating back 3,000 years that mention the demon of fury and wrath, Aeshma. Described as being a small and hairy demon, he excels at making men perform acts of cruelty and destruction. Said to be one of the seven archangels of the Persians, Aeshma's personal adversary is the angel of Obedience, Sraosha ("Lightning").

Sources: Hyatt, *Book of Demons*, 40; Jackson, *Zoroastrian Studies*, 89–90; Van der Toorn, *Dictionary of Deities and Demons*, 106.

Aesma Daeva

Variations: Aesma, AESHMA, Ashmadai, ASMODEUS, Æshma-deva

In Persian demonology Aesma Daeva ("covetous demon," "fury," "madness") is the king of demons. A species of DAEVAS, he is the personification of the only thing he loves: conflict, violence, and war. The demon of anger, fury, lust, revenge, and wrath, it is not uncommon for him to vent his aggression on herds of cattle. With the demon ASTO VIDATU, they chase the souls of the newly departed as they try to rise up to Heaven. Aesma Daeva's personal adversary is the angel of Obedience, Sraosha ("Lightning"). (See also ASMODEUS ZAVEHE.)

Sources: Barton, *Oxford Bible Commentary*, 629; Davies, *Cambridge History of Judaism*, 318; Icon, *Demons*, 136; Jackson, *Zoroastrian Studies*, 75.

Af

Created by God to execute His will, Af ("anger") is one of the ARCHANGELS OF PUNISHMENT and one of the three angels of Hell, Ema and MASHITH being the other two. He is under the direct command of the six Angels of Death over men, but has no dominion over children, young people, and kings. A demon of anger, he is described as being five hundred parasangs in height (1,789.5 miles) and that his body was forged out of chains made with black and red fire. Af resides in the seventh heaven and hates Moses because he did not observe the ritual of circumcision.

Sources: Ashley, *Complete Book of Devils and Demons*, 78; Davidson, *Dictionary of Angels*, 351; Singer, *Jewish Encyclopedia*, 593.

Afarorp

According to Christian demonology and the *Sacred Magic of Abramelin the Mage*, Afarorp ("breaking and rending") is one of the one hundred eleven SERVITORS OF AMAYMON, ARITON, ORIENS, AND PAYMON (see AMAYMON, ARITON, ORIENS, and PAYMON).

Sources: Belanger, *Dictionary of Demons*, 19; Mathers, *Book of Sacred Magic of Abramelin the Mage*, 114; Von Worms, *Book of Abramelin*, 256.

Afrasiab

Variations: Afra-Sia-Ab ("past the black river"), Afrosiyob, Alp Er Tonga ("Courageous Tiger Man"), Efrasiyab

Afrasiab is the name of a Scythian, demonic archfiend that looks like a snake (see AHRIMAN). It is also the name of an ancient city, several historical hero-kings, and a tribe of ancient people.

Sources: Bonnefoy, *Asian Mythologies*, 324, 337; Carus, *History of the Devil and the Idea of Evil*, 53; Johnson, *Dictator and the Devil*, 304.

Afray

Afray ("dust") is one of the fifty-three SERVITORS OF ASHTAROTH AND ASMODEUS (see ASHTAROTH and ASMODEUS).

Sources: Belanger, *Dictionary of Demons*, 19; Mathers, *Book of the Sacred Magic of Abramelin the Mage*, 116; Von Worms, *Book of Abramelin*, 248.

African Devils

Generally benign creatures, the devils of Africa are considered to be more of a nuisance than a threat. In their natural and true form they have one arm, one ear, one eye, and one leg, but they use their shape-shifting abilities to look human and are very fast runners. In this guise the devils live in villages blending in, assuming a name and a life, and even performing everyday tasks such as farming and hunting.

Sources: Conway, *Demonology and Devil-Lore*, 98, 217, 330; Nassau, *Fetishism in West Africa*, 41, 48, 100, 121; Summers, *History of Witchcraft and Demonology*, 163.

Afsus

Afsus is the demon of ungratefulness from Persian demonology. His name translates to mean "Alas!"

Sources: Hillmann, *Unity in the Ghazals of Hafez*, 59; Lambton, *Persian Grammar*, 355.

Agab

Variations: Zagal

According to the *Sacred Magic of Abramelin the Mage*, Agab ("beloved") is one of the eight SERVITORS OF ORIENS (see ORIENS).

Sources: Mathers, *Secret Magic of Abramelin the Mage*, 108; Susej, *Demonic Bible*, 259; Von Worms, *Book of Abramelin*, 257.

Agafali

Agafali ("age" or "reverence") is one of the fifteen SERVITORS OF PAYMON (see PAYMON).

Sources: Ford, *Bible of the Adversary*, 94; Mathers, *Secret Magic of Abramelin the Mage*, 108; Susej, *Demonic Bible*, 259; Von Worms, *Book of Abramelin*, 257.

Agaliarept

Variations: Agalierap, Agalierept

The eighteenth century book alleged to be written by Pope Honorius III, *Grimoire of Pope Honorius* (*Le Grimoire du Pape Honorius*), says that Agaliarept is the demon of anger, hate, vengeance, and war. He is the commander of the Secret Police of Hell and a grand general in the infernal army, commander of the 2nd Legion. Under his personal command are also four servitors. With the Tarihimal he shares commands of the servitor ELELOGAP (see SERVITORS OF AGALIAREPT). Sources conflict as to whose command he is under. Some claim that he is one of the two SERVITORS OF LUCIFER (SANTANACKIA being the other), while others say he is under

SAMMAEL. Agaliarept looks like a mature man with a thick handlebar moustache. He is summoned because of his ability to cause dissension in the enemy army by creating distrust among the men. Agaliarept can also discover the secrets of all the courts and council chambers of the world and from any time period; he holds sway over Europe and Asia Minor. His sign is that of two heads.

Sources: Baskin, *Sorcerer's Handbook*, 12; Diagram Group, *Dictionary of Unfamiliar Words*, 299; Mark, *Book of Hierarchies*, 28; Masters, *Devil's Dominion*, 131; Summers, *Witchcraft and Black Magic*, 135; Waite, *Book of Ceremonial Magic*, 187.

Agapiel

Agapiel is, according to *Theurgia Goetia*, the second book of the *Lemegeton*, the *Lesser Key of Solomon*, one of the fifteen SERVITORS OF ICOSIEL (see ICOSIEL). He has under his personal command 2,200 servitors and may be summoned any time of the day or night. Agapiel rules over the planet Mars.

Sources: Guiley, *Encyclopedia of Demons and Demonology*, 119; Peterson, *Lesser Key of Solomon*, 99; Trithemius, *Steganographia*, 69.

Agares

Variations: Agaros, Agreas, AGUARES, King of the East, TAMIEL ("perfection of God")

Agares is a grand duke of the eastern region of Hell and the prime minister of LUCIFER (see DUKES OF HELL and PRIME MINISTERS OF HELL). He is also responsible for distributing titles and prelacies. Sources vary as to whose service he falls directly under: LUCIFUGE ROFOCALE or MEPHISTOPHELES. Agares is also listed as being one of the seventy-two SPIRITS OF SOLOMON. One of the FALLEN ANGELS, formerly of the Order of Virtues, he swore allegiance to SAMIAZA and rebelled against God because he lusted after and took a human wife as his mate, fathering the NEPHILIM. He is the demon of courage and has thirty-one legions of servitors under his command, sharing an additional eighty-seven demons with SAMMAEL.

Agares is easily summoned but it is best to call him up during the month of March at the eleventh hour of the night when his power is at its peak. When he appears, Agares looks like a caring and kindly lord mounted upon a crocodile with a hawk perched upon his fist. He has a wide array of powers at his disposal such as causing earthquakes, destroying spiritual and temporal dignities, doling out power, granting titles, making terrestrial spirits dance, placing newfound courage in those who would flee before greater

21

Aggareth

numbers, scattering the enemy army, teaching languages, and other varied abilities.

Agares is mentioned in Christian demonology of Johann Wierus's *Pseudomonarchia Daemonum* (*False Monarchy of Demons*, 1583).

Sources: Baskin, *Sorcerer's Handbook*, 276; De Laurence, *Lesser Key of Solomon, Goetia*, 22; Laurence, *Foreign Quarterly Review*, Vol. 24, 370; Maberry, *Cryptopedia*, 42; Scott, *London Magazine*, Vol. 5, 378; Waite, *Unknown World 1894–1895*, 230; Wedeck, *Treasury of Witchcraft*, 96.

Agas

Agas is a female demon of illness from Persian demonology. Her name means "evil eye."

Sources: Littleton, *Gods, Goddesses, and Mythology*, Vol. 1, 402; Rose, *Spirits, Fairies, Gnomes, and Goblins*, 5, 350, 355.

Agathion

An agathion is a type of FAMILIAR demonic spirit and can appear as either an animal or a man. Once bound as a familiar, it lives inside a ring or talisman. Agathion are most powerful at mid-day.

Sources: Buckland, *Weiser Field Guide to Ghosts*, 136; Icon, *Familiarities*, 243; Spence, *Encyclopedia of Occultisim*, 6.

Agathodemon, plural: Agathodemons

Variations: Agathodaemon, Agathodaimon, Agathos Daimon

The mythology of the Agathodemon began back in Egypt; however, it is a Greek word. Its name translates to mean "the good god" or "good divinity." It was believed that every person was born with two personal, invisible guardians, the Agathodemons and the CACODAEMON. Agathodemons were said to be their good-natured protectors and CACODAEMON were their evil counterparts. Each demon encouraged its own impulses. Agathodemons are most often depicted as a snake with a human head, but on occasion they have been shown as a young man holding a basket full of ears of corn.

Agathodemons are most powerful on the first day after a new moon, a time when they are to be remembered for the duty they perform. They are given tribute daily and it is shown by the consumption of a glass of wine after a meal has been eaten. Agathodemons are the symbolic reminder to live a moral life and to always seek to improve oneself. The only time one of them would ever attack a person is if they were attempting to destroy a vineyard that was under their protection (see also ENOCHIAN CACODAEMONS).

Sources: De Claremont, *Ancient's Book of Magic*, 106; Osburn, *Monumental History of Egypt*, 289–91; Vaughan, *British Quarterly Review*, Vol. 7, 236.

Agb

According to Enochian lore, Agb is a CACODAEMON. His counterpart is the angel Gbal (ENOCHIAN CACODAEMONS).

Sources: Chopra, *Academic Dictionary of Mythology*, 12; Laycock, *Complete Enochian Dictionary*, 74.

Agchonion

Variations: Agchoniôn

In the *Testament of Solomon*, Agchonion is a demon that preys on infants (see SPIRITS OF SOLOMON). He lies in their bedding, waiting for an opportunity to strike. Agchonion is susceptible to banishment by the use of a cone spell using the word *lycurgos*, written out on a fig leaf.

Lycurgos
ycurgos
curgos
urgos
gos
os

Sources: Ashe, *Qabalah*, 51, 236; Belanger, *Dictionary of Demons*, 19; Bohak, *Ancient Jewish Magic*, 236–7; Conybeare, *Jewish Quarterly Review*, Vol. 11, 38.

Age of Demons, The

Hesiod (700 B.C.E.), a Greek oral poet whose writings serve as a major source on Greek mythology, calculated that demons live ten times longer than the phoenix, which in turn lives ten times longer than a human.

Plutarch (46–120 A.D.), a Roman citizen and Greek historian, biographer, and essayist, determined by his studies that demons are susceptible to disease, and therefore he estimated that the maximum age a demon could live to reach would be no more than 9,720 years.

Sources: Basin, *Dictionary of Satanism*, 18; Brenk, *Relighting the Souls*, 170–4; Jones, *Platonism of Plutarch*, 37–40.

Agei

Agei, whose name means "meditation" in Hebrew, is one of the fifty-three SERVITORS OF ASHTAROTH AND ASMODEUS (see ASHTAROTH and ASMODEUS).

Sources: Belanger, *Dictionary of Demons*, 20; Mathers, *Book of Sacred Magic of Abramelin the Mage*, 115; Von Worms, *Book of Abramelin*, 247.

Aggareth

Aggareth is one of the concubines that serve under the command of SATAN.

Sources: Carus, *Open Court*, Vol. 44, 517; Rudwin, *Devil in Legend and Literature*, 28, 98.

Aggelos Abussos

Variations: 'ABADDOWN, Apolluon

Aggelos abussos is Greek for "Angel of the Abyss," a title that is shared by APOLHUN and LUCIFER.

Sources: Oxford University Press, *Catholic Comparative New Testament*, 1683; Presutta, *Biblical Cosmos versus Modern Cosmology*, 167; Reiling, *Translator's Handbook on the Gospel of Luke*, 347.

Aggelos Hamartano

Aggelos hamartano is Greek for "angel of sin" or "bad angel." It is used in reference to a FALLEN ANGEL.

Source: Reiling, *Translator's Handbook on the Gospel of Luke*, 550, 778.

Aggelos Oxus Drepanon

Aggelos oxus drepanon is Greek for "angel with sharp sickle." It is used to refer to the Angel of Death, a title shared by ADRIEL, ASHMODAI, SAMAEL, and SARIEL.

Sources: Davidson, *Dictionary of Angels*, 26; Illes, *Encyclopedia of Spirits*, 218; Schwartz, *Tree of Souls*, 139.

Aggelos Phos

Aggelos phos is Greek for "angel of light." It may be a reference to LUCIFER.

Source: Reiling, *Translator's Handbook on the Gospel of Luke*, 707.

Aggelos Satanas

Aggelos satanas is Greek for "angel of the accuser." It may be a reference to the FALLEN ANGEL, MASTEMA, the Accusing Angel who tried to kill Moses in Exodus 4:24.

Sources: Price, *Pre–Nicene New Testament*, 375; Reiling, *Translator's Handbook on the Gospel of Luke*, 680–1.

Aggereth

Born the daughter of the Qliphothic witch MACHALOTH, Aggereth has snakes for hair and is depicted as being seated in a chariot that is being pulled by an ass and an ox. She, like her mother before her, is a demonic witch.

Sources: Crowley, *777 and Other Qabalistic Writings of Aleister Crowley*, 140; Ford, *First Book of Luciferian Tarot*, 174; Wise, *Origin of Christianity*, 95.

Aggrapart

Variations: Herod Agrippa

Aggrapart was a name that was used in the Middle Ages to refer to LUCIFER. It was a variation of the historical Jewish King Herod Agrippa, who in 7 B.C.E. most famously had his own son executed to appease the Roman Emperor Augustus.

Sources: Ewert, *French Studies*, Vols. 7–8, 133; Russell, *Lucifer, the Devil in the Middle Ages*, 249.

Agibol

Variations: Agibal

Agibol ("forcible love") is from Christian demonology and is mentioned in the *Sacred Magic of Abramelin the Mage*. He is one of the ten SERVITORS OF AMAIMON AND ARITON (see AMAIMON and ARITON).

Sources: Belanger, *Dictionary of Demons*, 20; Mathers, *Book of the Sacred Magic of Abramelin the Mage*, 106; Susej, *Demonic Bible*, 257.

Agiel

Agiel is a demonic spirit and a soldier in SATAN's army. His presence can be detected by signs of extreme violence on the battlefield. Agiel has the ability to invoke spirits that live in the firmament of the earth. He does not necessarily have dominion over fellow demons Asmodaï, Elubeb, and Haniel as he does the planet Saturn, but he has long been associated with them. It has been alleged that Agiel's name was engraved on a talisman that belonged to and was worn by Catherine de Medicis, Queen of France (April 13, 1519–January 5, 1589).

Sources: Guiley, *Encyclopedia of Magic and Alchemy*, 255; Jobes, *Outer Space*, 83; Regardie, *Tree of Life*, 89.

Agilas

From Christian demonology and as mentioned in the book *Sacred Magic of Abramelin the Mage*, Agilas ("sullen") is one of the sixty-five SERVITORS OF KORE AND MAGOTH.

Sources: Mathers, *Book of the Sacred Magic of Abramelin the Mage*, 107, 119.

Aglafos

Aglafos ("bright light") is one of the fifteen SERVITORS OF PAYMON (see PAYMON).

Sources: Belanger, *Dictionary of Demons*, 20; Mathers, *Sacred Magic of Abramelin*, 108; Von Worms, *Book of Abramelin*, 257.

Aglas

Aglas, a duke, is a nocturnal demon and one of the sixteen SERVITORS OF GEDEIL (DUKES OF HELL and GEDEIL).

Sources: Guiley, *Dictionary of Demons and Demonology*, 94; Peterson, *Lesser key of Solomon*, 72.

Aglasis

Aglasis is a demi-demon in service under NEBIROS. He has the ability to teleport anyone or anything from one location on the planet to another.

Sources: Kuriakos, *Grimoire Verum Ritual Book*, 12; Von Worms, *Book of Abramelin*, 260; Waite, *Book of Black Magic*, 288.

Agnan

According to Reginald Scott's *The Discovery of Witchcraft* (1584), Agnan is a devil who lives in America and breeds swine.

Sources: Boguet, *Examen of Witches*, 19; Gettings, *Dictionary of Demons*, 25; Grafton, *New Worlds, Ancient Text*, 92.

Agniel

Agniel is named in the *Book of Enoch* as one of the FALLEN ANGELS who swore an oath of allegiance to SAMIAZA, rebelled against God, took a human wife, and fathered the NEPHILIM. He also went on to teach mankind the "enchantments of roots," as well as how to use conjurations.

Sources: Davidson, *Dictionary of Angels*, 11; Kelly, *Who in Hell*, 8.

Agra

In the *Lemegeton, the Lesser Key of Solomon*, Agra, a nocturnal demon, is listed as one of the sixteen Duke SERVITORS OF GEDEIL (see DUKES OF HELL and GEDEIL).

Sources: Belanger, *Dictionary of Demons*, 20; Peterson, *Lesser Key of Solomon*, 72.

Agrat-Bat-Mahlaht

Variations: Angel of Prostitutes, Iggereth Bath Mahalath

The ARCH SHE-DEMON and SUCCUBUS Agrat-Bat-Mahlaht's origin lies in Jewish mysticism, and her name translates from Hebrew to mean "Spirit Daughter of Uncleanness." Named as one of the four DEMONS OF PROSTITUTION, she is also listed as one of the four wives of SAMMAEL (SATAN). Agrat-Bat-Mahlaht commands 180,000 demons of her own and is said to drive a chariot around the world on Wednesdays and Fridays. According to Talmudic lore, demons are mortal; however, it is said that Agrat-Bat-Mahlaht and LILITH will "continue to exist and plague man until the Messianic day, when God will finally extirpate uncleanliness and evil from the face of earth."

Sources: Davidson, *Dictionary of Angels*, 149; Godwin, *Godwin's Cabalistic Encyclopedia*, 11; Sperling, *The Zohar*, Vol. 5, 155.

Agrax

Agrax ("bone") is listed as one of the fifty-three SERVITORS OF ASHTAROTH AND ASMODEUS (see ASHTAROTH and ASMODEUS).

Sources: Belanger, *Dictionary of Demons*, 20; Mathers, *Book of Sacred Writings of Abramelin*, 116; Von Worms, *Book of Abramelin*, 248.

Agrimas

In Judaic lore and described in Midrashic literature, it is said that after the expulsion from the Garden of Eden, Adam and Eve separated from each other for a while. During this period, Piznia, a daughter of LILITH, met Adam and together they had many children, giving birth to a specific type of demonic half-breed known as Cambion Lutins. The first born child of their union was a son named Agrimas. Ninety-two thousand other children are said to have followed.

Using his status as a son of Adam, Agrimas sought out Methuselah the Righteous, who slew ninety thousand of his descendants in a single sword stroke. In exchange for peace, Agrimas gave Methuselah the names of his remaining descendants and the symbols of protection against them. The remaining LUTINS then sought refuge on the furthest mountains and in the deepest places in the sea.

Sources: Ginzberg, *Legends of the Jews*, 141; Hammer, *Jewish Book of Days*, 42; Scholem, *Kabbalah*, 357.

Aguares

Variations: AGARES

Aguares ("male") is the duke of the Eastern region of Hell, where he commands thirty-one legions of devils. He is described as riding a crocodile and carrying a sparrow hawk on his arm. Aguares is summoned for his ability to cause the enemy to flee and makes deserters return to their posts. He can also teach any language and causes earthquakes.

Sources: Ashley, *Complete Books of Demons*, 57; Bias, *Freedom from the World of Satanism and the Power of Satan*, 41; Ford, *Bible of the Adversary*, 79.

Ahazu

Variations: Ahazie, Seizer Demon of the Night

Named in ancient medical texts, Ahazu ("the Seizer") is a nocturnal lesser demon who causes diseases in humans, specifically those that cause seizures. It is said that a person will suffer from such an attack whenever this demon touches them.

Sources: De Claremont, *Ancient's Book of Magic*, 1060; Gettings, *Dictionary of Demons*, 27; Spence, *Encyclopedia of Occultism and Parapsychology*, 1016.

Aherom

Aherom ("separation") is listed as one of the one hundred eleven SERVITORS OF AMAYMON, ARITON, ORIENS, AND PAYMON (see AMAYMON, ARITON, ORIENS, and PAYMON).

Sources: Belanger, *Dictionary of Demons*, 22; Susej, *Demonic Bible*, 256.

Ahharu

An ahharu is a species of vampiric demon from Assyrian lore. Their nature is to be cunning and arrogant.

Sources: Baskin, *Dictionary of Satanism*, 20; Carus, *History of the Devil and the Idea of Evil*, 44.

Ahi

Variations: Demon of Drought, the Serpent of Ignorance, Verethra, VRITRA

Ahi is a demonic dragon god from Hindu mythology who brings about drought, egotism, and ignorance. He has the ability to control and alter the weather; typically this power is used to prevent rainfall. Ahi is described as looking like a snake, a spiderlike being, and a man with a snake rising from each shoulder. He has dominion over the sun.

Sources: Dange, *Bhāgavata Purāṇa*, 34; Perry, *Journal of the American Oriental Society*, Vol. 11, 199; MacDonnell, *Vedic Mythology*, 152, 158.

Ahlmakoh

From the demonology of the people of the Vancouver Islands comes the demonic terrestrial wood-spirit named Ahlmakoh. During a ritual ceremony his nasal mucus is collected in order to make amulets of invulnerability. He is described as being male.

Sources: Hastings, *Encyclopedia of Religion and Ethics*, 591, 592; Sapir, *Ethnology*, Vol. 4, 512, 514.

Ahpuch

Variations: Ah Puk, Ahpuk, Ahpuuc, Cizin, God-A, Hunahau, HUNHAU, Kimil, Kisin, Yum-Cimih, Yum-Cimil (Lord of Death), Yum-Kimil

Ahpuch is a demonic god from Mayan mythology. The demon of death, he is also the ruler of Mictlan, the lowest and the worst of the nine Hells. He is described as looking like a skeleton, seated upon a throne, holding a sacrificial knife. Dogs and owls are his sacred animals.

Sources: Evans, *Mayaad*, 91; Turner, *Dictionary of Ancient Deities*, 28; Van Scott, *Encyclopedia of Hell*, 68.

Ahriman

Variations: The Adversary, Afrasiâb, AHRIMANES, ANGRA MAINYU ("Destructive One"), ARIMANIUS, Farrusarrabba, Prince of Darkness, Prince of Lies

According to Zoroastrianism, Ahriman is the creator and leader of the DAEVAS as well as the 9,999 diseases he uses to plague the earth. He is described as looking like a soot-covered toad and is the eternal archenemy of Ahura Mazda, the "Wise Lord." Ahriman is destined to fail in his attempt to corrupt all things.

In Zoroastrianism all things have free will to choose between good and evil, and because Ahriman chooses to be evil, he is considered to be a demon.

Sources: Brucker, *History of Philosophy*, 44–5; Dhalla, *Zoroastrian Theology*, 157–9, 254–60, 337–8; Gettings, *Dictionary of Demons*, 27; Hyatt, *Book of Demons*, 56; Jackson, *Zoroastrian Studies*, 68–75.

Ahrimanes

In Chaldean and Persian demonology, Ahrimanes, a CACODAEMON (or FALLEN ANGEL, sources conflict), is ranked as the chief of the Cacodaemons and has command over all of the Cacodaemons (or Fallen Angels) who were expelled from Heaven. He and his followers live in Ahriman-abad, the space between Earth and the stars (see also GRIGORI and WATCHERS).

Sources: Heckethorn, *Secret Societies of all Ages and Countries*, 39; Volney, *The Ruins*, 115.

Ailo

Ailo is one of the many names of LILITH.

Sources: Gray, *Mythology of All Races*, 365; Hurwitz, *Lilith: The First Eve*, 39; Langdon, *Semitic Mythology*, 365.

Aim

Variations: Aini, ANIGUEL, Aym, Bast, HABORYM, Nacoriel, RÄUM

Christian demonology from the Middle Ages tells us that the demon of holocausts is Aim. Ranked as a fire duke, grand duke, and president (see DUKES OF HELL), he commands twenty-six legions, six chiefs, and six servitors. Aim is described as looking like a handsome man with three heads: one of a calf (or cat), one of a snake, and one of a man with two stars on his forehead. He carries a torch in his hand and rides upon a viper. Aim hopes to return to the Seventh Throne in 1,200 years.

Aim is summoned for his abilities to set cities on fire with his firebrand, make men witty, and honestly answer any question asked of him. Aim will also teach astrology and the liberal arts. He is most powerful during the month of July. His sacred color is deep blue and his zodiacal sign is Cancer.

Sources: Conway, *Demonology and Devil-Lore*, Vol. 299; De Laurence, *Lesser Key of Solomon*, *Goetia*, 29; Gettings, *Dictionary of Demons*, 27; Hall, *Secret Teachings of All Ages*, 297; Icon, *Demons*, 136; Scot, *Discoverie of Witchcraft*, 224.

Aisha Qandisha

Variations: Aiesheh Ghedishe, Aisha Qadisha, Ghedishe, Jinniya

Most likely, this vampiric and demonic goddess (a Jinniya) originated in the ancient city-state of Carthage. Her name, Aisha Qandisha, translates to "loving to be watered," as in to be covered with semen. Her name has been connected to Qadesha, the sexually free temple women of Canaan who served ASTARTE.

She, like the SUCCUBUS she is associated with, is described as being beautiful, but, along the northern coast of present-day Morocco, she is also said to have the feet of a goat. Then as now, she is found near wells and waterways, dancing wildly, bare-chested, lustfully enchanting anyone who will let her. Soon these unfortunate souls will find themselves her sexual slaves. Men whom she has seduced will be rendered impotent and lose interest in all other women. She has a constant companion, a DJINN named Hammu Qaiyu.

As a goddess, she cannot be destroyed, only driven away by plunging an iron knife as hard as one can deep into the ground before becoming entranced by her beauty. For a man to break the enchantment he must endure ritual sacrifice and enter into a trance where he must see for himself her cloven goat feet. Once he has, he must then stab an iron knife into the ground, breaking her hold over him.

Sources: Crapanzano, *The Hamadsha*; Gregg, *Culture and Identity*, 262; Gulick, *The Middle East*, 181; Westermarck, *Pagan Survivals*, 21–31.

Aitvaras

Variations: Damavikas ("house spirit"), Pukis ("dragon" or a toy kite)

In Lithuania, prior to the introduction of Christianity, Aitvaras was a nature spirit that lived in the sky or in the woods. It was said of it then that when it flew through the night sky, it looked like a meteorite. It was once considered to be a noble and divine being that regulated human wealth and relations. However, under the influence of Christianity, it was demonized and used as an antagonist in parables regarding ambition and greed. The Aitvaras became a type of demonic creature under the command of the DEVIL himself. It would make a nest for itself behind the stove and once it claimed a place as a home, it was very difficult to remove.

This demonic creature is often made into a FAMILIAR, which is either given to a person by the Devil in exchange for their soul, or it was patiently hatched from a seven-year-old rooster egg. If the Aitvaras is given as a Familiar, it will provide the corn, milk, and money that it stole from other people.

When indoors Aitvaras are described as looking like a black cat or black rooster; when outside they are said to take on the appearance of a fiery snake or flying dragon. They have the ability to heal themselves by touching earth. An infernal, immortal creature, the Aitvaras cannot be destroyed but can be prevented from attack by leaving offerings of food (they are partial to eating omelets).

Sources: DePorte, *Lithuanaia in the Last 30 Years*, 409; Grimal, *Larousse World Mythology*, 421; Icon, *Demons*, 136; Larson, *Myth in Indo-European Antiquity*, 89.

Aja-Mukhi

Variations: Aja-mukhee, Ajamukhee, Ajamukhi

In India, Aja-Mukhi is a DEMONESS. In Sanskrit, Aja means "unborn" and *mukhi* means "beautiful face."

Sources: Benfey, *Sanskrit-English Dictionary*, 710; Dogra, *Thought Provoking Hindu Names*, 18, 61; Gupta, *Indian Mysticism*, 93.

Ajatar

Variations: Ajattara, "The Devil of the Woods"

In Finnish demonology Ajatar is a demonic female dragon said to be the mother of the DEVIL. She breastfeeds serpents and spreads disease and pestilence. If a person sees her, they will instantly fall ill.

Sources: Icon, *Demons: Webster's Quotations*, 136; Rose, *Giants, Monsters, and Dragons*, 10; Turner, *Dictionary of Ancient Deities*, 31.

Aka Manah

Variations: ANGRA MAINYU

In Persian mythology Aka Manah ("evil mind") is a DAEVAS. He is the personification of sensual desire. Second in command to the host of demons, only his father, Angra Mainyu, is of higher rank. In service to AHRIMAN, Aka Manah, the demon of lust and sensual desire, commands a host of demons. His personal adversary is Vohu Manah.

Sources: Breck, *Spirit of Truth*, 62–3; Dhalla, *History of Zoroastrianism*, 91–2; Jackson, *Zoroastrian Studies*, 74, 74, 81.

Akaanga

Akaanga comes from the demonology of people of the Cook Islands. He is said to be the slave of the goddess MIRU. Using fishing nets, he catches the souls of those who have died a natural death and then half drowns those souls in a lake. He then takes them to the court of Miru where they are given kava root *(Piper mythisticum)* to drink before being placed in an oven to be cooked and eaten. Miru lives exclusively on human souls.

Sources: Conway, *Demonology and Devil-Lore*, 42–

3; Craig, *Dictionary of Polynesian Mythology*, 171; Gill, *Myths and Songs from the South Pacific*, 161–2, 175.

Akakasoh

In Burmese demonology, an akakasoh is a species of tree NAT that is known to attack anyone who hurts the tree it lives in by throwing stones at the offender. Living in the highest branches of a tree, it will also assault anyone who insults or injures it. Akakasoh can move faster than a man can run, but to prevent an attack from this type of demon, it is recommended to construct and maintain a small house for it to live in near the base of the tree.

Sources: Folkard, *Plant Lore, Legends, and Lyrics*, 80; Porteous, *Forest Folklore*, 125; Rose, *Spirits, Fairies, Gnomes, and Goblins*, 8; Scott, *The Burman*, 286.

Akanef

The *Sacred Magic of Abramelin the Mage* names Akanef ("a wing") as one of the fifty-three SERVITORS OF ASHTAROTH AND ASMODEUS (see ASHTAROTH and ASMODEUS).

Sources: Belanger, *Dictionary of Demons*, 22; Mathers, *Sacred Magic of Abramelin the Mage*, 106; Von Worms, *Book of Abramelin*, 247.

Akathartos

Akathartos is a word from the Greek language; it means "unclean," as in a person who has been possessed by a demon.

Sources: Meier, *A Marginal Jew*, 428; Turner, *Sacred Art*, 215; Van der Toorn, *Dictionary of Deities and Demons in the Bible*, 882.

Akathaso

In Burmese demonology, Akathaso is the name of a demonic spirit or Nat, which lives in trees.

Sources: De Claremont, *Ancient's Book of Magic*, 107; Icon, *Folklore*, 220; Hardiman, *Gazetteer of Upper Burma and the Shan States*, Vol. 2, Part 1, 136.

Akem Manah

Variations: AKA MANAH, AKOMAN, Akvan ("Evil Mind")

Shah-Nameh (*Book of Kings*), written by the Persian poet Firduasi in 1009, names Akem Manah ("evil intention") as the demon, or DIV, of discord and the physical evils of the world. In service to the DAEVAS, Akem Manah is described as having blue eyes, long hair, and a large head like an elephant with a wide mouth filled with tusks instead of teeth. He also has a long tail and wears a short skirt.

Akem Manah was the demon that asked ninety-nine questions of Zoroaster in an attempt to weaken his faith; not so surprising as this demon is known to cause men to lose the ability to make righteous decisions and to be able to tell what is good or evil. He also causes men to search for gross defects in others while hiding their own. He has unlimited power and incredible strength, but takes great pleasure in causing newborn infants to cry out at birth by showing them horrible images of the destiny of the world.

The personal adversary of Akem Manah is Vohu Manah, second of the Amesha Spentas. For all the evil of this Div, he has very little intelligence and a predictable personality; he always does the opposite of what is asked of him.

Sources: Carus, *Open Court*, Vol. 21, 165; Guthrie, *Hymns of Zoroaster*, 162; Mack, *Field Guide to Demons, Fairies, Fallen Angels, and Other Subversive Spirits*, 83–4; Mills, *Open Court*, Vol. 21, 165.

Akesoli

Akesoli ("pain bringers") is listed as one of the twenty SERVITORS OF AMAYMON (see AMAYMON).

Sources: Forgotten Books, *Book of the Sacred Magic of Abramelin the Mage*, 42–3; Mathers, *Sacred Magic of Abramelin the Mage*, 122.

Akhkhazu

Variations: Dimme-kur

Akhkhazu ("the seizer") originates from Akkadian mythology and was later adopted by the ancient Babylonians. Operating in tandem with LABARTU and LABASSU, this female demon grabs and holds its victims down, causing them to develop at best a fever, but at worst she will cause them to have the plague. She is personified as the demon of jaundice.

Sources: Icons, *Demons*, 136; Jastrow, *Religion of Babylonia and Assyria*, 260; Rogers, *Religion of Babylonia and Assyria*, 147; Sorensen, *Possession and Exorcism in the New Testament and Early Christianity*, 27–8.

Akibeel

Variations: Azibeel

The *Book of Enoch* names Akibeel as a CHIEF OF TENS, one of the FALLEN ANGELS who swore allegiance to SAMIAZA, rebelled against God, took a human as his wife, and fathered the NEPHILIM. He went on to teach mankind the meanings of portents and signs (see also GRIGORI and WATCHERS).

Sources: Barton, *Journal of Biblical Literature*, Vols. 30–31, 162; Gettings, *Dictionary of Demons*, 27; Laurence, *Book of Enoch, the Prophet*, 7; Laurence, *Foreign Quarterly Review*, Vol. 24, 370; Lévi, *History of Magic*, 38.

Akikel

First named in the *Book of Enoch* as one of the FALLEN ANGELS who swore allegiance to SAMIAZA, rebelled against God, took a human as his wife, and fathered the NEPHILIM, Akikel was given the rank of prime minister of Hell during the Middle Ages (see PRIME MINISTERS OF HELL). Most powerful during the tenth hour of the night, he commands six chiefs, six servitors, and eighty-seven additional demons which are also under SAMAEL'S command.

Sources: Baskin, *Dictionary of Satanism*, 22; Lane, *Thousand and One Nights*, 431.

Akium

Akium ("sure") is listed as one of the forty-nine SERVITORS OF BEELZEBUB (see BEELZEBUB).

Sources: Belanger, *Dictionary of Demons*, 22; Ford, *Bible of the Adversary*, 93; Mathers, *Book of the Sacred Magic of Abramelin the Mage*, 107.

Akoman

Variations: AKEM MANAH, Akvan

According to Zoroastrianism demonology, the demon Akoman is second in command under AHRIMAN. His name has Persian roots and translates to mean "the evil mind" or "evil thought." Created from the darkness, Akoman has a noticeable stench about him.

A demon of corruption and destruction, he is sent after only one specific person at a time and will do whatever it takes to corrupt them, sometimes by promoting false religions. Typically he will begin his task of corruption by weakening a man's ability to make righteous decisions, encouraging him to seek out and exploit the character flaws of others. Eventually, under his influence, his victims will lose the ability to tell the difference between good and evil. Akoman is a thoroughly convincing actor, even when he is pretending at being highly spiritual or seductive. He can only be driven off his prey by being fooled into believing that his task of corruption is complete.

Like AKEM MANAH, upon the birth of a child Akoman will appear to it and show it ghastly images of how the world will be reshaped under AHRIMAN's rule, causing the child to cry out with its first breath. Lore tells us that Akoman is riddled with character flaws but has always carefully hidden them.

Sources: Dhalla, *History of Zoroastrianism*, 399–400; Fernández-Armesto, *World of Myths*, 127; Horne, *Sacred Books and Early Literature of the East*, 183; Messadié, *History of the Devil*, 83.

Akop

From the demonology of the Philippines comes the demon Akop. Working in conjunction with the demon IBWA, it preys upon widows and widowers. Akop is described as having a large head and long slim arms and legs, but no torso. Akop attends funerals and attacks unguarded corpses, collecting the body fat that seeps out of a corpse preburial to collect and consume.

Sources: Ashley, *Complete Book of Devils and Demons*, 95; Cole, *Traditions of the Tinguian*, 180.

Akoros

The *Sacred Magic of Abramelin the Mage*, book two, names Akoros as one of the twenty SERVITORS OF AMAYMON (see AMAYMON). His name is Greek and translates to mean "overthrowers of authority."

Sources: Forgotten Books, *Book of the Sacred Magic of Abramelin the Mage*, 42–3; Mathers, *Book of the Sacred Magic of Abra-Melin*, 122.

Akton

First named in the *Testament of Solomon* (see SPIRITS OF SOLOMON), Akton is the demon of backaches and pains in the ribs. To prevent attack from this demon, one must make a talisman from a piece of copper that has been taken off a ship that has lost its anchor. Upon the copper, engrave the phrase "Marmaraôth, Sabaôth, pursue Akton" and wear it about the waist.

Sources: Conybeare, *Jewish Quarterly Review*, Vol. 11, 37; Ashe, *Qabalah*, 49; Belanger, *Dictionary of Demons*, 23.

Ala, plural: ale

Variations: Hala, plural: hali

Bulgarian, Macedonian, and Serbian demonology tell us of a species of AERIAL DEVIL known as ala. Demons of bad weather, ale, as they are collectively called, destroy and loot crops from the fields, send hail storms to destroy orchards and vineyards, and uproot trees. The ale also have the ability to cause crops not to ripen and remove the fertility from the land. Their favorite prey, however, is children and ale will use the elements to kill them if at all possible. In addition to their wanton destruction of food stock, the very presence of the ala is enough to cause a decline in a person's mental and physical health. After a person is weakened in such a way, an ala will possess their body.

Descriptions of this species of demon vary greatly and various sources claim that an ala looks like a wind, a female dragon, a large-mouthed human- or snakelike monster, an invisible being, a large creature of indistinguishable form, a large winged creature with a swordlike tail, a large creature with a horse head and a snake body, a raven, and a three-headed snake. Perhaps the confusion over their natural appearance can be explained by the demons' ability to shape-shift;

they are well known to assume the form of animals and humans.

Extremely gluttonous, even for a demon, the ala's attempt to devour the moon and the sun is made evident by periodic eclipses. When not consuming or destroying, ale are said to live in the clouds, gigantic trees, inhospitable mountain caves, lakes, remote places, and springs. To prevent being attacked by an ala, one must approach it with respect and trust. If one should win the favor of an ala, the demon will look after him, making him wealthy and seeing to his personal protection, even going as far as to save his life if necessary. For those not blessed, magical herbs called ala's herbs can be placed in the field where the plow turns around to prevent hailstorms from destroying crops.

The natural enemies of ale are dragons and eagles; Christianized tales tell of dragons and the saints fighting together against ale. There are also tales of humanlike ale that are strikingly similar to the Russian tales of Babba Yaga.

Sources: Books LLC, *Balkan Folklore*, 69; Monier-Williams, *Sanskrit-English Dictionary*, 1293; Turner, *Dictionary of ancient Deities*, 201.

Ala Demon

In Mesopotamian demonology an ala demon is a nocturnal demonic creature. Stalking the streets, it freely enters into a person's home. Appearing like an amorphous, cloudlike being, it preys upon sleeping men, causing them to have nocturnal emissions. If it envelopes a person in its cloudlike form, it will cause them to suffer from insomnia. Signs that a person has been attacked by this sort of demon include depression and loss of appetite.

Sources: Boulay, *Flying Serpents and Dragons*, 255; Pick, *Dreams and History*, 42; Sorensen, *Possession and Exorcism in the New Testament and Early Christianity*, 27–8.

Alagas

In the *Sacred Magic of Abramelin the Mage*, book two, Alagas ("wandering") is named as one of the one hundred eleven SERVITORS OF AMAYMON, ARITON, ORIENS, AND PAYMON. An AERIAL DEVIL, he and his court are constantly on the move, never staying in any one place for long (see also AMAYMON, ARITON, ORIENS, and PAYMON).

Sources: Belanger, *Dictionary of Demons*, 23; Susej, *Demonic Bible*, 256; Von Worms, *Book of Abramelin*, 255.

Alal

Variations: Alu

Alal ("destroyer" or "spirit") is one of a group of seven demons working in unison from Chaldean and Sumerian demonology. Named in the Magan Text as one of the servants of Ereshkigal, the goddess of death and gloom, this AERIAL DEVIL cannot be prevented from entering into a person's home, and when it does so will induce men to sin. He also has the ability to possess a person (see IRKALLA). Alal lives in the desert and in abandoned places of worship where sacrifices took place (see also GIGIM, IDPA, NAMTAR, TELAL, URUKU, and UTUK).

Sources: Baskin, *Sorcerer's Handbook*, 136; Icons, *Demons*, 136; Lenormant, *Chaldean Magic*, 24; Sorensen, *Possession and Exorcism in the New Testament and Early Christianity*, 27–8.

Alan

The *Sacred Magic of Abramelin the Mage*, book two, lists Alan ("a tree") as one of the thirty-two SERVITORS OF ASTAROT (see ASTAROT).

Sources: Belanger, *Dictionary of Demons*, 23; Ford, *Bible of the Adversary*, 91; Mathers, *Book of the Sacred Magic of Abramelin the Mage*, 106.

Alardi

Variations: "The winged one"

From the Ossetian people of the northern Caucasus Mountains in Europe comes the demonic spirit known as Alardi. He is known to inflict smallpox upon those individuals who hurt the women under his protection.

Sources: Baddeley, *Rugged Flanks of Caucasus*, 136–7; Field, *Contributions to the Anthropology of the Caucasus*, 69; Wieczynski, *Modern Encyclopedia of Russian and Soviet History*, 139.

Alastor

Variations: Alaster, Alastôr, Alastwr, Chalkis, "the Executioner"

From Greek mythology comes the demon Alastor ("avenger"). He is ranked as the executor of decrees handed down from SATAN'S court, as well as executioner and commissioner of public works. This AERIAL DEVIL under the command of ASMODEUS is the demon of blood feuds between families. Described as an avenging spirit, daimon, and a FALLEN ANGEL, Alastor was said to have been born a mortal man, the son of King Neleus of Pylos. He became a demon when he and his brothers were killed by Herakles. As a demon, Alastor is exceptionally cruel; he sees to it that the sins of the father are delivered onto the child, as well as tempting men to commit murder.

Sources: Chambers, *Book of Days*, 723; Chong-Gossard, *Gender and Communication in Euripides' Plays*, 94; Chopra, *Academic Dictionary of Mythology*, 20; Daniels, *Encyclopaedia of Superstitions, Folklore, and the Occult Sciences of the World*, 1420; Rudwin, *Devil in Legend and Literature*, 28.

Alath

Alath the demi-demon was named as one of the SPIRITS OF SOLOMON in the *Testament of Solomon*. He confessed to the king that he caused coughing and asthma in children, as well as disease. To prevent him from attacking, a talisman must be created and have the phrase "Rorêx, do thou pursue Alath" written on a piece of paper placed inside of it; then the charm must be worn around the neck. Another method is to call directly upon the angel Rorex for protection.

Sources: Ashe, *Qabalah*, 49; Conybeare, *Jewish Quarterly Review*, Vol. 11, 37; Davidson, *Dictionary of Angels*, 247; Giversen, *New Testament and Hellenistic Judaism*, 81; Unger, *Biblical Demonology*, 149.

Al-A'war

According to the Koran, Al-A'war ("the one-eyed") is a DJINN and one of the five SONS OF IBLIS. He is considered to be the demon of debauchery (see also IBLIS).

Sources: Cramer, *Devil Within*, 292; Singer, *Jewish Encyclopedia*, 521; Ṭabarī, *Sāsānids, the Byzantines, the Lakhmids, and Yemen*, 75.

Alcanor

Alcanor ("a harp") was named as one of the seventy-two SPIRITS OF SOLOMON in the *Testament of Solomon*. He is also named in Christian demonology as one of the forty-nine SERVITORS OF BEELZEBUB (see BEELZEBUB).

Sources: Belanger, *Dictionary of Demons*, 27; Ford, *Bible of the Adversary*, 93; Mathers, *Book of Sacred Magic of Abramelin the Mage*, 120.

Aldebaran

Aldebaran is, according to the *Book of Enoch*, one of the FALLEN ANGELS who swore allegiance to SAMIAZA, rebelled against God, took a human as his wife, and fathered the NEPHILIM. The star Aldebaran is the brightest star in the constellation Taurus.

Sources: Agrippa Von Nettesheim, *Three Books of Occult Philosophy*, 411; Greer, *New Encyclopedia of the Occult*, 509; Grimassi, *Italian Witchcraft*, 234.

Aldinach

In Egyptian demonology, Aldinach is a lesser demon who appears in the form of a woman. She is known to cause earthquakes, hail and rain storms, floods, and all sorts of natural disasters, as well as sinking ships.

Sources: Conner, *Cassell's Encyclopedia of Queer Myth, Symbol, and Spirit*, 48; Drury, *Dictionary of the Esoteric*, 8; Gettings, *Dictionary of Demons*, 28; Spence, *Encyclopædia of Occultism*, 13.

Alecto

In Greco–Roman mythology Alecto is a Fury, a type of demonic goddess. She is part of a trio, Meg[ae]ra and Tisiphone being the other two (see FURIES, THE). The name translates from Greek to generally mean "she who does not rest," "unceasing," or "unceasing in anger."

According to Hesiod, the great Greek epic poet, they are the daughters of the goddess Gaea. When her husband, Uranus, was murdered, the daughters came into being and sprang to life from his spilled blood. However, according to Aeschylus, the Greek playwright and tragedian, they were born to the goddess Nyx. Sophocles, the most influential writer of Ancient Greece, claimed them to be the children of Darkness and of Gaea.

No matter how they came into being, these sisters are demons of vengeance and are described as being monstrous, having bat wings, being DOG-headed, and having snakes for hair. Living in the underworld, they come to Earth and seek out unpunished criminals.

Sources: Gettings, *Dictionary of Demons*, 28; Parker, *Outlines of General History*, 348; Peterson, *Mythology in Our Midst*, 55; Rose, *Giants, Monsters and Dragons*, 126.

Alexh

Variations: Alex

The FALLEN ANGEL Alexh is one of eighteen demons that are quoted during exorcism and cases of collective possession (see LOUDUN POSSESSION).

Sources: Aikin, *General Biography*, 493; Bayle, *Historical and Critical Dictionary*, 262; Rudwin, *Devil in Legend and Literature*, 28; Ramsay, *Westminster Guide to the Books of the Bible*, 349; Voltaire, *Works of M. de Voltaire*, 193.

Alfar

Variations: Alb, Alberich, Alfa-blot

Originally seen as a half god and half dwarf, Alfar came from Scandinavian folklore and was named in the *Nibelungen Saga*. Later he evolved into the demon of diseases and NIGHTMARES.

Sources: Du Chaillu, *Viking Age*, 409–10; Keightley, *Fairy Mythology*, 108–9, 135; Turner, *Dictionary of Ancient Deities*, 166.

Algul

Variations: Alqul

Coming from Arabic lore, this vampiric demon, whose name translates as "horse-leech" or "bloodsucking DJINN," was immortalized as Amine in the tale *One Thousand and One Nights*, also known as *Arabian Nights*. There are other tales where an algul tricks a traveler into accompanying it and then upon reaching an isolated place, turns and attacks. Although its preferred prey is infants, an algul can survive from eating only a few grains of rice every day. Normally, this demon lives in cemeteries, but since it can pass for human, it occasionally marries and has children. An algul cannot die due to the effects of age or disease and is notoriously difficult to slay since it is impervious to attacks of bladed weapons. Since the creature is such a fierce combatant, magic is often employed to turn it into a less dangerous monster that can more easily be captured and burned down to ashes—the only way to destroy it.

Sources: Gore, *Gentleman's Magazine*, Vol. 275, 345; Guiley, *Encyclopedia of Demons and Demonology*, 6; Maberry, *Vampire Universe*, 12.

Alhoniel

Alhoniel is one of the twenty-eight demonic rulers of the lunar mansions (see ENOCHIAN RULERS OF THE LUNAR MANSIONS).

Sources: Gettings, *Dictionary of Demons*, 28; McLean, *Treatise on Angel Magic*, 42.

Aligar

Variations: Aligor

Aligar is one of the three SERVITORS OF FLEURETTY (see FLEURETTY).

Source: Baskin, *Sorcerer's Handbook*, 445.

Alilah

Variations: Allah

Alilah ("the deity") is a demonic goddess from ancient Babylon. Demon of the moon, she is most powerful when it is in a crescent shape.

Sources: Rudwin, *Devil in Legend and Literature*, 28; Turner, *Dictionary of Ancient Deities*, 422.

Allatu

Variations: Allatum, NAMTAR, Namtary

From Assyro-Babylonian religious texts comes the DEMONESS Allatu. Originally from the demonology of ancient Mesopotamia, Allatu was not only the Consort of Bel and NERGAL but also named as the Queen of the Underworld. Born the child of and answering only to Ereshkigal, the goddess of death and gloom, she is also the demon of sex (see IRKALLA). In pre–Islamic pantheon Allatu is the name given to the female counterpart of Allah.

Sources: Gettings, *Dictionary of Demons*, 28; King, *Babylonian Religion and Mythology*, 37, 42; Sorensen, *Possession and Exorcism in the New Testament and Early Christianity*, 27–8.

Alleborith

Named in the *Testament of Solomon*, Alleborith was one of the seventy-two SPIRITS OF SOLOMON. He is known for making people choke and swallow fish bones. To save yourself from one of his attacks, while choking, take a bone from the fish you are eating and cough on it; this will immediately banish Alleborith.

Sources: Ashe, *Qabalah*, 50; Belanger, *Dictionary of Demons*, 26; Conybeare, *Jewish Quarterly Review*, Vol. 11, 37; Fleg, *Life of Solomon*, 107.

Allocen

Variations: Alocas, Alocer, Allocer, Alloces, Alloien

According to Johann Wierus's *Pseudomonarchia Daemonum* (*False Monarchy of Demons*, 1583) Duke Allocen is a FALLEN ANGEL who commands thirty-six legions of demons (see DUKES OF HELL). He is described as looking like a soldier mounted upon a great horse. His face is very red and looks like a lion with flaming eyes. His voice is hoarse and he speaks very loudly. Allocen is summoned for his ability to give good FAMILIARs; he also teaches astronomy and liberal sciences. Some sources list Allocen as one of the seventy-two SPIRITS OF SOLOMON.

Sources: De Laurence, *Lesser Key of Solomon, Goetia*, 39; González-Wippler, *Complete Book of Spells, Ceremonies, and Magic*, 143; Poinsot, *Complete Book of the Occult and Fortune Telling*, 377; Waite, *Book of Ceremonial Magic*, 212; Scot, *Discoverie of Witchcraft*, 225.

Allu

The allu ("to connect") are a race of demons that were born of the union between Lilitu (LILITH) and human men while they slept or between the DEMONESS and one of her demonic servants. These faceless, hideous demonic creatures from Akkadian and Sumerian mythology destroy everything they encounter. If an allu was born from the union between Lilitu and a man, the demon will eventually return to his father and wait by his bedside as the man is about to die. Once there the demon will try to snatch up his soul as it leaves his body, making its father into a ghost, unable to pass over to the other side (see ALLU 2).

Sources: Black, *Concise Dictionary of Akkadian*, 13; Icon, *Waiting*, 434; Rogers, *Religion of Babylonia and Assyria*, 147; Turner, *Dictionary of Ancient Deities*, 291.

Allu 2

There is a second type of demon from mainstream Akkadian mythology that is called an allu ("to draw"), but it is different enough from the allu of Akkadian-Sumerian mythology to warrant its own entry (see ALLU). This vampiric demon is an infernal and immortal being; it was never human or created in any known way. Described as being faceless and desirous of destroying all life whenever the opportunity presents itself, the allu will possess a man when he is engaged in sexual intercourse with a SUCCUBUS. As the victim nears death, the allu will wait for the moment of expiration so that it may snatch up the fleeing soul and enslave it.

Sources: Muss-Arnolt, *Concise Dictionary of the Assyrian Language*, 39; Scurlock, *Diagnoses in Assyrian and Babylonian Medicine*, 505.

Alluph

Duke Alluph is named as one of the one hundred eleven SERVITORS OF AMAYMON, ARITON, ORIENS, AND PAYMON. His name is taken from Hebrew and it translates to mean "bull ox," as in the dominant animal of the herd (see also AMAYMON, ARITON, ORIENS, and PAYMON).

Sources: Mathers, *Book of Sacred Magic of Abramelin the Mage*, 112; Goodhugh, *Bible Cyclopædia*, 551; Susej, *Demonic Bible*, 256.

Alouqâ

Variations: Alouqua, Alouque

An alouqâ is a vampiric demon from ancient Hebrew lore. It is an infernal, immortal being that was never human. It exhausts men to death with its lovemaking (see SUCCUBUS) and drives them to commit suicide.

Sources: Langton, *La Démonologie*, 59; Masson, *Le Diable et la Possession Démoniaque*.

Alp

Variations: Alb, Alf, Alfemoe, Alpdaemon, Alpen, Alpes, Alpmann, Apsaras, BOCKSHEXE, BOCKSMARTE, Cauquemare, Chauche Vieille, Dochje, Dockele, Dockeli, Doggi, Druckerl, Drude, Drutt, Elbe, Fraueli, Inuus, Leeton, Lork, Mahr, Mahrt, Mar, Mara, Mare, Märt, Nachtmaennli, Nachtmahr, Nachtmanndli, Nachtmännlein, Night Terror, Quauquemaire, Sukkubus, Toggeli, Trud, Tudd, Walrider, Walriderske, and a host of others depending on the specific region one is in.

Originating from Germany, this vampiric demon does not have a single true form. Throughout the ages the only consistency in its description is that it is said to wear a white hat. Generally the alp is said to be male, and although there are a scant few reports of it being female, it should be noted that this creature has exceptional shapeshifting abilities. An alp can assume the form of any animal it pleases, but it is said to prefer that of birds, cats, demon dogs, dogs, mist, pigs, and snakes. It is very strong, can become invisible, can fly, and has the unique ability to spit butterflies and moths from its mouth. Because of its shape-shifting ability, the alp has been linked to werewolf lore in the Cologne, Germany, region.

Typically a demon is an infernal, immortal being that was never human, but this is not the case for the lecherous and ravenous alp. In fact, it became what it is through one of a few fairly mundane acts, such as when a newborn male child dies, when a child whose mother went through a particularly long and painful childbirth dies, or when a family member dies and his spirit simply just returns with no further explanation added.

At night the alp seeks out its most common prey, a sleeping woman, although it has been known to occasionally attack men and young boys, as well as cattle, geese, horses, and rabbits. Once the prey is selected, the alp shape-shifts into mist and slips into the person's home completely undetected. Next, it sits upon the victim's chest and compresses the air out of their lungs so that they cannot scream. Then the alp will drink blood (and milk if the victim is a woman who is lactating), which will cause her to have both horrible NIGHTMARES and erotic dreams. The next day the victim will have vivid memories of the attack and be left feeling drained of energy and miserable. The attack event in its entirety is called an *alpdrücke*. If a woman calls an alp to her, then the creature will be a gentle lover with her.

The alp, when it attacks a horse, is usually referred to as a *mare*. It will mount up and ride the animal to death. The alp, however, may also choose to crush the animal instead, as it is known to do when it crushes geese and rabbits to death in their pens. When an alp crushes cattle to death, it is called a *schrattl* attack.

Fortunately, as powerful as the alp is, its attacks can be fairly easily thwarted. To protect horses and cattle from being ridden or crushed to death, simply hang a pair of crossed measuring sticks in the barn or place a broom in the animal's stall.

There are numerous ways to prevent yourself or others from being attacked by an alp. According to lore, the alp's power is linked to its hat. If you can steal the hat off its head, it will lose its superhuman strength and the ability to become invisible. Desperate to have its hat back, the alp will greatly reward anyone who returns it, although with what or how this will happen specifically is not known.

Another way to keep an alp at bay is during the Festival of the Three Kings (January 6).

Draw a magical hexagram on your bedroom door with chalk and imbue it with the names of the three magi who visited the Christ child after his birth: Balthasar, Caspar, and Melchior. Variations of this preventive method say that the head of the household must make a pentagram on the bedroom door and empower it with names of the patriarchic prophets, Elias and Enoch.

Burying a stillborn child under the front door of your home will protect all the occupants who sleep there not only from alp attacks, but also from attacks by other species of vampires.

A less invasive defense is to keep your shoes at the side of your bed at night when you fall asleep. If the toes are pointed toward the bedroom door, it will keep the alp from entering. Also, sleeping with a mirror upon your chest will scare it off you should it somehow manage to enter into the room.

At one time there was the practice of singing a specific song at the hearth before the last person in the house went to bed for the night. Sadly, this method is no longer with us, as the words, melody, and even the name of the song have been lost to history; only the memory of once doing so remains.

If all preventive measures have been taken and alp attacks persist, there is hope to fend it off yet. If you should awaken during the attack and find yourself being pressed down upon by an alp, put your thumb in your hand and it will flee.

Occasionally a witch binds an alp to her in order to inflict harm upon others. Witches who have an alp in their possession have the telltale sign of letting their eyebrows grow together. They allow this to happen because the alp, in this instance, lives inside the witch's body when not in use. When it leaves her through an opening in her eyebrow, it takes on the guise of a moth or white butterfly. If it ever happens that you awaken in the night and see such an insect upon your chest, say to it, "Trud, come back tomorrow and I will lend you something." The insect should immediately fly away and the next day the alp, appearing as a human, will come to your home looking to borrow something. When that happens, give it nothing but say to it, "Come back tomorrow and drink with me." The alp will leave and the following day the witch who sent the alp to attack you will come to your home, seeking a drink. Give it to her and the attacks should stop.

Sometimes an alp will return night after night to assault the same person. Fortunately, there is a powerful, if not bizarre, way to prevent this from continuing. The victim needs to urinate into a clean, new bottle, which is then hung in a place where the sun can shine upon it for three days. Then, without saying a single word, carry the bottle to a running stream and throw it over your head into the water.

For all the trouble an alp can prove to be, it is as easy to kill as most every other form of vampire. Once it is captured, place a lemon in its mouth and set the creature ablaze.

Sources: Grimm, *Teutonic Mythology*, 423, 442, 463; Jones, *On the Nightmare*, 126; Nuzum, *Dead Travel Fast*, 234; Riccardo, *Liquid Dreams*, 139.

Alpan

Variations: Alpanu, Alpnu, La Bellaria ("Beautiful One of the Air")

As a goddess of the underworld, Alpan ("willing, with gladness"), was no doubt demonized with the rise of Christianity, her name pulled from Etruscan mythology. Alpan, one of the Lasas (Fate-Goddesses), was made into the demon of love, springtime, and the underworld. Her name translates to mean "gift" or "offering," but the implication is that the gift is made with a degree of implied willingness.

Commanding the underworld, she is depicted as a nude woman with wings, sometimes holding a bouquet of flowers or leaves, or a perfume-jar called an *alabastron*. She was most powerful during the season of spring.

Sources: De Grummond, *Etruscan Myth, Sacred History, and Legend*, 150, 163; Duston, *Invisible Made Visible*, 310; Lurker, *Routledge Dictionary of Gods and Goddesses, Devils and Demons*, 9–10.

Alpas

One of the SERVITORS OF AMAYMON, ARITON, ORIENS, AND PAYMON, Alpas's name translates from Greek to mean "yielding" (see also AMAYMON, ARITON, ORIENS, and PAYMON).

Sources: Belanger, *Dictionary of Demons*, 27; Guiley, *Encyclopedia of Demons and Demonology*, 7; Von Worms, *Book of Abramelin*, 255.

Alphun

Apollonius of Tyana's *Nuctemeron* (*Night Illuminated by Day*) named Alphun as the demon of doves. He was said to be most powerful during the eighth hour of the day.

Sources: Davidson, *Dictionary of Angels*, 14; Gettings, *Dictionary of Demons*, 29; Lévi, *Transcendental Magic*, 406.

Alpiel

According to the Talmud, Alpiel is the demon of fruit trees.

Sources: Davidson, *Dictionary of Angels*, 30; Gettings, *Dictionary of Demons*, 29; Spence, *Encyclopedia of Occultism*, 16.

Alrinach

Alrinach is described in E. Cobham Brewer's *Dictionary of Phrase and Fable*, 1898, as the demon of earthquakes, floods, hail and rain. When visible, this demon appears as a woman. She is known to cause shipwrecks.

Sources: Bassett, *Legends and Superstitions of the Sea and of Sailors*, 69; Brewer, *Dictionary of Phrase and Fable*, 38; Kelly, *Who in Hell*, 13; Poinsot, *Complete Book of the Occult and Fortune Telling*, 377.

Alrunes

Variations: Alioruns, Alurines, Alruna Wives

Originally a household goddess in ancient Germany and accredited with being the mother of the Huns, Alrunes ("secret") was demonized under Christian influence.

She has been described as both a magical wooden doll and a type of female sorcerer. As a magical wooden poppet, she can be asked questions regarding the future and she will answer with small motions of her head or by making faint sounds. Dolls of Alrunes stood about a foot tall, and each one was named and dressed in expensive clothing. Typically they were placed in a comfortable and dry niche somewhere in the main body of the house and served food and drink at every meal. If the doll built to honor Alrunes was neglected, it would bring misfortune down upon the household and cry out in anguish and anger.

As female sorcerers, they are said to have shape-changing abilities but cannot alter their sex.

Sources: Brewer, *Dictionary of Phrase and Fable*, 38; Ennemoser, *History of Magic*, Vol. 2, 89, 122; Witches' Almanac, *Magic Charms from A to Z*, 11.

Alü

Variations: Alu-Demon

Born a mortal man, Alü became a nocturnal demon according to Babylonian and Semitic demonology. Each night he was said to wander the dark streets seeking out prey, following a person back to their home and slipping inside behind them unseen. As the person is about to fall asleep, he appears and threatens to crush them to death with his enormous bulk if they close their eyes. Alü lurks in the corners of rooms, dark caves, and dimly lit streets.

Sources: Finkel, *Disease in Babylonia*, 90; Hurwitz, *Lilith: The First Eve*, 39, 131; Lenormant, *Chaldean Magic*, 24; Stol, *Epilepsy in Babylonia*, 41–2.

Alû

An invisible, demonic vampire from ancient Babylon, the alû is said to attack its victims (men) at night while they sleep. Its victims awake the next day ill and feeling drained of energy.

Sources: Curran, *Vampires*, 25; Jastrow, *Religion of Babylonia and Assyria*, 262; Turner, *Dictionary of Ancient Deities*, 28, 38, 146, 291; Van der Toorn, *Dictionary of Deities and Demons in the Bible*, 24.

Aluga

Variations: ALOUQÂ, Alouque, Alukah, Aluqa, Aulak

The aluga takes its name from the Hebrew word that is synonymous with vampirism and translates to mean "leech." This vampiric creature that originates from Mediterranean lore is considered by some sources to be nothing more than a blood-drinking demon, while others claim it to be the Demonic King of Vampires. A handful of references say that it is nothing more than a flesh-eating ghoul.

The aluga is mentioned in the Bible, Proverbs 30:15: "The horseleech hath two daughters, crying Give, give. There are three things that are never satisfied, yea, four things say not, It is enough: (16) the grave; and the barren womb; the earth that is not filled with water; and the fire that saith not, It is enough."

Sources: Bunson, *Vampire Encyclopedia*, 5; Hyatt, *Book of Demons*, 63; Preece, *New Encyclopaedia Britannica*, 461.

'Alukah A

Originally, 'Alukah A was a specific demon from ancient Babylonian lore that was absorbed into Hasidic lore. There, she became a SUCCUBUS and the mother of two demon daughters—Deber ("pestilence") and Keeb ("smiter"), the siblings who cry "Give" in the Book of Proverbs. Her name, 'Alukah A, closely resembles the Arabic word for horseleech, *'aulak*. She is credited as being the demon that tormented Saul.

It is said that the only way to protect oneself from her attack is through God's intervention, which can be evoked through the psalm "Shir shel Pega'im." In fact, the only way for 'Alukah A to be destroyed should she appear in our realm is by God smiting her through a supernatural means of His choosing (see also NERGAL).

Sources: Graves, *White Goddess*, 448; Masters, *Eros and Evil*, 181; Phillips, *Exploring Proverbs*, 557, 559.

Amaimon

Variations: AMAYMON, AMOYMON, Mahazael ("to consume"), Maimon, MAMMON, MAYMON

In *Theurgia Goetia*, book two of the *Lemegeton*, Amaimon, a devil, is ranked as the King of the East and was said to be one of the seventy-two SPIRITS OF SOLOMON. His name is most likely taken from Greek, and if so would probably translate to mean "terrible violence and vehemence."

Described as having deadly, fiery, and poisonous breath, it is necessary to use a magical ring, held up to one's mouth when speaking with him, to nullify his poisonous breath. Amaimon could be restrained from doing any evil from the third hour of the day until noon and then again from the ninth hour of the day until evening with the proper magical spell.

Sources: Ford, *Bible of the Adversary*, 90; Gettings, *Dictionary of Demons*, 29; Mathers, *Selected Occult Writings of S.L. MacGregor Mathers*, 96; McLean, *Treatise of Angel Magic*, 51; Von Worms, *Book of Abramelin*, 243.

Amaite-Rangi

From the demonology of Cook and Mangaia Islands comes the AERIAL DEVIL, Amaite-Rangi. The demon of the sky, it is said that he was ultimately defeated by the Polynesian cultural hero, Ngaru.

Sources: Sykes, *Who's Who in Non-Classical Mythology*, 8; Turner, *Dictionary of Ancient Deities*, 40.

Amalin

The *Ars Goetia*, the first book of the *Lemegeton*, names Amalin as one of the fifty-three SERVITORS OF ASHTAROTH AND ASMODEUS (see ASHTAROTH and ASMODEUS). His name is Chaldaic for "languidness."

Sources: Belanger, *Dictionary of Demons*, 28; Mathers, *Book of Sacred Magic of Abramelin the Mage*, 115; Susej, *Demonic Bible*, 257.

Aman

The *Sacred Magic of Abramelin the Mage*, book two, lists Aman ("to nourish") as one of the thirty-two SERVITORS OF ASTAROT as well as one of the fifty-three SERVITORS OF ASHTAROTH AND ASMODEUS (see ASHTAROTH, ASMODEUS, and ASTAROT). Although this demon has the ability to possess people, he is easily cast out. Aman is one of the demons who possessed Sister Jeanne des Anges. It was also the first demon she managed to cast out of herself (see LOUDUN POSSESSION).

Sources: Aikin, *General Biography*, 493; Bayle, *Historical and Critical Dictionary*, 262; Hsia, *World of Catholic Renewal*, 151; Rudwin, *Devil in Legend and Literature*, 28; Voltaire, *Works of M. de Voltaire*, 193.

Amand

A FALLEN ANGEL, formerly of the Order of Thrones, Amand is one of the entities that are often called upon during exorcism and cases of collective possession; he was one of the eighteen demons who possessed Sister Jeanne des Anges

in Loudun, France, in 1634 (see LOUDUN POSSESSION).

Sources: Aikin, *General Biography*, 493; Bayle, *Historical and Critical Dictionary*, 262; Hsia, *World of Catholic Renewal*, 151; Voltaire, *Works of M. de Voltaire*, 193.

Amane

In the *Book of Enoch*, Amane was named as a WATCHER angel, one of the GRIGORI. He later became a FALLEN ANGEL when he swore allegiance to SAMIAZA, rebelled against God, took a human as his wife, and fathered the NEPHILIM.

Source: Baskin, *Dictionary of Satanism*, 25.

Amaniel

In the *Sacred Magic of Abramelin the Mage*, book two, Amaniel ("nourishment of God") is listed as one of the fifty-three SERVITORS OF ASHTAROTH AND ASMODEUS (see ASHTAROTH, ASMODEUS, and ASMODEUS ZAVEHE).

Sources: Belanger, *Dictionary of Demons*, 30; Ford, *Bible of the Adversary*, 89; Mathers, *Book of the Sacred Magic of Abramelin the Mage*, 115.

Amaros

Variations: ARMAROS

In the *Book of Enoch*, Amaros was named as a FALLEN ANGEL when he swore allegiance to SAMIAZA, rebelled against God, took a human as his wife, and fathered the NEPHILIM. He went on to teach mankind "the resolving of enchantments."

Sources: Charles, *Book of Enoch*, 137; Davidson, *Dictionary of Angels*, 15; Horne, *Sacred Books and Early Literature of the East*, 114; Lumpkin, *Fallen Angels, the Watchers, and the Origins of Evil*, 31.

Amatia

Amatia ("ignorance") is one of the forty-nine SERVITORS OF BEELZEBUB (see BEELZEBUB).

Sources: Belanger, *Dictionary of Demons*, 40; Ford, *Bible of the Adversary*, 93; Mathers, *Sacred Magic of Abramelin the Mage*, 120.

Amaymon

Variations: AMAIMON, AMOYMON

According to the Christian demonology of the Middle Ages, Amaymon is ranked as a King of the West (or East, sources vary) and one of the PRINCES OF HELL (see also KINGS OF HELL). Although he does not necessarily have command or dominion over ASMODAI, he does have power over him. Amaymon casually breathes a deadly poison and only by wearing a blessed and consecrated silver ring on the middle finger can you be properly protected against it. If ever an exorcist is to attempt to cast this demon out of a person, he must remember to stand straight and to remove all coverings from his head as a show of respect; without doing this Amaymon cannot be exorcised.

Sources: De Laurence, *Lesser Key of Solomon, Goetia*, 32–3, 46; DuQuette, *Key to Solomon's Key*, 167, 176–7, 195, 197; Hyatt, *Book of Demons*, 48.

Amazarak

In the *Book of Enoch*, Amazarak is named as one of the FALLEN ANGELS who swore allegiance to SAMIAZA, rebelled against God, took a human as his wife, and fathered the NEPHILIM. After his fall, he went on to teach mankind geometry, sacred mathematics, and how to become a sorcerer.

Sources: Beard, *Autobiography of Satan*, 113; Blavatsky, *Secret Doctrine*, 376; Gettings, *Dictionary of Demons*, 29; Laurence, *Book of Enoch, the Prophet*, 7.

Ambolen

Variation: Ambolin

In the *Ars Goetia*, the first book of the *Lemegeton*, Ambolen ("tending unto nothingness") is named as one of the fifty-three SERVITORS OF ASHTAROTH AND ASMODEUS (see ASHTAROTH and ASMODEUS).

Sources: Belanger, *Dictionary of Demons*, 30; Ford, *Bible of the Adversary*, 89; Mathers, *Book of the Sacred Magic of Abramelin the Mage*, 115.

Ambolon

Ambolon is named in the *Sacred Magic of Abramelin the Mage*, book two, as one of the forty-nine SERVITORS OF BEELZEBUB (see BEELZEBUB). His name is Greek and translates to mean "earth thrown up" or "fresh turned," as in tilled soil.

Sources: Mathers, *Book of Sacred Magic of Abramelin the Mage*, 121; Susej, *Demonic Bible*, 259; Von Works, *Book of Abramelin*, 257.

Ambri

Ambri is ranked as a chief duke and is listed as one of the twelve SERVITORS OF CASPIEL (see CASPIEL and DUKES OF HELL).

Sources: Belanger, *Dictionary of Demons*, 30; Guiley, *Encyclopedia of Demons and Demonology*, 37; Peterson, *Lesser Key of Solomon*, 60.

Ambriel

In Heinrich Cornelius Agrippa Von Netteshim's *De Occulta Philosophia* (1531), Ambriel ("energy of God") is said to be the demon of the constellation Gemini.

Sources: Agrippa, *Three Books of Occult Philosophy*, 536; Peterson, *Lesser Key of Solomon*, 129; Scheible, *Sixth and Seventh Books of Moses*, 73.

Amchison

In the *Sacred Magic of Abramelin the Mage*, book two, Amchison is listed as one of the sixty-five SERVITORS OF KORE AND MAGOTH.

Sources: Belanger, *Dictionary of Demons*, 30; Ford, *Bible of the Adversary*, 92; Mathers, *Book of the Sacred Magic of Abramelin the Mage*, 107.

Amducias

Variations: Ambuscias, Amducious, Amdukias, Amduscas, Amduscias, Amdusias, Amukias, SAMIL, YOMAEL

Ranked as a duke and the musical director in Hell in Christian demonology, Amducias ("the destroyer") was originally one of the seventy-two SPIRITS OF SOLOMON. A FALLEN ANGEL and said to be the demon of music, as he is the most musically talented of the inhabitants of Hell, Amducias commands twenty-nine legions of demons, ten chiefs and 100 servitors. He appears before his summoner as a unicorn, but, if asked, will assume a human guise. He is tall, dark skinned, with long black hair, long fingers, rough hands, tan wings, and is physically strong. Amducias is summoned for ability to cause trees to go barren, bend, or become uprooted. He also gives excellent FAMILIARs, assists on secret missions, inspires music, and gives concerts. A nocturnal demon, he is most powerful during the sixth hour of the night.

As YOMAEL, he was one of the CHIEF OF TENS who swore allegiance to SAMIAZA and rebelled against God.

Sources: Collin de Plancy, *Dictionary of Witchcraft*, 16; De Laurence, *Lesser Key of Solomon, Goetia*, 43; Scott, *London Magazine*, Vol. 5, 378.

Amelouith

Amelouith was the demon of the Egyptian magicians. Together with the demon EPHIPPAS, they created a column out of some unknown purple substance that they raised out of the Red Sea. This is also the demon who hardened Pharaoh's heart when Moses asked him to set free the Israelites. When Moses and his people fled through the parting of the Red Sea, Amelouith traveled with Pharaoh's army to capture them. The sea closed up and washed away the army, but Amelouith was trapped beneath the water under the gigantic column he and Ephippas had created. He remained trapped until Ephippas found him and only with their combined strength were they able to lift it off him.

Sources: Belanger, *Dictionary of Demons*, 31; Calisch, *Fairy Tales from Grandfather's Big Book*, 127; Scott, *London Magazine*, 378.

Amenadiel

In *Theurgia Goetia*, the second book of the *Lemegeton*, Amenadiel ("treaty") is ranked as the King of the West. He commands 300 great dukes; 500 lesser dukes; 12 chief dukes; and 40,000,030,000,100,000 inferior spirits. Each of his dukes has 3,880 servants apiece (see SERVITORS OF AMENADIEL). Considered to be both a diurnal and nocturnal demon, Amenadiel is known for announcing secrets.

Sources: Guiley, *Encyclopedia of Demons and Demonology*, 7; Peterson, *Lesser Key of Solomon*, 62; Shah, *Occultism*, 68; Trithemius, *Steganographia*, 81.

Amentet

Variations: Ament, Amentit, Imentet, Set Amentet

From the religion of the ancient Egyptians comes the demon Amentet. His name translates to mean "the mountain of the underworld." This is a name that was commonly used for the cemeteries that were located in the mountains or in the desert along the western bank of the Nile River.

Sources: Horne, *Sacred Books and Early Literature of the East*, 166; Remler, *Egyptian Mythology A to Z*, 10; Turner, *Dictionary of Ancient Deities*, 44.

Amesiel

In the *Ars Paulina*, book three of the *Lemegeton*, Amesiel is ranked as a chief duke and is listed as one of the twelve SERVITORS OF AMENADIEL (see AMENADIEL and DUKES OF HELL). He commands three thousand servitors.

Sources: Peterson, *Lesser Key of Solomon*, 62.

Amezyarak

Variations: Amazarec, Amazaroc, AMIZIRAS, Semyaza

Amezyarak is one of the FALLEN ANGELS mentioned in the *Book of Enoch*. He is sometimes also referred to as a GRIGORI or a WATCHER. He was one of the two hundred angels who swore allegiance to SAMIAZA and rebelled against God. He lusted after and took a human wife, fathering the NEPHILIM. While he was on Earth he taught mankind the secrets of conjuration and herbology.

Sources: Ashley, *Complete Book of Devils and Demons*, 72; Barton, *Journal of Biblical Literature*, Vols. 30–31, 165; Davidson, *Dictionary of Angels*, 15; Penas, *Intertextual Dimension of Discourse*, 125.

Amiel

According to the *Theurgia Goetia*, the second book of the *Lemegeton*, the *Lesser Key of Solomon*, Amiel is one of the chief dukes of the SERVITORS OF ASYRIEL (see ASYRIEL). He is a nocturnal demon, good-natured and willing to obey those who summon him. Amiel has forty servitors of his own.

Sources: Belanger, *Dictionary of Demons*, 32; Guiley, *Encyclopedia of Demons and Demonology*, 20; Peterson, *Lesser Key of Solomon*, 73–4, 77.

Amisiel

Amisiel is an inferior demonic spirit who is most powerful during the fifth hour of the day. According to the *Lemegeton*, he is one of the ten SERVITORS OF SAZQUIEL (see SAZQUIEL).

Sources: Davidson, *Dictionary of Angels*, 16; Peterson, *Lesser Key of Solomon*, 114; Waite, *Book of Black Magic and Ceremonial Magic*, 67.

Amiziras

Variations: Amazarec, Semiaza, Semyaza, Shemhazai

According to the *Book of Enoch*, Amiziras was one of the FALLEN ANGELS who swore allegiance to SAMIAZA and rebelled against God, lusting after and taking a human woman as his wife, and fathering the NEPHILIM. Amiziras also taught mankind the art of conjuration and root-cutting (herbs).

Sources: Barton, *Journal of Biblical Literature*, Vols. 30–31, 162; Ashley, *Complete Book of Demons and Devils*, 72; Davidson, *Dictionary of Angels*, 15.

Amizires

Amizires is listed in several sources as the name of a demon, but no further information is ever given about him. It is possible that his name is a variation of the FALLEN ANGEL named AMIZIRAS.

Sources: Ashley, *Complete Book of Devils and Demons*, 72.

Ammiel

According to the *Ars Paulina*, book three of the *Lemegeton*, the *Lesser Key of Solomon*, Ammiel ("my people is God") is a chief and one of the eleven SERVITORS OF RAHAB (see RAHAB).

Sources: Bamberger, *Fallen Angels*, 279; Cheyne, *Encyclopaedia Biblica*, 39, 141; Waite, *The Book of Ceremonial Magic*, 67.

Ammit

Variations: Amit, Ammut

Ammit ("gobbler") is a demon of judgment mentioned in the ancient Egyptian's *Book of the Dead*. Her name translates to mean the "devourer of the dead," but is understood to mean that she is the "eater of the dead and the dweller in Amenta." She has the head of a crocodile, the body of a feral cat or lioness (as she is female), and the buttocks of a hippo.

Ammit stands in the Halls of Justice and weighs the newly deceased's heart on the Great Balance, a gigantic scale, against a feather of Maat, the goddess of justice and truth. If the heart is heavier than the feather, Ammit devours it, destroying the person's soul.

Sources: Applegate, *Egyptian Book of Life*, 114; Chopra, *Academic Dictionary of Mythology*, 23; Illes, *Encyclopedia of Spirits*, 168; Lurker, *Dictionary of Gods and Goddesses*, 22; Sutherland, *Putting God on Trial*, 72.

Ammon

Variations: AAMON, AMAIMON, AMAN, AMAYMON, Amo, AMOYMON, Amoyon, the Wolf

Originally Ammon was an ancient Egyptian god of the sun, but by the time his name appeared in the *Lemegeton*, he had been demonized by scholars. The King of the East and a Marquis of Hell, as well as one of the seventy-two SPIRITS OF SOLOMON, Ammon is the demon of life and reproduction, commanding forty legions of demonic servitors (see KINGS OF HELL and MARQUIS OF HELL). Ammon looks like a wolf with a snake for a tail but can shape-change to appear as a man with either a crow's (or owl's) head, his beak filled with doglike teeth. He is summoned because of his knowledge of all things that have ever happened. He can divine the future and reunite old friends who have become enemies.

Sources: Icons, *Legions*, 104; Maspero, *Popular Stories of Ancient Egypt*, 127; Rudwin, *Devil in Legend and Literature*, 28; Spence, *Encyclopedia of Occultism and Parapsychology*, 27.

Amnediel

Enochian lore tells us that Amnediel is one of the twenty-eight rulers of the lunar mansions. He presides over the mansion Alnaza ("misty clouds") and is known for his ability to imprison captives and repel mice (see ENOCHIAN RULERS OF THE LUNAR MANSIONS).

Sources: Barrett, *The Magus*, 57; Gettings, *Dictionary of Demons*, 30; Moura, *Mansions of the Moon for the Green Witch*, 42, 68; Webster, *Encyclopedia of Angels*, 10, 123.

Amnixiel

According to Enochian lore, Amnixiel is one of the twenty-eight rulers of the lunar mansions. He presides over the mansion Albotham and his sign is that of Pisces. He is known for his ability to cause the loss of treasure (see ENOCHIAN RULERS OF THE LUNAR MANSIONS).

Sources: Davidson, *Dictionary of Angels*, 16; Gettings, *Dictionary of Demons*, 30; McLean, *Treatise on Angel Magic*, 42; Scheible, *Sixth and Seventh Books of Moses*, 75; Von Goethe, *Goethe's Letters to Zelter*, 378; Webster, *Encyclopedia of Angels*, 10–11.

Amousias

Amousias, Greek for "without music," is the name of a demon or devil listed in many sources but with no other information given.

Source: Euripides, *Heracles of Euripides*, 41.

Amoymon

Variations: Amai'moit, AMAIMON, AMAYMON, Amoy'mon

King of the Eastern (or Western, depending on the source) portion of Hell as well as a Grand President of Eastern Hades, Amoymon has command over ASMODEUS, a lieutenant as well as one of his princes (see KINGS OF HELL and PRESIDENTS OF HELL). Amoymon is best summoned between the hours of 9 A.M. and noon and again later in the day from 3 P.M. till 6 P.M., when his powers are at their peak. When he appears to his summoner, he does so as a man with poisonous breath. It is so deadly that the other kings and PRINCES OF HELL are said to wear a silver ring on the middle finger of their left hand as a means of protecting themselves from it. When Amoymon appears, he will very often do so with ASMODEUS by his side. If proper respect is not paid to his favorite prince, Amoymon will deliberately foul any request made of him (see FOUR PRINCIPAL KINGS).

Sources: Daniels, *Encyclopaedia of Superstitions, Folklore, and the Occult Sciences of the World*, 1421; De Claremont, *Ancient's Book of Magic*, 111; Gilman, *New International Encyclopaedia*, Vol. 1, 147; Spence, *Encyclopædia of Occultism*, 23.

Amudiel

Heinrich Cornelius Agrippa Von Netteshim's book, *Naturalis et Innaturalis*, lists Amudiel as a FALLEN ANGEL and one of the seven ELECTORS OF HELL.

Sources: Butler, *Ritual Magic*, 162; Davidson, *Dictionary of Angels*, 104; Von Goethe, *Goethe's Letters to Zelter*, 377.

Amuku Sanniya

In Sinhalese demonology Amuku Sanniya is the demon of stomach disorders and vomiting as well as the diseases and illnesses that cause them. He is depicted in ceremonial masks as having a green face, large eyes wide open, and a tongue partially protruding from his mouth. Amuku Sanniya, like the other Sinhalese demons, is susceptible to the DAHA-ATA SANNIYA.

Sources: Illes, *Encyclopedia of Spirits*, 875; Tilakaratna, *Manners, Customs, and Ceremonies of Sri Lanka*, 121; Wirz, *Exorcism and the Art of Healing in Ceylon*, 44.

Amurru

Variations: Amorite, Martu

In ancient Akkadian demonology, Amurru was a demonic god of mountains and nomads. His sign was the gazelle and the shepherd's crook; his consort was the goddess Beletseri, queen of the underworld and keeper of the records of the dead.

Sources: Hadley, *Cult of Asherah in Ancient Israel and Judah*, 44; Leick, *Dictionary of Ancient Near Eastern Mythology*, 4; Van der Toorn, *Dictionary of Deities and Demons in the Bible*, 32.

Amutiel

Variations: Atliel

According to Enochian lore, Amutiel is one of the twenty-eight demonic rulers of the lunar mansions. He presides over the mansion Ahubene ("Horns of Scorpio") and is known to hinder journeys and wedlock. His zodiac sign is Scorpio (see ENOCHIAN RULERS OF THE LUNAR MANSIONS).

Sources: Barrett, *The Magus*, 57; Scheible, Sixth and Seventh Books of Moses, 75; Webster, *Encyclopedia of Angels*, 11, 125.

Amy

Variations: AMOUSIAS, Avnas, the fifty-eighth spirit

Amy is a president of Hell and the president of fire. A FALLEN ANGEL, formerly of the Order of Powers, Amy commands thirty-six legions. Appearing as a roaring fire or as a man, he is a nocturnal demon who can give the gift of knowledge of astrology and other liberal sciences. Amy also gives good FAMILIARs and will tell the locations of lost treasures that are otherwise protected by guardian spirits. One of the seventy-two SPIRITS OF SOLOMON, it is believed that at the end of 200,000 years of banishment, Amy will be allowed to return to Heaven and reassume his seat in the seventh throne.

Sources: Crowley, *The Goetia*, 59; De Laurence, *Lesser Key of Solomon, Goetia*, 41; DuQuette, *Key to Solomon's Key*, 189; Scott, *London Magazine*, Vol. 5, 378.

An

Variations: Anu; Lord of Constellations; King of Gods, Spirits, and Demons

In Sumerian mythology An ("High One") is a demonic god of the sky. He commands all other gods, spirits, and demons. Depicted as a jackal, he is diurnal, being most powerful at noon. An lives in the highest of the heavenly regions. He has the ability to judge those who commit crimes and he created the stars to be his soldiers whom he uses to punish the wicked. An was considered to be an active god by the ancient Sumerians and he was appealed to for assistance, especially in matters of justice. His sign is that of a royal tiara with bull horns and his planet is the sun (although technically the sun is a star and not a planet).

Sources: Cotterell, *Encyclopedia of World Mythology*, 28; Kirk, *Myth*, 121–3; Turner, *Dictionary of Ancient Deities*, 58.

Anader

Variations: Anadir

In the *Sacred Magic of Abramelin the Mage*, Anader ("flayer") is among the twenty-two SERVITORS OF ARITON (see ARITON).

Sources: Belanger, *Dictionary of Demons*, 32; Mathers, *Sacred Magic of Abramelin the Mage*, 96.

Anael

Anael is known as one of the "seven phantoms of flame," or as one of the seven demons "of the ignited spheres" in ancient Chaldean demonology. He is considered to be very powerful, able to cause earthquakes and to affect the economy. He and his cohorts are at war with the seven gods of the planets who govern the universe. More modern scholars have described him as both a retrograde spirit and as one of the seven PLANETARY PRINCES of Hell who live deep within the bowels of the earth (see DUKES OF HELL). His angelic overlord is Haniel.

Sources: Blavatsky, *Secret Doctrine Synthesis of Science*, 310; Marcus, *Jew in the Medieval World*, 245–6; Morrison, *Russian Opera and the Symbolist Movement*, 265.

Anagotos

In the *Sacred Magic of Abramelin the Mage*, Anagotos ("conducting") is listed as one of the sixty-five SERVITORS OF KORE AND MAGOTH.

Sources: Belanger, *Dictionary of Demons*, 33; Mathers, *Book of the Sacred Magic of Abralemin the Mage*, 107; Von Worms, *Book of Abramelin*, 256.

Anamalech

Variations: Anamelech, Anomylech

In Assyrian demonology Anamalech ("good King") was the demonic bearer of ill news. He was primarily worshipped at Sepharvaun, an ancient Assyrian town located on the Euphrates, about sixteen miles (25.75 kilometers) southwest of Baghdad and thirty miles (48.3 kilometers) due north of Opis. He was depicted as a quail but scholars vary as to the gender. Some sources claim that Anamalech is a moon goddess and Andramelech is her sun god.

Sources: Bell, *Bell's New Pantheon*, 14; Icons, *Demons*, 137; Layard, *Nineveh and its Remains*, 459;

Poinsot, *Complete Book of the Occult and Fortune Telling*, 377.

Ananel

Variations: Anane

The *Book of Enoch* lists Ananel as not just a FALLEN ANGEL but also as one of the CHIEF OF TENS who swore allegiance to SAMIAZA and rebelled against God. He lusted after and took a human wife, fathering the NEPHILIM (see also GRIGORI and WATCHERS).

Sources: Barton, *Journal of Biblical Literature*, Vols. 30–31, 162; Laurence, *Book of Enoch, the Prophet*, 6; Lévi, *History of Magic*, 38; Lumpkin, *Fallen Angels, the Watchers, and the Origins of Evil*, 31; Prophet, *Fallen Angels and the Origins of Evil*, 174.

Anarazel

Variations: Anazarel

Working in conjunction with FECOR and GAZIEL, Anarazel is a demon of buried treasure. Together these three demons work to protect the treasures they guard. When the bounty is close to discovery, it is Anarazel who moves it to a new location. In addition to being a tutelary demon, he has the ability to cause earthquakes, inspire fear, raise storms, ring bells at midnight, and summon ghosts.

Sources: De Claremont, *Ancient's Book of Magic*, 12; Hibbard, *Three Elizabethan Pamphlets*, 147; Nash, *Works of Thomas Nashe*, 232.

Anatreth

In the *Testament of Solomon*, Anatreth is the demon of fever and stomach pains. He was the twenty-fifth spirit to appear before Solomon confessing to him that if he heard the words "Arara, Charara" he would instantly flee (see SPIRITS OF SOLOMON).

Sources: Ashe, *Qabalah*, 49; Charlesworth, *Old Testament Pseudepigrapha*, Vol. 2, 980; Conybeare, *Jewish Quarterly Review*, Vol. 11, 37.

Anchancho

Variations: SUPAY

Anchancho are the demons of disease in the demonology of the Collao people of the Andes. According to their legends, Anchancho were born the children of a powerful prince named Malleu of Chacamita and his concubines. They are described as looking like black whirlwinds.

Anchancho are powerful at twilight but if there is a storm as well, their power greatly increases. Using the power of the evil eye they can charm a person, possess him, and once inside, drain the body of its blood directly from the heart. Fortunately, Anchancho live in isolated mountain areas and their presence can be detected easily because they make a noise similar to the sound of a braying mule. Their personal adversary is the god of plenty and wealth, Ekkekko.

Sources: Osborne, *South American Mythology*, 80; Senior, *Illustrated Who's Who in Mythology*, 24; Turner, *Dictionary of Ancient Deities*, 51.

Ancitif

During the Louviers Possessions, which took place in Normandy, France, in 1643, Ancitif was the name of the individual demon who possessed Sister Barbara of St. Michael. He caused in her the typical signs of possession such as wild contortions of the body, *glossolalia* (speaking in tongues), shouting obscene words, and the sudden appearance and disappearance of a wound upon the body.

Sources: Robbins, *Encyclopedia of Witchcraft and Demonology*, 128; Samuelson, *Visions of Tomorrow*, 101; Shepard, *Encyclopedia of Occultism and Parapsychology*, 51.

And

According to Enochian lore, And is a CACODAEMON. His counterpart is the angel Ndzn (ENOCHIAN CACODAEMONS).

Sources: Chopra, *Academic Dictionary of Mythology*, 26; Laycock, *Complete Enochian Dictionary*, 77.

Andhaka

Variations: Andhakasuravadhamurti

Andhaka ("Cosmos") is a demonic King from Hindu demonology. He was born blind and ugly from a drop of Lord Shiva's sweat. In art he is commonly shown as being impaled upon Lord Shiva's trident or as a dark-skinned skeletal being whose blood has been drained from his body. Andhaka is notably malevolent and incredibly fierce; he has a terrible roar that he uses in combat to frighten his opponents. If ever he is cut, as he bleeds, smaller versions of himself are created from the droplets of blood. He can only be destroyed after he decides to marry a beautiful woman who is like a mother to him.

Sources: Garg, *Encyclopaedia of the Hindu World*, Vol. 2, 449; Williams, *Handbook of Hindu Mythology*, 54–5.

Andras

Christian demonology says that Andras, the demon of quarrels, is a FALLEN ANGEL and Grand MARQUIS OF HELL who commands thirty legions, although conflicting sources claim him to be a prince (see PRINCES OF HELL). When summoned, he appears as a naked man with a set of angelic wings and the head of an owl. He rides upon the back of a black wolf and wields a saber.

Andras has little patience and will kill anyone who gives him the slightest provocation, especially those who are not constantly aware of his presence when he is around. Andras causes discord and has the ability to convince men to kill.

Sources: Collin de Plancy, *Dictionary of Witchcraft*, 16; De Laurence, *Lesser Key of Solomon, Goetia*, 42; Gettings, *Dictionary of Demons*, 31; Poinsot, *Complete Book of the Occult and Fortune Telling*, 377; Scot, *Discoverie of Witchcraft*, 224.

Andrealphus

Variations: Androalphus

In Johann Wierus's *Pseudomonarchia Daemonum (False Monarchy of Demons,* 1583), Andrealphus is listed as a marquis who commands thirty legions. A FALLEN ANGEL and lesser demon, he is also listed among the seventy-two SPIRITS OF SOLOMON (see MARQUIS OF HELL). Andrealphus will appear before his summoner as a peacock with an overly large beak, but, at his summoner's request, will assume the shape of a man. He is known for teaching astronomy, geometry, mathematics, and all sciences that involve measurements. Andrealphus also has the power to turn a man into a bird.

Sources: Crowley, *The Goetia*, 62; De Laurence, *Lesser Key of Solomon, Goetia*, 43; DuQuette, *Key to Solomon's Key*, 193; Scot, *Discoverie of Witchcraft*, 224; Waite, *Book of Black Magic*, 217.

Androcos

Androcos is Greek for "arranger of man" or "orderer of man." According to the *Sacred Magic of Abramelin the Mage*, he is one of the twenty-two SERVITORS OF ARITON (see ARITON).

Sources: Belanger, *Dictionary of Demons*, 33; Mathers, *Sacred Magic of Abramelin the Mage*, 108; Susej, *Demonic Bible*, 259.

Andromalius

Andromalius is listed as both a duke and an earl in traditional Christian demonology (see DUKES OF HELL and EARLS OF HELL). A FALLEN ANGEL and now a lesser demon, he is also listed as one of the seventy-two SPIRITS OF SOLOMON. Andromalius commands thirty-six legions of demons and punishes thieves and generally wicked people. Described as looking like a man holding a snake in his hands, Andromalius is summoned for his ability to find hidden treasures, return stolen items, and for uncovering underhanded dealings.

Sources: Crowley, *The Goetia*, 65; De Laurence, *Lesser Key of Solomon, Goetia*, 45–6; Godwin, *Godwin's Cabalistic Encyclopedia*, 22.

Andros

In the *Theurgia Goetia*, the second book of the *Lemegeton*, Andros ("man") is said to be an AERIAL DEVIL and one of the twelve SERVITORS OF MACARIEL (see MACARIEL). A chief duke who commands four hundred servitors, Andros can appear to his summoner in any number of forms but commonly appears as a dragon with a virgin's head. Both diurnal and nocturnal, he is good-natured and willing to obey those who summon him.

Sources: Krill, *Greek and Latin in English Today*, 44; Peterson, *Lesser Key of Solomon*, 103; Trithemius, *Steganographia*, 141; Waite, *Book of Black Magic and of Pacts*, 189.

Andrucha

Duke Andrucha is, according to the *Theurgia Goetia*, the second book of the *Lemegeton*, one of the ten SERVITORS OF BYDIEL (see BYDIEL). An AERIAL DEVIL, he commands 2,400 servitors. When summoned, Andrucha will have an attractive appearance. He is good-natured and willing to obey his summoner.

Source: Peterson, *Lesser Key of Solomon*, 105.

Andskoti

Andskoti is an ancient Norse word for the DEVIL or SATAN. Its literal translation is "one who shoots against us."

Sources: Grimm, *Teutonic Mythology*, Vol. 3, 989; McKinnell, *Fantastic in Old Norse/Icelandic Literature*, 119; Martin, *Investigation into Old Norse Concepts of the Fate of the God*, 121.

Angel of Edom

Variations: The angel of Rome, essentially another name for SATAN

The angel of Edom seeks to be "like the most high" and ascend into heaven to assume the very throne of God. The angel of Edom is the very same angel that Jacob saw in his dream ascending a ladder into the sky where he will almost reach Heaven, but God will cast him down. Each angel seen in the dream is a symbolic representation of a country that has come into power and eventually fallen. The four angels were Babylon, Persia, Greece, and Rome. According to legend, the angel of Edom will be destroyed when grabbed by the hair and slain by the prophet Elijah, spraying his blood upon the garments of the Lord.

Sources: Bamberger, *Fallen Angels*, 139–40; Davidson, *Dictionary of Angels*, 28; Quispel, *Studies in Gnosticism and Hellenistic Religions*, 84.

Angel-Peacock

Variations: IBLIS, Melek Taus, "the Peacock Angel," SATAN

The Moslem sects of Sunnite-Saafites believe

that the angel-peacock is a redeemed FALLEN ANGEL. His sacred color is blue.

Sources: Adams, *Persia by a Persian*, 503–5; Bolton, *Western Accounts of the History, Sociology and Linguistics of Chinese Secret Societies*, 160; Illes, *Encyclopedia of Spirits*, 824.

Angels of the Bottomless Pit, The

Variations: ABADDON, Apollyon ("one that exterminates"), "The destroyer," SATAN

The Book of Revelation 9:11 says that a bottomless pit will open at the sounding of the fifth trumpet of the seventh seal and in doing so will release the evil angels of Hell upon earth for the following five months. During that time the Angels of the Bottomless Pit are free to torture all of those people who do not have the seal of the Lord upon their foreheads (see SATAN).

Sources: Ballard, *Beasts of Eschatology and Related Subjects*, 38, 56; Prigent, *Commentary on the Apocalypse of St. John*, 282; Scott, *Holy Bible, Containing the Old and New Testaments*, 733.

Angels of Punishment, The

Variations: Malake Habbalah

There are seven Angels of Punishment listed in the *Testament of Solomon*. Their names are HUTRIEL ("rod of God"), KUSHIEL ("rigid one of God"), Lahatiel ("flaming one of God"), MAKATIEL ("plague of God"), PUSIEL or Puriel ("fire of God"), ROGZIEL ("wrath of God"), SHOFTIEL ("judge of God"). They are in service under the five ARCHANGELS OF PUNISHMENT.

Sources: Brewer, *Dictionary of Phrase and Fable*, 596; Davidson, *Dictionary of Angels*, 172; Mew, *Eclectic Magazine of Foreign Literature, Science, and Art*, Vol. 115, 407; Webster, *Encyclopedia of Angels*, 112.

Angra Mainyu

Variations: Angra Mainu, Angra Mainya, Angru Mainyu, AHRIMAN, Ako Mainyu

Angra Mainyu's name in Avestan, the language of Zoroastrian scripture, translates to mean "destructive one," "destructive spirit," or "fiendish spirit." A spirit of evil from the mythology of ancient Iran, Angra Mainyu is a demon of darkness and a destroyer of that which is good. Under the service of DRUJ, he commands dark forces. Angra Mainyu was fathered by the god Zurvan Akarana ("boundless time") and born the twin brother of Ahura Mazda ("wise lord"). He lives in Hell and his sign and sacred animal is the snake.

Unlike so many other demons, Angra Mainyu made the choice to be evil when he confessed, "It is not that I cannot create anything good, but that I will not." He causes diseases and created the serpent Aži Dahaka, frost in the winter, the peacock, and heat in the summer, as well as sixteen scourges to counter the sixteen lands that were created by his twin brother. Angra Mainyu also brought into being the demonic whore Jeh (see JAHI).

He leads his armies against the god of light, Spenta Mainyu ("holy spirit"), and his hosts. However, at the end of twelve millenniums, Saoshyant, another son of Zoroaster, will bring an era of peace and destroy Angra Mainyu.

Sources: Jackson, *Zoroastrian Studies*, 70–5; Jordan, *Encyclopedia of Gods*, 17; Messadié, *History of the Devil*, 83; Mills, *Zarathustra, Philo, the Achaemenids and Israel*, 277, 310.

Angry Ones, The

In Tibetan demonology the angry ones are demons that consume the flesh of man and serve fresh human brains in a skull chalice.

Sources: Kendra, *Imprints of Indian Thought and Culture Abroad*, 119; Li, *History of Tibetan Religion*, 211; Paul, *Sherpas of Nepal in the Tibetan Cultural Context*, 79.

Angul

Angul is from the demonology of the Philippines. He is known to kill people with an axe (see ARI-MASINGAN).

Source: Ashley, *Complete Book of Devils and Demons*, 95.

Aniel

Chief Duke Aniel is one of the twenty SERVITORS OF CABARIEL as well as one of the sixteen SERVITORS OF ASELIEL, according to the *Sacred Magic of Abramelin the Mage* (see ASELIEL and CABARIEL). Commanding fifty servitors of his own, Aniel, a diurnal demon, is obedient to his masters.

Sources: Belanger, *Dictionary of Demons*, 34; Guiley, *Encyclopedia of Demons and Demonology*, 36; Peterson, *Lesser Key of Solomon*, 84.

Aniguel

Variations: Anisel, the Serpent of Paradise

One of the ELECTORS OF HELL as well as a Grand Duke in service to Aini, Aniguel has the appearance of a ten-year-old boy. When invoking this demon, one must summon him three times. Aniguel is good at discovering buried treasure and mineral deposits. He also can fly very fast.

Sources: Conway, *Demonology and Devil-Lore*, 299; Hall, *Secret Teachings of All Ages*, 297; Rudwin, *Devil in Legend and Literature*, 28.

Anizel

One of the ELECTORS OF HELL and a Grand Duke, Anizel is under the command of ASHTAROTH.

Sources: Carus, *Open Court*, Vol. 43, 472; Rudwin, *Devil in Legend and Literature*, 28.

Anmael

Variations: Chnum, Khnum

Anmael is one of the FALLEN ANGELS who lusted after and took a human wife against God's will. According to lore, he was said to have made a bargain with a mortal woman named Istahar. In exchange for her sexual favors, he agreed that he would reveal to her the true name of God (see also AMEZYARAK, GRIGORI, and WATCHERS).

Sources: Davidson, *Dictionary of Angels*, 48; Illes, *Encyclopedia of Spirits*, 568; Jung, *Fallen Angels in Jewish, Christian and Mohammedan Literature*, 92.

Anneber

Variations: Anneberg

In German demonology, Anneber is a demon that lives in mines. He looks like a horse or a goat with a thick neck, poisonous breath, and terrifying eyes. According to one popular story, Anneber killed twelve miners with his toxic breath because they were working a silver vein that he had been charged to protect.

Source: Gettings, *Dictionary of Demons*, 33.

Annixiel

Heinrich Cornelius Agrippa Von Netteshim's book, *Naturalis et Innaturalis*, lists Annixiel as the eight ELECTORS OF HELL. All other grimoires and sources claim that there are only seven.

Source: Davidson, *Dictionary of Angels*, 104.

Anoster

Anoster is the twenty-ninth of the seventy-two SPIRITS OF SOLOMON. A demon that causes bladder troubles, he is easily banished. Grind into powder three laurel seeds and add it to pure oil, then, while rubbing it onto the body, say "I exorcise thee, Anostêr. Stop by Marmaraô." Marmaraô is the angelic adversary of Anoster.

Sources: Abrahams, *Jewish Quarterly Review*, Vol. 11, 37; Ashe, *Qabalah*, 50; Conybeare, *Jewish Quarterly Review*, Vol. 11, 37; Fleg, *Life of Solomon*, 107.

Ansitif

During the possession of the nuns of Louviers in 1643, Ansitif, a lesser demon, possessed the body of Sister Barbara of St. Michael.

Sources: Gettings, *Dictionary of Demons*, 33; Shepard, *Encyclopedia of Occultism and Parapsychology*, 48; Spence, *Encyclopedia of Occultism*, 27.

Antares

Antares is one of the FALLEN ANGELS who swore allegiance to SAMIAZA and rebelled against God. He lusted after and took a human wife and fathered the NEPHILIM.

Sources: Agrippa, *Three Books of Occult Philosophy*, 879; Greer, *New Encyclopedia of the Occult*, 509; Grimassi, *Italian Witchcraft*, 68.

Antichrist

Variations: Al-Daja, Al Daja'l, Al Maseeh, Antichristoi, Antichristos, Antichristos Tertullian, the "Ape of God," Ho Antichristos, Master of the Revel, the second Beast

Antichrist is a Greek word that translates to mean "in place of Christ" or "the opposite of Christ." Symbolically he is a vampire; whereas Christ shed his blood for all of mankind, the Antichrist feeds off the blood of man.

It is believed by many that the Antichrist will be born of the union between a virgin whose lineage can be traced back to the Tribe of Dan and the DEVIL. The child that will be born will look human in all ways and will rise to power as a major political leader who preaches peace. Seven years before the Apocalypse, he will come to power and stay there for forty-two months. Halfway through the Tribulation the Antichrist will be slain and resurrected by the DEVIL, who will then possess the body and finish out his rule. He will have the ability to draw down fire from the sky. The Antichrist will also be able to place a mark on the right hand or upon the head of a person to mark him as one of his followers. It is said that without this mark, a person will not be able to legally operate a business.

It is commonly accepted that the Antichrist's sacred number is six hundred sixty-six (666), also known as the Number of the Beast, an idea that came from the Book of Revelation in the New Testament of the Christian Bible (13:17–180) However, most scholars accept that the number is code for the Roman Emperor Nero. In 2005, however, scholars at Oxford University have translated the oldest known copy of the Book of Revelation, a 1,700-year-old papyrus, which has led them to conclude that six hundred sixteen (616) is the original Number of the Beast.

In the Book of Revelation the Antichrist is described as a creature rising up from the sea having seven heads. Each head has ten horns and each horn has upon it ten crowns. The body of this creature will be that of a jaguar, but with the large clawed feet of a bear, the vicious mouth of a lion, and all the power of a dragon.

Sources: Bousset, *Antichrist Legend*, 138–9, 145–7; Chambers, *Book of Days*, 723; McGinn, *Antichrist*, 4, 74, 83.

Antidikos

Variations: One of the many names of SATAN

Antidikos is a Greek name that translates to

mean "one who speaks against," "opponent in a lawsuit," an adversary. It was used as a replacement name for Satan in the testament of Peter: "Be sober-minded; be watchful. Your adversary the devil prowls around like a roaring lion, seeking someone to devour." The devil "devours" his prey by making accusations against a person in the Divine Court of Law.

Sources: Bremmer, *Apocryphal Acts of Andrew*, 49; Kelly, *Satan*, 135; Wells, *Sermon on the Mount*, 63.

Aor

According to Enochian lore, Aor is a CACO-DAEMON. His angelic counterpart is the angel Ormn (see ENOCHIAN CACODAEMONS).

Sources: Chopra, *Academic Dictionary of Mythology*, 30; Laycock, *Complete Enochian Dictionary*, 77.

Apa

According to Enochian lore, Apa is a CACO-DAEMON. His angelic counterpart is Paoc (see ENOCHIAN CACODAEMONS).

Sources: Chopra, *Academic Dictionary of Mythology*, 31; Laycock, *Complete Enochian Dictionary*, 78.

Apaosa

In Persian mythology Apaosa is considered to be a minor demon ("khord DAEVAS"). He rides upon a black-skinned horse with no hair, causing drought, famine, and heat waves as he travels. Apaosa, according to the myth, was defeated by the god Tistrya. He is similar to the Indian evil spirit VRITRA.

Sources: Ara, *Eschatology in the Indo-Iranian Traditions*, 181; Das, *Rgvedic India*, 481–2; Oldenberg, *Religion of the Veda*, 77.

Apaosha

Variations: Ab Osh "([having] the destruction of water)"; Apaush, the numbing frost; Aposh

Apaosha's name in Avestan, the language of Zoroastrian scripture, translates to mean "not thriving." A demon of drought and most powerful in the month of July, he looks like a black horse. Apaosha's personal adversary is the god of life-bringing rainfall, Tishtrya (see also APAOSA).

Sources: Darmesteter, *Avesta Khorda Avesta*, 56; Grey, *Mythology of All Races*, 268; Turner, *Dictionary of Ancient Deities*, 468.

Apelki

The *Sacred Magic of Abramelin the Mage* names Apelki as one of the twenty servitors of SERVITORS OF AMAYMON (see AMAYMON). His name is Greek and translates to mean "the misleaders" or "turners aside."

Sources: Forgotten Books, *Book of the Sacred Magic*

of Abramelin the Mage, 42–3; Lowry, *Under the Volcano*, 194; Mathers, *Book of the Sacred Magic of Abra-Melin*, 122.

Apep

Variations: Apap, Apepi, Apis, Apophis, Apopis, "Eater-up of Souls," Enemy of Ra, Evil Lizard, Rerek, Serpent from the Nile, World Encircler

In the religion of the ancient Egyptians, Apep ("great snake" or "he who was spat out") was the Lord of Darkness; he lived in the underworld. In service to the god Set, Apep was the personification of chaos and all that is evil. A fallen god himself, he commanded the demons Nak and Sebau. Apep has been depicted as a monstrous serpent, a crocodile, and in later times as a dragon. He is said to be sixteen yards long (14.6304 meters) with a head made of flint.

Apep, as well as various other nocturnal monsters from the ancient Egyptian beliefs, tries to prevent Ra from his daily passing across the sky by attacking him during the night when the sun is below the horizon. He tries to hypnotize souls who make it to the underworld and attempts to devour them while using his gigantic coils to stop the flow of the river they travel on.

Even though he is a fallen god, Apep is immortal. He has the ability to completely heal and rejuvenate the damage done daily to his body by Ra, his personal adversary. His roar is so loud it causes the entire underworld to shake. He has a magical gaze that can hypnotize Ra and those who travel with him. The power he releases in battle against Ra often causes earthquakes and thunderstorms. Whenever Apep is successful in swallowing Ra, during the day the absences of the sun god will be shown by an eclipse. Ra's imprisonment never lasts long, however, as he has many allies who rush to his aid to free him.

The ancient Egyptians were fearful of Apep and had developed a means by which to defend themselves against him. The *Book of Overthrowing Apep* is a definitive guide to fighting him. Within its pages it explains the process of how to create, dismember, and dispose of wax figures or drawings of the demon. The deceased were oftentimes buried with magical spells that would destroy Apep if he tried to devour them. Additionally, an annual rite called the Banishing of Apep was performed. In the ceremony the priest would make an effigy of Apep that contained all of the evil of Egypt within it. Then he would ritually destroy it.

Sources: Budge, *Gods of the Egyptians*, 61, 324–7; Chopra, *Academic Dictionary of Mythology*, 32; Godfrey,

Lake and Sea Monsters, 22–4; Remler, Egyptian Mythology A to Z, 20.

Apiel

Apiel is one of the twenty named Duke SERVITORS OF SYMIEL (see SYMIEL). He commands seven hundred ninety servitors of his own. A nocturnal demon, Apiel is disobedient, stubborn, and will not appear willingly to his summoner.

Sources: Belanger, Dictionary of Demons, 35; Guiley, Encyclopedia of Demons and Demonology, 253; Peterson, Lesser Key of Solomon, 89.

Apm

According to Enochian lore, Apm is a CACODAEMON. His angelic counterpart is the angel Pmox (see ENOCHIAN CACODAEMONS).

Sources: Chopra, Academic Dictionary of Mythology, 32; Laycock, Complete Enochian Dictionary, 78.

Apolhun

Variations: ABBADON, Angel of the Abyss, Angel of the Bottomless Pit, Apolluon, Apollyon ("one that exterminates"), Apollyn

Apolhun, Greek for "the destroyer," is one of the one hundred eleven SERVITORS OF AMAYMON, ARITON, ORIENS, AND PAYMON. According to the Book of Revelation he is the demonic spirit of locusts. (See also AGGELOS ABUSSOS, AMAYMON, ARITON, ORIENS, AND PAYMON.)

Sources: Belanger, Dictionary of Demons, 35; Mathers, Book of the Sacred Magic of Abramelin the Mage, 105; Von Worms, Book of Abramelin, 255.

Apormenos

Apormenos is named in the Sacred Magic of Abramelin the Mage ("uncertain") as a demonic spirit and one of the thirty-two SERVITORS OF ASTAROT (see ASTAROT).

Sources: Belanger, Dictionary of Demons, 36; Mathers, Book of the Sacred Magic of Abramelin the Mage, 106; Von Worms, Book of Abramelin, 249.

Apot

Hebrew for "tribute" as in a "treasure," Apot is listed in the Sacred Magic of Abramelin the Mage as one of the fifteen SERVITORS OF ASMODEUS AND MAGOTH (see ASMODEUS).

Sources: Belanger, Dictionary of Demons, 36; Ford, Bible of the Adversary, 91; Von Worms, Book of Abramelin, 248.

Apsu

Variations: Absu, ABZU, Apsû, Engur, KINGU

In the Sumero-Akkadian mythology, Apsu is the demonic god of the underworld ocean where he lives and is the consort of the demon TIAMAT. He is the demon of the primordial abyss of the saltwater of Chaos that is under the earth and the symbol of chaos. All lakes, rivers, springs, wells, and sources of freshwater are said to be drawn from him. According to the mythology, Apsu was placed under a magical spell that forced him into a deep sleep by the god Ea, who then slew him. Ea then took Apsu's decomposing body and used it to create the first human.

Sources: Hamilton, In the Beginning, 79–86; Leick, Dictionary of Ancient Near Eastern Mythology, 11–2; Van der Toorn, Dictionary of Demons and Deities in the Bible, 300.

Aqueous Devils

In Francesco Maria Guazzo's book Compendium Maleficarum (Compendium of Witches, 1628), he described seven different types of demons, one of which is the aqueous, or aquatic devil. He writes that as a species they appear as generally beautiful and seductive women who prey upon mankind, striking whenever an opportunity presents itself. They have the ability to drown swimmers, cause storms at sea, and sink ships. Naturally, one would encounter such a creature in lakes, oceans, and other bodies of water where they must live.

Sources: Kipfer, Order of Things, 255; Paine, Hierarchy of Hell, 69; Simons, Witchcraft World, 78; Summers, Witchcraft and Black Magic, 77.

Aquiel

Variations: Vel Aquiel

The eighteenth-century book alleged to be written by Pope Honorius III, Grimoire of Pope Honorius (Le Grimoire du Pape Honorius), says that Aquiel is the demon of all things that work against man keeping Sunday holy.

Sources: Belanger, Dictionary of Demons, 36; Poinsot, Complete Book of the Occult and Fortune Telling, 377; Shah, Occultism, 72.

Arachula

Arachula is an evil, demonic spirit of the air that comes from the area of China near the Siberian border.

Sources: Poinsot, Complete Book of the Occult and Fortune Telling, 377.

Araex

In the Sacred Magic of Abramelin the Mage, Araex is among the thirty-two SERVITORS OF ASTAROT (see ASTAROT). His name is Greek and translates to mean "shock."

Sources: Belanger, Dictionary of Demons, 36; Mathers, Book of Sacred Magic of Abramelin the Mage, 106; Susej, Demonic Bible, 257.

Arafes

Arafes is one of the twenty named Duke SERVITORS OF SYMIEL (see SYMIEL). He is a nocturnal demon that has command over seven hundred ninety servitors. He is by nature disobedient and stubborn, and will not appear willingly before his summoner.

Sources: Peterson, *Lesser Key of Solomon*, 88.

Arakh

Arakh is a vampiric demon from Cambodian demonology. An immortal demon, he was never human. Arakh is an overall powerful entity who possesses a person and persuades them to kill themselves. The only way to save one of his potential victims is to perform a successful ceremonial exorcism.

On a side note, *arakh* is also the word used in the Sumerian language for the eighth month, also known as the month of the scorpion.

Sources: Herbert, *South-East Asia*, 50; Steinberg, *Celebrating the Jewish Year*, Vol. 1, 19; Thompson, *Calling the Souls*, 153.

Arakiba

Variations: ARAKIEL, Arâkîba, Araqiel, AR-TAQIFA, URAKABARAMEEL

Arakiba is one of the CHIEF OF TENS who is mentioned in the *Book of Enoch*. He swore allegiance to SAMIAZA, rebelled against God, and lusted after and took a human wife against God's will. Arakiba is a FALLEN ANGEL, formerly of the Order of Angels. In addition to fathering the NEPHILIM, he taught geomancy and the signs of the earth to man. His name translates to mean "one who has dominion over the earth."

Sources: Charles, *Book of Enoch*, 137; Davidson, *Dictionary of Angels*, 50; Lumpkin, *Fallen Angels, the Watchers, and the Origins of Evil*, 31; Humphreys, *Lost Book of Enoch*, 4.

Arakiel

Variations: Arakab, ARAKIBA, Arâkîba, Araqiel, Araquel, Araquiel, Aretstikapha ("world of distortion") Aristiqifa, Arkas, ARTAQIFA, Artaquifa, Saraqaek, Saraquael, Urakaba, URAKABARAMEEL

In Enochian lore, Arakiel is one of the FALLEN ANGELS, formerly of the Order of Angels. He swore his allegiance to SAMIAZA, rebelled against God, and lusted after and took a human as his wife. He went on to teach mankind geomancy and geography and to father the NEPHILIM. His name translates to mean "earth of God," "one who has dominion over the earth," "the land of the mighty one," or "the land is mighty." Unlike other Fallen Angels, it is said that Arakiel still leads souls to their final judgment.

Sources: Barton, *Journal of Biblical Literature*, Vols. 30–31, 162; Charles, *Book of Enoch*, 16; Ginzberg, *Legends of the Jews*, 125.

Arallu

Variations: PAZUZU, UTUKKU

Arallu are a type of DJINN in Assryo-Babylonian demonology that were born from the bile of Ea (Enki) and the stagnant water under the KUR. They are described as "the storm, which breaks loose with fury in the skies" or "the rising wind, which casts darkness over the bright day" and are depicted as having a human male body, the head and paws of a lion, large wings, and small goat horns upon their head. Arallu are extremely powerful and immortal beings and have the power to cause disease, corrupt the unity of a family, inspire criminal acts, and kill livestock. When they possess a person it requires a very powerful exorcist to cast out the demons. Arallu hate mankind and there is no way to appease them.

They are the adversaries of the gods, especially the moon god, Sin (Nanna). According to mythology, an eclipse is caused when they attack him. They tie him up in a sack, causing him to have to fight his way out. Fortunately, there is a finite number of arallu, as they are all male and cannot reproduce.

Sources: Jastrow, *Religion of Babylonia and Assyria*, 260; Langdon, *Semitic Mythology*, 161; Rogers, *Religion of Babylonia and Assyria*, 147.

Araniel

In *Ars Paulina*, the third book of the *Lemegeton*, Araniel is one of the fifteen Duke SERVITORS OF SASQUIEL (see SASQUIEL) as well as one of the fifteen Duke SERVITORS OF SCOX (see SCOX). He has under his command 5,550 servitors.

Sources: Peterson, *Lesser Key of Solomon*, 114; Trithemius, *Steganographia*, 95.

Araon

In the *Theurgia Goetia*, book two of the *Lemegeton*, Araon is a duke and one of the sixteen SERVITORS OF GEDEIL. A FALLEN ANGEL, he is nocturnal (see DUKES OF HELL and GEDEIL).

Sources: Crowley, *The Goetia*, 82; Davidson, *Dictionary of Angels*, 85; Peterson, *Lesser Key of Solomon*, 202.

Arathaso

In Burmese demonology, an arathaso is a species of demon that lives in trees.

Sources: Gettings, *Dictionary of Demons*, 27.

Aratiel

Aratiel, a diurnal demon, is one of the sixteen SERVITORS OF ASELIEL, according to the *Sacred Magic of Abramelin the Mage*.

Sources: Belanger, *Dictionary of Demons*, 37; Peterson, *Lesser Key of Solomon*, 69.

Aratron

Variations: Arathron

In 1575 an unknown author published *Grimoire Arbatel de Magia Veterum* (*Arbatel of the Magic of the Ancients*) in Basel, Switzerland. In it was mentioned the demon Aratron, a chief under the domain of the demon CASSIEL and one of the seven OLYMPIAN SPIRITS. He is able to command those things which are astrologically attributed to Saturn; 17,640,000 spirits; 36,000 legions of spirits with each legion containing 490 spirits; 49 provinces; 49 kings; 42 princes; 35 presidents; 28 dukes; 21 ministers; 14 FAMILIARs; and seven messengers. He is at his peak of power on the first hour of the day on Saturdays.

Aratron would be summoned for his ability to bring together underworld spirits with men who seek them. He can also instantly turn to stone any living organism; cause men to become hairy; cure barrenness in women; give Familiars; grant long life; teach alchemy, how to become invisible, magic, and medicine; and transform coal into treasure and vice versa. He will also truthfully answer questions regarding his provinces and provincials.

Each of the Olympian Spirits rules, in succession, for a period of 490 years. Aratron is not due back into power until the year 2880.

Sources: Drury, *Dictionary of the Esoteric*, 16, 239; Gettings, *Dictionary of Demons*, 36; González-Wippler, *Complete Book of Spells*, 120; Konstantinos, *Summoning Spirits*, 176; Mathers, *Grimoire of Armadel*, 56.

Araziel

Variations: Arazjal, Arazyael, Arazyal, Asaradel, Atriel, Esdreel, Sahariel, Samuil, SARIEL, SERIEL

From the *Book of Enoch*, Araziel is one of the CHIEF OF TENS who swore allegiance to SAMIAZA and rebelled against God, lusting after and then taking a human as his wife. His name translates to mean "God is my noon," "light of God," "moon of God" or "my moon is God." He is said to have been the FALLEN ANGEL who taught men the course of the moon. Araziel commands the sign of Taurus. Araziel commands the sign of Taurus.

Sources: Behrens, *Lost Scrolls of King Solomon*, 283; Laurence, *Foreign Quarterly Review*, Vol. 24, 370; Lévi, *History of Magic*, 38.

Arbiel

Arbiel is listed as a chief duke in *Theurgia Goetia*, the second book of the *Lemegeton*, under the command of HYDRIEL, one of the eleven WANDERING PRINCES. An AERIAL DEVIL, Arbiel himself commands 1,320 servitors. He may be summoned any time of the day or night, as he is a very courteous demon and willing to obey his summoner. When he appears, he does so as a serpent with a virgin's face and head. Arbiel lives in or near water, marshes, and wetlands.

Sources: Belanger, *Dictionary of Demons*, 37; Guiley, *Encyclopedia of Demons and Demonology*, 115; Peterson, *Lesser Key of Solomon*, 95.

Arcan

The demon Arcan was first mentioned during the Elizabethan era, his name appearing in a book titled *An Elizabethan Devil-Worshiper's Prayer-Book*; it was quite possibly written by John Dee. Arcan's rank is given as being a king and he is described as being black-skinned with exposed fangs and saucerlike eyes. He carries a bow and arrow and rides upon a roe. He has dominion over the moon.

Sources: Anonymous, *Manuscripts and Books on Medicine, Alchemy, Astrology and Natural Sciences Arranged in Chronological Order*, 239; Gettings, *Dictionary of Demons*, 37; Summers, *A Popular History of Witchcraft*, 91.

Arch She-Demons

An arch she-demon is a female ARCHDEMON, and there are eight such named in all the various grimoires: AGRAT-BAT-MAHLAHT, ASTARTE, BARBELO, EISHETH ZENUNIM, LEVIATHAN, LILITH, NAAMAH, and Proserpine.

Sources: Greer, *New Encyclopedia of the Occult*, 191; Hanauer, *Folk-lore of the Holy Land*, 325; Hyatt, *Book of Demons*, 40, 43, 45, 52; Matthews, *Sophia*, 147–8; Voltaire, *Works of M. de Voltaire*, 193; Willis, *World Mythology*, 51; Wise, *Origin of Christianity*, 95.

Archaios Ophis

Variations: Ho Opis Ho Archaios ("the Ancient Serpent")

In Greek mythology, Archaios Ophis ("very old snake") is a demonic, primeval snake.

Sources: Gunkel, *Creation and Chaos in the Primeval Era and the Eschaton*, 238, 241; Kelly, *Satan*, 152; Mortenson, *Coming to Grips with Genesis*, 369.

Archangels of Punishment, The

There are five Archangels of Punishment listed in the *Testament of Solomon*. Their names are: AF, HEMAH, KEZEF, MASHITH, and MESHABBER. They are in service under the Angels of Death and command the ANGELS OF PUNISHMENT.

Sources: Ashley, *Complete Book of Demons and Devils*, 78; Davidson, Dictionary of Angels, 351; Singer, *Jewish Encyclopedia*, 593.

Archdemon

In Judeo-Christian and occult demonology, an archdemon is a leader of one of the demonic hosts. On occasion they are described as being a FALLEN ANGEL. Historically, the description of what an archdemon is and the names of those that exist have varied greatly throughout history; some examples of archdemons are Adam Belial, ASHTAROTH, ASMODEUS, and Lucifuge.

Sources: Hall, *Secret Teachings of all Ages*, 354; Harper, *Biblical World*, Vol. 41, 125–6; Meyer, *Ancient Christian Magic*, 108.

Archdemons, Ten

According to the Kabala, there are ten named archdemons and each of them commands an order of demons: ABBADON, ADRAMELECH, AGARES, ASHTAROTH, ASMODEUS, BAAL, Beelzebul (BEELZEBUB), BELIAL, LUCIFER, and MOLOCH.

Sources: Hall, *Secret Teachings of all Age*, 354; Hyatt, *Book of Demons*, 73; Oliphant, *Scientific Religion*, 226.

Archiel

Archiel is a chief under the service of the demon Tephros (see TEPHRAS).

Source: Trithemius, *Steganographia*, 88.

Arcisant

In the *Theurgia Goetia*, the second book of the *Lemegeton*, Arcisant is a chief duke and one of the sixteen SERVITORS OF ASYRIEL (see ASYRIEL). He is diurnal, good-natured, and willing to obey his summoners. He has command of twenty servitors.

Source: Peterson, *Lesser Key of Solomon*, 73–4, 77.

Arcisat

In *Theurgia Goetia*, the second book of the *Lemegeton*, Arcisat is ranked as a chief duke and listed as one of the sixteen SERVITORS OF ASYRIEL (see ASYRIEL). Arcisat is a diurnal demon, naturally good-natured, and willing to obey his summoners; he has command of twenty servitors.

Sources: Belanger, *Dictionary of Demons*, 37; Guiley, *Encyclopedia of Demons and Demonology*, 20; Peterson, *Lesser Key of Solomon*, 73.

Arcon

The *Sacred Magic of Abramelin the Mage* lists Arcon ("a ruler") as a demonic spirit and one of the forty-nine SERVITORS OF BEELZEBUB (see BEELZEBUB).

Sources: Belanger, *Dictionary of Demons*, 37; Mathers, *Book of the Sacred Magic of Abramelin the Mage*, 121; Von Worms, *Book of Abramelin*, 257.

Ardad

In numerous demonology sources, Ardad is said to be a demon who leads travelers astray. It is suspected by many sources that this demon may be one of the many guises of LILITH.

Sources: Ashley, *Complete Book of Devils and Demons*, 77; Poinsot, *Complete Book of the Occult and Fortune Telling*, 377; Trachtenberg, *Jewish Magic and Superstition*, 319.

Ardat-Lile

Variations: ARDAT-LILI, Ardat Lilî, Irdu, Lili

From ancient Babylonian, Hebrew, and Sumerian lore comes a species of vampiric demons known as ardat-lile; the name literally translates to mean "young females of marrying age now evil wanton spirits." It was common in the ancient Sumerian language that an individual word was used to convey a wide array of related concepts. Interestingly, there is no singular form of the word in its original language's translation.

This type of demon was never human but rather was always an infernal, immortal demon. Looking like a young female, when they could they would marry a man in order to wreak havoc in his life. They are known for their ravenous sexual appetite and for the delight that they take in doing harm to mankind. Ardat-lile are also responsible for causing nocturnal emissions, stealing the semen, and using it to give birth to demonic children (see SUCCUBUS). The ardat-lile are an early precursor to the demon LILITH, combined with a female storm demon.

Sources: Gettings, *Dictionary of Demons*, 37; Hyatt, *Book of Demons*, 35; Pick, *Dreams and History*, 42.

Ardat-Lili

Variations: Ardat, Ardat Lilî, Ardat Lile, LILITH

Originally a type of storm demon from Babylonian and Mesopotamian demonology, the ardat-lili evolved into a type of female nocturnal demon. Later, the book of Isaiah 34:14 changes the name to LILITH.

The ardat-lili are said to be known to swarm together in great numbers, and at night they would visit men while they slept in order to have sexual intercourse, conceive, and bear ghostly children. A telltale sign of their visitation is evidence of having experienced a nocturnal emission. The male equivalent of this type of demon is called *lilu*.

Sources: Hyatt, *Book of Demons*, 51; Jastrow, *Religion of Babylonia and Assyria*, 260; Pick, *Dreams and History*, 42; Rogers, *Religion of Babylonia and Assyria*, 147.

Ardesiel

Variations: Ardefiel, Ardifiel

According to Enochian lore, Ardesiel is one of the twenty-eight demonic rulers of the lunar mansions. Said to be one of the FALLEN ANGELS, he presides over the mansion Algelioche ("forehead of the lion") and is known for his ability to strengthen buildings (see ENOCHIAN RULERS OF THE LUNAR MANSIONS).

Sources: Moura, *Mansions of the Moon for the Green Witch*, 73; Scheible, Sixth and Seventh Books of Moses, 75; Webster, *Encyclopedia of Angels*, 20.

Arean

According to the book *Sacred Magic of Abramelin the Mage*, Arean is one of the sixteen SERVITORS OF ASELIEL (see ASELIEL). He is a diurnal demon.

Sources: Belanger, *Dictionary of Demons*, 37; Peterson, *Lesser Key of Solomon*, 69.

Aremata-Popoa

In Polynesian mythology, Aremata-Popoa ("short wave" or "tidal wave") is an immensely powerful demon of the ocean (see AQUEOUS DEVILS). Working in conjunction with another demon of the sea, AREMATA-RORUA, they prey upon sailors.

Sources: Andrews, *Dictionary of Nature Myths*, 223; Littleton, *Gods, Goddesses, and Mythology*, Vol. 1, 1274; Maberry, *They Bite*, 192–3.

Aremata-Rorua

In Polynesian mythology, Aremata-Rorua ("long wave") is an immensely powerful demon of the ocean (see AQUEOUS DEVILS). Working in conjunction with another demon of the sea, AREMATA-POPOA, they prey upon sailors.

Sources: Andrews, *Dictionary of Nature Myths*, 223; Littleton, *Gods, Goddesses, and Mythology*, Vol. 1, 1274; Maberry, *They Bite*, 192–3.

Argilon

In the second book of the *Sacred Magic of Abramelin the Mage*, Argilon ("clay") is listed as one of the thirty-two SERVITORS OF ASTAROT (see ASTAROT).

Sources: Mathers, *Book of the Sacred Magic of Abramelin the Mage*, 117; Susej, *Demonic Bible*, 257; Von Worms, *Book of Abramelin*, 257.

Ariaiel

Ariaiel ("Lion of God") is, according to the *Theurgia Goetia*, book two of the *Lemegeton*, one of the twelve Duke SERVITORS OF CASPIEL (see CASPIEL and DUKES OF HELL).

Sources: Agrippa, *Three Books of Occult Philosophy*,

553; De Claremont, *Ancient's Book of Magic*, 6; Hirsch, *Demon and the Angel*, 98–9.

Arias

Variations: Ariael, ARIEL ("Lion of God"), IALDABAOTH

Hebrew for "lion of God," Arias is, in the Gaelic tradition, one of the seven great princes who ruled over the waters of the earth (see PRINCES OF HELL). In Hasidic lore, however, he was originally an angel of the Order of Virtues who worked in conjunction with the angel Raphael ("healing one of God") to heal the sick. He is summoned for his ability to control other demons and he appears as a lion-headed angel.

Sources: Brewer, *Dictionary of Phrase and Fable*, 42; Davidson, *Dictionary of Angels*, 54; Kitto, *Cyclopædia of Biblical Literature*, 209; Von Goethe, *Goethe's Letters to Zelter*, 377.

Aridiel

Variations: ARIAIEL

The *Lesser Key of Solomon* describes Aridiel as being a rude and stubborn chief duke who commands 2,660 duke servitors. He is one of the twelve SERVITORS OF CASPIEL (see CASPIEL).

Sources: Eco, *Infinity of Lists*, 61; Peterson, *Lesser Key of Solomon*, 60.

Ariel

Variations: One of the seven demons "of the ignited spheres," one of the "seven phantoms of flame," Yà liè

Originally a demon from Chaldean demonology, Ariel ("lion of God") is now considered to be one of the FALLEN ANGELS, formerly of the Order of Virtues. He is said to be one of the retrograde spirits, moving against the regular path of the stars.

The seven spirits of the Abyss who live in the bowels of the earth are considered to be greater than all other demons in their collective power and in the terror and havoc they can cause. Among their powers is the ability to cause earthquakes, affect the economy, assist in finding hidden treasures, foretell the future, and have knowledge of the past. The spirits of the Abyss are overseen by the angelic overlord Michael, and they are continually thwarted by the seven gods of the planets who govern the universe.

Sources: Eco, *Infinity of Lists*, 61; Hirsch, *Demon and the Angel*, 98; Scheible, *Sixth and Seventh Books of Moses*, 73; Von Goethe, *Goethe's Letters to Zelter*, 377.

Arifel

Variations: Arifiel

In *Theurgia Goetia*, book two of the *Lemegeton*, Arifel is a duke and one of the twelve named

Duke SERVITORS OF CARNESIEL (see CARNESIEL and DUKES OF HELL).

Sources: Belanger, *Dictionary of Demons*, 39; Guiley, *Encyclopedia of Demons and Demonology*, 37; Peterson, *Lesser Key of Solomon*, 59.

Arimanius

Variations: AHRIMAN, ANGRA MAINYU, Angru Mainyu, Beelzeboul, SATAN

Arimanius is a demonic god in Zoroastrianism beliefs, the creator and leader of the deavas. He lives in a dimensional plane called Ariman-abad. His personal adversary is Ohrmazd.

Sources: Brucker, *History of Philosophy*, 44–5; Hyatt, *Book of Demons*, 56; Jortin, *Discourses Concerning the Truth of the Christian Religion*, 130.

Ari-Masingan

Variations: Agguiriguira, ANGUL

Ari-masingan is an invisible demon from the demonology of the Ibanag people of the Philippines. Most powerful at dusk and noontime, ari-masingans kill with their axe anyone who has disturbed, hurt, or offended them; such offenses include accidentally stepping or urinating on them. Even the touch of these demons is dangerous, as it causes *natukkal*, a Tagalog word that describes the act of a person's soul being startled and released from their body. If this should happen, the victim will suddenly become ill, fall into a coma, or have uncontrolled muscle spasms. Should an ari-masingan walk over a sleeping woman, she will become pregnant with a DOG or a snake.

The ari-masingans live along riverbanks, at crossroads, in deserted houses, in rivers, in trees, and on trails. To prevent attack from one of these demons, it is best not to walk near their dwelling without first asking permission to do so or leaving an offering of food and drink. Also, it is advised by the Ibanag people to never dress your children in bright colors, as it will attract an ari-masingan's attention.

Should a person find themselves under the attack of an ari-masingan, a complicated ritual must be performed to appease the offended demon. Offerings called *wari* must be made in hopes of appeasing it. The offering consists of biscuits, cigars, pieces of candy, and wine placed on red cloth or paper. If you experience goose bumps, the offering has been accepted.

Sources: Ashley, *Complete Book of Devils and Demons*, 95; Gatan, *Ibanag Indigenous Religious Beliefs*, 67, 113; Peters, *International Journal of Frontier Missions*, 69–80.

Arioch

Variations: Arioc, Ariukh, Arriwuk, Orioc, Oriockh

In Hebrew lore, Arioch ("Fierce Male Lion") is one of the FALLEN ANGELS under the command of SATAN. A demon of vengeance that is called upon for action, he is described as looking like a bat-winged demon.

Sources: Cooper, *Brewer's Book of Myth and Legend*, 19; Kelly, *Who in Hell*, 16; Rose, *Spirits, Fairies, Gnomes, and Goblins*, 20.

Arioth

The *Sacred Magic of Abramelin the Mage* lists Arioth ("lioness") as one of the sixty-five SERVITORS OF KORE AND MAGOTH.

Sources: Kitto, *A Cyclopedia of Biblical Literature*, 837; Mathers, *Book of the Sacred Magic of Abramelin the Mage*, 135; McClintock, *Cyclopædia of Biblical, Theological, and Ecclesiastical Literature*, 448.

Ariton

Variations: Egin, Egyn, Ozal

The Kabbalah tells us that Ariton is a demonic subprince with dominion over water. He commands twenty-two servitors (see SERVITORS OF ARITON and PRINCES OF HELL). The physical appearance of Ariton is so frightful that if the incantation to cause him to manifest were ever performed, the practitioner would suffer a fatal episode of apoplexy, epilepsy, or suffocation.

His name is possibly taken from Hebrew and if so would translate to mean "to delay," "to hinder," "to lay bare," "to make naked," and "to retard." However, if Ariton was taken from the Greek language it would translate as "mysterious" or "secret."

Sources: Ford, *Bible of the Adversary*, 90; Hyatt, *Book of Demons*, 48; Mathers, *Selected Occult Writings of S.L. MacGregor Mathers*, 96; Susej, *Demonic Bible*, 166; Von Worms, *Book of Abramelin*, 243.

Arizial

In Enochian lore Arizial is one of the FALLEN ANGELS who swore allegiance to SAMIAZA, rebelled against God, took a human woman as his wife, and fathered the NEPHILIM.

Sources: Gettings, *Dictionary of Demons*, 37; Spence, *Encyclopedia of Occultism*, 148.

Armadiel

In the *Theurgia Goetia*, book two of the *Lemegeton*, Armadiel is the Prince of the Northeast, who commands 100 servitors, fifteen of which are named chief dukes. The demon of keeping and delivering secret messages, Armadiel is one of the twelve SERVITORS OF DEMORIEL (see PRINCES OF HELL).

Sources: Gettings, *Dictionary of Demons*, 37; Peterson, *Lesser Key of Solomon*, 90; Shumaker, *Natural Magic and Modern Science*, 66; Trithemius, *Steganographia*, 81.

Ármány

In the *Theurgia Goetia*, book two of the *Lemegeton*, Ármány is listed as a duke and one of the twelve named Duke SERVITORS OF CARNESIEL (see CARNESIEL and DUKES OF HELL).

Sources: Eco, *Infinity of Lists*, 61; Guiely, *Encyclopedia of Demons and Demonology*, 37; Peterson, *Lesser Key of Solomon*, 69.

Ármány

Variations: Armani

Ármány ("deceive, intrigue") is essentially a nickname for the DEVIL in Hungarian.

Sources: Czigány, *Oxford History of Hungarian Literature*, 125–6, 531; Lurker, *Routledge Dictionary of Gods and Goddesses, Devils and Demons*, 16; Szabad, *Hungary, Past and Present*, 4.

Armarele

Armarele is listed as a chief in the *Lemegeton, the Lesser Key of Solomon*. He is one of the ten SERVITORS OF SAZQUIEL (see SAZQUIEL) and one of the fifteen SERVITORS OF SASQUIEL (see SASQUIEL).

Source: Waite, *Book of Ceremonial Magic*, 67.

Armaros

Variations: Aramaros, Armârôs, Armarus, ARMERS

Armaros ("accursed one," or "cursed one") is listed in the *Book of Enoch* as one of the CHIEF OF TENS, a GRIGORI, or WATCHERS as they are often called. He was one of the FALLEN ANGELS who swore allegiance to SAMIAZA, rebelled against God, took a human as his wife, and fathered the NEPHILIM. Armaros is also said to have taught mankind how to use magic.

In the poem "The Prophet Enoch," written by Mark Van Doren (1894–1972), Armaros is called ARMERS.

Sources: Barton, *Journal of Biblical Literature*, Vols. 30–31, 162; Eco, *Infinity of Lists*, 61; Laurence, *Book of Enoch, the Prophet*, 7; Laurence, *Foreign Quarterly Review*, Vol. 24, 370; Van Doren, *Spring Birth, and Other Poems*, 89.

Armbiel

In the *Theurgia Goetia*, book two of the *Lemegeton*, Armbiel is a chief duke, commands 1,140 servitors, and is one of the twelve SERVITORS OF DEMORIEL (see DEMORIEL and DUKES OF HELL).

Sources: Peterson, *Lesser Key of Solomon*, 63; Trithemius, *Steganographia*, 58.

Armen

In the *Book of Enoch*, Armen is one of the FALLEN ANGELS who swore allegiance to SAMI-AZA, rebelled against God, took a human as his wife, and fathered the NEPHILIM.

Sources: Barton, *Journal of Biblical Literature*, Vols. 30–31, 162; Laurence, *Foreign Quarterly Review*, Vol. 24, 370; Prophet, *Fallen Angels and the Origins of Evil*, 174.

Armenki

Variations: Armenci, Ermenki, Ermenlijki, Jermijki, Lehusnitsi ("devil"), Leusi, NAVI, S'rmjani

From southern Bulgarian folklore come the demonic ghosts known as armenki. This type of demon is created whenever a child is aborted, dies unbaptized, or comes into the world as a stillborn. An armenki can also be created when a woman dies and is not given a proper Christian burial or is not buried with the proper protective objects. One would suppose that the latter is the more common method of creation for this type of demon, as the name translates loosely to mean "Armenian women"; however, there is no connection. In all likelihood the name armenki probably came from the Greek word *eirmarmene*, which translates as "fate."

Armenki prey nearly exclusively on young mothers and their children. They leave their graves at night and call out to anyone who will listen, begging to be baptized.

Sources: Georgieva, *Bulgarian Mythology*, 102–3; MacDermott, *Bulgarian Folk Customs*, 81; Ugresic, *Baba Yaga Laid an Egg*, 307.

Armers

In the *Book of Enoch*, Armers is one of the FALLEN ANGELS who swore allegiance to SAMI-AZA, rebelled against God, took a human as his wife, and fathered the NEPHILIM.

Sources: Barton, *Journal of Biblical Literature*, Vols. 30–31, 162; Eco, *Infinity of Lists*, 61; Laurence, *Book of Enoch, the Prophet*, 7; Lévi, *History of Magic*, 38; Prophet, *Fallen Angels and the Origins of Evil*, 174.

Armilus

In Apollonius of Tyana's *Nuctemeron* (*Night Illuminated by Day*), Armilus is listed as the demon of the eighth hour of the day. Associated with the ANTICHRIST, it is said that he will be born from the union between a man and a feminine marble statute in Rome. Armilus will grow to become twelve ells long and two ells wide; he will have green footsteps, golden hair, slanted red eyes, and two skulls.

Sources: Baron, *Social and Religious History of the Jews*, 144–5; Gettings, *Dictionary of Demons*, 37; Singer, *Jewish Encyclopedia*, 296; Lévi, *Transcendental Magic*, 393.

Armisiel

In *Theurgia Goetia*, the second book of the *Lemegeton*, Duke Armisiel is one of the ten SERVITORS OF EMONIEL (see EMONIEL). An AERIAL DEVIL, he commands 1,320 lesser dukes and servitors. Armisiel is good-natured and willing to obey those who summon him. He lives in the woods.

Sources: Peterson, *Lesser Key of Solomon*, 97; Trithemius, *Steganographia*, 81.

Armoniel

In the *Theurgia Goetia*, the second book of the *Lemegeton*, Armoniel is listed as a duke and one of the ten SERVITORS OF BYDIEL. He is a good-natured demon, appearing in an attractive form, and willing to obey those who summon him. An AERIAL DEVIL, Armoniel commands 2,400 servitors (see BYDIEL).

Sources: Peterson, *Lesser Key of Solomon*, 105; Trithemius, *Steganographia*, 146.

Arogor

Arogor ("helper"), as listed in the *Sacred Magic of Abramelin the Mage*, is one of the forty-nine SERVITORS OF BEELZEBUB (see BEELZEBUB).

Sources: Belanger, *Dictionary of Demons*, 40; Ford, *Bible of the Adversary*, 93; Mathers, *Book of the Sacred Magic of Abramelin the Mage*, 107; Von worms, *Book of Abramelin*, 257.

Arolen

Arolen ("strongly agitated") is named in the *Sacred Magic of Abramelin the Mage* as one of the forty-nine SERVITORS OF BEELZEBUB (see BEELZEBUB).

Sources: Belanger, *Dictionary of Demons*, 40; Mathers, *Book of the Sacred Magic of Abramelin the Mage*, 120.

Arotor

In the *Sacred Magic of Abramelin the Mage*, book two, Arotor ("husbandman" or "ploughman") is listed as one of the sixty-nine SERVITORS OF KORE AND MAGOTH.

Sources: Belanger, *Dictionary of Demons*, 40; Bryce, *First Latin Book*, 93; Mathers, *Book of the Sacred Magic of Abramelin the Mage*, 118.

Arotosael

Variations: Arôtosael

In the *Testament of Solomon*, Arotosael is a demi-demon who causes injury to the eyes. He confessed to King Solomon that if ever he heard the words "Uriel, imprison Arotosael" that he would instantly retreat and flee (see SPIRITS OF SOLOMON).

Sources: Butler, *Ritual Magic*, 31; Conybeare, *Jewish Quarterly Review*, Vol. 11, 35; Fleg, *Life of Solomon*, 66.

Arphaxat

Arphaxat was a demon that possessed Louise de Pinterville, one of the nuns of Loudun. He was not, however, one of the eighteen demons involved in the 1634 possession of Sister Jeanne des Anges in Loudun, France.

There is also a story of a Persian sorcerer by the name of Arphaxat. Abdias of Babylon claims that the sorcerer was struck dead by a thunderbolt within an hour of St. Simon and St. Jude's martyrdom.

Sources: Aikin, *General Biography*, 493; Bayle, *Historical and Critical Dictionary*, 262; Voltaire, *Works of M. de Voltaire*, 193.

Arpiron

The *Sacred Magic of Abramelin the Mage*, book two, names Arpiron ("attempting straightway") among the sixty-five SERVITORS OF KORE AND MAGOTH.

Sources: Belanger, *Dictionary of Demons*, 41; Mathers, *Book of the Sacred Magic of Abramelin the Mage*, 118; Von Worms, *Book of Abramelin*, 256.

Arrabin

In the *Sacred Magic of Abramelin the Mage*, book two, Arrabin ("caution money," or "pledge") is one of the sixty-five SERVITORS OF KORE AND MAGOTH.

Sources: Belanger, *Dictionary of Demons*, 41; Ford, *Bible of the Adversary*, 92; Gordon, *Adventures in the Nearest East*, 12.

Arstikapha

Arstikapha is one of the FALLEN ANGELS mentioned in the *Book of Enoch* who swore allegiance to SAMIAZA, rebelled against God, took a human wife, and fathered the NEPHILIM.

Sources: Laurence, *Foreign Quarterly Review*, Vol. 24, 370; Laurence, *Book of Enoch, the Prophet*, 70; Prophet, *Fallen Angels and the Origins of Evil*, 174.

Artaqifa

Variations: Arakab, ARAKIBA, Aristiqifa, ARSTIKAPHA, Artaquifa

In the *Book of Enoch*, Artaqifa is one of the FALLEN ANGELS who swore allegiance to SAMIAZA, rebelled against God, took a human wife, and fathered the NEPHILIM.

Sources: Ashe, *Book of Enoch*, 57; Black, *Book of Enoch*, 119; Horne, *Sacred Books and Early Literature of the East*, 114; Laurence, *Foreign Quarterly Review*, Vol. 24, 370.

Arundhati

Variations: Lucifer-Venus, Phosphoros

In Hindu mythology, Arundhati ("bind" or "restrain") is the personification of the morning star; he was called Phosphoros or Lucifer-Venus by the ancient Greeks. Represented by the sign of a coiled serpent, he is one of the seven stars that make up the constellation of Ursa Major. Arundhati has the power to animate and bring to life that which would otherwise lie dormant in the void.

Sources: Garg, *Encyclopaedia of the Hindu World*, 648; Padfield, *Hindu at Home*, 132–3; Rosen, *Essential Hinduism*, 29.

Asa and Asael

According to the Talmud, Asa and ASAEL were the demons who taught King Solomon all the wisdom he had and all the knowledge of all the arts (see SPIRITS OF SOLOMON).

Sources: Lévi, *History of Magic*, 38; Laurence, *Book of Enoch, the Prophet* 6; Lumpkin, *Fallen Angels, the Watchers, and the Origins of Evil*, 31.

Asael

Variations: Asa'el, Azael ("whom God strengthens"), AZAZEL

The *Book of Enoch* lists Asael ("Creation of God" or "God has made") as having been one of the chiefs of the GRIGORI, of the Order of Angels; however, he became a FALLEN ANGEL when he swore allegiance to SAMIAZA, rebelled against God, took a human as his wife, and fathered the NEPHILIM. He is now under the command of AMEZYARAK or Semyaza (SAMIAZA). (See also CHIEF OF TENS and WATCHERS.)

Sources: Black, *Book of Enoch*, 121; Barton, *Journal of Biblical Literature*, Vols. 30–31, 162; Conway, *Demonology and Devil-Lore*, Vol. 299; Lévi, *History of Magic*, 38; Laurence, *Book of Enoch, the Prophet*, 6; Lumpkin, *Fallen Angels, the Watchers, and the Origins of Evil*, 31.

Asafoetida

Asafoetida is a Persian demon of compassion, love, lust, and relationships.

Sources: Ashley, *Complete Book of Demons and Devils*, 91; Laufer, *Chinese Contributions to the History of Civilization*, 353.

Asag

Variations: ABZU, ASAKKU, Dragon of the Abyss

The Sumerian mythological poem *Lugale* (*Lugal-e u me-lam-bi nir-gal, The Feats and Exploits of Ninurta*) mentions the demonic, underworld creature aptly named Asag ("demon that causes sickness"). Conceived on Earth and born from the union between the gods An and Ki, Asag was born a hideous, monstrous dragon. Although the poem speaks of him as if he were an actual being, it gives no true or definable description of him other than to say that he is so repulsive that his very presence in the water could boil fish. Asag commands an army of rock demons, his very own offspring created from his mating with a mountain.

The personification of the frigid cold of winter and a demon of disease and sickness, Asag attacks and kills mankind through drought, head fevers, and migraines. He also restrains and withholds the Primal waters that fill the Abyss, keeping them from flooding the earth.

Asag was said to live in the Abyss, or in the mountains. The poem *Lugale* alluded to all three places as his home. Just as unclear is Asag's fate. The poem reveals that he was attacked by the god Ninurta with his weapon, Sharur, but it doesn't explain whether Asag survived the assault or was slain.

Sources: Bienkowski, *Dictionary of the Ancient Near East*, 214; Journal of Near Eastern Studies, *Sumerian Mythology: A Review Article*, 128–152; Lurker, *Dictionary of Gods and Goddesses*, 38; Wakeman, *God's Battle with the Monster*, 7–8.

Asahel

In book two of the *Sacred Magic of Abramelin the Mage*, the diurnal servitors, Asahel ("God"), is said to be one of the sixteen SERVITORS OF ASELIEL (see ASELIEL).

Sources: Geikie, *Life and Words of Christ*, 610; Spivey, *Ecclesiastical Vocabulary and Apocryphal Code*, 26.

Asakku

Variations: ASAG

In Babylonian mythology asakku are demonic spirits and monsters. They attack their prey, humans, causing migraines so severe that they can kill. Their name translates to mean "land" or "mountain."

Sources: Abusch, *Mesopotamian Magic*, 50; Muss-Arnolt, *Concise Dictionary of the Assyrian Language*, 114; Wiggerman, *Mesopotamian Protective Spirits*, 162.

Asaredel

Variations: Saraquel, SARIEL, SURIEL ("command of God"), Zerachiel

According to the *Book of Enoch*, Asaredel was one of the FALLEN ANGELS who swore allegiance to SAMIAZA, rebelled against God, took a human for his wife, taught mankind the motions or course of the moon (possibly meaning astrology), and fathered the NEPHILIM.

Sources: Asher, *Charting the Supernatural Judgments of Planet Earth*, 108–9; Laurence, *Foreign Quarterly Review*, Vol. 24, 370; Stafford, *Function of Divine Manifestations*, 10.

Asasel

Variations: AZAZEL ("God strengthens" or "arrogant to God"), AZAZYEL

Asasel is a demonic spirit of the wilderness. He feeds upon the literal scapegoat, a male kid goat that is without blemish, that has been burdened to carry the sins of a community out into the wilderness.

Sources: Baerg, *Supernatural in the Modern German Drama*, 47–8; Lurker, *Dictionary of Gods and Goddesses*, 39; Prophet, *Fallen Angels and the Origins of Evil*, 174; Swedenborg, *The Apocalypse Explained*, 409.

Asbeel

Variations: Asb'el, Asheel, AZAZEL ("God strengthens" or "arrogant to God"), Kesabel

Asbeel ("God's deserter" or "the thought of God," sources conflict) was formerly of the Orders of Angels and according to the *Book of Enoch*, a Watcher angel as well. However, because he lusted after human women, he advised and misled the other WATCHERS that they too should rebel against God and swear allegiance to SAMIAZA. After his Fall (see FALLEN ANGELS), he taught mankind the secrets of the natural universe and fathered the NEPHILIM. Asbeel is oftentimes referred to as one of the FIVE SATANS.

Sources: Barton, *Journal of Biblical Literature*, Vols. 30–31, 162; Charles, *Book of Enoch*, 137; Ladd, *Commentary on the Book of Enoch*, 223; Prophet, *Fallen Angels and the Origins of Evil*, 174.

Ascaroth

In various grimoires, Ascaroth is listed as being the demon of informers and spies.

Sources: Fleay, *Macmillan's Magazine*, Vol. 31, 439; Jobes, *Dictionary of Mythology, Folklore and Symbols*, 96; Poinsot, *Complete Book of the Occult and Fortune Telling*, 377.

Aseliel

Aseliel is ranked as a king, a chief prince, or a duke (sources vary) under the command of CARNESIEL (see DUKES OF HELL, KINGS OF HELL, PRINCES OF HELL, and SERVITORS OF CARNESIEL). He himself commands eight diurnal and eight nocturnal servitors of his own (see SERVITORS OF ASELIEL).

Sources: Gettings, *Dictionary of Demons*, 232; Guiley, *Encyclopedia of Demons and Demonology*, 18; Peterson, *Lesser Key of Solomon*, 70.

Ash

According to Enochian lore, Ash is a CACODAEMON. His counterpart is the angel Shal (see ENOCHIAN CACODAEMONS).

Sources: Chopra, *Academic Dictionary of Mythology*, 37; Laycock, *Complete Enochian Dictionary*, 80.

Ashib

In the *Theurgia Goetia*, the second book of the *Lemegeton*, Ashib, a nocturnal demon, is one of the fifteen Duke SERVITORS OF BARMIEL (see BARMIEL and DUKES OF HELL).

Source: Peterson, *Lesser Key of Solomon*, 70.

Ashmodai

Variations: Ad, ADAD, Ashm'dai, "head of the devils," SAMAEL ("the angel of death")

In the Books of Kings, Ashmodai ("Ad is my name") is the King of Edom. He was born of the union between the female demon IGRAT, most likely a type of SUCCUBUS, and King David, who was visited by IGRAT in a dream one night while he slept in the desert. Ashmodai is known to kill people with deadly poison.

Ashmodai and the female demon LILITH bore a son together, a prince they named SWORD OF ASHMODAI THE KING, he who rules over 80,000 destroyers (see PRINCES OF HELL).

Sources: Illes, *Encyclopedia of Spirits*, 218; Isaac, *The Contributor*, 270–3; Schwartz, *Tree of Souls*, 139; Slifkin, *Sacred Monsters*, 197–8, 210–11.

Ashmogh

Variations: Ashemaogha, Ash-Mogh

From Persian demonology, the demon Ashmogh ("heretic") is one of the disciples of AHRIMAN. He is described as looking like a serpent with a camel's neck.

Sources: Blavatsky, *Secret Doctrine*, 205; Conway, *Demonology and Devil-Lore*, 65; Hyatt, *Book of Demons*, 56.

Ashtaroth, plural: ASTHAROTH

Variations: Amenodiel, ANAEL, ANARAZEL, ANIZEL, Arniniel, Aseroth, 'Ashtart, Ashtoreth, ASTAROT, ASTAROTH, ASTARTE, Asteroth, Astharthe, Astoreth, Atargatis, Ataroth, Azael ("whom God strengthens"), AZAZEL ("God strengthens" or "arrogant to God"), CORSON, DEMORIEL, Diabolus ("Flowing downwards"), Ishtar, MALGARAS.

Originally a Palestinian god, Ashtaroth ("Statues of Ashtoreth") was reimagined by Christian demonologists, first being named as a demonic goddess, then as a male demon of the First Hierarchy of Hell. As a demon he has been given a wide array of ranks and titles including Governor of Hell, Grand Duke of Western Hell (see DUKES OF HELL), Head of the Eighth Order of Hell, Lord Treasurer of Hell, Prince of Accusers and Inquisitors, and Prince of Thrones (see PRINCES OF HELL). He is also named as one of the seventy-two SPIRITS OF SOLOMON and a FALLEN ANGEL, formerly of the Order of Thrones, thereby making him a seraph.

A demon of lust, seduction, sloth, and vanity, Ashtaroth commands forty legions of demonic spirits and four servitors: AAMON, BARBATOS,

PRUSLAS, and RASHAVERAK (see SERVITORS OF ASHTAROTH).

Ashtaroth has been depicted as a naked man with dragon hands, feet, and wings riding upon a wolf. He has a second set of wings set behind the first, assumedly his angelic wings, as they are feathered. Upon his head he wears a crown and in one hand he holds a serpent. Sources that utilize this image of him also add that he has very bad breath. When summoned, Ashtaroth is said to, on occasion, appear as a human dressed only in black and white or, less frequently, as an ass. Back when Ashtaroth was a Phoenician moon goddess, she had two horns protruding from her head forming a crescent moon.

If one is to summon Ashtaroth, he is most powerful on Wednesdays in the month of August between the tenth and eleventh hours of the night. Once he appears, in whichever form he may take, he will answer any question asked of him honestly, as he knows all events of the past and the future. He wields great power and has the ability to give his summoner power over snakes, lead him to hidden treasures, and obtain for him and help him maintain the friendships of great lords. Ashtaroth is a patron of the liberal arts and most sciences; he will teach his summoner handicrafts, mathematics and science, and how to become invisible.

Ashtaroth seduces mankind by appealing to their laziness and vanity. He is fond of lecturing on the Creation and on the Fall of the angels, emphatically declaring himself to being punished unjustly and saying that one day he will retake his rightful place in heaven.

The personal adversary of Ashtaroth is St. Bartholomew. Numerous sources warn summoners that Ashtaroth smells so horrible that only holding a magical ring under your nose will allow you to breathe near him.

The plural form of the name Ashtaroth was taken from the King James Bible. Many scholars believe that Ashtaroth is a thinly veiled version of the goddess Ishtar. Medieval Christian sources say he lives in the Occident (America).

Sources: Gettings, *Dictionary of Demons*, 38; Jahn, *Jahn's Biblical Archaeology*, 524–5, 530; Prophet, *Fallen Angels and the Origins of Evil*, 174; Smith, *Comprehensive Dictionary of the Bible*, 73.

Asi

According to Enochian lore, Asi is a CACODAEMON. His counterpart is the angel Sisp (see ENOCHIAN CACODAEMONS).

Sources: Chopra, *Academic Dictionary of Mythology*, 39; Laycock, *Complete Enochian Dictionary*, 80.

Asima

Asima ("guardian," or "protector" or "he despaired," sources conflict) was the demon spoken of in 2 Kings 29–31: "And the men of Babylon made Succoth-benoth, and the men of Cuth made NERGAL, and the men of Hamath made Asima ["a goat with short hair"], and the Avvites made Nibhaz and Tartak, and the Sepharvites burnt their children in the fire to Adrammelech [ADRAMMELECH] and Anammelech, the gods of Sepharvaim."

Sources: Hyatt, *Book of Demons*, 73; Smith, *Dictionary of the Bible*, 258; Melton, *Encyclopedia of Occultism and Parapsychology*, 315.

Asimiel

Variations: Asimel

According to Christian demonology, Asimiel is one of the twenty SERVITORS OF CAMUEL (see CAMUEL). A nocturnal demon, he appears in a beautiful form and is known to be very courteous.

Sources: Guiley, *Encyclopedia of Demons and Demonology*, 36; Peterson, *Lesser Key of Solomon*, 67.

Asisiel

Variations: Amisiel

In the *Ars Paulina*, the third book of the *Lemegeton*, Asisiel is listed as one of the fifteen Duke SERVITORS OF SASQUIEL (see SASQUIEL). He commands 5,550 servitors.

Sources: Davidson, *Dictionary of Angels*, 16; Peterson, *Lesser Key of Solomon*, 114.

Asmadeus

Variations: ABBADON

Asmadeus ("the destroyer") was a demon mentioned in the *Book of Tobias*.

Sources: Herbermann, *Catholic Encyclopedia*, 792; Neusner, *History of the Jews in Babylonia*, 366–7.

Asmadiel

Variations: Amadiel

In the *Theurgia Goetia*, the second book of the *Lemegeton*, Asmadiel is said to be an AERIAL DEVIL and one of the twelve SERVITORS OF MACARIEL (see MACARIEL). A chief duke who commands four hundred servitors, Asmadiel can appear to his summoner in any number of forms but commonly appears as a dragon with a virgin's head. Both diurnal and nocturnal, he is good-natured and willing to obey those who summon him.

Sources: Belanger, *Dictionary of Demons*, 43; Peterson, *Lesser Key of Solomon*, 103; Trithemius, *Steganographia*, 141.

Asmenoth

Asmenoth is called a guider and ruler of the North by Friar Bacon; he is very likely a fictional demon.

Sources: Marlowe, *Tragical History of Dr. Faustus*, 261; West, *Invisible World*, 121, 133.

Asmiel

In the *Sacred Magic of Abramelin the Mage*, the AERIAL DEVIL Asmiel ("storing up") is one of the one hundred eleven SERVITORS OF AMAYMON, ARITON, ORIENS, AND PAYMON (see AMAYMON, ARITON, ORIENS, and PAYMON). He is also listed as one of the SERVITORS OF SYMIEL (see SYMIEL).

Sources: Guiley, *Encyclopedia of Demons and Demonology*, 253; Mathers, *Book of the Sacred Magic of Abramelin the Mage*, 113; Susej, *Demonic Bible*, 256.

Asmodai

Variations: Æshma, Æshma-dæva, Ashmadia, Ashmedai, ASHMODAI, Asmodaios, ASMODAY, Asmodee, Asmodée, Asmodei, Asmodeios, Asmodeous, Asmodeius, Asmodeo, Asmodeous, ASMODEUS, Asmodi, Chammaday, Chashmodai, the Great Bear, the Offspring of the Dragon, Sidonay, SYDONAI

In Avestan, the eastern Iranian language of Zoroastrian scripture, the name Asmodai translates to mean "wrath demon." This demon is mentioned in Christian demonology, Jewish folklore, Persian mythology, and Talmudic text as well as Zoroastrianism demonology. He has been assigned various titles and ranks, some of which include king, overseer of all the gambling houses in the court of Hell, prince of revenge, and the protector of male homosexuals.

For a short while Asmodai was under the command of King Solomon (see SPIRITS OF SOLOMON). In Christian demonology he is in service under LUCIFER and commands seventy-two legions of servitors, while in Mazdeism, he answers only to ANGRA MAINYU.

While Adam was still living with his first wife, LILITH, ancient Christian and Jewish lore tells us that Asmodai was conceived in a union between Adam and NAAMAH, the DEMONS OF PROSTITUTION.

Described as being strong and powerfully built, Asmodai has three heads; the first is that of a bull, the second is that of a ram, and the third is nothing more than the tail of a serpent. He has the ability to spit fire from both of his mouths. Asmodai rides a demonic dragon and carries with him a lance from which hangs his banner. Another description says that he has the chest of a man, legs of a rooster, a serpent tail, and three heads: one of a man vomiting up fire, one of a ram, and one of a bull. In this likeness he is described as riding upon a lion that has the neck and wings of a dragon. In the Talmud, Asmodai is described as being good-natured and a humorous companion.

With his ultimate goal being that of filling the world up with evil, Asmodai tempts men to leave their righteous lives behind and follow a life of evil; he does this by filling their hearts with anger and the desire for vengeance.

In addition to being able to belch forth fire and correctly predict the future, Asmodai has dominion over the zodiacal sign of Aquarius, but only between the dates of January 30 and February 8. He is most powerful during the month of November.

Like many demons, Asmodai has weaknesses that can be exploited. His personal adversary, according to Christian demonology, is St. John. Talmudic text tells us that he lusted after Bathsheba, one of King Solomon's wives. Another story involving King Solomon tells how the king tricked the demon into building his temple; another Solomonic tale tells of how Asmodai turned around and tricked the king in return, assuming the throne and ruling in his place for many years.

The *Book of Tobit* tells the story of how Asmodai fell in love with Sarah, daughter of Raguel. Each time the woman married, the demon would kill her husband on their wedding night before the marriage could be consummated. By doing this, keeping her a virgin, she was able to remarry again and again. Asmodai did this to the first seven of her bridegrooms. Her eighth husband, Tobias, was aided by the angel Raphael ("healing one of God"). Tobias was told to catch a fish and place its heart and liver over burning coals, creating a smoke and stench that would cause Asmodai to flee all the way to Egypt. Once there, Raphael bound him to the desert.

A final legend claims that Asmodai is married to Lilith the Younger, the daughter of SAMAEL and LILITH the Elder, the original wife of Adam.

Sources: Barton, *Journal of Biblical Literature*, Vols. 30–31, 162; Bear, *Quarterly Review of the Methodist Episcopal Church, South*, Vol. 7, 500–12; Christianson, *Ecclesiastes Through the Centuries*, 91–2; McLean, *Treatise of Angel Magic*, 51; Wise, *Origin of Christianity*, 95.

Asmoday

Variations: Aeshma daeva ("demon of lust" or "covetous demon"), Asamod, ("to destroy or exterminate"), Ashme Deus, ASHTAROTH, ASMODAI, Asmodaios, Asmodee, Asmodei, ASMODEUS, ASTARTE, Astoreth, Azmonden ("to tempt, to try or prove"), Chashmodai, the Destroyer, Sydonay

Although very similar to the demon Asmodai, Asmoday is different enough to be considered a separate individual. The name Asmoday is likely Hebrew or Persian, and he is mentioned in Jewish, Persian, Zoroastrian, and numerous other demonologies. He too has been given the rank of king and the overseer of the gambling houses in the Cabinet of Hell. Asmoday is a FALLEN ANGEL, formerly of the Order of Angels, according to Christian demonology. He is the first and most powerful demon under the command of AMAYMON.

Asmoday is the demon of adultery, impurity, lechery, luxury, passion, pleasure, and sensuality; he commands seventy-two legions. Asmoday arranges inappropriate marriages, causes chaos in monasteries by seducing the priests, and lures happily married couples into having affairs, sometimes with himself. Furthermore, he tempts people to buy fancy clothes and follow ridiculous fashion fads, as well as tempts people into overspending and wasting their assets.

Sources vary as to the creation of Asmoday. As a FALLEN ANGEL he would have been created by God. Some sources say that he was born the son of a mortal woman and an unnamed angel; some claim his mother to be the Demoness LILITH, and still others say that he is the incestuous result of an affair between Tubal-Cain and his sister Naafrfah (NAAMAH).

There are also several descriptions for Asmoday's appearance. One has him appearing before his summoner as a handsome and well-dressed man or a beautiful and elegantly dressed woman. Another description says that he appears to those who summon him as a bloated and animal-like man crouching as if readying himself to strike. A final description depicts him as having three heads: one of a bull, one of a ram, and one of a man vomiting fire. He also has a serpent tail, has webbed feet like a goose, and rides upon a dragon carrying a lance and banner.

Asmoday is summoned because he answers all questions asked of him and can grant the power of invincibility. He also has the ability to give his summoner the Ring of Virtues. Asmoday is credited with having invented carousels, dancing, music, plays, and recreational drug use. He grants matrimonial happiness; guards buried treasures if they are in the domain of AMAYMON; reveals the locations of buried treasures; and teaches art, astronomy, geometry, math, and science. He also possesses a stone that can cut ordinary stone with the greatest of ease.

When an exorcist calls on Asmoday, he must remain standing at all times and wear nothing on his head, as being seated or having his head covered will offend the demon. If while summoning Asmoday a being appears, ask immediately "Art thou Asmoday?" Asmoday cannot lie in answering this question and will eventually bow to the exorcist or the one who summoned him.

Sources: Crowley, *The Goethia*, 43; De Laurence, *Lesser Key of Solomon, Goetia*, 32; Diagram Group, *Little Giant Encyclopedia*, 506; Du Quette, *Key to Solomon's Key*, 176; Scot, *Discoverie of Witchcraft*, 220; Waite, *Book of Ceremonial Magic*, 205.

Asmodeus

Variations: Asmodee, Chashmodai

A sub–Prince and one of the seventy-two SPIRITS OF SOLOMON, Asmodeus ("to destroy or exterminate") is a demon of impurity and lechery (see PRINCES OF HELL). A FALLEN ANGEL, formerly from the Order of Thrones, Asmodeus is an ARCHDEMON and has dominion over the infernal hierarchy known as Golab. Like ASMODAY, Asmodeus was born of the incestuous relations between Tubal-Cain and his sister NAAMAH. His personal adversary is the angel Gabriel.

Asmodeus is often called upon during exorcisms and cases of collective possession. He is one of the eighteen demons who possessed Sister Jeanne des Anges in Loudun, France, in 1634 (see LOUDUN POSSESSION). When he worked cutting stone for Solomon's Temple, he used a stone that cut other stones most easily.

Sources: Aikin, *General Biography*, 493; Bayle, *Historical and Critical Dictionary*, 262; Chambers, *Book of Days*, 723; Conybeare, *Jewish Quarterly Review*, Vol. 11, 20–21; Hyatt, *Book of Demons*, 40–1; Robbins, *Encyclopedia of Witchcraft and Demonology*, 128; Voltaire, *Works of M. de Voltaire*, 193.

Asmodeus Zavehe

Variations: Areex, Ashmedai, ASIMA, ASMODAY, Chammadai, Charmeas, Sarindiel, SYDONAI, Sydonay, SYRACH, Zavehe

Asmodeus Zavehe ("King of Demons") was one of the FALLEN ANGELS who swore allegiance to SAMIAZA, rebelled against God, took a human wife, and fathered the NEPHILIM. He commands six chiefs, six servitors, and eighty-seven demons under SAMAEL.

Sources: Baskin, *Sorcerer's Handbook*, 628; Singer, *Jewish Encyclopedia*, 218; Voltaire, *Philosophical Dictionary*, 286.

Asmoug

Variations: Asmog

In Mazdean demonology, Asmoug is the chief emissary of AHRIMAN. A demon of discord, Asmoug starts conflicts and encourages warlike tensions between families and nations.

Sources: Bell, *Bell's New Pantheon*, 99; Hyatt, *Book*

of Demons, 56; McClintock, *Cyclopaedia of Biblical, Theological, and Ecclesiastical Literature*, Vol. 11, 240.

Asperim

Asperim ("dangerous," "perilous," "rigorous," or "rude") is one of the one hundred eleven SERVITORS OF AMAYMON, ARITON, ORIENS, AND PAYMON (see AMAYMON, ARITON, ORIENS, and PAYMON).

Sources: Belanger, *Dictionary of Demons*, 47; Mathers, *Book of the Sacred Magic of Abramelin the Mage*, 105; Susej, *Demonic Bible*, 256.

Asphiel

The *Sacred Magic of Abramelin the Mage*, book two, names the nocturnal demon Asphiel as one of the twenty SERVITORS OF ASELIEL (see ASELIEL).

Sources: Belanger, *Dictionary of Demons*, 47; Peterson, *Lesser Key of Solomon*, 69.

Aspiel

In the *Theurgia Goetia*, the second book of the *Lemegeton*, Chief Duke Aspiel is listed as one of the sixteen SERVITORS OF ASYRIEL (see ASYRIEL). A nocturnal demon, he is good-natured and willing to obey his summoner. Aspiel commands ten servitors of his own.

Sources: Belanger, *Dictionary of Demons*, 47; Peterson, *Lesser Key of Solomon*, 73–4, 77.

Assaba

In the *Theurgia Goetia*, the second book of the *Lemegeton*, Duke Assaba ("hit"), an AERIAL DEMON, is one of the sixteen SERVITORS OF GEDEIL (see DUKES OF HELL and GEDEIL).

Source: Peterson, *Lesser Key of Solomon*, 72.

Assistants of Ashtaroth

In Colin de Plancy's *Dictionaire Infernale* (1863), ASHTAROTH is credited with having four assistants: AAMON, BARBATOS, PRUSLAS, and RASHAVERAK (see also COUNTS OF HELL, and SERVITORS OF ASHTAROTH).

Sources: Jahn, *Jahn's Biblical Archaeology*, 524–5, 530; Prophet, *Fallen Angels and the Origins of Evil*, 174; Smith, *Comprehensive Dictionary of the Bible*, 73.

Assistants of Paymon

The *Ars Goetia*, book one of the *Lemegeton*, lists PAYMON as having only two assistants: ABALAM and BEBALL. Their ranks are given as being either kings or princes (see KINGS OF HELL and PRINCES OF HELL).

Sources: Agrippa, *Three Books of Occult Philosophy*, 536; Crowley, *The Goetia*, 31; De Laurence, *Lesser Key of Solomon, Goetia*, 24; McLean, *Treatise on Angel Magic*, 168; Waite, *Book of Black Magic and of Pacts*, 168.

Assyriel

In the *Theurgia Goetia*, the second book of the *Lemegeton*, Assyriel ("tenth") is credited as being the Prince of the Southwest. His is one of the twelve SERVITORS OF CASPIEL (see CASPIEL and PRINCES OF HELL).

Sources: Van der Toorn, *Dictionary of Deities and Demons*, 610.

Ast

According to Enochian lore, Ast is a CACO-DAEMON. His counterpart is the angel Stim (see ENOCHIAN CACODAEMONS).

Sources: Chopra, *Academic Dictionary of Mythology*, 39; Laycock, *Complete Enochian Dictionary*, 80.

Astarot

Variations: ASHTAROTH

In the *Grimoire of Pope Honorius* (*Le Grimoire du Pape Honorius*), an eighteenth-century book alleged to have been written by Pope Honorius III, the demon Astarot ("assemblies, crowds, or flocks") is listed as being a grand duke or sub-prince (see DUKES OF HELL and PRINCES OF HELL). This demonic spirit is one of the eighteen demons commonly called on during exorcism and cases of collective possession.

Sources: Botterweck, *Theological Dictionary of the Old Testament*, 431–2; Simon, *Papal Magic*, 116, 119; Van der Toorn, *Dictionary of Deities and Demons*, 113.

Astaroth

Astaroth was originally an ancient demonic goddess known as Astoreth to the Hebrews and as ASTARTE to the ancient Phoenicians. This re-imagination occurred during the medieval era and he was now described as looking like an ugly angel riding upon a dragon while holding a snake in his left hand. He is said to be a grand duke and the treasurer of Hell, commanding forty legions and the head of the hierarchy called GAM-CHICOTH. As a FALLEN ANGEL, he is a former prince of the Order of Thrones.

Astaroth is summoned for his ability to grant friendships to great lords; a nocturnal demon, he is most powerful on Wednesdays between the tenth and the eleventh hour of the night. Once this demon appears his summoner should not stand too close, as Astaroth gives off a deadly stench. He willingly answers all questions regarding the past, present, and future and will give up easily any secrets that he knows. Astaroth enjoys talking at length about the creation of the world, the Fall, and the faults of the angels, taking great care to point out how he is being punished unjustly.

An incredibly lazy demon, his personal adversary is Saint Bartholomew.

Sources: Chambers, *Book of Days*, 722; Collin de Plancy, *Dictionary of Witchcraft*, 18; Conway, *Demonology and Devil-Lore*, 299; De Laurence, *Lesser Key of Solomon, Goetia*, 30–1; Hyatt, *Book of Demons*, 74; McLean, *Treatise of Angel Magic*, 51; Scott, *London Magazine*, Vol. 5, 378.

Astarte

Variations: Asherah; Ashtart, Atargatis, Athirat (Lady of the Sea); Astarte-Astaroth in medieval Christian era; Astorath; Astroarche (Queen of the Stars); Athstar (Venus in the Morning) in Egypt; Athtarte (Lady of Heaven); "Morning Star of Heaven" in Aramaic; Progenitrix of the Gods, Queen of Heaven; wife of ASHTAROTH, wife of BAAL, wife of El, Mother of Heaven

Originally a Levantine deity, fertility goddess of the Semites, and war goddess of the Egyptians, Astarte was demonized and named one of the eight ARCH SHE-DEMONS. Her rank is given as being a queen. She is the demon of compassion, love, lust, and relationships. Astarte commands the spirits of the dead. She is described as having the head of a lioness and a woman's body. She drives a four-horse chariot. To prevent attack from Astarte, the blood of a sacrificed child is mixed with wine and offered to her in a chalice. Astarte's name also appears under the DUKES OF HELL.

Sources: Cornelius, *The Many Faces of the Goddess*, 93; Melton, *Encyclopedia of Occultism and Parapsychology*, 315; Pinch, *Egyptian Mythology*, 108–9; Willis, *World Mythology*, 51

Asteliel

In *Theurgia Goetia*, book two of the *Lemegeton*, Asteliel ("monument") is listed as the Prince of the South by Southeast (see PRINCES OF HELL). He is one of the twelve SERVITORS OF CASPIEL (see CASPIEL).

Source: Peterson, *Lesser Key of Solomon*, 69.

Astharoth, plural of Asthoreth

Astharoth is a collective name for the feminine Canaanite demonic deities.

Sources: Lemaire, *History and Traditions of Early Israel*, 20; Lurker, *Routledge Dictionary of Gods and Goddesses, Devils and Demons*, 22; Monaghan, *Encyclopedia of Goddesses and Heroines*, 83.

Asto Vidatu

Variations: Asto Vi' Datu, Astovidatu

In Persian and Zoroastrian demonology, Asto Vidatu ("dissolver of bones") is a demon of death. He works in conjunction with AESMA DAEVA. Using a noose, Asto Vidatu chases and tries to catch the souls of the recently deceased as they ascend to Heaven.

Sources: Cor de Vaan, *Avestan Vowels*, Vol. 12, 436; Khanam, *Demonology*, 136; Lurker, *Routledge Dictionary of Gods and Goddesses, Devils and Demons*, 23.

Astolit

According to the *Sacred Magic of Abramelin the Mage*, Astolit ("without garment") is one of the fifteen SERVITORS OF PAYMON (see PAYMON).

Sources: Belanger, *Dictionary of Demons*, 49; Mathers, *Book of the Sacred Magic of Abramelin the Mage*, 108.

Astor

In the *Theurgia Goetia*, the second book of the *Lemegeton*, Chief Duke Astor is listed as being one of the sixteen SERVITORS OF ASYRIEL (see ASYRIEL and DUKES OF HELL). He is diurnal, good-natured, and willing to obey his summoner. Astor commands forty servitors.

Sources: Guiley, *Encyclopedia of Demons and Demonology*, 20; Peterson, *Lesser Key of Solomon*, 73–4, 77.

Astrega

In the *Sacred Magic of Abramelin the Mage*, Astrega ("expeditions") is listed as being one of the one hundred eleven SERVITORS OF AMAYMON, ARITON, ORIENS, AND PAYMON (see AMAYMON, ARITON, ORIENS, and PAYMON).

Sources: Mathers, *Book of the Sacred Magic of Abramelin the Mage*, 114; Von Worms, *Book of Abremelin*, 255.

Asturel

In the *Sacred Magic of Abramelin the Mage*, Asturel ("bearing authority") is among the one hundred eleven SERVITORS OF AMAYMON, ARITON, ORIENS, AND PAYMON (see AMAYMON, ARITON, ORIENS, and PAYMON).

Sources: Belanger, *Dictionary of Demons*, 49; Ford, *Bible of the Adversary*, 88; Mathers, *Book of the Sacred Magic of Abramelin the Mage*, 113.

Asurakumara

In ancient Indian demonology, Asurakumara ("demon-Princes") is one of the first groups of Bhavanavasin gods. She is described as being black skinned and wearing red clothes and having the ability to make it rain and thunder. Asurakumara lives in the uppermost regions of the underworld.

Sources: Jordan, *Dictionary of Gods and Goddesses*, 34–5; Lurker, *Routledge Dictionary of Gods and Goddesses, Devils and Demons*, 23; Rose, *Spirits, Fairies, Gnomes, and Goblins*, 24.

Asuras

Variations: Ahura

In the Buddhism practiced in India, asuras ("life-force") are fighting demons, a type of fallen god comparable to the GRIGORI. The asuras are a primal group of gods and were born the children of Kasyapa. They were cast out of Heaven and thereafter were regarded as demons. Asuras are very strong and powerful demons, and they have dominion over secret wisdom. They constantly plot against the god INDRA and all the other gods who live atop Mt. Sumeru because they are jealous of them. Asuras live in a city beneath the ocean ruled by their king, Rahula.

Sources: Garg, *Encyclopaedia of the Hindu World*, 749; Heldreth, *Blood is the Life*, 49–50; Hyatt, *Book of Demons*, 15; MacDonnell, *Vedic Mythology*, 156–7.

Aswang Mandurugo

Variations: Danag, Mandragore

In the Philippines, the Capiz province is known as a haven for witches and for a species of rather elusive demonic vampires known as the aswang mandurugo. They appear as a beautiful woman during the day, but at night their true form, that of a monstrous winged being, is revealed. When it can, one of these creatures will marry a man to ensure that it has a constant supply of blood. It "kisses" the sustenance it needs nightly from its husband prey by inserting its barbed tongue into the victim's mouth and draining out the blood it needs. The only symptom that the husband may ever present is a gradual and unexplainable loss of weight. There is no test or discernable way to tell beforehand if a bride-to-be is one of these creatures. However, there is a preventive measure that may be taken. If the husband sleeps with a knife under his pillow, he may awake in time to see his attacker. If he is fast enough to draw the knife and stab the aswang mandurugo in the heart, it will be destroyed.

Sources: Curran, *Vampires*, 35–44; Lopez, *Handbook of Philippine Folklore*, 227; Ramos, *Aswang Syncrasy*, 3; University of San Carlos, *Philippine Quarterly*, Vol. 10–11, 213.

Aswang Tiyanak

Variations: Anak ni Janice, Tyanak

A vampiric demon from the Philippines, the aswang tiyanak is a species of CAMBION, as it is born the offspring between a woman and demon. However, it may also be created when a child dies without having been baptized or when a mother aborts her child; the fetus comes to life and brings mischief and hardships to the woman that should have been its mother. No matter how it was created, the aswang tiyanak is described as having red skin, being completely bald, and having glowing eyes. It preys on women, lying on the forest floor looking like an adorable, abandoned

baby. When a woman comes to its rescue and takes it into her home, it assumes its true form and attacks her, draining the woman dry of all her blood.

Sources: Demetrio, *Encyclopedia of Philippine Folk Beliefs*, 398; Jocano, *Folk Medicine*, 109, 169; Lopez, *Handbook of Philippine Festivals*, 146, 221, 227; University of the Philippines, *Asian Studies*, Vol. 8–9, 297.

Asyriel

In the *Theurgia Goetia*, book two of the *Lemegeton*, Asyriel is listed as being the King of the Southwest, third under the great Emperor of the South. He commands twenty chief duke servitors of the day and an additional twenty chief duke servitors of the night; however, only eight of each is named (see SERVITORS OF ASYRIEL).

Sources: Belanger, *Dictionary of Demons*, 86; Guiley, *Encyclopedia of Demons and Demonology*, 20; Peterson, *Lesser Key of Solomon*, 73.

Atabulus

Variations: Scirocco, Simoomn, Simoon, Sirocco

Atabulus is in all likelihood a fictional demon whose name in Latin translates to mean "a hot burning wind" or "southeastern wind."

Sources: D'Iseaeli, *New World*, Vol. 6, 72; Nettleship, *Contributions to Latin Lexicograph*, 339; Toynbee, *Concise Dictionary of Proper Names and Notable Matters*, 478.

Ataecina

From Iberian demonology comes Ataecina, the Queen of the Underworld. Originally she was an agrarian goddess, similar to the Eulalia and Proserpina. However, she was demonized during the Christian conversion.

Sources: Fear, *Rome and Baetica*, 261–2; Keay, *Roman Spain*, 161; NicMhacha, *Queen of the Night*, 110.

Ataliel

Variations: Atliel

Ataliel is a demon from Enochian lore. One of the twenty-eight demonic rulers of the lunar mansions, Ataliel rules over the mansion Agrapha ("covered flying"). He has dominion over the zodiacal sign Libra and is known to assist in the finding of buried treasures (see ENOCHIAN RULERS OF THE LUNAR MANSIONS).

Sources: Gettings, *Dictionary of Demons*, 41; Moura, *Mansions of the Moon for the Green Witch*, 10; Webster, *Encyclopedia of Angels*, 25, 124.

Atarculph

Variations: Atarculphegh

In the *Book of Enoch*, Atarculph is one of the FALLEN ANGELS who swore allegiance to SAMI-

AZA, rebelled against God, took a human as his wife, and fathered the NEPHILIM.

Sources: Ashley, *Complete Book of Devils and Demons*, 73; Davidson, *Dictionary of Angels*, 60; Voltaire, *Essays and Criticisms*, 106.

Atazoth

Atazoth is a demonic god from the pantheon of the Order of the Nine Angels. His name means "an increasing of azoth."

Sources: Carroll, *Liber Kaos*, 148; Ford, *Book of the Witch Moon Choronzon Edition*, 310.

Athanaton

In Reginald Scot's book, *The Discoverie of Witchcraft* (1584), Athanaton is named as a demonic leader who has "the power of the east." His name has Greek roots and translates to mean "deathlessness."

Sources: Frede, *Body and Soul in Ancient Philosophy*, 149; Gettings, *Dictionary of Demons*, 42.

Atheleberseth

Variations: Atheleberset

Alister Crowley mentions the demon Atheleberseth ("shiny" or "still") in his version of the Boneless Ritual. His number is 374, according to Crowley.

Sources: Betz, *Greek Magical Papyri in Translation*, 103; Crowley, *The Goetia*, 6; Scott-Moncrieff, *Paganism and Christianity in Egypt*, 44.

Athesiel

In the *Theurgia Goetia*, the second book of the *Lemegeton*, Chief Duke Athesiel is one of the fifteen SERVITORS OF ICOSIEL (see ICOSIEL). An AERIAL DEVIL, Athesiel is good-natured and obedient, doing exactly as his summoner asks. Both a diurnal and nocturnal demon, he is most easily summoned from within a house. Athesiel has dominion over the planet Mars and commands 2,200 servitors.

Sources: Belanger, *Dictionary of Demons*, 50; Guiley, *Encyclopedia of Demons and Demonology*, 118; Peterson, *Lesser Key of Solomon*, 99.

Atloton

In the *Sacred Magic of Abramelin the Mage*, book two, Atloton is among the one hundred eleven SERVITORS OF AMAYMON, ARITON, ORIENS, AND PAYMON. His name is Greek for "insufferable" (see AMAYMON, ARITON, ORIENS, and PAYMON).

Sources: Belanger, *Dictionary of Demons*, 50; Mathers, *Book of the Sacred Magic of Abramelin the Mage*, 114; Von Worms, *Book of Abramelin*, 256.

Ato

According to Enochian lore, Ato is a CACODAEMON. His counterpart is the angel Tott (see ENOCHIAN CACODAEMONS).

Sources: Chopra, *Academic Dictionary of Mythology*, 42.

Atrax

The *Testament of Solomon* tells us that Atrax was one of the seventy-two demons that King Solomon used in the construction of his Temple (SPIRITS OF SOLOMON). A demon of fevers, Atrax was made to perform heavy labor by the king, such as keeping the furnaces stoked for metalwork. He is described as having a shapeless head, like a DOG, but with the face of a bird, donkey, or ox.

To banish Atrax, chop up coriander and smear it on the lips of the person who has been inflicted with one of the demon's fevers. Then, recite the following charm: "The fever which is from dirt, I exorcise thee by the throne of the most high God, retreat from dirt and retreat from the creature fashioned by God."

Sources: Abrahams, *Jewish Quarterly Review*, Vol. 11, 36; Ash, *Qabalah*, 47, 61; Conybeare, *Jewish Quarterly Review*, Vol. 11, 36.

Augne-Baugauven

From Persian demonology comes the demon of fire, Augne-Baugauven. He is one of the eight AUSTATIKCO–PAULIGAUR who controls one of the eight sides of the world.

Sources: De Claremont, *Ancients' Book of Magic*, 118; Kindersley, *Specimens of Hindoo Literature*, 33; Spence, *Encyclopedia of Occultism*, 52.

Austatikco–Pauligaur

Variations: Aushta-tikcu-Pauligaur

From Persian demonology comes a class of daivergoel, DAIVERS, evil spirits, or DJINN called Austatikco–Pauligaur. They watch over the eight sides of the world. There are eight Austatikco–Pauligaur: AUGNE-BAUGAUVEN, EEMEN, ESSAUNIEN (or Shivven), GOOBEREN, INDIREN, NERUDEE, VAIVOO, and VAROONON.

Sources: Kindersley, *Specimens of Hindoo Literature*, 32–3; Smedley, *Occult Sciences*, 51; Spence, *Encyclopedia of Occultism*, 51.

Autothith

Autothith ("enmity") is one of the seventy-two spirits mentioned in the *Testament of Solomon* (see SPIRITS OF SOLOMON). He is the demon of arguments and grudges and causes arguments and grudges between friends. Autothith will flee if the words "Alpha and Omega" are written down in his presence.

Sources: Ashe, *Qabalah*, 51, 66; Conybeare, *Jewish Quarterly Review*, Vol. 11, 38; Davies, *A History of Magic Books*, 13.

Auza

Variations: Auzael, AZZA, Oza, Ozal

Auza was one of the CHIEF OF TENS who swore allegiance to SAMIAZA, rebelled against God, took a human wife, and fathered the anakim, also known as the NEPHILIM. Although he was born of the Elohim, Auza is still considered by scholars to be a FALLEN ANGEL. Auza, along with AZZAEL, are suspended between Heaven and Earth as a punishment for their part in the heavenly rebellion.

Sources: Davidson, *Dictionary of Angels*, 62; Dunlap, *Christian Examiner*, 79; Mathers, *Kabbalah Unveiled*, 249.

Ava

According to Enochian lore, Ava is a CACO-DAEMON. His counterpart is the angel Vasa (see ENOCHIAN CACODAEMONS).

Sources: Chopra, *Academic Dictionary of Mythology*, 43; Laycock, *Complete Enochian Dictionary*, 81.

Avarus

From the fifteenth century Christian manuscript *Librum de Nigromancia*, said to belong to a priest named Johannes Cunalis of Munich, Bavaria, comes the demon Avarus, a Latin name meaning "greedy" or "to crave." Avarus was said to be one of the three demons summoned by a French sorcerer in 1437 by the name of Jubertus of Bavaria, the other two demons being LUXU-RIOSUS and SUPERBUS. The demon of avarice, as his name would imply, he is described as having eyes glowing like sulfur-fueled fire. A diurnal demon, Avarus helped Jubertus of Bavaria discover and recover goods, but in exchange forbade him to ever drink holy water, do good deeds, or kiss the cross. Should he ever see the cross, he will flee from it.

Sources: Csonka-Takács, *Witchcraft Mythologies and Persecutions*, 66; Kieckhefer, *Forbidden Rites*, 30, 34, 38; Tigelaar, *Karolus Rex*, 191.

Aversier

Latin for "adversary," the demon Aversier is one of the many names of SATAN.

Sources: De Gubernatis, *Zoological Mythology*, 14; Home, *France*, 131; Russel, *Lucifer*, 249.

Awabi

A Japanese demon of the sea, Awabi ("abalone") is the guardian of large seashells containing pearls. Living in the sea near Nanao, he attacks fishermen (see AQUEOUS DEVIL).

Sources: Davis, *Myths and Legends of Japan*, 340–1; Roberts, *Japanese Mythology A to Z*, 9; Yolen, *Fish Prince and Other Stories*, 83.

Awaia

From the demonology of Myanmar comes the demon of NIGHTMARES, Awaia. He lives above and outside the main gate to a house.

Sources: Carey, *Chin Hills*, 197; Downie, *Anthologia Anthropologica*, 44; Hastings, *Encyclopedia of Religion and Ethics*, 25.

A'war

Variations: AL-A'WAR, Awar

In Arabic demonology, A'war ("One Eyed") is one of the five SONS OF IBLIS (see IBLIS). A DJINN, A'war is a demon of debauchery and laziness who tempts men into committing acts of debauchery. A ritual cleansing and fumigation will protect anyone who may have been exposed to this demon, as all the *shai'ans* (SHAITANS) enjoy dirt and refuse. Also saying the "takbir" formula will drive them off. Amulets may also be worn for protection.

Sources: Hughes, *Dictionary of Islam*, 135; Knowles, *Nineteenth Century*, Vol. 31, 449; Schimmel, *Islamic Names*, 50.

Awyrgda

Awyrgda, an ancient Anglo-Saxon name meaning "Accursed One," is essentially another name for the DEVIL.

Sources: Bosworth, *Anglo-Saxon Dictionary*, 64; Dendle, *Satan Unbound*, 21; Russell, *Lucifer*, 142.

Ayperor

Variations: AYPEROS, IPES

Ayperor is a count or prince (sources vary) who commands thirty-six legions. His name is mentioned in various grimoires of Christian demonology (see COUNTS OF HELL and PRINCES OF HELL).

Sources: De Claremont, *Ancients' Book of Magic*, 118; Shepard, *Encyclopedia of Occultism and Parapsychology*, 116; Spence, *Encyclopedia of Occultism*, 57.

Ayperos

Variations: AYPEROR, Ayphos, Ipos

The eighteenth-century book alleged to be written by Pope Honorius III, *Grimoire of Pope Honorius* (*Le Grimoire du Pape Honorius*), tells us that the lesser demon Ayperos appears before his summoner looking like a male eagle or vulture. He has the ability to see and foretell the future. Some sources list him as a count while others list him as a prince (see COUNTS OF HELL and PRINCES OF HELL). Commanding thirty-six legions of servitors, Ayperos is under the command of NEBIROS.

Sources: Baskin, *Sorcerer's Handbook*, 276; Waite, *Unknown World 1894–1895*, 230; Wedeck, *Treasury of Witchcraft*, 96.

Ays

In Armenian mythology Ays is a DEV of the wind, an immortal spirit. As a gust of wind Ays will enter into a human body where he will possess it. Then Ays will either cause the person to go insane or turn them into a demon.

Sources: Lurker, *Routledge Dictionary of Gods and Goddesses, Devils and Demons*, 26, 49; Maberry, *They Bite*, 49; Russell, *Zoroastrianism in Armenia*, 52, 475.

Az

In Persian and Zoroastrian demonology, Az ("avarice," "greediness," "progenitor of sin") is the mother of all demons and sin. She appears as a woman who is constantly eating; no matter how much she consumes, she can never experience the sensation of having a full belly. Az is a powerful and destructive demon. She tries to make people forget their divine origin so that they will forgo salvation.

Sources: Dhalla, *Zoroastrian Theology*, 268; Horne, *Sacred Books and Early Literature of the East*, 183; Messadié, *History of the Devil*, 83.

Azanigin

According to Satanic demonology, Azanigin is the mother of all demons. She lives on Earth in the pantheon of the Order of the Nine Angels.

Sources: Ford, *Book of the Moon Choronzon Edition*, 313, 379; Susej, *Demonic Bible*, 245.

Azaradel

In the *Book of Enoch* and Enochian lore, Azaradel is one of the FALLEN ANGELS who swore allegiance to SAMIAZA, rebelled against God, took a human as his wife, and fathered the NEPHILIM.

Sources: Heraud, *Judgement of the Flood*, 150, 290; Lévi, *History of Magic*, 55; Spence, *Encyclopedia of Occultism*, 148.

Azariel

In Enochian and Jewish lore Azariel is one of the twenty-eight demonic rulers of the lunar mansions; he rules the mansion Aldebaran ("eye of Taurus"). Azariel causes problems with buildings, fountains, gold mines, and wells and has dominion over all the water of the earth. (See ENOCHIAN RULERS OF THE LUNAR MANSIONS.)

Sources: Eco, *Infinity of Lists*, 61; Moura, *Mansions of the Moon for the Green Witch*, 57; Webster, *Encyclopedia of Angels*, 26–7.

Azazel

Variations: Akazazel, ASASEL, 'Asiz, Aza'zel, Azael ("whom God strengthens"), Azaël, AZARADEL, Azaze, Azâzêl, Azazello, AZAZIL, AZAZYEL, AZIEL ("whom God consoles"), AZZAEL, EBLIS ("despair"), IBLIS, Shaytan, Zazel

In the Jewish tradition, for the Feast of Expiation (also known as the Day of Atonement), two goats are selected for sacrifice. Lots are then drawn to determine their fate. One goat is sacrificed by the high priest to the Lord, the animal's blood serving as atonement for the people. The other goat is then charged by the high priest with the sins of the people, led out into the desert and abandoned, leaving their sin with it, knowing that the demon of the wilderness, the DJINN Azazel ("God strengthens" or "arrogant to God"), will soon discover and consume it.

Azazel is mentioned by name in Arabian, Canaanite, Enochian, and Islamic mythology. His name is Hebrew and translates to mean "arrogant towards God," "goat departure," or "strong one of God." He is the mate of NAAMAH and the father of the SEDIM, chief of the SE'IRIM (goat-demons). Azazel is described as looking like a dragon with the hands and feet of a man, having six wings on each side of his back. He has seven snake heads with two faces upon each.

In the *Book of Enoch*, Azazel is said to be one of the chiefs of the GRIGORI; he swore allegiance to SAMIAZA, rebelled against God, lusted after and took a human wife against God's will, and fathered the NEPHILIM. Additionally, he taught men how to make armor, cosmetics, and weapons, as well as how to use sorcery. He was punished for his transgression by the archangel Raphael ("healing one of God") who chained him hand and foot to a jagged rock in a place of darkness. On the Day of Judgment, AZAZEL will be destroyed with fire.

A FALLEN ANGEL, formerly of the Order of Cherubim, he was later given the title of standard-bearer of the army of Hell during the Middle Ages (see also CHIEF OF THE GRIGORI, and GRIGORI).

Sources: Barton, *Journal of Biblical Literature*, Vols. 30–31, 162; Crowley, *Book of the Goetia of Solomon the King*, 67; Eco, *Infinity of Lists*, 61; Hyatt, *Book of Demons*, 42; Prophet, *Fallen Angels and the Origins of Evil*, 174.

Azazil

Variations: ASAEL, AZAZEL ("God strengthens" or "arrogant to God"), Azaziel, AZAZYEL, IBLIS, SATAN, Uza

Heaven, Earth, and Hell are described as each

having levels to them. Azazil ("strong mountain" or "strongest of mountains") spent a thousand years worshipping God on each level, starting at the lowest in Hell and ascending upwards. On each level he was given a new angelic name. He was named Azazil upon reaching the fifth level of Heaven. He was so thorough in his devotions it was said that in Heaven not an area the size of a man's hand wasn't prayed upon by him. When God commanded that he worship at Adam, Azazil asked why a "son of fire should bow before a son of clay?" God cast him out of Heaven and changed his name to EBLIS, which means "despair." For three thousand years he waited at the Gates of Paradise for an opportunity to do harm to Adam and Eve; he has a deep hatred for them still.

Azazil, in Zoroastrian demonology, is named as being the lord of the DJINN and is described as once having had a pair of wings made of emerald. A powerful sorcerer, he has dominion over the zodiacal sign of Taurus.

Sources: Laurence, *Foreign Quarterly Review*, Vol. 24, 370; Lumpkin, *Fallen Angels, the Watchers, and the Origins of Evil*, 31; Prophet, *Fallen Angels and the Origins of Evil*, 174.

Azazyel

Variations: Azazyeel, AZZA, SATAN

In the Enochian lore, the *Book of Enoch* tells us that Azazyel was one of the FALLEN ANGELS who swore allegiance to SAMIAZA, rebelled against God, took a human as his wife, and fathered the NEPHILIM. Additionally, he taught man how to make and use armor, dyes, jewelry, knives, make-up, shields, and swords and is thereby particularly responsible for the corruption of mankind.

Azazyel was deemed to be the ringleader of the angels who rebelled, and his punishment was the greatest. The Lord ordered the angel Raphael ("healing one of God") to capture Azazyel, tie him up, take him to a place of darkness in the desert, make a hole and throw him in it face down, hurl upon him sharp stones, and to make sure he stayed there, denied of light, until the end of days, when he would finally be destroyed by fire. Those who followed Azazyel were also greatly punished. They were bound and buried as Azazyel was for seventy generations or until the end of days, whichever came first. Additionally, the children that the FALLEN ANGELS fathered were all slain.

The demon of corruption, fornication, and immorality, Azazyel planned on corrupting the earth.

Sources: Beard, *Autobiography of Satan*, 113; Grant, *Edgar Cayce on Angels, Archangels, and the Unseen Forces*, 135; Laurence, *Book of Enoch*, 10; Prophet, *Fallen Angels and the Origins of Evil*, 174; Voltaire, *Philosophical Dictionary*, 287.

Azemo

In Enochian lore, Azemo is one of the FALLEN ANGELS who swore allegiance to SAMIAZA, rebelled against God, took a human as his wife, and fathered the NEPHILIM. In Christian demonology Azemo is one of the nocturnal SERVITORS OF CAMUEL (see CAMUEL). When summoned, he appears in a beautiful form and is very courteous to his summoner.

Sources: Belanger, *Dictionary of Demons*, 53; Peterson, *Lesser Key of Solomon*, 68.

Azeruel

Variations: Atliel

According to Enochian lore, Azeruel is one of the twenty-eight rulers of the twenty-eight lunar mansions; he has dominion over the mansion Ahubene ("Horns of Scorpio") and the zodiacal sign of Scorpio. Azeruel hinders journeys and wedlock (see ENOCHIAN RULERS OF THE LUNAR MANSIONS).

Sources: Eco, *Infinity of Lists*, 61; Moura, *Mansions of the Moon for the Green Witch*, 87; Von Goethe, *Goethe's Letters to Zelter*, 378; Webster, *Encyclopedia of Angels*, 27, 124.

Azeuph

Apollonius of Tyana's *Nuctemeron* (*Night Illuminated by Day*) tells us that Azeuph is a type of demon known as a DJINN; he is most powerful during the tenth hour of the day and is a known destroyer of children.

Sources: Gettings, *Dictionary of Demons*, 43; Lévi, *Transcendental Magic*, 421.

Azhi-Dahak

Variations: Azi Dahaka; Azidahaka, the biting snake; Ezhdeha; Yim

In Iranian, Vedic, and Zoroastrian mythology, Azhi-Dahak ("fiendish snake") is a snakelike storm demon that has three heads and six eyes. In *Shah Namah*, he is described as a man with two snakes that grew up out of his shoulders from where AHRIMAN kissed him. He has been described as being a vested sovereign who looks like a dragon or snakelike creature. In some descriptions, he is described as having as many as three heads and six eyes. He is known to harm people and steal cattle. Although he is a storm demon, he is also part human (see CAMBION). His personal adversary is AHI.

Azhi-Dahak was captured by the warrior Thraetaona and was then placed in a prison on the top of Dermawend Mountain. At the time of the great renovation, he will be chained to Mount Demavand, but will inevitably break free and disturb creation. However, at Fraso-Kereti (the End of Time) he will die in Ayohsust, a river of fire.

Azhi-Dahak is the personification of the Babylonian oppression of Iran.

Sources: Charles, *Critical and Exegetical Commentary*, 311–2; Cox, *Mythology of the Aryan Nations*, 324, 362; Hastings, *Encyclopedia of Religion and Ethics*, 376, 387.

Azi

Variations: Æshma, Ashmedai, ASMODEUS, Asmodi

In the Mazdian religion, Azi is the demon of carnal desire and puts out household fires during the night. Sacrifices are made to trees and water in hopes of them yielding strength to resist his temptations.

Sources: Dhalla, *Zoroastrian Theology*, 171–2; Choksy, *Evil, Good and Gender*, 17; Horne, *Sacred Books and Early Literature of the East*, 133.

Aziel

According to Enochian lore, Aziel ("whom God consoles") is one of the twenty-eight demonic rulers of the lunar mansions. He presides over the mansion Sadalabra ("butterfly") and is known to cast spells that prevent copulation, encourage hostility and revenge, and prevent people from doing what they need to be doing (see ENOCHIAN RULERS OF THE LUNAR MANSIONS).

Sources: Conway, *Demonology and Devil-Lore*, 299; Eco, *Infinity of Lists*, 61; Moura, *Mansions of the Moon for the Green Witch*, 12; Scheible, *Sixth and Seventh Books of Moses*, 75; Webster, *Encyclopedia of Angels*, 26–7.

Azkeel

Variations: Ezeqeel

In the *Book of Enoch*, Azkeel, a FALLEN ANGEL, is listed as being one of the Chiefs of the Grigori (see CHIEF OF TENS) who swore allegiance to SAMIAZA, rebelled against God, took a human as his wife, and fathered the NEPHILIM.

Sources: Beard, *Autobiography of Satan*, 113; Davidson, *Dictionary of Angels*, 206, Laurence, *Book of Enoch, the Prophet*, 6; Lévi, *History of Magic*, 38.

Azza

Variations: AZAZEL, AZAZYEL, Samyaza, Semhaza, Semyaza, Shemhaza, Shemiaza, Uzza

In Enochian lore, the *Book of Enoch* tells the story of when Enoch was elevated from a mortal to an angelic being named Metatron and was given command of one of the two groups of Angels of Justice. Azza ("the strong one") is the angel who commanded the other group, protested the promotion, and was cast out of heaven for it. Now, as a FALLEN ANGEL, Azza is in a state of perpetually falling; one of his eyes is sealed shut while the other was left open so that he may see his plight and suffer all the more for it.

Some sources say that Azza was born of the union between the daughter of Lamech, NAAMAH, and the demon Azazel.

Sources: Boccaccini, *Enoch and Qumran Origins*, 157; Mathers, *Kabbalah Unveiled*, 249; Reed, *Fallen Angels and the History of Judaism and Christianity*, 256, 267–8.

Azzael

Variations: Azael ("whom God strengthens"), AZAZEL

In Enochian lore, in the *Book of Enoch*, Azzael ("God strengthens") is one of the FALLEN ANGELS who swore allegiance to SAMIAZA, rebelled against God, took a human wife, and fathered the NEPHILIM. Additionally, he taught the construction of jewelry; the use of cosmetics and dyes; a type of magic that would allow the moon, stars, and sun to move closer to the earth where they can be better worshipped; the science of metallurgy and minerals; and untold secrets of a sexual nature.

Through the power of the ring owned by King Solomon (see SPIRITS OF SOLOMON), Azzael was forced to reveal to the king the "heavenly mysteries." Azzael is portrayed as a scapegoat in the King James Version of the Bible since it was written that the Fallen Angels removed sin from the people under his protection and gave that sin to the Devil.

Azzael and Uzza are noted for having pierced noses; this was no doubt culturally significant. He and the Fallen Angel AZZA are chained with iron shackles to a mountain so remote that no bird can find it. The spot where they are chained is veiled in complete darkness.

Sources: Boccaccini, *Enoch and Qumran Origins*, 157; Lumpkin, *Book of Enoch*, 310; Reed, *Fallen Angels and the History of Judaism and Christianity*, 256, 267–8.

Baabal

In the *Theurgia Goetia*, the second book of the *Lemegeton*, Baabal, a diurnal demon, is one of the SERVITORS OF BARMIEL (see BARMIEL).

Sources: Peterson, *Lesser Key of Solomon*, 71; Trithemius, *Steganographia*, 17.

Baal, plural: "the Baalim"

Variations: ADON, Adonai, Aliyan Ha-ded, AMMON, Ba'al, Baal-Hammon ("the hidden god"), Baal-Tzephon ("god of the crypt"), BAEL, Baël, Baell, Bal, Bayal, Bel, Beth Ayin Lamed ("just lord"), Ha-ded, Haddu, Seth ("pillar" or "phallus")

In the language of the ancient Semites, the word *baal* translates as the title "lord," as in "the ruler" or "possessor" of a district. In Canaanite mythology, Baal was worshipped as a storm and fertility god. As a fertility god, he fought against his brother Mot. If Baal was victorious, the crops were plentiful. If Mot won, there was drought. He was believed to have lived on the mountain known as Sapan ("north"). This is possibly Mt. Jabal al-Aqra, located in Syria, 15 km north of Ugarit. Ancient worship of Baal required the sacrificial burning of children.

Baal was later demonized by Christian demonologists and made into an ARCHDEMON. He was mentioned in the *Lemegeton, the Lesser Key of Solomon*, and has been given various ranks including chief of Netzach, first monarch of Hell, general of the Infernal Armies, Grand Cross of the ORDER OF THE FLY, grand duke of Hell, king ruling in the East, and the second chief of staff of the Abyss.

Christian demonologists say that Baal, the demon of anger, hate, vengeance, and war, is in service under MEPHISTOPHELES or MOLOCH. He commands the armies of Hell and sixty-six legions and was one of the seventy-two SPIRITS OF SOLOMON. Summoners claim he appears as a portly, three-headed beast: one head is of a cat, one of a crowned man, and one of a toad. He has long spider legs that stem from his torso and speaks in a hoarse voice. Most powerful during the month of October, Baal is summoned because he has the ability to bestow onto his summoner the power to turn invisible at will; he can also heighten the summoner's perceptions and make him more cunning. Baal has the ability to shapeshift into a cat and a toad.

Sources: Chambers, *Book of Days*, 722; Conybeare, *Jewish Quarterly Review*, Vol. 11, 5; Lewis, *Origines Hebrææ*, 292–4; Melton, *Encyclopedia of Occultism and Parapsychology*, 315; Oort, *Worship of Baalim in Israel*, 35–65; Paine, *Hierarchy of Hell*, 71.

Baalam

Variations: BALAAM, BALAM, Balan

Baalam is listed in various grimoires as being either a king or duke, commanding forty legions of demons (see DUKES OF HELL and KINGS OF HELL). He is described as having three heads: one of a bull, one of a man, and the third of a ram. Baalam has flaming red eyes and a tail like a serpent and rides upon a bear carrying a hawk. He is also described by some sources simply as a naked man riding a bear. Baalam will answer any question his summoner puts to him honestly regarding the past, present, or future; he also teaches how to become invisible and makes men humorous.

Sources: De Giviry, *Witchcraft, Magic, and Alchemy*, 65; De Laurence, *Lesser Key of Solomon, Goetia*, 38–9; Icons, *Demons*, 139; Scott, *London Magazine*, Vol. 5, 378.

Baalberith

Variations: Baal-Berith, BAALAM, Baalberity, Baalphegor, Baalsebul, BAALZEPHON, BAEL, Baell, BALAM, Balan, BALBERITH, Beal, BELETH, Belberith, Belfagor, BELIAL, Beliar, BELPHEGOR, BERITH, Bilet, BILETH, BYLETH, Elberith

Originally a Canaanite god of the covenant, Baalberith ("Lord of the Covenant") was demonized by Christian demonologists and he was said to be one of the FALLEN ANGELS. He has been given various ranks including chief secretary of Hell, head of public archives, master of Ceremonies, master of the Infernal Alliance, and a pontiff of Hell. One of his major responsibilities is that of notarizing the pacts drafted between humans and demons. As the demon of blasphemy and murder, Baalberith, noted for being exceptionally talkative, is most powerful during the month of June.

Baalberith is listed as one of the demons who in 1612 possessed a nun in Aix-en-Provence. During the exorcism, he gave not only his own name freely, but the names of the other demons who were involved in the possession (ASHTAROTH, ASMODEUS, and BEELZEBUB) as well as a list of the saints who would be most effective against them.

Sources: Chambers, *Book of Days*, 722; Lewis, *Origines Hebrææ*, 295; Mayberry, *Cryptopedia*, 49; Scott, *London Magazine*, Vol. 5, 378.

Baal-Beryth

In Phoenician mythology Baal-Beryth was the god of the winter sun. He was later demonized by medieval scholars and made into one of the PRINCES OF HELL and the master of rituals and pacts.

Sources: Ford, *Book of the Moon Witch Chronozon Edition*, 359; Herbert, *Nimrod*, 253; Kitto, *Daily Bible Illustrations*, 207.

Baalimm

According to Father Zacharias Vicecomes's book *Complementum Artis Exorcistiae* (1608), Baalimm is one of thirty-two demons he catalogued that frequently take possession of humans.

Sources: Cobb, *Origines Judaicae*, 140–3; Melton, *Encyclopedia of Occultism and Parapsychology*, 315; Oort, *Worship of Baalim in Israle*, 35; Smedley, *Occult Sciences*, 176.

Baal-Peor

Variations: Baalpeor, Bel-Peor, BELPHEGOR, Beth-baal-peor, Beth-peor

Originally a Moabite god, Baal-Peor, or "Baal of Peor" ("Lord of Peor") as he is also known, took his name from Mount Peor, which is located on the left bank of the river Jordan. He was both a male sun god and a female moon goddess. He was said to appear as a beautiful young woman. It was during the Middle Ages that the name reemerged as BELPHEGOR and became synonymous with the Devil.

Sources: Calmet, *Dictionary of the Holy Bible*, 122–3; Faber, *Origin of Pagan Idolatry*, 250–2; Hyatt, *Book of Demons*, 46.

Baalzebub

Variations: Ba'al Zebûb, Baalzeboub, Beelzeboul, BEELZEBUB, Beelzebul

In Hebrew the name Baalzebub translates to mean "Lord of Zebûb" ("Lord of the Flies"); it is the name that is used for SATAN in the New Testament. Originally, in the Old Testament, Baalzebub was the name of the god worshiped in the ancient Philistine city of Ekron.

Sources: Cowan, *Curious Facts in the History of Insects*, 292–3; Lewis, *Origines Hebræ*, 296–7; Taylor, *Second Coming of Jesus*, 176–7.

Baalzephon

Variations: Aliyan Ba'l, Aliyan Haded ("most strong lord"), BAAL, Ba'al, Ba'al Tzaphon, Baalzephon, HADAD

Originally from Canaanite demonology, Baalzephon ("BAAL of the North") was listed among the demons in Johann Wierus's *Pseudomonarchia Daemonum* (*False Monarchy of Demons*, 1583) as the captain of the guard and sentinels of Hell, as well as the prime minister for Dispater (see PRIME MINISTERS OF HELL).

In the Book of Exodus, the name of the area where the Israelites camped before they crossed the Red Sea was called Baalzephon.

Sources: Krummacher, *Israel's Wanderings in the Wilderness*, 36, 44; Lewis, *Origines Hebræ*, 292–4; Thomas, *Hebrew and Semitic Studies*, 91.

Babael

Variations: "Keeper of Graves"

In various grimoires, Babael is listed as the demon of healing.

Sources: Laycock, *Complete Enochian Dictionary*, 83; Maberry, *Cryptopedia*, 49.

Babalon

Variations: Babalond (harlot), Babilu (Gateway of the Gods), Babylon the Great, Mother of Whores and Abominations of the Earth, The Scarlet Woman

In the Mystical System of Thelema, developed by the occultist Aleister Crowley, Babalon ("wicked") is a demonic earth goddess and demon of the female sexual impulse. She is described as carrying a sword and riding upon The Beast; in her right hand she holds its reigns, in the other, she carries a chalice.

Sources: Clark, *Royal Secret*, 315; Ford, *Book of the Witch Moon Choronzon Edition*, 97; Laycock, *Complete Enochian Dictionary*, 42, 83.

Babi

Variations: Bab, Babay, Bapho, Bebon, Seth

From the Old Kingdom of ancient Egypt, in the *Books of the Dead* and the *Book of Going Forth by Day*, Babi ("bull" as in the dominant male aggressor of the baboons) was the demonic god of darkness. The first born son of Osiris and Isis, and having the physical appearance of a baboon, he became the very symbol of aggression and virility. Babi controls the darkness and was called upon by the ancient Egyptians to give protection in the Underworld against snakes and dangerous waterways. His penis is the bolt on the doors that opens up the heavens and is also used as a mast on the Underworld ferry.

During the Weighing of the Heart ceremony, in the Hall of Double Truths, the deceased would use spells of protection against the vicious and bloodthirsty Babi, as he devoured human entrails and unworthy souls.

Sources: Hart, *Routledge Dictionary of Egyptian Gods and Goddesses*, 44; Jordan, *Dictionary of Gods and Goddesses*, 43; Lurker, *Dictionary of Gods and Goddesses*, 53; Pinch, *Egyptian Mythology*, 112–3, 138.

Babillo

Listed in various grimoires, the devil Babillo is the patron of painters.

Sources: Rudwin, *Devil in Legend and Literature*, 83.

Bacaron

The *Sacred Magic of Abramelin the Mage* lists Bacaron ("first born") among the fifteen SERVITORS OF ASMODEUS (see ASMODEUS). There are two lists of servitors to Asmodeus. One list has fifteen demons on it and the other has twelve; however, both lists contain the name Bacaron.

Sources: Belanger, *Dictionary of Demons*, 58; Mathers, *Book of the Sacred Magic of Abramelin the Mage*, 119; Von Worms, *Book of Abramelin*, 256.

Bachelor, The

The Bachelor is essentially a name that is applied to SATAN when he is in the guise of a great he-goat. It was alleged that he had sexual intercourse with witches in this form.

Sources: Michelet, *La Sorcière*, 171; Smedley, *Occult Sciences*, 56.

Bad

In Persian demonology Bad was a DJINN and the demon of tempests who could control the wind. He is most powerful on the twenty-second day of every month.

Sources: Drury, *Dictionary of the Esoteric*, 26.

Badad

In the *Sacred Magic of Abramelin the Mage*, book two, Badad ("Solitary") is among the one hundred eleven SERVITORS OF AMAYMON, ARITON, ORIENS, AND PAYMON (see AMAYMON, ARITON, ORIENS, and PAYMON).

Sources: Belanger, *Dictionary of Demons*, 57; Susej, *Demonic Bible*, 256; Von Worms, *Book of Abramelin*, 244.

Bael

Variations: BAAL, Baël, Baell, Beal, Bel, Bele, Belenus, Beli, Belinus, BELUS

In Johann Wierus's *Pseudomonarchia Daemonum* (*False Monarchy of Demons*, 1583), Bael ("Lord") is listed with the rank of First King of Hell of the Eastern Section, commanding sixty-six legions. He appears to his summoner as a cat, a toad (or crab), a man, or a conglomeration of all three at once and speaking with a hoarse voice. Bael is a good warrior and is known to grant the gift of alertness, cunning, and how to become invisible.

Sources: Baskin, *Sorcerer's Handbook*, 276; Collin de Plancy, *Dictionary of Witchcraft*, 22; De Laurence, *Lesser Key of Solomon, Goetia*, 22; McLean, *Treatise of Angel Magic*, 51; Melton, *Encyclopedia of Occultism and Parapsychology*, 315; Waite, *Unknown World 1894–1895*, 230; Wedeck, *Treasury of Witchcraft*, 96.

Bafamal

In the *Sacred Magic of Abramelin the Mage*, book two, Bafamal is listed as one of the thirty-two SERVITORS OF ASTAROT (see ASTAROT).

Sources: Ford, *Bible of the Adversary*, 91; Mathers, *Book of the Sacred Magic of Abramelin the Mage*, 116; Von Worms, *Book of Abramelin*, 249.

Baglis

Baglis, the demon of balance and measures, was mentioned in Apollonius of Tyana's *Nuctemeron* (*Night Illuminated by Day*). He is most powerful during the second hour of the day.

Sources: Davidson, *Dictionary of Angels*, 68; Gettings, *Dictionary of Demons*, 45; Webster, *Encyclopedia of Angels*, 31.

Bahak-Zivo

Variations: Bahak-ziwa, Father of the DJINN

In the *Codex Nazaraeus* (*Codex of the Nazarenes*, also known as the *Book of Adam*), Bahak-Zivo was the DJINN who called the world into existence, pulling it from the dark waters. He failed in the construction of creating life with a soul because he did not know ORCUS, the bottomless pit. Even calling upon a more pure spirit, Fetahil, he was still unable to create life with a soul.

Sources: Blavatsky, *Secret Doctrine*, 195; Dunlap, *Sôd*, 50–1; Norberg, *Codex Nasaraeus*, 149.

Bahal

In the *Sacred Magic of Abramelin the Mage*, book two, Bahal ("to disturb") is listed as one of the thirty-two SERVITORS OF ASTAROT (see ASTAROT).

Sources: Belanger, Dictionart of Demons, 58; Mathers, *Book of the Sacred Magic of Abramelin the Mage*, 106; Von Worms, Book of Abramelin, 249.

Bahaman

A DJINN from Persian demonology, Bahaman is the demon of appeasing anger. He has power over oxen, sheep, and all animals of a peaceful nature.

Sources: De Claremont, *Ancients' Book of Magic*, 119; Spence, *Encyclopedia of Occultism*, 62; Susej, *Demonic Bible*, 70.

Bairiron

The *Zodiac Qlippoth* lists Emperor Bairiron as a demon of balanced power and authority (see QLIPPOTHIC ORDERS OF DEMONS). He and the demons of his order are described as a dragon-like lion. Bairiron will assist the ANTICHRIST when he comes to being on earth. This demon gives feeling of empowerment and energy, helps write spells, and gain spell ideas. He teaches communication and wisdom to those who ask for it from him. Bairiron's sacred color is black and his zodiacal sign is Aries.

Sources: Ford, *Book of the Witch Moon Chorozon Edition*, 334; Mathers, *Sorcerer and his Apprentice*, 25.

Bâjang

In Malaysia witches and sorcerers have the ability through a magical ceremony to bring forth a vampiric demon. The ceremony involves the body of a stillborn child or the corpse of a family member. The demon, when called up, if male, is referred to as a bâjang; the female of the species is known as a langsuir. A strong enough caster can bind this demon to himself and keep it as a FAMILIAR, which will then be passed down his family line for generations. The bâjang is housed in a specially constructed container called a tabong; it is made of bamboo that is sealed with leaves and locked closed with a magical charm.

The sorcerer who possess the bâjang must personally feed it a diet of milk and eggs or else the demon will turn on its master and begin to feed itself on its favorite food—children.

The bâjang has the ability to shape-shift into three different forms: that of a cat, large lizard, or weasel. While in its cat form, if the demon mews at a baby, the child will die.

The witch who controls the bâjang will send it out as needed to do her bidding. When sent to bring harm to a person, the bâjang will inflict on its victim a mysterious disease for which there is no cure. The person grows weaker and weaker, suffering from convulsions and fainting spells until they eventually succumb to death.

There is no way to destroy a bâjang; however, there are charms that can be made and worn or purchased to keep it at bay. Perhaps the best way to deal with such a demonic creature would be to deal directly with the witch who commands it.

Sources: Clifford, *Dictionary of Malay Language*, 121; Gimlette, *Malay Poisons and Charms*, 47; Hobart, *People of Bali*, 116–17; Winstedt, *Malay Magician*, 25.

Balaam

Variations: BALAM, Balan

The demon of avarice, idol worship, and immorality, Duke Balaam commands thirty legions of demons. His name is taken from the Hebrew word for "avarice and greed" or for the word "foreigner."

Balaam is described as having three heads: one of a bull, one of a man, and one of a ram. He also has the tail of a snake and flaming eyes. He speaks with a hoarse voice and rides upon a bear and carries a goshawk on his wrist.

Balaam can only be summoned when the sun is in Sagittarius; when he arrives, he will have with him four kings and their entourage and armies. He is summoned because he will truthfully answer questions regarding the past, present, and future; give men the understanding of the language of birds, dogs, and other animals; reveal the locations of magical treasures hidden by magicians; reconcile friends and people in power; and teach those who ask him how to become invisible. Balaam was also one of the demons who possessed Sister Jeanne des Anges. It was said that Balaam's passion was "all the more dangerous because it seemed less evil" (see also BALALOS).

Sources: De Laurence, *Lesser Key of Solomon, Goetia*, 38–9; Dumas, *Crimes of Urbain Grandier and Others*, 81, 83; Grivy, *Witchcraft, Magic and Alchemy*, 65; Hsia, *World of Catholic Renewal*, 151; Scott, *London Magazine*, Vol. 5, 378.

Balaken

Variations: Balachem

The *Sacred Magic of Abramelin the Mage* names Balaken ("ravagers") as one of the six SERVITORS OF ORIENS (see ORIENS).

Sources: Belanger, *Dictionary of Demons*, 58; Mathers, *Book of the Sacred Magic of Abramelin the Mage*, 121; Von Worms, *Book of Abramelin*, 253.

Balalos

Balalos ("to throw") is listed in the *Sacred Magic of Abramelin the Mage* as one of the one hundred eleven SERVITORS OF AMAYMON, ARITON, ORIENS, AND PAYMON (see AMAYMON, ARITON, ORIENS, and PAYMON). The very powerful demon of finesse, middle courses, and ruses, Balalos commands forty legions of demons. He is described as having three heads: one of a bull, one of a man, and one of a ram. He also has the tail of a snake and flaming eyes. He rides upon a bear and carries a goshawk on his wrist.

Sources: Belanger, *Dictionary of Demons*, 58; Mathers, *Book of the Sacred Magic of Abramelin the Mage*, 114; Susej, *Demonic Bible*, 256.

Balam

Variations: BALAAM, Balamm, Balan, Balemm

Mayan for "jaguar," Balam, the demon of avarice and greed, is a FALLEN ANGEL, formerly of the Order of Dominions. He is ranked as a king or duke and commands forty legions. He is also listed as one of the seventy-two SPIRITS OF SOLOMON. He is described as having three heads: one of a bull, one of a man, and one of a ram. He has the tail of a snake and flaming eyes. Upon the ram's head, he wears a crown between his tall upturned horns and long, hairy ears. Speaking with a hoarse voice, he rides upon a bear and carries a goshawk on his wrist. His arms and legs are unnaturally long, as are his fingers and toes, which end in clawlike fingernails. Balam is a nocturnal demon who is most powerful during the month of December. His zodiacal sign is Sagittarius. Balam is summoned because he answers truthfully questions regarding the past, present, and future. He can also give the gifts of invisibility and wit.

This entity is often called upon during exorcism and cases of collective possession; he is also listed as one of the eighteen demons who possessed Sister Jeanne des Anges in Loudun, France, in 1634 (see LOUDUN POSSESSION).

Sources: Aikin, *General Biography*, 493; Bayle, *Historical and Critical Dictionary*, 262; De Laurence, *Lesser Key of Solomon, Goetia*, 38–9; Hyatt, *Book of Demons*, 75; Scot, *Discoverie of Witchcraft*, 225; Voltaire, *Works of M. de Voltaire*, 193.

Balban

Variations: Balbam

Balban is listed in various grimoires as the demon of delusions. He is also said to appear before humans in the guise of an angel who uses feigned sanctity to trick and manipulate.

Sources: Dingwall, *Some Human Oddities*, 33; Levack, *New Perspectives on Witchcraft, Magic, and Demonology*, 36; Waugh, *Christendom and Its Discontents*, 317.

Balberith

Variations: Ba'al Baal Davar, BAAL-PEOR, BAALAM, BAALBERITH, Baalphegor, Baalsebul, BAALZEPHON, BAEL, Baell, BALAM, Balan, Beal, Belberith, BELETH, Belfagor, BELIAL, Beliar, BELPHEGOR, BERITH, Bilet, BILETH, BYLETH, Elberith, "scriptor"

Originally from Canaanite demonology as the Lord of the covenant and later becoming a god of death, Balberith ("Covenant Lord") was eventually demonized and was listed among the seventy-two SPIRITS OF SOLOMON. He has been given the various ranks and titles of duke of Hell, grand pontiff and master of ceremonies, minister of foreign affairs, prince of Cherubim, and secretary of the archives of Hell (see DUKES OF HELL and PRINCES OF HELL). Among his various duties, he countersigns and notarizes pacts made with the DEVIL.

The demon of blasphemy and murder, Balberith is one of the FALLEN ANGELS, formerly of the order of Cherubim. He tempts men to commit homicides and be arguable, blasphemous, and quarrelsome. Balberith's personal adversary is the peacemaker St. Barnabas. He is also one of the demons who possessed the body of Sister Madeleine at Aix-en-Provence.

Sources: Allen, *Hosea, Malachi*, 16; Cuhulain, *Witch Hunts*, 206; Kelly, *Who in Hell*, 23; Guiley, *Encyclopedia of Angels*, 63; Scott, *London Magazine*, Vol. 5, 378.

Balewa

Balewa is a Sumero-Aryan word that translates to mean "baleful one" and "hateful and wicked one." This word is used to describe SATAN.

Sources: Bosworth, *Anglo-Saxon Dictionary*, 67; Russell, *Lucifer*, 142; Waddell, *Sumer Aryan Dictionary*, 27.

Balfori

In the *Sacred Magic of Abramelin the Mage*, book two, Balfori ("Lord of producing") is one

of the forty-nine SERVITORS OF BEELZEBUB (see BEELZEBUB).

Sources: Belanger, *Dictionary of Demons*, 58; Ford, *Bible of the Adversary*, 93; Mathers, *Book of the Sacred Magic of Abramelin the Mage*, 104.

Bali

A nocturnal demon of the Underworld, Bali is the king of the DAITYAS in Indian demonology. In service under the god Vishnu, Bali is known for his grand benevolence. He has the appearance of a donkey and once a year he returns to his people to light a million lamps to symbolize the darkness of anger, ego, greed, ignorance, jealousy, laziness, and lust being driven back by the light of friendship, harmony, knowledge, peace, and wisdom.

Bali grew so powerful that the other gods were afraid of him. So Vishnu went to the demon disguised as a dwarf and asked if he could have all the land he could cover in three steps. Bali agreed to the land grant and Vishnu revealed himself in all his glory. His first step covered all of the earth. His second step covered all of the heavens. Before he could take his third and final step, Bali offered his head to be stepped upon and crushed, compelling Vishnu to stop. Rather than kill him, the god kicked him down into the netherworld, but gave him a lamp and a promise that he may return to his people once a year.

Sources: Chopra, *Academic Dictionary of Mythology*, 47; Lurker, *Routledge Dictionary of Gods and Goddesses*, 30; Singh, *Encyclopaedia of Hinduism*, 2520, 2523; Turner, *Dictionary of Ancient Deities*, 91.

Balidet

In Enochian lore Balidet is a minister who is in service to MAMMON. An AERIAL DEVIL of the west, he is most powerful on Saturdays.

Sources: Davidson, *Dictionary of Angels*, 69; Kelly, *Who in Hell*, 24; McLean, *Treatise on Angel Magic*, 51.

Balkin

In Reginald Scot's *The Discoverie of Witchcraft* (1584), Balkin is listed as the king of the Northern Mountains of Hell. He commands the demons GLAURON and LURIDAN, as well as 1,500 legions of demons. Balkin rides upon a small goat and as he travels he is preceded by an innumerable company of dwarves riding chameleons. Known to perform acts of kindness and charity, Balkin will answer questions asked of him but he is also known to give quality FAMILIARs. They are described as being a span tall and will stay with the summoner for the rest of his life.

Sources: Davidson, *Dictionary of Angels*, 69; Gettings, *Dictionary of Demons*, 45; Kelly, *Who in Hell*, 24; Shah, *Occultism*, 206, 208.

Balphegor

Variations: BAAL-PEOR, Beelphegor, Belfagor

Originally a Moabite deity idol worshiped by the Israelites, Balphegor is listed in Collin de Plancy's *Dictionaire Infernale* (1863) as the ARCHDEMON of the Togarini and the sixth of the evil SEPHIROTHS. Hugo further adds that he is also the infernal ambassador to France and hides in the Louvre Museum.

The demon of ingenious discoveries and inventions, Balphegor appears to his summoner as either a giant phallus or as a beautiful young girl. He is known to give riches to his summoner, but only if he likes the person.

There is a medieval legend that tells of how Balphegor wanted to experience the happiness and dread of a married couple. He fled back to Hell in horror after living as a man, glad that there was no sexual intercourse in Hell.

Sources: Blavatsky, *Theosophist*, 275; Icon, *Demons*, 140; Gasparin, *Science vs. Modern Spiritualism*, 327; Melton, *Encyclopedia of Occultism and Parapsychology*, 315; Shepard, Encyclopedia of Occultism and Parapsychology, 440.

Balsur

In the *Ars Paulina*, book three of the *Lemegeton*, Balsur is one of the twelve chief duke SERVITORS OF AMENADIEL (see AMENADIEL and DUKES OF HELL). He commands three thousand servitors.

Sources: Belanger, *Dictionary of Demons*, 59; Guiley, *Encyclopedia of Demons and Demonology*, 7; Peterson, *Lesser Key of Solomon*, 62.

Baltazo

According to Jean Bodin's *Demonomania of Witches* (1581) the demon Baltazo, who possessed Nicole Aubry of Laon in 1566, had an aversion to water. According to legend, one evening Bodin went to dinner with the husband of Nicole Aubry under the pretense of protecting her from demonic possession. It was noted that during the meal, he did not drink, thereby Bodin deduced that demons are averse to water.

Sources: Calmet, *Phantom World*, 131; Collin de Plancy, *Dictionnaire Infernal*, 316, Summers; *Vampires in Europe*, 230.

Balternis

Variations: BATTERNIS

In the *Sacred Magic of Abramelin the Mage*, Balternis is listed as one of the sixty-five SERVITORS OF KORE AND MAGOTH.

Sources: Ford, *Bible of the Adversary*, 92; Mathers,

Book of the Sacred Magic of Abramelin the Mage, 119; Von Worms, *Book of Abramelin*, 251, 256.

Ba-Maguje

Ba-Maguje is a demonic spirit of drunkenness in the Hausa mythology. He has no physical description but is known to cause alcoholism by making the victim increasingly thirsty and eventually insensitive to the amount they have consumed.

Sources: Chopra, *Academic Dictionary of Mythology*, 44; Edgar, *Hausa Readings*, 61, 63–4; Tremearne, *Ban of the Bori*, 428.

Banim Shovavin

Variations: Banim Shovavim

In Judaic lore, banim shovavin ("backsliding children," "mischievous sons" or "wayward sons") is a type of CAMBION, born of the union between a human man and a SUCCUBUS. These demons show up at their father's deathbed or funeral claiming to be his son. Seeking their birthright, the banim shovavin will think nothing of physically harming and eliminating the legitimate heir if necessary to claim what they consider to be theirs.

The custom of circling the deceased at the graveyard came about in the seventeenth century to prevent demons from being at the graveside. It is also the reason in some communities that sons are not permitted to accompany their father's body to its grave, in the event that illegitimate half-brothers show up.

Sources: Dennis, *Encyclopedia of Jewish Myth, Magic and Mysticism*, 29; Koén-Sarano, *King Solomon and the Golden Fish*, 63; Scholem, *Kabbalah*, 322.

Baphomet

Variations: Baffomet, Bafomen, Bafoment, Bahemet, Baphoinet, Mahomet

It was suggested by Montague Summers that originally the name Baphomet came from the Greek words *baphe* and *metis*, read together translating as "absorption into wisdom." However, the Latin phrase *Templi omnium hominum pacis abhas* ("the father of universal peace among men") is translated as "Temp. ohp. Ab." and could also be a possible origin of the word. The word *baphomet* was first documented in twelfth-century France.

Baphomet is not so much a demon as it is the statue of the alleged god worshiped by the Knights Templars (properly named *Pauperes commilitis Christi et Templi Salomonis*).

The statue of Baphomet has been described as looking like a goat-headed demon; some reports claim it has a beard while others do not. It has also been said to be a man's skull, a statue of a three-faced demon, a monstrous head, and a goat. It is apparent that no one truly knows what the statue looked like or even what it was made of, as various sources each claim that the statue was made of wood, metal, stone, or crystal. Some accounts even claim it to have been a black and white painting. No matter what it looked like or what it was made of, all accounts agree that the statue itself was alleged to be magical.

Most common among its various appearances is the claim that a torch could be placed between the horns on the head and a pentagram painted on its forehead. The hands are in eccentric positions and point to two lunar crests, one black and the other white. The goat was picked to be the head of the creature because that animal has similar facial characteristics to a DOG, bull, and donkey, all animals common to the description of demons. The lower part of the statue was veiled and had a caduceus on it; however, its belly was scaled and painted green. It also had feminine breasts. The figure sat upon a cube, and for a footrest it used a ball.

Each aspect of the statue was highly symbolic. The torch was a symbol of the equalizing intelligence of the triad. The pentagram on the forehead was symbolic of human intelligence. The goat head represented the responsibility of penance for sins of the flesh and the nature of duality. The veil represented the mysteries of universal generation. The hands stood for the sanctity of labor. The two crests represented good and evil and mercy and justice. The breasts represented maternity, toil, and redemption.

To this day no one knows such a statue existed, and if it did what it looked like or how many of them there could have been. Descriptions were taken under the duress of torture and were largely later recanted by the knights who gave them.

Sources: Bailey, *Historical Dictionary of Witchcraft*, 12, 57; de Quincey, *Works of Thomas De Quincey*, 439–43; Grimassi, *Encyclopedia of Wicca and Witchcraft*, 41–2; Lewis, *Satanism Today*, 20–21; Melton, *Encyclopedia of Occultism and Parapsychology*, 315; Vinycomb, *Fictitious and Symbolic Creatures*, 221.

Bar Sheda

A young demon, Bar Sheda was the FAMILIAR to Rab Papa (died A.D. 375); he was the founder of the Talmud school at Neresch, near Sura in Babylonia.

Sources: Society of Biblical Archæology, *Proceedings of the Society of Biblical Archaeology*, 227.

Barakel

Variations: Baraqel, Baraq'el, Baraqijal, Baraqual, BARKAYAL, SARAKNYAL

In Enochian lore, the FALLEN ANGEL Barakel ("Lightning of God") was one of the CHIEF OF TENS (see GRIGORI and WATCHERS) who swore allegiance to SAMIAZA, rebelled against God, took a human as his wife, and fathered the NEPHILIM. One of his sons was named Mahway. Additionally, he taught astrology to men.

Sources: Barton, *Journal of Biblical Literature*, Vols. 30–31, 162; Beard, *Autobiography of Satan*, 113; Laurence, *Book of Enoch, the Prophet*, 7, 70; Lumpkin, *Fallen Angels, the Watchers, and the Origins of Evil*, 31; Prophet, *Fallen Angels and the Origins of Evil*, 174.

Barastir

Variations: Barastaer

In Central West Asia, specifically in the Caucasus region, it is believed that the demon Barastir commands the souls of the dead, directing them to either paradise or oblivion. He dwells in the Underworld.

Sources: Lurker, *Routledge Dictionary of Gods and Goddesses*, 30.

Barbas

Variations: MARBAS

In the *Ars Goetia*, Barbas ("beard") is listed as one of the PRESIDENTS OF HELL, commanding thirty-six legions. The demon of mechanics, Barbas appears as a great lion, but if his summoner asks, he will change form and shape-shift into that of a man. Known to answer questions honestly on the topic of hidden or secret things, he can also cause or cure diseases, change the appearance of men, and can, if asked, teach the mechanical arts.

Hellebore, a plant used in witchcraft for summoning demons, is called *barbas* in Latin.

Sources: Crowley, *The Goetia*, 68; De Laurence, *Lesser Key of Solomon, Goetia*, 23; Peterson, *Lesser Key of Solomon*, 261.

Barbatos

Variations: BARBAS, Barginiel, Brumiel, Lerajie, MARBAS

In the *Lemegeton, the Lesser Key of Solomon*, Barbatos ("bearded, old man, philosopher") is listed as a FALLEN ANGEL, formerly of the Order of the Virtues, whose rank is that of a count, duke, or earl, as it varies through editions (see COUNTS OF HELL, DUKES OF HELL and EARLS OF HELL). He is also listed as one of the seventy-two SPIRITS OF SOLOMON. Barbatos is one of the three SERVITORS OF SATANACHIA (see SATANACHIA) as well as one of the four ASSISTANTS OF ASHTAROTH (see ASHTAROTH). He commands four demonic kings and their legions, thirty legions of his own, the first legion of Hell, ten chiefs, one hundred servitors, and eighty-seven demons under SAMAEL.

Barbatos will only appear when the sun is in Sagittarius, but when he does appear he does so with four of his noble kings and three companies of troops. He dresses like a huntsman of the woods, wearing green and carrying a bow and a quiver. The arrows he shoots cause wounds that are extremely difficult to heal. He is summoned because he knows and reveals the location of treasures hidden with magic. He also knows the past and the future, reconciles friends and those who are in power, teaches all sciences, and also understands the language of the birds and other animals.

Sources: Baskin, *Sorcerer's Handbook*, 276; De Laurence, *Lesser Key of Solomon, Goetia*, 23–4; McLean, *Treatise of Angel Magic*, 52; Scott, *London Magazine*, Vol. 5, 378; Waite, *Unknown World 1894–1895*, 230; Wedeck, *Treasury of Witchcraft*, 96.

Barbelo

Variations: Achamoth, Athena, Istar, the Light-Maiden of the Pistis Sophia, the Maiden, Noe, Noria, Parthenos, Sophia, Wisdom

Gnostic texts list Barbelo as one of the eight ARCH SHE-DEMONS. Her worshippers were called *Barbelgnostics*.

Sources: Herbermann, *Catholic Encyclopedia*, 596; Lurker, *Routledge Dictionary of Gods and Goddesses*, 152; Matthews, *Sophia*, 147–8.

Barbiel

Variations: Barbuel, BARUEL

Originally from Chaldean demonology, in Enochian lore Barbiel ("illumination of God") is a FALLEN ANGEL, formerly of the Order of Virtues. He is considered to be an ARCHDEMON and a retrograde spirit. He is also listed as one of the seven PLANETARY PRINCES of Hell, one of the "seven phantoms of flame," and one of the seven ELECTORS OF HELL. In Heinrich Cornelius Agrippa Von Netteshim's *De Occulta Philosophia* (1531), he is named as one of the twenty-eight demonic rulers of the lunar mansions, commanding the mansion Archaam (see ENOCHIAN RULERS OF THE LUNAR MANSIONS). He is under the command of Zaphiel, an angelic overlord.

Living in the bowels of the earth, Barbiel causes problems with harvest and travelers and creates discord between people. He is more powerful than any other demon in his cosmology. He moves against the stars, affects the economy, and causes earthquakes.

There is also an angel with this name, but the two are separate entities.

Sources: Eco, *Infinity of Lists*, 61; Scheible, *Sixth and Seventh Books of Moses*, 73; Von Goethe, *Goethe's Letters to Zelter*, 378; Webster, *Encyclopedia of Angels*, 32.

Barbil

In the *Theurgia Goetia*, book two of the *Lemegeton*, the *Lesser Key of Solomon*, Barbil, a diurnal demon, is one of the fifteen named Duke SERVITORS OF BARMIEL (see BARMIEL and DUKES OF HELL).

Sources: Belanger, *Dictionary of Demons*, 60; Gettings, *Dictionary of Demons*, 47; Guiley, *Encyclopedia of Demons and Demonology*, 24; Trithemius, *Steganographia*, 17.

Barchiel

Variations: Bachiel

In the *Theurgia Goetia*, the second book of the *Lemegeton*, Barchiel, an AERIAL DEVIL, is a chief duke in service under HYDRIEL, one of the eleven WANDERING PRINCES. Commanding 1,320 servitors, he appears to his summoner as a serpent with a virgin's face and head, and he is very courteous and willing to obey. Barchiel is both a diurnal and nocturnal demon who lives in or near water, marshes, and wetlands.

Sources: Agrippa, *Three Books of Occult Philosophy*, 536; Eco, *Infinity of Lists*, 61; Gettings, *Dictionary of Demons*, 47.

Barcus

In Apollonius of Tyana's *Nuctemeron* (*Night Illuminated by Day*), Barcus is most powerful during the fifth hour.

Sources: Chisholm, *Encyclopedia Britannica*, Vol. 3, 399; Gettings, *Dictionary of Demons*, 47; Lévi, *Transcendental Magic*, 391.

Barfael

Variations: Barbuel

Ranked as one of the ELECTORS OF HELL and as a prince, Barfael ("demon of the long beard") appears to his summoner as a wild hog (see PRINCES OF HELL). He is very accommodating and appears quickly when summoned. He holds the secret of the Philosopher's Stone, is the master of all arts, and knows all secret knowledge.

Sources: Conway, *Demonology and Devil-lore*, 299; Rudwin, *Devil in Legend and Literature*, 79–80.

Bariel

In the *Ars Paulina*, book three of the *Lemegeton*, Duke Bariel is listed as one of the six SERVITORS OF TURAEL (see DUKES OF HELL and TURAEL).

Sources: Guiley, *Encyclopedia of Angels*, 63; Icon, *Demon*, 23; Peterson, *Lesser Key of Solomon*, 114.

Barkayal

Variations: Baraqel, Baraqijal, Barkaial

In Enochian lore Barkayal is one of the FALLEN ANGELS who swore allegiance to SAMIAZA, rebelled against God, took a human wife, and fathered the NEPHILIM. Additionally, he taught "the observers of the stars," meaning that either he taught the science of astrology or that he taught those who studied astronomy.

Sources: Blavtsky, *Secret Doctrine*, 393; Horne, *Sacred Books and Early Literature of the East*, 114; Laurence, *Book of Enoch, the Prophet*, 7; Lumpkin, *Fallen Angels, the Watchers, and the Origins of Evil*, 31.

Bar-Ligura

Variations: Bar-Lgura

In Semitic demonology Bar-Ligura is a demon who sits atop the roofs of houses and when the opportunity presents itself, leaps down, assaulting the inhabitants. Those who fall victim to his attacks are called *d'haregara*.

Sources: De Claremont, *Ancient's Book of Magic*, 120; Spence, *Encyclopaedia of Occultism*, 64.

Barma

Reginald Scot wrote in his book *The Discoverie of Witchcraft* (1584) that Emperor Barma is a FALLEN ANGEL, formerly of the Order of Seraphim. He has the ability to shape-change his summoner or anyone the summoner wishes and can transport anyone to a foreign country.

Sources: Laycock, *Complete Enochian Dictionary*, 85; Gettings, *Dictionary of Demons*, 48.

Barmiel

In *Theurgia Goetia*, the second book of the *Lemegeton*, Barmiel ("exception") is the Prince of the South, commanding ten dukes of the day and twenty dukes of the night (see PRINCES OF HELL). He is the demon of military surrenders and is one of the twelve SERVITORS OF CASPIEL (see CASPIEL).

Sources: Gettings, *Dictionary of Demons*, 232; Trithemius, *Steganographia*, 81.

Barq

Variations: Barku ("lightning"), Barqu

Various demonic grimoires name Barq as the demon who knows the secret of the Philosopher's Stone.

Sources: Gettings, *Dictionary of Demons*, 47; Flamel, *Nicholas Flamel and the Philosopher's Stone*, 4; Spence, *Encyclopedia of Occultism*, 163, 257.

Barsafael

According to the *Testament of Solomon*, Barsafael is one of the demonic spirits that Solomon used to build his Temple (see SPIRITS OF SOLOMON). While bound to King Solomon, he was made to do heavy labor, tending to the furnaces used for metalwork. He confessed to Solomon that he would immediately leave the area if he heard the words "Gabriel, imprison Barsafael."

The demon of migraines, he appears looking like a man but with a shapeless head, like a dog, and has a face like a bird, donkey, or oxen.

Sources: Ashe, *Qabalah*, 57; Charlesworth, *Old Testament Pseudepigrapha*, Vol. 2, 953; Conybeare, *Jewish Quarterly Review*, Vol. 11, 35.

Baruchas

In the *Lemegeton, the Lesser Key of Solomon*, Baruchas is listed as the prince of the East by Northeast. He is in service under DEMORIEL (see PRINCES OF HELL) and is a conveyor of secrets. Baruchas commands many dukes, both diurnal and nocturnal, but only fifteen in all are named. Each of his dukes has 7,040 servants to attend them.

Sources: Gettings, *Dictionary of Demons*, 232; Petterson, *Lesser Key of Solomon*, 93; Trithemius, *Steganographia*, 81.

Baruel

Variations: BARBIEL, Barbuel

In the *Sacred Magic of Abramelin the Mage*, Baruel ("Nourishment [food] from God") is named among the sixty-five SERVITORS OF KORE AND MAGOTH and one of the seven ELECTORS OF HELL. He appears before his summoner as a master workman wearing an apron. Baruel is the master of all arts and is able to teach more in a moment than all the master workmen in the world combined could teach in twenty years. When summoning this demon, it should be noted that he must be called upon three times before he will appear.

Sources: Butler, *Ritual Magic*, 96; Eco, *Infinity of Lists*, 61; Mathers, *Book of the Sacred Magic of Abramelin the Mage*, 133.

Barzabel

Variations: Barsabel

According to the demonologia *The Magus*, Barzabel, along with the Graphiel, are the demons of the planet Mars. His personal adversary is the archangel SAMAEL.

Sources: Agrippa, *Three Books of Occult Philosophy*, 748; McLean, *Treatises on Angel Magic*, 32; Redgrove, *Bygone Beliefs*, 72.

Basasael

Variations: Basasaeyal, Bezaliel, BUSASEJAL

In the *Book of Enoch*, Basasael ("Shadow of God") was named as one of the WATCHERS (see

CHIEF OF TENS) who swore allegiance to SAMI-AZA, rebelled against God, took a human wife, and fathered the NEPHILIM. He is a FALLEN ANGEL, formerly of the Order of Archangels.

Sources: Laurence, *Book of Enoch the Prophet*, 77; Prophet, *Fallen Angels and the Origins of Evil*, 174; Shuckford, *Sacred and Profane History of the World*, 125.

Batarel

Variations: Badariel, Batariel, BATARJAL, Batraal, Batrael, Metarel

In the *Book of Enoch*, Batarel ("Rain of God") was named as one of the CHIEF OF TENS (see GRIGORI and WATCHERS) who swore allegiance to SAMIAZA, rebelled against God, took a human wife, and fathered the NEPHILIM. He is a FALLEN ANGEL, formerly of the Order of Archangels. In various Christian grimoires he is ranked as a Duke (see DUKES OF HELL).

Sources: Barton, *Journal of Biblical Literature*, Vols. 30–31, 163; Beard, *Autobiography of Satan*, 113; Laurence, *Book of Enoch, the Prophet*, 6; Lumpkin, *Fallen Angels, the Watchers, and the Origins of Evil*, 31.

Batarjal

Variations: Bataryal

In Enochian lore Batarjal ("divider of God") is named as one of the FALLEN ANGELS (see also BATAREL).

Sources: Laurence, *Foreign Quarterly Review*, Vol. 24, 370; Lumpkin, *Fallen Angels, the Watchers, and the Origins of Evil*, 31; Prophet, *Fallen Angels and the Origins of Evil*, 174.

Bathim

Variations: Bathin, Bathsim, Bathym, Marthim, Mathim

Batha is an archaic word used to describe Ethiopians, as it was believed that demons could appear as a black-skinned man. It may also be derived from the Latin word "mathios," an herb believed to keep snakes young.

The eighteenth-century book alleged to be written by Pope Honorius III, *Grimoire of Pope Honorius* (*Le Grimoire du Pape Honorius*), says that Bathim is "of a deeper reach in the source of fire, the second after Lucifer's FAMILIAR, and hath not his fellow for agility and affableness in the whole Infernal Hierarchy." Other grimoires name him as a duke and a lieutenant general of the forces of Hell. Commanding thirty legions of demons, he is one of the three SERVITORS OF FLEURETTY (see FLEURETTY). Bathim is also listed as one of the DUKES OF HELL and one of the SPIRITS OF SOLOMON.

He appears before his summoner as a man with a serpent's tail, and according to some sources, rides upon a pale horse. He has the ability to tele-port and knows the properties of herbs and stones. His zodiacal sign is Gemini.

Sources: Baskin, *Sorcerer's Handbook*, 276; De Laurence, *Lesser Key of Solomon, Goetia*, 27; McLean, *Treatise of Angel Magic*, 52; Scott, *London Magazine*, Vol. 5, 378; Waite, *Unknown World 1894–1895*, 230; Wedeck, *Treasury of Witchcraft*, 96.

Batibat

Variations: Bangungot ("nightmare"), Fat Old Woman of the Post

From the demonology of the Ilocano people of the Philippines comes the batibat ("nightmare"); they are the demons of NIGHTMARES. Assuming the form of a huge, old, obese woman, these nocturnal demons prey upon those who cut down the tree that they live in so that it may be used as a support beam in a house or as a bedpost. They are territorial and vengeful demons who will not let anyone sleep near their home; if anyone should they will sit on their chest and suffocate them in their sleep. Batibat prefer to attack those individuals who sleep in a room alone.

Should the tree that a batibat lives in be cut down and used as a support beam in a house, the demon will not leave its tree but take its vengeance out on the inhabitants of the home, at the very least inflicting them with nightmares if not trying to kill them outright in their sleep. During a batibat-induced nightmare it is advised to bite your thumb or wiggle your toes to wake up and save yourself. Should a person survive a batibat attack, they are said to have become a *naluganan* ("something has taken hold") and have gained the ability to see and hear the supernatural.

Sources: Ramos, *Creatures of Philippine Lower Mythology*, 25, 30; Rosen, *Mythical Creatures Bible*, 220; Rubino, *Ilocano*, 222.

Ba-Toye

From the demonology of the Hausa people of West Africa comes the demon of fire, Ba-Toye. He is responsible for burning down fields, houses, and trees. To banish this demon, a specific ceremonial dance must be completed. A sacrifice must be offered as well, usually a bird of a specific color and gender pleasing to the demon.

Sources: Douglas, *Man in Africa*, 298; Knappert, *African Mythology*, 107; Tremearne, *Ban of the Bori*, 347.

Batternis

The *Sacred Magic of Abramelin the Mage*, book two, names Batternis as one of the sixty-five SERVITORS OF KORE AND MAGOTH.

Sources: Mathers, *Book of the Sacred Magic of Abramelin the Mage*, 107; Susej, *Demonic Bible*, 258.

Bayemon

In the *Grimoire of Pope Honorius* (*Le Grimoire du Pape Honorius*), a book alleged to be written by Pope Honorius III in the eighteenth century, Bayemon is named as the king of the western infernal regions (see KINGS OF HELL).

Sources: Collin de Plancy, *Dictionnaire Infernal*, 338–9; Kuriakos, *Grimoire Verum Ritual Book*, 15; Spence, *Encyclopedia of Occultism*, 65.

Bealphares

According to Johann Wierus's *Pseudomonarchia Daemonum* (*False Monarchy of Demons*, 1583) Bealphares is a benign duke of Hell, considered to be "the noblest carrier that ever did serve any man upon earth." This demon is not named in any other registries or listings of demons.

Sources: Davidson, *Dictionary of Angels*, 72; Gettings, *Dictionary of Demons*, 49; McLean, *Treatise of Angel Magic*, 51; Scot, *The Discoverie of Witchcraft*, 420.

Bearded Demon, The

The Bearded Demon, so named for his beard of remarkable note, is otherwise nameless. He is sought out for his knowledge regarding the secrets of the Philosopher's Stone, as King Solomon and Paracelsus are said to have done. This demon is often confused with the demons Barbatos and BARBAS, and Barbu.

Sources: De Claremont, *Ancient's Book of Magic*, 120; Lévi, *Transcendental Magic*, 309; Shepard, *Encyclopedia of Occultism and Parapsychology*, 136; Spence, *Encyclopedia of Occultism*, 65.

Beball

Variations: Beall, Bebal, BERITH, Labal

In Johann Wierus's *Pseudomonarchia Daemonum (False Monarchy of Demons*, 1583), Beball is ranked as a king or prince, sources vary, and is listed as one of the two SERVITORS OF PAYMON (see KINGS OF HELL, PAYMON, and PRINCES OF HELL). If offerings are made to PAYMON, Beball will attend well those who summon him.

Sources: Belanger, *Dictionary of Demons*, 65; Godwin, *Godwin's Cabalistic Encyclopedia*, 504; Icons, *Demons*, 140; Scot, *Discoverie of Witchcraft*, 220.

Bechard

Variations: BECHAUD

Bechard is the demon of the forces of nature, controlling the wind and lightning, and causing hail, rain, storms, and tempests. Under the command of ASMODEUS, he is most powerful on Fridays.

Sources: Bassett, *Legends and Superstitions of the Sea*, 40, 86; De Claremont, *Ancients' Book of Magic*, 120; Poinsot, *Complete Book of the Occult and Fortune Telling*, 378.

Bechaud

In the *Grimorium Vernum* (*Grimoire of Truth*), Bechaud is listed as one of the eighteen SERVITORS OF SYRACH (see SYRACH). The *Grimorium Vernum* was allegedly written by Alibek the Egyptian in Memphis, Egypt, in 1517, and was published in French and Latin. However, scholars generally agree that it was most likely written sometime during the eighteenth century, and in Rome, Italy. Arthur Waite translated and republished large portions of it in his own book, *The Book of Ceremonial Magic* (1911).

Sources: Masters, *Devil's Dominion*, 130; Sabellicus, *Magia Pratica*, 33.

Bechet

In various grimoires, Bechet is said to be the demon of Friday.

Sources: Flaubert, *Works*, Vol. 9, 266; Poinsot, *Complete Book of the Occult and Fortune Telling*, 378.

Bedary

In the *Theurgia Goetia*, book two of the *Lemegeton*, Bedary is one of the twelve named Duke SERVITORS OF CARNESIEL (see CARNESIEL and DUKES OF HELL).

Sources: Guiley, *Encyclopedia of Demons and Demonology*, 37; Peterson, *Lesser Key of Solomon*, 59.

Beelzebub

Variations: Achor, Archon Daimonion, BAAL the Prince, Baalsebul, Baal-zebub ("lord of the fly"), BAALZEBUB, Baalzebubg, Balzabouth, Beel d'boro, Beel-Zeboul ("god of the dwelling"), Beelzeboul ("Lord of the Earth"), Beel-Zebub ("god of flies"), Beelzebul, Beelzebus, Beelzebuth, Belzaboul, Belzebath, Belzebub, Belzebud, Belzebut, Belzebuth, Diabolos, Evil Chief of Binah, Lord of the Flies, Master of Calumny, Prince of Death, Prince of Demons

Originally he was known as Baal-zebub, the chief god of Ekron, a Philistine city. The priests of that city practiced divination based on the flight of flies. In contemporary Christianity, Beelzebub ("God of Flies," "Lord Fly of Flies") is an alternative name for SATAN or the DEVIL. He has been given a wide array of rank and titles including chief of false gods, the devil's chief of staff, founder of the ORDER OF THE FLY, grand chief, governor of hell, prime minister of the Infernal Spirits, prince, supreme chief of the Infernal Empire, and sub-prince. Demonic hierarchies have him under the command of SATAN (see PRIME MINISTERS and PRINCES OF HELL).

As a FALLEN ANGEL, formerly of the Order of Cherubim, he became the demon of gluttony, luck, money, the North, pride, and prosperity.

It is stated in many grimoires that after one summons Beelzebub, it would be best if the invocations to make him visible were not used, as most men would not survive the experience of looking upon his demonic form.

There are numerous descriptions of Beelzebub, most popular of which describe him as an enormous fly, a general monstrous form, a goat with a long tail, or as a misshapen calf.

Reynnier Gustave gives the most thorough description of Beelzebub in his book *De Marcelli Palingenii Stellati poetae Zodiaco* (1893). In it he describes the demon as being exceedingly tall, obvious even when seated upon his throne. A circle of fire hovers around his head from where two large horns protrude. His chest is large and puffed out; his face is swollen. Eyes and eyebrows give his countenance a menacing stare. He has exceptionally large nostrils, and a pair of bat wings jut out from his back. He has webbed ducklike feet, a lion's tail, and his body is completely covered with thick black fur.

Beelzebub has a wolflike howl and has the ability to send plagues of flies. He vomits up enormous amounts of water when angered. He was also one of the demons blamed for the demonic possessions at Aix-en-Provence in 1611 involving a nun by the name of Sister Madeleine de Demandolx de la Palud.

Sources: Chambers, *Book of Days*, 722; Conybeare, *Jewish Quarterly Review*, Vol. 11, 18–19; Hyatt, *Book of Demons*, 47; Lurker, *Dictionary of Gods and Goddesses*, 58; Melton, *Encyclopedia of Occultism and Parapsychology*, 315.

Behemiron

One of the twelve Princes of the Qlippoth, Behemiron is described as follows: "Whose arms are derived from BEHEMOTH, and their colors are black and brown, and their forms like those of awful beasts, like hippopotamus and an elephant, but crushed flat, or as if their skin was spread out flat over the body of a gigantic beetle or cockroach." He is under the command of (see QLIPPOTHIC ORDERS OF DEMONS).

Sources: Barton, *Journal of Biblical Literature*, Vols. 30–31, 164; Ford; *Book of the Witch Mooon Chronzon Edition*, 380; Greer, *New Encyclopedia of the Occult*, 129.

Behemoth

Variations: BEHEMIRON

In medieval demonology Behemoth ("several animals") is the nocturnal demon of indulgence and holds the ranks of caretaker of wine cellars, grand cupbearer of the royal household, and night watchman. He oversees the feasts of Hell and is responsible for serving the DEVIL his food and wine. He also entertains with song and music.

Described as a monstrous elephant with feet like a bear, he can also appear like a crocodile, hippopotamus, and whale. He is fairly stupid and his only concern is eating. Legend tells us that he was originally created by God to help stabilize the world, resting it on his back as he floated in the water, surrounded by cosmic darkness. Within his chest is an invisible desert called Dundayin.

Related to LEVIATHAN, when Behemoth is dealing with humans, he creates chaos in their lives. He can shape-change into a cat, DOG, fox, and a wolf.

According to Jewish tradition, only the creator of a Behemoth can destroy it; in this case, only Jehovah can destroy Behemoth. On the Day of Judgment, he will be slain by a whale and his body will provide the feast for the Celebration of Final Days and the Lord will distribute the meat to his followers.

This entity is often called upon during exorcism and cases of collective possession; he was one of the eighteen demons who possessed Sister Jeanne des Anges in Loudun, France, in 1634 (see LOUDUN POSSESSION).

Sources: Aikin, *General Biography*, 493; Bayle, *Historical and Critical Dictionary*, 262; Chambers, *Book of Days*, 723; Hsia, *World of Catholic Renewal*, 151; Hyatt, *Book of Demons*, 43; Robbins, *Encyclopedia of Witchcraft and Demonology*, 131; Voltaire, *Works of M. de Voltaire*, 193.

Beherit

Variations: Baal Bea, Beale, BERITH, Berithi, BOFRY, Bolfri, BOLFRY

Duke Beherit commands twenty-six legions of demons. He speaks with a clear and subtle voice and dresses like a soldier in a red uniform, wearing a golden crown upon his head and riding upon a red horse. He is summoned for his honesty in answering questions regarding the past, present and future, and for his ability to turn any metal into gold. However, it should be noted that when not answering a question, if he is speaking, he is lying. When summoned, the sorcerer must wear a silver ring and present it immediately to the demon upon his arrival. Beherit's personal adversary is St. Barnabas, the Patron Saint of Cyprus.

Sources: Drury, *Encyclopedia of the Esoteric*, 29; Icon, *Demons*, 31; Oesterreich, *Possession, Demoniacal and Other Among Primitive Races*, 18.

Belail

Variations: Baal ial ("Lord of Pride"), Baalial, Be'lal, Belhor, Beli ol ("yokeless"), Beli yo'il ("worthless"), Beliaal, BELIAL ("may have no rising"), Beliall, Beliar, Belias, Beliel, Lord of Arrogance, Matanbuchus, Mechembuchus, Meterbuchus

Originally worshipped by the Sidonians, inhabitants of the Phoenician city Sidon, Belail ("without worth") is named in the *Theurgia Goetia* as a prince over the Northern Reaches of Hell and the leader of the Sons of Darkness (see PRINCES OF HELL). He is a FALLEN ANGEL, referred to sometimes as an angel of confusion and lust.

Before the Fall, he had been created by God, the very next angel after the creation of LUCIFER. Belail was the first angel cast out of heaven because he was the angel who convinced LUCIFER to rebel against God. He was also the demon who encouraged Jochaneh and his brother, two Egyptian sorcerers, to oppose Moses and Aaron.

Belail controls the elements of earth and all earth elemental demons; he gives excellent FAMILIARs and is credited in some sources as being the father of LUCIFER. His personal adversary is St. Francis of Paola, the patron saint of boatmen. In the time of the ANTICHRIST, Belail will be unleashed upon Israel.

Sources: Barton, *Journal of Biblical Literature*, Vols. 30–31, 164; Kaye, *Devils and Demons*, 580; Poinsot, *Complete Book of the Occult and Fortune Telling*, 378; Scot, *Discoverie of Witchcraft*, 220.

Belbel

In the *Theurgia Goetia*, the second book of the *Lemegeton*, Belbel is listed as one of the thirty-six Elemental World Rulers. He was also one of the seventy-two SPIRITS OF SOLOMON that were used to build his temple. Belbel did much of the heavy physical labor on the Temple, including tending to the furnaces for the metalwork. He had the ability to distort the hearts and minds of man and is described as looking like a man with a shapeless head like a DOG's and a face like a bird, donkey, or oxen.

According to the *Testament of Solomon*, when the angelic name Kharael is said aloud, it will exorcise Belbel. He also admitted to King Solomon that if ever he heard the words "Araêl, imprison Belbel," he would immediately leave.

Sources: Charlesworth, *Old Testament Pseudepigrapha*, 978; Conybeare, *Jewish Quarterly Review*, Vol. 11, 35; Doresse, *Secret Books of the Egyptian Gnostics*, 203.

Beleth

Variations: Bilet, BILETH, BYLETH, the Mad King

Johann Wierus's *Pseudomonarchia Daemonum*

(*False Monarchy of Demons*, 1583) lists Beleth as a FALLEN ANGEL, formerly of the Order of Powers. A king who commands eighty-five legions of demons, he has been described as riding upon a pale horse. He is also listed among the seventy-two SPIRITS OF SOLOMON.

When summoned, Beleth is preceded by a parade that consists of every type of musician. Upon arrival, he will be furious and must be immediately commanded into a circle or triangle while the summoner's hazel wand is pointing southeast. Beleth must be spoken to courteously and paid homage. The summoner must also wear a silver ring upon his middle finger, which he must hold against his face while dealing with the demon. He is summoned because he has the ability to secure love between a man and a woman.

Beleth is a diurnal demon, most powerful during the month of May. His sacred color is red and he has sway over the planet Mercury. His zodiacal sign is Gemini.

Sources: Anderson, *Diary of Ancient Rites*, 207; De Laurence, *Lesser Key of Solomon, Goetia*, 25–6; Icons, *Demons*, 140; McLean, *Treatise of Angel Magic*, 52; Spence, *Encyclopedia of Occultism*, 119.

Belial

Variations: "The Beast," Beliall, Beliar, Beliel, Beliya'al ("worthless"), Beliyya'al, Bel'yya'al, Matanbuchus, Satanel

In Judeo-Christian demonology, Belial ("worthless one" or "may have no rising") is noted as being a particularly vicious demon. One medieval author wrote of him: "Never has Hell received a more dissolute, more heinous, more worthless spirit, or one more in love with vice for vice's sake!" A FALLEN ANGEL of the Order of Seraphim and of the Order of Virtues, he still retains some standing in these orders. He is also the leader of the order known as the Sons of Darkness. Belial, the demon of arrogance, deceit, hostility, and lies, is described as looking like a beautiful angel riding upon a chariot of flame. He commands eighty legions of demons and his domain is over all that falls in darkness. He is also listed as one of the seventy-two SPIRITS OF SOLOMON.

Like BELAIL, Belial was said to be the very next angel created after LUCIFER. He is also accredited as being the one who persuaded LUCIFER to rebel against God, as well as being the first angel to be cast out of heaven.

Belial, if given proper sacrifices, will answer any question posed to him truthfully. He is known to help politicians achieve high levels of office, acquire favors, and give excellent FAMIL-

IARs. A highly skilled orator, Belial tempts men to be disloyal and gossip, and he inspires rebellion in their hearts. He also tempts women to dress in finery, gossip in church, and overindulge their children. Belial openly accepts sacrifices, gifts, and offerings.

Most powerful during the month of February, his zodiacal sign is Pisces (see also FOUR PRINCIPAL KINGS).

Sources: Barton, *Journal of Biblical Literature*, Vols. 30–31, 164; Chambers, *Book of Days*, 723; Conway, *Demonology and Devil-Lore*, 299; De Laurence, *Lesser Key of Solomon, Goetia*, 44; Hyatt, *Book of Demons*, 76; Rachleff, *Occult in Art*, 224.

Belian

Variations: Belias

Belian is a Prince and a FALLEN ANGEL, formerly of the Order of Virtues (see PRINCES OF HELL). Abnormally small for an angel, he tempts men into being arrogant, women to dress haughty, and children to talk during mass.

Sources: Kaye, *Devils and Demons*, 580; Kelly, *Who in Hell*, 30; Rose, *Spirits, Fairies, Gnomes, and Goblins*, 350.

Belphegor

Variations: BAAL-PEOR, Baalphegor, Beelphegor, Bel-Phegor, Belphegore

Originally a Moabite god of sexual abandon, Belphegor ("Lord of the Opening") was worshipped on Mount Phegor. He was popularized in medieval grimoires. The Kabbalah says he is the ARCHDEMON of the Togarini. He has been given the rank of ambassador to France. A FALLEN ANGEL, formerly of the Order of Principalities, Belphegor is also one of the evil SEPHIROTHS, in service under MEPHISTOPHELES; he has dominion over the hierarchy named Togarini.

The demon of discovery, international rivalry, invention, laziness, pride, riches, sloth, and vanity, Belphegor is difficult to summon. When he does appear, it will be either as a beautiful young woman or a naked and hideous demonic being with a beard, horns, a gaping mouth, and sharp nails. He grants riches and empowers with discovery and ingenious inventions. Belphegor accepts offerings of excrement.

Sources: Chambers, *Book of Days*, 723; Collin de Plancy, *Dictionary of Witchcraft*, 24–5; Hyatt, *Book of Demons*, 46; Melton, *Encyclopedia of Occultism and Parapsychology*, 315.

Belu

A vampiric demon from the mythology of Burma, the belu is described as being gigantic in size.

Sources: Latham, *Descriptive Ethnology*, 164; Tremearne, *Ban of the Bori*, 470.

Belus

Buddhist literature tells us that the Belus are the demonic descendants of a legendary race that roamed India and Myanmar around 2000 B.C.E. They are diabolical, overbearing, and terrifying by nature. Shape-shifters, the Belus can assume different physical appearances at will.

Source: Turner, *Dictionary of Ancient Deities*, 97.

Ben Tamalion

According to Hasidic demonology, Ben Tamalion, a demon that appeared as a child, possessed the emperor's daughter. He was exorcized by Rabbi Simeon ben Yose. The Rabbi said aloud, "Ben Tamalion, leave her. Ben Tamalion, leave her," as he entered the room; soon thereafter, the demon departed.

Sources: Bell, *Deliver Us from Evil*, 76; Eve, *Jewish Context of Jesus' Miracles*, 345; Society of Biblical Archæology, *Proceedings of the Society of Biblical Archaeology*, 227.

Beng

Variations: O Beng

The name Beng ("frog") is essentially another name for SATAN used by the Kalderash and Romanian gypsies. Beng is said to often engage God in tests of strength, none of which he ever wins. Living in the woods, Beng prefers to conduct his mischief during the night.

Sources: Ashley, *Complete Book of Devils and Demons*, 100; Ficowski, *Gypsies in Poland*, 101; Gypsy Lore Society, *Journal of the Gypsy Lore Society*, 109; Lurker, *Dictionary of Gods and Goddesses*, 61.

Benoham

In the *Theurgia Goetia*, the second book of the *Lemegeton*, Benoham, an AERIAL DEVIL, is listed as one of the twelve named Duke SERVITORS OF CARNESIEL (see CARNESIEL and DUKES OF HELL).

Sources: Guiley, *Encyclopedia of Demons and Demonology*, 37; Peterson, *Lesser Key of Solomon*, 59; Trirthemius, *Steganographia*, 49.

Bensozia

Variations: Benzoria, Benzosiaj, Bona Socia, "the Diana of the Ancient Gauls," Herodias, NOCTICULA, "The Moon"

In the *Religion de Gaulois* (*The Religion of the Gauls*, 1727) written by Dom Jacques Martin (1684–1751), Bensozia ("friendly prosperous being") was demonized and made to be the consort to both ABEZETHIBOU and ASMODEUS. She is in service under ASMODEUS but is one of the twelve SERVITORS OF ABEZETHIBOU.

At night women would leave their homes on horseback and gather together to celebrate nighttime festivities of Bensozia. Each of these women had signed her name in a sabbatical book, and after performing a particular ceremony, believed that she would become a fairy. A manuscript discovered in the church at Couserans is alleged to be one of the books of Bensozia.

Sources: Baroja, *World of the Witches*, 66, 244; Grimm, *Teutonic Mythology*, 283; Spence, *Encyclopedia of Occultism*, 67.

Berbis

In the *Theurgia Goetia*, the second book of the *Lemegeton*, Berbis is listed as a nocturnal duke. He is one of the fifteen named SERVITORS OF BARMIEL (see BARMIEL and DUKES OF HELL).

Source: Peterson, *Lesser Key of Solomon*, 70.

Berith

Variations: Baal Berith, BALBERITH, Batraal, Beal, Beall, Beale, Bele, BELETH, Beratiel, Berithi; BILETH, Bofi, BOFRY, Bolfri, BOLFRY, BYLETH

Originally an ancient Mideastern deity, Berith was listed in the *Ars Goetia, the Lesser Key of Solomon* as a FALLEN ANGEL of the Order of Cherubim. Ranked as a duke, he was also tasked as the chief secretary and archivist of Hell as well as Hell's minister of foreign affairs. He is also listed as one of the DUKES OF HELL as well as one of the seventy-two SPIRITS OF SOLOMON.

The demon of blasphemy, disobedience, and murder, Berith commands twenty-six legions of demons. He appears before his summoner as a soldier in a red uniform wearing a crown on his head and riding upon a red horse; he speaks with a clear and subtle voice, accompanied by an orchestra. He is most powerful at noon on Mondays during July.

Berith is summoned because he will answer truthfully questions regarding the past, present, and future. It should be noted, however, that Berith is lying if he is speaking and not answering a question posed to him; additionally, his advice cannot be trusted. While being called for, the summoner must wear a very specific magical silver ring and immediately present it to him upon his arrival. Berith is able to turn any metal into gold and gives confirmed dignities, love spells, and beautiful singing voices. Berith has great alchemical knowledge that he is willing to impart and is capable of making men quarrelsome.

Berith's personal adversary is St. Barnabas, the peacemaker and Patron Saint of Cyprus.

Sources: Crone, *Poetics, Self, Place*, 282; De Laurence, *Lesser Key of Solomon, Goetia*, 30; Hyatt, *Book of Demons*, 77; McLean, *Treatise of Angel Magic*, 53; Melton, *Encyclopedia of Occultism and Parapsychology*, 315; Russell, *Connection of Sacred and Profane History*, 209; Paine, *Hierarchy of Hell*, 71.

Bernael

Variations: Azrael ("help of God"), Belhar

In Falashan lore Bernael is a FALLEN ANGEL and known as a demon of darkness. Bernael, who was cast out of Heaven by the archangel Michael, is identified or equated with Beliel (BELIAL). His personal adversary is the archangel Michael.

Sources: Davidson, *Dictionary of Angels*, 73; Patai, *Folklore Series*, Issue 13, 45–6; Schwarzbaum, *Jewish Folklore Between East and West*, 19, 22.

Bethage

According to *Complementum Artis Exorcistiae* (1608) written by Father Zacharias Vicecomes, Bethage is one of the names that the DEVIL uses when he is possessing a person. Other sources claim that Bethage is an individual entity under the command of MOLOCH, commanding nine legions.

Sources: Melton, *Encyclopedia of Occultism and Parapsychology*, 315; Shepard, *Encyclopedia of Occultism and Parapsychology*, 440; Smedley, *Occult Sciences*, 176.

Bethnael

Variations: Bethnel

In Enochian lore, Bethnael is one of the twenty-eight demonic rulers of the lunar mansions; he has dominion over the mansion Albelda ("defeat") (see ENOCHIAN RULERS OF THE LUNAR MANSIONS). Bethnael aids in expansion and causes divorce. His zodiacal sign is Capricorn.

Sources: Barrett, *The Magus*, 57; Moura, *Mansions of the Moon for the Green Witch*, 11; Von Goethe, *Goethe's Letters to Zelter*, 377; Webster, *Encyclopedia of Angels*, 35, 125.

Bethor

In the highly influential book *Arbatel de Magia Veterum* (*Arbatel of the Magic of the Ancients*) published in 1575 in Switzerland, Bethor is listed as one of the seven OLYMPIAN SPIRITS. The author of the book is unknown. Bethor commands 29,000 legions and rules 42 provinces and their kings, 35 princes, 28 dukes, 21 counselors, 14 ministers, and seven messengers. He also has dominion over the planet Jupiter.

Bethor answers truthfully questions posed to him and will assist his summoner in the acquisition of treasures. He can also bring together meetings between demons and men, extend a person's life by seven hundred years, create medicines that have miraculous healing properties, give FAMILIARs, help move people into noteworthy positions, and move precious stones.

Sources: Drury, *Dictionary of the Esoteric*, 239; González-Wippler, *Complete Book of Spells*, 120; Greer, *New Encyclopedia of the Occult*, 344.

Betryal

According to the *Book of Enoch*, Betryal is one of the FALLEN ANGELS. Soon after taking his human wife, his NEPHILIM son, Aristaqis, a well-known GRIGORI, was born. For reasons unexplained, Betryal lost interest in all things, left his family, and hid even from God.

Source: Guiley, *Encyclopedia of Angels*, 366.

Beyreva

Variations: Bhairava

In Indian demonology Beyreva is the demon of the souls that roam through space once they have been transformed into AERIAL DEVILs. He is described as having long crooked nails, which he once used to cut off one of Brahma's heads.

Sources: Collin de Plancy, *Dictionary of Witchcraft*, 25–6; Mahadevan, *Hymns of Sankara*, 98; Von Stietencron, *Hindu Myth, Hindu History, Religion, Art, and Politics*, 105–10.

Bhainsasura

In the Hindu folklore of India there is a demonic creature named Bhainsasura that lives in Lake Barewa in Mirzapur, India. He appears, accompanied by nagas, at the time of the rice harvest; if not given an offering of a pig and shown respect, he will destroy crops and fertile fields and terrorize the village. Bhainsasura is said to look like an enormous elephantine creature with the head of a water buffalo.

Fishermen will often make offerings of eggs, fowl, and goats so that they may have permission to fish in Lake Barewa without fear of reprisal from Bhainsasura. There is a story of how many water buffalos were once drowned in the lake. It is said that while a herdsman was watering his buffalos, a great flood swept through and drowned them all. Because Bhainsasura's evilness had permeated the water, all the buffalos returned as demonic creatures.

It should be noted that the demonic creature Bhainsasura is a derivative of another creature in Hindu mythology that is known as MAHISHA; it was slain by the goddess DURGA.

Sources: Crooke, *Popular Religion and Folk-Lore of Northern India*, 44; Hastings, *Encyclopedia of Religion and Ethics*, Part 24, 716; Rose, *Giants, Monsters, and Dragons*, 47.

Bhairava

Variations: BEYREVA, "Lord of Time-Death"

From Indian demonology comes the demon Bhairava. Created by the god Shiva, Bhairava looks like a human with long, crooked fingernails. His left hand has the skull of one of the Brahman's heads attached to it; he uses the skull as a begging bowl. Bhairava watches over the souls that wander through the space that is occupied by AERIAL DEVILs.

In one story Bhairava had insulted a god superior to himself. Brahma punished him by cutting off one of his five heads with the nail of his left thumb. This humiliated Bhairava, who quickly begged for forgiveness. Eswara forgave him and promised that even with four heads, Bhairava would still be respected.

Sources: Dwyer, *Divine and the Demonic*, 17; O'Flaherty, *Origins of Evil in Hindu Mythology*, 281, 301; Wijesekera, *Deities and Demons*, 163, 217.

Bhutadamara

Variations: Bhutadarma

In Buddhist demonology Bhutadamara ("Turmoil of the Spirits") is titled as the lord of the demons and keeps the other demons in check. A demonic god, he is described as having four arms and three eyes. Oftentimes he is depicted in art in the *alidha* pose, where his left knee is bent and his right held taut. He holds the thunderbolt scepter in his upper right hand and a noose in his left.

Sources: Chandra, *Encyclopedia of Hindu Gods and Goddesses*, 39; Jordan, *Encyclopedia of Gods and Goddesses*, 51; Lurker, *Routledge Dictionary of Gods and Goddesses*, 34.

Bhutamata

In Hindu demonology Bhutamata is a demonic goddess. She is a form of the goddess Parvati.

Sources: Bunce, *Hindu Deities*, 544; Chandra, *Encyclopedia of Hindu Gods and Goddesses*, 39; Jordan, *Dictionary of Gods and Goddesses*, 52.

Bialot

In the *Sacred Magic of Abramelin the Mage*, Bialot is listed as one of the fifty-three SERVITORS OF ASHTAROTH AND ASMODEUS (see ASHTAROTH and ASMODEUS).

Sources: Belanger, *Dictionary of Demons*, 71; Mathers, *Book of the Sacred Magic of Abramelin the Mage*, 115; Von Worms, *Book of Abramelin*, 247.

Bianakith

Bianakith is the demon of decomposition and disease; he causes flesh to decay and destroys houses. He hates the human body. To prevent this demon from attacking you, write on the front door of your home the words "Mêltô, Ardu, Anaath."

Sources: Ashe, *Qabalah*, 52; Belanger, *Dictionary of Demons*, 71; Conybeare, *Jewish Quarterly Review*, Vol. 11, 38.

Bidda

From the demonology of the Hausa people of West Africa comes the demon of stiffness, Bidda ("to search"). A specific magical dance is performed to determine the cause and the cure of the demonic attack. Usually an animal sacrifice is required, typically a bird of a specific gender and color.

Sources: Knappert, *African Mythology*, 106; Schön, *Dictionary of the Hausa Language*, 23; Tremearne, *Ban of the Bori*, 489.

Bidiel

In the *Theurgia Goetia*, second book of the *Lemegeton*, Bidiel, an AERIAL DEVIL, is one of the eleven WANDERING PRINCES (see PRINCES OF HELL). He commands twenty primary dukes, two hundred inferior dukes, and numerous servants. Most powerful during the first hour of the day, Bidiel appears in an attractive human form. Like all the WANDERING PRINCES, he and his court are constantly on the move; they never stay in any given place for more than a year.

Sources: Guiley, *Encyclopedia of Demons and Demonology*, 28; Peterson, *Lesser Key of Solomon*, 106; Trithemius, *Steganographia*, 81.

Bies, plural: Biesy

Variations: Bes; plural: Bies; Bisytysia ("to go mad"); Bisy (Ukrainian and always plural)

In Slavic mythology Bies ("Demon") was originally an evil spirit. Later he was associated with the DEVIL after the introduction of Christianity to the region.

Sources: Barford, *Early Slavs*, 192; Maberry, *Cryptopedia*, 232.

Biffant

Biffant is the povost for Dispater. He commands only one legion and has the power of possession. He and his legion possessed Denise de la Caille in Beauvais, France, in 1623. He was made to write out, using his claw as a pen, the verbal process of exorcisms.

Sources: De Claremont, *Ancient's Book of Magic*, 122; Shepard, *Encyclopedia of Occultism and Parapsychology*, 168; Spence, *Encyclopedia of Occultism*, 68.

Bifrons

Variations: Bierous, Bifrous, Bifrovs

A FALLEN ANGEL, Bifrons is the demon of death and is under the command of MEPHI-

STOPHELES. He has the rank of both count and earl and commands either twenty-six or sixty legions, sources vary (see COUNTS OF HELL and EARLS OF HELL). Appearing as a hideous demon, Bifrons is a nocturnal demon who is most powerful during the month of November. This demon is known to move bodies from one grave to another and cause corpse candles to float above graves. Bifrons, like many FALLEN ANGELS, is also a teacher; he teaches astrology, geometry, gemology, herbology, and numerous other arts and sciences. He has dominion over the planet Jupiter.

Sources: De Laurence, *Lesser Key of Solomon, Goetia*, 37; Godwin, *Godwin's Cabalistic Encyclopedia*, 373; Icons, *Demons*, 141; McLean, *Treatise of Angel Magic*, 52; Scot, *Discoverie of Witchcraft*, 223.

Biga

Variations: Beqa

Biga (Amharic for "good person") was originally the name of KASBEEL, one of the FALLEN ANGELS. As soon as this angel was created, he turned away from God, so his name was changed to Kasbeel, which means "he who lies to God."

Sources: Davidson, *Dictionary of Angles*, 165; Webster, *Encyclopedia of Angels*, 107.

Bihiri Sanniya

In Sinhalese demonology Bihiri Sanniya is the demon of deafness and causes in humans illnesses that can render a person deaf. Masks of him are made to look like a screaming face with a cobra emerging out of one eye and hands covering its ears. The cobra is emerging from the eye because it is believed that since the snake has no ears it must "hear" with its eyes. Bihiri Sanniya is susceptible to the DAHA-ATA SANNIYA.

Sources: Goonatilleka, *Masks and Mask Systems of Sri Lanka*, 30, 37; Scott, *Formations of Ritual*, 255; Wirz, *Exorcism and the Art of Healing in Ceylon*, 44.

Bile

Originally the Celtic god of Hell, Bile is named as the demon of courtesy in the Satanic bible.

Sources: Bailey, *Spiritual Warfare*, 94; Hopkins, *History of Religions*, 132; Susej, *Demonic Bible*, 77.

Bileth

Variations: BELETH, Bilet, BYLETH

In Enochian lore Bileth is named as one of the seventy-two SPIRITS OF SOLOMON and is one of the four chief demons that were imprisoned by the king in his brass vessel through the magic of his signet ring. However, it is from Johann Wierus's *Pseudomonarchia Daemonum* (*False Monarchy of Demons*, 1583) that we learn much more. Ranked as a king and a minister to Arcan, Bileth commands eighty-five legions of demons.

When summoned, as soon as Bileth appears, the summoner must be brave and, using a hazel wood wand, make a triangle in the air starting at the south, moving east, and then closing it. Then he must command the demon to enter into it. The summoner must be respectful and give the demon the honor due his rank. The summoner must also wear a silver ring on the middle finger of his left hand, and hold this ring up to the demon's face so it can be seen at all times. Bileth appears to the sounding of trumpets and rides upon a pale horse looking as frightening as possible in an attempt to scare his summoner. He is summoned because of his ability to cause love to happen between a man and a woman and for his talent in teaching mathematics. According to *Pseudomonarchia Daemonum*, it was shortly after the flood had passed that Noah's son, Cham, summoned this demon; together they wrote a book of mathematics.

Some sources claim that Bileth is a female demon, saying that she is a protector of Hell. In these sources she is described as looking like a winged she-wolf, whose wingspan is some twenty feet. A third eye, crystal-like, is located on her forehead between two long horns. She also has four tails.

Sources: Davidson, *Dictionary of Angles*, 76; Guiley, *Encyclopedia of Angels*, 69; McLean, *Treatise of Angel Magic*, 53.

Bilico

Variations: Lord of Manifestation

According to the *Sacred Magic of Abramelin the Mage*, Bilico, the demon of manifestations, is one of the forty-nine Servitors of Beelzebub (see Beelzebub).

Sources: Ford, *Bible of the Adversary*, 93; Mathers, *Book of the Sacred Magic of Abramelin the Mage*, 120; Von Worms, *Book of Abramelin*, 257.

Bilifares

Variations: Lord of Division

The *Sacred Magic of Abramelin the Mage* lists Bilifares, the Lord of Division, as one of the forty-nine Servitors of Beelzebub (see Beelzebub).

Sources: Belanger, *Dictionary of Demons*, 57; Churchill, *History and Practice of Magic*, 402; Mathers, *Book of the Sacred Magic of Abramelin the Mage*, 107.

Bilifor

Variations: Lord of Glory

According to the *Sacred Magic of Abramelin the Mage*, Bilifor, the Lord of Glory, is one of the forty-nine Servitors of Beelzebub (see Beelzebub).

Sources: Belanger, *Dictionary of Demons*, 74; Mathers, *Book of the Sacred Magic of Abramelin the Mage*, 116; Von Worms, *Book of Abramelin*, 257.

BiluBi

A species of vampiric demon from Burma, the bilu ("blue") is particularly difficult to detect because it looks exactly like a human, except that it has blood-red eyes and casts no shadow. A highly skilled predator with enormous teeth and corrosive touch, very few of its victims ever escape it.

Sources: Balfour, *Cyclopædia of India and of Eastern and Southern Asia*, 362; DeCaroli, *Haunting the Buddha*, 171; Seekins, *Historical Dictionary of Burma*, 110; Spiro, *Burmese Supernaturalism*, 44.

Bime

Variations: Bim, Bune

In the *Ars Goetia*, book one of the *Lemegeton*, Bime is named as a duke that commands thirty legions of demons. He appears before those who summon him as a dragon with three heads, a dog-headed griffon, or a man. He will answer truthfully any question asked of him, bestow riches and wisdom, move corpses from one grave to another, and create corpse candles.

Sources: Crowley, *The Goethia*, 39; De Laurence, *Lesser Key of Solomon, Goetia*, 29–30; Peterson, *Lesser Key of Solomon*, 18; Scott, *London Magazine*, Vol. 5, 378.

Bine

Variations: Bryth

In Akkadian demonology, Bine, similar to Cerberus in the Greek and Roman mythology, is the demonic guardian god. He was condemned to guard the gates of Hell because being something of a carpenter he supplied hand-crafted wings to all the demons of Hell, enabling them to escape. He constructed the wings from souls he captured; the more wings he added to a set of wings, the larger they would be.

Sources: Icons, *Guardians*, 256

Biqa

Biqa (Amharic for "good person") was original name of Kasbeel, one of the Fallen Angels. As soon as this angel was created, he turned away from God, so his name was changed to Kazbeel, which means "he who lies to God."

Sources: Davidson, *Dictionary of Angels*, 168; Fossum, *Name of God and the Angel of the Lord*, 273–4; Minchero, *Voice from the Jordan*, 68.

Biriel

Biriel ("Stronghold of God") is one of the fifteen Servitors of Asmodeus and Magoth (see ASMODEUS), according to the *Sacred Magic of Abramelin the Mage*.

Sources: Belanger, *Dictionary of Demons*, 74; Mathers, *Book of the Sacred Magic of Abramelin the Mage*, 116; Von Worms, *Book of Abramelin*, 248.

Bitru

Variations: SITRI, SYTRY

According to the demonologist Johann Wierus's book *Pseudomonarchia Daemonum* (*False Monarchy of Demons*, 1583), Bitru is one of the PRINCES OF HELL, commanding seventy legions of demons. He appears before his summoner as a leopard with griffon wings, a man of remarkable beauty, or as a winged man with a leopard's face. He creates lust in a man's heart, causes women to disclose their secrets, and makes people stand before him naked.

Sources: De Laurence, *Lesser Key of Solomon, Goetia*, 25; McIntosh, *Eliphas Lévi and the French Occult Revival*, 210; Scott, *London Magazine*, Vol. 5, 378; Spence, *Encyclopedia of Occultism*, 442.

Blackeman

During the Confessions of the Witches of Huntingdon, one of the witches confessed to having dealings with a devil under the command of SATAN by the name of Blackeman. This devil was described as looking like a man of varying heights, wearing black clothes with uncovered and ugly feet. It was said that Blackeman would appear to poor women and make a gift to them of two FAMILIARs in spirit form, GREEDIGUT and GRISSELL, who would, with or without permission, regularly bring them money. After delivering the FAMILIAR spirits, Blackeman would then aggressively solicit sex from the women. He also was said to have the power to make himself invisible.

Sources: Ashton, *Devil in Britain and America*, 237–8; Notestein, *History of Witchcraft in England*, 185; Wilby, *Cunning Folk and Familiar Spirits*, 6.

Blaomen

Mentioned in the *Apocryphon of John*, Chief Blaomen is the demon of fear.

Sources: Barnstone, *Gnostic Bible*, 55; Davies, *Secret Book of John*, 100; Ford, *Bible of the Adversary*, 74; Meyer, *Gnostic Gospels of Jesus*, 171.

Bobêl

Variations: Bobel, Bothothel

In the *Testament of Solomon*, Bobêl was one of the seventy-two SPIRITS OF SOLOMON; he was used by the king to assist in the building of his temple. A demon of diseases who causes nervous illnesses, his personal adversary is the angel Adonael. If he ever is to hear the words "Adon-

aêl, imprison Bothothêl," he will leave immediately.

Sources: Ashe, *Qabalah*, 48, 60; Conybeare, *Jewish Quarterly Review*, Vol. 11, 36.

Bockshexe

Variations: ALP

A male vampiric demon from the mythology of Germany, the bockshexe is essentially a subspecies of the ALP. A nocturnal demon with the ability to shape-shift into a goat, it seeks out a sleeping person, sits upon their chest, compresses the air out of their lungs so they cannot scream, and then bites into their chest, freely drinking its fill of blood. If the victim is a lactating woman, the demon will bite into her breast and drink in her blood and milk. During the process the victim suffers from horrific NIGHTMARES and erotic dreams. The following day the victim will have vivid memories of the assault and will feel tired and drained of energy (see also BOCKS-MARTE).

Source: Meyer, *Mythologie der Germanen*, 505.

BocksmarteBOX

Variations: ALP

A male vampiric demon from the mythology of Germany, the bocksmarte is essentially a subspecies of the ALP. A nocturnal demon, it seeks out a sleeping person, sits upon their chest, compresses the air out of their lungs so they cannot scream, and then bites into their chest, freely drinking its fill of blood. During the process the victim suffers from horrific NIGHTMARES and erotic dreams. The following day the victim will have vivid memories of the assault and will feel tired and drained of energy (see also BOCKSHEXE).

Sources: Meyer, *Mythologie der Germanen*, 134.

Bofar

In the *Sacred Magic of Abramelin the Mage*, book two, the nocturnal demon Bofar is listed as one of the sixteen SERVITORS OF ASELIEL (see ASELIEL).

Sources: Belanger, *Dictionary of Demons*, 74; Peterson, *Lesser Key of Solomon*, 69.

Bofry

Variations: Beal, Beale, BERITH, BOLFRY

Theurgia Goetia, the second book of the *Lemegeton*, says that Duke Bofry commands twenty-six legions of demons. He appears before his summoner as a solider wearing a red uniform and a gold crown upon his head, and riding a red horse. He will honestly answer any question regarding the past, present, or future and has the ability to transmute any metal into gold.

Sources: Crowley, *The Goethia*, 40; Peterson, *Lesser Key of Solomon*, 19; Paine, *Hierarchy of Hell*, 71.

Boginki

A vampiric demon from the mythology of Poland, the boginki ("little goddess") is found near riverbanks. Rather nymphlike in appearance, these beings were created by the original deities that prey upon the sky gods. Boginki attack mothers with newborn children, stealing the babies to eat and replacing them with a type of evil changeling called an *odmience* ("the changed one"). Only by making regular ritualistic sacrifices to them at the riverbank will the boginki be persuaded from attacking.

Sources: Georgieva, *Bulgarian Mythology*, 103; Icon Group International, *Sacrificing*, 232; Leary, *Wisconsin Folklore*, 445; Thomas, *Polish Peasant in Europe and America*, 238.

Bolfry

Variations: Baal Berith, Beal, Beale, Beall, BERITH, Berithi, BOFRY, Bolfri

Originally a Phoenician god, Bolfry was mentioned in Solomonic lore as one of the seventy-two SPIRITS OF SOLOMON that were used to build his temple. This duke of Hell is the demon of blasphemy and murder, commanding twenty-six legions. He speaks in a clear and subtle voice and appears as a red-skinned soldier in a red uniform, wearing a golden crown upon his head, and riding a red horse. When calling up this demon the summoner must wear a silver ring and hold it before Bolfry's face so that upon arrival the demon sees it immediately. He is summoned because he will honestly answer questions regarding the past, present, and future as well as for his ability to transmute any metal into gold. It should be noted, however, that if Bolfry is not answering a question but is speaking, then he is lying. He can also give confirmed dignities to men. Most powerful during the month of June, Bolfry's personal adversary is St. Barnabas, the patron of Cyprus.

Sources: Crowley, *The Goethia*, 40; Paine, *Hierarchy of Hell*, 71; Peterson, *Lesser Key of Solomon*, 19.

Bolla

Variations: Bullar

Bolla is a demonic dragon from Albanian folklore. It has a long serpentine body, four legs, silver, faceted eyes, and a pair of small wings. By the time it is twelve years old, it has grown nine tongues, horns, larger wings, spines down its back, and has fully developed its fire-breathing ability. At this point the creature is called a KULSHEDRA. Once a year, on Saint George's Day,

Bolla opens its eyes and will attack and consume the first person it sees upon awakening. Most countries that celebrate St. George's Day do so on April 23, the traditionally accepted day of his death. However, May 6 and November 23 are also days assigned to the saint.

Sources: Elsie, *Dictionary of Albanian Religion*, 46–7; Lurker, *Dictionary of Gods and Goddesses*, 66; Rose, *Giants, Monsters, and Dragons*, 54.

Bolrizohol

From the Kunimaipa of New Guinea comes the pig-demon of the Pacific Ocean, Bolrizohol. These demons live in caves, certain stones, pools and streams. Appearing either "hard" or "soft" in nature, they are said to cause severe gastrointestinal attacks.

Sources: Hogbin, *Anthropology in Oceania*, 172–4; Jones, *Evil in our Midst*, 187.

Boomasoh

In Burmese mythology Boomasoh is a demonic tree NAT. The infernal guardian of boats, houses, tribes, treasure, villages, and personal property, his presence is detected when the leaves on the trees move and there is no wind. Boomasoh lives in the roots of trees and as long as a *natsin* (nat shrine) is maintained at the base of a pagoda tree, he will not attack anyone.

Sources: Altman, *Sacred Trees*, 60; Folkard, *Plant Lore, Legends, and Lyrics*, 80; Porteous, *Forest Folklore*, 125.

Boniel

In Christian demonology Boniel is one of the twenty named Duke SERVITORS OF SYMIEL (see SYMIEL). Very obedient and quick to obey his summoner, he shares with the other diurnal Servitors of Symiel seven hundred twenty servitors between them.

Sources: Peterson, *Lesser Key of Solomon*, 88.

Boniface

Boniface and ORGEUIL were the two demons who had possessed Elisabeth Allier for twenty years before they were successfully exorcised from her in 1639 by Francois Faconne. They had entered into her body when she was seven by a crust of bread that they had her eat. They will flee at the sight of the holy sacrament.

Sources: American Psychiatric Association, *American Journal of Psychiatry*, Vol. 117, 148; Baskin, *Sorcerer's Handbook*, 100; Coumont, *Demonology and Witchcraft*, 200; Robbins, *Encyclopedia of Witchcraft and Demonology*, 27.

Boralim

In Reginald Scot's *The Discoverie of Witchcraft* (1584), Boralim is said to be the demon of the south; he is the personification of the south wind.

Sources: Gettings, *Dictionary of Demons*, 63; Shah, *Occultism*, 207.

Bori

Variations: Boree

From the demonology of the Hausa and Maguzawa people of West Africa comes the demonic spirit, or TERRESTRIAL DEVIL, known as the bori ("possessed"). The word *bori* is used when speaking of a coven of witches, a possession cult, and a secret society bearing that name.

The bori are demons of bad luck and disease and when they manifest they do so looking like a human with hoofed feet who acts oddly and has a distant and dreamy look to his eyes. They terrify people by appearing in a home and pretending to be the man of the house until the real husband comes home. They also scare people by shape-shifting into a headless person or the form of a python and race over people's feet.

Typically, however, the bori are not tricksters but rather possessor demons, seeking out a human host to occupy; they prefer women. The possessed person is called a *Mai-Bori* (dancer, plural *Maus-bori*) and it is not usually the goal to have the demon exorcised. They are called in or invited into a person when a ritualistic possession dance is performed or a magical potion is consumed. Once inside the body, the person will sometimes enter into a trancelike state, enabling the bori to speak using the host's voice.

The possessed person must perform certain specific dances to exorcise or at least placate the demon. Using drums and various other instruments, a trancelike state is achieved while sacrifices are made. Each demon is attuned to a particular rhythm, as well as to its own particular dance. Once the victim starts to dance, it can be determined by the victim's movements which demon has possessed the person. Victims who cannot appease a bori will die a slow and lingering death. While possessed, the Mai-Bori can divine the future.

Desperate and lonely demons, bori want to be wanted. They are easily repelled by iron; in fact, just saying the word *iron* several times in a row will scare them away. If an individual bori's true name is ever discovered, it will become the slave of the person who knows it.

When summoned for assistance rather than possession, they will work hard and always want to do more, but for a price. Bori are never vicious unless they are offended, which can happen by causing the sparks of a fire to singe a nearby and

invisible one or by taking its name in vain. Fortunately, they are easily appeased with offerings.

Sources: Hill, *Rural Hausa*, 212–3; Illes, *Encyclopedia of Spirits*, 881; Mack, *Field Guide to Demons, Fairies, Fallen Angels, and Other Subversive Spirits*, 102–3; Rsheim, *Animism, Magic, and the Divine King*, 166.

Borol

The *Sacred Magic of Abramelin the Mage* lists Borol ("to bury" or "a pit") as a demonic spirit and one of the forty-nine SERVITORS OF BEELZEBUB (see BEELZEBUB).

Sources: Ford, *Bible of the Adversary*, 93; Mathers, *Book of the Sacred Magic of Abramelin the Mage*, 108; Von Worms, *Book of Abramelin*, 257.

Boruta

Variations: Leśny, Lešny

In ancient Slavic mythology Boruta ("pine tree") was a god of hunting and the woods. After the introduction of Christianity, however, Boruta was demonized, given a rack of antlers, and portrayed as being surrounded by bears and a pack of wolves. Now considered to be a TERRESTRIAL DEVIL (see SPECIES OF DEVILS) who was tricked into building the church at Tum. Believing that he was building a tavern, when he realized the truth Boruta tried to tear the church down, grabbing hold of one of the towers. Unable to succeed, he left in a fury, but his clawed handmark is still visible upon the tower to this day. Modern Polish folklore says that he lives in the ruins of Lenezyca Castle.

Sources: William Curry, Jun. and Co., *Dublin University Magazine*, Vol. 70, 137; Hageneder, *Living Wisdom of Trees*, 143; Stallings, *Fodor's Poland*, 81.

Botis

Variations: Otis

Botis, a FALLEN ANGEL, is listed as both one of the four SERVITORS OF AGALIAREPT (see AGALIAREPT) as well as one of the seventy-two SPIRITS OF SOLOMON. His rank, which varies between sources as a count, earl, and president, allows for him to command the Second Legion of Hell as well as sixty legions of demons (see COUNTS OF HELL, EARLS OF HELL, and PRESIDENTS OF HELL). He is most powerful during the month of June and has dominion over the planet Saturn. His zodiacal sign is that of Gemini.

When summoned, Botis appears as a horned viper, but if commanded will take on the form of a human with large teeth or horns and carrying a sword. He will answer truthfully questions regarding the past, present, and future. He can bolster a man's courage, solve any world conflict successfully through warfare, ease tension in the home, help in making important decisions, protect against the hatred of others, and reconcile friends who have become enemies. He is a true warrior and a highly skilled combatant.

Sources: Baskin, *Sorcerer's Handbook*, 276; De Laurence, *Lesser Key of Solomon, Goetia*, 27; McLean, *Treatise of Angel Magic*, 52; Waite, *Unknown World 1894–1895*, 230; Wedeck, *Treasury of Witchcraft*, 96.

Bouge

In Johann Wierus's *Pseudomonarchia Daemonum* (*False Monarchy of Demons*, 1583) Bouge ("move") is listed as a servitor of Pluto.

Sources: Shepard, *Encyclopedia of Occultism and Parapsychology*, 404; Spence, *Encyclopedia of Occultism*, 120; Wier, *Praestigiis Daemonum*, 211.

Bramsiel

In the *Theurgia Goetia*, the second book of the *Lemegeton*, Bramsiel is one of the ten Duke SERVITORS OF BYDIEL (see BYDIEL). A good-natured AERIAL DEVIL who is willing to obey those who summon him, Bramsiel appears in an attractive form. He commands 2,400 servitors.

Sources: Belanger, *Dictionary of Demons*, 76; Guiley, *Encyclopedia of Demons and Demonology*, 28.

Broosha, El

In the Judeo-Christian folklore of Spain, el broosha is a vampiric demon that appears in the guise of a large black cat. By night, it hunts doe infants to drain dry of their blood.

There is a commonly believed folklore that cats can suck the breath out of a sleeping baby or that they will sleep across its face for warmth, thereby killing the infant. Essentially this demon is LILITH in cat form.

Sources: Conybeare, *Jewish Quarterly*, xi, 30; Howey, *Cat in Magic and Myth*, 173; Rose, *Giants, Monsters, and Dragons*, 382; Thompson, *Semitic Magic*, 42.

Broxa

From medieval Portuguese lore comes the demonic entity or demonic vampiric witch known as the broxa. Created through witchcraft, the broxa looks like a person, and flies through the night sky looking for people to attack, as it can only survive by living off human blood. It has an array of abilities that one would expect any sort of witch to have, such as the ability to divine the future, flight, hypnotism, mind reading, and shape-shifting. It is believed that the broxa as a demonic being is impossible to kill, no matter what form it assumes.

There is a creature in Hasidic folklore also named broxa, but it is described as a bird that attacks she-goats during the night, drinking their milk. It has been speculated by some scholars that over time the broxa bird myth evolved into the broxa vampiric witch of medieval Portugal.

Sources: Gaster, *Myth, Legend, and Custom*, 580; Masters, *Eros and Evil*, 181; Monaghan, *Women in Myth*, 51; Trachtenberg, *Jewish Magic*, 43.

Brufiel

Variations: Brusiel, Burfiel

In the *Theurgia Goetia*, the second book of the *Lemegeton*, Brufiel is named as one of the twelve named Duke SERVITORS OF MACARIEL (see MACARIEL). Good-natured and willing to obey, he commands four hundred servitors. An AERIAL DEVIL, Brufiel may be summoned any time of the day or night. He will appear in various forms but most often will assume the shape of a dragon with a virgin's head.

Sources: Guiley, *Encyclopedia of Demons and Demonology*, 159; Peterson, *Lesser Key of Solomon*, 103, 108; Trithemius, *Steganographia*, 141; Van der Toorn, *Dictionary of Gods and Goddesses*, 152.

Brulefer

Brulefer is one of the eight SERVITORS OF HALE AND SERGULATH. He is summoned because he has the ability to cause a woman to love a man.

Sources: Conway, *Demonology and Devil-Lore*, 59; Kuriakos, *Grimoire Verum Ritual Book*, 16; Masters, *Devil's Dominion*, 131; Waite, *Book of Black and Ceremonial Magic*, 193.

Bruxae

Variations: Xorguinae

According to the demonologist Alphonsus de Spina, the species of demon known as a bruxae are the demons that enable witches to fly to their sabbats. The word *bruxae* is possibly taken from a form of Latin, and if so, would translate as the word "broom." If this is true, this may be the origin of the idea that witches fly on brooms.

Sources: Broedel, *Malleus Maleficarum and the Construction of Witchcraft*, 50; Gettings, *Dictionary of Demons*, 64; Lea, *Materials Toward a History of Witchcraft*, 449.

Bubana

Variations: Bubanabub

In the *Sacred Magic of Abramelin the Mage*, Bubana ("emptiness") is named as one of the fifty-three SERVITORS OF ASHTAROTH AND ASMODEUS (see ASHTAROTH and ASMODEUS).

Sources: Mathers, *Book of the Sacred Magic of Abramelin the Mage*, 115; Von Worms, *Book of Abramelin*, 121.

Bucafas

In the *Theurgia Goetia*, book two of the *Lemegeton*, Bucafas, an AERIAL DEVIL, is named

as one of the twelve Duke SERVITORS OF CAR-
NESIEL (see CARNESIEL and DUKES OF HELL).

Sources: Peterson, *Lesser Key of Solomon*, 59;
Trithemius, *Steganographia*, 1.

Bucaphi

In Apollonius of Tyana's *Nuctemeron* (*Night Illuminated by Day*), Bucaphi is the demon of
stryges ("witches"). He is most powerful during
the tenth hour of the day, which according to
Apollonius "is the key of the astronomical cycle
and of the circular movement of human's life."

Sources: Gettings, *Dictionary of Demons*, 64; Lévi,
Transcendental Magic, 507.

Bucon

Variations: Bucom

Bucon is one of the eight SERVITORS OF HALE
AND SERGULATH. He is the demon of hatred,
causing hatred between a man and a woman.

Sources: Kuriakos, *Grimoire Verum Ritual Book*, 16;
Masters, *Devil's Dominion*, 131; Poinsot, *Complete Book
of the Occult and Fortune Telling*, 378; Waite, *Book of
Black and Ceremonial Magic*, 193.

Budar

In the *Theurgia Goetia*, the second book of the
Lemegeton, Budar is named as one of the sixteen
Duke SERVITORS OF ASYRIEL (see ASYRIEL). He
is good-natured and willing to obey, unusual for
a nocturnal demon.

Sources: Belanger, *Dictionary of Demons*, 77; Peterson, *Lesser Key of Solomon*, 74.

Budarim

Variations: Budarijm, Budarym, Femel

In the *Theurgia Goetia*, the second book of the
Lemegeton, Budarim is one of the twelve SERVI-
TORS OF CASPIEL (see CASPIEL). A rude and
stubborn demon, he commands 2,660 servitors
of his own.

Sources: McLean, *Treatise on Angel Magic*, 35; Peterson, *Lesser Key of Soloman*, 60; Trithemius,
Steganographia, 6.

Budiel

Budiel is one of the twenty SERVITORS OF CA-
MUEL (see CAMUEL). Appearing in a beautiful
form, this diurnal demon is known to be very
courteous.

Sources: Belanger, *Dictionary of Demons*, 77; Peterson, *Lesser Key of Soloman*, 68; Trithemius,
Steganographia, 73.

Budsturga

A dark, female demonic god, Budsturga is associated with the Order of the Nine Angels' 13th
path. She represents hidden wisdom that is po-

tentially dangerous to one's sanity. Appearing as
a blue ethereal mass, she is trapped in the vortex
between the causal spaces.

Source: Ford, *Book of the Moon Witch Chorozon Edition*, 315.

Buer

In demonology Buer has been named one of
the four SERVITORS OF AGALIAREPT (see
AGALIAREPT), one of the seventy-two SPIRITS
OF SOLOMON, as well as being a FALLEN ANGEL.
He holds the rank of president of the stars. A
demon of the second order, he commands the
Second Legion of Hell (see BOTIS), which contains fifty legions of demons as well as his own
personal ranks of an additional fifteen legions.

Buer is always described as being male but has
a number of appearances that he is known by: a
centaur carrying a bow and a quiver of arrows, a
five-spoke wheel that moves by rolling itself, a
man with the head of a lion and five goat legs
surrounding his body so that he can walk in any
direction, and a star.

A diurnal demon, Buer can only be successfully
summoned when the sun is in Sagittarius. He is
called upon for his ability to grant domestic fe-
licity, to give good FAMILIARs, and to heal the
sick. He also teaches philosophy and herbal medicine. He is most powerful in the month of May
and has dominion over the planet Mercury.

Although the etymology of the name is unknown, an ancient German city was named Buer
in what is now Gelsenkirchen in Westphalia,
Germany.

Sources: Baskin, *Sorcerer's Handbook*, 276; De Laurence, *Lesser Key of Solomon, Goetia*, 25; McLean, *Treatise of Angel Magic*, 53; Waite, *Unknown World 1894–
1895*, 230; Wedeck, *Treasury of Witchcraft*, 96.

Buk

The *Sacred Magic of Abramelin the Mage*, book
two, names Buk ("perplexity") as one of the fifty-
three SERVITORS OF ASHTAROTH AND AS-
MODEUS (see ASHTAROTH and ASMODEUS).

Sources: Belanger, *Dictionary of Demons*, 79; Mathers, *Book of the Sacred Magic of Abramelin the Mage*, 115.

Bukavac

From Slavic mythology comes the demonic
creature known as Bukavac ("noisy"). With its
gnarled horns and six legs, this nocturnal demon
leaves its watery home, a lake or pool, at night,
making a tremendous amount of noise. It leaps
upon animals and people alike and strangles them
to death.

Source: Hlobil, *Before You*, 106.

Buldumech

In the *Testament of Solomon* Buldumech is listed as one of the thirty-six Elemental World Rulers and one of the seventy-two SPIRITS OF SOLOMON. The demon of domestic discord, Buldumech causes grudges between husbands and wives. While bound by King Solomon, he did heavy labor for the construction of the temple, such as keeping the furnaces for metalwork stoked.

To keep this demon from entering into your home, on a piece of parchment paper write the words "The God of Abram, and the God of Isaac, and the God of Jacob commands thee— retire from this house in peace." Then place it in the antechamber of your home.

Sources: Ashe, *Qabalah*, 48; Conybeare, *Jewish Quarterly Review*, Vol. 11, 36.

Bune

Variations: BIME

Known as the Dragon Duke, Bune was one of the seventy-two SPIRITS OF SOLOMON (see DUKES OF HELL). A FALLEN ANGEL, he is under the service of ASMODEUS. Bune, a diurnal demon of death and necromancy, commands thirty legions of demons. The numerous demons under his direct command are called *Bunis*; they are considered exceedingly evil and practice their own brand of dark magic.

Bune appears to his summoner as either a human man with a pleasant voice or as a dragon with three heads, one of a DOG, one of a griffin, and one of a man. He is summoned for his honesty in answering any question put to him. He will also help in the acquisition of wealth, can gift a person with a flair for speaking, and impart sophistication and wisdom. He also changes the burial places of the dead and creates vampiric creatures known as corpse candles. He frequents cemeteries and is most powerful during the summer.

It should be noted that sources vary on Bune's communication ability. Some claim that he has a beautiful speaking voice, while others say that he only communicates through a type of sign language.

Sources: Crowley, *The Goetia*, 39; McLean, *Treatise of Angel Magic*, 53; Scott, *London Magazine*, Vol. 5, 378; Spence, *Encyclopedia of Occultism*, 81.

Buniel

In the *Theurgia Goetia*, the second book of the *Lemegeton*, Buniel is listed as one of the sixteen Duke SERVITORS OF ASYRIEL (see ASYRIEL). He is a diurnal demon and is said to be good-natured and willing to obey his summoners. Buniel commands forty legions of demons.

Source: Peterson, *Lesser Key of Solomon*, 73–4, 77.

Burasen

According to the *Sacred Magic of Abramelin the Mage*, book two, Burasen is one of the twenty SERVITORS OF AMAYMON (see AMAYMON). His name is Hebrew and translates to mean "destroys by stifling smoky breath."

Sources: Forgotten Books, *Book of the Sacred Magic of Abramelin the Mage*, 42–3; Mathers, *Book of the Sacred Magic of Abra-Melin*, 122.

Buriel

Theurgia Goetia, the second book of the *Lemegeton*, names Buriel as an Elemental Prince of the Air and one of the eleven WANDERING PRINCES (see PRINCES OF HELL). Described as looking like a serpent with a human head, this nocturnal AERIAL DEVIL commands twelve duke servitors (see SERVITORS OF BURIEL). He and his court are constantly on the move, never staying in any one place for long. Buriel is heliophobic and shuns the light (see HELIOPHOBIC DEVIL).

Sources: Gettings, *Dictionary of Demons*, 232; Shumaker, *Natural Magic and Modern Science*, 66; Spence, *Encyclopedia of Occultism*, 81; Trithemius, *Steganographia*, 81.

Buriol

The *Sacred Magic of Abramelin the Mage* names Buriol ("devouring fire of God") among the twenty SERVITORS OF AMAYMON (see AMAYMON).

Sources: Belanger, *Dictionary of Demons*, 81; Forgotten Books, *Book of the Sacred Magic of Abramelin the Mage*, 42–3; Mathers, *Book of the Sacred Magic of Abra-Melin*, 122.

Burisiel

Theurgia Goetia, the second book of the *Lemegeton*, lists Burisiel as one of the twelve Duke SERVITORS OF DEMORIEL (see DEMORIEL and DUKES OF HELL). He commands 1,140 servitors.

Sources: Belanger, *Dictionary of Demons*, 80; Guiley, *Encyclopedia of Demons and Demonology*, 60; Peterson, *Lesser Key of Solomon*, 63.

Buriul

Variations: Bur I Ul, Buriub

In the *Sacred Magic of Abramelin the Mage*, book two, Buriul ("in terror and trembling") is named as one of the fifty-three SERVITORS OF ASHTAROTH AND ASMODEUS (see ASHTAROTH and ASMODEUS).

Sources: Mathers, *Book of the Sacred Magic of*

Abramelin the Mage, 115; Von Worms, *Book of Abramelin*, 212, 247.

Busas

Variations: PRUflAS

Busas holds the rank of both duke and prince, commanding twenty-six legions of demons as well as half of the Order of Thrones, and half of the Order of Angels (see DUKES OF HELL and PRINCES OF HELL). He appears as a flame with the head of an owl and is summoned for his ability to create conflicts, lies, quarrels, and wars. Busas has a reputation for responding generously to requests made of him. His home is reported to be near the Tower of Babylon.

Sources: Collin de Plancy, *Dictionnaire Infernal*, 413; Shah, *Occultism*, 67.

Busasejal

Variations: BASASAEL, Bezaliel ("shadow of God")

According to Enochian lore, Busasejal ("damaged") was one of the FALLEN ANGELS who swore allegiance to SAMIAZA, rebelled against God, took a human wife, and fathered the NEPHILIM.

Sources: Ashe, *Book of Enoch*, 57; Ashley, *Complete Book of Devils and Demons*, 73; Charles, *Book of Enoch*, 137; Horne, *Sacred Books and Early Literature of the East*, 114.

Bushyasp

Variations: Bushyansia, "the fiend of decay," "the fiend of laziness," "the long-handed"

From Persian and Zoroastrian demonology comes the DEV of sloth, Bushyasp. He is most powerful in the mornings but can be driven off through prayer (see also DEVS WHO RESIDE IN MEN).

Sources: Ford, *Liber Hvhi*, 160; Wilson, *Pársí Religion as Contained in the Zand-Avastá*, 335.

Bushyasta

Variations: Bushasp, "the long-handed"

From Zoroastrian mythology comes the DAEVA known as Bushyasta ("sleep"). In service under AHRIMAN, he is the demon of lethargy and sloth.

Every day just before dawn Bushyasta attacks, leaving from the north, and rushes back into the darkness saying "Sleep on, O men! Sleep on, O sinners! Sleep on and live in sin" in the hopes that it will cause people to sleep through their religious obligations. He also causes procrastination.

Bushyasta is described as an evil genius with a gaunt body, long arms, and yellow skin. At dawn,

he must return back to his darkness; he will abandon his plans with the coming of dawn or at the sight of Mithra's mace.

Sources: Hyatt, *Book of Demons*, 56; Maberry, *Vampire Universe*, 64; Müller, *Sacred Books of the East*, 141–2, 193–4.

Buta

In Indonesian mythology there is a classification of Javanese demon that is particularly evil known as buta ("demon"). Buta spread disease and illness and it is the religious obligation of the *sanghuhu*, lower caste priests, to appease them.

Sources: Atmosumarto, *Learner's Comprehensive Dictionary of Indonesian*, 76; Gonda, *Sanskrit in Indonesia*, 300; Knappert, *Encyclopedia of Myth and Legend*, 38.

Buta Cakil

From Indonesian mythology come the demons known as buta cakil ("hook demons"), so named for their hooklike teeth. They attack animals and humans alike. It is the religious obligation of the *sanghuhu*, lower caste priests, to appease them (see BUTA).

Sources: Atmosumarto, *Learner's Comprehensive Dictionary of Indonesian*, 80; Knappert, *Pacific Mythology*, 38.

Buta Kala

Buta Kala ("demon spirit" or "demon animal") from Indonesian mythology is the judge of the dead. An earth spirit in service under Durga Sang Hyang Bathari (see TERRESTRIAL DEVILS), he is described as having large ears, a protruding chin, sharp teeth, a sparse beard, thin hair, and wide eyes. Buta Kala lingers near crossroads and causes trouble between friends if they do not maintain a good relationship. He also hides items that may start a family quarrel. It is the religious obligation of the *sanghuhu*, lower caste priests, to appease him. If he is given proper respect by being invited to partake in ceremonial offerings of cock fights, onions, meat, and spices, he will become helpful (see also BUTA).

Sources: Atmosumarto, *Learner's Comprehensive Dictionary of Indonesian*, 220; Becker, *Beyond Translation*, 60; Howe, *Changing World of Bali*, 58, 69–71; Wiener, *Visible and Invisible Realms*, 52–4.

Buta Macan

Little is known about this demon from Indonesian mythology. Buta Macan ("tiger demon"), like all buta demons, can be appeased by the *sanghuhu*, lower caste priests (see also BUTA).

Sources: Arnscheidt, *'Debating' Nature Conservation*, 53

Buta Sanniya

From Indonesian mythology come the demons known as Buta sanniya. They cause derangement, distortion, and the loss of the use of limbs, but it is the religious obligation of the *sanghuhu*, lower caste priests, to appease these demons (see also BUTA and DAHA-ATA SANNIYA).

Sources: Illes, *Encyclopedia of Spirits*, 875; Kapferer, *Celebration of Demons*, 231; Wijesekera, *Deities and Demons, Magic and Masks, Part 2*, 295, 299.

Buta Terong

Variations: Butoterong

From Indonesian mythology comes the demon known as Buta Terong ("eggplant nose demon"), so named for his exceptionally large and round nose. He also sports a double row of canine teeth and large eyes. No matter how much he eats, he can never be sated. A destroyer demon, Buta Terong spreads disease and illness. It is the religious obligation of the *sanghuhu*, lower caste priests, to appease him. Buta Terong is incapable of defeating a hero in a fight (see BUTA).

Sources: Becker, *Beyond Translation*, 60; Headley, *Durga's Mosque*, 501; Ras, *Shadow of the Ivory Tree*, 77.

Butarab

Butarab is one of the sixty-five SERVITORS OF KORE AND MAGOTH, according to the *Sacred Magic of Abramelin the Mage*, book two.

Sources: Belanger, *Dictionary of Demons*, 80; Mathers, *Book of the Sacred Magic of Abramein the Mage*, 118.

Butarah

The *Sacred Magic of Abramelin the Mage* names Butarah as one of the sixty-five SERVITORS OF KORE AND MAGOTH.

Sources: Ford, *Adversary of the Bible*, 92; Mathers, *Book of the Sacred Magic of Abramelin the Mage*, 118; Von Worms, *Book of Abramelin*, 250, 256.

Butatar

Apollonius of Tyana stated in his *Nuctemeron* (*Night Illuminated by Day*) that Butatar is demon of calculations. He has dominion over the third of the twelfth hour.

Sources: Davidson, *Dictionary of Angels*, 77; Lévi, *Transcendental Magic*, 404.

Buyasta

In Persian demonology, Buyasta is a demon of laziness. He prevents people from working.

Sources: Maberry, *Vampire Universe*, 64.

Bydiel

Bydiel is ranked as a PLANETARY PRINCE of Venus and one of the eleven WANDERING PRINCES (see PRINCES OF HELL). An AERIAL DEVIL, he commands twenty chief dukes, two hundred dukes, and a multitude of servitors. If asked by his summoner, he will appear in an attractive form. Bydiel is invoked for clothing and food. He is most powerful during the fifth hour of the day (see SERVITORS OF BYDIEL).

Sources: Belanger, *Dictionary of Demons*, 71; Gettings, *Dictionary of Demons*, 232; Peterson, *Lesser Key of Solomon*, 105.

Byleth

Variations: Ba'al, BELETH, Bilet

Originally a Phoenician goddess, King Byleth was named in the *Theurgia Goetia* as a FALLEN ANGEL formerly of the Order of Powers as well as one of the seventy-two SPIRITS OF SOLOMON. He commands eighty legions of demons. When summoned, he appears as a sorcerer riding upon a white horse with the sounding of trumpets announcing his arrival. It should be noted, however, that Byleth is said to have a very bad temper and enjoys drinking wine. When this demon was summoned by CHAM, son of Noah, they wrote a book of mathematics together.

Sources: Davidson, *Dictionary of Angels*, 76; Lea, *Materials Toward a History of Witchcraft*, 545; Peterson, *Lesser Key of Solomon*, 234.

Caacrinolaas

Variations: Caacrinoles, Caaerinolaas, Caasimolar, Caassimolar, Classyalabolas, Glassia-labolis, Glasya, Glasya Labolas, Glasyalabolas

According to medieval demonology and the grimoire *Ars Goetia*, Caacrinolaas is a president of Hell and titled the Author of Bloodshed and Manslaughter; however, some sources list him as an earl (see EARLS OF HELL and PRESIDENTS OF HELL). He commands thirty-six legions of demons. Caacrinolaas appears before his summoner as a godlike being with the wings of a griffon or as a DOG with the wings of a griffon. He is known to encourage acts of homicide, and he teaches the liberal arts and how to become invisible.

Sources: De Claremont, *Ancient's Book of Magic*, 122; Peterson, *Lesser Key of Solomon*, 223; Scott, *London Magazine*, Vol. 5, 378; Spence, *Encyclopedia of Occultism*, 83.

Cab

According to Enochian lore, Cab is a CACODAEMON. His angelic counterpart is unknown (see ENOCHIAN CACODAEMONS).

Sources: Chopra, *Academic Dictionary of Mythology*, 60; Laycock, *Complete Enochian Dictionary*, 92.

Cabariel

In the *Theurgia Goetia*, the second book of the *Lemegeton*, Cabariel is named as prince of the

North by Northwest (see PRINCES OF HELL). He is in service under the emperor of the West. Cabariel commands one hundred dukes, fifty of which are diurnal and fifty which are nocturnal; only ten from each are named (see SERVITORS OF CABARIEL). He is summoned for his ability to disclose betrayals.

Sources: Gettings, *Dictionary of Demons*, 232; Peterson, *Lesser Key of Solomon*, 84; Trithemius, *Steganographia*, 81.

Cabarim

Duke Cabarim is named in the *Theurgia Goetia*, the second book of the *Lemegeton*, as one of the twelve SERVITORS OF DEMORIEL (see DEMORIEL and DUKES OF HELL).

Sources: Guiley, *Encyclopedia of Demons and Demonology*, 60; Peterson, *Lesser Key of Solomon*, 63.

Cabiel

In Enochian lore Cabiel is one of the twenty-eight demonic rulers of the lunar mansions (see ENOCHIAN RULERS OF THE LUNAR MANSIONS).

Sources: Gettings, *Dictionary of Demons*, 65; McLean, *Treatise on Angel Magic*, 42; Scheible, *Sixth and Seventh Books of Moses*, 75.

Cac

According to Enochian lore, Cac is a CACODAEMON. His angelic counterpart is unknown (see ENOCHIAN CACODAEMONS and ENOCHIAN RULERS OF THE LUNAR MANSIONS).

Sources: Chopra, *Academic Dictionary of Mythology*, 60; Laycock, *Complete Enochian Dictionary*, 92.

Cacodaemon

Variations: Cacodemons, Kakadaimon, Kakodaimon, Kakos Daimon

Named for a Greek word meaning "bad demon" or "bad spirit" that crossed over into the Enochian language sometime in the sixteenth century, Cacodaemons were said by some sources to be the FALLEN ANGELS. Banished from Heaven and unable to find a place of their own to call home, they settled down to live in the space between the earth and the stars. They have been described as being large and powerfully built humanoids with dark-hued skin and also as a swirling black mass.

Cacodaemons are attracted to a particular person at birth; the demon attaches itself to that person and follows them through their life, controlling their impulses and personalities from time to time. They also act as a messenger between their charge and the gods.

Hostile by nature, they take pleasure in acting out revenge and causing injury. Some demonolo-

gists placed them under the command of the god Hades. Inferior demons, they have dominion over the twelfth house of the Zodiac. The opposite of a Cacodaemon is an agathodaemon (AGATHODEMON) or eudemon.

Sources: Hyatt, *Book of Demons*, 60; Russell, *Lucifer, the Devil in the Middle Ages*, 249; Wray, *Birth of Satan*, 25.

Cahor

Apollonius of Tyana's *Nuctemeron* (*Night Illuminated by Day*) lists Cahor as the demon of deception. He is most powerful during the third hour of the day.

Sources: Davidson, *Dictionary of Angels*, 79; De Givry, *Witchcraft, Magic, and Alchemy*, 12.

Caiga

In the *Theurgia Goetia*, the second book of the *Lemegeton*, Caiga is one of the sixteen SERVITORS OF ASYRIEL (see ASYRIEL). Commanding forty servitors, Caiga, a diurnal demon, is known to be good-natured and willing to obey his summoner.

Sources: Peterson, *Lesser Key of Solomon*, 73–4, 77.

Cagrino

Variations: Buecubu, Chagrin, GUECUBU, Harginn

Originally from the Gypsy demonology from northwestern India comes the demonic feylike creature Cagrino. Looking like a small yellow hedgehog that is a foot and half long and wide, he is known to mount horses and ride them to exhaustion, leaving them sick and weary with their manes tangled and their bodies covered in sweat.

To prevent Cagrino from stealing off with your horse, tie the animal to a stake that has been covered with garlic juice and then lay a red thread on the ground in the shape of a cross. Another method is to take some of the horse's hair, salt, meal, and the blood of a bat, make bread with it, and rub it on the horse's hoof. Then, take the bowl that the mixture was made in and hide it in a tree, saying the words "Tarry, pipkin, in this tree, till such time as full ye be."

Sources: Banis, *Charms, Spells, and Curses for the Millions*, 87; Leland, *Gypsy Sorcery and Fortune Telling*, 91; Spence, *Encyclopedia of Occultism*, 88.

Cailleach

Variations: Beira, Queen of Winter; Bheur Cailleach; the Black Queen; Cailleach nan Cruachan; Cailliach, the Goddess of Smallpox; Callech the Witch of Ben Cruachan

From Gaelic demonology comes the demon of

the late spring wind Cailleach ("old wife" or "veiled one"). An AERIAL DEVIL who commands gale storms and the winds, she has been described as looking like a blue-faced hag with boar tusks, bear teeth, and only one eye.

Not necessarily an evil being, Cailleach kills all that which is no longer needed. With her power at its peak in the springtime, she raises windstorms in an attempt to prevent summer from arriving. Cailleach has the ability to see beyond the duality of things. The day before May Day she leaves her staff under a holly tree and returns to her home in the Scottish Highlands, where she then turns herself into stone until Halloween. Cailleach created mountains and Loch Awe.

Sources: MacKillop, *Dictionary of Celtic Mythology*, 69; Rose, *Giants, Monsters, and Dragons*, 64; Turner, *Dictionary of Ancient Deities*, 112.

Caim

Variations: Camio, CAYM, CHAMOS, Chamus, Chium

In the *Ars Goetia*, the first book of the *Lemegeton*, Caim ("Cain") is given the ranks of both president and prince and has the titles of Grand Master of Hell and the Thrush President (see PRESIDENTS OF HELL and PRINCES OF HELL). He is also listed as one of the FALLEN ANGELS, formerly of the Order of Angels, and one of the seventy-two SPIRITS OF SOLOMON.

A nocturnal demon who is most powerful during the month of December, Caim commands thirty legions of demons. He has been described as looking like a blackbird, a man with a sharp sword, an elegant man with the head and wings of a blackbird, and a man with a peacock's tail wearing a tuft and many bracelets.

Caim is summoned for his willingness to answer honestly questions regarding the future, but it should be noted that they will not always be truthful. To ensure that what he says is the truth, make him stand in burning ashes or on hot coals, for while doing so he is incapable of lying. He is an expert at hydromancy and can give his summoner the understanding of the language of barking dogs, birdsong, lowing cattle, and water. His zodiacal sign is Sagittarius.

Sources: De Laurence, *Lesser Key of Solomon, Goetia*, 39; McLean, *Treatise of Angel Magic*, 53; Scot, *Discoverie of Witchcraft*, 223; Scott, *London Magazine*, Vol. 5, 378.

Calim

Variations: Calym

Theurgia Goetia, book two of the *Lemegeton*, Calim is one of the twenty SERVITORS OF CAMUEL (see CAMUEL). He appears before his summoner in a beautiful form. Calim has the reputation for being very courteous.

Sources: Belanger, *Dictionary of Demons*, 82; Guiley, *Encyclopedia of Demons and Demonology*, 36; Trithemius, *Steganographia*, 73.

Cam

According to Enochian lore, Cam is a CACODAEMON. His angelic counterpart is unknown (see ENOCHIAN CACODAEMONS). His name in Hebrew translates to mean "a spice used in incense."

Sources: Chopra, *Academic Dictionary of Mythology*, 61; Laycock, *Complete Enochian Dictionary*, 93.

Camal

In the *Sacred Magic of Abramelin the Mage*, Camal ("To desire God") is named as one of the thirty-two SERVITORS OF ASTAROT (see ASTAROT). A servitor of the Second Hierarchy, Camal is the demon of lust whose personal adversary is St. John the Evangelist, patron saint of the Freemasons.

There is also an archangel with this name that was mentioned in the Kabbalah.

Sources: Agrippa, *Three Books of Occult Philosophy*, 115; Belanger, *Dictionary of Demons*, 82; Sesej, *Demonic Bible*, 257.

Camaysar

According to Apollonius of Tyana's *Nuctemeron* (*Night Illuminated by Day*), Camaysar is the demon of the marriage of contraries. He is most powerful during the fifth hour of the day.

Sources: Davidson, *Dictionary of Angels*, 87; Gettings, *Dictionary of Demons*, 65; Lévi, *Transcendental Magic*, 391.

Cambions

Variations: Campions

From post-medieval European demonology comes the belief in the existence of a demonic hybrid offspring called a cambion. They were believed to be created when an INCUBUS and a human woman or when a SUCCUBUS and a human male had a child together. A cambion child can be easily detected, as it will be born with a deformity of some sort. Twins are especially suspect of being cambions as well.

The hybrid will develop the same as any child would, but before the age of seven they show little to no signs of life. These demonic offspring are not considered to be truly alive until they reach the age of seven years, and until that time, it is perfectly acceptable for a witch hunter to kill them. One may test a child by having a holy person touching him or her; a cambion will cry out.

As it grows into adulthood it will develop a

strong and incredibly dense physical form, growing tall and becoming well muscled. Its physical deformity, if not too severe to begin with, may well disappear altogether. By nature, it will be bold, arrogant, and wicked; however, there are some cambions who are not inclined to be evil and will live among humans peaceably enough. All cambions have some level of supernatural ability and they are likely to become wizards or sorcerers. Cambions usually find themselves discriminated against because of the circumstances surrounding their conception.

Throughout history there have been several famous individuals who were said to be cambions: Alexander the Great, Caesar Augustus, Martin Luther, Merlin (of King Arthur fame), Plato, Romulus and Remus, Scipio Africanus, and the father of William the Conqueror. All were suspected of having been fathered by an INCUBUS. Angela de Labarthe of Toulouse, France, was burned at the stake for allegedly giving birth to a child born with a wolf's head and a snake's tail in 1275; the reason given for her execution was that only a creature from hell, like an incubus, could have been the father.

Sources: Aylesworth, *Servants of the Devil*, 33; Buckland, *Weiser Field Guide to Ghosts*, 143, 145; Hugo, *Toilers of the Sea*, 47, 49; Maberry, *They Bite*, 301; Masters, *Eros and Evil*, 131; Spence, *Encyclopedia of Occultism*, 93.

Cambriel

In the *Theurgia Goetia*, the second book of the *Lemegeton*, Cambriel is named as one of the fifteen Duke SERVITORS OF ICOSIEL (see ICOSIEL). An AERIAL DEVIL who may be summoned any time of the day or night, Cambriel commands 2,200 servitors. Good-natured and willing to obey his summoner, he will do exactly what is asked of him. Cambriel is most easily summoned from inside a house, as he is fond of them. He has dominion over the planet Mars.

Sources: Agrippa, *Three Books of Occult Philosophy*, 536; Godwin, *Godwin's Cabalistic Encyclopedia*, 64; Peterson, *Lesser Key of Solomon*, 99; Trithemius, *Steganographia*, 69.

Came

According to the *Sacred Magic of Abramelin the Mage*, book two, the AERIAL DEVIL Came ("Tired") is one of the fifteen SERVITORS OF PAYMON (see PAYMON).

Sources: Mathers, *Book of the Sacred Magic of Abramelin the Mage*, 108, 121.

Camiel

Variations: Camael ("he who sees God")

In Christian demonology, Camiel has been given the rank of both a count and a duke (see COUNTS OF HELL and DUKES OF HELL). He has been named as one of the twelve Duke SERVITORS OF AMENADIEL (see AMENADIEL), one of the eleven WANDERING PRINCES of HYDRIEL, one of the named fifteen Duke SERVITORS OF SCOX (see SCOX) and one of the fifteen SERVITORS OF SASQUIEL (see SASQUIEL). An AERIAL DEVIL who commands 1,320 servitors (or 5,550 servitors, sources vary), he lives in or near water, marshes, and wetlands. Camiel may be summoned any time of the day or night, and when he appears will do so as a snake with a virgin's head and face. In spite of his appearance, Camiel has a reputation of being very courteous and willing to obey. His zodiacal sign is the fourth degree of Aquarius.

Sources: Belanger, *Dictionary of Demons*, 84; Davidson, *Dictionary of Angels*, 84; Peterson, *Lesser Key of Solomon*, 62, 114; Trithemius, *Steganographia*, 95.

Camonix

In the *Sacred Magic of Abramelin the Mage*, Camonix ("perseverance in combat") is among the thirty-two SERVITORS OF ASTAROT (see ASTAROT).

Sources: Belanger, *Dictionary of Demons*, 85; Mathers, *Book of the Sacred Magic of Abramelin the Mage*, 106; Von Worms, *Book of Abramelin*, 249.

Camor

Variations: CAMORY

Theurgia Goetia, book two of the *Lemegeton*, names Camor as one of the twelve Duke SERVITORS OF CASPIEL (see CASPIEL and DUKES OF HELL). A rude and stubborn AERIAL DEVIL, Camor commands 2,660 servitors.

Sources: Belanger, *Dictionary of Demons*, 85; Guiley, *Encyclopedia of Demons and Demonology*, 37; Peterson, *Lesser Key of Solomon*, 60; Shumaker, *Natural Magic and Modern Science*, 66.

Camory

Theurgia Goetia, book two of the *Lemegeton*, names Camory as one of the twelve Duke SERVITORS OF CASPIEL (see CASPIEL). A rude and stubborn AERIAL DEVIL, Camory commands 2,660 servitors.

Sources: Belanger, *Dictionary of Demons*, 85; Guiley, *Encyclopedia of Demons and Demonology*, 37; Peterson, *Lesser Key of Solomon*, 60.

Camuel

Theurgia Goetia, book two of the *Lemegeton*, names Camuel ("withered") as a Prince of the Southeast in service under CARNESIEL (see PRINCES OF HELL). He is known to be benevolent and has 60,000,000,000,000 duke servitors in all but only twelve are named (see SERVITORS OF CAMUEL).

Sources: Gettings, *Dictionary of Demons*, 232; McLean, *Treatise of Angel Magic*, 53; Trithemius, *Steganographia*, 81.

Camyel

Theurgia Goetia, book two of the *Lemegeton*, names Camyel as one of the twenty SERVITORS OF CAMUEL (see CAMUEL). A diurnal demon, he appears before his summoner in a very beautiful form. Camyel is known to be exceedingly courteous.

Sources: Guiley, *Encyclopedia of Demons and Demonology*, 36; Peterson, *Lesser Key of Solomon*, 67; Trithemius, *Steganographia*, 73.

Capriel

In *Theurgia Goetia*, book two of the *Lemegeton*, Capriel is named as one of the twelve Duke SERVITORS OF CARNESIEL (see CARNESIEL and DUKES OF HELL).

Sources: Belanger, *Dictionary of Demons*, 85; Peterson, *Lesser Key of Solomon*, 59.

Carabia

Variations: DECARABIA

Carabia is a Great Marquis from Christian demonology, commanding thirty legions of demons (see MARQUIS OF HELL). When summoned, he will appear as a pentagram but will take on a human guise at his summoner's request. He teaches both herbology and gemology and can shape-change into any type of bird.

Sources: De Laurence, *Lesser Key of Solomon, Goetia*, 44; Icon, *Demons*, 46; Scot, *Discoverie of Witchcraft*, 224.

Carasch

In the *Sacred Magic of Abramelin the Mage*, Carasch ("Voracity") is among the fifty-three SERVITORS OF ASHTAROTH AND ASMODEUS (see ASHTAROTH and ASMODEUS).

Sources: Belanger, *Dictionary of Demons*, 86; Mathers, *Book of the Sacred Magic of Abramelin the Mage*, 115.

Carelena

The *Sacred Magic of Abramelin the Mage* names Carelena ("to seize hair") as one of the forty-nine SERVITORS OF BEELZEBUB (see BEELZEBUB).

Sources: Ford, *Bible of the Adversary*, 93; Mathers, *Book of the Sacred Magic of Abramelin the Mage*, 107; Von Worms, *Book of Abramelin*, 257.

Carga

In the *Theurgia Goetia*, the second book of the *Lemegeton*, Carga is named as one of the sixteen Duke SERVITORS OF ASYRIEL (see ASYRIEL).

Commanding twenty demonic servitors, he is known to be good-natured and willing to obey his summoner.

Sources: Belanger, *Dictionary of Demons*, 86; Guiley, *Encyclopedia of Demons and Demonology*, 20; Peterson, *Lesser Key of Solomon*, 73.

Cariel

From Christian demonology comes the diurnal demon Cariel. One of the twenty SERVITORS OF CAMUEL, he will appear before his summoner in a beautiful form (see CAMUEL). He is known to be very courteous.

Sources: Belanger, *Dictionary of Demons*, 86; Peterson, *Lesser Key of Solomon*, 68; Trithemius, *Steganographia*, 30, 32, 73.

Carifas

In *Ars Paulina*, book three of the *Lemegeton*, Carifas is named as one of the twelve Duke SERVITORS OF AMENADIEL (see AMENADIEL and DUKES OF HELL). A nocturnal demon, he commands three thousand servitors.

Source: Belanger, *Dictionary of Demons*, 86.

Carnesiel

Variations: Carnesiell

In the *Theurgia Goetia*, the second book of the *Lemegeton*, Carnesiel ("radiant fire") is ranked as an emperor and king of the East. He is also said in various other Christian demonologies to be one of the thirty-six Elemental World Rulers as well as one of the seventy-two SPIRITS OF SOLOMON. An AERIAL DEVIL and demon of the east, Carnesiel commands 1,000 great dukes, 100 lesser dukes, 12 chief dukes, and 50,000,000,000,000 other demonic spirits (see SERVITORS OF CARNESIEL). When summoned, he will appear with 60,000,000,000,000 servitors of varying ranks.

Sources: Butler, *Ritual Magic*, 77; Gettings, *Dictionary of Demons*, 232; Pane, *Hierarchy of Hell*, 68; Peterson, *Lesser Key of Solomon*, 60.

Carnet

Variations: Carpid, Carpiel

In the *Theurgia Goetia*, the second book of the *Lemegeton*, Carnet, a nocturnal demon, is named as one of the fifteen SERVITORS OF BARMIEL (see BARMIEL and DUKES OF HELL).

Sources: Peterson, *Lesser Key of Solomon*, 70–1; Trithemius, *Steganographia*, 18.

Carnivean

Variations: Carniveau, CARREAU

In the *Histoire admirable de la possession d'une penitente* (1612) written by the French inquisitor and exorcist Father Sebastien Michaelis, Carnivean is a FALLEN ANGEL, formerly a Prince of the Order of Powers; but since his fall he has become a demon of the Second Hierarchy. The demon of lewd and obscene behavior, he gives boldness, confidence, and strength to the people he tempts into acting shamelessly. Carnivean is the demon who is invoked by witches during their sabbath meetings. His personal adversary is St. John the Evangelist, patron of art dealers, booksellers, and printers. Carnivean was one of the demons who possessed Sister Seraphica of Loudun.

Sources: Aikin, *General Biography*, 493; Bayle, *Historical and Critical Dictionary*, 262; Crisafulli, *Go to Hell*, 244; Cuhulain, *Witch Hunts*, 206; Kaye, *Devils and Demons*, 580; Voltaire, *Works of M. de Voltaire*, 193.

Carnodiel

In *Theurgia Goetia*, the second book of the *Lemegeton*, Carnodiel, an AERIAL DEVIL, is one of the ten SERVITORS OF EMONIEL (see EMONIEL). Good-natured and willing to obey, Carnodiel lives in the woods and commands 1,320 lesser dukes and servitors.

Sources: Peterson, *Lesser Key of Solomon*, 97; Trithemius, *Steganographia*, 67.

Carnol

According to *Theurgia Goetia*, book two of the *Lemegeton*, Carnol is one of twelve named SERVITORS OF DEMORIEL (see DEMORIEL and DUKES OF HELL).

Sources: Eco, *Infinity of Lists*, 67; Peterson, *Lesser Key of Solomon*, 63.

Caromos

Caromos ("joy") is named as one of the twenty-two SERVITORS OF ARITON (see ARITON) in the *Sacred Magic of Abramelin the Mage*.

Sources: Belanger, *Dictionary of Demons*, 86; Ford, *Bible of the Adversary*, 94; Mathers, *Book of the Sacred Magic of Abramelin the Mage*, 105.

Caron

Variations: Charon, the Ferryman of the dead

From Etruscan mythology and first mentioned in the epic poem *Minyad*, Caron is described as an old helmsman with a beard, standing upon his boat as he ferries the souls of the dead into Hades. In Christian demonology he is one of the twenty-two SERVITORS OF ARITON (see ARITON).

Sources: Mathers, *Book of the Sacred Magic of Abramelin the Mage*, 108; Susej, *Demonic Bible*, 259; Toynbee, *Concise Dictionary of Proper Names and Notable Matters*, 119–20.

Carpid

In the *Theurgia Goetia*, book two of the *Lemegeton*, Carpid, a diurnal demon, is named as one of the fifteen Duke SERVITORS OF BARMIEL (see BARMIEL and DUKES OF HELL).

Sources: Peterson, *Lesser Key of Solomon*, 70; Trithemius, *Steganographia*, 18.

Carreau

Variations: CARNIVEAN

In the *Histoire admirable de la possession d'une penitente* (1612) written by the French inquisitor and exorcist Father Sebastien Michaelis, Carreau is a FALLEN ANGEL, formerly a Prince of the Order of Powers. The demon of mercilessness, he causes people to harden their hearts and can give a person the ability to control his emotions.

Sources: Cuhulain, *Witch Hunts*, 206; Davidson, *Dictionary of Demons*, 82; Kaye, *Devils and Demons*, 580; Rachleff, *Occult in Art*, 224; Susej, *Demonic Bible*, 70.

Caspaniel

Variations: Oaspeniel

In the *Theurgia Goetia*, the second book of the *Lemegeton*, Caspaniel is named as one of the ten SERVITORS OF EMONIEL (see EMONIEL). Good-natured and willing to obey his summoner, Caspaniel is an AERIAL DEVIL who commands 1,320 lesser dukes and servitors. He lives in the woods.

Sources: Guiley, *Encyclopedia of Demons and Demonology*, 72; Peterson, *Lesser Key of Solomon*, 97.

Caspiel

In Enochian lore, Caspiel ("wonders") is ranked as an emperor and is named as the King of the South. He commands 400 lesser dukes, 200 great dukes, 12 named chief dukes, and 1,000,200,000,000 servitors (see SERVITORS OF CASPIEL).

Source: Gettings, *Dictionary of Demons*, 232.

Cassiel

In *Ars Paulina*, the third book of the *Lemegeton*, Cassiel is listed as one of the eleven SERVITORS OF RAHAB (see RAHAB). His rank is given as chief.

Sources: Britten, *Art Magic*, 297, 298; Diagram, *Little Giant Encyclopedia*, 291; De Laurance, *Occult Secrets*, 41.

Catabolignes

According to Lambert (?) Campester, a sixteenth-century theologian, Catabolignes are the Etruscan demons of destruction. After they have concluded their business with a person, they abduct him and crush him to death.

Sources: Baskin, *Sorcerer's Handbook*, 128; Shepard, *Encyclopedia of Occultism and Parapsychology*, 211; Spence, *Encyclopedia of Occultism*, 95.

Catgara

Variations: Sitgara

Catgara is one of the twenty SERVITORS OF CAMUEL (see CAMUEL). A diurnal demon, when summoned he appears in a beautiful form and is very courteous.

Source: Peterson, *Lesser Key of Solomon*, 67.

Cauchemar

Variations: Cauquemare, Chauche Vieille, Coche-Mares, Cochomaren, Cochomares, Couchemache, Couchemal, Gaukemares, Macouche, "pressing demon," Quauquemaire, "witch-riding"

A vampiric demon or vampiric witch from French lore and similar to the ALP, the cauchemar ("nightmare") is a nocturnal demon who usually attacks evil people. It slips into the victim's bed at night and has intercourse with them, draining them of their life and sexual energies much the way an INCUBUS or SUCCUBUS would, enslaving its victim with sexual pleasure.

Signs of having been attacked are waking up with drool descending from either side of the mouth, feeling overly tired, having leg cramps, and evidence of nocturnal emission during the night.

To prevent a cauchemar attack put salt under the pillow before you go to sleep each night. Other methods include placing beans under the bed, keeping a broom in the corner of the bedroom, saying your prayers before bedtime each night, sleeping on your stomach, keeping blessed religious items in the room, keeping stones under the bed and in a circle around it, and lastly, the most modern adaptation of putting screens in the windows.

If you find that you are unable to prevent a cauchemar attack from occurring, or if no one comes in the room and drives it away by touching you, the experience can be fatal.

Sources: *Living Age*, Vol. 4, 495; Mackay, *Gaelic Etymology*, 305; Masters, *Eros and Evil*, 181; Rose, *Spirits, Faries, Gnomes*, 212.

Causub

Apollonius of Tyana's *Nuctemeron* (*Night Illuminated by Day*) names Causub as the demon of snake charming. He is most powerful during the seventh hour.

Sources: Davidson, *Dictionary of Angels*, 82; Lévi, *Transcendental Magic*, 392, 406.

Caym

Variations: CAIM, Camio, DANEL, Gamiel

Caym's name may be a German derivative of the biblical Cain. In Christian demonology Caym is ranked as a chief of Hell and grand president commanding thirty legions of demons. He is also said to be a FALLEN ANGEL as well as one of the seventy-two SPIRITS OF SOLOMON.

When summoned and answering questions, he appears as a long-haired, bearded, and mustached human male carrying a sword and wearing bracelets and neat trousers and boots. He also takes the guise of a blackbird and a man wearing a headdress adorned with peacock feathers. In art he is depicted with both hands turned upward, a fierce facial expression, and a collection of animals and bits of wood at his feet.

Caym can imitate the sound and call of any animal. He is exceptionally wise and witty, and can teach how to communicate with animals and water. He has the ability to foretell the future and is a highly skilled logician. His voice will come from the smoke of a burning braiser. He is most powerful during the first hour of the night.

It should be noted that as the angel DANEL, he was one of the CHIEF OF TENS who swore allegiance to SAMIAZA, rebelled against God, took a human wife, and fathered the NEPHILIM (see FALLEN ANGELS).

Sources: Black, *Book of Enoch*, 119; Collin de Plancy, *Dictionary of Witchcraft*, 37; De Laurence, *Lesser Key of Solomon, Goetia*, 39; Laurence, *Book of Enoch, the Prophet*, 6.

Cédon

Variations: Cedon

This demonic entity is often called upon during exorcism and cases of collective possession. Cédon was one of the eighteen demons who possessed Sister Jeanne des Anges in Loudun, France, in 1634 (see LOUDUN POSSESSION).

Sources: Aikin, *General Biography*, 493; Bayle, *Historical and Critical Dictionary*, 262; Hsia, *World of Catholic Renewal*, 151; Ramsay, *Westminster Guide to the Books of the Bible*, 349; Voltaire, *Works of M. de Voltaire*, 193.

Celsus

This demonic entity is often called upon during exorcism and cases of collective possession. Celsus was one of the eighteen demons who possessed Sister Jeanne des Anges in Loudun, France, in 1634 (see LOUDUN POSSESSION).

Sources: Aikin, *General Biography*, 493; Bayle, *Historical and Critical Dictionary*, 262; Hsia, *World of Catholic Renewal*, 151; Ramsay, *Westminster Guide to the Books of the Bible*, 349; Voltaire, *Works of M. de Voltaire*, 193.

Chaigidel

Variations: Chaigidiel, Ghagiel, Ghogiel, Ogiel, Zogiel

In Judaic mysticism, Chaigidel ("Confusion of the Power of God") is named as one of the twelve Qliphoth, the beings that are the cause of all evil and suffering in the world who appear as empty shells or husks or as black giants with snakes entwined around them.

It is said in the *Clavicula Salomonis* that Chaigidel was cast down from Heaven after Adam and Eve ate from the Tree of Knowledge. His personal adversaries are the Auphanim, the spirits of Wisdom. When you feel as if you are being attacked by him, it is advised to meditate upon a circle that is filled with grey and white dots.

Christian demonology places Chaigidel under the command of BEELZEBUB (see SERVITORS OF BEELZEBUB).

Sources: Godwin, *Godwin's Cabalistic Encyclopedia*, 219; Horne, *Sacred Books and Early Literature of the East*, 163; Lévi, *Mysteries of Magic*, 110.

Chalkydri

Variations: Chalkadry, Kalkydra, Khalkedras

Chalkydri ("brazen serpents") in Gnostic lore are large, purple, flying demonic beings. Described in *Enoch 2* as looking like dragons with a crocodile-like head, lion feet, and twelve wings, they are said to be 900 measures long. Some translations claim that they are as "big as 900 mountains" or as "large as a mountain."

Sources: Charles, *Book of the Secrets of Enoch*, 31; Davidson, *Dictionary of Angels*, 84; Ginzberg, *Legends of the Jews*, 159; Kulik, *Baruch*, 228.

Cham

Cham is named among the FALLEN ANGELS, formerly of the Order of Thrones. He is often called upon during exorcism and cases of collective possession, and was one of the eighteen demons who possessed Sister Jeanne des Anges in Loudun, France, 1634 (see LOUDUN POSSESSION).

Sources: Aikin, *General Biography*, 493; Bayle, *Historical and Critical Dictionary*, 262; Hsia, *World of Catholic Renewal*, 151; Ramsay, *Westminster Guide to the Books of the Bible*, 349; Voltaire, *Works of M. de Voltaire*, 193.

Chamo

Variations: CHAMOS, Chamosh, CHEMOSH

Originally the god of the Moabites, Chamo was demonized, made into a subordinate demon, and named as the lord high chamberlain of Hell and a knight of the Fly, which would place him under the command of BEELZEBUB.

Sources: Collin de Plancy, *Dictionary Infernal*, 128; Melton, *Encyclopedia of Occultism and Parapsychology*, 315; Shepard, *Encyclopedia of Occultism and Parapsychology*, 440.

Chamoriel

Theurgia Goetia, the second book of the *Lemegeton*, names Chamoriel as being in service under HYDRIEL, one of the eleven WANDERING PRINCES. Ranked as a chief duke, he commands 1,320 servitors of his own (see DUKES OF HELL). Although he is an AERIAL DEVIL, Chamoriel lives in or near the water in marshes or in wetlands. He may be summoned any time of the day or night and when he appears will do so as a serpent with the face of a virgin. Chamoriel has a reputation as being very courteous and willing to obey his summoner.

Sources: Peterson, *Lesser Key of Solomon*, 95; Trithemius, *Steganographia*, 122.

Chamos

In the *Sacred Magic of Abramelin the Mage*, book two, Chamos, a nocturnal demon, is named as one of the sixteen SERVITORS OF ASELIEL (see ASELIEL).

Sources: Agrippa, *Three Books of Occult Philosophy*, 555; Chambers, *Book of Days*, 723.

Chaniel

In the *Theurgia Goetia*, the second book of the *Lemegeton*, Chaniel is named as one of the twelve Chief Duke SERVITORS OF MACARIEL (see MACARIEL). An AERIAL DEVIL who commands four hundred servitors of his own, he is constantly on the move, never staying in any one place for long. When summoned, Chaniel can appear in any form but typically will choose to do so in the form of a dragon with a virgin's head. He has a reputation as being good-natured and willing to obey his summoner.

Sources: Peterson, *Lesser Key of Solomon*, 103; Trithemius, *Steganographia*, 141.

Charas

The *Sacred Magic of Abramelin the Mage*, book two, lists Charas, a diurnal demon, as one of the sixteen SERVITORS OF ASELIEL (see ASELIEL).

Sources: Belanger, *Dictionary of Demons*, 92; Peterson, *Lesser Key of Solomon*, 69.

Chariel

In the *Theurgia Goetia*, the second book of the *Lemegeton*, Chariel is listed as one of the twelve SERVITORS OF CASPIEL and as one of the eleven WANDERING PRINCES (see CASPIEL). Ranked as a chief duke, Chariel is an AERIAL DEVIL who lives in or near the water in marshes and wetlands (see DUKES OF HELL). He commands 1,320 servitors of his own. Both a diurnal and nocturnal demon, when summoned, he will appear as a serpent with a virgin's face. He is known to be very courteous and willing to obey. Most powerful on Mondays, Chariel has dominion over the moon.

Sources: Belanger, *Dictionary of Demons*, 92; Peterson, *Lesser Key of Solomon*, 95.

Charobiel

In the *Theurgia Goetia*, the second book of the *Lemegeton*, Charobiel is named as one of the ten Duke SERVITORS OF BYDIEL (see BYDIEL). Commanding 2,400 servitors of his own, Charobiel, an AERIAL DEVIL, appears before his summoner in an attractive form and is known to be good-natured and willing to obey.

Sources: Peterson, *Lesser Key of Solomon*, 105; Trithemius, *Steganographia*, 220.

Charoel

Variations: Caroel

Theurgia Goetia, the second book of the *Lemegeton*, names Charoel as one of the twelve SERVITORS OF MACARIEL (see MACARIEL). Ranked as a chief duke, he commands four hundred servitors as his own. Both a diurnal and nocturnal AERIAL DEVIL, Charoel, when summoned, may appear in a variety of forms but commonly chooses to do so as a dragon with a virgin's head. He is known to be good-natured and willing to obey those who summon him. Like all AERIAL DEVILS, he is constantly on the move, never staying in any one place for long.

Sources: Guiley, *Encyclopedia of Demons and Demonology*, 159; Peterson, *Lesser Key of Solomon*, 100, 103; Trithemius, *Steganographia*, 141.

Charontes

Charontes are the demonic servitors of CHARUN from Etruscan demonology. Demons of death, they carry hammers and when commanded by Charun, attack those individuals who are dying, using their hammers to finish them off.

Sources: Lurker, *Routledge Dictionary of Gods and Goddesses*, 42; Rose, *Spirits, Fairies, Gnomes, and Goblins*, 65.

Charun

Variations: Caronte, Charon, Charu, Karun, Xaru, Xarun

Charun ("first lion") is one of the many psychopompoi of the ancient Etruscan underworld and should not be confused with Charon from ancient Greek mythology. Charun is death personified and guards the gateway to the underworld. He commands the CHARONTES as well as all the demons of the Etruscan underworld.

Charun is depicted in art as having blue skin to emphasize his deathly pallor. He has boar tusks, fiery eyes, large lips, pointed ears, snakes around his arms, a vulture's nose, and large wings. Some sources also depict him as having red hair and a black beard. Oftentimes he is shown carrying his sacred weapon and the sign of his office, a large war hammer or mallet. He is in service under the gods of the Etruscan underworld, Mantus and his wife Mania. Charun's consort is CULSU.

Sources: Bonfante, *Etruscan Myths*, 74; De Grummond, *Etruscan Myth, Sacred History, and Legend*, 215–17; Maberry, *They Bite*, 336.

Chax

Variations: SCOX, Shanm, Shassm, SHAX, Shaz

First published in 1563, Johann Wierus's *De Praestigiis Daemonum*, a catalogue of the HIERARCHY OF DEMONS and their powers, named the demon Chax as a grand duke consisting of thirty legions, whereas a single legion consists of 6,666 members. Nocturnal and looking like a stork that speaks with a faint and hoarse voice, Chax is described as capable of being a faithful and obedient demon but is well known also to be a liar. Occasionally he will grant a good FAMILIAR to one who summons him. He is more commonly used to render a person blind and deaf as well as to remove their ability to comprehend or understand. A thief, Chax steals horses as well as the gold of kings, which he then hides for a period of 1,200 years.

Sources: De Laurence, *Lesser Key of Solomon, Goetia*, 36; Guiley, *Encyclopedia of Demons and Demonology*, 233; Icon, *Demons*, 178.

Cheitan

In Arabic, Cheitan translates to mean "The DEVIL" and is essentially just another name for SATAN. Culturally, however, Cheitan is a DJINN and said to be the demon of smoke.

Sources: Poinsot, *Complete Book of the Occult and Fortune Telling*, 379.

Chemos

Variations: CHEMOSH, Keemosh

Originally the Moabite god of lust and war, Christian demonology of the Middle Ages made him into the demon of flattery and ranked him as the Grand Chamberlain of Hell.

Sources: Hunter, *Sacred Biography*, 169; Rudwin, *Devil in Legend and Literature*, 84.

Chemosh

Variations: "the abomination of Moab," Baalmaon, CHAMOS

Originally the Moabite god of war, Christian demonology of the Middle Ages named Chemosh ("the destroyer," "fish-god" or "subduer") as the demon of war. He allowed his people to become the vassals of Israel, but after his anger passed he ordered Mesha to rebel and thereby regained Moabite independence. When it was essential to have his favor, human sacrifice was performed and offered to him.

It is interesting to note that Chemosh was at some level worshipped by King Solomon, even if only for the sake of politics, as 1 Kings 11:7 reads: "Then Solomon built a high place for Chemosh the detestable idol of Moab, on the mountain which is east of Jerusalem, and for Molech the detestable idol of the sons of AMMON."

Sources: Hastings, *Encyclopedia of Religion and Ethics*, 761; McClintock, *Cyclopaedia of Biblical*, 475–6; Van der Toorn, *Dictionary of Deities and Demons*, 188.

Chemosit, plural: chemosisiek

From the demonology of the Nandi people of Kenya come the chemosisiek ("the strikers"). These demonic, elemental spirits were never human or created in any way; they have always been in existence. They are described as being one-legged half-bird, half-man creatures that use their walking sticks to strike cattle and humans, causing them to fall ill with disease. Masai folklore describes the chemosisiek as having nine buttocks, one leg, and a mouth that glows like fire.

Sources: Ashley, *Complete Book of Devils and Demons*, 100; Huntingford, *Nandi of Kenya*, 136, 143; Royal Institute of International Affairs, *International Affairs*, Vol. 32, 248.

Chernobog

Variations: Cernobog, Chernabog, Chernevog, Crnobog, Czernobog, Czernobóg, Czernobuh, Diabolous, Zcernoboch, Zernebog, Zherneboh

From *Chronica Slavorum*, a 12th-century book written by Father Helmold, a German priest, comes the nocturnal demon of death, evil, misfortune, and night, Chernobog ("black god"). Chernobog was originally a god of winter in Baltic and Slavic mythologies whose name was demonized during the introduction of Christianity.

Sources: Littleton, *Gods, Goddesses, and Mythology*, 1318–9; Lumpkin, *Fallen Angels, the Watchers, and the Origin of Evil*, 126; Maberry, *Cryptopedia*, 212; Turner, *Dictionary of Ancient Deities*, 135.

Cherti

Variations: Kherty

In the mythology of the ancient Egyptians, Cherti ("Lower One") was the ferryman of the dead. The *Pyramid Texts* describe this demonic god as looking like a man with the head of a ram. Ranked as a chieftain, he was the guardian of the pharaoh's tomb. Cherti lives in the underworld, Duat. His personal adversary is the god Re; the main center of worship was in Letopolis, northwest of Memphis.

Sources: Haney, *Russian Wondertales*, xv–xvi; Lurker, *Routledge Dictionary of Gods and Goddesses*, 43; Stookey, *Thematic Guide to World Mythology*, 109.

Cherufe

In Mapuche mythology there is a demon named Cherufe that lives in the magma pools of the volcanoes in Chile. Cherufe was said to cause earthquakes and volcanic eruptions unless offered a virgin human, who would be thrown into his volcano as a sacrifice. After consuming the choicest parts of his offering, he would ignite the head of his victim and launch it from the volcano.

It should be noted that there are actually some cryptozoologists who believe that this demon is based on actual sightings of an undiscovered and undocumented creature that can survive in pools of molten rock.

Sources: Faron, *Mapuche Indians of Chile*, 70; Lurker, *Dictionary of Gods and Goddesses*, 81; Maberry, *Vampire Universe*, 72; Porterfield, *Chile*, 44.

Chevaliers De L'enfer

French demonologists from the late Middle Ages have reported chevaliers de l'enfer, a type of diurnal demon, as being more powerful than demons with no title or rank, but not as powerful as those with title and rank.

Sources: Shepard, *Encyclopedia of Occultisim and Parapsychology*, 224; Spence, *Encyclopedia of Occultisim*, 1049.

Chief of Tens

In Enochian lore the *Book of Enoch* (1 Enoch 6:4–8:1) names twenty archangels with the rank of Chief of Tens: ANANEL (Anane, Anan'el), ARAKIBA, ARMAROS (ARMERS), ASAEL (Asa'el), Baraqijal (Baraq'el, SARAKNYAL), BATAREL (Batraal), DANEL (Dani'el), Ezeqeel (Azkee, EZEKEEL), JOMJAEL (Yomi'el, Yomyael), Kokabiel (AKIBEEL, Kawkabel, Kokab'el), Rameel (Ramt'el), RAMIEL (Ra'ma'el, Ramuel), SAMIAZA (Samyaza), SAMSAPEEL (Samsaveel), SARIEL (Arazyal), SATAREL (ERTAEL), TAMIEL ("perfection of God"), TURAEL (Turi'el), URAKABARAMEEL, and ZAQIEL (Zavebe).

These were the angels who initially decided to act upon the desire they felt for the human females. Knowing that there would be consequences for their actions and afraid to act individually, they gathered on top of a mountain they named Mount Hermond and collectively took a vow to one another that they all act upon their desires. Each of the Chief of Tens and the GRIGORI under them, two hundred in all, then chose for themselves a wife from which the race known as the NEPHILIM were born. Some of the Chief of Tens then went on to share with mankind knowledge that God had forbidden them to share, such as astrology, astrometry, geology, herbology, how to counter magical spells, magical incantations, and the art of weapon making, to name but a few. When God discovered their treachery, He punished them all, albeit some more than others. The Lord was outraged that his angels had defiled their bodies with humans but His true anger lay in the fact that they had created, in His eyes, unclean offspring.

There are many sources that list the names of the GRIGORI, but the *Book of Enoch* only names the twenty Chief of Tens. Other names mentioned as being one of the two hundred GRIGORI are: AGNIEL, ANMAEL, Araqiel, Araquiel, ARAZIEL, ASBEEL, Azael ("whom God strengthens"), AZAZEL, AZAZYEL, AZIEL ("whom God consoles"), Baraqel, Chazaqiel, EXAEL, Gadreel, Kakabel, KASADYA, Kashdejan, PENEMUE, Penemuel, Pharmoros, SAMIEL, SATANAIL, Shamsiel, TALMAIEL, URIEL, and USIEL (see also FALLEN ANGELS).

Sources: Black, *Book of Enoch*, 119; Davidson, *Dictionary of Angels*, 206; Laurence, *Book of Enoch, the Prophet*, 6; Lumpkin, *Fallen Angels, the Watchers, and the Origins of Evil*, 31; Martínez, *Dead Sea Scrolls Translated*, 247; Voltaire, *Essays and Criticisms*, 106.

Chiton

Variations: SEIKTHA

In Burmese demonology there is a type of demon known as a chiton that lives in groves, shrines, and trees. On occasion, one of these demons has been known to take on the role of village guardian or teacher. A shrine that has been made to it must be well maintained and supplied with drinks and food or it will abandon the village. These cults had become so widespread that at one time the chiton almost achieved godhead.

Sources: Rose, *Spirits, Fairies, Gnomes, and Goblins*, 287; Shepard, *Encyclopedia of Occultism and Parapsychology*, 187; Spence, *Encyclopedia of Occultism*, 81.

Chobaliel

In Enochian lore Chobaliel was named as one of the two hundred FALLEN ANGELS who swore allegiance to SAMIAZA and rebelled against God. He lusted after and took a human wife, fathering the NEPHILIM.

Source: Davidson, *Dictionary of Angels*, 88.

Chochoi

Variation: Yuqui

Chochoi is a demon that is mentioned in the demonology from Central Bolivia.

Sources: Jones, *Evil in Our Midst*, 108–9; Stearman, *Yuquí*, 131.

Chomiel

Variations: Chamiel, Chamiol

The *Theurgia Goetia*, the second book of the *Lemegeton*, names Chomiel as one of the twelve SERVITORS OF DEMORIEL (see DEMORIEL and DUKES OF HELL). Ranked as a chief duke, he commands 1,140 servitors of his own.

Sources: McLean, *Treatise of Angel Magic*, 54; Peterson, *Lesser Key of Solomon*, 63.

Chordeva

Variations: Chordewa, Cordewa

From the hill tribe of the Oraon people in Bengal, India, comes the vampiric demon or witch known as chordeva ("thief-demon"). It shape-shifts its soul into the form of a cat that then goes out and preys upon the sick by stealing their food and poisoning whatever small morsels it leaves behind. It is for this reason that all cats are kept away from a sick person even though the demon can be recognized for what it is by a very specific type of mewing sound it makes. While utilizing this form, the chordeva can kill a person simply by licking their lips.

Even though the chordeva has the ability to shape-shift into a werecat, it is still only as strong as the average person; however, while in this form it has the ability to place a person into a trance by making direct eye contact with them. It is completely indestructible while in its werecat form.

The chordeva is repelled by water of any kind, as well as by hawthorn. Any means that would kill a normal cat will also kill the demon when it is in its cat form. Any damage that is done to the cat form will also instantly appear on the chordeva's human body. When the demon is in its human guise, an iron or wooden stake driven through its heart will kill it, as will prolonged exposure to sunlight.

Sources: Briggs, *The Chamars*, 134; Crooke, *Religion and Folklore of Northern India*, 208; Meyer, *Sexual Life in Ancient India*, 392; Sinha, *Religious Life in Tribal India*, 41.

Choronzon

Variations: 333, Coronzom, Coronzon, Three-hundred thirty-three

The demon Choronzon first appeared in the writing of Edward Kelley in the 16th century and again later in John Dee's Enochian magic system. In the 20th century Aleister Crowley named this demon in the Holy Books of Thelema, the religious philosophy of Thelema system that he developed. Crowley claims that he summoned up this demon in the Algerian desert and then, some would say, it possessed the man for the rest of his life. When the demon appeared, he was shouting the words that would allegedly open the gates of hell: "Zazas, Zazas, Nasatanada, Zazas."

Choronzon, the demon of dispersion, is said to be the last obstacle between the adept and enlightenment. His sign is that of the crocodile.

Sources: Ford, *Book of the Witch Moon Chorozon Edition*, 30–1, 48; Laycock, *Complete Enochian Dictionary*, 98; Symonds, *Magic of Aleister Crowley*, 202–4.

Chort

Variations: Chert, Didko, Haspyda, Irod, Kutsyi

In Slavic demonology, Chort was born the son of the god CHERNOBOG and the goddess Mara. He has horns, hooves, a pig face, and a skinny tail. Chort allies himself with witches and warlocks.

Sources: Haney, *Russian Wondertales*, xv–xvi; Ouspensky, *Talks with a Devil*, 2; Putney, *Russian Devils and Diabolic Conditionality*, 57.

Chremo

In the *Theurgia Goetia*, the second book of the *Lemegeton*, Chremo is one of the ten SERVITORS OF BYDIEL (see BYDIEL). A duke, he commands 2,400 servitors of his own. Chremo is an AERIAL DEVIL who appears in an attractive form and is known to be good-natured and willing to obey his summoner.

Source: Peterson, *Lesser Key of Solomon*, 105.

Chrubas

Chrubas is one of the twenty Duke SERVITORS OF SYMIEL (see SYMIEL). A diurnal demon, he is known to be very good-natured and quick to obey his summoner. Chrubas commands seven hundred twenty servitors.

Sources: Peterson, *Lesser Key of Solomon*, 88; Trithemius, *Steganographia*, 42.

Chuiaels

Variations: Cijurreyls

The chuiaels is a vampiric demon that comes from Hindu lore. Created whenever a mother dies in childbirth, this demon looks like a beautiful woman, and it uses its lovely appearance to lure men into its bed. Once there, the chuiaels, much like the SUCCUBUS, has a reputation for being an exceedingly good lover according to the few men who have been lucky enough to survive the experience. These men claim that during the act of fellatio the demon literally drains away their life.

Source: Masters, *Eros and Evil*.

Church Condemned Angels

In the Church Council of 745, seven angels were removed from the list of angels recognized by the church. These angels were Inias, Raguel (RAGUHEL), Saboac, Simiel (Semibel), Tubuas, Tubuel (TOBIEL), and URIEL (Orbiel). Although their removal from the list does not automatically make them demons, according to legend, the angel Inias took the news badly and became an enemy of the Faith.

Sources: Guiley, *Encyclopedia of Angels*, 312; Hugo, *Toilers of the Sea*, Vol. 1, 6; Stafford, *Function of Divine Manifestations*, 10; Webster, *Encyclopedia of Angels*, 135.

Churibal

Theurgia Goetia, the second book of the *Lemegeton*, tells us that Churibal is one of the twelve SERVITORS OF DEMORIEL (see DEMORIEL and DUKES OF HELL). A chief duke and AERIAL DEVIL, he commands 1,140 servitors.

Sources: Peterson, *Lesser Key of Solomon*, 63; Trithemius, *Steganographia*, 115.

Chuschi

Variations: Cuschi

The *Sacred Magic of Abramelin the Mage* names Chuschi ("silent") as one of the one hundred eleven SERVITORS OF AMAYMON, ARITON, ORIENS, AND PAYMON (see AMAYMON, ARITON, ORIENS, and PAYMON).

Sources: Mathers, *Book of the Sacred Magic of Abramelin the Mage*, 105, 113; Von Worms, *Book of Abramelin*, 255.

Cihuateteo

Variations: Ciuatateo, Ciuateteo, Civapipltin, Civatateo

A type of vampiric, demonic demigoddess from the Aztec people of ancient Mexico, a cihuateteo ("right honorable mother") is created when a mother dies in childbirth or a child is stillborn. They fall under the command of the goddess of evil, lust, and sorcery, Tlazolteotl. Cihuateteo are depicted as having their arms, face, and hands as white as chalk. They live in the jungle, keeping to the dark places, as they are painfully susceptible to sunlight; long-term exposure to it will destroy them. Cihuateteo feed off lone travelers that they catch unaware as they fly through the jungle on their brooms. They prefer the blood of infants. The bite of the cihuateteo has a paralytic effect, allowing them to more easily feed.

Sources: Aguilar-Moreno, *Handbook of Life*, 147, 199, 258; Kanellos, *Handbook of Hispanic Culture*, 227; Salas, *Soldaderas*, 5–6, 34, 95; Stefoff, *Vampires, Zombies, and Shape-shifters*, 17; Turner, *Dictionary of Ancient Deities*, 129.

Cimejes

Variations: Cimeries, Cimeyes, Cymries, KIMARIS, Tuvries

Ars Goetia names Cimejes ("darkness of god") as a marquis who commands twenty legions of demons as well as all of the demons of Africa (see MARQUIS OF HELL). He is described as being strong and powerful looking, riding upon an equally fine black horse. He is summoned for his assistance in making a man into a good soldier and warrior and helps in the discovery of lost treasures. He also teaches logic, perfect grammar, and public speaking.

The name Cimejes possibly derived from the name Cumerians (Britons or possibly Cimmerians), mentioned by Homer as a warlike people.

Sources: De Laurence, *Lesser Key of Solomon, Goetia*, 43; McLean, *Treatise of Angel Magic*, 53; Scot, *Discoverie of Witchcraft*, 225

Cin

Variations: Cinler

Cin is a Turkish word used to describe a DJINN. They are invisible AERIAL DEVILS and considered to be the demons of madness.

Source: Eberhart, *Mysterious Creatures*, 136.

Cirecas

In the *Theurgia Goetia*, the second book of the *Lemegeton*, Cirecas is one of the sixteen SERVITORS OF GEDEIL (see DUKES OF HELL and GEDEIL). A nocturnal duke, this AERIAL DEVIL, when summoned, is very courteous, doting, and willing to serve.

Sources: Guiley, *Encyclopedia of Demons and Demonology*, 94; Peterson, *Lesser Key of Solomon*, 72.

Citipati

Variations: Charnel Lords, Chitipati

In Tibetan Buddhist folklore and demonology, Citipati means the "Funeral Pyre Lord" or "Lords of the Cemetery." The demon of the graveyard, Citipati was created when two monks who were so deep in a meditative trance were beheaded by a thief, they were not aware of their own deaths. They vowed eternal vengeance against thieves. The Citipati are depicted as dancing skeletons, usually a male and female, surrounded by flames; they symbolize the eternal dance of death and perfect awareness.

Sources: Bunce, *Encyclopaedia of Buddhist Deities, Demigods, Godlings, Saints, and Demons*, 107; Illes, *Encyclopedia of the Spirits*, 336; Linrothe, *Demonic Divine*, 126–8.

Ciuapipiltin

Variations: Totecujiooan Cioapipilti

In ancient Mexico, when an Aztec noblewoman died giving birth to her first child, she would become a type of vampiric, demonic demigoddess known as a Ciuapipiltin ("princess honored woman"). Like her less noble counterpart, the CIHUATETEO, the Ciuapipiltin fall under the command of the goddess Tlazolteotl, and like her followers, paint their arms, faces, and hands white. Truth be told, they are similar to the Cihuateteo in every way except for the fact that the Ciuapipiltin are royalty and can be beseeched not to attack. If offerings of bread or small bits of meteorites are left near an infant, Ciuapipiltin will accept them in place of the child's life. At one time temples were constructed at crossroads and at places where murders were committed to honor the Ciuapipiltin. Offerings of bread and meteorites were left for them in these places too, in the hopes of staving off attacks on travelers.

Sources: Bancroft, *Works of Hubert Howe Bancroft*, 362, 364, 366; Kanellos, *Handbook of Hispanic Cultures*, 227; Turner, *Dictionary of Ancient Deities*, 130.

Ciupipiltin

In ancient Mexico, when a woman died giving birth to her first child, she would become a type of vampiric, demonic demigoddess known as a ciupipiltin ("princess"). Like her noble counterpart, the CIUAPIPILTIN, the ciupipiltin falls under the command of the goddess Tlazolteotl, the goddess of sorcery, lust, and evil. They, like her followers, paint their arms, faces, and hands white. Ciupipiltin are similar to the ciuapipiltin in every way except for the fact that the ciupipiltin are not royalty and cannot be beseeched not to attack. Ciupipiltin have a paralytic bite, which they use when attacking infants, ensuring that they do not cry out, allowing the demon to feed by draining off their blood in peace. Ciupipiltin have the ability to fly, either of their own power or upon a broom. They are susceptible to sunlight and if left exposed to it will eventually be destroyed.

Sources: Bancroft, *Works of Hubert Howe Bancroft*, 362, 364, 366; Kanellos, *Handbook of Hispanic Cultures*, 227; Shepard, *Encyclopedia of Occultism and Parapsychology*, 1092; Spence, *Encyclopedia of Occultism*, 276.

Claniel

Variations: CHANIEL

In the *Theurgia Goetia*, the second book of the

Lemegeton, the AERIAL DEVIL Claniel is named as one of the twelve SERVITORS OF MACARIEL (see MACARIEL). Ranked as a chief duke, he commands four hundred servitors of his own. Claniel may be summoned any time of the day or night and will appear before his summoner in any one of a variety of forms; however, he most commonly appears as a dragon with a virgin's head. Said to be good-natured and willing to obey his summoner, Claniel is constantly on the move, never staying in any one place for long.

Sources: Belanger, *Dictionary of Demons*, 95; Peterson, *Lesser Key of Solomon*, 103; Trithemius, *Steganographia*, 141.

Clauneck

The *Grimoirium Verum* (*Grimoire of Truth*), allegedly written by Alibek the Egyptian in 1517, names the demon Clauneck as one of the eighteen SERVITORS OF C (see SYRACH). Well loved by LUCIFER, this demon is summoned because he has the ability to bestow wealth, either by bringing money over a great distance or by assisting in the discovery of hidden treasure. Clauneck is the demon of wealth, known to be obedient to his summoners, but only to those who show him the proper respect.

Sources: Collin de Plancy, *Dictionnaire Infernal*, 133; Kuriakos, *Grimoire Verum*, 17; Masters, *Devil's Dominion*, 130; Sabellicus, *Magia Pratica*, 35.

Cleansi

Variations: Chansi

In *Theurgia Goetia*, the second book of the *Lemegeton*, Cleansi is listed as one of the fifteen Duke SERVITORS OF BARMIEL (see BARMIEL and DUKES OF HELL). He is a diurnal demon.

Sources: Peterson, *Lesser Key of Solomon*, 70; Trithemius, *Steganographia*, 18.

Cleraca

The *Sacred Magic of Abramelin the Mage* names the demon Cleraca ("clerical") as one of the ten SERVITORS OF AMAYMON AND ARITON (see AMAYMON and ARITON). The name Cleraca is possibly a hybrid, coming from the combined Greek word *klerikos* and Latin word *clericus*.

Sources: Ford, *Bible of the Adversary*, 90; Mathers, *Book of Sacred Magic of Abramelin the Mage*, 106.

Clisthert

The *Grimoirium Verum* (*Grimoire of Truth*), allegedly written by Alibek the Egyptian in 1517, names the demon Clisthert as one of the eighteen SERVITORS OF SYRACH (see SYRACH). He is an inferior demon who can be summoned any time of the day or night. He has the ability to make day become the night.

Sources: Masters, *Devil's Dominion*, 130; Sabellicus, *Magia Pratica*, 35.

Clootie

The name Clootie is essentially another name for the DEVIL. In the Scottish language, *cloot* translates to mean a cleft hoof, a characteristic of the Devil.

Sources: Forsyth, *Demonologia*, 309; Henderson, *Scottish Fairy Belief*, 98, 214; Rose, *Spirits, Fairies, Gnomes, and Goblins*, 26.

Cms

According to Enochian lore, Cms is a CACODAEMON. His counterpart is the angel Msal (see ENOCHIAN CACODAEMONS).

Sources: Chopra, *Academic Dictionary of Mythology*, 71; Icon, *Counterparts*, 195; Kelley, *Complete Enochian Dictionary*, 96.

Cobel

Cobel ("chain") is named as one of the sixty-five SERVITORS OF KORE AND MAGOTH in the *Sacred Magic of Abramelin the Mage*, book two.

Sources: Ford, *Bible of the Adversary*, 92; Mathers, *Book of the Sacred Magic of Abramelin the Mage*, 118.

Cocornifer

Cocornifer ("hornbearer") was a word used in the Middle Ages for LUCIFER. It was a belief at that time that if a person said the name "Lucifer" aloud it would call the DEVIL to them, so oftentimes people made up nicknames to use when referencing the Devil.

Sources: Nicoll, *Masks, Mimes and Miracles*, 188; Russell, *Lucifer*, 249.

Codriel

The *Ars Paulina*, book three of the *Lemegeton*, names Codriel as one of the twelve SERVITORS OF AMENADIEL (see AMENADIEL and DUKES OF HELL). A chief duke, he commands three thousand servitors of his own.

Sources: Belanger, *Dictionary of Demons*, 96; Peterson, *Lesser Key of Solomon*, 62; Trithemius, *Steganographia*, 54.

Coelen

According to the *Sacred Magic of Abramelin the Mage*, Coelen ("Heavens") is one of the one hundred eleven SERVITORS OF AMAYMON, ARITON, ORIENS, AND PAYMON (see AMAYMON, ARITON, ORIENS, and PAYMON).

Sources: Mathers, *Book of the Sacred Magic of Abramelin the Mage*, 113; Susej, *Demonic Bible*, 256.

Colvam

In the *Sacred Magic of Abramelin the Mage*, book two, Colvam ("shame") is named as one of the sixty-five SERVITORS OF KORE AND MAGOTH.

Sources: Mathers, *Book of the Sacred Magic of Abramelin the Mage*, 118; Susej, *Demonic Bible*, 258.

Comadiel

The *Ars Paulina*, the third book of the *Lemegeton*, names Comadiel as one of the two hundred SERVITORS OF VEGUANIEL (see VEGUANIEL).

Sources: Peterson, *Lesser Key of Solomon*, 113; Trithemius, *Steganographia*, 91; Waite, *The Book of Ceremonial Magic*, 67.

Compusae PHOO

A compusae is an infernal, immortal vampiric demon. Essentially a SUCCUBUS, it was never human.

Source: Masters, *Eros and Evil*, 182.

Conferentes

A conferentes is a demonic god or type of INCUBUS.

Sources: Shepard, *Encyclopedia of Occultism and Parapsychology*, 258; Spence, *Encyclopedia of Occultism*, 109; Trithemius, *Steganographia*, 374.

Congo Zandor

Variations: Congo Savanne

Congo Zandor is a *gede*, a type of spirit of death and sexuality that is mentioned in Haitian vodun rites. He is an aggressive, malevolent, and violent blood-drinker.

Sources: Ashley, *Complete Book of Devils and Demons*, 66; University of California, Berkeley, *American Indian Quarterly*, Vol. 31, 553.

Cop

According to Enochian lore, Cop is a CACODAEMON. His counterpart is the angel Opna (see ENOCHIAN CACODAEMONS).

Sources: Chopra, *Academic Dictionary of Mythology*, 73; Laycock, *Complete Enochian Dictionary*, 97.

Corcaron

Corcaron ("noisy or "tumultuous") is named in the *Sacred Magic of Abramelin the Mage*, book two, as one of the fifty-three SERVITORS OF ASHTAROTH AND ASMODEUS (see ASHTAROTH and ASMODEUS).

Sources: Von Worms, *Book of Abramelin*, 247, 256.

Corilon

In the *Sacred Magic of Abramelin the Mage*, book two, Corilon is named as one of the forty-nine SERVITORS OF BEELZEBUB (see BEELZEBUB).

Sources: Ford, *Bible of the Adversary*, 93; Mathers, *Book of the Sacred Magic of Abramelin the Mage*, 120.

Corodon

In the *Sacred Magic of Abramelin the Mage*, book two, Corodon is named as one of the sixty-five SERVITORS OF KORE AND MAGOTH.

Sources: Ford, *Bible of the Adversary*, 92; Mathers, *Book of the Sacred Magic of Abramelin the Mage*, 107.

Corson

Variations: GORSON

Christian demonology has ranked the demon Corson as the bailiff for ABEZETHIBOU but is under the command of GERYON (see SERVITORS OF ABEZETHIBOU). He is also listed as the king of the South (or West, sources conflict). Corson, one of the FOUR PRINCIPAL KINGS, is also named as one of the seventy-two SPIRITS OF SOLOMON. It is ill-advised to ever summon this particular demon unless it is of great importance.

Sources: Icon, *Demons*, 145; Spence, *Encyclopedia of Occultism*, 109; Susej, *Demonic Bible*, 157.

Cotiel

In the *Theurgia Goetia*, the second book of the *Lemegeton*, the FALLEN ANGEL Cotiel is named as one of the sixteen Chief SERVITORS OF GEDEIL (see DUKES OF HELL and GEDEIL). He is a diurnal demon.

Sources: Peterson, *Lesser Key of Solomon*, 72.

Counts of Hell

There are seventeen named counts mentioned in the various grimoires. They are AYPEROR, AYPEROS, BARBATOS, BIFRONS, BOTIS, CAMIEL, FURFUR, IPES, MARAX, MURMUR, ORIAS, RÄUM, RENOVE, RONOBE, SALEOS, VINÉ, and ZAEBOS. Counts are considered to be demons of the Superior Order. The number of legions and servitors they command varies. They may be summoned any time of the day or night provided it is done in a wild and unused area.

Sources: Dix, *Black Baron*, 269; Icon, *Demons*, 176; Scott, *London Magazine*, Vol. 5, 378; Spence, *Encyclopedia of Occultism*, 110; *Transactions and Proceedings of the American Philological Association*, Vol. 101, 428; Von Goethe, *Goethe's Letters to Zelter*, 377.

Cozbi

Born the daughter of Zur, chief of the Midianites, Cozbi was one of the women killed when Moses gave the order to execute those guilty of the sin of whoredom in the town of BAAL-PEOR. She and an Israeli man were stabbed through the stomachs with a javelin while she was being introduced into his family. Cozbi and the other Midianite women were blamed for tempting Israeli men to commit the sin of idolatry. Her story is told in the book of Numbers 25:15.

Cozbi, whose name means "deceitful," "liar," "my lie," or "sliding away" in the Midianite language, became a lesser demon and the demon of idolatry. She is under the service of GERYON.

Sources: Masters, *Eros and Evil*, 118; Richards, *Every Woman in the Bible*, 76.

Cresil

Variations: GRESSIL

In Father Sebastien Michaelis's book, *Histoire admirable de la possession d'une penitente* (1612), Cresil is named as the demon of impurity and slovenliness.

Sources: Ashley, *Complete Book of Devils and Demons*, 58; Rachleff, *Occult in Art*, 224.

Crest of Dragons

Crest of Dragons is a three-headed dragon with human hands that was mentioned in the *Testament of Solomon*; he was made to make bricks for the construction of the king's temple. He is known to make unborn children blind, make children deaf and mute, and cause men to have seizures. This demon is frustrated by the writing of Golgotha.

Source: Ashe, *Qabalah*, 44.

Criminatores

Variations: Exploratores

Criminatores ("accusers" or "slanderers") is one of the eight orders of demons. As a demonic order, the Criminatores are evil archangels and ARCHDEMONs, the demons of calumny; they are under the domain of ASHTAROTH and Ishtar-Astaroth, better known as the WHORE OF BABYLON.

Sources: Coleman, *Dictionary of Mythology*, 254; McLean, *Treatise on Angel Magic*, 70.

Crocell

Variations: Crocelli, Crokell, PROCEL, Procell, Pucel

In the *Lemegeton*, Crocell is a FALLEN ANGEL, formerly a prince of the Order of Powers. He is named as one of the DUKES OF HELL and one of the seventy-two SPIRITS OF SOLOMON. As duke he commands forty-eight legions of demons. When summoned, he appears like an angel. He has the ability to instantly make boiling water freeze solid. He can also make the sound of rushing water and discover baths. He speaks mystically of hidden things and can teach geometry and any of the liberal sciences.

Sources: Crowley, *The Goetia*, 53; De Laurence, *Lesser Key of Solomon, Goetia*, 38; DuQuette, *Key to Solomon's Key*, 185; Peterson, *Lesser Key of Solomon*, 29.

Crucham

In the *Theurgia Goetia*, the second book of the *Lemegeton*, Crucham, an AERIAL DEVIL, is named as one of the ten SERVITORS OF BYDIEL (see BYDIEL). As a duke, he commands 2,400 servitors and when he is summoned he appears in an attractive form. He is said to be good-natured and willing to obey his summoner.

Sources: Peterson, *Lesser Key of Solomon*, 105.

Cruhiel

In the *Theurgia Goetia*, the second book of the *Lemegeton*, Cruhiel, an AERIAL DEVIL, is named as one of the ten SERVITORS OF EMONIEL (see EMONIEL). As a duke, Cruhiel commands 1,320 lesser dukes and servitors (see DUKES OF HELL). He lives in the woods, is good-natured, and is willing to obey his summoner.

Sources: Peterson, *Lesser Key of Solomon*, 97, Trithemius, *Steganographia*, 126.

Csc

According to Enochian lore, Csc is a CACODAEMON. His angelic counterpart is unknown (see ENOCHIAN CACODAEMONS).

Sources: Chopra, *Academic Dictionary of Mythology*, 75; Laycock, *Complete Enochian Dictionary*, 99.

Csúz

In Hungarian Magyar demonology, Csúz ("joint gout") is a demon of illness, specifically gout.

Sources: Kõiva, *Folk Belief Today*, 139; Orszagh, *Magyar*, 324.

Cubiel

The *Sacred Magic of Abramelin the Mage*, book two, names the nocturnal demon Cubiel as one of the sixteen SERVITORS OF ASELIEL (see ASELIEL).

Sources: Peterson, *Lesser Key of Solomon*, 70.

Culsu

Variations: Cul

In Etruscan mythology Culsu is the demon of gateways; she guards the entrance to the Underworld. Culsu is described as a female demon holding a burning torch and a pair of scissors. She is often depicted in art next to Culsans, the god of doors and doorways.

Sources: Bonfante, *Etruscan Myths*, 74; Lurker, Routledge, *Dictionary of Gods and Goddesses*, 45; Rose, *Spirits, Fairies, Gnomes and Goblins*, 74.

Cumariel

In the *Theurgia Goetia*, the second book of the *Lemegeton*, Cumariel, an AERIAL DEVIL, is named as one of the fifteen SERVITORS OF ICOSIEL (see ICOSIEL). A chief duke, he commands 2,200 servitors. Cumariel is most easily summoned from inside a house, as he has a fondness for them. He may be summoned any time of the day or night. He is good-natured and will obediently do whatever is asked of him by his summoner. Cumariel has dominion over the planet Mars.

Sources: Peterson, *Lesser Key of Solomon*, 99; Trithemius, *Steganographia*, 69.

Cumerzel

Variations: Cumeriel

In the *Theurgia Goetia*, the second book of the *Lemegeton*, Cumerzel is named as one of the twelve Duke SERVITORS OF CARNESIEL (see CARNESIEL and DUKES OF HELL). He commands between ten and three hundred servants.

Sources: Guiley, *Encyclopedia of Demons and Demonology*, 37; Peterson, *Lesser Key of Solomon*, 59.

Cuniali

In Apollonius of Tyana's book *Nuctemeron* (*Night Illuminated by Day*), Cuniali is named as the demon of association. He is most powerful during the eighth hour of the day.

Sources: Davidson, *Dictionary of Angels*, 90; Lévi, *Transcendental Magic*, 392.

Curiel

In the *Sacred Magic of Abramelin the Mage*, book two, Curiel is named as one of the SERVITORS OF ASELIEL (see ASELIEL). He is a nocturnal demon.

Sources: Agrippa, *Three Books of Occult Philosophy*, 553, Peterson, *Lesser Key of Solomon*, 69.

Curson

Variations: Pursan, PURSON

In the *Ars Goetia*, the first book of the *Lemegeton*, the *Lesser Key of Solomon*, Curson, an AERIAL DEVIL, is named as a KING OF HELL. A FALLEN ANGEL, formerly of the Order of Thrones, Curson commands twenty-two legions. He appears to his summoner as a man with the face of a lion carrying a viper in his hand while riding upon a bear. All around him are the sounds of many trumpets being played. He is summoned because he will answer questions honestly that are asked of him regarding the earth and its creation. He can assume a human body, tell where treasure is hidden, give good FAMILIARs, and can tell of past, present, and future events.

Sources: Davidson, *Dictionary of Angels*, 262; De Laurence, *Lesser Key of Solomon, Goetia*, 28; Peterson, *Lesser Key of Solomon*, 261, 262.

Cus

According to Enochian lore, Cus is a CACODAEMON. His counterpart is the angel Ussn (see ENOCHIAN CACODAEMONS).

Sources: Chopra, *Academic Dictionary of Mythology*, 76; Laycock, *Complete Enochian Dictionary*, 99.

Cusiel

In the *Theurgia Goetia*, the second book of the *Lemegeton*, Cusiel, a diurnal demon, is named as one of the sixteen SERVITORS OF ASYRIEL (see ASYRIEL). A chief duke, he commands twenty servitors of his own. When summoned, he is good-natured and willing to obey.

Sources: Belanger, *Dictionary of Demons*, 101; Guiley, *Dictionary of Demons and Demonology*, 20; Peterson, *Lesser Key of Solomon*, 73–4, 77.

Cusriel

In the *Theurgia Goetia*, the second book of the *Lemegeton*, Cusriel, a nocturnal demon, is named as one of the sixteen SERVITORS OF ASYRIEL (see ASYRIEL). When summoned, he is good-natured and willing to obey.

Source: Peterson, *Lesser Key of Solomon*, 74.

Czarnobog

Variations: Bielbog, Black God Koschey; Black God of the Dead; Cernobog; Chernevog; CHERNOBOG; Crnobog; Czarnobóg; Czerneboch; Czernobuh; God of Chaos and Night; Husband of Morena; Koschey; Ruler of Nav; Son of Zmey; Zcernoboch

Originally from Slavic mythology, Czarnobog ("black god"), a demonic god, was demonized during the introduction of Christianity. Named as the demon of evil, darkness, and night, he is similar to AHRIMAN, the Spirit of Evil. His personal adversary is Bylebog, the White God of the waxing year.

Sources: Hyatt, *Book of Demons*, 56; Sykes, *Who's Who in Non-Classical Mythology*, 33, 50, 179; Turner, *Dictionary of Ancient Deities*, 137.

Dabog

Variations: Daba, Dabo, Dajbog, Dajob, Dajboi, Dazbog, Dazbóg, Dažbog, Dazh'bog, Dazhbog, Dazhdbog, Hors Dazhbog, Hromi, Hromi Daba (Lame Daba), Lame, "shepherd of wolves," "the silver tsar," Vid, Zuariscici ("son of Svarog")

Dabog was originally a sun god and possibly a cultural hero in Slavic lore. The Russian epic *Slovo o polku Igoreve*, written in the 13th century, uses the phrase "grandchildren of Dazhbog" when referring to the people of Russia, making him an ancestral deity. Dabog's name translates to mean "the god who gives" or "giver of fortune."

He is mentioned in numerous medieval manuscripts and was born the son of the god Svarog. He was demonized with the arrival of Christianity to the region.

In Christian demonology Dabog was ranked as a demonic Lord, a demon of the underworld. He is described as looking like a lame and ugly shepherd of wolves and having a silver beard. Being lame was a common attribute given to Greek smith-gods because in ancient times weapon smiths used small amounts of arsenic in bronze to harden the metal. Low-level arsenic poisoning causes lameness and skin cancers. Dabog is associated with precious gems and smith work; his sacred metal is bronze. He lives in the underworld but can shape-shift into a wolf form that he uses to wander the mortal world at night. His personal adversary is the god of Christianity, and a Slavic saying goes "Dabog is tsar on earth, and the Lord God is in heaven."

Sources: Jones, *Encyclopedia of Religion*, Vol. 4, 2231; Jordan, *Dictionary of Gods and Goddesses*, 70; Lurker, *Routledge Dictionary of Gods and Goddesses*, 46; Sykes, *Who's Who in Non-Classical Mythology*, 51; Turner, *Dictionary of Ancient Deities*, 144; Warner, *Russian Myths*, 16.

Dabrinos

In the *Theurgia Goetia*, the second book of the *Lemegeton*, Dabrinos, an AERIAL DEVIL, is named as one of the twelve SERVITORS OF DEMORIEL (see DEMORIEL and DUKES OF HELL). As a chief duke, he commands 1,140 servitors.

Sources: Guiley, *Encyclopedia of Demons and Demonology*, 60; Peterson, *Lesser Key of Solomon*, 63.

Daemon

Variations: Dæmon, Daimon, DAIMONION

Originally in ancient Greek mythology daemons represented the divine influence that touched upon each person's fate. Historically, they were a small and nearly insignificant part of Greek mythology, mentioned in Greek literature. These tutelary spirits were bound to a particular person or location and were believed to serve the will of the higher gods. At birth, each person is assigned a daemon that is then charged with the task of protecting and guiding their person over the course of their lifetime. Although unable to take action themselves, the daemons were reported to give ideas, insight, or urges to their charges in the hopes of guiding them in the right direction. Offerings of wine were made daily to the daemons while milk and honey offerings were made on one's birthday. Living a good life honors your daemon, and conversely, living a dishonorable or reckless life disgraces it. The word *daemon* translates from Greek to mean "replete with knowledge" or "divine power."

It was through Roman and early Christian influences that the daemons were ultimately demonized as evil and infernal beings.

Sources: Lawson, *Modern Greek Folklore and Ancient Greek Religion*, 272–3, 290; McClintock, *Cyclopaedia of Biblical, Theological, and Ecclesiastical Literature*, 639–40; Wright, *Origin of Evil Spirits*, 212–13.

Daevas

Variations: Daaua, Daeuua, Daeva, Dews, Divs (DIV)

In ancient Persian and Zoroastrianism mythology the daevas ("false gods" or "wrong gods") were originally gods who were incapable of telling the difference between the truth and a lie and were rejected but still worshipped by people. The daevas deceive their followers, as well as themselves, but they are not doing so with evil intent. Eventually they lost their nativity and were perceived by the people as truly demonic beings they called DRUGS, capable of committing every conceivable type of evil.

Both nocturnal and diurnal, the daevas are now seen as the male demonic followers under the command of AHRIMAN; the female demonic followers of Ahriman are known as DRUG. Appearing as black-skinned beings, they cause diseases and plagues, encourage chaos, and fight against every form of religion. To prevent attack from the daevas one must recite the *Vendidad* aloud, but this preventive method is only effective between sunset and sunrise. The personal adversaries of the daevas are Ahuru Mazda and Amesha Spentas.

Sources: Hyatt, *Book of Demons*, 56; Messadié, *History of the Devil*, 83; Jackson, *Zoroastrian Studies*, 80–83.

Dagdagiron

The dagdagiron are one of the twelve QLIPPOTHIC ORDERS OF DEMONS. These demons take the form of large and devouring, flat-shaped fishes. Their color is a gleaming red.

Source: Mathers, *Sorcerer and his Apprentice*, 26.

Dagiel

Dagiel is one of the twenty SERVITORS OF SYMIEL (see SYMIEL). Known to be very good and quick to listen to those who summon him, Dagiel shares with his diurnal companions seven hundred twenty servitors.

Sources: Agrippa, *Fourth Book of Occult Philosophy*, 212; Barrett, *The Magus*, 125; Davidson, *Dictionary of Angels*, 93; Peterson, *Lesser Key of Solomon*, 88.

Daglas

Variations: Duglas

The *Sacred Magic of Abramelin the Mage*, book two, names Daglas among the sixty-five SERVITORS OF KORE AND MAGOTH.

Sources: Belanger, *Dictionary of Demons*, 103; Mathers, *Book of the Sacred Magic of Abramelin the Mage*, 107; Von Worms, *Book of Abramelin*, 256.

Dagon

Variations: Be-Dingir-Dingir ("Lord of the gods"), Bekalam ("Lord of the land"), Be-ka-na-na ("Lord of Canaan"), Dagan, Dagana, Dagn ("rain-cloud"), Dagon Marnas, Daguna, Dgn (Dagnu), Digan, Siton, Ti-lu ma-tim ("dew of the land"), Zeus Arotrios

Dagon ("fish" or "fishlike") was originally a Philistines and Semitic god of grain and agriculture. His consort was called Belatu ("Lady"), although some sources claim his wife to be the goddess Shala or the goddess Ishara. He was the primary god of the cities of Ma-Ne, Irim, Sipishu, Siwad, Tuttul, Uguash, and Zarad. Dagon was a powerful and war-minded protector as a god; he was described as having the lower body of a fish.

Dagon was later demonized during the introduction of Christianity; he was said to have been one of the FALLEN ANGELS, formerly of the Order of Archangels. He was ranked with various titles, both grand and superfluous, such as grand pantler of the royal household, judge of the dead, master baker of Hell, and prison guard of the seven children of Emmesharra. There is a story that says when the Philistines captured the Ark from the Israelites they placed it in a temple of Dagon's. The Ark then destroyed the statue of Dagon by destroying its upper half, leaving only its lower fish half intact.

Sources: Chambers, *Book of Days*, 723; Hastings, *Encyclopedia of Religion and Ethics*, Part 18, 843–890–1; Melton, *Encyclopedia of Occultism and Parapsychology*, 315; Rudwin, *Devil in Legend and Literature*, 86.

Dagular

Variations: Daguler

In the *Sacred Magic of Abramelin the Mage*, Dagular is one of the fifty-three SERVITORS OF ASHTAROTH AND ASMODEUS (see ASHTAROTH and ASMODEUS).

Sources: Belanger, *Dictionary of Demons*, 104; Mathers, *Book of the Sacred Magic of Abramelin the Mage*, 106; Von Worms, *Book of Abramelin*, 248.

Daha-Ata Sanniya

Sinhalese demonology utilized a dance ritual in their rites of exorcism known as the Daha-Ata Sanniya. An extremely colorful and energetic dance, the performers wear one of eighteen different masks to exorcise one of the eighteen different types of diseases that they believe can affect the human body. The Daha-Ata Sanniya will also lift the curse of the Evil Eye from anyone watching the dance while simultaneously blessing those who witness the performance. Because the cost of the ceremony is very expensive and the dance is extremely long and exhausting to perform, it is seldom done anymore.

The dance was created to counter the eighteen different demonic diseases that were brought into the world. The original story of the Daha-Ata Sanniya says that while King Sankapala was away at war his wife realized she was pregnant. The wife craved to eat a certain type of mango, and when it was acquired for her, her handmaiden asked for some. The queen refused and the overly vengeful maid told the king upon his return that his wife was unfaithful to him and that the child she carried was not his own. The king believed the lie the handmaid told and ordered his wife hung and her body cut in two. Due to the magic of the unborn child she carried, the mother's body reformed and carried the child to full term. When the child turned 16 years old he suddenly remembered the events of his birth. Using medicines and herbs he affixed to tablets, he created eighteen devils and led them to his father's kingdom where they spread diseases. The Daha-Ata Sanniya was created to counter these devils.

See also AMUKU SANNIYA, BIHIRI SANNIYA, DEMALA SANNIYA, DEVA SANNIYA, GINIJAL SANNIYA, GOLU SANNIYA, GULMA SANNIYA, KALA SANNIYA, KANA SANNIYA, KAPALA SANNIYA, KORA SANNIYA, MARU SANNIYA, MURTA SANNIYA, NAGA SANNIYA, PITA SANNIYA, SLESMA SANNIYA, VADI SANNIYA, and VATA SANNIYA.

Sources: Goonatilleka, *Masks and Mask Systems of Sri Lanka*, 24, 30, 33; Illes, *Encyclopedia of Spirits*, 875; Malik, *Mind, Man, and Mask*, 163–4; Wirts, *Exorcism and the Art of Healing in Ceylon*, 44.

Dahaka

Variations: Azi Dahaka, Dahak, ZAHHAK, Zohak

From ancient Persian and Zoroastrian mythology comes the demon Dahaka ("stinging"). Originally a god, Dahaka was later demonized and made into the demon of death, deceit, lies, and mendacity who takes pleasure in destroying all living things. He is depicted as having three heads; his body is covered with crawling lizards and poisonous scorpions.

Sources: Ford, *Liber Hvhi*, 94, 97; Rose, *Giants, Monsters, and Dragons*, 33; Turner, *Dictionary of Ancient Deities*, 85.

Daimon Pneuma

Daimon pneuma is a Greek phrase that translates to mean "demon spirits."

Source: Fahlbusch, *Encyclopedia of Christianity*, Vol. 5, 126.

Daimonian Hepta

Daimonian hepta is a Greek phrase that translates to mean "seven demons."

Source: Reiling, *Translator's Handbook on the Gospel of Luke*, 327, 507.

Daimonion

Variations: Daemonium, Daimon, Daimonizesthai, Demon-God, Demon of Demons, Transcendent Demon

Mentioned in the Old Testament, a daimonion is a type of immortal, vampiric demon that possessed people. Sometimes during the course of the possession, the afflicted would make utterances of prophecies. Daimonion, as a name, translates to mean "a knowing one," "something divine," "to be subject to an appointed fate," and "the divine spark within each of us."

People who were possessed by a demon were called *demoniacs*. More often than not these individuals already had some other sort of malady, be it a physical deformity or a disease.

Sources: Balfour, *Three Inquiries*, 94, 340, 358; Benardete, *Rhetoric of Morality and Philosophy*, 127–9; Collin de Plancy, *Dictionary of Witchcraft*, 48; Russell, *Prince of Darkness*, 25, 45.

Daimonion Akathartos

Daimonion akathartos is a Greek phrase that translates to mean "unclean demon-god."

Sources: Reiling, *Translator's Handbook on the Gospel of Luke*, 214; Van der Toorn, *Dictionary of Deities and Demons in the Bible*, 882.

Daimonion Poterion

Daimonion poterion is a Greek phrase that translates to mean "chalice of the demon-gods."

Source: Smith, *Comprehensive Dictionary of the Bible*, 197.

Daimonizomai

Daimonizomai ("DEMONIAC") is a Greek word for a person who is possessed by or under the power of a demon.

Sources: Boehm, *It's a Dark World*, 162; Kraft, *Defeating Dark Angels*, 35.

Daityas

Variations: Kratu-dvishas ("enemies of sacrifices")

In Hindu mythology, the gigantic, demonic spirits that were born from the goddess Diti and Kasyapa are known as daityas. Under the command of VRITRA, the dragon serpent, the daityas oppose sacrifice to the gods and will prevent it if they are able.

During Krita Yuga, the first age of the cosmos, these demons became so well armed and powerful that they were able to overpower and defeat the gods, and led by Vritra they scattered the gods across the cosmos. The gods pleaded to Brahma, who advised them to seek a demon-slaying weapon from Rishi, a sage. The gods did as they were advised and Rishi made a demon-slaying weapon he named *Vajra* from his own bones. It was placed in the hands of INDRA, who then led the gods to a victorious return to the heavens with it. In the course of the battle, Vritra was slain and the daityas who survived the battle were rounded up and banished by Indra to Patala, a realm deep beneath the ocean, where the serpent demons, NAGA, live. In their confinement the daityas gather and plot out their revenge.

Sources: Lurker, *Routledge Dictionary of Gods and Goddesses*, 47; Hyatt, *Book of Demons*, 23; Singh, *Encyclopaedia of Hinduism*, 2498, 2519–20; Turner, *Dictionary of Ancient Deities*, 140.

Daitya-Yuga

Daitya-yuga is an AGE OF DEMONS, said to last 12,000 divine years. Sources vary, but typically one year (365 days) equals one divine day; 365 divine days equal one divine year. The Daitya-yuga will last 1,555,200,000 actual years.

Sources: Clough, *Sinhalese English Dictionary*, 259; *Working Glossary for the Use of Students of Theosophical Literature*, 12.

Daivers

Variations: Daivergoel, Divs (DIV)

In Hindu mythology daivers are a species of demonic DJINN that have material and spiritual bodies as well as many human attributes, both good and evil. The daivers are under the command of their king, Daivuntren (or INDIREN, sources vary), their queen, Inderannee, and their prince, Seedcra-Hudderen. Daivers live in a world called Daiver Logum with those heroes and prophets who are not yet ready to dwell in the Shiva's paradise. They can also be found sitting in Daivuntren's audience chamber among the many other attendants. The mythology tells us that there are 330,000,000 daivers.

Sources: Kindersley, *Specimens of Hindoo Literature*,

33; Shepard, *Encyclopedia of Occultism and Parapsychology*, 327; Thompson, *Mysteries and Secrets of Magic*, 19.

Dajjal

Variations: Ad-Dajjal ("the false prophet" or "the impostor"), Dajal

The name or title Dajjal refers to the End-of-days deceiver in Islamic mythology, the ANTICHRIST, who will make himself known at Yawm al-Qiyamah ("The Day of Resurrection").

Sources: Smith, *Islamic Understanding of Death and Resurrection*, 67–9, 127–8; Waines, *Introduction to Islam*, 130.

Dakaki

Variations: The Drawer along the Stomach, MAI-JA-CHIKKI

From the demonology of the Hausa people of West Africa comes the demonic spirit of stomach ulcers known as Dakaki ("crawler"). Looking like a snake, he uses the Evil Eye to spread his disease upon mankind. High priestesses regularly make offerings of eggs and milk to keep him appeased, but on occasion he attacks anyway. When someone has fallen victim to him, only finding someone who is familiar with working with spirits can help. This person must perform a ritual dance to specifically determine which demon caused the illness; the process will also reveal to the dancer how to treat the illness as well. The cure typically involves the sacrifice of an animal of a specific color and gender.

Sources: Chopra, *Academic Dictionary of Mythology*, 78; Howey, *Encircled Serpent*, 239–40; Tremearne, *Ban of the Bori*, 328, 422.

Dakin

Variations: Dain, Dayan, Khandro

The Dakin of Tibet are a race of infernal, immortal, demonic vampire attendants to the goddess KALI. Many new age religions would have one believe that the Dakin are more like angelic beings, made of pure spiritual energy and not associated with any one god or goddess; this simply is not true. Their name has been translated by different sources to mean different things depending on the role that they are fulfilling. Common translations are "celestial woman," "cloud fairy," "sky dancer," and "space-goer."

Although the Dakin have the ability to shape-change and may choose to look like nearly any form they wish, they prefer to take on the guise of human females, as they enjoy being called upon to partake in tantric sex. The typical duty of the Dakin is to carry the souls of the deceased into the sky. There are many stories of the Buddha's former lives that mention them. Dakin, like

the SUCCUBUS, cause people to fall madly in love with them, which makes for a dangerous situation, as they are highly unpredictable by nature.

Sources: Blavatsky, *Theosophical Glossary*, 95; Bryant, *Handbook of Death and Dying*, 99; Lurker, *Dictionary of Gods and Goddesses*, 88.

Dala Kadavara

Variations: Gara Yaka

In the Singhalese mythology, Dala Kadavara was originally an elephant goddess but was demonized under the influence of Buddhism into a male demon of illness and misfortune. Classified as a Gara Demon, Dala Kadavara spreads diseases, illness, and misfortune.

Sources: Gooneratne, *On Demonology and Witchcraft in Ceylon*, 35; Lurker, *Dictionary of Gods and Goddesses*, 47; Rose, *Spirits, Fairies, Gnomes, and Goblins*, 78.

Dalaketnon

The dalaketnon is a type of *engkanto* (terrestrial) demon from Philippine demonology that commands some of the monstrous creatures of their mythology, such as the amalanhigs, aswangs, bal-bals, manananggals, tiktiks, and the wak waks. Dalaketnon are born from the royal blood of the evil engkantos and look like attractive, tall men and fashionably dressed women. Preying on humans, they try to blend in with human society so as to more easily abduct them. Once the humans are captured, dalaketnon take their prey to their world and force the victims to eat a special black rice, which will make them their slaves. When a dalaketnon's power manifests, their eyes and hair turn white, they have the gift of coño (telekinesis), and they have the ability to duplicate themselves indefinitely. If they so choose they also can transform a person into a dalaketnon like themselves. As a species, the dalaketnon are elitists and live in mansions both in their realm and in ours. Their personal adversaries are the good engkantos.

Source: Ramos, *Creatures of Philippine Lower Mythology*, 55–6.

Dala-Raja

Variations: Gara Yaka

In the Singhalese Buddhist mythology, Dala-Raja is the chief of the Gara Demons; he has command over all twelve of them. He is depicted as having three hooded cobras hovering over his head, ornamentation hanging from his ears, two tusks protruding from his mouth, and carrying a torch in each hand.

Although Dala-Raja and the rest of the Gara Demons are not specifically opposed to humans, they do prey upon them, casting the Evil Eye in their direction and making them "unclean." Offerings of drink, food, and money can prevent Dala-Raja from attacking a person, as well as observing the GARA-YAK-NATUMA ritual ceremony.

Sources: Lurker, *Dictionary of Gods and Goddesses*, 47; Raghavan, *Sinhala Natum*, 10; Sarachchandra, *Folk Drama of Ceylon*, 28–9.

Dalep

In the *Sacred Magic of Abramelin the Mage*, Dalep ("decaying in liquid," "putrefaction") is among the twenty SERVITORS OF AMAYMON (see AMAYMON).

Sources: Forgotten Books, *Book of the Sacred Magic of Abramelin the Mage*, 42–3; Mathers, *Book of the Sacred Magic of Abra-Melin*, 122.

Dalhan

Variations: Dahlan

The demon Dalhan is from Islamic mythology. He is described as a man riding upon an ostrich, devouring travelers and those who wash up on the shore from shipwrecks. He will even go so far as to attack ships if they venture too close to the shore. Dalhan can let loose with a cry that can cause disorientation in any who hear it. He lives on various named and unnamed islands.

Sources: Hughes, *Dictionary of Islam*, 137; Knowles, *Nineteenth Century*, Vol. 31, 449; Maberry, *They Bite*, 337; Turner, *Dictionary of Ancient Deities*, 141.

Dalkiel

Variations: Rugziel

Joseph Gikatilla ben Abraham (1248–1305) wrote in his book *Baraita de Massachet Gehinnom* that Dalkiel is an angel of Hell and the ruler of Sheol, a realm that is alleged to be four hundred twenty times hotter than fire. He is under the command of the demon DUMA. Dalkiel was named as the demon of Idolaters, Sabbath-breakers, and the uncircumcised. He is most powerful during the month of December.

Sources: Davidson, *Dictionary of Angels*, 94; Gaster, *Studies and Texts in Folklore*, 159; Guiley, *Encyclopedia of Angels*, 86; Mew, *Eclectic Magazine of Foreign Literature, Science, and Art*, Vol. 115, 407.

Damayas

Variations: DAITYAS, DANAVAS

The damayas are a race of demonic giants. They are opposed by ritualistic gods.

Sources: Bunce, *Hindu Deities, Demi-Gods, Godlings, Demons, and Heroes*, 978; Hyatt, *Book of Demons*, 23; Singh, *Encyclopaedia of Hinduism*, 2498, 2519.

Damiel

In the *Ars Paulina*, the third book of the *Lemegeton*, Damiel is named as one of the fifteen

SERVITORS OF SCOX (see SCOX) as well as one of the ten SERVITORS OF SAZQUIEL (see SAZQUIEL). A chief duke, he commands 5,550 servitors.

Sources: Trithemius, *Steganographia*, 95, 103; Peterson, *Lesser Key of Solomon*, 114; Waite, *Book of Ceremonial Magic*, 67.

Danavas

In Vedic mythology danavas are a type of AERIAL DEVIL, a race of the ASURAS. Born the sons of Danu, the immortal danavas are under the dominion of BALI. It was under his failed leadership on an attack against the gods that the danavas are now imprisoned in the deepest part of the ocean.

Sources: Hopkins, *Epic Mythology with Additions and Corrections*, 46–8; Hyatt, *Book of Demons*, 23; Singh, *Encyclopaedia of Hinduism*, 2518–9.

Danel

Variations: Dan'el

In Enochian lore Danel is one of the CHIEF OF TENS, a FALLEN ANGEL who swore allegiance to SAMIAZA, rebelled against God, took a human wife, and fathered the NEPHILIM (see also GRIGORI and WATCHERS).

Sources: Beard, *Autobiography of Satan*, 113; Black, *Book of Enoch*, 120; Barton, *Journal of Biblical Literature*, Vols. 30–31, 164; Laurence, *Book of Enoch, the Prophet*, 6; Lumpkin, *Fallen Angels, the Watchers, and the Origins of Evil*, 31.

Daniel

Variations: DANYUL

Daniel is one of the twenty SERVITORS OF CAMUEL (see CAMUEL) as well as one of the eleven SERVITORS OF RAHAB (see RAHAB) and one of the fifteen SERVITORS OF SASQUIEL (see SASQUIEL). A diurnal demon, Chief Daniel is a FALLEN ANGEL who appears to his summoner in a beautiful form. He is known to be very courteous. His name means "judged by God" or "judgment of God."

Sources: Guiley, *Encyclopedia of Demons and Demonology*, 36; Peterson, *Lesser Key of Solomon*, 68; Waite, *Book of Ceremonial Magic*, 67.

Danjal

Variations: DANIEL, Danjel, Danyal

In Enochian lore Danjal ("God is my judge") is named as one of the FALLEN ANGELS. He is said to be the demon in charge of the souls of lawyers.

Sources: Charles, *Book of Enoch*, 137; Horne, *Sacred Books and Early Literature of the East*, 114; Laurence, *Foreign Quarterly Review*, Vol. 24, 370; Prophet, *Fallen Angels and the Origins of Evil*, 174.

Dantalian

Variations: Dantalion, Dantallion, DANTANIAN, Dantelion

According to Christian demonology Dantalian is the Duke of Faces, commanding thirty-six legions of demons (see DUKES OF HELL). He can be summoned any time of the day or night and appears as a man with the faces of many men and women. In his right hand he is holding a book. He is summoned for his ability to encourage love, produce hallucinations, and reveal a person's innermost desires. He also knows what good advice a person would give to another and changes their mind about speaking. He can show the face of any person he so desires in a vision, and teaches all the arts and sciences. He is most powerful during the month of March and has dominion over the planet Mars. His zodiacal sign is Pisces. Dantalian is also named as one of the seventy-two SPIRITS OF SOLOMON.

Sources: De Laurence, *Lesser Key of Solomon, Goetia*, 45; Diagram, *Little Giant Encyclopedia*, 89; Kelly, *Who in Hell*, 66; Waite, *Book of Black Magic and of Pacts*, 188.

Dantanian

In Christian demonology, Dantanian is named as one of the many FALLEN ANGELS. He is said to have many faces.

Sources: Guiley, *Encyclopedia of Fallen Angels*, 89.

Danyul

In Christian demonology Danyul is named as one of the FALLEN ANGELS.

Sources: Charlesworth, *Old Testament Pseudepigrapha*, 47; Guiley, *Encyclopedia of Angels*, 366; Jackson, *Enochic Judaism*, 73.

Darascon

The *Sacred Magic of Abramelin the Mage* lists Darascon among the one hundred eleven SERVITORS OF AMAYMON, ARITON, ORIENS, AND PAYMON (see AMAYMON, ARITON, ORIENS, and PAYMON). His name is possibly Celtic in origin, and if so would translate to mean "turbulent."

Sources: Belanger, *Dictionary of Demons*, 105; Mathers, *Book of the Sacred Magic of Abramelin the Mage*, 114.

Darek

In the *Sacred Magic of Abramelin the Mage*, Darek ("path" or "way") is listed as one of the thirty-two SERVITORS OF ASTAROT (see ASTAROT).

Sources: Kirchmayer, *Un-Natural History*, 19; Mathers, *Book of the Sacred Magic of Abramelin the Mage*, 117; Von Worms, *Book of Abramelin*, 249.

Darokin

In the *Sacred Magic of Abramelin the Mage*, Darokin ("path" or "way") is one of the fifty-three SERVITORS OF ASHTAROTH AND ASMODEUS (see ASHTAROTH and ASMODEUS).

Sources: Mathers, *Book of the Sacred Magic of Abramelin the Mage*, 106; Von Worms, *Book of Abramelin*, 247.

Dasim

Dasim is a DJINN from Islamic mythology, the demon of hatred between man and wife. He was born one of the five SONS OF IBLIS.

Sources: Hughes, *Dictionary of Islam*, 135; Knowles, *Nineteenth Century*, Vol. 31, 449; Rose, *Spirits, Fairies, Gnomes, and Goblins*, 160.

Debam

In the *Sacred Magic of Abramelin the Mage*, book two, Debam ("strength") is one of the sixty-five SERVITORS OF KORE AND MAGOTH.

Sources: Mathers, *Book of the Sacred Magic of Abramelin the Mage*, 118.

Deber

Originally called NERGAL, he was once the god of midsummer, but during his demonization his name was changed to Deber ("pestilence") and was made into the nocturnal demon of plagues. Deber was named as one of the servitors of God and said to be used by the Lord to deliver plagues to earth as a means of punishment. To prevent attack from this demon, one must chant the psalm "Shir shel Pega'im."

Sources: Blair, *De-demonizing the Old Testament*, 35, 37; King, *Babylonian Religion and Mythology*, 37, 42; Van der Toorn, *Dictionary of Deities and Demons in the Bible*, 231–2.

Decarabia

Variations: CARABIA, Decarbia, Narcoriel, Nestoriel

Decarabia is a FALLEN ANGEL who commands six chiefs, six subalterns, thirty legions, and eighty-seven demonic servitors. Ranked as a marquis, he is under the command of SAMAEL, one of the seventy-two SPIRITS OF SOLOMON (see MARQUIS OF HELL). When summoned, he appears as a pentagram, but if commanded to do so by his summoner he will take on the guise of a man. A nocturnal demon, Decarabia is summoned for his ability to grant knowledge of magic as well as for his ability to teach gemology and herbology. He also has the ability to create illusions of birds, and gives birds as FAMILIARs. His sign is that of a star in a pentagram and he is most powerful during the month of March.

Sources: De Laurence, *Lesser Key of Solomon, Goetia*, 44; Godwin, *Godwin's Cabalistic Encyclopedia*, 87; Waite, *Book of Black and Ceremonial Magic*, 218; Scott, *London Magazine*, Vol. 5, 378.

Deccal

In the *Sacred Magic of Abramelin the Mage*, book two, Deccal ("dreadful" or "to fear") is one

of the one hundred eleven SERVITORS OF AMAY-
MON, ARITON, ORIENS, AND PAYMON (see
AMAYMON, ARITON, ORIENS, and PAYMON).

Sources: Mathers, *Book of the Sacred Magic of
Abramelin the Mage*, 113; Von Worms, *Book of
Abramelin*, 255.

Deception

Named in Babylonian, Jewish, and Solominic
lore, Deception was one of the demonic goddesses
who was bound by King Solomon and made to
dig the foundation of his Temple (see SPIRITS OF
SOLOMON). She is named as the second of the
SEVEN HEAVENLY BODIES and as one of the
thirty-three (or thirty-six, sources vary) elements
of the cosmic rulers of the darkness.

In the *Testament of Solomon*, Deception is described as one of seven female spirits, all fair in
appearance, bound and woven together, represented as a cluster of stars in the heavens (see
SPIRITS OF SOLOMON). They travel about sometimes living in Lydia, or Olympus, or on a great
mountain. Deception is known for ability to deceive, excite and whet heresies, and the weaving
of snares. Her personal adversary is the angel
Lamechalal.

Sources: Abrahams, *Jewish Quarterly Review*, Vol.
11, 25; Charlesworth, *Old Testament Pseudepigrapha*,
935; Conybeare, *Jewish Quarterly Review*, Vol. 11, 24–
6.

Demala Sanniya

In Singhalese demonology Demala Sanniya
("Tamil demon") is the demon of bad dreams and
madness that distorts the body. He is known to
cause disease, play pranks, and make muttering
sounds. Fortunately he is susceptible to the
DAHA-ATA SANNIYA.

Sources: Illes, *Encyclopedia of Spirits*, 875; Kapferer,
Celebration of Demons, 231; Wirz, *Exorcism and the Art
of Healing in Ceylon*, 44.

Demogorgon

Variations: "God of the Earth," GORGO, Master of the Fates

Although *Demogorgon* is a Greek word meaning "demon-Gorgon," or "terrible demon," the
idea of this demonic being may have been in-
fluenced by the Orient, as originally it was a deity
of the Underworld. The Demogorgon is a powerful being who created all the gods and the universe. Speaking his name aloud is taboo and
doing so will cause a great calamity to happen.

Sources: Debus, *Alchemy and Early Modern Chemistry*, 312, 313; Lowe, *Magic in Greek and Latin Literature*, 55, 65–6; Lumpkin, *Fallen Angels, the Watchers,
and the Origin of Evil*, 126; Scudder, *Atlantic Monthly*,
Vol. 70, 267–8, 272.

Demoness

Demoness is a word used to describe a female
demon.

Sources: Cavendish, *Man, Myth and Magic*, 862;
Cooley, *Dictionary of English Language Exhibiting Orthography*, 141.

Demonette

Demonette is a French word that translates to
mean "a little demon." It is sometimes used when
referring to imps or FAMILIARs.

Sources: Grambs, *Endangered English Dictionary*,
49.

Demoniac

Variations: Daimonakos, Daimonikos, Demo-
niak, Demoniaque

The word *demoniac* has its etymology traced
back to Middle English and it means simply "one
possessed by a demon."

Sources: De Givry, *Pictorial Anthology of Witchcraft,
Magic and Alchemy*, 155; Graham, *Standard-Phonographic Dictionary*, 102; Ogilvie, *Imperial Dictionary of
the English Language*, 698; Partridge, *Origins*, 147;
Stratmann, *Middle-English Dictionary*, 158.

Demoniacal

To be *demoniacal* is to be demonic, that which
resembles or is possessed by a demon.

Sources: Graham, *Standard-Phonographic
Dictionary*, 102; Ogilvie, *Imperial Dictionary of the English Language*, 698; Oesterreich, *Possession, Demoniacal
and Other, Among Primitive Races*, 26, 83–5.

Demoniacally

The word *demoniacally* means to be or act in a
demonic manner.

Sources: Cambridge University Press, *Cambridge
Advanced Learner's Dictionary*, 372; Ogilvie, *Imperial
Dictionary of the English Language*, 698.

Demoniacism

The word *demoniacism* means "to be in a demonic state of being."

Sources: Graham, *Standard-Phonographic
Dictionary*, 102; Gras, *Studies in Elizabethan Audience
Response to the Theater*, 191–2; Ogilvie, *Imperial Dic-
tionary of the English Language*, 698.

Demonial

Demonial is an archaic word from Middle English that means "demonic."

Sources: Ogilvie, *Imperial Dictionary of the English
Language*, 698; Whitney, *Century Dictionary and Cyclopedia*, 1528.

Demoniality

The word *demoniality* refers to demons collectively, as well as the nature of a demon and the
state of being demonic.

Sources: Ogilvie, *Imperial Dictionary of the English Language*, 698; Sinistrari, *Demoniality; or, Incubi and Succubi*, 15, 17.

Demonian

Demonian refers to characteristics that are like or that refer to a demon.

Sources: Graham, *Standard-Phonographic Dictionary*, 102; Ogilvie, *Imperial Dictionary of the English Language*, 698; Whitney, *Century Dictionary and Cyclopedia*, 1528.

Demonianism

The word *demonianism* means "the condition of being possessed by a demon."

Sources: Graham, *Standard-Phonographic Dictionary*, 102; Ogilvie, *Imperial Dictionary of the English Language*, 698; Whitney, *Century Dictionary and Cyclopedia*, 1528.

Demonic

The word *demonic* means that which refers to or originates from a demon; to be inspired, like, of, or possessed by a demon.

Sources: Cambridge University Press, *Cambridge Advanced Learner's Dictionary*, 372; Ogilvie, *Imperial Dictionary of the English Language*, 698; Whitney, *Century Dictionary and Cyclopedia*, 1528.

Demonic Possession

The oldest known records of demonic possession come from ancient Sumerian texts, and since that earliest time, very little has changed in the way it has been described. Historically, it has been reported that a person's physical appearance changes when they are possessed; such noted changes are eyes changing color, foam frothing from the mouth, limbs shaking, skin pigmentation taking on a bluish tint, and sores suddenly appearing on the body, to name the most common.

The symptoms of demonic possession beyond the noted physical changes that may not ever occur are similar to those of a variety of mental diseases; the person may suddenly have a deep fear or hatred of holy objects, be unwilling or unable to say the names of the saints or utter the name "Christ," they may blaspheme or cry out obscenities in a language previously unknown to them, vomit up foreign objects, or even show signs of pain or rage when hearing prayers. (Most often it is only people who are possessed; however, Christian beliefs allow for the possession of animals such as cats and goats.)

As difficult as it may be to fully determine if a person is a victim of demonic possession, it is even more difficult to prevent, as no people or religion has ever made the claim to have a surefire means of prevention. Even the most devout person may become possessed, as there are reports of cases of possession occurring when a person unknowingly ate a bit of food that a demon was using as a means to enter into their body. Fortunately, many religions do have a ceremonial exorcism that can be performed to drive the demon, or demons, from an individual. Unfortunately, it is a common belief that if the exorcism is not properly performed, the demon can return or leave the person vulnerable to being possessed again.

While playing host, either willingly or not, to a demonic spirit, a person typically cannot exercise their own free will, or if they can, may only do so with tremendous effort. While possessed, the person gains the ability through the demon to accurately give the location of lost items, divine the future, read minds, and speak a language previously unknown to the person.

Every religion that has the belief of spiritlike entities allows for possession, and not all religions see possession as an evil occurrence or undesirable state of being. In fact, there are religious practices that encourage and invite such an event to happen.

Sources: Kaplan, *Understanding Popular Culture*, 134, 139–42; Klaits, *Servants of Satan*, 111–2, 115–6; Manual, *Encyclopedia of Phobias, Fears, and Anxieties*, 224, 510.

Demonic Prophecy

A demonic prophecy is a prediction or bit of insight that is given by a person who is believed to be possessed by a demon. Some sources claim that demons are incapable of predicting the future and that what these demons are doing is announcing the Devil's intent.

Sources: Chajes, *Between Worlds*, 135; Evans, *Prophetic Ministry, Misery, and Mishaps*, 25–6.

Demonifuge

A demonifuge is that which is designed to avert and be used against demons.

Sources: Ogilvie, *Imperial Dictionary of the English Language*, 698; Whitney, *Century Dictionary and Cyclopedia*, 1528.

Demonism

Demonism is a modernization of the archaic word *demonolatry*; it is the belief in demons.

Sources: Graham, *Standard-Phonographic Dictionary*, 102; Ogilvie, *Imperial Dictionary of the English Language*, 698; Whitney, *Century Dictionary and Cyclopedia*, 1528.

Demonist

1. A demonist is one who deals or has dealings with a demon. 2. One who lives under demonic

rule or influence or one who is subjected to demonic rule or influence.

Sources: Baretti, *New Dictionary of the Italian and English Languages*, 153; Ogilvie, *Imperial Dictionary of the English Language*, 698; Whitney, *Century Dictionary and Cyclopedia*, 1528.

Demonize

To demonize is to make someone or something demonic, to say that it has been put under the influence of a demon. To demonize something is to infer that it is evil.

Sources: Cambridge University Press, *Cambridge Advanced Learner's Dictionary*, 372; Ogilvie, *Imperial Dictionary of the English Language*, 698.

Demonocracy

The Greek word *demonocracy* translates to mean "the rule of demons;" it is used most frequently when describing the HIERARCHY OF DEMONS. Although not commonly used, *demonocracy* also refers to a religion where there is a reverence of demons.

Sources: Graham, *Standard-Phonographic Dictionary*, 102; Ogilvie, *Imperial Dictionary of the English Language*, 698; Whitney, *Century Dictionary and Cyclopedia*, 1528.

Demonographer

A demonographer, also known as a demonologist, is one who is knowledgeable and versed in demonology, one who records the descriptions and histories of demons.

Sources: Ogilvie, *Imperial Dictionary of the English Language*, 698; Whitney, *Century Dictionary and Cyclopedia*, 1528.

Demonography

Demonography is the recording of the descriptions and histories of demons. It is applied to the written works on demonology and demons.

Sources: Ogilvie, *Imperial Dictionary of the English Language*, 698; Whitney, *Century Dictionary and Cyclopedia*, 1528.

Demonolator, feminine: demonolatress

A demonolator is one who practices the worship of demons. It should be noted that a demonolator is not a Satanist.

Sources: Ogilvie, *Imperial Dictionary of the English Language*, 698; Whitney, *Century Dictionary and Cyclopedia*, 1528.

Demonolatry

Demonolatry is the act of worshiping demons. To practice demonolatry is not the same as practicing Satanism.

Sources: Ogilvie, *Imperial Dictionary of the English Language*, 698; Whitney, *Century Dictionary and Cyclopedia*, 1528.

Demonologia

A demonologia is a dissertation or treatises on demons.

Sources: Baretti, *New Dictionary of the Italian and English Languages*, 153; Ogilvie, *Imperial Dictionary of the English Language*, 698.

Demonologic

Variations: Demonological

Any person or object that pertains to demonology is said to be a demonologic; to behave in a demonological manner.

Sources: Ogilvie, *Imperial Dictionary of the English Language*, 698; Whitney, *Century Dictionary and Cyclopedia*, 1528.

Demonologist

Variations: Demonologer

A demonologist is one who studies demonology, is practiced in removing demonic influences, or catalogues demons.

Sources: Baretti, *New Dictionary of the Italian and English Languages*, 153; Ogilvie, *Imperial Dictionary of the English Language*, 698; Whitney, *Century Dictionary and Cyclopedia*, 1528.

Demonology

Demonology, simply put, is the study of demons.

Sources: Baretti, *New Dictionary of the Italian and English Languages*, 153; Ogilvie, *Imperial Dictionary of the English Language*, 698; Whitney, *Century Dictionary and Cyclopedia*, 1528.

Demonomagy

The type of magic or sorcery that involves the use of demons is called *demonomagy*.

Sources: Ogilvie, *Imperial Dictionary of the English Language*, 698; Whitney, *Century Dictionary and Cyclopedia*, 1528.

Demonomancy

The word *demonomancy* is Greek and it translates to mean "to raise demons"; it is used to describe the means of divining the future through the use of demons.

Sources: Ogilvie, *Imperial Dictionary of the English Language*, 698; Spence, *Encyclopedia of Occultism*, 120.

Demonomania

Demonomania is a psychological condition; it is the pathological fear of demons. A person who is fearful of demons to the point of being phobic is said to suffer from demonophobia.

Sources: Ogilvie, *Imperial Dictionary of the English Language*, 698; Spence, *Encyclopedia of Occultism*, 120.

Demonomy

Demonomy refers to the dominion of demons.

Sources: Baretti, *New Dictionary of the Italian and*

English Languages, 153; Graham, *Standard-Phonographic Dictionary*, 102; Ogilvie, *Imperial Dictionary of the English Language*, 698; Whitney, *Century Dictionary and Cyclopedia*, 1528.

Demonopathy

Demonopathy is the state of feeling sympathy for or feeling an emotional connection to demons.

Sources: Anonymous, *Intellectual Observer*, Vol. 7, 374; Ogilvie, *Imperial Dictionary of the English Language*, 698.

Demons of the Grimoire

There are 298 demons mentioned in traditional grimoires, hierarchies, and research books that other than a having a name, have no other additional information known about them. They are Abdicuel, Aceruel, Acoroba, Acreba, Acteror, Adadiel, Aesthesis-Ouchepiptoe, Afiniel, Afmadiel, Agor, Akephalos, Ahisdophies, Aknim, Alhemiel, Al-Kazwini, Alexandros, Altib, Amniel, Angingnars, Anoyrbulon, Anticif, Apactiel, Apadiel, Aphakat, Araciel, Arfaxat, Armanos, Arphakat, Arzikki Boboniya, Asiel, Assardiel, Armodiel, Atogbo, Atolaglaeca ("Cruel Wretch"), Atoti, Auchiadiel, Avabo, Azcall, Azdra, Azer, Azimo, Badiol, Ballisargon, Bara, Baras, Baratron, Baraque ("lightning"), Barbarin, Barbis, Barbu, Barfas, Bariol, Barman, Barron, Bbemo, Bealowesgast ("Spirit of Evil"), Beamot, Beherith, Belmagel, Bellie, Bestarbeto, Bludohn, Boras, Boul, Brazglavac, Brendly, Buder, Budu, Bufar, Burchas, Bussajel, Cafphiel, Calconix, Caniel, Cameron, Camniel, Capfiel, Carievan, Carpiel, Carnaziel, Carniean, Casadiel, Casdiel, Cedin, Cedor, Cedron, Charustea, Chobabies, Chomie, Chu Kwai, Cocao, Colchan, Coachtiel, Coradiel, Craffiel, Cusion, Cyamintho, Dasarach, Datzepher, Delmuson, Djata, Dorothiel, Drekavac, Drufiel, Dua, Dur, Eltzen, Earmaglaeca ("Miserable Wretch"), Easa, Eesaunien, Elmoyn, Ema, Ergediel, Erlick, Eusi, Evomiel, Evoviel, Feondaldor ("Prince of Fiends"), Fergalus, Floron, Foudre, Fracasso, Frauenzorn ("Woman's Wrath"), Frightful Ones, Funkeldune, Galast, Galifas, Gambgyn, Gaonim, Gadara, Germiciel, Gidan Jama'a ("House of Jama'a"), Gidan Kuri, Go, Godesandsaca ("God's Adversary"), Greissmodel, Grongade, Hantu Apu, Hantu Cika, Hantu Daguk, Hantu Kayung, Hantu Kocong, Hantu Lembong, Hantu Malayu, Hantu Wewer, Hanty Penyardin, Hargin, Hashothea, Hekakontalithos, Herefiel; Heros, Hermoni ("sophistry"), Hicacth, Hogos, Hunapi, Icu, Iophiel, Induren, Ischscadabadiel, Joseph, Jrtum, Jubanladance, Judal, Jurupar, Katrax, Karteel, Keriel, Kirotiel, Kniedadiel, Kniedatiel, Krutli, Kutrub, Lafusi, Lafuti; Lamaston, Laraie, Larthy-Tytiral, Lausi, Lauski, Lehusnici, Leontophron, Lisegangl, Lykketape, Macarul, Madine, Madyn, Magajin Yaura, Mahoumet, Malecic, Malic, Malichac, Malichic, Malicic, Malitac, Malizaz, Maljak, Maljik, Mamalic, Manjinjorg, Marbuel, Marcail, Marquus, Maslak, Masmalic, Massariol, Masvalic, Matr'el, Maynom, Mazzamauro, Mazzariol, Mazzemarielle, Melany, Moelay, Morborgran, Nacheshiron, Nadannies, Nakada, Nal-Gab, Napalaixlan, Napur, Nas, Nasash, Nasush ("concupiscence"), Nasnas, Nekrstenci, Nekrsteni, Nekrsteniki, Nenkir, Nevidimici, Nevidncici, Nicholas, Niu Mo Wang, Nott, Nyd, Oberycorn, Orho Oshurmy, Marino, Orko, Orpeniel, Orphaxat, Osphadiel, Panalcarp, Paradiel, Pavoys, Peano, Phazan, Qematial, Qentall, Radiel, Rama-Umi, Rashoone Taroone, Ratri, Rebel, Sahr'el ("moon of God"), Salaah, Sargantanas, Sentait, She-Strangler, Sislam, Sims'el ("sun of God"), Sithwa'el ("winter of God"), Siva, Sokar, Solday, Soleuiel, Soleviel, Sondennath, Sumnici, Svoyator, Syrrhichiel, Tamm'el ("God has completed"), Tando Ashanti, Tempeste, Tentellino, Thafloyn, Tintilin, Tintilinic, Tinto, Titilin, Tracson, Tsianphiel, Tugaroso, Umayya ("slave girl"), Valanu, Yah-Li-Yah, Yammel ("sea of God"), Yetzirhara, Zachriel; Zaciel Parmar, Zaheve, Zedex, Zehorel ("brighteness of God"), Zemen, Zenumim, Zeveac, Zeveak, Zhive, Zikiel ("fireball"), Zofiel, and Zoxim.

Sources: Black, *Book of Enoch*, 123; Butler, *Ritual Magic*, 33; Baskin, *Dictionary of Satanism*, 157; Baskin, *Sorcerer's Handbook*, 264; Choksy, *Evil, Good and Gender*, 17; Fleg, *Life of Solomon*, 66; Gettings, *Dictionary of Demons*, 232; Kindersley, *Specimens of Hindoo Literature*, 33; Knowles, *Nineteenth Century*, Vol. 31, 449; Lumpkin, *Fallen Angels, the Watchers and the Origin of Evil*, 16; Rudwin, *Devil in Legend and Literature*, 86; Russell, *Witchcraft in the Middle Ages*, 256; Schimmel, *Islamic Names*, 50; Shumaker, *Natural Magic and Modern Science*, 66; Spence, *Encyclopedia of Occultism and Parapsychology*, 315; Trithemius, *Steganographia*, 17, 69, 81; Wedeck, *Treasury of Witchcraft*, 135.

Demons of Prostitution

There are four named demonic angels of prostitution in Jewish mysticism: AGRAT-BAT-MAHLAT, EISHETH ZENUNIM, LILITH, and NAAMAH. Each one is a SUCCUBUS and one of the wives of SATAN. They are ranked as the demons of prostitutes and whores.

Sources: Dennys, *Heraldic Imagination*, 91; Gettings, *Dictionary of Demons*, 23, 25; Illes, *Encyclopedia of Spirits*, 639, 734, 929; Ringdal, *Love for Sale*, 51.

Demonship

Demonship is defined as the title or condition of a demon.

Sources: Ogilvie, *Imperial Dictionary of the English Language*, 698; Singh, *Psychotherapy in India*, 20.

Demoriel

Variations: Emperor of the North

Theurgia Goetia, the second book of the *Lemegeton*, ranks Demoriel ("blood of the lion") as an emperor and the king of the North. He has at his command 400 great dukes, 12 chief dukes, 600 lesser dukes, and 70,000,080,000,900,000 (or 700,000,800,000,900,000, sources vary) servitors (see SERVITORS OF DEMORIEL).

Sources: Gettings, *Dictionary of Demons*, 232; McLean, *Treatise on Angel Magic*, 54; Trithemius, *Steganographia*, 81.

Deofol

Deofol was an Old English name for the DEVIL.

Sources: Cook, *Exercises in Old English*, 44; Hall, *Elves in Anglo-Saxon England*, 127.

Deumas

Variations: Deumo, Deumus, Dumo

From the demonology of Calicut, Malabar, India (now called Kozhikode, Kerala, India) comes the she-devil Deumas. Also mentioned in Collin de Plancy's *Dictionaire Infernale* (1863), she is described as having four horns and wearing a crown atop her head. Her enormous mouth has only four crooked teeth, her nose is bent and pointed, and she has roosterlike feet. In Deumas's clawed hand she holds a human soul.

Sources: Collin de Plancy, *Dictionnaire Infernal*, 208; Corbey, *Alterity, Identity, Image*, 160; Mitter, *Much Maligned Monsters*, 16–8.

Dev

Variations: Divs (DIV), Drauga, DRUJ, Durugh

In Persian mythology a dev is a demon (DJINN) of war. They were created by ANGRA MAINYU, are immoral and ruthless, and intended to be the counterparts to the Amesha Spentas.

Sources: Blavatsky, *Isis Unveiled*, 482; Ford, *Luciferian Witchcraft*, 288; Turner, *Dictionary of Ancient Deties*, 147–8.

Deva Sanniya

In Sinhalese demonology Deva Sanniya is the demon of madness, nocturnal emissions, and epidemic disease. It is described as having wide eyes, flared nostrils, thin lips, a closed mouth, and an oval-shaped head. Known to spread epidemic diseases, it is susceptible to the DAHA-ATA SANNIYA.

Sources: Illes, *Encyclopedia of Spirits*, 875; Sarachchandra, *Folk Drama of Ceylon*, 28; Wirz, *Exorcism and the Art of Healing in Ceylon*, 44.

Dever

Variations: Pestilence That Walks by Night, Terror by Night

Dever ("pestilence") is the demon of plague. He is mentioned by name in Psalm 91:3: "Surely he will save you from the fowler's snare and from the deadly pestilence."

Sources: Dennis, *Encyclopedia of Jewish Myth, Magic and Mysticism*, 68; Hunter, *Magickal Judaism*, 87; Isaacs, *Why Hebrew Goes from Right to Left*, 50.

Devil

The word *devil* is often incorrectly used interchangeably with the word *demon*. A devil is a higher order of spirit compared to a demon. *Devil* ("accusers" or "slanderers") directly refers to the FALLEN ANGELS who rebelled against God and are, according to various grimoires, under the service of LUCIFER.

Sources: Davies, *Supplementary English Glossary*, 180; Hunter, *Encyclopaedic Dictionary*, 12; Rose, *Spirits, Fairies, Gnomes, and Goblins*, 161.

Devil, The

Variations: Auld ("Old"), Auld Chied, Auld CLOOTIE, Auld Harry, Auld Nic, Auld Nick, Auld Sandy, Beelzebul, the Black Fiend, DJALL, Dreqi, Hal Holt, KUL, Kul-Ater, LUCIFER, Old Evil, OLD NICK, SATAN, Se Werega ("Wretched One"), Se werga gast ("wretched spirit")

In the Judeo-Christian mythology, the Devil is the ruler of Hell, commanding all other demons and devils. An anointed FALLEN ANGEL created by God to enact His divine will, he rebelled and is now considered to be the source of all evil, the supreme adversary of God and man alike, an expert tempter and tormenter, a master of deceit.

Before the sixth century there was no physical description for the Devil, after which he was described as a small, black, impish figure. As pagan religions were demonized, the Devil began to take on aspects of the god Pan, cloven-hoofed and bearded.

The Devil, as both a name and concept, is used interchangeably with LUCIFER and SATAN.

Sources: Greer, *New Encyclopedia of the Occult*, 131–2; Messadié, *History of the Devil*, 251–70; Spence, *Encyclopedia of Occultism*, 810–17.

Devilet

A devilet is a type of IMP. This small demon delights in causing mischief but is largely considered to be harmless.

Sources: Davies, *Supplementary English Glossary*, 181; Hunter, *Encyclopaedic Dictionary*, 12.

Devil's Mark

Variations: Devil mark (stigmata diabolic), Devil's seal (sigillum diaboli)

A Devil's mark is a supernatural brand placed on a witch's body by the Devil for the sake of identification and to seal a demonic pact. There are numerous descriptions of what a Devil's mark looks like that have been reported by witch hunters, some of which include birthmarks, moles, scars, tattoos, and warts. However, it was not always the case that the Devil's mark be a physical malformation, as it was claimed by some witch hunters that it could be invisible and present itself only as a small place on a person's body that did not feel the prick of a pin or was a place on the body that did not bleed when stuck with a pin. Typically this mark, whether it can be seen or not, is located on a private and highly concealed part of the body such as under the eyelids or in the arm pit.

It is interesting to note that nearly all references to a Devil's mark originate from witch trials and various inquisitions and are often confused with and wrongly called a witch's mark. A witch's mark is a mole or other protrusion on the body that a witch would use to suckle her FAMILIAR with.

Sources: Adams, *Dwellers on the Threshold*, 272; Guazzo, *Compendium Maleficarum*, 57; Muchembled, *History of the Devil*, 63–6; Summers, *Witchcraft and Black Magic*, 193–4.

Devils of Adam

According to Rabi Elias's *Thisbi*, there are four principal devils of Adam: LILIS, MACHALAS, NAOME, and OGÉRE. These she-devils are said to be under the command of SATAN. During the one hundred thirty years before Adam was married to Eve, it is said that he fathered many offspring with these four she-devils.

Sources: Smedley, *Encyclopaedia Metropolitana*, 725; Spence, *Encyclopædia of Occultism*, 152; Van der Toorn, *Dictionary of Deities and Demons*, 246.

Devs Who Reside in Men

In Persian and Zoroastrian demonology it is said that there are ten DEVS who reside in man: Âz, BUSHYASP, DÊR, Hisham, KHASHM, Niyâz, PADMOZ, PAS, RISHK, and VARAN.

Sources: Ford, *Liber Hvhi*, 116, 160; Wilson, *Pársí Religion as Contained in the Zand-Avastá*, 335.

Diablesse, La

Variations: Lajables

There is a vampiric demon that exists in the folklore of France, Trinidad, and Tobago that tells of a beautiful vampiric woman wearing a large hat and carrying a fan. Known as *La Dia-blesse* ("Devil Woman"), it roams the quiet roads in the form of a woman wearing a long billowing dress to hide her one leg that ends in a cloven hoof.

Any man that La Diablesse meets, she will attempt to charm and lure off the path with sweet promises of a discreet indiscretion. If she succeeds, she will drain the man dry of his blood, leaving his nude body to be found up in a tree or atop a grave in a cemetery. More modern tellings of this vampire say it no longer is content to wander down seldom-used roads but has learned it can slip unnoticed into celebrations to hunt for men.

Sources: Besson, *Folklore and Legends*, 12; Cartey, *The West Indies*, 43; Jones, *Evil in Our Midst*, 122; Parson, *Folk-lore of the Antilles*, 75.

Diabolic Hosts

Johann Wierus's *Pseudomonarchia Daemonum* (*False Monarchy of Demons*, 1583) claimed that there are seventy-two infernal princes and 7,405,926 devils that make up the diabolic monarchy. They are grouped in 1,111 legions of 6,666 souls each. Weirus also defined six species of demons: igneous demons are those that never descend to the earth; AERIAL DEVILS are those who roam through the air and appear on occasion as men; TERRESTRIAL DEVILS dwell in secret among men or set snares for hunters and travelers; aquatic demons are those who cause storms at sea; subterranean demons dwell in caves and are very spiteful; and Lucifuges are those who shun the light of day and assume corporeal features by night.

Sources: Gijswijt-Hofstra, *Witchcraft and Magic in Europe*, 215; Lazarus, *Comparative Religion for Dummies*, 292; Penwyche, *World of Angels*, 51; Roper, *Witch Craze*, 74; Waite, *Eradicating the Devil's Minions*, 25.

Diabolic Pact

A diabolic pact is a contractual agreement, either written or spoken, that is made between the DEVIL and a mortal. Although each pact varies depending on each person's needs, wants, and desires, all pacts have five points in common. First, there must be some sort of preparation before attempting to summon a demon, such as abstaining from sex or not eating meat. Next, a ritual invocation must be performed that includes a sacrifice. A complex set of formulas must be followed precisely, and if all is done correctly, the Devil will appear. The bargain will be struck and the pact itself must be signed with blood drawn from the left arm. If the pact was successful, the person will no longer cast a shadow or have a reflection in a mirror.

Sources: Broedel, *Malleus Maleficarum and the Construction of Witchcraft*, 123–4. 130, 147; Gijswijt-Hofstra, *Witchcraft and Magic in Europe*, 225, 231; Roper, *Witch Craze*, 94–95, 116–7.

Diabolical Signature

Variations: Demonic seal

In 1575 an unknown author published *Grimoire Arbatel de Magia Veterum* (*Arbatel of the Magic of the Ancients*) in Basel, Switzerland. It defined a diabolical signature as the unique signature of a devil, demon, or similar type spirit that is designed to conceal their actual name. It is described as looking like complicated lineal drawings written in a circle, similar to how Egyptian royalty placed their names in a cartouche. These signatures are typically rendered in blood.

It should be mentioned that some demons have more than one signature and many demonic seals contain the cross, which is supposed to frighten and repel demons according to alchemists, cabalists, priests, scientists, and theologians of the Renaissance era.

Sources: Caciola, *Divine and Demonic Possession in the Middle Age*, 47; Davies, *Grimoires*, 115; Roper, *Witch Craze*, 212; Mathers, *Grimoire of Armadel*, 12, 44, 50.

Dibeil

Variations: Dobriel

Dibeil is one of the twenty SERVITORS OF CAMUEL (see CAMUEL). A nocturnal demon, he appears before his summoner in a beautiful form and has a reputation for being very courteous.

Sources: Guiley, *Encyclopedia of Demons and Demonology*, 36; Peterson, *Lesser Key of Solomon*, 68.

Dimirag

Dimirag ("driving forward," "impulsion") is named as one of the forty-nine SERVITORS OF BEELZEBUB (see BEELZEBUB) in the *Sacred Magic of Abramelin the Mage*, book two. His name originates from Chaldaic mythology.

Sources: Ford, *Bible of the Adversary*, 93; Mathers, *Book of the Sacred Magic of Abramelin the Mage*, 107; Von Worms, *Book of Abramelin*, 257.

Dimme

Variations: Lamashtu, "the seven witches"

According to Mesopotamian mythology, the DEMONESS Dimme was born the daughter of the Sky god An. She is described as having the head of a lion and is depicted in art as kneeling on the back of a donkey while carrying a two-headed snake in each hand; a DOG is suckling from her right breast while a piglet suckles from her left. She infects infants and men with diseases, killing men to drink their blood and eat their flesh.

Dimme causes NIGHTMARES, destroys crops, infects infants with diseases, makes pregnant women miscarry, and poisons rivers.

Sources: Chopra, *Academic Dictionary of Mythology*, 170; Doniger, *Merriam-Webster's Encyclopedia of World Religions*, 353; Sorensen, *Possession and Exorcism in the New Testament and Early Christianity*, 27–8.

Dimurgos

Ars Goetia, the first book of the *Lemegeton*, the *Lesser Key of Solomon*, names Dimurgos ("artisan" or "workman") as one of the fifty-three SERVITORS OF ASHTAROTH AND ASMODEUS (see ASHTAROTH and ASMODEUS).

Sources: Mathers, *Book of the Sacred Magic of Abramelin the Mage*, 128; Von Worms, *Book of Abramelin*, 247.

Diopos

In the *Sacred Magic of Abramelin the Mage*, book two, Diopos ("an overseer") is named as one of the fifteen SERVITORS OF ASMODEUS AND MAGOTH (see ASMODEUS). However, in the language of the ancient Etruscans, Diopos means "he who looks stealthily."

Sources: Belanger, *Dictionary of Demons*, 110; Mathers, *Book of the Sacred Magic of Abramelin the Mage*, 106; Torelli, *The Etruscans*, 232.

Dioron

The *Sacred Magic of Abramelin the Mage*, book two, names Dioron ("delay") as one of the fifty-three SERVITORS OF ASHTAROTH AND ASMODEUS (see ASHTAROTH and ASMODEUS).

Sources: Belanger, *Dictionary of Demons*, 110; Mathers, *Book of the Sacred Magic of Abramelin the Mage*, 115.

Dirachiel

In Enochian and Jewish lore, Dirachiel, a FALLEN ANGEL, is named as one of the seven ELECTORS OF HELL. He is also one of the twenty-eight demonic rulers of the lunar mansions, having dominion over the mansion Athanna (also known as Alchaya the "little star of great light") (see ENOCHIAN RULERS OF THE LUNAR MANSIONS). Dirachiel is known to destroy harvests and prevent physicians from helping people.

Sources: Moura, *Mansions of the Moon for the Green Witch*, 42; Scheible, *Sixth and Seventh Books of Moses*, 75; Von Goethe, *Goethe's Letters to Zelter*, 377; Webster, *Encyclopedia of Angels*, 50.

Diralisen

Variations: Diralison

In the *Sacred Magic of Abramelin the Mage*, book two, Diralisen ("the ridge of a rock") is named as one of the forty-nine SERVITORS OF BEELZEBUB (see BEELZEBUB).

Sources: Belanger, *Dictionary of Demons*, 110; Ford, *Bible of the Adversary*, 93; Susej, *Demonic Bible*, 258.

Diriel

In the *Theurgia Goetia*, book two of the *Lemegeton*, Diriel is ranked as a duke and is named as one of the twelve SERVITORS OF DEMORIEL (see DEMORIEL and DUKES OF HELL).

Sources: McLean, *Treatise of Angel Magic*, 34, 54; Peterson, *Lesser Key of Solomon*, 89.

Dis

Variations: Deius Piter, Dis Pater ("Wealthy Father"), Dispater, Father Dis, ORCUS, Pluto, Sucellus, Vedionis

In ancient Greek, Roman, and Slavic mythology, Dis ("Wealthy") was born one of the three sons of Saturn and Ops; his brothers are Jupiter and Neptune, and his wife is Proserpina. Dis is also the name of one of the cities in Hell.

Dis has three faces: one black, one red, and one white. The demon of death and the ruler of the Underworld, only oaths and curses sworn while striking the ground can reach him. Black sheep were sacrificed to him and the Roman Senate declared that every one hundred years a special three-day-long festival would be held to honor Dis and his wife. He commands the demons ARIOCH, BAALZEPHON, BIFFANT, BITRU, Furcas (see FORCAS), Merodach, and Titivulus (see TITIVILLUS).

Sources: Beeton, *Beeton's Classical Dictionary*, 110; Daly, *Greek and Roman Mythology A to Z*, 43; Turner, *Dictionary of Ancient Deities*, 43.

Disolel

The *Sacred Magic of Abramelin the Mage*, book two, names Disolel as one of the fifteen SERVITORS OF ASMODEUS AND MAGOTH (see ASMODEUS).

Sources: Matters, *Book of the Sacred Magic of Abramelin the Mage*, 113; Von Worms, *Book of Abramelin*, 248.

Dison

Dison ("divided") is one of the fifteen SERVITORS OF PAYMON (see PAYMON) In the *Sacred Magic of Abramelin the Mage*, book two.

Sources: Belanger, *Dictionary of Demons*, 110; Von Worms, *Book of Abramelin*, 257.

Div, plural: divs

Variations: Daivres, devas

From the demonology of ancient Persia and in Zoroastrian mythology comes a species of demon known as the div; the word translates from ancient Iranian to mean "false god." Under the command of Aherman these demons prey upon animals, crops, man, and plants. Divs have the ability to shape-shift into devils, giants, ogres, snakes, and other various forms. Female divs are known as perris; however, male divs are considered to be the more dangerous and evil of the two genders. All divs are subject to human frailties and weaknesses.

Divs live high up in the mountains in caves but can also be found wandering in the desert. Their capital city, Ahermanabad, is located on mount Kaf. The god Mithra is their personal adversary.

Sources: Spence, *Encyclopedia of Occultism*, 129; Turner, *Dictionary of Ancient Deities*, 147; Yadav, *Global Encyclopaedia of Education*, 513.

Div Sepid

In ancient Iranian mythology Div Sepid ("white demon") was a DIV that was said to live in a cave in Mazandaran.

Sources: Blavatsky, *Secret Doctrine,* 407; Curtis, *Persian Myths*, 49.

Djall, plural: djaj

Variations: Dreqi

Djall is an Albanian demon of death and evil. The word is also used as another name for the DEVIL.

Sources: Lurker, *Routledge Dictionary of Gods and Goddesses*, 214; Rose, *Spirits, Fairies, Gnomes, and Goblins*, 87.

Djinn

Variations: Ajnan (male), Ande, CIN, Cinler, the "concealed ones," the "dark ones," DIV, Djin, Djinnee, Djinni, Djinny, Dschin, Duh, Dzin, Dzsinn, Genii, GENIE, Génie, Gênio, GHADDAR, Ginn, Haltija, Hengetär, JANN, Jin, Jinn, Jinnee, (plural: Jineeyeh), Jinni, Jinniyah (female), Jinnie, Jinniy, Ka-Jinn ("fire demon"), Kijini, MARID, Mareed, Maride, Nar, Nara, QUTRUB, SE'IRIM, Skyddsande, Szellem, Xhind

In Islamic mythology the djinn ("angry, possessed") are a race of demons that are divided into two species. The first has five classes: Afreet, GHILAN, Jann, Marid, and the Sheitan. The other has only three: GHUL, IFRIT, and SILA. They were created by Allah out of smokeless fire and were given permission to attempt to seduce and tempt men away from God's teachings. They are immortal and unless slain they will live indefinitely. When a djinn has been mortally wounded it bleeds fire; eventually the flames will consume the demon. They will also avoid direct sunlight, salt, and steel. These demons fear the "falling stars" that God can throw at them and the sound of singing. In general they are known to be quick-tempered and vain.

All djinn were ruled by a succession of seventy-two kings or "Suleyman." Their homeland is called Jinnistan; its capital city is called the City of Jewels and its main district is called the Country of Delight. Outside of their homeland they live in abandoned buildings, caves, graveyards, places of darkness, and underground. If a djinn is near, cattle will refuse to drink if driven to water.

Nocturnal demons of fire, the djinn have the ability to shape-change into a variety of animals, insects, inanimate objects, and reptiles, frogs, heavily muscled youths, lizards, scorpions, snakes, and wrinkled old men. They will even take the form of a hybrid animal, such as a hyena-wolf crossbreed. Additionally, djinn can become invisible, cause insanity, foretell the future, possess inanimate objects, and spread diseases.

Djinn are capable of PROCREATION with their own species as well as with humans. They have INCUBUS-like tendencies and the offspring of a djinn and human coupling take the best attributes of each parent. These children are very cunning and are considered dangerous, and like all djinn, are immortal unless slain.

Unlike other demons, djinn have free will, and with it they have the ability to choose to be good or evil. Evil djinn can be redeemed if they are converted to Islam. King Solomon is said to have gained control over the djinn by use of magical spells given to him by an archangel (see IBLIS, JAN-IBN-JAN, and SPIRITS OF SOLOMON).

Sources: Hughes, *Dictionary of Islam*, 135; Hyatt, *Book of Demons*, 54–5; Knowles, *Nineteenth Century*, Vol. 31, 449.

Dog

Variations: The Devil's accomplice

Although traditionally dogs are remembered for their loyalty and faithfulness, there is a little known and ancient belief that says that dogs are commonly the companion of a necromancer. Dogs that are solid black were especially suspect because it was also believed that this was one of the forms that the DEVIL would adopt so that he could be closer to the necromancer he was assisting without arousing too much suspicion. In ancient times black dogs were sacrificed to infernal entities.

Sources: Baskin, *Sorcerer's Handbook*, 180, Collin de Plancy, *Dictionary of Witchcraft*, 55; Conway, *Demonology and Devil-lore*, 137.

Döghalál

Döghalál ("plague-like") is a Hungarian demon of cholera and numerous other plagues.

Sources: Herczegh, *Magyar Családi És Öröklési Jog*, 168.

Dommiel

Dommiel is the demon of terror and trembling. He is the Guardian of the Gates of Hell.

Sources: Netzley, *Angels*, 67.

Dorak

In the *Sacred Magic of Abramelin the Mage*, book two, Dorak ("proceeding," "walking forward") is among the forty-nine SERVITORS OF BEELZEBUB (see BEELZEBUB).

Sources: Ford, *Bible of the Adversary*, 93; Mathers, *Book of the Sacred Magic of Abramelin the Mage*, 120; Von Worms, *Book of Abramelin*, 257.

Dorje Phangmo

Variations: Vajra Varahi

According to the ancient Tibetan text *Kangi Karchhak*, Dorje Phangmo is the red-skinned demonic consort, or wife, of Demchhok. Identified with DURGA, she lives on the snow-capped mountain of Tijun.

Sources: Bedi, *Kailas and Manasarovar After 22 Years in Shiva's Domain*, 4; Turner, *Dictionary of Ancient Deities*, 489.

Dorochiel

In the *Theurgia Goetia*, the second book of the *Lemegeton*, Dorochiel ("trampling") is ranked as prince of the West by Northwest (see PRINCES OF HELL). One of the twelve SERVITORS OF AMENADIEL, he commands forty diurnal dukes, forty nocturnal dukes, twenty-four diurnal chief dukes, twenty-four nocturnal chief dukes, and an innumerable amount of servitors.

Sources: Guiley, *Encylopedia of Demons and Demonology*, 69; Peterson, *Lesser Key of Solomon*, 89.

Douens

From the mythology of the Republic of Trinidad and Tobago comes a species of demon known as douens. They are created whenever a child dies before it has been baptized, and when they return they look like genderless, faceless, naked children with small mouths and backward-turned feet. They stand no more than three feet tall and wear floppy straw hats. Douens crave the love of a family but have been damned to wander the earth, lost and alone, forever.

Douens prey upon unbaptized children, luring them out into the woods with a mesmerizing whooping sound until they are lost. It is advised never to call out a child's name, as the douens will use it to lure the child away. These demons are pranksters and cry at the front door of homes at night. Douens will eat food out of people's gardens and have a bizarre fondness for water crabs.

These demons, which live in the forest and near rivers, have been known to assist animals that are being hunted, are injured, or are caught in a trap.

Sources: Ahye, *Golden Heritage*, 154–6; Carter, *Myth and Superstition in Spanish-Caribbean Literature*, 248–9.

Dousheta

Variations: Opyri, Oupir

Bulgarian folklore claims that if a child dies before it can be baptized, then it will become a type of vampiric demon known as a dousheta.

Sources: Bryant, *Handbook of Death*, 99; Georgieva, *Bulgarian Mythology*, 102; MacPherson, *Blood of His Servants*, 25.

Draca

In Celtic mythology the draca ("drake") is a demonic spirit that lives in lakes and rivers and preys upon women. It lures them into the water where it then devours them.

Sources: Whitney, *Century Dictionary and Cyclopedia*, 2229.

Dragon at the Apocalypse

Variations: Apocalyptic Beast, Dabba, Dragon of the Apocalypse, Dragon of Revelation, Hydra of the Apocalypse, the old serpent, Red Beast of the Apocalypse, SATAN

The Book of Revelation names the Dragon at the Apocalypse as the demon of sin. This red being has seven heads with ten horns and seven crowns upon each head. This demon's personal adversary in Heaven is the archangel Michael; on earth it is St. George.

Sources: Rose, *Giants, Monsters, and Dragon*s, 106–7; Smith, *Prophecies of Daniel and the Revelation*, 562, 564.

Drakul

Variations: Dracul

In the Moldavia and Rumania languages the word *drakul* means "the dragon" or "demon nearly" and it is used to describe a type of vampiric demon that possesses the body of a deceased person and animates it. Once the demon has possession of the corpse, it makes it walk around naked, carrying its coffin on its head while looking for humans to prey upon. Fortunately, if the burial shroud of the person is destroyed, the demon will lose its hold on the body.

Sources: Andreescu, *Vlad the Impaler*, 183; McNally, *In Search of Dracula*, 21; Twitchell, *Living Dead*, 16.

Dramas

In *Ars Goetia*, the first book of the *Lemegeton*, Dramas ("action") is named as one of the fifty-three SERVITORS OF ASHTAROTH AND ASMODEUS (see ASHTAROTH and ASMODEUS).

Sources: Guiley, *Encyclopedia of Demons and Demonology*, 246; Spence, *Encyclopedia of Occultism*, 187.

Dramiel

In the *Theurgia Goetia*, the second book of the *Lemegeton*, Dramiel, an AERIAL DEVIL, is named as one of the ten Duke SERVITORS OF EMONIEL (see EMONIEL). Good-natured and willing to obey his summoner, he commands 1,320 lesser dukes and servitors. Dramiel lives in the woods.

Sources: Bellanger, *Dictionary of Demons*, 112; Peterson, *Lesser a Key of Solomon*, 67, 97; Trithemius, *Steganographia*, 23.

Drelmeth

In the *Ars Paulina*, the third book of the *Lemegeton*, Drelmeth is named as being one of the FALLEN ANGELS and one of the twenty chiefs. He is most powerful during the third hour of the day. Drelmeth is one of the SERVITORS OF VEGUANIEL (see VEGUANIEL).

Sources: Davidson, *Dictionary of Angels*, 98; Waite, *The Book of Ceremonial Magic*, 67.

Dresop

In the *Sacred Magic of Abramelin the Mage*, Dresop ("they who attack their prey by tremulous motion") is among the twenty SERVITORS OF AMAYMON (see AMAYMON).

Sources: Forgotten Books, *Book of the Sacred Magic of Abramelin the Mage*, 42–3; Lowry, *Under the Volcano*, 194; Mathers, *Book of the Sacred Magic of Abra-Melin*, 122.

Drouk

Drouk is a Celtic word that translates to mean "DEVIL."

Sources: Bellanger, *Dictionary of Demons*, 112; Mathers, *Book of the Sacred Magic of Abramelin the Mage*, 109.

Drsmiel

Drsmiel is an evil angel who is summoned to separate a husband from his wife (see also IABIEL).

Sources: Davidson, *Dictionary of Angels*, 98; Gaster, *Sword of Moses*, 52.

Druden

Variations: Perchten, Trotha, Truden, Walküren

From the demonology of South Germany and Austria comes the druden ("ghosts" or "powers"). Originally they were seen as AERIAL DEVILS, demonic witches, or evil spirits that were believed to have escaped from the Land of the Dead in order to plague mankind.

At night it was believed that a druden would try to sneak into a man's room through a small opening, like a keyhole or window crack; then it would sit upon his chest and "ride" him, oftentimes causing NIGHTMARES. Should the victim awake during the assault he would see what would look like a heavyset, old, and ugly woman. Fortunately, they can be easily warded off with the sign of the pentagram. In more persistent cases a beloved household pet must be offered to the druden in place of the man. Should the offering be accepted, the animal will be found dead.

Druden were said to be active participants in the Wild Hunt; however, after the introduction of Christianity, they were reduced to nursery bogies.

Sources: Lurker, *Routledge Encyclopedia of Gods and Goddesses*, 53; Spence, *Encyclopedia of Occultism*, 297.

Drug

Variations: Drauga, DRUH, DRUJ

According to ancient Iranian mythology, the god ANGRA MAINYU created a type of DAEVAS called *drug* ("lie," as to deceive). Appearing as a woman, this nocturnal demon of lies preyed upon licentious men. Her sacred animal was the snake, and she was most powerful in the winter. Drug's personal adversary is Asha Vahishta (see also DRUJ NASU).

Sources: Lurker, *Dictionary of Gods and Goddesses*, 100; Messadié, *History of the Devil*, 83.

Druh

In Iranian mythology, Druh ("harm") is the demon of lies. He lives in dark caves.

Sources: Petrie, *Journal of the Transactions of the Victoria Institute*, Vol. 14, 328; Woodard, *Cambridge Companion to Greek Mythology*, 129, 161.

Druj

Variations: Drauga, DRUG, DRUH, Druje

In ancient Iranian mythology the nocturnal demon of lies, Druj ("lie," as to deceive), was originally a singular individual, but in later periods, she became a DAEVAS and was considered to be the personification of evil. Most powerful during winter months, Druj is in service to AHRIMAN. Her personal adversary is Asha (see DRUJ NASU).

Sources: Dhalla, *Zoroastrian Theology*, 164–6; Ford, *Liber Hvhi*, 123; Horne, *Sacred Books and Early Literature of the East*, 135.

Druj Nasu

In ancient Iranian mythology, Druj Nasu ("Liar nasu") was the demon of uncleanness of the body. Named as a DAEVAS in the Avestan texts, this female demon feeds off human corpses. As soon as a person's soul leaves their body, if the corpse is guarded by only one person, Druj Nasu will swoop down from Aresura, her mountain home, in the form of a fly. Then she will seize the corpse and attack the lone mourner. Druj Nasu can be warded off with the use of specific holy spells or by the gaze of a yellow dog with four eyes (having a dark spot over each of its eyes) or a white dog with yellow ears (see also DRUG, DRUJ).

Sources: Choksy, *Evil, Good and Gender*, 17; Dhalla, *Zoroastrian Theology*, 165; Horne, *Sacred Books and Early Literature of the East*, 93–4.

Drusiel

In the *Theurgia Goetia*, book two of the *Lemegeton*, Drusiel is named as one of the twelve Chief Duke SERVITORS OF MACARIEL (see MACARIEL). He commands four hundred servitors. Drusiel is both a diurnal and nocturnal demon, and when summoned will appear in a variety of forms, but will do so most commonly as a dragon with the head of a virgin. Said to be good-natured and willing to obey his summoner, Drusiel, like all AERIAL DEVILS, is constantly on the move, never staying in any one place for long.

Sources: Guiley, *Encyclopedia of Demons and Demonology*, 35; Peterson, *Lesser Key of Solomon*, 103; Trithemius, *Steganographia*, 141.

Dubbiel

Variations: Angel of Persia, Dobiel, Dubiel, Prince of the kingdom of Persia

Dubbiel ("bear-god") had once overseen Heaven for twenty-one days while the archangel Gabriel was temporarily removed from the position because he was in a momentary state of disgrace. While Dubbiel was in power, he became corrupt through national bias and elevated Persia in favor over Israel, the country that was under Gabriel's protection. When Gabriel was returned to power he restored Israel to the position of most favored. In many grimoires Dubbiel is counted as one of the FALLEN ANGELS.

Sources: Davidson, *Dictionary of Angels*, 98; Guiley, *Encyclopedia of Angels*, 109; Trithemius, *Steganographia*, 73.

Dubilon

In the *Theurgia Goetia*, the second book of the *Lemegeton*, Dubilon is one of the twelve Chief Duke SERVITORS OF DEMORIEL (see DEMORIEL and DUKES OF HELL). An AERIAL DEVIL, he commands 1,140 servitors.

Sources: Guiley, *Encyclopedia of Demons and Demonology*, 60, Peterson, *Lesser Key of Solomon*, 63.

Ducci

Variations: The DEVIL, Ducii

Ducci ("sweet") is the name of an INCUBUS

from medieval folklore. Appearing as a handsome young man to sleeping women, this nocturnal demon would have sexual relations with women while they slept; he would either drain them of nearly all their life energies or possess them.

Sources: Edwards, *Melbourne Review*, Vol. 7, 256; Gettings, *Dictionary of Demons*, 99; Robbins, *Encyclopedia of Witchcraft and Demonology*, 45.

Dud

In Tibetan mythology Dud ("smoke" or "to bow") is an AERIAL DEVIL. Described as being black in color, he lives in a black castle.

Sources: Labdrön, *Machik's Complete Explanation*, 334; Norbu, *Drung, Deu, and Bön*, 90, 171; Waddell, *Buddhism of Tibet, or Lamaism*, 538.

Dukes of Hell

There are one hundred eighteen named dukes mentioned in the various grimoires. They are ABIGOR, ABRULGES, ACEREBA, ACLEROR, AGARES, AGLAS, AGRA, AIM, Alocer (ALLOCEN), AMBRI, Amduscias (Amudcias), AMESIEL, ANAEL, Aneyr, ARAON, ARIAIEL, ARIFEL, ARMANY, ARMBIEL, ASHIB, ASHTAROTH, ASSABA, ASTARTE, ASTOR, Ba'al, Baabel, BALSUR, BARBATOS, BARBIL, BARIEL, BATHIM, BEDARY, BENOHAM, BERBIS, BERITH, Bonoham, BUCAFAS, Budarijm, BUNE, BURISIEL, CABARIM, CAMIEL, CAMOR, Camorr, CAPRIEL, CARIFAS, CARNET, CARNOL, CARPID, CHARIEL, CHOMIEL, CHURIBAL, CIRECAS, CLEANSI, CODRIEL, COTIEL, CROCELL, CRUHIEL, CUMERZEL, DABRINOS, DANTALIAN, DIRIEL, DUBILON, EBRA, Flauros (HAURAS), FURCALOR, GABIR, GERIEL, GOMORY, HAMORPHOL, ITRASBIEL, Itules, KIRIEL, LAMAEL, LAPHOR, LARMOL, LUZIEL, MADRES, Madriel, MANSI, MARAS, MARQUES, MISHEL, Moder, Monandor, MORCAZA, MURMUR, MUSIRIEL, Myrezyn, NADROC, NAPHULA (Valupa), NARAS, ORMENU, ORVICH, Otiel, PRUFLAS, RABLION, RANTIEL, RAPSEL, RECIEL, SABAS, SADIEL, SARIEL, SOCHAS, SOTHEANS, SYRACH, Temol, TIGARA, UVALL, VADRAS, VADRIEL, Valefor, Vepar (SEPAR), VRIEL, Vusiel, Wall, ZABRIEL, Zepar, and ZOENIEL.

Sources: De Laurence, *Lesser Key of Solomon, Goetia*, 35–6; Poinsot, McLean, *Treatise of Angel Magic*, 51; *Complete Book of the Occult and Fortune Telling*, 377; Scot, *Discoverie of Witchcraft*, 225; Waite, *Manual of Cartomancy and Occult Divination*, 97.

Dulid

The *Sacred Magic of Abramelin the Mage*, book two, Dulid is included as one of the sixty-five SERVITORS OF KORE AND MAGOTH.

Sources: Belanger, *Dictionary of Demons*; 114; Mathers, *Book of the Sacred Magic of Abramelin the Mage*, 118.

Duma

Variations: Douma, Dumah, the Guardian of Egypt, Keeper of the Three Keys to the Three Gates of Hell

Originally a Sumerian god of vegetation from Yiddish folklore, Duma ("dumbness" or "silence") is said to be the chief of the demons in Gehinnom (the hell for outspoken sinners). He is also one of the seven PRINCES OF HELL as well as the national guardian angel of Egypt (see PRINCES OF HELL). An angel of vindication or FALLEN ANGEL, Duma is the demon of the silence of death and commands the PRESIDENTS OF HELL, 12,000 servitors, and tens of thousands of angels of destruction. He is described as having a thousand eyes and carries a flaming sword.

Sources: Davidson, *Dictionary of Angels*, 99; Guiley, *Encyclopedia of Angels*, 109; Olyan, *Thousand Thousands Served Him*, 75.

Durga

Variations: Sang Hyang Bathari

According to contemporary Javanese mythology, Durga, a death goddess, is the female ruler of the spirit world and the consort to Bathara Guru. She commands all of the dangerous and demonic free-floating spirits that she uses as her "army." Appearing as a beautiful young woman, she protects her chosen city from dark powers, such as death and disease. Durga lives in the woods and can be found wandering in cremation grounds.

Sources: Chopra, *Academic Dictionary of Mythology*, 92; Jinruigaku, *Asian Folklore Studies*, Vol. 56, 255–6; Monaghan, *Encyclopedia of Goddesses and Heroines*, 152–3, 171–2.

Durzi

In Zoroastrian demonology, Durzi is the demon of falsehood and vanity. He is one of the commanders of the demonic army. Durzi breaks down order by causing chaos and confusion. He has the ability to shape-shift and spread death, illness, and pestilence.

Sources: Abdul-Rahman, *Islam*, 111.

Dus

In Celtic lore there is a species of hairy vampiric demons called dus ("specter") that consume the flesh and blood of humans. They are believed to live in the woods.

Sources: Gettings, *Dictionary of Demons*, 84; Turner, *Dictionary of Ancient Deities*, 159; Whitney, *Century Dictionary and Cyclopedia*, 1576.

Duses, plural: dusii

Variations: LUTINS

In Gaulish mythology a duses ("demon") is a

type of INCUBUS. Dusii, as they are called collectively, live in caves in the woods and have sexual relations with witches and young maidens. In ancient times, Gaul was a region of land in Western Europe that is made up of modern-day Belgium, France, northern Italy, western Switzerland, and those parts of Germany and the Netherlands that touch upon the river Rhine.

Sources: Buckingham, *New England Magazine*, Vol. 5, 7; Masters, *Eros and Evil*, 65; Sinistrari, *Demoniality*, 21; Stephens, *Demon Lovers*, 81.

Dusins

Variations: Dehuset

The word *dusins* is vulgar slang for "deuce take you." *Duce* is Gaulish for the DEVIL.

Sources: Anonymous, *Guernsey Magazine*, Vol. 10, n.p.; Shepard, *Encyclopedia of Occultism and Paraschology*, 327; Spence, *Encyclopedia of Occultism*, 121.

Dusiriel

In the *Theurgia Goetia*, the second book of the *Lemegeton*, Dusiriel is one of the eleven chief dukes of HYDRIEL (see DUKES OF HELL). Described as looking like a serpent with a virgin's face and head, Dusiriel is an AERIAL DEVIL who may be summoned any time of the day or night. Said to be very courteous and willing to obey his summoner, he commands 1,320 servitors and is said to live in or near water, marshes, and wetlands.

Sources: Belanger, *Dictionary of Demons*, 114; Peterson, *Lesser Key of Solomon*, 95.

Dwopi

In Myanmar demonology a dwopi demon causes madness. It is believed to live above the doorway to a house.

Sources: Carey, *Chin Hills*, 197; Hastings, *Encyclopaedia of Religion and Ethics*, Vol. 3, 25; Scott, *Burma*, 404.

Dyavo

Dyavo is a Serbian word that translates to mean "the DEVIL."

Sources: Sykes, *Who's Who in Non-Classical Mythology*, 58; Turner, *Dictionary of Ancient Deities*, 160.

Dybbuk, plural: dybbukim

Variations: Gilgul ("clinging soul")

The concept of the dybbuk first entered into Judaism by means of the mysticism that was practiced in the eighth century. Jews were forbidden to practice the art of mysticism for fear that it would weaken their faith. However, by the twelfth century mysticism was an accepted part of the kabala, and by the sixteenth century mysticism was completely embraced.

The dybbuk ("cleaving" or "clinging"), an evil and restless vampiric spirit, was said by some sources to be one of the children born of LILITH; others say that it was created through an act of sorcery. Earliest beliefs in the dybbuk claimed that it was a demon, but later that origin was changed to be the soul of a person attempting to escape final justice. Its description remained the same, that of a hairy, unclean, goatlike demon.

For the dybbuk to survive, it must gain entry into a human body. It may allow itself to be breathed in through incense or it may embed itself in a piece of food about to be eaten, but typically it will make its own way into the body by force if necessary, through the nostril, although any orifice will suffice. Once it has gained access, the dybbuk will possess the person and begin to feed off the person's life force, taking up residence in their pinky finger or one of the toes.

While it is in the body, the dybbuk will drive the person to consume candy and other such treats, as it has a sweet tooth. The person will begin to tire and soon fall ill. They may even develop a twitch and start to vomit up a foamy white substance. After a little while the dybbuk will start to cause mental illness, and with the person weak and broken down, the dybbuk will become the dominant personality. Eventually the dybbuk will leave the body, as it can only occupy a body for a limited amount of time. The possessed person may be saved by a rabbi who has specialized training to perform a complex ritual to drive the dybbuk away.

Amulets made of wax or iron may be worn or hung in the home to ward it off. Repeating certain ritual incantations may work as well. Red ribbons and garlic tied to a baby's crib will protect a child. Leaving almonds, candy, raisins, and the like for the dybbuk to find will cause it to leave a baby alone as well.

When not possessing a person, dybbukim, as they are collectively called, live in caves, dust storms, whirlwinds, and buildings that have been abandoned for some time.

Sources: Dennis, *Encyclopedia of Jewish Myth*, 72–3; Loewenthal, *Religion, Culture and Mental Health*, 119–20; Mack, *Field Guide to Demons*, 241; Schwartz, *Reimagining the Bible*, 72–77.

Eac

According to Enochian lore, Eac is a CACODAEMON. His counterpart is the angel Acae (see ENOCHIAN CACODAEMONS).

Sources: Chopra, *Academic Dictionary of Mythology*, 94; Laycock, *Complete Enochian Dictionary*, 106.

Earls of Hell

There are twenty named earls mentioned in the various grimoires. They are ANDROMALIUS, BARBATOS, BIFRONS, BOTIS, CAACRINOLAAS, FORAII, FORFAX, FURFUR, GLACIA LABOLAS, GLASSYALABOLAS, HALPHAS, IPES, MARAX, MORAX, MURMUR, RÄUM, RONOBE, SALEOS, VINÉ, and ZAEBOS.

Sources: Ashley, *Complete Book of Devils and Demons*, 60, 74; De Claremont, *Ancient's Book of Magic*; Diagram Group, *Little Giant Encyclopedia*, 504; Scott, *London Magazine*, Vol. 5, 378.

Ebaron

In the *Sacred Magic of Abramelin the Mage*, Ebaron ("not burdensome") is among the fifteen SERVITORS OF PAYMON (see PAYMON).

Sources: Mathers, *Book of the Secret Magic of Abramelin the Mage*, 108; Von Worms, *Book of Abramelin*, 257.

Eblis

Variations: AZAZEL, the Father of Devils, the Great SATAN, Haris, Iblees, IBLIS, the SATAN of Mohammed

There are two stories of Eblis ("despair"). The first has him as an angel who resided in Azaze, the Heaven nearest God, but he refused to bow down to Adam and acknowledge him as a superior creation. He joined the rebel angels and after the battle he was banished to Hell. There he was transformed into a SHAITAN, condemned to haunt ruins and eat unblessed food until Judgment Day.

In the other story of Eblis, he was a DJINN who was captured in the great war between the Djinn and the angels. He was taken back to Heaven, re-educated, and gained angelic status. He became the Treasurer of the Heavenly Paradise. When Eblis learned that his brother Djinn had regrouped and were preparing for another attack on Heaven, Eblis, seeking even more power, broke free from the angels and returned to his fellow DJINN to lead them. He became the chief of all the DJINN, and according to Arabic and Persian mythology he commands all of the evil Djinn. Like all Djinn, he was created by God out of smokeless fire. As a FALLEN ANGEL he has been given the rank and title of Chief of Those Who Rebelled. He was the angel who taught men how to make tools and develop skills that were forbidden to them.

Sources: Ashley, *Complete Book of Devils and Demons*, 92; Brewer, *Character Sketches of Romance, Fiction and the Drama*, 90–1, 201; Daniels, *Encyclopaedia of Superstitions, Folklore, and the Occult Sciences of the World*, 1250; Horne, *Sacred Books and Early Literature of the East*, 114.

Ebra

According to the *Theurgia Goetia*, the second book of the *Lemegeton*, Duke Ebra is one of the eleven named SERVITORS OF PAMERSIEL (see DUKES OF HELL and PAMERSIEL). A nocturnal AERIAL DEVIL, Ebra is known as being a very useful demon when it comes to driving out spirits from haunted places. He is an expert liar and cannot keep a secret. Ebra is arrogant and stubborn and when summoned it must be done from the second floor of a home or in a wide open space.

Sources: Guiley, *Encyclopedia of Demons and Demonolgy*, 196; McLean, *Treatise on Angel Magic*, 36; Peterson, *Lesser Key of Solomon*, 64; Waite, *Manual of Cartomancy and Occult Divination*, 97.

Edimmu

Variations: Êdimmu, Êkimmu, Ekimmu

An edimmu is a species of ghost from Sumerian mythology. Its name translates to mean "the seizer." Akin to many AERIAL DEVILS, the edimmu are invisible and noncorporeal. Created when a person does not receive proper burial rites, these demonic ghosts hate the living and are known for draining away the life of children while they sleep and attacking the "middle part" of men. Edimmu have the ability to possess someone who has broken certain taboos, such as the consumption of ox meat; they can also cause disease and inspire criminal behavior. Edimmu live in the underworld in the kingdom of Ereshkigal, the goddess of death and gloom, where they are favored subjects (see IRKALLA). Fortunately, the destruction of this type of demon is easy enough, as performing a proper funeral rite for the body of the deceased will dissolve the demonic being.

Sources: Jastrow, *Religion of Babylonia and Assyria*, 260; Thompson, *Semitic Magic*, 3, 26, 3; turner, *Dictionary of Ancient Deities*, 4879.

Edriel

Duke Edriel is named as one of the ten SERVITORS OF EMONIEL in the *Theurgia Goetia*, the second book of the *Lemegeton* (see EMONIEL). He is said to be a good-natured AERIAL DEVIL and willing to obey his summoner. Edriel commands 1,320 lesser dukes and servitors and lives in the woods.

Sources: Peterson, *Lesser Key of Solomon*, 97, 119; Trithemius, *Steganographia*, 67.

Eemen

The king of death and Hell, Eemen is one of the eight AUSTATIKCO-PAULIGAUR who rule over one of the eight sides of the world, according to Persian mythology. This demonic spirit rules over his Hell, Narekah, which is filled with the wicked souls that the DIV take there.

Sources: Kindersley, *Specimens of Hindoo Literature*, 33; Shepard, *Encyclopedia of Occultism* and Parapsychology, 72; Spence, *Encyclopedia of Occultism*, 129.

Eequiel

Eequiel is an angel of Hell and a planetary spirit. He holds the rank of ELECTOR OF HELL.

Sources: Davidson, *Dictionary of Angels*, 104; Von Goethe, *Goethe's Letters to Zelter*, 377.

Effrigis

The *Sacred Magic of Abramelin the Mage* names Effrigis as one of the twenty SERVITORS OF AMAYMON (see AMAYMON). His name translates from Greek to mean "one who quivers in a horrible manner."

Sources: Forgotten Books, *Book of the Sacred Magic of Abramelin the Mage*, 42–3; Lowry, *Under the Volcano*, 194; Mathers, *Book of the Sacred Magic of Abra-Melin*, 122.

Egakireh

According to the *Sacred Magic of Abramelin the Mage*, book two, Egakireh is one of the sixty-five SERVITORS OF KORE AND MAGOTH.

Sources: Belanger, *Dictionary of Demons*, 116; Von Worms, *Book of Abramelin*, 256.

Egestes

Variations: Acestes ("pleasing goat")

In Roman mythology Egestes is the demon of poverty. Sources vary as to the gender, but this demon resides in the Underworld.

Sources: Drew, *Wiccan Bible*, 264.

Egibiel

Egibiel is, in Enochian lore, one of the twenty-eight demonic rulers of the lunar mansions. He rules the mansion named Alchas (Heart of Scorpio) and is known to cause conspiracies against princes, discord, and sedition (see ENOCHIAN RULERS OF THE LUNAR MANSIONS).

Sources: Barrett, *The Magus*, 57; Von Goethe, *Goethe's Letters to Zelter*, 378; Webster, *Encyclopedia of Angels*, 53, 125.

Egym

Variations: Egin

According to the *Grimoire of Pope Honorius*, an eighteenth-century book alleged to be written by Pope Honorius III, Egym is the demonic king of the South.

Sources: Agrippa, *Three Books of Occult Philosophy*, 536; Cavendish, *Man, Myth and Magic*, 640; González-Wippler, *Complete Book of Spells*, 131.

Eirenus

Apollonius of Tyana stated in his *Nuctemeron* (*Night Illuminated by Day*) that Eirenus is the demon of idols. He is most powerful during the third hour of the day.

Sources: Gettings, *Dictionary of Demons*, 100.

Eirnilus

In Apollonius of Tyana's *Nuctemeron* (*Night Illuminated by Day*), Eirnilus is named as the demon of fruit. He is said to be most powerful during the sixth hour.

Sources: Lévi, *Transcendental Magic*, 391; Salmonson, *Encyclopedia of Amazons*, 191.

Eisheth Zenunim

Variations: Eisheth

In Jewish mysticism and written of in the *Zoharistic Kabbalah*, Eisheth Zenunim is named as one of the four wives of SATAN. An arch she-demon, this SUCCUBUS is one of the four DEMONS OF PROSTITUTION, patron to prostitutes and whores.

Sources: Greer, *New Encyclopedia of the Occult*, 191; Guiley, *Encyclopedia of Angels*, 40; Mason, *Necronomicon Gnosis*, 151; Salmonson, *Encyclopedia of Amazons*, 191.

Ekalike

The *Sacred Magic of Abramelin the Mage*, book two, names Ekalike ("at rest" or "quiet") as one of the one hundred eleven SERVITORS OF AMAYMON, ARITON, ORIENS, AND PAYMON (see AMAYMON, ARITON, ORIENS, and PAYMON).

Sources: Mathers, *Book of the Sacred Magic of Abramelin the Mage*, 114; Von Worms, *Book of Abramelin*, 255.

Ekdulon

The *Sacred Magic of Abramelin the Mage*, book two, includes Ekdulon ("to despoil") as one of the one hundred eleven SERVITORS OF AMAYMON, ARITON, ORIENS, AND PAYMON (see AMAYMON, ARITON, ORIENS, and PAYMON).

Sources: Mathers, *Book of the Sacred Magic of Abramelin the Mage*, 112; Von Worms, *Book of Abramelin*, 255.

Ekorok

Ekorok is one of the twenty-two SERVITORS OF ARITON. His name translates from Hebrew to mean "thy breaking," or "thy barrenness" (see ARITON).

Sources: Mathers, *Book of the Sacred Magic of Abramelin the Mage*, 108; Von Worms, *Book of Abramelin*, 257.

Elafon

In the *Sacred Magic of Abramelin the Mage*, book two, Elafon ("stag") is named as one of the ten SERVITORS OF AMAYMON AND ARITON (see AMAYMON and ARITON).

Sources: Mathers, *Book of the Sacred Magic of Abramelin the Mage*, 106; Susej, *Demonic Bible*, 257.

Elathan

According to Gaelic mythology and described in the *Book of the Dun Cow* (*Lebor Na H-Uidhri*), an ancient Irish manuscript compiled around the year 1100 C.E., Elathan is a chief among the Fomorians and is considered by some to be a demon of darkness. Like all Fomorians, he has the body of a man and the head of a goat; however, Elathan was said to be very handsome. He and all of his kind were defeated by the Tuatha de Denann and driven into the sea.

Sources: Knox, *History of the County of Mayo*, 329; Moore, *The Unicorn*, 71, 72; Squire, *Celtic Myth and Legend*, 33, 51.

Elaton

In the *Sacred Magic of Abramelin the Mage*, book two, Elaton ("borne away" or "sublime") is among the ten SERVITORS OF AMAYMON AND ARITON (see AMAYMON and ARITON).

Sources: Mathers, *Book of the Sacred Magic of Abramelin the Mage*, 106; Susej, *Demonic Bible*, 257.

Elcar

Elcar is one of the twenty SERVITORS OF CAMUEL (see CAMUEL). A diurnal demon, he appears before his summoner in a beautiful form and is said to be very courteous.

Sources: Peterson, *Lesser Key of Solomon*, 68; Trithemius, *Steganographia*, 73.

Elder Lilith

Variations: Lilith the Elder, the "shell of the moon," Lilith Savta

In Cabalistic lore Elder Lilith was the wife of SAMAEL; together they were originally a mere root under the throne of God that grew and became independent through an emanation of God's power. She is described as looking like a woman with an ever-changing face, and she is a sexually veracious demon. There is a rivalry between the Elder Lilith and her daughter, YOUNGER LILITH, because her demonic husband, Samael, is sexually aroused by their daughter. ASMODEUS, the husband of Younger Lilith, is constantly fighting with Samael because of his unsolicited sexual advances. Of note, there is an old belief that on holy days Elder Lilith and Younger Lilith hold screaming contests.

Sources: Dan, *Jewish Mysticism*, 210; Patai, *Hebrew Goddess*, 228, 246, 253; Scheiber, *Occident and Orient*, 62.

Electors of Hell

An Elector of Hell is more commonly referred to as an angel of Hell, or, less commonly, as a planetary spirit. Although nearly all grimoires agree that there are seven Electors of Hell, none of them agree on who those demons are; however, there are five electors that appear commonly on the list: Amudiel, Annixiel, Barbiel, Barfael, and Dirachiel. Presented here is a list of the fifteen named Electors of Hell that were gathered from various Sources: ACIEL, AMNIXIEL, AMUDIEL, ANIGUEL, ANIZEL, ANNIXIEL, BARBIEL, BARFAEL, BARUEL, DIRACHIEL, EEQUIEL, ENEDIEL, GANAEL, GELIEL, and GENIEL.

Sources: Davidson, *Dictionary of Angels*, 104; Hall, Secret Teachings of All Ages, 297; Von Goethe, *Goethe's Letters to Zelter*, 377.

Elel

In Argentinean demonology Elel is the demon of death, illness, and storms.

Sources: Lurker, *Rutledge Dictionary of Gods and Goddesses*, 56; Rose, *Spirits, Fairies, Gnomes and Goblins*, 98; Steward, *Handbook of South American Indians*, Vol. 1, 166.

Elelogap

The *Grimoirium Verum* (*Grimoire of Truth*) is alleged to have been written by Alibek the Egyptian in 1517; however, it is now commonly believed to have been written in the eighteenth century and translated by Arthur Waite. This grimoire names Elelogap as the demon of water, a servitor of AGALIAREPT and Taralimal, but who is under the command of SAMMAEL. Having control over the element of water, Elelogap causes floods and tsunamis.

Sources: Belanger, *Dictionary of Demons*, 117; Masters, *Devil's Dominion*, 131; Waite, *Book of Black Magic*, 188.

Elerion

The *Sacred Magic of Abramelin the Mage*, book two, names Elerion ("laugher" or "mocker") as one of the twenty-two SERVITORS OF ARITON (see ARITON).

Sources: Belanger, *Dictionary of Demons*, 117; Mathers, *Book of the Sacred Magic of Abramelin the Mage*, 108, 122.

Eligor

Variations: ABIGOR, Eligos, Ertrael, Jefischa

Eligor is called the Knightly Duke; he is in service under SAMIAZA. He commands sixty legions, six chiefs, and six servitors. Eligor is described as looking like a knight carrying a lance, scepter, and standard. He is summoned for his ability to cause wars, find things that have been hidden, and kindle love and lust, especially with members of the upper classes and royalty. He is most powerful during the fourth hour of the night during the month of June. His zodiacal sign is Gemini.

As a FALLEN ANGEL he is said to have been one of the leaders of the two hundred angels who swore allegiance to SAMIAZA and rebelled against God.

Sources: Baskin, *Sorcerer's Handbook*, 276; De Laurence, *Lesser Key of Solomon, Goetia*, 27; Lévi, *History of Magic*, 38; Waite, *Unknown World 1894–1895*, 230; Wedeck, *Treasury of Witchcraft*, 96.

Elmis

In the *Sacred Magic of Abramelin the Mage*, book two, Elmis ("flying") is among the one hundred eleven SERVITORS OF AMAYMON, ARITON, ORIENS, AND PAYMON (see AMAYMON, ARITON, ORIENS, AND PAYMON).

Sources: Mathers, *Book of the Sacred Magic of Abramelin the Mage*, 105, 113; Von Worms, *Book of Abramelin*, 255.

Eloah Va-Daath

Eloah Va-Daath is one of the NINE MYSTIC NAMES used to summon demons; it translates from Hebrew to mean "Lord God of all Knowledge."

Sources: Crowley, *The Goetia*, 72; Greer, *New Encyclopedia of the Occult*, 149; Mathers, *Key of Solomon the King*, 26.

Elohim Gibor

Variations: Eloh Geburah

Elohim Gibor is one of the NINE MYSTIC NAMES used to summon demons; it translates from Hebrew to mean "Heavenly Warrior," "Lord of Battles," or "Mother Warrior."

Sources: Agrippa, *Three Books of Occult Philosophy*, 758; Crowley, *The Goetia*, 72, 91; Mathers, *Key of Solomon the King*, 26, 97; Pullen-Burry, *Qabalism*, 40, 68.

Elohim Tzabaoth

Elohim Tzabaoth is one of the NINE MYSTIC NAMES used to summon demons; it translates from Hebrew to mean "Elohim of Hosts."

Sources: Crowley, *The Goetia*, 72; Peterson, *Lesser Key of Solomon*, 141; Pullen-Burry, *Qabalism*, 40, 69, 73.

Elponen

The *Sacred Magic of Abramelin the Mage*, book two, includes Elponen ("force of hope") as one of

the forty-nine SERVITORS OF BEELZEBUB (see BEELZEBUB).

Sources: Ford, *Bible of the Adversary*, 93; Mathers, *Book of the Sacred Magic of Abramelin the Mage*, 107; Von Worms, *Book of Abramelin*, 257.

Elzagan

Variations: Elzegan

In the *Sacred Magic of Abramelin the Mage*, book two, Elzagan ("turning aside") is named as one of the one hundred eleven SERVITORS OF AMAYMON, ARITON, ORIENS, AND PAYMON (see AMAYMON, ARITON, ORIENS, and PAYMON).

Sources: Mathers, *Book of the Sacred Magic of Abramelin the Mage*, 114; Von Worms, *Book of Abramelin*, 255.

Emarfiel

In the *Ars Paulina*, the third book of the *Lemegeton*, Emarfiel is listed as one of the eleven SERVITORS OF RAHAB (see RAHAB).

Sources: Waite, *The Book of Ceremonial Magic*, 67; Trithemius, *Steganographia*, 93.

Emma-O

Variations: Emma, Judge of Souls, King of the Dead, Lord of Shadows

Emma-O is a demon from Japanese mythology. He is ranked as the ruler and chief judge of hell.

Sources: Parker, *Mythology*, 366; Russell, *Prince of Darkness*, 12; Turner, *Dictionary of Ancient Deities*, 251.

Emoniel

Emoniel is named in the *Theurgia Goetia*, the second book of the *Lemegeton*, as both a PLANETARY PRINCE of Jupiter and one of the eleven WANDERING PRINCES (see PRINCES OF HELL). He is an AERIAL DEVIL with dominion over the planet Jupiter. Emoniel commands one hundred princes and chief dukes, twenty lesser dukes, twelve named dukes, and a multitude of servitors (see SERVITORS OF EMONIEL). He is invoked for the assistance he gives in acquiring luxuries and property and for his willingness to do or give anything asked of him. Like all the WANDERING PRINCES, he and his court are constantly on the move, never staying in any one place for long.

Sources: Gettings, *Dictionary of Demons*, 232; Trithemius, *Steganographia*, 81.

Emperors of Hell

Various grimoires have named different demons with the rank of emperor. Typically when this is done, there are four emperors, one for each of the cardinal points. The ten demons that have been assigned the rank of emperor are AMENADIEL of the West, BAIRIRON, BARMA,

CARNESIEL of the East, CASPIEL of the South, DEMORIEL of the North, LUCIFER, PADIEL, SAMAEL, and SYMIEL.

Sources: Butler, *Ritual Magic*, 77; Ford, *Book of the Witch Moon Chorozon Edition*, 334; Gettings, *Dictionary of Demons*, 232; Laycock, *Complete Enochian Dictionary*, 85; Shah, *Occultism*, 68.

Emphastison

Emphastison ("image," "representation") is named in the *Sacred Magic of Abramelin the Mage*, book two, as one of the one hundred eleven SERVITORS OF AMAYMON, ARITON, ORIENS, AND PAYMON (see AMAYMON, ARITON, ORIENS, and PAYMON).

Sources: Mathers, *Book of the Sacred Magic of Abramelin the Mage*, 113; Von Worms, *Book of Abramelin*, 255.

Empouse, plural: empousai

Variations: Démon du Midi ("mid-day demon"), Empusa, Empusae, Empusas, Empuse, Empusen, Mormo, Moromolykiai, "She who moves on one leg"

In Greek, the word *empouse* translates as "vampire," but technically, it was considered to be a demon by the ancient Greeks' own mythological standards of classification. They defined a demon as any creature born in another world but with the ability to appear in the human world as a being of flesh. In spite of this, the word was understood to mean a vampire; therefore, the empouse is considered by some scholars to be the oldest recorded vampire myth.

In Greek mythology the empouse, or *empousai* as they are referred to collectively, are born the red-headed daughters of the witch goddess Hecate and act as her attendants. Their legs are mulelike and shod with bronze shoes. Along with its powers of illusion and shape-shifting, an empouse will also use its persuasive abilities to cause a man to have sexual relations with it. During the act it will drain him of his life and, on occasion, make a meal of his flesh, much like a SUCCUBUS.

Avoiding an attack from an empouse is fairly easy, as long as one does not fall victim to its allurements. A thin-skinned and sensitive creature, it will shriek in pain and flee as quickly as it can if confronted for what it is, with use of insults and profanities. Outrunning the vampire is also possible, as all references to it describe the empouse's fastest gait as being comically slow.

In Russian folklore, the empouse appears at harvest time as a widow. It breaks the arms and legs of every harvester it can lay hands on.

Sources: Challice, *French Authors at Home*, 240;

Curl, *Egyptian Revival*, 403; Oinas, *Essays on Russian Folklore and Mythology*, 117; Time-Life Books, *Transformations*, 110.

Enaia

The *Sacred Magic of Abramelin the Mage*, book two, includes Enaia ("afflicted," "poor") as one of the one hundred eleven SERVITORS OF AMAYMON, ARITON, ORIENS, AND PAYMON (see AMAYMON, ARITON, ORIENS, and PAYMON).

Sources: Belanger, *Dictionary of Demons*, 120; Mathers, *Book of the Sacred Magic of Abramelin the Mage*, 112; Susej, *Demonic Bible*, 256.

Enediel

The FALLEN ANGEL Enediel, according to Enochian lore, is one of the ELECTORS OF HELL and one of the twenty-eight demonic rulers of the lunar mansions (see ENOCHIAN RULERS OF THE LUNAR MANSIONS). He has dominion over the mansion Allothaim ("Belly of Aries"). Known to cause discord, his zodiacal sign is Aries.

Sources: Moura, *Mansions of the Moon for the Green Witch*, 41; McLean, *Treatise on Angel Magic*, 42.

Enenuth

In the *Testament of Solomon* Enenuth is listed as one of the thirty-six Elemental World Rulers as well as one of the seventy-two SPIRITS OF SOLOMON that were used to build his temple. Enenuth is described as looking like a man with a shapeless head, similar to that of a DOG's, and having a face like a bird, donkey, or oxen. He is known to change men's hearts, steal their minds, and cause them to become toothless. While Enenuth was bound to King Solomon, he was made to do heavy labor, tending to the furnaces used for metalwork. To banish this demon, write the words "Allazool pursue Enenuth" on a piece of paper and then tie it around your neck.

Sources: Ashe, *Qabalah*, 50; Conybeare, *Jewish Quarterly Review*, Vol. 11, 37.

Enepsigos

Variations: Kronos

The FALLEN ANGEL Enepsigos appears as a woman, but on each of her shoulders is another head; each head has control over its own set of arms. After her audience with King Solomon (see SPIRITS OF SOLOMON) where she foretold the destruction of his temple as well as the crucifixion of Jesus, Enepsigos was imprisoned in a water jug, which was placed under the temple, where it remained until its destruction. She currently resides on the moon. Her personal adversary is the angel Rathanael.

Sources: Butler, *Ritual Magic*, 33; Conybeare, *Jewish Quarterly Review*, Vol. 11, 3.

Eniuri

Eniuri ("found in") is named in the *Sacred Magic of Abramelin the Mage*, book two, as one of the sixteen SERVITORS OF ASMODEUS (see ASMODEUS).

Sources: Mathers, *Book of the Sacred Magic of Abramelin the Mage*, 119; Von Worms, *Book of Abramelin*, 256.

Enochian Cacodaemons

The word *cacodaemon* first appeared in the sixteeth century. There are fifty-seven CACODAEMONS named in Enochian lore. In most cases very little is known about them except for who their angelic adversary is. These demons are Aax, Adi, Agb, And, Aor, Apa, Apm, Ash, Asi, Ast, Ato, Ava, Cab, Cac, Cam, Cms, Cop, Csc, Cus, Eac, Erg, Ern, Exr, Hbr, Hru, Hua, Idalam, Mgm, Miz, Mma, Moc, Mop, Mto, Oap, Odo, Oec, Oia, Ona, Onh, Onp, Pdi, Pfm, Pia, Piz, Rad, Rda, Rpa, Rrb, Rrl, Rsi, Rxp, Xai, Xcz, Xdz, Xii, Xom, Xoy, and Xpa.

Sources: Agrippa, *Three Books of Occult Philosophy*, 885; Icon, *Constructing*, 185; Tyson, *Enochian Magic for Beginners*, 210, 310.

Enochian Rulers of the Lunar Mansions

In Enochian lore there are twenty-eight demonic rulers of lunar mansions. Although nearly all sources agree on the number of rulers, very often AMNIXIEL and DIRACHIEL are listed twice. It is unknown if this is an error dating back to the original source or if there are two demons who share the same name. The rulers of lunar mansions are ABDUXUEL, ABRINAEL, ALHONIEL, AMNEDIEL, AMNIXIEL, AMUTIEL, ARDESIEL, ATALIEL, AZARIEL, AZERUEL, AZIEL, BARBIEL, BETHNAEL, CABIEL, DIRACHIEL, EGIBIEL, ENEDIEL, ERGODIEL, GELIEL, GENIEL, JAZERIEL, KIRIEL, NOCIEL, REQUIEL, SCHELIEL, and TAGRIEL.

Sources: Moura, *Mansions of the Moon for the Green Witch*, 13–18; Lewis, *Astrology Book*, 418–19, 463–4 Scheible, *Sixth and Seventh Books of Moses*, 75.

Envy

Variations: Phtheneoth

The demon Envy was one of the seventy-two SPIRITS OF SOLOMON that were used to build Solomon's Temple. He is described in the *Testament of Solomon* as a headless man. Desiring a head of his own, he finds a head that he would want for himself, removes it from the victim, and then consumes it. He haunts crossroads, creating sores, mutilating feet, and making children deaf and mute. Envy is repelled by a flash of lightning.

Sources: Ashe, *Qabalah*, 37, 52; Davidson, *Dictionary of Angels*, 33, 147.

Ephata

Variations: Targumic

In Aramaic lore there is a vampiric demon, an ephata, which appears as a shadow. It is formed when the body of a deceased person did not properly decay, forcing their spirit to stay with the body, bound to this world. At night the ephata leaves the corpse and seeks out humans to drain of their blood. If the corpse should ever be destroyed, then the demon will be released to pass on to the next world. The word *ephata* is the Aramaic feminine plural form of the word for "night shadows."

Sources: Cross, *Phoenician Incantations*, 42; Donner, *Kanaanaishe*, 44; Fauth, *S-s-m bn P-d-s-a*, 299; Hurwitz, *Lilith, the First Eve*, 67.

Ephélés

Variations: Éphialte, Ephialtes

First conceived in ancient Greece and later adopted by ancient Rome, the ephélés ("one who leaps upon") was a vampiric demon with hooked talons. Created when a person died before his time or was murdered, the ephélés was a bringer of NIGHTMARES. At night it would sit on a person's chest, grabbing hold tightly with its hooks and sending forth bad dreams.

The ephélés was identified with the gods Artemis and Pan (Diana and Faunus in Roman times) as well as the satyrs, sirens, and silvani. During the reign of Augustine, the ephélés were directly tied to the INCUBUS, SUCCUBUS, and the god Pan, who, apart from having dominion over flocks and shepherds, was also the giver of bad dreams.

Sources: Hillman, *Pan and the Nightmare*, 97; Hufford, *Terror That Comes in the Night*, 131, 229; Rose, *Handbook of Greek Mythology*, 62; Royal Anthropological Institute, *Man*, 134.

Ephememphi

Named in the *Apocryphon of John*, Ephememphi is the demon of delights.

Sources: Dunderberg, *Myth, Lifestyle, and Society in the School of Valentinus*, 110; Lumpkin, *Fallen Angels, the Watchers and the Origin of Evil*, 16; Smith, *Dictionary of Gnosticism*, 83, 87.

Ephippas

In the *Testament of Solomon* the king gave his ring and a wineskin to a boy and sent him to the land of Arabia, where the demon Ephippas was harassing the people. There, the boy held the empty bag up to the wind and held the ring near the mouth of the bag, which pulled the demon into it. Ephippas was named as one of the seventy-two SPIRITS OF SOLOMON that were bound to build his temple. While bound to the king, he carried stones to the building site. This was the demon that was used to lift a stone that was originally rejected by the builders as too heavy; it was later used as the cornerstone to the entrance of the temple.

Ephippas confessed to the king that he causes death, moves mountains, overthrows kings, sets fires, and withers trees. Together with the demon of the Red Sea, AMELOUITH, they miraculously created a column out of some unknown purple substance they raised out of the Red Sea.

Sources: Calisch, *Fairy Tales from Grandfather's Big Book*, 127; Conybeare, *Jewish Quarterly Review*, Vol. 11, 4, 22; Rappoport, *Myth and Legend of Ancient Israel*, Vol. 1, 95, 100, 107.

Er Mo

According to Szechuan demonology, Er Mo is the king of demons.

Sources: Ashley, *Complete Book of Devils and Demons*, 100; Graham, *Customs and Religion of the Ch'iang*, 96.

Eratoath

Variations: RABDOS

In the *Testament of Solomon*, Eratoath ("scepter") was one of the seventy-two SPIRITS OF SOLOMON that were bound to build his temple; he was made to supply green cut marble from a mountainous region. Eratoath was once a mortal sage but was changed into a large hound when he became a demon. His personal adversary is the angel Brieus.

Source: Conybeare, *Jewish Quarterly Review*, Vol. 11, 27–28.

Erekia

In the *Sacred Magic of Abramelin the Mage*, Erekia ("one who tears asunder") is named as one of the twenty SERVITORS OF AMAYMON (see AMAYMON).

Sources: Belanger, *Dictionary of Demons*, 122; Forgotten Books, *Book of the Sacred Magic of Abramelin the Mage*, 42–3; Mathers, *Book of the Sacred Magic of Abra-Melin*, 122.

Erenutes

In the *Sacred Magic of Abramelin the Mage*, Erenutes ("receiving") is among the one hundred eleven SERVITORS OF AMAYMON, ARITON, ORIENS, AND PAYMON (see AMAYMON, ARITON, ORIENS, and PAYMON).

Sources: Mathers, *Book of the Sacred Magic of*

Abramelin the Mage, 114; Von worms, *Book of Abramelin*, 256.

Erg

According to Enochian lore, Erg is a CACODAEMON. His counterpart is the angel Rgan (see ENOCHIAN CACODAEMONS).

Sources: Chopra, *Academic Dictionary of Mythology*, 102; Laycock, *Complete Enochian Dictionary*, 108.

Ergamen

In the *Sacred Magic of Abramelin the Mage*, Ergamen ("busy") is named as one of the forty-nine SERVITORS OF BEELZEBUB (see BEELZEBUB).

Sources: Ford, *Bible of the Adversary*, 93; Mathers, *Book of the Sacred Magic of Abramelin the Mage*, 107; Von Worms, *Book of Abramelin*, 257.

Erge

Variations: Deo Erge, Erge Deo, Erge deo Andossus

From Basque mythology comes the demon Erge ("taker"). The intangible and invisible demon of death, he takes a person's life when he feels that their time is right.

Sources: Lurker, *Routledge Dictionary of Gods and Goddesses*, 59; Rose, *Spirits, Fairies, Gomes, and Gobblins*, 102.

Ergodiel

Variations: Ciriel

In Enochian lore, Ergodiel is one of the twenty-eight demonic rulers of the lunar mansions.

Sources: Chopra, *Academic Dictionary of Mythology*, 102; Laycock, *Complete Enochian Dictionary*, 108; McLean, *Treatise on Angel Magic*, 42.

Erinnyes

Variations: "The ANGRY ONES," Dirae ("the Terrible"), Erinyes, Eumenides, the Fatal Sisters, FURIAE, FURIES, the Kindly Ones, the Solemn Ones

In ancient Greek and Roman mythology the erinnyes were demons of vengeance. Born from the blood of Uranus when he was castrated, they are described as winged, black-skinned female demons donning black robes. They have fiery eyes, snakes in their hair, and doglike faces. There are three erinnyes in all: ALECTO, Megaera, and Tisiphone.

The erinnyes, whose name translates from Greek to mean "a punisher," "punishing," or "to punish," would seek out those who have committed murder in order to enact justice upon them by causing the criminal to go insane. Usually victims of the erinnyes commit suicide. If they feel that someone is about to escape from them, they can call upon the goddess of justice, Dike, for divine assistance. These demons are particularly devoted to their cause, especially when the crime is matricide. There is no amount of prayer or sacrifice that can be offered that will deter them from their relentless pursuit of unyielding justice.

The erinnyes live in the underworld. Some sources claim they dwell at the entrance to Tartarus while others say that they live in Erbus, the darkest pit of the underworld. When home they torment those who have not yet atoned for their sins.

Sources: Baynes, *Encyclopedia Britannica*, Vol. 17, 699, 730, 827–8; Bjerregaard, *Great Mother*, 268, 271; Keightley, *Mythology of Ancient Greece and Italy*, 38, 174–5, 302–3.

Ermeniel

The *Theurgia Goetia*, the second book of the *Lemegeton*, names Ermeniel as one of the ten Duke SERVITORS OF EMONIEL (see EMONIEL). An AERIAL DEVIL, he commands 1,320 lesser dukes and servitors. Ermeniel is said to be good-natured and willing to obey his summoner. He lives in the woods.

Sources: Gettings, *Dictionary of Demons*, 232; Trithemius, *Steganographia*, 81.

Ern

According to Enochian lore, Ern is a CACO-DAEMON. His counterpart is the angel Rnil (see ENOCHIAN CACODAEMONS).

Sources: Chopra, *Academic Dictionary of Mythology*, 104; Laycock, *Complete Enochian Dictionary*, 108.

Error

The demon Error is mentioned in Babylonian, Jewish, and Solomonic lore. She is ranked as the sixth of the SEVEN HEAVENLY BODIES as well as one of the thirty-three (or thirty-six, sources vary) elements of the Cosmic Ruler of the Darkness. She was said to be one of the SPIRITS OF SOLOMON as well, made to dig the foundation of the temple. She claimed to be the demon that caused King Solomon to slay his own brother. This demonic goddess appears as one of the seven beautiful female spirits that are bound together; collectively they represent a cluster of stars in the sky. Together they travel about, sometimes living in Lydia, or Olympus, or on a great mountain.

Error is summoned because she is known to assist necromancers in placing spirits into corpses. She also causes people to err, leads errant souls from piety, and has many other unnamed evil traits. Her personal adversary is the angel Uriel, not to be confused with the demon of the same name (see URIEL).

Sources: Abrahams, *Jewish Quarterly Review*, Vol. 11, 25; Charlesworth, *Old Testament Pseudepigrapha*, 935; Conybeare, *Jewish Quarterly Review*, Vol. 11, 24–6.

Ertael

Variations: Ertrael

Ertael is, according to Enochian lore, one of the FALLEN ANGELS who swore allegiance to SAMIAZA, rebelled against God, lusted after and took a human woman as his wife, and fathered the NEPHILIM.

Sources: Beard, *Autobiography of Satan*, 113; Laurence, *Book of Enoch, the Prophet* 6; Lévi, *History of Magic*, 38.

Essas

This entity is often called upon during exorcism and cases of collective possession; he is also listed as one of the eighteen demons who possessed Sister Jeanne des Anges in Loudun, France, in 1634 (see LOUDUN POSSESSION).

Sources: Aikin, *General Biography*, 493; Bayle, *Historical and Critical Dictionary*, 262; Hsia, *World of Catholic Renewal*, 151; Ramsay, *Westminster Guide to the Books of the Bible*, 349; Voltaire, *Works of M. de Voltaire*, 193.

Essaunien

Variations: Shivven

In Persian mythology Essaunien is said to be one of the eight AUSTATIKCO-PAULIGAUR, a type of demonic spirit, DJINN, or DIV. These demons are said to preside over one of the eight sides of the world. With Veeshnoo, the supreme god in the Vaishnavite tradition of Hinduism, they decide if a hero is worthy of entering paradise yet.

Sources: De Claremont, *Ancient's Book of Magic*, 118; Smeadly, *Occult Sciences*, 51; *Encyclopedia of Occultism*, 113.

Estrie

The estrie is a species of demon from the Hasidic lore of the medieval era. They are considered to be vampiric demons or vampiric spirits and are described as looking like a noncorporeal mass of evil that can assume a human female form. These SUCCUBUS-like demons take up residence in a community to ensure themselves a constant supply of blood. At night the estrie will engage in sexual activity with men, draining them dry of their blood. As long as these demons are able to drink blood and consume human flesh, they will be able to maintain their human form.

If an estrie should ever become injured or seen in its true form by a person, it must eat some of that person's bread and salt or it will lose its abilities and be rendered helpless. Eating bread and salt will also heal any damage that its form has received.

Should a woman ever be suspected of being an estrie, when she dies, her mouth must be filled with dirt, as this will prevent her from rising up from her grave.

Sources: Hurwitz, *Lilith, the First Eve*, 43; Masters, *Eros and Evil*, 183; Robinson, *Myths and Legends of All Nations*, 197; Trachtenberg, *Jewish Magic and Superstition*, 43.

Etaliz

Ars Goetia, the first book of the *Lemegeton*, names Etaliz ("the furrow of a plow") as the demon of agriculture and one of the fifty-three SERVITORS OF ASHTAROTH AND ASMODEUS (see ASHTAROTH and ASMODEUS).

Sources: Mathers, *Book of the Sacred Magic of Abramelin the Mage*, 106; Von Worms, *Book of Abramelin*, 247.

Ethan

Ars Goetia, the first book of the *Lemegeton*, names Ethan ("an ass") as one of the fifty-three SERVITORS OF ASHTAROTH AND ASMODEUS (see ASHTAROTH and ASMODEUS).

Sources: Mathers, *Book of the Sacred Magic of Abramelin the Mage*, 115; Von Worms, *Book of Abramelin*, 247.

Ethanim

Ethanim is included among the one hundred eleven SERVITORS OF AMAYMON, ARITON, ORIENS, AND PAYMON (see AMAYMON, ARITON, ORIENS, and PAYMON), in the *Sacred Magic of Abramelin the Mage*, book two. In Hebrew his name translates to mean "an ass," or a furnace.

Sources: Mathers, *Book of the Sacred Magic of Abramelin the Mage*, 113; Susej, *Demonic Bible*, 256; Von Worms, *Book of Abramelin*, 255.

Euronymous

Variations: Eurynomous, EURYNOME

Euronymous, a blue-black skinned corpse eater, was originally from the mythology of the ancient Greeks but was demonized under Christian influence into the demon of cannibalism. He was said to be a member of the Grand Cross of the ORDER OF THE FLY and was ranked as a prince of death (see KNIGHTS OF HELL and PRINCES OF HELL).

Sources: Chambers, *Book of Days*, 722; Collin de Plancy, *Dictionary of Witchcraft*, 57–8; Jobes, *Dictionary of Mythology, Folklore and Symbols*, Vol. 1, 98, 192; Waite, *Book of Black Magic*, 181.

Eurynome

Variations: Eurymone, Eurynomos, Eurynomus

Collin de Plancy's *Dictionaire Infernale* (1863) named Eurynome as a Knight of the ORDER OF THE FLY, and ranked him as a prince (see KNIGHTS OF HELL and PRINCES OF HELL). Said to be the demon of death who preys carrion-like on corpses, he is described as having impossibly long wolflike teeth and a hideous black-skinned body covered with open sores, and wearing fox-skin clothing. In art Eurynome is depicted as sitting on a vulture pelt.

Sources: Chambers, *Book of Days*, 722; Collin de Plancy, *Dictionnaire Infernal*, 186–7; De Givry, *Pictorial Anthology of Witchcraft, Magic and Alchemy*, 132, 141; Leeming, *Goddess*, 51, 53, 116.

Ewah

Variations: Ew'ah, the Spirit of Madness, Underground Panther

From the Cherokee folklore of East Tennessee and Western North Carolina comes the demon of madness, Ewah. The very sight of this nocturnal demon is enough to cause permanent, irreversible insanity. He feeds upon the dreams of children and lives in the forest. Ewah is afraid only of the Wampas Mask, a magical mask made from the preserved head of a bobcat. It is said that he was ultimately destroyed by a Native American woman named Running Deer.

Sources: Coleman, *Ghosts and Haunts of Tennessee*, 37; Price, *Demon in the Woods*, 8–14.

Exael

According to Enochian lore, Exael is one of the FALLEN ANGELS who swore allegiance to SAMIAZA, rebelled against God, took a human woman as his wife, and fathered the NEPHILIM. He also taught mankind how to make engines of war, perfume, and to work with gold and silver to make jewelry. Additionally, he taught the skill of gemology.

Sources: Conway, *Guides, Guardians and Angels*, 129; Davidson, *Dictionary of Angels*, 108; Kelly, *Who in Hell*, 86.

Exr

According to Enochian lore, Exr is a CACODAEMON. His counterpart is the angel Ernh (see ENOCHIAN CACODAEMONS).

Sources: Chopra, *Academic Dictionary of Mythology*, 107; Laycock, *Complete Enochian Dictionary*, 109.

Exteron

Exteron is listed as one of the fifty-three SERVITORS OF ASHTAROTH AND ASMODEUS (see ASHTAROTH and ASMODEUS). His name is Latin and translates to mean "distant," "foreign," and "without."

Sources: Mathers, *Book of the Sacred Magic of*

Abramelin the Mage, 115; Von Worms, *Book of Abramelin*, 247.

Ezekeel

Variations: AZKEEL, Ezekiel (God will strengthen"), Ezeqeel, Ezequiel, Ezequeel ("strength of God"), NEQAEL

Ezekeel ("strength of God") is, according to Enochian lore, one of the CHIEF OF TENS (see GRIGORI) who swore allegiance to SAMIAZA, rebelled against God, took a human woman as his wife, and fathered the NEPHILIM. This FALLEN ANGEL went on to teach mankind how to foretell the future by the patterns of the clouds, but this may possibly be an attempt to explain early meteorology.

Sources: Barton, *Journal of Biblical Literature*, Vols. 30–31, 164; Conway, *Guides, Guardians and Angels*, 129; Davidson, *Dictionary of Angels*, 206; Lumpkin, *Fallen Angels, the Watchers, and the Origins of Evil*, 31.

Fagani

The *Sacred Magic of Abramelin the Mage* names Fagani ("devourers") as one of the thirty-two SERVITORS OF ASTAROT (see ASTAROT).

Source Mathers, *Book of the Sacred Magic of Abramelin the Mage*, 106; Von Worms, *Book of Abramelin*, 258.

Fallen Angels

Variations: GRIGORI, WATCHERS

A fallen angel is an angel who has fallen out of the grace of God for having committed a sin or transgression; in some instances, the condition of being a fallen angel is temporary. There are three spheres, or levels, of fallen angels. Each sphere has three categories under it.

The first sphere consists of the original fallen angels, those angels who were made by God in the beginning, before he constructed the Heavens and Earth. The three subcategories under this heading are the Seraphim, the Cherubim, and the Thrones. These angels acted as heavenly councilors. The second sphere contains the Dominions, the Virtues, and the Powers. These angels acted as heavenly governors. The third and final sphere contains the Principalities, the Archangels, and the Angels. Angels in this sphere acted as heavenly messengers.

In the first heavenly rebellion, it is said that LUCIFER was the first and most powerful of the angels ever created. His intelligence and beauty were unmatched among his peers. Eventually, he succumbed to the sin of pride as he grew ambitious and self-centered and ultimately declared himself God's equal. Gathering like-minded angels to his cause, nearly one third of the heavenly host, a rebellion followed that ended in God's victory over LUCIFER and those who followed him. They were all expelled from Heaven and sent to live in the lower worlds.

A second rebellion occurred not from a power-play but rather out of a lust-driven pack mentality. The GRIGORI, or the WATCHER angels as they were also called, were supposed to assist the Archangels in the construction and maintenance of Eden. However, it was these angels who were the first to fall. These WATCHER angels came to find that they desired to live among the humans, even lusting after the women. Afraid to act on their impulses, it was decided that if they acted as a group that God would certainly not punish them all. Making a pact among themselves, they descended from Heaven to reside on Earth and live among the humans, marrying human women and having children with them. They even taught mankind certain skills that God forbade humans to know, such as astrology, cosmotology, gemology, sorcery, and weaponsmithing.

Regardless of their reasons for doing so, the actions of this group of angels were in direct opposition of God's desire. The worst sin they committed was having children and diluting their most pure and holy bloodline. As punishment for their actions, God cursed the rebel angels, exiled them from Heaven, and in some cases, physically punished them. They were made mortal and demonic. In a final act to clean the world of their sin, God sent a great flood to cleanse the land of their half-breed children, the NEPHILIM, who were by their very nature destructive and murderous. The Hebrew word for *giants* is NEPHILIM, whose root word is "to fall."

Some sources say that the fallen angels (fallen because they fell from their state of grace) are bound to wander the Earth until Judgment Day and thereafter they will be banished to Hell. However, very early church teachings claim that by the practice of virtue the fallen angels, as well as demons, can return to a state of grace and become an angel again through God's eternal love and mercy.

There is no true or complete list of all the fallen angels, as names have been pulled from various sources through the millennium. What follows is a list of two hundred sixty-three angelic beings collected from various religions and mythologies that are in a fallen state of grace: AATXE, ABADDON, ABAROS, ABBADON, ABEZETHIBOU, ABIGOR, ACAOS, ACHAS, ADIRAEL, ADRAMELECH, AGARES, AGNIEL, AHRIMANES, AKIBEEL, AKIKEL, ALASTOR, ALDE-

BARAN, ALEXH, ALLOCEN, AMAND, AMANE, AMAROS, AMAZARAK, AMDUCIAS, AMEZYARAK, AMIZIRAS, AMUDIEL, AMY, ANANEL, ANDRAS, ANDREALPHUS, ANDROMALIUS, ANGEL-PEACOCK, ANMAEL, ANTARES, ARAKIBA, ARAKIEL, ARAON, ARAZIEL, ARDESIEL, ARIEL, ARIOCH, ARIZIAL, ARMAROS, ARMEN, ARMERS, ARSTIKAPHA, ARTAQIFA, ASAEL, ASAREDEL, ASBEEL, ASHTAROTH, ASMODAY, ASMODEUS, ASMODEUS ZAVEHE, ATARCULPH, AUZA, AZARADEL, AZAZEL, AZAZYEL, AZEMO, AZKEEL, AZZA, AZZAEL, BAALBERITH, BALAM, BALBERITH, BARAKEL, BARBATOS, BARBIEL, BARKAYAL, BARMA, BASASAEL, BATAREL, BATARJAL, Beelzeboul, BEELZEBUB, BELAIL, BELETH, BELIAL, BELIAN, BELPHEGOR, BERITH, BERNAEL, BETRYAL, BIFRONS, BIGA, BOTIS, BUER, BUNE, BUSASEJAL, BYLETH, CAIM, CARNIVEAN, CARREAU, CHAM, CHOBALIEL, COTIEL, CROCELL, CURSON, DAGON, DANEL ("Judge of God"), DANIEL, DANJAL, DANTANIAN, DANYUL, DIRACHIEL, DRELMETH, DUBBIEL, DUMA, EBLIS, ELIGOR, ENEDIEL, ENEPSIGOS, ERTAEL, EXAEL, EZEKEEL, FIRNEUS, FOCALAR, Foe, FOMALHAUT, Forneas, FORNEUS, FURCALOR, GAAP, GADER'EL, GENIEL, GERYON, GOAP, GRÉSIL, GRESSIL, GURSON, GUSION, HAKAEL, HANANEL, HARUT, HAURES, HIVVAH, Hiyyah, HOSAMPSICH, IALDABAOTH, IBLIS, IELAHIAH, IMAMIAH, Iniaes, IOMUEL, IUVART, JEQON, JETREL, JOMJAEL, Jove, JUNIER, KAEL, KAKABAEL, KASADYA, KASBEEL, Kathazel, Kawkabel, KEZEF, Kokabel, LAHASH, Lahatiel, LAUVIAH, LEVIATHAN, LUCIFER, MAAMAH, MAHONIN, MAKATIEL, MALIK, MAMMON, MARCHOSIAS, MAROU, MARUT, MASTEMA, MEPHISTOPHELES, MERESIN, MERIHIM, MERIRIM, MISHEL, MOLOCH, MURMUR, NAAMAH, NACHIEL, NAHEMA, NELCHAEL, NEQAEL, NILAIHAH, NISROC, NISROCH, NITHAEL, OEILLET, OG, OLIVER, OMAEL, ONIEL, OPHIS, OUZA, PAYMON, PENEMUE, PHARMAROS, PHARZUPH, PHENEX, PINEM'E, POSRIEL, PROCEL, PURSON, RABDOS, RAHAB, RAMIEL, RÄUM, RECIEL, REMIEL, RIMMON, ROSIER, RUMAEL, SABAS, SADIEL, SALIKOTAL, SAMAEL, Samathael, Sameveel, SAMIAZA, SAMIEL, Samjaza, SAMMAEL, SAMSAPEEL, SARAKNYAL, Sarfael, SARIEL, SATAN, SATAREL, SATHARIEL, SEALIAH, SEMAZAS, SENCINER, SERIEL, SHAITAN, SHAMDAN, SHAMSHIEL, SIMAPESIEL, SONNEILLON, SURIEL, TABAET, TAMIEL, TAREL, THAMMUS, THAUSAEL, TIRIL, TUMAEL, TURAEL, URAKABARAMEEL, USIEL, UVALL, UZZIEL, VERRIER, VERRIN, VODYANOI, XAPHAN, YEQON, YETAREL, YOMAEL, ZAGIEL, and ZAQIEL.

Sources: Beard, *Autobiography of Satan*, 113; Charles, *Book of Enoch*, 137; Laurence, *Foreign Quarterly Review*, Vol. 24, 370; Lumpkin, *Fallen Angels, the Watchers, and the Origins of Evil*, 31; Mew, *Eclectic Magazine of Foreign Literature, Science, and Art*, Vol. 115, 407; Prophet, *Fallen Angels and the Origins of Evil*, 174; Scott, *London Magazine*, Vol. 5, 378; Voltaire, *Essays and Criticisms*, 106; Von Goethe, *Goethe's Letters to Zelter*, 377.

Fallen Principality

A principality is a ranking or hierarchy of angel. Although it is reasonable to assert that the word *principality* refers more to a title or function of the angelic being, rather than the kind of being, there is no way to be certain. There are four named Fallen Principalities: ACHAS, Alex, CHAM, and ZABULON (see also FALLEN ANGELS).

Sources: De Givry, *Pictorial Anthology of Witchcraft, Magic and Alchemy*, 128; Ramsay, *Westminster Guide to the Books of the Bible*, 349; Spence, *Encyclopedia of Occultism*, 385.

Familiar

Variations: Familiar spirit

Christian demonology of the Middle Ages defined a familiar as a demonic spirit that acted as an attendant or assistant to a conjuror, demonologist, or witch in both domestic duties as well in practicing their magical craft. It was given to them by the demon or devil that they made the pact with soon after the contract was signed. This demonic being typically took on the guise of an animal companion but lore claims that it would usually have the ability to shape-shift into a human or dwarf.

Sources: De Puy, *Encyclopædia Britannica*, Vol. 7, 63; Maggi, *In the Company of Demons*, 100–103; Russell, *Witchcraft in the Middle Ages*, 14, 55, 187.

Faraii

The *Grand Grimoire*, alleged to have been written by Alibek the Egyptian and published in Cairo in 1522, names Faraii as one of the three SERVITORS OF SARGATANAS (see SARGATANAS).

Sources: Baskin, *Sorcerer's Handbook*, 276; Waite, *Book of Black Magic and Ceremonial Magic*, 188; Waite, *Book of Black Magic and of Pacts*, 158; Waite, *Unknown World 1894–1895*, 230; Wedeck, *Treasury of Witchcraft*, 96.

Faseua

Named in the *Theurgia Goetia*, the second book of the *Lemegeton*, as one of the sixteen SERVITORS OF ASYRIEL, Faseua is a nocturnal demon (see ASYRIEL). It is said that he is good-natured and willing to obey his summoners.

Sources: Guiley, *Encyclopedia of Demons and Demonology*, 20; Peterson, *Lesser Key of Solomon*, 74.

Faturab

In the *Sacred Magic of Abramelin the Mage*, book two, Faturab is named as one of the sixty-five SERVITORS OF KORE AND MAGOTH. His name is most likely taken from Hebrew, and if so, would translate to mean "interpretation."

Sources: Mathers, *Book of the Sacred Magic of Abramelin the Mage*, Von Worms, *Book of Abramelin*, 118, 123, 249.

Fecor

The demon Fecor has the ability to call up tempests, cause fear, cause ghosts to appear, ring the bells at midnight, and shake the foundations of homes. He is known to work in conjunction with ANARAZEL and GAZIEL.

Sources: De Claremont, *Ancient's Book of Magic*, 12; Hibbard, *Three Elizabethan Pamphlets*, 147; Nash, *Works of Thomas Nashe*, 232.

Federwisch

Variations: One of the names for the DEVIL

The devil Federwisch is said to be the demon of vanity. His name was often used in the Middle Ages as a synonym for the Devil (SATAN).

Sources: Muchembled, *History of the Devil*, 15; Russell, *Prince of Darkness*, 112; Russell, *Witchcraft in the Middle Ages*, 256.

Femol

In the *Theurgia Goetia*, the second book of the *Lemegeton*, Femol is ranked as a chief duke who commands 2,660 duke servitors of his own. Listed as one of the SERVITORS OF CASPIEL (see CASPIEL), he has a reputation for being rude and stubborn.

Source: Peterson, *Lesser Key of Solomon*, 60.

Fene

From Hungarian mythology comes the demon of illness and tumors in humans, Fene ("damn[ed]"). His personal adversary is Isten, the god of light. There is a Hungarian curse that goes "*egye meg a fene*"; it translates as "Fene eat you!"

Sources: Dodson, *Uglier Than a Monkey's Armpit*, n.p.; Lurker, *Routledge Dictionary of Gods and Goddesses*, 62; Szabó, *Hungarian Practical Dictionary*, 391.

Fersebus

According to the *Sacred Magic of Abramelin the Mage*, book two, Fersebus ("bringer of veneration") is one of the sixty-five SERVITORS OF KORE AND MAGOTH.

Sources: Mathers, *Book of the Sacred Magic of Abramelin the Mage*, 118; Von Worms, *Book of Abramelin*, 249.

Feurety

Variations: Flauros, Flavros, Flereous, HAURAS, HAURES, Havres

In the *Ars Goetia*, the first book of the *Lemegeton*, Feurety is ranked as a duke, grand general, and lieutenant commander who is possibly in service under ANDROS. He commands either twenty or thirty-six legions of demons; sources vary. Feurety, the demon of fire and wrath, will appear before his summoner in the form of a leopard; however, at the summoner's request he will take on the form of a man with fiery eyes. In art, he is often depicted as a humanoid with large claws. He is also the symbol of passion, personality, power, will, and wrath.

Feurety is summoned for his ability to burn and destroy the enemies of the one who summoned him. He will also answer honestly questions regarding the past, present, and future. He will also speak openly about the creation of the world and the fall of the angels—on the provision that he has been commanded into a triangle. Otherwise he will lie very convincingly to the summoner.

Sources: Crowley, *The Goetia*, 61; Collin de Plancy, *Dictionary of Witchcraft*, 62; De Laurence, *Lesser Key of Solomon, Goetia*, 42–3; Scot, *Discoverie of Witchcraft*, 225; Scott, *London Magazine*, Vol. 5, 378.

Finaxos

In the *Sacred Magic of Abramelin the Mage*, Finaxos is one of the fifty-three SERVITORS OF ASHTAROTH AND ASMODEUS (see ASHTAROTH and ASMODEUS). His name likely came from the Greek language, and if it did would translate to mean "worthy in appearance."

Sources: Mathers, *Book of the Sacred Magic of Abramelin the Mage*, 116; Susej, *Demonic Bible*, 257; Von Worms, *Book of Abramelin*, 247.

Fire Devils

Friar Francesco Maria Guazzo's *Compendium Maleficarum* (1628) describes fire devils as one of the six species of demons (or devils) in Hell. In service to the DEVIL, these servitor demons of fire are the most powerful of all the species and therefore command the five other SPECIES OF DEVILS: AERIAL DEVIL, AQUEOUS DEVILS, HELIOPHOBIC DEVILS, subterranean devils, and TERRESTRIAL DEVILS. Fire demons, according to Friar Guazzo, live in the upper air.

Source: Kipfer, *Order of Things*, 255.

Firneus

Variations: Forneaus, FORNEUS

Firneus is named in the *Theurgia Goetia*, the second book of the *Lemegeton*, as one of the seventy-two SPIRITS OF SOLOMON. Ranked as a marquis, this FALLEN ANGEL formerly of the Order of Thrones commands twenty-nine legions (see MARQUIS OF HELL). He is described as looking like a sea monster but is said to have the ability to give men a good name and make them well liked. He may also give them the ability to speak many languages and bless them with the gift of rhetoric. Firneus's name is Latin for "oven."

Sources: Crowley, *The Goetia*, 42; Guiley, *Encyclopedia of Angels*, 142; Peterson, *Lesser Key of Solomon*, 262.

Five Satans, The

Variations: The Five Giants, the Five Titans

The *Book of Enoch* refers to the collection of five FALLEN ANGELS, Asb'el, GADER'EL, KASADYA, PINEM'E, and YEQON, as the Five Satans. Their actions were in part responsible for the series of events that incited God to flood the earth.

Sources: Guiley, *Encyclopedia of Demons and Demonology*, 265; Hastings, *Dictionary of the Bible*, 556; Icon, *Sin*, 398.

Flagel

In Christian demonology, Flagel is a devil and the patron of lawyers.

Source: Rudwin, *Devil in Legend and Literature*, 28, 83.

Flaxon

In the *Sacred Magic of Abramelin the Mage*, book two, Flaxon is named as one of the twenty-two SERVITORS OF ARITON (see ARITON). His name is Greek and translates to mean "about to rend" or "to be rent asunder."

Sources: Mathers, *Book of the Sacred Magic of Abramelin the Mage*, 122; Von Worms, *Book of Abramelin*, 257.

Fleuretty

Variations: Fleurity, VADRIEL

In the *Legemeton*, Fleuretty is ranked as the lieutenant general of the Legions of Hell and listed as one of the twelve SERVITORS OF ABEZETHIBOU (see ABEZETHIBOU). He commands ten chiefs, one hundred servitors, and the demon Pursan (PURSON). Fleuretty, a diurnal demon, is most powerful during the ninth hour of the day.

Sources: Mark, *Book of Hierarchies*, 28; Shah, *Occultism*, 62; Wedick, *Treasury of Witchcraft*, 97.

Fleurety

Christian demonology ranks the demon of lust, Fleurety, as the commander of Africa and a lieutenant general of the Army of Hell. He personally commands numerous legions and the demons Bathsin, ELIGOR, and Pursan (PURSON). In service under BEELZEBUB, this nocturnal demon is an expert in hallucinatory herbs and poisonous plants; he can also perform any labor during the night and cause hail storms (see SERVITORS OF BEELZEBUB).

Sources: Baskin, *Sorcerer's Handbook*, 276; Waite, *Unknown World 1894–1895*, 230; Wedeck, *Treasury of Witchcraft*, 96.

Focalar

Variations: Forcalor, FURCALOR, LUCIFUGE ROFOCALE, Rofocale

Focalar is ranked as a duke and seneschal who is under the command of the demon MAMMON; he has also been listed as one of the seventy-two SPIRITS OF SOLOMON. Appearing as a man with feathered wings, this FALLEN ANGEL, formerly of the Order of Thrones, is said to command thirty legions. Focalar has a reputation for drowning men, as he has power over the oceanic winds and the seas, which he uses to sink warships. Fortunately he will not harm anyone if he is commanded to do the contrary. Focalar has hopes that he will be able to return to the Seventh Throne after one thousand fifty years of banishment.

Sources: Davidson, *Dictionary of Angels*, 113; McLean, *Treatise of Angel Magic*, 54; Peterson, *Lesser Key of Solomon*, 26.

Fomalhaut

According to the *Book of Enoch*, Fomalhaut ("mouth of the whale") is one of the FALLEN ANGELs who swore allegiance to SAMIAZA, rebelled against God, took a human as his wife, and fathered the NEPHILIM.

Sources: Bumbly, *Museum of Unnatural History*, 82; Clemen, *Primitive Christianity and its Non-Jewish Sources*, 100; Greer, *New Encyclopedia of the Occult*, 509; Icon, *Quartering*, 311.

Fomorian, plural: Fomorians or Fomors

Variations: Fomori, Fomóiri, Fomóraig, Fomors

The *Book of the Dun Cow* (*Lebor Na H-Uidhri*), an ancient Irish manuscript compiled around the year 1100, tells us of the subaquatic demonic race of beings known as the Fomorians ("dark of the sea") in Celtic lore. Some sources say that the Fomors were born the offspring of Noah's son Ham, while other stories say they were born before the gods came into existence and were the children of Chaos and the Old Night. Usually they are described as having the body of a man and the head of a goat, but they always will have some other such distinctive physical characteristic, if not the head of a goat, then it may be that they have only one eye, or that they are missing an arm or leg. On a few more rare occasions they are said to be very beautiful, having metallic feathers, or even three heads.

The Fomors were one of the four races that were defeated by the Tuatha De Danaan in the conquest of Ireland. Since their defeat they have resided under the sea on an island called Lochlan. Historically, the Fomors are the symbol of chaos and wild nature.

Sources: Bourke, *Pre-Christian Ireland*, 53–55; O'-Grady, *History of Ireland*, 62–3; O'Hanlon, *Irish Folk Lore*, 114, 172–80.

Foraii

Variations: MARAX

Ars Goetia, the first book of the *Lemegeton*, names Foraii as an earl and president who commands thirty-six or thirty-two legions; sources vary (see EARLS OF HELL and PRESIDENTS OF HELL). Described as being a large bull with the face of a man, this demon is summoned for his ability to give good FAMILIARs that know herbology and gemology; he also teaches astronomy and liberal sciences. Foraii's name is taken from Latin and means "that delays" or "that stops."

Sources: Guiley, *Encyclopedia of Demons and Demonology*, 179; Peterson, *Lesser Key of Solomon*, 262; Wedeck, *Treasury of Witchcraft*, 97.

Foras

Variations: FORCAS, Forras, Furcas

Listed as one of the seventy-two SPIRITS OF SOLOMON, Foras, a President of Hell, commands twenty-nine legions (see PRESIDENTS OF HELL). A diurnal demon, he is summoned for his ability to grant the gift of invisibility and long life. He will also disclose the hiding place of lost treasure as well as teach ethics, eloquence, gemology, herbology, logic, palmistry, pyromancy, and rhetoric. Most powerful during the month of August, Foras appears before his summoner as a strong-looking man or as an old man with a long white beard. His name is taken from Latin and means "out" or "outside."

Sources: De Laurence, *Lesser Key of Solomon, Goetia*, 31; DuQuette, *Key to Solomon's Key*, 175; McLean, *Treatise of Angel Magic*, 54; Scot, *Discoverie of Witchcraft*, 221.

Forau

The *Grimoire of Pope Honorius* (*Le Grimoire du Pape Honorius*) was written in the eighteenth century, allegedly by Pope Honorius III; in it the demi-demon Forau is listed as one of the three SERVITORS OF SARGATANAS and ranked as a brigadier general.

Sources: Drury, *Dictionary of the Esoteric*, 109; Wedeck, *Treasury of Witchcraft*, 96.

Forcas

Variations: FORAS, Forras, Furcas

In medieval demonology Forcas was ranked as a grand president, knight, master of the devil's stables, and a senator. Under the command of ASMODEUS, he is said to command twenty or twenty-nine legions of demons; sources vary. He is summoned for his ability to make objects invisible at will; he can also give his summoner power over the opposite sex as well as teach him logic, palm reading, pyromancy, and rhetoric. He is described as looking like a robust white-haired man carrying a sharp weapon in his hand while riding a pale horse.

Sources: Conway, *Guides, Guardians and Angels*, 129; Collin de Plancy, *Dictionary of Witchcraft*, 62; Drury, *Dictionary of the Esoteric*, 109; González-Wippler, *Complete Book of Spells, Ceremonies, and Magic*, 188; Scot, *Discoverie of Witchcraft*, 221; Shah, *Occultism*, 66.

Forfax

Variations: FORAII, MARAX

Forfax is said to be one of the seventy-two SPIRITS OF SOLOMON; he holds the rank of both earl and president and commands thirty-six legions of demons (see EARLS OF HELL and PRESIDENTS OF HELL). Forfax is summoned for his ability to give good FAMILIARs and for teaching astronomy, gemology, liberal sciences, and herbology.

Sources: Davidson, *Dictionary of Angels*, 113–14; Diagram Group, *Little Giant Encyclopedia*, 499, 502; Guiley, *Dictionary of Demons and Demonology*, 179.

Forneus

Variations: FIRNEUS, Fornjotr

In *Theurgia Goetia*, the second book of the *Lemegeton*, Forneus is named as one of the seventy-two SPIRITS OF SOLOMON. A FALLEN ANGEL, formerly of the Order of Thrones, demonology of the Middle Ages ranked him as a marquis (see MARQUIS OF HELL). He is sometimes described as looking like a sea monster.

Sources: Conway, *Guides, Guardians and Angels*, 129; De Laurence, *Lesser Key of Solomon, Goetia*, 31; DuQuette, *Key to Solomon's Key*, 175; Lurker, *Dictionary of Gods and Goddesses*, 120.

Forteson

Variations: Fortison

In the *Sacred Magic of Abramelin the Mage*, book two, Forteson is among the sixty-five

SERVITORS OF KORE AND MAGOTH. His name is Greek for "burdened."

Sources: Ford, *Bible of the Adversary*, 92; Mathers, *Book of the Sacred Magic of Abramelin the Mage*, 118; Susej, *Demonic Bible*, 258.

Four Principal Kings

In demonology there are traditionally four principal kings, one for each of the four cardinal points; however, sources vary as to who exactly those kings are. Three lists are commonly cited. The first names the four kings as AMAYMON, King of the East; CORSON, King of the South; GAAP, King of the West; and Ziminiar, King of the North. The second list of commonly cited kings is made up of ASMODAI, BELETH, BELIAL, and GAAP. The third and final list names AMAYMON, King of the South; Egyn, King of the North; PAYMON, King of the West; and Uricus, King of the East.

Sources: De Laurence, *Lesser Key of Solomon, Goetia*, 32–3; González-Wippler, *Complete Book of Spells, Ceremonies, and Magic*, 146; Icon, *Demons*, 190; McLean, *Treatise of Angel Magic*, 52; Spence, *Encyclopedia of Occultism*, 109.

Friar Rush

Variations: Brüder Rausch, Brother Tipple, RUSH

In medieval German folklore Friar Rush was said to be the bartender of Hell and the demon of drunkenness. He would enter into monasteries and cause trouble by confusing the monks, tempting them to drink too much, and playing pranks on them, such as turning on the wine taps in the cellar. In some versions of the folklore Friar Rush is said to be none other than the DEVIL himself disguised as a friar.

Sources: Brewer, *Dictionary of Phrase and Fable*, 318; Briggs, *Dictionary of British Folk-Tales in the English Language*, 204–6; Hazlitt, *Tales and Legends of National Origin*, 134–55.

Frimost

Variations: FURCALOR

In the *Grimoirium Verum* (*Grimoire of Truth*) allegedly written by Alibek the Egyptian in 1517, Frimost is listed as one of the eighteen SERVITORS OF SYRACH (see SYRACH). Most powerful on Tuesdays between the hours of nine and ten at night, this demon requires that he be given the first pebble that was found during the day as part of his summoning ritual. He has the ability to possess the minds and bodies of young women.

Sources: Kelly, *Who in Hell*, 96; Kuriakos, *Grimoire Verum Ritual Book*, 20; Waite, *Book of Black Magic*, 184, 283.

Frucissiere

Variations: Frucisiere

In the *Grimoirium Verum* (*Grimoire of Truth*) allegedly written by Alibek the Egyptian in 1517, Frucissiere is listed as one of the eighteen SERVITORS OF SYRACH (see SYRACH). Although he does not, this demi-demon appears to have the power to raise the dead.

Sources: Kuriakos, *Grimoire Verum Ritual Book*, 20; Masters, *Devil's Dominion*, 131; Sabellicus, *Magia Pratica*, 35.

Frutimiere

In the *Grimoirium Verum* (*Grimoire of Truth*) allegedly written by Alibek the Egyptian in 1517, Frutimiere is listed as one of the eighteen SERVITORS OF SYRACH (see SYRACH). He has the ability to create any feast you desire.

Sources: Kuriakos, *Grimoire Verum Ritual Book*, 21; Sabellicus, *Magia Pratica*, 35; Waite, *Book of Black Magic*, 187.

Ftheboth

Ftheboth is a demon that casts the evil eye.

Source: Sabellicus, *Magia Pratica*, Vol. 1, 150.

Fuchsin

Variations: Vixen

Fuchsin is a SUCCUBUS from German lore. According to the story, Johannes Junius, a literate and wealthy man as well as the former burgomaster of his town, was recently widowed, as his wife was condemned to death for being a witch. While lamenting her execution he was approached by what he believed at the time to be a beautiful woman who enticed him into having sexual relations with her. After the event, she changed into the form of a goat and demanded that he renounce God or she would break his neck. Junius cried out to God for help, which caused the demon to flee for a moment, but when it returned it had numerous people with it. The group was then able to bully him into renouncing God, after which they baptized him into their evil fold and renamed him "Krix." The SUCCUBUS Fuchsin then demanded that he kill his daughters and his youngest son, but instead Junius killed his horse with the powers she gave him. Even with all his wealth and money, his status and influence, he confessed to being a witch after days of torture and was promptly executed.

Source: Baskin, *Sorcerer's Handbook*, 230, 324.

Fujin

In Japanese demonology Fujin is a demonic and the eldest of the Shinto gods. Demon of the wind and present when the world was created, he appears as a dark and terrifying figure. He carries a large bag filled with wind over his shoulder. He wears leopard-skin clothes.

Sources: Ashkenazi, *Handbook of Japanese Mythology*, 154–5; Maberry, *Cryptopedia*, 206; Turner, *Dictionary of Ancient Deities*, 182.

Fumaroth

Folklore of the Middle Ages tells us that once, during childbirth, a woman forgot to make the sign of the cross before drinking a cup of water; this simple act enabled the demon Fumaroth to enter into her body.

Sources: Baskin, *Satanism*, 136; Graf, *Story of the Devil*, 89; Kelly, *Who in Hell*, 96.

Furcalor

Variations: Focalor, Forcalor

In the *Ars Goetia*, the first book of the *Lemegeton*, Furcalor is a FALLEN ANGEL formerly of the Order of Thrones and is ranked as the Duke of Water (see DUKES OF HELL). He is said to command either three or thirty legions of demons; sources vary. It is said that Furcalor had hoped to be able to return to Heaven after a thousand years of exile, but he had been misled into believing this. Described as looking like a man with the wings of a griffon, Furcalor feeds his murderous tendencies by drowning men and sinking warships with his command over the sea and wind. He is casually violent, so when summoned he must be commanded not to harm any man or living thing.

It is believed by some scholars that Rofocale is an anagram for the demon Furcalor.

Sources: Crowley, *The Goetia*, 49; De Laurence, *Lesser Key of Solomon, Goetia*, 35; Scot, *Discoverie of Witchcraft*, 223; Scott, *London Magazine*, Vol. 5, 378.

Fureas

Duke Fureas, a lesser demon, is described as looking like an old man riding upon a horse and carrying a spear. Although he is particularly malevolent, he is summoned for his ability to teach philosophy and the sciences.

Sources: Brewer, *Dictionary of Phrase and Fable*, 494; Guiley, *Encyclopedia of Demons and Demonology*, 91.

Furfur

Variations: Eureur, Faraji, Farris, Furfures, Furtur

In Johann Wierus's *Pseudomonarchia Daemonum* (*False Monarchy of Demons*, 1583) Furfur ("brand"), the demon of storms, is ranked as a count or an earl who commands twenty-six legions of demons, six chiefs, and six servitors; he is also listed as one of the seventy-two SPIRITS OF SOLOMON (see COUNTS OF HELL and EARLS OF HELL). Most powerful during the second hour of the night, when summoned he appears as an angel who speaks in a hoarse voice or as a winged stag with human arms and a flaming tail. He is summoned for his ability to create marital love and will answer truthfully any questions asked of him regarding the divine or secret knowledge. He can also create lightning, powerful winds, and thunder. Unless Furfur is bound inside a magical triangle, he cannot be trusted to speak the truth.

Sources: Collin de Plancy, *Dictionnaire Infernal*, 290; De Laurence, *Lesser Key of Solomon, Goetia*, 33; Scot, *Discoverie of Witchcraft*, 221.

Furia

Variations: Furiel

In the *Ars Paulina*, the third book of the *Lemegeton*, Furia is listed as one of the two hundred SERVITORS OF VEGUANIEL (see VEGUANIEL).

Sources: Gettings, *Dictionary of Demons*, 112; Waite, *Book of Ceremonial Magic*, 67.

Furiae

Variations: The Seminatrices Malorum

The Furiae is one of the seven orders of demons; they are under the command of ABADDON. Demons of this order create destruction, discord, mischief, and wars.

Sources: Coleman, *Dictionary of Mythology*, 391; Gettings, *Dictionary of Demons*, 112; McLean, *Treatise on Angel Magic*, 70, 102.

Furies, The

Variations: Dirae ("the terrible"), Erinyes, Eumenides ("kind ones"), the Furor, the Maniae ("the madnesses"), the Potniae ("the awful ones"), the Praxidikae ("the vengeful ones"), Semnai ("the venerable ones"), Semnai Theai ("venerable goddesses")

In Greco-Roman mythology the Furies were originally the ghosts of murdered people but later evolved into the three demonic goddesses of vengeance: ALECTO ("She who does not rest" or "Unceasing in Anger"), Megaera ("The envious one" or "Jealous"), and Tisiphone ("Avenger of Murder").

According to the ancient Greek dramatist Aeschylus, the Furies were born the daughters of the goddess Nyx. The Greek poet Hesiod said they were born when the life-blood of Uranus mixed with his wife, Gaea. Sophocles, one of the most influential writers of Ancient Greece, believed them to be the daughters of Darkness and Gaea. It was Euripides, the last of the three great tragedians of classical Athens, who was the first to say that the Furies' total number was three. No matter how it was that these demons came into existence, they were described as being blood-covered, their eyes weeping with blood, and living snakes for their hair. In the older myths, they were said to have the body of a DOG and the wings of a bat.

The Furies are the personification of curses and vengeance, preying upon anyone who broke the "natural laws," particularly those who committed fratricide, patricide, or other types of family-related murder, as it was believed that mortal men did not have the right or the authority to enforce justice on that type of criminal. Although their typical victim was usually human, the Furies did strike Xanthus, a magical horse, dumb for rebuking the hero Achilles. Typically the Furies would drive their victims insane. They lived in the Underworld and when they were there, they would torture the souls of the damned.

Sources: Daly, *Greek and Roman Mythology A to Z*, 58; Tresidder, *Complete Dictionary of Symbols*, 197; Walsh, *Heroes and Heroines of Fiction*, 115.

Fustiel

Variations: FUTINIEL

In the *Ars Paulina*, the third book of the *Lemegeton*, Fustiel is named as one of the fifteen Duke SERVITORS OF SCOX (see SCOX). Most powerful during the fifth hour of the day, he commands 5,550 servitors. As Futiniel, he is named as one of the ten inferior servitor spirits of SAZQUIEL (see SERVITORS OF SAZQUIEL).

Sources: Davidson, *Dictionary of Angels*, 115; Peterson, *Lesser Key of Solomon*, 114; Trithemius, *Steganographia*, 95.

Futiniel

Futiniel is listed as one of the six lesser servitor spirits of SAZQUIEL in the *Lemegeton, the Lesser Key of Solomon*.

Source: Waite, *Book of Ceremonial Magic*, 67.

Gaap

Variations: GOAP, GORSON, Tap, Zaazonash, Zazel

A FALLEN ANGEL formerly of the Order of Potentates, Gaap holds many ranks, some of which include King of the West, president, Prince of Hell, Prince of the West, and one of the FOUR PRINCIPAL KINGS (see KINGS OF HELL and PRESIDENTS OF HELL). This nocturnal demon is in service to AMAYMON and commands sixty-six legions of his own. In Solomonic lore Gaap was listed as one of the SPIRITS OF SOLOMON and was trapped inside a brass vessel.

Gaap is summoned for his willingness to answer truthfully questions regarding the past, present, and future; he also gives FAMILIARs, which he will take from their current master, and he will transport a person from one place to another instantly. Additionally, he can cause insanity, stir up the loves and hates in men, teach the liberal sciences as well as philosophy, and give instructions on how to bless items and devote them to his king, AMAYMON.

When Gaap appears before his summoner he will do so in the guise of a man, but on occasion he will also have huge batlike wings. This is an extremely proud demon and unless bound inside a magical triangle he will not speak a word of truth. Burning offerings and sacrifices to him will greatly reduce the chance of him attacking.

Sources: Crowley, *The Goetia*, 44; De Laurence, *Lesser Key of Solomon, Goetia*, 32–3; McLean, *Treatise of Angel Magic*, 54.

Gabir

Variations: Jabir

In the *Theurgia Goetia*, the second book of the *Lemegeton*, Gabir, a nocturnal demon, is listed as one of the fifteen SERVITORS OF BARMIEL (see BARMIEL). He holds the rank of duke (see DUKES OF HELL).

Sources: Peterson, *Lesser Key of Solomon*, 71; Trithemius, *Steganographia*, 17.

Gader'el

Variations: Gadreel, Gadrel, Gadriel

The *Book of Enoch* names Gader'el as one of the FALLEN ANGELS who swore allegiance to SAMIAZA, rebelled against God, took a human as his wife, and fathered the NEPHILIM. He went on to teach mankind how to make breastplates, shields, and swords and how to effectively use these items. His name is taken from Hebrew and means "God is my helper." Christian demonology claims that this demon once had sexual relations with Eve (see also FIVE SATANS, KASADYA, PINEM'E, and YEQON).

Sources: Barton, *Journal of Biblical Literature*, Vols. 30–31, 164; Charles, *Book of Enoch*, 137; Choice, *Secular and the Sacred Harmonized*, 116, 120; Laurence, *Book of Enoch, the Prophet*, 70.

Gagalin

In the *Sacred Magic of Abramelin the Mage*, book two, Gagalin ("ganglion, swelling, tumor") is one of the ten SERVITORS OF AMAYMON AND ARITON (see AMAYMON and ARITON). He is the demon of tumors.

Sources: Belanger, *Dictionary of Demons*, 134; Mathers, *Book of the Sacred Magic of Abramelin the Mage*, 106; Susej, *Demonic Bible*, 257.

Gagalos

The *Sacred Magic of Abramelin the Mage* names Gagalos among the fifty-three SERVITORS OF ASHTAROTH AND ASMODEUS (see ASHTAROTH and ASMODEUS). His name is likely Greek and if so would translate to mean "tumor."

Sources: Mathers, *Book of the Sacred Magic of Abramelin the Mage*, 106; Susej, *Demonic Bible*, 257.

Gagh Shekelah

Variations: AGNIEL, AZIEL ("whom God consoles"), Charariel, GAMCHICOTH, Gog Sheklah ("disturber of all things"), Gashekla, Gha'agsheblah

The Gagh Shekelah lives in the second of the seven Palaces of Evil according to Kabbalaic mysticism. Their name in Hebrew means "the disturbing ones." In service under the Chesed, the fourth Sephirah on the tree of life in the Kabbalah, their symbolic appearance is that of black cat-headed giants.

Sources: Davidson, *Dictionary of Angels*, xvii, 349; Godwin, *Godwin's Cabalistic Encyclopedia*, 129, 242; Greer, *New Encyclopedia of the Occult*, 187.

Gagison

In the *Sacred Magic of Abramelin the Mage*, Gagison is among the SERVITORS OF ORIENS (ORIENS). His name in Hebrew means "spread out flat."

Sources: Mathers, *Book of the Sacred Magic of Abramelin the Mage*, 108; Von Worms, *Book of Abramelin*, 257.

Ga-Git

From the mythology of the Haida Indians of the Queen Charlotte Islands off the west coast of North America comes the demonic creature known as the ga-git. It is said that when a man survives a canoe wreck at sea and he makes it back to shore, there is the chance that in a daze he may wander off into the woods where he will survive off berries, moss, and roots. Eventually he will discard his clothing and gain the power of flight and superhuman strength, shortly thereafter fully transforming into a ga-git. Should this creature intentionally breathe on a person's face, the transformation process will begin immediately and take only a few days to complete. Basically humanoid in appearance, its body is covered in heavy black fur with taloned hands and feet. The creature emits a deep, continuous, rumbling growl; it smells of filth and rotting meat.

A nocturnal demon, it hunts by night, attacking anyone it happens upon. Ga-git are known to shake houses and uproot trees. Occasionally one will venture near a village and cast a magical spell that causes a very deep sleep to fall over a house. Once this happens, it will slip inside and carry away its occupants. Ga-git also have the ability to change their shape at will. Although they have the ability to fly, only the very old and powerful ones can fly high enough to clear the top of a house; the rest can only rise up a few yards off the ground.

These demons live in caves in the woods. If ever you are chased by a ga-git, immediately run to the nearest body of water, as they are phobic of it and will not follow.

Sources: Harrison, *Ancient Warriors of the North Pacific*, 133–5; Jones, *Evil in Our Midst*, 19–22.

Galak

In the *Sacred Magic of Abramelin the Mage*, book two, Galak is included among the twenty-two SERVITORS OF ARITON (see ARITON). His name comes from the Greek language and means "milky."

Sources: Mathers, *Book of the Sacred Magic of Abramelin the Mage*, 108; Von Worms, *Book of Abramelin*, 257.

Galla

Variations: Gallu

In Sumerian demonology the galla were the messengers and the seven attendants of the death goddess Ereshkigal (see IRKALLA). They were the only beings in Sumerian mythology who had the ability to travel back and forth from Kur, the underworld. These demons are incorruptible as they cannot be bribed, have no need to eat or drink, and have no sexual desires. They are described as having claws and fangs and carrying axes. One Sumerian line of text reads, "Small galla are like the reeds in a low reed fence, large galla are like the reeds in a high reed fence." Galla hunt the earth terrorizing mankind and occasionally bringing a person back to the underworld with them. They especially hate children.

Sources: Hyatt, *Book of Demons*, 36; Lurker, *Dictionary of Gods and Goddesses*, 125; Sorensen, *Possession and Exorcism in the New Testament and Early Christianity*, 27–8.

Gallu

Variations: GALLA, gallû

The gallu is a violent, nocturnal demon from Assyrian, Babylonian, Chaldean, and Sumerian mythology. Looking like a bull, it wanders in cities by night, attacking anyone it sees and dragging the bodies back to the Underworld with it. Although it lives in the Underworld, it will use its shape-changing abilities to take shelter in dark places. Scholars are uncertain if there is one demon named Gallu or if the gallu is a species of demon.

Sources: Sources: Hurwitz, *Lilith: The First Eve*, 38–41; Jastrow, *Religion of Babylonia and Assyria*, 260; Lenormant, *Chaldean Magic*, 24; Sorensen, *Possession and Exorcism in the New Testament and Early Christianity*, 27–8.

Galtxagorriak

Variations: Galtzagorri, Prakagorris

A galtxagorriak is an *iratxoak* (IMP) from Basque mythology. The word translates to mean "red pants," a fitting enough name as these little demons are described as wearing them. There is a popular story from the region of a lazy man who was once instructed where to go and purchase a box of galtxagorriak. When he got home he opened the box and many of the little demons came out and asked, "What can we do?" He gave them a list of chores and within a few minutes the chores were completed. Again the galtxagorriak asked, "What can we do?" and the man gave them more chores, which were again completed in a few moments. Again the galtxagorriak asked, "What can we do?" but there were no chores left so the lazy man replied, "Nothing." The galtxagorriak became furious and immediately set out to undo all the work they had done. The man managed to somehow get them all back in the box and resolved never to use them again.

Sources: Aulestia, *Basque-English, English-Basque Dictionary*, 142; de Barandiarán, *Selected Writings of José Miguel de Barandiarán*, 127; Facaros, *Bilbao and the Basque Lands*, 45.

Gamaliel

The gamaliel are the demons of death, according to the *Qlippoth*. Born of and in service under the demonness LILITH, the gamaliel ("polluted of God") are described as being misshapen and twisted beings. They live in the Palace of Yesod.

Sources: Greer, *New Encyclopedia of the Occult*, 188; Guiley, *Encyclopedia of Magic and Alchemy*, 159, 257; Mason, *Necronomicon Gnosis*, 151.

Gamchicoth

Variations: Agshekeloh, Breakers into Pieces, the Disturbers of Souls, Ga'ashekelah, Gog Sheklah

In Cabalistic lore the gamchicoth ("breakers") are placed in the fourth Sephirah of the Tree of Life and are in the order of "Devourers." These demons waste the substance and thought of creation and are said to be under the command of ASHTAROTH. Their personal adversaries are the Spirits of Gedulah (see also GAMIGIN).

Sources: Greer, *New Encyclopedia of the Occult*, 187; Horne, *Sacred Books and Early Literature of the East*, 163; Waite, *Doctrine and Literature of the Kabalah*, 80.

Gamigin

Variations: Gamigm, Gamygyn, SAMIGINA

Listed as one of the seventy-two SPIRITS OF SOLOMON, Gamigin commands thirty legions of demons. This diurnal demon is most powerful in the month of April, and when summoned he will appear before his caster looking like a donkey or a small horse; however, by request, he will alter his appearance to look like a man. When he speaks he will do so with a rough voice. Gamigin is known to take his time with anyone who summons him, as he is never in a rush to leave the earth realm, but he will attack if the scorcerer is not wearing the seal of GAMCHICOTH. This demon is summoned not only for his ability to answer any questions asked of him and his willingness to teach the liberal sciences, but also because he keeps track of all the souls who died in a state of sin as well as those who died at sea.

Sources: De Laurence, *Lesser Key of Solomon, Goetia*, 22–23; DuQuette, *Key to Solomon's Key*, 162; McLean, *Treatise of Angel Magic*, 55; Scot, *Discoverie of Witchcraft*, 223.

Gamori

Variations: Gamory, Gremory

Gamori is the Duke of Songs and commands twenty-six legions of demons. Listed as one of the seventy-two SPIRITS OF SOLOMON, this demon appears as a beautiful woman with the crown of a duchess tied to her waist. She rides upon a large camel. Gamori knows all things from the past, present, and future. She knows where treasure is hidden and can secure the love of a woman to a man.

Sources: De Laurence, *Lesser Key of Solomon, Goetia*, 40; Godwin, *Godwin's Cabalistic Encyclopedia*, 117; Susej, *Demonic Bible*, 200.

Ganael

From Acadian, Assyrian, and Chaldean demonology comes the demon Ganael. He is ranked as an ELECTOR OF HELL and a planetary ruler under the command of Apadiel and Camael (see CAMIEL and DEMONS OF THE GRIMOIRE). This demon is one of the seven spirits of the Abyss, one of the "seven phantoms of flame," and a retrograde spirit. Ganael has the ability to cause earthquakes and is said to be more powerful and terrifying than any other species of demon. He lives in the bowels of the earth.

Sources: Butler, *Ritual Magic*, 161; Davidson, *Dictionary of Angels*, 121; Von Goethe, *Goethe's Letters to Zelter*, 377.

Gandarewa

Variations: "Golden heeled," Kundraw

Gandarewa is a demonic dragon from Persian and Sumerian demonology that is described as being so incredibly large that his upper body could be in the clouds while his lower body was on the bottom of the sea. An aquatic demon who eats humans, Gandarewa is titled as the Lord of the Abyss; he is answerable only to the god of dragons, Azhi Dahaki. This demon constantly tries to devour all the good things of creation; however, he has had streaks of charity, such as when he gives the gift of Haoma plants to mankind. The guardian of the other dragons, Gandarewa lives in Vourukasha, the cosmic sea. His personal adversary is the hero Keresaspa.

Sources: Gray, *Mythology of all Races*, Vol. 6, 58–9, 279; Lurker, *Routledge Dictionary of Gods and Goddesses*, 65; Turner, *Dictionary of Ancient Deities*, 185.

Ganga-Gramma

Variations: Bhagirathi, Ganga, Ganges, Jahnavi (daughter of Jahnu)

Collin de Plancy's *Dictionaire Infernale* (1863) mentions this Vedic goddess, the second wife of Shiva. Ganga-Gramma is the demon of waters and there are an assortment of tales explaining how she came into being. In the first, the sacred water in Brahma's water vessel transformed the maiden; another version has the water that Brahma saved after washing the feet of Vishnu transformed into Ganga; and the third version claims she was born the daughter of the King of the Mountains, Himavan, and his consort Mena. Ganga-Gramma is a four-armed, beautiful and voluptuous woman. In her left hand she holds a bowl, symbolic of abundant life and fertility, and in her right she carries a three-pronged fork. She is depicted in art riding astride a *makara*, a crocodile with the tail of a fish. This goddess, arrogant and vain as she may be, purifies souls so that they may pass on to Heaven. Sacrifice of buffalos, goats, and the occasional human will prevent her from attacking mankind.

Sources: Anonymous, *Missionary Magazine for 1802*, 238; Bell, *Bell's New Pantheon*, 348–9; Collin de Plancy, *Dictionnaire Infernal*, 295–6.

Gara-Demons, plural: gara-yakku; singular: gara-yaka

In the Singhalese Buddhist mythology, gara-yakku, as they are known collectively, are a group of twelve demons that are not innately hostile to humans. During the GARA-YAK-NATUMA ceremony they are summoned and invited to remove the evils of the body while not harming the person in the process and accepting the sacrificial offerings of confections, drink, food, and money. These demons have the ability to cast *vas-dos* (the evil eye).

Sources: Gooneratne, *On Demonology and Witchcraft in Ceylon*, 35–6; Lurker, *Routledge Dictionary of Gods and Goddesses*, 47; Obeyesekere, *Cult of the Goddess Pattini*, 175, 177.

Garadiel

In the *Theurgia Goetia*, the second book of the *Lemegeton*, Garadiel is ranked as a chief; he is also one of the eleven WANDERING PRINCES (see PRINCES OF HELL). This AERIAL DEVIL commands 18,150 servitors, none of which are dukes or princes. Garadiel is both diurnal and nocturnal, and depending on the time of day that he is summoned, he will bring a different number of his servitors with him, all of which are good-natured and willing to obey.

Dawn is the start of the day and marks the beginning of the first hour, so if summoned in the two first hours of the day and the two second hours of the night, he will arrive with 470 servitors. If summoned in the two second hours of the day and the two third hours of the night he will arrive with 590 servitors. If summoned in the two third hours of the day and the two fourth hours of the night he will arrive with 930 servitors. If summoned in the two fourth hours of the day and the two fifth hours of the night he will arrive with 1,560 servitors. If summoned in the two fifth hours of the day and the two sixth hours of the night he will arrive with 13,710 servitors. In the last two hours of the day and the first two hours of the night, if summoned, he will arrive with 1,560 servitors.

Sources: Guiley, *Encyclopedia of Demons and Demonology*, 94; Peterson, *Lesser Key of Solomon*, 92–3; Shumaker, *Natural Magic and Modern Science*, 66.

Gara-Yak-Natuma

In the Singhalese Buddhist mythology the gara-yak-natuma ("dance of the gara-yakku") is a ceremonial religious dance performed at the end of annual ceremonies, such as the peraheras and the tovil. It wards off the *vas-dos* (the evil eye) that is cast by the GARA-DEMONS. The participants of the ceremony wear highly decorated and expensive masks representing each of the twelve different GARA-DEMONS. Because the masks that are necessary to perform the dance are so expensive, the ritual is performed only once or twice a year. During the ceremonial dance, the demons are summoned and invited to remove the evils of the body while not harming the person in the process and accepting the sacrificial offerings in exchange.

Sources: Obeyesekere, *Cult of the Goddess Pattini*, 173–4, Wirx, *Exorcism and the Art of Healing in Ceylon*, 163.

Gasarons

In the *Sacred Magic of Abramelin the Mage*, Gasarons is listed as one of the SERVITORS OF ORIENS (see ORIENS).

Sources: Belanger, *Dictionary of Demons*, 136; Mathers, *Book of the Sacred Magic of Abramelin the Mage*, 108.

Gaziel

Variations: Gaxiel

The demon Gaziel commands eleven legions and works in conjunction with ANARAZEL and FECOR. He has the ability to call up tempests, cause fear, cause ghosts to appear, ring the bells at midnight, and shake the foundations of homes.

Sources: De Claremont, *Ancient's Book of Magic*, 12; Hibbard, *Three Elizabethan Pamphlets*, 147; Nash, *Works of Thomas Nashe*, 232.

Gedeil

Variations: Gediel

In the *Theurgia Goetia*, the second book of the *Lemegeton*, Gedeil is ranked as the Prince of the South by Southwest (see PRINCES OF HELL). He is said to command twenty diurnal and twenty nocturnal servitors; however, only eight dukes are named for each. His name is likely taken from Hebrew, and if so would mean "baby goat." Gedeil is known for his ability to give timely warnings of danger.

Sources: Gettings, *Dictionary of Demons*, 232; Scheible, *Sixth and Seventh Books of Moses*, 73; Trithemius, *Steganographia*, 81.

Gelal

From the demonology of the ancient Sumerians comes a demon they referred to as a gelal (INCUBUS). There has yet to be a physical description for this demon; however, it has been described as having a "male" feeling. The gelal assaults a woman sexually while she sleeps, stealing energy from her. Its victims will not be awakened but will experience the encounter through an erotic dream.

Sources: Jones, *On the Nightmare*, 119; Lenormant, *Chaldean Magic*, 38; Masters, *Eros and Evil*, 174.

Geliel

Heinrich Cornelius Agrippa Von Netteshim's book *Naturalis et Innaturalis* mentions Geliel, ranking him as a duke. In Enochian lore and Christian demonology he is also said to be an ELECTOR OF HELL and one of the twenty-eight demonic rulers of the lunar mansions; he has dominion over the mansion Sadahacha, also called Zodeboluch (see ENOCHIAN RULERS OF THE LUNAR MANSIONS). In service under CASPIEL, Geliel commands twenty diurnal and nocturnal servitors but only eight are named for each (see SERVITORS OF GELIEL). This demon is summoned for the assistance he will give in helping prisoners to escape. His zodiacal sign is Capricorn.

Sources: Moura, *Mansions of the Moon for the Green Witch*, 45; Von Goethe, *Goethe's Letters to Zelter*, 377; Webster, *Encyclopedia of Angels*, 69.

Gello

Variations: Drakaena, Drakos, GALLU, Gallû, Ghello, Gillo, Gyllo, Gyllou, Gylo, the Lady of Darkness, Lamashtu, LAMIA, LILITH, Lilitu

Originating in Graeco-Byzantine and Sumerian mythology, the most famous of the ancient Greek women poets, Sappo, wrote of the DEMONESS Gello in the text *Apotrofe tes miaras kai akazartu Gyllus* (*Averting of the Wicked and Impure Gylu*). It is both a cautionary tale and a spell for defeating the demon.

According to the story, Gello was a maiden from the isle of Lesbos who opposed divine law and took a stance against it using her willpower and magic to get her way. She compounded her sin by having died leaving no heirs or descendants, which caused her to become a demon. At night Gello would return, shape-shift into her maiden form, find a female child, and play with it. When the game was over, she would consume the child. Eventually it took three angels—Senoy, Sansenoy, and Semangeloph (or three saints: Sinisius, Sines, and Sinodorus from the Byzantine period)—to finally defeat her. The three first captured her and she immediately began to beg for her life, saying she would do whatever was asked of her, promising if they let her go she would run and not stop until she was three thousand miles away. They beat her soundly until she confessed her twelve and a half names to them; by doing this she made herself powerless against them. They demanded that she return the children she consumed. Gello confessed that to do so she would first have to breast-feed from the tit of a woman whose child she had eaten. After feeding, she vomited up the child, whole and alive. Once all the children were returned, Gello was stoned to death.

The twelve and a half names of Gello are Anavadalaia ("soaring"), Apletou ("insatiable"), Byzou ("bloodsucker"), Chamodracaena ("snake"), Gulou, Marmarou ("stony-hearted"), Mora,

Paidopniktia ("child strangler"), Pelagia ("sea creature"), Petasia ("winged one"), Psychanaspastria ("soul catcher"), Strigla, and Vordona ("swooping like a hawk").

Sources: Bremmer, *Early Greek Concept of the Soul*, 101; Cumont, *Afterlife in Roman Paganism*, 128–47; Hartnup, *On the Beliefs of the Greeks*, 110; Hurwitz, *Lilith: The First Eve*, 41, 131; Jastrow, *Religion of Babylonia and Assyria*, 260; Oeconomides, *International Congress for Folk Narrative Research in Athens*, 328–34.

Geloma

The *Sacred Magic of Abramelin the Mage*, book two, lists Geloma as one of the one hundred eleven SERVITORS OF AMAYMON, ARITON, ORIENS, AND PAYMON (see AMAYMON, ARITON, ORIENS, and PAYMON). His name is Hebrew and means "wrapped" or "wound together."

Sources: Mathers, *Book of the Sacred Magic of Abramelin the Mage*, 105; Susej, *Demonic Bible*, 256.

Genie

Variations: DJINN, Dyinyinga, Genii

From the demonology of the Mende people of Sierra Leone comes the genie. Originally Mende ancestral spirits, genies evolved into generic good or evil spirits, then nature spirits, and in some places, demonic spirits. They are described as looking like a person of Portuguese descent and being white skinned. Genies live deep in the forest or on isolated mountainsides or where Islam is practiced (see also NDOGBOJUSUI and TINGOI).

Genies have well-defined human emotions and passions. They are highly receptive to flattery and are notoriously fickle. They have the ability to shape-shift into animals and people and are also capable of causing good fortune to enter into a person's life by use of their innate magical abilities. Occasionally they will have sexual relations with humans or visit one while they sleep, but a genie will only attack when it is displeased with the personality of the Mende it encounters. There is no formulated approach on how to deal with a genie who has been angered except to act boldly. If dominance is not quickly established, it will claim dominance and have power over you. If this should happen, to escape out from under a genie's power, a sacrifice of something dearly loved or treasured must be offered, such as the life of your firstborn son. If a person becomes possessed by a genie, a magical Mende ceremony must be performed.

Sources: Forde, *African Worlds*, 115, 124, 137; Hughes, *Dictionary of Islam*, 135; Rose, *Spirits, Fairies, Gnomes, and Goblins*, 96.

Geniel

According to Enochian lore, the FALLEN ANGEL Geniel is one of the twenty-eight demonic rulers of the lunar mansions; he has dominion over the mansion Alnath ("Horn of Aries"). He is ranked in Christian demonology as one of the ELECTORS OF HELL.

Sources: McLean, *Treatise on Angel Magic*, 42; Webster, *Encyclopedia of Angels*, 121.

Gerevil

In the *Sacred Magic of Abramelin the Mage*, book two, Gerevil is named as one of the one hundred eleven Servitors of AMAYMON, ARITON, ORIENS, and PAYMON (see AMAYMON, ARITON, ORIENS, and PAYMON). His name is taken from Hebrew and translates to mean "divining lot" or "sortilege."

Sources: Masters, *Book of the Sacred Magic of Abramelin the Mage*, 113; Von Worms, *Book of Abramelin*, 255.

Geriel

Variations: Geriol

In the *Theurgia Goetia*, the second book of the *Lemegeton*, Geriel is named as one of the twelve SERVITORS OF CASPIEL (see CASPIEL). Ranked as a rude and stubborn chief duke, he commands 2,660 duke servitors (see DUKES OF HELL).

Sources: Belanger, *Dictionary of Demons*, 138; Peterson, *Lesser Key of Solomon*, 80.

Geryon

Variations: Geryones, Geyron, Ghruonh, Ghruwn, Gusayn, Guseyn, GUSION, GUSOYN, Osgarbial, Pirsoyn, Urakabarameek, URAKABARAMEEL

In Christian demonology and Enochian lore, Geryon is listed among the FALLEN ANGELS one of the CHIEF OF TENS who, under the name Urakabarameel, swore allegiance to SAMIAZA, rebelled against God, took a human as his wife, and fathered the NEPHILIM (see also GRIGORI and WATCHERS). Geryon, grand duke, is said to command many chiefs and servitors, including COZBI, FECOR, GORSON, Herodias, and MACHALAS. A demon of death, he has the ability to grant positions of honor and power. He is most powerful during the eighth hour of the day.

In *Dante's Inferno* Geryon was the monster that carried Dante and Virgil from the third ring of the seventh circle to the Malebolge in the eighth circle. There is also a monster in Greek mythology bearing this name and therefore this demon's name is possibly Greek; if so it would translate to mean "earth" or "singing."

Sources: Beard, *Autobiography of Satan*, 113; Cooper,

Brewer's Book of Myth and Legend, 108; Walsh, *Heroes and Heroines of Fiction*, 122–3; Saini, *Satan vs. God*, 251.

Ghaddar

Variations: Gharra

From Islamic mythology comes the demon Ghaddar ("goat" or "hound"), born one of the children from the union between IBLIS and a wife whom God created especially for him out of the fire of the Samum. Ghaddar's gender is uncertain, but many scholars believe female. Hideously ugly, this demon preys upon travelers, capturing them and torturing them with mutilation; eventually death comes when she devours their genitals. Ghaddar lives in the desert in the countries near the Red Sea.

Sources: Hughes, *Dictionary of Islam*, 137–8; Knowles, *Nineteenth Century*, Vol. 31, 449, Rose, *Giants, Monsters, and Dragons*, 136.

Ghilan

Variations: ALGUL, Ghillan, Ghoul, GHUL

From Islamic mythology and mentioned in the Koran are two genuses of DJINN. The first is divided into five classes: Afreet, Ghilan, JANN, MARID, Sheitan. In their genus, they are the fourth strongest of the DJINN.

The ghilan are born the children of IBLIS. They have innate magical abilities and are expert shape-shifters; no matter the form they choose to appear in, they will always have hooves rather than feet. They use their shape-shifting to take on the appearance of a beautiful woman to lure a traveler away from his companions, at which point the ghilan will kill and consume him. Grave robbers, ghilan live in cemeteries. They are capable of being destroyed, but they must be hit hard enough to be killed with a single blow; a second assault will restore a ghilan to full health.

Sources: Houtsma, *E.J. Brill's First Encyclopaedia of Islam*, 165; Oesterley, *Immortality and the Unseen World*, 33.

Ghole

Variations: Gholi, Ghoûl, Ghoulas, Goule, Gouli, Labasu

Covered in thick hair, the ghole from Arabic lore also has long tusks, one large cyclopean eye, and a long neck like an ostrich. Using its ability to shape-shift into a human of either sex, it lures lone travelers to a secluded place where it may then consume their flesh and drink their blood. On occasion it has been known to fall in love with a human, and when it does, it will capture that person and take them on as a mate. It is said that the offspring from such couplings produces a new type of ghole, a monstrous being that is a fast, savage, extremely effective predator that takes delight in killing and raping.

Sources: Collin de Plancy, *Dictionnaire Infernal*, 70; Gustafson, *Foundation of Death*, 32–33; Jones, *On the Nightmare*, 112; Smedley, *Occult Sciences*, 70; Summers, *Vampire: His Kith and Kin*, 204.

Ghoreb Zereq

Variations: Aarab Tzereq ("Ravens of Dispersion"), Getzphiel

Originating in cabalistic teaching and the *Grimoirium Verum (Grimoire of Truth)*, Ghoreb Zereq are hideous demon-headed ravens under the command of Baal Chanan or Netzach who rule the hierarchy known as Harab. They live in volcanoes and are located on the seventh Sephirah of the Tree of Life. Their name in Hebrew means "dispersing ravens."

Sources: Greer, *New Encyclopedia of the Occult*, 1.

Ghul

In Muslim folklore there is a female vampiric demon known as a ghul that eats only the flesh of the dead. It breaks into the graves of those properly buried and feeds off their corpses. If it cannot find an easy meal in a graveyard, it shape-shifts into a beautiful woman in order to trick male travelers into thinking that it is a prostitute. Then, once alone with a man, she kills him.

Sources: Delcourt, *Oedipe*, 108–9; Gibb, *Shorter Encyclopaedia of Islam*, 114, 159; Stetkevych, *Mute Immortals Speak*, 95–99; Villeneuve, *Le Musée des Vampires*, 368.

Gian Ben Gian

Variations: Gnan, Gyan, Gyan-ben-Gian, Jnana

In ancient Persian mythology, Gian Ben Gian, the chieftain of the female *peris* (see DIV), was said to have been the governor of the world for the two thousand years after the creation of Adam. She carries a shield that is impervious to all forms of black or evil magic. Her personal adversary is Eblis, against whom her shield is useless. Her name is Arabic and means "occult wisdom" or "true wisdom."

Sources: Blavatsky, *Secret Doctrine*, 394; Brewer, *Dictionary of Phrase and Fable*, 339.

Giang Shi

Variations: Chang Kuei, Chiang-Shih, Kiang-Shi, Kuang-Shii, Xianh-Shi

As far back as 600 B.C.E. there are records of a vampiric demon called the giang shi. Said to take possession of the new corpse of a person who died a violent death or committed suicide, it leaps up out of the grave, attacking travelers.

The giang shi is described as having two different forms. The first is that of a tall corpse with green or white hair. It has red eyes, serrated teeth, and long claws on its fingertips. Its other form passes for human until it does something to give itself away, such as obviously retreating from garlic or shape-shifting into a wolf.

The breath of the giang shi is so foul that it will literally send a man staggering back a full twenty feet. If it is successful enough to mature, as told by when its hair is long and white, it will develop the ability to fly. Once it has achieved maturity, only the sound of an extremely loud thunderclap can destroy it.

Since there is no way to prevent a giang shi from possessing a corpse, destruction is the only option. The vampire cannot cross running water, and during moonlit nights, it can be trapped in a circle made of rice. Once captured, it must be reburied and given proper burial rites.

Sources: Bush, *Asian Horror Encyclopedia*, 96; Glut, *Dracula Book*, 25; Groot, *Religion of the Chinese*, 76–77; Summers, *Vampire: His Kith and Kin*, 213.

Gid-Dim

Variations: Gidim

The demonic spirit of sickness, Gid-Dim originates from Sumerian demonology. His name translates to mean "black approaching" or "eclipsed." He causes all forms of physical and mental illnesses.

Ritual prayers to the gods asking for protection from his demonic possession are the only way to prevent attack from this demon; however, if a person should be possessed by him, only an exorcism performed by an *ashipu* (sorcerer) can save them.

Sources: Black, *Gods, Demons, and Symbols of Ancient Mesopotamia*, 88–9; Icons, *Demons*, 35; Pu, *Rethinking Ghosts in World Religions*, 26, 32.

Gigim

Gigim, an AERIAL DEVIL, is one of a group of seven demons working in unison who are in service to Ereshkigal, the goddess of death and gloom (see IRKALLA). Detailed in the *Magan Text* of ancient Sumerian demonology, Gigim is said to enter into a person's home and attack their bowels or possess them. There is no known way to prevent this demon from entering into a home. Gigim lives in the desert and in abandoned places of worship where sacrifices took place. His name in Sumerian translates to mean "evil" (see also ALAL, IDPA, NAMTAR, TELAL, URUKU, and UTUK).

Sources: Gray, *Mythology of All Races*, 355, 364; Lenormant, *Chaldean Magic*, 24; Turner, *Dictionary of Ancient Deities*, 64.

Gilarion

According to the *Sacred Magic of Abramelin the Mage*, book two, Gilarion is one of the sixteen SERVITORS OF ASMODEUS (see ASMODEUS).

Sources: Mathers, *Book of the Sacred Magic of Abramelin the Mage*, 107; Von Worms, *Book of Abramelin*, 256.

Ginar

The *Sacred Magic of Abramelin the Mage* names Ginar as one of the thirty-two SERVITORS OF ASTAROT (see ASTAROT). His name is possibly Chaldaic and if so would mean "to finish" or "to perfect."

Sources: Mathers, *Book of the Sacred Magic of Abramelin the Mage*, 117; Von Worms, *Book of Abramelin*, 249.

Ginijal Sanniya

In Sinhalese demonology Ginijal Sanniya is the demon of fevers. He is depicted in ceremonial masks as having a wide nose and tusked mouth. Ginijal Sanniya has the ability to cause excess heat and like the other Sinhalese demons, he is susceptible to the DAHA-ATA SANNIYA.

Sources: Illes, *Encyclopedia of Spirits*, 875; Wirz, *Exorcism and the Art of Healing in Ceylon*, 44.

Giri

In Singhalese Buddhist mythology the giri are the female aspect of the GARA-DEMONS. Their name translates from Singhalese to mean "a hard rock" or "to scream." During the GARA-YAK-NA-TUMA ceremony they are summoned and invited to remove the evils of the body while not harming the person in the process and accepting the sacrificial offerings of confections, drink, food, and money. These demons have the ability to cast *vas-dos* (the evil eye) (see also DALA-RAJA).

Sources: Conway, *Demonology and Devil-Lore*, 153; Obeyesekere, *Cult of the Goddess Pattini*, 64–6.

Glacia Labolas

Variations: Caasimolar, Caassimolar, Glasya, Glasya Labolas, Glasyalabolas

Ars Goetia, the first book of the *Lemegeton*, ranks Glacia Labolas as an earl, president, and master of murderers; he is under the service of NEBIROS and commands thirty-six legions of demons (see EARLS OF HELL and PRESIDENTS OF HELL). When this diurnal demon is summoned, he appears as a DOG with feathered wings. Glacia Labolas has the ability to create love between friends and enemies, disclose past events, foretell the future, grant invisibility, and inspire murder. He is an expert teacher in arts, killing techniques, and the various sciences (see also CAACRINOLAAS).

Sources: Crowley, *The Goetia*, 39; De Laurence, *Lesser Key of Solomon, Goetia*, 29; McLean, *Treatise of Angel Magic*, 55.

Glassyalabolas

Variations: CAACRINOLAAS, Caassimolar, Classyalabolas, Glassia-labolis, Glasya Labolas, Glasya-Labolas, Glasyabolis

In the *Lesser Key of Solomon*, Glassyalabolas is listed as one of the eighteen SERVITORS OF FLEURETTY, LUCIFUGE, NEBIROS, SARGATANAS, AND SATANACHIA (see FLEURETTY, LUCIFUGE, NEBIROS, SARGATANAS, and SATANACHIA). He is ranked in Christian demonology as an earl or president; sources vary (see EARLS OF HELL and PRESIDENTS OF HELL). The demon of bloodshed and manslaughter, he commands thirty-six legions of demons. When summoned he appears as a dog with the wings of a griffin. He has the power to cause love between enemies, incite homicides, foretell the past and future, and can make a man invisible.

Sources: Baskin, *Sorcerer's Handbook*, 276; Peterson, *Lesser Key of Solomon*, 18, 233, 262; Waite, *Unknown World 1894–1895*, 230; Wedeck, *Treasury of Witchcraft*, 96.

Glauron

Reginald Scot's *The Discoverie of Witchcraft* (1584) names Glauron as the demon of the North and the chief of the AERIAL DEVILS. Known as a pacifist, this demon is called upon during the summoning of LURIDAN.

Sources: Gettings, *Dictionary of Demons*, 117; Shah, *Black and White Magic*, 206.

Glesi

Glesi is named in the *Sacred Magic of Abramelin the Mage* as one of the twenty SERVITORS OF AMAYMON (see AMAYMON). His name is Hebrew and means "one who glistens horribly like an insect."

Sources: Forgotten Books, *Book of the Sacred Magic of Abramelin the Mage*, 42–3; Lowry, *Under the Volcano*, 194; Mathers, *Book of the Sacred Magic of Abra-Melin*, 122.

Glmarij

In the *Ars Paulina*, the third book of the *Lemegeton*, Glmarij is named as one of the two hundred SERVITORS OF VEGUANIEL (see VEGUANIEL).

Sources: Davidson, *Dictionary of Angels*, 135; Waite, *The Book of Ceremonial Magic*, 67.

Glykon

Variations: Glycon

In Gnostic-Mithraic demonology, Glykon ("the sweet one") is believed to be an incarnation of Asclepius. He is described as having a human head with the body of a snake.

Sources: Charlesworth, *Good and Evil Serpent*, 151; Meyer, *Ancient Mysteries*, 42.

Gnod-Sbyin

Variations: Gnod Sbyin Mo, Gnodsbyin, YAKSHA

The gnod-sbyin of Tibet preys exclusively on people who live a holy or spiritual life. Its name, *gnod-sbyin*, translates literally to mean "doer of harm," and this demonic vampiric spirit does everything it can to live up to its name. Apart from its immense strength and its ability to cause and spread disease on an epidemic scale, it has a wide array of unspecified supernatural powers at its disposal. It has INCUBUS- and SUCCUBUS-like behaviors that it indulges in whenever the opportunity presents itself. It takes great pleasure in the hurt it causes people and it delights in making noises that disrupt the meditation of the monks and nuns, but its silence can be purchased with the regular offerings of proper sacrifices. Described as having black skin, the gnod-sbyin is usually found living in difficult to reach and isolated places in the mountains.

Sources: Bellezza, *Spirit-Mediums*, 292; Beyer, *Cult of Tara*, 252, 253, 293, 294, 342, 416; Dagyab, *Tibetan Religious Art*, 19, 70; Nebesky-Wojkowitz, *Oracles and Demons of Tibet*, 30, 32.

Goap

Variations: GAAP, Göap, Tap

A FALLEN ANGEL, formerly of the Order of Thrones (or Powers, sources vary), Goap is ranked as one of the PRINCES OF HELL, Prince of the West, one of the four regents of Hell, and one of the eleven PRESIDENTS OF HELL. According to Christian demonologies, he is also one of the seventy-two SPIRITS OF SOLOMON.

Sources: Beard, *Autobiography of Satan*, 46; Davidson, *Dictionary of Angels*, 125; Gaspey, *The Witch-Finder*, 201; Scot, *Discoverie of Witchcraft*, 226; Spence, *Encyclopedia of Occultism*, 119.

Gog and Magog

Variations: Goemagot, Goemot, Gogmagog, Gogmagog and Corineus, Ma'juj wa Ya'juj, Yajuj was Majuj

Demonic giants Gog and MAGOG are mentioned in various mythologies, but according to the *Historia Regum Brittaniae* (*The History of the Kings of Britain*) written in 1136 by Geoffrey of Monmouth, they are the traditional guardians of the city of London. The legend tells us that the Roman Emperor Diocletian had thirty-three evil daughters whom he sought to marry off. Alba, the eldest, led her sisters in a plot to murder their father (or their husbands, sources vary). They were caught and for their punishment were set adrift at sea. The ship landed on an island inhabited by demons. Alba changed her name to Albion, and there she and her sisters chose husbands from the demons and gave birth to a race of giants. As the last two survivors of the sons of the thirty-three sisters and their demon husbands, Gog and MAGOG were captured and placed in chains fastened to the palace gates in Guildhall to act as guardians.

Depending on the various sources and mythologies that cite and reference Gog and Magog throughout history, the pair have been a race of people from Central Asia, demons, FALLEN ANGELS, giants, lands, and nations.

Sources: Brewer, *Reader's Handbook of Famous Names in Fiction*, 433; Larkin, *Book of Revelation*, 191; Rose, *Giants, Monsters, and Dragons*, 145–6.

Goleg

The *Ars Goetia*, the first book of the *Lemegeton*, names Goleg as one of the fifty-three SERVITORS OF ASHTAROTH AND ASMODEUS (see ASHTAROTH and ASMODEUS). His name is possibly a Hebrew word meaning "whirling."

Sources: Belanger, *Dictionary of Demons*, 141; Susej, *Demonic Bible*, 257.

Golen

In the *Sacred Magic of Abramelin the Mage*, Golen is among the thirty-two SERVITORS OF ASTAROT (see ASTAROT). His name is Greek, meaning "a cavern."

Sources: Mathers, *Book of the Sacred Magic of Abramelin the Mage*, 106, 117; Von Worms, *Book of Abramelin*, 249.

Golu Sanniya

In Sinhalese demonology Golu Sanniya is the demon of disease. He causes mental illness and the inability to hear and speak. Golu Sanniya, like the other Sinhalese demons, is susceptible to the DAHA-ATA SANNIYA.

Sources: Illes, *Encyclopedia of Spirits*, 875; Wirz, *Exorcism and the Art of Healing in Ceylon*, 44.

Gomory

Variations: GAMORI, Gamory, Gemory, Gomory, Gremory

Gomory, described as looking like a beautiful woman wearing a crown tied around her waist and riding upon a camel, is one of the seventy-two SPIRITS OF SOLOMON; she commands twenty-six legions of demons. A nocturnal demon most powerful during the month of December, Gomory is summoned for her ability to

discover the location of treasures; foretell the past, present, and future; and obtain love for a woman. She is named as one of the DUKES OF HELL.

Sources: Guiley, *Encyclopedia of Demons and Demonology*, 94; Kelly, *Who in Hell*, 100; Scot, *Discoverie of Witchcraft*, 224; Scott, *London Magazine*, Vol. 5, 378.

Gong Gong

Variations: Gong Qinwang, I-Hsin, Kang Hui, Kung Ch'in-wang, Kung Kung

In Chinese demonology Gong Gong ("quarrelsome") is a demonic god who, along with his associate XIANG YAO, causes widescale flooding. He is said to look like a dragon or a gigantic baboon. In Chinese legend Gong Gong declared war against Zhu-Rong for the rulership of the heavens. Gong Gong lost, and since he was denied the gift of speech by the gods, he could not cry out his rage. In his anger and depression he banged his head against one of the pillars that held up the heavens, which caused the heavens to tilt and spill a great flood upon the earth. The goddess Nüwa was able to correct the problem and righted heaven again, but it was not perfect, and now occasionally floodwaters will wash over the land. His personal adversary is Zhu-Rong. Christian demonology names him as the superintendent of public works.

Sources: Kelly, *Who in Hell*, 100; Lurker, *Dictionary of Gods and Goddesses*, 132; Qu, *Tian Wen*, 105–6; Rose, *Giants, Monsters, and Dragons*, 147.

Gonogin

The *Sacred Magic of Abramelin the Mage* names Gonogin as one of the thirty-two SERVITORS OF ASTAROT (see ASTAROT). His name is Hebrew for "delights" or "pleasures."

Sources: Belanger, *Dictionary of Demons*, 141; Susej, *Demonic Bible*, 257.

Gooberen

Gooberen is one of the eight AUSTATIKCO-PAULIGAUR, a type of demonic spirit or DIV from Persian mythology. The demon of riches, he presides over one of the eight sides of the world.

Sources: De Claremont, *Ancient's Book of Magic*, 118; Kindersley, *Specimens of Hindoo Literature*, 33; Spence, *Encyclopedia of Occultism*, 51.

Gorgo

Gorgo is a diminutive form of the word *demogorogon*, another name for SATAN.

Sources: Brown, *The Unicorn*, 49; *Chambers Dictionary*, 431; Powell, *Classical Myth*, 349–50.

Gorgons

Variations: The Phorcydes

The Gorgons ("the grim ones") were three demonic creatures from Greek mythology; their names were Euryale ("the far-springer"), Medusa ("the queen"), and Stheno ("the mighty"). These sisters were born the daughters of the sea gods Phorcys and Ceto and they were priestesses in the temple of Athena. Medusa had sexual relations with the god Poseidon in the temple and in a fit of rage Athena transformed the three sisters into the monstrous Gorgons. They were cursed with boarlike tusks; bronze claws; long, razor-sharp teeth; pockmarked faces; snakes for hair; and leathery wings. They were so hideously ugly that for a mortal to look directly at them would turn a man to stone. Medusa was the only mortal Gorgon and the blood from her beheading birthed Chrysaor and Pegasus. Blood taken from the right side of a Gorgon could bring the dead back to life, while blood from the left was an instantly fatal poison. The remaining Gorgons, Euryale and Stheno, live in the Underworld or on an island far out to sea.

Sources: Fontenrose, *Python*, 283–6, 288–9; Illes, *Encyclopedia of Spirits*, 488–9; Reed, *Demon-lovers and Their Victims in British Fiction*, 30.

Gorilon

Gorilon is listed among one hundred eleven Servitors of AMAYMON, ARITON, ORIENS, AND PAYMON (see AMAYMON, ARITON, ORIENS, and PAYMON) in the *Sacred Magic of Abramelin the Mage*, book two. His name is Coptic Egyptian and means "axe," "cleaving asunder," or "cleaving bones."

Sources: Belanger, *Dictionary of Demons*, 141; Susej, *Demonic Bible*, 256.

Gorson

Variations: Gorsou, GURSON

Gorson is the King of the South and was titled as the King of the Southern Maze. He is one of the chiefs of GERYON, one of the twelve SERVITORS OF ABEZETHIBOU, a servitor to Amaymon, as well as a servitor to Lucifer (SATAN). (See AMAYMON and also ABEZETHIBOU, GAAP, GERYON, and GURSON.)

Sources: Beard, *Autobiography of Satan*, 46; Gaspey, *The Witch-Finder*, 201; Scot, *Discoverie of Witchcraft*, 226.

Gosegas

In the *Sacred Magic of Abramelin the Mage*, book two, Gosegas is named as one of the one hundred eleven SERVITORS OF AMAYMON, ARITON, ORIENS, AND PAYMON (see AMAYMON, ARITON, ORIENS, and PAYMON). His name is possibly a Hebrew and Chaldaic hybrid meaning "shaking strongly."

Sources: Mathers, *Book of the Sacred Magic of Abramelin the Mage*, 114; Von Worms, *Book of Abramelin*, 245.

Gotifan

In the *Sacred Magic of Abramelin the Mage*, book two, Gotifan is as among the one of the forty-nine SERVITORS OF BEELZEBUB (see BEELZEBUB). His name is likely Hebrew and means "crushing" and "turning over."

Sources: Ford, *Bible of the Adversary*, 93; Mathers, *Book of the Sacred Magic of Abramelin the Mage*, 107; Von Worms, *Book of Abramelin*, 257.

Gramon

The *Sacred Magic of Abramelin the Mage*, book two, lists Gramon ("writing") as among the one of the forty-nine SERVITORS OF BEELZEBUB (see BEELZEBUB).

Sources: Ford, *Bible of the Adversary*, 93; Mathers, *Book of the Sacred Magic of Abramelin the Mage*, 108; Von Worms, *Book of Abramelin*, 257.

Grasemin

The *Sacred Magic of Abramelin the Mage*, book two, names Grasemin as one of the ten SERVITORS OF AMAYMON AND ARITON (see AMAYMON and ARITON). His name is likely Hebrew and may mean "a bone."

Sources: Mathers, *Book of the Sacred Magic of Abramelin the Mage*, 106; Von Worms, *Book of Abramelin*, 248.

Greedigut

The demonic FAMILIAR Greedigut was first mentioned in the confessions of the Witches of Huntingdon in 1645. He was described as looking like a DOG with hoglike bristled hair upon its back. As a FAMILIAR he works in tandem with the demon GRISSELL, and at the request of their master they will bring anything that is asked for. If they are not sent off on occasional tasks, they will seek out a random person to physically assault and rob, bringing the unsolicited money back to their master. Reports of men being pulled off their horses by two large dogs are telltale signs of a Greedigut and GRISSELL attack. Both of these demons are under the command of the demon BLACKEMAN and need to regularly suckle off their master.

Sources: Ashton, *Devil in Britain and America*, 237–8; Notestein, *History of Witchcraft in England*, 185; Wilby, *Cunning Folk and Familiar Spirits*, 61.

Gremial

Variations: Germel, Gerniel, Gremiel

In the *Theurgia Goetia*, the second book of the *Lemegeton*, Gremial is one of the twelve named

SERVITORS OF MACARIEL (see MACARIEL). Ranked as a chief duke, this AERIAL DEVIL commands four hundred servitors. When summoned he can appear in any form but typically will do so in the form of a dragon with a virgin's head. Good-natured and willing to obey his summoner, Gremial is constantly on the move, never staying in any one place for long.

Sources: Guiley, *Encyclopedia of Demons and Demonology*, 159; Peterson, *Lesser Key of Solomon*, 103; Trithemius, *Steganographia*, 141.

Grésil

Variations: Gresil

A FALLEN ANGEL formerly of the Order of Thrones, Grésil is the demon of impurity and pride. He is often called upon during exorcisms and cases of collective possession. He was one of the eighteen demons who possessed Sister Jeanne des Anges in Loudun, France, in 1634 (see LOUDUN POSSESSION).

Sources: Aikin, *General Biography*, 493; Bayle, *Historical and Critical Dictionary*, 262; Hsia, *World of Catholic Renewal*, 151; Robbins, *Encyclopedia of Witchcraft and Demonology*, 22; Voltaire, *Works of M. de Voltaire*, 193.

Gressil

Variations: CRESIL

In 1612 the French exorcist Father Sebastien Michaelis named Gressil as a FALLEN ANGEL, former prince in the Order of Thrones. He tempts men with impurity and slothfulness. He himself is said to be prone to lechery.

Sources: Cuhulain, *Witch Hunts*, 206; Davidson, *Dictionary of Angels*, 357; Maberry, *Cryptopedia*, 77.

Griffael

Griffael is ranked as a clerk of devils; he is described as looking like a small black figure.

Source: Rudwin, *Devil in Legend and Literature*, 28.

Grigori

Variations: FALLEN ANGELS, Irin, The Old Ones, Sentinels, Sons of God (bene-ha-Elohim), WATCHERS

In Judeo-Christian demonology and mentioned in the books of Daniel, Enoch, and Jubilees, the Grigori are a collection of FALLEN ANGELS who were once in servitude to God. These were the angels who banded together, swore a collective oath, and under the direction of Samyaza went directly against God's will by choosing to marry human women and father a race of children known as the NEPHILIM, who by nature were destructive and murderous. The Grigori went on to teach humans the secrets of Heaven, such as astrology, cosmotology, gemol-ogy, and weaponsmithing. For these sins they were exiled from Heaven, hunted down, and punished. Some sources say that the Grigori are bound to wander the earth until Judgment Day when they will be banished to Hell.

Most sources say that there are two hundred Grigori but typically only name the leaders, the CHIEF OF TENS. They are described as looking like large humans who never slept and usually remained silent.

Sources: Davidson, *Dictionary of Angels*, 126–7; Ford, *Bible of the Adversary*, 76; Guiley, *Encyclopedia of Angels*, 365–7; Voltaire, *Essays and Criticisms*, 106; Webster, *Encyclopedia of Angels*, 100.

Grissell

The demonic FAMILIAR Grissell was first mentioned in the confessions of the witches of Huntingdon in 1645. He was described as looking like a DOG with hoglike bristled hair upon its back. As a FAMILIAR he worked in tandem with the demon GREEDIGUT. At the request of their master they will bring anything that is asked for. If they are not sent off on occasional tasks, they will seek out a random person to physically assault and rob, bringing the unsolicited money back to their master. Reports of men being pulled off their horses by two large dogs are telltale signs of a Greedigut and Grissell attack. Both of these demons are under the command of the demon BLACKEMAN and need to regularly suckle off their master.

Sources: Ashton, *Devil in Britain and America*, 237–8; Notestein, *History of Witchcraft in England*, 185; Wilby, *Cunning Folk and Familiar Spirits*, 61.

Gromenis

In the *Sacred Magic of Abramelin the Mage* Gromenis ("to mark out") is listed as one of the thirty-two SERVITORS OF ASTAROT (see ASTAROT).

Sources: Ford, *Bible of the Adversary*, 91; Mathers, *Book of the Sacred Magic of Abramelin the Mage*, 106.

Guagamon

In the *Ars Goetia*, the first book of the *Lemegeton*, Guagamon ("net") is listed as one of the SERVITORS OF ASHTAROTH AND ASMODEUS (see ASHTAROTH and ASMODEUS).

Sources: Mathers, *Book of the Sacred Magic of Abramelin the Mage*, 106; Von Worms, *Book of Abramelin*, 247.

Gualichu

Variations: Gualicho

In the Mapuche mythology Gualichu is a demonic spirit. A purely spiritual being, he has no physical form or description, although some believe that the thorn tree is Gualichu incarnate, which makes it both venerated and feared. This demon, who lives underground, causes and creates every calamity, disease, or evil thing that happens; he also possesses objects and people. The only way to prevent attack from Gualichu is by placing sacrifices on his altar, which is found beneath gnarled and permanently windswept thorn trees bent toward the northeast. The sacrifices are hung from the thorny branches and consist of things no longer useful to man but would otherwise be pleasing to Gualichu, such as animal skins, broken horse bridles, spearheads, worn-out clothing, and in modern times, plastic wrappings and tin cans. Should a person become possessed by Gualichu, only a timely exorcism can save them. The Argentinean and Chilean saying "it has Gualichu" is to say that something has been cursed or jinxed. The word *gualichu* is used as both a noun and a verb.

Sources: Featherman, *Social History of the Races of Mankind*, 498–500; Icon, *Exorcising*, 21; Peck, *International Cyclopaedia*, 375.

Guaricana

In the demonology of the Yurimagua people of Brazil and Peru the demon Guaricana preys upon young men, flogging them until they bleed. To prevent attack from this demon, the men of the community must worship him in a special hut that is forbidden to children and women.

Sources: Ashley, *Complete Book of Devils and Demons*, 100; Krickeberg, *Pre-Columbian American Religions*, 284; Steward, *Handbook of South American Indians*, 704.

Guayota

The demonology of the Guanche people of the Canary Islands tells us of Guayota, the king of evil genies (DJINN, see also GENIE). He looks like a black dog accompanied by a host of demons, called *tibicenas*, who are also disguised as dogs (see DOG). Guayota and his entourage live in the volcano Mount Teide on Tenerife. His personal adversary is the god Achamán.

Sources: Month, *Scenes in Tenerife*, 555; Prichard, *Natural History of Man*, 237.

Guecubu

In the Mapuche mythology of Chile, South America, comes a species of demonic spirits known as guecubu. They do everything they can to foil the Great Spirit Togin and his ministers.

Source: Spence, *Encyclopedia of Occultism*, 196.

Guédé

Variations: Ghede, Guede

In Haitian voodoo there is a vampiric Ioa named Guédé. He is one of thirty different spirits who are members of the spirit family headed by Baron Samdi. Guédé, who dresses like an undertaker, presides over death, sex, and tomfoolery. He is a healer to the sick and protector of children, as well as being a font of knowledge when it comes to death and those who have died. Guédé also has the power to return a zombie back to a living human. During ceremonies he freely possesses his followers, particularly those who cross-dress or wear the traditional elaborate costuming consisting of dark glasses, large hats, and walking sticks.

Sources: Deren, *Divine Horsemen*, 267; Huxley, *The Invisibles*, 220; Laguerre, *Voodoo Heritage*, 100; Rigaud, *Secrets of Voodoo*, 67–8.

Gugonix

In the *Ars Goetia*, the first book of the *Lemegeton*, Gugonix is listed as one of the fifty-three SERVITORS OF ASHTAROTH AND ASMODEUS (see ASHTAROTH and ASMODEUS).

Sources: Mathers, *Book of the Sacred Magic of Abramelin the Mage*, 106; Susej, *Demonic Bible*, 257; Von Worms, *Book of Abramelin*, 248.

Guland

Variations: Nabam

In the *Grimoirium Verum* (*Grimoire of Truth*) allegedly written by Alibek the Egyptian in 1517, Guland is listed as the demon of disease and illness who is in service under ASMODEUS. He is most powerful on Saturdays.

Sources: Kuriakos, *Grimoire Verum Ritual Book*, 22; Masters, *Devil's Dominion*, 131; Sabellicus, *Magia Pratica*, 35.

Gulma Sanniya

In Sinhalese demonology, Gulma Sanniya is the demon that causes diarrhea, nausea, parasitic worms, and vomiting. He, like the other Sinhalese demons, is susceptible to the DAHA-ATA SANNIYA.

Source: Wirz, *Exorcism and the Art of Healing in Ceylon*.

Gurson

Variations: GORSON, Gorsou

In the *Book of Enoch*, Gurson is listed as one of the FALLEN ANGELS who swore allegiance to SAMIAZA, rebelled against God, took a human as his wife, and fathered the NEPHILIM.

Sources: Davidson, *Dictionary of Angels*, 125; Spence, *Encyclopedia of Occultism*, 119.

Gusion

Variations: Gusayn, Guseyn, Gusoin, GUSOYN

In Johann Wierus's *Pseudomonarchia Dae-*

monum (*False Monarchy of Demons*, 1583) Gusion, the Wise Duke, is named as one of the four SERVITORS OF AGALIAREPT (see AGALIAREPT). A FALLEN ANGEL, he commands forty legions of demons. A diurnal demon who looks like a cynocephalus, Gusion is summoned for his ability to answer any question asked; divine the past, present and future; grant dignity and honor; and reconcile enemies. He is most powerful in the month of May and his zodiacal sign is Taurus.

Sources: De Laurence, *Lesser Key of Solomon, Goetia*, 25; DuQuette, *Key to Solomon's Key*, 166; Scott, *London Magazine*, Vol. 5, 378.

Gusoyn

Variations: Geryones, Geyron, Ghruonh, Ghruwn, Gusayn, Guseyn, GUSION, Gusoin, Gusoyn, Osgarbial, Pirsoyn, URAKABARAMEEL

Named in both the *Grimoire of Pope Honorius* and the *Pseudomonarchia Daemonum* (*False Monarchy of Demons*) (1583), Gusoyn is listed as one of the three SERVITORS OF AGALIAREPT and as one of the eighteen named subordinate spirits, or servitors as they are also called (see also AGALIAREPT, ELELOGAP, and HIERARCHY OF DEMONS).

Sources: Baskin, *Sorcerer's Handbook*, 12; De Laurence, *Lesser Key of Solomon, Goetia*, 25; Wedeck, *Treasury of Witchcraft*, 97.

Gustoyn

Gustoyn is one of the eighteen SERVITORS OF FLEURETTY, LUCIFUGE, NEBIROS, SARGATANAS, AND SATANACHIA (see FLEURETTY, LUCIFUGE, NEBIROS, SARGATANAS, and SATANACHIA).

Sources: Baskin, *Sorcerer's Handbook*, 276; Waite, *Unknown World 1894–1895*, 230; Wedeck, *Treasury of Witchcraft*, 96.

Guta

Guta is the Hungarian demon of heart attacks and strokes, caused when he beats his victims to death. His name translates to mean "apoplexy" or "strike down." The Hungarian saying "he has been beaten by Guta" means that the person has died suddenly of internal hemorrhage in the brain or has died because of a stroke.

Sources: Kõiva, *Folk Belief Today*, 139; Lurker, *Routledge Dictionary of Gods and Goddesses*, 71; Rose, *Spirits, Fairies, Gnomes, and Goblins*, 137.

Guzalu

Variations: Guzallu, Ninurta

In Sumerian mythology the demon Guzalu ("throne-bearer") is a messenger in service to NERGAL.

Sources: Muss-Arnolt, *Concise Dictionary of the Assyrian Language*, Vol. 1, 214–5; Thompson, *Semitic Magic*, 256.

Gyík

In Hungarian mythology Gyík ("lizard") is the demon of diphtheria and sore throats.

Sources: Yolland, *Dictionary of the Hungarian and English Languages*, 326.

Haagenti

Variations: Hagenit, Hagenith, Hagenti, Zagan, Zagum

Haagenti is known as the Winged President, as he appears before his summoner as a winged bull; however, he will assume a human form if asked to do so. He has the ability to grant wisdom and can transmute any type of metal into gold, and transform water into wine and vice versa. He also teaches a wide variety of subjects. Listed as one of the seventy-two SPIRITS OF SOLOMON, he commands thirty-three legions.

Sources: De Laurence, *Lesser Key of Solomon, Goetia*, 38; Scot, *Discoverie of Witchcraft*, 225; Scott, *London Magazine*, Vol. 5, 378.

Haatan

Haatan is mentioned in Apollonius of Tyana's *Nuctemeron* (*Night Illuminated by Day*) as the demon of concealed treasures. He is most powerful during the sixth hour.

Sources: Gettings, *Dictionary of Demons*, 128; Kelly, *Who in Hell*, 103; Lévi, *Transcendental Magic*, 391.

Habergeiss

Variations: Schrattl, Ziegenmelker

A vampiric demon from Serbia, the habergeiss looks like a three-legged birdlike creature. It uses its shape-shifting ability to appear like various types of animals. In its disguised form it attacks cattle during the night to feed off their blood. The cry of the habergeiss is considered to be a death omen.

Sources: Folkard, *Plant Lore*, 84; Friend, *Flowers and Flower Lore*, Vol. 1, 64; Hillman, *Pan and the Nightmare*, 127; Jones, *On the Nightmare*, 108; Róheim, *Riddle of the Sphinx*, 55.

Habhi

The *Sacred Magic of Abramelin the Mage*, book two, lists Habhi ("hidden") among the one hundred eleven SERVITORS OF AMAYMON, ARITON, ORIENS, AND PAYMON (see AMAYMON, ARITON, ORIENS, and PAYMON).

Sources: Belanger, *Dictionary of Demons*, 149; Mathers, *Book of the Sacred Magic of Abramelin the Mage*, 112; Susej, *Demonic Bible*, 256.

Haborym

Variations: AIM, Aym, Haborgm, Haborim, RÄUM

Haborym, demon of holocausts, is a duke of

Hell who commands twenty-six legions of demons. He is summoned for his willingness to answer truthfully questions regarding private matters and for making men witty. He appears before his summoner with three heads—one of a cat, one of a man, and one of a snake. He sits upon a serpent holding a torch in his hand, which he uses to catch castles and cities on fire. Other sources say that Haborym's body is very handsome and his three heads are that of a calf, a man with two stars on his forehead, and a serpent.

Sources: Ashley, *Complete Book of Devils and Demons*, 60, 74; De Laurence, *Lesser Key of Solomon, Goetia*, 35; DuQuette, *Key to Solomon's Key*, 180–1; Ford, *Bible of the Adversary*, 81; Icon, *Demons*, 174.

Hacamuli

In the *Sacred Magic of Abramelin the Mage*, book two, Hacamuli is listed as one of the forty-nine SERVITORS OF BEELZEBUB (see BEELZEBUB). His name is Hebrew for "fading" or "withering."

Sources: Belanger, *Dictionary of Demons*, 150; Ford, *Bible of the Adversary*, 93; Susej, *Demonic Bible*, 259.

Hael

The demon Hael causes the creation of gossip; he reveals secrets and teaches the art of languages, letter writing, and tactics. In service under NEBIROS, Hael commands eight demonic servitors with the demon Sergulath (see SERVITORS OF HALE AND SERGULATH).

Sources: Belanger, *Dictionary of Demons*, 150, 153; Sabellicus, *Magia Pratica*, Vol. 2, 37; Waite, *Book of Black Magic*, 188.

Hagion

Hagion ("sacred") is listed as one of the sixty-five SERVITORS OF KORE AND MAGOTH in the *Sacred Magic of Abramelin the Mage*, book two.

Sources: Mathers, *Book of the Sacred Magic of Abramelin the Mage*, 107; Von Worms, *Book of Abramelin*, 256.

Hagith

Variations: Haggit, Haggith

Hagith first appeared in late Renaissance era books of magic including the grimoire *Arbatel de Magia Veterum* (*Arbatel of the Magic of the Ancients*) published in Basel, Switzerland, in 1575 by an unknown author. One of the seven OLYMPIAN SPIRITS, he is in service under the demon CASSIEL. A nocturnal demon, Hagith commands four thousand legions and twenty-one infernal provinces. He is summoned for his ability to give the gift of beauty and faithful FAMILIARs, as well as revealing a person's destiny and transmuting copper into gold. He has dominion over the planet Venus.

It should be noted that each of the OLYMPIAN SPIRITS rules, in succession, for a period of 490 years. Hagith was last in power from 1410–1900 and will be back in power in 4840.

Sources: Drury, *Dictionary of the Esoteric*, 239; González-Wippler, *Complete Book of Spells*, 120; Kelly, *Who in Hell*, 104.

Hagog

In the *Sacred Magic of Abramelin the Mage*, book two, Hagog is named as one of the sixty-five SERVITORS OF KORE AND MAGOTH. His name translates from Hebrew to mean "the name of GOG."

Sources: Mathers, *Book of the Sacred Magic of Abramelin the Mage*, 107; Susej, *Demonic Bible*, 258; Von Worms, *Book of Abramelin*, 251, 256.

Hahab

Apollonius of Tyana's *Nuctemeron* (*Night Illuminated by Day*) named Hahab as the demon of royal tables. He is most powerful during the twelfth hour of the day.

Sources: Gettings, *Dictionary of Demons*, 129; Lévi, *Transcendental Magic*, 509.

Hahabi

Apollonius of Tyana's *Nuctemeron* (*Night Illuminated by Day*) named Hahabi as the demon of fear. He is most powerful during the third hour of the day.

Sources: Gettings, *Dictionary of Demons*, 129; Kelly, *Who in Hell*, 104.

Hakael

Variations: "The seventh SATAN"

According to the *Book of Enoch*, Hakael is listed as one of the FALLEN ANGELS who swore allegiance to SAMIAZA, rebelled against God, took a human as his wife, and fathered the NEPHILIM.

Sources: Ashley, *Complete Book of Devils and Demons*, 73; Charles, *Book of Enoch*, 138; Davidson, *Dictionary of Angels*, 133, 269, 353.

Halacho

In Apollonius of Tyana's *Nuctemeron* (*Night Illuminated by Day*), Halacho is listed as the demon of sympathies. He is one of the seven demons of the eleventh hour; however, some sources list him as a DJINN.

Sources: Davidson, *Dictionary of Angels*, 7; Gettings, *Dictionary of Demons*, 27; Lévi, *Transcendental Magic*, 422.

Haligax

In *Ars Goetia*, the first book of the *Lemegeton*, Haligax is named as one of the fifty-three SERVI-

TORS OF ASHTAROTH AND ASMODEUS (see ASHTAROTH and ASMODEUS).

Sources: Ford, *Bible of the Adversary*, 90; Mathers, *Book of the Sacred Magic of Abramelin the Mage*, 116.

Halphas

Variations: Halpas, Malthus, Mathas

Christian demonology ranks Halphas as an earl and lists him as one of the seventy-two SPIRITS OF SOLOMON (SEE ALSO EARLS OF HELL and PRESIDENTS OF HELL). Commanding twenty-six legions, this nocturnal demon appears before his summoner as a stork and speaks with a hoarse voice. He has the ability to teleport men to battlefields, cause wars, fill towns with soldiers looking to fight, and is known to stockpile weapons. Destructive, warlike Halphas attacks with a sword and sets towns ablaze. His zodiac sign is Libra.

Sources: De Laurence, *Lesser Key of Solomon, Goetia*, 34; DuQuette, *Key to Solomon's Key*, 179–80; Icon, *Demons*, 165; Scott, *London Magazine*, Vol. 5, 378.

Ham

In the Scandinavian *Saga Grettir*, also known as *The Saga of Grettir the Strong*, Ham is a storm demon in service under Helgi (see AERIAL DEVIL). He is described as an eagle with black wings.

Sources: De Claremont, *Ancients' Book of Magic*, 127; Spence, *Encyclopedia of Occultism*, 410.

Hamas

In *Theurgia Goetia*, the second book of the *Lemegeton*, Hamas is ranked as a chief duke and is listed as one of the sixteen SERVITORS OF ASYRIEL (see ASYRIEL). A nocturnal demon, he is good-natured and willing to obey his summoner.

Sources: Belanger, *Dictionary of Demons*, 152; Guiley, *Encyclopedia of Demons and Demonology*, 20; Peterson, *Lesser Key of Solomon*, 74.

Hamorphol

In *Theurgia Goetia*, the second book of the *Lemegeton*, Hamorphol is ranked as one of the eleven named SERVITORS OF PAMERSIEL (see PAMERSIEL). Ranked as a duke, this nocturnal AERIAL DEVIL is known to be very useful at driving out spirits from haunted places. He is also an expert liar and tells secrets. An arrogant and stubborn demon, Hamorphol must be summoned from the second floor of a home or in a wide open space.

Sources: Waite, *Manual of Cartomancy and Occult Divination*, 97.

Hamou Ukaiou

Hamou Ukaiou is the husband to the DJINN Aicha Kandida in Moroccan folklore. A nocturnal demon, he preys upon women who travel alone at night, stalking and then devouring them. Sharpening a knife on the ground in his presence will prevent him from attacking.

Sources: Illes, *Encyclopedia of Spirits*, 145; Rose, *Giants, Monsters, and Dragons*, 20.

Hananel

Variations: Anai, ANANEL, Khananel

Hananel ("mercy of God") is named in the *Book of Enoch* as one of the FALLEN ANGELS who swore allegiance to SAMIAZA, rebelled against God, took a human wife, and fathered the NEPHILIM. His name means "glory or grace of God."

Sources: Charles, *Book of Enoch*, 137; Laurence, *Foreign Quarterly Review*, Vol. 24, 370; Lumpkin, *Fallen Angels, the Watchers, and the Origins of Evil*, 31.

Hanbi

Variations: Hanpa

Akkadian and Sumerian mythology names Hanbi as the Lord of the Evil Wind Demons. He is the father of the demon PAZUZU.

Sources: Black, *Gods, Demons, and Symbols of Ancient Mesopotamia*, 148; Finkel, *Sumerian Gods and Their Representations*, 143; Icons, *Demons*, 171.

Hannya

Variations: Akeru, Hannya-Shin-Kyo ("emptiness of forms")

A vampiric demon from Japan, the *hannya* ("empty") feeds exclusively off truly beautiful women and infants. It is described as having a large chin, long fangs and horns, green scales, a snakelike forked tongue, and eyes that burn like twin flames.

Normally, the hannya lives near the sea or wells, but it is never too far from humans, as it can sneak unseen into any house that has a potential victim (a sleeping woman) inside. Just before it attacks, the hannya lets loose with a horrible shriek. While the woman is in a state of being startled, the vampire possesses her, slowly driving her insane and physically altering her body into that of a hideous monster. Eventually, it drives her to attack a child, drink its blood, and eat its flesh.

There is no known potential weakness to exploit, but there is a Buddhist sutra that renders humans invisible to spirits and demons. In Japanese No (Noh) theater, young men are depicted as the favorite victims of an especially vicious and vindictive hannya.

Sources: Louis-Frédéric, *Japan Encyclopedia*, 287–88; Pollack, *Reading Against Culture*, 50; Toki, *Japanese Nō Plays*, 40

Hantiel

In *Ars Paulina*, the third book of the *Lemegeton*, Hantiel is listed as one of the two hundred SERVITORS OF VEGUANIEL (see VEGUANIEL).

Sources: Davidson, *Dictionary of Demons*, 135; Waite, *The Book of Ceremonial Magic*, 67.

Hantu

In Malaysian folklore a hantu is a demonic ancestral spirit. There are three classifications of hantu: minor, medium, and greater. All hantu are nocturnal demons of lesser dangers and retributions who prey upon mankind. Usually they are invisible and can only be heard. Hantu cause diseases and insanity in humans, as well as possess people and herald IBLIS. When not harassing man, they live on Pulau Hantu ("Ghost Island"). The word *hantu* means "demon," "ghost," or "spirit."

There is a hantu for every evil, malady, and event that can be imagined, each with its own additional strengths and specific weaknesses, all of which vary from town to town and even from person to person.

Lesser known hantus include Hantu Air ("water ghost in rivers, lakes and swimming pools"), Hantu Anak Gua Batu ("water spirit"), Hantu Ayer ("spirit of the waters"), Hantu Balung Bidai ("ghost with a rooster crest screen"), Hantu Bandan ("spirit of the waterfall"), Hantu Batu ("stone-throwing spirit," the Malay equivalent of the poltergeist), Hantu Beruk ("ghost moth"), Hantu Bisa ("ghost venom"), Hantu Bujang ("bachelor ghost"), Hantu Bukit ("ghost that haunts the hilly area"), Hantu Bulu ("body hair ghost"), Hantu Bunyi-Bunyian ("ghosts that are heard but not seen"), Hantu Burong ("ghost bird"), Hantu Buta ("ghost that causes blindness"), Hantu Chika ("ghost that causes pain in the head and abdomen"), Hantu Dapur ("kitchen ghost"), Hantu Doman ("ghost plucking coconuts"), Hantu Golek ("rolling ghost"), Hantu Gulung ("scroll ghost"), Hantu Gunung ("mountain ghost"), Hantu-Hantuan ("echoing ghost"), Hantu Harimau ("tiger ghost"), Hantu Hitam ("desert ghost"), Hantu Jamuan ("reception ghost," a FAMILIAR spirit), Hantu Jembalang ("possessing spirits"; a three day ceremony called Main Puteri can exorcise them), Hantu Jerambang ("will-o'-the-wisp ghost"), Hantu Jerangkung ("skeleton ghost"), Hantu Jinjang ("rude ghost"), Hantu Kamang ("ghost that causes swelling in the legs and feet"), Hantu Kambong ("ghost that causes pain in the abdomen and head"), Hantu Kangkang ("squatting ghost"), Hantu Kayu ("tree ghosts"), Hantu Kemang ("ghost that lives in the placenta and torments newborn babies"), Hantu Kembung ("ghost that causes stomach aches"), Hantu Keramat ("holy ghost"), Hantu Ketumbuhan ("ghost that causes smallpox"), Hantu Kuang ("ghost with a hundred eyes"), Hantu Kuda ("ghost horse"), Hantu Kubur ("ghost that haunts the cemetery"), Hantu Laut ("sea spirit"), Hantu Lemong ("lemon tree ghost"), Hantu Lilin ("candle ghost"), Hantu Lubang ("hole ghost"), Hantu Orang ("ghost of a man killed by the police, either by accident or on purpose"), Hantu Orang Mati Di-Bunoh ("ghost of a murdered man"), Hantu Pancur ("spitting ghost"), Hantu Pari-Pari ("fairy ghost"), Hantu Pekak ("ghost of deafness"), Hantu Pelak ("ghost of place where a horrible crime has been committed"), Hantu Penyakit ("ghost of illness"), Hantu Puaka ("evil ghost"), Hantu Pusaka ("heirloom ghost"), Hantu Sugu ("sex fiend demon"), Hantu Tanah ("spirit of the earth" or the "sand ghost"), and Hantu Uri ("placenta ghost").

Sources: Dennys, *Descriptive Dictionary of British Malaya*, 151–2; McHugh, *Hantu Hantu*, 123–4; Porteous, *Forest Folklore*, 130; Skeat, *Malay Magic*, 101–6; Werner, *Bomoh-Poyang*, 552.

Hantu Ban Dan

Hantu Ban Dan ("demon of the waterfall") is a HANTU from Malay demonology that looks like a copper cooking pot floating on the water surface near rocks. One of the AQUEOUS DEVILS, it lives in and near rivers.

Sources: Lunge-Larsen, *Hidden Folk*, 9; Rose, *Spirits, Fairies, Gnomes, and Goblins*, 143.

Hantu Bangkit

Hantu Bangkit ("rising ghost") is a HANTU from Malay demonology that looks like a person under a long and winding sheet, but it cannot walk because its sheet is too tightly wrapped around its body. It is seen in cemeteries. To avoid being attacked by this demonic ghost, simply do not get within its reach.

Sources: Endicott, *Analysis of Malay Magic*, 74–5; McHugh, *Hantu Hantu*, 124; Osman, *Malaysian World-View*, 116, 117; Wilkinson, *Malay Beliefs*, 23.

Hantu Belian

In Selangor Malay demonology, hantu belian is a tiger demon that looks like a *chenchawi* (a king crow). It is an excellent FAMILIAR to the person who summons and binds it, as it is an expert diamond thief. While sitting on the back of a tiger it will pluck out bits of fur and swallow it, not allowing any hairs to fall to the ground (see HANTU).

Sources: Maberry, *Vampire Universe*, 149; McHugh, *Hantu Hantu*, 105–6; Skeat, *Malay Magic*, 104.

Hantu Blian

Variations: Blian

Hantu blian ("tiger devil") is from Malaysian folklore; it is the demon of the common people. To prevent this HANTU from attacking you, call it a "blian" as opposed to a "hantu blain," which upsets it.

Sources: Clifford, *Dictionary of the Malay Language*, 258; Frazer, *Golden Bough*, Vol. 9, 199; Swettenham, *Malay Sketches*, 157.

Hantu B'rok

Variations: The "cocoa-nut monkey"

Hantu B'rok is an invisible baboon HANTU from Malay demonology who can become visible. He possesses people and causes them to dance and perform amazing feats of climbing. He lives in the forest.

Sources: Bellingham, *Goddesses, Heroes, and Shamans*, 123; Rose, *Spirits, Fairies, Gnomes, and Goblins*, 350; Skeat, *Malay Magic*, 104.

Hantu Bungkus

Variations: Hantu Golek ("rolling ghost"), Hantu Kochong, Hantu Pochong, HANTU POCONG, Pocong

In Malaysian Muslim folklore hantu bungkus ("wrapped-up ghost") is a demonic ghost that looks like a person who is wrapped in a funeral cloth called *kain kapan*. Its face is obscured and it wanders about villages as if it is looking for something. This HANTU can make 100-meter leaps and will only attack people who try to block its path.

Sources: Endicott, *Analysis of Malay Magic*, 74–5; McHugh, *Hantu Hantu*, 90, 121; Wilkinson, *Malay Beliefs*, 23.

Hantu Denai

The hantu denai ("ghost of the tracks") of Malay demonology is the demon of hunting. Preying on hunters, it lies in wait in the tracks left by wild animals; when opportunity presents itself, it attacks the hunter as he is following his prey.

Sources: Rose, *Spirits, Fairies, Gnomes, and Goblins*, 350; Wilkinson, *Malay Beliefs*, 31.

Hantu Dondong

Hantu dondong ("ghost box") is a cave demon from Malaysian folklore. Using a blowgun, it kills dogs and wild pigs.

Sources: Dennys, *Descriptive Dictionary of British Malaya*, 151; Skeat, *Pagan Races of the Malay Peninsula*, 323.

Hantu Gaharu

Hantu gaharu is a nocturnal, aquatic demon from West Malaysian folklore; its name translates to mean "ghost of the aloe wood tree." When an aloe tree is needed to be cut down, this HANTU will visit the axeman in his dream and demand a human sacrifice from him. The person will then select a victim who is asleep and mark him by smearing his head with lime juice. Then the hantu gaharu will come and consume the victim's soul.

Sources: Frazer, *Golden Bough*, 404; Porteous, *Forest Folklore*, 130; Rose, *Spirits, Fairies, Gnomes, and Goblins*, 144, 350.

Hantu Galah

Hantu galah ("tall ghost") is from Malaysian folklore. It is described as looking like a human but as you walk nearer it seems to grow taller until you can only see its legs. If you look up to try to see its face, your head will be stuck in that position. This demon will only attack if you try to walk between its legs.

Sources: McHugh, *Hantu Hantu*, 38, 124; Osman, *Malay Folk Beliefs*, 87.

Hantu Gharu

West Malaysian folklore tells us of the hantu gharu ("ghost of the eagle wood tree"). The demonic protector of the eagle wood tree (also known as the Agar wood or Agila wood tree), it will attack anyone who tries to cut its tree down. Should it fail in preventing its tree from being felled, as soon as the tree hits the ground it will take the opportunity to lash out and attack the people responsible.

Sources: Rose, *Spirits, Fairies, Gnomes, and Goblins*, 144, 350; Skeat, *Malay Magic*, 612.

Hantu Hutan

Variations: HANTU JARANG GIGI ("Snaggle-Toothed Ghost"), Hantu Siaran Gigi, Orang Dalam

The hantu hutan ("forest demon") is a twelve-foot-tall hairy humanoid from Malaysian folklore who lives in the rain forest and preys upon fish.

Sources: McHugh, *Hantu Hantu*, 40–1; Porteous, *Forest Folklore*, 127; Rose, *Spirits, Fairies, Gnomes, and Goblins*, 144, 350; Werner, *Bomoh-Poyang*, 554.

Hantu Jarang Gigi

Variations: Bigfoot, Gigi, Hantu Jarang, Mawas, Siamang

Hantu jarang gigi is a TERRESTRIAL DEVIL from Malaysian folklore; its name means "ghost with widely spaced teeth," "snaggle-toothed ghost" or "thin tooth ghost." It looks like an ape-man covered in black fur, standing between six and ten feet tall. It lives in the southern rainforests of Malaysia, most often seen during the fruiting and monsoon seasons.

Sources: Eberhart, *Mysterious Creatures*, 409; Werner, *Bomoh-Poyang*, 549.

Hantu Jepun

The Hantu Jepun ("Japanese ghost") are AERIAL DEVILS from Malaysian folklore. They were created when Japanese soldiers died during their occupation of Southeast Asia during World War II. They look like men wearing the imperial army uniform, carrying a rifle, samurai sword, or both; usually they are headless.

Sources: Sue, *Blood on Borneo*, 191, 198.

Hantu Kertau

Variations: Hantu Kepala Babi

In Malaysian folklore hantu kertaus are demonic spirits that live in Perak, Malaysia. They have the body of a deer and the head of a boar with large tusks.

Sources: Wilkinson, *Abridged Malay-English Dictionary*, 109; Winstedt, *Malay Magician*, 24.

Hantu Kopek

Variations: HANTU TETEK, Nightmare

Hantu kopeks ("flaccid breast ghost") are large-breasted nocturnal female spirits from Malaysian folklore. They prey upon children who are trying to fall asleep and they wake up those who are sleeping. They use their large breasts to suffocate children. Hantu kopeks linger in playgrounds.

Sources: McHugh, *Hantu Hantu*, 101–2; Skeat, *Malay Magic*, 106.

Hantu Kuali

Looking like a frying pan, the hantu kuali of Malaysian folklore can cause trouble at any time, but it is more dangerous during the night. Found in the kitchen of a home, it will not properly fry fish and will break the yoke of fried eggs. It will burn anyone who mistakes it for a normal pan and bangs it on the stove.

Source: Burgess, *Malayan Trilogy*, 622.

Hantu Kubor

The hantu kubor ("grave spirit") of Malaysian folklore is a nocturnal demon who preys upon both the living and the dead. This demon is created when a person has died, was buried, and their soul has already risen into Heaven or descended into Hell but the evil of that person remained behind in their grave and manifested. This HANTU looks like the person it was in life but is dressed in a white burial shroud. It lives in

cemeteries where bodies are interred. Offerings of food and water and a fire kept alit on its grave will keep it from attacking.

Sources: McHugh, *Hantu Hantu*, 90, 122; Skeat, *Pagan Races of the Malay Peninsula*, 98.

Hantu Kum Kum

Hantu Kum Kum of Malaysian folklore is a singular entity and looks like a woman carrying a tombstone as if it were a baby, asking for milk. She preys upon menstruating virgins. According to the story, there was once an ugly woman who wanted to be beautiful so she visited a sorcerer. His magic worked and made her the most beautiful woman in the village; however, the spell required that she not look into a mirror for forty-four days. Unable to resist the temptation, she looked in a mirror and instantly broke the spell, making her more ugly than ever before. The sorcerer said that in order to restore the spell, she needed to drink the blood of virgins for forty-four days. Fortunately, she cannot enter into a house without the owner's permission.

Source: Munan, *Culture Shock! Borneo*, 78.

Hantu Langsuir

Variations: Hantu Pennanggalan

A vampiric demon from Malaysia, the hantu langsuir looks like a beautiful woman or a floating woman's head with a tail made of entrails and spinal column that hangs down from its severed neck. It is most difficult to keep this vampire from entering into your home, as it can squeeze through even the smallest opening or crack.

A picky eater, the hantu langsuir has a very specific order to the victims it preys on. Of all the sources of blood that a vampire can choose from, the hantu langsuir prefers the blood of a newborn male child. If none is available, then the blood of a newborn female will suffice. The entrails of either gender are consumed as well. When the hantu langsuir manages to find a suitable victim, it bites a tiny hole in their neck from which it draws the blood.

On occasion, it will drink milk from any available source and will lick the blood off a sanitary napkin. If it does so, the woman to whom the pad belonged will start to grow weak as her life-energy is being mystically drained away.

Should the hantu langsuir be caught in the act of feeding, the head will detach from its body and fly off to safety as it shape-shifts into an owl, emitting an ear-piercing screech as it flees. Both parts of the vampire, the discarded body and the head, must be captured and burned to ash if the creature is ever to be destroyed.

There are some women who have the ability

to see the hantu langsuir, as it is invisible during the day.

Sources: Annandale, *Fasciculi Malayenses*, 23; Guiley, *The Complete Vampire Companion*, 24; Laderman, *Wives and Midwives*, 126; McHugh, *Hantu-Hantu*, 125–28, 131, 201; Skeat, *Pagan Races of the Malay Peninsula*, 697.

Hantu Langut

The hantu langut ("ghost of the jungle") is from Malaysian folklore. It lives in the jungles of Pahang, Malaysia, and is described as having its head permanently tilted upwards.

Sources: McHugh, *Hantu Hantu*, 23, 25, 31; Werner, *Bomoh-Poyang*, 209.

Hantu Longgok

In Malaysian folklore the hantu longgok ("spirit of the rubbish heaps") is the demon of disease. Living in garbage heaps or dumps, its victim's head is tilted back all the time, as if looking upward, while foaming at the mouth.

Sources: Rose, *Spirits, Fairies, Gnomes, and Goblins*, 144, 350.

Hantu Orang Minyak

Variations: Orang minyak ("oily men")

Originating from the Malaysian folklore of the 1960s, the hantu orang minyak ("ghost of the oily man") is described as looking like a human man with a dark complexion. He appears to his victims completely nude with oiled-down skin, which, according to reports, was to make his physical apprehension that much more difficult. According to the folklore, this HANTU was created when a human demonic operative was able to rape twenty-one virgins in a seven-day period so that SATAN would grant his worldly desires.

Numerous versions of the story exist and a wide array of abilities have been given to the assailant, such as his assault caused muteness in his victim during the rape, that he was invisible to non-virgins, and that he caused sleep paralysis. It was believed that the use of a type of Malay medium called a *bomoh* could chase the orang minyak away, as well as biting your left thumb during the attack and covering it with a *batik*, a generic word for a type of fabric that has been dyed in a "resistance" method. During this reign of fear and terror, women were also wearing sweaty clothes to bed so that the orang minyak would mistake them for a man in the dark.

Sources: Moss, *Distant Archipelagos*, 55; McHugh, *Hantu Hantu*, 110; Munan, *Culture Shock! Borneo*, 78; Roff, *Kelantan*, 227.

Hantu Parl

From Indian and Malaysian folklore comes the nocturnal hantu parl, a demon that scavenges battlefields to lap up the blood of dying and newly dead. It is also said to appear in hospitals.

Source: Konstantinos, *Vampires*, 25.

Hantu Pemburu

Hantu pemburu ("ghost huntsman") is the demon of the hunt from Malaysian folklore; it commands spectral hunting hounds that appear as a flock of birds. He is described as looking like a massive humanoid whose body is completely covered with plants and his head permanently tilted upward. He stalks the jungle seeking his impossible prey, a pregnant male deer, but will kill and leave the body of any other living being he happens upon. Passing too near this HANTU will infect a person with cholera.

According to the story, this hantu was originally a man, and one day he was asked by his pregnant wife to bring her some deer meat. He left the home vowing that he would not return until he was able to grant her request. Unfortunately, the husband had misheard his wife's words and began hunting for a pregnant male mouse deer. He sent his hunting dogs up into the sky so they would have a better vantage point to find the quarry, and after years of continually looking upwards, he was unable to lower his head.

Carcasses found on jungle paths are the telltale sign of the hantu pemburu having passed that way. By listening for the cries of the birik birik bird, which warns of the hantu pemburu's approach, you will be forewarned of its proximity. When it nears, shout out the words "*nenek, bawa hati nia*" ("Great-grandfather, bring us their hearts"). The idea is to trick the demon into thinking that you are related to it so that it will spare you. The hantu pemburu will only attack what it can see, so it is advised to sleep at the foot of a tree rather than up in the branches.

Sources: McHugh, *Hantu Hantu*, 31, 121; Skeat, *Malay Magic*, 112, 594.

Hantu Penyardin

Originally a Malaysian vampiric demon, the hantu penyardin has spread to the Polynesian Islands. It looks like a DOG-headed demon and lives in caves in and near the sea. The hantu penyardin feeds off human souls.

Sources: Aylesworth, *Story of Vampires*, 5; Flynn, *Cinematic Vampires*, 2; Spence, *Encyclopædia of Occultism*, 220.

Hantu Pocong

In an Islamic burial ritual the burial shroud, called a *kain kafan*, is tied in several places to keep it in place during the body's journey to its gravesite. When the body is placed in the grave, the knots must be undone or the corpse will animate and be known as a hantu pocong. It is described as looking like a human enshrouded in a burial cloth and moves by hopping or rolling along the ground. While running away from a hantu pocong, if the victim looks back for any reason, when they face forward again, the demon will be right in front of them. This demon can be destroyed if the knots tying its shroud closed are undone.

Sources: Bush, *Asian Horror Encyclopedia*, 151; Dalton, *Indonesia Handbook*, 548; Torchia, *Indonesian Idioms and Expressions*, 163.

Hantu Puteri

Hantu puteri ("princess ghost") is a singular entity from Malaysian folklore. Looking like a beautiful woman and using the art of seduction, she lures men deep into the jungle where they are forever lost. If, however, they should return, these victims have become insane or have had their memory erased. Occasionally she is in a playful mood and will disappear before the man can catch her. She lives in the jungle.

Sources: Knappert, *Pacific Mythology*, 90; McHugh, *Hantu Hantu*, 124.

Hantu Putung

Variations: HANTU BUNGKUS ("wrapped-up ghost"), Hantu Pochong, HANTU POCONG, Pocong

In Malaysian folklore hantu putung is a nocturnal demon that is described as a glowing man wrapped in a white burial shroud. It moves itself by jumping down the middle of the road.

Sources: McHugh, *Hantu Hantu*, 90, 121.

Hantu Ranges

The hantu ranges ("FAMILIAR ghost") of Malaysian folklore looks like a green-colored man of average height, carrying an axe. He has the ability to fly.

Sources: Laderman, *Wives and Midwives*, 125.

Hantu Raya

Originating from the folklore of West Malaysia, the hantu raya ("large ghost") is a type of AERIAL DEVIL that is bound to a Malaysian black magic practitioner who uses it as a FAMILIAR. The practitioner forms a pact with a DJINN who gives one, or he has inherited it from a previous generation. The act of passing down the hantu raya is a legacy known as *saka*. If not passed down to a new practitioner, it will take on the guise of its last master and haunt the area seeking food and a new master of its own choosing. If the hantu raya is not passed down to a new practitioner before its current one dies, the practitioner's death will be particularly long and painful and he will most likely return as a zombie.

This nocturnal demon can look like any person or object. It will attack anyone its handler sends it after but left to its own accord will assault anyone who travels at night and passes through a crossroads. It has the ability to assume the form of its practitioner, thereby giving him an alibi when he needs one. It brings wealth to his practitioner, possesses others, and when it shapeshifts into a person it will be a flawless impersonation. A hantu raya is subject to following its master's orders.

Frequent and regular food offerings of *acak*, a type of cake made of eggs, rice cakes, roasted chicken, yellow glutinous rice, and a doll will prevent a hantu raya from attacking. The occasional offering of animal blood is also required.

Sources: Eberhart, *Mysterious Creatures*, 230; Laderman, *Wives and Midwives*, 125; McHugh, *Hantu Hantu*, 38, 53; Peletz, *Reason and Passion*, 251, 370; Skeat, *Malay Magic*, 104.

Hantu Ribut

In the folklore of the West Malaysian people the hantu ribut ("ghost of the violent storm") is a storm demon that creates violent storms and whirlwinds.

Sources: Maberry, *Vampire Universe*, 149; McHugh, *Hantu Hantu*, 122; Skeat, *Malay Magic*, 103.

Hantu Saburo

The hantu saburo ("black hunter ghost") of Malaysian folklore is accompanied by three dogs all named Sokom and a bird called Bere-Bere. The dogs are used to chase men through the forest, and when they are caught, the dogs will drink their blood. This HANTU lives in lakes and rivers. To prevent being attacked by this demon, whenever the bird Bere-Bere is sighted, knock together pieces of wood or metal loud enough to frighten away the dogs, which are always nearby.

Sources: Dennys, *Descriptive Dictionary of British Malaya*, 151; Wright, *Book of Vampires*, 64.

Hantu Sawan

In the folklore of West Malaysia the hantu sawan ("epilepsy ghost") is the demon of convulsions; it causes children to suffer from epileptic seizures.

Sources: McHugh, *Hantu Hantu*, 86, 121; Skeat, *Malay Magic*, 102.

Hantu Si Buru

In the folklore of the people of West Malaysia comes the hantu si buru ("ghost that hunts"). According to legend there was once a wife who asked her husband to bring her the meat of a pregnant deer in order to guarantee that her own child would be born a son. The husband vowed he would not return until he did so, but he misheard his wife and killed a male deer that was standing near a fawn. Unable to fulfill his wife's wishes, he wandered the woods with a pack of dogs until he became a demon. Hantu si buru is a nocturnal demon who is especially effective during the new moon. Looking upon this demon is fatal; it is an omen of death and sickness. The birik-birik bird will cry out in alarm whenever it is near. Offerings made to honor this HANTU may cure those who were made ill by his passing.

Sources: Rose, *Spirits, Fairies, Gnomes, and Goblins*, 144, 350; Skeat, *Pagan Races of the Malay Peninsula*, 303.

Hantu Songkei

The hantu songkei ("loosening demon") of Malaysian folklore has an enormous nose and large eyes that can stretch all the way around its head. It is invisible from the waist down. This HANTU sets off the animal traps that hunters place.

Sources: McHugh, *Hantu Hantu*, 122; Swettenham, *Malay Sketches*, 157.

Hantu Tetek

Hantu tetek ("breast ghost") is from Malaysian folklore and some sources claim this to be a type of Balinese witch. It is described as a woman with large breasts; various sources claim that the breasts are on its back. Most powerful during evening twilight, it preys on children, suffocating them to death by pressing them into her breasts.

Sources: Cheo, *Baba Folk Beliefs and Superstitions*, 17; McHugh, *Hantu Hantu*, 101–2.

Hantu Tiga Beranak

The hantu tiga beranak of Malaysian folklore has the ability to shape-change into a taller version of itself, as it hates to be looked down at by tall people.

Source: Kasimin, *Religion and Social Change Among the Indigenous People of the Malay Peninsula*, 213.

Hantu Tinggi

Variations: HANTU GALAH, Hantu Terulung

The folklore of West Malaysia tells us of the hantu tinggi ("tall ghost"); it grows taller as a person approaches it. After it has gained height, if the victim and the hantu tinggi make eye contact, the person will slowly die of a mysterious disease. If it grabs its prey they are immediately teleported to some other nearby place where the person will land disoriented. To prevent being attacked, walk directly at the HANTU and do not look at it; if you do your neck will be permanently tilted upwards.

Sources: McHugh, *Hantu Hantu*, 122; Skeat, *Pagan Races of the Malay Peninsula*, 323.

Harab Serapel

Variations: A'arab Tzereq ("The Ravens of Dispersion"), "Ravens of the Burning of God"

In the cabbalistic tradition and according to the Qliphoth, the harab serapel ("ravens of death") are the seventh of the ten demons of the Asiatic world. Under the command of Baal Chanan and Theuniel, they oversee an infernal region of Hell. These demonic ravens live in a volcano. In Hebrew this word is related to *khorev seraphim* (kho-REV se-RAF, "flaming raven").

Sources: Davidson, *Dictionary of Angels*, 135; Horne, *Sacred Books and Early Literature of the East*, 163.

Harembrub

Variations: HAROMBRUB

The *Sacred Magic of Abramelin the Mage*, book two, includes Harembrub ("exalted in greatness") as one of the twenty-two SERVITORS OF ARITON (see ARITON).

Sources: Mathers, *Book of the Sacred Magic of Abramelin the Mage*, 108; Susej, *Demonic Bible*, 259; Von Worms, Book of Abramelin, 2574, 257.

Haril

In the *Sacred Magic of Abramelin the Mage*, book two, Haril ("thorny") is among the one hundred eleven SERVITORS OF AMAYMON, ARITON, ORIENS, AND PAYMON (see AMAYMON, ARITON, ORIENS, and PAYMON).

Sources: Mathers, *Book of the Sacred Magic of Abramelin the Mage*, 114; Von Worms, *Book of Abramelin*, 255.

Haristum

In the *Grimoirium Verum* (*Grimoire of Truth*) allegedly written by Alibek the Egyptian in 1517, Haristum is said to have the ability to grant immunity to fire. He is in service to the demons HAEL and Sergulath.

Sources: Kelly, *Who in Hell*, 106–7; Masters, *Devil's Dominion*, 131; Waite, *Book of Black and Ceremonial Magic*, 193.

Hariti

Variations: Kangimo ("Bringer of happiness"), Karitei, Kariteimo, Kishibojin ("Giver of Children and Easy Delivery"), Kishi-mojin, Kishimo-jin, KISHIMOJIN, Koyasu, the Rapacious One

Originally from Buddhist and Japanese mythology, the story of Hariti ("green" or "stealing") is mentioned in both Vedic and Puranic texts. According to the story, this DEMONESS would abduct and kill children in order to feed her own brood whom she greatly loved and doted over. The Buddha took the youngest of her five hundred children and hid it under his begging cup to show her the pain that she was causing in other mothers. Having seen the error of her ways, the Buddha was then able to convince her to become the patron goddess of children. Her consort is Pancika.

Sources: Illes, *Encyclopedia of Spirits*, 464; Indira Gandhi National Center for the Arts, *Iconography of the Buddhist Sculpture of Orissa*, 332–4; Wangu, *Images of Indian Goddesses*, 58–62.

Harombrub

In the *Sacred Magic of Abramelin the Mage*, book two, Harombrub is among the twenty-two SERVITORS OF ARITON (see ARITON).

Sources: Mathers, *Book of the Sacred Magic of Abramelin the Mage*, 108; Susej, *Demonic Bible*, 259.

Harpax

In the *Testament of Solomon*, Harpax was one of the demons bound by Solomon to build his temple; he was made to do heavy work such as tending the furnace for the metalworkers. The demon of insomnia, he is described as looking like a man with a doglike head and the face of a bird, donkey, or oxen. To prevent this demon from attacking you, write the word *Kokphnêdismos* on a piece of paper and secure it to your head.

Sources: Ashe, *Qabalah*, 50; Conybeare, *Jewish Quarterly Review*, Vol. 11, 37; Fleg, *Life of Solomon*, 107.

Harut

Variations: Haroth, Haruvatat, HATU-ATU-TOPUN, Hetu-Ahin

In Islamic mythology Harut is one of the FALLEN ANGELS; he and MARUT were sent to earth by God to see how well they would be able to resist human temptations. They were immediately seduced by the women of earth and killed the man who witnessed their seduction. They admitted their crimes to God and were condemned to hang in a well by their feet until Judgment Day.

Most powerful at sunrise and sunset, Harut knows the powerful and secret name of God and is summoned for his ability to establish a government and teach sorcery. He never begins a lesson in sorcery without first saying to his student, "We have been sent to deceive you."

Sources: Abdul-Rahman, *Meaning and Explanation of the Glorious Qur'an*, Vol. 1, 188–90; Davidson, *Dictionary of Angels*, 353; Jung, *Fallen Angels in Jewish, Christian and Mohammedan Literature*, 91, 127–40; Knappert, *Islamic Legends*, 4, 59–62.

Hatipus

In Apollonius of Tyana's *Nuctemeron* (*Night Illuminated by Day*), Hatipus is named as the demon of attire. He is most powerful during the sixth hour of the day.

Sources: Gettings, *Dictionary of Demons*, 130.

Hatu-Atu-Topun

Variations: Hetu-Ahin

Hatu-Atu-Topun is a female demon from Polynesian demonology that stalks her victims at sunrise and sunset.

Sources: Ashley, *Complete Book of Devils and Demons*, 62.

Hatuibwari

Melanesian mythology tells of the half demonic and half divine being known as Hatuibwari. Her upper body is female with four eyes and four breasts; the lower half is a huge serpent with a pair of wings. She is said to be the progenitor of the human race: she used her breasts to give nourishment to everything.

Sources: Riesenfeld, *Megalithic Culture of Melanesia*, 151–3; Rose, *Giants, Monsters, and Dragons*, 169; Turner, *Dictionary of Ancient Deities*, 206.

Hauges

The *Sacred Magic of Abramelin the Mage*, book two, names Hauges ("brilliance") as one of the ten SERVITORS OF AMAIMON AND ARITON (see AMAIMON and ARITON).

Sources: Mathers, *Book of the Sacred Magic of Abramelin the Mage*, 106; Von Worms, *Book of Abramelin*, 248.

Hauras

Variations: HAURES, Haurus, Havres, Flauros

In the *Ars Goetia*, the first book of the *Lemegeton*, the *Lesser Key of Solomon*, Hauras is named as the Leopard Duke (DUKES OF HELL). He is described as looking like a leopard but at the request of his summoner will take on the appearance of a man with fiery eyes and a frightening face or a combination of both. He is called upon to answer questions regarding the past, present, and future; to divine the truth about any event from the past or in the future; and for his willingness to share his knowledge of how the world was created, the nature of divinities, and how the angels fell from Heaven. He will also, by request of the summoner, use fire to kill anyone the sorcerer desires and will protect him from being attacked by demons that others may have sent against him. He commands thirty-six or twenty legions, sources vary. Hauras is also one of the seventy-two SPIRITS OF SOLOMON. He was bound in a brass vessel and thrown into a lake.

Sources: Conway, *Guides, Guardians and Angels*, 129; Crowley, *The Goetia*, 61; Davidson, *Dictionary of Angels*, 137; De Laurence, *Lesser Key of Solomon, Goetia*, 42–3; Scott, *London Magazine*, Vol. 5, 378.

Haures

The *Book of Enoch* names Haures as one of the FALLEN ANGELS who swore allegiance to SAMIAZA, rebelled against God, took a human as his wife, and fathered the NEPHILIM. He went on to teach mankind astrology and fortune telling.

Sources: Crowley, *The Goetia*, 61–2; De Laurence, *Lesser Key of Solomon, Goetia*, 42–3; Forrest, *Isis Magic*, 199.

Haussibut

According to the court records of the trial of Jelianne de Brigue, the demon Haussibut was under her command. He was said to cause deadly illnesses, divine the future, find lost and stolen property, make a man fall in love with a woman, and teach how to divine the future. Trial records say that the day before this demon is to be called upon the summoner cannot cross himself, use holy water, or wash his hands. From within a circle the summoner must call upon the Holy Trinity to force this demon to appear. For the promise of his continued service he requires a gift, such as bequeathing him your arm at the time of your death.

Sources: Cawthorne, *Witches*, 37; Robbins, *Encyclopedia of Witchcraft and Demonology*, 380; Russell, *Witchcraft in the Middle Ages*, 53, 111, 215.

Haven

Haven is named in Apollonius of Tyana's *Nuctemeron* (*Night Illuminated by Day*) as the demon of dignity. He is most powerful during the first hour of the day.

Sources: Cawthorne, *Witches*, 37; Robbins, *Encyclopedia of Witchcraft and Demonology*, 380; Russell, *Witchcraft in the Middle Ages*, 53, 111, 215.

Hbr

According to Enochian lore Hbr is a CACODAEMON. His counterpart is the angel Brap (see ENOCHIAN CACODAEMONS).

Sources: Chopra, *Academic Dictionary of Mythology*, 131; Laycock, *Complete Enochian Dictionary*, 117.

Head of the Dragons

Head of the Dragons is one of the seventy-two SPIRITS OF SOLOMON who was made to make bricks for the temple. A three-headed dragon with human hands, he causes blindness, deafness, and muteness in children and epilepsy in adults, and gives the location of lost treasure. His personal adversary is an angel of the Wonderful Counselor.

Sources: Charlesworth, *Old Testament Pseudepigrapha*, Vol. 2, 936; Guiley, *Encyclopedia of Angels*, 161; Timmons, *Everything About the Bible That You Never Had Time to Look Up*, 236.

Heart Devourers

In Russian folklore there is a tale of a once-brave man whose heart was removed by a demon wielding a magical wand made of aspen wood. The organ was consumed and replaced with a rabbit's heart, causing the man to thereafter be a coward.

Sources: Conway, *Demonology and Devil-Lore*, Vol. 1, 51; Wright, *Book of Vampires*, 123.

Hedammu

Hedammu is a demonic creature from Hurrian mythology that is described in Kumarbi Cycle's *Song of the Sea*. An AQUEOUS DEVIL, it was born the reptilian child of Kumarbi and the daughter of a sea-god. Snakelike in its appearance and raging with its insatiable appetite, it attacked anything that came into its territory. According to the tale, the creature was lured to the shore with music, beautiful dancing women, and offerings of blood that was tainted with a sleeping elixir. Once ashore, he consumed the blood offerings and was then possibly slain by Sausga, sister of Tessub, or by Istar, but it will remain a mystery, as the original source is incomplete.

Sources: Cotterell, *Encyclopedia of World Mythology*, 26, 29; Foley, *Companion to Ancient Epic*, 261; Rose, *Giants, Monsters, and Dragons*, 170.

Heiglot

In Apollonius of Tyana's *Nuctemeron* (*Night Illuminated by Day*), Heiglot is named as the demon of snowstorms. He is most powerful during the first hour of the day.

Sources: Davidson, *Dictionary of Angels*, 138; Kelly, *Who in Hell*, 109; Lévi, *Transcendental Magic*, 417, 502.

Hekura

Variations: Hekula

From the demonology of the Yanomami people of Central Brazil comes a species of domesticatable AERIAL DEVIL known as hekura. Said to be small and very bright in appearance, these devils live in the jungle. A Yanomami shaman will travel out into the jungle to capture and tame a hekura, making it into something like his FAMILIAR. Once it is trained, the hekura will only attach to whom or what its shaman tells it to. Domesticated hekura live in the chests of Yanomami shamans. It hangs its little hammock between the man's ribs. The shaman will sniff some *yopo* powder (the dried and pulverized seeds of the *Anadenanthera colubrine*) to activate his hekura, and will use it to cure a disease or deliver a magical attack that the shaman wishes to send forth. A shaman may be in possession of several hekura, each one trained in curing a different illness. Each hekura has its own song that the shaman must learn in order to use his hekura properly. When the song or chant is done properly, it is the devil's voice that is really heard and the hekura will do as it is asked. If the song is performed incorrectly, the hekura may turn on its shaman or do the opposite of what was asked of it.

Wild hekura live deep in the jungle and do not like noisy places. They will attack anyone if the mood strikes them, if not with a physical blow then by causing some disease to befall their prey; however, it should be noted that these devils never assault children.

Sources: Ember, *Encyclopedia of Medical Anthropology*, 1023–4; Jones, *Evil in our Midst*, 104–6; Lizot, *Tales of the Yanomami*, 12–3, 75–7, 88–90.

Heliophobic Devil

Francesco Maria Guazzo's *Compendium Maleficarum* (*Compendium of Witches*) published in 1628 catalogued Heliophobic devils, strictly nocturnal servitors of the Devil, as they are terrified of light.

Source: Kipfer, *Order of Things*, 255.

Hellmouth

A hellmouth is created by the willful act of God allowing the earth to open and swallow in those he sees fit to descend into Hell. It has been associated with the LEVIATHAN of Job 41:1 and is mentioned in the Old Testament in Numbers 16:28–33. The scripture reads: "28 And Moses said, 'Hereby you shall know that the Lord has sent me to do all these works, and that it has not been of my own accord. 29 If these men die as all men die, or if they are visited by the fate of all mankind, then the Lord has not sent me. 30 But if the Lord creates something new, and the ground opens its mouth and swallows them up with all that belongs to them, and they go down alive into Sheol, then you shall know that these men have despised the Lord.' 31 And as soon as he had finished speaking all these words, the ground under them split apart. 32 And the earth opened its mouth and swallowed them up, with their households and all the people who belonged to Korah and all their goods. 33 So they and all that belonged to them went down alive into Sheol, and the earth closed over them, and they perished from the midst of the assembly."

Sources: Bildhauer, *Monstrous Middle Ages*, 161–2, 171–2; Crisafulli, *Go to Hell*, 27–9; Van Scott, *Encyclopedia of Hell*, 159–61.

Hemah

Hemah ("wrath") is named as one of the five ARCHANGELS OF PUNISHMENT in Hasidic lore; he is the demon of the death of domestic animals. Created by God's will at the beginning of the world to do his will, Hemah commands seven chiefs and seventy under-chiefs. He is described as being 500 parasangs (about 3,000,000 meters) tall, forged with chains of black and red fire.

With the other two Archangels of Punishment, AF and MASHITH, they prey upon those who commit the sins of idolatry, incest, and murder.

Sources: Ashley, *Complete Book of Devils and Demons*, 78; Davidson, *Dictionary of Angels*, 351.

Hemis

In the *Sacred Magic of Abramelin the Mage*, book two, Hemis ("halfway") is included as one of the sixty-five SERVITORS OF KORE AND MAGOTH.

Sources: Mathers, *Book of the Sacred Magic of Abramelin the Mage*, 118; Von Worms, *Book of Abramelin*, 256.

Hephesimireth

Named as one of the SPIRITS OF SOLOMON, Hephesimireth is the demon of lingering diseases. He confessed to the king that if his victims rubbed salt in their hands, mixed it into oil, and then smeared it onto themselves while saying "Seraphim, Cherubim, help me!" he would immediately flee.

Sources: Ashe, *Qabalah*, 51, 65; Belanger, *Dictionary of Demons*, 155.

Hepogon

In the *Sacred Magic of Abramelin the Mage*, book two, Hepogon is named as one of the sixty-five SERVITORS OF KORE AND MAGOTH. His name is possibly Greek and if so would loosely translate to mean "saddle cloth."

Sources: Mathers, *Book of the Sacred Magic of Abramelin the Mage*, 107; Von Worms, *Book of Abramelin*, 256.

Heramael

The *Grimoirium Verum* (*Grimoire of Truth*), allegedly to have been written by Alibek the Egyptian in 1517, names Heramael as one of the forty-four SERVITORS OF SATANACHIA AND SA-

TANICIAE, ranking him as a chief (see SA-
TANACHIA and SATANICIAE). This demon is helpful and quick to act upon his summoner's bidding.
He is known for his perfect and complete knowledge of botany, diseases, healing, herbalism,
medicine, plants, and radical medical cures.

Sources: Kelly, *Who in Hell*, 111; Masters, *Devil's
Dominion*, 131; Waite, *Book of Black Magic and of Pacts*,
162, 187.

Herensugue

Variations: Dragoi, Edaansuge, Edeinsuge,
Edensuge, Egansuge, Erensuge, Errensuge, Er-
suge, Hensuge, Herainsuge, Herensuge, Herren-
Surge, Iguensuge, Iraunsuge, Sierpe

Herensugue is a subterranean demon described
in Basque mythology as being a snake with seven
heads and sporting a pair of wings that make a
ghastly sound when it flies. His name aptly translates to mean "end snake" or "one-third snake."
He is under the command of the dragon-line
deity of storms, Sugaar.

Preying on herd animals and humans by using
its breath to lure cattle to it, Herensugue lives in
caves generally speaking but has definite homes
in the mountain ranges of Ahuski, in Aralar, in
Muragain, and in Ezpeleta.

Each year it grows a new head, and at the end
of seven years it self-combusts and is reborn in
Itxasgorrieta, the "region of the red seas." Anyone
who sees this demonic creature and lives to tell
the tale will have bad luck until the day it is reborn. Herensugue can be appeased with human
sacrifice, and although it is said that he is susceptible to poison, he can only be slain by a hero
or through divine intervention.

Sources: Ashely, *Complete Book of Devils and
Demons*, 101; Kelly, *Who in Hell*, 111; Lurker, *Routledge
Dictionary of Gods and Goddesses*, 253; Rose, *Giants,
Monsters, and Dragons*, 172.

Heresiel

In the *Theurgia Goetia*, the second book of the
Lemegeton, Heresiel is named as one of the fifteen
SERVITORS OF ICOSIEL (see ICOSIEL). Ranked as
a chief duke, this AERIAL DEVIL commands 2,200
servitors. Heresiel can be summoned any time of
the day or night and is known as being good-natured and obedient, doing exactly as the summoner
asks. He is most easily summoned from inside a
house. Heresiel has dominion over the planet Mars.

Sources: Belanger, *Dictionary of Demons*, 155; Peterson, *Lesser Key of Solomon*, 99.

Herg

The *Sacred Magic of Abramelin the Mage* names
Herg ("to slay") as one of the thirty-two SERVI-
TORS OF ASTAROT (see ASTAROT).

Sources: Mathers, *Book of the Sacred Magic of
Abramelin the Mage*, 106; Von Worms, *Book of Abramelin*,
249.

Hergotis

In the *Sacred Magic of Abramelin the Mage*, Hergotis ("a laborer") is included as one of the twenty
SERVITORS OF AMAYMON (see AMAYMON).

Sources: Mathers, *Book of the Sacred Magic of Abra-
Melin*, 109; Von Worms, *Book of Abramelin*, 257.

Hermiala

In the *Ars Goetia*, the first book of the *Lemege-
ton*, Hermiala is named as one of the fifty-three
SERVITORS OF ASHTAROTH AND ASMODEUS (see
ASHTAROTH and ASMODEUS).

Sources: Mathers, *Book of the Sacred Magic of
Abramelin the Mage*, 106; Von Worms, *Book of Abramelin*,
248.

Heyd

Heyd is a storm demon or sea witch alluded to
in the *Friðþjófs saga hins frœkna*, written sometime
in the 1300s. According to Norwegian mythology, this demon looks like a white bear and has
control over the weather. Heyd often works in
tandem with another storm demon named HAM.

Sources: Bassett, *Legends and Superstitions of the Sea
and of Sailors*, 88; De Claremont, *Ancient's Book of
Magic*, 127; Kelly, *Who in Hell*, 113.

Hez

Variations: The arrow that flies by day

According to Hebrew demonology, Hez
("arrow") is a type of demon known as a MAZZ-
IKIM ("afflicters or damagers"). He preys upon Israelites who have forsaken the Lord in preference
to "foreign gods" by using a bow that shoots arrows of fire. He is powerless to hurt anyone who
is under protection of the Lord (see also DEVER).

Sources: Dennis, *Encyclopedia of Jewish Myth, Magic
and Mysticism*, 68; Hunter, *Magickal Judaism*, 87;
Isaacs, *Why Hebrew Goes from Right to Left*, 50.

Hicpacth

Variations: Hiepacth

The *Grimoirium Verum* (*Grimoire of Truth*), allegedly written by Alibek the Egyptian in 1517,
lists Hicpacth as being under the command of
Aerial. This demon has the ability to transport a
person to his summoner instantly, no matter the
distance.

Sources: Kelly, *Who in Hell*, 113; Masters, *Devil's
Dominion*, 130; Waite, *Book of Black and Ceremonial
Magic*, 190.

Hidimba

Variations: Hdimba, Hidimb, Hidimbasura

Hidimba was an ASURAS, PISACHA, or RAK-

SHASA (sources vary) from Vedic demonology and mentioned in *The Mahabharata*, one of the two major Sanskrit epics of ancient India; authorship is traditionally attributed to Vyasa. Hidimba and his beautiful sister, Hidimbaa, lived in a bone-strewn cave in the forest. He would use his sister to lure travelers away with the promise of a meal. He was slain by the giant and hero Bhima.

Sources: Buitenen, *Mahābhārata*, Vol. 1, 294–300; Husain, *Demons, Gods and Holy Men*, 98; Rose, *Giants, Monsters, and Dragons*, 172.

Hierarchy of Demons

In man's attempt to catalogue all accumulated knowledge so that it can be better assimilated and utilized to avoid chaos, the idea of a hierarchy was conceived. During the Middle Ages demonologists began assigning ranks and titles to those demons who, historically up until then, did not have any.

Emperor, great kings, kings, great princes, princes, great marquises, marquises, great dukes, dukes, great earls, earls, great presidents, presidents, knights, and great marshals are the ranks that are most often given. Other positions and job titles are used, such as chief, head physician, or flag bearer. All demons placed in the hierarchy are a servitor to some other demon. Traditionally, the ranks of baronet, baron, viscount, and viceroy are not used.

Abramelin the Mage claims there are two halves to the primary hierarchy. The first is made up of the four chief spirits: BELIAL, LEVIATHAN, LUCIFER, and SATAN. The second half is made up of eight sub-princes: AMAIMON, ARITON, Asmodee, ASTAROT, Belzebud, MAGOT, ORIENS, and PAYMON. All other demons are servitors to them.

According to Johann Weirus' hierarchy, Beelzebuth (BEELZEBUB) is supreme chieftain and SATAN holds an unnamed position as his second. The third plane of power holds the sixty-six princes. Each prince commands 6,666 legions, and each legion contains 6,666 devils. The fourth place holds the commander of the Armies of Hell: ADRAMELECH, ASHTAROTH, BAAL, BAAL-BERITH, BEHEMOTH, CHAMOS, DAGON, MELCHOM, NERGAL, and Proserpine. Other positions of note are the ANTICHRIST, mime and juggler of Hell; ASMODEUS, who runs the gambling houses; and Belial, demonic ambassador to England; to name but a few.

There is also the system of tiers used to explain the hierarchy. In this system, there are four tiers. On the first tier, and listed in order of rank, are Lucifer, emperor; Beelzebub, prime minister; and Astorath, grand duke. On the second tier, in order of rank and answerable only to the first tier are Lucifuge, prime minister; SATANACHIA, grand general; AGALIAREPT, grand general; FLEURETTY, lieutenant general; SARGATANAS, brigadier; and NEBIROS, field marshal. On the third tier are the eighteen subordinates who answer directly to those on the second: AAMON, ABIGAR, AGARES, AYPEROS, BAEL, BARBATOS, BATHIM, BOTIS, BUER, FORAU, Glasyabolas (GLASSYALABOLAS), GUSOYN, LORAY, MARBAS, NUBERUS, PRUSLAS, Pursan (PURSON), and VALEFAR. On the fourth tier are millions of subordinates and make up the legions of servitors.

In addition to the four widely cited hierarchies listed above, there are numerous interpretations of the hierarchies listed in innumerable grimoires.

Sources: Baglio, *The Rite*, 185–6; Baglio, *Encyclopædia of Religion and Ethics*, Vol. 8, 272, 304; Diagram Group, *Little Giant Encyclopedia*, 86; Icon, *Hierarchy*, 223; Wedeck, *Treasury of Witchcraft*, 96.

Hifarion

Hifarion ("pony") is named as one of the sixteen SERVITORS OF ASMODEUS (see ASMODEUS) in the *Sacred Magic of Abramelin the Mage*, book two.

Sources: Mathers, *Book of the Sacred Magic of Abramelin the Mage*, 119; Von Worms, *Book of Abramelin*, 256.

Hiisi, plural: Hiiet

Variations: Hiite, Hisi

Hiisi is a demonic giant, hideous and beardless with lopsided eyes and no eyelids. He is the personification of the North wind in Finnish mythology. A tribal chief and the demon of the forces of nature, he was under the command of the demon LEMPO. In Estonian his name means "sacred forest." Hiisi was born in Pohjola, the mythical northern polarity mentioned in the Finnish national epic, *Kalevala*.

Dressing slovenly, he is accompanied everywhere he goes by his entire household: his wife, their many children, household servants and their horses, dogs, and cat. One of his servants, Hiisi-hejmolainen, is in charge of the mountains, while his other servant, Wesi-Hiisi, is in charge of the waters. His bird, Hiiden-Lintu, carries evil through the air. His cat, Hiiden-kissa, although fierce, sometimes forces thieves to confess to their crimes. His horse, Hiiden-Ruuna, runs over the planes spreading diseases. To hear its hoofs is an omen of imminent disaster. Fortunately, he cannot enter into a blessed or urban area. In less populated regions it was believed that Hiisi could not open a door and enter into a house, but if one was left open he considered it an invitation to enter.

Traveling in a loud procession, Hiisi and his entourage spread death and evil, killing anyone, animals and humans alike, in their path. Large boulders seemingly placed in the middle of a field were placed there by him. Hiisi uses the North wind to freeze animals and people to death as well as to overturn ships; he also makes axe heads loose and causes people to cut themselves. When not on the march, he is said to live at notable geographical features such as large boulders, deep crevasses, or isolated peninsulas.

When translating from English into Finnish, the word *goblin* is often translated to *hiisi*.

Sources: Abercromby, *Pre- and Proto-historic Finns*, 292–9; Hyatt, *Book of Demons*, 81; Korpela, *World of Ladoga*, 88–9, 92–6; Lurker, *Dictionary of Gods and Goddesses*, 153.

Hipoles

Variations: HIPOLOS

In the *Sacred Magic of Abramelin the Mage*, Hipoles ("goat herd") is ranked as one of the thirty-two SERVITORS OF ASHTAROTH (see ASHTAROTH).

Sources: Ford, *Bible of the Adversary*, 91; Mathers, *Book of the Sacred Magic of Abramelin the Mage*, 106; Von Worms, *Book of Abramelin*, 249, 256.

Hipolos

In the *Sacred Magic of Abramelin the Mage*, Hipolos is ranked as one of the thirty-two SERVITORS OF ASTAROT (see ASTAROT).

Sources: Mathers, *Book of the Sacred Magic of Abramelin the Mage*, 106; Von Worms, *Book of Abramelin*, 249.

Hiranyakashipu

Variations: Hiranyakasipu

According to the Puranic scriptures and Vedic mythology, Hiranyakashipu, a king, is both an ASURAS and a RAKSHASA. His name in Sanskrit means "one who is wrapped in gold." Born the son of Sage Kashyapa and his wife, Diti, Hiranyakashipu was conceived at sunset, an unfavorable time. This demon, who is arrogant, exceedingly cruel, and materialistic by nature, is married to Leelavathi, his "sinless" wife. Together they have a son, Prahlada. He is the symbol of the futility of power over others.

HIRANYAKSHA and his brother Hiranyakashipu are one of the three incarnations of Jaya and Vijaya, the gatekeepers of the Vaikuntha who are serving out the conditions of a curse.

Through a boon granted to him by Brahma, Hiranyakashipu cannot be killed by any animal, deva, or human; in the day or night; indoors or out; not on the earth or in space; or by any object animate or inanimate. Because he preyed upon the followers of Vishnu, this demon was eventually slain by the Narasimha avatar of Vishnu at twilight, at a threshold, on his lap, with his fingernails.

Sources: Chopra, *Academic Dictionary of Mythology*, 136, 200; Mack, *Field Guide to Demons*, 196–7; Turner, *Dictionary of Ancient Deities*, 219, 256.

Hiranyaksha

Hiranyaksha ("goldeneye"), an ASURAS, is the king of the world in Vedic mythology, born the son of Sage Kashyapa and his wife, Diti. Tyrannical at best, this demon preyed upon the earth itself, including all the animals and people on it. Through a boon granted by Brahma, no animal or person who he could name in one sitting would be able to harm him. It was during his rule of terror that he dragged the earth to the bottom of the ocean. Eventually, because of his reign of terror, Vishnu took the form of a sow and in a battle that lasted one thousand years, finally slew him.

Sources: Knappert, *Indian Mythology*, 54, 119, 257; Turner, *Dictionary of Ancient Deities*, 219.

Hivvah

In the sixth and seventh *Books of Moses*, Hivvah is named as one of the two sons of the FALLEN ANGEL Semyaza; his brother's name was Hiyyah (also known as Ahiah). It was a common belief at one time that angels could not reproduce their own kind unless they had become corrupt, or Fallen. An angelic hybrid, he consumed each day one thousand camels, horses, and oxen each. His name translates to mean "spoke" or "female serpent."

Sources: Davidson, *Dictionary of Angels*, 141; Jung, *Fallen Angels in Jewish, Christian and Mohammedan Literature*, 114.

Hizarbin

In Apollonius of Tyana's *Nuctemeron* (*Night Illuminated by Day*), Hizarbin is named as the demon of the seas. He is most powerful during the second hour of the day.

Sources: Davidson, *Dictionary of Angels*, 141; Kelly, *Who in Hell*, 114; Lévi, *Transcendental Magic*, 404.

Hmin Nat

Hmin Nat ("forest demon") is the demon of malaria in Burmese demonology, and on occasion, he is a village guardian. Offerings of drink and food at his shrines will keep him from attacking. It is believed that he is present when the leaves of a tree move when all else is still. He lives in the groves or trees and violently shakes people until they go insane.

Sources: Folkard, *Plant Lore, Legends, and Lyrics*, 80; Spence, *Encyclopedia of Occultism*, 81; Turner, *Dictionary of Ancient Deities*, 220.

Hminza Tase

In Burma, there is a vampiric spirit that attacks the people in the village where it used to live. The people it pays particular attention to are those who caused it the most strife during its human life. The hminza tase will possess the body of a crocodile, dog, or tiger and use it to attack people (see DOG). There are death dance rituals and sacrifices that can be made to prevent its return, but these do not always work. If the spirit returns, remove its grave marker in the hopes that the vampire will forget who it was since it only haunts the place it used to live and attacks the people it used to know.

Sources: Burma Research Society, *Journal of Burma*, Vol. 46–47, 4; Hastings, *Encyclopedia of Religion and Ethics*, 30; Hyatt, *Book of Demons*, 29; Jobes, *Dictionary of Mythology*, 1537; Leach, *Funk and Wagnalls*, 1104.

Hoberdidance

Variations: Haberdidance, Hobbididance, Hopdance

Hoberdidance is the demon of the English folk dance called the Morris (Moorish) dance, specifically, from Elizabethan demonology. In sixteenth-century English his name translates to mean "Satan's scarecrow." In Shakespeare's *King Lear* he was entitled the "Prince of Dumbness."

Sources: Rudwin, *Devil in Legend and Literature*, 84; Schmidt, *Shakespeare-Lexicon*, 1464; Winkler, *O Let Us Howle Some Heavy Note*, 38.

Holastri

In the *Sacred Magic of Abramelin the Mage*, book two, Holastri is named as one of the forty-nine SERVITORS OF BEELZEBUB (see BEELZEBUB). His name is possibly Coptic and may mean "to surround."

Sources: Ford, *Bible of the Adversary*, 93; Mathers, *Book of the Sacred Magic of Abramelin the Mage*, 120; Von Worms, *Book of Abramelin*, 257.

Holba

In the *Sacred Magic of Abramelin the Mage*, book two, Holba ("fatness") is one of the sixteen SERVITORS OF ASMODEUS (see ASMODEUS).

Sources: Belanger, *Dictionary of Demons*, 158; Mathers, *Book of the Sacred Magic of Abramelin the Mage*, 120.

Horamar

In the *Ars Goetia*, the first book of the *Lemegeton*, Horamar is one of the fifty-three SERVITORS

OF ASHTAROTH AND ASMODEUS (see ASHTAROTH and ASMODEUS).

Sources: Belanger, *Dictionary of Demons*, 158; Von Worms, *Book of Abramelin*, 247.

Horanar

In the *Ars Goetia*, the first book of the *Lemegeton*, Horanar is one of the fifty-three SERVITORS OF ASHTAROTH AND ASMODEUS (see ASHTAROTH and ASMODEUS).

Sources: Mathers, *Book of the Sacred Magic of Abramelin the Mage*, 106; Von Worms, *Book of Abramelin*, 247.

Horminos

The *Sacred Magic of Abramelin the Mage*, book two, includes Horminos ("stirrer up") as one of the sixty-five SERVITORS OF KORE AND MAGOTH.

Sources: Mathers, *Book of the Sacred Magic of Abramelin the Mage*, 107; Susej, *Demonic Bible*, 258.

Hornblas

Hornblas is the demon of musical discord and is ranked as a trumpeter; he blows the trumpet that calls together the Ministry of Hell.

Sources: Guggenheimer, *Jewish Family Names and Their Origins*, 347; Rudwin, *Devil in Lore and Literature*, 123.

Horse Faces

Variations: Horse Head

In Chinese mythology Horse Faces, along with OX HEADS, are the guardians of the Underworld and the messengers for the King of Hell, YAN LUO WANG.

A mortal who once held an official position in life, he was rewarded for his incorruptible integrity in death by being given a position in the nether world befitting his honesty and virtue. Higher in rank than Ox-Head, Horse Faces has the title of Constable and First Torturer.

Horse Faces stands on the king's right and in art he is portrayed as a human figure with a white horse head standing in the "breathing defiance" pose. He is often depicted as having numerous magical charms and talismans and, carrying a pronged fork or trident in his grip, brings magicians and sorcerers to their appropriate punishment. Horse Faces was once worshipped as a god of divination in Japan and a god of vengeance in China.

Sources: Asiatic Society of Japan, *Transactions of the Asiatic Society of Japan*, Vols. 10–11, 266–70, 272; DuBose, *Dragon, Image, and Demon*, 306–7.

Hosampsich

In the *Book of Enoch* Hosampsich is listed as one of the FALLEN ANGELS who swore allegiance to SAMIAZA, rebelled against God, took a human as his wife, and fathered the NEPHILIM. He went on to teach mankind astrology and fortune-telling.

Sources: Davidson, *Dictionary of Angels*, 142; Voltaire, *Essays and Criticisms*, 106.

Hosen

In the *Sacred Magic of Abramelin the Mage*, book two, Hosen ("powerful, strong, and vigorous") is among the one hundred eleven SERVITORS OF AMAYMON, ARITON, ORIENS, AND PAYMON (see AMAYMON, ARITON, ORIENS, and PAYMON).

Sources: Mathers, *Book of the Sacred Magic of Abramelin the Mage*, 111; Von Worms, *Book of Abramelin*, 255.

Hotua Poro

Hotua Poro is an INCUBUS from Samoan demonology. At night, he comes and has sexual relations with a sleeping person while causing NIGHTMARES and suffocating them; on occasion he will also impregnate a woman. Tell-tale signs of attack from this demon are waking up feeling totally exhausted.

Sources: Hastings, *Encyclopedia of Religion and Ethics*, Part 10, 687; Rose, *Spirits, Fairies, Leprechauns, and Goblins*, 155; Sagan, *Demon-Haunted World*, 124.

Hru

According to Enochian lore, Hru is a CACODAEMON. His counterpart is the angel Rroi (see also ENOCHIAN CACODAEMONS).

Sources: Chopra, *Academic Dictionary of Mythology*, 139; Laycock, *Complete Enochian Dictionary*, 118.

Hsa

According to Enochian lore, Hsa is a CACODAEMON. His counterpart is the angel Saiz (see also ENOCHIAN CACODAEMONS).

Sources: Laycock, *Complete Enochian Dictionary*, 118.

Hsi-Hsue-Kue

Variations: Hsi-Hsue-Keui

The hsi-hsue-kue is a type of vampiric demon from China. Its name translates to mean "suck-blood demon."

Sources: Bunson, *Vampire Encyclopedia*, 126; Colloquium on Violence and Religion, *Contagion*, 32; Crowell, *Farewell My Colony*, 182; Maberry, *Vampire Universe*, 152.

Hsu Hao

Originating from the Tang dynasty period, Hsu Hao is a demon from Chinese demonology who is very small and wears red pants but no shoes. His name means "to desire emptiness and desolation." Living on Mount Li in Shensi, China, this demon causes fevers and delirium. His personal adversary is Chung Kuei.

Sources: Hensman, *More Hong Kong Tale-Spinners*, 309; Hyatt, *Book of Demons*, 27; Werner, *Myths and Legends of China*, 169.

Hua

According to Enochian lore, Hua is a CACODAEMON. His counterpart is the angel Vsag (see also ENOCHIAN CACODAEMONS).

Sources: Chopra, *Academic Dictionary of Mythology*, 139; Laycock, *Complete Enochian Dictionary*, 119.

Huictiigaras

Grimoirium Verum (*Grimoire of Truth*), allegedly written by Alibek the Egyptian in 1517, names Huictiigaras as one of the eighteen SERVITORS OF SYRACH (see SYRACH).

Sources: Kuriakos, *Grimoire Verum Ritual Book*, 24; Sabellicus, *Magia Pratica*, 35.

Huli Jing

There are many tales of the huli jing ("fox fairy") in Chinese demonology. A nocturnal *kuie* (ghostly demon), they are immortal shape-shifters who usually choose to appear as an animal, a deceased relative, an old or handsome man, or a seductive woman. They must, however, consume human souls to maintain their immortality. They also have the power to pass through the walls of a house, fly, and become invisible at will.

Huli jing are especially fond of attacking virtuous scholars, as reasonable and virtuous people enrage them. They also make people believe that something is the opposite of what it is. At night they emerge from the ground and hunt from rooftops looking for prey; then they shape-change into attractive people to seduce their prey in order to steal their vital essences that are released during sexual intercourse. Those who succumb to their temptation soon wither and die. During the day they sleep in the ground at graveyards.

Sources: Brill, *Nan Nü*, 97; Jones, *Evil in Our Midst*, 158–61; Leonard, *Asian Pacific American Heritage*, 452; Pomfret, *Chinese Lessons*, 143.

Humots

In the *Grimoirium Verum* (*Grimoire of Truth*), allegedly written by Alibek the Egyptian in 1517, Humots is listed as one of the eighteen SERVITORS OF SYRACH (see SYRACH). He has the ability to give his summoner any book he desires.

Sources: Kuriakos, *Grimoire Verum Ritual Book*, 24; Sabellicus, *Magia Pratica*, 35.

Hunhau

Variations: Ah Puch, Hunahau, Yum Cimil

Hunhau is possibly a demonic manifestation of the god Ah Puch in Mayan demonology. Ranked as a chief, this demon of death is under the command of Ah Puch. He has dominion over Mitnal, the ninth level of the Mayan underworld.

Sources: Evans, *Mayaad*, 91; Turner, *Dictionary of Amncient Deities*, 28; Van Scott, *Encyclopedia of Hell*, 68.

Hutgin

Variations: Ein Hedeckin, Hödecken, Hudgin, Hutjin

From the folklore of the diocese of Hildeshiem, a city in Lower Saxony, Germany, Hutgin is said to be the ambassador to Italy. In service under MEPHISTOPHELES, he commands two legions. Described as wearing a hood and a cloak, he preys upon those whom he is able to gain the trust of but only physically assaults those who first assault him. Hutgin acts as an advisor or protector, persuading men to do favors for him. Although he will give warning when his patience is being tested, this demon is extremely vengeful, even for an infernal being. He is summoned for his ability to grant knowledge. Hutgin can become invisible at will and is found living among the company of men.

Sources: Cameron, *Enchanted Europe*, 44; Chambers, *Book of Days*, 723; Ritson, *Fairy Tales, now First Collected*, 72–5.

Hutriel

Variations: ANAEL, Hamiel, ONIEL, Onoel

According to Gnostic lore, Hutriel ("rod of God") is one of the seven ANGELS OF PUNISHMENT. In the *Theurgia Goetia*, the second book of the *Lemegeton*, he is said to be hostile by nature and is ranked as the supervisor of the fifth division of Hell. Hutriel is described as looking like an ass.

Sources: Conway, *Guides, Guardians and Angels*, 130; Gaster, *Studies and Texts in Folklore*, 159; Guiley, *Encyclopedia of Angels*, 173; Webster, *Encyclopedia of Angels*, 155.

Huwawa

The *Epic of Gilgamesh*, an ancient poem from Mesopotamia written on twelve clay tablets, names Huwawa as the demon of the cedar mountain forest. A tutelary demon, a demonic storm god and the personification of volcanoes, Huwawa is under the command of the god Enlil. Mesopotamian demonology describes him as being enormously large with a hideous face made up of twisted intestines; his mouth is filled with fire. He is so incredibly ugly that his appearance strikes terror into the hearts of men. Virtually indestructible and having poisonous breath, Huwawa is eventually slain by the hero Gilgamesh but is beheaded by the hero's friend and companion Enkidu.

Sources: Sources: Black, *Gods, Demons, and Symbols of Ancient Mesopotamia*, 89–90, 106; Forsyth, *Old Enemy*, 21–36; Mack, *Field Guide to Demons, Fairies, Fallen Angels, and Other Subversive Spirits*, 55–7.

Hydriel

Duke Hydriel is named in the *Theurgia Goetia*, the second book of the *Lemegeton*, as one of the eleven WANDERING PRINCES and the Elemental Prince of Water (see PRINCES OF HELL). An AERIAL DEVIL who proclaims watery affairs, he commands 100 great dukes; 200 lesser dukes; 12 chief dukes who each have 1,320 servitors; and innumerable servitors. He is described as a serpent with a human head.

Sources: Gettings, *Dictionary of Demons*, 232; Shumaker, *Natural Magic and Modern Science*, 66; Trithemius, *Steganographia*, 81.

Hyenas

In the demonology from East Africa, hyenas are considered to be the allies of evil sorcerers and witches. Nocturnal animals, they are believed to be used as mounts and can be sent out to hunt and kill the enemies of the sorcerer who commands it. These animals are said to be able to imitate human voices and their eyes glow yellow when they are possessed by a spirit. From their anal gland they secrete a substance known as "hyena butter," which is collected and used as a fuel source in the gourd torch that witches carry.

Sources: Goodrich, *Illustrated Natural History of the Animal Kingdom*, 284; Middleton, *Witchcraft and Sorcery in East Africa*, 167.

Iabiel

Iabiel is an evil angel who is summoned to separate a husband from his wife (see DRSMIEL).

Sources: Sources: Davidson, *Dictionary of Angels*, 147; Kelly, *Who in Hell*, 119; Wedeck, *Treasury of Witchcraft*, 74.

Ialdabaoth

Variations: Iadalbaoth, Ialdaboath, Iao, Iidabaoth, Jaldabaoth, Ptahil, 'Yaldabaoth,' Yao

In alchemy, gnostic, Hebrew, and Phoenician mythology, Ialdabaoth is one of the seven elohim (angels) who created the visible universe, the demiurges directly below the "unknown father." His name means "artisan" in ancient Greek, and "child of chaos" in Hebrew.

A FALLEN ANGEL, formerly of the Order of

Thrones and a supreme archon, he is said to have the head of a lion. He is said to have created the Lower world, the physical aspects of the universe, and the physical aspects of humanity as well as seven elohim (angels) in his own image. Ignorant, proud, and vengeful, he now resides in the darkness of matter.

According to the Ophites doctrine, Ialdabaoth was born the child of Sophia, Christ's sister.

Sources: Seligmann, *Magic, Supernaturalism, and Religion*, 147.

Ialus

From the mythology of the Ulithi of the Ulithi Atoll of the Pacific Islands comes a species of demons known as the ialus. Their name literally translates to mean "demon." They live in small communities and set up a system of rules that they expect the humans of the area to figure out and learn to live by. For instance, the rules an ialus in a swamp garden may establish is that any woman who is barren, menstruating, or mourning may enter into the swamp garden; no man who has caught a fish with the use of a metal hook in the past four days or has dug a grave in the last five months may enter the swamp garden. Occasionally they are seen hovering a few inches off the ground. They are sticklers for details, waiting eagerly to attack anyone who has broken one of their rules by afflicting them with boils or an assault by a swarm of insects.

The ialus can mimic any sound, shape-shift into anything, and speak numerous languages. These demons are very difficult to defend against.

Sources: Lessa, *More Tales from Ulithi Atoll*, 18, 34, 74, 83; Lessa, *Tales from Ulithi Atoll*, 57.

Iamai

In the *Sacred Magic of Abramelin the Mage*, book two, Iamai is one of the forty-nine SERVITORS OF BEELZEBUB (see BEELZEBUB). His name is possibly taken from Hebrew and may translate to mean "days," as in a period of time.

Sources: Ford, *Bible of the Adversary*, 93; Mathers, *Book of the Sacred Magic of Abramelin the Mage*, 107; Von Worms, *Book of Abramelin*, 257.

Iaresin

The *Sacred Magic of Abramelin the Mage*, book two, lists Iaresin ("possessing") among the one hundred eleven SERVITORS OF AMAYMON, ARITON, ORIENS, AND PAYMON (see AMAYMON, ARITON, ORIENS, and PAYMON).

Sources: Mathers, *Book of the Sacred Magic of Abramelin the Mage*, 113; Von Worms, *Book of Abramelin*, 255.

Iblis

Variations: "The Bruised One," El-Harith, Enais, "Father of the Sheitans," Haris, SHAITAN, Shaytan, Sheitan

Originating in Hasidic and Muslim lore and adopted into Christian demonology, Iblis ("despair") has been mentioned in the Book of Revelation, the *Book of the Yezidi*, and the Koran. He has been called the chief of the spirits of evil and the Ruler of Hell, as well as a FALLEN ANGEL and a DJINN. He is often depicted as having the head of a donkey and wearing a peacock-feathered headdress, or as a hermaphrodite.

Created by God and created out of the element of fire, Iblis is the father of five evil DJINN sons. Sworn to tempt mankind until Judgment Day, he has the ability to lay eggs from which demons are born, can shape-shift into any form, self-impregnate to give birth to evildoers, and knows the three sacred words that grant immortality. Proud Iblis loves the idea of divinity, but he is powerless against Allah and his followers.

Sources: Guiley, *Encyclopedia of Demons and Demonology*, 67, 117–8; Houtsma, *E.J. Brill's First Encyclopaedia of Islam*, 187, 296, 351; Hyatt, *Book of Demons*, 53; McHugh, *Hantu Hantu*, 121.

Ibwa

Originally a benign spirit in Philippine demonology, Ibwa was once given a drink that he consumed, which was made from the body fat that had seeped out of a corpse for the seven days prior to burial. Ever since then, he and his companion, AKOP, have been stealing the clothes of the deceased and trying to consume corpses.

Sources: Guiley, *Encyclopedia of Demons and Demonology*, 67, 117–8; Houtsma, *E.J. Brill's First Encyclopaedia of Islam*, 187, 296, 351; Hyatt, *Book of Demons*, 53; McHugh, *Hantu Hantu*, 121.

Ichthion

Ichthion is one of the seventy-two SPIRITS OF SOLOMON that were named in the *Testament of Solomon*, which the king used to build his temple; he was made to perform heavy labor, such as keeping the furnaces for metalwork stoked. This demon, one of the thirty-six Elemental World Rulers, is described as having a shapeless head like a dog with a face of a bird, donkey, or ox. He has the ability to paralyze muscles. Ichthion's personal adversary is the angel Adonaeth and will immediately flee if he hears the cry "Adonaêth, help!"

Sources: Ashe, *Qabalah*, 51, 66; Conybeare, *Jewish Quarterly Review*, Vol. 11, 38; Davidson, *Dictionary of Angels*, 8.

Icosiel

In the *Theurgia Goetia,* the second book of the *Lemegeton,* Icosiel is named as the PLANETARY PRINCE of Mars and one of the eleven WANDERING PRINCES. He commands one hundred dukes, fifteen chief dukes, three hundred companions, and innumerable servitors (see PRINCES OF HELL). This demon is invoked for assistance with tools and weapons, but Icosiel is known to become his summoner's personal spirit slave from time to time. He and his court are, like all AERIAL DEVILS, constantly on the move, never staying in any one place for long.

Sources: Gettings, *Dictionary of Demons,* 232; Peterson, *Lesser Key of Solomon,* 98; Trithemius, *Steganographia,* 69.

Idalam

In Enochian lore, Idalam commands the CACODAEMONS of Earth and Water. His name is the reversal of the angelic name Maladi (see also ENOCHIAN CACODAEMONS).

Sources: Chopra, *Academic Dictionary of Mythology,* 147; Laycock, *Complete Enochian Dictionary,* 122.

Idpa

Idpa ("fever") is one of seven demons working in unison from Sumerian demonology, mentioned in the Magan Text. This AERIAL DEVIL is under the command of Ereshkigal, the goddess of death and gloom (see IRKALLA). He cannot be prevented from entering into a person's home, and once inside he possesses one of the occupants by entering into the body through the head. He lives in the desert and in abandoned places of worship where sacrifices took place (see also ALAL, GIGIM, NAMTAR, TELAL, URUKU, and UTUK).

Sources: Castellani, *Manual of Tropical Medicine,* 4; Seligmann, *Magic, Supernaturalism, and Religion,* 1; Spradlin, *Search for Certainty,* 37.

Ielahiah

Variations: Jeliabian, Yelaiah

A FALLEN ANGEL, formerly of the Order of Virtues, Ielahiah protects magistrates and renders decisions in legal suits. He is one of the seventy-two Schemamphoras, the angels bearing the name of God.

Sources: Ashley, *Complete Book of Devils and Demons,* 73; Davidson, *Dictionary of Angels,* 148; Webster, *Encyclopedia of Angels,* 94.

Ieropael

Variations: Ieropaêl

Ieropael was named in the *Testament of Solomon* as one of the seventy-two SPIRITS OF SOLOMON that the king used to build his temple;

he was made to perform heavy labor. The demon of convulsions and cramps, he knocks a person down and then sits on their stomach, causing cramps and convulsions, typically while they are bathing or traveling. Ieropael, described as having a shapeless head like a DOG and the face of a bird, donkey, or ox, is also one of the thirty-six Elemental World Rulers. He is easily banished by saying in the right ear of one of his victims the phrase "*Iudarizê, Sabunê, Denôê*" three times; he will immediately retreat.

Sources: Ashe, *Qabalah,* 48, 61; Belanger, *Dictionary of Demons,* 162.

Ifrit

Variations: Afreet, Afrit, Afrite, Efreet, Ifreet

The ifrit is a species of DJINN from Arabic mythology. A subterranean spirit, it looks like an enormous, winged demon made of smoke. Cunning, immortal, and strong, its veins flow with fire, not blood. When an ifrit is mortally wounded, it combusts into flames. Ifrit live underground and in ruins in a structured tribal society under the command of their tribal leader. The female of the species is known as an ifritah. These demons fear lightning bolts.

Sources: Hyatt, *Book of Demons,* 55; Merriam-Webster, Inc., *Merriam-Webster's Encyclopedia of World Religions,* 498; Rose, *Giants, Monsters, and Dragons,* 6.

Ifrita

In Arabic mythology an ifrita is a type of DJINN that looks like a woman with huge breasts and large buttocks. A natural seductress, it can shape-shift into a beautiful woman.

Sources: Gibb, *Shorter Encyclopaedia of Islam,* 159; Knappert, *Encyclopaedia of Middle Eastern Mythology and Religion,* 154.

Igarak

In the *Sacred Magic of Abramelin the Mage,* book two, Igarak is among the hundred eleven SERVITORS OF AMAYMON, ARITON, ORIENS, AND PAYMON (see AMAYMON, ARITON, ORIENS, and PAYMON). His name is possibly Celtic and may mean "terrible."

Sources: Mathers, *Book of the Sacred Magic of Abramelin the Mage,* 114; Von Worms, *Book of Abramelin,* 255.

Igilon

The *Sacred Magic of Abramelin the Mage,* book two, names Igilon as one of the one hundred eleven SERVITORS OF AMAYMON, ARITON, ORIENS, AND PAYMON (see AMAYMON, ARITON, ORIENS, and PAYMON). His name is possibly Greek and may mean "after the fashion of Eikelos."

Sources: Mathers, *Book of the Sacred Magic of Abramelin the Mage*, 114; Von Worms, *Book of Abramelin*, 255.

Igis

In the *Sacred Magic of Abramelin the Mage*, book two, Igis is one of the one hundred eleven SERVITORS OF AMAYMON, ARITON, ORIENS, AND PAYMON (see AMAYMON, ARITON, ORIENS, and PAYMON). His name is possibly Greek and may mean "coming."

Sources: Belanger, *Dictionary of Demons*, 163; Mathers, *Book of the Sacred Magic of Abramelin the Mage*, 114; Von Worms, *Book of Abramelin*, 255.

Igrat

Igrat is a SUCCUBUS and although female in appearance, is ranked as the king of the demons. This nocturnal demon travels with LILITH, Mahalath, and NAAMAH and commands ADAD, the king of Edom, and ASHMODAI. A story of her tells that she visited King David in a dream, conceived a son by him and named the CAMBION offspring Adad. Once, when asked his name, Adad replied, "*Sh'mi Ad, Ad Sh'mi*" ("My name is Adad, Adad is my name"). He came to be called Ashm'dai, and later Ashmodai.

Sources: Agrippa, *Three Books of Occult Philosophy*, 514; Koltuv, *Book of Lilith*, 35; Patai, *Gates to the Old City*, 460.

Igurim

The *Sacred Magic of Abramelin the Mage*, book two, includes Igurim ("fears") as one of the forty-nine SERVITORS OF BEELZEBUB (see BEELZEBUB).

Sources: Ford, *Bible of the Adversary*, 93; Mathers, *Book of the Sacred Magic of Abramelin the Mage*, 107; Von Worms, *Book of Abramelin*, 257.

Igymeth

Igymeth is listed as one of the concubines of SATAN.

Sources: Leven, *Satan, His Psychotherapy and Cure*, 394; Rudwin, *Devil in Legend and Literature*, 98.

Ijedtség

According to Hungarian demonology, Ijedtség is the demon of physical disease. His name means "fright."

Sources: Szabó, *Hungarian Practical Dictionary*, 431.

Ika-Zuchi-No-Kami

Variations: Ikazuchinokami

According to Japanese demonology, Ika-Zuchi-No-Kami is one of the seven Shinto demons. A subterranean spirit who lives in the underworld, his rumblings can be heard through volcanic earthquakes and eruptions.

Source: Roberts, *Japanese Mythology A to Z*, 57.

Ikonok

The *Sacred Magic of Abramelin the Mage*, book two, lists Ikonok ("phantasmal") as one of the forty-nine SERVITORS OF BEELZEBUB (see BEELZEBUB).

Sources: Ford, *Bible of the Adversary*, 93; Mathers, *Book of the Sacred Magic of Abramelin the Mage*, 107; Von Worms, *Book of Abramelin*, 257.

Ikwaokinyapippilele

In the Cunas cosmology, Ikwaokinyapippilele is the nocturnal demon of headaches and the Guardian of the night, preying on the devils that cause diseases. Known to be rash, this demon is an excellent marksman; he shoots the "friendly whales" that bring ocean water to pregnant women and throws his spear at heroes during battle. Ikwaokinyapippilele appears in the night sky as two of the three bright stars that are in a row in the constellation Orion.

Sources: Ashley, *Complete Book of Devils and Demons*, 64; Keeler, *Secrets of the Cuna Earthmother*, 84–5, 245.

Ilagas

Variations: Iligas

In the *Sacred Magic of Abramelin the Mage*, book two, Ilagas ("have obtained" or "obtaining") is named as one of the one hundred eleven SERVITORS OF AMAYMON, ARITON, ORIENS, AND PAYMON (see AMAYMON, ARITON, ORIENS, and PAYMON).

Sources: Mathers, *Book of the Sacred Magic of Abramelin the Mage*, 114; Von Worms, *Book of Abramelin*, 255.

Ilarax

Ilarax is named as one of the sixty-five SERVITORS OF KORE AND MAGOTH, in the *Sacred Magic of Abramelin the Mage*, book two. His name is possibly Greek and may mean "cheerful."

Sources: Mathers, *Book of the Sacred Magic of Abramelin the Mage*, 107; Von Worms, *Book of Abramelin*, 256.

Ilemlis

In the *Sacred Magic of Abramelin the Mage*, book two, Ilemlis is named among the twenty-two SERVITORS OF ARITON (see ARITON).

Sources: Mathers, *Book of the Sacred Magic of Abramelin the Mage*, 108; Von Worms, *Book of Abramelin*, 257.

Ileson

In the *Sacred Magic of Abramelin the Mage*, Ileson ("enveloping") is listed among the thirty-two SERVITORS OF ASTAROT (see ASTAROT).

Sources: Mathers, *Book of the Sacred Magic of*

Abramelin the Mage, 106; Von Worms, *Book of Abramelin*, 249.

Illirikim

The *Sacred Magic of Abramelin the Mage* includes Illirikim among the twenty SERVITORS OF AMAYMON (see AMAYMON). His name means "they who shriek with a long drawn-out cry" in Hebrew.

Sources: Lowry, *Under the Volcano*, 194; Mathers, *Book of the Sacred Magic of Abramelin the Mage*, 122.

Ilmenos

Variations: ILEMLIS

In the *Sacred Magic of Abramelin the Mage*, book two, Ilmenos ("silent lion") is named as one of the twenty-two SERVITORS OF ARITON (see ARITON).

Sources: Mathers, *Book of the Sacred Magic of Abramelin the Mage*, 108; Von Worms, *Book of Abramelin*, 254, 257.

Imamiah

Variations: A'amamiah, Amamiah, Imamaih

The Cabbala names Imamiah as one of the seventy-two angels who bear the mystical name of God, SHEMHAMPHORAE. Currently, he is a FALLEN ANGEL, formerly of the Order of Principalities, who bears adversity with patience and courage. He is fond of work and forceful when necessary; however, he is also blasphemous and wicked. Imamiah controls and oversees voyages. He destroys and humiliates enemies both when invoked to do so or by whimsy. He also protects prisoners who turn to him and gives them a means to gain their freedom. His name is Hebrew for "God elevated above all things."

Sources: Davidson, *Dictionary of Angels*, 149; Encausse, *Qabalah*, 284; Webster, *Encyclopedia of Angels*, 95.

Imdugud

Variations: Anzû (Akkadian), Anzu ("Rain Cloud") or ZU (Babylonian)

In the Mesopotamian mythology of ancient Sumeria, Imdugud was described in the Sumerian poem *Ninurta and the Turtle* as being half deity and half demon, an enormous black eagle with a lion's head. He had a sawlike beak and the beat of his wings caused sandstorms. He stole the Tablets of Destiny and returned with them to his nest atop a holy mountain (or a sacred tree, sources are unclear). Eventually, Imdugud was slain by the hero Ninurta. His name in Sumerian translates to mean "heavy rain" or "stone."

Sources: Black, *Gods, Demons, and Symbols of Ancient Mesopotamia*, 43, 74; Conway, *Magickal Mystical Crea-*tures, 73–5; Lurker, *Dictionary of Gods and Goddesses*, 164; Rose, *Giants, Monsters, and Dragons*, 189.

Imink

The *Sacred Magic of Abramelin the Mage*, book two, names Imink among the one hundred eleven SERVITORS OF AMAYMON, ARITON, ORIENS, AND PAYMON (see AMAYMON, ARITON, ORIENS, and PAYMON). His name is possibly Coptic and may mean "devouring."

Sources: Mathers, *Book of the Sacred Magic of Abramelin the Mage*, 113; Von Worms, *Book of Abramelin*, 255.

Imp

Variations: DJINN, GENIE

Imps originated in Germanic folklore as messenger spirits, but sometime during the Middle Ages, the words *imp* and *FAMILIAR became interchangeable with one another and were thereafter associated with witches and warlocks. Imps were summoned to assist in witches' magical practices. An imp is a type of lesser demon, a small and unattractive creature that was believed to be an evil offshoot of the DEVIL*, who has the ability to heal and knows alchemy. Said to be mischievous and not necessarily evil, they have a wild and uncontrollable nature, much like the fay. Imps left unattended will lead travelers astray and spank babies until they cry. This type of demon is oftentimes bound and kept in a bottle or ring until needed, much like in the lore connected to the DJINN.

Sources: Davies, *Witchcraft, Magic and Culture*, 182–4; Guiley, *Encyclopedia of Witches and Witchcraft*, 172; Robbins, *Encyclopedia of Witchcraft and Demonology*, 190.

Incubus, plural: incubi

Variations: Ag Rog ("old hag"), Agumangia, ALP, Aufhöcker, Barychnas ("the heavy breather"), Buhlgeist, Cauchmar ("trampling ogre"), Da Chor, Dab ("nightmare"), DUCCI, Duendes, EPHÉLÉS, Haegte, Haegtesse, Haehtisse, Hagge, Hegge, Hexendrücken, Hmong, Ka wi Nulita ("scissors pressed"), Kanashibara ("to tie with iron rope"), Kikimora, Kokma, Mab, Maere, Mair, Mar, Mara, Mare-Hag, Molong, More, Morúsi, Móry, Muera, Ngarat, Nightmare, Phi Kau ("ghost possessed"), Phi Um ("ghost covered"), Pnigalion ("the choker"), Preyts, Raukshehs, Tsog ("evil spirit"), Tsog Tsuam ("evil spirit who smothers"), Ukomiarik, Urum, Védomec, Zmora

All cultures from all over the world and from all time periods have reports of a type of vampiric demon that feeds off the sexual energy of humans. The incubus is generally described by its female victims as "feeling" male. At night this demonic vampire assaults a woman while she is asleep, stealing her sexual energy from her. She seldom wakes during the attack but will experience the event as if it were an erotic dream.

Once an incubus has locked on to a woman (it prefers nuns), it can be very difficult to drive away, although there are many recommendations that the church offers in order to ward it off, such as performing an exorcism, relocating, repeatedly making the sign of the cross, or, as a last resort, performing an excommunication on the woman being assaulted. Traditional lore says that to hang garlic and a druidstone (a stone with a natural hole through it) next to your bed will keep an incubus away.

Incubi can father children with their female victims; these offspring are known as CAMBIONS. There is a report of a man from Bologna, Italy, who staffed his entire brothel with incubi and the female equivalent of this vampiric creature, succubi (see SUCCUBUS).

Sources: Cohn, *Europe's Inner Demons*, 235; Doniger, *Britannica Encyclopedia of World Religions*, 503; Jones, *On the Nightmare*; Robbins, *Encyclopedia of Witchcraft and Demonology*, 28, 125.

Indiren

Indiren is, according to Persian mythology, the king of the eight AUSTATIKCO-PAULIGAUR.

Sources: De Claremont, *Ancient's Book of Magic*, 118; Smedley, *Occult Sciences*, 51; Spence, *Encyclopedia of Occultism*, 113.

Indra

Indra is a DAEVAS, the personification of apostasy in Persian demonology. His personal adversary is Arashtat. The demon Indra is not to be confused with Indira, the Aryan god of thunder.

Sources: Jackson, *Zoroastrian Studies*, 84–7; Messadié, *History of the Devil*, 83.

Inferus

French printer, publisher, and writer Simon Blocquel wrote a book under the nom de plume of Frinellan in 1844 titled *Le Triple Vocabulaire Infernal Manuel de Demonomane*. In it he ranks the demon Inferus as one of the demons of Hell and claims that if a person spits three times on the ground in his presence, that demon will have no power over you. It will also break all demonic pacts made with him or members of his court.

Sources: Peschke, *International Encyclopedia of Pseudonyms*, 306.

Inhuman Spirit

Occasionally manifesting as a genderless, half-human half-animal being, an inhuman spirit is an immortal being that was never human. By nature they are defiant, jealous, and prone to fits of rage with an extreme hatred toward humans. They seek to break a person's will and then possess the body. They cause welts and lesions and can levitate objects. They are very strong and physically attack people by biting, pushing, and scratching. It is said that an inhuman spirit is near whenever you hear a frightening sound that seems to be coming from every direction, or if you smell the stench of rotting meat. Seeing a dense fog or the temperature in a room rising several degrees are other signs an inhuman spirit is near. Roaming the earth, these demons are unpredictable in where and when they will strike, but one thing is certain: when they do, it will be done with a measure of extremity. The only way to save a victim of an inhuman spirit is to perform a successful exorcism.

Sources: Brittle, *The Demonologist*, 2, 48, 84; Dunwich, *Witch's Guide to Ghosts and the Supernatural*, 217; Hawkins, *Getting Started in Paranormal Investigation*, 88–90.

Inmai

In Myanmar demonology, Inmai is the demon that causes people to be injured with thorns. He lives in the front part of a house (see also BATIBAT).

Sources: Ashley, *Complete Book of Devils and Demons*, 67; Hastings, *Encyclopedia of Religion and Ethics* Part 5, 25.

Inokos

The *Sacred Magic of Abramelin the Mage*, book two, names Inokos as one of the fifteen SERVITORS OF ASMODEUS AND MAGOTH (see ASMODEUS). His name is possibly Latin and may mean "rake the earth of newly sown seed."

Sources: Mathers, *Book of the Sacred Magic of Abramelin the Mage*, 111; Von Worms, *Book of Abramelin*, 248.

Intxixu

Variations: Inntxixu, Inttxixu, Intxix, Intxixa, Intxixua, Intxixue, Intxixui, Intxixuo, Intxoxu, Intxxiu, Inxtixu, Itnxixu, Mairu

In Basque mythology an intxixu is a type of small half human and half *betizu*, a breed of wild cow found in the Basque region of Spain. Mischievous yet shy, it will occasionally offer to help humans. It lives in deserted mines and is said to build megalithic monuments on the Aiako Harria Mountain.

Sources: Aulestia, *Basque-English, English-Basque Dictionary*, 274; Miguel de Barandiarán, *Selected Writings of José Miguel de Barandiarán*, 88; Whitmore, *Trials of the Moon*, 73.

Iogion

In the *Sacred Magic of Abramelin the Mage*, book two, Iogion is named as one of the one hundred eleven SERVITORS OF AMAYMON, ARITON, ORIENS, AND PAYMON (see AMAYMON, ARITON, ORIENS, and PAYMON). His name is possibly taken from the Greek language and may mean "noise of battle."

Sources: Belanger, *Dictionary of Demons*, 165; Mathers, *Book of the Sacred Magic of Abramelin the Mage*, 105.

Iomuel

Iomuel is named by Moïse Schwab in his book, *Vocabulaire de l'Angelologie* (1897) as one of the FALLEN ANGELS who swore allegiance to SAMIAZA, rebelled against God, took a human wife, and fathered the NEPHILIM.

Source: Davidson, *Dictionary of Angels*, 150.

Ipakol

In the *Sacred Magic of Abramelin the Mage*, book two, Ipakol ("breathing forth") is among the one hundred eleven SERVITORS OF AMAYMON, ARITON, ORIENS, AND PAYMON (see AMAYMON, ARITON, ORIENS, and PAYMON).

Sources: Mathers, *Book of the Sacred Magic of Abramelin the Mage*, 105; Von Worms, *Book of Abramelin*, 255.

Iparkas

The *Sacred Magic of Abramelin the Mage*, book two, includes Iparkas as one of the one hundred eleven SERVITORS OF AMAYMON, ARITON, ORIENS, AND PAYMON (see AMAYMON, ARITON, ORIENS, and PAYMON). His name is possibly taken from the Greek language and may mean "a commander or cavalry" or "leader of horse."

Sources: Mathers, *Book of the Sacred Magic of Abramelin the Mage*, 112; Von Worms, *Book of Abramelin*, 244, 255.

Ipes

Variations: Aiperos, Aypeos, Ayporos, Ipos

According to Johann Wierus's *Pseudomonarchia Daemonum* (*False Monarchy of Demons*, 1583), Ipes is one of the seventy-two SPIRITS OF SOLOMON. He is ranked as an earl (or count, sources vary) and prince (or duke, sources vary) who commands thirty-six legions (see COUNTS OF HELL, DUKES OF HELL, EARLS OF HELL, and PRINCES OF HELL). When he appears before his summoner he looks like an angel with the head of a lion, a goose's foot, and a rabbit's tail; occasionally he manifests as a lion, and on very rare occasions, as a vulture. He is summoned for his knowledge on all things, past, present, and future, as well as for his ability to make men bold and witty.

Sources: De Laurence, *Lesser Key of Solomon, Goetia*, 28; DuQuette, *Key to Solomon's Key*, 171.

Ira-Kewa

From the demonology of the Maori people of New Zealand comes Ira-Kewa, a demon who causes confusion, disorientation, and death. One legend of this demon claims that Ira-Kewa was called up against the Maruiwi tribe. Under his influence as they traveled in familiar territory one night, they became confused and disoriented. Only a few members of the tribe survived the deadly fall from the precipice near Tohue that they walked right off of.

Sources: Orbell, *Illustrated Encyclopedia of Māori Myth and Legend*, 75–6; Rose, *Spirits, Fairies, Leprechauns, and Goblins*, 163.

Irix

In the *Sacred Magic of Abramelin the Mage*, book two, Irix ("falcon" or "hawk") is named as one of the sixty-five SERVITORS OF KORE AND MAGOTH.

Sources: Mathers, *Book of the Sacred Magic of Abramelin the Mage*, 107; Von Worms, *Book of Abramelin*, 250, 256.

Irkalla

Variations: ALLATU, Ereshkigal ("mistress of the great earth"), Ir-Kalla, Irkalia

Originating from the Akkadian, Babylonian, and Sumerian mythology, Irkalla is the queen of the Underworld and guardian and patroness of the Dark City, and has the ability to raise the dead. Her name translates from ancient Sumerian to mean "the big land" or literally "Underworld."

Demonic goddess of the Underworld, she has the body of a woman with the head of a lioness. In art she is depicted as holding a serpent in her hand. In the Sumerian myth she is married to Gugalanna, but her consort is NERGAL and she is passionately in love with him. Irkalla is bitter, dark, and violent by nature, but mortuary offerings and being praised in hymns can prevent her from turning her aggression toward mankind.

Sources: Colum, *Myths of the World*, 34–6; King, *Babylonian Religion and Mythology*, 37, 42; Turner, *Dictionary of Ancient Deities*, 241.

Irmenos

The *Sacred Magic of Abramelin the Mage*, book two, includes Irmenos as one of the twenty-two SERVITORS OF ARITON (see ARITON). His name is possibly Greek and may mean "an expounder."

Sources: Mathers, *Book of the Sacred Magic of Abramelin the Mage*, 108; Von Worms, *Book of Abramelin*, 124, 257.

Irminon

In the *Sacred Magic of Abramelin the Mage*, book two, Irminon is among the one hundred eleven SERVITORS OF AMAYMON, ARITON, ORIENS, AND PAYMON (see AMAYMON, ARITON, ORIENS, and PAYMON). His name is taken from the Greek language and means "supporting."

Sources: Mathers, *Book of the Sacred Magic of Abramelin the Mage*, 105, 113; Von Worms, *Book of Abramelin*, 119, 245, 255.

Irroron

Irroron ("sprinkling with dew") is among the one hundred eleven SERVITORS OF AMAYMON, ARITON, ORIENS, AND PAYMON (see AMAYMON, ARITON, ORIENS, and PAYMON) named in the *Sacred Magic of Abramelin the Mage*, book two.

Sources: Mathers, *Book of the Sacred Magic of Abramelin the Mage*, 105, 114; Von Worms, *Book of Abramelin*, 246, 256.

Irvene

Irvene is from the demonology of the Guanches of Tenerifer and Las Palmas of the Canary Islands. This devil looks like a large and woolly dog and lives at the Peak of Teyde (see DOG). Irvene appears to ancestors during ceremonial offerings made at burial sites.

Sources: Ashley, *Complete Book of Devils and Demons*, 101; Hooton, *Ancient Inhabitants of the Canary Islands*, 55.

Isaacharum

According to the grimoire the *Red Lilly*, Isaacharum is a devil that is said to be mighty, but not as powerful as ASMODEUS.

Sources: France, *On Life and Letters*, 220; Rudwin, *Devil in Lore and Literature*, 28, 86.

Isacaaron

Isacaaron is the demon of blind lust who causes people to have licentious thoughts. He appears as a three-legged DOG. This demon is said to abhor pain, be blind to reason, prone to extremes, and violently passionate. Isacaaron is often called upon during exorcisms and cases of collective possession; he was one of the eighteen demons who possessed Sister Jeanne des Anges in Loudun, France, in 1634 (see LOUDUN POSSESSION).

Sources: Aikin, *General Biography*, 493; Bayle, *Historical and Critical Dictionary*, 262; Hsia, *World of Catholic Renewal*, 151; Voltaire, *Works of M. de Voltaire*, 193.

Ischigas

In the *Sacred Magic of Abramelin the Mage*, Ischigas is listed as one of the thirty-two SERVI-

TORS OF ASTAROT (see ASTAROT). His name is possibly Hebrew and may mean "to aid" or "to save."

Sources: Mathers, *Book of the Sacred Magic of Abramelin the Mage*, 106, 117; Von Worms, *Book of Abramelin*, 249, 256.

Ischiron

In the *Sacred Magic of Abramelin the Mage*, book two, Ischiron ("mighty" or "strong") is among the sixty-five named SERVITORS OF KORE AND MAGOTH.

Sources: Ford, *Bible of the Adversary*, 92; Mathers, *Book of the Sacred Magic of Abramelin the Mage*, 118.

Isekel

The *Sacred Magic of Abramelin the Mage*, book two, names Isekel ("anointed") among the one hundred eleven SERVITORS OF AMAYMON, ARITON, ORIENS, AND PAYMON (see AMAYMON, ARITON, ORIENS, and PAYMON).

Sources: Mathers, *Book of the Sacred Magic of Abramelin the Mage*, 105, 114; Von Worms, *Book of Abramelin*, 246, 255.

Isiamon

In the *Sacred Magic of Abramelin the Mage*, Isiamon ("desolation") is named as one of the thirty-two SERVITORS OF ASTAROT (see ASTAROT).

Sources: Mathers, *Book of the Sacred Magic of Abramelin the Mage*, 106, 117; Von Worms, *Book of Abramelin*, 249, 256.

Isigi

In the *Ars Goetia*, the first book of the *Lemegeton*, Isigi is named as one of the fifty-three SERVITORS OF ASHTAROTH AND ASMODEUS (see ASHTAROTH and ASMODEUS). His name is possibly Hebrew and may mean "err" or "error."

Sources: Mathers, *Book of the Sacred Magic of Abramelin the Mage*, 115; Von Worms, *Book of Abramelin*, 247, 256.

Itrasbiel

Variations: Itules

In the *Theurgia Goetia*, the second book of the *Lemegeton*, Itrasbiel is ranked as a duke and is listed as one of the one thousand SERVITORS OF PAMERSIEL (see DUKES OF HELL and PAMERSIEL). A nocturnal AERIAL DEVIL, Itrasbiel is known to be very useful at driving out spirits from haunted places as well as an expert liar. Arrogant, stubborn, and unable to keep a secret, this demon can be temporarily bound in a crystal stone or glass receptacle. It should be noted that when summoning him, it must be done from the second floor of a home or in a wide open space.

Sources: Findlen, *Athanasius Kircher*, 262; Peterson,

Lesser Key of Solomon, 64; Trithemius, *Steganographia*, 1.

Itzcoliuhqui

Variations: Itzlacoliuhqui

In the demonology of the ancient Aztec people of Mexico, Itzcoliuhqui was a demonic god, an aspect of Quetzalcoatl or Tezcatlipoca, sources vary. His name in the Nahuatl language means "twisted obsidian one." Itzcoliuhqui is the demon of darkness, destruction, extreme cold, volcanic eruptions, and possibly dryness.

Sources: Ashley, *Complete Book of Devils and Demons*, 64; Burland, *Gods of Mexico*, ix; Hyatt, *Book of Demons*, 90–3; Turner, *Dictionary of Ancient Deities*, 244.

Iudal

Iudal was one of the SPIRITS OF SOLOMON that was used to build his temple; he was made to tend the furnaces for metalwork. The demon of deafness, he will immediately retreat if he hears the phrase "Uruel Iudal." Like many of the demons summoned forth by Solomon, Iudal is described as having a shapeless head like a dog with a face like a bird, donkey, or ox.

Sources: Ashe, *Qabalah*, 57; Belanger, *Dictionary of Demons*, 167; Conybeare, *Jewish Quarterly Review*, Vol. 11, 35.

Iuvart

Iuvart is a FALLEN ANGEL, formerly a Prince of the Order of Angels. Currently he is of the third hierarchy of Hell and ranked as the Prince of the FALLEN ANGELS (see PRINCES OF HELL). Iuvart is the demon of sin and vices not covered by the other demons and devils.

Sources: Davidson, *Dictionary of Angels*, 154; Donovan, *Never on a Broomstick*, 138; Robbins, *Encyclopedia of Witchcraft and Demonology*, 129.

Iya

Variations: Eya

Originating from the mythology of the Sioux Indians of North America, Iya ("evil spirit") is the demon of all things. Born the child of Inyan and Unk and looking like a giant with foul breath, this demon preys upon the Dakota, Lakota, Nakota, and Pte people, devouring and maiming them as well as animals. He causes sickness; creates sores; rouses anger, greed, passions, and vanity in men; and steals food during hard times. Iya, through an incestuous relationship with his mother, Unk, fathered the very beautiful, deceitful, and enticing demon Gnaski. He lives to the east near a large body of water.

Legend tells us that his personal adversary is Wakinyan but that he was slain by Stone Child

and the trickster god Iktomi. Lakota mythology describes a Stone Child as a perfectly round stone. Iya's lifeblood formed the Great Salt Lake.

Sources: Dooling, *Sons of the Wind*, 8–11; Erdoes, *American Indian Myths and Legends*, 337–8; Lurker, *Dictionary of Gods and Goddesses*, 172; Walker, *Anthropological Papers of the American Museum of Natural History*, Vol. 16, 198.

Íz

Íz, the demon of illness, is from Hungarian Magyar demonology. His name means "joint gout," "shade" or "the shadow-spirit" in old Hungarian.

Sources: Kõiva, *Folk Belief Today*, 139.

Jahi

Variations: Baba Yaga, Jeh, Jezebel, Jezibaba, the "polluting whore," "the Whore"

In Zoroastrian demonology Jahi is the queen of Hell, the daughter and wife of AHRIMAN, the demon of lasciviousness and prostitutes. This demon preys primarily on women, as she controls menstrual cycles, and she causes grief in their lives. Her goal is to defile all women. She is a seductress and looks like a beautiful woman with wet curly hair and a body covered with filth, giving off a horrible stench. Her gaze is powerful enough to kill. Jahi steals and consumes Haoma's sacrificial offerings. Her personal adversary is Ohrmazd. Her name in Avestan translates to mean "adultery," "libertine," "menstruation," or "one who leads a licentious life."

Sources: Hyatt, *Book of Demons*, 56; Illes, *Encyclopedia of Spirits*, 520; Kloppenborg, *Female Stereotypes in Religious Traditions*, 27–31; Messadié, *History of the Devil*, 83.

Jameriel

Variations: Jamersil

In the *Ars Paulina*, the third book of the *Lemegeton*, Jameriel is ranked as being one of the fifteen SERVITORS OF SCOX (see SCOX). He is also listed as one of the ten SERVITORS OF SAZQUIEL (see SAZQUIEL). Ranked as a duke, he commands 5,550 servitors.

Sources: Peterson, *Lesser Key of Solomon*, 114; Waite, *Book of Ceremonial Magic*, 67.

Jan-Ibn-Jan

Variations: Jan bin Jan, Jann al-Jann

The last of the seventy-two Suleymans (kings) of the DJINN, Jan-Ibn-Jan is the ruler of Jinnestan with command over all of his kind, according to Arabic mythology. His name means "Jan son of Jan." Builder of the great pyramids of Egypt, his shield was a powerful magical item that came into the hands of King Solomon, allowing him to bind demons. This demon's personal adversary is the angel Iblis, not to be confused with the demonic king of the SHAITANS, IBLIS.

Sources: Hyatt, *Book of Demons*, 54; Keightley, *Fairy Mythology*, 18, 25; Lieber, *Encyclopædia Americana*, Vol. 5, 412.

Jann

Variations: Jan

There are two classes of DJINN in Islamic mythology. The first and higher class is divided into five genera: the Afreet, GHILAN, Jann, MARID, and the Sheitan. Born the children of IBLIS, the jann ("spirit") are the weakest of their genus. A type of FAMILIAR spirit, these demons steal animals from farmers.

The author of *One Thousand and One Arabian Nights*, Sir Richard F. Burton, considered the word *jann* to be the plural form of the word GENIE.

Sources: Borges, *Book of Imaginary Beings*, 133–4; Eberhart, *Mysterious Creatures*, 136; Mercatante, *Good and Evil*, 69.

Jaracas

Variations: Jaracaca

In Brazil there is a vampiric demon known as a jaracas. It assumes the form of a snake when it is time to feed, slithers up to a mother while she is asleep, and attaches itself to her breast, draining her breast milk. During the attack, the jaracas slips the end of its tail into the baby's mouth to prevent it from crying and waking its mother. When it attacks a sleeping man, it will bite him in his upper arm, taking a survivable amount of blood. Victims will eventually begin to grow weaker as the attacks continue and will never be able to fully recover until the jaracas has moved on to other prey. Mothers will discover that their milk has dried up.

A jaracas can only be driven off if one hopes to save its victims, as it cannot be destroyed. Catholic prayers to the saints are said to work, as will the blessing of a Catholic priest. There are also several ancient and traditional incantations, spells, and talismans that can be purchased or made to ward it off.

Sources: Masters, *Natural History of the Vampire*, 51; Volta, *The Vampire*, 85.

Jato

Variations: Jakada, Janzari, Janziri

From the demonology of the Hausa people of West Africa comes a demon who lives in gutters and sewers known as Jato. His name in the Hausa language means "a vegetable poison used by smearing on arrows." This demon causes venereal disease that leads to insanity and makes men eat dung. He is the patron to the *masubori* ("madmen"). A specific dance must be performed accompanied by a specific animal sacrifice in order to banish Jato.

Sources: Knappert, *African Mythology*, 107; Oesterreich, *Possession*, 258, 260; Robinson, *Dictionary of the Hausa Language*, Vol. 1, 148; Tremearne, *Ban of the Bori*, 141, 294.

Jazer

In Apollonius of Tyana's *Nuctemeron* (*Night Illuminated by Day*) Jazer is the demon who compels one to love. He is most powerful during the seventh hour.

Sources: Kelly, *Who in Hell*, 125; Lévi, *Transcendental Magic*, 392.

Jazeriel

Variations: Jareriel

Jazeriel is one of the twenty-eight demonic rulers of the lunar mansions from Enochian lore; he has dominion over the mansion Alhalre ("Wings of Virgo"). He is summoned for his willingness to help prisoners to gain their freedom. His zodiacal sign is Virgo (see ENOCHIAN RULERS OF THE LUNAR MANSIONS).

Sources: Moura, *Mansions of the Moon for the Green Witch*, 43; Scheible, Sixth and Seventh Books of Moses, 75; Webster, *Encyclopedia of Angels*, 100, 124.

Jealousy

From Babylonian, Jewish, and Solominic lore comes the demonic goddess Jealousy, the fourth of the SEVEN HEAVENLY BODIES, one of the thirty-three (or thirty-six, sources vary) elements of the cosmic ruler of the darkness. In the *Testament of Solomon* she was named as one of the seventy-two SPIRITS OF SOLOMON; she was made to dig the foundation of the temple. Described as being a female spirit, fair in appearance, she is bound and woven together with other female spirits as part of the Seven Heavenly Bodies, which are represented as a cluster of stars in the heavens. They travel about sometimes living in Lydia, or Olympus, or on a great mountain. Working in tandem with the demon STRIFE, they cause husbands to leave their wives, cause men to forget their moderation and sobriety, create rifts between brothers and sisters, divide groups of men into different factions, and separate children from their parents. Jealousy's personal adversary is the angel Balthial.

Sources: Ashe, *Qabalah*, 26; Conybeare, *Jewish Quarterly Review*, Vol. 11, 24–6.

Jeqon

Variations: Yekun ("Rebel"), YEQON, Yikon

In the *Book of Noah* Jeqon is named as one of the FALLEN ANGELS who swore allegiance to SAMIAZA, rebelled against God, took a human wife, and fathered the NEPHILIM. His name is possibly Hebrew and may mean "inciter."

Sources: Charles, *Book of Enoch*, 137; Horne, *Sacred Books and Early Literature of the East*, 115; Lumpkin, *Lost Books of Enoch*, 84; Russell, *The Devil*, 206.

Jetrel

Variations: YETAREL

In the *Book of Enoch* Jetrel is named as one of the FALLEN ANGELS who swore allegiance to SAMIAZA, rebelled against God, took a human wife, and fathered the NEPHILIM.

Sources: Charles, *Book of Enoch*, 137; Horne, *Sacred Books and Early Literature of the East*, 114; Laurence, *Book of Enoch, the Prophet*, 70.

Jezebeth

Variations: Iezabel ("chaste, intact"), Iyzebel ("unchaste" or "without cohabitation"), Jezebel

Jezebeth is the demon of falsehoods and lies.

Sources: Ashley, *Complete Book of Devils and Demons*, 59; Lumpkin, *Fallen Angels, the Watchers, and the Origin of Evil*, 128.

Jigo, plural: jiguna

Variations: Gausami, Jihu, Maker of Orphans

From the demonology of the Hausa people of West Africa comes a type of AERIAL DEVIL called a jigo, or jiguna when referred to collectively. The word in the Hausa language means "beam" or "long pole." These demons cause fever, prickly heat, and shivering. To cure a person afflicted by this demon a specific dance must be performed accompanied by a specific animal sacrifice.

Sources: Knappert, *Swahili Culture*, Vol. 2, 653; Robbison, *Dictionary of the Hausa Language*, Vol. 1, 15; Tremearne, *Ban of the Bori*, 34, 344–5.

Jikininki

In Japanese Buddhist demonology there is a species of demon known as a jikininki ("human-eating ghosts"); they are a *preta* (supernatural being) of the twenty-sixth class, considered by some to be a type of RAKSHASA or gaki. These demons are created when greedy, impious, or selfish individuals are cursed to return as a jikininki after death. They are fully aware of what they have become and hate themselves and their uncontrollable craving for corpse flesh. Looking like a decomposing cadaver with claws and glowing eyes, these nocturnal demons are the symbol of avarice, as they feed upon rotting human flesh. Scavenging the burial grounds, they live in for fresh corpses to consume, they will also steal items left as mortuary offerings in order to bribe local officials to leave them alone. Anyone who sees a jikininki will freeze with fear. They also have the magical ability to disguise themselves by day to blend into the community. The only way a jikininki can be saved is to destroy what it has become by performing a Segaki service when the opportunity arrives in the summertime and by offering remembrance prayers.

Sources: Hearn, *Oriental Ghost Stories*, 55–58; Maberry, *Zombie CSU*, 106; Roberts, *Japanese Mythology A to Z*, 62.

Jilaiya

Variations: Jilaiya of Bihār, Jalwaiya, Marchiriya

The jilaiya is a nocturnal vampiric creature or vampiric demon from the demonology of India. At night it shape-shifts into a bird and flies into a home where it drains blood from sleeping mothers and their children; however, it can only drink the blood of children whose names it hears. Because of this, mothers are careful not to call out the names of their children after dark for fear that this demon may be listening. If the jilaiya flies over the head of a pregnant woman, it will cause her to miscarry or, should the child survive, it will be born sickly and weak. These children are referred to as *jalwaiya ke chhual*.

Sources: Ashley, *Complete Book of Devils and Demons*, 67; Crooke, *Popular Religion and Folk-Lore of Northern India*, Vol. 1, 264; Griffiths, *Modern India*, 35.

Jin Laut

Jin Laut is an AQUEOUS DEVIL from Javanese mythology who is in service under the goddess of the southern ocean, Gusti Kangjeng Ratu Kidul ("Her Majesty Queen of the South"). This demon kills by sitting on a person's chest and pressing them to death. It lives in the southern oceans of Indonesia.

Sources: Fraser, *Rusembilan*, 188; Maxwell, *In Malay Forests*, 300; McHugh, *Hantu Hantu*, 122.

Joachimken

A joachimken is a type of vampiric demon from Germany.

Source: Sturm, *Von denen Vampiren oder Menschen-saugern*.

Jochmus

From the mythology of the people of the Norman Archipelago comes the AQUEOUS DEMON known as Jochmus. This demon pretended to be Saint Maclou and sat, reading books, upon the Ortach, a large square rock in the channel harbor of St. Peter's Port between Aurigny Isle and Caskets Isle. When seen there by fishermen, they would stop what they were doing and kneel to him as they passed by.

Sources: Hugo, *Toilers of the Sea*, Vol. 1, 6; Morvan, *Legends of the Sea*, 96; Rappoport, *Superstitions of Sailors*, 136; Rudwin, *Devil in Legend and Literature*, 62.

Jomjael

Variations: Yomyael ("Day of God")

Jomjael ("Day of God") is listed in the *Book of Enoch* as one of the CHIEF OF TENS who swore allegiance to SAMIAZA, rebelled against God, took a human wife, and fathered the NEPHILIM (see also FALLEN ANGELS, GRIGORI, and WATCHERS).

Sources: Beard, *Autobiography of Satan*, 113; Laurence, *Book of Enoch, the Prophet* 6; Lumpkin, *Fallen Angels, the Watchers, and the Origins of Evil*, 31.

Jove

Jove is named in the *Book of Enoch* as one of the FALLEN ANGELS who swore allegiance to SAMIAZA, rebelled against God, took a human wife, and fathered the NEPHILIM.

Source: Davidson, *Dictionary of Angels*, 161.

Julana

In Australian demonology Julana is the demon of lust.

Sources: Róheim, *Eternal Ones of the Dream*, 259–62; Savill, *Pears Encyclopaedia of Myths and Legends*, 88.

Junier

In the *Book of Enoch*, Junier is named as one of the FALLEN ANGELS who swore allegiance to SAMIAZA, rebelled against God, took a human wife, and fathered the NEPHILIM. Formerly a prince of the Order of Angels, he is now considered to be a demonic angel.

Source: Davidson, *Dictionary of Demons*, 161.

Jurasetsu-Nyo

Variations: Jurasetsu Nyoshin, Jyu-Rasetsu-Nyo, Rasetsu-nyo, Ten Cannibal Demon Women

Originating in Japanese and Buddhist demonology, Jurasetsu-Nyo ("ten demon daughters") are seen as a collection of tutelary demons, a type of RASETSU, or female RAKSHASAS who are under the service of KISHIMOJIN. These demons are said to look like beautiful women dressed in courtly attire bearing weapons or holy items, and having a mouth full of fangs. They chant magical incantations and spells collectively known as *dharanis*.

Sources vary as to the creation of these demons. Some say they were born the daughters of Kishimojin back before her conversion when she was the demon HARITI, while other sources claim they are Rakshasa or Rasetsu demons. These demons stole and murdered children to feed the children of Kishimojin. When Kishimojin converted to Buddhism so did they, vowing to protect women who practiced Lotus Sutra. The names of the ten Jurasetsu-Nyo are: Black Teeth, in her right hand she holds the Abhaya mudra, in her she left holds a halberd; Crooked Teeth holds a tray of flowers in her left hand while her right selects a flower; Flowery Teeth holds a Varada mudra pendant in her right hand and a wish-fulfilling gem in her left; Insatiable holds a scepter in her right hand and a flower vase in her left; Kunti holds a spear; Lamba wields a sword in her right hand and a sutra in her left; Many Tresses wields a halberd in her right hand and holds the Abhaya mudra in her left; Necklace Holder holds garland with both hands; Spirit Snatcher (also known as Plunderer-of-Vital-Energy-of-All-Beings) holds a staff in her right hand and wields a club in her left; and Vilamba holds cymbals in her hands.

Sources: Bakshi, *Hindu Divinities in Japanese Buddhist Pantheon*, 137, 147, 152; Hackin, *Asiatic Mythology 1932*, 435; Rosenfield, *Journey of the Three Jewels*, 59; Turner, *Dictionary of Ancient Deities*, 272.

Jutas

The *Kalevala*, the nineteenth-century epic poem comprised of Finnish and Karelian folklore and mythology and compiled by Elias Lönnrot, names Jutas as the companion or henchman to the demon LEMPO. Working in conjunction with HIISI, LEMPO, and PIRU, Jutas commands the demons and evil spirits of the forests as well as a fierce herd of moose that he turned on the hero Väinämöinen. The word *jutas* is a mild Finnish swear word.

Sources: Bray, *World of Myths*, 42; Crawford, *The Kalevala*, 739, 742; Redfield, *Gods*, 143, 160.

Kabada

Kabada is one of the forty-nine SERVITORS OF BEELZEBUB (see BEELZEBUB) listed in the *Sacred Magic of Abramelin the Mage*, book two. His name means "dullness" or "heaviness."

Sources: Ford, *Bible of the Adversary*, 93; Mathers, *Book of the Sacred Magic of Abramelin the Mage*, 108, 121; Von Worms, *Book of Abramelin*, 252, 257.

Kabandha

Variations: Danu

From Hindu mythology, Kabandha ("barrel") was originally a gandharva, a type of male nature spirit, but later became a RAKSHASA. Born the son of the goddess Sri, this demon has a very large, barrel-shaped body that is covered with hair. He has one eye and a gigantic mouth located in the middle of his chest that is filled with fierce teeth. His arms were a league long and sometimes he is depicted as having eight legs. Some sources say he became deformed when INDRA struck him with a thunderbolt; others claim he was cursed by a sage. Eventually Kabandha was slain by Rama.

Sources: Parmeshwaranand, *Encyclopaedic Dictionary of Purāṇas*, 711–12; Roveda, *Sacred Angkor*, 166–7; Williams, *Handbook of Hindu Mythology*, 166–7.

Kabersa

In the *Sacred Magic of Abramelin the Mage*, Kabersa ("wider measure") is listed as one of the fifteen SERVITORS OF PAYMON (see PAYMON).

Sources: Mathers, *Book of the Sacred Magic of Abramelin the Mage*, 108, 121; Von Worms, *Book of Abramelin*, 253, 257.

Kabhanda

Kabhanda ("rain cloud") is a RAKSHASA from Hindu mythology. He looks like a large, hair-covered, barrel-shaped being with eight arms, each a mile long, and he walks on them like a spider. He has a large and wide mouth filled with sharp teeth and only one eye. Kabhanda received his unique appearance at the hands of the god INDRA. A blow to the top of his head relocated it to the middle of his torso; Indra also cut off his legs in the same battle.

Living in the forest outside of Lanka, Kabhanda begged the hero Rama to immolate him. The fire reduced Kabhanda to ash and he was instantly reborn as a good spirit.

Sources: Baring-Gould, *Book of Were-Wolves*, 178; Icon, *Mentioning*, 247; Mack, *Field Guide to Demons, Fairies, Fallen Angels, and Other Subversive Spirits*, 131; Roveda, *Images of the Gods*, 371, 509.

Kabo Mandalat

From the demonology of the Maori people of New Caledonia comes the demonic goddess Kabo Mandalat, the demon of disease; she causes and cures elephantiasis. She looks like a female hermit crab with legs as big as coconut trees, living in the shell of an enormous litiopa melanostoma. Pott Island has a sacred place called *Tsiabouat* devoted to her and sacrificial offerings left there for her are said to prevent her from attacking.

Sources: Guirand, *New Larousse Encyclopedia of Mythology*, 450; Layard, *Stone Men of Malekula*, Vol. 1, 228; Turner, *Dictionary of Ancient Deities*, 255.

Kabotermannekens

Kabotermannekens is an AERIAL DEVIL from Flemish mythology who preys on female dairy workers by playing tricks on them.

Sources: Franklyn, *A Survey of the Occult*, 157; Shepard, *Encyclopedia of Occultism* and Parapsychology, 489; Spence, *Encyclopedia of Occultism*, 242.

Kabrakan

Kabrakan ("earthquake") is the demon of earthquakes and disappearing mountains in Mayan mythology. This gigantic being was born the son of the demonic god VUCUB CAQUIX. His brother, Zipakna, creates mountains through the use of earthquakes.

Sources: Jordan, *Dictionary of Gods and Goddesses*, 360; Lurker, *Routdelge Dictionary of Gods and Goddesses*, 209; Editors of Thelema Press, *Gnostic Kabbalah 1*, 79.

Kadolon

The *Sacred Magic of Abramelin the Mage*, book two, Kadolon listed among the one hundred eleven SERVITORS OF AMAYMON, ARITON, ORIENS, AND PAYMON (see AMAYMON, ARITON, ORIENS, and PAYMON). His name is possibly taken from Greek and may mean "a small vase or urn."

Sources: Mathers, *Book of the Sacred Magic of Abramelin the Mage*, 105, 114; Von Worms, *Book of Abramelin*, 246, 255.

Kael

Enochian lore names Kael as one of the FALLEN ANGELS who swore allegiance to SAMIAZA, rebelled against God, took a human wife, and fathered the NEPHILIM.

Sources: Godwin, *Godwin's Cabalistic Encyclopedia*, 517; Laurence, *Book of Enoch, the Prophet*, 70; Prophet, *Fallen Angels and the Origin of Evil*, 174.

Kaia

Originally a type of creation spirit, kaia became demons of destruction in Melanesian mythology. Bent on the destruction of mankind, these demons have shape-shifting abilities and take on the appearance to the natives of eels, snakes, wild pigs, or humanoid hybrids, but they prefer human form. They live in underground caves beneath volcanoes.

Sources: Hastings, *Encyclopædia of Religion and Ethics*, Vol. 9, 337; Lurker, *Dictionary of Gods and Goddesses*, 182; Mackenzie, *Myths from Melanesia and Indonesia*, 35–7; Rivers, *Medicine, Magic, and Religion*, 14–16.

Kaiamunu

Variations: Kai'a-Imunu, Kaiemunu

From the mythology of the tribal people in the Purari Delta in New Guinea, Kaiamunu appears as a piece of wickerwork, typically, a large basket with four legs, nine to twelve feet long, a tubelike body and a gaping maw; his voice is the thunder. His name in Papuan possibly means "sky" or "thunder."

Kaiamunu is the symbol of the passage from childhood to manhood. During the initiation ceremony into manhood, the spirit of Kaiamunu swallows whole young boys and then vomits them up as adult men. The ceremony is performed where there are enough boys of age in the village whose parents can afford the ceremony and the replacement of the wicker Kaiamunu. Boys are taken up river by a male relative from the mother's side of the family. They cut cane and drink the sap from it, allowing the spirit of Kaiamunu to enter into their bodies. When they return, the old wicker form of Kaiamunu is broken by the boys, burned, and then a new one is immediately built. A fire is made from the old form and its heat is used to stoke the new one. Ashes from the fire are used to mark the boys and the new wickerwork. The boys and men go back up river and spend a night there. In the morning the boys paddle back to the village and are given dog teeth necklaces. Feasting pigs are given to the relatives who sponsored the boys on their journey into manhood. Now that they are considered men, they assist in pushing a cannibal victim through the new wicker Kaiamunu. The body is then lightly roasted, followed by feasting.

Sources: Lurker, *Routledge Dictionary of Gods and Goddesses, Devils and Demons*, 98; Rose, *Spirits, Fairies, Leprechauns, and Goblins*, 174.

Kaitabha

Kaitabha is an ASURAS from Hindu mythology; it was one of the two demons born from the ear wax of the god Vishnu. With his brother, MADHU, he intended to kill the Brahma while he slept. They were slain by the god Vishnu or the goddess Uma, sources vary. After their deaths, the bodies disintegrated into twelve pieces (two heads, two torsos, four arms, and four legs), which were then thrown into the ocean where they produced a great deal of fat and marrow. These elements were used to sculpt the twelve seismic plates of the earth.

Sources: Parmeshwaranand, *Encyclopaedic Dictionary of Purānas*, Vol. 3, 716–7; Schrader, *Introduction to the Pañcaratra and the Ahirbudhnya Samhita*, 44, 127; Williams, *Handbook of Hindu Mythology*, 169.

Kaitar

In the *Sacred Magic of Abramelin the Mage*, book two, Kaitar is among the sixty-five SERVITORS OF KORE AND MAGOTH. He commands 365,000 servitors of his own. Kaitar's name is possibly Hebrew and may mean "a crown or summit."

Sources: Mathers, *Book of the Sacred Magic of*

Abramelin the Mage, 107, 119; Von Worms, *Book of Abramelin*, 250, 256.

Kakabael

Variations: AKIBEEL, Cocabel, Kakabael, Kakabael, Kakabel, Kawkabel, Kochbiel, Kokabel ("star of God"), Kokabiel, Kokb'ael, Kokos

Enochian lore names Kakabael as one of the FALLEN ANGELS who swore allegiance to SAMIAZA, rebelled against God, took a human wife, and fathered the NEPHILIM. His name is possibly Hebrew and may mean "star of God."

Some sources list him among the CHIEF OF TENS and say that he was a former angelic prince of the Order of Principalities, as well as prince regent of the stars and constellations (see GRIGORI and WATCHERS). After his fall, he became the demon of the constellations and stars and went on to teach mankind astrology, the science of the constellations.

Sources: Black, *Book of Enoch*, 120; Barton, *Journal of Biblical Literature*, Vols. 30–31, 165; Horne, *Sacred Books and Early Literature of the East*, 114; Lumpkin, *Fallen Angels, the Watchers, and the Origins of Evil*, 31; Prophet, *Fallen Angels and the Origins of Evil*, 174.

Kala Sanniya

In Sinhalese demonology Kala Sanniya creates the "black death." Like the other Sinhalese demons, he is susceptible to the DAHA-ATA SANNIYA.

Sources: Illes, *Encyclopedia of Spirits*, 875; Wirz, *Exorcism and the Art of Healing in Ceylon*, 44.

Kalab

Apollonius of Tyana's *Nuctemeron* (*Night Illuminated by Day*) names Kalab as the demon of sacred vessels. He is most powerful during the twelfth hour. His name in Egyptian translates to mean "a key."

Sources: Le Plongeon, *The Word*, 349; Lévi, *Transcendental Magic*, 509.

Kalengu

In the mythology of Northern Cameroon, *kalengu* is a word that essentially means "demons."

Source: Jones, *Evil in our Midst*, 138.

Kalevanpojat

Kalevanpojat is a type of demonic giant from Finnish mythology; the name translates from Finnish to mean "sons of Kaleva." These demons of destruction were born the sons of the giant Kaleva. They have the ability to make fertile lands barren and turn forests into swamps.

Sources: Lurker, *Routledge Dictionary of Gods and Goddesses*, 98–9; Rose, *Giants, Monsters, and Dragons*, 202.

Kali

Variations: Cause of Time, Force of Time, Kalaratri, Kali Ma ("Black Mother"), Kalikamata, Kottavei, Maha Kali, Mother of Karma, Nitya Kali, Raksha Kali, She Who is Beyond Time, Shyama Kali, Smashana Kali ("Lady of the Dead"), The Terrible

Kali is the vampiric goddess of Change and Destruction in the Hindu religion. She is attended to by the DAKIN, collectively known as the asrapas. Kali is described as having an exceptionally long tongue that she uses to drink blood with, eyes and eyebrows the color of blood, jet-black skin, and long, loose hair. She has four arms and each hand wields a sword. The only thing she wears is a necklace of human skulls and a belt made of severed arms.

Kali, whose name means "black," became a blood drinker only out of necessity. She was fighting a demon named RAKTAVIJA, and each time a drop of his blood was shed, a thousand new demons came into being and added themselves to the confrontation against the goddess. Finally, in order to defeat Raktavija and his ever-increasing horde of minions, she had to drain him dry of his blood.

Kali is a destroyer of ignorance and only kills in order to maintain the cosmic balance to things. Whenever she acts in violence, change comes in her wake. It is said that her image can be seen on a battlefield after a particularly long and bloody engagement.

As recently as the 1880s a tribe called Thugee worshipped Kali with human sacrifices. It was estimated that they were responsible for some 30,000 deaths each year that were offered in honor to the goddess. Thugee were said to garrote their victims, rob them of any valuables, drain their blood, and roast the bodies over an open fire before an image of Kali. The British claim that they were able to put a stop to that brand of worship by something short of tribal genocide. However, it has been alleged that small pockets of worshippers still practice human sacrifice to their goddess in remote areas of India.

Sources: Crooke, *Introduction to the Popular Religion*, 31, 43, 50, 78, 81–82, 91–92, 105, 152; Hyatt, *Book of Demons*, 16–7; Leeming, *Goddess*, 22–25; Masters, *Natural History of the Vampire*, 171; Turner, *Dictionary of Ancient Deities*, 257.

Kallikantzaros

Variations: Callicantzaro, Kalkes

The myth of the vampiric creature kallikantzaros is specific to the Aegean, Crete, and Messenia regions of Greece. It is believed that when a child is conceived on the Day of the Annunciation (March 25), a holy day, that exactly nine months later on Christmas Day (December 25) or anytime during the Feast of Saturnalia (December 17–23), a kallikantzaros child will be born. If the child is not immediately bound up in garlic and straw and then held over a fire until its toes are blackened, it will quickly develop into this type of vampiric creature. It will have black skin, fangs, horns, hooves, a tail, talons, or any combination of animal parts. In the Greek language, *kallikantzaros* translates to mean "beautiful centaur."

Once a year, starting on the winter solstice and then every night for the next sixteen days, the vampire is free to roam the world doing evil. By day it will hide in an underground lair away from the lethal rays of the sun. By night, it will "ride" people, much the same way that the ALP of German folklore does, stealing their sexual energy. It is also blamed for putting out hearth fires, urinating on the food stores, and sawing away at the roots of the Tree of the World.

Fortunately, for as dangerous as a kallikantzaros can be, it is balanced by having a great number of weaknesses. It is most susceptible to sunlight, and any direct exposure will kill it, as will throwing it into a bonfire. It will only willingly count as high as two, but if it can be tricked into counting to three, a holy number, it will combust into flames. Placing a colander or a knotted ball of string on your doorstep will prevent it from entering your home, as it is compelled to count the holes in the colander and untie the knots. The idea of this is to occupy its attention long enough for the sun to rise and destroy it.

The sound of church bells or Christmas carols will drive it away. Burning a handful of salt and an old shoe in the fireplace will keep it from entering your home through the chimney, as the smell of these objects burning will keep it at bay. Also, hanging the jaw of a pig on your door or over the chimney will ward it off as well.

Sources: Anthiasm, *Cyprus Village Tales*, 11–12; Blum, *The Dangerous Hour*, 46, 120; Ginzburg, *Ecstasies*, 168–69; Jackson, *Compleat Vampyre*.

Kalona

Variations: Raven Mockers

The kalona are a demonic, undead creature from the mythology of the Cherokee Indian Tribes of North Carolina, Oklahoma, and Tennessee. Created when an *adawehi*—a magical warrior who is vastly powerful and a knowledgeable conjuror or medicine man—dies, these man-sized birdlike creatures have a foot-long black beak but have the ability to shape-shift to look like a very old man or woman.

Usually nocturnal, the kalona consume the blood and entrails of the dying and those near death, most typically the elderly, grabbing up their body and throwing it around until it is badly broken, taking enjoyment in the fear and terror they cause.

At night, when flying in human form, its outstretched arms look like they are traced in fire. The kalona must constantly renew their life force or they face oblivion.

Sources: Fox, *Under the Rattlesnake*, 35; Jones, *Evil in Our Midst*, 5–9; Kilpatrick, *Night Has a Naked Soul*, 9.

Kamusil

The *Sacred Magic of Abramelin the Mage*, book two, lists Kamusil ("like a raising or elevation") among the sixty-five SERVITORS OF KORE AND MAGOTH.

Sources: Ford, *Bible of the Adversary*, 92; Mathers, *Book of the Sacred Magic of Abramelin the Mage*, 107, 118.

Kana Sanniya

In Sinhalese demonology Kana Sanniya is the demon of blindness. Masks representing this demon typically have no eyes. Like the other Sinhalese demons, he is susceptible to the DAHA-ATA SANNIYA.

Sources: Illes, *Encyclopedia of Spirits*, 875; Wirz, *Exorcism and the Art of Healing in Ceylon*, 44.

Kaous

A kaous ("burner") is a type of demonic fay. Malevolent and troublesome beings, they mount on the backs of people and ride them across the countryside, beating them with a stick. It is believed in Greek lore that if a child is conceived on March 25, it will be born on Christmas Eve as a kaous.

Source: Weigel, *Lawrence Durrell*, 34.

Kapala Sanniya

In Sinhalese demonology Kapala Sanniya is the demon of insanity. Like the other Sinhalese demons, he is susceptible to the DAHA-ATA SANNIYA.

Sources: Illes, *Encyclopedia of Spirits*, 875; Wirz, *Exorcism and the Art of Healing in Ceylon*, 44.

Kappa

Variations: Kawako

In Japan there is a vampiric creature that lives in ponds called a *kappa* ("river child"). It looks like a green child with a long nose, round eyes, tortoise shell on its back, webbed fingers and toes, and smells like fish. However, its most interesting physical feature is a dent in the top of its head deep enough to hold water. The water that sits in the dent is representative of its power. Should a kappa attempt to attack you, quickly bow to it. As it is a stickler for courteousness and ritual, the kappa will take pause to return the bow. When it does so, the water in the dent will spill out, rendering the creature powerless.

The kappa hunts from its home in the water. It waits until a cow or horse comes to drink and then it pulls the animal down into the water. As the animal drowns, the kappa bites into the animal's anus to drain it of its blood. The only time a kappa will leave its watery home is to steal cucumbers and melons, rape women, and to rip the liver out of people.

The kappa is incredibly strong and a highly skilled sumo wrestler. It is also a skilled teacher in the art of bone setting and medical skills.

It may well be that the kappa is the only vampire that has a cucumber fetish. No matter what may be happening all around it, a kappa will stop whatever it is doing to steal away with one should the opportunity arise. By writing one's family name on a cucumber and giving it to a kappa, the entire family will be temporarily protected from its attacks.

Kappas can be surprisingly courteous, honorable, and trustworthy beings. They are highly respectful of ritual and tradition, even going so far as to challenge one of its would-be victims to a wrestling match. A kappa can even be bargained with, willing to enter into contractual agreements not to attack certain people.

Sources: Davis, *Myths and Legends of Japan*, 350–52; Hyatt, *Book of Demons*, 30; Mack, *Field Guide to Demons, Fairies, Fallen Angels, and Other Subversive Spirits*, 17–18; Rowthorn, *Japan*, 511.

Karaisaba

Variations: Great Jungle Lord, Ogre Big-Eye, Ogre Eye-Extractor, Ogre Moon-Eye

In the demonology of the Warao people of Venezuela, the nocturnal Karaisaba attacks anyone who walks through or is alone in the jungle at night. If he finds someone asleep in the jungle, this demon will place them in a deep trance, then he'll place his mouth over the victim's eyes one at a time and suck them out of their head. He is described as having a large light glowing in the middle of his forehead.

Sources: Jones, *Evil in Our Midsts*, 101–3; Wilbert, *Folk Literature of the Warao Indians*, 68–70.

Karakondzol

Variations: Karakondzula

A nocturnal demon from Bulgarian lore, the

karakondzol lives in the underworld, but on the "nonbaptized" days of January 7–19 it roams the earth.

Sources: Klaniczay, *Christian Demonology and Popular Mythology*, 204; McClelland, *Slayers and their Vampires*, 57; Ugrešić, *Baba Yaga Laid an Egg*, 253.

Karasu Tengu

Variations: Demonic Crow Tengu, Kotengu, Minor Tengu

Originally, there were two types of *TENGU* ("sky dog") demons in Japan: the karasu tengu and the *YAMABUSHI TENGU*. However, as time passed, the two species of tengu demons became intertwined and developed into a singular entity.

The karasu tengu is a demon in the truest sense of the word in that it was never a human; it was always an immortal being. It looks like a small humanoid with a green face but has the beak, claws, and wings of a crow. It lives in the mountains and is malicious and fiercely territorial, attacking anyone who nears. It is particularly fond of the flesh of children, stealing them to get it if it must.

Able to shape-shift into the forms of a man, woman, or child, it is often seen carrying a ring-tipped staff called a *shakujos* that aids it in exorcisms and protects it from magic. Known for its unusual sense of humor, the karasu tengu can possess people and speak through them. An offering of bean paste and rice can appease it.

Sources: Blomberg, *Heart of the Warrior*, 35; Davis, *Myths and Legends of Japan*, 170; Hyatt, *Book of Demons*, 31; Louis-Frédéric, *Japan Encyclopedia*, 958; McNally, *Clutch of Vampire*.

Karau

Variations: Mashiramu ("bush spirit")

In the demonology of the Yupas people of Columbia, Panama, and Venezuela, Karau is the demon of devastation. He has a humanoid body that is covered in hair and has backward-turned feet, cold hands, and very large teeth. A nocturnal demon who commonly preys on women, he is said to have brought death into the world. He is a very dangerous demon who rapes and kills women, eating their flesh.

Sources: Varner, *Creatures in the Mist*, 79, 193; Wilbert, *Yupa Folktales*, 139.

Kardiakos

Kardiakos is a demon that causes gastric afflictions.

Sources: Ashley, *Complete Book of Devils and Demons*, 101; Clifford, *Malevolent Koklir*, 314; Simons, *Culture-Bound Syndromes*, 180; Society of Biblical Archæology, *Proceedings of the Society of Biblical Archaeology*, Vol. 9, 227.

Kasadya

Variations: Beqa; Kasdaya; Kasdaye; Kasdeja; Kasdeya; Kasdeys; Kashdejan; Kasyade ("observer of the hands"); Kesdeja; Kesdeya; Kisdeja, the son of the serpent; Taba'ta

In the *Book of Enoch*, Kasadya is generally believed to be female, almost human looking and having a long head of hair. She is ranked as one of the FIVE SATANS and is the physician of the WATCHERS, possibly a Cherubim before becoming a FALLEN ANGEL and the demon of abortions, snake bites, and sunstrokes (see GRIGORI). She taught mankind herbology; how to perform abortions and cure various diseases, including those of the mind; how to fight against spirits and demons; and is thought to be the creator of the blood magic that was used throughout the Middle Ages. She is the symbol of fire. Kasadya's greatest sin is considered to be her teachings of how to cure the illnesses of the mind.

Sources: Barton, *Journal of Biblical Literature*, Vols. 30–31, 164; Charlesworth, *Old Testament Pseudepigrapha*, Vol. 2, 48; Sorensen, *Possession and Exorcism in the New Testament and Early Christianity*, 60.

Kasbeel

Variations: Called BIQA ("good person") before his fall, the "angel of the oath"; Kasbel, Kazbiel

Kasbeel, "he who lies to God," is a FALLEN ANGEL who is ranked as the chief of the Oath. In Enochian lore it is said that he once asked the archangel Michael for the hidden name of God. Not surprisingly, his personal adversary is the archangel Michael.

Sources: Bamberger, *Fallen Angels*, 264; Horne, *Sacred Books and Early Literature of the East*, 115; Webster, *Encyclopedia of Angels*, 107.

Katakhana

Variations: Katakhanádes, Katalkanas, Katalkanás

On the mountainous Greek island of Crete there is a vampiric demonic spirit called a *katakhana*; its very name means *vampire*. It is created when an evil person or someone who has been excommunicated by the church dies. It is believed that after burial, a demonic spirit inhabits the body and for the next forty days is able to occupy the corpse and use it to attack islanders.

Although it can be frightened off by gunfire, the katakhana must be found, decapitated, and the head boiled in vinegar as quickly as possible to ensure its destruction. Forty days after its creation, the vampire is indestructible.

Sources: Belanger, *Sacred Hunger*, 21; Neale, *History of the Holy Eastern Church*, 1021; Rodd, *Customs and Lore*, 197; Summers, *Vampire in Europe*, 268.

Katanikethal

Variations: Katanikotael, Katanikotaêl

Katanikethal is the demon of domestic troubles and, according to the *Testament of Solomon*, creates feuds and strife in the home. To cast this demon from an area you write upon seven laurel leaves the phrase "Angel, Eae, Iae, Ieô, sons of Sabaôth, in the name of the great God let him shut up Katanikethal." Then, wash the leaves in water and sprinkle the water from the leaves throughout the house.

Sources: Ashe, *Qabalah*, 59; Belanger, *Dictionary of Demons*, 172; Conybeare, *Jewish Quarterly Review*, Vol. 11, 35.

Kataraomai

Kataraomai is a demon named in the New Testament in a curse incantation. His name is Greek and means "accursed one" or to "imprecate evil upon" or "to pray against"; however, in Hebrew it means "to curse." The main biblical terminology for the curse, words said aloud with the intent that they are empowered by forces to do the harm spoken, contain the words *kataraomai*, *katara* and *epikataratos* as well as *anathematizou* and *anathema*. The first group of words is the malediction where an agent, such as Kataraomai, is sent forth to do harm.

Sources: Middelkoop, *Curse, Retribution, Enmity as Data in Natural Religion*, 94; Reiling, *Translator's Handbook on the Gospel of Luke*, 274.

Kataris

In Apollonius of Tyana's *Nuctemeron* (*Night Illuminated by Day*), Kataris is the demon of dogs and that which is profane. He is most powerful during the tenth hour.

Source: Lévi, *Transcendental Magic*, 393, 507.

Kataron

In the *Sacred Magic of Abramelin the Mage*, Kataron ("casting down") is listed as one of the thirty-two SERVITORS OF ASTAROT (see ASTAROT).

Sources: Mathers, *Book of the Sacred Magic of Abramelin the Mage*, 106, 117; Von Worms, *Book of Abramelin*, 121, 249.

Katini

Katini ("tunic") is among the one hundred eleven SERVITORS OF AMAYMON, ARITON, ORIENS, AND PAYMON (see AMAYMON, ARITON, ORIENS, and PAYMON) named in the *Sacred Magic of Abramelin the Mage*, book two.

Sources: Mathers, *Book of the Sacred Magic of Abramelin the Mage*, 105, 113; Von Worms, *Book of Abramelin*, 244, 255.

Katolin

In the *Sacred Magic of Abramelin the Mage*, book two, Katolin ("walls") is one of the sixty-five SERVITORS OF KORE AND MAGOTH.

Sources: Mathers, *Book of the Sacred Magic of Abramelin the Mage*, 107, 118; Von Worms, *Book of Abramelin*, 249, 256.

Kawancha

In Hindu mythology Kawancha is a demon under the command of KALI and Shiva.

Sources: Koizumi, *Dance and Music in South Asian Drama*, 12, 169.

K'daai

Variations: K'daai Maqsin

In the demonology of the Yakut people of Siberia, K'daai is a fire demon and a premier blacksmith; it was he who created the art of iron working. A demon of fire, he typically heals the broken bones of heroes and tempers the souls of shamans during their initiation process. He lives in the underworld in an iron house surrounded by fire. His name is taken from Sakha, a Turkish variant.

Sources: American Folklore Society, *Journal of American Folklore*, Vol. 46, 260, 263; Illes, *Encyclopedia of Spirits*, 1041; Turner, *Dictionary of Ancient Deities*, 265.

Kele

In the *Sacred Magic of Abramelin the Mage*, book two, Kele ("to consume") is named as one of the fifteen SERVITORS OF ASMODEUS AND MAGOTH (ASMODEUS).

Sources: Mathers, *Book of the Sacred Magic of Abramelin the Mage*, 117; Von Worms, *Book of Abramelin*, 248.

Kelen

According to the *Sacred Magic of Abramelin the Mage*, book two, Kelen is one of the one hundred eleven SERVITORS OF AMAYMON, ARITON, ORIENS, AND PAYMON (see AMAYMON, ARITON, ORIENS, and PAYMON). His name is Greek and means "going swiftly, as in a race."

Sources: Mathers, *Book of the Sacred Magic of Abramelin the Mage*, 105; Von Worms, *Book of Abramelin*, 244, 256.

Kelets

Variations: Ke'lets

In the mythology of the Chukchi people of Siberia, Kelets is the demon of death. He is accompanied by his pack of hunting dogs as he preys upon mankind.

Sources: Fitzhugh, *Crossroads of Continents*, 245; Lurker, *Routledge Dictionary of Gods and Goddesses*, 101.

Kemal

The *Sacred Magic of Abramelin the Mage*, book two, includes Kemal ("desire of God") as one of the forty-nine SERVITORS OF BEELZEBUB (see BEELZEBUB).

Sources: Ford, *Bible of the Adversary*, 93; Mathers, *Book of the Sacred Magic of Abramelin the Mage*, 120; Von Worms, *Book of Abramelin*, 252, 257.

Kenaimas

In the demonology of the Macusi people of British Guiana, kenaimas are a species of AERIAL DEVIL in service under *peay-men,* or mediums, who summon them to answer questions. Said to be large, winged animal shapes, they accept offerings of tobacco water. Once summoned, these demons must be driven off by a *piai* (shaman).

Sources: Jones, *Evil in Our Midst*, 97–100; Thurn, *Among the Indians of Guiana*, 328–333.

Kephn

Variations: Swamx

The Karen people of Burma fear a demonic vampire called a kephn. It is believed to be created through the use of dark or evil magic. It is described as looking like both the floating head of a wizard, dangling its stomach beneath, or as a DOG-headed water demon. Both descriptions are always hungry for human blood and souls.

Sources: Conway, *Demonology and Devil-lore*, 41–43; Spence, *Encyclopædia of Occultism*, 421; Summers, *Vampire: His Kith and Kin*, 224.

Ker, plural: keres

Variations: Letum, Tenebrae

In ancient Greece a ker was believed to be the vampiric spirit of a deceased person who had escaped the funeral jar that it was buried in. Keres are described as hideous women wearing red robes over their dark-skinned bodies. They were said to have black wings and long white fangs and nails.

The keres are under the control of the Fates, killing only those that they are permitted to kill. The vampires begin their attack with a bloodcurdling scream, and then they dive down and drink the blood of the dying on the battlefield and rip the souls from the bodies of the dying. Vengeful, plague-carrying beings, the keres have been known to control heroes on the battlefield. It was said that the Olympian gods themselves would stand invisibly on the battlefield and swat at incoming keres to keep them off their favorite heroes.

Tar was often painted on doorways to keep a ker from entering into a home. The idea was that the tar would stick to the ker if it tried to enter into the home and it would be stuck in the door-way. To destroy one, it must be exorcised by ritual incantations.

Keres played a prominent role in Homer's *The Iliad*. On March 4, a three-day ritual called *anthesteria* was held to honor the keres, keeping them from attacking.

Sources: Berens, *Myths and Legends*, 149; Lawson, *Modern Greek Folklore*, 290; Turner, *Dictionary of Ancient Deities*, 266; Widengren, *Historia Religionum*.

Keron-Kenken

In the demonology of Patagonia, Argentina, Keron-Kenken is a species of demon known as a keren. They eat newborn children and drink the tears of their grieving mothers. The word *keren* is used to imply an evil spirit.

Sources: Ashley, *Complete Book of Devils and Demons*, 101; Hastings, *Encyclopedia of Religion and Ethics*, 669.

Kerthiel

Kerthiel ("cut off from God") is an evil and averse SEPHIROTH from the *Qlippoth* in service under Kether. He looks like a black giant.

Sources: Ford, *Liber Hvhi*, 74; Hyatt, *Book of Demons*, 49.

Keteb

Variations: Keteb Meriri, Ketev ("destruction that wastes at noonday"), the Midday demon

Keteb ("destruction") is a demon from the Jewish tradition who first appeared in the Middle Ages. The personification of the sun's heat, this demon is most powerful at midday between the 17th of *Tammuz* (July) and the 9th of *Av* (August), the twenty-one days known as *bein hameitzarim* ("between the narrow places"). Covered with hair and scales, he sees out of only one eye, the other is set in the middle of his heart. He rolls up into a ball and stalks his prey, those out in direct moonlight or sunlight during his season. He causes his victims to become overcome with exhaustion; anyone who sees him will fall down on their face. This demon lives the rest of the year walking the borderline between shadow and sun. He is only powerful in the space between darkness and sunlight.

An example of one such keteb story goes that the demon once approached a group of children on their way to school at noon, killing all but two instantly; the survivors suffered through extremely long illnesses.

It is difficult to determine if Keteb and Keteb-Meriri are two different demons or the same demon with two names.

Sources: Hammer, *Jewish Book of Days*, 356; Oesterley, *Immortality and the Unseen World*, 44–5.

Kezef

According to Hasidic lore, Kezef ("destructive anger" or "indignation") is one of the five ARCHANGELS OF PUNISHMENT and is under the command of the Angels of Death. An archangel of destruction and wrath, he commands seven divisions of Hell and 90,000 servitors. He lives at the far end of Heaven and cannot leave there, but is able to inflict punishment on the wicked. He fled when Moses cried out, "Remember Abraham, Isaac, and Israel." Kezef is not a FALLEN ANGEL.

Sources: Ashely, *Complete Book of Demons and Devils*, 78; Davidson, *Dictionary of Angels*, 351; Singer, *Jewish Encyclopedia*, 593.

Khado

Variations: Khadomas ("sky going female")

Originating in Tibetan lore, the khado are a type of dakini. They are mindless, naked, elemental female beings with green or red eyes but sporadically they will appear as an old woman. The symbol of primordial spontaneity, they operate only by their animal-like instincts, seeking out holy men in meditation to disturb them by causing flashes of inspiration and spontaneity. They live in the highest parts of mountains.

Sources: Blavatsky, *Secret Doctrine*, 271, 285; Das, *Tibetan-English Dictionary*, 112; Turner, *Dictionary of Ancient Deities*, 268.

Khanzab

Variations: Khunzab ("devil")

In Muslim demonology the khanzab is a type of Sheitan that preys upon praying Muslims by disturbing them and causing a lack of concentration. To prevent them from assault, you must ask for the protection of Allah and spit over your left shoulder three times. The word *khanzab* is Arabic and may translate to mean "strange." According to Muslim tradition, the name khanzab is forbidden to be said aloud.

Sources: Crooke, *Popular Religion and Folk-lore of Northern India*, Vol. 2, 22; Hughes, *Dictionary of Islam*, 84.

Kharisiri

Variations: Cholas, Ñakaq, PISHTACO

The Kallawaya tribes of the Andes Mountains in Bolivia never had a vampire in their mythology or lore until they encountered the Spanish and were invaded. From the start of the Spanish occupation, the Kallawaya suddenly had vampiric attacks upon their people, and the vampiric demon they named kharisiri suddenly became woven into their culture and mythology.

A kharisiri is said to attack when a person is intoxicated. It will cut a small hole near the person's liver and enter into their body. Once inside, it eats away at the fatty tissue. What it does not eat, the kharisiri gathers together and sells to bishops and hospitals.

If a person has this vampiric demon inside of them, they will run a high fever and behave oddly. Sometimes there is also a small scar on their body near the liver. Chewing on cocoa leaves is said to have the magical ability to ward off a wide variety of evil beings, including the kharisiri.

Sources: Crandon-Malamud, *From the Fat of Our Souls*, 119–23; Jones, *Evil in Our Midst*, 67–70; Kolata, *Valley of the Spirits*, 25–26; Wachtel, *Gods and Vampires*, 52–71, 146.

Khashm

Variations: Æshma dev, Khashm-dev; essentially another name for ASMODAI

In Persian and Zoroastrian demonology khashm is a DEV (see also DEVS WHO RESIDE IN MEN).

Sources: Ford, *Liber Hivi*, 70; Singer, *Jewish Encyclopedia*, Vol. 1, 220.

Khil

The *Grimoirium Verum* (*Grimoire of Truth*) allegedly written by Alibek the Egyptian in 1517, Khil is named as one of the eighteen SERVITORS OF SYRACH (see SYRACH). He has the ability to cause earthquakes.

Sources: Kuriakos, *Grimoire Verum Ritual Book*, 25; Sabellicus, *Magia Pratica*, 35.

Khism

Khism is the demon of anger and wrath in Middle Eastern demonology.

Source: Gettings, *Dictionary of Demons*, 142.

Kiel-Gelal

Variations: Ardat, Dusii, GELAL, KIEL-UDDA-KARRA, Lil, Lilhit, Nightmare; essentially another name for LILITH

In Acadian and Chaldean demonology Kiel-Gelal is a SUCCUBUS. She causes nocturnal emissions, sleepless nights, and sexual attraction between men and women.

Sources: Lea, *History of the Inquisition of the Middle Ages*, Vol. 3, 383; Masters, *Eros and Evil*, 174; Shah, *Oriental Magic*, 16.

Kiel-Udda-Karra

Variations: Ardat, Ardat-lilt ("the servant"), the concubine of the night

In Accadian demonology Kiel-Udda-Karra is a SUCCUBUS who engages in sexual intercourse with human men in order to produce offspring.

Her name in Accadian means "she who sets forth to conceive a child."

Sources: Lenormant, *Beginnings of History According to the Bible and the Traditions of Oriental Peoples*, 323; Thompson, *Semitic Magic*, 65–6.

Kigatilik

In Inuit mythology kigatilik are a species of vicious and violent fanged demons who prey upon shamans. These demons are similar to a tribe of spirits known as Claw People.

Sources: Grimal, *Larousse World Mythology*, 447; Maberry, *Vampire Universe*, 175; Turner, *Dictionary of Ancient Deties*, 271.

Kikituk

Variations: Qivittoq, Tupilak, Tupilaq, Tupilat

From the demonology of the Inuit of Alaska, North America, comes the demonic creature known as the kikituk. Using animal flesh and bones, cloth, and human flesh and bones, a sorcerer makes a *peat* doll. Then a magical charm is sung over it and as the doll becomes a living being and grows larger, it must be suckled on the sorcerer's sexual organs. Each kikituk looks different, as the sorcerer makes its creature to suit his needs or fancy. These demons are usually sent to kill the enemies of the sorcerer who made it; however, if made by a shaman, it will seek out the demon of illness who is attacking his people. Only a truly evil or utterly reckless sorcerer would set a kikituk free by releasing it into a body of water in order to cause random terror to those who walk along the shore.

This demonic creature is very similar to the Tupilak of the Inuit of Greenland.

Sources: Jones, *Evil in Our Midst*, 26–31; Kleivan, *Eskimos, Greenland and Canada*, 21–2; Lyon, *Encyclopedia of Native American Healing*, 17, 135.

Kiligil

In the *Sacred Magic of Abramelin the Mage*, book two, Kiligil is listed as one of the sixty-five SERVITORS OF KORE AND MAGOTH.

Sources: Mathers, *Book of the Sacred Magic of Abramelin the Mage*, 119; Von Worms, *Book of Abramelin*, 250, 256.

Kilik

In the *Sacred Magic of Abramelin the Mage*, book two, Kilik ("wrinkled with age") is among the one hundred eleven SERVITORS OF AMAYMON, ARITON, ORIENS, AND PAYMON (see AMAYMON, ARITON, ORIENS, and PAYMON).

Sources: Mathers, *Book of the Sacred Magic of Abramelin the Mage*, 105; Von Worms, *Book of Abramelin*, 182, 255.

Kimaris

Variations: Cimeies, CIMEJES, Cimeries, Cymries, Khem-our ("black light"), Tuvries

In the *Ars Goetia*, the first book of the *Lemegeton*, Kimaris, a nocturnal demon, is ranked as a marquis and commands twenty legions and all the demonic spirits of Africa (see MARQUIS OF HELL). He is summoned for his ability to assist people crossing rivers and seas quickly. He also finds lost and hidden treasures; teaches grammar, logic, and rhetoric; and trains men to be warriors like himself. A good combatant, this demon appears before his summoner as a warrior riding upon a black horse. His zodiacal sign is Capricorn.

There is some uncertainty as to the etymology of Kimaris's name. If it is Hebrew it would mean "darkness of God," but if it is Sanskrit it would translate to mean "without words" or "wordless."

Sources: Crowley, *The Goetia*, 63; De Laurence, *Lesser Key of Solomon, Goetia*, 43; DuQuette, *The Key to Solomon's Key*, 193; Godwin, *Godwin's Cabalistic Encyclopedia*, 163.

Kings of Hell

There are eighty-nine named kings mentioned in the various grimoires and demonologies. They are ABADDON, ABALAM, ABRASAX, ADRAMALECK, ADRAMELECH, ADRAMELECH, AESMA DAEVA, AGARES, ALUGA, AMAIMON, AMAYMON, AMENADIEL, AMMON, AMOYMON, AMY, AN, ANDHAKA, ARCAN, ASELIEL, ASHMODAI, ASMODAI, ASMODAY, ASMODEUS ZAVEHE, ASYRIEL, BAAL, BAALAM, BAEL, BALAM, BALI, BALKIN, BARBAS (MARBAS), BAYEMON, BEBALL, BELETH, BILETH, BOTIS, BUER, BYLETH, CAACRINOLAAS, CAIM, CARNESIEL, CASPIEL, CORSON, CURSON, DEMORIEL, EEMEN, EGYM, EMMA-O, ER MO, FORCAS, FORFAX, GAAP, GLACIA LABOLAS, GOAP, GORSON, GUAYOTA, HAAGENTI, HIRANYAKASHIPU, HIRANYAKSHA, IGRAT, INDIREN, KUBERA, LAVNASURA, MADHU, MAHASURA, MALPHAS, MAYMON, MORAX, NERGAL, OG, ORIENS, OSE, PAYMON, PAZUZU, PURSON, RAJA HANTU, RAVANA, REAHU, SAMMAEL, SATAN, SUTH, Valac (UALAC), VARSAVARTI, VINÉ, Yama, YEN WANG, ZAGAM, ZAPAN, ZIMIMAR.

Sources: Hyatt, *Book of Demons*, 73; Illes, *Encyclopedia of Spirits*, 572; Scott, *London Magazine*, Vol. 5, 378.

Kingu

Variations: Qingu

In Babylonian and Sumerian demonology Kingu is the second consort of and commands the army of the demonic goddess TIAMAT. According to the Babylonian creation epic *Enuma*

Elish, which may date back as far as 1100 B.C.E., he was gifted the Tablets of Destiny by Tiamat. Eventually he was slain by the god Marduk and his blood was used to create mankind so that he could not be resurrected. His name in ancient Akkadian means "unskilled laborer."

Sources: Budge, *Babylonian Legends of Creation*, 17–9; Jastrow, *Religion of Babylonia and Assyria*, 420–3; Jeremias, *Old Testament in the Light of the Ancient East*, Vol. 1, 145–51; Lurker, *Dictionary of Gods and Goddesses*, 190.

Kipokis

The *Sacred Magic of Abramelin the Mage*, book two, includes Kipokis ("like overflowing") as one of the forty-nine SERVITORS OF BEELZEBUB (see BEELZEBUB).

Sources: Ford, *Bible of the Adversary*, 93; Mathers, *Book of the Sacred Magic of Abramelin the Mage*, 108; Von Worms, *Book of Abramelin*, 252.

Kiriel

Variations: Ciriel

The *Theurgia Goetia*, the second book of the *Lemegeton*, names Kiriel as one of the fifteen SERVITORS OF BARMIEL (see BARMIEL). A diurnal duke, he is also one of the twenty-eight demonic rulers of the lunar mansions (see also ENOCHIAN RULERS OF THE LUNAR MANSIONS and DUKES OF HELL).

Sources: Gettings, *Dictionary of Demons*, 142; McLean, *Treatise on Angel Magic*, 42; Von Goethe, *Goethe's Letters to Zelter*, 377.

Kirik

In *Ars Goetia*, the first book of the *Lemegeton*, Kirik ("mantle or stole") is one of the fifty-three SERVITORS OF ASHTAROTH AND ASMODEUS (see ASHTAROTH and ASMODEUS).

Sources: Mathers, *Book of the Sacred Magic of Abramelin the Mage*, 115; Von Worms, *Book of Abramelin*, 121, 247.

Kishi

The Kimbundu people of Angola believe in a fast and agile vampiric AQUEOUS DEMON named kishi. In its true form it has two heads or appears as a hyena with large teeth and powerful jaws. It can shape-shift into a man or a skull. In its human guise it will take a wife and impregnate her as quickly as possible. After she gives birth to its child, the kishi will kill her. It will then raise the two-headed monstrosity (one head of a man and the other of a hyena) in its home under the sea, where the child will become a flesh eater like its father.

Sources: Chatelain, *Folk-Tales of Angola*, 57, 85, 97; Mack, *Field Guide to Demons, Fairies, Fallen Angels,*

and Other Subversive Spirits, 70–71; Stookey, *Thematic Guide to World Mythology*, 138.

Kishimojin

Variations: Kali Devi, Kangimo, Karitei, Karitei-mo, Kishibojin, Kishimo-Jin, Mother of Demons Who Repents and Convert to Buddhism. Her demon name is Hariti ("mother of demons")

Originating in India and absorbed into Japanese and Buddhist demonology, Kishimojin ("Mother goddess of the demons") was converted by the Buddha and is now considered to be a goddess, the patron deity of little children and easy childbirth.

As a demon she had a monstrous aspect, but as a goddess she is portrayed as a mother nursing a child while holding a pomegranate in her hand, the symbol of love and feminine fertility. Kishimojin represents the Buddha's appeal to compassion. When she was a demon, she preyed upon children whenever the opportunity presented itself, abducting them and feeding them to her own children; sources vary widely on the number of children she had, with numbers ranging from fifty to 10,000. With so many mouths to feed, she often recruited the assistance of the JURASETSU-NYO.

Sources: Hackin, *Asiatic Mythology 1932*, 435; Roberts, *Japanese Mythology from A to Z*, 69; Rose, *Giants, Monsters, and Dragons*, 168, 204.

Kiskil

Variations: Ki-sikil-lil-la-ke ("Lila's maiden, or beloved"), Ki-sikil-ud-da-ka-ra ("the maiden who has stolen the light"), Kiskil-Lilla

Possibly another name for LILITH, Kiskil is a nocturnal female demon from Sumerian demonology. She was named as a "gladdener of all hearts" and "maiden who screeches constantly" in the ancient Mesopotamian poem *The Epic of Gilgamesh*, dating back possibly as far as 2150 B.C.E. She had dominion over the moon and was eventually slain by the cultural hero Gilgamesh.

Sources: Hurwitz, *Lilith: The First Eve*, 50–1; Langdon, *Semitic Mythology*, 362; Lurker, *Routledge Dictionary of Gods and Goddesses*, 103.

Kitsune

Variations: HULI JING

The kitsune, a type of lewd and wanton species of demon from Japanese demonology, is rarely seen in its true form, that of a fox or humanoid fox, as it usually appears as a beautiful woman in order to better prey upon men. This demonic creature commits terrible acts of mischief, such as cutting off women's hair and shaving men's heads while they sleep. It lures travelers astray and possesses humans. If, while in human form, a kitsune drinks too much wine, it will revert to its true form.

These beings have the ability to cast magic and cause rain during bright and sunny days. It can shape-shift into human form if it twitches its tail, places a skull on its head, and bows to the moon. If the skull does not fall off, it becomes a bewitchingly beautiful woman. Once transformed, it will seduce a man and drain his energy from him.

An annual festival called *Kitsune-okuri* ("fox-expelling") is held in the Totomi province of Japan each January 14 to prevent their attacks for the coming year. Priests lead a procession of villagers carrying straw foxes that are taken outside of town and buried.

Sources: Bathgate, *Fox's Craft in Japanese Religion and Folklore*, 18–20, 34; Mack, *Field Guide to Demons, Fairies, Fallen Angels, and Other Subversive Spirits*, 128–30; Rosen, *Mythical Creatures Bible*, 255, 370.

Klepoth

In the *Grimoirium Verum* (*Grimoire of Truth*) allegedly written by Alibek the Egyptian in 1517, Klepoth is named as one of the eighteen SERVITORS OF SYRACH (see SYRACH).

Sources: Kuriakos, *Grimoire Verum Ritual Book*, 25; Sabellicus, *Magia Pratica*, 35.

Klothod

Variations: Klothon

In Babylonian, Jewish, and Solominic lore, the demonic goddess Klothod ("battle") is ranked as the third of the SEVEN HEAVENLY BODIES and one of the thirty-three (or thirty-six, sources vary) elements of the Cosmic Ruler of the Darkness. In the *Testament of Solomon* she was said to be one of the demons that were bound to work on the temple, digging its foundations (see SPIRITS OF SOLOMON). She is one of seven female spirits that are fair in appearance and bound and woven together, and represented as a cluster of stars in the heavens. They travel about sometimes living in Lydia, or Olympus, or on a great mountain. Klothod has the ability to cause the well-behaved to scatter and fall afoul of one another. Her personal adversary is the angel Marmarath.

Sources: Conybeare, *Jewish Quarterly Review*, Vol. 11, 24–6; Fleg, *Life of Solomon*, 107.

Knights of Hell

Only four named demons hold the official rank of knight in the various demonic hierarchies and grimoires: CHAMO, ELIGOR, FORCAS, and LEONARD. However, ABIGOR and EURYNOME are described as appearing before their summoner dressed as knights.

Sources: Belanger, *Dictionary of Demons*, 129; Guiley, *The Encyclopedia of Demons and Demonology*, 2; Lewis, *Encyclopedia of Religion, Folklore, and Popular Culture*, 18; Melton, *Encyclopedia of Occultism and Parapsychology*, 315; Wedeck, *Treasury of Witchcraft*, 96.

Kobal

The demon Kobal is a dramatist and manager of the infernal theater; he holds the position of entertainment director of Hell and stage manager of the Masters of the Revels. An INCUBUS and the demon patron of comedians, he tempts men with fraud and pretense. Kobal is under the command of LILITH.

Sources: Belanger, *Dictionary of Demons*, 176; Chambers, *Book of Days*, 723; Ripley, *The American Cyclopaedia: A Popular Dictionary of General Knowledge*, 795.

Kok-Lir

Variations: Dyaks, Koklir, Langsuyar, PONTIANAK

In the demonology of the Indonesian archipelago and Malay, a kok-lir is a species of demonic vampire. Created when a woman dies in parturition or postpartum, it enacts its vengeance of having died by tearing off its male prey's penis and testicles and consuming his sexual vitality.

Sources: Ashley, *Complete Book of Devils and Demons*, 67; Becker, *Imagination of Reality*, 155; McHugh, *Hantu Hantu*, 121.

Kolam

In the *Sacred Magic of Abramelin the Mage*, book two, Kolam ("shame" or "to be ashamed") is listed as one of the sixty-five SERVITORS OF KORE AND MAGOTH.

Sources: Mathers, *Book of the Sacred Magic of Abramelin the Mage*, 109, 119; Von Worms, *Book of Abramelin*, 250, 256.

Kolofe

Kolofe ("height of achievement" or "summit") is one of the thirty-two SERVITORS OF ASTAROT (see ASTAROT) named in the *Sacred Magic of Abramelin the Mage*.

Sources: Mathers, *Book of the Sacred Magic of Abramelin the Mage*, 106, 117; Von Worms, *Book of Abramelin*, 249, 256.

Kommasso

Kommasso is a TERRESTRIAL DEVIL from Burmese demonology. The demon of trees, he lives in trees.

Sources: Shepard, *Encyclopedia of Occultism and Parapsychology*, 729; Spence, *Encyclopedia of Occultism*, 82, 244.

Kora Sanniya

In Sinhalese demonology Kora Sanniya is the demon of lameness and paralysis. He is depicted in ceremonial masks as having one side of his face slack and loose, as if motion there were lost due to a stroke. Kora Sanniya, like the other Sinhalese demons, are susceptible to the DAHA-ATA SAN-NIYA.

Sources: Illes, *Encyclopedia of Spirits*, 875; Wirz, *Exorcism and the Art of Healing in Ceylon*, 44.

Koschei the Deathless

Variations: Koshchei, Kostchtchie

In Russian folklore Koschei the Deathless is a greedy demonic being who is described as having a skull for a head and a fleshless body with a pulsing yellow heart. He wears a black hood and cape and carries an iron club that he uses to beat anyone he sees. His name in Russian means "immortal."

It is said in folklore that his death has been transferred to the inside of a needle that has been inserted inside an egg which has been placed in a box that has been hidden inside a tree. When the needle is broken, he will die. Koschei is attracted to beautiful women and hates anyone prosperous. He lives in the Caucasus and Koskel mountains with his treasure hoard.

Sources: Coxwell, *Siberian and Other Folk-Tales*, 768–75; Dixon-Kennedy, *Encyclopedia of Russian and Slavic Myth and Legend*, 154–5; Yearsley, *Folklore of Fairytale*, 131–2, 143.

Kosh

In the demonology of the people of the southern Congo region, Kosh is a TERRESTRIAL DEMON of the forest.

Source: Spence, *Encyclopedia of Occult and Parapsychology*, 730.

Kravyad

In India the word *kravyad* ("flesh eater") refers to anything that consumes flesh, including animals, cannibals, and funeral pyres. There is also a type of vampiric spirit that is called kravyad because it feeds off human flesh. It is said to be a hideously ugly thing with teeth made of iron.

Sources: Dowson, *Classical Dictionary of Hindu Mythology and Religion, Geography, History, and Literature*, 160; Feller, *Sanskrit Epics' Representation of Vedic Myths*, 91, 117; Macdonell, *Vedic Mythology*, 164; Roy, *The Later Vedic Economy*, 223–34; Singh, *Vedic Mythology*, 34–5, 117; Turner, *Dictionary of Ancient Deities*, 26, 275.

Kubera

Variations: Dhanapati, Kuber, Kuvera

Originally the chief of all evil creatures living in darkness, Kubera later became a god in Hindu mythology, the guardian of the treasures of the gods, the world guardian, and king of the Yakshas. He is also one of the eight guardians of the world, the Ashta-Dikpalas. He is described as looking like a hideous dwarf with pasty white skin, three legs, and eight teeth, who rides upon a magical flying chariot called Pushpak. He is an opportunist, but has difficulty moving because of his physical deformities.

Kubera has a host of servitor attendants. The males are called Kinnaras, the female counterparts are called the Kinnoris. He lives in an opulent palace on Mount Kailash in the Himalayas.

Sources: Hyatt, *Book of Demons*, 20; Shashi, *Encyclopaedia Indica*, 1112–3; Sutherland, *Disguises of the Demon*, 20, 33, 40, 51–54.

Kucedre

Variations: KULSHEDRA

Kucedre is an aquatic, demonic hag with enormous, pendulous breasts from Albanian mythology (see AQUEOUS DEVIL) but she has the ability to shape-shift into a flying dragon that spits fire. No matter her appearance, Kucedre uses her urine to contaminate water supplies and cause drought. She lives in or near water sources. Offerings of human sacrifices are made in hopes of appeasing her.

Sources: Elsie, *Dictionary of Albanian Religion, Mythology, and Folk Culture*, 154–6; Isaacs, *Dragons or Dinosaurs*, 122; Lurker, *Dictionary of Gods and Goddesses*, 197; Rose, *Giants, Monsters, and Dragons*, 214, 240.

Kud

Kud is the demon of darkness and evil in Korean mythology. His personal adversary is the god of light, Palk.

Sources: Littleton, *Gods, Goddesses, and Mythology*, Vol. 6, 792; Lurker, *Routledge Dictionary of Ancient Deities*, 105.

Kuei

Variations: K'uei

In China, there is a vampiric demon known as a kuei. Horrific in appearance, it possesses and animates the corpse of the recently deceased. It seeks out bodies that did not have proper burial rites said for them or performed properly. As it ages, the kuei gains the ability to fly with its corpse, but until that time, it is limited as to how it can attack. The kuei is incapable of climbing over even the simplest of walls or fencing.

Sources: Latourette, *The Chinese*, 36, 164; Strickmann, *Chinese Magical Medicine*, 24–26, 72–75; Summers, *Vampire: His Kith and Kin*, 237; Werne, *China of the Chinese*, 231–33.

Kuk

Variations: Bringer of Light, Keku

In the Ogdoad cosmogony of ancient Egypt,

Kuk ("darkness") is the demonic god of chaos, obscurity, and the unknown. Androgynous in appearance, the female aspect is known as Kauket or Keket and is depicted as a snake-headed woman; the male aspect is depicted as a frog-headed man. Kuk is the symbol of the primordial concept of darkness.

Sources: Lurker, *Routledge Dictionary of Gods and Goddesses*, 105, 142; *Studies in the History of Religions*, Vol. 26, 113.

Kukudhi

Variations: Kukuth

A kukudhi ("elfin") is a female demon of disease and pestilence in Albanian mythology created whenever an evil miser dies. These demons carry and spread the plague. Kukudhi is also a word used to describe a vampire that has been undead for more than thirty years.

Sources: Elsie, *Dictionary of Albanian Religion, Mythology, and Folk Culture*, 153; Lurker, *Routledge Dictionary of Ancient Gods and Goddesses*, 106.

Kul

Variations: Hal, Holt, Kul-Ancs, Kul-Ater

In Hungarian mythology Kul ("death" or "sickness") is a species of demonic insect that will attack anyone who walks through the forest. It drops down from a tree branch, lands atop the head of its victim, and from there it begins to bore through the skull and into the brain.

Sources: Maberry, *They Bite*, 355; Sri RAM, *Theosophist Magazine*, January 1962–August 1962, 42–3.

Kulshedra

Variations: BOLLA, Bullar, KUCEDRE

Kulshedra is a demonic dragon with faceted silver eyes, four legs, a long, serpentine body, and small wings. When it is 12 years old it grows horns and nine tongues, its wings increase in size, and it gains the ability to breathe fire. Occasionally it is described as an enormous woman covered with hair and having very large breasts. Human sacrifices were once made to this creature to prevent it from attacking.

This demon of drought from Albanian mythology sleeps all year, waking only on Saint George's Day (April 23) to kill the first human it sees and then it returns to sleep. Of note, Saint George's Day marks the beginning of summer and the new year in ancient Albania. In more modern times it is celebrated on May 6.

Sources: Elsie, *Dictionary of Albanian Religion, Mythology, and Folk Culture*, 154–6; Lurker, *Routledge Dictionary of Gods and Goddesses*, 106; Rose, *Spirits, Fairies, Gnomes, and Goblins*, 188, 244.

Kumbhakarna

Kumbhakarna is a RAKSHASA that is said to stand 420,000 meters (1,377,952.75 feet) tall. Because he was once tongue-tied, he misspoke a boon granted to him; this caused him to sleep for six months and to be awake only for a day. When he awakens he is ravenously hungry. Nearly invulnerable, even sliced-off pieces of him can still fight in battle.

Sources: Macdonald, *Iliad of the East*, 269–83; Mack, *Field Guide to Demons, Fairies, Fallen Angels, and Other Subversive Spirits*, 119–20; Williams, *Handbook of Hindu Mythology*, 192.

Kumeatêl

Variations: Kumateal, Kumeatel

In the *Testament of Solomon*, Kumeatêl is named as one of the seventy-two SPIRITS OF SOLOMON. He is one of the thirty-six demons of disease. Kumeatêl is the demon of drowsiness and shivering and will immediately leave if he hears the phrase "Zôrôêl, imprison Kumeatêl."

Sources: Ashe, *Qabalah*, 47, 60; Belanger, *Dictionary of Demons*, 177; Conybeare, *Jewish Quarterly Review*, Vol. 11, 36.

Kunopegos

The AQUEOUS DEVIL Kunopegos ("dog-flow" or "cruel sea-horse demon") looks like a seahorse and preys upon the ships of the sea, causing seasickness. His personal adversary is the angel Jameth.

Sources: Butler, *Ritual Magic*, 33; Frankfurter, *Evil Incarnate*, 25; Paine, *Hierarchy of Hell*, 65.

Kunospaston

Variations: Kunos Paston, Kunospaston Kunopaston

In Solomonic lore, Kunospaston is the demon of the sea (see AQUEOUS DEVIL); he is in service under Beelzeboul and was listed among the SPIRITS OF SOLOMON. Appearing as a seahorse with a powerful speaking voice, this greedy demon preys upon sailing vessels carrying numerous men and cargos of gold or silver. He causes problems for those who sail the sea; in wave form he crashes down on vessels in order to sink them, offering the crew up to Beelzeboul and keeping the cargo of gold and silver for himself. Kunospaston has the ability to cause seasickness and can shapeshift into a human or a giant wave, and he can create whirlpools.

Without water, he cannot stay on this plane for more than three days. Solomon put him in a phial with ten jugs of seawater and sealed them with his ring. Then he placed the container in the temple. Kunospaston's personal adversary is the angel Iameth.

Sources: Conybeare, *Testament of Solomon*, 1–45; Davidson, *Dictionary of Angels*, 168.

Kupe-Dyeb

Kupe-Dyeb are a race of nocturnal, subterranean, demonic batlike people from the mythology of the Apinaye people of the Amazon rainforest. These demons feed upon corpses and prefer to encourage the Apinaye people to go to war so there will be bodies littering the jungle floor. If the Apinaye are not at war, the Kupe-Dyeb will hunt them. Living in the caves of Bat Mountain located in the Sierra of Sao Vicente, the lair of the Kupe-Dyeb is distinctive, as it is located at the base of the mountain and has a large windowlike opening above the entrance.

Sources: Jones, *Evil in Our Midst*, 71–75; Wilbert, *Folk Literature of the Gê Indians*, 327–8.

Kur

Variations: Körmöcz

Kur is both the personification of the evil entity that spreads illness as well as personifying the home of the dead, the river of the dead, and the space between the primeval sea and Earth (Ma) in Sumerian mythology. The demon of disease and sickness, he is described as having a monstrous appearance.

In Sumerian, Kur's name translates literally as "mountain"; in Finnish and Hungarian it is essentially another name for SATAN but it can also refer to a mountain or the staircase that ascends from the underworld to Heaven.

Sources: Black, *Gods, Demons, and Symbols of Ancient Mesopotamia*, 36, 114; Johnston, *Religions of the Ancient World*, 478; Kramer, *Sumerian Mythology*, 110–19.

Kuri

Variations: Yandu, YERRO

Kuri is the demon of paralysis in the demonology of the Hausa people of West Africa. He appears as a black hyena spirit. A specific dance must be performed and specific animal sacrifices must be offered in order to save one of his victims.

Sources: Oesterreich, *Possession, Demoniacal and Other Among Primitive Races*, 261–3; Tremearne, *Ban of the Bori*, 270–281.

Kurtael

Variations: Kurtaêl

The *Testament of Solomon* names Kurtael as one of the seventy-two SPIRITS OF SOLOMON that were bound into service and made to build his temple. This demon causes colic and pains in the bowels but will leave immediately if he hears the phrase "Iaôth, imprison Kurtaêl."

Sources: Butler, *Ritual Magic*, 31; Conybeare, *Jewish Quarterly Review*, Vol. 11, 35; Fleg, *Life of Solomon*, 66.

Kushiel

Kushiel ("rigid one of God") is one of the seven ANGELS OF PUNISHMENT who are under the command of the ARCHANGELS OF PUNISHMENT, according to Jewish folklore. A presiding angel of Hell, Kushiel punishes the nations with his whip of fire. He is said to live in the third heaven.

Sources: Davidson, Dictionary of Angels, 351; Mew, *Eclectic Magazine of Foreign Literature, Science, and Art*, Vol. 115, 407.

Kworrom

Kworrom is a TERRESTRIAL DEVIL from the demonology of the Hausa people of West Africa. He causes people to trip and stumble and lives under the roots of trees.

Sources: Knappert, *African Mythology*, 106; Tremearne, *Ban of the Bori*, 342.

Labartu

Variations: Lamashtu, referred to as the "seven witches" in magical incantations

Labartu ("hag demon") is a demonic ghost from Assyrian demonology. Born the daughter of Anu, a sky god, this demon who lives in the marshes and mountains blights plants, causes NIGHTMARES and miscarriages, consumes human flesh and blood, dries up rivers and streams, sends disease, and steals children.

On magical amulets Labartu is portrayed as a lion-headed or bird-headed woman kneeling on a donkey, while holding a serpent in each hand and suckling dogs or pigs at her breasts. Wearing a charm of protection will work against her if the mother and newborn child are kept together at all times. Similar to the Sumerian DIMME, Labartu may be an early interpretation of LILITH.

Sources: Jastrow, *Religion of Babylonia and Assyria*, 260; Sorensen, *Possession and Exorcism in the New Testament and Early Christianity*, 27–8.

Labassu

Variations: Dimmea, Labasu

Labassu is a female demonic phantom from Assyrian demonology and is often associated with being a member of a trio of female demons along with Ahchazu and LABARTU. Labassu is known to be particularly evil, although scholars are not sure as to against whom or what. In art, this demon may be depicted as a goat. An Assyrian demon, her name may possibly be Sumerian and mean "to be clothed."

Sources: Jastrow, *Religion of Babylonia and Assyri*, 260; Rogers, *Religion of Babylonia and Assyria*, 147.

Labezerin

In Apollonius of Tyana's *Nuctemeron* (*Night Illuminated by Day*), Labezerin is the demon of success. He is most powerful during the second hour.

Sources: Kelly, *Who in Hell*, 137; Lévi, *Transcendental Magic*, 404.

Labisi

In the *Sacred Magic of Abramelin the Mage*, Labisi ("the flesh in clothed") is listed as one of the twenty SERVITORS OF AMAYMON (see AMAYMON).

Sources: Sources: Mathers, *Book of the Sacred Magic of Abramelin the Mage*, 109, 122; Von Worms, *Book of Abramelin*, 124, 255, 257.

Laboneton

In the *Sacred Magic of Abramelin the Mage*, book two, Laboneton is listed as one of the sixty-five SERVITORS OF KORE AND MAGOTH. His name is possibly Greek and may mean "to grasp or seize."

Sources: Mathers, *Book of the Sacred Magic of Abramelin the Mage*, 107, 118; Von Worms, *Book of Abramelin*, 123, 250.

Laboux

In the *Ars Goetia*, the first book of the *Lemegeton*, Laboux is listed as one of the fifty-three SERVITORS OF ASHTAROTH AND ASMODEUS (see ASHTAROTH and ASMODEUS). Possibly Latin, his name may mean "laborious."

Sources: Mathers, *Book of the Sacred Magic of Abramelin the Mage*, 115; Von Worms, *Book of Abramelin*, 247, 256.

Labus

Apollonius of Tyana's *Nuctemeron* (*Night Illuminated by Day*) lists Labus as the demon of inquisitions. He is most powerful during the twelfth hour.

Sources: Gettings, *Dictionary of Demons*, 144; Lévi, *Transcendental Magic*, 509.

Lagasuf

The *Sacred Magic of Abramelin the Mage*, book two, lists Lagasuf as one of the one hundred eleven SERVITORS OF AMAYMON, ARITON, ORIENS, AND PAYMON (see AMAYMON, ARITON, ORIENS, and PAYMON). This name is possibly Hebrew in origin and may mean "in paleness; pining away."

Sources: Mathers, *Book of the Sacred Magic of Abramelin the Mage*, 105, 114; Von Worms, *Book of Abramelin*, 246, 256.

Laginx

In *Ars Goetia*, the first book of the *Lemegeton*, Laginx is listed as one of the fifty-three SERVITORS OF ASHTAROTH AND ASMODEUS (see ASHTAROTH and ASMODEUS).

Sources: Mathers, *Book of the Sacred Magic of Abramelin the Mage*, 106, 115; Von Worms, *Book of Abramelin*, 247, 256.

Lahash

Lahash and fellow angel Zakum commanded one hundred eighty-four myriads of angels. Lahash was the angel who tried to intercept Moses's prayer to God; however, he had a change of heart and admitted his crime. For attempting to intervene in the will of God, Lahash was bound in chains of fire, given sixty lashes with a whip of fire, and cast out of Heaven by SAMMAEL (see FALLEN ANGELS). It is unknown what punishment ZAKUN and the angels he led received.

Sources: Davidson, *Dictionary of Angels*, 325; Ginzberg, *Legends of the Jews*, Vol. 3, 434.

Laila

Variations: Lailahel, Lajil, Layla ("night"), Leliel ("jaws of God")

In Cabalistic lore Laila ("night"), the prince of conception, was appointed to guard the spirits of newborn children at their birth. He is the equal of LILITH, the DEMONESS of conception. A nocturnal demon, he physically fought for Abraham when he was battling kings. Although he is cited as being the demon of the night, scholars are uncertain if Laila is a good or evil angel.

Sources: Davidson, *Dictionary of Angels*, 172; Hurwitz, *Lilith, the First Eve*, 53, 87.

Lamael

In the *Ars Paulina*, book three of the *Lemegeton*, Lamael is ranked as a chief duke who commands three thousand servitors (see DUKES OF HELL). He is listed as one of the twelve SERVITORS OF AMENADIEL (see AMENADIEL).

Sources: Guiley, *Encyclopedia of Demons and Demonology*, 7; Peterson, *Lesser Key of Solomon*, 62; Trithemius, *Steganographia*, 7.

Lamalon

In the *Sacred Magic of Abramelin the Mage*, book two, Lamalon is listed among the forty-nine SERVITORS OF BEELZEBUB (see BEELZEBUB). His name is likely Hebrew and means "declining" or "turning aside."

Sources: Ford, *Bible of the Adversary*, 93; Mathers, *Book of the Sacred Magic of Abramelin the Mage*, 120; Von Worms, *Book of Abramelin*, 252, 257.

Lamarion

In the *Sacred Magic of Abramelin the Mage*, book two, Lamarion is one of the forty-nine SERVITORS OF BEELZEBUB (see BEELZEBUB).

Sources: Ford, *Bible of the Adversary*, 93; Mathers, *Book of the Sacred Magic of Abramelin the Mage*, 107, 120; Von Worms, *Book of Abramelin*, 251, 257.

Lamašhtu

Variations: DIMME, Lamashto, Lamastu, Lamatu; in incantations Lamašhtu is referred to as "the Seven Witches"

At least four thousand years ago in ancient Babylon, there was a vampiric, demonic goddess by the name of Lamašhtu. She was born the daughter of the sky god Anu and was described as a woman with a hairy body, the head of a lioness (or bird), the ears and teeth of a donkey, wings, and long eagle talons for fingers. She was said to ride upon an ass, carrying a double-headed snake in each hand. In art she was depicted as suckling dogs and pigs at her breasts.

If crops failed or rivers ran dry it was believed to be her doing. When Lamašhtu grew hungry she would seek out a pregnant woman and touch her belly seven times, causing the woman to miscarry. Then Lamašhtu would eat the aborted fetus. If opportunity presented itself, she would kidnap a newborn child and nurse it from her own poisoned breast.

The most feared goddess of her time because she was known as a remorseless baby-killer, Lamašhtu would also strike down men at random, as well as send haunting NIGHTMARES and fatal diseases.

Pregnant mothers would often wear the amulet of PAZUZU, a wind demon, as he would often clash with the goddess. Mothers who did not want the protection of a demon had the option of offering Lamašhtu gifts of broaches, centipedes, combs, and fibulae. These gifts, along with a clay image of the goddess, would be put in a model boat, and in ritualistic fashion be set adrift down a river in the hopes that it would reach Lamašhtu in her underworld home.

For all the fear the goddess inspired, archeologists have never discovered any evidence of a single sanctuary, shrine, or temple erected to her; not even a mention of one exists in any writings that were left behind. There have, however, been numerous prayers that can be said to invoke against Lamašhtu; here is an example of one:

Great is the daughter of Heaven who tortures
    babies
Her hand is a net, her embrace is death
She is cruel, raging, angry, predatory

A runner, a thief is the daughter of Heaven
She touches the bellies of women in labor
She pulls out the pregnant woman's baby
The daughter of Heaven is one of the gods,
    her brothers
With no child of her own.
Her head is a lion's head
Her body is a donkey's body
She roars like a lion
She constantly howls like a demon-dog.

Sources: McNally, *Clutch of Vampires*; Nemet-Nejat, *Daily Life in Ancient Mesopotamia*, 128–32; Schwartz, *Tree of Souls*, 216; Sorensen, *Possession and Exorcism in the New Testament and Early Christianity*, 27–8; Turner, *Dictionary of Ancient Deities*, 285–86.

Lamassu

Variations: Ach-Chazu, Alu, Dimmea, Dimme-Kur, GALLU, Labashu, Lama, Lamastu, Lammassu, Mula, Mulla

From Acadian, Babylonian, and Mesopotamian demonology comes the protective deity, demon, or creature known as Lamassu. In Acadia she was described as a bare-chested woman suckling a DOG or a pig who inflicted infants with diseases and fevers. In Babylon she was said to have a bull's body, eagle wings, and a human head, and she was considered to be a protective being. In Mesopotamia, however, she was considered a creature with eagle wings, a lion's body, and a human man's head, and she guarded temples and attacked anyone who was not either of the purest good or of the purest evil.

Lamassu's name is possibly Sumerian in origin. Her male counterpart is called Alad (Sêdu in Acadian).

Sources: Jastrow, *Religion of Babylonia and Assyria*, 260; Lenormant, *Chaldean Magic*, 24.

Lameniel

The *Theurgia Goetia*, the second book of the *Lemegeton*, names Lameniel as being under the command of HYDRIEL, one of the eleven WANDERING PRINCES. An AERIAL DEVIL, this chief duke commands 1,320 servitors. Lameniel can be summoned any time of the day or night, and when he appears before his summoner he looks like a serpent with a virgin's face and head. Known to be very courteous and willing to obey, he lives in or near water in marshes and wetlands.

Sources: Guiley, *Encyclopedia of Demons and Demonology*, 28, 115; Peterson, *Lesser Key of Solomon*, 105; Trithemius, *Steganographia*, 88.

Lameros

In the *Ars Paulina*, the third book of the *Lemegeton*, Lameros is ranked as a duke and commands 5,550 servitors of his own. He is also listed as one of the fifteen SERVITORS OF SCOX (see SCOX) as well as one of the fifteen SERVITORS OF SASQUIEL (see SASQUIEL).

Sources: Peterson, *Lesser Key of Solomon*, 114; Trithemius, *Steganographia*, 95.

Lamia

Variations: Lamie, Lamien, Lamies, Leecher, Swallower, Vrukalakos

In ancient Greece there was a singular and specific type of vampiric demon known as Lamia. Her name was used in early versions of the Bible to mean "screech owl" and "sea monster." She was said to be a monstrous creature that fed exclusively on the flesh and blood of children each night. There are a number of vampiric beings, creatures, revenants, and the like throughout ancient times that share the name *Lamia*, which translates as "dangerous lone-shark."

In Greek mythology Lamia was born daughter of the king of Lybia, BELUS, and eventually, because of her beauty, she became a lover to the god Zeus. When his wife, the goddess Hera, found out, she stole Lamia's children. Driven insane by the grief over the loss of her children, Lamia went on a killing spree, becoming a hideously ugly demon and murdering the children of her kingdom. She had the ability to shape-shift and used it to become a beautiful woman again so that she could lure men into isolated places, have sex with them, and then drain them of their blood. In her state of embitterment, Lamia aligned herself with a group of demons known as the EMPOUSE, the wicked children of the goddess Hecate. Zeus, in an act of compassion for what had happened to his former lover, granted her a boon—she was able to remove her eyes so that she would not have to look upon herself; however, it also made her vulnerable, as she could be slain when they were removed.

Sources: Flint, *Witchcraft and Magic in Europe*, 24, 131, 293; Thorndike, *History of Magic and Experimental Science*, 515–17; Turner, *Dictionary of Ancient Deities*, 286.

Lamiastu

Variations: LAMIA, Lamastu

In Akkadian mythology the demon Lamiastu is described as being a bare-breasted and pale-faced female with donkey ears and poisoned claws. Preying upon women in childbirth, she steals children while they are suckling from their mothers.

Sources: Cunningham, *Deliver Me from Evil*, 106–8; Stol, *Birth in Babylonia and the Bible*, 222–3, 230–2.

Lamolon

In the *Sacred Magic of Abramelin the Mage*, book two, Lamolon ("with detestation") is one of the forty-nine SERVITORS OF BEELZEBUB (see BEELZEBUB).

Sources: Ford, *Bible of the Adversary*, 93; Mathers, *Book of the Sacred Magic of Abramelin the Mage*, 108, 121; Von Worms, *Book of Abramelin*, 253, 257.

Laousnicheta

Laousnicheta is a type of vampiric demon from Bulgarian mythology that is created when a child dies before it has been baptized.

Sources: Georgieva, *Bulgarian Mythology*, 102.

Laousnitsi

Laousnitsi is a type of vampiric demon from Bulgarian mythology that is created when a woman dies in childbirth.

Sources: Georgieva, *Bulgarian Mythology*, 102.

Laphor

The *Theurgia Goetia*, the second book of the *Lemegeton*, is ranked as a chief duke who commands between ten and three hundred servitors. An AERIAL DEVIL, he is also listed as one of the twelve named Duke SERVITORS OF CARNESIEL (see CARNESIEL and DUKES OF HELL).

Sources: Eco, *Infinity of Lists*, 61; Guiley, *Encyclopedia of Demons and Demonology*, 37; Peterson, *Lesser Key of Solomon*, 59.

Larael

Duke Larael is one of the twenty SERVITORS OF SYMIEL (see SYMIEL). He, along with the other diurnal SERVITORS OF SYMIEL shares the use of seven hundred twenty servitors. Larael is said to be very good-natured and willing to obey his summoners.

Sources: Peterson, *Lesser Key of Solomon*, 88; Trithemius, *Steganographia*, 85.

Larmiel

In Jewish folklore and medieval Christian demonology Larmiel is ranked as a chief, one of the eleven SERVITORS OF RAHAB (see RAHAB).

Sources: Sources: Peterson, *Lesser Key of Solomon*, 144; Waite, *The Book of Ceremonial Magic*, 67.

Larmol

Variations: Camorr, Larmel

In the *Theurgia Goetia*, the second book of the *Lemegeton*, Larmol is a chief duke who commands 2,660 duke servitors (see DUKES OF HELL). In service under CASPIEL, this demon is said to be rude and stubborn (see SERVITORS OF CASPIEL).

Sources: McLean, *Treatise on Angel Magic*, 35; Peterson, *Lesser Key of Solomon*, 60, 101.

Larphiel

In the *Theurgia Goetia*, the second book of the *Lemegeton*, Larphiel is ranked as a duke who commands 2,200 servitors. An AERIAL DEVIL, he is listed as one of the fifteen SERVITORS OF ICOSIEL (see ICOSIEL).

Sources: Peterson, *Lesser Key of Solomon*, 99; Trithemius, *Steganographia*, 69.

Lasterlein

Lasterlein is the German demon of robbery.

Source: Rudwin, *Devil in Legend and Literature*, 28.

Lauviah

Variations: Lauiah, Laviah, Lavviah, Leviha, Luviah

A FALLEN ANGEL, formerly of the Order of Thrones and the Order of Cherubim, Lauviah ("may God be praised and exalted") is also one of the seventy-two Schemhamphoras. Together with BERITH, MAROU, and SALIKOTAL, they plotted against mankind and placed the Forbidden Tree in the Garden of Eden because Lauviah was jealous of humankind. Lauviah is the demon of geniuses and people of greatness, influencing evil men and savants. Most powerful during the month of May, his zodiacal sign is Virgo.

Sources: Maberry, *Cryptopedia*, 78, 80; Waite, *Book of Destiny*, 89; Webster, *Encyclopedia of Angels*, 112.

Lavnasura

Variations: Lavanasura

The ancient Sanskirt epic *Ramayana*, ascribed to the Hindu sage Valmiki and dating back as far as perhaps the fourth century B.C.E., names Lavnasura as the demon king of Mathura, holder of the divine trishula (trident) of Lord Shiva. Born the son of King Madhu and his wife, Kumbhini, Lavnasura was unable to be slain or to be stopped from committing sinful activities. Eventually he was killed by the hero Shatrughna with an arrow empowered by Vishnu.

Sources: Kr Singh, *Ramayana in Kathakali Dance Drama*, 22, 24; Mittal, *History of Ancient India*, 304; Prabhupād, *Srimād Bhagavatam*, 287.

Lecherous Spirit of a Giant

The *Testament of Solomon* names the demon Lecherous Spirit of a Giant as one of the demons bound by King Solomon (see SPIRITS OF SOLOMON). Described as being a shadowy form of a man with gleaming eyes who carried a sword, this demon caused insanity and possession. Also, if he sat near the dead in their tomb at midnight,

he could assume their form. This demon lived in inaccessible places. Eventually he was slain in a massacre during the age of the giants.

Sources: Charlesworth, *Old Testament Pseudepigrapha*, 936; Schwartz, *Tree of Souls*, 459; Stephens, *Giants in Those Days*, 77.

Legion

Variations: Gadarenes Demon, the Gerasene Demon, Gergesenes Demon

The Christian New Testament gospels of Mark, Luke, and Matthew each describe a similar story where Jesus was walking in a town near the Sea of Galilee. There he encountered a possessed man who came running out of a nearby graveyard, forbidding anyone to pass. Jesus confronted the demon within the man, demanding to know its name, to which the response was "My name is Legion, for we are many." Jesus then cast out the thousands of demons that were housed within the DEMONIAC, sending the beings into a herd of swine. The animals panicked and ran off a ledge into the water, drowning.

The word *legion* infers "a number of 2,000 or more."

Sources: Mack, *Field Guide to Demons*, 233–4; Sorensen, *Possession and Exorcism*, 125–9; Van der Toorn, *Dictionary of Deities and Demons in the Bible*, 237, 239–40.

Lemel

In the *Ars Goetia*, the first book of the *Lemegeton*, Lemel ("for speech" or "unto fullness," sources vary) is listed as one of the fifty-three SERVITORS OF ASHTAROTH AND ASMODEUS (see ASHTAROTH and ASMODEUS).

Sources: Mathers, *Book of the Sacred Magic of Abramelin the Mage*, 106, 115, 219; Von Worms, *Book of Abramelin*, 247, 256.

Lemodac

Variations: Alboneÿ, Aromusij, Aromusÿ

In the *Theurgia Goetia*, the second book of the *Lemegeton*, Lemodac is ranked as a chief duke who commands four hundred servitors; he is also listed as one of the twelve named SERVITORS OF MACARIEL (see MACARIEL). Lemodac appears before his summoner in various forms but will commonly appear as a dragon with a virgin's head. Both a diurnal and nocturnal demon, he is said to be good-natured and willing to obey his summoners. Like all AERIAL DEVILS, he is constantly on the move, never staying in any one place for long.

Sources: Peterson, *Lesser Key of Solomon*, 103; Trithemius, *Steganographia*, 141.

Lemoniel

Variations: LAMENIEL

In the *Theurgia Goetia*, the second book of the *Lemegeton*, Lemoniel is ranked as a duke; he commands 2,400 servitors. Listed as one of the ten SERVITORS OF BYDIEL, he appears to his summoner in an attractive form (see BYDIEL). Lemoniel is said to be good-natured and willing to obey.

Sources: Peterson, *Lesser Key of Solomon*, 95, 105; Trithemius, *Steganographia*, 79.

Lempo

Variations: Juntas, JUTAS, Pääpiru ("Head of the Demons")

In the *Kalevala*, a nineteenth-century epic poem compiled by Elias Lönnrot which consists of Finnish and Karelian folklore and mythology, Lempo is described as a TERRESTRIAL DEVIL; however, some sources say that this demon may also represent the dark side of the Finnish cultural hero Lemminkäinen. It is also possible that in the original Finnish mythology Lempo was the god of archery, confusion, cruelty, love, wickedness, and the wilderness. His name is a mild swear word in the Finnish language.

Lempo works in conjunction with the demons he commands: HIISI, JUTAS, and PIRU, as well as the evil spirits of the forests, and a fierce herd of moose. This demon is also the leader of the demonic forest spirits that seek to slay Väinämöinen.

Sources: Abercromby, *Pre- and Proto-historic Finns*, 296–300; Folklore Society, *Folklore*, Vol. 3, 55, 58; Turner, *Dictionary of Ancient Deities*, 216, 29.

Leohtberende

Variations: LUCIFER

Leohtberende ("lightbearer") is an Old English word that was used in referring to the DEVIL, or LUCIFER.

Sources: Finnegan, *Christ and Satan*, 79, 137; Roberts, *Thesaurus of Old English*, 1142.

Leonard

Variations: BAPHOMET, Goat of Mendes, "Le Grand Negre" (The Black Man), Leraie, LERAIEL, Leraikha, Leraje, Master Leonard, URIAN

The demon Leonard holds many ranks and titles, such as the chief of the subaltern demons, grand master of the Witches' Sabbaths, inspector general of black magic and sorcery, Knight of the Fly, and marquis. Possibly in service under AZAZEL, this demon commands thirty legions (see KNIGHTS OF HELL and MARQUIS OF HELL).

Leonard has three different appearances: that of a three-horned, black goat with the head of a fox or man; as an archer wearing green clothes, carrying a bow and quiver; and as a goat's body from the waist up, with three horns, foxlike ears, flaming eyes, goose feet, and a second face on his bottom. Normally Leonard is said to have a melancholy and reserved attitude, unless he is presiding over a witch's Sabbath when he is commanding and powerful.

This demon is summoned for his ability to cause battles and contests to break out as well as for his skill at teaching black magic and sorcery. He is able to shape-shift into a black bird, bloodhound, steer, and tree trunk with a sad face upon it. His zodiacal sign is Sagittarius.

Sources: Chambers, *Book of Days*, 722; Collin de Plancy, *Dictionary of Witchcraft*, 27; Guiley, *Encyclopedia of Magic and Alchemy*, 249; Icon, *Leonard*, 370; Lewis, *Encyclopedia of Religion, Folklore, and Popular Culture*, 18.

Leosiel

In the *Ars Paulina*, the third book of the *Lemegeton*, Leosiel is listed as one of the twenty SERVITORS OF VEGUANIEL (see VEGUANIEL).

Sources: Waite, *The Book of Ceremonial Magic*, 67.

Lepaca

The *Sacred Magic of Abramelin the Mage* names Lepaca ("for opening or disclosing") as one of the thirty-two SERVITORS OF ASTAROT (see ASTAROT).

Sources: Mathers, *Book of the Sacred Magic of Abramelin the Mage*, 106; Von Worms, *Book of Abramelin*, 249, 256.

Leraiel

Variations: Larajie, LEONARD, Leraie, Leraikha, Leraje, Leraye, LORAY, Oray

In the *Ars Goetia*, the first book of the *Lemegeton*, the *Lesser Key of Solomon*, Leraiel is ranked as a marquis; he commands thirty legions (see MARQUIS OF HELL). When summoned for his ability to cause battles and contests to break out, he appears as a handsome archer wearing all green clothing and carrying a bow and quiver. This demon can also purify wounds made by arrowheads. His zodiacal sign is Sagittarius.

Sources: De Laurence, *Lesser Key of Solomon, Goetia*, 26; DuQuette, *Key to Solomon's Key*, 168; Scott, *London Magazine*, Vol. 5, 378.

Leshy, plural: lechies

Variations: Lešak, Leshii, Lesiy, Lesní mužík, Lesnik, Lesný mužík ("forest man"), Lesny mužik/ded, Lesovij, Lesovik, Lesovy, Lesun, Lešý, Leszi, Leszy

Originally a god or spirit of the forest in

Slavonic mythology, a leshy ("forest") was named as a type of TERRESTRIAL DEVIL in Colin de Plancy's *Dictionaire Infernale* (1818, 1863). Satyr-like humans from the waist up with notable beards, ears, and the horns of a she-goat, these demons used their ability to imitate voices as a way to lure people back to their caves. Once the victim was inside, they would be tickled to death. Lechies, as they are called in numbers, have a bansheelike cry and the ability to shrink down to the height of grass when marching through fields. They can also grow as tall as a tree when running through the forest where it lives.

Sources: Johnson, *Slavic Sorcery*, 8, 88; Mack, *Field Guide to Demons, Fairies, Fallen Angels, and Other Subversive Spirits*, 111–13; Varner, *Mythic Forest*, 30–1.

Leviathan

Variations: Behemah ("beast"), Livyatan, Liwyātān ("Twisted Coil"), Levitan, LOTAN, Taninim

Originating in ancient Hebrew lore and popularized in medieval demonology, Leviathan, the demon of envy and faith, was an aquatic, ARCH SHE-DEMON; she was also said to be a FALLEN ANGEL of the Order of Seraphim. Her name in Hebrew means "the crooked (or piercing) serpent (or dragon)" or "whale."

Created by God on the fifth day of Creation, Leviathan is described as a monstrous female sea creature three hundred miles long with eyes glowing as brightly as twin suns. She is the symbol of chaos. Using her supernatural strength, she hunted and ate a whale a day. Her breath was so foul that to breathe it in was enough to kill. She could send a wave of intense heat from her mouth that could boil water instantly.

Especially mean-natured, even for a demon, this demon was fearful of a species of sea-worm called a *kilbit*, as it clings to the gills. She was said to have lived in the Mediterranean Sea, but God slew the female leviathan, salted it, and fed it to His people so that it could not reproduce with its mate. The hide of the beast was used to make the tent the feast was held under. The male species of this demon is known as BEHEMOTH (see also LOUDUN POSSESSION).

Sources: Aikin, *General Biography*, 493; Barton, *Journal of Biblical Literature*, Vols. 30–31, 165; Hyatt, *Book of Demons*, 43, 45; Bayle, *Historical and Critical Dictionary*, 262; Melton, *Encyclopedia of Occultism and Parapsychology*, 315; Voltaire, *Works of M. de Voltaire*, 193.

Lhamayin

Variations: Lha Ma Yin

In Tibetan demonology, lhamayin ("not a god") are demonic beings that consume the understanding of innocent and unsuspecting people. Living below the mountain Meru and said to be very powerful, their personal adversaries are the devas.

Sources: Blavatsky, *Secret Doctrine*, 16, 63; Das, *Tibetan-English Dictionary*, 1334; Schlagintweit, *Buddhism in Tibet*, 92, 109, 115.

Lhamo

Variations: Gyelmo Maksorma "The Victorious One Who Turns Back Enemies," Lha-mo, Machik Pelha Shiwai Nyamchen, Palden Lamo, Palden Lhamo, Remati, Shri Devi, Ukin Tengri

In Tibetan mythology Lhamo is the principal protector of Tibet, protector of the Dalai Lama lineage, and the consort of Mahakala. Originally a demon and one of the Wrathful Deities, she was converted to Buddhism.

Described as having dark blue skin, three eyes, and red hair, Lhamo rides upon a white mule as she drinks from a chalice. The mule has an extra eye on its rump and the saddle Lhamo sits upon is made of the flesh of her son.

Sources: Beér, *Encyclopedia of Tibetan Symbols and Motifs*, 305–7; Das, *Tibetan-English Dictionary*, 790; Dowman, *Power-Places of Central Tibet*, 78.

Librabis

In Apollonius of Tyana's *Nuctemeron* (*Night Illuminated by Day*) Librabis is the demon of hidden gold. He is most powerful during the seventh hour.

Sources: Davidson, *Dictionary of Angels*, 174; Frey, *Hebrew, Latin, and English, Dictionary*, 1297; Lévi, *Transcendental Magic*, 392, 505.

Licanen

In the *Sacred Magic of Abramelin the Mage*, book two, Licanen is one of the forty-nine SERVITORS OF BEELZEBUB (see BEELZEBUB). His name is possibly Greek and may mean "a winnowing fan."

Sources: Ford, *Bible of the Adversary*, 93; Mathers, *Book of the Sacred Magic of Abramelin the Mage*, 107; Von Worms, *Book of Abramelin*, 252, 257.

Lidérc

Variations: Lüderc

In Hungary there is a vampiric creature that is very similar to the INCUBUS and SUCCUBUS in that it drains off the blood and life energies of a person through sexual intercourse. Called a lidérc, it is created by placing the first egg laid by a black hen under your armpit and keeping it there until it hatches. The lidérc also acts as something of a FAMILIAR, as it is known for its ability to find treasure. It can shape-shift into a chicken or into a person who has one foot that is a chicken's foot. The lidérc will ask to do odd jobs for the person who hatched it. It is always asking for more to do, never satisfied with its given task and wanting to move on to the next one as quickly as possible. Keeping a lidérc out of your home so that it cannot assault you during the night as you sleep is as easy as hanging garlic on your bedroom doorknob. Killing a lidérc is also easy, if you know how. Simply give it an impossible task to complete, such as cutting an odd length of rope or dehydrating water into a powder. The little vampiric creature will try its hardest, but eventually it will become so frustrated that it will suffer a stroke and die.

Sources: Dömötör, *Hungarian Folk Beliefs*, 83; Hoppál, *Eros in Folklore*, 129; Pócs, *Between the Living and the Dead*, 48–49.

Lilim

Variations: LILIN, LILIS, Liln

According to Jewish folklore, LILITH, the first wife of Adam, left her husband and their children to be with the demon SAMMAEL. Together they dwelt in and near the Red Sea where Lilith became a demon herself. Every day she gave birth to one hundred demonic offspring. These vampiric demons, her children, are called *lilim*, although some sources say that all of her female children, even those she had with her first husband, Adam, were called the lilim. Some sources say that if the demon was male, it was called lili or SHAITAN. The ancient Greeks called these beings lilim lamiae, EMPOUSE, and the daughters of Hecate. Ancient Christians referred to them as the Harlots of Hell and SUCCUBUS.

Lilim are said to feed their blood lust by attacking children, deer, fish, menstruating women, pregnant women, and men who have fantasies about having sex with a woman who is not his wife while engaging in intercourse with his wife. Lilim also have the right to plague newborn male children for eight days or until they have been circumcised, as well as being allowed to attack newborn females until they are twenty days old, kidnapping them to consume if the opportunity presents itself. When lilim attack adults, they have succubus-like tendencies. They also have the interesting ability to look into a person's eyes and see what, if any, doubts they may have about anything.

To prevent attack, monks who have taken a vow of celibacy must sleep with their hands over their genitals, clutching a crucifix. Wearing Hasidic amulets of protection are said to work as well. Lilim can only be destroyed by God, as He

had decreed that one hundred lilim a day will die until Lilith returns to her husband.

Sources: Eason, *Fabulous Creatures*, 26–27; Hyatt, *Book of Demons*, 51, 59; Koén-Sarano, *King Solomon and the Golden Fish*, 63; Koltuv, *Book of Lilith*, 35; Turner, *Dictionary of Ancient Deities*, 166.

Lilin, singular: Lili

Variations: LILIM, Lil-in

In Jewish folklore the lilin are a species of SUCCUBUS. They were born the daughters of Adam and LILITH. These nocturnal demons prey upon newborn baby boys until they are eight days old and newborn girls until they are twenty days old. The lilin will also attack menstruating virgins, pregnant women, and the children of men who fantasize about other women while having sexual intercourse with their wives. These demons cause barrenness, complications during childbirth, and miscarriages. These nocturnal demons can be kept from attacking if potential victims wear a protective amulet.

Sources: Hyatt, *Book of Demons*, 51; Hurwitz, *Lilith: The First Eve*, 72, 88; Rogers, *Religion of Babylonia and Assyria*, 147.

Lilis

Variations: LILITH

In Hassidic demonology Lilis, a devil, is the wife of SATAN. One of the four DEVILS OF ADAM, she commands the demons MACHALAS, NAOME, and OGÉRE. During the one hundred thirty years before Adam was married to Eve, he fathered many offspring with these demons.

Sources: Khanam, *Demonology*, 128; Smedley, *Occult Sciences*, 173; Spence, *Encyclopedia of Occultism*, 152.

Lilith

Variations: Abeko, ABITO, ABRO, Abyzu, AILO, Alio, Alu, ALÚ, Amiz, Amizo, Amizu, Ardad Lili, ARDAT-LILE ("Maid of Desolation"), ARDAT-LILI, Astaribo, ASTARTE, Avitu, Avitue, Baalat ("Divine Lady"), Bat Zuge, Batna, Belili, Belit-Ili, Bituah, Bogey Wolf, BROXA, Child Stealing Witch, Dianae, Eilo, Elio, End of All Flesh, End of Days, Eostre, Flying DEMONESS, Flying One, GALLU, GELLO, Gelou,Gilou, Gilû, Heva, Hilthot, IK, 'Ik, 'Ils, Ita, Izorpo, Kakash, Kakos ("evil"), Kalee, Kalee,' KALI, Kea, Kema, KIEL-GELAL, KISKIL, Kokos, LABARTU, Lalla, Lamashtu, LAMASSU, Lavia, Lavil, Lilatou, Lilats, Lildtha, Lili, LILIS, Lilit, Lilithu, Lilitu, Lilla, Lillake, Lillu, Lilu, Mahalat, Maid of Desolation, Maid of Lilla, Night Hag, Nightjar, OBIZUTH, ODAM, Odem, Ostra, Partasah, Partasha, Petrota, Podia ("feet"), Podo, Pods, Ptrotk, Queen of Sheba, Queen of Zemargad, Raphi,

Satrina, Satrinah, Screech Owl, She-Wolf, Talto, Thilthoh, WERZELYA, Winged, Woman of Harlotry, Zahriel, Zariel, Zefonith, Zephonith

Titles: The Ancient, Bogey-Wolf, Chief of the Succubi, Daughter of Night, the Devil's Consort, the Flying One, The Foolish Woman, Grand Duchess of the Eighth Hell, Maid of Desolation, Night Hag, Night Jar, the Night Monster, the Northerner, Princess of Demons, Princess of Hell, the Queen of Hell, Queen of the Succubi, Queen of Zemargad

From the earliest records of man, there is a story of an ancient being that preyed upon children. It was suspected to be female and demonic, and killed not only children but also women who were with child and men as well, seducing them and draining them of their blood. Over the eons, it has had many names and many titles, but today, we call it Lilith.

In ancient Assyria she was called Lilitu and described as a DEMONESS with wings and a hairy body, much like the DJINN of Arabic lore. In the Babylonian tradition, she was one of a trio of demons. Lilith was believed to have aligned herself with the other two demons after she had been banished from the Sumerian goddess Innana's garden. She is mentioned in the Sumerian telling of Gilgamesh and was said to live in a willow tree.

In Hebrew texts it was said that King Solomon had at first mistook the Queen of Sheba for Lilitu, as she had unshaven legs, reminding him of the DJINN of Arabian tales. In the Hebrew Bible, Psalm 91, she was called the "terror of the night." In Isaiah 34:14, she was called the "night devil."

In the Talmud, it is not Lilith's hatred for infants that causes her to kill them, but rather her love for them. Infertile and unable to have a child of her own, it is said that she slips into a nursery and gently picks up the infant to hold against her breast. Eventually her desperation to be a mother to a child of her own becomes much too distressing and Lilith accidentally smothers the baby to death as she presses it against her.

Because there are so many ancient texts and beliefs that have Lilith in their mythology, her story is a difficult one to exactly set straight. But the most familiar story of Lilith, as well as the oldest record of her, comes from the anonymously written Hebrew text *The Alphabet of Ben Sira*. There has been much speculation as to when the text was originally written. Some sources claim that it is as old as the seventh century and as young as the eleventh century, but most scholars are content to split the difference and say the ninth.

The text tells the story of the birth and education of Rabbi Ben Sira. The final section of the text is written as taking place in the palace of Babylonian King Nebuchadnezzar. The king asks the prophet a series of questions that must be answered by telling a story. There are twenty-two questions posed, one for each letter of the Hebrew alphabet, hence, the name of the book. In the fifth passage, King Nebuchadnezzar demands that his son, who is suffering from a mysterious illness, be cured. Ben Sira responds with the tale of Lilith, the first wife of Adam.

It says that she was Adam's first wife, created from filth and mud. They were joined physically back to back, but she complained so insistently that God separated them. Still, she was not content with her lot as Adam's subservient wife and mother to their children. Wanting equality, she left her husband to live with a group of demons outside Paradise. By crying out the name of God, she was given the ability to fly, and did so, leaving Adam far behind. God was not pleased with Lilith's new life and sent three angels to speak with her: Sanvi, Sansanvi, and Semangalef. Their job was to persuade Lilith to return to Adam and their children. She adamantly refused and was punished for it—cursed so that none of her children would survive their infancy. With Lilith on the brink of suicide, the angels took pity on her and a compromise was struck: she would be given power over newborn boys for the first eight days of their lives, and the first twenty days of life for newborn girls. In exchange, she promised not to harm any child who had the names of the angels written near them. Lilith wandered the world and came to be near the Red Sea, where she met the demon SAMMAEL. Bound by their mutual hatred for humanity, they spawned a race of demonic beings, the LILIM.

There are as many variations to the story of Lilith as she has aliases and titles combined. It is believed by many that it was Lilith and SAMMAEL who plotted the downfall of Adam and Eve. In fact, numerous pieces of art depict a woman, Lilith, offering the forbidden fruit to Adam and Eve. She is also said to be one of the ARCHDEMONS and has dominion over the infernal hierarchy known as GAMALIEL.

There have been hundreds of books written about Lilith, who she was, what she means, and how to interpret her story; equally as numerous are the points of view accompanying each. Some are Christian, some Jewish, some are from a purely historic point of view, while others yet have taken such a wild interpretation and speculative spin that she has become lost in their message. Suffice it to say that no matter what you are looking for in the Lilith story, there is an interpretation of it to suit your needs.

Sources: Conybeare, *Jewish Quarterly*, xi, 30; Hanauer, *Folk-lore of the Holy Land*, 325; Hyatt, *Book of Demons*, 52; Leeming, *Goddess*, 111–15.

Lilith the Lesser

Variations: Lesser Lilith, Lilith the Maiden, Mehetabel ("immersed"), YOUNGER LILITH

In Jewish demonology and Kabbalistic lore Lilith the Lesser was born the daughter of the demons LILITH and SAMMAEL and grew to be the mate to ASMODEUS. The *Treaties of the Left Emanation* written by Rabbi Isaac Ben Jacob Ha-Kohen in the first half of the thirteenth century describes Lilith the Lesser as being a beautiful woman from the waist up; from the waist down she is made of fire. Her intentions are never good, as she seeks to incite war.

Sources: Dan, *Early Kabbalah*, 175, 179–80; Dennis, *Encyclopedia of Jewish Myth, Magic and Mysticism*, 22; Schwartz, *Tree of Souls*, 139.

Lilot, The

Variations: BANIM SHOVAVIN ("mischievous sons")

The demonology of the Middle Ages describes the lilot as a species of incubi and succubi who were born the children of LILITH (See INCUBUS and SUCCUBUS). Their name is taken from Hebrew and it translates as a plural form of the name LILITH. These demons hate humans and are especially spiteful, preying on infants and mothers in labor. Amulets of protection against the lilot have the names of the angels Sanvi, Sansanvi, and Semangalef inscribed upon them.

Source: Dennis, *Encyclopedia of Jewish Myth, Magic and Mysticism*, 35.

Lima

Lima is a demon that is worshipped in Haitian demonology.

Source: Turner, *Dictionary of Ancient Deities*, 234.

Limos

Variations: Fames, Limus

In ancient Greek mythology Limos ("famine") is the demon of famine, hunger, and starvation. Born one of the sons of the goddess Eris ("discord") and the god Zeus, this demon has coarse hair, crusted white lips, parchment-colored skin, a sallow face, swollen joints, and withered hips. He lives near the entrance of Orcus and attacks men who do not work the fields. Limos's personal adversaries are Demeter, a goddess of food, and her personal daimon, Ploutos ("plenty").

Sources: Garnsey, *Famine and Food Supply in the Graeco-Roman World*, 18, 19, 199; Scull, *Greek Mythology Systematized*, 42.

Lingelson

Lingelson is a demon that is worshipped in Haitian demonology. To prevent his attacks, sacrifices are made to appease him.

Sources: Ashley, *Complete Book of Devils and Demons*, 66.

Lion-Demon

Variations: God with Scimitar, Lion-centaur, Ugallu (big weather creature)

In Neo-Assyrian and Neo-Babylonian mythology, the Lion-Demon is a tutelary demonic spirit described as having the lower body, including all four legs, of a lion with the upper body of a man. Oftentimes he is described as wearing a horned hat that denotes divinity. This demon preys upon evil demons and illness.

Sources: Conway, *Magickal Mystical Creatures*, 113–4; Stol, *Birth in Babylonia and the Bible*, 223–4, 146–7; Wiggermann, *Mesopotamian Protective Spirits*, 72, 171–2.

Lirion

In the *Sacred Magic of Abramelin the Mage*, book two, Lirion ("lilly") is among the one hundred eleven SERVITORS OF AMAYMON, ARITON, ORIENS, AND PAYMON (see AMAYMON, ARITON, ORIENS, and PAYMON).

Sources: Mathers, *Book of the Sacred Magic of Abramelin the Mage*, 105; Von Worms, *Book of Abramelin*, 245, 255.

Lirochi

The *Sacred Magic of Abramelin the Mage*, book two, names Lirochi ("in tenderness") as one of the forty-nine SERVITORS OF BEELZEBUB (BEELZEBUB).

Sources: Ford, *Bible of the Adversary*, 93; Von Worms, *Book of Abramelin*, 252, 257.

Listheret

Listheret is from the *Book of Black Magic and of Pacts* written by Arthur Edward Waite in 1898. This demon is said to be able to make it daytime or nighttime at the summoner's request.

Source: Waite, *Book of Black Magic and of Pacts*, 185.

Lithobolia

Variations: The Stone Throwing Devil

According to a written account by Richard Chamberlain, the secretary of the colony of New Hampshire and an agent to the Walton family, the demon Lithobolia was believed to have been summoned by an elderly neighbor woman to haunt and harass the family from June to September in 1682.

George and Alice Walton lived on Great Island, New Hampshire. Their neighbor, the elderly woman, was said to be embittered due to the loss of a piece of property that she believed she rightfully owned but was given to the Waltons in a land dispute settlement. It is said that after losing the case she used witchcraft to curse the family. For four months the Walton family, their servants, and houseguests were pelted with stones both in their field and inside their home; the largest one reported being found in the home was thirty pounds. The demon responsible for this, Lithobolia, also threw bric-a-brac, bricks, domestic utensils, hammers, iron-crows, mauls, spits, and a stirrup. He broke gates off their hinges, shattered the windows by throwing rocks through them, and rang alarms out in the night. Stones fell from the ceilings inside the home upon the family. Lithobolia, both a diurnal and nocturnal demon, was invisible, intangible, and could teleport short distances. Whenever the demon showed himself he did so in the form of a black cat.

The assaults only ended when stones fell from a great height, broke the planks of the boat Mr. Walton was in, and one fatally struck him in the head.

Sources: Broome, *Is Your House Haunted?* 143–4; Clough, *American Imagination at Work*, 71–75; Jehlen, *English Literatures of America*, 388–99.

Lix Tetrax

The *Testament of Solomon* names Lix Tetrax as a demon of the wind, born the child of and in service to the Great One. It should be noted that the Great One may be a reference to the Greek goddess Artemis who was referred to as The Great in Testament of Solomon 7:6. His name may be a Greek term that is possibly a reference to utilizing a field in each of the four seasons.

Lix Tetrax causes household chaos, creates divisions between men, makes whirlwinds, sets fields ablaze, starts fires, and cures those with the "day-and-a-half-fever" who chant to him "*Baltala, Thallal, Melchal.*" This demon has dominion over the moon and is most powerful in the summer. His personal adversary is the archangel Azae.

Sources: Arnold, *Powers of Darkness*, 99; Charlesworth, *Old Testament Pseudepigrapha*, 935, 954, 969; Icons, *Demons*, 164.

Ljubi

In Albanian demonology Ljubi is the demon of drought. She lives in a magnificent vegetable garden. To prevent her from causing drought to befall the land, a virgin was sacrificed to her.

Sources: Lurker, *Routledge Dictionary of Gods and Goddesses*, 112; Rose, *Spirits, Fairies, Gnomes, and Goblins*, 201.

Llorona, La

Variations: Ciguanabana, La Pucullén, La Sucia ("the dirty woman"), La Tulivieja, Maria, Weeping Woman, Woman in White

In Hispanic folklore, particularly in the regions of Chile, El Salvador, Guatemala, Honduras, Panama, parts of Mexico, and New Mexico, Montana and Texas in the United States comes the folklore of la Llorona, the Crying Woman.

There are numerous versions of this cautionary tale, but all the stories have the same basic element: Maria, a beautiful woman who has three children, typically two boys and a girl, and her man. In most versions the couple is married, occasionally they are wed in secret because of some sort of cultural, social, or economic reason. Reasons vary accordingly but the man always leaves or rejects Maria, who in a fit of rage kills the children and then herself. Maria's body is then found by local villagers, but those of her children are never recovered. Next, Maria returns to the land of the living as la Llorona (she who weeps), the Crying Woman, a type of aquatic, demonic ghost (see AQUEOUS DEVIL).

Some versions of the tale claim she cries because God will not allow her to enter Heaven without her children, while others say her restless ghost sits at the bank of a river and cries in grief over her actions, and yet another explanation has her walking along river banks looking for the bodies of her children.

More modern renditions of the story have Maria as a young widow with many children who falls in love with a man who has no interest in children. In order to keep her man, she stabs her children to death and throws their bodies in the Rio Grande, but when her lover discovers what she has done, he rejects her. Maria suddenly realizes the gravity of her actions and throws herself into the Rio Grande, where her ghost wanders in search of the children she desperately wants back.

Yet another version claims Maria was a widowed mother who left her children alone one night, presumably to be with a man. A sudden flash flood swept the house and children away. Maria walks the banks eternally looking for them.

Still another version claims she was a prostitute who would abort her unwanted children and throw the bodies into the Tecpan River. Upon her death God told her she could not enter into Heaven without finding all of her children and sent her back to earth in a white dress to find them.

A final adaptation says that while she was out, again, presumably with a man, her children died in a house fire. Although she searched the rubble and was severely burned herself, she wanders the streets in black rags looking for her children.

La Llorona is classically described as being dressed in either all black or all white clothing. Sometimes she is said to have no eyes, while other times she is described as a skeletal form. One story even describes her as having the head of a horse. In the Panamanian version she was cursed by God to be a hideously ugly woman with a pockmarked face, her body covered with hair, and having the feet of a chicken. In Chilean lore she can only be seen by those who are about to die and dogs.

A nocturnal death omen, la Llorona will drown children who are unattended by bodies of water (including pool and laundry tubs), children who are disrespectful to their parents, and men. In some tellings of her tale this demon has the ability to assume the form of a person that her prey is familiar with. She also has a wailing cry that can be heard for miles and men who see her may go insane. La Llorona can be driven away by prayer. If she is invisible she can be seen by rubbing the tears of a dog into your eyes.

Some of the cries she is said to call out in the night are *"Toma mi teta, que soy tu nana"* ("Drink my tits, for I am your mother"); *"¿Has visto a mis hijos?"* ("Have you seen my children?"); *"¡Ay mis hijos!"* or *"¡O hijos mios!"* ("O my children!"); *"Mis ninos, mis ninos!"* ("My children, my children!"); *"Donde estan mis hijos?"* or *"¿Donde estan mis hijos?"* ("Where are my children?").

Sources: Pacheco, *Ghosts-Murder-Mayhem*, 20–22; Ruíz, *Latinas in the United States: A Historical Encyclopedia*, Vol. 1, 362–63; Vigil, *Eagle on the Cactus*, 17–21.

Locater

In the *Sacred Magic of Abramelin the Mage*, book two, Locater is listed as one of the sixty-five SERVITORS OF KORE AND MAGOTH.

Sources: Mathers, *Book of the Sacred Magic of Abramelin the Mage*, 107, 119; Von Worms, *Book of Abramelin*, 251, 256.

Locyta

During the witch trials of Elfdale and Mora, Sweden, in 1668, Locyta was named as a jovial and plump devil who preyed upon children on the nights of the Sabbath. The victims of this demon would fall into a deep sleeplike trance and their spirits would leave their bodies, flying upon broomsticks to Sabbath meetings where in addition to dancing and feasting they were taught how to perform magical spells and ride upon flying brooms.

Sources: Jackson, *Mysteries of Witchcraft and the Occult*, 71, 75–6; Spence, *Encyclopedia of Occultism*, 347; Wright, *Narratives of Sorcery and Magic*, 249.

Lomiol

In the *Sacred Magic of Abramelin the Mage*, book two, Lomiol is among the one hundred eleven SERVITORS OF AMAYMON, ARITON, ORIENS, AND PAYMON (see AMAYMON, ARITON, ORIENS, and PAYMON). His name is possibly Hebrew meaning "binding" or "bitter."

Sources: Mathers, *Book of the Sacred Magic of Abramelin the Mage*, 105, 113; Von Worms, *Book of Abramelin*, 121, 245.

Loray

The *Grimoire of Pope Honorius* (*Le Grimoire du Pape Honorius*), alleged to have been written by Pope Honorius III in the eighteenth century, names Loray as one of the three SERVITORS OF SAEGATANAS (see FORAU, SAEGATANAS, and VALAFAR).

Sources: Baskin, *Satanism*, 200; *Dublin University Magazine*, Vol. 66, 521; Wedeck, *Treasury of Witchcraft*, 96, 97.

Loriol

In the *Ars Goetia*, the first book of the *Lemegeton*, Loriol ("unto horror") was named as one of the fifty-three SERVITORS OF ASHTAROTH AND ASMODEUS (see ASHTAROTH and ASMODEUS).

Sources: Mathers, *Book of the Sacred Magic of Abramelin the Mage*, 115; Von Worms, *Book of Abramelin*, 247, 256.

Losimon

Losimon is one of the one hundred eleven SERVITORS OF AMAYMON, ARITON, ORIENS, AND PAYMON (see AMAYMON, ARITON, ORIENS, and PAYMON) listed in the *Sacred Magic of Abramelin the Mage*, book two. His name is possibly Coptic and means "understanding of restriction."

Sources: Mathers, *Book of the Sacred Magic of Abramelin the Mage*, 105, 114; Von Worms, *Book of Abramelin*, 121, 255

Lotan

Variations: "The Coiling Serpent," "The Fleeing Serpent," Lawtan, LEVIATHAN, Lotanu, "The serpent of Lot," TANNIN

In Canaanite and Judaic demonology Lotan is

an aspect of the god Yaw. The demon of destruction, Lotan causes destructive floods. He appears as a sea serpent or a seven-headed dragon. The symbol of primordial chaos, this demon lives in the sea. His personal adversary is the god Baal Hadad.

Sources: Day, *God's Conflict with the Dragon and the Sea*; Isaacs, *Animals in Jewish Thought and Tradition*, 180; Stone, *When God Was a Woman*, 68, 109.

Loudun Possession

In 1634, Cardinal Richelieu had wanted to raze the castle of Loudun. It had been an orthodox holding before being taken over by the Church, but the charismatic and handsome Father Grandier openly opposed him and his plan, perhaps even going so far as to write a pamphlet against the cardinal. In response, Richelieu likely manipulated the mother superior, Sister Jeanne des Anges, who whipped her nuns up into a case of hystero-demonopathy.

A respected priest, Father Urbain Grandier was accused of using evil spells, practicing sorcery, and causing the possession of some of the Ursuline nuns. Accusations began with Sister Jeanne des Anges, who claimed having demonic and illicit dreams of Grandier. Other nuns soon followed suit, claiming of having similar dreams of their own, barking, blaspheming, contorting their bodies, and screaming. Most people believed they were possessed by an army of devils. Father Mignon and his assistant began exorcisms. Grandier wrote to the archbishop of Bordeaux, who sent a doctor to examine the nuns who were in isolation; the good doctor found them not to be possessed. Grandier's enemies, Father Mignon among them, had him arrested on charges of witchcraft. Alleged lovers of Grandier came forward with stories of his adultery, incest, and sacrilege. Meanwhile, the nuns added to the hysteria, crying out names of the devils within them. One nun even suffered a psychosomatic pregnancy.

Ultimately Grandier was found guilty and sentenced to death by the testimony of seventy-two witnesses. He was burned alive, but the nuns were still possessed. Famed exorcist Father Surin (who later became insane) was able to successfully exorcize the nuns. However, the public by this point suspected fraud, especially as the story the nuns told began to degenerate.

In 1638 the mother superior, Sister Jeanne des Anges, claimed she had a vision that traveling to the tomb of St. François of Assise would banish the devils once and for all. It apparently worked.

The names of the eighteen demons who pos-

sessed Sister Jeanne des Anges in Loudun, France, 1634, are ACAOS, ACHAS, ALEXH, AMAND, ASHTAROTH, ASMODEUS, Behemot, Beherie, Cedon, CELSUS, CHAM, Easas, GRESIL, ISACAARON, Leviatom, Naphthalim, Ureil, and ZABULON. These entities are often called upon during exorcism and cases of collective possession.

Sources: Aikin, *General Biography*, 493; Bayle, *Historical and Critical Dictionary*, 262; Collin de Plancy, *Dictionary of Witchcraft*, 71–2; Hsia, *World of Catholic Renewal*, 150–1; Hyatt, *Book of Demons*, 133; Ramsay, *Westminster Guide to the Books of the Bible*, 349; Voltaire, *Works of M. de Voltaire*, 193.

Luciel

In the *Theurgia Goetia*, the second book of the *Lemegeton*, Luciel is ranked as a chief duke who is in service under HYDRIEL (see DUKES OF HELL and SERVITORS OF HYDRIEL). An AERIAL DEVIL, he commands 1,320 servitors. When summoned, he appears before his summoner as a serpent with a virgin's face and head. Said to be very courteous and willing to obey, this demon may be summoned any time of the day or night. He lives in or near water, marshes, and wetlands.

Source: Guiley, *Encyclopedia of Demons and Demonology*, 115.

Lucifer

Variations: the Adversary, the Angel of the Abyss, Angel of Light, the Arch-Fiend, Bearer of Fire, Bearer of Light, the Enemy of All Good, the Evil One, the Father of Lies, the Giver of Light, the Great Dragon, Heylel Ben Shacher, His Satanic Majesty, LEOHTBERENDE ("Lightbearer"), Lightbeard, Los, Lucibel, Luciper, Lucipher, Lussibiaus, Morning Star, Murderer, the Oppressor of the Saints, the Proud One, Roaring Lion, Sata, Son of the Morning (Helel ben Shahar), the Sower of Discord, the Tempter, That Ancient Serpent, ZU

Lucifer, named in various religious texts, is often considered to be the font of all earthly evil. In Christian demonology he is said to be an ARCHDEMON, one of the FALLEN ANGELS, formerly of the Order of Cherubim, once a Seraphim. He holds many ranks, including emperor, minister of justice of Hell, Prince of Darkness, Prince of Demons, PRINCE OF HELL, Prince of Pandemonium, Prince of the Power of the Air, prince of this world (or Age) (see PRINCES OF HELL). The demon of pride, he commands the Infernal armies.

Lucifer had a history of being arrogant, proud, and unsettled. Created by God, he sought to be God's equal; he tried to sit on the Divine Throne and refused to be subservient to mankind. Eventually he was cast out of Heaven for leading a rebellion. His name is Latin for "light bearer" or "he who shuns the light."

Appearing as an attractive male youth, he tempts man by appealing to his pride and own selfish interests. Lucifer is summoned for his ability to share knowledge, tell secrets, and teach sorcery. He is most powerful Mondays at dawn.

It should be noted that all information in this entry refers only to Lucifer in the sense of his demonic being. In the Book of Isaiah Chapter 14, verse 12, Lucifer was mistakenly identified with SATAN; however, the passage refers to King Nebuchednezzar: "How art thou fallen from heaven, O Lucifer, son of the morning! How art thou cut down to the ground, which didst weaken the nations!"

Sources: Chambers, *Book of Days*, 723; Melton, *Encyclopedia of Occultism and Parapsychology*, 315.

Lucifuge Rofocale

Variations: Lucifage, Lucifuge, Lucifer Rofocale

In the Christian demonology Lucifuge Rofocale holds many ranks, some of which include the evil chief of Chokmah (Wisdom), chief of the Treasury, prime minister, Prince of Hell, and the ruler of the Qliphoth Satariel. His name is taken from Latin and translates to mean "He who flees the light, Rofocale." However, it is believed by some scholars that Rofocale is an anagram for the demon FURCALOR.

The demon of anger, hate, vengeance, and war, Lucifuge Rofocale is in service under LUCIFER. He commands the demons AGUARES, BAAL, and MARBAS.

A nocturnal demon, he avoids the light and can only assume a solid form at nighttime. When summoned, he takes a human form. He has the ability to cause deformity and disease; he also controls all the treasure in the world.

Sources: Butler, *Ritual Magic*, 87–89; Waite, *Book of Black Magic and of Pacts*, 157, 225, 229; Wedeck, *Treasury of Witchcraft*, 98, 100.

Luesaf

In the *Sacred Magic of Abramelin the Mage*, book two, Luesaf ("unto loss or destruction") is listed as one of the sixty-five SERVITORS OF KORE AND MAGOTH.

Sources: Mathers, *Book of the Sacred Magic of Abramelin the Mage*, 118; Von Worms, *Book of Abramelin*, 149, 256.

Lukezi

In Hittite demonology Lukezi is a black-skinned INCUBUS. His name is possibly taken from Akkadian, Nesili, or Sumerian, and it may mean "bright."

Sources: Knappert, *Encyclopaedia of Middle Eastern Mythology and Religion*, 158; Sturtevant, *Comparative Grammar of the Hittite Language*, 116.

Lundo

In the *Sacred Magic of Abramelin the Mage*, book two, Lundo is listed as one of the fifteen SERVITORS OF ASMODEUS AND MAGOTH (see ASMODEUS).

Sources: Mathers, *Book of the Sacred Magic of Abramelin the Mage*, 106; Von Worms, *Book of Abramelin*, 248, 256.

Luridan

Variations: Belelah, Elgin, Urthin, Wadd

From the demonology of the people of Pomonia Island, the Orkneys, Scotland, Luridan is a type of demonic fay or brownie. This demon claims that he once resided in the lands of residence in the days of Solomon and David and that he instructed the Welsh bards how to write poetry and give prophesies. He is in service to the demon GLAURON.

The conjuration of this demon requires drawing a fiery mountain inside of a magical circle. Once called up, Luridan performs domestic household chores such as making a fire in the hearth, sweeping rooms, and washing dishes while people sleep.

Sources: Davidson, *Dictionary of Angels*, 69; Folklore Society, *County Folk-Lore*, Vol. 49; Monaghan, *Encyclopedia of Celtic Mythology and Folklore*, 299–300; Scot, *Discovery of Witchcraft*.

Lutins

Variations: Bon Garçon ("Good Boy"), Nain Rouge ("red dwarf")

In Scandinavian demonology lutins are a type of DUSES or goblinoid that were born the children of Adam and PIZNAI, a daughter of LILITH. The females of the species are known as *lutines*. These demons tie the manes and tails of horses together, braids the hair of young maidens together so tightly the hair must be cut to release them, and when they shape-shift into horse form they buck their rider and throw them into a ditch or marsh. To prevent them from attacking, pour a line of salt across a barn door and scatter flaxseed in it.

Sources: Evans-Wentz, *Fairy-Faith in Celtic Countries*, 206–7; Parent, *Of Kings and Fools*, 49, 69, 196; Sherman, *Trickster Tales*, 149.

Luxuriosus

Luxuriosus was first named in a fifteenth-century manuscript titled *Librum de Nigromancia*, which was said to belong to a priest named Johannes Cunalis of Munich, Bavaria. This devil is one of three that were summoned by a French sorcerer, Jubertus of Bavaria, in 1437, the other two devils being AVARUS and SUPERBUS.

A devil of lust, rape, and seduction, Luxuriosus was described as looking like a charming twelve-year-old girl but with eyes that glowed like sulphurous fire. A nocturnal devil, she was also a lover to Jubertus and forbade him to drink holy water, do good deeds, or kiss the cross as the very sight of it filled her with terror, causing her to flee.

At night Jubertus worshipped her like a god. He would face the east, make the sign of the cross, defecate, spit, and urinate on it, then deny God, thus committing his body and soul to Luxuriosus after his own death. The sorcerer would give Luxuriosus three or five pence on Holy Friday.

Sources: Csonka-Takács, *Witchcraft Mythologies and Persecutions*, 66; Kieckhefer, *Forbidden Rites*, 30, 31, 34; Tigelaar, *Karolus Rex*, 191.

Luziel

In *Ars Paulina*, book three of the *Lemegeton*, Luziel is ranked as a chief duke and is listed as one of the twelve SERVITORS OF AMENADIEL (see AMENADIEL and DUKES OF HELL). He commands three thousand servitors.

Sources: Peterson, *Lesser Key of Solomon*, 62; Trithemius, *Steganographicos*, 54.

Maamah

Variations: NAAMAH ("pleasant"), Na'amah, Nahemah, Malkuth

In Jewish mysticism, Maamah ("hiding place"), both a FALLEN ANGEL and SUCCUBUS, is the mother of the demon ASMODAI; she is also one of the four DEMONS OF PROSTITUTION. Maamah appears as a woman with an animal-like body; she is often depicted as crouching and eating the earth. The demon of divination and music, she is consort to LILITH THE LESSER, the mate of SAMAEL.

Sources: Davenport, *The Koran*, 52; Ford, *Book of the Witch Moon Choronzon*, 356; Mason, *Necronomicon Gnosis*, 151.

Mabakiel

The *Sacred Magic of Abramelin the Mage*, book two, names Mabakiel ("lamentation, weeping") as one of the fifteen SERVITORS OF ASMODEUS AND MAGOTH (see ASMODEUS).

Sources: Mathers, *Book of the Sacred Magic of Abramelin the Mage*, 106, 117; Von Worms, *Book of Abramelin*, 248, 256.

Macariel

In the *Theurgia Goetia*, the second book of the *Lemegeton*, Macariel is ranked as a PLANETARY PRINCE of Mercury, a prince, and one of the eleven WANDERING PRINCES (see PRINCES OF HELL). He commands forty dukes, twelve named chief dukes, and a host of servitors. This devil is invoked for assistance with books and puzzles and will convey secrets reliably. Like all AERIAL DEVILS, he and his court are constantly on the move, never staying in any one place for long.

Sources: Gettings, *Dictionary of Demons*, 232; Peterson, *Lesser Key of Solomon*, 102; Trithemius, *Steganographia*, 81.

Machalas

According to Hassidic demonology, Machalas was one of the four devils who had children with Adam during the one hundred thirty years before his marriage to Eve (see DEVILS OF ADAM). During that time, he fathered many offspring with her (see CAMBION). She is under the command of LILIS, and her name may translate to mean "illness."

Sources: Guiley, *Encyclopedia of Demonology*, 159; Peterson, *Lesser Key of Solomon*, 99, 102; Trithemius, *Steganographia*, 69, 141.

Machaloth

Machaloth is a demonic witch that looks like a serpent-skinned woman with burning eyes. She rides upon a serpent scorpion demon (see also AGGERETH).

Sources: MacGregor, *Sorcerer and His Apprentice*, 25; Wise, *Origin of Christianity*, 95.

Machariel

In the *Theurgia Goetia*, the second book of the *Lemegeton*, Machariel is ranked as a duke and one of the seven PLANETARY PRINCES as well as one of the eleven WANDERING PRINCES (see DUKES OF HELL and PRINCES OF HELL). He is listed as one of the fifteen SERVITORS OF ICOSIEL. An AERIAL DEVIL, he commands numerous dukes, twelve named chief dukes, and numerous inferior servitors. This demon is easily summoned to houses. His zodiacal sign is Mercury.

Sources: Guiley, *Encyclopedia of Demonology*, 159; Peterson, *Lesser Key of Solomon*, 99, 102; Trithemius, *Steganographia*, 69, 141.

Machlath

Variations: Agrath bath Machlath, LILITH, Mahalath

In Hassidic demonology Machlath ("the dancer") is one of the concubines of SATAN. Described as being a beautiful woman with long flowing hair, this nocturnal demon is most powerful on Wednesdays and Saturdays.

Sources: Rudwin, *Devil in Legend and Literature*, 98; Salmonson, *Encyclopedia of Amazons*, 191.

Macic

Variations: Macaklic, Machic, Matic

The Dalmatian folklore, specifically from Poljice and the islands of Brac, Hvar, Korcula, and Peljesac, has a type of demon called a macic. Hatched from an egg, this demon appears during the noon hour. Throughout the night it assumes the form of a donkey and will attack anyone who tries to ride it.

Source: Neale, *Notes Ecclesiological and Picturesque*, 181.

Madail

In the *Sacred Magic of Abramelin the Mage*, book two, Madail ("drawing out") is listed as one of the sixty-five SERVITORS OF KORE AND MAGOTH.

Sources: Mathers, *Book of the Sacred Magic of Abramelin the Mage*, 118; Von Worms, *Book of Abramelin*, 250, 256.

Madame White

According to Taoist lore, Madame White is a demon that preys upon young men. Her true form is that of a white python but she takes on the form of a beautiful woman with cherry-red lips, dainty features, small feet, and a tiny waist, who is all dressed in white; she is accompanied by a maiden dressed in all blue (who is actually a blue fish). Living in or near lakes, this demon is most often seen on holidays like Quing Ming, the Festival of the Dead. She is said to be a possessive demon and when stressed will revert to her true form. There are no known common remedies to drive her off a man whose affection she seeks; a professional must be consulted.

Sources: Chang, *Chinese Literature*, 205–62; Daigaku, *Asian Folklore Studies*, Vol. 56, 335; Larrington, *Feminist Companion to Mythology*, 238–9; Mack, *Field Guide to Demons, Fairies, Fallen Angels, and Other Subversive Spirits*, 26–8.

Madhu

Madhu ("nectar") is an ASURAS from Hindu mythology. The demon of darkness, he is one of the two gigantic demons born from the ear wax of the god Vishnu. Ranked as a king, he is cruel and has committed many atrocities. With his brother, KAITABHA, they intended to kill the Brahma while he slept. This king lives with his wife, Kumbhini, in his kingdom, Madhuvana. He is the father of LAVANASURA.

Eventually the brothers were slain by Krishna, the god Vishnu, or the goddess Uma; sources vary. After their deaths, the bodies disintegrated into twelve pieces (two heads, two torsos, four arms, and four legs), which were then thrown into the ocean where they produced a great deal of fat and marrow. These elements were used to sculpt the twelve seismic plates of the earth.

Sources: Parmeshwaranand, *Encyclopaedic Dictionary of Purāṇas*, Vol. 3, 716–7; Schrader, *Introduction to the Pāñcarātra and the Ahirbudhnya Saṃhitā*, 44, 127; Williams, *Handbook of Hindu Mythology*, 169.

Madime

Madime is the demon of Tuesdays. He has dominion over the planet Mars.

Sources: Gettings, *Dictionary of Demons*, 154; Waite, *Book of Black Magic and of Pacts*, 122.

Madres

In the *Theurgia Goetia*, the second book of the *Lemegeton*, Duke Madres is listed as one of the eleven SERVITORS OF PAMERSIEL (see DUKES OF HELL and PAMERSIEL). A nocturnal AERIAL DEVIL, he is known to be very useful at driving out and exorcising spirits from haunted places. Arrogant and stubborn, he is also an expert liar and freely tells secrets he has learned. Madres, when summoned, must be called from the second floor of a home or in a wide open space.

Sources: Johnson, *Landscape Ethnoecology*, 147; Peterson, *Lesser Key of Solomon*, 64.

Maereboe

In the Brazilian demonology of the Bororo people, Maereboe ("bad") is a species of nocturnal AERIAL DEVIL known as a *bope*. Created when an evil *bari* (shaman) dies, the soul becomes this type of demonic spirit. The demons of death and decay, they command flies, lesser bope, and mosquitoes. Described as being three feet tall and humanoid in appearance, they have fiery eyes, glassy-black skin, cloven hooves, and matted hair growing in patches upon their body.

These demons consume human souls, attacking a single target, an entire family, or even an entire village. They move in while the victim is asleep. Then the Maereboe steals an item that is beloved by the victim so that their soul will leave the body and follow after it. Then the demon catches the soul, flies into the air with it, sets it on fire, and sends it hurling back down to the earth where it feeds upon the shattered and charred remains. Sometimes it will rape the soul before destroying it.

Maereboe are said to cause eclipses, horrific NIGHTMARES, meteor showers, rainstorms, and wind gusts. They can also spit fire and change children into small animals in order to more easily consume them. Greedy beings by nature, they can be prevented from attacking by making offerings of hand-rolled cigarettes.

Source: Jones, *Evil in Our Midst*, 80–4.

Mafalac

According to the *Sacred Magic of Abramelin the Mage*, Mafalac ("fragment") is one of the eight SERVITORS OF ORIENS (see ORIENS).

Sources: Mathers, *Book of the Sacred Magic of Abramelin the Mage*, 108, 121; Von Worms, *Book of Abramelin*, 253, 257.

Mafrus

Christian demonology ranks Mafrus as a duke and lists him as one of the twenty SERVITORS OF SYMIEL (see SYMIEL). He shares the seven hundred ninety servitors that are at the disposal of all of SYMIEL's servitors. Mafrus is disobedient, stubborn, and will not appear willingly when summoned.

Sources: Guiley, *Encyclopedia of Demons and Demonology*, 253; Peterson, *Lesser Key of Solomon*, 88–9; Trithemius, *Steganographia*, 42.

Magalast

In the *Sacred Magic of Abramelin the Mage*, book two, Magalast ("greatly") is one of the forty-nine SERVITORS OF BEELZEBUB (see BEELZEBUB).

Sources: Ford, *Bible of the Adversary*, 93; Mathers, *Book of the Sacred Magic of Abramelin the Mage*, 108, 120; Von Worms, *Book of Abramelin*, 253, 257.

Maggid

The *Sacred Magic of Abramelin the Mage*, book two, includes Maggid ("precious things") as one of the sixteen SERVITORS OF ASMODEUS (see AS-MODEUS).

Sources: Mathers, *Book of the Sacred Magic of Abramelin the Mage*, 107, 119; Von Worms, *Book of Abramelin*, 251, 256.

Magiros

In the *Sacred Magic of Abramelin the Mage*, book two, Magiros ("cook") is listed as one of the fifteen SERVITORS OF ASMODEUS AND MAGOTH (see ASMODEUS).

Sources: Mathers, *Book of the Sacred Magic of Abramelin the Mage*, 106; Von Worms, *Book of Abramelin*, 248, 256.

Magog

Variations: Magon

In the *Sacred Magic of Abramelin the Mage*, book two, Magog, a devil, is among the fifteen SERVITORS OF ASMODEUS AND MAGOTH (see ASMODEUS).

It should be noted that Ezekiel 38 and 39 are not references to demonic entities. GOG is a reference to a person, specifically the chief prince of Meshech and Tubal. Magog is a reference to a place, the Land of Magog.

Sources: France, *On Life and Letters*, 220; Mathers, *Book of the Sacred Magic of Abramelin the Mage*, 116; Rudwin, *Devil in Legend and Literature*, 86; Von Worms, *Book of Abramelin*, 221, 248.

Magot

Variations: Magos, Maguth, Maguth Gutrix

Liber Iuratus Honorii (*The Sworne Booke of Honorius*), a thirteenth-century grimoire that is considered by many scholars to be one of the foundation works of European magical practices, names Magot as an infernal minister who is under the command of the demon Guth. The demon of hidden treasures, he is most powerful on Thursdays and has dominion over the planet Jupiter. Magot's name may be Hebrew in origin and if so would translate to mean "small stones."

Sources: Belanger, *Dictionary of Demons*, 141; Von Worms, *Book of Abramelin*, 248.

Mahalbiya

From the demonology of the Hausa people of West Africa, Mahalbiya ("markswoman") is the demon of skin diseases; however, she is sometimes considered to be a goddess. Born the daughter of the demon JIGO, she causes fevers, sores, and topical ulcers. To cure someone who has been afflicted by her, a specific magical dance is performed to determine the cause and the cure of the demonic attack. Usually an animal sacrifice is required, typically a bird of a specific gender and color.

Sources: Knappert, *African Mythology*, 107; Tremearme, *Ban of the Bori*, 346.

Mahasohon

Variations: Maha-sohon

In Sri Lanka there is belief in a gigantic, hairy vampiric demon known as the mahasohon, which hunts not only humans but elephants as well. The mahasohon waits at the crossroads at night for someone to pass by; when they do, it leaps out and attacks, draining them dry of their blood and then eating most of the corpse. There is a demon dance ceremony that can be performed to drive it away called *Mahasohon Samayama*.

Sources: Goonatilleka, *Masks and Mask Systems of Sri Lanka*, 10, 15, 19–20; Jayatilaka, *Dictionary of the Sinhalese Language*, 762; Kapferer, *Celebration of Demons*, 206; Pranāndu, *Rituals*, 180.

Mahasura

Variations: Daitya Raja ("King of the Demons"), the great ASURAS

Mahasura ("great demon not-god") is an

ASURAS from Hindu demonology. Said to be very strong, he is often referred to as the SATAN of Hinduism.

Sources: Blavatsky, *Secret Doctrine: Anthropogenesis*, 237; Hopkins, *Epic Mythology with Additions and Corrections*, 501, 62.

Mahisha

Variations: BHAINSASURA, Mahisha-Asura, Mahishasura ("the buffalo demon")

In Hindu and Tantric mythology, Mahisha ("buffalo") is an ASURAS, according to the *Markandeya Purana*, one of the eighteen *mahapuranas*, a type of Hindu religious text. The demon of death, Mahisha was born the son of Ramba and a demon in the guise of a buffalo, or as the son of a mother buffalo and a demon. This buffalo-headed demon who had the ability to shape-shift into a buffalo, elephant, human, lion, and create a million copies of himself had once received a boon from Brahma in which no male could kill him. Mahisha was an expansionistic, greedy, lusty, malevolent, and slow-witted individual who was prone to sloth. He was eventually slain by the goddess DURGA, an aspect of KALI.

Sources: Mack, *Field Guide to Demons, Fairies, Fallen Angels, and Other Subversive Spirits*, 73–6; Narayan, *Gods, Demons, and Others*, 50–61; Williams, *Handbook of Hindu Mythology*, 205–6.

Mahonin

Variations: Mahonim

Named during a Catholic exorcism at Auch, France (1618 to 1622 or 1625), the devil and Mahonin preyed upon a French countess and her servants daily for about five years. Said to be under the command of Brother Natal, a Franciscan confessor, Mahonin claimed to have been born in Beziers, a town in Languedon, France. This devil was once an angel, formerly of the third hierarchy and the second order of archangels (see FALLEN ANGELS). His personal adversary is St. Mark the Evangelist.

During the exorcism of the countess, the priest was able to discover that the demon entered the body on the third Tuesday of the previous Easter; that it was sent to her by the Franciscan confessor Brother Natal; and that should it be compelled to leave the body, it would signal its defeat by throwing a stone off the tower into the moat below.

Sources: Gettings, *Dictionary of Demons*, 159; Paine, *Hierarchy of Hell*, 79; Robbins, *Encyclopedia of Witchcraft and Demonology*, 128, 185; Sands, *Demon Possession in Elizabethan England*, 48.

Mai-Gangaddi

Variations: The nodding one, Sarikin Barchi

In the demonology of the Hausa people of West Africa, the demon Mai-Gangaddi causes sleeping sickness. To save those who have fallen victim to this demon a specific magical dance is performed to determine the cause and the cure of the demonic attack. The shaman will dance and suddenly fall down to the floor as if asleep, and rise and dance and fall again. Usually an animal sacrifice is required, typically a bird of a specific gender and color.

Sources: Knappert, *Swahili Culture*, Vol. 2, 653; Tremearne, *Ban of the Bori*, 337–9.

Mai-Ja-Chikki

Variations: DAKAKI

In the demonology of the Hausa people of West Africa, the demon Mai-Ja-Chikki appears as a serpent and is said to cause the evil eye and stomach ulcers. His attacks can be prevented with regular offerings of eggs and milk, but if a person does fall prey to this demon, a specific magical dance is performed to determine the cause and the cure of the demonic attack. Usually an animal sacrifice is required, typically a bird of a specific gender and color.

Sources: Howey, *Encircled Serpent: A Study of Serpent Symbolism*, 239–40; Oesterreich, *Possession, Demoniacal and Other Among Primitive Races*, 257–8; Tremearne, *Ban of the Bori*, 174, 178, 228.

Maisadul

The *Sacred Magic of Abramelin the Mage*, book two, lists Maisadul as one of the sixty-five SERVITORS OF KORE AND MAGOTH.

Sources: Mathers, *Book of the Sacred Magic of Abramelin the Mage*, 107, 119; Von Worms, *Book of Abramelin*, 250, 256.

Makalos

In the *Sacred Magic of Abramelin the Mage*, book two, Makalos is among the sixty-five SERVITORS OF KORE AND MAGOTH. The etymology of this name is possibly Chaldaic and could mean "attenuated, wasted."

Sources: Mathers, *Book of the Sacred Magic of Abramelin the Mage*, 107, 119; Von Worms, *Book of Abramelin*, 251, 256.

Makatiel

Variations: Matniel

In Jewish demonology Makatiel ("plague of God") is ranked as one of the seven ANGELS OF PUNISHMENT of the ten nations. He is under the command of the ARCHANGELS OF PUNISHMENT. This FALLEN ANGEL is the demon of punishment and trees. He lives in the fourth lodge of Hell.

Sources: Ashley, *Complete Book of Devils and Demons*, 78; Davidson, *Dictionary of Angels*, 41; Gaster, *Studies and Texts in Folklore*, 159.

Makeri

In the demonology of the Hausa people of West Africa, Makeri ("blacksmith") preys specifically upon craftsmen by causing back, arm, and work related illness in craftspeople. For those afflicted, a specific magical dance is performed to determine the cause and the cure of the demonic attack. Usually an animal sacrifice is required, typically a bird of a specific gender and color.

Sources: Knappert, *African Mythology*, 107; Tremearne, *Ban of the Bori*, 352, 487.

Malad

As one of the twenty Duke SERVITORS OF SYMIEL (see SYMIEL), Malad is disobedient, stubborn, and will not appear willingly before his summoner. He shares with the other nocturnal SERVITORS OF SYMIEL seven hundred ninety servitors among them.

Source: Peterson, *Lesser Key of Solomon*, 88.

Malgaras

In the *Theurgia Goetia*, the second book of the *Lemegeton*, Malgaras is ranked as the Prince of the West, demon of the southwest, and is one of the twelve SERVITORS OF AMENADIEL (see AMENADIEL and PRINCES OF HELL). He keeps hidden the affairs of friends. Malgaras' name may be Hebrew and translate to mean "award-head."

Sources: Gettings, *Dictionary of Demons*, 232; Trithemius, *Steganographia*, 81.

Malgron

As one of the twenty Duke SERVITORS OF SYMIEL (see SYMIEL), Malgron is very obedient and quick to obey his summoner. He shares with the other diurnal SERVITORS OF SYMIEL seven hundred twenty servitors among them.

Sources: Guiley, *Encyclopedia of Demons and Demonology*, 253; Peterson, *Lesser Key of Solomon*, 88.

Malguel

In the *Theurgia Goetia*, the second book of the *Lemegeton*, Malguel is ranked as a chief duke and is listed as one of the sixteen SERVITORS OF ASYRIEL (see ASYRIEL). A diurnal demon, he commands twenty servitors and is said to be good-natured and willing to obey his summoner.

Source: Peterson, *Lesser Key of Solomon*, 73.

Malik

Variations: Malac, Malek, Melik

In Arabic demonology, Malik ("King") is said to be a *zabaniya* (guardian) who preys upon sinners who denied the truth when it was revealed to them. A FALLEN ANGEL, Malik stokes the fires of Hell and taunts those he guards over.

Sources: Davidson, *Dictionary of Angels*, 182; Hastings, *Encyclopædia of Religion and Ethics*, Vol. 4, 346–7, 618; Khanam, *Demonology*, 195.

Malogra, La

Variations: La Malora ("The evil one")

In Hispanic folklore *la malogra* ("evil hour") is a heliophobic, nocturnal, TERRESTRIAL DEMON that appears to look like a large piece of wool or the entire fleece of a sheep; very rarely is it described as taking human form. Typically attacking travelers who pass through the crossroads, anyone who sees this demon runs a chance of being driven insane (see HELIOPHOBIC DEVIL). *La malogra*, considered to be a death omen, can change its size and is wholly evil.

Sources: Aquino, *Reader in Latina Feminist Theology*, 69; Gebhardt, *Female Mythologies in Contemporary Chicana Literature*, 94; McNeil, *Ghastly Ghost Stories*, 64.

Malpas

Variations: MALPHAS

In Solomonic lore Malpas is one of the seventy-two SPIRITS OF SOLOMON. He appears as a huge black bird. This demon builds things by supernatural means. He has the ability to destroy the desires and thoughts of the enemy and gives good FAMILIARs.

Sources: Diagram Group, *Little Giant Encyclopedia*, 502; Gettings, *Dictionary of Demons*, 160; Icon, *Demons*, 165; Scot, *Discoverie of Witchcraft*, 221.

Malphas

Variations: HALPHAS, Malthous, Malthus

In Christian demonology and written of in various grimoires, Malphas is ranked as a grand president or prince. He is said to be the president of deceivers and commands forty legions (see PRESIDENTS OF HELL and PRINCES OF HELL). Typically he is depicted as a crow, but at the request of his summoner will shape-shift into the form of a man and will speak in a hoarse voice. Malphas is summoned for his ability to build houses, high towers, and strongholds. He destroys the enemies' desires and disrupts their thoughts, razes their buildings, and gives his summoner the enemy's plans. Malphas can also grant good FAMILIARs and quickly brings together skilled craftsmen to one place from all places of the world.

Malphas requires that he be given a sacrifice so as not to attack his summoner and will accept it with much kindness; however, after accepting it he will lie or otherwise deceive the summoner.

Sources: Collin de Plancy, *Dictionary of Witchcraft*, 87; De Laurence, *Lesser Key of Solomon, Goetia*, 34; DuQuette, *Key to Solomon's Key*, 180.

Malutens

In the *Sacred Magic of Abramelin the Mage*, book two, Malutens is one of the one hundred eleven SERVITORS OF AMAYMON, ARITON, ORIENS, AND PAYMON (see AMAYMON, ARITON, ORIENS, and PAYMON). His name is possibly Hebrew and means "to lie, deceive, or prevaricate."

Sources: Mathers, *Book of the Sacred Magic of Abramelin the Mage*, 105, 112; Von Worms, *Book of Abramelin*, 244, 255.

Mama Dlo

Variations: Mama Dglo, Mama Glow, Maman de l'eau

In the mythology of the people from the Republic of Trinidad and Tobago comes the AQUATIC DEVIL Mama Dlo ("Mother of the Water"). She has the head and shoulders of a beautiful woman with long hair and the body of a snake. This demon uses her beauty to lure men off to their deaths by crushing their bodies during her lovemaking, restoring them back to life and killing them anew, for all time her sex slaves. Although she will prey upon any man she can get, Mama Dlo particularly hunts out those who destroy the natural swamp habitat where she lives. Telltale signs of Mama Dlo's presence in an area are reports of men on work crews disappearing. Survivors also say that they heard a loud cracking sound, which is said to be the noise she makes with her tail as she slaps it on the surface of a mountain pool or a still lagoon. Should this demon ever be encountered, remove your left shoe and place it upside down on the path before you, then, walking backwards, quickly return to your home.

Sources: Jones, *Evil in Our Midst*, 126–9; Lewis, *Guinea's Other Suns*, 179; Philpott, *Trinidad and Tobago*, 53, 89.

Mames

In the *Sacred Magic of Abramelin the Mage*, Mames ("they who move by backward motion") is listed as one of the twenty SERVITORS OF AMAYMON (see AMAYMON).

Sources: Lowry, *Under the Volcano*, 194; Mathers, *Book of the Sacred Magic of Abramelin the Mage*, 109, 122; Von Worms, *Book of Abramelin*, 255, 257.

Mammon

According to medieval demonology, Mammon ("money") is the demon of avarice. Ranked as the prince of tempters and Hell's ambassador to England, he is described as looking wolflike (see PRINCES OF HELL). Mammon is an ARCHDEMON, a FALLEN ANGEL, formerly of the Order of Thrones.

Sources: Chambers, *Book of Days*, 723; Crane, *Great Exorcism*, 49; Nicoll, *Masks, Mimes and Miracles*, 188.

Manasael

In the *Theurgia Goetia*, the second book of the *Lemegeton*, Manasael is ranked as a duke who commands 2,400 servitors and is listed as being one of the ten SERVITORS OF BYDIEL (see BYDIEL). This AERIAL DEVIL has an attractive form and is said to be good-natured and willing to obey his summoner.

Source: Peterson, *Lesser Key of Solomon*, 105.

Mandragora

A mandragora is a type of FAMILIAR who is given to a sorcerer by the DEVIL. It looks like a small man with black-colored skin. Sources vary as to whether it is bearded. They are also described as looking like little dolls or figurines made from withered plants or wax. These demons act as a consultant and assistant to a sorcerer in times of need or in performing magic. Secretly they live among human populations causing mischief, as they can become invisible and cause madness in any animal or man its sorcerer wishes. Mandragora are said to live in the root of the mandrake plant when not being used by their sorcerer. The wearing of various charms and talismans for protection will ward off this demonic being.

Sources: Collin de Plancy, *Dictionary of Witchcraft*, 87–8; Dunwich, *Wicca Garden*, 101; Gettings, *Dictionary of Demons*, 161–2; Olcott, *People from the Other World*, 336; Spence, *Encyclopaedia of Occultism*, 266.

Manó, plural: manók

In Hungarian demonology a manó (or manók as they are called in numbers) is a species of subterranean devil that lives underground. The word translates to mean "devil" or "naughty."

Sources: Chambers, *Chambers's Encyclopædia*, 359; Gaskell, *Dictionary of the Sacred Languages*, 36–7.

Mansi

In the *Theurgia Goetia*, the second book of the *Lemegeton*, Mansi is a diurnal duke that is listed as one of the fifteen SERVITORS OF BARMIEL (BARMIEL and DUKES OF HELL).

Sources: Peterson, *Lesser Key of Solomon*, 70–1.

Mantahungal

In the demonology of the Tagbanua people of the Philippines the mantahungal is a creature that lives in the forests on top of high mountains. Described as being a hornless, shaggy cow with a monstrous mouth and tusklike incisors, it rips humans apart with its tusks.

Source: Ramos, *Creatures of Philippine Lower Mythology*, 344.

Mantan

Mantan is one of the sixty-five SERVITORS OF KORE AND MAGOTH named in the *Sacred Magic of Abramelin the Mage*, book two.

Sources: Mathers, *Book of the Sacred Magic of Abramelin the Mage*, 118; Von Worms, *Book of Abramelin*, 250, 256.

Mantiens

The *Sacred Magic of Abramelin the Mage*, book two, includes Mantiens ("prophesying") as one of the one hundred eleven SERVITORS OF AMAYMON, ARITON, ORIENS, AND PAYMON (see AMAYMON, ARITON, ORIENS, and PAYMON).

Sources: Susej, *Demonic Bible*, 256; Von Worms, *Book of Abramelin*, 244, 255.

Manuval

In the demonology of New Guinea, Manuval is a demon of the night.

Sources: Ashley, *Complete Book of Devils and Demons*, 64; Hastings, *Encyclopedia of Religion and Ethics*, 361.

Marag

In the *Sacred Magic of Abramelin the Mage*, book two, Marag ("to drive forward") is listed as one of the sixty-five SERVITORS OF KORE AND MAGOTH.

Sources: Mathers, *Book of the Sacred Magic of Abramelin the Mage*, 118; Von Worms, *Book of Abramelin*, 250, 256.

Marakayikas

Variations: Ma ("goblins")

In Buddhist demonology, Marakayikas, born one of the children of Mara the Evil One, is said to be under the command of the demon PAPIYAN.

Sources: Carus, *History of the Devil and the Idea of Evil*, 105; Grünwedel, *Buddhist Art in India*, 39, 92; Soothill, *Dictionary of Chinese Buddhist Terms*, 266; Turner, *Dictionary of Ancient Deities*, 308.

Maranton

The *Sacred Magic of Abramelin the Mage*, book two, lists Maranton ("having extinguished, quenched") among the twenty-two SERVITORS OF ARITON (see ARITON).

Sources: Mathers, *Book of the Sacred Magic of Abramelin the Mage*, 108, 122; Von Worms, *Book of Abramelin*, 124, 254.

Maras

The *Theurgia Goetia*, the second book of the *Lemegeton*, ranks Maras as a chief duke in service under CASPIEL (see DUKES OF HELL and SERVI-TORS OF CASPIEL). Rude and stubborn, this demon commands 2,660 duke servitors.

Sources: Guiley, *Encyclopedia of Demons and Demonology*, 37, 169; Peterson, *Lesser Key of Solomon*, 60, 67.

Marax

Variations: FORAII, FORFAX, MORAX

Johann Wierus's *Pseudomonarchia Daemonum* (*False Monarchy of Demons*, 1583) describes Marax ("that delays, that stops") as a large bull with the face of a man. This demon is ranked as an earl (or count, sources conflict) and president who commands thirty (or thirty-six, sources vary) legions (see COUNTS OF HELL, EARLS OF HELL and PRESIDENTS OF HELL). He is summoned for his ability to teach astronomy and the liberal sciences as well as for his willingness to give good and wise FAMILIARs that know gemology and herbology. It should be noted that when summoned, Marax's seal must be worn by the demonologist.

Sources: De Laurence, *Lesser Key of Solomon, Goetia*, 28; DuQuette, *Key to Solomon's Key*, 170–1; Scott, *London Magazine*, Vol. 5, 378.

Marbas

Variations: BARBAS

In the *Ars Goetia*, Marbas is ranked as a president and the Master of the Seal; he commands thirty-six legions. When summoned he appears as a powerful lion but at the summoner's request will shape-shift into a man. He answers truthfully any question asked of him about the location of hidden treasures and secrets. He can also cause and cure diseases, change men into other shapes, give the knowledge of handicrafts and the mechanical arts, and make men wise.

Sources: Baskin, *Sorcerer's Handbook*, 276; De Laurence, *Lesser Key of Solomon, Goetia*, 23; DuQuette, *Key to Solomon's Key*, 162–3; Waite, *Unknown World 1894–1895*, 230; Wedeck, *Treasury of Witchcraft*, 96.

Marchosias

Variations: Marchocias, Marchoias

According to medieval demonology, Marchosias is a FALLEN ANGEL, formerly of the Order of Dominions. Ranked as a prince or grand marquis (sources vary), he commands thirty legions (see PRINCES OF HELL and MARQUIS OF HELL).

Although this is a male demon, he appears before his summoner as a she-wolf or an ox with griffin wings and a serpent for a tail; however, at the request of his summoner he will shape-shift into the form of a man. Said to be honest and faithful to the one who summons him forth, Marchosias will answer all questions put to him truthfully. He has the ability to spit fire and is a strong combatant. Marchosias told Solomon that after 1,200 years he hopes to be able to return unto the Seventh Heaven (see SPIRITS OF SOLOMON).

Sources: De Laurence, *Lesser Key of Solomon, Goetia*, 33–4; DuQuette, *Key to Solomon's Key*, 178; Lurker, *Dictionary of Gods and Goddesses*, 222; McLean, *Treatise of Angel Magic*, 55; Scot, *Discoverie of Witchcraft*, 221; Scott, *London Magazine*, Vol. 5, 378.

Mardero

Mardero is the demon of fevers. He appears as a man with the shapeless head of a dog and the face of a bird, donkey, or ox. This demon, who causes incurable fevers, was condemned to heavy labor tending the furnaces used for metalworking on the Temple of Solomon (see SPIRITS OF SOLOMON). To save a person who has been assaulted by this demon, write the words "Sphener Rafael retire drag me not about flay me not" and wear it around the neck. His personal adversary is the angel Sphener.

Sources: Ashe, *Qabalah*, 48; Charlesworth, *Old Testament Pseudepigrapha*, 980; Conybeare, *Jewish Quarterly Review*, Vol. 11, 37; Pilch, *Cultural Dictionary of the Bible*, 162.

Marfiel

In the *Ars Paulina*, the third book of the *Lemegeton*, Marfiel is listed as one of the eleven SERVITORS OF RAHAB (see RAHAB).

Sources: Peterson, *Lesser Key of Solomon*, 114; Trithemius, *Steganographia*, 93; Waite, *The Book of Ceremonial Magic*, 67.

Marianu

Marianu is one of the twenty SERVITORS OF SYMIEL, a disobedient and stubborn demon who will not appear willingly before his summoner. He shares with the other nocturnal SERVITORS OF SYMIEL seven hundred ninety servitors among them.

Sources: Eco, *Infinity of Lists*, 61; Peterson, *Lesser Key of Solomon*, 88.

Maricha

In the *Ramayana*, an ancient Sanskrit epic ascribed to the Hindu sage Valmiki and possibly dating from the fourth century B.C.E., Maricha was originally a YAKSHA, born the son of TATAKA, but he was cursed to become an ASURAS. Along with his brother, SUBAHU, they disrupted the Vedic rituals by throwing unclean meat and blood into the oblation fire. He had the ability to shape-shift into a golden stag. Eventually he was slain by Rama with an arrow.

Sources: Buck, *Ramayana*, 161–8; Coomaraswamy,

Myths of the Hindus and Buddhists, 20, 27, 55; Sehgal, *Encyclopaedia of Hinduism*, 44–8.

Marid

Islamic mythology tells us that the Marid ("rebellious") are the favored troops of IBLIS, as they are the most powerful of all the species of DJINN even if they are the least numerous. Unique for a demon, they are said to have free will. Marid are arrogant and proud, and as such can be compelled to perform chores. They are physically powerful and knowledgeable and very evil. They can grant wishes to mortals but it involves battle, imprisonment, rituals, or copious amounts of flattery.

Sources: Hughes, *Dictionary of Islam*, 134; Mack, *Field Guide to Demons, Fairies, Fallen Angels, and Other Subversive Spirits*, 146; Waardenburg, *Islam: Historical, Social, and Political Perspectives*, 39.

Mariel

Mariel, a diurnal demon, is one of the sixteen SERVITORS OF ASELIEL (see ASELIEL) named in the *Sacred Magic of Abramelin the Mage*, book two.

Sources: Davidson, *Dictionary of Angels*, 164; Peterson, *Lesser Key of Solomon*, 69; Trithemius, *Steganographia*, 101.

Marnes

In Apollonius of Tyana's *Nuctemeron* (*Night Illuminated by Day*) Marnes is named as the demon of discernment of spirits. He is said to be most powerful during the twelfth hour.

Sources: Gettings, *Dictionary of Demons*, 162; Lévi, *Transcendental Magic*, 422.

Marock

Variations: Maroch

In the *Ars Paulina*, the third book of the *Lemegeton*, Marock is ranked as a chief and is listed as one of the SERVITORS OF SCOX (see SCOX). He is also listed as one of the ten SERVITORS OF SAZQUIEL (see SAZQUIEL).

Sources: Davidson, *Dictionary of Angels*, 184; Peterson, *Lesser Key of Solomon*, 114; Trithemius, *Steganographia*, 95; Waite, *Book of Black Magic and Ceremonial Magic*, 67.

Maroth

The *Theurgia Goetia*, the second book of the *Lemegeton*, ranks Maroth as a chief duke and is listed as one of the sixteen SERVITORS OF ASYRIEL (see ASYRIEL). A nocturnal demon, he is said to be good-natured and willing to obey his summoner.

Sources: Davidson, *Dictionary of Angels*, 184; Peterson, *Lesser Key of Solomon*, 74.

Marou

Marou is a FALLEN ANGEL, formerly of the Order of Cherubim. Along with BERITH, LAU-

VIAH, and SALIKOTAL, this demon helped place the Tree of Knowledge in the Garden of Eden. In the trial of Urbain Grandier, Marou was cited as one of the six demons that possessed Elizabeth Blanchard.

Sources: Davidson, *Dictionary of Angels*, 184; Maberry, *Cryptopedia*, 78, 80.

Marques

The *Theurgia Goetia*, the second book of the *Lemegeton*, ranks Marques as a nocturnal duke and lists him as one of the fifteen SERVITORS OF BARMIEL (see BARMIEL and DUKES OF HELL).

Source: Peterson, *Lesser Key of Solomon*, 70.

Marquis of Hell

There are twenty-two named marquis mentioned in the various grimoires. They are AAMON, AMMON, ANDRAS, ANDREALPHUS, CARABIA, CIMEJES, DECARABIA, FIRNEUS, FORNEUS, KIMARIS, LEONARD, LERAIEL, MARCHOSIAS, NABERUS, ORIAS, PHENEX, RENOVE, RONOBE, SABANACK, SAMIGINA, SCOX, and SHAX.

Sources: De Laurence, *Lesser Key of Solomon, Goetia*, 22–23; Scott, *London Magazine*, Vol. 5, 378.

Maru Sanniya

In Sinhalese demonology Maru Sanniya ("Tamil demon") is the demon of delirium. He is depicted in ceremonial masks as having a black face with a low forehead and protruding eyes, tongue, and tusks; his head is topped with strands of yellow rope to represent unkempt hair. This demon has the ability to cause death, delirium, and the fear of death. Like the other Sinhalese demons, Maru Sanniya is susceptible to the DAHA-ATA SANNIYA.

Sources: Illes, *Encyclopedia of Spirits*, 875; Wirz, *Exorcism and the Art of Healing in Ceylon*, 44.

Marut

In Islamic mythology Marut is a FALLEN ANGEL who knows the powerful and secret name of God. He taught mankind how to establish a government and sorcery.

HARUT and Marut were sent to earth by God to see how well they would be able to resist human temptations. They were immediately seduced by the women of earth and killed the man who witnessed their seduction. The angels admitted their crimes to God and were condemned to hang in a well by their feet until Judgment Day.

Neither one of these two FALLEN ANGELS will ever begin a lesson in sorcery without first saying to their students, "We have been sent to deceive you."

Sources: Abdul-Rahman, *Meaning and Explanation of the Glorious Qur'an*, Vol. 1, 188–90; Davidson, *Dictionary of Angels*, 353; Jung, *Fallen Angels in Jewish, Christian and Mohammedan Literature*, 91, 127–40; Knappert, *Islamic Legends*, 4, 59–62.

Masaki

From the demonology of the Hausa people of West Africa comes the demon Masaki ("weaver"). Preying upon craftsmen, he causes back, arm, and work related illnesses in craftspeople. A specific magical dance is performed to determine the cause and the cure of the demonic attack. Usually an animal sacrifice is required, typically a bird of a specific gender and color.

Sources: Knappert, *African Mythology*, 107; Robinson, *Dictionary of the Hausa Language*, Vol. 1, 209; Tremearne, *Ban of the Bori*, 352–3.

Masaub

In the *Sacred Magic of Abramelin the Mage*, book two, Masaub ("circuit") is among the sixty-five SERVITORS OF KORE AND MAGOTH.

Sources: Mathers, *Book of the Sacred Magic of Abramelin the Mage*, 118; Von Worms, *Book of Abramelin*, 249, 256.

Mascarvin

Variations: Mascarum

In Apollonius of Tyana's *Nuctemeron* (*Night Illuminated by Day*), Mascarvin is the demon of death. He is most powerful during the third hour of the day.

Sources: Gettings, *Dictionary of Demons*, 162.

Maseriel

In the *Theurgia Goetia*, the second book of the *Lemegeton*, Maseriel ("deliver") is ranked as the Prince of the West by Southwest. He is one of the twelve SERVITORS OF AMENADIEL (see AMENADIEL and PRINCES OF HELL). He is summoned for his knowledge in magic, necromancy, and philosophy.

Sources: Belanger, *Dictionary of Demons*, 115; Gettings, *Dictionary of Demons*, 232; Guiley, *Encyclopedia of Demons and Demonology*, 169.

Mashith

One of the four ANGELS OF PUNISHMENT from Cabalistic lore, Mashith ("destroyer") is in service to the Angels of Death. The demon of punishment, it is with AF and Hema that he punishes those who are guilty of idolatry, incest, and murder.

Sources: Ashley, *Complete Book of Devils and Demons*, 78; Greenburg, *Haggadah According to the Rite of Yemen*, 31; Levertoff, *The Zohar*, Vol. 1, 105.

Masinel

Variations: Nasiniel

In the *Theurgia Goetia*, the second book of the *Lemegeton*, Masinel is ranked as a duke and is listed as one of the ten SERVITORS OF EMONIEL (see EMONIEL). He commands 1,320 lesser dukes and servitors. An AERIAL DEVIL who lives in the woods, he is said to be good-natured and willing to obey his summoner.

Sources: Peterson, *Lesser Key of Solomon*, 97.

Maskim

Variations: The Terror of the Earth's Mass

A Sumerian class of demon, the seven maskim ("ensnarers" or "layers of ambush") live in both the bowels of the earth and high up in the mountains. Ancient Sumerian tablets describe them as being neither male nor female but rather "stretch themselves out like chains"; they do not reproduce their own kind, answer prayers, or show any sort of mercy whatsoever. These demons have powers that enable them to go against the natural course of things, even being able to reverse the course of the stars. Typically, maskim attack humans with their magical spells and cause evil to befall their prey.

Sources: Hyatt, *Book of Demons*, 37; Lenormant, *Chaldean Magic*, 24.

Mastema

Variations: The Accusing Angel, the Angel of Adversity, the Angel of Hostility, Mansemat

Mentioned in the *Book of Jubilees*, Mastema ("animosity") is an executioner and tempter, and the prince of condemnation, evil, and injustice (see PRINCES OF HELL). This FALLEN ANGEL is in service under God and commanded the off-spring of the FALLEN ANGELS, the NEPHILIM.

Mastema appears throughout the Bible. In Exodus 4:24 he tried to kill Moses; he hardened Pharaoh's heart against the plight of the Jews; he assisted the Egyptian sorcerer in performing magic tricks when Moses and Aaron came before Pharaoh; and when God decided to flood the world he convinced the Lord to spare some of the demons so that he could continue with his work, tempting mankind. Mastema was allowed to maintain one-tenth of those under his command.

Sources: Davidson, *Dictionary of Angels*, 185–6; Kelly, *Satan*, 35–47; Lewis, *Satanism Today*, 164.

Mastho

In Apollonius of Tyana's *Nuctemeron* (*Night Illuminated by Day*), Mastho is the demon of delusive appearances. He is most powerful during the tenth hour.

Sources: Davidson, *Dictionary of Angels*, 186; Gettings, *Dictionary of Demons*, 162; Lévi, *Transcendental Magic*, 507.

Mastinim

Variations: "The greatest angels of the nations"

The Mastinim ("accuser") is the collective name for the flight of accuser angels who are under the command of SAMMAEL. They accuse sinners by reading aloud their sins from the *Book of Life*.

Sources: Bamberger, *Fallen Angels*, 124, 138; Davidson, *Dictionary of Angels*, 186.

Mastuel

Variations: Nastuel, Naustuel, Naystuel

The *Theurgia Goetia*, the second book of the *Lemegeton*, ranks Mastuel as a chief duke who commands four hundred servitors and lists him as one of the twelve SERVITORS OF MACARIEL (see MACARIEL). This demon can be summoned any time of the day or the night and when he appears may do so in various forms; however, he commonly chooses to appear as a dragon with a virgin's head. He is said to be good-natured and willing to obey his summoner. An AERIAL DEVIL, he is constantly on the move, never staying in any one place for long.

Sources: Peterson, *Lesser Key of Solomon*, 103; Trithemius, *Steganographia*, 141.

Maymon

Maymon is a demon who originated in Elizabethan demonology. The first appearance of his name was in a book titled *An Elizabethan Devil-Worshiper's Prayer-Book*, which was possibly written by John Dee. In it, Maymon was ranked as a king, under the command of a demon named VERCAN. Described as a black-skinned, humanoid devil with two bird heads who rides upon a dragonlike creature, Maymon was credited with dominion over the planet Saturn.

Sources: Anonymous, *Manuscripts and Books on Medicine, Alchemy, Astrology and Natural Sciences Arranged in Chronological Order*, 239; Summers, *A Popular History of Witchcraft*, 91.

Mazzikim

In both Jewish and Zohar mythology the demon Mazzikim is said to have been born the child of Adam and LILITH, conceived at twilight on the Sabbath. He takes advantage of human carelessness.

Mazzikim's name is Hebrew and means "afflictors" or "damagers." The Hebrew words SHEDIM and *mazzikim* were used interchangeably for demons, but the latter became more widely used in the Middle Ages.

Sources: Ashley, *Complete Book of Devils and Demons*, 51; Lurker, *Dictionary of Gods and Goddesses*, 227; Mack, *Field Guide to Demons, Fairies, Fallen Angels, and Other Subversive Spirits*, 125; Smith, *Cornhill Magazine*, Vol. 32, 205.

Mbulu

In the demonology of the Xhosas and Zulu people of Africa, a mbulu is a type of AQUEOUS DEVIL with a humanoid appearance. Covered with scales, this devil has a very long tail that has a mouth of its own located on its tip that is filled with sharp teeth. The tail has a mind of its own and is always hungry. Preying most often on travelers, the mbulu is a trickster and uses people's fears against them. As long as it can keep its tail hidden or under control, this devil can pass itself off as human.

Sources: Jordan, *Tales from Southern Africa*, 155–78; Mack, *Field Guide to Demons, Fairies, Fallen Angels, and Other Subversive Spirits*, 42; Theal, *History and Ethnography of Africa South of the Zambesi*, 141–3.

Mebbesser

In the *Sacred Magic of Abramelin the Mage*, book two, Mebbesser ("of fleh") is one of the sixteen SERVITORS OF ASMODEUS (see ASMODEUS). His name is taken from either Chaldee or Hebrew and may mean "to reject" or "flesh."

Sources: Mathers, *Book of the Sacred Magic of Abramelin the Mage*, 107, 119; Von Worms, *Book of Abramelin*, 256.

Mediac

Variations: Modiac

Mediac is a demon who originated in Elizabethan demonology. The first appearance of his name was in a book titled *An Elizabethan Devil-Worshiper's Prayer-Book*, which was possibly written by John Dee. In it, Mediac is said to be in the service of a demon named VERCAN. Described as a red-skinned humanoid who wears a suit of armor and rides upon a bear, Mediac was credited with dominion over the planet Mercury.

Sources: Anonymous, *Manuscripts and Books on Medicine, Alchemy, Astrology and Natural Sciences Arranged in Chronological Order*, 239; Summers, *A Popular History of Witchcraft*, 91.

Megalak

In the *Sacred Magic of Abramelin the Mage*, book two, Megalak ("cutting off") is ranked as one of the sixty-five SERVITORS OF KORE AND MAGOTH.

Sources: Mathers, *Book of the Sacred Magic of Abramelin the Mage*, 118; Von Worms, *Book of Abramelin*, 250, 256.

Megalosin

The *Sacred Magic of Abramelin the Mage*, book two, ranks Megalosin ("in great things") as one of the twenty-two SERVITORS OF ARITON (see ARITON).

Sources: Mathers, *Book of the Sacred Magic of Abramelin the Mage*, 108; Von Worms, *Book of Abramelin*, 254, 257.

Meklboc

In the *Sacred Magic of Abramelin the Mage*, book two, Meklboc is among the sixty-five SERVITORS OF KORE AND MAGOTH. His name is possibly Hebrew and may mean "like a dog."

Sources: Mathers, *Book of the Sacred Magic of Abramelin the Mage*, 118; Von Worms, *Book of Abramelin*, 251.

Melamud

In the *Sacred Magic of Abramelin the Mage*, book two, Melamud ("stimulus to exertion") is ranked as one of the one hundred eleven SERVITORS OF AMAYMON, ARITON, ORIENS, AND PAYMON (see AMAYMON, ARITON, ORIENS, and PAYMON).

Sources: Mathers, *Book of the Sacred Magic of Abramelin the Mage*, 105, 115; Von Worms, *Book of Abramelin*, 244, 255.

Melas

The *Sacred Magic of Abramelin the Mage*, book two, names Melas, a nocturnal demon, among the sixteen SERVITORS OF ASELIEL (see ASELIEL).

Source: Mathers, *Book of the Sacred Magic of Abramelin the Mage*, 200.

Melchom

Variations: "He who carries the purse," Malcam, MALIK, Malk, Malkekem ("your King"), Melech, Melek ("King"), Milcom, Milkom, Molech, Molek, MOLOCH, "the abomination of the Ammonites"

Originally a West-Semitic deity, the god or idol of the Ammonites, and part of Canaanite and Phoenician mythology, Melchom ("unearthly king") is now considered to be a lesser demon. At one time child sacrifices were made to him in the valley at the base of Mount of Olives. Ranked as Hell's paymaster and SATAN's treasurer, Melchom is the demon of greed, according to Collin de Plancy's *Dictionaire Infernale* (1863).

Commanding many servitors, this demon has the ability to make men greedy and can appear before his summoner as an artist, a fat medieval merchant, a rich nobleman, or as a tall soldier. Melchom loves the world so much that he wants to own it all.

Sources: Chambers, *Book of Days*, 723; Collin de Plancy, *Dictionnaire Infernal*, 453.

Melhaer

Variations: Melher

In the *Sacred Magic of Abramelin the Mage*, book two, Melhaer is one of the one hundred eleven SERVITORS OF AMAYMON, ARITON, ORIENS, AND PAYMON (see AMAYMON, ARITON, ORIENS, and PAYMON).

Sources: Mathers, *Book of the Sacred Magic of Abramelin the Mage*, 105, 112; Von Worms, *Book of Abramelin*, 244, 255.

Melna

Melna one of the one hundred eleven SERVITORS OF AMAYMON, ARITON, ORIENS, AND PAYMON (see AMAYMON, ARITON, ORIENS, and PAYMON) included in the *Sacred Magic of Abramelin the Mage*, book two. His name is possibly Hebrew and means "to abide" or "rest."

Sources: Mathers, *Book of the Sacred Magic of Abramelin the Mage*, 105, 112; Von Worms, *Book of Abramelin*, 244, 255.

Memuneh, plural: memunim

In Jewish ceremonial magic, memunim are the oftentimes malicious demonic dispensers of dreams. The name memuneh is Hebrew for "appointed one."

Sources: Davidson, *Dictionary of Angels*, 189; Minchero, *Voice from the Jordan*, 68.

Menolik

In the *Sacred Magic of Abramelin the Mage*, Menolik is one of the fifteen SERVITORS OF PAYMON (see PAYMON). His name is possibly taken from Greek and may mean "winnowing with fury."

Sources: Mathers, *Book of the Sacred Magic of Abramelin the Mage*, 108, 121; Von Worms, *Book of Abramelin*, 257.

Mephistopheles

Variations: "the Destroyer," Mephisto, Mephistophiel, Mephistophilis, Mephistophilus, Mephostopheles

The demon Mephistopheles is purely a fictional creation by the anonymous author of *Faustbuch* (published in 1587) and has ever since been associated as the DEVIL. The name has its roots in Greek and Hebrew and means "destroyer liar" or "he who loves not the light." Although this demon is the fictional creation of an author, it did not stop medieval scholars and demonologists from adding him to their hierarchies.

Medieval literature says that this fictional demon is one of the PRINCES OF HELL, one of the FALLEN ANGELS, and formerly of the Order of Archangels, who now stands under the planet Jupiter. His personal adversary is Zadkiel ("righteousness of God"), an equally fictitious enthroned angel.

Sources: Butler, *Ritual Magic*, 160–1, 164, 167; Gettings, *Dictionary of Demons*, 163; Hyatt, *Book of Demons*, 35, 135.

Meras

Christian demonology lists Meras as one of the twenty SERVITORS OF CAMUEL (see CAMUEL). Beautiful in his appearance, this nocturnal demon is said to be very courteous.

Sources: Guiley, *Encyclopedia of Demons and Demonology*, 36; Trithemius, *Steganographia*, 73.

Meresin

Variations: Merasin, MERIRIM, MERIHIM, Meris, Metiris, Mererim

In medieval Christian demonology Meresin was ranked and titled as the chief of the Aerial Power, lord of thunder and lightning, and a prince of the Air (see PRINCES OF HELL). Said to be one of the FALLEN ANGELS, Meresin has control and power over the air as well as the ability to cause fire, plagues, and thunder. As the demon Mererim, he is alleged to be one of the four holy Angels of Revelation.

Sources: Crane, *Great Exorcism*, 49; Davidson, *Dictionary of Angels*, 190, 353; Ripley, *American Cyclopædia*, Vol. 5, 794.

Merihim

Variations: Merasin, MERESIN, MERIRIM, Meris, Metiris

The lord of lightning and thunder in Hell and the prince of evil and war, Merihim is the demon of the spirits of harassment and pestilence (see PRINCES OF HELL). He is an AERIAL DEVIL and one of the FALLEN ANGELS.

Sources: Davidson, *Dictionary of Angels*, 190; Gettings, *Dictionary of Demons*, 163; Ripley, *New American Cyclopaedia*, Vol. 6, 369.

Meririm

Variations: Merasin, Mererim, MERESIN, MERIHIM, Meris, Metiris

In medieval demonology Meririm is ranked as the chief of the aerial powers and the lord of lightning and thunder in Hell; he is also one of the seven PRINCES OF HELL and the prince of air and pestilence. Most powerful during the noon hour, Meririm is an AERIAL DEVIL and a FALLEN ANGEL, but some sources also say that he is a boiling spirit and a meridian devil.

Sources: Davidson, *Dictionary of Angels*, 190; Kelly, *Who in Hell*, 155; Sepharial, *Book of Charms and Talismans*, 78; Summers, *Witchcraft and Black Magic*, 168.

Merizim

Variations: Meerihim

In Enochian lore, Prince Merizim is the AER-
IAL DEVIL who commands the AERIAE POTES-
TATES (see PRINCES OF HELL). Demon of the air
and of the South, he lives in the air.

Sources: Gettings, *Dictionary of Demons*, 23;
McLean, *Treatise on Angel Magic*, 70; Thompson, *Mysteries and Secrets of Magic*, 111.

Mermo

The *Sacred Magic of Abramelin the Mage*, book
two, nanes Mermo ("across the water") as one of
the one hundred eleven SERVITORS OF AMAY-
MON, ARITON, ORIENS, AND PAYMON (see
AMAYMON, ARITON, ORIENS, and PAYMON).

Sources: Mathers, *Book of the Sacred Magic of
Abramelin the Mage*, 105, 112; Von Worms, *Book of
Abramelin*, 244, 255.

Mersilde

The *Grimorium Vernum* (*Grimoire of Truth*) allegedly written by Alibek the Egyptian in 1517
names Mersilde as one of the eighteen SERVITORS
OF SYRACH (see SYRACH).

Sources: Masters, *Devil's Dominion*, 130; Sabellicus,
Magia Pratica, 35; Waite, *Book of Black Magic*, 184.

Meshabber

The *Testament of Solomon* names Meshabber
as an archangel and the commander of the five
ANGELS OF PUNISHMENT. He is in service to the
Angels of Death.

Sources: Ashley, *Complete Book of Demons and
Devils*, 78; Wace, *Holy Bible, According to the Authorized
Version*, 181.

Metafel

In the *Sacred Magic of Abramelin the Mage*,
book two, Metafel ("to fasten") is listed as one of
the one hundred eleven SERVITORS OF AMAY-
MON, ARITON, ORIENS, AND PAYMON (see
AMAYMON, ARITON, ORIENS, and PAYMON).

Sources: Mathers, *Book of the Sacred Magic of
Abramelin the Mage*, 105, 114; Von Worms, *Book of
Abramelin*, 246, 256.

Metathiax

In the *Testament of Solomon*, Metathiax is
named as the demon of disease and pain of the
kidneys. His personal adversary is the angel
Adonael, and he flees if he hears the words "Adô-
naêl, imprison Metathiax."

Sources: Conybeare, *Jewish Quarterly Review*, Vol.
11, 35; Fleg, *Life of Solomon*, 107.

Mgm

According to Enochian lore, Mgm is a CACO-
DAEMON. His counterpart is the angel Gmnm.
(See also ENOCHIAN CACODAEMONS).

Sources: Chopra, *Academic Dictionary of Mythology*,
189; Laycock, *Complete Enochian Dictionary*, 134.

Mictantecutli

Mictantecutli is the great Lord of Hell in the
Aztec pantheon under whom all other demons
operate. He captures the souls of evil people, tortures them, and then locks them up forever in the
darkest recesses of his realm. A picture of Mictantecutli from the *Codex Vaticanus A*, written by
Halian monks in the sixteenth century, depict
him as looking like an animated skeleton; his
throne bears the symbols of sorcery and
witchcraft and is encircled with a bundle of desert
grass, a corpse, a dish filled with human hearts,
and an owl. Mictantecutli is associated with
everything to do with the North, the region of
death and misfortune. Most powerful at midnight, Mictantecutli would open the door of Hell
and let malign spirits wander the world to do as
they pleased until sunrise.

Source: Hyatt, *Book of Demons*, 94.

Miliom

The *Sacred Magic of Abramelin the Mage*, book
two, lists Miliom as one of the twenty-two
SERVITORS OF ARITON (see ARITON). His name
is Hebrew and it means "destroyer of day" or "the
ender."

Sources: Mathers, *Book of the Sacred Magic of
Abramelin the Mage*, 122; Von Worms, *Book of
Abramelin*, 254, 257.

Mimosa

In the *Sacred Magic of Abramelin the Mage*,
book two, Mimosa is one of the sixty-five SERVI-
TORS OF KORE AND MAGOTH. His name is possibly Greek and it means "imitator."

Sources: Mathers, *Book of the Sacred Magic of
Abramelin the Mage*, 122; Von Worms, *Book of
Abramelin*, 254, 257.

Minoson

The *Grimorium Vernum* (*Grimoire of Truth*),
allegedly written by Alibek the Egyptian in 1517,
names Minoson as one of the eight SERVITORS
OF HALE AND SERGULATH. This demon is said
to be very powerful.

Sources: Masters, *Devil's Dominion*, 131; Waite, *Book
of Black and Ceremonial Magic*, 193.

Miru

Variations: Miru Kura, Miru-the-ruddy, Muru

From the demonology of the Mangaia people,

traditionally known as Auau Enua ("terraced"), who live on the Cook Islands, Miru is the Mistress of the Invisible World. A demonic goddess of the underworld, this devil is extremely ugly, the very personification of it; her cheeks are perpetually aglow from the heat of her ovens.

Souls are captured by her slave, AKAANGA, and then are taken before her and forced to drink kava root (*Piper mythisticum*), which reduces their willpower and makes them unable to resist. First they are fattened up by being fed black beetles, crabs, small blackbirds, and red earthworms; next they are hauled off to the ovens to be cooked and later consumed by her and her beautiful daughters. They are especially fond of the souls of those who died natural deaths.

Sources: Conway, *Demonology and Devil-Lore*, Vol. 1, 42–3; Gill, *Myths and Songs from the South Pacific*, 161–2, 175.

Mishel

The *Theurgia Goetia*, the second book of the *Lemegeton*, ranks Mishel as a nocturnal duke and lists him as a FALLEN ANGEL and one of the sixteen SERVITORS OF GEDIEL (see DUKES OF HELL and GEDEIL).

Source: Belanger, *Dictionary of Demons*, 127.

Misran

In Apollonius of Tyana's *Nuctemeron* (*Night Illuminated by Day*), Misran is said to be the demon of persecution. He is most powerful during the twelfth hour.

Sources: Gettings, *Dictionary of Demons*, 169; Lévi, *Transcendental Magic*, 509.

Mitox

Variations: Mitixt

Zoroastrian demonology said that Mitox is the demon of the falsely spoken word, a DAEVA, and a servitor of AHRIMAN.

Sources: Davidson, *Dictionary of Angels*, 197; Seligmann, *Magic, Supernaturalism, and Religion*, 14.

Miz (MITZ)

According to Enochian lore, Miz ("oppressor") is a CACODAEMON. His counterpart is the angel Izxp (see also ENOCHIAN CACODAEMONS).

Sources: Chopra, *Academic Dictionary of Mythology*, 191; Laycock, *Complete Enochian Dictionary*, 135.

Mizgitari

In Apollonius of Tyana's *Nuctemeron* (*Night Illuminated by Day*), Mizgitari is the demon of eagles. He is most powerful during the seventh hour.

Sources: Gettings, *Dictionary of Demons*, 169; Lévi, *Transcendental Magic*, 392.

Mizkun

In Apollonius of Tyana's *Nuctemeron* (*Night Illuminated by Day*), Mizkun is the demon of amulets. He is most powerful during the first hour.

Sources: Davidson, *Dictionary of Angels*, 198; Gettings, *Dictionary of Demons*, 169; Lévi, *Transcendental Magic*, 417.

Mma

According to Enochian lore, Mma is a CACODAEMON. His counterpart is the angel Magm. (See also ENOCHIAN CACODAEMONS).

Sources: Chopra, *Academic Dictionary of Mythology*, 191; Laycock, *Complete Enochian Dictionary*, 135.

Moc (MOK)

According to Enochian lore, Moc is a CACODAEMON. His counterpart is the angel Ocnm (ENOCHIAN CACODAEMONS).

Sources: Chopra, *Academic Dictionary of Mythology*, 191; Laycock, *Complete Enochian Dictionary*, 135.

Molael

Molael is one of the twenty SERVITORS OF SYMIEL (see SYMIEL). He shares with the other nocturnal SERVITORS OF SYMIEL seven hundred ninety servitors among them. Like many nocturnal demons, he is said to be disobedient, stubborn, and not so willing to appear before his summoner.

Sources: Guiley, *Dictionary of Demons and Demonology*, 253; Peterson, *Lesser Key of Solomon*, 88.

Molin

The *Sacred Magic of Abramelin the Mage*, book two, includes Molin ("abiding in a place") as one of the one hundred eleven SERVITORS OF AMAYMON, ARITON, ORIENS, AND PAYMON (see AMAYMON, ARITON, ORIENS, and PAYMON).

Sources: Mathers, *Book of the Sacred Magic of Abramelin the Mage*, 114; Von Worms, *Book of Abramelin*, 246, 256.

Moloch

Variations: "the abomination of the children of AMMON," Malach-bel Molech, MALIK, Molek, Molekh, Moloc, MULACH

From Assyrian, Babylonian, Canaanite, Egyptian, Hebrew, and Phoenician demonology comes the demon Moloch ("to rule"). Originally a Canaanite god, he became an ARCHDEMON and FALLEN ANGEL, formerly of the Order of Archangels, in Christian demonology. The demon of fire, he is ranked as the Prince of the Land of Tears (see PRINCES OF HELL).

In ancient times Moloch was represented by a huge bronze hollow statue of a bull-headed man with upturned hands. Some descriptions say the statue had seven compartments for holding various sacrifices. The idol was heated until it glowed red, then firstborn children were sacrificed to him by placing them on its hands, which then moved and deposited them through the mouth and into the furnace within which they were cremated and their lives used to renew the power of the sun. His center of worship was in Tophet in the valley of Geennom. In Kings 11:7 King Solomon built a temple to Moloch: 'Then Solomon built a temple for Chamos the idol of Moab, on the hill that is over against Jerusalem, and for Moloch the idol of the children of AMMON.'

Sources: Chambers, *Book of Days*, 722; Conybeare, *Jewish Quarterly Review*, Vol. 11, 4, 5; Hyatt, *Book of Demons*, 49; Nicoll, *Masks, Mimes and Miracles*, 188; Melton, *Encyclopedia of Occultism*, 69, 120, 153.

Mop

According to Enochian lore, Mop is a CACO-DAEMON. His counterpart is the angel Opmn (ENOCHIAN CACODAEMONS).

Sources: Chopra, *Academic Dictionary of Mythology*, 192; Laycock, *Complete Enochian Dictionary*, 136.

Morail

The *Grimorium Vernum* (*Grimoire of Truth*), allegedly written by Alibek the Egyptian in 1517, names Morail as one of the eighteen SERVITORS OF SYRACH (see SYRACH).

Sources: Masters, *Devil's Dominion*, 131; Sabellicus, *Magia Pratica*, 35.

Morax

Variations: FORAII, Forax, MARAX

Morax is ranked as an earl and president who commands thirty-six legions; he is also listed as one of the seventy-two SPIRITS OF SOLOMON (SEE EARLS OF HELL and PRESIDENTS OF HELL). Appearing before his summoner as a minotaur, he is summoned for his ability to teach astrology, knowledge of the use magical herbs and stones, and knowledge of the various sciences. This demon also gives good FAMILIARs.

Sources: De Laurence, *Lesser Key of Solomon, Goetia*, 28; Gettings, *Dictionary of Demons*, 171; Guiley, *Encyclopedia of Demons and Demonology*, 179; Scott, *London Magazine*, Vol. 5, 378.

Morcaza

The *Theurgia Goetia*, the second book of the *Lemegeton*, names Duke Morcaza, a nocturnal demon, as one of the fifteen SERVITORS OF BARMIEL (see and DUKES OF HELL).

Sources: Guiley, *Encyclopedia of Demons and Demonology*, 24; Peterson, *Lesser Key of Solomon*, 70.

Morel

The *Sacred Magic of Abramelin the Mage*, book two, lists Morel as one of the one hundred eleven SERVITORS OF AMAYMON, ARITON, ORIENS, AND PAYMON (see AMAYMON, ARITON, ORIENS, and PAYMON). His name is possibly Hebrew and means "to rebel."

Sources: Mathers, *Book of the Sacred Magic of Abramelin the Mage*, 112; Von Worms, *Book of Abramelin*, 244, 255.

Morete

Variations: Kopiletije, Kukumavce Nekrstenici

In the demonology of Pirot, Serbia, a morete is a type of nocturnal demon that is created when an unbaptized child dies. It looks like a glowing ball of light.

Sources: McClelland, *Slayers and their Vampires*, 55.

Moriel

Moriel is one of the twenty SERVITORS OF CAMUEL (see CAMUEL). This nocturnal demon appears before his summoner in a beautiful form. He is said to be very courteous.

Sources: Davidson, *Dictionary of Angels*, 198; Peterson, *Lesser Key of Solomon*, 67–8; Trithemius, *Steganographia*, 73.

Morilen

In the *Sacred Magic of Abramelin the Mage*, book two, Morilen is among the one hundred eleven SERVITORS OF AMAYMON, ARITON, ORIENS, AND PAYMON (see AMAYMON, ARITON, ORIENS, and PAYMON). Possibly Greek, his name may mean "foolish speaking."

Sources: Ford, *Bible of the Adversary*, 89; Mathers, *Book of the Sacred Magic of Abramelin the Mage*, 114; Von Worms, *Book of Abramelin*, 249, 256.

Mortaiel

The *Lesser Key of Solomon* lists Duke Mortaiel as one of the twelve SERVITORS OF HYDRIEL (see HYDRIEL).

Sources: Peterson, *Lesser Key of Solomon*, 95; Trithemius, *Steganographia*, 202.

Moschel

The *Sacred Magic of Abramelin the Mage*, book two, lists Moschel ("to move oneself about") as one of the one hundred eleven SERVITORS OF AMAYMON, ARITON, ORIENS, AND PAYMON (see AMAYMON, ARITON, ORIENS, and PAYMON).

Sources: Mathers, *Book of the Sacred Magic of Abramelin the Mage*, 105, 113; Von Worms, *Book of Abramelin*, 244, 258.

Mrx

According to Enochian lore, Mrx is a CACO-DAEMON. His counterpart is the angel Rxnl (see ENOCHIAN CACODAEMONS).

Source: Laycock, *Complete Enochian Dictionary*, 136.

Mto (M'TO)

According to Enochian lore, Mto ("his death") is a CACODAEMON. His counterpart is the angel Toco (see ENOCHIAN CACODAEMONS).

Sources: Chopra, *Academic Dictionary of Mythology*, 193; Laycock, *Complete Enochian Dictionary*, 137.

Mudriel

The *Theurgia Goetia*, the second book of the *Lemegeton*, lists Duke Mudriel, commander of 2,400 servitors, as one of the ten SERVITORS OF BYDIEL (see BYDIEL). This AERIAL DEVIL appears before his summoner in an attractive form and is said to be good-natured and willing to obey.

Source: Peterson, *Lesser Key of Solomon*, 105.

Mukil-Res-Lemutti

Variations: Urmahlullu ("lion-man")

Originating in neo-Assyrian and neo-Babylonian mythology, Mukil-Res-Lemutti is the demon of headaches. He has the body of a lion and the head, torso, arms, and hands of a man; he wears the horned cap of divinity. The name Mukil-Res-Lemutti is Assyrian and translates to mean "evil-attendant," "he who offers misfortune," "provider of evil" or "the holder of the head of evil" or "upholder of evil."

Sources: Black, *Gods, Demons, and Symbols of Ancient Mesopotamia*, 119; Oppenheim, *Ancient Mesopotamia*, 204; Stol, *Epilepsy in Babylonia*, 75, 82.

Mulach

Variations: MOLOCH

In the *Sacred Magic of Abramelin the Mage*, book two, Mulach ("to rule") is one of the one hundred eleven SERVITORS OF AMAYMON, ARITON, ORIENS, AND PAYMON (see AMAYMON, ARITON, ORIENS, and PAYMON).

Sources: Lewis, *Satanism Today*, 178–9; Mathers, *Book of the Sacred Magic of Abramelin the Mage*, 112; Von Worms, *Book of Abramelin*, 255.

Mullin

According to Christian demonology Mullin is a lieutenant of LEONARD; he is also ranked as the servant of the House of Princes, a valet de chamber.

Sources: Ashley, *Complete Book of Devils and Demons*, 59; Bias, *Freedom from the World of Satanism and the Power of Satan*, 42; Chambers, *Book of Days*, 723; Ripley, *American Cyclopaedia*, 795.

Munuane

Munuane, master of fish, is from the demonology of the Sikuani people of South America. A tutelary demon, he is described as being a large, grey-haired and toothless humanoid with his eyes located in his knees; additionally he is said to be slow-witted. This demon preys upon greedy fishermen and hunters most of the time, but he considers all humans to be both destructive and edible.

Munuane floats downriver on a raft, appearing only where the fishing is good, carrying a bow and one arrow. Exceptionally charismatic, he lures his victims to him. When shooting with his arrow, he never misses his target. This demon can only be destroyed if sufficient damage is delivered to him; however, he can only be harmed by shooting him in his knees.

Sources: Mack, *Field Guide to Demons, Fairies, Fallen Angels, and Other Subversive Spirits*, 22–3; Wilbert, *Folk Literature of the Sikuani Indians*, 446–7.

Murahe

Duke Murahe is one of the twenty SERVITORS OF SYMIEL (see SYMIEL). Murahe is disobedient, stubborn, and will not appear willingly to his summoner. He shares with the other nocturnal SERVITORS OF SYMIEL seven hundred ninety servitors between them.

Sources: Peterson, *Lesser Key of Solomon*, 88; Trithemius, *Steganographia*, 85.

Murmur

Variations: Murmus, Murmuur, Murmux

Christian demonology ranks Murmur ("noise, murmur, whisper") as a count, duke, and earl who commands thirty legions (see COUNTS OF HELL, DUKES OF HELL, and EARLS OF HELL). A FALLEN ANGEL, formerly of the Order of Thrones, he is summoned for his ability to teach philosophy and make prophecy. Appearing as a warrior wearing a ducal crown, he rides upon a griffin or vulture; sources conflict. Two ministers blasting trumpets come first to herald him. He has the ability to call the souls of the deceased up before him to answer questions.

Sources: De Laurence, *Lesser Key of Solomon, Goetia*, 39–40; McLean, *Treatise of Angel Magic*, 55; Scot, *Discoverie of Witchcraft*, 223.

Murries

Ars Paulina, the third book of the *Lemegeton*, ranks Murries as a chief and lists him as one of the twenty SERVITORS OF VEGUANIEL (see VEGUANIEL).

Sources: Davidson, *Dictionary of Demons*, 199; Waite, *Book of Black and Ceremonial Magic*, 67.

Murta Sanniya

In Sinhalese demonology, Murta Sanniya ("swooning demon") is the demon of unconsciousness, as he causes swooning and a loss of consciousness. Victims of his assaults must have an exorcist perform a healing ritual over them called a *tovil*. This demon frequents the forest.

Sources: Illes, *Encyclopedia of Spirits*, 875; Wirz, *Exorcism and the Art of Healing in Ceylon*, 44.

Mush

Variations: Mūsh

Originating in Iranian demonology and absorbed into Zoroastrianism, the demon of darkness and eclipses, Mush ("rat"), causes meteors to fall from the sky. He is a type of demon called *pairikās duzhyairay* and is known for destroying crops.

Sources: Ashley, *Complete Book of Devils and Demons*, 64; Fisher, *Cambridge History of Iran*, 679.

Musiniel

The *Theurgia Goetia*, the second book of the *Lemegeton*, ranks Musiniel as a duke who commands 1,320 servitors and lists him as one of the ten SERVITORS OF EMONIEL (see EMONIEL). He is described as being good-natured and willing to obey his summoner. This demon lives in the woods.

Sources: Guiley, *Encyclopedia of Demons and Demonology*, 72; Peterson, *Lesser Key of Solomon*, 97.

Musiriel

In the *Ars Paulina*, book three of the *Lemegeton*, Musiriel is ranked as a chief duke, commanding three thousand servitors (see DUKES OF HELL). He is listed as one of the twelve SERVITORS OF AMENADIEL (see AMENADIEL).

Sources: Guiley, *Encyclopedia of Demons and Demonology*, 7; Peterson, *Lesser Key of Solomon*, 62.

Musisin

The *Grimorium Vernum* (*Grimoire of Truth*), allegedly written by Alibek the Egyptian in 1517, names Musisin as one of the eighteen SERVITORS OF SYRACH (see SYRACH).

Sources: Sabellicus, *Magia Pratica*, 35; Waite, *Book of Black Magic and Pacts*, 159.

Musor

Musor is one of the twenty SERVITORS OF SYMIEL (see SYMIEL). He shares with the other diurnal SERVITORS OF SYMIEL seven hundred twenty servitors among them. Like many diurnal demons, he is said to be very obedient and quick to listen to his summoner. The word *musor* means "garbage" in Russian.

Sources: Guiley, *Encyclopedia of Demons and Demonology*, 253; Peterson, *Lesser Key of Solomon*, 88.

Musuziel

In the *Theurgia Goetia*, the second book of the *Lemegeton*, Musuziel is ranked as duke who commands 1,320 servitors and is listed as one of the twelve SERVITORS OF HYDRIEL (see HYDRIEL and DUKES OF HELL). This demon can be summoned any time of the day or night and when he appears takes on the guise of a serpent with a virgin's face. Said to be very courteous and willing to obey, Musuziel lives in or near water, marshes, and wetlands.

Sources: Guiley, *Encyclopedia of Demons and Demonology*, 115; Peterson, *Lesser Key of Solomon*, 95.

Naamah

Variations: Na'amah, Nahemah

Babylonian mythology, Christian demonology, and Jewish mysticism all make mention of the demon Naamah ("darling" or "pleasurable"), one of the four DEMONS OF PROSTITUTION and consort of LILITH THE LESSER.

Born the daughter of Lamech, this female demon is said to be under the command of LILITH and has been described as being a type of ARCH SHE-DEMON, FALLEN ANGEL, and SUCCUBUS.

The demon of seduction, she is the patron of divination, music, prostitutes, and whores. Naamah seduces men in their sleep and learns what their desires are. Then, she makes her way into their lives, ruins their hopes, and has many children with them who are in truth evil spirits. She also is known to throttle babies.

Living in the waves of the sea, Naamah is the mother of ASMODEUS; and as the one-time mate of Adam, together they bore many children known collectively as the Plagues of Mankind. With her one-time mate Cain, they bore a child named Tubal-Cain who introduced weapons of war into the world.

Sources: Hyatt, *Book of Demons*, 40; Mason, *Necronomicon Gnosis*, 151; Wise, *Origin of Christianity*, 95.

Naberrs

In the *Ars Goetia*, the first book of the *Lemegeton*, Naberrs is listed as one of the eighteen SERVITORS OF FLEURETTY, Lucifuge, NEBIROS, SARGATANAS, AND SATANACHIA (see FLEURETTY, LUCIFUGE ROFOCALE, NEBIROS, SARGATANAS, and SATANACHIA).

Sources: Waite, *Book of Black Magic and of Pacts*, 183; Wedeck, *Treasury of Witchcraft*, 96.

Naberus

Variations: Cerbere, Cerberus, Naberius, Naburus, NEBIROS

In Johann Wierus's *Pseudomonarchia Dae-*

monum (*False Monarchy of Demons,* 1583) Naberus is ranked as a marquis who commands nineteen legions (see MARQUIS OF HELL). He appears before his summoner as a black crane, a raven, a rooster unable to stand upright, a monstrous three-headed bird creature with a deafening voice, or as a three-headed DOG. A diurnal demon, Naberus presents himself as amiable and eloquent and is known to be especially valiant. He is summoned for his ability to restore lost honor and privileges as well as for his ability to teach the art of graceful living, persuasion, and logic. Most powerful during the month of November, he has dominion over the mood. His zodiacal sign is Scorpio.

Naberus is mentioned for the first time in print in the *Pseudomonarchia Daemonum*; Weirus considered this demon and the Greek mythological creature Cerberus to be the same individual.

Sources: Baskin, *Dictionary of Satanism*, 252; Bowyer, *Encyclopedia of Mystical Terminology*, 88; Chaplin, *Dictionary of the Occult and Paranormal*, 105; Peterson, *Lesser Key of Solomon*, 233; Scott, *London Magazine*, Vol. 5, 378; Shah, *Occultism*, 62, 66.

Nachashiron

The nachashiron are one of the twelve QLIP-POTHIC ORDERS OF DEMONS; their colors are like those of the serpents, and they look like DOG-headed snakes.

Source: Mathers, *Sorcerer and his Apprentice*, 26.

Nacheran

In the *Sacred Magic of Abramelin the Mage*, book two, Nacheran is among the sixty-five SERVITORS OF KORE AND MAGOTH. His name is possibly Hebrew and means "nostrils."

Sources: Mathers, *Book of the Sacred Magic of Abramelin the Mage*, 107, 118; Von Worms, *Book of Abramelin*, 123, 249.

Nachiel

Variations: Nakhiel, Nakiel

Mentioned in both Cabalistic ceremonial magic as well as in *Paracelsus' Doctrine of Talismans*, written in the fifteenth century by physician Theophrastus Paracelsus, Nachiel is said to be one of the FALLEN ANGELS. He has dominion over the sun and his zodiacal sign is Leo. Sorath, the angel and not the demon who shares this name, is Nachiel's personal adversary.

Sources: Greer, *New Encyclopedia of the Occult*, 319; Tyson, *Ritual Magic*, 72.

Nadroc

In the *Ars Paulina*, book three of the *Lemegeton*, Nadroc is a chief duke who commands three thousand servitors of his own (see DUKES OF

HELL). He is listed as one of the twelve SERVITORS OF AMENADIEL (see AMENADIEL).

Sources: Peterson, *Lesser Key of Solomon*, 62; Trithemius, *Steganographia*, 54.

Naga

Variations: Nāga, Nagis

In Hindu mythology the nagas are demonic beings, members of a demonic race that was born of the union between the sage Kasyapa and Kadru, the daughter of Daksha, according to *The Mahabharata*, one of the two major Sanskrit epics of Ancient India. The female of the species are called *nagini*. Their name translates from Sanskrit to mean "a hooded snake" or "those who do not walk, who creep."

The nagas are described as being human with the lower body of a snake. Sometimes they are said to have as many as seven heads. A precious gem is embedded into their head or throat that grants them magical powers. Typically they only attack humans when they have been mistreated, but they are known to prey upon wealthy individuals, singling them out and attacking with their venom, and then stealing the victims' wealth. Especially greedy, nagas hoard jewels and precious metals in their underwater homes. They have the ability to shape-shift into a cobra or dragon, and they possess an array of undefined magical abilities from the gem embedded in their head.

The homeland of the naga is called Patala and is located on the bottom of the ocean. The personal adversary of the naga is their cousin, the god Garuda.

Sources: Allardice, *Myths, Gods, and Fantasy*, 1990; Dange, *Myths from the Mahābhārata*, 26, 41, 126; Hyatt, *Book of Demons*, 19, 24; Turner, *Dictionary of Ancient Deities*, 498.

Naga Sanniya

In Sinhalese demonology Naga Sanniya ("mania") is the demon of boils and skin diseases. He is depicted in ceremonial masks as having skin lesions and carbuncles on his face. Signs of having been attacked by him are an aching body, bloodshot eyes, peeling skin, and a swollen face. A nocturnal demon, he causes dreams in which snakes attack. Like the other Sinhalese demons, he is susceptible to the DAHA-ATA SANNIYA.

Sources: Ames, *Tovil*, 42–9; Conway, *Magickal, Mystical Creatures*, 122; Illes, *Encyclopedia of Spirits*, 875; Kapferer, *Celebration of Demons*, 231, 346; Wirz, *Exorcism and the Art of Healing in Ceylon*, 44.

Nagid

The *Sacred Magic of Abramelin the Mage*, book two, names Nagid ("a leader") among the one hundred eleven SERVITORS OF AMAYMON, ARITON, ORIENS, AND PAYMON (see AMAYMON, ARITON, ORIENS, and PAYMON).

Sources: Mathers, *Sacred Magic of Abramelin the Mage*, 105–113; Spence, *Encyclopaedia of Occultism*, 119; Von Worms, *Book of Abramlin*, 119, 245, 255.

Nahema

Variations: Na'amah, NAAMAH, Nahemah, Namaah

Originating in Babylonian mythology and absorbed into Jewish mysticism, the SUCCUBUS Nahema ("pleasant") was said to be a concubine of SATAN, chief of Malkuth, princess of all the succubi, and one of the four angels of prostitution (see FALLEN ANGELs). She has dominion over the infernal hierarchy known as Nahemoth. The demon of abortion and debauchery and considered to be the inventor of divination, Nahema, born the daughter of Lamech, is generally regarded to be an aspect or relation of LILITH. This demon engaged in sexual intercourse with Adam and is said to be the mother of ASMODAI.

Sources: Ford, *Liber Hvhi*, 71, 79, 80, 86; Guiley, *Encyclopedia of Demons and Demonology*, 140; Mathers, *Key of Solomon*, 123.

Nâi-Batar

In Zoroastrian demonology, Nâi-Batar is a nocturnal DAEVAS that appears as a black shadow in the forms of a bat, predatory bird, raven, or a wolf. Once this demon is summoned, it will assist in the draining of the power of others to give to his summoner. He also strengthens auras and assists in crimes of emotional and spiritual vampirism.

Source: Ford, *Gates of Dozak*, 98.

Naiwun and Nokpi

In Myanmar demonology the demons Naiwun and Nokpi cause women to become barren. They are said to live on the front porch of a house.

Sources: Hastings, *Encyclopedia of Religion and Ethics Part 5*, 25; Scott, *Burma*, 404.

Najin

The *Sacred Magic of Abramelin the Mage*, book two, names Najin ("propagating") as one of the one hundred eleven SERVITORS OF AMAYMON, ARITON, ORIENS, AND PAYMON (see AMAYMON, ARITON, ORIENS, and PAYMON).

Sources: Mathers, *Book of the Sacred Magic of Abramelin the Mage*, 105; Susej, *Demonic Bible*, 197; Von Worms, *Book of Abramelin*, 245, 256.

Näkki

Variations: Nacken, Nak, Nakk, Neck, Nikr, Vesihiisi, Vetehinen

Originating in Estonian, Finnish, Lap, and Swedish mythology, a näkki is a type of demonic fay that appears as a floating tree trunk, a large black horse, a hound, a silvery fish, a beautiful woman with three breasts, or as an ugly fisherman. Preying upon bathers and children trying to see their reflection in the water, the näkki will grab hold of them and pull them under the water, drowning them. They are said to live under bridges that cross rivers, docks, and piers and in murky pools and wells. This AQUEOUS DEVIL can be warded off by reciting a magical spell three times in a row before entering the water, wearing a charm made of iron, or by keeping a knife nearby when bathing.

Sources: Gray, *Mythology of All Races*, 206; Meurger, *Lake Monster Traditions*, 156, 158, 318; Philological Society, *Transactions of the Philological Society*, 12; Rose, *Giants, Monsters, and Dragons*, 87; Rose, *Spirits, Fairies, Leprechauns, and Goblins*, 239.

Namiros

In the *Sacred Magic of Abramelin the Mage*, book two, Namiros ("nautical" or "naval") is listed as one of the forty-nine SERVITORS OF BEELZEBUB (see BEELZEBUB).

Sources: Ford, *Bible of the Adversary*, 93; Mathers, *Book of the Sacred Magic of Abramelin the Mage*, 108, 120; Von Worms, *Book of Abramelin*, 123, 252, 257.

Namorodo

The Aboriginal people of West Arnhem Land, Australia, have in their mythology a vampiric demon called a namorodo. It is said to be a skeletal humanoid that is held together by ligaments and has long, razor-sharp finger bones. Inactive by day, at night it flies through the sky seeking prey. The namorodo will enter a home and when it finds a sleeping person, it attacks and drains them of their blood. If it is so inclined, it has the ability to create more of its own kind. The namorodo are associated with shooting stars and sorcery.

Sources: McLeish, *Myth*, 407; Rose, *Giants, Monsters, and Dragons*, 263; Tresidder, *Complete Dictionary of Symbols*, 335.

Namtar

Variations: Namtaru

Originating in Sumerian demonology, Namtar ("fate") was the messenger of Ereshkigal, the goddess of death and gloom and queen of the underworld, but has since has been made into the demon of plagues in Christian demonology (see IRKALLA). Born the offspring of the guardian of the fount of life and having no true form, this demon is in service under NERGAL and is ranked as the chief minister. Namtar grabs men by the hair and drags them down to the Underworld; he has the ability to spread sixty different types of disease and can enter into a man's body through their heart. He is said to live in desolate places and sacrificial grounds.

Nana Ayesha

Variations: Grinder of the Corn, Nana Ayesha Karama

In North and West African demonology Nana Ayesha is the demon of eye sores and smallpox. Born the daughter of Zanzanna, she can be persuaded to not spread her diseases by the sacrificial offering of speckled fowls. Nana Ayesha is represented in dance by wearing red, white, and punk clothing with two kerchiefs tied on the head. Dancing wildly, clapping hands, and scratching themselves, eventually Nana Ayesha's representatives will sit and sob until someone gives them a bit of sugar; revived, they begin to dance anew.

Sources: Caillois, *Man, Play, and Games*, 94; Oesterreich, *Possession, Demoniacal and Other Among Primitive Races*, 260; Tremearne, *Ban of the Bori*, 377.

Nanghaithya

Variations: Nanqaithya, Naonhaitya, Nasatya

Originally a Vedic deity, Nanghaithya was demonized by Zoroastrianism. Her name means "discontentment." In service under ANGRA MAINYU, Nanghaithya is a DAEVAS, DRUG, as well as one of seven arch-demons; she is the personification of discontentment. This demon causes diseases and plagues. She fights and opposes every form of religion. Her personal adversary is the angel Armaiti.

Sources: Burrell, *Religions of the World*, 69; Chisholm, *Encyclopaedia Britannica*, 1041; Cohn, *Cosmos, Chaos, and the World to Come*, 92, 93.

Nantur

In Apollonius of Tyana's *Nuctemeron* (*Night Illuminated by Day*), Nantur is the demon of writing. He is most powerful during the eighth hour.

Sources: Lévi, *Transcendental Magic*, 392, 506.

Naome

In Hassidic demonology Naome ("my joy" or "like Namoi") is one of the four devils who had children with Adam. She is under the command of LILIS (see DEVILS OF ADAM). Naome visited Adam during the one hundred thirty years before his marriage to Eve; he fathered many offspring with her.

Sources: *Encyclopædia Metropolitan*, 173; Spence, *Encyclopaedia of Occultism*, 152.

Naoth

Naoth ("knees") is one of the thirty-six Elemental World Rulers bound by King Solomon (see SPIRITS OF SOLOMON). Said to look like a man with the shapeless head of a DOG and having the face of a bird, donkey, or oxen, this demon sits on the knees of man. To stop Naoth from attacking, on a piece of paper write the words "Phnunoboêol, depart Nathath, and touch thou not the neck."

Sources: Ashe, *Qabalah*, 48; Conybeare, *Jewish Quarterly Review*, Vol. 11, 36.

Naphula

Variations: Valupa, Vapul

In *Ars Goetia*, the first book of the *Lemegeton*, the *Lesser Key of Solomon*, Naphula is ranked as a duke who commands thirty-six legions (see DUKES OF HELL). He appears as a griffon-winged lion. He is summoned for his ability to teach mechanics, philosophy, and sciences.

Sources: Crowley, *The Goetia*, 59; De Laurence, *Lesser Key of Solomon, Goetia*, 41–2; Godwin, *Godwin's Cabalistic Encyclopedia*, 524.

Naras

In *Ars Goetia*, the first book of the *Lemegeton*, the *Lesser Key of Solomon*, Duke Naras commands twenty servitors and is listed as one of the diurnal SERVITORS OF GEDEIL (see DUKES OF HELL and GEDEIL). He is said to be courteous, loving, and eager to serve his summoner.

Sources: Guiley, *Encyclopedia of Demons and Demonology*, 94; Peterson, *Lesser Key of Solomon*, 72.

Narbas

The *Grimoire of Pope Honorius* (*Le Grimoire du Pape Honorius*), alleged to be written by Pope Honorius III in the eighteenth century, names Narbas as a servitor demon.

Sources: De Givry, *Witchcraft, Magic, and Alchemy*, 26.

Nari

Nari are a species of demonic being from Slavic lore said to be created from the souls of children.

Source: Turner, *Dictionary of Ancient Deities*, 309, 337.

Narzad

Duke Narzad is one of the twenty SERVITORS OF SYMIEL (see SYMIEL). Disobedient, stubborn, and not willing to appear before his summoner, Narzad shares with the other nocturnal SERVITORS OF SYMIEL seven hundred ninety servitors among them.

Source: Peterson, *Lesser Key of Solomon*, 88.

Nasu

Variations: Drug Nasu ("demon of dead matter")

In Zoroastrian demonology, Nasu ("corpse") is the demon of bodily decomposition, decay, and pollution. This demon is said to look like a monstrous, speckled, female fly with backward-facing knees and a large stinger. Nasu has the ability to possess a corpse and makes his presence felt through decomposition and infection. Should a body be assaulted by him, an extremely complicated cleansing ritual that lasts nine days must take place.

Sources: Catholic University of America, *Catholic University Bulletin*, 269–70; Darmesteter, Vol. 3 of *Sacred Books of the East*, 26, 75–77, 190; Jackson, *Zoroaster: The Prophet of Ancient Iran*, 52; Lincoln, *Religion, Empire, and Torture*, 91–93, 140; Müller, *Sacred Books of the East*, 49.

Natalis

In the *Sacred Magic of Abramelin the Mage*, book two, Natalis ("a birthday") is listed as one of the forty-nine SERVITORS OF BEELZEBUB (see BEELZEBUB).

Sources: Ford, *Bible of the Adversary*, 93; Mathers, *Book of the Sacred Magic of Abramelin the Mage*, 108, 120; Murray's Magazine, *Early British Periodicals*, 669.

Nathriel

In *Theurgia Goetia*, the second book of the *Lemegeton*, Nathriel is ranked as a chief duke who commands 2,200 servants and is listed as one of the fifteen SERVITORS OF ICOSIEL (see ICOSIEL). This demon appears most easily for a summoner who invokes him from inside a home.

Sources: Peterson, *Lesser Key of Solomon*, 99; Trithemius, *Steganographia*, 69.

Naush

In Persian mythology and Zoroastrian demonology Naush is a race of demons known as a DRUG ("to lie"). Said to come from "the north," the sources and homeland of all evil, they appear as female mottled flies. They are the personification of the corruption of corpses.

Sources: Curtis, *Persian Myths*, 21; Fernández-Armesto, *World of Myths*, 97, 397; Garnier, *Worship of the Dead*, 235.

Navi

Variations: Látawci, Navj, Navjaci, Navje, Navki, Navyatsi, Opyr, Opyri, Oupir, Oupire ("bloodsucker")

A vampiric demon from Bulgaria, Poland, Russia, and Slovenia, a navi is said to be created whenever a child dies before they are baptized or when a person drowns. It returns to the world looking like a common enough bird. It searches the countryside looking for its mother and calling out to anyone who will listen that it wants to be baptized. Never knowing its own mother's love, it will attack women who are about to give birth, cutting them just deep enough to draw blood so it may take a drink. For seven years the navi can wander the earth calling out to others to help it. If it manages to persuade someone to baptize it, its spirit will be able to rest; if not it will forever remain a demon.

Sources: Georgieva, *Bulgarian Mythology*, 102–3; MacDermott, *Bulgarian Folk Customs*, 81; McClelland, *Slayers and Their Vampires*, 110; Ugresic, *Baba Yaga Laid an Egg*, 307.

Ndogbojusui

In the demonology of Sierra Leone, Ndogbojusui is a TERRESTRIAL DEVIL that appears as a pale white man with yellow hair and a long white beard. He preys upon travelers who stray from the path, luring them deeper and deeper into the forest all the while asking them questions aimed at discovering what his prey is thinking. This demon lives in the mountaintops by day and in the forests below at night. If ever you should think that you are in his company, remember to never give him a direct answer or admit what you are thinking; rather, reply to his questions with contrary answers. If you are able to do so long enough, he will leave you a gift (see also GENIE and TINGOI).

Sources: Cotterell, *Dictionary of World Mythology*, 211; Dooling, *White Man's Grave*, 93; Forde, *African Worlds*, 125; Gittins, *Mende Religion*, 76, 83; Rose, *Spirits, Fairies, Leprechauns, and Goblins*, 96.

Neabaz

Neabaz is a devil, one of the twelve SERVITORS OF ABEZETHIBOU (see ABEZETHIBOU). He is commonly named as the possessing devil in demonic cases.

Sources: Gettings, *Dictionary of Demons*, 246; Melton, *Encyclopedia of Occultism and Parapsychology*, 315; Spence, *Encyclopædia of Occultism*, 1553.

Nebiros

Variations: Cerberus, Naberius, Naberro, Nebirots

The *Grimoire of Pope Honorius* (*Le Grimoire du Pape Honorius*), alleged to have been written by Pope Honorius III in the eighteenth century, ranks Nebiros as a field marshal and an inspector general in service under ASTAROTH. The demon of North America, anger, hate, vengeance, and war, he commands the demons Aperos, Glasyabolas ("GLASSYALABOLAS") and NABERUS.

Appearing as a three-headed cock, this demon is summoned because he is a great necromancer, can make animals perform nefarious acts, can inflict harm on whomever he wishes, can predict the future, and can teach rhetoric and the properties of things.

Sources: Baskin, *Sorcerer's Handbook*, 276; Smith, *Edinburgh Review*, 122; Mark, *Book of Hierarchies*, 28; Waite, *Book of Black Magic and of Pacts*, 181–2; Wedeck, *Treasury of Witchcraft*, 96.

Necheshethiron

Necheshethiron is one of the twelve princes of the Qlippoth (see QLIPPOTHIC ORDERS OF DEMONS); he, like all the demons of his order, are said to look like a copper colored, human headed insect. His zodiacal sign is Scorpio.

Sources: Ford, *Bible of the Adversary*, 121; Mathers, *Sorcerer and His Apprentice*, 26.

Nefthada

Variations: Neftihadu

The *Theurgia Goetia*, the second book of the *Lemegeton*, lists Nefthada as one of the thirty-six Elemental World Rulers and one of the seventy-two SPIRITS OF SOLOMON that were used in the construction of the temple. This demon was made to do much of the heavy physical labor on the temple, including tending to the furnaces used for metalworking. The demon of kidney disease, Nefthada appears as a man with a shapeless head like a dog and a face like a bird, donkey, or oxen. He causes pain in the kidneys and heart, and painful urination. If ever afflicted by this demon, write the words "Iathôth, Uruêl, Nephthada" on a plate of tin and wear it next to your loins.

Sources: Ashe, *Qabalah*, 49; Conybeare, *Jewish Quarterly Review*, Vol. 11, 37.

Negarsanel

Variations: Der Fürst des Gehinnom (Prince of Gehinnom), Nagazdiel, Nagdasgiel, Nagrasagiel, Nasragiel

In Hasidic lore Negarsanel is a tutelary demon described as having the head of a lion and ranked as one of the PRINCES OF HELL. Along with KIPOD and Nairyo Sangha, he guards the upper gate to Gehinnom and was the demon who escorted Moses on his tour of Gehinnom.

Sources: Davidson, *Dictionary of Angels*, 205.

Nehemoth

In Jewish mystical lore the demon Nehemoth ("whisper") creates frightening sounds and causes the mind to rationalize its fears.

Source: Prasad, *Lilitu*, xii.

Nelchael

Variations: Once one of the seventy-two angels who bore the mystical name of God, SHEMHAMPHORAE; Nelakhel, Nelokhiel

A FALLEN ANGEL, formerly of the Order of Thrones, Nelchael is a diurnal demon who taught astronomy, geography, and mathematics to other FALLEN ANGELS. He is most powerful in the month of July and his zodiacal sign is Cancer. His personal adversary is the angel Sith.

Sources: Anderson, *Diary of Ancient Rites*, 196; Conway, *Guides, Guardians and Angels*, 131; Davidson, *Dictionary of Fallen Angels*, 205; Godwin, *Godwin's Cabalistic Encyclopedia*, 210; Gould, *Bizarre Notes and Queries*, 347; Maberry, *Cryptopedia*, 79; Scheible, *Sixth and Seventh Books of Moses*, 63; Webster, *Encyclopedia of Angels*, 7, 140.

Nenetophni

In the *Apocryphon of John*, Nenetophni is the demon of grief.

Sources: Dunderberg, *Myth, Lifestyle, and Society in the School of Valentinus*, 110; Lumpkin, *Fallen Angels, the Watchers and the Origin of Evil*, 16.

Nenisem

Nenisem is one of the sixty-five SERVITORS OF KORE AND MAGOTH named in the *Sacred Magic of Abramelin the Mage*, book two. His name is possibly Hebrew and means "displaying" or "waving."

Sources: Mathers, *Book of the Sacred Magic of Abramelin the Mage*, 107, 118; Susej, *Demonic Bible*, 258; Von Worms, *Book of Abramelin*, 250, 256.

Nephilim

Variations: Fallen Ones, the "giants of Canaan," N'philim, Nefilim, Neflim, Nephel (plural: Nephelim), Nephelin, Nephites (plural: Nephi'im)

In the Book of Genesis, the Book of Numbers, and noncanonical Christian and Jewish writings, we are told that the Nephilim ("rejects") are a race of evil giants who were born the offspring of human women and FALLEN ANGELS, making them semidivine beings. Their name in Hebrew means "fallen ones." Most sources describe them as being extraordinarily large when compared to the height of a man and being warlike by nature. There are six different types of Nephilim: Anakim ("Long-necked" or "Wearers of Necklaces"), Awwim ("Devastators" or "Serpents"), Emim ("Terrors"), Gibborim ("Giant Heroes"), Repha'im ("Weakeners"), and the Zamzummim ("Achievers").

The Nephilim were destroyed in the great flood that God sent to wipe the world clean of sin; however, He allowed ten percent of the disembodied spirits of the race to remain upon the earth in order to act as demons. They are to attempt to lead mankind astray until the final judgment.

Sources: Eberhart, *Mysterious Creatures*, 373; Icke, *Biggest Secret*, 41, 43, 46; Mathers, *Kabbalah Unveiled*, 249; Schwartz, *Tree of Souls*, 454–9; Shuker, *Mysteries of Planet Earth*, 126–31; Smith, Book of Deuteronomy, 19; Zimmerer, *Chronology of Genesis*, 77.

Nephtalius

Nephtalius was mentioned at the seventeenth-century trial of Urbain Grandier. This entity is often called upon during exorcism and cases of collective possession. He is also one of the eighteen demons who possessed Sister Jeanne des Anges in Loudun, France, in 1634 (see LOUDUN POSSESSION).

Sources: Aikin, *General Biography*, 493; Bayle, *Historical and Critical Dictionary*, 262; de Givry, *Witchcraft, Magic and Alchemy*, 128; Ramsay, *Layman's Guide to the New Testament*, 67; Ramsay, *Westminster Guide to the Books of the Bible*, 349; Voltaire, *Works of M. de Voltaire*, 193.

Neptuni

In French demonology, Neptuni is an aquatic demon.

Sources: Gerhardt, *Old Men of the Sea*, 31; Watkins, *History and the Supernatural in Medieval England*, 61.

Neqael

Variations: Ezeqeel, KAEL, Nuqael

In Enochian and Judaic lore, Neqael is one of the FALLEN ANGELS who swore allegiance to SAMIAZA, rebelled against God, took a human wife, and fathered the NEPHILIM. He is now considered to be the demon of the clouds.

Sources: Barton, *Journal of Biblical Literature*, Vols. 30–31, 165; Black, *Book of Enoch, or, I Enoch*, 64; Davidson, *Dictionary of Angels*, 206; Hoffmann, *Destroyer and the Lamb*, 57; Princeton Theological Seminary, *Princeton Theological Review*, Vol. 21, 190.

Neqa'el

Originating in Egyptian and Greek demonology, Neqa'el is a demonic god who was once worshipped by assassins in ancient Egypt. Preying on anyone who harmed a cat and fighting only when necessary, his victims were tortured for a month before they were finally killed. Having canine teeth and a quick wit, it was Neqa'el's saliva that spawned the sun god Ra.

Sources: Black, *Book of Enoch, or, I Enoch*, 121; Charlesworth, *Old Testament, Pseudepigrapha*, 47.

Nercamay

In the *Sacred Magic of Abramelin the Mage*, book two, Nercamay ("a boy or companion") is among the one hundred eleven SERVITORS OF AMAYMON, ARITON, ORIENS, AND PAYMON (see AMAYMON, ARITON, ORIENS, and PAYMON).

Sources: Mathers, *Book of the Sacred Magic of Abramelin the Mage*, 105, 112; Von Worms, *Book of Abramelin*, 244, 255.

Nergal

Variations: Lord of the decree of Uruk, Ne-uru-gal (lord of the great dwelling), Nergel, Nirgal, Nirgali, the crouching one, the "furious one," the "glowing flame," "the raging King"

Originating in Babylonian, Mesopotamian and Sumerian god of the underworld, Nergal ("great lord") was born the son of the god Enlil and became the ruler of the underworld, a subterranean cave known as Aralu (or IRKALLA); married to Allotu or Ereshkigal, the goddess of death and gloom (sources conflict; see IRKALLA); and consort to Laz. He was often said to be the father of the god Ninazu.

Nergal was later demonized and said to be the chief of the Secret Police of Hell and honorary spy in service under Belzebuth in Christian demonology. Titled the demon of destruction, fire, pestilence, and war, it is said that when he appears he does so as a grim warrior. He is portrayed in art as carrying a mace with a lion's head. Nergal is said to be most powerful at noontime in the summer, especially during the summer solstice.

This demon has destructive tendencies and a fiery nature, although he is patient when it comes to vengeance. He is summoned for his ability to destroy soil so it cannot grow food. He has dominion over the planet Mars and his sacred animal is the lion. Nergal lives in the area where he fell to earth, in the desert.

Nergal is mentioned in the Bible (2 Kings 17:30) as the god of the city of Cuth (Cuthah): "And the men of Babylon made Succoth-benoth, and the men of Cuth made Nergal" (see also ASIMA).

Sources: Chambers, *Book of Days*, 722; Jastrow, *Civilization of Babylonia and Assyria*, 206, 207, 211, 232, 239, 261, 417; Prince, *Journal of the American Oriental Society*, Vol. 28, 168–82; Melton, *Encyclopedia of Occultism and Parapsychology*, 315; Van der Toorn, *Dictionary of Deities and Demons in the Bible*, 621–2; Victoria Institute, *Journal of the Transactions of the Victoria Institute*, 16–17.

Neriel

Neriel is one of the twenty SERVITORS OF CAMUEL (see CAMUEL). This diurnal demon appears before his summoner in a beautiful form and is said to be very courteous.

Sources: Scheible, *Sixth and Seventh Books of Moses*, 75; Trithemius, *Steganographia*, 73.

Nerudee

In Persian mythology Nerudee is one of the eight AUSTATIKCO-PAULIGAUR, a type of demonic spirit. He is said to preside over one of the eight sides of the world (see also DIV).

Sources: De Claremont, *Ancient's Book of Magic*, 118; Kindersley, *Specimens of Hindoo Literature*, 33; Smedley, *Occult Sciences*, 51; Melton, *Encyclopedia of Occultism and Parapsychology*, 209, 253.

Nesbiros

Nesbiros, along with SAGATANA, is one of the two SERVITORS OF ASTAROTH (see ASTAROTH).

Sources: Kuriakos, *Grimoire Verum Ritual Book*, 30; Masters, *Devil's Dominion*, 130.

Neshimiron

In Cabalistic lore the neshimiron are one of the twelve QLIPPOTHIC ORDERS OF DEMONS. These demons appear as skeletally thin glowing women whose bodies have been fused with fish and snakes. They are known to copulate with gigantic fish and snakes.

Sources: Gilbert, *Sorcerer and His Apprentice*, 26; Greer, *Monsters*, 165.

Nesnas

Variations: Nesnás

Arabic and Judaic traditions refer to the nesnas as both a race of man and apes as well as a species of demonic creature or hybrid. The nesnas were born the offspring of a SHIKK and of a human being. The creature appears as a human with half a head, half a body, one arm, and one leg on which it very agilely hops quickly. It eats grass. The nesnas's appearance causes fear. It is said to live in the woods of El-Yemen. A species of winged nesnas is said to inhabit the island of Raij in the sea of Es-Seen. The people of Hadramót eat this creature and claim that its meat is sweet.

Sources: Burton, *Arabian Nights*, 354; Knowles, *Nineteenth Century*, Vol. 31, 449; Lane, *Arab Society in the Time of the Thousand and One Nights*, 45; Placzek, *Popular Science*, September 1882, 160–1; Poole, *The Thousand and One Nights*, 33; *Popular Science Monthly*, 660–1.

Nexroth

In Father Zacharias Vicecomes' *Complementum Artis Exorcistiae* (1608), Nexroth is a devil that commonly possesses people.

Sources: Spence, *Encyclopaedia of Occultism*, 153; Melton, *Encyclopedia of Occultism and Parapsychology*, 315.

Nia'gwai'he'gowa

According to the mythology of the Seneca tribe of North America, Nia'gwai'he'gowa ("bear monster") is a demonic beast with magical powers and the ability to shape-shift to what appears to its victims as a scrawny old man. It attempts to trick mortals into racing him and betting their life against a year's worth of its own power. Living in the shade of the hemlock tree, it has only one vulnerable place on its body—a tender spot on the heel of its right foot.

Sources: Jones, *Evil in Our Midst*, 55; Parker, *Code of Handsome Lake*, 125.

Nickar

Variations: Hnickars, Nicor, Nickur, Nikke

Originating in Saxon, Scandinavian, and Teutonic mythology, the demon of death and destruction, Nickar, was at one time considered to be a lesser form of the god Odin. They were the descendants of the nymphs of the Elbe and the Gaal.

According to Collin de Plancy's *Dictionaire Infernale* (1863), these demons are said to be able to command the water; they have the ability to cause blizzards, hailstorms, hurricanes, and tempests. They are described as having long fishlike tails, long blond or green hair, and wearing seaweed. They are often described as combing their hair, playing a harp, or singing. If anyone should see them and the Nickar notice, they will pull that person down into the water with them and drown them there. They also have a reputation for using their power over the sea to cause death and destruction by capsizing boats, tormenting fishermen, and throwing people into shore-side trees.

Nickars, a type of AQUEOUS DEVIL, are similar to mermaids, mermen, necks, nixies, sirens, stromkarls, and undine.

Sources: Collin de Plancy, *Dictionnaire Infernal*, 492; Percy, *Mirror of Literature, Amusement, and Instruction*, 69; Rose, *Spirits, Fairies, Leprechauns, and Goblins*, 236.

Nightmares

According to Alphonse de Spina's book, *Fortalitium Fidei* (*Fortress of Faith*) published in 1467, the nightmare is a species of demon that disrupts one's natural sleep with disturbing dreams. De Spina claimed that there are ten species of demons and 133,306,668 individual demonic beings in all (see NUMBER OF DEMONS).

Sources: Ashley, *Amazing World of Superstition, Prophecy, Luck, Magic and Witchcraft*, 198; Ashley, *What's in a Name*, 214.

Nihasa

Anton LeVey claimed that Nihasa was the Native American word for "SATAN"; however, he did not indicate which tribe used this word.

Sources: Bailey, *Spiritual Warfare*, 95; Susej, *Demonic Bible*, 72, 79.

Nilaihah

Variations: Nith-Haiah, Nithaiah, Nithhaja

Nilaihah is a FALLEN ANGEL, formerly of the Order of Dominions and also one of the seventy-two Schemnamphoras. The demon of occult sciences, he has influence over those who love peace and solitude. He will reveal prophecies in the form of poetry. This demon is said to be most powerful in the month of July. To summon Nilaihah, speak aloud one of the names of God and recite Psalm 9, *Thanksgiving for God's Justice*.

Sources: Ashley, *Complete Book of Devils and Demons*, 74; Davidson, *Dictionary of Angels*, 207; Webster, *Encyclopedia of Angels*, 142.

Nile

Variations: NILEN

Nile is among the one hundred eleven SERVITORS OF AMAYMON, ARITON, ORIENS, AND PAYMON (see AMAYMON, ARITON, ORIENS, and PAYMON) named in the *Sacred Magic of Abramelin the Mage*, book two.

Sources: Mathers, *Book of the Sacred Magic of Abramelin the Mage*, 112; Von Worms, *Book of Abramelin*, 244, 255.

Nilen

In the *Sacred Magic of Abramelin the Mage*, book two, Nilen is listed as one of the one hundred eleven SERVITORS OF AMAYMON, ARITON, ORIENS, AND PAYMON (see AMAYMON, ARITON, ORIENS, and PAYMON). His name is possibly Greek or Latin and may translate to mean "the river," as in the River Nile.

Sources: Mathers, *Selected Occult Writings of S.L. MacGregor Mathers*, 112; Susej, *Demonic Bible*, 256.

Nilima

In the *Sacred Magic of Abramelin the Mage*, Nilima ("evil questioners") is among the twenty SERVITORS OF AMAYMON (see AMAYMON).

Sources: Mathers, *Book of the Sacred Magic of Abra-Melin*, 122; Susej, *Demonic Bible*, 259.

Nimalon

In the *Ars Goetia*, the first book of the *Lemegeton*, Nimalon is listed as one of the fifty-three SERVITORS OF ASHTAROTH AND ASMODEUS (see ASHTAROTH and ASMODEUS). His name is possibly Hebrew and means "circumcision."

Source: Susej, *Demonic Bible*, 198.

Nimerix

In the *Sacred Magic of Abramelin the Mage*, Nimerix is listed as one of the thirty-two SERVITORS OF ASTAROT (see ASTAROT). The etymology of his name is possibly Celtic.

Sources: Mathers, *Book of the Sacred Magic of Abramelin the Mage*, 117; Susej, *Demonic Bible*, 257; Von Worms, *Book of Abramelin*, 249, 256.

Nimorup

In the *Sacred Magic of Abramelin the Mage*, book two, Nimorup is one of the forty-nine SERVITORS OF BEELZEBUB (see BEELZEBUB).

Sources: Cavendish, *The Powers of Evil in Western Religion, Magic and Folk Belief*, 253.

Nimrod

Variations: Nimrod the Giant

Born of the union between a NEPHILIM and a Nephilim-human woman named Semiramis, Nimrod ("he rebelled") is described as being a black-skinned giant. It is possible that he later took Semiramis as his wife. This NEPHILIM was the individual who commissioned the Tower of Babel. Said to be a great hunter and incredibly strong, he and his wife are the progenitors of the Cushite (Ethiopian) race. Nimrod was noted for being exceptionally cruel; he required the blood sacrifice of the firstborn son from his people.

Source: Garnier, *Worship of the Dead*, 196, 197, 198, 209, 211, 331.

Nine Mystic Names

Originating in medieval demonology, these nine mystical names are said to be used when summoning demons in order to gain control over them. The names are Ehieh, El, El Adonai Tzabaoth, ELOAH VA-DAATH, ELOHIM GIBOR, ELOHIM TZABAOTH, Iod, Shaddai, and Tetragrammaton Elohim.

Sources: Baskin, *Satanism*, 238; Cavendish, *Man, Myth and Magic*, 865; Chaplin, *Dictionary of the Occult and Paranormal*, 89.

Nirgalli

According to the demonology from ancient Assyria, nirgalli ("winged lions") are types of demonic guardians stationed at the entranceways to the royal palace. Always appearing in pairs, these lion-headed humans with the legs of eagles fight one another with clubs and daggers. Magical incantations that mention the nirgalli say that "the evil demons should get out; they should mutually kill one another."

Sources: Carus, *History of the Devil and the Idea of Evil*, 39–40; Cheyne, *Prophecies of Isaiah*, 299; Methodist Book Concern, *Methodist Review*, Vol. 35, 118.

Nisroc

Variations: The Great Eagle, NYSROCK

Originating in ancient Assyria, Nisroc was the Guardian of the Tree and was worshipped as a god. When he was absorbed into Judeo-Christian demonology he was labeled as a FALLEN ANGEL and made into the chief cook of Hell. He is the demon of fatality and hatred.

Sources: Davidson, *Dictionary of Angels*, 41.

Nisroch

Variations: DAGON

Originally an ancient Assyrian god of agriculture, some religious authors consider Nisroch ("eagle") as a FALLEN ANGEL, formerly of the Order of Principalities. In Collin de Plancy's *Dictionaire Infernale* (1863) and Johann Wierus's *Pseudomonarchia Daemonum* (*False Monarchy of Demons*, 1583) he is ranked as the chief of cuisine to the princes in Hell. The demon of cooking, he is said to be an associate to BELPHEGOR.

Sources: Weyer, *Witches, Devils, and Doctors in the Renaissance*, 13.

Nisumba

Born the twin brother of SUMBHA in Hindu mythology, Nisumba, an ASURAS, was a giant who was impervious to harm from any of the gods. Eventually, he was slain by his personal adversary KALI and her powerful army.

Sources: Harper, *Roots of Tantra*, 30; Kondos, *On the Ethos of Hindu Women*, 187; Parmeshwaranand, *Encyclopaedic Dictionary of Purāṇas*, 460; Shastri, *Ancient Indian Tradition and Mythology*, 1651; Vergati, *Gods and Masks of the Kāthmāṇḍu Valley*, 92.

Nithael

Nithael is, according to the Kabbalah, one of the seventy-two angels who bear the mystical name of God, SHEMHAMPHORAE. A FALLEN ANGEL, formerly of the Order of Principalities, he commands human emperors, kings, high-ranking clergy, and the civilians of Hell. He is most powerful during the month of December. His zodiacal sign is Sagittarius.

Sources: Anderson, *Diary of Ancient Rites*, 114; Davidson, *Dictionary of Angels*, 208; Gould, *Bizarre Notes and Queries*, 347; Webster, *Encyclopedia of Angels*, 74, 141, 142, 180.

Nitibus

Nitibus is listed in Apollonius of Tyana's *Nuctemeron* (*Night Illuminated by Day*) as the demon of stars. He is most powerful during the second hour.

Sources: Davidson, *Dictionary of Angels*, 209; Kelly, *Who in Hell*, 167.

Nitika

In Apollonius of Tyana's *Nuctemeron* (*Night Illuminated by Day*) Nitika is listed as the demon of precious stones. He is said to be most powerful during the sixth hour.

Sources: Davidson, *Dictionary of Angels*, 209; Kelly, *Who in Hell*, 167; Lévi, *Transcendental Magic*, 391, 505.

Niyaz

Variations: He who causes distress, Niyâz ("Indigent")

Originating in Persian and Zoroastrian demonology, Niyaz ("want") is a DEV mentioned in Manichaean, Middle Persian, Zoroastrian, and Zuwanite texts. Destructive and powerful, this demon causes distress during times of change in a person's life. Niyaz cannot ever be filled, fulfilled, or satisfied. His personal adversary is Atar, god of fire (see also DEVS WHO RESIDE IN MEN).

Sources: Dhalla, *Zoroastrian Theology*, 268; Ford, *Bible of the Adversary*, 141; Ford, *Luciferian Witchcraft*, 262; West, *Sacred Books of the East*, 28.

Nociel

Variations: Ciriel

In Enochian lore Nociel is one of the twenty-eight demonic rulers of the lunar mansions (see ENOCHIAN RULERS OF THE LUNAR MANSIONS).

Sources: Gettings, *Dictionary of Demons*, 176; McLean, *Treatise on Angel Magic*, 42.

Nocticula

Variations: "The Diana of the Ancient Gauls," Herodiade, "The Moon"

Nocticula is a vampiric, demonic goddess from France, a singular entity. Her followers were said to be most active during the twelfth and thirteenth centuries. Nocticula, a consort to both ASMODEUS and BEELZEBUB, demanded human sacrifices be made in her name to the goddess Lamiae. These sacrifices, usually children, were cut into little pieces and fed to Lamiae, who devoured them but would quickly regurgitate them back up. Then it was believed that Nocticula, in a show of mercy, would restore the children's bodies and place their souls back in, returning them to life. Then her followers would take the babies back to where they had been stolen from.

Nocticula followers were usually women, and while completely naked, they rode horses to their meeting place to pay homage to their goddess. Followers wrote their names in a Book of Shadows and thereafter no longer considered themselves to be human women, but rather, fay. Only one book of Nocticula has ever been found, and it was discovered in the ruins of one of her temples in the eighteenth century. Apart from the names of her followers, the book also contained the names of sorcerers and other magic users.

It has been speculated by some scholars that she may be a reinterpretation of a much older deity called BENSOZIA.

Sources: Alford, *Folklore*, Vol. 46; Baroja, *World of Witches*, 62, 64; Clifton, *Paganism Reader*, 171; Gardner, *Meaning of Witchcraft*, 101; Grimm, *Teutonic Mythology*, 1057; Lederer, *Fear of Women*, 197; McClintock, *Cyclopaedia of Biblical, Theological, and Ecclesiastical Literature*, 824.

Nodar

In Christian demonology Nodar is one of the twenty SERVITORS OF CAMUEL (see CAMUEL). This nocturnal demon appears before his summoner in a beautiful form and is known to be very courteous.

Sources: Guiley, *Encyclopedia of Demons and Demonology*, 36; Peterson, *Lesser Key of Solomon*, 68; Trithemius, *Steganographia*, 73.

Nogar

The *Sacred Magic of Abramelin the Mage*, book two, names Nogar ("flowing") as one of the one hundred eleven SERVITORS OF AMAYMON, ARITON, ORIENS, AND PAYMON (see AMAYMON, ARITON, ORIENS, and PAYMON).

Sources: Ford, *Bible of the Adversary*, 88; Mathers, *Book of the Sacred Magic of Abramelin the Mage*, 105; Von Worms, *Book of Abramelin*, 245.

Nogen

In the *Sacred Magic of Abramelin the Mage*, book two, Nogen ("to strike a musical instrument") is included among the one hundred eleven SERVITORS OF AMAYMON, ARITON, ORIENS, AND PAYMON (see AMAYMON, ARITON, ORIENS, and PAYMON).

Sources: Mathers, *Book of the Sacred Magic of Abramelin the Mage*, 105; Susej, *Demonic Bible*, 197; Von Worms, *Book of Abramelin*, 246.

Nokondisi

The mythology of the Gururumba village of Miruma, located in the Asaro Valley of New Guinea, tells of the demonic nature spirits known as nokondisi. Demons of the Pacific Ocean, they normally appear as fog, haze, or mist. Nokondisi are all male and can take the form of half-bat and half-human creatures, their bodies covered in fur, with a set of large bat wings, a mouthful of sharp and pointy teeth, and an eerily, whispery voice.

Opportunity hunters, these demons prey on women, violently raping them and partially consuming anyone who dares to enter into their sanctuary, as they are highly territorial. If the demon should impregnate a woman, she will give birth to a child with a deformed face. Nokondisi have the ability to assume a human form as well as being able to turn animals into stones.

Nokondisi live in the upper-land forests in crevices in rock faces, mounds of boulders, or in the tangled exposed roots of old trees. The only way to prevent attack from one of these demons is to try to appeal to its sense of reciprocity. By building a spirit house for the nokondisi in a garden and fencing off some territory for it to claim as well as by leaving offerings of food and gifts, the nokondisi will then, in exchange, protect a person's pigs and yam gardens.

The nokondisi differ only slightly from the demonic gwomai in that they live in the lowlands in the reed banks along rivers. Some sources claim that the gwomai use lightning to knock down the trees on the property of weak men, thereby causing them to fall ill.

Sources: Jones, *Evil in Our Midst*, 179–82; Savill, *Pears Encyclopaedia of Myths and Legends*, 99; Spradley, *Conformity and Conflict*, 414; Varner, *Creatures in the Mist*, 191.

Nominon

In the *Sacred Magic of Abramelin the Mage*, book two, Nominon ("conventional) is among the forty-nine SERVITORS OF BEELZEBUB (see BEELZEBUB). According to Alister Crowley, Nominon looks like "a large red spongy jellyfish with one greenish luminous spot."

Sources: Cavendish, *The Powers of Evil in Western Religion, Magic and Folk Belief*, 254; Crowley, *Confessions*, 408; Ford, *Bible of the Adversary*, 93; Mathers, *Book of the Sacred Magic of Abramelin the Mage*, 120.

Nopperabo

Variations: Mujina, Noppera-bō

In Japanese demonology nopperabo demons typically appear as women with a perfectly featureless and smooth faces. Sometimes one will impersonate someone familiar to the victim before revealing itself for what it truly is. Exceptionally frightening to experience, nopperabo are otherwise harmless.

It should be noted that there is a type of creature called the mujina, which are small furry shape-shifting beings that frequently take on the guise of nopperabo to frighten people.

Sources: Bush, *Asian Horror Encyclopedia*, 136; Frédéric, *Japan Encyclopedia*, 727; Hearn, *Kwaidan*, 42.

Notiser

In the *Sacred Magic of Abramelin the Mage*, book two, Notiser is one of the twenty-two SERVITORS OF ARITON (see ARITON). His name is possibly Greek and may mean "putter to flight."

Sources: Ford, *Bible of the Adversary*, 94; Susej, *Demonic Bible*, 259; Von Worms, *Book of Abramelin*, 254.

Nuberus

The *Grimoire of Pope Honorius* (*Le Grimoire du Pape Honorius*), alleged to have been written in the eighteenth century by Pope Honorius III, says that Nuberus is a subordinate spirit, a servitor.

Sources: Baskin, *Dictionary of Satanism*, 160; de Givry, *Witchcraft, Magic and Alchemy*, 128; Wedeck, *Treasury of Witchcraft*, 97.

Nuditon

Variations: Nudatus, Nudition

In the *Sacred Magic of Abramelin the Mage*, book two, Nuditon ("nakedness") is listed as one of the one hundred eleven SERVITORS OF AMAYMON, ARITON, ORIENS, AND PAYMON (see AMAYMON, ARITON, ORIENS, and PAYMON).

Sources: Mathers, *Book of the Sacred Magic of Abramelin the Mage*, 105, 112; Von Worms, *Book of Abramelin*, 244, 255.

Nujaitun

Possibly originating in Persian demonology, Nujaitun is the demon of asthma and madness.

Sources: Society of Biblical Archæology, *Proceedings of the Society of Biblical Archaeology*, Vol. 9, 227.

Number of Demons

Alfonso de Spina calculated that of the 400 million angels, one-third were demons as attributed to the Book of Revelation 12:3–9. In 1467 de Spina gave the number of demons at 133,316,666.

Daniel 7:10, Hebrews 12:22, and Revelation 5:11 all assert that the number of angels is countless; however, Revelation 12:4–9 says that one third of them are FALLEN ANGELS.

Fromenteau in his book *Le cabinet du Roy de France* (1581) claims that sorcerers have counted the number of demons at 7,409,127 with seventy-two princes.

Johann Wierus, author of *De Praestigiis Daemonum* published in 1568, claims that there are 7,451,926 demons divided into 111 legions of 6,666 demons each and that each legion is ruled over by the seventy-two demonic PRINCES OF HELL. His *Pseudomonarchia Daemonum* (*False Monarchy of Demons*, 1583) estimates the number of demons to be 44,435,622. They are divided into 666 legions, each legion consisting of 6,666 demons. The legions are ruled over by the 66 infernal dukes, kings, and princes; however, their number is not added into his original total. In later editions of this book he changes these numbers, now claiming that there are 6 legions with 66 cohorts each, which are divided into 666 companies consisting of 6,666 individuals, for a total of 1,758,640,176 in all. In this breakdown the legions are led by one emperor, seven kings, 10 counts, 11 presidents, 13 marquis, and 23 dukes.

Talmudic tradition states that there are 7,405,926 demons.

Gregory of Nyssa said that demons fathered children with mortal women, thereby continuously adding to the number of existing demons.

The cardinal bishop of Tusculum (fifteenth century) estimated the number of FALLEN ANGELS to be 133,306,668. According to the Book of Revelation, one third of the angelic hosts fell, an event that took place over nine days.

Sources: Bailey, *Historical Dictionary of Witchcraft*, 36; Chambers, *Book of Days*, 723; De Givry, *Witchcraft, Magic, and Alchemy*, 124–5; Eliade, *Encyclopedia of Religion*, Vol. 5, 380; Icons, *Demons*, 130; Lea, *Materials Toward a History of Witchcraft*, 99; Schneck, *History of Psychiatry*, 41.

Nuthon

The *Sacred Magic of Abramelin the Mage*, book two, names Nuthon as one of the one hundred eleven SERVITORS OF AMAYMON, ARITON, ORIENS, AND PAYMON (see AMAYMON, ARITON, ORIENS, and PAYMON). His name is possibly Coptic or Greek and may mean "God-like" or "piercing."

Sources: Ford, *Bible of the Adversary*, 88; Mathers, *Book of the Sacred Magic of Abramelin the Mage*, 105; Von Worms, *Book of Abramelin*, 245.

Nyavaja

Variations: Nyavalya ("falling sickness")

Nyavaja is the demon of illness in Hungarian demonology. His name means "diseases" or "a great illness."

Sources: Gyarmathi, *Uralic and Altaic Series*, Vol. 95, 168; Kõiva, *Folk Belief Today*, 139; Sherekh, *Prehistory of Slavic*, 70; Sinor, *Inner Asia*, 168.

Nybbas

Variations: Nebachas, Nebahaz, Nybras

In Collin de Plancy's *Dictionaire Infernale* (1863), Nybbas holds several infernal posts, including chief mimic of the Masters of the Revels, the court fool of Hell, grand publicist of the pleasures of Hell, the great parodist, and the ruler of dreams. This low-ranking servitor of VAPULA is in service under LILITH, as he is an INCUBUS of the inferior order. The demon who advertises the pleasures of Hell, he was born the son of either SAMAEL or URIEL (sources conflict) and is described as looking like a winged lion or as a man with a sickening grinning face whose eyes are hidden behind a hat or veil. Nybbas dehumanizes and desensitizes humanity, and manages the dreams and visions of mankind. This natural-born liar is both disdainful and manipulative. He is known to strangle his lovers while they sleep.

Sources: Chambers, *Book of Days*, 723; Collin de Plancy, *Dictionnaire Infernal*, 496; Kelly, *Who in Hell*, 168; Shah, *Occultism*, 64; Waite, *Book of Black Magic and Ceremonial Magic*, 187; Wall, *Devils*, 26.

Nysrock

Variations: NISROC, Nysrogh

Nysrock is the demon of the pleasures of the table. The chief cook in the kitchen of Hell, he is ranked as a second order of demon.

Source: Collin de Plancy, *Dictionnaire Infernal*, 389.

Oap

According to Enochian lore Oap is a CACODAEMON. His counterpart is the angel Apst (ENOCHIAN CACODAEMONS).

Sources: Chopra, *Academic Dictionary of Mythology*, 213; Laycock, *Complete Enochian Dictionary*, 143.

Obedama

In the *Sacred Magic of Abramelin the Mage*, book two, Obedama ("woman-servant" or "mother") is among the one hundred eleven SERVITORS OF AMAYMON, ARITON, ORIENS, AND PAYMON (see AMAYMON, ARITON, ORIENS, and PAYMON).

Sources: Ford, *Bible of the Adversary*, 88; Mathers, *Book of the Sacred Magic of Abra-Melin*, 112; Susej, *Demonic Bible*, 197.

Obiriron

The obiriron are one of the twelve demons of the QLIPPOTHIC ORDERS OF DEMONS. Looking like bloated goblins, the Obiriron colors are "like the clouds."

Sources: Mathers, *Sorcerer and his Apprentice*, 26.

Obizuth

Variations: Obyzouth; Admits in the text that she has many names but describes none

In the *Testament of Solomon*, Obizuth is a nocturnal DEMONESS who admits to the king that she has many appearances but describes none of them; she appears before Solomon cloaked in shadow with bright eyes, wild hair, a clear voice, and no apparent limbs. At night she preys upon women she finds in childbirth. If she does not kill their newborns outright, she renders them blind, deaf, mentally deficient, or some other such birth defect. Every night this demon must inflict harm to at least one child or she cannot rest.

Although she was bound by King Solomon's seal, he could not make Obizuth work on the construction of his temple, so he ordered her hair bound and hung her by it on the temple doors. Her personal adversary is the angel Afarol (Raphael). To prevent her from attacking, write the angelic name Afarol on an amulet and wear it during labor to protect the child.

Many scholars speculate that Obizuth and LILITH are in fact the same demon; if this is true, then this is the earliest reference of amulets being used to ward her off.

Sources: Conybeare, *Jewish Quarterly Review*, Vol. 11, 3, 30; Folklore Society, *Folklore*, Vol. 11, 160; Gaster, *Studies and Texts in Folklore*, 1034; Koltuv, *Book of Lilith*, 59; Lacks, *Women and Judaism*, 44; Langond, *Lilith*, 362–65; Schwartz, *Lilith's Cave*, 7.

Och

The grimoire *Arbatel de Magia Veterum* (*Arbatel of the Magic of the Ancients*) written by an unknown author and published in 1575 in Basel, Switzerland, ranks Och as one of the seven OLYMPIAN SPIRITS. A planetary spirit, Och is the demon of alchemy, magic, and medicine. Commanding 36,536 legions and twenty-eight provinces, as well has having dominion over the sun, this demon causes the one he possesses to be worshipped as a god. He is known to create medicine; give excellent FAMILIAR spirits, gold, money, and wisdom; transform any substance into the purest precious gem or metal; as well as extend a person's life with perfect health for six hundred years (see also ARATRON, BETHOR, HAGITH, OPHIEL, PHALEG, and PHUL).

Sources: Drury, *Dictionary of the Esoteric*, 16, 239; González-Wippler, *Complete Book of Spells*,120; Greer, *New Encyclopedia of the Occult*, 339; McLean, *Magical Calendar*, 110; Webster, *Encyclopedia of Angels*, 143.

Ochnotinos

Ochnotinos is the demon of fevers in Judaic demonology who is called upon to remove them when his name is chanted in a reduction:

Ochnotinos
Chnotinos
Notinos
Tinos
Inos
Nos
Os

Sources: Baskin, *Sorcerer's Handbook*, 219; Goldwag, *Beliefnet Guide to the Kabbalah*, 107; Isaacs, *Divination, Magic, and Healing*, 88; Wedeck, *Treasury of Witchcraft*, 28.

Ochus Bochus

Variations: Oker Boker

Ochus Bochus is a demonic sorcerer from Norse mythology who is said to live in the forest. Many magic users and sorcerors over the centuries have used the words "ochus bochus" when wielding their magic, leaving some scholars to believe that the phrase is not invoking the demonic sorcerer of Norse lore but is rather a corruption of some other name, word, or phrase, such as: Bacchus (Bochus), the god of conjuration; the Welsh phrase "*hovea pwca*," which is used to describe a trick played on one by a will-o'-the-wisp named Pwca; or perhaps a corruption of a Latin phrase said during the Catholic mass, "*Hoc est corpus.*" Additionally, several jugglers in Tudor, England, used Ochus Bochus as their stage name, as mentioned in the French Royal Dictionary.

Sources: Dickens, *All the Year Round*, 158; Mitchell, *Significant Etymology*, 224.

Odam

Odam is one of the many secret names of LILITH.

Sources: Ashley, *Complete Book of Devils and Demons*, 77; Folklore Society, *Folklore*, Vol. 11, 148; Pereira, *Lilith*, 52, 65; University of Pennsylvania University Museum, *Publications of the Babylonian Section*, Vol. 3, 260, 262.

Odax

In the *Sacred Magic of Abramelin the Mage*, book two, Odax ("biting") is listed as one of the sixty-five SERVITORS OF KORE AND MAGOTH.

Sources: Ford, *Bible of the Adversary*, 92; Mathers, *Book of the Sacred Magic of Abra-Melin*, 107; Von Worms, *Book of Abramelin*, 250.

Odiel

Odiel, a nocturnal demon, is one of the sixteen SERVITORS OF ASELIEL (see ASELIEL) named in the *Sacred Magic of Abramelin the Mage*, book two.

Sources: Peterson, *Lesser Key of Solomon*, 69.

Odiosus

An Odiosus ("hateful") demon appears as a human female with large butterfly wings. They haunt and torment an individual or a family line. These demons have the ability to possess inanimate objects. Odiosus demons have free will and are immortal; they cannot be killed by the individual or family line that they are bound to.

Source: Stormonth, *Etymological and Pronouncing Dictionary of the English Language*, 398.

Odo

According to Enochian lore, Odo is a CACO-DAEMON. His counterpart is the angel Doop (ENOCHIAN CACODAEMONS).

Sources: Chopra, *Academic Dictionary of Mythology*, 214; Laycock, *Complete Enochian Dictionary*, 144.

Oec

According to Enochian lore, Oec is the CA-CODAEMON of earth and fire. His counterpart is the angel Ecop (see ENOCHIAN CACODAEMONS).

Sources: Chopra, *Academic Dictionary of Mythology*, 215; Laycock, *Complete Enochian Dictionary*, 145.

Oeillet

Variations: Oelliet, Oiellet

In Father Sebastien Michaelis's *Histoire admirable de la possession et conversion d'une penitente* (1612), Oeillet ("carnation") is listed as a FALLEN ANGEL, formerly of the Order of Dominions. The demon of luck, money, and prosperity, he is known to tempt monks to break their vow of poverty. His personal adversary is St. Martin.

Sources: Ashley, *Complete Book of Devils and Demons*, 61; Gettings, *Dictionary of Demons*, 180; Robbins, *Encyclopedia of Witchcraft and Demonology*, 129.

Og

Variations: Palit

Og was the king of Bashan, according to Hebrew lore. The last of the Refaim race and a descendant of the NEPHILIM, he was said to have been born the son of Ahijah and grandson of Sham-Hazai, one of the FALLEN ANGELS. His birth was before the time of the Great Flood, and Jewish folklore says that he was allowed to survive by clinging to the side of Noah's ark.

Og was described as being a giant. Deuteronomy 3:11 says that Og's bed was made of iron and was more than nine cubits (thirteen and a half feet) long and four cubits (six feet) wide. Eventually, Og was slain by Moses with a blow to his ankle.

Sources: Bamberger, *Fallen Angels*, 59; Davidson, *Dictionary of Angels*, xxiv, 274; Pulszky, *Tales and Traditions of Hungary*, 81; Schwarts, *Tree of Souls*, 461.

Ogére

Originating in Hassidic demonology, Ogére is one of the four devils who had children with Adam (see DEVILS OF ADAM). Under the command of LILIS, this devil visited Adam during the one hundred thirty years before his marriage to Eve, when he fathered many offspring with her.

Sources: Oxford Journals, *Notes and Queries*, 495; Smedley, *Occult Sciences*, 173; Spence, *Encyclopaedia of Occultism*, 152.

Ogilen

In the *Sacred Magic of Abramelin the Mage*, book two, Ogilen ("round" or "wheel") is listed as one of the one hundred eleven SERVITORS OF AMAYMON, ARITON, ORIENS, AND PAYMON (see AMAYMON, ARITON, ORIENS, and PAYMON).

Sources: Mathers, *Book of the Sacred Magic of Abramelin the Mage*, 10; Von Worms, *Book of Abramelin*, 245.

Oia

According to Enochian lore, Oia is a CACO-DAEMON. His counterpart is the angel Iaba (see ENOCHIAN CACODAEMONS).

Sources: Chopra, *Academic Dictionary of Mythology*, 216; Laycock, *Complete Enochian Dictionary*, 145.

Okeus

Variations: Oke, Oki

From the demonology of the Powhatan people of Virginia, Okeus was a malevolent if not demonic god. If not obeyed, he would destroy crops, enable enemies to conquer them, or cause natural disasters. He always prevailed. Child scarifices were offered to him. At his main temple, the Uttamussac Indians would toss pieces of copper, pearls, and puccoon in the water as they paddled their canoes by to appease him.

Sources: Lang, *Making of Religion*, 231; Matthews, *World Religions*, 20, 406; Price, *Love and Hate in Jamestown*, 175.

Okiri

In the *Sacred Magic of Abramelin the Mage*, Okiri ("to cause to sink or fail") is among the thirty-two SERVITORS OF ASTAROT (see ASTAROT).

Sources: Mathers, *Book of the Sacred Magic of Abramelin the Mage*, 106, 117; Susej, *Demonic Bible*, 257; Von Worms, *Book of Abramelin*, 249.

Old Nick

Variations: Nekker, Nikker ("to wash")

Old Nick is a colloquialism for "the Devil" taken from the German word *kikker*, which was originally in German mythology as a Teutonic water sprite. Old Nick's appearance to a sailor was considered to be a death omen.

Sources: Baskin, *Dictionary of Satanism*, 243; *Encyclopedia Britannica*, Vol. 19, 719; Grimm, *Teutonic Mythology*, 488; Stallybrass, *Teutonic Mythology*, Vol. 4, 235.

Olisermon

In the *Sacred Magic of Abramelin the Mage*, book two, Olisermon is one of the sixty-five SERVITORS OF KORE AND MAGOTH. His name is possibly either Greek or Latin and may mean "of short speech."

Sources: Ford, *Bible of the Adversary*, 92; Susej, *Demonic Bible*, 258; Von Worms, *Book of Abramelin*, 256.

Oliver

Variations: Olivier

In the Christian demonology of Sebastien Michaelis's *Histoire admirable de la possession et conversion d'une penitente* (1612), Oliver was ranked as the prince of the demonic archangels, a FALLEN ANGEL and archangel himself (see also ARCHDEMONS and PRINCES OF HELL).

Sources: Cuhulain, *Witch Hunts*, 206; Gettings, *Dictionary of Demons*, 181; Rachleff, *Occult in Art*, 224.

Olympian Spirits

Variations: Olympic Spirits, Olympick Spirits

First mentioned during the Renaissance and written of in post–Renaissance books of ceremonial and ritual magic, the Olympian Spirits are a collection of seven individual spirits: ARATRON, BETHOR, HAGITH, OCH, OPHIEL, PHALEG, and PHUL. Each of the Olympians rules a set number of provinces. They are said to live in the firmament and in the stars of the firmament from where they administer fatal charms and tell people their destinies. Each of the Olympian spirits is rivaled by one of the traditional seven archangels.

Sources: Davidson, *Dictionary of Angels*, 212; Drury, *Dictionary of the Esoteric*, 239; Gettings, *Dictionary of Demons*, 181; Hall, *Secret Teachings of All Ages*, 103–4.

Omael

Variations: Avamel, Evamel

Omael was once one of the seventy-two angels who bore the mystical name of God, SHEMHAMPHORAE. He is possibly one of the FALLEN ANGELS, formerly a member of the Order of Dominions. Currently, he is ranked as the regent of alchemy. Omael is said to operate in both Heaven and in Hell. He helps humans and animals to procreate, influences chemists, multiplies species, and perpetuates races. He is most powerful during the month of August. Omael's name is possibly Hebrew and may mean "hope" or "God of patience."

Sources: Davidson, *Dictionary of Angels*, 212; Godwin, *Godwin's Cabalistic Encyclopedia*, 34; Peterson, *Lesser Key of Solomon*, 79; Waite, *Book of Destiny*, 95; Webster, *Encyclopedia of Angels*, 144.

Omages

Variations: Ho Magos

In the *Ars Goetia*, the first book of the *Lemegeton*, Omages is listed as one of the fifty-three SERVITORS OF ASHTAROTH AND ASMODEUS (see ASHTAROTH and ASMODEUS). The etymology of this name is possibly Greek and may mean "the magician."

Sources: Ford, *Bible of the Adversary*, 90; Mathers, *Book of the Sacred Magic of Abra-Melin*, 106; Susej, *Demonic Bible*, 257; Von Worms, *Book of Abramelin*, 256.

Oman

In the *Ars Goetia*, the first book of the *Lemegeton*, Oman is listed as one of the fifty-three SERVITORS OF ASHTAROTH AND ASMODEUS (see ASHTAROTH and ASMODEUS). The etymology of this name is possibly Chaldaic and may mean "to cover, obscure."

Sources: Mathers, *Book of the Sacred Magic of Abramelin the Mage*, 115; Von Worms, *Book of Abramelin*, 247; Zabara, *Book of Delight*, 147.

Ombalat

The *Sacred Magic of Abramelin the Mage* lists Ombalat is as one of the thirty-two SERVITORS OF ASTAROT (see ASTAROT).

Sources: Ford, *Bible of the Adversary*, 91; Mathers, *Book of the Sacred Magic of Abra-Melin*, 106; Susej, *Demonic Bible*, 258; Von Worms, *Book of Abramelin*, 256.

Omerach

In the *Ars Paulina*, the third book of the *Lemegeton*, Omerach is listed as one of the fifteen SERVITORS OF SCOX (see SCOX) as well as one of the fifteen SERVITORS OF SASQUIEL (see SASQUIEL). A duke, he commands 5,550 servitors.

Sources: Peterson, *Lesser Key of Solomon*, 114; Trithemius, *Steganographia*, 95.

Omiel

In the *Theurgia Goetia*, the second book of the *Lemegeton*, Omiel is a chief duke and one of the sixteen SERVITORS OF ASYRIEL (see ASYRIEL). A nocturnal demon, he is said to be good-natured and willing to obey his summoner.

Sources: Guiley, *Encyclopedia of Demons and Demonology*, 20; Peterson, *Lesser Key of Solomon*, 73, 80.

Omyel

In Christian demonology Omyel is ranked as one of the twenty SERVITORS OF CAMUEL (see CAMUEL). This diurnal servitor appears before his summoner in a beautiful form and is known for being very courteous.

Sources: Guiley, *Encyclopedia of Demons and Demonology*, 36; Peterson, *Lesser Key of Solomon*, 68; Trithemius, *Steganographia*, 73.

Ona

According to Enochian lore, Ona is a CACODAEMON (see ENOCHIAN CACODAEMONS).

Sources: Chopra, *Academic Dictionary of Mythology*, 217; Laycock, *Complete Enochian Dictionary*, 148.

Onei

The *Sacred Magic of Abramelin the Mage*, book two, names Onei ("one" or "purchase") as one of

the sixteen SERVITORS OF ASMODEUS (see ASMODEUS).

Sources: Mathers, *Book of the Sacred Magic of Abra-Melin*, 119; Von Worms, *Book of Abramelin*, 256.

Oneskelis

Variations: Oinopole, Onokole, Onopole, Onoskelis, "The Fain One of the Mountains or the Nereid, Onoskelis"

Oneskelis ("she with the ass's legs") is one of the seventy-two SPIRITS OF SOLOMON. She was bound by the king to spin hemp into rope for the construction of his temple. Oneskelis appears as a beautiful woman with a fair complexion and the legs of a mule and is described in the *Testament of Solomon* 4:8 as being created "from an unexpected voice which is called a voice of the echo of a black heaven, emitted in matter."

A type of empusa, satyra (female satyr), or a SUCCUBUS, this demon from Greek and Hebrew demonology enjoys preying upon men but is an indiscriminate murderer. Oneskelis admitted to being especially fond of the ones with "honey-colored" skin, and that she would attempt to pervert them from their true nature or kill them by strangulation. Having the ability to give gold to her followers, she admits that she gives them very little. Oneskelis travels stealthily, perhaps due to her shape-shifting, and lives in the caves along cliffs and ravines, which she seldom leaves; some sources say her cave is filled with or made of gold. She is said to be most powerful during the nights of the full moon, the celestial body she has dominion over.

Sources: Butler, *Ritual Magic*, 31; Fontenrose, *Python*, 117, 186; Larson, *Greek Nymphs*, 63; Rappoport, *Myth and Legend of Ancient Israel*, 88, 92; Schwartz, *Tree of Souls*, 228.

Onh

According to Enochian lore, Onh is a CACODAEMON (see ENOCHIAN CACODAEMONS).

Sources: Chopra, *Academic Dictionary of Mythology*, 218; Laycock, *Complete Enochian Dictionary*, 148.

Oni

In Japanese demonology the oni ("to hide or conceal") were originally invisible spirits who later evolved into gigantic humanoid beings with horns, sharp nails, and wild hair. Occasionally these demons were depicted in art with a number of eyes, fingers, and toes. Their skin is commonly red or blue but can be any color; they wear tiger-skin loincloths and carry a kanabō, a heavy oak wood club with iron spikes or studs on one end.

Oni have the ability to cause earthquakes, eclipses, and allow enemy invasions. Seasonal ceremonies and festivals are held to drive the oni away. Monkey statues ward against oni approaching. These demons prey upon the souls of evil people; only by performing a ceremony called *oni-yarabi* can that soul be saved. The sage Nichiren ("sun-lotus") created a special school of Buddhism to combat the oni and reform his people.

Sources: Bush, *Asian Horror Encyclopedia*, 141; Hackin, *Asiatic Mythology*, 443–4; Mack, *Field Guide to Demons, Fairies, Fallen Angels, and Other Subversive Spirits*, 116–8; Sosnoski, *Introduction to Japanese Culture*, 9; Turner, *Dictionary of Ancient Deities*, 363.

Oniel

Variations: ANAEL, Hamiel, Haniel, Onoel

Oniel is a FALLEN ANGEL and the supervisor of the Fifth Division of Hell.

Sources: Gaster, *Studies and Texts in Folklore*, 159; Davidson, *Dictionary of Angels*, 213.

Onp

According to Enochian lore, Onp is a CACO-DAEMON. His counterpart is the angel Npat (see ENOCHIAN CACODAEMONS).

Sources: Chopra, *Academic Dictionary of Mythology*, 218; Laycock, *Complete Enochian Dictionary*, 148.

Ophiel

In the grimoire *Arbatel de Magia Veterum (Arbatel of the Magic of the Ancients)*, published in Latin in 1575 in Switzerland by an unknown author, Ophiel is ranked the sixth of the seven OLYMPIAN SPIRITS, commanding 100,000 legions, fourteen provinces, and all things attributed to the planet Mercury as well as the zodiacal sign. It is said that he has the ability to enable his summoner to be able to change quicksilver into the Philosopher's Stone. Ophiel gives FAMILIARs and teaches all the arts.

Sources: Davidson, *Dictionary of Angels*, 213; Drury, *Dictionary of the Esoteric*, 239; González-Wippler, *Complete Book of Spells*, 120; Hall, *Secret Teachings of All Ages*, 103–4; Waite, *Book of Ceremonial Magic*, 33; Webster, *Encyclopedia of Angels*, 145.

Ophis

Originating in Assyrian demonology, Ophis ("serpent") was said to be not only a FALLEN ANGEL in Cornelius Agrippa's *Three Books of Occult Philosophy*, but the very one who successfully tempted Adam and Eve in the Garden of Eden.

Sources: Barrett, *The Magus*, 47; Blavatsky, *Secret Doctrine*, 445; Davidson, *Dictionary of Angels*, 213; Watson, *Biblical and Theological Dictionary*, 910.

Opilm

Variations: Opilim

In the *Ars Goetia*, the first book of the *Lemege-*ton, Opilm ("citadels, eminences") is listed as one of the fifty-three SERVITORS OF ASHTAROTH AND ASMODEUS (see ASHTAROTH and ASMODEUS).

Sources: Forgotten Books, *Book of the Sacred Magic of Abramelin the Mage*, 130; Mathers, *Book of the Sacred Magic of Abra-Melin*, 116.

Opun

In the *Sacred Magic of Abramelin the Mage*, book two, Opun ("wheel") is listed as one of the fifteen SERVITORS OF ASMODEUS AND MAGOTH (see ASMODEUS).

Sources: Forgotten Books, *Book of the Sacred Magic of Abramelin the Mage*, 350; Von Worms, *Book of Abramelin*, 256.

Orage

Orage is a devil who was first mentioned in Middle Age demonology.

Source: Russell, *Lucifer, the Devil in the Middle Ages*, 250.

Oration

Variations: Ormion

The *Sacred Magic of Abramelin the Mage*, book two, lists Oration as one of the sixteen SERVITORS OF ASMODEUS (see ASMODEUS). This demon's name is possibly Greek and may mean "fastened securely" or "moored."

Sources: Forgotten Books, *Book of the Sacred Magic of Abramelin the Mage*, 136; Mathers, *Book of the Sacred Magic of Abra-Melin*, 45.

Orcus

Variations: DIS, Dis Pater, Ditis, Uragus, Urgus

Possibly originating in Etruscan mythology, Orcus ("oath") was the god of the underworld who appeared as a hairy, bearded giant and acted as a reaper who would take pity on those suffering and gently take them away to the afterlife. Later he became the Roman god of the underworld and a punisher of broken oaths. When absorbed into Christian demonology, he was ranked as the prince of the Undead and the demon of death who commands the underworld (see PRINCES OF HELL).

Sources: Frazer, *Golden Bough*, 231; Gray, *Mythology of all Races*, 303, 319; Hansen, *Classical Mythology*, 179, 183; Keightley, *Mythology of ancient Greece and Italy*, 470, 493–4; Turner, *Dictionary of Ancient Deties*, 153, 201.

Order of the Fly, the Knights of Beelzebub

In Johann Wierus's *Pseudomonarchia Daemonum (False Monarchy of Demons*, 1583) the

Order of the Fly is an order of infernal, demonic knights who are under the command of BEELZE-BUB, the chief lieutenant of LUCIFER, the emperor of Hell.

Sources: Chambers, *Book of Days*, 722; Ripley, *New American Cyclopædia*, 369; Rudwin, *Devil in Legend and Literature*, 76.

Ordog

Variations: Ördög, Urdung ("lord of the dead")

Originating in possibly ancient Mesopotamian and Sumerian demonology, Ordog was initially a Hungarian tutelary spirit that was demonized under Christian influences. Ordog, Lord of the Dead, commands the dark and evil forces of the world, but is himself subject to Isten (God).

Sources: Gettings, *Dictionary of Demons*, 109; Leger, *History of Austro-Hungary from the Earliest Time to the Year 1889*, 61; Lurker, *Routledge Dictionary of Gods and Goddesses, Devils and Demons*, 143.

Orgeuil

Orgeuil ("pride") and BONIFARCE were the two demons who possessed Elisabeth Allier for twenty years and were successfully exorcised from her in 1639 by Francois Faconne. They had entered her when she was seven by hiding on a crust of bread that they had her eat. These demons will flee at the sight of the holy sacrament.

Sources: American Psychiatric Association, *American Journal of Psychiatry*, Vol. 117, 148; Baskin, *Sorcerer's Handbook*, 100; Coumont, *Demonology and Witchcraft*, 200; Robbins, *Encyclopedia of Witchcraft and Demonology*, 27.

Orgosil

In the *Sacred Magic of Abramelin the Mage*, book two, Orgosil ("tumultuous") is among the forty-nine SERVITORS OF BEELZEBUB (see BEELZEBUB).

Sources: Ford, *Bible of the Adversary*, 49; Forgotten Books, *Book of the Sacred Magic of Abramelin the Mage*, 139; Mathers, *Book of the Sacred Magic of Abra-Melin*, 108; Susej, *Demonic Bible*, 259.

Orias

Variations: Oriax

One of the seventy-two SPIRITS OF SOLOMON, Orias is also listed as a count of Hell and a marquis who commands thirty legions (see COUNTS OF HELL and MARQUIS OF HELL). The demon of divination, he is said to appear before his summoner as either a lion or as a lion-faced man, riding a horse with a snake for a tail. In each hand he is carrying a snake or two snakes in his right hand; sources vary. This demon is invoked because he is an expert in astrology and by the use of metamorphosis can change the appearance of any man. Additionally, he can also grant dignities and prelacies with confirmation as well as foster relations with friends and foes.

Sources: Ashley, *Complete Book of Devils and Demons*, 60; Cavendish, *Man, Myth and Magic*, Vol. 7, 3376; De Laurence, *Lesser Key of Solomon, Goetia*, 41; Dix, *Black Baron*, 269; Ford, *Bible of the Adversary*, 81; Gettings, *Dictionary of Demons*, 182; Scot, *Discoverie of Witchcraft*, 224.

Oribel

Variations: URIEL

Originally a saint, Oribel's canonization was removed by Pope Zachary in 745 C.E. when he "unearthed and turned out of the saintly calendar" those demons who had been passing themselves off as saints, namely Oribel, RAGUHEL, and TOBIEL (see CHURCH CONDEMNED ANGELS).

Sources: Davidson, *Dictionary of Angels*, 238; Hugo, *Toilers of the Sea*, Vol. 1, 6; Rudwin, *Devil in Legend and Literature*, 28, 62.

Oriel

Variations: Otiel

In *Theurgia Goetia*, the second book of the *Lemegeton*, Chief Duke Oriel is listed as one of the twelve SERVITORS OF CASPIEL (see CASPIEL). Commanding 2,660 duke servitors, this demon is known to be rude and stubborn.

Sources: Davidson, *Encyclopedia of Angels*, 283; Peterson, *Lesser Key of Solomon*, 118.

Oriens

Variations: Uriens ("to burn or devour with flame"), Urieus, SAMAEL

Oriens ("eastern" or "rising") is listed in the *Sacred Magic of Abramelin the Mage* as the king of the eastern quarter of the infernal world. This sub-prince is the demon of communication and knowledge, and commands eight servitors directly (see SERVITORS OF ORIENS and PRINCES OF HELL). An AERIAL DEVIL, he has an array of powers including the ability to force any spirit to appear in any form, as well as being able to summon armed men to appear. Oriens can also obtain information concerning propositions and doubtful sciences and tell how to summon and keep FAMILIARs. He can also supply a person with as much gold and silver as they wish, give the gift of flight, cause visions, answer any question asked of him, as he knows everything from the past and the future that God allows, and restore life to the dead for seven years.

Sources: Ford, *Luciferian Goetia*, 15; Forgotten Books, *Book of the Sacred Magic of Abramelin the Mage*, 110; Kuriakos, *Grimoire Verum Ritual Book*, 30; Rapacki, *Satanism*, 59; Sloat, *Texas Ritualistic Crime*

Information Network Occult Crime Manual, 14; Susej, *Demonic Bible*, 165.

Orinel

In the *Ars Goetia*, the first book of the *Lemegeton*, Orinel ("Ornament of God") is listed as one of the fifty-three SERVITORS OF ASHTAROTH AND ASMODEUS (see ASHTAROTH and ASMODEUS).

Sources: Ford, *Bible of the Adversary*, 89; Mathers, *Book of the Sacred Magic of Abra-Melin*, 115; Von Worms, *Book of Abramelin*, 256.

Ormenu

In the *Theurgia Goetia*, the second book of the *Lemegeton*, Ormenu is ranked as duke and listed as one of the eleven SERVITORS OF PAMERSIEL (see DUKES OF HELL and PAMERSIEL). A nocturnal AERIAL DEVIL, this demon is known to be very useful at driving out spirits from haunted places. An expert liar and willing to tell secrets that he knows, Ormenu is arrogant and stubborn. Summoning this demon must be done from the second floor of a home or in a wide open space.

Sources: Lehrich, *Language of Demons and Angels*, 191; Peterson, *Lesser Key of Solomon*, 64.

Ormijel

In *Ars Paulina*, the third book of the *Lemegeton*, Ormijel is ranked as a chief and is listed as one of the eleven SERVITORS OF RAHAB (see RAHAB).

Source: Waite, *The Book of Ceremonial Magic*, 67.

Ornias

In ancient Hebrew lore, there is a vampiric demon known as Ornias. He was one of many demons mentioned in the *Testament of Solomon*. Said to appear before his summoner in the form of fire, a lion, or a horrid winged creature, he has the ability to shape-shift into a beautiful woman and trick men into having sex with him, draining their sexual energy and potency much like an INCUBUS or SUCCUBUS. Ornias seeks out men whose zodiac sign is Aquarius and strangles them to death, leaching off their life-energy as he does so. It is believed he does this because he resides in the constellation of Aquarius. It is further believed that the only way to save one of his victims before they die is to press the Seal of Solomon against the demon's chest.

During the construction of King Solomon's temple, Ornias appeared to one of the laborers, stealing half his wages as well as draining the life-energy from one of his sons. The laborer sought the king for help and Solomon prayed to God for insight or intervention on the matter. His prayers were answered; the archangel Michael delivered to Solomon a ring with the seal of God upon it, giving the bearer power over demons. Solomon used the ring not only to stop Ornias from his daily muggings and assaults but also to bind other demons and use them as part of his labor force to build his temple.

Occasionally Ornias is summoned by magicians and witches who seek to divine the future, as this demon can be persuaded to fly up into the heavens and glean the future as it is written in the stars. It was said that Ornias looked like a shooting star as he descended back to Earth. Continued use of his abilities would cause his summoner to waste away.

Sources: Conybeare, *Jewish Quarterly Review*, Vol. 11, 15–18, 18; Ginzberg, *Legends of the Jews*, 151–53; James, *Old Testament Legends*, 109; Rappoport, *Myth and Legend of Ancient Israel*, 88–90; Wedeck, *A Treasury of Witchcraft*, 172.

Oroan

Variations: Olozan, The dark-browed enemy of man

Originating in Guyana demonology, specifically from the Akawoios, Arekunas, and Taulipangs tribes, the demon of eclipses and darkness, Oroan ("dark spirit"), appears scorched and blackened as he regularly tries to seize the sun and quench its fire and devour the moon. During an eclipse, the men in the village rush from their houses and shout repeatedly at the sky which will, hopefully, frighten Oroan away.

Sources: Ashley, *Complete Book of Devils and Demons*, 64; Brett, *Legends and Myths of the Aboriginal Indians of British Guiana*, 89–90; Goeje, *Philosophy, Initiation and Myths of the Indians of Guiana and Adjacent Countries*, 9, 40; Smithsonian Institution, *Thirteenth Annual Report of the Bureau of American Ethnology*, 254–5.

Orobas

Variations: Orobos

Orobas, the Prince of Horses, appears before his summoner as a beautiful horse but will assume a human form if commanded to do so. He commands twenty legions (see PRINCES OF HELL). Orobas is invoked for his willingness to answer truthfully questions put to him about the creation of the world and divinity as well as events from the past, present, or future. This demon will also assist in a person's advancements by giving them titles and helping them gain the favor of friends and foes. Orobas is faithful to the one who summons him and will even go as far as to defend his summoner against invading spirits. His name is Latin in origin and refers to a type of incense.

Sources: De Laurence, *Lesser Key of Solomon, Goetia*, 40; Gettings, *Dictionary of Demons*, 226; Rose, *Spirits,*

Oroias 246

Fairies, Gnomes, and Goblins, 250; Scot, *Discoverie of Witchcraft*, 224; Scott, *London Magazine*, Vol. 5, 378; Shah, *Black and White Magic*, 67.

Oroias

The *Sacred Magic of Abramelin the Mage*, book two, names Oroias among the one hundred eleven SERVITORS OF AMAYMON, ARITON, ORIENS, AND PAYMON (see AMAYMON, ARITON, ORIENS, and PAYMON). The etymology of this name is possibly Greek and may mean "returning in due season."

Sources: Forgotten Books, *Book of the Sacred Magic of Abramelin the Mage*, 121; Ryan, *Bathhouse at Midnight*, 62; Susej, *Demonic Bible*, 167.

Orpemiel

Orpemiel is one of the twenty SERVITORS OF CAMUEL (see CAMUEL). This diurnal servitor is said to be very courteous and appears before his summoner in a beautiful form.

Source: Peterson, *Lesser Key of Solomon*, 68.

Orphiel

Orphiel is a servitor who is under the command of Tephros (see TEPHRAS).

Sources: Brann, *Trithemius and Magical Theology*, 200; Davidson, *Dictionary of Angels*, 51; Scheible, *Sixth and Seventh Books of Moses*, 138; Trithemius, *Steganographia*, 88.

Orthon

Originating in medieval folklore, the AERIAL DEVIL Orthon is said to have been the FAMILIAR to both the Comte de Foix, an independent medieval fief in southern France, and to the Comte de Corasse. He was given to them by BOTIS. A nocturnal being, he has been described as being invisible, as looking like two straws tumbling about in the wind, and as a lean and bony sow with long ears and snout.

Orthon travels very quickly and wanders about various countries, such as England, Germany, and Scotland, and then two or three times a week reports his findings to his master. Like a poltergeist, this devil can do no harm, as he cannot commit an act of violence, but he wakes sleeping people and has the gift of speech. Orthon will stay with his charge as long as his charge does nothing to displease him. The only way this devil can be destroyed is to destroy the physical form that he has assumed.

Sources: Froissart, *Stories from Froissart*, 249–65; Knight, *Penny Magazine of the Society for the Diffusion of Useful Knowledge*, Vol. 11, 458–9; Yonge, *Lances of Lynwood*, 196–9.

Orusula

In Costa Rican demonology, Orusula is a demonic giant pig; the froth from its mouth causes a rash that can kill. Living in lagoons and muddy swamps, Orusula cuts off the heads of people.

Sources: Ashley, *Complete Book of Devils and Demons*, 101; Stone, *Talamancan Tribes of Costa Rica*, 52.

Orvich

In the *Theurgia Goetia*, book two of the *Lemegeton*, Orvich is ranked as a duke and is listed as one of the twelve named SERVITORS OF CARNESIEL (see CARNESIEL and DUKES OF HELL). Commanding 2,060 servitors, this ill-natured and stubborn demon will appear with as few as ten but with as many as three hundred of them.

Source: Peterson, *Lesser Key of Solomon*, 58.

Ose

Variations: Osé, Oso, Oze, Voso

Ose, the leopard president, commands three or thirty legions; sources vary. His name is Latin for "mouth" or "that who abhors." This nocturnal demon, said to be one of the seventy-two SPIRITS OF SOLOMON, will appear before his summoner as a leopard but will if asked change to the form of a man. Ose is summoned for his willingness to answer truthfully questions that are put to him. He can also cause delusions and insanity in men, and will teach the liberal sciences.

Sources: De Laurence, *Lesser Key of Solomon, Goetia*, 40; Gettings, *Dictionary of Demons*, 183; Icon, *Demons*, 170; McLean, *Treatise of Angel Magic*, 55; Scot, *Discoverie of Witchcraft*, 224.

Othiel

Variations: Gothiel

In the *Sacred Magic of Abramelin the Mage*, book two, Othiel is listed as one of the sixteen SERVITORS OF ASELIEL (see ASELIEL). This nocturnal demon appears as a black, bloated man-insect hybrid that is wider than he is long. Othiel unites the forces adverse to Binah, the second intellectual Sephirah on the tree of life.

Sources: Ford, *Liber Hvhi*, 76; Peterson, *Lesser Key of Solomon*, 69.

Ouza

Variations: AZZA, AZZAEL, Ouzza, Oza, USIEL, Uzza ("strength")

According to rabbinical lore, Ouza is the tutelary guardian angel of Egypt. He has a pierced nose, punishment for his sin of having had sexual relations with human women (see FALLEN ANGELS).

Ouza and Azza, who although considered to have been fallen, still resided in Heaven. They openly opposed Enoch being transformed into the angel Metatron. Because of the tension between them, Metatron ultimately had them cast out of Heaven.

Sources: Davidson, *Dictionary of Angels*, 216; Ginzberg, *Legends of the Jews*, Vol. 1 and 2, 170; Ginzberg, *Legends of the Jews*, Vol. 3 and 4, 293; Mathers, *Kabbalah Unveiled*, 249; Vermès, *Discovery in the Judean Desert*, 211.

Ox Heads

Variations: Bull Head, Cow's Head, Niú Tóu

In Chinese mythology, Ox Heads, along with HORSE FACES, is the guardian of the Underworld and the messenger for the king of Hell, YAN LUO WANG.

This demon was created when an ox who was worked to death reached Hell and had pity taken upon it by Yan Luo Wang, who made it one of his soldiers. As the name would imply, this demon has the head of an ox. Ox Heads is seen as the symbol of sickness and only preys upon those who are about to die, as he is sent out by his master to collect the soul from a dying person. Then, he escorts the soul to Hell to see if they will be punished for the life they led or if they will be reincarnated.

Sources: Crisafulli, *Go to Hell*, 282; Hackin, *Asiatic Mythology*, 288, 371; Maspero, *Taoism and Chinese Religion*, 110; Turner, *Dictionary of Ancient Deities*, 298.

Oyasi

From the mythology of the Ainu people of Sakhalin and Japan comes oyasi ("demon") shapeshifters that specialize in transforming themselves into birds with catlike eyes, goldenflecked feathers, and long talons, although they can take any form. Some of the oyasi are eternal, demonic beings that were never created, while others are the estranged souls that have been created by a seemingly innocent act, such as when a tool that is no longer wanted or needed is not broken and its soul becomes angry and seeks to kill its owner.

Normally oyasi are invisible and use the emotions of others to amplify their own powers. When one assumes the form of a bird, its nocturnal call can cause insanity. No matter what form they are in, these demons are strong enough to knock over a house.

Vicious and vindictive, extreme in their revenge, even for a demon, the oyasi are said to be undefeatable, although if a person has become possessed by one, a demonic exorcism can drive it away. It is said that the skulls of sacrificed puppies will bark when one of these demons is near.

Sources: Jones, *Evil in Our Midst*, 156–7; Tierney, *Illness and Healing Among the Sakhalin Ainu*, 70.

Ozibuth

Variations: "The destroyer of children"

Ozibuth is a female demon from Christian demonology. Her personal adversary is the angel Afriel.

Source: Davidson, *Dictionary of Angels*, 10.

Pacheil

In the *Ars Goetia*, the first book of the *Lemegeton*, Pacheil is listed as one of the fifty-three SERVITORS OF ASHTAROTH AND ASMODEUS (see ASHTAROTH AND ASMODEUS).

Sources: Mathers, *Book of the Sacred Magic of Abramelin the Mage*, 106, 116; Susej, *Demonic Bible*, 257, 256.

Pachid

Pachid ("fear") is among the one hundred eleven SERVITORS OF AMAYMON, ARITON, ORIENS, AND PAYMON (see AMAYMON, ARITON, ORIENS, and PAYMON) named in the *Sacred Magic of Abramelin the Mage*, book two.

Sources: Ford, *Bible of the Adversary*, 88; Mathers, *Book of the Sacred Magic of Abramelin the Mage*, 105; Von Worms, *Book of Abramelin*, 244.

Pachiel

In *Ars Goetia*, the first book of the *Lemegeton*, Pachiel is listed as one of the fifty-three SERVITORS OF ASHTAROTH AND ASMODEUS (see ASHTAROTH and ASMODEUS). This name is possibly Greek and may mean "coarse, thick."

Sources: Forgotten Books, *Book of the Sacred Magic of Abramelin the Mage*, 130; Susej, *Demonic Bible*, 257; Trithemius, *Steganographia*, 81.

Padiel

Variations: Phadihel

Johannes Trithemius's *Steganographia*, written in 1499 but published in 1606 in Frankfurt, Germany, names Padiel as the Prince of the East by Southeast who is under the command of the Emperor of the East (see PRINCES OF HELL). Padiel has a reputation for being unfriendly and unreliable; he commands the southeastern section of Hell as well as ten thousand diurnal spirits and twenty thousand nocturnal ones. This demon is summoned for his ability to carry written messages from one person to another. His name is possibly Hebrew and may mean "fruit."

Sources: Davidson, *Dictionary of Angels*, 219; Gettings, *Dictionary of Demons*, 232; Higley, *Hildegard of Bingen's Unknown Language*, 54, 59, 60; Peterson, *Lesser Key of Solomon*, 66–7; Von Goethe, *Goethe's Letters to Zelter*, 377; Woolley, *Queen's Conjurer*, 66, 68.

Padmoz

In both Persian and Zoroastrian demonology, the DEV Padmoz is said to be one of the ten principal demons that reside within men (see DEVS WHO RESIDE IN MEN). He makes mankind want more, to become something advanced. His name means "to put on," as in to don clothes.

Sources: Boyce, *Word-List of Manichaean Middle Persian and Parthian*, 68; Ford, *Liber Hvhi*, 116.

Pafesla

In the *Sacred Magic of Abramelin the Mage*, book two, Pafesla is among the ten SERVITORS OF AMAIMON AND ARITON (see AMAIMON and ARITON). The etymology of this name is possibly from the Hebrew word for "idol," *pesel*, and may mean "a sculptured image."

Sources: Ford, *Book of Abramelin*, 90; Forgotten Books, *Book of the Sacred Magic of Abramelin the Mage*, 130; Mathers, *Book of the Sacred Magic of Abra-Melin*, 106; Von Worms, *Book of Abramelin*, 256.

Pahaunui

Variations: Pahuanui

In Tahitian demonology Pahaunui is the demon of the sea.

Sources: Kindersley, *Specimens of Hindoo Literature*, 28, 146; Melton, *Encyclopedia of Occultism and Parapsychology*, 973; Smedley, *Occult Sciences*, 54; Spence, *Encyclopaedia of Occultism*, 312.

Paigoels

Paigoels are, according to Hindu demonology, a species of devil originally created as diabolic beings or were banished from heaven because of their sins; sources vary. Their numbers increase every time an evil person dies. They have the ability to possess a person bodily and they tempt mankind into committing sin, but fortunately, they are forbidden all communication with the upper worlds except for Earth. Paigoels who are assigned to specific sins typically have a name. There is a proverb that goes, "The mind of a woman resembles that of a Paigoels."

Sources: Kindersley, *Specimens of Hindoo Literature*, 28; Smeadly, *Occult Sciences*, 54; Spence, *Encyclopedia of Occultism*, 312.

Pairaka

Variations: Pari

In Persian mythology pairaka are a type of devil or demonic fay that appear as beautiful women. Nocturnal, they prey upon men, seducing and placing spells upon them; they also have the ability to shape-shift into various forms, such as rats and shooting stars. Their personal adversaries are the god Mithra and the sun goddess Mitra.

Sources: Curtis, *Persian Myths*, 21; Parker, *Mythology*, 332.

Palas Aron Azinomas

Variations: "Bagahi Iaca Bachabe," "Xilka, Xilka, Besa, Besa"

"Palas aron azinomas" is a magical formula for invoking demons.

Sources: Baskin, *Sorcerer's Handbook*, 306, 447; de Givry, *Witchcraft, Magic and Alchemy*, 102; Wedeck, *Treasury of Witchcraft*, 87.

Pamersiel

Prince of the East, Pamersiel is one of the twelve named Duke SERVITORS OF CARNESIEL; he commands one thousand servitors (see CARNESIEL and PRINCES OF HELL). His name is possibly Hebrew and may translate to mean "exempt."

Sources: Gettings, *Dictionary of Demons*, 232; Peterson, *Lesser Key of Solomon*, 66; Shah, *Occultism*, 68; Waite, *Manual of Cartomancy and Occult Divination*, 97.

Pandiel

In the *Theurgia Goetia*, the second book of the *Lemegeton*, Pandiel is a duke who is listed as one of the ten SERVITORS OF EMONIEL (see EMONIEL); he commands 1,320 lesser dukes and servitors. Good-natured and willing to obey, this AERIAL DEVIL lives in the woods.

Sources: Peterson, *Lesser Key of Solomon*, 97; Trithemius, *Steganographia*, 126.

Pandoli

In the *Sacred Magic of Abramelin the Mage*, book two, Pandoli ("altogether a slave") is listed as one of the sixty-five SERVITORS OF KORE AND MAGOTH.

Sources: Mathers, *Book of the Sacred Magic of Abra-Melin*, 118; Susej, *Demonic Bible*, 258; *Book of Abramelin*, 250.

Pantagruel

The demon Pantagruel first appeared in the writings of the late fifteenth century. Pantagruel is also the name of the drunken, gigantic, jovial, and rowdy son in Rabelais's book *Gargantua and Pantagruel*.

Sources: Brewer, *Reader's Handbook of Famous Names in Fiction*, 801–2; Craig, *Routledge Encyclopedia of Philosophy*, 15–7.

Panuel

Variations: Phanuel ("face of God")

In the *Theurgia Goetia*, the second book of the *Lemegeton*, Panuel is ranked as a duke who commands 1,320 lesser dukes and servitors. He is listed as one of the ten SERVITORS OF EMONIEL (see EMONIEL). An AERIAL DEVIL, it is said that this demon lives in the woods and is good-natured and willing to obey.

Source: Peterson, *Lesser Key of Solomon*, 97.

Papiyan

Variations: Mara ("death" or "thirst"), Mara Papiyan, the Murderer, Namuche ("not letting go the waters"), Pisuna, the Tempter, VARSAVARTI ("he who fulfills desires"), Wicked One

In Buddhist demonology, Papiyan, whose name translates from Sanskrit to mean "evil one," "more wicked," or "wicked one," was originally the king of the Heaven of Sensual Delight before his conversion to Buddhism. He was the demon of the fulfillment of desire or the triple thirst (the desire for existence, pleasure, and power) and he commanded an army of demons as well as his three daughters, Lust, Thirst, and Delight.

As a demon, Papiyan was described as having one hundred arms and a monstrous form but would on occasion shape-shift into the guise of a vulture; in art he is depicted as riding an elephant attended to by MARAKAYIKAS. This demon captured the souls of the dying as he wandered the earth, homeless. He had the ability to control rainstorms and whirlwinds and could make it rain hot ashes, mud, red-hot coal, rocks, sand, and weapons. Papiyan also caused darkness to surround a person.

After his conversion to Buddhism, Papiyan became a Dharma-protector of the Buddha.

Sources: Carus, *History of the Devil and the Idea of Evil*, 105; Grünwedel, *Buddhist Art in India*, 39, 92; Soothill, *Dictionary of Chinese Buddhist Terms*, 266.

Papus

In Apollonius of Tyana's *Nuctemeron* (*Night Illuminated by Day*) the demon Papus is said to be most powerful during the first hour.

Source: Lévi, *Transcendental Magic*, 502.

Paramor

Variations: Paramore

In the *Sacred Magic of Abramelin the Mage*, book two, Paramor is among the sixty-five SERVITORS OF KORE AND MAGOTH.

Sources: Ford, *Bible of the Adversary*, 92; Mathers, *Book of the Sacred Magic of Abramelin the Mage*, 107; Susej, *Demonic Bible*, 258; Von Worms, *Book of Abramelin*, 256.

Paraseh

In the *Sacred Magic of Abramelin the Mage*, book two, Paraseh ("divided") is listed as one of the one hundred eleven SERVITORS OF AMAYMON, ARITON, ORIENS, AND PAYMON (see AMAYMON, ARITON, ORIENS, and PAYMON).

Sources: Ford, *Bible of the Adversary*, 88; Mathers, *Book of the Sacred Magic of Abramelin the Mage*, 105; Susej, *Demonic Bible*, 197.

Pareht

According to the *Sacred Magic of Abramelin the Mage*, book two, Pareht ("fruit") is one of the one hundred eleven SERVITORS OF AMAYMON, ARITON, ORIENS, AND PAYMON (see AMAYMON, ARITON, ORIENS, and PAYMON).

Sources: Ford, *Bible of the Adversary*, 88; Mathers, *Book of the Sacred Magic of Abramelin the Mage*, 105; Von Worms, *Book of Abramelin*, 255.

Parek

In the *Sacred Magic of Abramelin the Mage*, book two, Parek ("roughness" or "savage") is one of the one hundred eleven SERVITORS OF AMAYMON, ARITON, ORIENS, AND PAYMON (see AMAYMON, ARITON, ORIENS, and PAYMON).

Sources: Ford, *Bible of the Adversary*, 88; Susej, *Demonic Bible*, 197; Von Worms, *Book of Abramelin*, 255.

Pariel

Pariel is one of the twenty SERVITORS OF CAMUEL (see CAMUEL). Appearing before his summoner in a beautiful form, this diurnal demon is known to be very courteous.

Source: Trithemius, *Steganographia*, 73.

Parmatus

The *Sacred Magic of Abramelin the Mage*, book two, Parmatus ("shield bearing") is among the one hundred eleven SERVITORS OF AMAYMON, ARITON, ORIENS, AND PAYMON (see AMAYMON, ARITON, ORIENS, and PAYMON).

Sources: Mathers, *Book of the Sacred Magic of Abramelin the Mage*, 105; Susej, *Demonic Bible*, 256; Von Worms, *Book of Abramelin*, 254.

Parmiel

In *Ars Paulina*, the third book of the *Lemegeton*, Parmiel is listed as one of the two hundred SERVITORS OF VEGUANIEL (see VEGUANIEL).

Sources: Davidson, *Dictionary of Angels*, 221; Waite, *Book of Black Magic and Ceremonial Magic*, 67.

Parniel

In the *Sacred Magic of Abramelin the Mage*, book two, Parniel, a diurnal demon, is one of the sixteen SERVITORS OF ASELIEL (see ASELIEL).

Sources: Peterson, *Lesser Key of Solomon*, 69; Trithemius, *Steganographia*, 91.

Parusur

According to the *Sacred Magic of Abramelin the Mage*, book two, Parusur ("present to assist") is among the one hundred eleven SERVITORS OF AMAYMON, ARITON, ORIENS, AND PAYMON (see AMAYMON, ARITON, ORIENS, and PAYMON).

Sources: Mathers, *Book of the Sacred Magic of*

Abramelin the Mage, 105; Susej, *Demonic Bible*, 197; Von Worms, *Book of Abramelin*, 245.

Pas

In Persian and Zoroastrian demonology, Pas ("calumniator") is a DEV who uses its word to influence or defame (see DEVS WHO RESIDE IN MEN).

Source: Ford, *Liber Hvhi*, 116.

Pashittu

In Akkadian and Sumerian demonology, Pashittu ("extinguisher") is a female demon who preys on newborn children in order to keep the human population down. She answers only to the Sumerian god Enki.

Sources: Bottéro, *Ancestor of the West*, 59; Jacobsen, *Treasures of Darkness*, 120; Kensky, *Studies in Bible and Feminist Criticism*, 354; Stol, *Birth in Babylonia and the Bible*, 236–7; Van der Toorn, *Dictionary of Deities and Demons in the Bible*, 236.

Patid

In the *Sacred Magic of Abramelin the Mage*, book two, Patid ("topaz") is listed as one of the one hundred eleven SERVITORS OF AMAYMON, ARITON, ORIENS, AND PAYMON (see AMAYMON, ARITON, ORIENS, and PAYMON).

Sources: Ford, *Bible of the Adversary*, 88; Forgotten Books, *Book of the Sacred Magic of Abramelin the Mage*, 105; Susej, *Demonic Bible*, 256; Von Worms, *Book of Abramelin*, 245.

Patupaiarehe

Variations: Pakepakehā, Patu-Paiarehe, Tūrehu

From the demonology of the Maori people of New Zealand comes a race of demonic fay known as the patupaiarehe. Seldom seen, they are light skinned with blond or red hair, and have either blue or black eyes. A patupaiarehe will never have a tattoo. Their height varies from very small to human sized to twice as tall as a person. Most active at twilight and all through the night, as they are fearful of light, a patupaiarehe will lure a person who offended it into danger with the sound of its flute playing and then take him or her prisoner to be tortured (see HELIOPHOBIC DEVIL).

Patupaiarehe speak their own language, although whoever encounters them will instantly be able to understand them. The patupaiarehe live in the forests and in the mountaintops, but incantations and magical rites can be performed to keep them away.

Sources: Cowan, *Journal of the Polynesian Society*, Vol. 30, 96–102, 142–151; Grace, *Folk-Tales of the Maori*, 195–207; Jones, *Evil in Our Midst*, 194–7.

Paymon

Variations: Paimon, Paimonia

Paymon ("bell") is a king as well as the master of ceremonies of Hell. In service under LUCIFER, he is also, according to Collin de Plancy's *Dictionaire Infernale* (1863), one of the seventy-two SPIRITS OF SOLOMON. A FALLEN ANGEL, formerly of the Order of Dominions, he commands two hundred twenty legions, half of which are from the Angelic Order and half from the Order of Powers. Living in the northwest region of Hell and known as the demon of the northwest, Paymon is arrogant and craves knowledge, wanting to be like God.

An offering or sacrifice must be made to this demon when he is invoked; upon his arrival Paymon must be allowed to ask any question he wishes of his summoner and he must be answered honestly and directly. When summoned, Paymon appears as a crowned man with a feminine face. Seated upon a dromedary, he is surrounded by musicians. He speaks with a loud and roaring voice that is sometimes difficult to understand. If this demon is summoned with sacrifice or libation, he may appear accompanied by the infernal princes ABALAM and Bebal (or ABALI and Labal or Abalam and BEBALL; sources vary). Paymon, a diurnal demon, is summoned for his knack of answering clearly questions put to him. He can also make men subject to the will of the one who summons him. He gives and confirms dignities as well as good FAMILIARs, teaches all the arts and the sciences, and tells secrets he knows.

The name Paymon may etymologically be Hebrew, and if so may translate to mean "tinkling sound."

Sources: Crowley, *The Goetia*, 31; Davidson, *Dictionary of Angels*, 220; De Laurence, *Lesser Key of Solomon, Goetia*, 24; McLean, *Treatise on Angel Magic*, 168; Mathers, *Book of the Sacred Magic of Abramelin the Mage*, 246; Scot, *Discoverie of Witchcraft*, 220; Waite, *Book of Black Magic and of Pacts*, 168.

Pazuzu

Variations: "Bringer of Plague," "Lord of Fevers and Plagues"

In ancient Assyrian, Babylonian, and Mesopotamian demonology, Pazuzu is a demonic god and is known as the Lord of the Wind demons. The demon of diseases, recklessness, and the southeast storm winds, he is said to have been born the son of Hanpa, the king of the evil spirits of the air. This demon is described as having a deformed canine head, bulging eyes, scaly body, snake-headed penis, four eagle wings, lion claws on his hands and feet, and a scorpion tail. His roar can make even the mountains tremble. He causes malaria and spreads various diseases with his dry and fiery breath. This demon lives in the desert and is noted for protecting pregnant women from the demon Lamastu (LAMAŠTU), who steals their babies from the womb.

Sources: Marple, *Domain of Devils*, 18; Russell, *The Devil*, 91; Woods, *History of the Devil*, 72.

Pdi

According to Enochian lore Pdi is a CACODAEMON. His counterpart is the angel Diri (see also ENOCHIAN CACODAEMONS).

Sources: Chopra, *Academic Dictionary of Mythology*, 227; Laycock, *Complete Enochian Dictionary*, 155.

Pedaré

In Malaysian demonology a demonic ghost known as a pedaré is created whenever a person does not have their proper funeral rites said for them. Returning in the form of a shadow, this demon is now an unbound spirit, forever to roam the earth in want of a resting place. Pedaré inadvertently interferes with a person's well-being, but their attacks can be prevented with magical spells. These demons can be destroyed by discovering who they were in life and then performing a proper funeral rite for them. The name pedaré means "ghost" or "haunting spirit" in Malaysian.

Sources: Smedal, *Lom-Indonesian-English and English-Lom Wordlists*, 124.

Pekar

Variations: Butcher's Horse, Pehar

In Tibetan demonology Pekar is a prince, the regent of the northerly quarter of Hell (see PRINCES OF HELL). A tutelary spirit who lives in a realm called Petahor, he was born the reincarnation of the demon Mudu Tankhar. Pekar has three faces and six arms and he rides upon a white tiger or lion; sources vary. He has five aspects—Activity, Body, Knowledge, Mind, and Speech—and each has a different appearance.

In his Activity aspect he is known as Thinley gyi Gyalpo. He has three faces and six arms. In his first right hand he holds a hook, in his second an arrow, and in his third a sword. His first left hand he holds a knife, in his second a bow, and in his third a staff. He wears a leopard skin skirt, a *tipshu*, and a white shawl; he rides upon a snow leopard. His sacred color is navy blue.

In his Body aspect he is known as Kui Gyalpo. He has one face. In his right hand he holds a vajra and in his left is a single cymbal. Riding atop a black bear, he wears a golden, round, cymbal-shaped hat. His sacred color is dark blue.

In his Knowledge aspect he is known as

Yonten kyi Gyalpo. In his right hand he holds an axe, in his left is a demon lasso. Wearing a tiger-skin shawl and black snakeskin, he rides upon a dragon. His sacred color is black.

In his Mind aspect he is known as Tuk ki Gyalpo. He has one face and two arms. In his right hand he holds a spear; in his left is a doubled-edged sword and lasso. He wears a brown bear skin and a black turban. He rides an elephant. His sacred color is brown.

In his Speech aspect he is known as Sung gi Gyalpo. In his right hand he holds a staff and in his left is a club made of sandalwood. He rides upon a wolf and wears black robes. His sacred color is dark brown.

Sources: Bharati, *Realm of the Extra-Human*, 214; Fisher, *Himalayan Anthropology*, 295–7; Lurker, *Routledge Dictionary of Gods and Goddesses, Devils and Demons*, 278.

Pelariel

In the *Lesser Key of Solomon*, Pelariel is listed as one of the twelve SERVITORS OF HYDRIEL (see HYDRIEL). This duke is an AERIAL DEVIL who commands 1,320 servitors. Pelariel can be summoned any time of the day or night, and when he appears will do so as a serpent with a virgin's face and head. Known to be very courteous and willing to obey his summoner, Pelariel lives in or near marshes, water, and wetlands.

Sources: Guiley, *Encyclopedia of Demons and Demonology*, 115; Peterson, *Lesser Key of Solomon*, 95.

Pellipis

Pellipis is one of the forty-nine SERVITORS OF BEELZEBUB (see BEELZEBUB), according to the *Sacred Magic of Abramelin the Mage*, book two. His name is possibly Greek and may mean "oppressing."

Sources: Ford, *Bible of the Adversary*, 93; Mathers, *Book of the Sacred Magic of Abra-Melin*, 108; Susej, *Demonic Bible*, 259; Von Worms, *Book of Abramelin*, 257.

Penemue

Variations: Penemuel

In Enochian lore Penemue is said to be one of the FALLEN ANGELS, formerly from the order of Cherubim, as he was one of the GRIGORI who swore allegiance to SAMIAZA, rebelled against God, took a human wife, and fathered the NEPHILIM (see also WATCHERS). He went on to teach mankind "the bitter and the sweet and the secrets of wisdom" and how to write with ink and paper.

Penemue's teaching men to write was not his crime but teaching men to write on paper—as opposed to animal skin, parchment, pottery, or stone—was. It is said that when using paper, man recorded "evil ideas," which were then allowed to spread.

The name Penemue translates to mean "the inside" or "the pearl before God"; sources vary.

Sources: Barton, *Journal of Biblical Literature*, Vols. 30–31, 165; Charles, *Apocrypha and Pseudepigrapha of the Old Testament*, 179; Davidson, *Dictionary of Angels*, 222; Ladd, *Commentary on the Book of Enoch*, 40, 165, 223; Webster, *Encyclopedia of Angels*, 149.

Pentagony

Variations: Pentagnony, Pentagnuny

The *Grimoirium Verum* (*Grimoire of Truth*), allegedly written by Alibek the Egyptian in 1517, lists Pentagony as being powerful and one of the eight SERVITORS OF HALE AND SERGULATH. He has the ability to give the power of invisibility as well as being able to make one beloved by great lords.

Sources: Masters, *Devil's Dominion*, 131; Waite, *Book of Black Magic*, 188.

Penunggu

Variations: Keramat, Pulaka

In Malaysian demonology the penunggu is a tutelary demon. His name means "attendant, guard, or watchman." Taking the form of cobras, crocodiles, frogs, lizards, and pythons, these demons guard specific places or things, such as an abandoned house, a cave, a lake, an old tree, or a large stone. Their presence is marked by suddenly feeling cold or smelling something sweet. In order to prevent attack from this type of demon, one needs to ask for its permission when passing by or resting at a location they guard.

Sources: Leee, *Tanah Tujuh*, 92, 100, 101; Osman, *Indigenous, Hindu, and Islamic Elements in Malay Folk Beliefs*, 130, 198, 241; Osman, *Malay Folk Beliefs*, 89, 131, 159.

Pereuch

In the *Sacred Magic of Abramelin the Mage*, book two, Pereuch is listed as one of the one hundred eleven SERVITORS OF AMAYMON, ARITON, ORIENS, AND PAYMON (see AMAYMON, ARITON, ORIENS, and PAYMON). His name is possibly Greek and may mean "concerning prayer" or "given unto prayer."

Sources: Ford, *Bible of the Adversary*, 88; Forgotten Books, *Book of the Sacred Magic of Abramelin the Mage*, 112, 123; Mathers, *Selected Occult Writings of S.L. Mac-Gregor Mathers*, 105; Susej, *Demonic Bible*, 197; Von Worms, *Book of Abramelin*, 244.

Permiel

In the *Ars Paulina*, the third book of the *Lemegeton*, Permiel is ranked as a chief and is listed as one of the eleven SERVITORS OF RAHAB (see RAHAB).

Sources: Davidson, *Dictionary of Angels*, 222; Peterson, *Lesser Key of Solomon*, 114; Trithemius, *Steganographia*, 93; Waite, *The Book of Ceremonial Magic*, 67.

Perrier

According to Christian demonology, Perrier is a prince of the principalities who is under the command of SATAN (see PRINCES OF HELL). He is said to be most powerful on Wednesdays and Saturdays.

Sources: Aylesworth, *Servants of the Devil*, 55; Spence, *Encyclopædia of Occultism*, 251; Susej, *Demonic Bible*, 285.

Persifiel

In the *Theurgia Goetia*, the second book of the *Lemegeton*, Persifiel is ranked as a duke who commands 2,400 servitors and is himself listed as one of the ten SERVITORS OF BYDIEL (see BYDIEL). An AERIAL DEVIL, when summoned he appears in an attractive form and is known to be good-natured and willing to obey his summoner.

Source: Peterson, *Lesser Key of Solomon*, 105.

Petunof

In the *Sacred Magic of Abramelin the Mage*, book two, Petunof ("exciting") is among the sixty-five SERVITORS OF KORE AND MAGOTH.

Sources: Mathers, *Book of the Sacred Magic of Abramelin*, 170; Susej, *Demonic Bible*, 258; Von Worms, *Book of Abramelin*, 250.

Pey

The pey are a species of vampiric demons from the lore of Sri Lanka and Tamil, India. They feed off the blood from wounded warriors that they find on battlefields. A pey first drains the warrior of his blood and then takes the body back to its home, where the corpse is cooked and eaten.

Sources: Blavatsky, *Isis Unveiled*, 447; Hikosaka, *Encyclopaedia of Tamil Literature*, 67, 79, 30; Maberry, *Vampire Universe*, 247; Selby, *Tamil Geographies*, 194–95; Waghorne, *Gods of Flesh, Gods of Stone*, 197.

Pfm

According to Enochian lore, Pfm is a CACODAEMON. His counterpart is the angel Fmna (ENOCHIAN CACODAEMONS).

Source: Chopra, *Academic Dictionary of Mythology*, 229.

Phaldor

In Apollonius of Tyana's *Nuctemeron* (*Night Illuminated by Day*), Phaldor is the demon of oracles. He is said to be most powerful during the eleventh hour.

Sources: Davidson, *Dictionary of Angels*, 7; Gettings, *Dictionary of Demons*, 23; Lévi, *Transcendental Magic*, 422.

Phaleg

Variations: Phalec, Pharos, "the War-Lord"

The grimoire *Arbatel de Magia Veterum* (*Arbatel of the Magic of the Ancients*), which was published in Switzerland by an unknown author in 1575, lists Phaleg as one of the seven OLYMPIAN SPIRITS. The demon of war, Phaleg commands thirty-five provinces.

Sources: Drury, *Dictionary of the Esoteric*, 16, 239; González-Wippler, *Complete Book of Spells*, 120; Greer, *New Encyclopedia of the Occult*, 370; McLean, *Magical Calendar*, 110; Webster, *Encyclopedia of Angels*, 5, 150.

Phalgus

In Apollonius of Tyana's *Nuctemeron* (*Night Illuminated by Day*), Phalgus is listed as being a DJINN and the demon of judgment. He is most powerful during the fourth hour.

Sources: Crowley, *777 Revised*, 33; Davidson, *Dictionary of Angels*, 224; Gettings, *Dictionary of Demons*, 190; Lévi, *Transcendental Magic*, 404.

Phaniel

Phaniel is one of the twenty SERVITORS OF CAMUEL (see CAMUEL). A nocturnal demon, he appears before his summoner in a beautiful form and is known to be very courteous.

Sources: Guiley, *Encyclopedia of Demons and Demonology*, 36; Peterson, *Lesser Key of Solomon*, 68.

Pharmaros

Variations: ABAROS, Arearos, ARMAROS, ARMERS

According to Enochian lore, Pharmaros is one of the FALLEN ANGELS who swore allegiance to SAMIAZA, rebelled against God, took a human wife, and fathered the NEPHILIM. He went on to teach mankind how to diagnose an illness, as well as the art of herbal, pharmaceutical, and practical medicine.

Sources: Laurence, *Foreign Quarterly Review*, Vol. 24, 370; Society for Jewish Study, *Journal of Jewish Studies*, Vols. 34–35, 142.

Pharzuph

Apollonius of Tyana's *Nuctemeron* (*Night Illuminated by Day*) lists Pharzuph as a FALLEN ANGEL. The demon of delights, fornication, and lust, he is said to be most powerful during the fourth hour. His name translated from Hebrew means "hypocritical" or "two-faced."

Sources: Davidson, *Dictionary of Angels*, 224; Lévi, *Transcendental Magic*, 418.

Phenex

Variations: Phenix, Pheynix, Phoenix

Phenex is a FALLEN ANGEL, formerly of the Order of Thrones, who ranks as a marquis of Hell, commanding twenty legions (see MARQUIS OF HELL). This nocturnal demon, when summoned, will appear as a phoenix and speak with the voice of a child. It is said that he has a sweet singing voice, is a good poet, and is willing to take requests from his summoner. He has the ability to teach all the sciences. As soon as this demon is summoned, do not listen to his melodious song but rather command that he take a human form. In the *Testament of Solomon*, he told the king that he hopes to return to the Seventh Throne after another 1,200 years.

Sources: Davidson, *Dictionary of Angels*, 224; De Laurence, *Lesser Key of Solomon, Goetia*, 34; DuQuette, *Key to Solomon's Key*, 179; Maberry, *Cryptopedia*, 79; Scot, *Discoverie of Witchcraft*, 225.

Pheth

Variations: Phêth (Axiôphêth)

In the *Testament of Solomon*, Pheth is described as having the shapeless head of a DOG with the face of a bird, donkey, or ox. The demon of hemorrhoids and tuberculosis, Pheth is exorcized by making the victim drink a mixture of sweet-smelling, unmixed wine.

Sources: Ashe, *Qabalah*, 50; Conybeare, *Jewish Quarterly Review*, Vol. 11, 37.

Philotanus

Variations: Philatanus

In Christian demonology Philotanus is named as one of the assistants of BELIAL. This demon tempts mankind to engage in pederasty and sodomy.

Sources: Ashley, *Complete Book of Devils and Demons*, 60, 66; Baskin, *Dictionary of Satanism*, 258.

Phlogabitus

In Apollonius of Tyana's *Nuctemeron* (*Night Illuminated by Day*), Phlogabitus is the demon of adornments. He is most powerful during the third hour.

Sources: Crowley, *777 and Other Qabalistic Writings*, 34; Gettings, *Dictionary of Demons*, 190; Lévi, *Transcendental Magic*, 418.

Phthenoth

In the *Testament of Solomon*, Phthenoth is listed as one of the seventy-two SPIRITS OF SOLOMON. Described as appearing as a man with the shapeless head of a DOG and the face of a bird, donkey, or ox, he has the ability to cast the evil eye. Wearing a talisman of protection against evil eye will ward this demon off.

Sources: Conybeare, *Jewish Quarterly Review*, Vol. 11; Vasilakē, *Images of the Mother of God*, 257.

Phul

In the grimoire *Arbatel de Magia Veterum* (*Arbatel of the Magic of the Ancients*), published in Switzerland by an unknown author in 1575, Phul is listed as one of the seven OLYMPIAN SPIRITS and named the lord of the powers of the moon and supreme lord of the waters. He is said to command the seven provinces and ruled over the earth from 1040 to 550 B.C.E. Phul will return to power in 2390, ruling until 2880 C.E.

A nocturnal demon with dominion over the moon, Phul is said to have the ability to change any metal into pure silver. He can extend a person's life by three hundred years, heal dropsy (also known as edema, the noticeable swelling caused by fluid build-up in body tissues), govern lunar concerns, become invisible at will, and provide spirits of water.

Sources: Drury, *Dictionary of the Esoteric*, 239; González-Wippler, *Complete Book of Spells*, 120; Webster, *Encyclopedia of Angels*, 144, 150.

Pia

According to Enochian demonology, Pia is a CACODAEMON. His personal adversary is the angel Iahl (ENOCHIAN CACODAEMONS).

Sources: Chopra, *Academic Dictionary of Mythology*, 231; Laycock, *Complete Enochian Dictionary*, 156.

Picollus

Variations: Pikulis, Poccolus

Originally a Prussian god of winter, Picollus ("winter") was demonized in Colin de Plancy's *Dictionaire Infernale* (1863). He is described as wearing seventh-century garb, complete with a wide ruff and cloak; however, traditional descriptions say he is a pale, well-dressed old man with a large nose and long white beard. This demon appears to important people during their final days. Offerings of human blood, the severed head of a dead man, and tallow will prevent him from attacking. De Plancy's description of Picollus is exactly like the popular Victorian era puppet Punch, of "Punch and Judy" fame.

Sources: *Classical Manual*, 583; Gettings, *Dictionary of Demons*, 190; Kelly, *Who in Hell*, 183.

Pinel

In Christian demonology, Pinel is said to be one of the servitors of SATAN.

Sources: Spence, *Encyclopedia of Occultism*, 120.

Pinem'e

Pinem'e is one of the FALLEN ANGELS who swore allegiance to SAMIAZA, rebelled against God, took a human wife, and fathered the NEPHILIM. He went on to teach mankind how to write with ink on papyrus.

Sources: Choice, *Secular and the Sacred Harmonized*, 116; Davis, *Antithesis of the Ages*, 110; Fröhlich, *Time and Times and Half a Time*, 69.

Pirichiel

The *Theurgia Goetia*, the second book of the *Lemegeton*, ranks Pirichiel as one of the eleven WANDERING PRINCES (see PRINCES OF HELL). This AERIAL DEVIL commands eight knights: Almasor, Cardiel, Cuprisiel, Damarsiel, Demediel, Hursiel, Menariel, and Nemariel. Each of these knights has two thousand servitors each.

Sources: Bellanger, *Dictionary of Demons*, 108; Peterson, *Lesser Key of Solomon*, 96.

Piru

Variations: Pääpiru ("Headpiru")

In Finnish mythology Piru is, according to the *Kalevala*, the companion or henchman to LEMPO. Piru is a type of TERRESTRIAL DEVIL who lives in the forest and commands the demons and evil spirits of the forests as well as a fierce herd of moose.

Working in conjunction with HIISI, JUTAS, and LEMPO, the demon Piru preys upon anyone walking through the forest, trapping them, and forcing them to answer riddles or forfeit their life. When these demons were fighting the hero Väinämöinen, HIISI made his axe wobble and made a simple cut that bled heavily.

Sources: Carlyle, *Gods of the Earth*, 530; Pentikäinen, *Nordic Dead-Child Tradition*, 234.

Pisacas, The

Variations: Kravyad, Picacas, Pisachi (feminine form), Pisakas, Pishachas, Pishashas

In ancient India it is said that there is a demonic race of vampiric ASURAS known as the pisacas. They are dangerous, evil, and malignant by nature, the most vile of all the demons, and they chatter incessantly. Although aligned with the RAKSHASAS, pisacas are ranked beneath them. The pisacas often war against the Aryans, Daitayas, and Nagas. They eat the flesh and drink the blood of both the living and the dead, being particularly fond of pregnant women. Pisacas live in abandoned places, burial grounds, and charnel houses but have been known to hunt the jungle spreading diseases while looking for humans to afflict with insanity or to consume. Carrying iron or a piece of the neem tree will ward off a pisacas.

The bhuts and the chutas are species of PISACHA. The demon HIDIMBA and the DEMONESS Picacu are Pisacha.

Sources: De Gubernatis, *Zoological Mythology*, 376; Hyatt, *Book of Demons*, 15; Keith, *Religion and Philosophy*, 384; Meyer, *Sexual Life in Ancient India*, 94; Rose, *Spirits, Fairies, Leprechauns, and Goblins*, 261.

Pisacha

Variations: Kapisa

In India, the word *pisacha* ("bloodthirsty savages" and "eaters of raw flesh") is used to refer collectively to all ghosts and vampires. There is a demonic spirit called a pisacha that was created by Brahma from the stray droplets of water that created gods, gandharvas, and men. Typically female and hideous in appearance, the pisacha looks like the fading remnants of a human form. Ranked lower than the RAKSHASAS and VETALA, the pisacha preys on men, causing them to develop various illnesses. Should a man fall victim, the only way to rid himself of the disease is to make an offering of rice to the pisacha at the crossroads in a ceremony for four consecutive days.

Pisacha live in charnel grounds and at crossroads throughout central Asia. These demons are barbaric, bloodthirsty, and cruel. They possess a great deal of arcane and mystical knowledge and are often captured and enslaved by sorcerers because of it. The symbol of marriage by rape, these demons are nearly impossible to destroy. Only their physical form can be damaged beyond usage; their spirit will continue to haunt an area. Only a sage who knows and uses its true name—a nearly impossible bit of knowledge to discover—in an ancient and complex ritual can force the pisacha to move on to its final spiritual destination.

Sources: Asiatic Society, *Bibliotheca Indica*, 255–6; Dowson, *Classical Dictionary of Hindu Mythology and Religion, Geography, History, and Literature*, 235; Maberry, *Vampire Universe*, 248–9.

Pisatji

In Javanese demonology there is a type of *memedis*, a frightening spirit that is basically harmless, known as a pisatji ("wanderers"). It is difficult even with the proper talent to see such things, but it is said to look like a ghostly child. These demonic spirits wander through cemeteries, as they have no fixed location and are always on the lookout for a place to live. When the opportunity presents itself, the pisatji will turn someone into a child and torment them until the pisatji become bored and wander off, thereby breaking the spell.

Should a person ever want to summon one of these demons, they would have to go to a cemetery at night and place toys and candies on a child's grave. When these items move of their own accord, the pisatji are present. Before the demons move on or otherwise become distracted, quickly ask them to seek revenge for you with promises of more toys and candies.

Sources: Geertz, *Religion of Java*, 17; Jones, *Evil in Our Midst*, 169–72.

Pischiel

In the *Theurgia Goetia*, the second book of the *Lemegeton*, Pischiel is ranked as a duke and is listed as one of the fifteen SERVITORS OF ICOSIEL (see ICOSIEL). This AERIAL DEVIL commands 2,200 servitors and has a reputation for being good-natured and willing to obey his summoner.

Sources: Peterson, *Lesser Key of Solomon*, 99.

Pishtaco

Variations: Phistako

Originally an Andean legend, Pishtaco is now a Peruvian nursery bogey that is said to represent the dark side of the cultural Latino male persona. A vampiric demon, the pishtaco is said to look like a tall white man wearing a long white coat, which hides the knife he carries. It is said to sleep too much and drink great quantities of milk. This imagery has appeared on the ceramic work of the ancient Nazca people. The pishtaco, said to be overly aggressive and unnaturally overendowed, captures children and severs the limbs and heads so that all remains are the torsos. Then the pishtaco removes the body fat, which it then sells to make large bells for the church, run machinery, and contribute to paying off the country's huge international debt.

As recently as April 8, 1998, police received an anonymous tip that led them to discover the mangled bodies of two men. The bodies were described as having been flayed and all of their body fat removed. The autopsy named the cause of death as cardiac arrest caused by lack of blood. The skins of the men were never found.

Sources: Campion-Vincent, *Organ Theft Legends*, 153–56, 168; Gow, *Amazonian Myth and Its History*, 256–59; Llosa, *Death in the Andes*, 12–13, 18–19, 28, 33, 52–58, 80–85, 98–101.

Pita Sanniya

In Sinhalese demonology the Pita Sanniya ("bile demon") causes bile-related diseases that cause continuous sleep, headaches, NIGHTMARES, and vomiting. Pita Sanniya, like the other Sinhalese demons, are susceptible to the DAHA-ATA SANNIYA.

Sources: Ames, *Tovil*, 42–9; Illes, *Encyclopedia of Spirits*, 875; Kapferer, *Celebration of Demons*, 231; Wirz, *Exorcism and the Art of Healing in Ceylon*, 44.

Pithius

Variations: Pythius, Pytho

Pithius is a prince who commands the liar-spirits (see PRINCES OF HELL). Appearing like a snake, he gives false prophecies. This name is possibly Greek and may be a variant on the word *pythoness*.

Sources: Barrett, *The Magus*, 49; Icon, *Demons*, 172; Pepin, *Vatican Mythographers*, 55.

Pitkis

Pitkis is the demon of the night in Baltic demonology.

Source: Ashley, *Complete Book of Devils and Demons*, 64.

Pitua

In Polynesian Maori demonology, the demon Pitua appears as an attractive woman with a long tail. Some sources say that the pitua is a species of demonic creatures that resemble mermaids and not a single entity.

Source: Knappert, *Pacific Mythology*, 206.

Piz

According to Enochian lore, Piz is a CACO-DAEMON (see ENOCHIAN CACODAEMONS).

Sources: Chopra, *Academic Dictionary of Mythology*, 232; Laycock, *Complete Enochian Dictionary*, 157.

Piznai

The DEMONESS Piznai is a type of SUCCUBUS in Judaic mythology. She was born the daughter of LILITH. Through sexual relations with Adam, she became the progenitor of a lesser race of demons known as LUTINS when she gave birth to 92,000 of them. The firstborn Lutins son between Piznai and Adam was named AGRIMAS.

Sources: Dennis, *Encyclopedia of Jewish Myth, Magic and Mysticism*, 202; Ginzberg, *Legends of the Jews*, Vol. 5, 166; Scholem, *Kabbalah*, 357.

Planetary Princes

Variations: Planetary demons

According to the *Theurgia Goetia*, the second book of the *Lemegeton*, there are seven planetary princes: BYDIEL, prince of Venus; EMONIEL, prince of Jupiter; ICOSIEL, prince of Mars; MACARIEL, prince of Mercury; Monadiel, prince of the Moon; SOLERIEL, prince of the Sun; and URIEL, prince of Saturn.

Agrippa's list of planetary *daemonia* (demons) is different from that in the *Theurgia Goetia*. His list is used in the post-medieval demonic traditions as follows: Barbazel, prince of Mars; Hismael, prince of Jupiter; Kedemel, prince of Venus; Schedbarschemoth, prince of the Moon;

SORATH, prince of the Sun; Taphthartharath, prince of Mercury; and Zazel, prince of Saturn.

Source: Gettings, *Dictionary of Demons*, 138, 191.

Platien

The *Sacred Magic of Abramelin the Mage*, book two, lists Platien ("broad" or "flat") as one of the one hundred eleven SERVITORS OF AMAYMON, ARITON, ORIENS, AND PAYMON (see AMAYMON, ARITON, ORIENS, and PAYMON).

Sources: Mathers, *Book of the Sacred Magic of Abramelin the Mage*, 105; Susej, *Demonic Bible*, 256; Von Worms, *Book of Abramelin*, 256.

Plegit

The *Sacred Magic of Abramelin the Mage*, book two, lists Plegit as one of the one hundred eleven SERVITORS OF AMAYMON, ARITON, ORIENS, AND PAYMON (see AMAYMON, ARITON, ORIENS, and PAYMON). His name is possibly Greek and may mean "smiting" or "smitten."

Sources: Mathers, *Book of the Sacred Magic of Abramelin the Mage*, 105; Susej, *Demonic Bible*, 256; Von Worms, *Book of Abramelin*, 245.

Pleiades

In the *Testament of Solomon*, the Pleiades are, collectively, one of the seventy-two SPIRITS OF SOLOMON; they were bound by the king and made to dig the foundation of his temple. They appeared before Solomon as seven beautiful women all bound together. Their name is Greek and it means "to sail." They travel about sometimes living in Lydia, or Olympus, or on a great mountain and are represented in the heavens as a cluster of stars (see also PLEIADES DECEPTION, PLEIADES ERROR, PLEIADES JEALOUSY, PLEIADES KLOTHOD, PLEIADES POWER, PLEIADES STRIFE, and PLEIADES "THE WORST OF ALL").

Sources: Butler, *Ritual Magic*, 31; Conybeare, *Jewish Quarterly Review*, Vol. 11, 24–6; Frazer, *Golden Bough*, 311; Hastings, *Dictionary of the Bible*, 895–6.

Pleiades Deception

In the *Testament of Solomon*, the PLEIADES are, collectively, one of the seventy-two SPIRITS OF SOLOMON; they were bound by the king and made to dig the foundation of his temple. The demon Deception admitted to the king that she deceives men by weaving snares for them to trap themselves in, as well as inciting and instigating heresies. Her personal adversary is the angel Lamechalal.

Sources: Charlesworth, *Old Testament Pseudepigrapha*, 935; Conybeare, *Jewish Quarterly Review*, Vol. 11, 24–6.

Pleiades Error

In the *Testament of Solomon*, the PLEIADES are, collectively, one of the seventy-two SPIRITS OF SOLOMON; they were bound by the king and made to dig the foundation of his temple. The demon Error admitted to the king that she led men astray and into committing the crime of grave robbery. Her personal adversary is the angel URIEL.

Sources: Charlesworth, *Old Testament Pseudepigrapha*, 935; Conybeare, *Jewish Quarterly Review*, Vol. 11, 24–6.

Pleiades Jealousy

In the *Testament of Solomon*, the PLEIADES are, collectively, one of the seventy-two SPIRITS OF SOLOMON; they were bound by the king and made to dig the foundation of his temple. The demon Jealousy admitted to the king that she causes men to forget moderation and sobriety and that she splits men into factions as well as dividing families. Her personal adversary is the angel Balthial.

Sources: Conybeare, *Jewish Quarterly Review*, Vol. 11, 24–6.

Pleiades Klothod

In the *Testament of Solomon*, the PLEIADES are, collectively, one of the seventy-two SPIRITS OF SOLOMON; they were bound by the king and made to dig the foundation of his Temple. The demon Klothod ("battle") admitted to the king that she causes war and that her personal adversary is the angel Marmarath.

Sources: Conybeare, *Jewish Quarterly Review*, Vol. 11, 24–6; Fleg, *Life of Solomon*, 107.

Pleiades Power

In the *Testament of Solomon*, the PLEIADES are, collectively, one of the seventy-two SPIRITS OF SOLOMON; they were bound by the king and made to dig the foundation of his temple. The demon Power admitted to the king that she supplies rebels with power, raises up tyrants, and tears down kings. Her personal adversary is the angel Asteraoth.

Sources: Charlesworth, *Old Testament Pseudepigrapha*, 935; Conybeare, *Jewish Quarterly Review*, Vol. 11, 24–6.

Pleiades Strife

In the *Testament of Solomon*, the PLEIADES are, collectively, one of the seventy-two SPIRITS OF SOLOMON; they were bound by the king and made to dig the foundation of his temple. The demon Strife admitted to the king that she brings hangers, stones, timbers, and weapons. Her personal adversary is the angel Baruchiachel.

Sources: Charlesworth, *Old Testament Pseudepigrapha*, 935; Conybeare, *Jewish Quarterly Review*, Vol. 11, 24–6.

Pleiades "The Worst of All"

In the *Testament of Solomon*, the PLEIADES are, collectively, one of the seventy-two SPIRITS OF SOLOMON; they were bound by the king and made to dig the foundation of his temple. The demon WORST OF ALL admitted to the king that she imposes the bonds of Artemis and makes men worse off than they already are. Her personal adversary is the locust.

Sources: Charlesworth, *Old Testament Pseudepigrapha*, 935; Conybeare, *Jewish Quarterly Review*, Vol. 11, 24–6.

Plirok

In the *Sacred Magic of Abramelin the Mage*, book two, Plirok is listed as one of the one hundred eleven SERVITORS OF AMAYMON, ARITON, ORIENS, AND PAYMON (see AMAYMON, ARITON, ORIENS, and PAYMON). This name is possibly Coptic and could mean "burning up."

Sources: Ford, *Bible of the Adversary*, 89; Forgotten Books, *Book of the Sacred Magic of Abramelin the Mage*, 112; Mathers, *Book of the Sacred Magic of Abra-Melin*, 113; Von Worms, *Book of Abramelin*, 245.

Plison

In the *Sacred Magic of Abramelin the Mage*, book two, Plison is one of the forty-nine SERVITORS OF BEELZEBUB (see BEELZEBUB). This name is possibly Greek and may mean "to swim."

Sources: Mathers, *Book of the Sacred Magic of Abra-Melin*, 120; Susej, *Demonic Bible*, 259; Von Worms, *Book of Abramelin*, 257.

Poludnica

Variations: Lady Midday, Poludniowka, Polunditsa ("noon-wife"), PSEZPOLNICA, Rzanica

In Slovenia there is a vampiric demon that looks like a beautiful, tall woman wearing white or dressed as if in mourning. In either guise, a poludnica ("noon") is said to be carrying a scythe or shears. During harvest time, right around noon, a poludnica attacks laborers who are working and not taking their proper rest, causing them to be afflicted with heat stroke or madness if they are lucky. If not, the poludnica will lure them off with her beauty and when she has them in a secluded place, attack viciously, draining them of their blood. It has also been said that she will break the arms and legs of anyone she happens to come across. If a poludnica comes up to a field worker, she will ask him difficult questions. As soon as he cannot answer one, she will chop off his head. It was said that if a poludnica was seen, immediately drop to the ground and lie perfectly still until it meanders off. The male version of the poludnica is called polevoy.

Typically a bundle of grain is decorated when harvest starts to keep poludnica at bay, and when harvest is over, the effigy is burned.

In addition to attacking laborers, she is said to also steal children that she finds wandering unattended as the adults work. Most likely the poludnica is a nursery bogey used by parents to keep their children from wandering off and damaging the crops. It is also an excellent story for a worker who wants to take a break.

Sources: Grey, *Mythology of All Races*, 267; Oinas, *Essays on Russian Folklore and Mythology*, 103–10; Roucek, *Slavonic Encyclopaedia*, 237.

Polunocnica

Variations: Gwiazda Polnoca, Polunochnitsa, Zorya Polunochnaya, Zwezda Polnoca

Polunocnica ("Lady Midnight") is a pendulous-breasted nocturnal demon from Slavic mythology who preys upon children by tormenting them in the middle of the night. Living in the swamp, this demon is oftentimes the forgotten third aspect of the triple goddess Zorya.

Sources: Deck-Partyka, *Poland: A Unique Country and Its People*, 281; Oinas, *Essays on Russian Folklore and Mythology*, 107.

Pontianak

Variations: Buo, Kuntilanak, Mati-anak, Pontipinnak

In the folklore of Indonesia and Malaya there is a vampiric demon known as a pontianak. It is believed that when a woman dies in childbirth, dies as a virgin, or is the victim of a pontianak attack, she will then transform into this type of vampire unless specific burial rites are followed. Glass beads must be placed in the corpse's mouth, an egg in each armpit, and needles driven into the palms and soles of the feet.

A pontianak can pass as a human woman except for a hole in the back of its neck and smelling exactly like the tropically sweet frangipani flower. It will also announce its presence with a call that sounds like a crying baby.

At night, it leaves its home in a banana tree and shape-shifts into a bird. Then the pontianak flies out looking for prey. Although any person will do, it truly prefers the blood of infants and pregnant women, as it is filled with hatred for never having been a mother itself. When it finds a suitable target, the pontianak then changes back into its human guise and detaches its head from its body, dangling its organs beneath as it flies back to where it saw its prey. If it can, it will rip the unborn child right out of the mother's body, eating it on the spot.

The pontianak has a unique fear among vampire kind. It will flee in terror from anyone who manages to pull a hair out of its head. It is also believed that if a nail can be placed into the hole in the back of the neck, it will change into a beautiful woman and remain that way until someone pulls the nail back out. It is fortunate to know that the pontianak has these weaknesses, because there is no known method for destroying one.

Sources: Laderman, *Wives and Midwives*, 126–27; McHugh, *Hantu-Hantu*, 74; Skeat, *Malay Magic*, 326–28.

Poraii

The demon Poraii was named in the *Grimoire of Pope Honorius* (*Le Grimoire du Pape Honorius*) as one of the nineteen servitor spirits.

Sources: de Givry, *Witchcraft, Magic and Alchemy*, 128.

Posriel

Variations: Hadriel

One of the FALLEN ANGELS, Posriel is said to command the sixth lodge of Hell where the prophet Micah resides.

Sources: Davidson, *Dictionary of Angels*, 227.

Po-Tangotango

The personification of a moonless night, the DEMONESS Po-Tangotango ("very dark night") is the thoughtless wife of Bangi. According to Maori mythology she was born the child of the god Hine-nui-te Po.

Sources: Reed, *Treasury of Maori Folklore*, 48, 163, 174; Tregear, *Maori-Polynesian Comparative Dictionary*, 322, 342, 467.

Poter

In the *Sacred Magic of Abramelin the Mage*, book two, Poter ("a drinking cup or vase") is included among the one hundred eleven SERVITORS OF AMAYMON, ARITON, ORIENS, AND PAYMON (see AMAYMON, ARITON, ORIENS, and PAYMON).

Sources: Mathers, *Book of the Sacred Magic of Abramelin the Mage*, 112; Susej, *Demonic Bible*, 197.

Power

Originally a goddess in Babylonian mythology when she was absorbed into Jewish and Solominic lore, the DEMONESS Power became the fifth of the SEVEN HEAVENLY BODIES, one of the thirty-three (or thirty-six, sources vary) Elements of the Cosmic Ruler of the Darkness. In the *Testament of Solomon* she was named as one of the PLEIADES, a collection of seven beautiful women bound together who are represented in the sky as a cluster of stars; they were made to dig the foundation of the temple (see SPIRITS OF SOLOMON).

The DEMONESS Power admitted to the king that she supplies rebels with power, raises up tyrants, and tears down kings. Her personal adversary is the angel Asteraoth.

Source: Abrahams, *Jewish Quarterly Review*, Vol. 11, 25.

Praestigiatores

Variations: Diviner, enchanter, Lamiae, magi, Sortilgi, Tricksters, Venefici

The Italian word *Praestigiatores* refers to users of black magic as well as the demons who are used by them. These magicians and demons alike have the ability to imitate miracles by use of demonic deception. The sorcerer is able to confuse the senses of men and make them believe that they are actually performing cures and that a legitimate miracle has occurred. They are of the fifth order of demons and are under the command of SATAN, the caco-magi and malefic.

Sources: Lea, *Materials Toward a History of Witchcraft*, 763, 765, 837, 842; Thorndike, *History of Magic and Experimental Science*, Part 12, 251, 252; Gettings, *Dictionary of Demons*, 194; Shumaker, *Occult Sciences in the Renaissance*, 92.

Preches

In the *Sacred Magic of Abramelin the Mage*, book two, Preches is listed as one of the sixteen SERVITORS OF ASMODEUS (see ASMODEUS). His name is possibly Greek and may mean "to swell out."

Sources: Eckley, *Children's Lore in Finnegans Wake*, 158; Mathers, *Book of the Sacred Magic of Abra-Melin*, 119; Von Worms, *Book of Abramelin*, 256.

Presidents of Hell

There are twenty-seven named presidents mentioned in the various grimoires. They are ADRAMALECK, AIM, AMOYMON, AMY, BARBAS, Beur, BOTIS, BUER, CAACRINOLAAS, CAIM, CAYM, FORAII, FORAS, FORCAS, FORFAX, GAAP, GLACIA LABOLAS, GLASSYALABOLAS, GOAP, HAAGENTI, MALPHAS, MARAX, MARBAS, MORAX, OSE, UALAC, and ZAGAM.

Sources: Ashley, *Complete Book of Devils and Demons*, 61; Belanger, *Dictionary of Demons*, 129; De Laurence, *Lesser Key of Solomon, Goetia*, 40; Gettings, *Dictionary of Demons*, 171; Godwin, *Godwin's Cabalistic Encyclopedia*, 324; Wedeck, *Treasury of Witchcraft*, 96.

Pretas

Pretas ("ghosts") are the demonic spirits of people who committed criminal deeds and have been sent to the circle of perpetual hunger. According to Hindu mythology, there are thirty-six types of these demons of hunger and thirst. Although they are typically depicted as having bloated stomachs, overly large mouths, and constricted throats, other forms of these demons include animated corpses' skeletons and *yeaks* ("giants"). There are those pretas who are slightly taller than average and wear pig masks. The ones that live on the earth are only visible at night as they fly through the air; the rest reside in Preta-Loka, the realm of tortured spirits, as the servants of YAMA, the king of the Underworld.

These souls that have been condemned to perpetual hunger and thirst cannot enter into a new body and will not go into a house where God-fearing people live. The symbol of unfulfilled hunger and thirst, it is said they will even eat excrement in an attempt to feel full and sated. Pretas have the ability to animate corpses left exposed in graveyards. Some can belch fire and others have long nails and teeth. All species of these demons can easily influence people with weak minds. Attack from these demons can be prevented by performing the Hindu Bodhisattvas ceremony of feeding the pretas.

Sources: Chandra, *Encyclopaedia of Hindu Gods and Goddesses*, 71; Hastings, *Encyclopedia of Religion and Ethics*, Vol. 11, 831–2; Hyatt, *Book of Demons*, 25; Williams, *Buddhism in Its Connexion with Brāhmanism and Hinduism*, 121, 218–9.

Prime Ministers of Hell

According to the various grimoires and miscellaneous medieval hierarchies, there are six prime ministers of Hell: ABEZETHIBOU, AGARES, AKIKEL, BAALZEPHON, BEELZEBUB, and LUCIFUGE ROFOCALE.

Sources: Crowley, *Aleister Crowley's Illustrated Goetia: Sexual Evocation*, 75; Ford, *Liber Hvhi*, 76.

Princes of Hell

Johann Wierus said in his *Pseudomonarchia Daemonum* (1583) that there are sixty-nine princes of Hell. Samuel L. MacGregor Mathers's 1904 *The Goetia: The Lesser Key of Solomon the King* added three, bringing the total to seventy-two. However, when combining those mentioned in various grimoires and hierarchies, there are one hundred four named princes in all: ABALAM, ADRAMALECK, Aeradiel, AMAYMON, AMOYMON, ANDRAS, ARIAS, ARITON, ARMADIEL, ASELIEL, ASHTAROTH, ASMODEUS, ASSYRIEL, ASTAROT, ASTELIEL, AYPEROR, AYPEROS, BAAL-BERYTH, Baal-zebub, BALBERITH, BARFAEL, BARMIEL, BARUCHAS, BEBALL, BELAIL, BELIAN, BIDIEL, BITRU, BURIEL, BUSAS, BYDIEL, CABARIEL,

CAIM, CAMUEL, DOROCHIEL, DUMA, EMONIEL, EURONYMOUS, EURYNOME, GAAP, GARADIEL, GEDEIL, GOAP, HYDRIEL, ICOSIEL, IPES, IUVART, LUCIFER, LUCIFUGE ROFOCALE, MACARIEL, MACHARIEL, MALGARAS, MALPHAS, MAMMON, MARCHOSIAS, MASERIEL, MASTEMA, Menadile, MERESIN, MERIHIM, MERIRIM, MERIZIM, MOLOCH, Monadiel, MUSUZIEL, NEGARSANEL, OLIVER, ORCUS, ORIENS, OROBAS, PADIEL, PAMERSIEL, Pekat, PERRIER, PIRICHIEL, PITHIUS, PRUFLAS, PUTA, PYRICHIEL, PYRO, PYTHON, RAHAB, RASIEL, RHOTOMAGO, RIMMON, ROSIER, SAMAEL, SAMIL, SAMMAEL, SARIEL, SATAN, SEERE, SITRI, SOLERIEL, STOLAS, SURIEL, SWORD OF ASHMODAI THE KING, SYMIEL, SYTRY, URIEL, USIEL, VASSAGO, VERRIER, and YOMAEL.

Sources: Belanger, *Dictionary of Demons*, 13; Bailey, *Spiritual Warfare*, 71–2; Kiely, *Dark Sacrament*, 375–6; Laurence, *Foreign Quarterly Review*, Vol. 24, 370; Scott, *London Magazine*, Vol. 5, 378; Trithemius, *Steganographia*, 81.

Principal Kings of Hell

According to the *Pseudomonarchia Daemonum*, there are four principal kings, each of which is under the command of MAMMON: AMAYMON, king of an unspecified direction; CORSON, king of the West; GAAP, king of an unspecified direction; and ZIMINIAR, king of the North (see FOUR PRINCIPAL KINGS).

Sources: De Laurence, *Lesser Key of Solomon, Goetia*, 32–3; González-Wippler, *Complete Book of Spells, Ceremonies, and Magic*, 146; Icon, *Demons*, 190; McLean, *Treatise of Angel Magic*, 52; Spence, *Encyclopedia of Occultism*, 109.

Procel

Variations: CROCELL, Crokel, Procell, PROCULO, Prucel, Pucel

In the *Ars Goetia*, the first book of the *Lemegeton*, the *Lesser Key of Solomon*, Procel is ranked as a duke under the command of NEBIROS, one of the seventy-two SPIRITS OF SOLOMON. This FALLEN ANGEL, formerly of the Order of Powers, commands forty-eight legions. When summoned, Procel will appear as an angel. He has the ability to place a person into a deep sleep that will last up to forty-eight hours. He can also grant and teach illusions as well as teach geometry and the liberal sciences. This demon speaks of hidden things, people's tempers, and warms baths, and by the request of his summoner will make a sound like a great rush of water.

Sources: Crowley, *The Goetia*, 53; DuQuette, *Key to Solomon's Key*, 185; Gettings, *Dictionary of Demons*, 194; Scot, *Discoverie of Witchcraft*, 223; Webster, *Encyclopedia of Angels*, 44.

Procreation, demonic

Variations: Insceafte

While some sources claim that demons are quite capable of siring their own kind—SAMMAEL and his four demonic wives are quite prolific—others claim that the INCUBUS and SUCCUBUS must steal human seed to create more demons.

Sources: Elmer, *Challenges to Authority*, 277; Kluttz, *Return of the King*, 59–60; Levack, *New Perspectives on Witchcraft, Magic, and Demonology*, 59; Powell, *Apocryphal Texts and Traditions in Anglo-Saxon England*, 132.

Proculo

According to the *Grimoirium Verum* (*Grimoire of Truth*), allegedly written by Alibek the Egyptian in 1517, Proculo is listed as one of the eight SERVITORS OF HALE AND SERGULATH. The demon of dreams and sleep, he has the ability to cause a person to sleep for a full twenty-four hours.

Sources: Masters, *Devil's Dominion*, 131; Waite, *The Book of Ceremonial Magic*, 168.

Promakos

The *Sacred Magic of Abramelin the Mage*, book two, includes Promakos ("a fighter in the front of conflict") as one of the one hundred eleven SERVITORS OF AMAYMON, ARITON, ORIENS, AND PAYMON (see AMAYMON, ARITON, ORIENS, and PAYMON).

Sources: Ford, *Bible of the Adversary*, 89; Forgotten Books, *Book of the Sacred Magic of Abramelin the Mage*, 112; Mathers, *Book of the Sacred Magic of Abra-Melin*, 105; Susej, *Demonic Bible*, 197; Von Worms, *Book of Abramelin*, 246.

Proxosos

Proxosos is among one hundred eleven SERVITORS OF AMAYMON, ARITON, ORIENS, AND PAYMON (see AMAYMON, ARITON, ORIENS, and PAYMON), according to the *Sacred Magic of Abramelin the Mage*, book two. This name is possibly Greek and may mean "a kid."

Sources: Ford, *Bible of the Adversary*, 88; Mathers, *Book of the Sacred Magic of Abra-Melin*, 112; Susej, *Demonic Bible*, 256; Von Worms, *Book of Abramelin*, 244.

Pruflas

Variations: Bufas, Busas, VASSAGO

Originating in Babylonian demonology, Pruflas was absorbed into Christian demonology and named in Johann Wierus's *Pseudomonarchia Daemonum* (*False Monarchy of Demons*, 1583) as a grand duke and grand prince who commands twenty-six legions, half from the Order of Thrones and half from the Order of Angels (see

DUKES OF HELL and PRINCES OF HELL). He appears before his summoner as a man with the head of an owl or hawk and is known to respond generously to any request asked of him, such as giving lengthy answers to questions. He encourages mankind to lie, starts quarrels and wars, and stirs up strife. This demon once lived in the Tower of Babel, and while he did so appeared as a lick of flame. Unlike other demons, Pruflas may not be admitted into every place.

Pruflas was accidently left out of Reginald Scot's English translation of Johann Wierus's *Pseudomonarchia Daemonum*.

Sources: Collin de Plancy, *Dictionnaire Infernal*, 413; De Laurence, *Lesser Key of Solomon, Goetia*, 22; Icon, *Demons*, 134, 135, 173, 543; Peterson, *Lesser Key of Solomon*, 229; Shah, *Occultism*, 67.

Pruslas

The *Grimoire of Pope Honorius* (*Le Grimoire du Pape Honorius*), alleged to be written by Pope Honorius III in the eighteenth century, ranks Pruslas as a servitor demon who collaborates with SATAN in seducing women. He is also listed as one of the ASHTAROTH assistants and one of the three SERVITORS OF SATANACHIA (see SATANACHIA).

Sources: Baskin, *Sorcerer's Handbook*, 275, 276, 445; de Givry, *Witchcraft, Magic and Alchemy*, 128; Icon, *Seducing*, 50; Waite, *Unknown World 1894–1895*, 230; Wedeck, *Treasury of Witchcraft*, 96.

Pscipolnitsa

Variations: Kornwief ("woman of the corn"), Kornwyf ("lady of the grain plants"), Mittagsfrau, Polednice, POLUDNICA, Poludnitsa, Roggenmuhme ("lady of the rye")

The personification of sunstroke in Slavic demonology, Pscipolnitsa ("Lady Midday") appears as a young woman dressed in white, sometimes said to be carrying a scythe; she is also described as a twelve-year-old girl, an old hag, and a whirling dust cloud. Most powerful at noontime in the summer, this demon preys upon field workers and women who have already given birth. Anyone who cannot answer her difficult questions will be beheaded or struck with an illness such as heatstroke, madness, or neck pains (see also PSEZPOLNICA).

Sources: Icon, *Roaming*, 90; Lurker, *Routledge Dictionary of Gods and Goddesses, Devils and Demons*, 155; Mednick, *Take a Nap*, 4; Oinas, *Essays on Russian Folklore and Mythology*, 103–7; Roucek, *Slavonic Encyclopaedia*, 327; Soucková, *Czech Romantics*, 112.

Pseudothei

The pseudothei are in service to BEELZEBUB. They are from the first Order of Demons.

Seeking to usurp God's name, they want to be worshipped as gods themselves, to have adorations and sacrifices made to them. The word *pseudothei* is possibly Greek and likely means "false gods."

Sources: McLean, *Treatise on Angel Magic*, 69, 102; Gettings, *Dictionary of Demons*, 195.

Psezpolnica

In Serbian lore Psezpolnica ("Woman of the Midday") is a demon who appears during the harvest and beheads field workers or drives them mad. Most powerful at noontime, she is described as looking like a woman or a dervish (see also PSCIPOLNITSA).

Sources: Lurker, *Dictionary of Gods and Goddesses*, 290; Messadié, *History of the Devil*, 197.

Psoglav

Psoglav ("doghead") is a demonic creature from Slavic lore that is described as looking like a man with horse legs, a DOG's head, a mouth filled with teeth of iron, and one eye on its forehead. An opportunity hunter, it excavates graves and consumes the dead. It is said to live in caves that have gemstones throughout Bosnia and Montenegro.

Source: Doirievich, *Srpski etnografski zbornik 66*, 106–7.

Pua Tu Tahi

Pua Tu Tahi ("coral rock standing alone") is an AQUEOUS DEVIL from Tahitian demonology who lives in the sea.

Sources: Craig, *Dictionary of Polynesian Mythology*, 217; Henry, *Ancient Tahiti*, 469, Maberry, *Cryptopedia*, 32.

Pubrisiel

In the *Lemegeton*, the *Lesser Key of Solomon*, Pubrisiel is ranked as one of the ten named chiefs under the command of SAZQUIEL (see SERVITORS OF SAZQUIEL).

Source: Waite, *Book of Black Magic and Ceremonial Magic*, 67.

Puk

Variations: Draug ("living dead person")

The AQUEOUS DEVIL Puk of Norwegian lore is the demon of impending disaster. He appears to fishermen as a headless fisherman dressed in oilskins. Living in the water, he is said to be exceptionally malevolent and sinister, even for a demon.

Sources: *Athenaeum*, Part 1, 324; Christiansen, *Folktales of Norway*, 259; *Norwegian-American Studies and Records*, Vol. 12, 40–1.

Puloman

Puloman, the father of Indrani and Sivasri, is a type of ASURAS in the Hindu religion. He is slain by INDRA when he wished to curse him for having raped his daughter.

Sources: Balfour, *Cyclopædia of India and of Eastern and Southern Asia*, 309; Chandra, *Encyclopaedia of Hindu Gods and Goddesses*, 154; Dowson, *Classical Dictionary of Hindu Mythology and Religion, Geography, History, and Literature*, 74, 126, 244; Gupta, *From Daityas to Devatas in Hindu Mythology*, 36–7.

Purson

Variations: CURSON, PRUFLAS, Pursan, Pusron

Appearing in many books of Christian demonology, such as the *Grimoire of Pope Honorius* (*Le Grimoire du Pape Honorius*), Purson is ranked as a king and the lieutenant general of the legions of Hell. He is also said to be one of the three SERVITORS OF FLEURETTY, as well as one of the seventy-two SPIRITS OF SOLOMON (see FLEURETTY). One of the FALLEN ANGELS, formerly of the Order of Virtues, this demon commands twenty-two legions, half of which are from the Order of Virtues and the other half from the Order of Thrones. When summoned, Purson appears to the sound of many trumpets looking like a lion-headed man riding a bear and carrying a snake in his hand. He is known for his willingness to truthfully answer any question asked of him. He also discovers treasures, gives good FAMILIARs, and knows the location of all hidden things. Purson also knows the creation of the world and will reveal events from the past, present, and future.

Sources: Baskin, *Sorcerer's Handbook*, 276; De Laurence, *Lesser Key of Solomon, Goetia*, 28; Waite, *Unknown World 1894–1895*, 230; Wedeck, *Treasury of Witchcraft*, 96.

Pusiel

Variations: Puriel ("Fire of God"), Puruel, Pyriel

Pusiel is one of the ARCHANGELS OF PUNISHMENT who is described as being "fiery and pitiless." He lives in the northern section of the third Heaven.

Sources: Baskin, *Sorcerer's Handbook*, 276, 445; de Givry, *Witchcraft, Magic and Alchemy*, 128; Gaster, *Studies and Texts in Folklore*, 159; Wedeck, *Treasury of Witchcraft*, 96.

Put Satanachia

The commander-in-chief of the armies of Hell, Put Satanachia directly commands the demons AAMON, BARBATOS, HERAMAEL, PRUSLAS, Sergutthy (SERGUTHY), SUSTUGRIEL, and TRIMASAEL, as well as forty-five (or fifty-four, sources conflict) additional demons. He himself is in service to LUCIFER. This demon can enforce his will over maidens and wives and has power over mothers. He has immense knowledge of the planets and provides witches with their animal FAMILIARs. Put Satanachia is known to frequent the continents of Asia and Europe.

Sources: Kelly, *Who in Hell*, 189; Masters, *Devil's Dominion*, 29; Waite, *Book of Black Magic and Ceremonial Magic*, 186; Waite, *Book of Black Magic and of Pacts*, 156.

Puta

Variations: The Prince of Forgetfulness, Purah

Prince Puta is the demon of forgetfulness. He is the same demon that is named in the incantatory formula that is incanted before drinking the Habdalah wine (see PRINCES OF HELL).

Sources: Brück, *Pharisäische Volkssitten*, 121; Singer, *Jewish Encyclopedia*, 520.

Putah Rangas

Putah rangas ("FAMILIAR spirits") are a type of demon in Malaysian demonology.

Sources: Smedal, *Order and Difference*, 50.

Putana

Variations: Poothani ("killer of infants"), Pūtanā ("devoid of virtue")

In Hindu mythology, Putana ("putrefaction") is a demonic *raksasis* ("giant"). She is referred to in the *Bhagavata Purana* with the rarely used word *yātudhānī* ("evil spirit"). Putana has a gigantic body, some six miles long, and she dresses in rags. She is described as being black skinned with an abdomen like a dried-up lake, breasts like small hills, and eye sockets like deep wells. She has long reddish bushlike hair, hands like bridges, nostrils like caves, teeth like plows, and thighs like the banks of two rivers. This demon also has the ability to assume the form of a beautiful woman.

The symbol of infantile diseases, Putana preys upon babies and small children using her black magic; however, offerings of alcohol, crow dung, fish, ground sesame, and a rice dish will prevent her from attacking. When Putana is eventually slain, her body is cut into pieces, boiled, and eaten.

Sources: Dimmitt, *Classical Hindu Mythology*, 111–2; Herbert, *Encyclopaedia Indica*, 842–4; White, *Kiss of the Yogini*, 51–3.

Puting Anak

Puting Anak ("child of a whirlwind") is a species of HANTU known as antu anak from Malaysian demonology that specialize in attacking the hearts and testicles of men. Making a sound like a laughing woman, this demon attacks men's testicles, causing them to perpetually itch.

Eating a boiled egg provides some protection against these demons.

Sources: Bernstein, *Spirits Captured in Stone*, 57, 94; Swettenham, *Vocabulary of the English and Malay Languages*, 4.

Putisiel

In the *Ars Paulina*, the third book of the *Lemegeton*, Putisiel is ranked as a duke and is listed as one of the fifteen SERVITORS OF SCOX (see SCOX) as well as one of the fifteen SERVITORS OF SASQUIEL (see SASQUIEL). He commands 5,550 servitors.

Source: Peterson, *Lesser Key of Solomon*, 114.

Pyrichiel

In the *Theurgia Goetia*, the second book of the *Lemegeton*, Pyrichiel is ranked as the elemental prince of fire. He is described as looking like a serpent with a human head (see PRINCES OF HELL). He is concerned with fire and flames.

Sources: Gettings, *Dictionary of Demons*, 196, 233; Trithemius, *Steganographia*, 81.

Pyro

Variations: PYTHON

Pyro is the prince of falsehood and the demon of deceit and lies (see PRINCES OF HELL).

Sources: Ashley, *Complete Book of Devils and Demons*, 60; Bias, *Freedom from the World of Satanism and the Power of Satan*, 42.

Python

Originally a tutelary demon of the oracular cult at Delphi, when absorbed into Christian demonology Python became the prince of the Lying Spirits (see PRINCES OF HELL). One of the five ARCHDEMONS of Hell, he is also the demon of control and pride. Appearing as a dragon or great snake, Python is a soothsayer.

Sources: Alexander, *Demonic Possession in the New Testament*, 99; Blavatsky, *Secret Doctrine*, Vol. 2, 259; McLean, *Treatise on Angel Magic*, 69.

Qandias

Variations: 'Aisa Qandisa, Qandiša

Qandias is a demonic goddess from the demonology of Northern Morocco, an older version of the goddess ASTARTE. The demon of lust, Qandias appears as a beautiful woman, but sometimes she has the feet of a mare or mule. Preying on handsome young men, she seduces them, driving them insane in the process; however, sacrifices made to her on the summer solstice will prevent her from attacking. She is said to live in rivers and springs.

Sources: Manfred, *Dictionary of Gods and Goddesses, Devils and Demons*, 293; Westermarck, *Belief in Spirits in Morocco*, 123, 151; Westermarck, *Ritual and Belief in Morocco*, Vol. 1, 393–4.

Qlippothic Orders of Demons, Twelve

Variations: The Lords of Unbalanced Forces

There are twelve qlippothic orders of demons, according to Cabalistic demonology: ADIMIRON, who looks like a lion-lizard hybrid; Airiron, who looks like a dragon-lion hybrid; BEHEMIRON, who looks like the hippopotamus or the elephant but crushed flat, or as if their skin was flayed and covered the body of a cockroach or gigantic beetle; DAGDAGIRON, whose form is like a vast and devouring flat-shaped fish; NACHASHIRON, who looks like DOG-headed serpents; NECHESHETH-IRON, who looks like human-headed insects; NESHIMIRON, who looks like hideous skeletal women with the bodies of fish and serpents; OBIRIRON, who looks goblinlike; SCHECHIRION, the hybrids of insects, reptiles, and shellfish with demonic faces; SHELHABIRON, who looks like merciless wolves and jackals; TZELLADIMIRON, who looks like savage triangular-headed dogs; and the TZEPHARIRON, who are living yet decaying corpses.

Sources: Ford, *Bible of the Adversary*, 112–14; Greer, *New Encyclopedia of the Occult*, 129; Mathers, *Sorcerer and His Apprentice*, 25–6.

Quartas

In the *Sacred Magic of Abramelin the Mage*, Quartas ("fourth") is listed as one of the thirty-two SERVITORS OF ASTAROT (see ASTAROT).

Sources: Ford, *Bible of the Adversary*, 91; Von Worms, *Book of Abramelin*, 256.

Quedbaschmod

Variations: Alphabet of the Celestial Language, Alphabet of Genii

The word *quedbaschmod* refers to the sigils that represent the alphabet of demons.

Sources: Gettings, *Dictionary of Demons*, 29, 197; McLean, *Treatise on Angel Magic*, 87.

Quoriel

In *Ars Paulina*, the third book of the *Lemegeton*, Quoriel is ranked as a chief and is listed as one of the eleven SERVITORS OF RAHAB (see RAHAB).

Sources: Davidson, *Dictionary of Demons*, 234, Peterson, *Lesser Key of Solomon*, 113; Waite, *The Book of Ceremonial Magic*, 67.

Qutrub

Originating in pre–Islamic demonology, qutrub are the male demonic ghouls or DJINN that are born from eggs as the children of IBLIS and a wife created especially for him by God out of the fire of Samun. The females are called ghul. Qutrub wander graveyards consuming human corpses.

Sources: Hughes, *Dictionary of Islam*, 137; Knappert, *Encyclopaedia of Middle Eastern Mythology and Religion*, 234; Rose, *Spirits, Fairies, Leprechauns, and Goblins*, 126; Turner, *Dictionary of Ancient Deities*, 251.

Rabas

In the *Theurgia Goetia*, the second book of the *Lemegeton*, Rabas is listed as one of the sixteen SERVITORS OF ASYRIEL (see ASYRIEL). A diurnal demon, he commands twenty servitors. Rabas is said to be good-natured and willing to obey his summoner.

Source: Peterson, *Lesser Key of Solomon*, 73–4, 77.

Rabdos

Variations: Rabdos the Strangler, Rhabdis

Originally the wand of the Greek god Hermes that was later demonized in Solominic lore into a being, Rabdos is listed as one of the seventy-two SPIRITS OF SOLOMON, bound by the king to cut marble. This demon showed Solomon the location of a great emerald that later was used to adorn the temple. Some sources say he was an angel powerful enough to stop the stars in the heavens, and fell when he did so (see FALLEN ANGELS). Other sources claim that he was born a mortal man who became a powerful mage and once "restrained the stars of heaven."

Said to appear before his summoner in the form of a man with the face of a DOG or in the form of a gigantic dog, Rabdos leads men into acts of stupidity. As a Fallen Angel, he is known to strangle his victims. His personal adversary is the angel Brieus.

Rabdos's sign is the phallus, rod, scepter, and wand. His name in Hebrew translates to mean "staff," but it literally means an ebony stick.

Sources: Cavendish, *The Black Arts*, 223; Conybeare, *Jewish Quarterly Review*, Vol. 11, 27–28; Davidson, *Dictionary of Angels*, 237; Ginzberg, *Legends of the Jews*, 152; McCown, *Testament of Solomon*, 45, 88; Rappoport, *Myth and Legend of Ancient Israel*, Vol. 1, 88; Van der Toorn, *Dictionary of Deities and Demons in the Bible*, 409.

Rabinu

Variations: Rabanu, Rabi, Rabianu

Rabinu is a demon from ancient Mesopotamian demonology. From the shadows he leaps out and overpowers his victims.

Source: Baskin, *Satanism*, 271.

Rabisu

Variations: "The Croucher," "the seizer," "the vagabond"

Originating in Akkadian mythology, there is a species of demons known as the rabisu ("demon lurking") that are dispatched by God to punish a person, but they will also attack without provocation when not under God's direct orders. These demons hide near the entrances to alleys, dark corners, and houses, waiting to leap out and attack their victims. Rubbing the area of the body they wish to affect with their hands, these demons cause an array of medical problems such as arthritis, bloody gums, blunt force trauma to the head and abdomen, difficulty breathing, dragging the left foot when walking, gout, Hepatitis A, an inability to talk, severe drooling, strokes, stiff feet, trembling hands, and twitching. A sure telltale sign that one has been attacked by this sort of demon is bruising on the temple and upper abdomen, the loss of consciousness, peripheral cyanosis ("black hands"), and severe strokes.

In hell the rabisu live in the Desert of Anguish, attacking new souls as they arrive on the Road of Bone, which leads to the City of the Dead. On earth they hide in lavatories, near rivers, and in shadows.

These demons are susceptible to pure sea salt; a person can bar them from crossing a threshold by pouring it in a line across it. It is advised not to step onto their footprints, as this will cause them to attack. Performing the Shurpu ritual and prayers to the god Marduk is said to banish these demons (see also ŠULAK).

Sources: Jastrow, *Religion of Babylonia and Assyri*, 260; Scurlock, *Diagnoses in Assyrian and Babylonian Medicine*, 162, 254, 287, 292, 328, 330, 451, 460; Thompson, *Semitic Magic*, 30–40, 44, 100; Widengren, *Accadian and Hebrew Psalms of Lamentation as Religious Documents*, 198, 202, 283.

Rablion

In the *Theurgia Goetia*, the second book of the *Lemegeton*, Duke Rablion is listed as one of the eleven SERVITORS OF PAMERSIEL (see DUKES OF HELL and PAMERSIEL). A nocturnal AERIAL DEVIL, this demon is known to be very useful at driving out spirits from haunted places, as it has the ability to exorcise lesser spirits; however, he is also an expert liar and easily tells any secrets he knows. Arrogant and stubborn, this demon must be summoned from the second floor of a home or in a wide open space.

Sources: Guiley, *The Encyclopedia of Demons and Demonology*, 196; Mathers, *The Goetia: Lesser Key of Solomon*, 64; Mysticalgod, *Magical Advice*, Part 5, 28; Peterson, *Lesser Key of Solomon*, 64.

Rachiar

The *Sacred Magic of Abramelin the Mage*, book two, names Rachiar ("the sea breaking on the

rocks") as one of the one hundred eleven SERVI-
TORS OF AMAYMON, ARITON, ORIENS, AND PAY-
MON (see AMAYMON, ARITON, ORIENS, and
PAYMON).

Sources: Ford, *Bible of the Adversary*, 88; Mathers,
Book of the Sacred Magic of Abra-Melin, 113; Von
Worms, *Book of Abramelin*, 244.

Rad

According to Enochian lore, Rad is a CACO-
DAEMON (see ENOCHIAN CACODAEMONS).

Source: Chopra, *Academic Dictionary of Mythology*,
242.

Raderaf

In the *Sacred Magic of Abramelin the Mage*,
book two, Raderaf is listed as one of the forty-
nine SERVITORS OF BEELZEBUB (see BEELZE-
BUB). This name is possibly Greek and may mean
"a rose bearer."

Sources: Ford, *Bible of the Adversary*, 93; Mathers,
Book of the Sacred Magic of Abra-Melin, 108; Susej, *Demonic Bible*, 259; Von Worms, *Book of Abramelin*, 253.

Ragalim

In *Ars Goetia*, the first book of the *Lemegeton*,
Ragalim ("feet") is listed as one of the fifty-three
SERVITORS OF ASHTAROTH AND ASMODEUS (see
ASHTAROTH and ASMODEUS).

Sources: Ford, *Bible of the Adversary*, 90; Mathers,
Book of the Sacred Magic of Abra-Melin, 106; Susej, *Demonic Bible*, 257; Von Worms, *Book of Abramelin*, 256.

Ragamuffin

Variations: Alud Muffy, Rag mna's roll, Rag
of Muffian, Rag of Muffin, Ragamoffin, Ragamoffyn, Raggamouff (1591), Raggedemuffins
(1622), Raggmuffin ("dangerous scoundrel"),
Rigmarole

The word *ragamuffin* (Ragamoffyn) first appeared in text in 1393 in the poem *Piers Plowman*
(1360–1387) by William Langland, as the name
of a demon whose "bel-syre" is BELIAL.

Sources: Liberman, *Analytic Dictionary of English
Etymology*, 181, 182; Liberman, *Word Origins and How
We Know Them*, 74; Russell, *Lucifer, the Devil in the
Middle Ages*, 249; Wray, *Birth of Satan*, 25.

Ragaras

In the *Sacred Magic of Abramelin the Mage*,
book two, Ragaras is among the one hundred
eleven SERVITORS OF AMAYMON, ARITON,
ORIENS, AND PAYMON (see AMAYMON, ARITON,
ORIENS, and PAYMON). His name is possibly
Coptic and may translate to mean "bow the head"
or "to incline."

Sources: Ford, *Bible of the Adversary*, 89; Mathers,
Book of the Sacred Magic of Abra-Melin, 105; Susej, *Demonic Bible*, 197; Von Worms, *Book of Abramelin*, 245.

Raghoshi

Variations: Rakoshi, RAKSHASA

Raghoshi is a RAKSHASA in Filipino demonology. He has the ability to shape-shift into
the form of someone you know and trust in order
to get what he wants from you.

Sources: Fansler, *Filipino Popular Tales*, 53.

Raguhel

Originally a saint, Raguhel's canonization was
removed by Pope Zachary in 745 C.E., when
Zachary "unearthed and turned out of the saintly
calendar" demons who had been passing themselves off as saints, such as ORIBEL, Raguhel, and
TOBIEL (see CHURCH CONDEMNED ANGELS).

Sources: Davidson, *Dictionary of Angels*, 238; Hugo,
Toilers of the Sea, Vol. 1, 6; Rudwin, *Devil in Legend
and Literature*, 28, 62.

Rahab

Variations: The Angel of the Sea, The Angel
of Violence, "the crooked serpent," "Dragon of
Darkness," "Dragon of the Moon," Rahab Seriel,
Ramuel, SERIEL, VACHMIEL; may also be the
demon TANNIN

Named in the Book of Job, the Talmud, and
various medieval hierarchies, the demon Rahab
is ranked as the guardian angel of Egypt, one of
the seven PRINCES OF HELL, and the prince of
the ocean. He commands ten chiefs, one hundred
servitors, the sea, and the demons AMMIEL,
CASSIEL, DANIEL, EMARFIEL, LARMIEL,
MARFIEL, ORMIJEL, PERMIEL, QUORIEL,
SARDIEL, and STURBIEL. In Enochian lore he is
known as Ramuel, one of the two hundred angels
who aligned themselves with SAMIAZA. It was
Rahab who rescued the book of the angel Raziel
("secret of God") when it had been thrown into
the ocean by envious angels who did not want
Adam to have the knowledge it contained.

The demon of the sea, Rahab, whose name
means "arrogance," "large," "noise," and "tumult"
in Hebrew, is said to have existed at the creation
of the world. He appears before his summoner as
a woman riding upon a donkey, as a water-
dragon, or as a whirlwind. Most powerful during
the fourth hour, he attacks like a raging monster,
creating huge waves and causing the ocean to roar
(see LEVIATHAN and TIAMAT). Possibly having
lived in the Red Sea, Rahab suffers with unbe-
lievable pride and insolence, so much so that it
is said in some sources that he was kicked to
death by God for his disobedience.

Sources: Barton, *Journal of Biblical Literature*, Vols.
30–31, 165; Dalley, *Myths of Mesopotamia*, 228–77;
Fishbane, *Great Dragon Battle and the Talmudic Redaction*, 41–55; Schwartz, *Tree of Souls*, 36, 106–7, 116.

Rahu

Variations: Abhra-pisacha ("demon of the sky"), the Crooked Serpent, Rahu Ketu, the Tormentor

Rahu ("to abandon" or "void") is an ASURAS in Vedic demonology. The prince of the DAITYAS, Rahu was born the son of Viprachitta and Sinhika. Disguised as a god, a snake demon sat between the sun and moon while gods and demons alike came together to produce the nectar of immortality. Lord Visnu saw the snake and cut its head off but it had already consumed a drop of the nectar; the head was called Rahu and the body Ketu.

Rahu has an unquenchable hatred for the powers of righteousness. He rides a chariot with his mouth open, ready to eat the moon or sun, his personal adversaries. The chariot he rides is pulled by eight black horses. Occasionally he is depicted as riding an owl or reclining in a sedan. He has been described as a dragon head without a body or a black man riding a lion. In Tibet he is portrayed as having nine heads and the body of a snake.

Rahu causes lunar and solar eclipses and the worship of him prevents attacks from other evil spirits. Unable to slay him, Visnu exiled him to the heavens and made him into the constellation Draco.

Sources: Hyatt, *Book of Demons*, 18, 23; Koppedrayer, *Contacts Between Cultures*, 134, 132; Walker, *Hindu World*, 272; Wilkins, *Hindu Mythology, Vedic and Purānic*, 363, 366–7.

Rai Na'in

The rai na'in ("lords of the earth") are a demonic race from the demonology of the Tetum people of Eastern Timor. Considered to be the demons of all the bounty of the earth, they are described as having large knuckled hands; powerful, long arms; and stubby legs. Rai na'in consume human souls, preferring those of children and women. They sit upon a person's chest at night and squeeze their neck until the victim falls unconscious. Sure sign of an attack from one of these demons is waking up with bruises on your chest, neck, and shoulders. The rai na'in live in sacred realms in ancient trees, bamboo groves, chasms, caves, hills, forests, strange-looking rocks, and whirlpools. The easiest way to keep them from attacking is to stay off their sacred groves and respect them with offerings.

Sources: Hicks, *Tetum Ghosts and Kin*, 35, 38, 40, 128; Jones, *Evil in Our Midst*, 173–6; Royal Anthropological Institute, *Journal of the Royal Anthropological Institute*, Vol. 13, 42.

Raiju

Companion of Raijin, Shinto god of lightning, the raiju ("thunder animal" or "thunder beast") is a demonic creature in Japanese demonology. The demon of lightning, a raiju is described as looking like a cat, badger, ball of fire, ball of lightning, monkey, *tanuki* (Japanese raccoon dog), weasel, a white and blue wolf, and a wolf wrapped in lightning (its body is made of lightning and its cry sounds like thunder).

Attacking only during thunderstorms, the raiju is normally calm and harmless, but if it falls asleep in its favorite place, inside a person's navel, Raiden, god of thunder and lightning, will shoot bolts at it to wake it up, usually killing the person. These creatures become extremely agitated during thunderstorms, jumping from tree to tree. Lightning strikes on trees and houses are said to be the claw marks of the raiju.

Sources: Ashkenazi, *Handbook of Japanese Mythology*, 276; Chopra, *Academic Dictionary of Mythology*, 243; Hearn, *Glimpses of Unfamiliar Japan*, 116; Littleton, *Gods, Goddesses, and Mythology*, Vol. 1, 406; Smith, *Complete Idiot's Guide to World Mythology*, 280.

Raja Hantu

Variations: Batara Guru, HANTU PEMBURU ("ghost huntsman")

In Malay demonology, Raja Hantu, also known as the "King of Specters," is a type of TERRESTRIAL DEVIL. His assaults can be prevented by leaving offerings of cooked eggs for him and raw eggs for his followers.

Sources: Hastings, *Encyclopedia of Religion and Ethics*, 355; National Psychological Association, *Psychoanalytic Review*, Vol. 20, 48; Skeat, *Malay Magic*, 418; Smedal, *Order and Difference*, 40, 42.

Rako

From the demonology of the Hausa people of West Africa comes a species of AERIAL DEVIL known as rako ("escorting"). A demon of illness, it has no physical form and preys on the elderly, causing them to feel sleepy and weak. To save a rako victim, someone knowledgeable of them must perform their spirit dance during which the cause and cure will be discovered. Cures usually involve animal sacrifice, typically a bird, but of a specific age, gender, and color.

Sources: Knappert, *African Mythology*, 106; Newman, *Hausa-English Dictionary*, 166; Robinson, *Dictionary of the Hausa Language*, Vol. 1, 286; Tremearne, *Ban of the Bori*, 341.

Raksas

Variations: Raksasa, Raksava, Srin Po

The raksas ("to protect") is a demonic race in Vedic demonology. They appear as dogs or birds, usually owls or vultures. These nocturnal demons who eat raw animal and human flesh cause bad luck, illness, madness, and muteness in people. Making offerings and sacrifices while chanting "Eat the one to whom you belong, eat him who has sent you, eat your own flesh" is the only way to save someone who has fallen prey to the raksas. Shape-shifters and users of magic, they are sometimes kept as a FAMILIAR by particularly evil magicians. They are especially powerful under the light of the new moon and during childbirth, funerals, and marriage ceremonies.

The collective adversaries of the raksas are the devas. These demons are also driven back and repelled by sunlight and are powerless in the east. Interestingly, they have the odd disadvantage of not being able to step over shrubbery, stones, or water, or to cross a meadow.

In Vedic mythology there are no named raksas, although there are some that are alleged not to be evil.

Sources: Griswold, *Religion of the Rigveda*, 92, 95, 240; Oldenberg, *Religion of the Veda*, 133, 257, 259; Shendge, *Civilized Demons*, 107, 124.

Rakshasas

Variations: Ramayana

In the Hinduism practiced in India, there is a vampiric race of demons known as the rakshasas that was created by Brahma to protect the ocean from those who sought to steal the secret elixir of immortality. These demons are part human and part animal, but the human-to-animal ratio varies widely depending on the source being cited. Most often the animal mix is said to be tiger. The *Vedas,* a Hindu religious text, describes the beings as having five legs and a body completely covered in blood. Modern descriptions of rakshasas add that they have fangs and the ability to use magic.

When not protecting the elixir of immortality, the rakshasas are said to live in the treetops; however, they will often wander in cemeteries where they will disrupt services and religious incantations. When hunting for humans to feed upon, the male of the species will stay up in the treetops and wait for its favorite prey to pass underneath: infants or pregnant women. Then, the rakshasas will vomit down onto them, killing them. Female rakshasas, called rakshasis, have the ability to shape-shift into beautiful women, and in that guise will lure men off to a discreet location in order to attack them, draining them of their blood.

There is a belief that if a child can be persuaded to eat human brains, he will transform into this vampiric creature. A type of sorcerer is said to exist that follows the rakshasas' activities closely, as they will consume the uneaten remains of a rakshasas kill. This act is called *yatu-dhana.*

Rakshasas can be killed if an exorcism is performed on them, but prolonged exposure to sunlight and burning them to ash works as well (see also RAVANA).

Sources: Crooke, *Introduction to the Popular Religion,* 124, 154–58, 234, 320; Curran, *Vampires,* 137; Hyatt, *Book of Demons,* 15, 20, 22; Knapp, *Machine, Metaphor, and the Writer,* 161–62, 171; Walker, *Hindu World,* 277, 280, 292.

Raktavija

Variations: Raktabhija, Raktabij, Raktabija

In Vedic demonology Raktavija ("blood seed") is an ASURAS. This general commands a mighty army of elephants, horses, and men and used them when he fought with Shumbha and Nishumbha against DURGA and KALI. Raktavija was very difficult to kill because whenever a drop of his blood was spilled, as soon as it hit the ground a duplicate of him was formed. Eventually he was slain by the goddess Kali, who drank up his blood as it was shed in combat.

Sources: Srivastava, *Iconography of Sakti,* 75, 111; Wilkins, *Hindu Gods and Goddesses,* 305; Wilkins, *Hindu Mythology, Vedic and Purānic,* 255.

Ralaratri

There is a vampiric witch in India that is called a *ralaratri* ("black night"). Accompanied by cats, one of which is her FAMILIAR, she is described as having eyebrows that have grown together, full lips, large cheeks, and suspiciously large and predominant teeth. Beyond having her own type of witchcraft, the ralaratri has an array of abilities, including controlling storms, prophesying, potion brewing, and shape-shifting into a tiger. It is usually in her tiger form that the ralaratri will hunt for humans to kill, but she will revert to her human self to eat their flesh.

The ralaratri in tiger form is notoriously difficult, as well as dangerous, to kill. It is suggested that the better route would be to follow or track the tiger back to the ralaratri's home and wait until she has assumed her human form. Then, before she can cast her magic or shape-shift again, her teeth must be smashed in, as this will remove her powers. Once stripped of her magic and abilities, the ralaratri is completely helpless and can be killed by any method that would kill a human.

Sources: Baskin, *Dictionary of Satanism,* 272; Masters, *Eros and Evil,* 188; Spence, *Encyclopædia of Occultism,* 226; Wedeck, *Dictionary of Pagan Religions,* 77.

Ramaratz

In the *Sacred Magic of Abramelin the Mage*, book two, Ramaratz ("raised ground or earth") is among the one hundred eleven SERVITORS OF AMAYMON, ARITON, ORIENS, AND PAYMON (see AMAYMON, ARITON, ORIENS, and PAYMON).

Sources: Ford, *Bible of the Adversary*, 89; Forgotten Books, *Book of the Sacred Magic of Abramelin the Mage*, 127; Mathers, *Book of the Sacred Magic of Abra-Melin*, 105; Susej, *Demonic Bible*, 197.

Rameriel

In the *Ars Paulina*, the third book of the *Lemegeton*, Rameriel is listed as one of the fifteen Duke SERVITORS OF SCOX (see SCOX) as well as one of the fifteen SERVITORS OF SASQUIEL (see SASQUIEL). He commands 5,550 servitors of his own.

Sources: Charles, *Book of Enoch*, 67; Ladd, *Commentary on the Book of Enoch*, 222; Lévi, *History of Magic*, 38; Peterson, *Lesser Key of Solomon*, 114; Trithemius, *Steganographia*, 95.

Ramiel

Variations: Rameel ("Evening of God"), Râmîêl, REMIHIL, Rumael, Rumjal

In Enochian lore, Ramiel ("thunder of God") is said to be one of the CHIEF OF TENS who swore allegiance to SAMIAZA, rebelled against God, took a human wife, and fathered the NEPHILIM (see FALLEN ANGELS, GRIGORI, and WATCHERS). Ramiel was formerly of the Order of Archangels.

Sources: Barton, *Journal of Biblical Literature*, Vols. 30–31, 165; Laurence, *Foreign Quarterly Review*, Vol. 24, 370; Horne, *Sacred Books and Early Literature of the East*, 114; Lumpkin, *Fallen Angels, the Watchers, and the Origins of Evil*, 31.

Ramisiel

Ranked as a chief in the *Lemegeton, the Lesser Key of Solomon*, Ramisiel is listed as one of the fifteen SERVITORS OF SCOX (see SCOX) one of the ten SERVITORS OF SAZQUIEL (see SAZQUIEL).

Sources: Waite, *The Book of Ceremonial Magic*, 67.

Ramison

The *Sacred Magic of Abramelin the Mage* names Ramison as one of the twenty SERVITORS OF AMAYMON (see AMAYMON). His name is Hebrew and translates to mean "creepers," or rather "to move with a particular creeping motion."

Sources: Forgotten Books, *Book of the Sacred Magic of Abramelin the Mage*, 42–3; Mathers, *Book of the Sacred Magic of Abra-Melin*, 122; Von Worms, *Book of Abramelin*, 257.

Raner

In the *Ars Goetia*, the first book of the *Lemegeton*, Raner is listed as one of the fifty-three SERVITORS OF ASHTAROTH AND ASMODEUS (see ASHTAROTH and ASMODEUS). This name is possibly Greek or Hebrew and may translate as "singing" or "watering."

Sources: Ford, *Bible of the Adversary*, 89; Mathers, *Book of the Sacred Magic of Abra-Melin*, 115; Von Worms, *Book of Abramelin*, 256.

Rantiel

Variations: RECIEL

In the *Lesser Key of Solomon*, Rantiel is ranked as a duke and listed as one of the sixteen SERVITORS OF GEDEIL (see DUKES OF HELL and GEDEIL). This nocturnal demon commands twenty servitors.

Source: Peterson, *Lesser Key of Solomon*, 72.

Rapganmea

Variations: LABARTU

In Acadian demonology a rapganmea is a type of demonic spirit that is frightening to look upon.

Sources: Jastrow, *Religion of Babylonia and Assyria*, 260; Lenormant, *Chaldean Magic*, 37.

Rapganmekhab

Variations: Akhkharu

In Chaldean demonology a rapganmekhab is a type of demonic ghost that preys on humans for their blood. Demons of hunger, they drink blood from their victims in the hopes that if they consume enough of it that one day, they will be transformed into humans.

Sources: Conway, *Demonology and Devil-Lore*, Vol. 1, 49, 55; Lenormant, *Chaldean Magic*, 37; Sayce, *Lectures on the Origin and Growth of Religion*, 308; Susej, *Demonic Bible*, 240.

Rapsel

In *Ars Paulina*, book three of the *Lemegeton*, Rapsel is one of the twelve chief dukes of AMENADIEL (see DUKES OF HELL and SERVITORS OF AMENADIEL). He commands three thousand servitors.

Source: Peterson, *Lesser Key of Solomon*, 62.

Rasetsu

In Vedic demonology Rasetsu is a tutelary deity that was once introduced to Buddhism; it is essentially a RAKSAS or an ONI demon. The name is Japanese and means "to castrate," more literally "to cut the penis."

The rasetsu prey upon those who were evil in life, torturing them and feeding upon their flesh. They can be found near the outer wall of kongo-kai and taizo-kai mandala (see also JURASETSU-NYO).

Sources: Bakshi, *Hindu Divinities in Japanese Buddhist Pantheon*, 137, 147, 152; Hepburn, *Japanese-English and English-Japanese Dictionary*, 498; Thakur, *India and Japan*, 39; Ury, *Tales of Times Now Past*, 28.

Rashaverak

In the *Theurgia Goetia*, the second book of the *Lemegeton*, Rashaverak is said to be one of the four ASSISTANTS OF ASHTAROTH (see also SERVITORS OF ASHTAROTH).

Source: Maberry, *Cryptopedia*, 48, 73.

Rasiel

Variations: Raysiel

The *Theurgia Goetia*, the second book of the *Lemegeton*, ranks Rasiel as the prince of the North and lists him as one of the six SERVITORS OF TURAEL (see PRINCES OF HELL and TURAEL). This demon of the North commands fifty duke servitors of the day and as many for the night. Rasiel is known to announce secrets in surrenders.

Sources: Gettings, *Dictionary of Demons*, 208; Peterson, *Lesser Key of Solomon*, 85.

Rasphuia

Apollonius of Tyana's *Nuctemeron* (*Night Illuminated by Day*) names Rasphuia as the demon of necromancy. He is most powerful during the first hour.

Source: Lévi, *Transcendental Magic*, 502.

Rath

According to the *Testament of Solomon*, Rath was one of the seventy-two SPIRITS OF SOLOMON that was bound by the king and made to work on the construction of his temple. Rath was made to carry wood. This demon commands an undisclosed number of servitors and has the ability to cause illness and exorcize demons. Appearing as a lion, his personal adversary is the angel Emmanuel.

Sources: Abrahams, *Jewish Quarterly Review*, Vol. 11, 28; Ashe, *Qabalah*, 33.

Rattle Jaguar

From the demonology of the Warao people of Venezuela comes Rattle Jaguar. He is described as looking like a jaguar reclining in a hammock surrounded by human bones. As he rests in the hammock this demon cuts the strings, making a rattle sound that is both hypnotic and compelling to any who hear it.

Sources: Jones, *Evil in Our Midst*, 103; Olsen, *Music of the Warao of Venezuela*, 105–6; Wilbert, *Folk Literature of the Warao Indians*, 463.

Räum

Variations: Aym, HABORYM, Raim, Raum, Raym

According to the *Lemegeton*, Räum ("empty space") is a count and an earl who commands thirty legions. A FALLEN ANGEL, formerly of the Order of Thrones, he is also listed as one of the seventy-two SPIRITS OF SOLOMON (see also COUNTS OF HELL and EARLS OF HELL). The demon of destruction and theft, Räum appears as a blackbird or crow but will take a human form at his summoner's request. He is invoked for his willingness to answer truthfully questions about the past, present, and future, detect a thief, detail out love spells, destroy cities and reputations, reconcile enemies, and steal from the treasury of the king.

Sources: Ashley, *Complete Book of Devils and Demons*, 60, 74; De Laurence, *Lesser Key of Solomon, Goetia*, 35; DuQuette, *Key to Solomon's Key*, 180–1; Ford, *Bible of the Adversary*, 81; Icon, *Demons*, 174; Scott, *London Magazine*, Vol. 5, 378.

Ravana

Variations: The King of (Sri) Lanka

Ravana ("one of terrifying roar"), according to Hindu lore, was once the king of Lanka, faithful to his god, and ruler of a prosperous kingdom. He was said to be brave, courageous, smart, and knew how to use every type of weapon with a degree of skill. It was said that only Lord Shiva himself could kill him. He was further blessed with the ability of flight and invisibility, and could make it rain water, fire, or thousands of arrows. Despite all of this, in his heart Ravana was a pleasure seeker who sought to use his abilities and gifts for his own personal satisfaction, which in turn caused him to become lustful, proud, quick to anger, and filled with jealousy.

Open to corruption, he succumbed and fell from his status as human and devolved into a ten-headed and twenty-armed demon that became the king of the RAKSHASAS. As a demon, he is now driven by his compulsion to drink human blood. A highly skilled shape-shifter, he is also strong enough to split a mountain with his bare hands. Ravana can rip a man's soul right from his body and regenerate lost limbs, and is immune to all the elements of this plane of existence. Should by some means an attack reach his only vulnerable place, his heart, Ravana can be struck dead by any blow or attack that would destroy a human heart. However, he can be resurrected by pouring blood into his mouth.

Sources: Chopra, *Academic Dictionary of Mythology*, 129, 245; Hyatt, *Book of Demons*, 20–1; Lumpkin, *Fallen Angels, the Watchers, and the Origin of Evil*, 126;

Shashi, *Encyclopedia Indica*, 418–39; Summers, *Vampire: His Kith and Kin*, 300; Turner, *Dictionary of Ancient Deities*, 335.

Rax

In the *Sacred Magic of Abramelin the Mage*, Rax ("grape seed") is listed as one of the thirty-two SERVITORS OF ASTAROT (see ASTAROT).

Sources: Ford, *Bible of the Adversary*, 91; Mathers, *Book of the Sacred Magic of Abra-Melin*, 106; Von Worms, *Book of Abramelin*, 256.

Razanil

In Apollonius of Tyana's *Nuctemeron* (*Night Illuminated by Day*) Razanil is named as the demon of onyx. He is most powerful during the tenth hour.

Source: Lévi, *Transcendental Magic*, 507.

Rda

According to Enochian lore, Rda is a CACODAEMON (see ENOCHIAN CACODAEMONS).

Source: Chopra, *Academic Dictionary of Mythology*, 246.

Reahu

Variations: RAHU, Rahu a'surin

Originating in Brahmanist and Buddhist legend and adopted into the demonology of the Khmer people of Cambodia, Reahu is named as the king of the demons and all that is evil. Described as being a round, floating head with bulbous eyes, a lion's nose, and clawlike hands, this tutelary guardian of temples chases the moon and sun on his silver chariot through the sky in order to catch and consume them. When he catches one it causes an eclipse but because he has no body it passes through, causing him to begin his pursuit again.

Sources: Lurker, *Routlege Dictionary of Gods and Goddesses, Devils and Demons*, 300; Rose, *Spirits, Fairies, Leprechauns, and Goblins*, 273, 275; Zepp, *Field Guide to Cambodian Pagodas*, 10, 73.

Reciel

In the *Theurgia Goetia*, the second book of the *Lemegeton*, Reciel, a FALLEN ANGEL, is ranked as a duke and is listed as one of the sixteen SERVITORS OF GEDEIL (see DUKES OF HELL and GEDEIL). This demon is a diurnal AERIAL DEVIL.

Sources: Mysticalgod, *Magical Advice*, Part 5, 32; Peterson, *Lesser Key of Solomon*, 72.

Red Man

Variations: The Red Specter of the Tuileries, Red Spirit (L'Homme Rouge), Redcap, Redcomb

There is a French legend of a demon known as the Red Man. Dressed in red clothes, he is described as having a humped back, cloven feet, one eye, misshapen mouth, prodigious tongue, and small, piercing eyes. This demon of tempests who can command the elements seldom speaks. He is said to appear at Louvre or Tuileries on the eve of a great disaster and disappears as soon as his presence is noticed.

Enraged when his solitude is disrupted, legend says that he lives in old castles and places that were once the scene of crimes or tyranny. The Red Man was last seen during the last day of the Commune by a concierge of the Louvre in 1871 a few hours before Tuileries was burnt to the ground.

Sources: Baskin, *Sorcerer's Handbook*, 495; Daw, *McBrides Monthly Magazine*, Vol. 43, 759–60; Spence, *Encyclopaedia of Occultism*, 335; Wheeler, *Dictionary of the Noted Names of Fiction*, 315.

Reginon

In the *Sacred Magic of Abramelin the Mage*, book two, Reginon ("vigorous ones") is included as one of the twenty-two SERVITORS OF ARITON (see ARITON).

Sources: Forgotten Books, *Book of the Sacred Magic of Abramelin the Mage*, 117; Susej, *Demonic Bible*, 259.

Remiel

Variations: Jeremiel, Râmîêl, URIEL

In Christian and Jewish demonology Remiel is ranked as "Lord of souls awaiting resurrection" and is said to be the leader of the Apostates. His name is among the two hundred angels who swore allegiance to SAMIAZA, rebelled against God, took a human wife, and fathered the NEPHILIM (see FALLEN ANGELS). Remiel is also believed to be an archangel in Islamic traditions. His name is Hebrew and means "compassion of God," "mercy of God," or "thunder of God."

Sources: Charles, *Book of Enoch*, 46; Landman, *Universal Jewish Encyclopedia*, 310; Van der Toorn, *Dictionary of Deities and Demons in the Bible*, 81.

Remmon

Variations: RIMMON

The demon Remmon is only referenced by name and translation, as in 2 Kings 5:18: "In this matter may the LORD pardon your servant: when my master goes into the house of Rimmon to worship there, and he leans on my hand and I bow myself in the house of Rimmon, when I bow myself in the house of Rimmon, the LORD pardon your servant in this matter." Remmon was possibly originally a Syrian deity.

Sources: Ashley, *Complete Book of Devils and Demons*, 76; Jamieson, *Commentary, Critical and Explanatory, on the Old and New Testaments*, Vol. 2, 621;

Weyer, *Witches, Devils, and Doctors in the Renaissance*, 14.

Remoron

In the *Sacred Magic of Abramelin the Mage*, book two, Remoron ("hindering" or "to stay") is listed as one of the one hundred eleven SERVITORS OF AMAYMON, ARITON, ORIENS, AND PAYMON (see AMAYMON, ARITON, ORIENS, and PAYMON).

Sources: Ford, *Bible of the Adversary*, 89; Mathers, *Selected Occult Writings of S.L. MacGregor Mathers*, 105; Susej, *Demonic Bible*, 197; Von Worms, *Book of Abramelin*, 246.

Renove

Variations: Roneue, Roneve

Renove is a count and marquis and is listed among the seventy-two SPIRITS OF SOLOMON. He is summoned for his ability to teach languages (see also COUNTS OF HELL and MARQUIS OF HELL).

Sources: Diagram, *Little Giant Encyclopedia*, 87; Peterson, *Lesser Key of Solomon*, 19, 239; Scott, *London Magazine*, Vol. 5, 378; Shah, *Occultism*, 67.

Requiel

Variations: Zequiel ("swallowing")

According to Enochian lore, Requiel is one of the twenty-eight demonic rulers of the lunar mansions; he has dominion over the mansion Zabadola. This demon encourages unhappy couples to divorce and helps prisoners gain freedom (see also ENOCHIAN RULERS OF THE LUNAR MANSIONS).

Sources: Moura, *Mansions of the Moon for the Green Witch*, 12; Von Goethe, *Goethe's Letters to Zelter*, 377.

Rhotomago

Rhotomago was one of the numerous "farfadets, goblins, and imps" that tormented Alexis-Vincent-Charles Berbiguier de Terre-Neuve du Thym (1765–December 3, 1851), a French author and demonologist who wrote at length on this subject in his bibliography *Les farfadets ou Tous les démons ne sont pas de l'autre monde* (*The Imps or, All the Demons Are Not from the Other World*). It was published in three volumes between 1818 and 1820. In it, Rhotomago is said to be the demonic prince of time who serves under BEELZEBUB. This demon is described as carrying a pitchfork and utilizing weather magic (see PRINCES OF HELL).

Sources: Culianu, *Eros and Magic in the Renaissance*, 155; de Givry, *Witchcraft, Magic and Alchemy*, 143, 145; Dingwall, *Some Human Oddities*, 62.

Ribesal

In Colin de Plancy's *Dictionaire Infernale* (1863), the drawing of Ribesal depicts him as somewhat humanoid, with a very long and pointed nose, arms like that of a lobster but with the left claw missing, his left foot like a rooster's, and his other foot like a goat's. A demonic spirit, this demon causes localized tempests and covers his mountaintop home on the summit of Mount Risemberg with clouds. De Plancy claims that Ribesal is the same entity as Rubezal, who is the prince of the Gnomes.

Sources: Gettings, *Dictionary of Demons*, 209; Kelly, *Who in Hell*, 198.

Richel

As one of the twenty Duke SERVITORS OF SYMIEL (see SYMIEL), Richel is very disobedient, stubborn, and will not appear willingly to his summoner. He shares with the other nocturnal Servitors of Symiel seven hundred ninety servitors among them.

Source: Peterson, *Lesser Key of Solomon*, 88.

Rigios

The *Sacred Magic of Abramelin the Mage* names Rigios ("horrible, terrible") as one of the thirty-two SERVITORS OF ASTAROT (see ASTAROT).

Sources: Mathers, *Book of the Sacred Magic of Abramelin the Mage*, 106; Susej, *Demonic Bible*, 257; Von Worms, *Book of Abramelin*, 256.

Rigolin

Variations: Rigolen

In the *Sacred Magic of Abramelin the Mage*, book two, Rigolin is listed as one of the ten SERVITORS OF AMAIMON AND ARITON (see AMAIMON and ARITON). His name is possibly taken from Hebrew and may mean "to drag down."

Sources: Mathers, *Book of the Sacred Magic of Abramelin the Mage*, 116; Von Worms, *Book of Abramelin*, 121, 248.

Rimmon

Variations: Barku ("lightning"), Damas, REMMON, Rimum, Rimun

Originally an Aramaean deity worshipped at Damascus, a Syrian god of healing, and a Babylonian storm god during the medieval demonology craze, Rimmon ("exalted" or "roarer") was demonized and made into the infernal ambassador in Russia, prince of lightning and storms, and the only doctor in Hell. He is said to be under the command of SAMAEL and RAHAB (see PRINCES OF HELL). Rimmon is a FALLEN ANGEL, formerly of the Order of Archangels. His sign is the pomegranate.

Sources: Chambers, *Book of Days*, 723; Lenormant, *Chaldean Magic*, 182, 205; Patai, *Hebrew Goddess*, 19; Ripley, *American Cyclopaedia*, 795; Severus, *Sixth Book of the Select Letters of Severus*, 274.

Rimog

In the *Sacred Magic of Abramelin the Mage*, book two, Rimog is listed as one of the sixty-five SERVITORS OF KORE AND MAGOTH. His name is possibly taken from Hebrew and may mean "a mare."

Sources: Ford, *Bible of the Adversary*, 92; Forgotten Books, *Book of the Sacred Magic of Abramelin the Mage*, 136; Susej, *Demonic Bible*, 258; Von Worms, *Book of Abramelin*, 251.

Rishk

In Persian and Zoroastrian demonology Rishk is a DEV, the demon of jealousy or the want for more (see also DEVS WHO RESIDE IN MEN).

Source: Ford, *Liber Hvhi*, 116.

Risnuch

In Apollonius of Tyana's *Nuctemeron* (*Night Illuminated by Day*) Risnuch is said to be the demon of agriculture. He is most powerful during the ninth hour.

Source: Lévi, *Transcendental Magic*, 393.

Rocots

In Jean Bodin's *De La Demonomanie Des Sorciers* (*On the Demon Worship of Sorcerers*) published in 1581, rocots are said to be a demonic species born the offspring of women and Incubi (see CAMBION and INCUBUS).

Source: Bodin, *Le Fleau des Demons et Sorciers*, 5, 22.

Roêlêd

Variations: Roelad

One of the seventy-two SPIRITS OF SOLOMON, Roêlêd causes cold and frost as well as pains in the stomach. If the phrase "Iax, bide not, be not warmed, for Solomon is fairer than eleven fathers" is said aloud, this demon will flee.

Sources: Ashe, *Qabalah*, 60; Davidson, *Dictionary of Angels*, 246.

Roffles

According to the *Sacred Magic of Abramelin the Mage*, Roffles ("the lion trembling") is one of the fifteen SERVITORS OF PAYMON (see PAYMON). The name Roffles seems to come from a Hebrew word that means "trembling lion."

Sources: Forgotten Books, *Book of the Sacred Magic of Abramelin the Mage*, 140; Mathers, *Book of the Sacred Magic of Abra-Melin*, 121; Susej, *Demonic Bible*, 259; Von Worms, *Book of Abramelin*, 257.

Roggiol

In the *Ars Goetia*, the first book of the *Lemegeton*, Roggiol is listed as one of the fifty-three SERVITORS OF ASHTAROTH AND ASMODEUS (see ASHTAROTH and ASMODEUS). His name is possibly taken from Hebrew and may mean "to drag down."

Sources: Ford, *Bible of the Adversary*, 90; Mathers, *Book of the Sacred Magic of Abra-Melin*, 115; Susej, *Demonic Bible*, 257; Von Worms, *Book of Abramelin*, 256.

Rogo-Tumu-Here

Rogo-Tumu-Here is a demonic creature from Hawaiian mythology. While Turi-a-faumea and his wife, Hina-arau-riki, were surfing, Rogo-Tumu-Here grabbed Hina and fled to the bottom of the ocean. Tangaroa, a Polynesian god, built Turi a canoe, which they used to sail out over Rogo's home. Baiting a hook with sacred red feathers, they caught the demon and pulled him on the boat, cutting off his tentacles one at a time, until Tangaroa beheaded him, releasing Hina in a font of slime.

Sources: Beckwith, *Hawaiian Mythology*, 268; Turner, *Dictionary of Ancient Deities*, 178.

Rogziel

According to the *Testament of Solomon*, Rogziel ("wrath of God") is one of the seven ANGELS OF PUNISHMENT who are under the command of the ARCHANGELS OF PUNISHMENT. Rogziel is also called the demon of wrath.

Sources: Ashley, *Complete Book of Devils and Demons*, 78; Dennis, *Encyclopedia of Jewish Myth, Magic and Mysticism*, 222; Webster, *Encyclopedia of Angels*, 155.

Rokuro-Kubi

Variations: Rokurokubi

Rokuro-kubi are demonic creatures in Japanese demonology. Thought to have once been humans, through an act of karma they were transformed for their transgressions. Usually appearing as human females by day, at night their faces become horrific and their necks stretch to great lengths or, in some cases, detach from their bodies. Who a rokuro-kubi preys upon varies upon the individual creature's preference; some attack those who broke a particular Buddhist doctrine while others only attack men. At night, the rokuro-kubi's neck elongates or detaches from the body, allowing it to spy on its prey before attacking. As it flies it makes the traditional ghost laughing sound of *kèta-kèta!*

Tricksters by nature, they are compelled to frighten and spy on humans; these demons feed off life energy and drink lamp oil. Some rokuro-kubi live human lives, keeping their demonic nature a secret. Some revel in their nature, and others are not even aware that they are anything other than human.

Sources: Hearn, *Kwaidan*, 81–100; Hearn, *Oriental Ghost Stories*, 63–72; Hearn, *Romance of the Milky Way*, 36–7; Japan Society of London, *Transactions and Proceedings of the Japan Society, London*, Vol. 9, 33–4.

Roler

In the *Sacred Magic of Abramelin the Mage*, book two, Roler is listed as one of the sixty-five SERVITORS OF KORE AND MAGOTH.

Sources: Mathers, *Book of the Sacred Magic of Abramelin the Mage*, 107, 118; Von Worms, *Book of Abramelin*, 250, 256.

Romages

The *Sacred Magic of Abramelin the Mage*, book two, lists Romages as one of the one hundred eleven SERVITORS OF AMAYMON, ARITON, ORIENS, AND PAYMON (see AMAYMON, ARITON, ORIENS, and PAYMON). This name is possibly taken from Hebrew and may mean "to throw and touch."

Sources: Mathers, *Book of the Sacred Magic of Abramelin the Mage*, 105; Susej, *Demonic Bible*, 256; Von Worms, *Book of Abramelin*, 246.

Romerac

The *Sacred Magic of Abramelin the Mage* names Romerac ("violent thunder") as one of the twenty SERVITORS OF AMAYMON (see AMAYMON).

Sources: Forgotten Books, *Book of the Sacred Magic of Abramelin the Mage*, 142; Mathers, *Book of the Sacred Magic of Abra-Melin*, 122.

Romiel

As one of the twenty Duke SERVITORS OF SYMIEL (see SYMIEL), Romiel is very obedient and quick to obey his summoner. He shares with the other diurnal SERVITORS OF SYMIEL seven hundred twenty servitors among them.

Source: Peterson, *Lesser Key of Solomon*, 88.

Romyel

Variations: Remijel, Remÿel, Romÿel

In *Theurgia Goetia*, the second book of the *Lemegeton*, Romyel is ranked as a chief duke and is listed as one of the twelve named SERVITORS OF MACARIEL (see MACARIEL). Commanding four hundred servitors, this demon appears before his summoner in a variety of forms but most typically will choose that of a dragon with a virgin's head. Romyel can be summoned any time of the day or night and is said to be good-natured and willing to obey. Like all AERIAL DEVILS, he is constantly on the move, never staying in any one place for long.

Sources: Peterson, *Lesser Key of Solomon*, 103; Trithemius, *Steganographia*, 141.

Ronobe

Variations: Roneve, Ronove, Ronové, Ronwe

In Christian demonology, Ronobe is ranked as both an earl (or count) and a marquis, commanding twenty (or nineteen, sources vary) legions (see also COUNTS OF HELL, EARLS OF HELL, and MARQUIS OF HELL). He is also listed among the seventy-two SPIRITS OF SOLOMON. Appearing before his summoner in a monstrous form and holding a staff, he is called up for his ability to give good and loyal servants, grant the knowledge of tongues and understanding, humble one's enemies, and to teach the arts and rhetoric. Ronobe has dominion over the planet Jupiter and is most powerful during the month of August. His zodiacal sign is Leo. Ronobe is known as a taker of souls, harvesting them from dying animals and humans.

Sources: Collin de Plancy, *Dictionary of Witchcraft*, 105; Diagram Group, *Little Giant Encyclopedia*, 504; Gettings, *Dictionary of Demons*, 209; Kelly, *Who in Hell*, 203; Waite, *Book of Black Magic and of Pacts*, 173; Wippler, *Complete Book of Spells, Ceremonies, and Magic*, 104.

Rosabis

In Apollonius of Tyana's *Nuctemeron* (*Night Illuminated by Day*), Rosabis is the demon of metals. He is most powerful during the eleventh hour.

Sources: Davidson, *Dictionary of Angels*, 7; Gettings, *Dictionary of Demons*, 23; Lévi, *Transcendental Magic*, 422.

Rosaran

In the *Sacred Magic of Abramelin the Mage*, book two, Rosaran is listed as one of the twenty-two SERVITORS OF ARITON (see ARITON). His name is possibly Hebrew and may mean "evil and wicked."

Sources: Ford, *Bible of the Adversary*, 94; Forgotten Books, *Book of the Sacred Magic of Abramelin the Mage*, 117; Mathers, *Book of the Sacred Magic of Abramelin the Mage*, 108; Susej, *Demonic Bible*, 259; Von Worms, *Book of Abramelin*, 254.

Rosenkranz

In medieval-era German demonology, Rosenkranz ("rose wreath") was said to be the confrere of Kranzlein ("little wreath").

Sources: Carus, *Open Court*, Vol. 43, 472; Rudwin, *Devil in Legend and Literature*, 28, 84, 257; Walker, *Woman's Encyclopedia of Myth and Secrets*, 865.

Rosier

In Father Sebastien Michaelis's *Histoire admirable de la Possession et conversion d'une penitente* (1612), he named the ARCHDEMON Rosier as the patron devil of seduction and the prince of the demonic Order of Dominations (see PRINCES OF HELL). One of the FALLEN ANGELS, formerly of the Order of Dominions, Rosier is the demon of love, lust, seduction, and tainted love. When summoned he appears as a stunningly beautiful man or woman, assuming this guise whenever possible in order to tempt people to fall in love so that they will sin. Rosier has the ability to cause people to fall hopelessly in love, turning them from God and their spouse; he also gives the gift of fanciful and romantic speech. The personal adversary of this demon is Saint Basil.

Sources: Ashley, *Complete Book of Devils and Demons*, 61, 74; Icon, *Demons*, 175; Kaye, *Devils and Demons*, 581; Rachleff, *Occult in Art*, 224; Rose, *Spirits, Fairies, Leprechauns, and Goblins*, 84, 350.

Rpa

According to Enochian lore, Rpa is a CACODAEMON (see ENOCHIAN CACODAEMONS).

Sources: Chopra, *Academic Dictionary of Mythology*, 248; Laycock, *Complete Enochian Dictionary*, 164, 203.

Rrb

According to Enochian lore, Rrb is a CACODAEMON (see ENOCHIAN CACODAEMONS).

Sources: Chopra, *Academic Dictionary of Mythology*, 248; Laycock, *Complete Enochian Dictionary*, 164.

Rrl

According to Enochian lore, Rrl is a CACODAEMON (see ENOCHIAN CACODAEMONS).

Sources: Chopra, *Academic Dictionary of Mythology*, 248; Laycock, *Complete Enochian Dictionary*, 164.

Rsi

According to Enochian lore Rsi is a CACODAEMON (see ENOCHIAN CACODAEMONS).

Sources: Chopra, *Academic Dictionary of Mythology*, 248; Laycock, *Complete Enochian Dictionary*, 164.

Ruach

The *Sacred Magic of Abramelin the Mage*, book two, includes Ruach ("spirit") as one of the one hundred eleven SERVITORS OF AMAYMON, ARITON, ORIENS, AND PAYMON (see AMAYMON, ARITON, ORIENS, and PAYMON).

Sources: Mathers, *Book of the Sacred Magic of Abra-Melin*, 112; Susej, *Demonic Bible*, 256; Von Worms, *Book of Abramelin*, 244.

Ruaniel

In *Ars Paulina*, the third book of the *Lemegeton*, Ruaniel is ranked as a duke and has command of 5,500 servitors. He is listed as one of the fifteen SERVITORS OF SASQUIEL (see SASQUIEL).

Source: Peterson, *Lesser Key of Solomon*, 114.

Ruax

In the *Testament of Solomon*, chapter eighteen specifically, Ruax is named as the first deacon of the zodiac and the demon of headaches, causing migraines and making people think slowly. He is one of the seventy-two SPIRITS OF SOLOMON. Saying the phrase "Michael, imprison Ruax" will cause him to flee.

Sources: Ashe, *Qabalah*, 44, 57; Fleg, *Life of Solomon*, 66; Gager, *Curse Tablets and Binding Spells from the Ancient World*, 59; Porter, *Lost Bible*, 77.

Rudra

Variations: Shiva-Rudra

Tibetan demonology tells us that Shiva, having broken his tantric vow in a previous life, was reborn as the demonic god Rudra ("howler, terrible and horrible"), bringer of storms and violent, egoistical anger and pride. Extremely violent and malevolent, this demon kills the Vedic people and their cattle, befouls their sacrifices to the gods, and destroys grain supplies.

Unable to see his evil ways, Rudra had a horse forced into his rectum which charged through his body, clearing out all impurities as it exploded out of the top of his head. The horse's body was turned green and its mane orange. After his forced conversion, Rudra became known as Hayasrica, The Horse Necked One.

Sources: Chakravarti, *Concept of Rudra-Siva Through the Ages*, 5, 27, 47, 52; Huntington, *Circle of Bliss*, 99, 100, 503; Singh, *Encyclopaedia of Hinduism*, 1086.

Ruffo

In medieval demonology and in various grimoires, Ruffo is listed as the demon of robbery.

Sources: Carus, *Open Court*, Vol. 43, 472; Rudwin, *Devil in Legend and Literature*, 84.

Rukum

In the *Sacred Magic of Abramelin the Mage*, Rukum ("diversified") is listed as one of the fifteen SERVITORS OF PAYMON (see PAYMON).

Sources: Ford, *Bible of the Adversary*, 94; Forgotten Books, *Book of the Sacred Magic of Abramelin the Mage*, 116; Mathers, *Book of the Sacred Magic of Abra-Melin*, 108, Susej, *Demonic Bible*, 259.

Rumael

Variations: Raamiel, RAMIEL, Râmîêl, Ramuel, REMIEL, Rumael, Rumel, Rum'el, Rumyal, Rumyel

Rumael ("thunder of God") is a FALLEN ANGEL, formerly of the Third Sphere in Enochian lore. He swore allegiance to SAMIAZA, rebelled against God, took a human wife, and fathered the NEPHILIM.

Sources: Anonymous, *Book of Enoch*, 55; Barton, *Journal of Biblical Literature*, Vols. 30–31, 165; Laurence, *Book of Enoch, the Prophet*, 6, 70; Prophet, *Fallen Angels and the Origins of Evil*, 174; Schodde, *Book of Enoch*, 168.

Ruruhi-Kerepo

Variations: Ruruhikerepo

From the demonology of the Maori people of New Zealand comes the perpetually hungry demon Ruruhi-Kerepo ("blind old woman"). Appearing in isolated and lonely places as an emaciated old and blind woman who cries tears of blood, she lures victims close to her and then unhinges her jaw to consume them, ripping them apart limb by limb; the bones of her victims protrude from her stomach. This demon emits a shrill cry loud enough to stagger a man to his knees. She can also leap long distances, and when she does so it looks as if she were flying.

Sources: Best, *The Maori*, Vol. 1, 212; Jones, *Evil in Our Midst*, 198–200; Reed, *Treasury of Maori Folklore*, 175, 247–8; Simmons, *The Role of the Aged in Primitive Society*, 72.

Rusalka, plural: Rusalki

A rusalka is a species of SUCCUBUS-like water nymph from Slavic lore. Its name loosely translates to mean "mermaid." Rusalki are seen as the demons of the dualistic quality of nature, created when a woman dies an unnatural death, such as in a drowning, dying unbaptized, dying a virgin, or having committed suicide. They are described as looking like pale, lithe, startlingly beautiful women with loose and wild-looking green hair, or as ugly, large-breasted creatures. Most commonly seen in the summer and winter, rusalki prey upon men, using their charms to lure them into the water where they tickle them to death. Controlling the cycles of the moon, these demonic creatures are also said to direct the clouds across the sky, as well as control the weather and the amount of rain that falls. The rusalki are the symbol of life and death and are said to live in the forest near the edge of a river or lake during spring and summer months; they live in the water in the winter months. Each individual rusalka is a unique person with her own tale.

Sources: Andrews, *Dictionary of Nature Myths*, 165; Mack, *Field Guide to Demons, Fairies, Fallen Angels, and Other Subversive Spirits*, 19–21; Phillips, *Forests of the Vampire*, 67; Riasanovsky, *California Slavic Studies*, Vol. 11, 65–6; *Slavic and East European Folklore Association Journal*, Vol. 3, Issue 2, 59, 62.

Rush

Variations: FRIAR RUSH

Rush is a devil from British folklore who is under the command of LUCIFER. Appearing as a young man, he presents himself to religious houses and works there, earning the trust and favor of those within. Once he has won them over, he enables them to sin by providing secrecy and discretion to cover up their lust and greed.

Sources: Briggs, *Dictionary of British Folk-Tales in the English Language*, 255–8; Hazlitt, *National Tales and Legends*, 136.

RuwachRa'

Variations: Ruwach ("breath")

Ruwach is a word that appears in the Old Testament; it is translated from Hebrew to mean "breath." However, since it can be interpreted to mean "a violent exhalation," in rare instances this word has also been used to mean "evil spirit or foul wind" in reference to demons.

Sources: Barnes, *People's Bible Encyclopedia*, 1050; Eubank, *Secrets of the Bible*, 221; Scobie, *Ways of our God*, 242.

RuwachSheqer

Ruwach sheqer is a word that appears in some versions of the Old Testament; it is translated from Hebrew to mean "false or lying spirit" and refers to demons.

Sources: Harris, *Theological Wordbook of the Old Testament*, Vol. 2, 956, Scobie, *Ways of our God*, 242; Van der Torn, *Dictionary of Deities and Demons in the Bible*, 771.

Rxp

According to Enochian lore Rxp is a CACODAEMON (see ENOCHIAN CACODAEMONS).

Sources: Chopra, *Academic Dictionary of Mythology*, 249; Laycock, *Complete Enochian Dictionary*, 164.

Sabanack

Variations: Sab Nac, Sabnac, Sabnach, Sabnack, Sabnacke, Sabnak, Sabnock, Sabrock, Saburac, Saburnac, Salmac, Savnock, Savnok

In the *Ars Goetia*, the first book of the *Lemegeton*, Sabanack is ranked as a marquis and commands fifty legions (see MARQUIS OF HELL). Appearing before his summoner as an armed soldier with a lion head and riding a pale horse, this nocturnal demon is known for his ability to build and fortify camps, cities, and towers. He can also cause incurable wounds and give good FAMILIARs.

Sources: Booth, *Witches of Early America*, 17; De Laurence, *Lesser Key of Solomon, Goetia*, 36; Godwin, *Godwin's Cabalistic Encyclopedia*, 702; Icon, *Demons*, 176; Susej, *Demonic Bible*, 194; Waite, *Book of Black Magic and of Pacts*, 207.

Sabas

In the *Theurgia Goetia*, the second book of the *Lemegeton*, Sabas, a FALLEN ANGEL, is ranked as

a duke and is listed as one of the sixteen SERVI-
TORS OF GEDEIL (see DUKES OF HELL and
GEDEIL). He is a diurnal demon.

Sources: Guiley, *Encyclopedia of Demons and Demonology*, 94; Peterson, *Lesser Key of Solomon*, 72.

Sabrus

In Apollonius of Tyana's *Nuctemeron* (*Night Illuminated by Day*), Sabrus is said to be most powerful during the seventh hour.

Sources: Gettings, *Dictionary of Demons*, 211; Lévi,
Transcendental Magic, 392.

Sachiel

Variations: Zadkiel ("righteousness of God")

In the *Sacred Magic of Abramelin the Mage*,
book two, Sachiel ("covering of God," "to
trample down," or "price of God") is said to be
the angel of the planet Jupiter and one of the one
hundred eleven SERVITORS OF AMAYMON, ARI-
TON, ORIENS, AND PAYMON (see AMAYMON,
ARITON, ORIENS, and PAYMON). This demon is
most powerful on Thursdays.

Sources: Davidson, *Dictionary of Angels*, 252; God-
win, *Godwin's Cabalistic Encyclopedia*, 255; Rose,
Spirits, Fairies, Leprechauns, and Goblins, 345; Susej,
Demonic Bible, 197.

Sachluph

In Apollonius of Tyana's *Nuctemeron* (*Night Illuminated by Day*), Sachluph is the demon of
plants and is most powerful during the second
hour of the day.

Sources: Davidson, *Dictionary of Angels*, 252; Gettings, *Dictionary of Demons*, 211; Lévi, *Transcendental
Magic*, 404.

Sadiel

In *Theurgia Goetia*, the second book of the
Lemegeton, Sadiel is ranked as a duke and is listed
as one of the sixteen SERVITORS OF GEDEIL (see
DUKES OF HELL and GEDEIL). This FALLEN
ANGEL is considered to be a diurnal demon.

Sources: Davidson, *Dictionary of Angels*, 252; Peterson, *Lesser Key of Solomon*, 72; Shadduck, *England's
Amorous Angels*, 347; Trithemius, *Steganographia*, 20.

Saegatanas

Variations: Sargatanas

The *Grimoire of Pope Honorius* (*Le Grimoire du
Pape Honorius*), written in the eighteenth century
allegedly by Pope Honorius III, ranks the demon
Saegatanas as a brigadier general. His demonic
seal resembles a moth or other such winged
insect. He commands three servitor demons,
FORAU, LORAY, and VALAFAR.

Sources: de Givry, *Witchcraft, Magic, amnd Alchemy*,
26, 30; Shah, *Occultism*, 61, 62; Wedeck, *Treasury of
Witchcraft*, 97.

Sagares

In *Ars Goetia*, the first book of the *Lemegeton*,
Sagares is listed as one of the fifty-three SERVI-
TORS OF ASHTAROTH AND ASMODEUS (see
ASHTAROTH and ASMODEUS). His name is
Greek and it translates to mean a "double-headed
axe," specifically like the type used by the Ama-
zons and the Sacae (Scythians).

Sources: Cary, *Herodotus*, 434; Mathers, *Book of the
Sacred Magic of Abramelin the Mage*, 106, 116; Von
Worms, *Book of Abramelin*, 248, 256.

Sagatana

Sagatana, along with NESBIROS, is one of the
two SERVITORS OF ASTAROTH (see ASTAROTH).

Sources: Kuriakos, *Grimoire Verum Ritual Book*, 33;
Masters, *Devil's Dominion*, 130.

Sahirim

Variations: Sa'iyr, Se irim, SE'IRIM

In Hebrew demonology Sahirim ("hairy") is a
demon who is described in the Old Testament as
looking like a goat or satyr.

Sources: Lurker, *Routledge Dictionary of Gods and
Goddesses, Devils and Demons*, 169; Rose, *Spirits, Fairies,
Leprechauns, and Goblins*, 350, 354, 362.

Sair

In Apollonius of Tyana's *Nuctemeron* (*Night Illuminated by Day*), Sair is the demon of "stibium
of the sages," an alchemical term whose exact
meaning has been lost to time. He is said to be
most powerful during the fifth hour.

Sources: Dumas, *Histoire de la Magie*, 81; Lévi,
Transcendental Magic, 391.

Sakhar

Variations: Sakhr ("rock")

According to Arabic lore, Solomon once removed his ring and entrusted it to a favored concubine, Amina, while he bathed. The demon
Sakhar assumed the guise of the king and gained
possession of the ring from her, and thereby assumed the throne. To ensure his rule, the demon
altered Solomon's features by magic, which reduced the king to begging. For forty days the
demon ran amuck in his kingdom. Sakhar,
hoping to ensure his falsely gained power, threw
the ring into the river, believing it would be lost
forever. The ring was eaten by a fish that was later
caught by Solomon. Using the power of the ring,
the king was able to regain his throne. A great
stone was tied around Sakhar's neck and he was
tossed into a deep lake. Other versions say the
demon was sealed in a copper jar and placed between two rocks in the Lake of Tiberias.

Sources: Iliowizi, *Weird Orient*, 197; Seymour, *Tales*

of King Solomon, 180; Schimmel, *Islamic Names*, 50; Tyson, *Power of the Word*, 93.

Sakinis

In Hindu demonology the sakinis ("able ones") are the female attendants of DURGA.

Sources: Daniélou, *Myths and Gods of India*, 288; Dowson, *Classical Dictionary of Hindu Mythology and Religion, Geography, History, and Literature*, 247; Heremann-Pfandt, *Wild Goddesses in India and Nepal*, 39–70; Monier-Williams, *Brahmanism and Hinduism*, 189.

Saleos

Variations: Sallos, ZAEBOS, Zaleos

Saleos is a duke (earl, or grand-count, sources conflict) who commands thirty legions. He appears before his summoner as a crowned brave, gallant, and handsome soldier, riding upon a crocodile. This demon has a peaceable nature and is known for his ability to create love between men and women. He will, if asked, give his summoner love spells (see also COUNTS OF HELL, DUKES OF HELL, and EARLS OF HELL).

Sources: Crowley, *The Goetia*, 36; De Laurence, *Lesser Key of Solomon, Goetia*, 27–8; Godwin, *Godwin's Cabalistic Encyclopedia*, 259; Icon, *Demons*, 176; Peterson, *Lesser Key of Solomon*, 15; Scot, *Discoverie of Witchcraft*, 225; Waite, *Book of Black Magic and Ceremonial Magic*, 201.

Salikotal

A FALLEN ANGEL formerly of the Order of Cherubim, Salikotal, along with BERITH, LAUVIAH, and MAROU, helped place the Tree of Knowledge in the Garden of Eden.

Sources: Icons, *Experimenting*, 343; Maberry, *Cryptopedia*, 78.

Salilus

In Apollonius of Tyana's *Nuctemeron* (*Night Illuminated by Day*), Salilus is the demon of opening doors. He is most powerful during the seventh hour.

Sources: Davidson, *Dictionary of Angels*, 254; Gettings, *Dictionary of Demons*, 211; Lévi, *Transcendental Magic*, 391, 502.

Samael

Variations: ABBADON, "the Adversary," Aminadar, Angel of Death, Angel of Poison, Angel of the Bottomless Pit, Apolloyon, "the Destroyer," Diabolus, EBLIS, Esau-Samael ("Hairy Samael"), IBLIS, "Light Bearer," LUCIFER, Melek Taus, Prince of the Accusers and the Evil Inclination, Salamiel, Samael Aun Weor ("Samael, sexual strength and light"), SAMIAZA, SAMMAEL, Samuel ("heard of God"), SATAN, Satanael ("adversary of God"), Satannael, SHAITAN, URIEL

Originating in Jewish demonology, Samael ("a figure, idol, or image," "poisoned angel," or "venom of God") has been given many titles and ranks, including emperor of Hell, guardian of the third gate in the valley of Ben Hinnom opposite Zion and Jerusalem, the leader of demon locusts from Revelation, and one of the three great princes of Gehenna (see PRINCES OF HELL). Samael is said to be a diurnal FALLEN ANGEL, formerly of the First Sphere, and is called the demon of death. He is an accuser, a destroyer, and a seducer.

Commanding four hundred forty-four servitors, he also has under his service all the spirits of America and Europe as well as the individual demons AGALIAREPT, ELELOGAP, LUCIFER, PUT SATANACHIA, and Tari Himal, or Agrat Bat Mahlat, EISHETH ZENUNIM, LILITH, and NAAMAH (sources vary). He has dominion over the planet Mars and his sacred animal is the snake. It is said that Samael has a deep appreciation of art.

Samael is described as being a handsome, red-headed young man, so attractive in fact that it is difficult for females to resist his charms. He was the seducer of Eve in rabbinical traditions, and when they had intercourse, he injected his filth into her, after which she conceived Cain. It was also Samael who wrestled with the Hebrew patriarch Jacob. His personal adversaries are the angel Metatron and Peter the Apostle.

Sources: Barrett, *The Magus*, 116, 118, 119, 120, 139; Blavatsky, *Secret Doctrine*, 388, 409, 417–8; Dowley, *Introduction to the History of Christianity*, 255; Ginzberg, *Legends of the Jews*, 230, 235; Hall, *Secret Teachings of All Ages*, 298, 351, 356; Lumpkin, *Fallen Angels, the Watchers, and the Origin of Evil*, 126; Schwartz, *Tree of Souls*, 139.

Samalo

In the *Sacred Magic of Abramelin the Mage*, book two, Samalo is listed as one of the forty-nine SERVITORS OF BEELZEBUB (see BEELZEBUB). This name is possibly taken from Hebrew and it may translate to mean "his image."

Sources: Ford, *Bible of the Adversary*, 93; Mathers, *Book of the Sacred Magic of Abramelin the Mage*, 120.

Samana

Variations: Akhu-demon

In ancient Egyptian, Mesopotamian, and Sumerian demonology, there is a species of demon known as the samana that preys upon prostitutes, young men, and women. These demons have dragonlike teeth, eagle claws, lion mouths, and the tail of a scorpion. They block the virility of young men, cause fevers and an infectious disease, prevent prostitutes from performing their services, and put a stop to the menstruation of young girls.

Sources: Black, *Gods, Demons, and Symbols of Ancient Mesopotamia*, 153; Golan, *Prehistoric Religion*, 269; Leick, *Sex and Eroticism in Mesopotamian Literature*, 223; Najovits, *Trunk of the Tree*, 93; Pinch, *Magic in Ancient Egypt*, 45.

Samax

Samax is a demon who originated in Elizabethan demonology and appears for the first time in print in a book titled *An Elizabethan Devil-Worshiper's Prayer-Book*, which was possibly written by John Dee. Samax is said to be under the command of the demon VERCAN. He is described as having a rack of antlers upon his head and rides upon a pantherlike animal that has a bushy tail. Samax has dominion over the planet Mars.

Sources: Anonymous, *Manuscripts and Books on Medicine, Alchemy, Astrology and Natural Sciences Arranged in Chronological Order*, 239; Summers, *A Popular History of Witchcraft*, 91.

Sameveel

Variations: SAMAEL, SAMMAEL

Enochian lore names Sameveel as one of the FALLEN ANGELS who swore allegiance to SAMIAZA, rebelled against God, took a human wife, and fathered the NEPHILIM.

Sources: Davidson, *Dictionary of Angels*, 256; Spence, *Encyclopaedia of Occultism*, 148.

Samiaza

Variations: AMAZARAK, Amezarak, AMEZYARAK, Azaziel, AZZA, Samiazaz, Samiyaza, Samjaza, Samjâzâ, Samlazaz, SAMMAEL, Samyasa, Samyaza, Semiaxas, Sêmîazâz, Semihazah, Semiyaza, Semjâzâ, Semyazah, ShamHazai, Shamhazzai, Shemhazai, Shemyaza, Shemyazaz, Shenhazai, Uzza

In Christian and Jewish demonology, Samiaza is a FALLEN ANGEL, formerly of the Order of Seraphim. He was the CHIEF OF TENS who, along with two hundred other angels, swore allegiance in a rebellion against God (see CHIEF OF THE GRIGORI and WATCHERS). His coupling with human women resulted in giant offspring, the NEPHILIM. He went on to teach mankind botany, enchantments, herbology, and root-cuttings. After Anah (Ishtar or NAAMAH; sources vary), the granddaughter of Cain, revealed her explicit name to him, Samiaza carried her off to live on another planet. Samiaza's name is taken from Hebrew and is translated in various ways to mean "famous arrogance," "he sees the name," "infamous rebellion," "named the strong," or "the name Azza or Uzza."

The archangel Michael bound Samiaza and his co-conspirators, and then the archangel incited a war among the Nephilim knowing that they would kill one another. The rebellious angels were held in custody for seventy generations in the valleys of the earth until their judgment day; then they were cast into an abyss of eternal fire for all eternity.

Sources: Ashe, *Qabalah*, 14; Charles, *Apocrypha and Pseudepigrapha of the Old Testament*, 191, 192, 193, 194; Fordham, *Collected Works*, 412–22; Horne, *Sacred Books and Early Literature of the East*, 56; Langton, *Essentials of Demonology*, 109–10, 122; Laurence, *Foreign Quarterly Review*, Vol. 24, 370; Lumpkin, *Fallen Angels, the Watchers, and the Origins of Evil*, 31; Voltaire, *Essays and Criticisms*, 106.

Samiel

In the *Theurgia Goetia*, the second book of the *Lemegeton*, Samiel ("blind god") is a chief duke who is listed as one of the twelve SERVITORS OF HYDRIEL (see HYDRIEL). Samiel is a FALLEN ANGEL, and according to the Apocryphal of Peter, an "immortal angel of God." Commanding 1,320 servitors, this demon appears before his summoner as a serpent with a virgin's face and head or as a blind, evil, and malformed being. Able to be summoned any time of the day or the night, Samiel is said to be very courteous and willing to obey. He can usually be found in or near marshes, water, or wetlands.

Sources: Davidson, *Dictionary of Angels*, 256; Peterson, *Lesser Key of Solomon*, 90, 95; Voltaire, *Essays and Criticisms*, 106.

Samigina

Variations: GAMIGIN

Samigina is a marquis who commands thirty legions (see MARQUIS OF HELL). When summoned he appears as a donkey or small horse but will take a human guise at his summoner's request. He speaks with a hoarse voice. This demon is known for his willingness to answer questions asked of him but in his own time. He will also give an account of all the souls that died in sin or drowned at sea, teach the liberal sciences, and make those souls that dwell in purgatory appear in a ghostly form.

Sources: Crowley, *The Goetia*, 29; De Laurence, *Lesser Key of Solomon, Goetia*, 22–23; DuQuette, *Key to Solomon's Key*, 162.

Samil

Variations: Salmael, SAMMAEL, SATAN, Satanil, Seir

In the *Lemegeton*, Samil ("poisoned angel") is the demon of death and is ranked as the chief of the Satans, magician, Prince of Demons, and ruler of the sixth hour of the day (see PRINCES OF HELL). Samil, a diurnal demon, commands ten chiefs, five of which are Araebel, Charuch, Medussusiel, Nathaniel ("gift of God"), and Perniel; as well as one hundred servitors, among which are Farsiel, Jamiel, Joustriel, Sameon, and Zamion.

Sources: Bastow, *Biblical Dictionary*, 375; Davidson, *Dictionary of Angels*, 84, 161, 187, 255, 256; Lumpkin, *Fallen Angels, the Watchers, and the Origin of Evil*, 127; Trithemius, *Steganographia*, 97; Waite, *Book of Black Magic and Ceremonial Magic*, 67.

Sammael

Variations: Ophiomorphus, Salmael, SAMAEL, SAMIEL, SAMIL, SATAN, Satanael ("adversary of God"), Satanil, Seir, Simoon, Smoel, Sumiel, Zamael

Originating in Rabbinical lore, Sammael ("poisoned angel" or "venom of god") has been ranked by various grimoires as the Angel of Egypt, chief of all the Satans, executioner, king of volcanoes, prince of air, and prince of demons (see PRINCES OF HELL). Historically, this storm demon has been called a FALLEN ANGEL, but new sources claim that he is still in service to God. When he was an angel, it is said that he had twelve wings and carried a gall-tipped sword. This demon of death is the mate to AGRAT-BAT-MAHLAHT, EISHETH ZENUNIM, LILITH, NAAMAH, and all angels of prostitution. Having dominion over the planet Mars, Sammael is an accuser, destroyer, and seducer. He once led a group of angels to earth to trick Adam into sinning; in the guise of the serpent, he tempted Eve in paradise. He accused Abraham of selfish piety and brought about the death of Moses. Sammael carries out the death sentences ordered by God. He is said to fly through the air like a bird.

As one of the uncircumcised mates of LILITH, Sammael fathered a huge family of demons. The dark patches seen on the moon's surface are said to be his excrement.

Sources: Davidson, *Dictionary of Angels*, 255; Dowley, *Introduction to the History of Christianity*, 255; Hyatt, *Book of Demons*, 50; Lewis, *Satanism Today*, 238; Lumpkin, *Fallen Angels, the Watchers, and the Origin of Evil*, 127; Priest, *Anti-Universalist*, 334; Voltaire, *Essays and Criticisms*, 106.

Samnu

Although listed as a demon from central Asia in Anton S. LeVey's *Satanic Bible*, "samnu" is most likely an oil used in religious ceremonies and not a demonic being.

Sources: Haldar, *Associations of Cult Prophets Among the Ancient Semites*, 64, 204; King, *Babylonian Magic and Sorcery*, 65, 178; LeVey, *Satanic Bible*, 60.

Samsapeel

Variations: Samsapeel Samsaveel, Samsawiel, SHAMSHIEL ("light of day"), SIMAPESIEL, Simapisiel, Simipesiel

In Enochian lore Samsapeel ("harkens to the mouth of God") is said to be a CHIEF OF TENS, one the FALLEN ANGELS who swore allegiance to SAMIAZA, rebelled against God, took a human wife, and fathered the NEPHILIM (see GRIGORI and WATCHERS). He went on to teach mankind about the eclipses, equinoxes, and solstices.

Sources: Barton, *Journal of Biblical Literature*, Vols. 30–31, 165; Beard, *Autobiography of Satan*, 113; Davidson, *Dictionary of Angels*, 256; Lévi, *History of Magic*, 38; Montgomery, *Journal of Biblical Literature*, 165, 166; Laurence, *Book of Enoch, the Prophet*, 6; Lumpkin, *Fallen Angels, the Watchers, and the Origins of Evil*, 31.

Sanguisuga

In medieval times, in Latin, the word *sanguisuga* was translated as "bloodsucking corpse." It is Italian for "bloodsucker" or "leech." In medieval England, however, Sanguisuga was thought to be a vampiric demon who was also a disease carrier.

Sources: Bunson, *Vampire Encyclopedia*, 5, 231; Davies, *Magic, Divination, and Demonology Among the Hebrews and Their Neighbours*, 96; Summers, *Vampire: His Kith and Kin*, 202.

Sangye Khado

Sangye Khado is the queen of the KHADO (the female DJINN). She is a SUCCUBUS-like Djinn who can fly through the air and is especially kind to humans. This demon does not have a human-like mind but rather acts on animal instinct. She is essentially the Buddha Dakini from Hindu lore and LILITH of Hebrew lore.

Sources: Blavatsky, *Secret Doctrine*, 298; Schlagintweit, *Buddhism in Tibet*, 248; Turner, *Dictionary of Ancient Deities*, 268, 414.

Santanackia

Variations: SATANACHIA

Santanackia is said to be one of the two SERVITORS OF LUCIFER (see LUCIFER).

Sources: Waite, *Unknown World 1894–1895*, 230; Wedeck, *Treasury of Witchcraft*, 96.

Sapason

In the *Sacred Magic of Abramelin the Mage*, book two, Sapason is listed as one of the twenty-two SERVITORS OF ARITON (see ARITON). His name is possibly taken from Greek and means "to putrefy."

Sources: Ford, *Bible of the Adversary*, 94; Mathers, *Book of the Sacred Magic of Abramelin the Mage*, 122; Susej, *Demonic Bible*, 259; Von Worms, *Book of Abramelin*, 254.

Saphathorael

Saphathorael, the demon of drunkenness, causes drunken stupors, inspires strong political views to be spoken aloud, and causes stumbling. His personal adversaries are the angels Bae, Iacô, Iealô, Iôelet, Ithoth, and Sabaôth. To ward this demon off, on a piece of paper write the angelic names of his adversaries, fold the paper, and then wear it against your ear or around your neck. As Saphathorael leaves, the drunken stupor will dissipate.

Sources: Conybeare, *Jewish Quarterly Review*, Vol. 11, 36; Lamb, *Magic, Witchcraft and the Occult*, 27; Paine, *Hierarchy of Hell*, 65.

Sarabotres

Sarabotres first appeared in Elizabethan demonology in a book titled *An Elizabethan Devil-Worshiper's Prayer-Book*, which was possibly written by John Dee. In service to VERCAN, Sarabotres is described as being green skinned, carrying a scepter, and riding upon a roe. He has dominion over the planet Venus.

Sources: Anonymous, *Manuscripts and Books on Medicine, Alchemy, Astrology and Natural Sciences Arranged in Chronological Order*, 239; Summers, *A Popular History of Witchcraft*, 91.

Saraknyal

Variations: Sarakuyal

According to Enochian lore, Saraknyal was the FALLEN ANGEL who swore allegiance to SAMIAZA, rebelled against God, took a human wife, and fathered the NEPHILIM.

Sources: Davidson, *Dictionary of Angels*, 258; Laurence, *The Book of Enoch, the Prophet*, 6; Lévi, *History of Magic*, 38; Prophet, *Fallen Angels and the Origins of Evil*, 105.

Saraph

In the *Sacred Magic of Abramelin the Mage*, book two, Saraph is listed as one of the one hundred eleven SERVITORS OF AMAYMON, ARITON, ORIENS, AND PAYMON (see AMAYMON, ARITON, ORIENS, and PAYMON). His name means "to burn" or "to devour with fire" in Hebrew.

Sources: Ford, *Bible of the Adversary*, 88; Mathers, *Selected Occult Writings of S.L. MacGregor Mathers*, 105; Susej, *Demonic Bible*, 197; Von Worms, *Book of Abramelin*, 244.

Saraphiel

Variations: Serapiel

In *Ars Paulina*, the third book of the *Lemegeton*, Saraphiel is ranked as a duke who commands 5,550 servitors and is listed as one of the fifteen SERVITORS OF SCOX (see SCOX). He is also listed as one of the ten SERVITORS OF SAZQUIEL (see SAZQUIEL).

Sources: Davidson, *Dictionary of Angels*, 357; Peterson, *Lesser Key of Solomon*, 114; Waite, *Book of Black and Ceremonial Magic*, 67.

Sardiel

In *Ars Paulina*, the third book of the *Lemegeton*, Sardiel is ranked as a chief and is listed as one of the eleven SERVITORS OF RAHAB (see RAHAB).

Sources: Peterson, *Lesser Key of Solomon*, 127; Waite, *The Book of Ceremonial Magic*, 67.

Sardiniel

In *Ars Paulina*, the third book of the *Lemegeton*, Sardiniel is ranked as a chief and is listed as one of the twenty SERVITORS OF VEGUANIEL (see VEGUANIEL).

Source: Waite, *The Book of Ceremonial Magic*, 67.

Sargatanas

Sargatanas is a brigadier major and the general of the Infernal Spirits; with no legions of his own, he does have command over the demons FARAII (FORAU), LORAY, and VALEFAR (VALAFAR). He is under the command of ASHTAROTH. This demon is summoned for his brainwashing abilities, mind reading, and memory erasing and stealing, but he can also give the gift of invisibility and the skill of lovemaking. He can also open locks and transport people to distant places.

Sources: Baskin, *Sorcerer's Handbook*, 276; Chaplin, *Dictionary of the Occult and Paranormal*, 136; Diagram Group, *Dictionary of Unfamiliar Words*, 299; Mark, *Book of Hierarchies*, 28; Waite, *The Book of Ceremonial Magic*, 162; Waite, *Unknown World 1894–1895*, 230; Wedeck, *Treasury of Witchcraft*, 96, 97.

Sariel

Variations: ARIEL ("Lion of God"), Asaradel, Cyril, Esdreel, Juriel, Sahariel, Sarakiel, Saraqel, Sauriel, Seraquel, SERIEL, SURIEL ("command of God"), "Suriel the Angel of Death," "Suriel the Trumpeter," Suriyel, Surya, URIEL, Zerachiel

In Enochian, Islamic, and Judaic lore, it is said that Sariel is one of the FALLEN ANGELS who swore allegiance to SAMIAZA, rebelled against God, took a human wife, and fathered the NEPHILIM. He went on to teach mankind how to use the moon for planting times, how to plot the phases of the moon, and what eclipses really are. In the various lores, this demon holds the ranks of CHIEF OF TENS, duke, prince of the moon, and one of the seven PRINCES OF HELL (see DUKES OF HELL). His name means "command of God," but it has also been translated as "light of God" and "moon of God." Some sources claim that Sariel is feminine.

The name Sariel is also mentioned in the *Sacred Magic of Abramelin the Mage*, book two, where he is listed as a nocturnal demon and as one of the sixteen SERVITORS OF ASELIE (see ASELIE).

Sources: Black, *Book of Enoch, or, I Enoch*, 129; Hayward, *Interpretations of the Name Israel in Ancient Judaism and Some Early Christian Writings*, 297–8; Laurence, *Foreign Quarterly Review*, Vol. 24, 370; Lumpkin, *Fallen Angels, the Watchers, and the Origins of Evil*, 31; Neusner, *Christianity, Judaism and Other Greco-Roman Cults*, 159–65.

Sarikin Bakka

Variations: Ali

From the demonology of the Hausa people of West Africa comes the demon Sarikin Bakka. His name translates to mean "Chief of the bow" or "Chief huntsman." This demonic nature spirit has command over the animals of the forest and can cause madness in humans that can only be cured with a ceremonial dance and the proper animal offered up in sacrifice. The Hausa routinely make sacrifices of a red rooster and a white hen to this demon before the start of a hunting expedition. It is said that Sarikin Bakka lives in a small iron bow.

Sources: Knappert, *African Mythology*, 107; Knappert, *Swahili Culture*, Vol. 2, 653; Tremearne, *Ban of the Bori*, 204, 343.

Saris

In the *Sacred Magic of Abramelin the Mage*, book two, Saris ("a pike or spear") is listed as one of the twenty-two SERVITORS OF ARITON (see ARITON).

Sources: Ford, *Bible of the Adversary*, 94; Mathers, *Selected Occult Writings of S.L. MacGregor Mathers*, 108; Susej, *Demonic Bible*, 259; Von Worms, *Book of Abramelin*, 254.

Sarisel

In the *Sacred Magic of Abramelin the Mage*, Sarisel ("minister of God") is listed as one of the eight SERVITORS OF ORIENS (see ORIENS).

Sources: Ford, *Bible of the Adversary*, 94; Mathers, *Book of the Sacred Magic of Abramelin the Mage*, 108; Susej, *Demonic Bible*, 259; Von Worms, *Book of Abramelin*, 253.

Sarkany

Sarkany is a demon of weather in Hungarian folklore. Born the son of the witch Boszorkany, he has either seven, eight, nine, or twelve heads (sources vary) and wields a morning star and sword. Mounted upon his charger, he rides through the thunderclouds, oftentimes accompanied by a magician. Sarkany ("a dragon") lives in the underworld and has the power to turn people into stone. As his power lies in his heads, he becomes weaker with the decapitation of each head.

Sources: Hoppál, *Studies on Mythology and Uralic Shamanism*, 66; Lurker, *Routledg Dictionary of Gods and Goddesses, Devils and Demons*, 310; Rose, *Spirits, Fairies, Leprechauns, and Goblins*, 350.

Sarra

In the *Sacred Magic of Abramelin the Mage*, book two, Sarra ("to strike") is listed as one of the sixteen SERVITORS OF ASMODEUS (see ASMODEUS).

Sources: Mathers, *Book of the Sacred Magic of Abramelin*, 119; Von Worms, *Book of Abramelin*, 256.

Sartabakim

Variations: Sartabakins

In the *Sacred Magic of Abramelin the Mage*, book two, Sarabakim ("the zodiac Cancer") is listed as one of the fifteen SERVITORS OF ASMODEUS AND MAGOTH (see ASMODEUS).

Sources: Mathers, *Book of the Sacred Magic of Abramelin the Mage*, 106, 117; Von Worms, *Book of Abramelin*, 248, 256.

Sasabonsam

Variations: Asanbonsam, Asasabonsam, Kongamato, Obboney

In the demonic lore from the Ashanti people of Africa, as well as from the Jamaicans of their own island, comes a vampiric, demonic creature called a sasabonsam. Said to have come to the region from "another land," this bearded man-faced demon stands about five feet tall and has a mouth full of fanged teeth, a row of scaly ridges over its bloodshot eyes, and a small horn that protrudes from the top of its head. Its very long arms are like gigantic bat wings that have a twenty-foot span. Its torso is skeletally thin, its legs are permanently bent, and there are three toes on each of its feet. The sasabonsam's body is covered with black and white spots, adding to its camouflage as it sits in the cotton tree, dangling its stringy legs below. When a person walks underneath, if the legs are brushed against, it snatches up the person, pulling them into the tree and biting off their head, then drinking up the blood. The belief that the sasabonsam lives in the *ceiba*, the great silk-cotton trees, is prevailing, as can be proven by the great height that these trees grow to—everyone is afraid to cut them down.

Sasabonsam, who live off fruit and human blood, are said to cause sickness in a person just by looking at them. These demons are believed to work in tandem with the *mmoatia* (dwarf sorcerers) and the *obayifo* (witchcraft experts).

An article written in 1939 for *The West African Review* reported that a sasabonsam had been successfully hunted down and killed. The sasabonsam is similar to the Cornish myth of the "Owlman."

Sources: Jahoda, *Psychology of Superstition*, 12; Rattray, *Ashanti Proverbs*, 48; Shuker, *Beasts That Hide from Man*, 103–5; Williams, *Psychic Phenomena of Jamaica*, 16–18.

Sasquiel

Variations: Sasquiel

In *Ars Paulina*, the third book of the *Lemegeton*, Sasquiel is said to command ten chief dukes, one hundred lesser dukes, and a multitude of servitors. He is most powerful during the fifth hour (see SERVITORS OF SASQUIEL).

Sources: Guiley, *Encyclopedia of Angels*, 318; Peterson, *Lesser Key of Solomon*, 114.

Satan

Variations: ABADDON ("Destruction"), Abatōn, Accuser, Accuser of our brethren, Adversary, al-Shaitan ("the adversary"), ANGEL OF EDOM, Angel of light, Angel of the bottomless pit, Anointed covering cherub, ANTICHRIST, Apollyon ("one that exterminates"), Apostate, Archfiend, Ascmedai, ASMODEUS, AVERSIER ("adversary"), AZAZEL, BAAL, Baker, Beast, BEELZEBUB, BEHEMOTH, Béherit, Beliar, Beliel, Blacafeond, Beliel, Blacafeond, Black Bogey, Black Donald, Black Fiend, Black Man, Black Star of Morning, Bogey, Bogeyman, Boogeyman, Bugbear, Charlot, Creature of Judgment, Cunning over Blood, Dark Prince, Deceiver, Deceiver of Mankind, Dick, Dickens, Dicon, DJALL, DRAGON AT THE APOCALYPSE, DUMA, Enemy, Evil One, Father of Lies, Father of the Night, FEDERWISCH, Gadreel, Gentleman Jack, God of this age, Good Fellow, GORGO, Gorgorant Great Dragon, Ha borm, Ha satan, Haborm, Hammerlin, Hämmerlin, Harry, HAUSSIBUT, Heinekin, Hellhundt ("Hell Hound"), Hinkebein, Hornli, Horny, Horny One, Jack, Joker, King of Babylon, King of the bottomless pit, King of Tyre, Knecht Ruprecht, Lawless one, LEVIATHAN, Liar, Little horn, Lord of Flies, LUCIFER ("Day star"), Lusty Dick, Man of sin, Mansemat, MASTEMA, MEPHISTOPHELES, Murderer, Nekker, Nick, Nicker, NIHASA, Old Bogie, Old Gentleman, Old Hairy, Old Horny, OLD NICK, Old One, Old Scratch, Old Splitfoot, O-Yama, Pater Pseutes, Poker, Potentate of the Pit, Power of darkness, Prince of Darkness, Prince of Deluders, Prince of the Pit, Prince of the power of the air, Prince of this World, Prince without throne, Pwcca, Roaring lion, Robin Goodfellow, Robin Hood, Rofocale, Ruler of demons, Ruler of this world, Rulers of the darkness, Rumpelstiltskin, Sabbathai, Saitan, SAMMAEL, Satanas, Seducer of Mankind, Serpent, Serpent of old, SHAITAN, Sheitan, Sir Urien, Socothbenoth, Son of perdition, Son of the morning, Spigelglantz ("Mirror Gleam"), Splitfoot, Stan, Star, Stoker, TCHORT, Tempter, Tenebrifer ("Shadowbearer"), TERRYTOP, Teufel, Thief, Thief of Paradise, Tryphön, Wicked One, and Without a Master, to name but a few

BEELZEBUB, the DEVIL, LUCIFER, and Satan are considered, by various religious and academic sources, to be separate and independent entities as well as the same single being with varied and numerous names. The mythology of the most evil archfiend is, at best, blurred.

The name Satan ("adversary") originates in Jewish demonology, and it is used in the Old Testament and the Talmud alike. Christian demonology, with its apparent need to categorize and order, has in various grimoires given Satan a variety of ranks and titles, only some of which are the chief of Kether, grand general of the infernal spirits, lord of fire, lord of Hell, lord of the Underworld, prince of deluders, and the vice president of Hell (see PRINCES OF HELL and PRESIDENTS OF HELL). In these same references, Satan is sometimes said to be under the command of the DEVIL, a demon of anger who himself commands the demons AAMON, BARBATOS, and PRUSLAS. This demon is believed to have the power to make women completely submissive to his will as well as tempting all of mankind to commit every sin imaginable, especially those involving anger.

A FALLEN ANGEL of the First Sphere, this twelve-winged Seraphim created by God has been credited as being the serpent who tempted Eve in the Garden of Eden, the evil that delivered misfortunes onto Job, and the devil who tempted Jesus in the desert.

Sources: Barton, *Journal of Biblical Literature*, Vols. 30–31, 165; Lumpkin, *Fallen Angels, the Watchers, and the Origin of Evil*, 127; Russell, *Lucifer, the Devil in the Middle Ages*, 66, 249; Melton, *Encyclopedia of Occultism and Parapsychology*, 315.

Satanachia

Variations: Charpon, Kasdeya, PUT SATANACHIA, Sarakmyal, Sarquamich, Satanchia, Sataniachia, Satanicæ, "The Supreme"

Originating in Enochian lore, Satanachia was one of the FALLEN ANGELS who swore allegiance to SAMIAZA, rebelled against God, took a human wife, and fathered the NEPHILIM. He was first named and listed as a principal demon by the church during one of its Council of Braga meetings that were held during the Middle Ages. Ranked as a commander in chief and a grand general, sources conflict as to whether Satanachia commands the demons AAMON, BARBATOS, and Pralas or if he answers to them. The number of demons he commands varies widely from source to source as well. Popular names and numbers are forty-five or fifty-four; the First Legion of Hell; six chiefs; six subalterns; eighty-seven demons under SAMAEL; and the individual demons BOTIS, HERAMAEL, PRUSLAS, SERGUTHY (Sergutthy), SUSTUGRIEL, and TRIMASAEL.

Best summoned during the third hour of the night, Satanachia has profound knowledge of all the planets, has power over virgins, makes women submissive, and can teach men the secrets of destruction.

Sources: Baskin, *Sorcerer's Handbook*, 276; Black, *Edinburgh Review*, Vol. 107, 240; Mark, *Book of Hierarchies*, 28; Shah, *Occultism*, 61; Trithemius, *Steganographia*, 88; Waite, *Book of Black Magic and Ceremonial Magic*, 187; Wedeck, *Treasury of Witchcraft*, 96.

Satanail

Variations: Salamiel, Satanail, Satomail, Sotona

Originating in Bogomilism and Enochian lore, Satanail and several other angels were already being punished for an unnamed crime they had committed before the WATCHERS conspired together to take human wives. This prince of the GRIGORI believed that he could become more powerful than God.

Sources: Charles, *Book of the Secrets of Enoch*, 21; Davidson, *Dictionary of Angels*, 262; Wright, *Origin of Evil Spirits*, 142.

Sataniciae

The *Grimoirium Verum* (*The True Grimoire*) says that along with SATANACHIA, Sataniciae commands either forty-five or fifty-five servitors (sources vary) but only two of which are chiefs, the rest being of no consequence (see SERVITORS OF SATANACHIA AND SATANICIAE).

Sources: Kuriakos, *Grimoire Verum Ritual Book*, 36, 39–40; Trithemius, *Steganographia*, 88; Waite, *Book of Black Magic*, 187.

Satarel

Variations: ERTAEL, Sataral

Enochian lore names Satarel ("God's side") as a CHIEF OF TENS and one of the FALLEN ANGELS who swore allegiance to SAMIAZA, rebelled against God, took a human wife, and fathered the NEPHILIM (see also GRIGORI and WATCHERS). In service under ASHTAROTH, he has dominion over the planet Jupiter and has con-

trol over "hidden things" (the secrets of nature). (See also SERVITORS OF ASHTAROTH.)

Sources: Ford, *Liber Hvhi*, 76; Ginzberg, *Legends of the Jews*, Vol. 5, 153; Laurence, *Foreign Quarterly Review*, Vol. 24, 370; Lumpkin, *Fallen Angels, the Watchers, and the Origins of Evil*, 31; Mathers, *Key of Solomon the King*, 122.

Sathariel

Sathariel ("concealment of God") is a FALLEN ANGEL, formerly a Sephirah.

Sources: Ashley, *Complete Book of Devils and Demons*, 72; Davidson, *Dictionary of Angels*, 262; Waite, *Holy Kabbalah*, 257.

Satorial

Variations: Harasiel, SERIEL

The demon Satorial is described as having a gigantic black veiled horned head and hideous eyes that can be seen through the veil. A concealer and destroyer, he commands evil centaurs and falls under the service of Binah ("understanding").

Sources: Fusco, *Insegnamenti Magici Della Golden Dawn*, 151; Gettings, *Dictionary of Demons*, 93.

Saurva

Variations: Sauru, Savar, Sharva

In Zoroastrian demonology Saurva, a type of DAEVAS, is the chief of the DEVS. A demon of hunger, he commits acts that are evil, lawless, oppressive, tyrannical, and violent. To keep from being victimized by Saurva, he must be rejected outright in deed, thought, and word. His personal adversary is the angel Khshathra Vairya. His name in Avestian may mean "archer."

Sources: Boyce, *A History of Zoroastrianism*, 54, 251; Dhalla, *History of Zoroastrianism*, 269; Ford, *Bible of the Adversary*, 138; Horne, *Sacred Books and Early Literature of the East*, 183; Jackson, *Zoroastrian Studies*, 85–7.

Sazquiel

According to the *Lemegeton*, Sazquiel commands four superior servitor spirits, also know as chiefs; their names are ARMARELE, DAMIEL, Maroch, and Serapiel (SARAPHIEL). He also commands one hundred lesser servitor spirits, six of which are named AMISIEL, FUSTIEL, FUTINIEL, Jamersil (JAMERIEL), PUBRISIEL, and RAMISIEL. This demon is said to be most powerful during the fifth hour.

Sources: Davidson, *Dictionary of Angels*, 262; Peterson, *Lesser Key of Solomon*, 114; Waite, *The Book of Ceremonial Magic*, 67.

Sbarionat

Variations: Sbarronat

In the *Sacred Magic of Abramelin the Mage*,

book two, Sbarionat is listed as one of the sixteen SERVITORS OF ASMODEUS (see ASMODEUS). His name is possibly Coptic and may mean "a little friend."

Sources: Ford, *Bible of the Adversary*, 93; Mathers, *Book of the Sacred Magic of Abra-Melin*, 119; Susej, *Demonic Bible*, 258; Von Worms, *Book of Abramelin*, 256.

Schabuach

In the *Sacred Magic of Abramelin the Mage*, book two, Schabuach ("to assuage") is listed as one of the one hundred eleven SERVITORS OF AMAYMON, ARITON, ORIENS, AND PAYMON (see AMAYMON, ARITON, ORIENS, and PAYMON).

Sources: Mathers, *Book of the Sacred Magic of Abramelin the Mage*, 112; Susej, *Demonic Bible*, 256.

Schachlil

In Apollonius of Tyana's *Nuctemeron* (*Night Illuminated by Day*), Schachlil is the demon of the sun's rays. He is most powerful during the ninth hour.

Sources: Davidson, *Dictionary of Angels*, 262; Gettings, *Dictionary of Demons*, 216; Lévi, *Transcendental Magic*, 393.

Scharak

In the *Sacred Magic of Abramelin the Mage*, book two, Scharak ("to twine about or to wind") is listed as one of the sixty-five SERVITORS OF KORE AND MAGOTH.

Sources: Ford, *Bible of the Adversary*, 92; Mathers, *Book of the Sacred Magic of Abramelin the Mage*, 107; Susej, *Demonic Bible*, 258; Von Worms, *Book of Abramelin*, 250.

Schechirion

Schechirion is a monstrous black-colored demonic creature (see QLIPPOTHIC ORDERS OF DEMONS). It is a hybrid of insect, reptile, and shellfish; it has a demonic face.

Sources: Ford, *Bible of the Adversary*, 121; Mathers, *Sorcerer and his Apprentice*, 26.

Sched

In the *Sacred Magic of Abramelin the Mage*, book two, Sched ("demons") is listed as one of the one hundred eleven SERVITORS OF AMAYMON, ARITON, ORIENS, AND PAYMON (see AMAYMON, ARITON, ORIENS, and PAYMON). His name in Hebrew means "to shed" and signifies a female breast.

Sources: Ford, *Bible of the Adversary*, 88; Mathers, *Book of the Sacred Magic of Abramelin the Mage*, 105; Susej, *Demonic Bible*, 197; Von Worms, *Book of Abramelin*, 244.

Schedim

In Hebrew the word *schedim* essentially means "demons" or "to be violent," and there is no singular form. They are said to be innumerable. In the Talmud and in Hebrew demonology, the schedim are a demonic species that were born the children of Adam and LILITH during the one hundred years he was apart from his second wife, Eve. Other legends say they were created on the sixth day by God, but the sun set before their bodies could be created, causing these beings to remain half human and half spirit; yet others claim that they are the descendants of snakes or are demons in the form of snakes. A final creation story claims that after the Tower of Babel fell, some people were transformed into schedim.

Schedim have angelic wings and they can fly from world to world. They know the future by listening from behind the veil that the angels have permitted them to use. Some sources claim they have the hands and feet of roosters. Like men, schedim must eat and drink; they can reproduce more of their kind and are mortal with a fixed lifespan. In general, they are malevolent; however, in ancient Assyrian and Babylonian lore the schedim could be summoned as either a force of evil or good.

These demonic beings hover around dead bodies and graves and live in deserted or "unclean" places. To test if schedim are around, toss ashes on the ground; if they are present, their footprints will become visible.

Animal and child sacrifices will keep these demons from attacking. Some sources claim that sinful people offered their daughters to the schedim, but the sources are unclear if this was an offering of life, sexuality, or something else. Whistling attracts them, as does saying the word "schedim" aloud.

Sources: *Atlantic Monthly*, Vol. 54, 462, 464; Burton, *Magic, Mystery, and Science*, 120; Farmer, *Dissertation on Miracles*, 248, 250; Plaut, *The Torah*, 1403.

Schelagon

In the *Sacred Magic of Abramelin the Mage*, Schelagon ("like snow") is listed as one of the thirty-two SERVITORS OF ASTAROT (see ASTAROT).

Sources: Ford, *Bible of the Adversary*, 91; Susej, *Demonic Bible*, 257; Von Worms, *Book of Abramelin*, 249.

Scheliel

According to Enochian lore, Scheliel is one of the twenty-eight demonic rulers of the lunar mansions; he has dominion over the mansion Aldimiach (see ENOCHIAN RULERS OF THE

LUNAR MANSIONS). This demon works against people in authority.

Sources: Davidson, *Dictionary of Angels*, 348; Scheible, Sixth and Seventh Books of Moses, 75; Webster, *Encyclopedia of Angels*, 176.

Schiekrom

In Apollonius of Tyana's *Nuctemeron* (*Night Illuminated by Day*) Schiekrom is said to be the demon of bestial love. He is most powerful during the fourth hour.

Sources: Davidson, *Dictionary of Angels*, 263; Lévi, *Transcendental Magic*, 418.

Schonspigel

Schonspigel ("Pretty Mirror") is the demon of vanity.

Sources: Carus, *Open Court*, Vol. 43, 472; Rudwin, *Devil in Legend and Literature*, 28; Russell, *Lucifer, the Devil in the Middle Ages*, 249; Wray, *Birth of Satan*, 25.

Schorbrandt

In German demonology Schorbrandt is the demon of conflicts and discord.

Sources: Carus, *Open Court*, Vol. 43, 472; Grimm, *Teutonic Mythology*, 1064; Rudwin, *Devil in Legend and Literature*, 28, 84.

Sclavak

In the *Sacred Magic of Abramelin the Mage*, book two, Sclavak is listed as one of the sixteen SERVITORS OF ASMODEUS (see ASMODEUS). This name is possibly Coptic and means "pain and torture."

Sources: Mathers, *Book of the Sacred Magic of Abra-Melin*, 119; Susej, *Demonic Bible*, 258.

Scox

Variations: CHAX, Samsavael, SAZQUIEL, Shass, SHAX, Shaz, Spax

In *Ars Goetia*, book one of the *Lemegeton*, Scox is ranked as a duke and a marquis and commands thirty legions of demons, ten chiefs, and a hundred servitors (see MARQUIS OF HELL). When summoned, he appears as a bird and speaks with a hoarse voice. A known liar and thief, Scox is called upon for his ability to cause blindness, deafness, and muteness; he reveals the location of hidden treasure not protected by evil spirits but if he steals anything he will return it after two hundred years. Scox has a reputation for completing all tasks given to him (see also SERVITORS OF SCOX).

Sources: Ashley, *Complete Book of Devils and Demons*, 58; Chaplin, *Dictionary of the Occult and Paranormal*, 137; Icon, *Demons*, 178; Shah, *Occultism*, 67.

Scrilis

In the *Sacred Magic of Abramelin the Mage*, Scrilis is listed as one of the twenty SERVITORS OF AMAYMON (see AMAYMON). This name is possibly taken from Latin and may mean "offense" or "sacrilegious."

Sources: Ford, *Bible of the Adversary*, 95; Mathers, *Book of the Sacred Magic of Abramelin the Mage*, 122; Susej, *Demonic Bible*, 259; Von Worms, *Book of Abramelin*, 257.

Sealah

Variations: DJINN, Saaláh, Sealáh

A sealah is a demonic species of creature in Arabic lore. It is a type of Djinn that was born the offspring of a human and a Djinn that ate human flesh. Absolutely hideous in its appearance, the sealah prey upon men, hunting and capturing them, forcing them to dance, torturing them, and using them to practice their hunting techniques.

Sealah live in the forests, and ancient Arabic geographers named an island off the coast of China "the island of the sealah," believing it was populated by these demons.

Hated by wolves, when attacked by one the sealah will cry out "Come to my help, for the wolf devoureth me!" or "Who will liberate me? I have a hundred deenars, and he shall receive them!" But do not answer its call for help. The wolf will destroy the demon and consume its body.

Sources: Campbell, *Popular Tales of the West Highlands*, 297; Chambers's Encyclopaedia: A Dictionary of Universal Knowledge, 749; Poole, *The Thousand and One Nights*, 32–3.

Sealiah

Variations: Saeliah, Seeliah

The demon of plants that grow in the forest as well as vegetables, Sealiah is a FALLEN ANGEL, formerly of the Order of Virtues. Sealiah is most powerful in the month of November. When invoking this demon, recite a verse from Psalms.

Sources: Anderson, *Diary of Ancient Rites*, 198; Davidson, *Dictionary of Angels*, 264.

Sebettu

Variations: The PLEIADES

Originating in Akkadian and Babylonian demonology, Sebettu ("the seven") appear as two sets of seven demons each, one benign and the other evil. They were born the children of the sky god An and are under the command of Erra, a plague god. The Sebettu cause lunar eclipses.

Sources: Lurker, *Dictionary of Gods and Goddesses, Devils and Demons*, 313–4; Rose, *Spirits, Fairies, Leprechauns, and Goblins*, 286.

Seddim

Seddim is the demon of destruction.
Source: Baskin, *Dictionary of Satanism*, 293.

Sedim

Variations: Demonic goblins, SE'IRIM

In Hasidic demonology the sedim were born of the union between the archangel Azael ("whom God strengthens") and the human woman NAAMAH, and became the tutelary spirits of Assyria. They have magical powers and live in abandoned places. Child sacrifices were once made to them. The word *sedim* in Hebrew possibly translates to mean "the hairy one, the he-goat," or more likely "foreign demons," as they are referred to in Deuteronomy 32:17 "They sacrificed to demons, which are not God—gods they had not known, gods that recently appeared, gods your fathers did not fear."
Sources: Anderson, *Diary of Ancient Rites*, Vol. 2, 107; Deluge, *Beginnings of History*, 326; Gray, *Mythology of All Races*, 361; Ryken, *Dictionary of Biblical Imagery*, 203.

Sedu

Sedu are guardian demons in Assyrian demonology. They are described as looking like a LAMIA or a winged man-headed bull.
Source: Herbermann, *Catholic Encyclopedia*, 712.

Seera

Seera is the demon of time; he has the ability to control it.
Source: Kelly, *Who in Hell*, 210.

Seere

Variations: Sear, Seir, Seire

In the *Lemegeton*, Seere is ranked as a prince commanding twenty-six legions of demons that are under the service of AMAYMON (see PRINCES OF HELL and SERVITORS OF AMAYMON). He is also listed as one of the seventy-two SPIRITS OF SOLOMON. When summoned he appears as a handsome man riding upon a winged horse. Willing to do whatever his summoner asks of him, Seere is best at finding lost treasures and discovering theft. He has the ability to travel to any place on the planet in just a few seconds. Seere is said to be good-natured and mostly indifferent to evil.
Sources: Baskin, *Dictionary of Satanism*, 293; Crowley, *The Goetia*, 64; De Laurence, *Lesser Key of Solomon, Goetia*, 44–5; Peterson, *Lesser Key of Solomon*, 38; Waite, *Book of Black Magic and of Pacts*, 188.

Segal

The *Grimoirium Verum* (*Grimoire of Truth*), allegedly written by Alibek the Egyptian in 1517, lists Segal as one of the eighteen SERVITORS OF SYRACH (see SYRACH). He is said to cause prodigies to appear and is willing to demonstrate the differences between natural and supernatural phenomenon.
Sources: Kuriakos, *Grimoire Verum Ritual Book*, 35; Sabellicus, *Magia Pratica*, 35.

Seiktha

Variations: Nat

Born of nature and innumerable in number, the seiktha of Burmese demonology is a species of demonic animal. Typically malign, on occasion these creatures become tutelary spirits to a village; some even go on to achieve godhead. Animalistic in nature, the seiktha usually live in groves but have the ability to possess shrines. Offerings of drink and food will keep them sated and prevent them from attacking.
Sources: Rose, *Spirits, Fairies, Leprechauns, and Goblins*, 287; Shepard, *Encyclopedia of Occultism and Parapsychology*, 187; Spence, *Encyclopædia of Occultism*, 81.

Se'irim

Variations: Goat demons, goat idols, SAHIRIM

Se'irim ("hairy ones") are demonic creatures from ancient Arabic lore. A se'irim looks like a hairy calf or goat. Believed to be part animal and part spiritual creature, they live in desolate places. Leviticus 17:7 speaks of the se'irim, "They must no longer offer any of their sacrifices to the goat idols to whom they prostitute themselves. This is to be a lasting ordinance for them and for the generations to come."
Sources: Herzog, *New Schaff-Herzog Encyclopedia of Religious Knowledge*, 400, 401; Mould, *Essentials of Bible History*, 119; Oesterley, *Immortality and the Unseen World*, 37–8; Plumptre, *Bible Educator*, 99.

Sekabin

In the *Sacred Magic of Abramelin the Mage*, book two, Sekabin ("casters down") is listed as one of the twenty-two SERVITORS OF ARITON (see ARITON).
Sources: Ford, *Bible of the Adversary*, 94; Mathers, *Selected Occult Writings of S.L. MacGregor Mathers*, 108; Von Worms, *Book of Abramelin*, 257.

Sellen

In Apollonius of Tyana's *Nuctemeron* (*Night Illuminated by Day*), Sellen is the demon of great favors and is most powerful during the twelfth hour.
Sources: Gettings, *Dictionary of Demons*, 220; Lévi, *Transcendental Magic*, 422.

Semazas

Variations: Semiaza,' Semiazas,' Semiazas, Shamhazai, Shem'sa,' Shemyaza, Shemyazai, Smyz

In the *Book of Enoch*, Semazas ("the name sees" or "God sees") is one of the FALLEN ANGELS who swore allegiance to SAMIAZA, rebelled against God, took a human wife, and fathered the NEPHILIM. He told his human wife, Istahar, the name of God, an ability that empowered him with the ability to ascend into the constellation Draco. For his sins, Semazas has suspended himself upside down between Heaven and earth, making up part of the constellation Orion.

Sources: Lewis, *Satanism Today*, 247; Owen, *Sanctorale Catholicum*, 7; Reicke, *Disobedient Spirits and Christian Baptism*, 83.

Semlin

In the *Ars Goetia,* the first book of the *Lemegeton*, Semlin ("appearances") is listed as one of the fifty-three SERVITORS OF ASHTAROTH AND ASMODEUS (see ASHTAROTH and ASMODEUS).

Sources: Mathers, *Book of the Sacred Magic of Abramelin the Mage*, 105, 115; Von Worms, *Book of Abramelin*, 247, 256.

Senciner

Senciner is a FALLEN ANGEL, formerly of the Order of Virtues.

Source: Ashley, *Complete Book of Devils and Demons*, 74.

Separ

Variations: Vepar, Vephar, Zepar

The *Ars Goetia*, book one of the *Lemegeton*, ranks Separ as the Sea Duke, commanding twenty-nine legions (see DUKES OF HELL). He is also said to be one of the seventy-two SPIRITS OF SOLOMON. When summoned, Separ appears wearing red clothing and is armed like a soldier, or he appears before his summoner as a mermaid. This demon has the ability to make calm waters rough and stormy and look to be filled with ships; he can act as a guide for ammunition and warships. Separ can also cause women to fall in love with men, changing their shape to make them more pleasing. He causes wounds to putrefy or can heal them instantly.

Sources: De Claremont, *Ancient's Book of Magic*, 136; Diagram Group, *Little Giant Encyclopedia*, 506; De Laurence, *Lesser Key of Solomon, Goetia*, 27; Diagram Group, *Little Giant Encyclopedia*, 506; Scott, *London Magazine*, Vol. 5, 378.

Sephiroth, the Ten Evil

Variations: The Ten Evil Enumerations, the Ten Seraphs of Darkness

According to the Cabalistic lore of the thirteenth century, there are ten evil sephiroths: ADRAMELECH, ASHTAROTH, ASMODEUS, BAAL, BEELZEBUB, BELPHEGOR, LILITH, Lucifuge, MOLOCH and SATAN (as a pair), and NAAMAH. These sephiroths are under the command of the ARCHDEMONS and SAMMAEL. Working constantly to destroy and undo all that God has created, they are destroyed when the human spirit triumphs against them through goodness and morality.

Sources: Carus, *Open Court*, Vol. 35, 28; Cavendish, *The Black Arts*, 252; Gilman, *New International Encyclopaedia*, Vol. 3, 764.

Serguliath

Variations: Serguiath, Seruglath

Serguliath has the ability to give means of speculation and strategy to his summoner. He is under the command of NEBIROS.

Sources: DeGivry, *Witchcraft, Magic, and Alchemy*, 30; Shah, *Occultism*, 66; Waite, *Book of Black and Ceremonial Magic*, 181.

Serguthy

Variations: Sergutthy

The *Grimoirium Verum* (*Grimoire of Truth*), allegedly written by Alibek the Egyptian in 1517, ranks Serguthy as a chief and lists him as one of the four SERVITORS OF SATANACHIA (see SATANACHIA). This demon, who has power over wives and virgins, acts quickly once summoned, provided that he is content with the summoner.

Sources: Kuriakos, *Grimoire Verum Ritual Book*, 36; Masters, *Devil's Dominion*, 131; Waite, *Book of Black Magic and of Pacts*, 187.

Seriel

Variations: SARIEL

According to Enochian lore, Seriel is one of the FALLEN ANGELS who swore allegiance to SAMIAZA, rebelled against God, took a human wife, and fathered the NEPHILIM. He went on to teach mankind the signs of the moon.

Sources: *Christian Examiner*, Vol. 66–7, 367; Ford, *Bible of the Adversary*, 76; Ginzberg, *Legends of the Jews*, 1204; Laurence, *Foreign Quarterly Review*, Vol. 24, 370.

Sermeot

In the *Sacred Magic of Abramelin the Mage*, book two, Sermeot ("death to the flesh") is listed as one of the twenty-two SERVITORS OF ARITON (see ARITON).

Sources: Ford, *Bible of the Adversary*, 95; Mathers, *Book of the Sacred Magic of Abra-Melin*, 108; Susej, *Demonic Bible*, 259; Von Worms, *Book of Abramelin*, 257.

Serviel

In *Ars Paulina*, the third book of the *Lemegeton*, Serviel is listed as one of the two hundred SERVITORS OF VEGUANIEL (see VEGUANIEL).

Source: Waite, *Book of Ceremonial Magic*, 67.

Servitors of Abezethibou

Johann Wierus's *Pseudomonarchia Daemonum* (*False Monarchy of Demons*, 1583) says that there are twelve servitors of ABEZETHIBOU, but only eight of them are named and ranked. They are: ABIGOR, a duke; BENSOZIA, a consort; CORSON, a bailiff; FLEURETTY, a lieutenant general; GORSON, a king; NEABAZ; Tartiamache; and ZEPHAR, a duke.

Sources: Conybeare, *Jewish Quarterly Review*, Vol. 11, 4; Guiley, *Encyclopedia of Demons and Demonology*, 2; Pietersma, *Apocryphon of Jannes and Jambres*, 31, 194, 193; Webster, *Encyclopedia of Angels*, 3.

Servitors of Agaliarept

There are four Servitors of AGALIAREPT. They are: BOTIS, BUER, ELELOGAP, and GUSOYN.

Sources: Baskin, *Satanism*, 17; Shah, *Occultism*, 61; Waite, *Unknown World 1894–1895*, 230; Wedeck, *Treasury of Witchcraft*, 96.

Servitors of Amaimon and Ariton

The *Sacred Magic of Abramelin the Mage*, book two, names ten servitors for the demons AMAIMON and ARITON. They are AGIBOL, CLERACA, ELAFON, ELATON, GAGALIN, GRASEMIN, HAUGES, PAFESLA, RIGOLIN, and TRISAGA.

Sources: Ford, *Bible of the Adversary*, 90; Mathers, *Selected Occult Writings of S.L. MacGregor Mathers*, 96; Susej, *Demonic Bible*, 166; Von Worms, *Book of Abramelin*, 243.

Servitors of Amaymon

The *Sacred Magic of Abramelin the Mage* says there are twenty servitors for the demon AMAYMON. They are AKESOLI, AKOROS, APELKI, BURASEN, BURIOL, DALEP, DRESOP, EFFRIGIS, EREKIA, GLESI, HERGOTIS, ILLIRIKIM, LABISI, MAMES, Niliuma, RAMISON, ROMERAC, SCRILIS, TARALIM, and VISION.

Sources: De Laurence, *Lesser Key of Solomon, Goetia*, 32–3, 46; DuQuette, *Key to Solomon's Key*, 167, 176–7, 195, 197; Hyatt, *Book of Demons*, 48; Waite, *Book of Black Magic and of Pacts*, 158.

Servitors of Amaymon, Ariton, Oriens, and Paymon

Although some demonologists claim that there are only fifty servitors to these demons, the *Sacred Magic of Abramelin the Mage*, book two, says there are one hundred eleven servitors of AMAYMON, ARITON, ORIENS, and PAYMON. They are ACUAR, ADON, AFARORP, AHEROM, ALAGAS, ALLUPH, ALPAS, APOLHUN, ASMIEL, ASPERIM, ASTREGA, ASTUREL, ATLOTON, BADAD, BALALOS, CHUSCHI, COELEN, DARASCON, DECCAL, EKALIKE, EKDULON, ELMIS, ELZAGAN, EMPHASTISON, ENAIA, ERENUTES, ETHANIM, GELOMA, GEREVIL, GORILON, GOSEGAS, HABHI, HARIL, HOSEN, IARESIN, IGARAK, IGILON, IGIS, ILAGAS, IMINK, IOGION, IPAKOL, IPARKAS, IRMINON, IRRORON, ISEKEL, KADOLON, KATINI, KELEN, KILIK, LAGASUF, LIRION, LOMIOL, LOSIMON, MALUTENS, MANTIENS, MELAMUD, MELHAER, MELNA, MERMO, METAFEL, MOLIN, MOREL, MORILEN, MOSCHEL, Mulach, NAGID, NAJIN, NERCAMAY, NILEN, NOGAR, NOGEN, NUDITON, NUTHON, OBEDAMA, OGILEN, Oroia, PACHID, PARASEH, PAREHT, PAREK, PARMATUS, PARUSUR, PATID, PEREUCH, PLATIEN, PLEGIT, PLIROK, POTER, PROMAKOS, PROXOSOS, RACHIAR, RAGARAS, RAMARATZ, REMORON, ROMAGES, RUACH, SACHIEL, SARAPH, SCHABUACH, SCHED, SOTERION, TAGNON, TARADOS, TASMA, TIRANA, TORFORA, TRACI, TRAPIS, TULOT, and ZARAGIL.

Sources: Hyatt, *Book of Demons*, 48; Kuriakos, *Grimoire Verum Ritual Book*, 30; Mathers, *Book of the Sacred Magic of Abramelin the Mage*, 111–17; McLean, *Treatise on Angel Magic*, 168; Rapacki, *Satanism*, 59; Scot, *Discoverie of Witchcraft*, 220.

Servitors of Amenadiel

In the *Ars Paulina*, book three of the *Lemegeton*, twelve chief duke servitors of Amenadiel are listed. Each of these demons commands three thousand servitors of their own. They are Almesiel, BALSUR, CAMIEL, CODRIEL, Curifas, LAMAEL, LUZIEL, MUSIRIEL, NADROC, Rapsiel, Vadros, and ZOENIEL.

Sources: Belanger, *Dictionary of Demons*, 59, 84, 96; Davidson, *Dictionary of Angels*, 84; Guiley, *Encyclopedia of Demons and Demonology*, 7; Peterson, *Lesser Key of Solomon*, 62, 114; Shah, *Occultism*, 68; Trithemius, *Steganographia*, 7, 54, 81, 91, 95.

Servitors of Ariton

The *Sacred Magic of Abramelin the Mage*, book two, lists twenty-two servitors of ARITON: ANADER, ANDROCOS, CAROMOS, CARON, EKOROK, ELERION, FLAXON, GALAK, HAROMBRUB, ILEMLIS, IRMENOS, MARANTON, MEGALOSIN, MILIOM, NOTISER, REGINON, ROSARAN, SAPASON, SARIS, SEKABIN, SERMEOT, and SIBOLAS.

Sources: Ford, *Bible of the Adversary*, 90, 94,95; Hyatt, *Book of Demons*, 48; Mathers, *Book of the Sacred Magic of Abramelin the Mage*, 96, 105, 108, 121–2; Toynbee, *Concise Dictionary of Proper Names and Notable Matters*, 119–20; Von Worms, *Book of Abramelin*, 124, 243, 254, 257.

Servitors of Armadiel

The *Theurgia Goetia*, the second book of the *Lemegeton*, lists fifteen chief dukes as being in the service of ARMADIEL, each of which commands

1,260 servitors of their own: Alferiel, Asbibiel, Asmael, Caluarnia, Carasiba, Haziel, Laiel, Mafayr, Massar, Oeniel, Orariel, Orin, PANDIEL, Parabiel, and SAMIEL.

Sources: Eco, *Infinity of Lists*, 61; Shumaker, *Natural Magic and Modern Science*, 66.

Servitors of Aseliel

In the *Sacred Magic of Abramelin the Mage*, book two, there are sixteen Servitors of ASELIEL listed. They are: ANIEL, of the day; ARATIEL, of the day; AREAN, of the day; ASAHEL, of the day; ASPHIEL, of the night; BOFAR, of the night; CHAMOS, of the night; CHARAS, of the day; CUBIEL, of the day; CURIEL, of the night; MARIEL, of the day; MELAS, of the night; ODIEL, of the night; OTHIEL, of the night; PARNIEL, of the day; and SARIEL, of the night.

Sources: Agrippa, *Three Books of Occult Philosophy*, 553, 555; Black, *Book of Enoch, or, I Enoch*, 129; Chambers, *Book of Days*, 723; Geikie, *Life and Words of Christ*, 610; Hayward, *Interpretations of the Name Israel in Ancient Judaism and Some Early Christian Writings*, 297–8; Laurence, *Foreign Quarterly Review*, Vol. 24, 370; Mathers, *Book of the Sacred Magic of Abramelin the Mage*, 200; Trithemius, *Steganographia*, 91, 101.

Servitors of Ashtaroth

There are four servitors of ASHTAROTH. They are AAMON, BARBATOS, PRUSLAS, and RASHAVERAK.

Sources: de Givry, *Witchcraft, Magic and Alchemy*, 128; De Laurence, *Lesser Key of Solomon, Goetia*, 23–4; Jahn, *Jahn's Biblical Archaeology*, 524–5, 530; McLean, *Treatise of Angel Magic*, 52; Prophet, *Fallen Angels and the Origins of Evil*, 174; Scott, *London Magazine*, Vol. 5, 378; Smith, *Comprehensive Dictionary of the Bible*, 73; Wedeck, *Treasury of Witchcraft*, 96–7.

Servitors of Ashtaroth and Asmodeus

The *Ars Goetia*, the first book of the *Lemegeton*, names fifty-three servitors of Ashtaroth and Asmodeus: ABAHIN, ABUTES, AFRAY, AGEI, AGRAX, AKANEF, AMALIN, AMANIEL, Ambolin, BIALOT, BUBANA, BUK, BURIUL, CARASCH, CORCARON, DAGULAR, DAROKIN, DIMURGOS, DIORON (or Dablat), DRAMAS, ETALIZ, ETHAN, EXTERON, FINAXOS, GAGALOS, GOLEG, GUAGAMON, GUGONIX, HALIGAX, HERMIALA, HORANAR, ISIGI, KIRIK, LABOUX, LAGINX, LEMEL, LORIOL, NIMALON, OMAGES, OMAN, OPILM, ORINEL, PACHEIL, RAGALIM, RANER, ROGGIOL, SAGARES, SEMLIN, TABLAT, TARET, TIMIRA, UDAMAN, and UGALES.

Sources: Aikin, *General Biography*, 493; Bayle, *Historical and Critical Dictionary*, 262; Chambers, *Book of Days*, 723; Conybeare, *Jewish Quarterly Review*, Vol. 11, 20–21; Hyatt, *Book of Demons*, 40–1; Jahn, *Jahn's Biblical Archaeology*, 524–5, 530; Mathers, *Book of the*

Sacred Magic of Abramelin the Mage, 114; Prophet, *Fallen Angels and the Origins of Evil*, 174; Robbins, *Encyclopedia of Witchcraft and Demonology*, 128; Smith, *Comprehensive Dictionary of the Bible*, 73; Voltaire, *Works of M. de Voltaire*, 193.

Servitors of Asmodeus

In the *Sacred Magic of Abramelin the Mage*, book two, sixteen servitors of ASMODEUS are listed: ABADIR, BACARON, ENIURI, GILARION, HIFARION, HOLBA, MAGGID, MEBBESSER, Omet, ONEI, ORATION, PRECHES, SARRA, SBARIONAT, SCLAVAK, and UTIFA.

Sources: Bayle, *Historical and Critical Dictionary*, 262; Bryant, *New System*, 201; Chambers, *Book of Days*, 723; Eckley, *Children's Lore in Finnegans Wake*, 158; Howey, *Encircled Serpent*, 31; Hyatt, *Book of Demons*, 40–1; Jennings, *Ophiolatreia*, 3; Mathers, *Book of the Sacred Magic of Abramelin the Mage*, 107, 119, 120; Robbins, *Encyclopedia of Witchcraft and Demonology*, 128.

Servitors of Asmodeus and Magoth

In the *Sacred Magic of Abramelin the Mage*, book two, fifteen servitors of ASMODEUS and Magoth are listed: APOT, BIRIEL, DIOPOS, DISOLEL, INOKOS, KELE, LUNDO, MABAKIEL, MAGIROS, MAGOG, OPUN, SARTABAKIM, SIFON, SOBE, and TOUN.

Sources: Conybeare, *Jewish Quarterly Review*, Vol. 11, 20–21; Hyatt, *Book of Demons*, 40–1; Mathers, *Book of the Sacred Magic of Abramelin the Mage*, 118; Voltaire, *Works of M. de Voltaire*, 193; Von Worms, *Book of Abramelin*, 250.

Servitors of Astarot

The *Sacred Magic of Abramelin the Mage* lists thirty-two servitors of ASTAROT. They are ALAN, AMAN, APORMENOS, ARAEX, ARGILON, BAFAMAL, BAHAL, CAMAL, CAMONIX, DAREK, FAGANI, GINAR, GOLEN, GONOGIN, GROMENIS, HERG, HIPOLOS, ILESON, ISCHIGAS, ISIAMON, KATARON, KOLOFE, LEPACA, NIMERIX, OKIRI, OMBALAT, QUARTAS, RAX, RIGIOS, SCHELAGON, TOXAI, and UGIRPEN.

Sources: Agrippa, *Three Books of Occult Philosophy*, 115; Aikin, *General Biography*, 493; Bayle, *Historical and Critical Dictionary*, 262; Botterweck, *Theological Dictionary of the Old Testament*, 431–2; Hsia, *World of Catholic Renewal*, 151; Kirchmayer, *Un-Natural History*, 19; Mathers, *Book of the Sacred Magic of Abramelin the Mage*, 106, 117; Rudwin, *Devil in Legend and Literature*, 28; Simon, *Papal Magic*, 116, 119; Van der Toorn, *Dictionary of Deities and Demons*, 113; Voltaire, *Works of M. de Voltaire*, 193; Von Worms, *Book of Abramelin*, 121, 249, 256–8.

Servitors of Asyriel

The *Theurgia Goetia*, the second book of the *Lemegeton*, names sixteen chief duke servitors for ASYRIEL, eight diurnal and eight nocturnal. They are AARIEL, of the day; AMIEL, of the night; AR-CISAT, of the day; ASPIEL, of the night; ASTOR, of the day; BUDAR, of the night; BUNIEL, of the day; CARGA, of the day; CUSIEL, of the day; CUS-RIEL, of the night; FASEUA, of the night; HAMAS, of the night; MALGUEL, of the day; MAROTH, of the night; OMIEL, of the night; and RABAS, of the day.

Sources: Belanger, *Dictionary of Demons*, 32, 37, 47, 77, 86, 152; Davidson, *A Dictionary of Angels: Including the Fallen Angels*, 1, 184; Guiley, *Encyclopedia of Demons and Demonology*, 20; Peterson, *Lesser Key of Solomon*, 73–4, 77, 80.

Servitors of Barmiel

There are fifteen servitors for BARMIEL, eight named dukes of the night and seven for the day: ACEREBA, of the night; Aclerorv (ACLEROR), of the day; ASHIB, of the night; BAABAL, of the night; BARBIL, of the day; BERBIS, of the night; CARNET, of the night; CARPID, of the day; CLEANSI, of the day; GABIR, of the night; KIRIEL, of the day; MAR-QUES, of the night; MORCAZA, of the night; SO-CHAS, of the day; and TIGARA, of the day.

Sources: Gettings, *Encyclopedia of Demons and Demonology*, 24, 47, 142; Leslau, *Arabic Loanwords in Ethiopian Semitic*, 367; Mathers, *Book of the Sacred Magic of Abra-Melin*, 107; McLean, *Treatise on Angel Magic*, 42; Peterson, *Lesser Key of Solomon*, 70–1; Trithemius, *Steganographia*, 17–8; Von Goethe, *Goethe's Letters to Zelter*, 377.

Servitors of Beelzebub

The *Sacred Magic of Abramelin the Mage*, book two, lists forty-nine servitors under the command of BEELZEBUB. They are ADIRAEL, AKIUM, AL-CANOR, AMATIA, AMBOLON, ARCON, AROGOR, AROLEN, BALFORI, BILICO, BILIFARES, BILIFOR, BOROL, CARELENA, CORILON, DIMIRAG, DI-RALISEN, DORAK, ELPONEN, ERGAMEN, GOTI-FAN, GRAMON, HACAMULI, HOLASTRI, IAMAI, IGURIM, IKONOK, KABADA, KEMAL, KIPOKIS, LAMALON, LAMARION, LAMOLON, LICANEN, LIROCHI, MAGALAST, NAMIROS, NATALIS, NI-MORUP, NOMINON, ORGOSIL, PELLIPIS, PLISON, RADERAF, SAMALO, SOROSMA, TACHAN, TROMES, and ZAGALO.

Sources: Cavendish, *The Powers of Evil in Western Religion, Magic and Folk Belief*, 253–4; Chambers, *Book of Days*, 722; Churchill, *History and Practice of Magic*, 402; Hyatt, *Book of Demons*, 47; Mathers, *Book of Sacred Magic of Abramelin the Mage*, 104, 107–8, 116, 120–1; Mathers, *Magia Della Cabala*, 136; Melton, *Encyclopedia of Occultism and Parapsychology*, 315; *Murray's Magazine, Early British Periodicals*, 669.

Servitors of Buriel

Twelve chief dukes are in service under Buriel. Each of them commands eight hundred servitors

of their own. Appearing before their summoner as a snake with a virgin's head and sounding like a man when they speak, these nocturnal demons are all evil-natured, hated by the other demons, and heliophobic (see HELIOPHOBIC DEVIL). They are Almadiel, Bufiel, Carniel, Casbriel, Cupriel, Drubiel, DRUSIEL, Futiel, Merosiel, Nastros, Nedriel, and Sarviel.

Source: Peterson, *Lesser Key of Solomon*, 93, 103.

Servitors of Bydiel

The *Theurgia Goetia*, the second book of the *Lemegeton*, lists ten dukes in service to BYDIEL. Each one appears before his summoner in an attractive form, commands 2,400 servitors of his own, and is said to be good-natured and willing to obey. Bydiel's servitors are ANDRUCHA, AR-MONIEL, BRAMSIEL, CHAROBIEL, CHREMO, CRUCHAM, LEMONIEL, MANASAEL, MUDRIEL, and PERSIFIEL.

Sources: Belanger, *Dictionary of Demons*, 71, 76; Gettings, *Dictionary of Demons*, 232; Guiley, *Encyclopedia of Demons and Demonology*, 28; Peterson, *Lesser Key of Solomon*, 95, 105; Trithemius, *Steganographia*, 79, 146, 220.

Servitors of Cabariel

There are one hundred chief duke servitors of CABARIEL, but only ten diurnal and ten nocturnal are named for each. Each of these demons commands fifty servitors of his own. The diurnal servitors are said to be obedient to their summoner, but the nocturnal ones are disobedient and evil by nature, and will try to deceive at every opportunity. Cabariel's servitors are ANIEL, of the day; Asoriel, of the day; Cazul, of the night; Clyssan, of the day; Cugiel, of the night; Cuphal, of the day; Dubiel (DUBBIEL), of the night; Elitel, of the day; Etimiel, of the day; Godiel, of the day; Ladiel, of the night; Mador, of the night; Morias, of the night; Otim, of the night; Pandor, of the night; Parius, of the day; Peniel ("face of God"), of the night; Satifiel, of the day; Taros, of the day; and Thalbus, of the night.

Sources: Belanger, *Dictionary of Demons*, 34; Davidson, *Dictionary of Angels*, 98; Guiley, *Encyclopedia of Angels*, 109; Guiley, *Encyclopedia of Demons and Demonology*, 36, 232; Peterson, *Lesser Key of Solomon*, 84; Trithemius, *Steganographia*, 73, 81.

Servitors of Camuel

The twenty servitors of CAMUEL appear before their summoner in a beautiful form and are said to be very courteous. They are ASIMIEL (Asimel), of the night; AZEMO, of the night; BUDIEL, of the day; CALIM (Calym), of the night; CAMYEL, of the day; CARIEL, of the day; Citgara (Sitgara), of the day; DANIEL, of the day; Dobiel (DUB-

BIEL), of the night; ELCAR, of the day; MERAS, of the night; MORIEL, of the night; NERIEL, of the day; NODAR, of the night; OMYEL, of the day; ORPEMIEL, of the day; PARIEL, of the day; PHANIEL, of the night; TEDIEL, of the night; and TUGAROS, of the night.

Sources: Peterson, *Lesser Key of Solomon*, 67–8; Scheible, *Sixth and Seventh Books of Moses*, 75; Trithemius, *Steganographia*, 12, 30, 32, 73; Waite, *Book of Ceremonial Magic*, 67.

Servitors of Carnesiel

The *Theurgia Goetia*, book two of the *Lemegeton*, says there are 60,000,000,000,000 duke servitors of CARNESIEL, but it only names twelve of them: Arifiel, ARMANY, BEDARY, BENOHAM, BUCAFAS, CAPRIEL, CUMERZEL, LAPHOR, Myrezyn, Ornich, VADRIEL, and ZABRIEL.

Sources: Butler, *Ritual Magic*, 77; Eco, *Infinity of Lists*, 61; Gettings, *Dictionary of Demons*, 232; Pane, *Hierarchy of Hell*, 68; Peterson, *Lesser Key of Solomon*, 59–60, 69; Trirthemius, *Steganographia*, 1, 49; Waite, *Manual of Cartomancy and Occult Divination*, 97.

Servitors of Caspiel

According to the *Lesser Key of Solomon*, there are twelve chief duke servitors of CASPIEL. Each one commands 2,660 duke servitors of his own and is said to be rude and stubborn. They are AMBRI, ARIDIEL (ARIAIEL), BUDARIM (Budarijm, Budarym, and Femel), CAMOR, CAMORY, CHARIEL, FEMOL, GERIEL (Geriol), LARMOL (Camorr, Larmel), MARAS, ORIEL (Otiel), and URSIEL (USIEL).

Sources: Belanger, *Dictionary of Demons*, 89, 138; Davidson, *Encyclopedia of Angels*, 283; McLean, *Treatise on Angel Magic*, 35, 53; Peterson, *Lesser Key of Solomon*, 70.

Servitors of Demoriel

The *Theurgia Goetia*, the second book of the *Lemegeton*, says there are twelve chief duke servitors of DEMORIEL; each one commands 1,140 servitors of his own. Demoriel's servitors are ARMBIEL, BURISIEL, CABARIM, CARNOL, CHOMIEL, CHURIBAL, DABRINOS, DIRIEL, DUBILON, Mador, Moder, and Monandor.

Sources: Guiley, *Encyclopedia of Demons and Demonology*, 60; McLean, *Treatise of Angel Magic*, 34, 54; Peterson, *Lesser Key of Solomon*, 63; Trithemius, *Steganographia*, 58.

Servitors of Ereshkigal

Originating in Babylonian, Chaldean, and Sumerian demonology and written of in the *Magan Text*, Ereshkigal, the goddess of death and gloom, is said to have seven gigantic larvae servitors: ALAL, GIGIM, IDPA, NAMTAR, TELAL, URUKU, and UTUK.

Sources: Crisafulli, *Go to Hell*, 222; Gray, *Mythology of All Races*, 355, 364; King, *The Supernatural*, 296; Lenormant, *Chaldean Magic*, 24, 37; Myer, *Qabbalah*, 453; Seligmann, *Magic, Supernaturalism, and Religion*, 1; Sorensen, *Possession and Exorcism in the New Testament and Early Christianity*, 27–8; Spradlin, *Search for Certainty*, 37.

Servitors of Emoniel

The *Theurgia Goetia*, the second book of the *Lemegeton*, lists twelve duke servitors under the command of EMONIEL. Each of these demons commands 1,320 lesser dukes. They are said to be good-natured and willing to obey their summoner, and they live in the woods. They are ARMISIEL, CARNODIEL, CASPANIEL (Oaspeniel), CRUHIEL, DRAMIEL, EDRIEL, ERMENIEL, MASINEL (Nasiniel), MUSINIEL, PANDIEL, PANUEL (Phanuel), and VASENEL.

Sources: Gettings, *Dictionary of Demons*, 232; Peterson, *Lesser a Key of Solomon*, 67, 97, 119; Trithemius, *Steganographia*, 23, 67, 81, 126.

Servitors of Fleuretty

Johann Wierus's *Pseudomonarchia Daemonum* (*False Monarchy of Demons*, 1583) lists three servitors to the demon FLEURETTY: ALIGAR, BATHIM, and PURSON.

Sources: Baskin, *Sorcerer's Handbook*, 276, 245; De Laurence, *Lesser Key of Solomon, Goetia*, 27–8; Waite, *Unknown World 1894–1895*, 230; Wedick, *Treasury of Witchcraft*, 96–7.

Servitors of Fleuretty, Lucifuge, Nebiros, Sargatanas, and Satanachia

There are eighteen servitors of FLEURETTY, Lucifuge (LUCIFUGE ROFOCALE), NEBIROS, SARGATANAS, and SATANACHIA. They are AAMON, AGARES, AYPEROS, BAEL, BARBATOS, BATHIM, BOTIS, BUER, ELIGOR, FARAII, GLASSYALABOLAS, GUSTOYN, MARBAS, NABERRS, PRUSLAS, Pursan (PURSON), VALEFAR, and ZORAY.

Sources: Baskin, *Dictionary of Satanism*, 9, 275–6, 445; Butler, *Ritual Magic*, 87–89; De Laurence, *Lesser Key of Solomon, Goetia*, 22–5, 27–8; DuQuette, *Key to Solomon's Key*, 162–3; McLean, *Treatise of Angel Magic*, 52–3; Peterson, *Lesser Key of Solomon*, 18, 233, 262; Shah, *Occultism*, 61–2; Waite, *Book of Black Magic and Ceremonial Magic*, 157, 187–8, 225, 229; Wedeck, *Treasury of Witchcraft*, 96–8, 100, 296.

Servitors of Gedeil

The *Theurgia Goetia*, the second book of the *Lemegeton*, lists GEDEIL as having sixteen duke servitors: AGLAS, of the night; AGRA, of the day; ANAEL, of the day; ARAON, of the night; ASSABA, of the day; BARIEL, of the night; CIRECAS, of the night; COTIEL, of the day; MISHEL, of the night; NARAS, of the day; RANTIEL, of the night; RECIEL, of the day; SABAS, of the day; SADIEL, of the day; SARIEL, of the night; and VRIEL, of the night.

Sources: Black, *Book of Enoch, or, I Enoch*, 129; Laurence, *Foreign Quarterly Review*, Vol. 24, 370; Lumpkin, *Fallen Angels, the Watchers, and the Origins of Evil*, 31; Marcus, *Jew in the Medieval World*, 245–6; Neusner, *Christianity, Judaism and Other Greco-Roman Cults*, 159–65; Peterson, *Lesser Key of Solomon*, 72, 114, 202; Shadduck, *England's Amorous Angels*, 347; Trithemius, *Steganographia*, 20, 81.

Servitors of Hale and Sergulath

The *Grimoirium Verum* (*Grimoire of Truth*), alleged to have been written by Alibek the Egyptian in 1517, says there are eight servitors of Hale and Sergulath. Said to be powerful in their own right, their names are AGLASIS, BRULEFER, BUCON, HARISTUM, MINOSON, PENTAGONY, PROCULO, and Sidragrisam.

Sources: Conway, *Demonology and Devil-Lore*, 59; Kelly, *Who in Hell*, 106–7; Kuriakos, *Grimoire Verum Ritual Book*, 12, 16; Masters, *Devil's Dominion*, 131; Poinsot, *Complete Book of the Occult and Fortune Telling*, 378; Von Worms, *Book of Abramelin*, 260; Waite, *Book of Black Magic*, 188, 288.

Servitors of Icosiel

The *Theurgia Goetia*, the second book of the *Lemegeton*, names fifteen chief duke servitors who are under the command of ICOSIEL. Each of these demons are said to have 2,200 servitors of their own. Able to be summoned any time of the day or night, they are said to be good natured and obedient, doing exactly as the summoner asks. Most easily summoned from inside a house, their names are AGAPIEL, Amediel, ATHESIEL, CAMBRIEL, CUMARIEL, HERESIEL, LARPHIEL, MACHARIEL, Munefiel, NATHRIEL, PISCHIEL, THANATIEL, URBANIEL, ZACHARIEL, and Zosie.

Sources: Agrippa, *Three Books of Occult Philosophy*, 536; Gettings, *Dictionary of Demons*, 232; Godwin, *Godwin's Cabalistic Encyclopedia*, 64; Peterson, *Lesser Key of Solomon*, 98–9, 102; Trithemius, *Steganographia*, 69, 141; Von Goethe, *Goethe's Letters to Zelter*, 378; Webster, *Encyclopedia of Angels*, 219.

Servitors of Kore and Magoth

The *Sacred Magic of Abramelin the Mage*, book two, lists sixty-five servitors for Kore and Magoth. Many of the various grimoires list Kore and Magoth; however, none of them list these demons separately or tell any other information about them. Their names are ABAGIRON, AGILAS, AMCHISON, ANAGOTOS, ARIOTH, AROTOR, ARPIRON, ARRABIN, BARUEL, BATTERNIS, BUTARAB, COBEL, COLVAM, CORODON, DAGLAS, DEBAM, DULID, EGAKIREH, FATURAB, FERSEBUS, FORTESON, HAGION, HAGOG, HEMIS, HEPOGON, HORMINOS, ILARAX, IRIX, ISCHIRON, KAITAR, KAMUSIL, KATOLIN, KILIGIL, KOLAM, LABONETON, LOCATER, LUESAF, MADAIL, MAISADUL, MAKALOS, MANTAN, MARAG, MASAUB, MEGALAK, MEKLBOC, MIMOSA, NACHERAN, NENISEM, ODAX, OLISERMON, PANDOLI, PARAMOR, PETUNOF, RIMOG, ROLER, SCHARAK, SIKASTIN, SOBEL, SORRIOLENEN, SUPIPAS, TAGORA, TIGRAFON, TIRAIM, UBARIN, and URIGO.

Sources: Belanger, *Dictionary of Demons*, 30, 33, 40–1, 80, 103, 114, 116; Bryce, *First Latin Book*, 93; Butler, *Ritual Magic*, 96; Eco, *Infinity of Lists*, 61; Ford, *Bible of the Adversary*, 92; Gordon, *Adventures in the Nearest East*, 12; Kitto, *A Cyclopedia of Biblical Literature*, 837; Mathers, *Book of the Sacred Magic of Abralemin the Mage*, 107, 109, 118–22, 133, 135; McClintock, *Cyclopædia of Biblical, Theological, and Ecclesiastical Literature*, 448; Susej *Demonic Bible*, 258; Von Worms, *Book of Abramelin*, 118, 123, 249–51, 254, 256.

Servitors of Lucifer

There are two servitors of Lucifer, AGALIAREPT and SANTANACKIA.

Sources: Baskin, *Sorcerer's Handbook*, 12; Mark, *Book of Hierarchies*, 28; Masters, *Devil's Dominion*, 131; Roberts, *Magician of the Golden Dawn*, 80; Summers, *Witchcraft and Black Magic*, 135; Waite, *Book of Ceremonial Magic*, 187; Wedeck, *Treasury of Witchcraft*, 96.

Servitors of Macariel

In the *Theurgia Goetia*, the second book of the *Lemegeton*, there are twelve named chief duke servitors of MACHARIEL. Each of these demons commands four hundred of his own servitors, and when summoned they will appear in a variety of forms, but most commonly will do so as a dragon with a virgin's head. Able to be summoned any time of the day or night, they are said to be good-natured and willing to obey. The names of MACHARIEL's servitors are ANDROS, ASMADIEL, BRUFIEL, CHAROEL, CLANIEL, DRUSIEL, GREMIAL, LEMODAC, MASTUEL, ROMYEL, THURIEL, and VARPIEL.

Sources: Belanger, *Dictionary of Demons*, 43, 95; Gettings, *Dictionary of Demons*, 232; Guiley, *Encyclopedia of Demons and Demonology*, 35, 159; Krill, *Greek and Latin in English Today*, 44; Peterson, *Lesser Key of Solomon*, 100, 102, 103, 108; Trithemius, *Steganographia*, 81, 141; Van der Toorn, *Dictionary of Gods and Goddesses*, 152; Waite, *Book of Black Magic and of Pacts*, 189.

Servitors of Oriens

In the *Sacred Magic of Abramelin the Mage*, eight servitors are listed for ORIENS. They are AGAB (Zagal), BALAKEN (Balachem), GAGISON, GASARONS (Gazaron), MAFALAC, SARISEL, SOROSMA, and TURITEL.

Sources: Belanger, *Dictionary of Demons*, 58, 136; Ford, *Bible of the Adversary*, 93–4; Mathers, *Book of the Sacred Magic of Abramelin the Mage*, 108, 121–22; Susej, *Demonic Bible*, 259; Von Worms, *Book of Abramelin*, 253, 257.

Servitors of Pamersiel

The *Theurgia Goetia*, the second book of the *Lemegeton*, says that there are eleven servitors of Pamersiel. Nocturnal and known to be very useful for driving out spirits of haunted places, they have a reputation for being arrogant and stubborn as well as expert liars. When summoned, these demons must be invoked from the second floor of a home or in a wide open space. Pamersiel's servitors are ABRULGES, Aneyr, EBRA, HAMORPHOL, ITRASBIEL, Itules, MADRES, Madriel, ORMENU, RABLION, and SOTHEANS.

Sources: Findlen, *Athanasius Kircher*, 262; Johnson, *Landscape Ethnoecology*, 147; Lehrich, *Language of Demons and Angels*, 191; McLean, *Treatise on Angel Magic*, 36; Peterson, *Lesser Key of Solomon*, 64; Rasula, *Imagining Language*, 130–1; Trithemius, *Steganographia*, 1; Waite, *Manual of Cartomancy and Occult Divination*, 97.

Servitors of Paymon

The *Sacred Magic of Abramelin the Mage* lists fifteen servitors for PAYMON, named ACHANIEL, AGAFALI, AGLAFOS, ASTOLIT, CAME, DISON, EBARON, KABERSA, MENOLIK, ROFFLES, Rukum, SUDORON, TACAROS, UGOLA, and ZALANES.

Sources: Belanger, *Dictionary of Demons*, 20, 49, 110, 150; Ford, *Bible of the Adversary*, 94; Mathers, *Book of the Sacred Magic of Abramelin the Mage*, 108, 121; Susej, *Demonic Bible*, 259; Von Worms, *Book of Abramelin*, 253, 257.

Servitors of Rahab

Ars Paulina, the third book of the *Lemegeton*, lists eleven servitors of RAHAB: AMMIEL, a chief; CASSIEL, a chief; DANIEL; EMARFIEL; LARMIEL, a chief; MARFIEL, a chief; ORMIJEL, a chief; PERMIEL; QUORIEL; SARDIEL, a chief; and STURBIEL.

Sources: Barton, *Journal of Biblical Literature*, Vols. 30–31, 165; Fishbane, *Great Dragon Battle and the Talmudic Redaction*, 41–55; Peterson, *Lesser Key of Solomon*, 68, 113–4, 127, 144; Schwartz, *Tree of Souls*, 36, 106–7, 116; Trithemius, *Steganographia*, 93; Waite, *Book of Ceremonial Magic*, 67.

Servitors of Raysiel

The *Theurgia Goetia*, the second book of the *Lemegeton*, names thirty chief dukes for Raysiel. The diurnal servitors are good-natured and willing to obey their summoner, but the nocturnal servitors are disobedient, naturally evil, stubborn, and will not obey their summoner willingly. They are Albhadur, of the day; Aleasi, of the night;

Arayl, of the night; Arepach, of the night; Armena, of the day; Astael, of the day; Baciar, of the day; Belsay, of the night; Betasiel, of the day; Chanaei, of the day; Culmar, of the night; Dubarus, of the day; Fursiel, of the day; Lamas, of the night; Lazaba, of the night; Melcha, of the day; Morael, of the night; Paras, of the night; Quibda, of the night; Ramica, of the day; Sadar, of the day; Sarach, of the night; Sebach, of the night; Sequiel, of the day; Terath, of the day; Tharas, of the day; Thariel, of the night; Thoac, of the day; Thurcal, of the night; and VRIEL, of the day.

Of the diurnal servitors, Betasiel, Chanaei, Fursiel, Melcha, Tharas, and Vriel have thirty servitors each; Albhadur, Armena, Astael, Baciar, Dubarus, Ramica, Sadar, Sequiel, Tharas, and Thoac have fifty each.

Of the nocturnal servitors, Arayl, Culmar, Paras, and Thariel have forty servitors; Aleasi, Lazaba, Quibda, and Sebach have twenty; Arepach, Belsay, Lamas, Morael, and Thurcal have ten.

Sources: Guiley, *Encyclopedia of Demons and Demonology*, 206; Peterson, *Lesser Key of Solomon*, 86; Trithemius, *Steganographia*, 81.

Servitors of Saegatanas

The *Grimoire of Pope Honorius* (*Le Grimoire du Pape Honorius*), alleged to have been written by Pope Honorius III in the eighteenth century, names Saegatanas as having three servitors: FORAU, LORAY, and VALAFAR.

Sources: Drury, *Dictionary of the Esoteric*, 109; *Dublin University Magazine*, Vol. 66, 521; Knappert, *Encyclopaedia of Middle Eastern Mythology and Religion*, 288; McLean, *Treatise of Angel Magic*, 57; Wedeck, *Treasury of Witchcraft*, 96.

Servitors of Sargatanas

According to the *Grimoire of Pope Honorius*, there are three servitors for Sargatanas: FORAU, LORAY, and VALAFAR.

Sources: Baglio, *Encyclopædia of Religion and Ethics*, Vol. 8, 272, 304; Baskin, *Sorcerer's Handbook*, 276; Chaplin, *Dictionary of the Occult and Paranormal*, 136; Drury, *Dictionary of the Esoteric*, 109; Mark, *Book of Hierarchies*, 28; Wedeck, *Treasury of Witchcraft*, 96, 97.

Servitors of Sasquiel

The *Ars Paulina*, the third book of the *Lemegeton*, lists fifteen duke servitors for SASQUIEL. Each of these demons has 5,550 servitors. SASQUIEL's servitors are ARANIEL (ARMARELE), ASISIEL (AMISIEL), CAMIEL, DAMIEL, FUSTIEL, Futiniel, JAMERIEL, LAMEROS, Maroch, OMERACH, PUTISIEL (PUBRISIEL), RAMERIEL, RUANIEL, Serapiel (SARAPHIEL), and ZACHIEL.

Sources: Charles, *Book of Enoch*, 67; Davidson, *Dictionary of Angels*, 16, 84, 115, 184, 357; Ladd, *Commentary on the Book of Enoch*, 222; Lévi, *History of Magic*, 38; Peterson, *Lesser Key of Solomon*, 62, 99, 114; Trithemius, *Steganographia*, 95, 103; Waite, *Book of Black and Ceremonial Magic*, 67; Waite, *The Book of Ceremonial Magic*, 67.

Servitors of Satanachia

The *Grimoirium Verum* (*Grimoire of Truth*), allegedly written by Alibek the Egyptian in 1517, says there are four servitors to the demon SATANACHIA. Each is ranked a chief, and their names are HERAMAEL, SERGUTHY, SUSTUGRIEL, and TRIMASAEL.

Sources: Kelly, *Who in Hell*, 111; Kuriakos, *Grimoire Verum Ritual Book*, 34, 36, 39–40; Masters, *Devil's Dominion*, 131; Waite, *Book of Black Magic and of Pacts*, 162–3, 187.

Servitors of Satanachia and Sataniciae

Although there are fifty-five (or forty-five, sources vary) servitors for SATANACHIA and SATANICIAE, only four of them are named: HERAMAEL, Sergutthy (SERGUTHY), SUSTUGRIEL, and TRIMASAEL. Ranked as chiefs, these servitors are summoned for their willingness to give good FAMILIARs, furnish mandragores (mandrake plants), and teach the magical arts. They are known to act quickly and without causing any trouble to their summoner, provided that they are content with him.

Sources: Black, *Edinburgh Review*, Vol. 107, 240; Kuriakos, *Grimoire Verum Ritual Book*, 36, 39–40; Mark, *Book of Hierarchies*, 28; Masters, *Devil's Dominion*, 131; Trithemius, *Steganographia*, 88.

Servitors of Sazquiel

The *Lemegeton* lists Sazquiel as having ten chief servitors. ARMARELE, DAMIEL, Maroch, and Serapiel are his superior servitor spirits, while AMISIEL, FUSTIEL, FUTINIEL, JAMERIEL (Jamersil), PUBRISIEL, and RAMISIEL are his inferior servitor spirits.

Sources: Davidson, *Dictionary of Angels*, 16, 115, 184, 357; Peterson, *Lesser Key of Solomon*, 114; Trithemius, *Steganographia*, 95, 103; Waite, *Book of Black and Ceremonial Magic*, 67.

Servitors of Scox

The *Ars Paulina*, the third book of the *Lemegeton*, lists fifteen duke servitors for SCOX: AMISIEL, ARANIEL, CAMIEL, DAMIEL, FUSTIEL, Futiniel, JAMERIEL, LAMEROS, Maroch, OMERACH, PUTISIEL, RAMERIEL, SARAPHIEL, URANIEL, and ZACHIEL.

Sources: Charles, *Book of Enoch*, 67; Davidson, *Dictionary of Angels*, 16, 84, 115, 184, 357; Ladd, *Commentary on the Book of Enoch*, 222; Lévi, *History of Magic*,

38; Peterson, *Lesser Key of Solomon*, 62, 99, 114; Trithemius, *Steganographia*, 95, 103; Waite, *Book of Ceremonial Magic*, 67.

Servitors of Symiel

There are one thousand servitors under the command of SYMIEL, but only twenty of them are named, ten dukes for the day and as many for the night. They are ACHOT, of the day; APIEL, of the night; ARAFES, of the night; ASMIEL, of the day; BONIEL, of the day; CHRUBAS, of the day; CURIEL, of the night; DAGIEL, of the day; LARAEL, of the day; MAFRUS, of the night; MALAD, of the night; MALGRON, of the day; MARIANU, of the night; MOLAEL, of the night; MURAHE, of the night; MUSOR, of the day; NARZAD, of the night; RICHEL, of the night; ROMIEL, of the day; and Vaslos of the day.

The servitors of the day have collectively under them seven hundred twenty lesser servitors that they share; they are said to be very good-natured and quick to obey their summoner. The servitors of the night have seven hundred ninety lesser servitors to divide among them; they are disobedient, stubborn, and will not appear willingly when summoned.

Sources: Agrippa, *Fourth Book of Occult Philosophy*, 212, 553; Barrett, *The Magus*, 125; Davidson, *Dictionary of Angels*, 93; Eco, *Infinity of Lists*, 61; Hoffman, *And God Said*, 163–4; Mathers, *Book of the Sacred Magic of Abramelin the Mage*, 113; Peterson, *Lesser Key of Solomon*, 69, 88–9, 99; Trithemius, *Steganographia*, 42, 69, 85.

Servitors of Syrach

The *Grimoirium Verum* (*Grimoire of Truth*), allegedly written by Alibek the Egyptian in 1517, says there are eighteen servitors to the demon SYRACH. They are BECHAUD, CLAUNECK, CLISTHERT, FRIMOST, FRUCISSIERE, FRUTIMIERE, GULAND, HICPACTH, HUICTIIGARAS, HUMOTS, KHIL, KLEPOTH, MERSILDE, MORAIL, MUSISIN, SEGAL, SIRCHADE, and SURGAT.

Sources: Butler, *Ritual Magic*, 81, 94; Collin de Plancy, *Dictionnaire Infernal*, 133; Kelly, *Who in Hell*, 96, 113; Kuriakos, *Grimoire Verum Ritual Book*, 17, 20–5, 35, 38–9; Masters, *Devil's Dominion*, 130–1; Sabellicus, *Magia Pratica*, 33, 35; Waite, *Book of Black Magic and of Pacts*, 159, 184, 187, 190, 283.

Servitors of Turael

There are six servitors for the demon TURAEL. Their names are BARIEL, BEHEMOTH, BELIAL, Beliar, RASIEL, and ZIMINAR.

Sources: Barton, *Journal of Biblical Literature*, Vols. 30–31, 164; Horne, *Sacred Books and Early Literature of the East*, 114; Chambers, *Book of Days*, 723; Conway, *Demonology and Devil-Lore*, 299; De Laurence, *Lesser Key of Solomon, Goetia*, 44.

Servitors of Vachmiel

There are five named chiefs in service under the demonic ruler of the fourth hour, VACHMIEL; their names are AMMIEL, LARMIEL, MARFIEL, ORMIJEL, and SARDIEL. Although VACHMIEL has one hundred lesser servitors, only five of them are named: DANIEL, EMARFIEL, PERMIEL, QUORIEL, and STURBIEL. All the servitors of Vachmiel have numerous servitors of their own.

Sources: Davidson, *Dictionary of Angels*, 303; Peterson, *Lesser Key of Solomon*, 113; Waite, *Book of Ceremonial Magic*, 67.

Servitors of Vadriel

The *Sacred Magic of Abramelin the Mage* lists ten servitors for the demon VADRIEL: Astroniel, Brasiel, Charms, Dameil, Kromos, Madriel, Meros, Nafarin, Pamerif, and Zoigiel.

Source: Waite, *Manual of Cartomancy and Occult Divination*, 97.

Servitors of Veguaniel

The *Ars Paulina*, the third book of the *Lemegeton*, names ten servitors for VEGUANIEL. They are COMADIEL; DRELMETH, a chief; FURIA; GLMARIJ; HANTIEL; Lessiel, a chief; Murriel, a chief; PARMIEL; SARDINIEL, a chief; and Servile.

Sources: Davidson, *Dictionary of Angels*, 98, 135, 221; Gettings, *Dictionary of Demons*, 112; Peterson, *Lesser Key of Solomon*, 113; Trithemius, *Steganographia*, 91; Waite, *Book of Black Magic and Ceremonial Magic*, 67.

Seven Demons, The

Variations: Seven and Seven, Seven Times Seven

In ancient Mesopotamia, Sumerian mythology claimed that the Seven Demons were the offspring of the god of the underworld and earth, An, and goddess of the sky, Ki. The Seven Demons were the personifications of the violent and deadly forces of nature. These immortal demons who survive on human blood are a collection, considered to be a single entity, and seldom act independently of one another. They are mentioned in several holy texts and demonic banishing rites. They will not go into temples because they are afraid of the images of the Sumer gods, such as Anshar, Enki, Enlil, and Ereshkigal (see IRKALLA).

Sources: Dalley, *Myths of Mesopotamia*, 224; Harris, *Gender and Aging in Mesopotamia*, 133; Horowitz, *Mesopotamian Cosmic Geography*, 219; Mackenzie, *Myths of Babylonia and Assyria*, 34.

Seven Heavenly Bodies, The

In Babylonian, Jewish, and Solominic lore, the Seven Heavenly Bodies are one of the thirty-three (or thirty-six, sources vary) elements of the cosmic ruler of the darkness. Named as one of the seventy-two SPIRITS OF SOLOMON who were bound to the king and made to dig the foundations of his temple, these demonic goddesses are in all likelihood a variation of the PLEIADES. Described as a collection of seven female spirits, fair in appearance, bound and woven together, represented as a cluster of stars in the heavens, the Seven Heavenly Bodies each have their own personal angelic adversary. This demon travels about sometimes living in Lydia, or Olympus, or on a great mountain.

Sources: Conybeare, *Jewish Quarterly Review*, Vol. 11, 24–6; Charlesworth, *Old Testament Pseudepigrapha*, 935; Guiley, *Encyclopedia of Angels*, 163.

Sezarbil

In Apollonius of Tyana's *Nuctemeron* (*Night Illuminated by Day*), Sezarbil is named as the demon of hostility. He is said to be most powerful during the tenth hour.

Sources: Gettings, *Dictionary of Demons*, 223; Lévi, *Transcendental Magic*, 393, 507.

Shabriri

Shabriri is the demon of blindness in Jewish lore. He rests atop uncovered water at night, including pools and rivers, and causes blindness in anyone who drinks it. He is especially attracted to clear and shining vessels. To render Shabriri powerless before drinking, say the incantation "Shabriri. Beriri. Riri. Jiri. Ri. I am thirsty for water in a white glass." The reduction of his name causes him to shrink in size and vanish. His name in Hebrew translates to mean "dazzling glare" or more literally, "breaker of the eyesight."

Sources: Bias, *Freedom from the World of Satanism and the Power of Satan*, 42; Thompson, *Semitic Magic*, 30; Trachtenberg, *Jewish Magic and Superstition*, 119; Van Loopik, *Ways of the Sages and the Way of the World*, 156–7.

Shadow Ghost

Variations: Shadow People

A shadow ghost is a type of demonic entity that is most typically found inside of homes; it looks like featureless black mist. Birds and cats are especially sensitive to its presence.

Source: Dunwich, *Witch's Guide to Ghosts and the Supernatural*, 228.

Shaitan

Variations: IBLIS, Shatana, Shatian, Shaytan IBLIS, Sheitan

From Rabanic lore comes a type of demon known as a shaitan. According to the Koran, they are FALLEN ANGELS. In Hebrew the word *shaitan* means "SATAN" or "enemy."

Sources: Crowley, *Magick*, lxiv; Davidson, *Dictionary of Angels*, 270; Knowles, *Nineteenth Century*, Vol. 31, 449; Leeming, *Oxford Companion to World Mythology*, 347; Mack, *Field Guide to Demons, Fairies, Fallen Angels, and Other Subversive Spirits*, 151.

Shaitans

Variations: Shaytans, Shedeem, SHEDIM, Sheitan, Sheytan, Mazikeen

Created by the fire of Allah, the shaitans, a type of DJINN, appear in their natural form as wisps of smoke, very ugly, and with the feet of a rooster, although they do have the ability to take on a solid form, according to Arabic lore, shape-shifting to look like an animal, a regular person, or a seductive woman. Ruled by IBLIS, king of the shaitans, their behavior varies from mildly mischievous to purely evil (see SONS OF IBLIS). The purpose of the shaitans is to tempt mankind into sin; however, some of these beings have been converted to Islam and are faithful servants of Allah.

Living off a diet of dirt and excrement, the shaitans send tempting and unclean thoughts to those who miss morning prayers. These demons have the ability to create mental illusions, sending visions of pleasure to entice mankind to sin. If a person does not wash their hands after supper and goes to bed without having done so, the shaitans will lick their hands to bloody stumps. They can also possess a corpse or a person. Shaitans have an aversion to water. The word in Arabic means "the heat from the sun."

Sources: Davidson, *Dictionary of Angels*, 270; Hughes, *Dictionary of Islam*, 134; Mack, *Field Guide to Demons, Fairies, Fallen Angels, and Other Subversive Spirits*, 151.

Shamdan

Variations: Ashamdon, Sham'dan

According to Jewish lore, the FALLEN ANGEL Shamdan took NAAMAH, the "lovely sister of Tubal-Cain," as his wife; their union produced the demon ASMODEUS.

Sources: Davidson, *Dictionary of Angels*, 270; Ginzberg, *Legends of the Jews*, Vol. 5, 147; Monaghan, *Encyclopedia of Goddesses and Heroines*, 90; Pearson, *Gnosticism, Judaism, and Egyptian Christianity*, 90.

Shamshiel

Variations: SAMSAPEEL, Samsaweel, Shamshiel, Shamsiel, Shemuiel, TAMIEL ("perfection of God")

In Enochian lore, Shamshiel is said to have been chief of the WATCHERS; he was one of the FALLEN ANGELS who swore allegiance to SAMI-AZA, rebelled against God, took a human wife, and fathered the NEPHILIM. He went on to teach mankind the "signs of the sun" (the zodiac).

Sources: Adler, *Jewish Quarterly Review*, Vol. 12, 174; Davidson, *Dictionary of Angels*, xxvi, xxvii, 33; Dennis, *Encyclopedia of Jewish Myth, Magic and Mysticism*, 238; Ginzberg, *Legends of the Jews*, Vol. 2, 314–5; Laurence, *Foreign Quarterly Review*, Vol. 24, 370.

Shax

Variations: CHAX, SCOX, Shan, Shass, Shaz

According to the *Lemegeton*, Shax is ranked as a marquis or duke who commands thirty legions, and he is also said to be one of the seventy-two SPIRITS OF SOLOMON (see DUKE OF HELL and MARQUIS OF HELL). He appears before his summoner as a dove or stork and speaks with a subtle but hoarse voice. Thought to be faithful and obedient, he will lie and deceive if not commanded to stand inside a triangle by the summoner.

Shax is invoked for his ability to discover the location of anything that is hidden and not guarded by spirits and to bring the summoner anything he asks for, and is able to transport anything any distance. He can also remove the hearing, sight, or understanding from anyone his summoner asks him to, is an expert horse thief, and will steal money from kings; however, he will return it 1,200 years later. Shax usually gives good FAMILIARs.

Sources: Crowley, *The Goetia*, 51; De Laurence, *Lesser Key of Solomon, Goetia*, 36; Icon, *Demons*, 178; Kelly, *Who in Hell*, 213.

Shed

Variations: Shaddim, Shedu

Originally a class of storm-demons from Chaldean mythology, the shed were absorbed into Jewish demonology where they were said to be the descendants of Adam and LILITH or the descendants of serpents. Another Jewish legend says that God created them but had to stop when the Sabbath came and never finished making them. The word translates to mean "demon" or "destroyer."

Typically shedim, as they are called in numbers, are described as having the legs and feet of a rooster and are often depicted as bulls or as having bull horns. They have the ability to possess inanimate objects such as statues. To determine if shedim are in the area, spread ashes on the ground; if they are present, their tracks will become visible. They follow the dead and linger near graves.

There is a belief that sinners in an attempt to purify themselves would sacrifice their daughters to the shedim, but it is uncertain if this was a blood, life, sexuality, or some other kind of sacrifice (see SCHEDIM). It should be noted that at one time benevolent SHEDIM were used in Cabalistic ceremonies.

Sources: Jastrow, *Religion of Babylonia and Assyria*, 260; Rogers, *Religion of Babylonia and Assyria*, 147.

Shedim

The shedim are a species of demon from Jewish lore, described as looking like hairy humanoids with horns upon their heads, wide mouths, and lolling tongues. Prone to fall for acts of human good-heartedness and trickery, the shedim live in the woods and in uninhabitable places. To prevent them from attacking, make the gesture known as "to fig," as it is a powerful repellent. This is done by bending the thumb and placing it between the index and second finger, then making a fist. Spitting three times will also drive them away.

Sources: Hunter, *Magickal Judaism*, 87; Mack, *Field Guide to Demons, Fairies, Fallen Angels, and Other Subversive Spirits*, 125–6.

Sheerree

Variations: Strix Nocturna

The Berber people of the High Atlas Mountains in Morocco have in their mythology a vampiric demonic bird with a woman's breasts and nipples. Said to prey on newborn and nursing children, the sheerree ("owl") hunts at night. The fate of the child depends entirely on which breast it is drawn to. If the child suckles from the correct breast, it will live; if it chooses incorrectly, it will die. A sign that a child has fed from this demon is oozing nostrils.

Sources: American Philological Association, *Transactions and Proceedings*, 138; Knappert, *Aquarian Guide to African Mythology*, 39; Tate, *Flights of Fancy*, 94–95.

Shekkasoh

Variations: Skekkasoh

In Burma there is a *nat* (a tree spirit) that causes fever and malaria; it is known as a shekkasoh. These demons live in the trunks of trees, and when the leaves of a tree move when all else is still, it is said that the shekkasoh are present. Should a person fall victim to one of these demons, they must go to the last tree they rested under and leave offerings, then an exorcism must be performed on the person.

Sources: Altman, *Sacred Trees*, 60; Folkard, *Plant Lore, Legends, and Lyrics*, 80; Porteous, *Forest Folklore, Mythology and Romance*, 125; Scott, *Burman, His Life and Notions*, 237.

Shelhabiron

The shelhabiron are under the command of AHRIMAN. They are one of the twelve QLIPPOTHIC ORDERS OF DEMONS. The shelhabiron are described as looking like the shadow forms of jackals and wolves, according to the Qlippoth. Most powerful from July 23 to August 22, their zodiacal sign is Leo; their colors are firery and yellow.

Sources: Ford, *Bible of the Adversary*, 121; Mathers, *Sorcerer and his Apprentice*, 26.

Shemhamphorae, The

Variation: Shem ha-Mephorash, Shem ha-Mephoresh, Shem Hamitfaresh, Shemahamphorasch, Shemhamforash, Shemhamphorash, Shemhamphoresch, Shemhamphoresh

The Kabala tells us that there were once seventy-two angels who bore the mystical name of God, Shemhamphorae ("the divine name"). The demons IMAMIAH, NELCHAEL, NITHAEL, and OMAEL, are FALLEN ANGELS were once members of the Shemhamphorae. The names are Aehaiah, Aladiah, ANIEL, Annauel, ARIEL, Asaliah, Cahethel, Caliel, Chavakiak, Damabiah, DANIEL, Eiael, Elemiah, Haaiah, Haamiah, Habuiah, Hahahel, Hahaziah, Hahuiah, Haiaiel, Hakamiah, Harahel, Hariel, Haziel, Iahhel, Iehuiah, Ieiaiel, Ieiazel, Ieilael, Ielahiah, Ieliel, Ierathel, Ihiazel, Iibamiah, Imamiah, Lauiah, Lecabel, Lehahiah, Lelahel, Leuuiah, Leviah, Mahasiah, Mebahel, Mebahiah, Mehekiel, Melahel, Meniel, Michael, Mihael, Mizrael, Monadel, Mumiah, Nanael, Nelchael, Nemamaih, Nithael, Nithaiah (NILAIHAH), Omael, Pahaliah, Poiel, Rehael, Reiiel, Rochel, Sealiah, Seehiah, Sitael, Umabel, Vasiariah, Vehuel, Vehuiah, and Vevaliah.

Sources: *Bizarre Notes and Queries*, 347; Davidson, *Dictionary of Angels*, 345; Eco, *Infinity of Lists*, 61.

Shikigami

Variations: Shiki No Kami, Shikijin

A shikigami is a type of demonic FAMILIAR that is in service to a sorcerer in Japanese mythology. Shikigami are neither good nor evil but do whatever their sorcerers ask of them, be it a common household task, placing a curse, or killing someone. Normally invisible, these demons can take on a wide variety of forms.

Sources: Bush, *Asian Horror Encyclopedia*, 164; Havens, *Encyclopedia of Shinto*, 84, 100; Illes, *Encyclopedia of Spirits*, 904.

Shikk

Variations: Shiq, Shiqq

The shikk ("the half" or "one sided") is a demonic creature from Arabic lore. Its body is literally divided longitudinally, one half human, the other half demon. Offspring of a shikk and of a human being is called a NESNAS. The shikk preys on travelers.

Sources: Burton, *Arabian Nights, in 16 Volumes*, 354; Forbes, *Dictionary, Hindustani and English*, 504; Knowles, *Nineteenth Century*, Vol. 31, 449; Poole, *Thousand and One Nights*, 33.

Shiyu

Variations: Chiyou

Shiyu is a demonic god in Chinese mythology, the inventor of weapons. Appearing as a cow-human hybrid, he was eventually defeated by Huang-Ti. According to lore, this demon has either seventy-two or eighty-one siblings.

Sources: Leeming, *Dictionary of Asian Mythology*, 40; Roberts, *Chinese Mythology A to Z*, 40.

Shoftiel

Shoftiel ("judge of God") is one of the seven ANGELS OF PUNISHMENT who are under the command of the ARCHANGELS OF PUNISHMENT, according to the *Book of Enoch*. He is said to live in the north of the third heaven.

Sources: Ashley, *Complete Book of Devils and Demons*, 78; Davidson, *Dictionary of Angels*, 41; Dennis, *Encyclopedia of Jewish Myth, Magic and Mysticism*, 241; Webster, *Encyclopedia of Angels*, 155.

Sholmos

Variations: Shudkher

Sholmoses are a type of demon in the Mongol-Buriat demonology. Appearing as humanoids, their personal adversary is the god Burkhan.

Sources: Leach, *The Beginning*, 200–201; Sproul, *Primal Myths*, 219.

Shony

Variations: Shellycoat, Shoney, Shoney of the Lews, Sjofn

Shony, the demon of death in ancient Scottish lore, was originally a sea demon described as a large man with thick, shaggy hair covering his head and a ridge of fins running down his back. Yearly human sacrifices were once made to him by slitting the throat of a crewman and throwing him overboard. Ship builders would bind a man to the logs used to roll a new boat into the water in the hopes that it would please him. Shony then evolved into a god of the sea who appeared on land, wearing strands of shells that clattered, announcing his presence. Offerings of ale were made to Shony at Hallowtide in hopes that he would let seaweed wash up on the shore. Evolving yet again, this time into a trickster, he would pretend to be a drowning man and when about to be rescued would laugh and swim away.

Preying on fishermen and sailors, Shony keeps the souls he captures in his castle of jagged coral that lies on the ocean floor in the North Sea. Sometimes he is said to be off the coast of Scotland.

It was the ancient custom not to try to rescue a man who fell overboard because Shony had to receive his annual quota of souls. If an attempt was made it was said that Shony would take the rescuer and leave the would-be victim alive in his place.

Shony is similar to, and possibly the predecessor of, Davey Jones and "the old John" in that he keeps those who drown at sea eternally in his realm.

Sources: Evans, *Fairy-Faith in Celtic Countries*, 93; Henderson, *Norse Influence on Celtic Scotland*, 101; Hyatt, *Book of Demons*, 83; MacKenzie, *Scottish Folk-Lore and Folk Life*, 252–3; Spence, *Magic Arts in Celtic Britain*, 91.

Shtabai

The Shtabai are serpentine demons from Mayan demonology that have the ability to shape-shift into a human appearance. The females are known seducers of men and can cause their ruin. Shtabai are said to live in caves.

Sources: Alexander, *Mythology of All Races*, 141; Turner, *Dictionary of Ancient Deities*, 373.

Shui-Mu

Variations: Old Mother of the Water, Shui-mu Niang-niang

In Chinese demonology, possibly with Buddhist origins, Shui-Mu ("water mother") is an AQUEOUS DEVIL whose personal adversary is Yo Huang, the lord of the skies. She is said to cause the annual floods in and around the town of Ssu Chou, in Anhui Province, bringing death, desolation, and famine until it finally was so flooded it became a lake in 1574. This lake is now called Lake of Hung-tse.

According to the legend, Kuan-yin Pusa, a powerful and good sorceress, disguised herself as a noodle vender and let Shui-Mu eat her inventory. Then she turned the noodles into chains that wrapped around the demon's entrails and removed her magical powers. Weakened, Shui-Mu was chained for all time at the bottom of a deep well at the foot of a mountain in Hsü-i Hsien province. To this day, it is said that when the water is low in the well, the chains that bind the demon can be seen.

Sources: Dyson, *Forgotten Tales of Ancient China*, 301–2; Hyatt, *Book of Demons*, 28; Werner, *Myths and Legends of China*, 220–22.

Sialul

Apollonius of Tyana's *Nuctemeron* (*Night Illuminated by Day*) lists Sialul as the demon of prosperity. He is said to be most powerful during the seventh hour.

Sources: Davidson, *Dictionary of Angels*, 274; Lévi, *Transcendental Magic*, 392.

Sibolas

Variation: Sibolis

In the *Sacred Magic of Abramelin the Mage*, book two, Sibolas ("a rushing lion") is listed as one of the twenty-two SERVITORS OF ARITON (see ARITON).

Sources: Mathers, *Book of the Sacred Magic of Abra-Melin*, 108; Von Worms, *Book of Abramelin*, 254.

Siddim

Siddim are a type of demonic, terrestrial nature spirit from Canaanite demonology who can be kept from attacking with regular offerings of blood sacrifices. The word *siddim* in Hebrew translates to mean "to drag" or "to plow a furrow."

Sources: Faber, *Many Mansions of the House of the Father*, 260; Ginzberg, *Legends of the Jews*, 122.

Sidragasum

Variations: Sidragosam, Sidragrism, Sidragrosam, Sydragasum

Sidragasum is one of the eight SERVITORS OF HALE AND SERGULATH. He is said to assist SATAN in luring women to dance on the Sabbath, seducing them, and making them believe that they are more beautiful than they really are. He has the power to make women dance naked.

Sources: Icon, *Collaborates*, 228; Laurent, *Magica Sexualis 1934*, 34; Masters, *Devil's Dominion*, 131; Waite, *Book of Black Magic and of Pacts*, 188.

Sifon

In the *Sacred Magic of Abramelin the Mage*, book two, Sifon ("to cover up") is listed as one of the fifteen SERVITORS OF ASMODEUS AND MAGOTH (see ASMODEUS).

Sources: Mathers, *Book of the Sacred Magic of Abra-Melin*, 106; Von Worms, *Book of Abramelin*, 256.

Sigbin

The sigbin is a demonic creature from Philippine Visayan lore. It is said to be a companion animal to the aswang vampire. Although descriptions of this demon vary because it has the ability to shape-shift, it is usually described as being a doglike creature with long back legs, similar to a rabbit or kangaroo; as having the body of a crow but with grasshopper legs; or as a giant bat with sharp teeth and long floppy ears.

A nocturnal demon, the sigbin bites the shadow of its victim, usually children, in the neck area to mystically drink their blood. Should a victim survive the attack, he must be treated with a special herbal rub. Sigbin also eat charcoal. These demons cause illness and can kill with their bite or by the smell of their flatulence. If it has large ears, it can clap them together like giant hands. Should its aswang master have a child, the sigbin will have an offspring itself for the aswang child.

Having the power to become invisible, the sigbin is most visible during the last phases of the moon; however, applying the tears of a dog to your eyes will let you see a sigbin for what it is. Although a sigbin cannot be drowned, once it has been slain it must be burned down to the very last hair or its aswang witch will be able to call it back to life.

Sources: Icon, *Victims*, 492; Lieban, *Cebuano Sorcery*, 68.

Siho I Salo

From the demonology of the Solomon Islands comes the demon Siho I Salo ("descended from the sky"). Said to have appeared from out of a storm, he looks like a man with ears like giant pandanus leaves; he wraps himself up in one and lies down on the other when going to sleep.

Siho I Salo is a greedy cannibal greatly feared for his voracious appetite. It is said that once, long ago, a sorcerer placed a spell on him that made Siho I Salo the guardian of vegetable plots, keeping other spirits away. In return for his protection, a share of the fishermen's catch is made to him. His sacred animal is the crocodile.

Sources: Poignant, *Myths of Polynesia, Micronesia, Melanesia, Australia*, 109; Rose, *Spirits, Fairies, Leprechauns, and Goblins*, 293.

Sikastin

In the *Sacred Magic of Abramelin the Mage*, book two, Sikastin is listed as one of the sixty-five SERVITORS OF KORE AND MAGOTH.

Sources: Ford, *Bible of the Adversary*, 92; Mathers, *Book of the Sacred Magic of Abramelin the Mage*, 107; Von Worms, *Book of Abramelin*, 250.

Sila

Variations: Si'lah

Sila are said to be the weakest of all the types of the DJINN. They have the ability to appear in any form.

Sources: Britannica, *Students' Britannica India*, Vols. 1–5, 142; Carta, *Djinn Summoning*, 26; Hughes, *Dictionary of Islam*, 135; Knowles, *Nineteenth Century*, Vol. 31, 449; Rose, *Spirits, Fairies, Leprechauns, and Goblins*, 363.

Si'lat, plural: Sa'āli

Variations: Si'la

A si'lat is an invisible, demonic creature or DJINN from Arabic lore. Sa'āli, as they are called in numbers, are shape-shifters who commonly choose to appear as women. These demons capture men and force them to dance for their pleasure. Sa'āli are hated by wolves and when attacked they will cry out for help, even going so far as to offer vast sums of money to anyone who would rescue them. It is said that the Arabic clan, 'Amr b.Yarbu, are descended from a si'lat (see also SILA).

Sources: Hastings, *Encyclopedia of Religion and Ethics*, Part 2, 670; Hughes, *Dictionary of Islam*, 137; Thompson, *Semitic Magic*, 70; Zwemer, *Influence of Animism on Islam*, 126.

Silcharde

Variations: Sicharde

The *Grimorium Vernum* (*Grimoire of Truth*), allegedly written by Alibek the Egyptian in 1517, names Silcharde as one of the eighteen SERVITORS OF SYRACH (see SYRACH). This demon, whose presence makes people feel happy, appears before his summoner looking like a king and is invoked for his ability to discover lost treasure. He can also make a person able to see all magical and mundane animals. Easily summoned by necromancers and accepting offerings of bread, he is most powerful between three and four in the morning on Thursdays.

Sources: Baskin, *Satanism*, 297; Butler, *Ritual Magic*, 94; Masello, *Raising Hell*, 16; Waite, *The Book of Ceremonial Magic*, 290.

Simapesiel

Variations: Simapiseel, Sipwese'el

Enochian lore names Simapesiel as one of the FALLEN ANGELS who swore allegiance to SAMIAZA, rebelled against God, took a human wife, and fathered the NEPHILIM.

Sources: Charles, *Book of Enoch or One Enoch*, 137; Davidson, *Dictionary of Angels*, 353; Horne, *Sacred Books and Early Literature of the East*, 114; Prophet, *Fallen Angels and the Origins of Evil*, 174.

Sinbuck

Variations: "The Judge"

Apollonius of Tyana's *Nuctemeron* (*Night Illuminated by Day*) says that Sinbuck is most powerful during the first hour.

Source: Lévi, *Transcendental Magic*, 502.

Sirchade

The *Grimorium Vernum* (*Grimoire of Truth*), allegedly written by Alibek the Egyptian in 1517, names Sirchade as one of the eighteen SERVITORS OF SYRACH (see SYRACH).

Source: Masters, *Devil's Dominion*, 130.

Sisera

Apollonius of Tyana's *Nuctemeron* (*Night Illuminated by Day*) lists Sisera as the demon of desire. He is most powerful during the second hour.

Sources: Davidson, *Dictionary of Angels*, 275; Lévi, *Transcendental Magic*, 404.

Sislau

Apollonius of Tyana's *Nuctemeron* (*Night Illuminated by Day*) lists Sislau as the demon of poisons. He is most powerful during the fourth hour.

Sources: Davidson, *Dictionary of Angels*, 275; Lévi, *Transcendental Magic*, 391.

Sitri

Variations: BITRU, SYTRY

According to the *Lemegeton*, Sitri is ranked as the Beautiful Prince and commands sixty legions (see PRINCES OF HELL). Appearing as a man with a leopard's head and griffon wings, at his summoner's request he will take on the guise of a handsome man. This demon is invoked for his ability to enflame men and women with love, to reveal women's secrets, and to make people expose their naked bodies. Sitri is also listed as one of the seventy-two SPIRITS OF SOLOMON.

Sources: Crowley, *The Goetia*, 34; De Laurence, *Lesser Key of Solomon, Goetia*, 25; DuQuette, *Angels, Demons and Gods of the New Millennium*, 159; McLean, *Treatise of Angel Magic*, 55; Scott, *London Magazine*, Vol. 5, 378.

Skrzak

Variations: Skrzat

In Polish and Wendish mythology, a skrzak is a species of IMP.

Sources: Icon, *Flies*, 565; Kmietowicz, *Slavic Mythical Beliefs*, 13, 199; MacCulloch, *Celtic Mythology*, 245; Shailer, *Dictionary of Religion and Ethics*, 415.

Slange

Slange ("snakey") is a word from Middle English that essentially is another name for the DEVIL.

Sources: Russell, *Lucifer, the Devil in the Middle Ages*, 249.

Slesma Sanniya

In Sinhalese demonology Slesma Sanniya is the demon of illness, affecting the mucous membranes and causing anxiety attacks, epileptic seizures, and mucous to seep from the anus and mouth. Like the other Sinhalese demons, they are susceptible to the DAHA-ATA SANNIYA.

Sources: Illes, *Encyclopedia of Spirits*, 875; Wirz, *Exorcism and the Art of Healing in Ceylon*, 44.

Sobe

In the *Sacred Magic of Abramelin the Mage*, book two, Sobe is listed as one of the fifteen SERVITORS OF ASMODEUS AND MAGOTH (see ASMODEUS). His name in Greek means "the tail of a horse" or "a fly flap."

Sources: Mathers, *Book of the Sacred Magic of Abramelin the Mage*, 117; Von Worms, *Book of Abramelin*, 256.

Sobel

In the *Sacred Magic of Abramelin the Mage*, book two, Sobel ("a burden") is listed as one of the sixty-five SERVITORS OF KORE AND MAGOTH.

Sources: Mathers, *Book of the Sacred Magic of Abramelin the Mage*, 118; Von Worms, *Book of Abramelin*, 250.

Sochas

The *Theurgia Goetia*, the second book of the *Lemegeton*, ranks Sochas as a diurnal duke who commands twenty servitors and lists him as one of the fifteen SERVITORS OF BARMIEL (see BARMIEL and DUKES OF HELL).

Sources: Peterson, *Lesser Key of Solomon*, 70; Trithemius, *Steganographia*, 17.

Sodzu-Baba

Variations: The Old Woman of the Three Roads

Appearing as an old woman with small eyes, white hair and skin, a strangely wrinkled face, and wearing a pale blue robe, Sodzu-Baba sits at the left side of EMMA-O, according to Japanese demonology. Living at the banks of the River of the Three Roads with her husband, Ten Datsu-Ba, Sodzu-Baba takes the burial clothes of those who cannot pay her three rin fee. The clothes she collects are hung in a nearby tree.

Sources: China Society of Science and Arts, *China Journal*, Vol. 23, 72; Davis, *Myths and Legends of Japan*, 222; Hearn, *Glimpses of Unfamiliar Japan*, 23, 25–6.

Soleriel

The *Theurgia Goetia*, the second book of the *Lemegeton*, Soleriel is one of the eleven WANDERING PRINCES and is the PLANETARY PRINCE of the Sun (see PRINCES OF HELL). Soleriel commands two dukes, two-hundred servitors, and twelve named chief dukes: Almodar, Amriel, Axosiel, CHAROEL, Cobusiel, Moracha, Mursiel, NACHIEL, Nadrusiel, Penador, Prasiel, and Praxeel. This demon is invoked for his ability in athletics and games.

Source: Peterson, *Lesser Key of Solomon*, 99.

Sonneillon

Variations: Lady of Hatred, Sonnelion, Sonnilion, Sonnillon, Sunnillon

Originally an Armenian goddess of hate, Sonneillon is now considered to be a FALLEN ANGEL, formerly of the Order of Thrones. As the demon of hate and lies, he tempts men with hatred to use against his enemies. His personal adversary

is St. Stephen. Sonneillon is said to be one of the three devils that possessed Sister Louise Capeau in the sixteenth century.

Sources: Cuhulain, *Witch Hunts*, 206; Davidson, *Dictionary of Angels*, 353; Icon, *Demons*, 179; Kelly, *Who in Hell*, 215; Robbins, *Encyclopedia of Witchcraft and Demonology*, 22.

Sons of Iblis

According to the Koran, there are five sons of IBLIS: AL-A'WAR, Dasimn, Sut, Tir (Ir), and ZALAMBUR. These DJINN or SHAITANS are indestructible, but Arabic demonology says that they will all die the day that their father, Iblis, dies. To prevent them from attacking in the meanwhile, say the *takbir* formula aloud to drive them away: "Allah akbar" (Allah is very great). Wearing protective amulets also works.

Sources: Hughes, *Dictionary of Islam*, 84, 135; Knowles, *Nineteenth Century*, Vol. 31, 449.

Sorath

The Cabbala tells us that Sorath is the demon of the sun and that his personal adversary is the angel Mikael. His zodiacal sign is Leo.

Sources: Gettings, *Dictionary of Demons*, 228; Guénon, *King of the World*, 19; Steiner, *Apocalypse of St. John*, 6, 200.

Sorosma

In the *Sacred Magic of Abramelin the Mage*, book two, Sorosma is listed as one of the forty-nine SERVITORS OF BEELZEBUB and as one of the eight SERVITORS OF ORIENS (see BEELZEBUB and ORIENS). This name is possibly Greek and may mean "a funeral bearer or urn."

Sources: Ford, *Bible of the Adversary*, 93; Mathers, *Book of the Sacred Magic of Abra-Melin*, 108; Susej, *Demonic Bible*, 259; Von Worms, *Book of Abramelin*, 253.

Sorriolenen

In the *Sacred Magic of Abramelin the Mage*, book two, Sorriolenen is listed as one of the sixty-five SERVITORS OF KORE AND MAGOTH.

Sources: Mathers, *Book of the Sacred Magic of Abra-Melin*, 107; Susej, *Demonic Bible*, 258; Von Worms, *Book of Abramelin*, 250.

Soterion

In the *Sacred Magic of Abramelin the Mage*, book two, Soterion ("delivering" or "saving") is named among the one hundred eleven SERVITORS OF AMAYMON, ARITON, ORIENS, AND PAYMON (see AMAYMON, ARITON, ORIENS, and PAYMON).

Sources: Mathers, *Book of the Sacred Magic of Abramelin the Mage*, 105; Von Worms, *Book of Abramelin*, 246.

Sotheans

Variations: Sotheano

In the *Theurgia Goetia*, the second book of the *Lemegeton*, Sotheans is listed as one of the eleven SERVITORS OF PAMERSIEL (see PAMERSIEL). A nocturnal duke, this demon is known to be very useful at driving out spirits from haunted places (see DUKES OF HELL). Arrogant and stubborn, Sotheans is an expert liar and tells any secrets he knows. This demon must be summoned from the second floor of a home or in a wide open space.

Source: Peterson, *Lesser Key of Solomon*, 64.

Species of Demons

Ten different species of demons are described by Alphonse de Spina (1467), a Franciscan Catholic bishop and the author of the *Fortalitium Fidei* (*Fortress of Faith*). The species are: demons formed from stolen human semen; demons who assail the saintly; demons who instigate witchcraft; disguised demons; FAMILIARs, who assist witches; fates, who alter destiny; incubi and succubi, who stimulate lust and perversion (see INCUBUS and SUCCUBUS); marching hordes, who bring about war; NIGHTMARES, who disturb sleep through bad dreams; and poltergeists, who cause mischief.

Source: de Spina, *Fortalitium Fidei*.

Species of Devils

Six species of devils are described by Friar Francesco Maria Guazzo in his book *Compendium Maleficarum* (1628): AERIAL DEVILS live in the air around humans and have the most direct access to us; AQUEOUS DEVILS live in lakes, rivers, and seas; FIRE DEVILS live in the upper air and help supervise the other five groups, they are the most powerful; HELIOPHOBIC DEVILs hate the light and are only active at night; subterranean devils live in caves and under ground; and TERRESTRIAL DEVILS live in the fields, forests, and woods.

Source: Kipfer, *Order of Things*, 255.

Sphandor

Variations: Sphandôr

Sphandor is one of the thousands of Egyptian demons that were worshipped as gods. According to the *Testament of Solomon* this demon breaks and bruises the bones in the neck, sucking out their marrow. He paralyzes the nerves in the hands and weakens the shoulders, making them tremble. His personal adversary is the angel 'Araêl, and if he hears the words "Araêl, imprison Sphandor," he will immediately leave.

Sources: Charlesworth, *Old Testament Pseude-pigrapha*, Vol. 2, 978–9; Conybeare, *Jewish Quarterly Review*, Vol. 11, 35; Fleg, *Life of Solomon*, 66; Frankfurter, *Evil Incarnate*, 25.

Sphendonael

In Solomonic lore Sphendonael is one of the thirty-six elemental world rulers; he is also listed as one of the seventy-two SPIRITS OF SOLOMON, bound to heavy work on the temple tending the furnace for metalwork. Described as having a shapeless head like a DOG with a face like a bird, donkey, or ox, he causes tumors in the parotid gland, inflammations in the tonsils, and tetanic recurvation. His personal adversary is the angel Sabrael, who can cure the diseases Sphendonael causes.

Sources: Conybeare, *Jewish Quarterly Review*, Vol. 11, 35; Butler, *Ritual Magic*, Vol. 1998, Part 2, 31; Charlesworth, *Old Testament Pseudepigrapha*, Vol. 2, 978–9; Fleg, *Life of Solomon*, 66; Good, *Study of Medicine*, 352.

Spirits of Solomon

The Spirits of Solomon are demons that were invoked by King Solomon, made to stand before him where they told him their name, what they were good for, and how to banish them. These demons were then bound by the king to work on the construction of his temple. They were held in a brass container that was sealed with magical sigils.

The *Lesser Key of Solomon* (*Clavicula Salomonis*) is a seventeenth-century grimoire that was purported to have been written by King Solomon himself; however, this is obviously not true and historically impossible, as the ranks of earl and marquis were not in use during the time that Solomon was in power, around 967 B.C.E. This is nearly a thousand years before Jesus lived, so the prayers contained within that beseech the son of God and make reference to the Holy Trinity only add to the fact it was not written by the biblical king.

The *Testament of Solomon* is an Old Testament catalog of fifty-two demons that were summoned by King Solomon. It explains what each demon does and how demons can be thwarted by invoking the angel they most fear. The demons are: "a lascivious spirit;" Agchoniôn; AKTON; ALATH; ALLEBORITH; ANATRETH; Anostêr; Arôtosael (AROTOSAEL); ASMODEUS; ATRAX; BARSAFAEL; Beelzeboul; BELBEL; BIANAKITH; BOBÊL; Buldumêch; CREST OF DRAGONS; ENENUTH; Enêpsigos; ENVY; EPHIPPAS; HARPAX; HEPHESIMIRETH; ICHTHION; Ieropaêl; IUDAL; Katanikotaêl (KATANIKETHAL); KUMEATÊL; Kuno[s]paston; Kurtaêl (KURTAEL); Lionbearer

(RATH); Marderô; METATHIAX; Naôth; NEFTHADA; OBIZUTH (LILITH); Onoskelis; OR-NIAS; Phêth; PHTHENOTH; RABDOS; ROÊLÊD; Ruax; Saphathoraél; Sphandôr; Sphendonaêl; TEPHRAS; the ram; the thirty-three elements of the cosmic ruler of the darkness (DECEPTION, ERROR, JEALOUSY, KLOTHOD, POWER, STRIFE, and WORST OF ALL; see PLEIADES); the thirty-six elements; the world-rulers of this darkness; and Winged Dragon.

The demons listed in this text are not the same as the demons listed in Johann Wierus's *Pseudo-monarchia Daemonum* or the *Lesser Key of Solomon* (*Clavicula Salomonis*), two often cited grimoires of the late Middle Ages. Although the ranking and the spelling of the demons listed in these books vary slightly, basically they are the same. The seventy-two demons mentioned are AGARES, a duke; AIM, a duke; Alloces, a duke; Amdusias, a duke; Amon (AAMON), a marquis; AMY, a president; ANDRAS, a marquis; ANDREALPHUS, a marquis; ANDROMALIUS, an earl; ASHTAROTH, a duke; ASMODAY, a king; BAEL, a king; BALAM, a king; BARBATOS, a duke; Bathin (BATHIM), a duke; BELETH, a king; BELIAL, a king; BERITH, a duke; BIFRONS, a count; BOTIS, a count/president; BUER, a president; Buné, a duke; CAIM, a president; Cimeies (KIMARIS), a marquis; CRO-CELL, a duke; DANTALIAN, a duke; DECARABIA, a marquis; Eligos (ELIGOR), a duke; FORAS, a president; Forneas, a marquis; FURCALOR, a duke; Furcas (FORCAS), a knight; FURFUR, a count; Gäap, a prince/president; Glasya-Labolas, a count/president; Gremory, a duke; GUSION, a duke; Häagenti, a president; HALPHAS, a count; HAURES, a duke; Ipos (IPES), a count/prince; Leraje, a marquis; MALPHAS, a president; MARAX, a count/president; MARBAS, a president; MARCHOSIAS, a marquis; MURMUR, a duke/count; Naberius (NABERUS), a marquis; ORIAS, a marquis; OROBAS, a prince; OSE, a president; PAYMON, a king; PHENEX, a marquis; PURSON, a king; RÄUM, a count; Ronové (RONOBE), a marquis/count; Sabnock (SABANACK), a marquis; Sallos (SALEOS, ZAEBOS), a duke; SAMIGINA, a marquis; SEERE, a prince; SHAX, a marquis; SITRI, a prince; STOLAS, a prince; Valac (UALAC), a president; Valefor, a duke; Vapula, a duke; VAS-SAGO, a prince; Vepar (SEPAR), a duke; VINÉ, a king/count; Vual (UVALL), a duke; Zagan, a king/president; and Zepar, a duke.

Sources: Butler, *Ritual Magic*, 33; Conybeare, *Jewish Quarterly Review*, Vol. 11, 1–45; De Laurence, *Lesser Key of Solomon, Goetia*, 22–46; Fleg, *Life of Solomon*, 107; McLean, *Treatise of Angel Magic*, 52; Scot, *Discoverie of Witchcraft*, 224–5.

Spiritus Mendaciorum

The *spiritus mendaciorum* ("spirits of lying") are a classification of demons that prey upon diviners, oracles, and those who seek answers from them. These deceptive demons are in service under PYTHON.

Sources: Gettings, *Dictionary of Demons*, 231; McLean, *Treatise on Angel Magic*, 69.

Srat

In the demonology of the Western Slavs, Srat is a domestic demon who appears as a domesticated animal or as a fiery figure. The demon of fortune, he helps one family with gifts of food and needed materials that he has stolen from another.

Sources: Lurker, *Dictionary of Gods and Goddesses, Devils and Demons*, 330; Rose, *Spirits, Fairies, Leprechauns, and Goblins*, 300.

Sri

Variations: Srin

Originating in the Bon religion of Tibet, the sri is a demonic subterranean vampiric being. A corpse eater, it is especially fond of consuming children, chasing them down and when it catches them, devouring them. Sri live underground and linger in places where corpses have been laid out. They have the ability to possess a person, and when one does, a sri-pressing exorcism must be performed to force the demon to return to the underworld until it has received "the Bodhisattiva mind."

Sources: Jäschke, *Tibetan-English Dictionary*, 581; Kloppenborg, *Female Stereotypes in Religious Traditions*, 182, 192; Lurker, *Dictionary of Gods and Goddesses, Devils and Demons*, 176; Mumford, *Himalayan Dialogue*, 148.

Stihi

The stihi is a demonic creature from southern Italo-Albanian demonology. This female fire-breathing dragon greedily guards her treasure trove.

Sources: Elsie, *Dictionary of Albanian Religion, Mythology, and Folk Culture*, 241; Lurker, *Dictionary of Gods and Goddesses, Devils and Demons*, 330; Maberry, *Vampire Universe*, 272; Rose, *Giants, Monsters, and Dragons*, 345.

Stolas

Variations: Solas, Stolos

Stolas is the Raven Prince, commanding twenty-six legions, according to Johann Wierus's *Pseudomonarchia Daemonum* (*False Monarchy of Demons*, 1583; see PRINCES OF HELL). Appearing before his summoner as a raven or crowned owl, this powerful, diurnal demon will, if asked by his summoner, take on the semblance of a man. He is invoked for his ability to teach astronomy, prophecy based on the study of plants, and how to judge the value of gems. He is one of the SPIRITS OF SOLOMON.

Sources: Conybeare, *Jewish Quarterly Review*, Vol. 11, 24–6; Crowley, *The Goetia*, 47: De Laurence, *Lesser Key of Solomon, Goetia*, 34; DuQuette, *Key to Solomon's Key*, 178–9; Godwin, *Godwin's Cabalistic Encyclopedia*, 297; Scott, *London Magazine*, Vol. 5, 378.

Strife

Strife is named in the *Testament of Solomon* as the second of the SEVEN HEAVENLY BODIES, one of the thirty-three (or thirty-six, sources vary) elements of the cosmic ruler of the darkness. She was bound by the king and made to dig the foundations of his temple. A demonic goddess in Babylonian lore and fair in appearance, Strife is one of the seven female spirits that are bound and woven together, represented as a cluster of stars in the heavens. Her personal adversary is the angel Baruchiachel. She and the other PLEIADES travel about, sometimes living in Lydia, or Olympus, or on a great mountain (see PLEIADES STRIFE).

Source: Conybeare, *Jewish Quarterly Review*, Vol. 11, 24–6.

Strix

Variations: SHEERREE, Shre

The strix mythology originated in ancient Rome, even being catalogued by Pliny in his *Natural History*, who commented that they must be imaginary creatures since the bat is the only "bird" that breast feeds its young. The strix did not become a demonic creature linked to SATAN until medieval times. The word *strix* translates as "owl" in Greek, but it has come to mean "witch" in Italian.

The strixes of medieval demonology, as described in Saint Isidore of Seville's *Etymologiae*, are demonic subterranean creatures under the command of SATAN. A strix is created when a person turns to SATAN and renounces their humanity; they are then transformed into this unnatural creature, a birdlike monster with huge talons and human breasts.

Working to bring about the downfall of mankind, these spiteful, nocturnal demons live in caves and prey upon nursing babies. Susceptible to garlic and hawthorn, when one is killed, during its dissection, its entrails can be read to discern who it was in life. After the dissection, the body of the strix must then be cremated.

Source: De Gubernatis, *Zoological Mythology*, 202;

Maggi, *In the Company of Demons*, 34; McDonough, *Transactions of the American Philological Association*, 315–44; Oliphant, *Transactions and Proceedings of the American Philological Association*, Vol. 44, 133–49.

Sturbiel

In *Ars Paulina*, the third book of the *Lemegeton*, Sturbiel is ranked as a chief and is listed as one of the eleven SERVITORS OF RAHAB (see RAHAB).

Source: Waite, *Book of Ceremonial Magic*, 67.

Subahu

Variations: Sawahu

In the Ramayana epic of Indian mythology, Subahu was an ASURAS. With his brother, MARICHA, they disrupted the Vedic rituals by throwing unclean meat and blood into the oblation fire. Eventually, this demon was slain by Rama with a divine missile (see TATAKA).

Sources: Buck, *Ramayana*, 50; Parmeshwaranand, *Dictionary of Purāṇas*, Vol. 1, 1124, 1262.

Succor

Variations: Benoth, Succor-Beloth, Succor-benoth, Succoth Benoth ("hidden daughters"), Tonsils Succor-Beneth

Succor is the chief of the eunuchs, the favored one of Proserpine. The demon of jealousy, he presides over the DEVIL's harem, working in the palace of PRINCES OF HELL. He protects bridges and gates and tempts men to lechery.

In ancient Babylon, Succoth Benoth was a temple structure where Babylonian women would prostitute themselves to strangers at least once in their lifetime, offering up the service as a gift to their goddess.

Sources: Chambers, *Book of Days*, 723; Hugu, *Toilers of the Sea*, 10; Waite, *Book of Black Magic*, 181.

Succubus, plural: succubi

Variations: ALUGA, Alukah, Aulak, Belili, Buhlgeist, COMPUSAE, Daitja, EPHÉLÉS, Hyphialtes, KIEL-GELAL, LILIN, Lilit, Pishauchees, RUSALKA, Succuba, Succumbus, Unterliegerinnen

Men have been assaulted by the vampiric demon known as the succubus ("spirit bride" or "to lie under") as far back as ancient Akkadia, Summeria, and Greece, where it was clearly defined and described. The male counterpart to the succubus is known as an INCUBUS, and according to medieval lore, the incubi outnumber the succubi by a ratio of nine to one. The princess of all the succubi is Nahemah (see MAAMAH, NAAMAH, and NAHEMA).

At night succubi, as they are collectively called, appear as beautiful women. They can be very alluring and persuasive. They seek out sleeping men to have sexual intercourse with and, according to medieval lore, are particularly fond of monks. During the sex act, the succubi are said to drain off a number of vital essences and fluids, such as blood, breath, life-energy, and semen to the point of their victim's death. A succubus need not even be physically in the room for the assault to take place, as it can visit a man in his dreams, causing his body to fall into a state of sleep paralysis. Succubi are specifically interested in semen, taking it and implanting it into unsuspecting and innocent women.

If a man wanted an encounter with a succubus, he need not wait in hopeful anticipation for one to show, as it is a demonic being and can be summoned to appear by use of magical incantations. Likewise, if a man is desirous of ridding himself of its assaults, he must seek help through the church.

If a child is conceived by a succubus, it will be born a half demonic being known as a CAMBION.

Sources: Bullough, *Human Sexuality*, 298–99; Cavendish, *The Powers of Evil in Western Religion, Magic and Folk Belief*, 103–5; Doniger, *Britannica Encyclopedia of World Religions*, 503, 1035; Jones, *On the Nightmare*, 125, 243, 320.

Suclagus

In Apollonius of Tyana's *Nuctemeron* (*Night Illuminated by Day*), Suclagus is the demon of fire. He is most powerful during the ninth hour.

Sources: Gettings, *Dictionary of Demons*, 237; Lévi, *Transcendental Magic*, 393.

Sudoron

In the *Sacred Magic of Abramelin the Mage*, Sudoron ("false gift") is listed as one of the fifteen SERVITORS OF PAYMON (see PAYMON).

Sources: Ford, *Bible of the Adversary*, 94; Mathers, *Book of the Sacred Magic of Abramelin the Mage*, 108; Susej, *Demonic Bible*, 259; Von Worms, *Book of Abramelin*, 257.

Süly

Süly ("scurvy") is the demon of illness in Hungarian Magyar demonology, specifically scurvy.

Source: Kõiva, *Folk Belief Today*, 139.

Šulak

Variations: The Hitter, the Lurker, Sulak

A šulak is a type of RABISU demon from Akkadian mythology. Appearing as a lion, it hides near the entrances to alleys, dark corners, and houses waiting to leap out and attack its victims, rubbing the part of the body it wishes to affect, leaving the victim suffering with severe stroke on the right side of the body. Signs of a šulak attack are

noticeable bruising on both temples and a loss of consciousness. Performing the Shurpu ritual immediately after the attack will banish this demon. These demons prefer to assault people as they are en route to empty their bowels; images of lions and *urmahlullû* (lion-men) in the lavatories will ward them off. Šulak are also susceptible to pure sea salt.

Sources: Jastrow, *Religion of Babylonia and Assyri*, 260; Scurlock, *Diagnoses in Assyrian and Babylonian Medicine*, 328, 477; Stol, *Epilepsy in Babylonia*, 17, 71, 76; Wiggermann, *Mesopotamian Protective Spirits*, 98.

Sumbha

Born the twin brother of NISUMBA, Sumbha is a giant ASURAS who was made impervious to harm by any of the gods, according to Hindu mythology. Eventually, he was slain by the god Kail and her powerful army.

Sources: Harper, *Roots of Tantra*, 30; Kondos, *On the Ethos of Hindu Women*, 187; Parmeshwaranand, *Encyclopaedic Dictionary of Purāṇas*, 460; Shastri, *Ancient Indian Tradition and Mythology*, Vol. 4, 1651; Vergati, *Gods and Masks of the Kāthmāṇḍu Valley*, 92.

Sundelbolong

Variations: Kuntianak, PONTIANAK, Sundel Bolong

The sundelbolong is a type of demon known as a Peri in Javanese folklore. The name translates to mean "prostitute with a hole in her," but the literal translation is "to push up through a hole." These female demons appear as a beautiful woman with a hole in her back that is covered with long, black hair. They lack genitalia. Sundelbolong are said to laugh freely and loudly, a quality attributed to prostitutes in Javanese culture. Preying on young men, one of these demons will attempt to lure one away for an indiscretion; if the man does not run from her in terror but rather goes with her, the demon will castrate him.

Sources: Couperus, *Hidden Force*, 249; Geertz, *Religion of Java*, 18; Weiss, *Folk Psychology of the Javanese of Ponorogo*, Vol. 2, 595.

Suoyator

The *Kalevala*, the nineteenth-century epic poem comprised of Finnish and Karelian folklore and mythology that was compiled by Elias Lönnrot, names Suoyator as a demon whose saliva created the serpent of sin.

Sources: Baskin, *Dictionary of Satanism*, 308; Blavatsky, *Theosophical Glossary*, 313; Wedeck, *Dictionary of Pagan Religions*, 309.

Supay

From the demonology of the Quechua-speaking Incas of Peru comes Supay, the lord of mineral wealth who commands the evil spirits of the dismal underworld, Uca Pacha. In modern times the Catholic Indians of Bolivia and Peru use the word to mean "the DEVIL."

Supay is a monstrous being having a lion's body, ram hooves and horns, tigerlike teeth, and smelling of sulfur. When he is angry he roars like a wild boar or grunts like a pig. Although he is not considered to be evil, he is sinister and voracious and unable to experience any sort of joyful emotion; he has an insatiable appetite. Only a child sacrifice can temporarily sate him.

This demon has the ability to shape-shift into a cat, owl, pig, or an attractive young man or woman. He causes earthquakes, epilepsy, hurricanes, madness, and storms. Supay can also change veins of silver to quartz and veins of gold to pyrites.

Sources: LeVey, *Satanic Bible*, 196; Osborne, *South American Mythology*, 80; Réville, *Native Religions of Mexico and Peru*, 197–8.

Superbus

A fifteenth-century manuscript, *Librum de Nigromancia*, said to have belonged to a priest named Johannes Cunalis of Munich, Bavaria, lists Superbus as one of three devils once summoned by a French sorcerer, Jubertus of Bavaria, in 1437 (the other two were AVARUS and LUXURIOSUS). Said to have eyes that glowed like sulfurous fire, this diurnal devil forbids his sorcerer to drink holy water, do good deeds, or kiss the cross. At dawn the sorcerer would worship him like a god; first he would face the east, make the sign of the cross, then defecate, spit, and urinate on it, denying God. The sorcerer would give Superbus all of his uneaten food. This devil would flee from the cross.

Sources: Baskin, *Dictionary of Satanism*, 308; Csonka-Takács, *Mythologies and Persecutions*, 67; Kieckhefer, *Forbidden Rites*, 30, 31, 34, 38.

Suphlatus

In Apollonius of Tyana's *Nuctemeron* (*Night Illuminated by Day*), Suphlatus is said to be the demon of fire. He is most powerful during the ninth hour.

Sources: Davidson, *Dictionary of Angels*, 280; Gettings, *Dictionary of Demons*, 237; Lévi, *Transcendental Magic*, 391.

Supipas

In the *Sacred Magic of Abramelin the Mage*, book two, Supipas is listed as one of the sixty-five SERVITORS OF KORE AND MAGOTH. His name is possibly Greek and may mean "relating to swine."

Sources: Ford, *Bible of the Adversary*, 92; Forgotten Books, *Book of the Sacred Magic of Abramelin the Mage*, 134; Susej, *Demonic Bible*, 258; Von Worms, *Book of Abramelin*, 256.

Surgat

Variation: AQUIEL

The eighteenth-century book purportedly written by Pope Honorius III, *Grimoire of Pope Honorius* (*Le Grimoire du Pape Honorius*), says that Surgat ("arise") is a nocturnal demon, most powerful on Sundays the hour before and after midnight. In service under SYRACH, this demon will demand a hair from your head before he will assist in any task or command. Rather than give one of your own, make him take the hair of a fox instead (see SERVITORS OF SYRACH). This demon is invoked for his ability to open any lock or to discover and transport treasure, and if asked, he will give his summoner a magical stone.

Sources: Butler, *Ritual Magic*, 81, 94; Icon, *Ceremonies*, 460; Kuriakos, *Grimoire Verum Ritual Book*, 38; Masters, *Devil's Dominion*, 131; Sabellicus, *Magia Pratica*, 35; Waite, *Book of Black Magic and of Pacts*, 289.

Suriel

Variations: Arazyal, ARIEL ("Lion of God"), Esdreel, Juriel, Sahariel, Sarakiel, Saraqel, SARIEL, Sauriel, Seraquel, SERIEL, Suriyel, Surjan, Surya, URIEL, Zerachiel

Originating in Enochian, Judaic, and Islamic lore and mentioned in numerous medieval hierarchies, Suriel ("God's command" or possibly "Moon of God") is ranked as the prince of the moon (see PRINCES OF HELL). He is also said to be one of the FALLEN ANGELS who swore allegiance to SAMIAZA, rebelled against God, took a human wife, and fathered the NEPHILIM. Sources vary and have Suriel listed as both an angel and a FALLEN ANGEL. His zodiacal sign is Aries.

Sources: Davidson, *Dictionary of Angels*, 280; Laurence, *Foreign Quarterly Review*, Vol. 24, 370; Schodde, *Book of Enoch*, 74; Van der Toorn, *Dictionary of Deities and Demons in the Bible*, 570, 886.

Susabo

Apollonius of Tyana's *Nuctemeron* (*Night Illuminated by Day*) names Susabo as the demon of voyages. He is most powerful during the sixth hour.

Sources: Gettings, *Dictionary of Demons*, 237; Lévi, *Transcendental Magic*, 391.

Sustugriel

Sustugriel is a chief and is listed as one of the four SERVITORS OF SATANACHIA AND SATANICIAE (see SATANACHIA and SATANICIAE). This demon is invoked for his ability to give FAMILIARs, furnish mandragores, and teach the magical arts.

Sources: Kuriakos, *Grimoire Verum Ritual Book*, 39; Masters, *Devil's Dominion*, 131; Waite, *Book of Black Magic and of Pacts*, 162–3.

Suth

Named in *An Elizabethan Devil-Worshiper's Prayer-Book*, possibly written by John Dee, Suth is ranked as a king who is under the command of VERCAN. This demon has brown skin, carries a sword, and rides upon a stag. He has dominion over the planet Jupiter.

Sources: Anonymous, *Manuscripts and Books on Medicine, Alchemy, Astrology and Natural Sciences Arranged in Chronological Order*, 239; Summers, *A Popular History of Witchcraft*, 91.

Sword of Ashmodai the King

Variations: Harba di ashm'dai (Ashmodai's Sword)

Born the offspring of ASHMODAI and LILITH THE LESSER, the demon named the Sword of Ashmodai the King has a face that "flames like the fire of flame." He is an infernal prince and commands eighty thousand servitors, according to Cabalistic lore and Isaac Ha-Cohen's *Treatise on the Left Handed Emanation* (1320). (See PRINCES OF HELL.)

Sources: Dequeker, *Expulsion of the Jews*, 15; Patai, *Gates to the Old City*, 464, 469.

Sybacco

Variations: ORTHON

Sybacco was the FAMILIAR to the Comte de Corasse, the Comte de Foix, and Adriano Lemmi. Described as having bull horns and three eyes in his forehead, he is under the command of the demon BOTIS.

Source: Ashley, *Amazing World of Superstition, Prophecy, Luck, Magic and Witchcraft*, 18.

Sydonai

Variations: Chammadaï

Sydonai is a lieutenant of Hell. With Chammada, Dele Tear, and Remedod, he is one of the four named lieutenants under ASMODAY.

Source: Masters, *Eros and Evil*, 302.

Symiel

Symiel is the prince of the North by Northeast and is under the command of the emperor of the North (see PRINCES OF HELL). He commands ten dukes of the day and one thousand dukes of the night (see SERVITORS OF SYMIEL).

Sources: Gettings, *Dictionary of Demons*, 237; Peterson, *Lesser Key of Solomon*, 87–8; Trithemius, *Steganographia*, 81.

Syrach

Syrach is a duke who commands eighteen servitors servitors (see DUKES OF HELL and SERVITORS OF SYRACH). He forced other demons to honor their summoners' requests.

Source: Kuriakos, *Grimoire Verum Ritual Book*, 39.

Sytry

Variations: BITRU

A prince who commands seventy legions, Sytry is listed in the *Pseudomonarchia Daemonum* (1583) as being one of the SPIRITS OF SOLOMON (see PRINCES OF HELL). Appearing before his summoner as a winged human with the head of a leopard, he will, at the summoner's request, appear as a handsome man. This demon is invoked for his ability to cause both love and lust, and he can make women expose themselves.

Sources: Diagram Group, *Little Giant Encyclopedia*, 506; Spence, *Encyclopædia of Occultism*, 68; Waite, *Book of Black Magic and Ceremonial Magic*, 99.

Tabaet

Variations: LEVIATHAN, the Noon-tide Serpent, Taba'et, TIAMAT

Originating in Enochian and Hebrew lore, the demon of chaos, Tabaet, a CHIEF OF TENS and FALLEN ANGEL, tempts mankind to accept the gift of the Black Flame in the form of an apple. Kasdeja (see KASADYA) taught mankind how to perform abortions, the secret of the Noon-tide Serpent, and the art of summoning and working with demons. Tabaet ("male" or "strong") is the Noon-tide Serpent.

Sources: Barton, *Journal of the American Oriental Society*, Vol. 15, 20; Davis, *Genesis and Semitic Tradition*, 69; Knnibb, *Ethiopic Book of Enoch*, 162; Moore, *Journal of the American Oriental Society*, Vol. 21, 124.

Tablat

Variations: Tioron

In the *Ars Goetia*, the first book of the *Lemegeton*, Tablat is listed as one of the fifty-three SERVITORS OF ASHTAROTH AND ASMODEUS (see ASHTAROTH and ASMODEUS). His name is possibly Hebrew and may mean "immersions."

Sources: Mathers, *Book of the Sacred Magic of Abramelin the Mage*, 115; Von Worms, *Book of Abramelin*, 247, 256.

Tablibik

In Apollonius of Tyana's *Nuctemeron* (*Night Illuminated by Day*), Tablibik is listed as the demon of fascination. He is said to be most powerful during the fifth hour.

Sources: Kelly, *Who in Hell*, 219; Gettings, *Dictionary of Demons*, 238; Lévi, *Transcendental Magic*, 391

Tabris

Apollonius of Tyana's *Nuctemeron* (*Night Illuminated by Day*) lists Tabris as the demon of free will. He is most powerful during the sixth hour.

Sources: Kelly, *Who in Hell*, 219; Lévi, *Transcendental Magic*, 391.

Tacaros

In the *Sacred Magic of Abramelin the Mage*, Tacaros ("soft, tender") is listed as one of the fifteen SERVITORS OF PAYMON (see PAYMON).

Sources: Ford, *Bible of the Adversary*, 94; Mathers, *Book of the Sacred Magic of Abramelin the Mage*, 108, 121; Susej, *Demonic Bible*, 259; Von Worms, *Book of Abramelin*, 257.

Tachan

In the *Sacred Magic of Abramelin the Mage*, book two, Tachan ("grinding to powder") is listed as one of the forty-nine SERVITORS OF BEELZEBUB (see BEELZEBUB).

Sources: Ford, *Bible of the Adversary*, 93; Mathers, *Book of the Sacred Magic of Abramelin the Mage*, 120; Susej, *Demonic Bible*, 258; Von Worms, *Book of Abramelin*, 257.

Tacritan

Apollonius of Tyana's *Nuctemeron* (*Night Illuminated by Day*) lists Tacritan as the demon of geotic magic. He is most powerful during the fifth hour.

Source: Gettings, *Dictionary of Demons*, 238.

Tagaririm

Variations: Targaririm, Tageriron, Togaririm

In Judaic demonology Tagaririm ("those who bellow grief and tears") is in service under BELPHEGOR. He builds ugliness and then groans about it. This demon lives in Tiphereth, a place of great beauty.

More modern sources describe the tagaririm (and translate the word to mean "the disputers," or "the hagglers") as a group of demons under the command of Belphegor. Their personal adversaries are the spirits of the Tiphereth, the Malachim.

Sources: Ford, *Liber Hvhi*, 77; Godwin, *Godwin's Cabalistic Encyclopedia*, 262, 308; Lévi, *Mysteries of Magic*, 111; Mathers, *Key of Solomon the King*, 122.

Tagnon

In the *Sacred Magic of Abramelin the Mage*, book two, Tagnon is listed as one of the one hundred eleven SERVITORS OF AMAYMON, ARITON, ORIENS, AND PAYMON (see AMAYMON, ARITON, ORIENS, and PAYMON). This name is possibly Greek and may mean "heating."

Sources: Ford, *Bible of the Adversary*, 88; Mathers,

Book of the Sacred Magic of Abramelin the Mage, 105; Susej, *Demonic Bible*, 256; Von Worms, *Book of Abramelin*, 245.

Tagora

In the *Sacred Magic of Abramelin the Mage*, book two, Tagora ("assembly") is listed as one of the sixty-five SERVITORS OF KORE AND MAGOTH.

Sources: Mathers, *Book of the Sacred Magic of Abramelin the Mage*, 118; Susej, *Demonic Bible*, 258; Von Worms, *Book of Abramelin*, 250.

Tagriel

Tagriel ("spout of the urn") is the chief guard in the sixth or seventh Heaven; he is also listed as one of the twenty-eight demonic rulers of the lunar mansions, having dominion over the mansion Alpharg (see ENOCHIAN RULERS OF THE LUNAR MANSIONS). This demon has the ability to destroy prisons, and his zodiacal sign is Aquarius-Pisces.

Sources: Barrett, *The Magus*, 57; Moura, *Mansions of the Moon for the Green Witch*, 46; Scheible, *Sixth and Seventh Books of Moses*, 75; Von Goethe, *Goethe's Letters to Zelter*, 377; Webster, *Encyclopedia of Angels*, 165.

Taiki, plural: tayaka

Variations: Possibly Mai-Jan-Ruwa

From the demonology of the Hausa tribe of West Africa comes a species of demons called tayaka. These demons, who have no description, cause "the swelling of the stomach" (food poisoning). When a taiki attacks a person, a specific ritualistic dance with the sacrifice of a pair of black chickens must be performed. The ritual involves tapping lightly on the stomach with iron implements, as these demons have an aversion to it. The word *taiki* in the Hausa language means "complimentary phrase" or a "hide-bag," as in the type used for pack animals.

Sources: Fletcher, *Hausa Sayings and Folklore*, 35; Knappert, *African Mythology*, 106; Newman, *Hausa-English Dictionary*, 194; Tremearne, *Ban of the Bori*, 340.

Talmaiel

Talmaiel, a NEPHILIM, was born a descendent of the GRIGORI. He escaped both the flood and the swords of the avenging angels, although sources do not say how.

Source: Ford, *Bible of the Adversary*, 77.

Tamboree

According to the demonology of the Dusun people of Borneo, tamboree ("disease-givers") are the demons of all aspects of nature. They are believed to be eternal, immortal beings that have existed since the beginning of time itself. Unless a person has the gift of "second sight" and is able to see demons for what they really are, the tamboree look just like normal people. These demons prey upon people who violate the rules of the natural world or commit an act of *tapun* (the refusal of an act of friendship), which creates a negative spiritual state of being. The tamboree will make the person look like a fool before killing them, usually with a fatal disease. They are often accompanied in their vengeance by the *ragun* (souls of the dead).

Sources: Jones, *Evil in Our Midst*, 162–4; Williams, *The Dusun*, 18.

Tamiel

Variations: Kasdeja, Kasyade ("observer of the hands"), Rampel, Tamel, Tamuel, Temel, TUMAEL

Tamiel ("perfection of God") carries the titles of the Angel of the Deep, Angel of the Sea, and was once a CHIEF OF THE GRIGORI. As a CHIEF OF TENS, he was one of the FALLEN ANGELS who swore allegiance to SAMIAZA, rebelled against God, took a human wife, and fathered the NEPHILIM (see WATCHERS). Tamiel went on to teach mankind astronomy; how to perform abortions; the secret of the noon-tide serpent, TABAET; and the art of summoning and working with demons.

Sources: Bacon, *Journal of Biblical Literature*, Vols. 31–32, 166; Barton, *Journal of Biblical Literature*, Vols. 30–31, 166; Ginzberg, *Legends of the Jews*, Vol. 11, 120; Laurence, *Foreign Quarterly Review*, Vol. 24, 370; Voltaire, *Philosophical Dictionary*, 77.

T'an Mo

In Chinese demonology, T'an Mo is the demon of covetousness and desire.

Sources: Awn, *Satan's Tragedy and Redemption*, 23; de Jésus-Marie, *Satan*, 133, 145; Jackson, *Researches in Manichaeism*, 107; Susej, *Demonic Bible*, 80.

Taninniver

Variations: Tanin'iver

The early Kabbalistic work titled *Treatise on the Left Emanation*, written in the first half of the thirteenth century, names Taninniver ("blind dragon") as the steed of LILITH. An evil Sefiroth, he is a cosmic and blind dragon, completely eyeless, and a mechanism by which evil is activated. If he were to ever manifest in the flesh, his presence would destroy the world. Castrated, Taninniver brings about the union of LILITH with SAMAEL.

Sources: Dan, *Early Kabbalah*, 180; Dennis, *Encyclopedia of Jewish Myth, Magic and Mysticism*, 71, 154, 254.

Tannin

Variations: Associated with Asaszarim, LEVIATHAN, RAHAB, and TIAMAT; Tannanu

Tannin is the Dragon of the Sea, the demon of chaos in Jewish demonology. Living in the sea, he looks like a dragon or great serpent. His name in Hebrew translates to mean "alligator" or "crocodile."

Sources: Icon, *Folklore*, 244; Van der Toorn, *Dictionary of Deities and Demons in the Bible*, 265, 512.

Tarab

Apollonius of Tyana's *Nuctemeron* (*Night Illuminated by Day*) lists Tarab as the demon of extortion. He is most powerful during the twelfth hour.

Sources: Gettings, *Dictionary of Demons*, 238; Lévi, *Transcendental Magic*, 509.

Tarados

In the *Sacred Magic of Abramelin the Mage*, book two, Tarados is listed among the one hundred eleven SERVITORS OF AMAYMON, ARITON, ORIENS, AND PAYMON (see AMAYMON, ARITON, ORIENS, and PAYMON). This name is possibly Coptic and may mean "dispersion."

Sources: Mathers, *Book of the Sacred Magic of Abramelin*, 105; Susej, *Demonic Bible*, 256; Von Worms, *Book of Abramelin*, 245.

Taraka

Variations: Tarakâ

Taraka was an ASURAS from Hindu mythology who was feared by the gods. He knew all divine knowledge and had occult powers. Taraka forcibly carried off the wives of the gods and sought to subjugate the world; however, he was slain by Skanda (Karttikeya), a god of war.

Taraka, it should be noted, was also the name of a female RAKSHASA that was slain by Rama.

Sources: Doniger, *Hindu Myths*, 154–6; Kramrisch, *Presence of Siva*, 350–1.

Taralim

In the *Sacred Magic of Abramelin the Mage*, Taralim ("mighty stronghold") is listed as one of the twenty SERVITORS OF AMAYMON (see AMAYMON).

Sources: Ford, *Bible of the Adversary*, 95; Forgotten Books, *Book of the Sacred Magic of Abramelin the Mage*, 42–3; Mathers, *Book of the Sacred Magic of Abramelin the Mage*, 122; Susej, *Demonic Bible*, 259; Von Worms, *Book of Abramelin*, 257.

Tarchimache

The *Grand Grimoire*, alleged to have been written by Alibek the Egyptian in 1522, lists Tarchimache as one of the two commanders of

BEELZEBUB, the other being FLEURETTY. He is said to live in Africa.

The *Sacred Magic of Abramelin the Mage*, however, says that BEELZEBUB has forty-nine servitors and Tarchimache is not among them (see SERVITORS OF BEELZEBUB).

Sources: Masters, *Devil's Dominion*, 103; Waite, *Book of Black Magic and of Pacts*, 180.

Tarel

Enochian lore tells us that Tarel is one of the FALLEN ANGELS.

Sources: Charles, *Book of Enoch*, 178; Laurence, *Foreign Quarterly Review*, Vol. 24, 370; Prophet, *Fallen Angels and the Origins of Evil*, 74.

Taret

Variations: Ta Re T

In the *Ars Goetia*, the first book of the *Lemegeton*, Taret is listed as one of the fifty-three SERVITORS OF ASHTAROTH AND ASMODEUS (see ASHTAROTH and ASMODEUS). The name is possibly Hebrew and may mean "dampness, tending to corruption."

Sources: Ford, *Bible of the Adversary*, 90; Mathers, *Book of the Sacred Magic of Abra-Melin*, 115; Von Worms, *Book of Abramelin*, 256.

Tartach

Originally the demonic god of the Hevites, Tartach ("the enchained") is ranked as a Legat who serves under MOLOCH.

Sources: Ashley, *Complete Book of Devils and Demons*, 76; Smedley, *Occult Sciences*, 176; Weyer, *Witches, Devils, and Doctors in the Renaissance*, 13.

Tartaruchus, plural: tartaruchi

In the *Apocalypse of Paul*, the tartaruchi are angels of torments, a species of demon, and they are ranked among the Keepers of Hell until Judgment Day. The only tartaruchus ("shiver") named in the text is TEMELUCHUS. The tartaruchus uses one hand to choke damned souls and with the other uses an "iron of three hooks" to pierce entrails.

Source: Davidson, *Dictionary of Angels*, 44.

Tasma

In the *Sacred Magic of Abramelin the Mage*, book two, Tasma is among the one hundred eleven SERVITORS OF AMAYMON, ARITON, ORIENS, AND PAYMON (see AMAYMON, ARITON, ORIENS, and PAYMON). The name is both Chadian and Hebrew and means "weak."

Sources: Ford, *Bible of the Adversary*, 88; Mathers, *Book of the Sacred Magic of Abramelin the Mage*, 105, 113; Susej, *Demonic Bible*, 105, 256; Von Worms, *Book of Abramelin*, 244.

Tataka

Tataka is the wife of Sunda and the mother of MARICHA. She was a godling who was cursed and changed into a rakshasi by Agestya (see RAKSHASAS). This DEMONESS can raise clouds of dust, rain down rocks, shape-shift into any form she wishes, turn invisible, and is said to have the strength of a thousand elephants. She lives in the forest (see also SUBAHU).

Sources: Kurup, *Ramayana*, 13–5; Paswan, *Encyclopaedia of Dalits in India*, 58–9; Prime, *Ramayana*, 9–11.

Tavogivogi

The tavogivogi are a species of demon associated with a mysterious species of snake called mae in the demonology of the New Hebrides Islands. The name means "changeling," as they have the ability to shape-change into various animal forms. Appearing as a youthful and attractive person with a small patch of snake skin on its lower neck, such a demon seduces and kills its lover. Wherever a tavogivogi touches a person it will cause boils and oozing sores to open up. In snake form the demon cannot help itself and obviously behaves in a manner very much not like a snake, such as barking at approaching strangers, bathing its young, and singing to children. To test if someone is a tavogivogi, ask them the name of a tree; if it is a demon it will instantly transform into a bird and fly off.

Sources: Codrington, *the Melanesians*, 172; Jones, *Evil in Our Midst*, 201–3.

Tawrich

Variations: Tauriz, Taurvi

In Ancient Iranian demonology, Persian lore, and Zoroastrian demonology, Tawrich ("hunger"), who appears as a woman, is a DAEVAS, the personification of hunger. This demon of hunger is obsessed with blood. Her personal adversary is Haurvatat, one of the seven Amesha Spentas.

Sources: Ford, *Luciferian Witchcraft*, 24; Jackson, *Zoroastrian Studies*, 84–5.

Tcalyel

Variations: The Darkness

Tcalyel is a demon from Navajo demonology who commands the night when "there is more of whatever is bad." He has the ability to go anywhere without making a sound.

Sources: American Folklore Society, *Journal of American Folklore*, Vol. 1–2, 91; Ashley, *Complete Book of Devils and Demons*, 64.

Tchort

Tchort, whose name means the "Black God" in Russian, is essentially another name for SATAN.

Sources: Grimm, *Teutonic Mythology*, Vol. 4, 1541; Susej, *Demonic Bible*, 80.

Tediel

Tediel is one of the twenty SERVITORS OF CAMUEL (see CAMUEL). A nocturnal demon, he appears before his summoner in a beautiful form and is known to be very courteous.

Sources: Trithemius, *Steganographia*, 73.

Tege

Made by the god Ugatame when he made the universe, tege demons are a part of the natural world according to the demonology of the Kapauku people of New Guinea. These demons cause death and sickness but a shaman can harness their power and use it as his own to cause and cure illness as well as to kill. Tege live in the plants in the forest.

Sources: Jones, *Evil in Our Midst*, 183–5; Pospisil, *Kapauku Papuans and Their Law*, 12, 24; Pospisil, *Kapauku Papuans of West New Guinea*, 82, 86.

Telal

Telal ("spirit," "warrior," and "wicked demon") is one of a group of seven demons working in unison from Sumerian demonology. The *Magan Text* says that he is in service under Ereshkigal, the goddess of death and gloom (see IRKALLA). This demon will enter into a person's home and possess their hands, making them commit an act of thugery and violence. Telal cannot be prevented from entering into a home. This demon lives in the desert and in abandoned places of worship where sacrifices took place (see also ALAL, GIGIM, IDPA, NAMTAR, URUKU, and UTUK).

Sources: Burton, *Lady Burton's Edition of Her Husband's Arabian Nights*, 49; Crisafulli, *Go to Hell*, 222; King, *The Supernatural*, 296; Lenormant, *Chaldean Magic*, 24.

Temeluchus

Variations: Abtelmoluchos, Merciless Angel of Fire, TARTARUCHUS ("Keeper of Hell"), Tatirokos, Temeluchus, Temleyakos

In the *Apocalypse of Peter*, Temeluchus is said to be the Angel of Gehenna (Hell); he torments the souls in Hell. This name is possibly Greek and may translate to mean "caretaking."

Sources: Robinson, *Gospel According to Peter, and the Revelation of Peter*, 65; Salmon, *Historical Introduction to the Study of the Books of the New Testament*, 510, 513.

Tenebrion

Tenebrion ("idea") is the demon of darkness.

Sources: *Merriam-Webster's Collegiate Dictionary*, Edition 11, 1287; Poinsot, *Encyclopedia of Occult Sciences*, 305.

Tengu

Variations: Ten-Gu, Tien-Kou

Originating in eighth-century Japanese chronicles, tengu ("celestial dogs") are omens of catastrophes and war. In medieval times it was believed that haughty, insincere Buddhist monks were reborn as tengu demons. They are typically described as looking like a crow, a crow with a long beak and claws, or as a man with a crow's beak. In human form they have a large nose and a red face. It is said that the larger the beak or nose, the more powerful the demon. They speak through telepathy.

Tengu do not have a definite preference for any specific evil, but they are very imaginative and will exploit any situation; they are particularly fond of harassing children and monks who retire to the mountains to meditate. They struggle with feelings of compassion and vengeance.

These demons cause rock slides, collapse buildings, fell trees, and set forest fires. They are very quick and have the ability to bewitch humans and become invisible. They have magical powers and are renowned martial artists and storytellers.

Tengu live in the mountains and to hear the sound of falling timber or to see bird droppings on mats are a sign that tengu are near. With proper gifts and offerings a tengu demon may lend its powers to a human, aiding him with a magical amulet or spell, knowledge of the mountain, a mantra to render someone invisible, stamina, or swordsmanship. A tengu demon can only be slain by a power greater than its own or by a superior martial combatant.

Sources: Ashkenazi, *Handbook of Japanese Mythology*, 271; Bonnefoy, *Asian Mythologies*, 285–7; Hyatt, *Book of Demons*, 31; Mack, *Field Guide to Demons, Fairies, Fallen Angels, and Other Subversive Spirits*, 58–60.

Tentatores

Tentatores are FAMILIARs and servitors to evil men and necromancers, according to medieval demonology. A type of DJINN or devil, their bodies are made of air, fire, or water. These devils have the ability to create more of their own kind through sexual intercourse. Their attack can be prevented by calling out for Jesus to drive them back, by shaking bells or keys, by sounding an alarm, by using an herbal concoction mixed with red coral, or by using fire or swords against their bodies.

Sources: Sluhovsky, *Believe Not Every Spirit*, 180; Waite, *Book of Ceremonial Magic*, 298.

Tentatores Maligenii

Variations: Diaboli, infidiatores

The Tentatores Maligenii is the name of the

ninth order of demons. These demons of temptation are under the command of MAMMON.

Sources: Coleman, *Dictionary of Mythology*, 1000; McLean, *Treatise on Angel Magic*, 70–1; Thorndike, *History of Magic and Experimental Science*, Part 10, 405.

Tephras

Variations: EPHIPPAS, Tephros

Born the offspring of "the great one," Tephras, the demon of ashes, is listed as one of the SPIRITS OF SOLOMON, bound to work on the temple carrying stones. This demon may be summoned any time of the day or night, and is most powerful during the summer months. Tephras creeps into the corners of walls and is known to bring darkness to man, cause convulsions and fevers, destroy homesteads, and set fields on fire. His personal adversary is the archangel Azael ("whom God strengthens"). His name is Greek for "the ashes of a funeral pyre."

Sources: Conybeare, *Jewish Quarterly Review*, Vol. 11, 23–24; Ashe, *Qabalah*, 31–33; Guazzo, *Compendium Maleficarum*, Part 2, 73; Inman, *Ancient Faiths Embodied in Ancient Names*, Part 3, 869; West, *Invisible World*, 23.

Terrestrial Devils

Friar Francesco Maria Guazzo's book *Compendium Maleficarum* (1628) said that terrestrial demons were cast out of Heaven for their sins and now live in the fields, forests, and woods. They attack those who wander in the woods, lay snares for hunters, and lead astray those who travel at night.

Source: Kipfer, *Order of Things*, 255.

Terrytop

Terrytop is a devil from the Cornish folk tale "Duffy and the Devil." In the story a young maiden named Duffy is beaten by her stepmother for romping about town with boys rather than tending to her knitting. A handsome squire, having seen the beating take place, is instantly smitten by her good looks and takes Duffy back to his home. There, the old woman who runs his household sets Duffy to spinning and knitting. Angry at having to work, she curses at the spinning wheel, which summons up a devil. The devil then offers to do her work and fulfill any wish she has if at the end of three years she becomes his, but only if by that time she cannot correctly guess his name. Duffy agrees to the bargain.

The squire soon marries Duffy and they have a wonderful life, but as end of the three-year contract she made with the devil draws near, Duffy grows more and more despondent. The day before her time is up the squire tells his wife of a sight he saw in the woods with the hopes it will cheer her up. He tells her he saw a devil dancing in a circle around a coven of witches singing a song that went "Duffy, my lady, you'll never know—what? That my name is Terrytop, Terrytop, top!" The next day when the devil appears he taunts Duffy and gives her three guesses at his name. She plays with him, pretending to be nervous and tossing out two names she knows will not work, but on her last try uses the correct name. Enraged, the devil leaves in a flash of fire, taking his knitting and spinning wheel with him.

Sources: Cooper, *Fairy Tales*, 70; Folklore Society, *Folk-Lore Journal*, Vol. 7, 143–4; Hunt, *Popular Romances of the West of England*, 239–47.

Thagrinus

Apollonius of Tyana's *Nuctemeron* (*Night Illuminated by Day*) lists Thagrinus as the demon of confusion. He is most powerful during the fourth hour.

Sources: Gettings, *Dictionary of Demons*, 241; Lévi, *Book of Hermes*, 404.

Thamiel

Variations: Double-Headed Ones, Thaumiel

In Solomonic lore the thamiel are an order of lesser demons under the command of MOLOCH and SATAN, who are constantly at odds with one another. Demons of anarchy and revolt, they are described as having two giant heads with batlike wings. These demons continuously try to unite themselves with the bodies of other beings and forces. The personal adversaries of the thamiel ("duality of God" or "the polluted of God") are the Chaioth Ha-Qadesh, the Intelligences of the Divine Tetragram.

Sources: Lévi, *Mysteries of Magic*, 110; Mathers, *Key of Solomon the King*, 121.

Thammus

Variations: Tammus, Tammuz, Tamuz, Thammuz, Thamuz, Zagreus

Originally a Sumerian god, when absorbed into Christian demonology Thammus became a FALLEN ANGEL, formerly of the Order of Archangels, and was assigned the infernal task of being the ambassador of Hell to Spain. This demon is said to have been the one who created the Holy Inquisition and invented artillery; he causes men to desire to hurt one another. He is most powerful during the month of September.

Sources: Chambers, *Book of Days*, 723; *Greek Mythology*, 113; Seisenberger, *Practical Handbook for the Study of the Bible and of Bible Literature*, 65.

Thanatiel

In the *Theurgia Goetia*, the second book of the *Lemegeton*, Thanatiel is ranked as a duke who commands 2,200 servitors and is listed as one of the fifteen SERVITORS OF ICOSIEL (see ICOSIEL). Said to be good-natured, he will do whatever his summoner asks of him. He prefers to be summoned from inside of a house.

Sources: Peterson, *Lesser Key of Solomon*, 99; Trithemius, *Steganographia*, 69.

Thausael

Enochian lore names Thausael as one of the FALLEN ANGELS who swore allegiance to SAMI-AZA, rebelled against God, took a human wife, and fathered the NEPHILIM.

Sources: Baty, *Book of Enoch the Prophet*, 51; *Foreign Quarterly Review*, Vols. 24–25, 205; Laurence, *Foreign Quarterly Review*, Vol. 24, 370; Voltaire, *Philosophy of History*, 293; Voltaire, *Essays and Criticisms*, 106.

Theutus

Originating from the demonology of Cornelius Agrippa, Theutus was a misinterpretation of the Egyptian god Thoth. The demon of cards, dice, and gambling as well as the inventor of all things evil and wicked, this demon is from an order of demons known as the Vessels of Iniquity.

Thoth was demonized because he was the god that taught humans about numbers and how to use them, which in the Middle Ages was immediately associated with gambling for money, an activity that was looked upon as evil by the bulk of the European population.

Sources: Hibbert, *Sketches of the Philosophy of Apparitions*, 186; McLean, *Treatise on Angel Magic*, 96; Morley, *Cornelius Agrippa*, 195.

Th'uban

Variations: Al-Tinnin, Tinnin

The demon Th'uban ("serpent") from Islamic demonology looks like an enormous fire-breathing dragon with many heads.

Sources: Allen, *Star-Names and their Meanings*, 208; Hargreaves, Lurker, *Routledge Dictionary of Gods and Goddesses, Devils and Demons*, 184; Rose, *Giants, Monsters, and Dragons*, 359.

Thuriel

Variations: Thirciel, Thirsiel

In *Theurgia Goetia*, the second book of the *Lemegeton*, Thuriel is ranked as a chief duke who commands four hundred servitors and is listed as one of the twelve named SERVITORS OF MACARIEL (see MACARIEL). This demon can be summoned from any time of the day or night and appears in any variety of forms, but most commonly as a dragon with a virgin's head. Thuriel is known to be good-natured and willing to obey his summoner.

Sources: Peterson, *Lesser Key of Solomon*, 103; Trithemius, *Steganographia*, 141.

Thursir

Variations: "Frost giants," Hrimthurses, Thurses

Thursir is a demonic giant from Norse mythology who was created at the beginning of the world from the melting ice. He is said to have large ears and a body covered with long hair. Thursir causes illness and steals man's ability to comprehend. It was after the introduction of Christianity that Thursir was demonized, said to be malicious and a bringer of misfortune.

Sources: Lurker, *Routledge Dictionary of Gods and Goddesses, Devils and Demons*, 184; Rose, *Giants, Monsters, and Dragons*, 359.

Tiamat

Tiamat, a winged cosmic serpent, is a demonic goddess from the Babylonian creation epic. She is the demon of the sea, the personification of chaos and saltwater. Tiamat gave birth to all the bull-men, demons, fish-men, gods, horned snakes, and monsters. APSU is her consort, and he is the personification of fresh water. Tiamat was slain by her great-great grandson, the solar god Marduk; he then used her slain body to create the heavens and the earth, clouds, fog, mountains, rain, and rivers.

Sources: Mack, *Field Guide to Demons, Fairies, Fallen Angels, and Other Subversive Spirits*, 7–9.

Tiawath

Variations: Damkina, Dawkina, "Mother Hubur," Mummu-Tiamat, Tauthe, Thauatth, TIAMAT, Tiawthu

Tiawath ("the sea"), a great dragon, was the DEMONESS of chaos, confusion, and evil in Babylonian mythology; she existed before there was time. Living in the primeval ocean that surrounded the earth and sky, she brought into being a wide array of horrific monsters and created weapons for her followers: a horde of fish men, giant serpents, raging dogs, scorpion men, and other terrible beings. Tiawath declared war against the higher gods, feeling that they were a threat to her and the lower gods. She had possessed the Tablets of Fate and used her charms and magical incantations in battle. Eventually she was slain by the god Belus (Bel-Merodach); her body was divided to create the earth and the sky.

Sources: Pinches, *Religion of Babylonia and Assyria*, Vol. 8, 33–8; Spence, *Encyclopædia of Occultism*, 122.

Tigara

Variations: Tigora

In the *Theurgia Goetia*, the second book of the *Lemegeton*, Tigara ("wander about"), a diurnal demon, is ranked as a duke and is listed as one of the fifteen SERVITORS OF BARMIEL (see BARMIEL and DUKES OF HELL).

Sources: Leslau, *Arabic Loanwords in Ethiopian Semitic*, 367; Mathers, *Book of the Sacred Magic of Abra-Melin*, 107; Trithemius, *Steganographia*, 17.

Tigrafon

In the *Sacred Magic of Abramelin the Mage*, book two, Tigrafon is listed as one of the sixty-five SERVITORS OF KORE AND MAGOTH. His name is possibly Greek and may translate to mean "capable of writing."

Sources: Mathers, *Book of the Sacred Magic of Abra-Melin*, 107; Susej, *Demonic Bible*, 258; Von Worms, *Book of Abramelin*, 250.

Tii

Variations: Tiki

Tii is a demon from Maori demonology whose name means "to come for a thing," "to retrieve a thing," or "to go for a thing." More literally, it is used when referring to driving a demon out of a possessed person.

Sources: Tregear, *Maori-Polynesian Comparative Dictionary*, 306, 510–11; Turner, *Dictionary of Ancient Deities*, 467.

Tikbalang

Variations: Binangunan (Negrito), Tigbalan, Tigbalang, Tikbalan, Tulung, Tuwung

A tikbalang is a species of demonic creature from the Philippines. These demons are created whenever a fetus is aborted and they look like a tall man with a horse head. Typically they are black-skinned but in rare instances they are white. White tikbalang have greater magical properties. They have thick manes with spines, clawed feet, an enlarged penis, a large mouth full of teeth, and long hair. Their legs are so long that when they sit, their knees are over their head. Nocturnal demons, they kidnap women and hold them captive in bamboo cages until they murder them. They also lead travelers astray.

The tikbalang spread death, misfortune, and sickness. They can assume any form or size they wish. They can also bewilder, blind, and cause insanity; disappear in a dusty cloud and falling stones; cause fevers and invisibility; shape-shift into humans; and steal rosary beads from Christians.

Tikbalang live atop balete and kalumpang trees; in balete, banana, and bamboo groves; and in the pitcher plant (*Sterculia foetida*). They are also found beneath bridges, near hot springs, or in any sparsely populated, foliage-overgrown area.

The call of the tikbalang can be heard when one is near: "Tik-tik." To prevent an attack by these demons, when passing through the territory of one, first ask for permission by saying "By your leave" or by wearing your shirt inside out. Using a specially prepared rope, a person may jump onto its back and hang on while the tikbalang tries to throw him off; when it is completely exhausted it will admit defeat. Then, pluck the three thickest spines in its mane, as they can be made into a talisman to make the tikbalang into your servant. These demons have a magic jewel that is the source of its power. It will give up if captured in exchange for its freedom.

Sources: Ramos, *Creatures of Midnight*, 17; Rosen, *Mythical Creatures Bible*, 103.

Tikoloshe

A short, humanoid amphibian, the tikoloshe is covered with hair and swings his arms when he walks. This demon of the Xhosa people of South Africa preys nightly on women, appearing at dances and community gatherings dressed like someone from a neighboring village. The demon will offer to do household chores for a woman in exchange for sexual favors, meanwhile weaving a spell over his prey and further adding to his charm. If the woman does not succumb, he will take her by force. Tikoloshe are extremely charming and seductive demons with voracious sexual appetites.

In Chinese lore there is a demonic creature similar to the tikoloshe called WHITE MONKEY.

Sources: Knappert, *Bantu Myths and Other Tales*, 173; Mack, *Field Guide to Demons, Fairies, Fallen Angels, and Other Subversive Spirits*, 35–6.

Timira

In the *Ars Goetia*, the first book of the *Lemegeton*, Timira ("palm") is one of the fifty-three SERVITORS OF ASHTAROTH AND ASMODEUS (see ASHTAROTH and ASMODEUS).

Sources: Ford, *Bible of the Adversary*, 89; Mathers, *Book of the Sacred Magic of Abra-Melin*, 115; Susej, *Demonic Bible*, 257; Von Worms, *Book of Abramelin*, 256.

Tin Tin

The tin tin is a vampiric demon from Ecuador who preys upon adolescent girls. It whistles to get its prey's attention. Then, as soon as it can, it takes the girl to its cave and rapes her, typically impregnating her. This demon hunts only when the moon is out.

Sources: Eberhart, *Mysterious Creatures*, 82; Guiley, *Encyclopedia of Vampires, Werewolves, and other Monsters*, 280.

Tingoi

Variations: Dyinyinga

Originating in the Mende tribe of Sierra Leone, the tingoi are beautiful, mermaidlike demonic creatures with white skin but smelling of rotting fish. Living in deep rivers, the ocean, and deep ponds, they sit on rocks combing out their long hair with golden combs. If one's comb is stolen, the tingoi will beg rather desperately and pathetically for it to be returned; however, if it is returned, the thief will suffer poverty for the rest of his life. The only way to break the curse is for the comb to be burned and its ashes spread over your cooking stones. If tingoi are approached at exactly the right time and in the proper way, they will be pleasant and polite and will give their guest a present (see also NDOGBOJUSUI).

Sources: Rose, *Spirits, Fairies, Leprechauns, and Goblins*, 96, 309; Schön, *Vocabulary of the Mende Language*, 139.

Tipua

Variations: Tupua

A tipua is a species of shape-shifting demons from Māori mythology. They can become any common item with an unusual shape, such as rocks and trees. These demons are known to travel from location to location, and there are many stories of tipua using hunting dogs. To keep from being attacked, travelers will leave an offering at a known tipua location or risk being harassed by the demon. The Māori word *tipua* is understood to mean "demon," but more literally it means "uncanny thing."

Sources: Djiwandono, *Journal of the Polynesian Society*, Vol. 15, 27–8; White, *Ancient History of the Maori*, 190.

Tiraim

In the *Sacred Magic of Abramelin the Mage*, book two, Tiraim ("filling up") is listed as one of the sixty-five SERVITORS OF KORE AND MAGOTH.

Sources: Ford, *Bible of the Adversary*, 92; Mathers, *Book of the Sacred Magic of Abramelin the Mage*, 118; Susej, *Demonic Bible*, 258; Von Worms, *Book of Abramelin*, 250.

Tirana

In the *Sacred Magic of Abramelin the Mage*, book two, Tirana is one of the one hundred eleven SERVITORS OF AMAYMON, ARITON, ORIENS, AND PAYMON (see AMAYMON, ARITON, ORIENS, and PAYMON). The name is possibly Hebrew and it may mean "an apple tree" or "a mast of a ship."

Sources: Ford, *Bible of the Adversary*, 88; Susej, *Demonic Bible*, 256; Von Worms, *Book of Abramelin*, 255.

Tiril

Voltaire's *Of Angels, Genii, and Devils* names Tiril as one of the FALLEN ANGELS who swore allegiance to SAMIAZA, rebelled against God, took a human wife, and fathered the NEPHILIM. Voltaire's list of fallen angels is different from that of the Enochian tradition.

Sources: Davidson, *Dictionary of Angels*, 290; Voltaire, *Philosophy of History*, 293; Voltaire, *Essays and Criticisms*, 106.

Titivillus

Variations: Titivil, Titivulus, Tutivillus

The Christian demonologist John of Wales, also known as Johannes Galensis, wrote *Tractatus de Penitentia* in 1285; in it he named Titivillus as the demon of calligraphy artists, gossips, and scribes. Believed to be a servitor under the command of BELPHEGOR, LUCIFER, or SATAN, Titivillus preys upon calligraphy artists and scribes, causing them to make copying errors. He also collects idle chit-chat from the congregation of church gossips and the mumbled or skipped words that priests leave out during church services to use against them on Judgment Day.

Sources: Drogin, *Medieval Calligraphy*, 17–20; Icon, *Demons*, 183; McKean, *Verbatim*, 227.

Tobiel

Variations: Tubuel

Originally a saint, Tobiel's canonization was removed by Pope Zachary in 745 when he "unearthed and turned out of the saintly calendar" demons who had been passing themselves off as saints, such as ORIBEL and RAGUHEL (see also CHURCH CONDEMNED ANGELS).

Sources: Davidson, *Dictionary of Angels*, 238; Hugo, *Toilers of the Sea*, 62; Rudwin, *Devil in Legend and Literature*, 28, 62.

Toglas

In Apollonius of Tyana's *Nuctemeron* (*Night Illuminated by Day*), Toglas is the demon of hidden treasures. He is most powerful during the eighth hour.

Source: Lévi, *Transcendental Magic*, 392.

Toia

Toia is a demon from the mythology of the Native Americans of Florida and Louisiana. He sends NIGHTMARES and horrific visions.

Sources: Baskin, *Satanism*, 320; Pitrat, *Pagan Origin of Partialist Doctrines*, 63.

Tokebi

Tokebi is a one-legged demon in Korean demonology who preys upon those in authority.

Playful, he spends most of his time drinking and eating. He has superhuman powers and can bring good fortune. This demon causes a little chaos and some mayhem but seldom does any actual damage.

Sources: Fukuoka, *Lives of Young Koreans in Japan*, 74; Maberry, *Vampire Universe*, 278–9.

Tonga-Hiti

Variations: Big-eyed Tonga-hiti, Jovial-faced Tonga-hiti, Tongahiti

Tonga-Hiti ("glow of the South") is a type of demon known as a *ponaturi* in Polynesian mythology. He is the demon of headaches. This demon has the ability to shape-shift into a very small bird or a sooty albatross. Living in the ocean, he can only be destroyed by direct sunlight.

Sources: Craig, *Dictionary of Polynesian Mythology*, 228; Tregear, *Maori-Polynesian Comparative Dictionary*, 532; White, *Ancient History of the Maori*, Vol. 1, 101–2; White, *Ancient History of the Maori*, Vol. 7, 89–90.

Torfora

In the *Sacred Magic of Abramelin the Mage*, book two, Torfora ("a small knife" or "lancet") is one of the one hundred eleven SERVITORS OF AMAYMON, ARITON, ORIENS, AND PAYMON (see AMAYMON, ARITON, ORIENS, and PAYMON).

Sources: Ford, *Bible of the Adversary*, 88; Mathers, *Book of the Sacred Magic of Abramelin the Mage*, 105; Susej, *Demonic Bible*, 256; Von Worms; *Book of Abramelin*, 244.

Torvatus

Apollonius of Tyana's *Nuctemeron* (*Night Illuminated by Day*) lists Torvatus as the demon of discord. He is most powerful during the second hour of the day.

Sources: Gettings, *Dictionary of Demons*, 242; Kelly, *Who in Hell*, 227; Lévi, *Transcendental Magic*, 418.

Toun

In the *Sacred Magic of Abramelin the Mage*, book two, Toun is listed as one of the fifteen SERVITORS OF ASMODEUS AND MAGOTH (see ASMODEUS). This name is possibly Hebrew and may translate to mean "hire" or "price."

Sources: Mathers, *Book of the Sacred Magic of Abramelin the Mage*, 116; Von Worms, *Book of Abramelin*, 256.

Toxai

In the *Sacred Magic of Abramelin the Mage*, book two, Toxai is listed as one of the thirty-two SERVITORS OF ASTAROT (see ASTAROT). This name means "archery" in Greek and "poison" in Latin.

Sources: Mathers, *Book of the Sacred Magic of Abramelin the Mage*, 106, 117; Von Worms, *Book of Abramelin*, 249, 256.

Toyol

Variations: Tuyul

A vampiric demon in Malaysian lore, the *toyol* ("elevated") is created by magic and used by a witch to be her FAMILIAR; they also appear in the demonology of Indonesia, Singapore, and Thailand. Taking the body of a deceased baby, the witch performs a ceremony that allows a demonic spirit to possess and animate the corpse, binding it to her to do her bidding. Looking like the green-skinned baby with red eyes that it is, the toyol is usually kept in an earthenware jar called *tempayan*, which is stored under the witch's home until it is needed, as the toyol is rather mischievous when left to its own devices. It is also something of an accomplished thief, but unless it is told to go and steal something, it only takes half of what it was told to.

Sources: Fogelson, *Anthropology of Power*, 282; Icon, *Deads*, 542; Robbins, *Global Problems*, 62.

Traci

In the *Sacred Magic of Abramelin the Mage*, book two, Traci ("harsh" or "rude") is one of the one hundred eleven SERVITORS OF AMAYMON, ARITON, ORIENS, AND PAYMON (see AMAYMON, ARITON, ORIENS, and PAYMON).

Sources: Ford, *Bible of the Adversary*, 88; Mathers, *Selected Occult Writings of S.L. MacGregor Mathers*, 105; Susej, *Demonic Bible*, 256; Von Worms, *Book of Abramelin*, 244.

Trapis

In the *Sacred Magic of Abramelin the Mage*, book two, Trapis ("turning") is one of the one hundred eleven SERVITORS OF AMAYMON, ARITON, ORIENS, AND PAYMON (see AMAYMON, ARITON, ORIENS, and PAYMON).

Sources: Ford, *Bible of the Adversary*, 88; Mathers, *Selected Occult Writings of S.L. MacGregor Mathers*, 105; Susej, *Demonic Bible*, 256; Von Worms, *Book of Abramelin*, 245.

Trimasael

Variations: Trimasel

The *Grimoirium Verum* (*Grimoire of Truth*), allegedly written by Alibek the Egyptian in 1517, names the demon Trimasael as a chief under the command of of SATANACHIA and SATANICIAE (see SERVITORS OF SATANACHIA and SATANICIAE). This demon is summoned for his ability to teach alchemy, chemistry, illusions, and sleight of hand, and how to burn base metals into silver and gold. When invoked, if Trimasael is not content with his summoner, this demon will not impart onto him the secrets of changing base metals.

Sources: Kuriakos, *Grimoire Verum Ritual Book*, 40; Masters, *Devil's Dominion*, 131; Waite, *Book of Black Magic and of Pacts*, 162–3.

Trisaga

In the *Sacred Magic of Abramelin the Mage*, book two, Trisaga ("directing by triads") is listed as one of the ten SERVITORS OF AMAIMON AND ARITON (see AMAIMON and ARITON).

Sources: Susej, *Demonic Bible*, 257; Von Worms, *Book of Abramelin*, 256.

Troian

Troian is a nocturnal demon from the demonology of the Baltic region of Russia. He is described only as having "waxen wings."

Source: Ashley, *Complete Book of Devils and Demons*, 64.

Tromes

In the *Sacred Magic of Abramelin the Mage*, book two, Tromes ("disaster" or "wound") is listed as one of the forty-nine SERVITORS OF BEELZEBUB (see BEELZEBUB).

Sources: Ford, *Bible of the Adversary*, 93; Von Worms, *Book of Abramelin*, 257.

Tsan

Tsan is a Chinese word that translates to mean "devil."

Sources: Morrison, *Dictionary of the Chinese Language*, 234; Waddell, *Tibetan Buddhism*, 474.

Tsi Sgili

From the demonology of the Cherokee tribes of North Carolina, Tennessee and Oklahoma comes a type of demonic witch known as a *tsi sgili* ("owl" and "witch"). These witches have a wide array of psychic powers called *ane li sqi* ("one who thinks") that they use to kill or maim, oftentimes consuming the flesh of their prey afterwards. They have the ability to shape-shift into animal form and will at some point take on an apprentice to train. Cherokee mythology says that anyone can become a witch and that when they do they are no longer considered human, but rather some sort of nonhuman or dead creature.

Source: Jones, *Evil in Our Midst*, 10–4.

Tü

On the Polynesian islands there is a vampiric demon known as a *tü* ("war" or "to stand"). When a person wants the power to communicate with the dead, they eat a piece of the corpse belonging to the person they wish to converse with. The

spirit, the tü, that once resided in the body will return and appear to the person, seeking to start a friendship with them. As a show of good faith and wanting to make friends, the tü will offer to do favors for the person, such as attacking those who would do its potential new friend harm and drinking their blood.

Sources: Carlyon, *A Guide to the Gods*, 382; Fornander, *Account of the Polynesian Race*, 170; Handy, *Polynesian Religion*, 265.

Tugaros

Tugaros is one of the twenty SERVITORS OF CAMUEL (see CAMUEL). A nocturnal demon, he appears in a beautiful form and is known for being very courteous.

Sources: Peterson, *Lesser Key of Solomon*, 68; Trithemius, *Steganographia*, 12.

Tukiphat

Apollonius of Tyana's *Nuctemeron* (*Night Illuminated by Day*) lists Tukiphat as the demon of schamir (a magical worm that can cut stone). He is most powerful during the eighth hour.

Source: Lévi, *Transcendental Magic*, 392.

Tulot

The *Sacred Magic of Abramelin the Mage*, book two, lists Tulot ("triple") as one of the one hundred eleven SERVITORS OF AMAYMON, ARITON, ORIENS, AND PAYMON (see AMAYMON, ARITON, ORIENS, and PAYMON).

Sources: Mathers, *Book of the Sacred Magic of Abra-Melin*, 105; Susej, *Demonic Bible*, 256; Von Worms, *Book of Abramelin*, 245.

Tumael

Variations: Tuma'el

Enochian lore names Tumael as one of the FALLEN ANGELS who swore allegiance to SAMIAZA, rebelled against God, took a human wife, and fathered the NEPHILIM.

Sources: Horne, *Sacred Books and Early Literature of the East*, 114; Laurence, *Book of Enoch the Prophet*, 77; Prophet, *Fallen Angels and the Origins of Evil*, 174.

Tunrida

Tunrida is a devil from Scandinavian demonology said to look like an old woman. He was created through a pact with the DEVIL. This name translates as "hedge-rider" or "house-rider" and essentially means a witch.

Sources: Bailey, *Spiritual Warfare*, 96; Kelly, *Who in Hell*, 227; Susek, *Demonic Bible*, 80.

Tupapau

A tupapau ("spirit of the dead") is an ancestral spirit in Polynesian demonology who appears as a ghostly apparition or a fiery serpent. A nocturnal demon, it comes at night to torment people and the local priest, causing mischief. A tupapau attacks a person's eyes, causes sickness, damages crops and trees, and kills young children. These demons live in burial places. Polynesian lore suggests not going into burial places or approaching a newly deceased body until a priest has laid a small pig next to it, lest you risk a tupapau attack. Night travel should be in large groups and with lanterns, as this demon avoids the lights and will not attack people in numbers.

Sources: *Religious and Cosmic Beliefs of Central Polynesia*, 396, 398; Wood, *Natural History of Man*, 424.

Turael

Variations: Terel, Turel, Tur'el, Turyal

Enochian lore names Turael ("rock of God") as one of the CHIEF OF TENS (see GRIGORI and WATCHERS). A FALLEN ANGEL, he swore allegiance to SAMIAZA, rebelled against God, took a human wife, and fathered the NEPHILIM.

Sources: Beard, *Autobiography of Satan*, 113; Horne, *Sacred Books and Early Literature of the East*, 114; Laurence, *Book of Enoch, the Prophet*, 6; Lumpkin, *Fallen Angels, the Watchers, and the Origins of Evil*, 31; Prophet, *Fallen Angels and the Origins of Evil*, 174.

Turitel

In the *Sacred Magic of Abramelin the Mage*, Turitel ("mountain cast down") is listed as one of the eight SERVITORS OF ORIENS (see ORIENS).

Sources: Ford, *Bible of the Adversary*, 94; Mathers, *Book of the Sacred Magic of Abra-Melin*, 108; Susej, *Demonic Bible*, 259; Von Worms, *Book of Abramelin*, 257.

Tzelladimiron

In Cabalistic demonology, Tzelladimiron is one of the twelve QLIPPOTHIC ORDERS OF DEMONS. Demons of this order look like savage triangle-headed dogs; their colors are bronze, crimson, limped blood and tzelil.

Sources: Ford, *Bible of the Adversary*, 112–14; Greer, *New Encyclopedia of the Occult*, 129; Mathers, *Sorcerer and His Apprentice*, 26.

Tzephariron

In cabalistic demonology the tzephariron are one of the twelve QLIPPOTHIC ORDERS OF DEMONS. They appear as a living yet decaying corpse. Their colors are like those of the earth.

Sources: Ford, *Liber Hvhi*, 66; Greer, *New Encyclopedia of the Occult*, 129; Mathers, *Sorcerer and His Apprentice*, 26.

Tzitzimitl, plural: tzitzimimeh

A tzitzimitl is a species of celestial demon from Aztec demonology. Its name translates to mean "monsters descending from above." Tzitzimimeh, as they are called in numbers, appear as skeletal females wearing skirts with a skull and crossbones pattern. Nocturnal demons, during solar eclipses the tzitzimimeh would descend to the earth to devour humans. Prior to Aztec conquest the tzitzimimeh were considered to be fertility gods and were worshipped by midwives.

Sources: de Sahagún, *Primeros Memoriales*, 153; Taube, *Aztec and Maya Myths*, 40–1.

Uahti

In South America, all along the Amazon River and in the nearby jungle, there lives a type of vampiric demon called uahti. It is a small and hairy creature with an enlarged penis, large belly, and toeless feet. Following behind a colony of bats, the uahti sexually assaults adolescent girls and adult men, draining away their sexual and life-energy during the assault.

Sources: Reichel-Dolmatoff, *Shaman and the Jaguar*, 72, 83, 85; Roth, *American Elves*, 106, 107, 108; Wicker, *From the Ground Up*, 33.

Ualac

Variations: Valac, Valak, Valax, Valic, Valu, Volac

The *Lesser Key of Solomon* ranks Ualac as the dragon president who commands thirty (or thirty-eight, sources vary) legions. Appearing as a cherubim riding upon a two-headed dragon, he is summoned for his ability to answer questions put to him truthfully concerning the location of hidden treasures and where snakes are. He can make snakes listless in the summoner's hands.

Sources: Crowley, *The Goetia*, 60; De Laurence, *Lesser Key of Solomon, Goetia*, 42; Godwin, *Godwin's Cabalistic Encyclopedia*, 324; McLean, *Treatise of Angel Magic*, 57; Peterson, *Lesser Key of Solomon*, 35; Scot, *Discoverie of Witchcraft*, 224.

Ubarin

In the *Sacred Magic of Abramelin the Mage*, book two, Ubarin ("insult, outrage") is listed as one of the sixty-five SERVITORS OF KORE AND MAGOTH.

Sources: Ford, *Bible of the Adversary*, 92; Mathers, *Book of the Sacred Magic of Abra-Melin*, 107; Susej, *Demonic Bible*, 258; Von Worms, *Book of Abramelin*, 250.

Udaman

Ars Goetia, the first book of the *Lemegeton*, names Udaman as one of the fifty-three SERVITORS OF ASHTAROTH AND ASMODEUS (see ASHTAROTH and ASMODEUS). His name is possibly Greek and means "fortunate."

Sources: Ford, *Bible of the Adversary*, 90; Mathers, *Book of the Sacred Magic of Abra-Melin*, 115; Von Worms, *Book of Abramelin*, 247.

Udu

Variations: Udug, UTUKKU

Udu, one of the evil SEBETTU, was one of seven children born to the sky god Anu, according to Mesopotamian demonology. Assistant to the plague god Erra, Udu lives in deserted places or in graveyards. Sebettu is Akkadian for "the seven."

Sources: Jastrow, *Religion of Babylonia and Assyria*, 260; Lurker, *Dictionary of Gods and Goddesses, Devils and Demons*, 314, 364; Rogers, *Religion of Babylonia and Assyria*, 147; Russell, *The Devil*, 92.

Ugales

In the *Ars Goetia*, the first book of the *Lemegeton*, Ugales is listed as one of the fifty-three SERVITORS OF ASHTAROTH AND ASMODEUS (see ASHTAROTH and ASMODEUS). His name is possibly Greek and may translate to mean "calm."

Sources: Ford, *Bible of the Adversary*, 90; Mathers, *Book of the Sacred Magic of Abra-Melin*, 116; Von Worms, *Book of Abramelin*, 248.

Ugirpen

In the *Sacred Magic of Abramelin the Mage*, Ugirpen is listed as one of the thirty-two SERVITORS OF ASTAROT (see ASTAROT).

Sources: Mathers, *Book of the Sacred Magic of Abramelin the Mage*, 106; Von Worms, *Book of Abramelin*, 249, 256.

Ugola

In the *Sacred Magic of Abramelin the Mage*, Ugola ("fluent in speech") is listed as one of the fifteen SERVITORS OF PAYMON (see PAYMON).

Sources: Mathers, *Book of the Sacred Magic of Abra-Melin*, 121; Von Worms, *Book of Abramelin*, 257.

Ukobach

Variations: UROBACH

In Collin de Plancy's *Dictionaire Infernale* (1863), Ukobach is ranked as the stationary engineer of Hell in service under BEELZEBUB; his job is to replenish the cauldrons of Hell with oil. A fire demon, Ukobach appears as a man wrapped in flames. He created the art of frying food and invented fireworks.

Sources: Ashley, *Complete Book of Devils and Demons*, 60; Cavendish, *Man, Myth and Magic*, Vol. 5, 861; Collin de Plancy, *Dictionary of Witchcraft*, 118; Knappert, *Encyclopaedia of Middle Eastern Mythology and Religion*, 282; Robbins, *Encyclopedia of Witchcraft and Demonology*, 337.

Ultores Scelorum

Variations: Revengers of Wickedness

Ultores scelorum are of the fourth order of demons. They are the demons of revenge and are under the command of ASMODEUS.

Sources: Coleman, *Dictionary of Mythology*, 1057; McLean, *Treatise on Angel Magic*, 70.

Ulu Tojon

Variations: Arson Duolai ("Ruler of the Dead"), Chief of the black spirits, Syga Tojon

From the demonology of the Yakut people comes the demon lord and thunder god Ulu Tojon ("powerful Lord"); he commands all nine clans of the abassy and rules the underworld (see ABAASI). Preying on human souls and spreading diseases, he appears as a humanoid with his mouth on his forehead and his eyes on his temples.

An autumn festival called *abasy-yayakh*, which is full of games and blood sacrifices, is held in his honor and hosted by nine male and nine female shamans in the hopes of pleasing him into peace for another year.

Sources: Grimal, *Larousse World Mythology*, 434; Shoolbraid, *Oral Epic of Siberia and Central Asia*, 9, 157; Sinorm, *Uralic and Altaic Series*, Vol. 1–150, 9; Turner, *Dictionary of Ancient Deities*, 70.

Unkcegila

Variations: The spirit of the land

The mythology of the Lakota-speaking Oglala tribe of North America tells of a demon called Unkcegila. He is under the command of Wakan Sica. Responsible for unexplained deaths and disappearances, this demon is repelled by the smell of sage, sweetgrass, and pipe smoke. Unkcegila's power resides in his brittle horns and tail and may be warded off with rituals.

Sources: Jones, *Evil in Our Midst*, 47–50; Powers, *Oglala Religion*, 55, 79.

Uphir

Variations: Ufir, Uphor

Uphir is the apothecary and physician of Hell. He has secret knowledge of medicine and is known to dissect human bodies in graveyards.

Sources: Ashley, *Complete Book of Devils and Demons*, 60; Knappert, *Encyclopaedia of Middle Eastern Mythology and Religion*, 282.

Ura

Ura ("perfect servant of the gods"), a demonic god of disease, is one of the forms of NERGAL, the god of famine, plague, war, and destruction in general from Babylonian demonology. His councilor is the god Ishun. Ura commands seven evil spirits and wishes to destroy "the dark-heads" (mankind). He can utter an "unloosable curse" that kills domestic animals and humans with disease. He can be prevented from attacking by reciting a formula that praises his bravery and power.

Sources: Hastings, *Encyclopedia of Religion and Ethics*, Part 12, 645; Thompson, *Devils and Evil Spirits of Babylonia*, xlvii.

Urakabarameel

Enochian lore names Urakabarameel as a CHIEF OF THE GRIGORI and one of the CHIEF OF TENS who became one of the FALLEN ANGELS when he swore allegiance to SAMIAZA, rebelled against God, took a human wife, and fathered the NEPHILIM (see GRIGORI and WATCHERS). His name is a combination of the names Arakib and RAMIEL.

Sources: Laurence, *Foreign Quarterly Review*, Vol. 24, 370; Spence, *Encyclopædia of Occultism*, 148; Voltaire, *Philosophical Dictionary*, Vol. 1, 152.

Uraniel

In the *Ars Paulina*, the third book of the *Lemegeton*, Uraniel is ranked as a duke and listed as one of the fifteen SERVITORS OF SCOX (see SCOX).

Sources: Peterson, *Lesser Key of Solomon*, 114; Trithemius, *Steganographia*, 95.

Urbaniel

In the *Theurgia Goetia*, the second book of the *Lemegeton*, Urbaniel is ranked as a duke who commands 2,200 servitors. Listed as one of the fifteen SERVITORS OF ICOSIEL, he is most powerful for the two hours before sunrise (see ICOSIEL). He is said to be good-natured and willing to do as his summoner asks.

Sources: Peterson, *Lesser Key of Solomon*, 99.

Urian

Variations: LEONARD, SATAN

The demon Urian is the inspector general of black magic and sorcery and has dominion over all witches, according to German mythology. Appearing as a giant black goat, this demon copulates with witches and presides over their sabbaths.

In a German folktale, Urian crossed the Rhine at Dusseldorf with a large pack on his back filled with evil to destroy Aix-la-Chapelle. As he climbed the embankment to enter the city he was frightened by an elderly woman and dropped his pack. To this day the bank in that region is known as Looseburg.

Sources: Ashley, *Complete Book of Devils and Demons*, 59; Percy, *Mirror of Literature, Amusement, and Instruction*, Vol. 39, 263; Tait, *European Life, Legend, and Landscape*, 102.

Uriel

Uriel ("fire of God" or "sun of God") is a PRINCE OF HELL, a PLANETARY PRINCE of Sat-

urn, and one of the eleven WANDERING PRINCES. Commanding ten chief dukes and one hundred lesser dukes, he is invoked for the assistance he can give with walls and barriers; he will also carry messages for his summoner. A steganographic demon, Uriel is often called upon during exorcism and in cases of collective possession. He was one of the eighteen demons who possessed Sister Jeanne des Anges in Loudun, France, in 1634 (see LOUDUN POSSESSION). Additionally, Uriel the demon is not to be confused with Uriel the archangel.

Sources: Black, *Book of Enoch*, 119; Aikin, *General Biography*, 493; Bayle, *Historical and Critical Dictionary*, 262; France, *On Life and Letters*, 220; Gettings, *Dictionary of Demons*, 231–3, 244; Harkness, *John Dee's Conversations with Angels*, 50; Voltaire, *Works of M. de Voltaire*, 193.

Urigo

In the *Sacred Magic of Abramelin the Mage*, book two, Urigo ("spoiled, unfit food") is listed as one of the sixty-five SERVITORS OF KORE AND MAGOTH.

Sources: Mathers, *Book of the Sacred Magic of Abra-Melin*, 118; Von Worms, *Book of Abramelin*, 256.

Urnell

According to medieval German demonology, Urnell is the demon of drunkenness.

Sources: Carus, *Open Court*, Vol. 43, 473; Rudwin, *Devil in Legend and Literature*, 85.

Urobach

Collin de Plancy's *Dictionaire Infernale* (1863) lists Urobach as a being from a low order of demons.

Sources: Robbins, *Encyclopedia of Witchcraft and Demonology*, 337.

Ursiel

Variations: USIEL, Vusiel

In the *Theurgia Goetia*, the second book of the *Lemegeton*, Ursiel is a chief duke who commands 2,660 duke servitors. He is one of the twelve SERVITORS OF CASPIEL (see CASPIEL) and is known to be rude and stubborn.

Sources: Guiley, *Encyclopedia of Demons and Demonology*, 37; Peterson, *Lesser Key of Solomon*, 60.

Uruku

Uruku ("larvae") is from Babylonian, Chaldean, and Sumerian demonology, and is one of a group of seven demons working in unison in service under Ereshkigal, the goddess of death and gloom (see IRKALLA). Appearing as a gigantic larvae, uruku enters into a person's home and attacks them for their blood. There is no way to prevent these demons from entering into a home. They also have the ability to possess a person and spread disease. Uruku live in the desert and in abandoned places of worship where sacrifices took place (see also ALAL, GIGIM, IDPA, NAMTAR, TELAL, and UTUK).

Sources: Lenormant, *Chaldean Magic*, 37; Myer, *Qabbalah*, 453; Sorensen, *Possession and Exorcism in the New Testament and Early Christianity*, 27–8.

Usiel

Variations: Uziel, UZZIEL ("power of God")

Usiel ("strength of God") is the prince of the Northwest and is one of the twelve SERVITORS OF AMENADIEL (see AMENADIEL and PRINCES OF HELL). Enochian lore has him as one of the FALLEN ANGELS, formerly of the Order of Virtues, who swore allegiance to SAMIAZA, rebelled against God, took a human wife, and fathered the NEPHILIM. Commanding forty diurnal and nocturnal servitors, only fourteen of each are named.

Sources: Davidson, *Dictionary of Angels*, 299–301; Peterson, *Less Key of Solomon*, 83.

Utifa

In the *Sacred Magic of Abramelin the Mage*, book two, Utifa is one of the sixteen SERVITORS OF ASMODEUS (see ASMODEUS).

Sources: Ford, *Bible of the Adversary*, 93; Mathers, *Book of the Sacred Magic of Abra-Melin*, 119; Von Worms, *Book of Abramelin*, 256.

Utuk

Utuk ("spirit") is from Babylonian, Chaldean, and Sumerian demonology, one of a group of seven demons working in unison in service under Ereshkigal, the goddess of death and gloom (see IRKALLA). Appearing as a gigantic larvae, Utuk enters into a home and attacks a person's head. There is no way to prevent this demon from entering into a home. It also has the ability to possess a person and spread disease. Utuk lives in the desert and in abandoned places of worship where sacrifices took place (see also ALAL, GIGIM, IDPA, NAMTAR, TELAL, and URUKU).

Sources: Sorensen, *Possession and Exorcism in the New Testament and Early Christianity*, 27–8.

Utukku

In ancient Akkadian, Assyrian, and Babylonian mythology there are two types of demons known as utukku.

The first type of utukku is a returned soul that cannot rest until it is appeased. These demons can be recruited to be a force of good. The more these demons kill, the longer they can stay in this world.

The other is a being of pure evil born of the bile of a god. These beings of evil are horrific human and animal hybrids with claws and horns. They spread disease and send criminal thoughts to inspire sinful acts to be committed. These utukku live in caverns, holes in rocks, and isolated ruins.

Both utukku assault those who break certain taboos, such as eating ox meat. Wearing protective amulets can prevent them from attacking.

Sources: Abusch, *Mesopotamian Magic*, 49; Jastrow, *Religion of Babylonia and Assyria*, 260; Justi, *History of All Nations*, Vol. 1, 185; Maberry, *Vampire Universe*, 289–91; Rogers, *Religion of Babylonia and Assyria*, 147.

Utuq

In Assyrian demonology the utuq demons live in the desert and may be a force for good or for evil. Good and evil utuq are each other's adversary.

Sources: Allen, *History of Civilization*, Vol. 2, 384; Lenormant, *Chaldean Magic*, 148; Wesleyan-Methodist Magazine, Vol. 63, 1006.

Uvall

Variations: Uval, Vuall, Voval, Vual, Wal, Wall

Uvall is the duke of sands and waste. He is a FALLEN ANGEL, formerly of the Order of Potestates or Powers, and is said to command thirty-seven legions (see DUKES OF HELL). Johann Wierus's *Pseudomonarchia Daemonum (False Monarchy of Demons, 1583)* describes him as a large camel, but at the summoner's request he will shape-shift into a strong man who speaks imperfect Egyptian. This demon has the ability to ensure friendship between friends and enemies, ensures the love between a man and woman, and foretells the past, present, and future.

Sources: Crowley, *The Goetia*, 52; Davidson, *Dictionary of Angels*, 301; De Laurence, *Lesser Key of Solomon, Goetia*, 37; DuQuette, *Key to Solomon's Key*, 184; Ford, *Luciferian Witchcraft*, 191; McLean, *Treatise of Angel Magic*, 57.

Uzziel

Variations: USIEL

Enochian lore names Uzziel ("power of God" or "strength of God") as one of the FALLEN ANGELS, formerly of the Order of Virtues, who swore allegiance to SAMIAZA, rebelled against God, took a human wife, and fathered the NEPHILIM.

Source: Davidson, *Dictionary of Angels*, 299–301.

Vachmiel

Variations: Vathmiel

The ruler of the fourth hour, Vachmiel demon commands ten chiefs and one hundred lesser de-

monic servitors (see SERVITORS OF VACHMIEL).
Vachmiel is likely the demon RAHAB.

Sources: Davidson, *Dictionary of Angels*, 303; Peterson, *Lesser Key of Solomon*, 113; Waite, *Book of Ceremonial Magic*, 67.

Vadataja

Using its shape-shifting abilities, the demon Vadataja ("leading to nowhere") of Latvian mythology lures travelers into dangerous swamps, pits, quicksand, and off cliff sides; he causes travelers to become lost at crossroads. Vadataja also causes a person to stray from their religious beliefs.

Sources: Kelly, *Who in Hell*, 233; Lurker, *Dictionary of Gods and Goddesses, Devils and Demons*, 363; Maberry, *Vampire Universe*, 290.

Vadi Sanniya

In Sinhalese demonology Vadi Sanniya is the demon of body sores and contagious diseases. He carries a bow and arrow and causes people to dream of guns and shootings. Vadi Sanniya, like the other Sinhalese demons, is susceptible to the DAHA-ATA SANNIYA.

Sources: Illes, *Encyclopedia of Spirits*, 875; Wirz, *Exorcism and the Art of Healing in Ceylon*, 44.

Vadras

In the *Ars Paulina*, book three of the *Lemegeton*, Vadras is a chief duke who commands three thousand servitors. He is listed as one of the twelve SERVITORS OF AMENADIEL (see AMENADIEL and DUKES OF HELL).

Source: Peterson, *Lesser Key of Solomon*, 62.

Vadriel

Vadriel is one of the twelve named Duke SERVITORS OF CARNESIEL (see CARNESIEL and DUKES OF HELL). He commands ten chiefs and one hundred servitors and is most powerful during the ninth hour of the day.

Sources: Davidson, *Dictionary of Angels*, 60, 84, 94, 180, 191, 303, 330; Gettings, *Dictionary of Demons*, 188, 245; Peterson, *Lesser Key of Solomon*, 59; Waite, *The Book of Ceremonial Magic*, 68.

Vaivoo

From Persian demonology comes the demon of the air and wind, Vaivoo. He is one of the eight AUSTATIKCO-PAULIGAUR, a type of demonic spirit or DIV, who controls one of the eight sides of the world.

Sources: Kindersley, *Specimens of Hindoo Literature*, 33; Smedley, *Occult Sciences*, 51; Spence, *Encyclopædia of Occultism*, 129.

Valafar

Variations: Malaphar, Malapher, Malephar, VALEFAR, Valefor

The *Grand Grimoire*, alleged to have been written by Alibek the Egyptian and published in Cairo in 1522, names Valafar as the Duke of Thieves, one of the three SERVITORS OF SARGATANAS (see SARGATANAS); he is also listed as one of the SPIRITS OF SOLOMON. The demon of brigands and robbers, Valafar commands ten legions. He appears before his summoner as a man with the head of a thief or mule and the body of a lion. He is invoked for his ability to make people commit theft, as well as giving good FAMILIAR spirits and teaching occult medicine. Valafar is loyal to his followers until they are caught, then he abandons them.

Sources: Ashley, *Complete Book of Devils and Demons*, 61; De Laurence, *Lesser Key of Solomon, Goetia*, 23; Ford, *Bible of the Adversary*, 81; Knappert, *Encyclopaedia of Middle Eastern Mythology and Religion*, 288; McLean, *Treatise of Angel Magic*, 57.

Valefar

Variations: VALAFAR

In *Ars Goetia*, the first book of the *Lemegeton*, Valefar is listed as one of the eighteen SERVITORS OF FLEURETTY, LUCIFUGE, NEBIROS, SARGATANAS, AND SATANACHIA (see FLEURETTY, LUCIFUGE ROFOCALE, NEBIROS, SARGATANAS, and SATANACHIA).

Sources: Scott, *London Magazine*, Vol. 5, 378; Waite, *Book of Black Magic and of Pacts*, 158; Wedeck, *Treasury of Witchcraft*, 97.

Vanth

The herald of death in Etruscan demonology, Vanth is the companion to CHARUN. She is described as a winged woman with eyes on her wings and in art she is depicted as having a stern face and carrying a snake. Preying on the dying and sick, Vanth guides the souls of the dead from their deathbed to the Underworld where she lives. Omnipresent, her symbol is the key and torch.

Sources: De Grummond, *Guide to Etruscan Mirrors*, 126; De Grummond, *Religion of the Etruscans*, 61; Lurker, *Dictionary of Gods and Goddesses, Devils and Demons*, 366–7.

Vaotere

Variations: Vao-tere

Vaotere ("moving-recess") is the demon of the ironwood tree in Polynesian mythology. A horrific visage to behold with his mouth full of jagged teeth, this demon maliciously attacks anyone who tries to cut down or otherwise use the ironwood tree. Vaotere is eventually slain by the hero Ono with his magical spade, Rua-i-paku ("the hole where it must fall").

Sources: Agnew, *Foreign Literature*, Vol. 46, 226; Gill, *Myths and Songs from the South Pacific*, 82, 84–5.

Vapula

Variations: NAPHULA

Vapula is the Lion Duke, commanding thirty-six legions. Appearing before his summoner as a winged lion, he is invoked for his ability to teach all handicraft professions and skills, mechanics, philosophy, and other sciences.

Sources: Crowley, *The Goetia*, 59; Scot, *The Discoverie of Witchcraft*, 225; Peterson, *Lesser Key of Solomon*, 34, 41; Scott, *London Magazine*, Vol. 5, 378; Waite, *Book of Black Magic and of Pacts*, 215.

Varan

Varan, a DEV from Persian and Zoroastrian demonology, is the demon of gluttony, heresy, lust on the physical plane, and the misuse of intellect on the spiritual plane (see DEVS WHO RESIDE IN MEN). He attacks mankind's physical nature and reason and is described as wearing a garment made of "self-will." His sign is the white boar and his personal adversaries are the warrior god Vay and the god of wisdom Xrat.

Sources: Dobbins, *False Gods or the Idol Worship of the World*, 301; Zaehner, *Zurvan*, 124, 175.

Varoonon

From Persian demonology comes Varoonon, the demon of clouds and rain. He is one of the eight AUSTATIKCO-PAULIGAUR, a type of demonic spirit or DIV who controls one of the eight sides of the world.

Sources: Gettings, *Dictionary of Demons*, 42, 245; Kindersley, *Specimens of Hindoo Literature*, 33.

Varpiel

Variations: Varpil, Verpiel

In the *Theurgia Goetia*, the second book of the *Lemegeton*, Varpiel is one of the twelve named Chief Duke SERVITORS OF MACARIEL, commanding four hundred servitors (see MACARIEL). When summoned he will appear in a variety of forms but most commonly choses that of a dragon with a virgin's head. Both diurnal and nocturnal, Varpiel has a reputation for being good-natured and willing to obey his summoner.

Sources: Peterson, *Lesser Key of Solomon*, 103; Trithemius, *Steganographia*, 141.

Varsavarti

Variations: the Evil One, Mara ("death" or "thirst"), the Murderer, PAPIYAN ("more wicked"), Paranimmita, the Tempter, Vasavatlti ("bringing into subjection that which is created by others"), the Wicked One

Varsavarti ("he who fulfills desires") is the king of the Heaven of Sensual Delight in Buddhist demonology. The demon of death, sin, and temptation, he captures and collects the souls of those dying. He also enables man to fulfill his "triple thirst": existence, pleasure, and power. Occasionally Varsavarti will shape-shift into a vulture as he wanders the earth homeless.

Sources: Baskin, *Dictionary of Satanism*, 328; Carus, *History of the Devil and the Idea of Evil*, 105; *Word Monthly Magazine*, Vol. 3, 233.

Varuna

Originally a god and then reduced to a demigod in Vedic mythology, Varuna was ultimately demoted to an ASURAS or yaksa and made to be the demon of the sea. Varuna was demoted from a solar deity to demon by degrees. Apart from having an unlikeable personality, he punished sinners with vengeance, torturing their consciousness, causing sudden death and withholding water; the latter was said to have caused the disease edema to develop, a condition that causes bodily tissues to retain excess water.

Presiding over the West, he uses *maya* (illusions) and is described as being a judgmental and punishing bald and bucktoothed man with yellow eyes who carries a water pot.

Sources: Littell, *Littell's Living Age*, Vol. 143, 223–30; Sutherland, *Disguises of the Demon*, 76–7, 81–2, 85–6.

Vasa Inquitatis

Variations: Vessels of Anger, Vessels of Death, Vessels of Fury, Vessels of Iniquity, Vessels of Killing, Vessels of Destruction

The Vasa Inquitatis ("vessels of iniquity") are a class of demon under the command of BELIAL. These are the demons of anger, of all deformity, malice, and wickedness; they are the inventors of mischief and of all the evil arts. Plato claimed that one of these demons was named THEUTUS and that he played card and dice games and taught plays.

Sources: Coleman, *Dictionary of Mythology*, 1074; McLean, *Treatise on Angel Magic*, 69.

Vasenel

Variations: Phanuel ("face of God")

In the *Theurgia Goetia*, the second book of the *Lemegeton*, Vasenel is listed as one of the ten Duke SERVITORS OF EMONIEL (see EMONIEL). Commanding 1,320 lesser dukes and servitors of his own, Vasenel is said to be good-natured and willing to obey his summoner. He lives in the woods.

Sources: Guiley, *Demons and Demonology*, 72; Peterson, *Lesser Key of Solomon*, 97.

Vassago

Variations: BUSAS, PRUFLAS

The *Lemegeton* ranks Vassago as a prince who commands twenty-six legions and is under the command of Baro (see PRINCES OF HELL). He is also said to be one of the SPIRITS OF SOLOMON. Vassago, good-natured and willing to obey his summoner, is invoked for his ability to discover hidden and lost things; foretell the past, present, and future; and for telling a woman's deepest secret. He is most easily invoked by crystal gazers.

Sources: Crowley, *The Goetia*, 28; Davidson, *Dictionary of Angels*, 304; De Laurence, *Lesser Key of Solomon, Goetia*, 22; DuQuette, *Key to Solomon's Key*, 162; Peterson, *Lesser Key of Solomon*, 8.

Vata Sanniya

In Sinhalese demonology Vata Sanniya is the demon of illness, causing anxiety, burning of limbs, epileptic seizures, flatulence, indigestion, mucous secretion from mouth and anus, and rheumatism. Like the other Sinhalese demons, he is susceptible to the DAHA-ATA SANNIYA.

Sources: Goonatilleka, *Masks and Mask Systems of Sri Lanka*, 39; Illes, *Encyclopedia of Spirits*, 875; Lommel, *Masks: Their Meaning and Function*, 81; Wirz, *Exorcism and the Art of Healing in Ceylon*, 44.

Vazarush

Variations: Vizaresha

Vazarush ("the dragger away") is one of the ten DEVS that reside in man, according to Persian and Zoroastrian demonology (see DEVS WHO RESIDE IN MEN). The demon of separation, Vazarush preys upon the *urvan* ("souls") of those judged to be wicked. After a soul has been judged wicked at the Gates of Heaven, Vazarush drags it down to the bottomless pit of Hell. To prevent Vazarush from fulfilling his duty, burn a fire for three days near the body of a person whom you suspect may be denied entry into Heaven, as the flames will repel this demon.

Sources: Conway, *Demonology and Devil-Lore*, 289; Dhalla, *Zoroastrian Theology*, 169; Segal, *Life after Death*, 186.

Veguaniel

In the *Ars Paulina*, book three of the *Lemegeton*, Veguaniel is most powerful during the third hour of the day. He commands twenty chiefs, of which only four are named (DRELMETH, LEOSIEL, Murriel, SARDINIEL), two hundred lesser officers, of which six are named (COMADIEL, Furiel, GLMARIJ, HANTIEL, PARMIEL, SERVIEL), and a host of servitors.

Sources: Davidson, *Dictionary of Angels*, 304; Trithemius, *Steganographia*, 91, Waite, *The Book of Ceremonial Magic*, 67.

Velns

Variations: Jod

Velns ("devil") is the husband to Ragana in Latvian mythology. She is unintelligent and easily outwitted.

Sources: Encyclopaedia Britannica, *Encyclopedia of World Religions*, 109; Green, *Folklore*, 841.

Veltis

Veltis is a spirit who originated in Babylonian lore and was absorbed into Christian demonology. He assaulted and was overcome by Saint Margaret of Cortona, who after defeating the demon asked who it was and where it came from, to which it replied: "My name is Veltis, and I am one of those whom Solomon by virtue of his spells, confined in a copper cauldron at Babylon, but when the Babylonians, in the hope of finding treasure dug up the cauldron and opened it, we all made our escape. Since that time our efforts have been directed to the destruction of righteous persons, and I have long been striving to turn thee from the course thou hast embraced."

Sources: Spence, *Encyclopædia of Occultism*, 422.

Vercan

The demon Vercan was first mentioned during the Elizabethan era, his name appearing in a book titled *An Elizabethan Devil-Worshiper's Prayer-Book*; it was quite possibly written by John Dee. Vercan's rank was not given but he was described as appearing in various forms, including a monstrous humanoid with bird feet, a grotesque face, a hairy body, and horns upon his head; also as having three heads and riding upon a bear. He is summoned by the power that belongs to the names of sacred things, and if his invoker wishes not to be immediately attacked when he appears, he must stand within the protection of a magical circle. Vercan is the most powerful of the seven demons mentioned in *An Elizabethan Devil-Worshiper's Prayer-Book*.

Sources: Anonymous, *Manuscripts and Books on Medicine, Alchemy, Astrology and Natural Sciences Arranged in Chronological Order*, 239; Summers, *A Popular History of Witchcraft*, 91.

Verdelet

Variations: Jolybois, Maitre Persil ("Master Parsley"), Sainte-Buisson, Sante-Buisson, Verd-Joli

The demonic FAMILIAR Verdelet was named during the French witchcraft trials as being a grand master of ceremonies. A demon of the second order and under the command of SATAN, it was his duty to see to it that the witches arrived to the Sabbath ceremonies on time. He has the ability to entice women into doing his bidding.

Sources: Chambers, *Book of Days*, 723; Lea, *Materials Toward a History of Witchcraft*, Part 2, 606; Masello, *Fallen Angels and Spirits of the Dark*, 44; Summers, *Vampires in Lore and Legend*, 165.

Verrier

Variations: Verrine

A former Prince and a FALLEN ANGEL, formerly of the Order of Principalities, Verrier is now the demon of disobedience, according to Father Sebastien Michaelis's *Histoire admirable de la Possession et conversion d'une penitente* (1612). (See PRINCES OF HELL.) Verrier makes man's neck stiff so that it cannot bow to the yoke of obedience.

Sources: Cuhulain, *Witch Hunts*, 206; Davidson, *Dictionary of Angels*, 353; Kelly, *Who in Hell*, 235; Robbins, *Encyclopedia of Witchcraft and Demonology*, 129.

Verrin

Variations: Verin, Verrine

Verrin is a FALLEN ANGEL, formerly of the Order of Thrones. He is the demon of impatience.

Sources: Cuhulain, *Witch Hunts*, 206; Ashley, *Complete Book of Devils and Demons*, 61; Bias, *Freedom from the World of Satanism and the Power of Satan*, 42; Ford, *Bible of Adversary*, 81; Robbins, *Encyclopedia of Witchcraft and Demonology*, 22.

Vetala

Variations: Baital, Baitala, Betail, Bhut

In India, there is a vampiric demon that is called a vetala. One is created every time a child dies and does not receive proper funeral rites. When a vetala possesses a corpse it causes a hideous transformation to take place: the feet and hands twist backward; the face twists about until it resembles a fruit bat with slitted eyes; the skin becomes discolored by turning either green, light brown, or white; and the fingernails grow long and carry a poison on them. While the vetala possesses the corpse, it is able to animate it and will use its magic to find human blood to drink, for as long as it does so regularly, the body that the vetala is possessing will not decompose. It will call to it a green horse that it will use as its mount.

Using its magic, the vetala will enter into a home by use of an enchanted thread being fed down a chimney. Typically it preys on those who are asleep, using the opportunity to drain them of their blood, but it will also take advantage of a person who has passed out drunk. Women who have gone insane are also fed upon, the idea being who would believe them if they reported it? But above all, its favorite prey is children. Regardless of whom it attacks, the vetala mostly feeds on their intestines and excrement.

Vetalas can cause insanity and miscarriages, and anyone who survives one of its attacks will first suffer through a severe illness before they can begin to recover. However, because of the vetala's ability to see into the past, present, and future, as well as its deep insight into human nature, it is often the goal of a sorcerer to capture one and use it for his or her own intent.

When not seeking out prey, vetalas are at rest hanging upside-down from trees in cemeteries, dark forests, or any deserted place. They may be appeased with offerings of gifts, but should that not work, they can be driven off with the use of magical spells. Should all else fail, the body of the child that caused the creation of the vetala must be found. Then proper funeral rites must be performed over it, essentially destroying the vetala.

Sources: Crooke, *Introduction to the Popular Religion*, 67, 97, 152; Cuevas, *Travels in the Netherworld*, 95–97; Saletore, *Indian Witchcraft*, 83.

Vetis

Variations: Vedius, Veiovis, Veive

Originally an Etruscan god written of on the Zagreb mummy wrappings, Vetis was later demonized. He is said to be a beardless youth with goatlike features, carrying arrows and wearing a laurel wreath on his head. He corrupts and tempts the holy.

Sources: Ashley, *Complete Book of Devils and Demons*, 61; Bias, *Freedom from the World of Satanism and the Power of Satan*, 42; Bonfante, *Etruscan Language*, 210; Bonnefoy, *Roman and European Mythologies*, 36; Lurker, *Dictionary of Gods and Goddesses, Devils and Demons*, 368.

Vilas

In Bulgarian mythology the Vilas are the returned souls of deceased children and virgins. They appear as beautiful maidens wearing white robes. Living in lakes, mountains, and the woods, they will shoot with arrows any man who disrupts their exquisite dancing and singing; however, offerings of flowers, fruits, or garments will prevent them from attacking. They cause apoplexy, blindness, and deafness. On occasion, they will have sexual relations with men.

Sources: Hastings, *Encyclopedia of Religion and Ethics*, Vol. 4, 628; McClelland, *Slayers and Their Vampires*, 41.

Vinc

Variations: "Foe of Emmanuel," Leontophoron, "Ruler of Legions," VEGUANIEL

Vinc commands twenty chiefs and two hundred servitors, only seven of which are named: COMADIEL, DRELMETH, GLMARIJ, LEOSIEL, Murriel, PARMIEL, and SARDINIEL. Appearing as a lion, Vinc is summoned for his ability to cause destruction; he also knows and can tell the true name of sorcerers and witches. He is most powerful during the third hour of the day.

Sources: Butler, *Ritual Magic*, 33; Davidson, *Dictionary of Angels*, 304; Gettings, *Dictionary of Demons*, 188, 246.

Viné

Variations: Vin, Vine, Vinea

Viné is ranked as a count (or earl) and king and is listed as one of the SPIRITS OF SOLOMON (see also COUNTS OF HELL, EARLS OF HELL, and KINGS OF HELL). The demon of storms at sea, he commands thirty-six legions. Viné is monstrous in appearance, even for a demon, but will take on a human guise if asked to do so by his summoner. He has also been described as appearing as a lion or as a man with a lion's head riding upon a black horse and carrying a viper in his hand. He is invoked for his ability to control storms at sea, discover hidden things, expose witches, and foretell the past, present, and future. At his summoner's request he will build a fortress or destroy walls.

A viné is a type of ancient war machine that is made of wood and covered with branches and leather; it was used to overthrow walls.

Sources: Crowley, *The Goetia*, 51; De Laurence, *Lesser Key of Solomon, Goetia*, 36–7; Peterson, *Lesser Key of Solomon*, 2247; Scot, *Discoverie of Witchcraft*, 223; *Transactions and Proceedings of the American Philological Association*, Vol. 101, 428.

Vision

In the *Sacred Magic of Abramelin the Mage*, Vision is listed as one of the twenty SERVITORS OF AMAYMON (see AMAYMON).

Sources: Forgotten Books, *Book of the Sacred Magic of Abramelin the Mage*, 42–4; Mathers, *Book of the Sacred Magic of Abra-Melin*, 122.

Vjeshitza

Vjeshitza are the incubi and succubi under the service of LILITH (see INCUBUS and SUCCUBUS). The succubi appear as women with flaming wings and the incubi as men with a dragon's hands and feet. Preying at night, they climb on the chest of a sleeping person, engage them in a sexual embrace, and then suffocate them. Their personal adversary is the angel Bazazatu.

Sources: Baskin, *Dictionary of Satanism*, 330; Kelly, *Who in Hell*, 236.

Vodnik

Variations: Hastrman, Morskoj Tsar, Nyks, Povodnji, Topislec, Vodjanoj, Vodny

Vodnik is the lord of the water in Slavonic folklore, the demon of aquatic birds and the water. There is usually one in each body of water, created when an unbaptized child drowns there. He can appear as a fish, a human with green clothes and hair, or a stripling. In his human guise water always flows from the edges of his clothes. Most powerful during the middle of the day, he lures people into the water and holds them under until they drown; most commonly he preys upon children. Vodnik will take a bride for himself from a selection of drowned women, sometimes adopting drowned children as his own as well.

This demon can shape-change into a brook and travel to a new location where he will then create a new body of water to live in. He can also shape-shift into a DOG, fish, frog, horse, or known person. Vodnik will give timely warning to those he is on good terms with of upcoming floods. Vodnik enjoys strong drink and when drunk will disrupt the flow of streams.

Mills often interfere with his activity, so in fits of rage he will lash out against them. Offerings will keep Vodnik's anger at bay, general offerings of live chickens are always welcome; beekeepers offer bees and honey to him; fishermen offer bread, salt, tobacco, and the first catch of the day; goose herdsmen make an offering of a goose each autumn; millers who work closest to him make the largest offering, that of a horse and fatty pork. Originally when a new mill was constructed a human sacrifice was made to the local Vodnik.

Sources: Hastings, *Encyclopedia of Religion and Ethics*, Part 8, 629; Kelly, *Who in Hell*, 237; Lurker, *Dictionary of Gods and Goddesses, Devils and Demons*, 374.

Vodyanoi

Cast out of Heaven by the archangel Michael, Vodyanoi is a FALLEN ANGEL who has command of all the fish and spirits that live in the pond he occupies. Sometimes referred to as the lord of the rivers, he appears as an old man covered in mulch, with a greenish beard; sometimes he is said to have scales, a tail, or even appear as a half-fish and half-man creature.

Vodyanoi rarely comes all the way to the surface, living in the depths of freshwater lakes and ponds. On the bottom he has a palace, complete with furnishings. He lingers near the dam or at the mill wheel and preys upon anyone who enters the water in his area with the exception of the miller and a scant few fishermen he allows to work there. All others he drowns, as he is easily aggravated and highly territorial. Any attempt to retrieve the body of someone he drowned will result in his attacking the would-be rescuer. Making the sign of the cross before entering the water will reduce the chance that he will attack.

When a mill is built he will kill at least one person on the site for disturbing his pond. Although he prefers human sacrifice, he will accept a black rooster or chicken in their place. Fishermen must make an offering of bread, salt, tobacco, and vodka. It is believed that millers will make an annual sacrifice of a drunkard to Vodyanoi. Vodyanoi only leaves the water to inspect his herd of black cattle.

Sources: Gilchrist, *Russian Magic*, 238–9; Mack, *Field Guide to Demons, Fairies, Fallen Angels, and Other Subversive Spirits*, 42.

Vriel

In the *Theurgia Goetia*, the second book of the *Lemegeton*, Vriel is ranked as a nocturnal duke and listed as one of the sixteen SERVITORS OF GEDEIL (see DUKES OF HELL and GEDEIL).

Sources: Peterson, *Lesser Key of Solomon*, 72; Trithemius, *Steganographia*, 81.

Vritra

Variations: A'hi, Vrtra

Vritra ("enveloper") is the leader of the demons in Vedic mythology. The demon of drought and commanding ninety-nine fortresses, he imprisons the storm clouds that bring rain. He appears as a dragon or serpent so large that he can encircle mountains and still have his head touch the sky. He is the personification of the rain.

When Vritra was the human King Chitraketu he was cursed to be reborn as a demon in his next incarnation for making a disparaging remark about the Ardha-Nari form of Lord Shiva. He was reborn as the son of Tvashta, who misspoke a word during a magical ceremony, making him vulnerable to the god INDRA's attacks.

An enemy to all the gods, Vritra is the personal adversary to the god INDRA. Eventually he is slain by INDRA with sea foam that was actually Lord Vishnu incarnate (or with a thunderbolt, sources conflict). Other sources say Vritra was slain by the goddess Sarasvati.

Sources: Balfour, *Cyclopædia of India and of Eastern and Southern Asia*, 52–3; Cox, *Mythology of the Aryan Nations*, 29, 162, 238, 536; Hyatt, *Book of Demons*, 23; Lumpkin, *Fallen Angels, the Watchers, and the Origin of Evil*, 127; Williams, *Handbook of Hindu Mythology*, 303.

Vrykolaka

Variations: Alastores, Barbalakos, Borbolakas, Bordoukas, Bourbolakas, Bourboulakas, Bourdoulakos, Brykolakas, Kalakhanos, Upirina, Vrukolakes, Vrykolokas, Vurkokalas, Vurvukalas

A vampiric demon from Greek lore, the *vrykolaka* ("vampire" or "wolf fairy") possesses the corpse of a person who died a violent death, was improperly buried, was cursed to undeath by a priest, or was excommunicated by the church. When it rises from the grave it looks every bit like the bloated animated corpse that it is. It will go to the homes of the people it knew in life, its former friends and family, and knock upon their doors. Whoever has the misfortune to answer, the vrykolaka, a bloodthirsty and ravenous thing, will ruthlessly attack by day or by night.

Victims who happen to survive the attack of a vrykolaka will become this type of vampire themselves when they die unless they eat some of the dirt from the grave of the body that attacked them.

The vrykolaka can be prevented from attacking if its resting place is found. Then driving a stake through the body it has possessed and into the coffin it is resting in will ensure that it will be unable to rise up ever again. However, if you already know where the vampire is, killing it would at that point be just as easy as affixing it to the earth. Decapitating the vampire and hiding its head where it cannot be found is used in modern times, but the traditional method of rendering the body to ash is both the most certain and effective. The only way to destroy a vrykolaka that was created through excommunication is to have a priest perform a special ceremony over the body followed immediately by either of the methods of destruction previously mentioned.

Originally the vrykolaka was not an evil vampiric being but rather a restless spirit that needed to fulfill a task or see to a need before it could rest in peace. It could be anything from a simple chore to as complex as packing a bag, moving to another part of the country, marrying, having children, and living out what would have been the rest of its natural life. It was not until the Greek Orthodox Church became influential enough to sway cultural beliefs that the vrykolaka was considered an implement of the devil. It was deemed that only a proper church burial could absolutely prevent the vrykolaka from rising from its grave and doing evil. Being excommunicated from the church absolutely guaranteed that a person would become a vampire.

Sources: Aylesworth, *Story of Vampires*, 5; Calmet, *Phantom World*, 113–19; Davenport, *Sketches of Imposture*, 278.

Vualdat

Vualdat is only mentioned by name as having been recorded by Abdias, the bishop of Babylon in Johann Wierus's *De Praestigiis Daemonum*. Beyond that, there is no other information known about this demon.

Sources: Weyer, *Witches, Devils, and Doctors in the Renaissance*, 14.

Vucub Caquix

Variations: Gucup-Cakix, Itzamna Yeh ("Bringer of Magic"), Vucab-Cakix, Vucab-Came, Vucub Camé, Vukub-Cakix

Vucub Caquix ("seven macaw") was the first wizard of the Mayan cosmos and the demon of the Underworld. The husband of Chimalmat and father of the giants KABRAKAN and Zipakna (earthquake demons), Vucub Caquix is described as a large birdlike demon and is represented by the seven stars of the Big Dipper. Exceedingly vain, he was a false moon, sun, and twilight. Vucub Caquix was slain by the twins Hunahpu and Ixbalangue to avenge their father's death.

Sources: Brennan, *Hidden Maya*, 130–1; Guernsey, *Ritual and Power in Stone*, 112; Lurker, *Dictionary of Gods and Goddesses*, 375; Stookey, *Thematic Guide to World Mythology*, 193; Tedlock, *Popol Vuh*, 93.

Wahini Hal

Wahini Hal is a demonic mother figure in Polynesian demonology, appearing as a woman with protruding eyes and a tongue that hangs down to the ground. A nocturnal predator, she preys upon small children, stealing and consuming them.

Source: Turner, *Dictionary of Ancient Deities*, 271.

Wahwee

A wahwee is a demonic creature from the lore of the Aboriginal people of Australia. An amphibious creature about thirty feet long with a froglike head, long tail, and three legs on each side of its body, this creature preys upon bush animals, such as kangaroos, wallaby, and wombats, as well as humans. After everyone in camp is asleep, the wahwee with its insatiable appetite creeps in and consumes its victims whole. Living in deep water holes, this demon creates droughts, floods, and rains.

Sources: Anthropological Institute of Great Britain and Ireland, *Journal of the Royal Anthropological Institute of Great Britain and Ireland*, Vol. 25, 301; Folklore Society, *Folklore*, Vol. 9, 314; Mack, *Field Guide to Demons, Fairies, Fallen Angels, and Other Subversive Spirits*, 24–5.

Wamu

Variations: "Owner of Poisons"

All diseases and illnesses reside in Wamu's body, according to the Arawak-speaking Baniwa people of Brazil. Wamu ("black sloth") is described as being slow moving and having discolored saliva, a lolling tongue, matted fur, and vicious eyes; it smells like rotting meat. Magic and magical incantations may stave off Wamu for a short while but ultimately he will succeed.

Sources: Jones, *Evil in Our Midst*, 76–9; Wright, *Cosmos, Self, and History in Baniwa Religion*, 47.

Wandering Princes

Variations: Wandering Dukes

According to the various grimoires such as the *Theurgia Goetia*, the second book of the *Lemegeton*, and miscellaneous medieval hierarchies, there are eleven Wandering Princes. Although referred to collectively as the Wandering Princes, in their individual conjuring, each demon is a prince in his own right and many have dukes serving them. The Wandering Princes are Bidiel, BURIEL, EMONIEL, GARADIEL, HYDRIEL, ICOSIEL, MACARIEL, Menadiel, PIRICHIEL, SOLERIEL, and URIEL.

Sources: Peterson, *Lesser Key of Solomon*, 92; Trithemius, *Steganographia*, 81.

Wang Liang

Variations: Wangxiang

Wang Liang ("shadowy phantom") is a demonic fay or *tsing* (mountain spirit) in Chinese mythology. This demon of pestilence is described as having one leg or as looking like a child with long ears and hair, red and black skin, and red eyes. Wang Liang eats the brains and livers of the deceased and, using its ability to imitate human voices, it leads travelers astray, confusing them. This demon lives in forests, hills, marshes, mountains, rivers, rocks, and trees.

Sources: Bodde, *Festivals in Classical China*, 220; Maspero, *China in Antiquity*, 95; Shar, *Coming to Terms with Chinese Buddhism*, 160, 174; Sterckx, *Animal and the Daemon in Early China*, 312.

Wannein Nat

Wannein Nat is a forest *nat* ("spirit") in Burmese demonology. Having animalistic characteristics and considered to be malign, on occasion this demon acts as a tutelary village guardian. Living in groves and trees, Wannein Nat accepts offerings of drink and food at his shrines.

Source: Spence, *Encyclopædia of Occultism*, 81, 425.

Watchers, The

Variations: Benei Ha-Elohim ("Sons of God"), GRIGORI, Irin

The *Book of Enoch*, where their story originates from, names only twenty of the two hundred Watchers; however, over the years, various sources, texts, and grimoires have added to the list of names.

The Watcher angels were one of the seven orders of angels created by God to oversee the first generation of humans and teach them how to properly survive. They were described to be large, like giants. They were made CHIEF OF TENS, meaning that each of them had ten angels under his command. It was not so long after they went to work on Earth that the Watchers began to lust after human women. Under the leadership and instigation of the angel SAMIAZA, they gathered together to form a pact among themselves. As a group they acted against the will of God and took human women as their wives, assuming that God would not punish them all. They then taught their spouses and their families the arts of astrology, astronomy, botany, divination, healing, and magic as well as how to make cosmetics, mirrors, and weapons. The Watchers fathered the NEPHILIM, semidivine offspring that were generally violent, cannibalistic, and evil by nature. However, a few of the NEPHILIM became great artisans, poets, and priests. For their numerous sins, God punished all the angels involved, casting them out of Heaven (see FALLEN ANGELS).

Sources: Black, *Book of Enoch, or, I Enoch*, 27–35; *Book of Enoch the Prophet*, 11–21; *Journal of Theological Studies*, Vol. 8, 444–7.

Water Babies

Water babies are nocturnal, demonic creatures from the demonology of the Washo people of Lake Tahoe, Nevada, United States. Described as being small, hideous, humanoid creatures with the "body of an old man and long hair like a girl," they are said to live in the lakes, springs, and large bodies of water throughout Nevada. At night it makes a crying or whimpering sound to lure people to the shoreline or out into the water. Once the prey has fallen for the trick, the water baby grabs them and, pulling them into the water, drowns them. To prevent these demonic creatures from attacking, a shaman must communicate with the water babies and explain to them why his tribe needs to use their water. To speak of them is taboo, as they are considered an omen of death. Offerings of baskets filled with cord and pine nuts that are weighted and sealed are thrown into the lake.

Sources: Downs, *Two Worlds of the Washo*, 62; Jones, *Evil in Our Midst*, 6–4; Oesterle, *Weird Las Vegas and Nevada*, 44; Roth, *American Elves*, 66, 128.

Werzelya

From Ethiopia comes the tale of a female vampiric demon known as Werzelya. In life Werzelya was the sister of Saint Susenyos, but unlike her sainted brother, she dedicated her life to evil. Werzelya had taken SATAN as her lover and through their union, she gave birth to a daughter. Assuming that the child would have some magical ability since her father was the devil, Werzelya killed the child and drank her blood, gaining the ability to shape-shift into a bird or snake. When Susenyos learned that his sister had relations with the devil, killed her child, and drank the child's blood, he confronted and killed Werzelya. However, she returned as a vampiric demon and began killing the children of the region, including Susenyos's own newborn son. Susenyos mounted his horse and with a spear in his right hand killed her again, as well as her demonic entourage and as many of the evil magicians as he could find. With her dying breath, Werzelya swore that any child who wore Susenyos's medal would be safe from her future assaults should she ever return.

Sources: Budge, *Amulets and Superstitions*, 182; Budge, *History of Ethiopia*, 590; Hastings, *Encyclopedia of Religion and Ethics*, 339.

White Monkey

Exceptionally large and evil, White Monkey is a virtually unstoppable demon from Chinese lore that preys upon women. At night he kidnaps them and takes them to his cave in the most remote part of the mountains, where he adds them to his harem. White Monkey can be driven off by the sound of exploding firecrackers. He is fond of consuming dogs and drinking wine.

Sources: Chihling, *Traditional Chinese Tales*, 85–7; Mack, *Field Guide to Demons, Fairies, Fallen Angels, and Other Subversive Spirits*, 85–7.

Whore of Babylon

Variations: "The great whore"

The Whore of Babylon from the Book of Revelation is associated with the ANTICHRIST and the Beast of Revelation; she is an allegorical figure of evil. A drunken woman dressed in purple and scarlet, wearing gold, pearls, and precious stones, she is holding a golden cup in her hand. Her clothes have the blood of martyrs and saints on them. Written on her forehead are the words "Mystery, Babylon the Great, the Mother of Harlots and Abominations of the Earth." Her downfall will come at the hands of the beast with seven heads and ten horns.

Sources: Jeffrey, *Dictionary of Biblical Tradition in English Literature*, 826–8; Streete, *Strange Women*, 4–7, 152–3, 155–8.

Wi-Lu-Gho-Yuk

Wi-lu-gho-yuk are a *tunerak*, a type of demonic creature from the demonology of the Inuit of Alaska. Small mouselike creatures, they are attracted to their prey by movement. Moving through the ice, they gnaw a hole into a person's shoe, scamper over their body, burrow into their chest, and then consume their heart. A mortal man cannot withstand the attacks of a *tunerak*; however, if the victim sees the wi-lu-gho-yuk before it attacks and stands perfectly still, it will ignore him and the victim will instead become a successful hunter, and his first new kill will be this demon. These creatures can be slain by any attack that would kill a small animal.

Sources: Jones, *Evil in Our Midst*, 32–4; Sproul, *Primal Myths*, 226.

Win

Variations: The transforming witch

A win ("witch") is a demonic witch from the demonology of the Quiche people of Mexico. He is in service to the DEVIL. One is created when a lazy and unethical man sleeps in a cemetery for nine consecutive nights, praying to the Devil the whole time. On the tenth day the Devil will appear to him and challenge him to a fight. If the Devil wins, the man will die within a week; if the man wins the Devil will give him the power of win—this is the ability to shape-change.

Typically male, when a win is in his animal form he has a particular quality to him, such as being exceptionally ugly or having overly large eyes. In animal form he will break into homes, kill the head of the household, rape sleeping women, and steal valuables. Win are driven by base emotions such as envy, greed, lust, or revenge. Susceptible to "The Lord's Prayer" chanted backward, a win can only be killed in his animal form in a bare-handed fight.

Sources: Jones, *Evil in Our Midst*, 51–4; Orellana, *Indian Medicine in Highland Guatemala*, 51; Walker, *Witchcraft and Sorcery of the American Native Peoples*, 268.

Windigo

Variations: "He Who Lives Alone," Upayokawitigo ("the Hermit"), Weendigo, Wendigo, Wetikoo, Wiitigo, Witiko

The windigo is a demonic creature from the demonology of the Ojibwa and Saulteaux Manitoba people of Canada. Its name means "cannibal" and "evil spirit" in Algonquin. For a human to become a windigo he must travel into the creature's region and make offerings to it of flesh and prayers. The windigo will either consume the person, thereby ending his petition, or adopt him. Once adopted the man's heart will turn to ice, his hair will grow all over his body, and the craving for human flesh will begin. Almost immediately he will chew off his own lips in a desperate act

to consume flesh. Windigos created in this fashion are never as tall as those who are natural born.

Typically male, these cannibalistic giants are described as having an apelike face, bloodshot eyes, huge jagged teeth, and a heart made of ice. They are addicted to human flesh and said to be as tall as pine trees with long hair covering their entire bodies. Their long and narrow feet have one toe each and pointed heels; they smell horrible.

Windigo hunt the subarctic forests in search of humans to consume. When it cannot find humans, it will eat parts of its own body; when it can no longer do that it will consume carrion, moss, and rotten wood. Eventually it will turn on its own family, eating its youngest children first. Blizzards accompany the windigo as it travels. On occasion they hunt in packs. These demons are known to run madcap through the woods, screaming in rage and tearing up earth and trees with superhuman strength.

These demonic creatures are impervious to all human weapons and the natural elements; it is speculated that either decapitation or melting its heart may kill it. Their assaults can be prevented with shamanistic conjurations. If a person has become a windigo, they must be captured, bound up, and held over an open fire so that the heat and smoke will drive the evil away and melt their heart of ice. If this method does not work, the person is typically slain.

Sources: Gilmore, *Monsters*, 75–90; Jones, *Evil in Our Midst*, 43–6.

"Worst of All"

Named in Babylonian, Jewish, and Solominic lore, "Worst of All" was one of the demonic goddesses who was bound by King Solomon and made to dig the foundation of his Temple (see SPIRITS OF SOLOMON). She is named as the last of the SEVEN HEAVENLY BODIES and as one of the thirty-three (or thirty-six, sources vary) Elements of the Cosmic Rulers of the Darkness.

In the *Testament of Solomon*, "Worst of All" is described as one of seven female spirits, all fair in appearance, bound and woven together, represented as a cluster of stars in the heavens. They travel about sometimes living in Lydia, or Olympus, or on a great mountain. "Worst of All" imposes the bonds of Artemis and makes a bad situation worse. She can be appeased, however, with a sacrifice of five locusts.

Source: Ashe, *Qabalah*, 33.

Xai

According to Enochian lore, Xai is a CACODAEMON (see ENOCHIAN CACODAEMONS).

Source: Chopra, *Academic Dictionary of Mythology*, 306.

Xa-Mul

Xa-Mul is a demon from Philippine demonology who swallows people whole without chewing.

Source: Ashley, *Complete Book of Devils and Demons*, 95.

Xaphan

Variations: Guzfan, Xaphon, Zephon

Xaphan is a demon of the second order who is under the command of SATAN, according to Collin de Plancy's *Dictionaire Infernale* (1863). A FALLEN ANGEL forever cast out of Heaven to live in Hell, he is said to have a creative mind; in fact, it was during the revolt against God that Xaphan tried to set fire to Heaven. He keeps the fires of Hell lit with his hands and mouth; his sign is a pair of bellows. The name Xaphan is possibly Hebrew or Phoenician and it may translate to mean "rabbit."

Sources: Anthon, *Classical Dictionary*, 634; Baskin, *Satanism*, 341; Collin de Plancy, *Dictionary of Witchcraft*, 123; Davidson, *Dictionary of Angels*, 315; Kelly, *Who in Hell*, 247.

Xcz

According to Enochian lore, Xcz is a CACODAEMON (see ENOCHIAN CACODAEMONS).

Source: Chopra, *Academic Dictionary of Mythology*, 306.

Xdz

According to Enochian lore, Xdz is a CACODAEMON (see ENOCHIAN CACODAEMONS).

Source: Chopra, *Academic Dictionary of Mythology*, 306.

Xezbeth

Variations: Al-Kathab ("The Liar"), Shezbeth

Xezbeth is the demon of fairy tales, legends, and lies.

Sources: Baskin, *Satanism*, 341; Icon, *Demons*, 189; Knappert, *Encyclopaedia of Middle Eastern Mythology and Religion*, 256.

Xiang Yao

The Chinese demon Xiang Yao ("to want") has a snakelike body with nine human heads. Working in tandem with the demon GONG GONG, they create floods. The excrement of Xiang Yao makes lakes and rivers into putrid swamps.

Sources: Lurker, *Dictionary of Gods and Goddesses, Devils and Demons*, 132; Rose, *Giants, Monsters, and Dragons*, 401; Rose, *Spirits, Fairies, Leprechauns, and Goblins*, 339.

Xii

According to Enochian lore, Xii is a CACODAEMON (see ENOCHIAN CACODAEMONS).

Source: Chopra, *Academic Dictionary of Mythology*, 306.

Xilka

Xilka is an ancient formula for summoning a demon that was on a cuneiform tablet from the ancient city of Nineveh. The chant in its entirety is "Xilka, Xilka, Besa, Besa."

Sources: Baskin, *Satanism*, 341; de Givry, *Witchcraft, Magic and Alchemy*, 102; Randi, *Encyclopedia of Claims, Frauds, and Hoaxes of the Occult and Supernatural*, 129.

Xipe Totec

A demonic ghost who makes his appearance wherever there is bloodshed, Xipe Totec sucks the blood out of those who fall asleep when they are supposed to be performing their penance. Originally worshipped by the Aztecs as a god of penitence, Xipe Totec once had prisoners of war scarified to him by slicing open their legs and tongues and letting them bleed to death. He is renowned as a heinous trickster. On one occasion while pretending to be a prophet, he tricked an entire village into falling off a cliff.

Source: Hyatt, *Book of Demons*, 94.

Xom

According to Enochian lore, Xom is a CACODAEMON (see ENOCHIAN CACODAEMONS).

Source: Chopra, *Academic Dictionary of Mythology*, 306.

Xoy

According to Enochian lore, Xoy is a CACODAEMON (see ENOCHIAN CACODAEMONS).

Source: Chopra, *Academic Dictionary of Mythology*, 306.

Yacuruna

Yacuruna ("river person") is the master of the river in the demonology of the Iquitos people of the Peruvian Amazon. He is a tutelary spirit of lakes and rivers. Appearing as a humanoid amphibian, typically that of a toad or as a beautiful boy with golden skin, he creates inescapable whirlpools, flies into the sky to create terrible storms, and uproots trees with his hands. Yacuruna preys on people who drown; bodies that are lost to the river and never recovered are said to be his victims. He lives in a magnificent and inverted city on the bottom of the deepest whirlpool.

Sources: Gow, *Of Mixed Blood*, 192; Jones, *Evil in Our Midst*, 85–7; Pócs, *Fairies and Witches at the Boundary of South-Eastern and Central Europe*, 83.

Yaka, plural: yaku

Variations: Yaksa

A yaka ("demon") is a type of FAMILIAR to the shamans who summon them in the demonology of Sri Lanka. Demons of disease, yaku, as they are called in numbers, have deformed bodies that are covered in dark fur. They have bulging bloodshot eyes, flared nostrils, pointy animal-like noses, sharp curved teeth, and thick inverted lips. When summoned by a shaman they utilize his body and speak through his mouth. Yaku are bloodthirsty demons that crave human flesh and are filled with sexual desire. Very strong and capable of possessing a person, they can be warded off with burnt offerings.

Source: Gilmore, *Monsters*, 123.

Yaksas

The yaksas are a *hirsute*, a species of demon from the mythology of the Newars people of Nepal. Horned carnivores with wide mouths filled with teeth and voracious appetites, they live in the kingdom Kamrup.

Sources: Mack, *Field Guide to Demons, Fairies, Fallen Angels, and Other Subversive Spirits*, 85–7.

Yaksha

Variations: Ba-lu, Yakkha, Yakṣa, Yasha, Yè Chā

Originally tutelary gods of forests and villages, yaksha are chthonic beings in Hindu mythology, half god and half demon. Under the command of KUBERA, the god of wealth who rules them from his kingdom, Alaka, the male yaksha are fierce dwarflike warriors; females, referred to as yaksi or yaksini, are beautiful young women with full breasts and hips and innocent, round faces. They live under the Himalayas and guard the wealth of the earth: gems, gold, and silver. Generally they are benevolent and nonviolent.

Sources: Singh, *History of Ancient and Early Medieval India*, 430, 510, 538; Sutherland, *Disguises of the Demon*, 93–6.

Yamabushi Tengu

Variations: Mountain goblin, pride-fallen monks

Yamabushi Tengu ("mountain priest tengu") are a vampiric TENGU demon from Chinese demonology. Looking like a barefoot priest with a very long nose, these demons carry a staff or mallet. As they age, their feet become more wrinkled. Yamabushi Tengus walk through the mountains and use their magic to fight corruption.

Sources: Bonnefoy, *Asian Mythologies*, 286; Pauley, *Pauley's Guide*, 197; Wakabayashi, *Tengu*, 155.

Yamo

Yamo ("wind") are demonic creatures that are commonly used as messengers by Tipu in the demonology of the Lango people of Uganda. Usually they are seen as being an elflike or ratlike creature between six and eighteen inches tall. Yamo prey upon those who have thwarted the will of their master, Tipu. They are numerous and unpredictable demons of all things negative. They can cause illness, possess people, and shapeshift into any form that a person can imagine. Anyone who has contracted a disease from one of these demons must perform a *mako yamo* ("catching the wind") ceremony to save himself. Yamo live in humanlike communities on hilltops or near rocks, springs, and streams. Motivated by their greed, they are extremely desirous of clothing, food, and money.

Sources: Curley, *Elders, Shades, and Women*, 160–1, 178; Jones, *Evil in Our Midst*, 141–3.

Yan-Gant-Y-Tan

Yan-Gant-Y-Tan is an aqueous, nocturnal demon from the demonology of Brittany. He hunts at night, lighting his way with his candle-like fingers. The female equivalent that specializes in drowning children is called Bête Havette.

Sources: Collin de Plancy, *Dictionary of Witchcraft*, 124; Saunders, *National Magazine*, Vol. 5–6, 87; Shah, *Occultism*, 160.

Yan Luo Wang

Variations: Yama Raja, Yan Wang, Yen-Lo-Wang

Yan Luo Wang ("god of Hell") is the ruler of Hell in Chinese mythology. Essentially Yama, the god of death and king of demons, Yan Luo Wang commands numerous assistants. When a person dies, his or her soul is brought to him for judgment by Bullheads and HORSE FACES.

Sources: Lurker, *Dictionary of Gods and Goddesses, Devils and Demons*, 365; Mao, *Writings of Mao Zedong*, 65, Wilhelm, *Chinese Fairy Book*, 114.

Yaoguai

Variations: Yao-gui, Yaojing, Yaomo

Yaoguai is a Chinese word that translates as "demon."

Source: Von Glahn, *Sinister Way*, 86.

Yauhahu

Variations: Hebo, Yauwahu

The yauhahu are a type of demon from the demonology of the Indians of British Guiana who only attack those who offend them. Unceasingly active in the pursuit of evil, these demons shoot invisible arrows of illness and disease. They also destroy cooking utensils, despoil food, and inflict misery. To save a person who has fallen ill to one of their attacks, a *semicici* ("sorcerer") must perform a several-day-long ceremony, continually burning tobacco leaves, which they are particularly fond of. The semicici will ultimately place his lips on the inflicted body part and suck out some item that the yauhahu has inserted into the victim that is causing the illness, such as a fish bone, snake tooth, or thorn.

Sources: Brett, *Indian Missions in Guiana*, 62, 244–5, 249; Gray, *Mythology of All Races in Thirteen Volumes*, Vol. 11, 261; Spence, *Encyclopædia of Occultism*, 21, 338.

Yen Wang

Variations: Yen-lo, Yen-lo Wang

Yen Wang is the king of hell and the emperor and final judge of the Underworld in Buddhist and Chinese demonology, very similar to the god Yama. Yen Wang controls the manner and time of a person's death. He enforces the laws of retribution and is the tormentor of the most terrible souls. His powers only extend to the lower realms of existence; he has no power over those who pass into the realm of incarnate thought.

Sources: Hastings, *Encyclopedia of Religion and Ethics*, Part 8, 578; Sykes, *Who's Who in Non-Classical Mythology*, 216.

Yeqon

Variations: Yekum, Yikon ("inciter"), JEQON

Yeqon ("led astray" or "rebel") is a fallen archangel in Enochian lore; he is labeled as one of the FIVE SATANS (see FALLEN ANGEL). Yeqon was the WATCHER who, with Asb'el, led all the others to earth to copulate with human women.

Sources: Barton, *Journal of Biblical Literature*, Vols. 30–31, 166; Black, *Book of Enoch, or, I Enoch*, 65, 245–6; Davidson, *Dictionary of Angels*, 159, 320.

Yerro

Variations: KURI, Yandu

Yerro is a demonic spirit in the form of a black hyena in the demonology of the Hausa people of West Africa. He is the demon of paralysis. To banish Yerro, a specific ceremonial dance must be completed. A sacrifice must be offered as well, usually a bird of a specific color and gender pleasing to the demon.

Sources: Knappert, *Aquarian Guide to African Mythology*, 106; Tremearne, *Ban of the Bori*, 334–5.

Yetarel

Variations: Yeter'el

Enochian lore names Yetarel as one of the FALLEN ANGELS who swore allegiance to SAMIAZA, rebelled against God, took a human wife, and fathered the NEPHILIM.

Sources: Horne, *Sacred Books and Early Literature of the East*, 114; Laurence, *The Book of Enoch, the Prophet*, 77; Prophet, *Fallen Angels and the Origins of Evil*, 174; Sparks, *Apocryphal Old Testament*, 241.

Yezer Ha-Ra

A vampiric demon from Hebrew lore, the *Yezer Ha-Ra* ("the evil inclination in man's nature from birth") only attacks worshippers as they exit the synagogue on Friday nights. It possesses a person's body and drains away their life-energy over a period of some time until the victim dies or the vampire has been successfully exorcised by a rabbi. As long as the demon remains in the person's body, it will be harassing its victim by sending them explicit and intense lustful thoughts.

Sources: Curran, *Vampires*, 100; Gaster, *Ma'aseh Book*, 279–300; Macdonell, *Vedic Reader for Students*, 245.

Yoko

According to the *Apocryphon of John*, Yoko is the demon of desire.

Sources: Dunderberg, *Beyond Gnosticism*, 110; Ford, *Bible of the Adversary*, 74; Kelly, *Who in Hell*, 251; Lumpkin, *Fallen Angels, the Watchers and the Origin of Evil*, 16; Robinson, *Facsimile Edition of the Nag Hammadi Codices*, Vol. 12, 109.

Yōkai

Yōkai is a type of demonic creature in Japanese folklore. Generally these demons have both animal and human features, the ability to shape-shift, and an array of supernatural powers. *Yōkai* means "apparitions," "demons," or "spirits" and is a broad term used to include virtually all fantastical creatures and supernatural beings.

Sources: Bathgate, *Fox's Craft in Japanese Religion and Folklore*, 20; Li, *Ambiguous Bodies*, 142, 166.

Yomael

Variations: Jomiael, JOMJAEL, Yom'el, Yomiel, Yomyael ("Day of God")

Enochian lore names Yomael, prince of the seventh Heaven, as a CHIEF OF TENS and one of the FALLEN ANGELS who swore allegiance to SAMIAZA, rebelled against God, took a human wife, and fathered the NEPHILIM (see CHIEF OF THE GRIGORI, GRIGORI, PRINCES OF HELL, and WATCHERS).

Sources: Barton, *Journal of Biblical Literature*, Vols. 30–31, 166; Baskin, *Satanism*, 344; Davidson, *Dictionary of Angels*, 161, 320; Kelly, *Who in Hell*, 252; Laurence, *Foreign Quarterly Review*, Vol. 24, 370; Lévi, *History of Magic*, 38; Lumpkin, *Fallen Angels, the Watchers, and the Origins of Evil*, 31.

Younger Lilith

Variations: Lesser Lilith, Lilith the Younger, Mehetabel ("immersed")

Younger Lilith is a demon who looks like a woman from the waist up and fire (or a man) from the waist down. Her chariot is drawn by a winged horse and winged lion. She is the wife of ASMODAI and the mother of Harba di Ashm'dai ("Ashmodai's Sword") (see LILITH THE LESSER and SWORD OF ASMODAI).

Sources: Ford, *Liber Hvhi*, 24; Patai, *Hebrew Goddess*, 247; Scholem, *Origins of the Kabbalah*, 296.

Yuki-Onna

Variations: Yuki Onna, Yuki-Onne

In Japanese lore there is a type of vampiric spirit known as a *yuki-onna* ("snow woman"). It levitates rather than walks and appears to its victims as a tall and beautiful woman with impossibly long hair and inhumanly pale skin. Sometimes a yuki ona will show itself wearing a pure white kimono, but other times it will appear in the nude. On occasion, it will be holding a child in its arms. A yuki-onna is perfectly camouflaged against a snowy backdrop, and combined with its ability to shape-shift into a cloud of mist or falling snow, it can be impossible to find.

The yuki-onna is only active in the winter months as its hunting methods require. It will lead travelers astray, assuring they die from exposure or by breathing on them with its icy breath to make sure they meet the same death, but more quickly. It will appear before parents who are looking for their child; the yuki-onna will seem to be holding it, beckoning for them to come and claim it. As soon as they do, taking it into their arms, the yuki-onna turns them into ice. It has also been known to be aggressive, and although under normal circumstances it must be invited into a home, it will burst into a person's home by sending a gust of icy wind, freezing the occupants, especially the sleeping ones, to death. Not afraid to use its beauty as a lure, it will tempt men into having sexual intercourse with it, and all the while the yuki ona will drain them of their life-energy, pleasuring them until they die. When it wishes to, one look into its eyes will cause a person to go insane. With each death it causes, it absorbs the life-energy of its victims.

It is only on the very rare occasion that a yuki-onna will allow a potential victim to live, but they must beg for their life and be so moving and convincing when promising that it will never tell anyone about the encounter that even the icy heart of the yuki-onna is moved.

Sources: Davis, *Myths and Legends of Japan*, 149–53, 391; Mack, *Field Guide to Demons, Fairies, Fallen Angels, and Other Subversive Spirits*, 64; Perez, *Beings*, 35; Smith, *Ancient Tales and Folklore of Japan*, 307–11.

Yukshee

Yukshee is a singular and specific vampiric demon from the Hindu lore of India, and she is said to be the most beautiful and sexually insatiable of all the succubi (see SUCCUBUS). If a man has survived an encounter with her, he will be rendered impotent for the rest of his life, as she will have consumed all of his sex drive.

Sources: Edwardes, *Jewel in the Lotus*, 108; Riccardo, *Liquid Dreams*, 51; Tyson, *Sexual Alchemy*, 10.

Zabriel

In the *Sacred Magic of Abramelin the Mage*, Zabriel is a duke and is one of the twelve named Duke SERVITORS OF CARNESIEL (see CARNESIEL and DUKES OF HELL). Zabriel commands no less than ten but no more than three hundred servitors.

Source: Peterson, *Lesser Key of Solomon*, 59.

Zabulon

Zabulon is a FALLEN PRINCIPALITY. It was said that he was sent by Father Urbain Grandier to possess a lay sister in Loudon, France, in 1634. Zabulon is often called upon during exorcisms and cases of collective possession (see LOUDUN POSSESSION).

Sources: Aikin, *General Biography*, 493; Bayle, *Historical and Critical Dictionary*, 262; Bare, *Do You Still Believe in the Devil*, 50–1; De Givry, *Witchcraft, Magic and Alchemy*, 25–6; Ramsay, *Westminster Guide to the Books of the Bible*, 349; Spence, *Encyclopædia of Occultism*, 438; Voltaire, *Works of M. de Voltaire*, 193.

Zachariel

In the *Theurgia Goetia*, the second book of the *Lemegeton*, Zachariel is ranked as a chief duke and is listed as one of the fifteen SERVITORS OF ICOSIEL (see ICOSIEL). Commanding 2,200 servitors, he is said to be good-natured and willing to obey his summoner. This demon prefers to be summoned from inside a house.

Sources: Davidson, *Dictionary of Angels*, 43; Peterson, *Lesser Key of Solomon*, 99; Webster, *Encyclopedia of Angels*, 219.

Zachiel

In the *Ars Paulina*, the third book of the *Lemegeton*, Zachiel is ranked as a duke and is listed as one of the fifteen SERVITORS OF SASQUIEL and one of the fifteen SERVITORS OF SCOX (see SASQUIEL and SCOX). He commands 5,550 servitors.

Sources: Peterson, *Lesser Key of Solomon*, 99, 114; Trithemius, *Steganographia*, 95.

Zaebos

Variations: SALEOS, Sallos, Zabos, Zaebros, Zaleos

Zaebos is a grand count, duke, or earl, sources conflict, who commands thirty legions (see also COUNTS OF HELL, DUKES OF HELL, and EARLS OF HELL). Appearing before his summoner as a handsome soldier mounted on a crocodile, he wears on his head a ducal coronet, the traditional crown for a duke. Some sources describe him as having a human head wearing a ducal coronet and having the body of a crocodile. Known to have a genteel disposition and to be a fierce warrior, Zaebos is summoned for his ability to create love between men and women. He is also listed as one of the SPIRITS OF SOLOMON.

Sources: Ashley, *Complete Book of Devils and Demons*, 61; De Claremont, *Ancient's Book of Magic*, 439; Gettings, *Dictionary of Demons*, 211, 252; Scott, *London Magazine*, Vol. 5, 378.

Zagalo

In the *Sacred Magic of Abramelin the Mage*, book two, Zagalo is listed as one of the forty-nine SERVITORS OF BEELZEBUB (see BEELZEBUB). His name is Greek and possibly means "a reaping hook."

Sources: Mathers, *Book of the Sacred Magic of Abra-Melin*, 108; Susej, *Demonic Bible*, 256; Von Worms, *Book of Abramelin*, 257.

Zagam

Variations: Zagan

Zagam is a king and president, the demon of counterfeiting, deceit, and lies. Commanding thirty legions (or thirty-three, sources vary), he appears before his summoner as a bull with griffon wings. Witty by nature, he is summoned for his ability to change blood into oil, copper into gold, lead into silver, metals into coins, and water into wine. He can also make a fool into a wise man and make any man witty. He is listed as one of the SPIRITS OF SOLOMON.

Sources: Ashley, *Complete Book of Devils and Demons*, 61; De Claremont, *Ancient's Book of Magic*, 136; De Laurence, *Lesser Key of Solomon, Goetia*, 42; Peterson, *Lesser Key of Solomon*, 248; Scott, *London Magazine*, Vol. 5, 378.

Zagiel

Enochian lore names Zagiel ("scattering") as a FALLEN ANGEL, formerly of the Order of Archangels. He swore allegiance to SAMIAZA, rebelled against God, took a human wife, and fathered the NEPHILIM.

Source: Davidson, *Dictionary of Angels*, 324.

Zahhak

Variations: Aži Dahaka, Aži Dahāka ("Dragon Man"), Bēvar-Asp ("[He who has] 10,000 horses"), Dahāg ("Having ten sins"), Dahak, Zahhāk, Zahhāk-e Tāzi ("the Arabian Zahhāk"), Zohak, Zohhāk

Zahhak is a demonic dragon in the lore of ancient Persian and Zoroastrian mythology who is in the service of ANGRA MAINYU. He is the personification of evil. Born the child of an Arab ruler named Merdas and a woman named Wadag (or Ōdag) who was a great sinner, she went on to take her son, Zahhak, as a lover.

He was originally described as a monstrous dragon with six eyes, three heads (one of which is human), and three mouths; texts later describe him as a human with a snake growing off each shoulder. Zahhak is cunning and possesses evil counsels and all possible sins. He controls disease and storms, is exceptionally strong, and when cut, he bleeds scorpions, snakes, and other venomous creatures.

Zahhak lives in an inaccessible fortress of Kuuirinta in the land of Baßri (Babylon). He was defeated by Θraētaona, son of Aθßiya, who chained and imprisoned him on the mythical Mt. Damāvand. At the end of the world Zahhak will break his bonds and consume one in three humans and livestock. The hero Az ī Srūwar (also known as Feridun and Thraetaona) will come back to life to slay him.

Sources: Russell, *The Devil*, 116; Turner, *Dictionary of Ancient Deities*, 524; Yamamoto, *Oral Background of Persian Epics*, 115, 129.

Zahun

Apollonius of Tyana's *Nuctemeron* (*Night Illuminated by Day*) lists Zahun as the demon of scandal. He is most powerful during the first hour.

Source: Lévi, *Transcendental Magic*, 502.

Zakun

Zakun, a FALLEN ANGEL, along with LAHASH, led one hundred eighty-four myriads of angels and tried to intercept Moses's prayer to God. For attempting to intervene in the will of God, LAHASH was bound in chains of fire, given sixty lashes with a whip of fire, and cast out of Heaven by SAMMAEL. It is unknown what punishment, if any, Zakun and the angels he led received.

Sources: Davidson, *Dictionary of Angels*, 325; Ginzberg, *Legends of the Jews*, Vol. 3.

Zalambur

Zalambur is the demon of mercantile dishonesty in the demonology of Islam. He was born one of the five SONS OF ILBIS. This demon causes quarrels, makes men believe the nonsense and false oaths that merchants use to describe their goods, and causes men to cheat.

Sources: Brewer, *Dictionary of Phrase and Fable*, 643; Davidson, *Dictionary of Angels*, 281; Knowles, *Nineteenth Century*, Vol. 31, 449; Zwemer, *Childhood in the Moslem World*, 124.

Zalanes

In the *Sacred Magic of Abramelin the Mage*, Zalanes ("trouble bringer") is listed as one of the fifteen SERVITORS OF PAYMON (see PAYMON).

Sources: Ford, *Bible of the Adversary*, 94; Mathers, *Book of the Sacred Magic of Abramelin the Mage*, 108; Susej, *Demonic Bible*, 259; Von Worms, *Book of Abramelin*, 257.

Zalburis

Apollonius of Tyana's *Nuctemeron* (*Night Illuminated by Day*) names Zalburis as the demon of therapeutics. He is said to be most powerful during the eighth hour.

Source: Lévi, *Transcendental Magic*, 392.

Zapan

According to Johann Wierus's *Pseudomonarchia Daemonum* (*False Monarchy of Demons*, 1583), Zapan is a KING OF HELL who commands four legions.

Source: Spence, *Encyclopædia of Occultism*, 439.

Zaqiel

Variations: Zavebe, Zavehe

Enochian lore names Zaqiel as a CHIEF OF THE GRIGORI and one of the FALLEN ANGELS who swore allegiance to SAMIAZA, rebelled against God, took a human wife, and fathered the NEPHILIM (see GRIGORI and WATCHERS).

Sources: Beard, *Autobiography of Satan*, 113; Gettings, *Dictionary of Demons*, 102–105, 252; Laurence, *Book of Enoch, the Prophet*, 6; Voltaire, *Philosophical Dictionary*, 77; Lumpkin, *Fallen Angels, the Watchers, and the Origins of Evil*, 31; Laurence, *Book of Enoch, the Prophet*, 6.

Zaragil

In the *Sacred Magic of Abramelin the Mage*, book two, Zaragil is listed as one of the one hundred eleven SERVITORS OF AMAYMON, ARITON, ORIENS, AND PAYMON (see AMAYMON, ARITON, ORIENS, and PAYMON). This name is possibly Hebrew and may mean "scattering."

Sources: Ford, *Bible of the Adversary*, 89; Mathers, *Selected Occult Writings of S.L. MacGregor Mathers*, 105; Susej, *Demonic Bible*, 256; Von Worms, *Book of Abramelin*, 246.

Zaren

Apollonius of Tyana's *Nuctemeron* (*Night Illuminated by Day*) names Zaren as the demon of vengeance choice. He is most powerful during the sixth hour.

Source: Lévi, *Transcendental Magic*, 391.

Zarich

Variations: Zairik ("conquering," "jaundice," or "yellowish, greenish")

Zarich ("age") is a female DAEVAS, the personification of aging in Zoroastrian demonology. Although female, this demon is very masculine in appearance and action. She is one of the seven archdemons of AHRIMAN. Her personal adversary is Ameretat.

Sources: Eliade, *Encyclopedia of Religion*, Vol. 1, 158; Ford, *Luciferian Witchcraft*, 20; Reiterer, *Angels*, 27.

Zarobi

Apollonius of Tyana's *Nuctemeron* (*Night Illuminated by Day*) names Zarobi as the demon of precipices. He is most powerful during the third hour.

Sources: Gettings, *Dictionary of Demons*, 252; Kelly, *Who in Hell*, 255.

Zeffar

Apollonius of Tyana's *Nuctemeron* (*Night Illuminated by Day*) names Zeffar as the demon of irrevocable choice. He is most powerful during the ninth hour.

Source: Lévi, *Transcendental Magic*, 393.

Zeirna

Apollonius of Tyana's *Nuctemeron* (*Night Illuminated by Day*) names Zeirna as the demon of infirmities. He is most powerful during the fifth hour.

Source: Lévi, *Transcendental Magic*, 391.

Zelinda

Variations: Zelinda the Fair

Zelinda, born one of the daughters of LILITH, is the wife of Cain in Jewish folklore.

Source: Rudwin, *Devil in Legend and Literature*, 28, 96.

Zephar

Variations: BELIAL, Zepar

Zephar, the Red Duke, commands twenty-eight legions and is one of the twelve SERVITORS OF ABEZETHIBOU (see ABEZETHIBOU). When summoned, he appears as a soldier wearing red armor or clothes and gives love spells. He also induces pederasty (a sexual relationship between an older man and an adolescent boy who is not a family member), and teaches how to shape-shift.

Sources: Ashley, *Complete Book of Devils and Demons*, 58; Kelly, *Who in Hell*, 255; Maberry, *Cryptopedia*, 65; Susej, *Demonic Bible*, 71.

Zimimar

Variations: Zemimar, Zimmar, Zimmimar, Zinimar

Zimimar is the king of the North, one of the FOUR PRINCIPAL KINGS that has power over the seventy-two SPIRITS OF SOLOMON, according to Johann Wierus's *Pseudomonarchia Daemonum* (*False Monarchy of Demons*, 1583). In service under MAMMON, Zimimar commands six legions.

Sources: Beard, *Autobiography of Satan*, 46; Davidson, *Dictionary of Angels*, 328; Gaspey, *The Witch-Finder*, 201; Scot, *Discoverie of Witchcraft*, 226; Spence, *Encyclopaedia of Occultism*, 119.

Ziminar

Ziminar is one of the six SERVITORS OF TURAEL (see TURAEL).

Sources: Gettings, *Dictionary of Demons*, 252; González-Wippler, *Complete Book of Spells, Ceremonies, and Magic*, 146.

Zizuph

Apollonius of Tyana's *Nuctemeron* (*Night Illuminated by Day*) names Zizuph as the demon of mysteries. He is most powerful during the eighth hour.

Source: Lévi, *Transcendental Magic*, 392.

Zoeniel

In *Ars Paulina*, book three of the *Lemegeton*, Zoeniel is a chief duke who commands three thousand servitors and one of the twelve SERVITORS OF AMENADIEL (see AMENADIEL and DUKES OF HELL).

Sources: Peterson, *Lesser Key of Solomon*, 62; Trithemius, *Steganographia*, 91.

Zophas

Apollonius of Tyana's *Nuctemeron* (*Night Illuminated by Day*) names Zophas as the demon of pentacles. He is most powerful during the eleventh hour.

Sources: Davidson, *Dictionary of Angels*, 7; Gettings, *Dictionary of Demons*, 23; Lévi, *Transcendental Magic*, 422.

Zoray

The *Grand Grimoire*, alleged to have been written by Alibek the Egyptian and published in Cairo in 1522, names Zoray as one of the three SERVITORS OF SARGATANAS (see SARGATANAS).

Sources: Baskin, *Sorcerer's Handbook*, 276; Waite, *Unknown World 1894–1895*, 230; Wedeck, *Treasury of Witchcraft*, 96.

Zosiel

Theurgia Goetia, the second book of the *Lemegeton*, ranks Zosiel as a chief duke who commands 2,200 servitors and lists him as one of the fifteen SERVITORS OF ICOSIEL (see ICOSIEL). This demon is said to be good-natured and willing to obey his summoner. He prefers to be invoked from inside a house.

Source: Peterson, *Lesser Key of Solomon*, 99.

Zozo

Along with the demons Mimi and Crapoulet, Zozo bewitched a young girl in the town of Teilly in northern France in 1816. It was said that when the girl walked on all fours that the demon Zozo was right behind her.

Sources: Collin de Plancy, *Dictionary of Witchcraft*, 125; Fowler, *The King's English*, 271; Lowell, *Writings of James Russell Lowell in Prose and Poetry*, 387–8.

Zu

Variations: Anzu, IMDUGUD

A divine storm-bird, Zu was the chief worker of evil in Sumero-Akkadian mythology; he was the personification of the southern wind and the thunder clouds. Zu lived in an inaccessible recess in a mountain. His personal adversaries were the gods En-Lil and Shamash. This half-man, half-bird demon stole the Tablets of Destiny from Enlil and hid them on a mountaintop, causing the gods to fear him and the power he had over their fate while he was in possession of the tablets. Eventually, Zu was slain by Marduk or the arrows of the god Ninurta; sources conflict.

Sources: Gray, *Mythology of All Races in Thirteen Volumes*, Vol. 6, 264, 269; Jastrow, *Religion of Babylonia and Assyria*, 525, 537–8, 540, 542.

Zuphlas

Apollonius of Tyana's *Nuctemeron* (*Night Illuminated by Day*) names Zuphlas as the demon of forests. He is most powerful during the eleventh hour.

Sources: Davidson, *Dictionary of Angels*, 7; Gettings, *Dictionary of Demons*, 23; Lévi, *Transcendental Magic*, 422.

Bibliography

Abdul-Rahman, Muhammad Saed. *Islam: Questions and Answers; Schools of Thought, Religions and Sects*, Vol. 8. London: MSA, 2003.
_____. *The Meaning and Explanation of the Glorious Qur'an*, Vol. 1. London: MSA, 2009.

Abercromby, John. *Pre- and Proto-Historic Finns: Both Eastern and Western with the Magic Songs of the West Finns*. London: David Nutt, 1898.

Abrahams, Israel. "The Testament of Solomon," *The Jewish Quarterly Review*, Vol. 11, pages 8–46. London: Macmillan, 1899.

Abusch, I. Tzvi, and K. van der Toorn. *Mesopotamian Magic: Textual, Historical, and Interpretative Perspectives*. Leiden: Brill, 1999.

Adams, Isaac. *Persia by a Persian: Being Personal Experiences, Manners, Customs, Habits, Religious and Social Life in Persia*. London: E. Stock, 1906.

Adams, William Henry Davenport. *Dwellers on the Threshold; or, Magic and Magicians, With Some Illustrations of Human Error and Imposture*. London: John Maxwell, 1864.

Adler, Cyrus, Dropsie College for Hebrew and Cognate Learning, Dropsie University, Annenberg Research Institute, University of Pennsylvania, and the Center for Judaic Studies. *The Jewish Quarterly Review*, Vol. 12. Philadelphia: Dropsie College for Hebrew and Cognate Learning, 1922.

Agnew, John Holmes, and Walter Hilliard Bidwell. *Eclectic Magazine: Foreign Literature*, Vol. 46. New York: E.R. Pelton, 1887.

Agrippa, Henry Cornelius, and Donald Tyson. *The Fourth Book of Occult Philosophy: The Companion to Three Books of Occult Philosophy*. St. Paul: Llewellyn, 2009.

Agrippa von Nettesheim, Heinrich Cornelius, James Freake, and Donald Tyson. *Three Books of Occult Philosophy*. St. Paul: Llewellyn, 1993.

Ahye, Molly. *Golden Heritage: The Dance in Trinidad and Tobago*. Tobago: Heritage Cultures, 1978.

Aikin, John, and William Enfield. *General Biography; or, Lives, Critical and Historical, of the Most Eminent Persons of All Ages, Countries, Conditions and Professions, Chiefly Composed by J. Aikin and W. Enfield*, Vol. 4. London: Robinson, 1803.

Alexander, Hartley Burr. *The Mythology of All Races in Thirteen Volumes*, Vol. 11, *Latin-America*. Boston: Marshall Jones, 1920.

Alexander, William Menzies. *Demonic Possession in the New Testament: Its Historical, Medical, and Theological Aspects*. Edinburgh: T. and T. Clark, 1902.

Allardice, Pamela. *Myths, Gods, and Fantasy*. Garden City Park: Avery, 1990.

Allen, Clifton J. *Hosea, Malachi*. Nashville: Broadman, 1972.

Allen, Emory Adams. *History of Civilization*, Vol. 2. Cincinnati: Central Publishing House, 1889.

Allen, Richard Hinckley. *Star-Names and Their Meanings*. New York: G.E. Stechert, 1899.

Altman, Nathaniel. *Sacred Trees*. San Francisco: Sierra Club Books, 1994.

American Folklore Society. *Journal of American Folklore*, Vol. 46. New York: Houghton, Mifflin, 1933.

American Indian Quarterly, Vol. 31. Berkeley: Southwestern American Indian Society, 2007.

American Philological Association. *Transactions and Proceedings of the American Philological Association*, Vol. 44. Cleveland: Case Western Reserve University, 1913.

American Philological Association, Philological Association of the Pacific Coast. *Transactions and Proceedings of the American Philological Association*, Vol. 101. Cleveland: Press of Case Western Reserve University, 1970.

American Psychiatric Association. *The American Journal of Psychiatry*, Vol. 117. Palo Alto: High Wire Press, 1961.

Ames, Michael. "Tovil: Exorcism by White Magic." *Natural History*, January 1978, Vol. 87, No. 1, pp. 42–49.

Anderson, Melissa E. *Diary of Ancient Rites: A Guide for the Serious Practitioner*. Raleigh: Lulu, 2006.
_____. *Diary of Ancient Rites, Vol. 2: Living a Magical Life*. Sandy: Aardvark Global, 2007.

Andrews, Tamra. *Dictionary of Nature Myths: Legends of the Earth, Sea, and Sky*. New York: Oxford University Press, 2000.

Antares. Tanah Tujuh: Close Encounters with the Temuan Mythos. Kuala Lumpur: Silverfish Books, 2007.

Anthon, Charles. *A Classical Dictionary: Containing an Account of the Principal Proper Names Mentioned in Ancient Authors and Intended to Elucidate All the Important Points Connected with the Geography, History, Biography, Mythology, and Fine Arts of the Greeks and Romans. Together with an Account of Coins Weights and Measures with Tabular Values of the Same*. New York: Harper and Brothers, 1886.

Anthropological Institute of Great Britain and Ireland, JSTOR. *Journal of the Royal Anthropological Institute of Great Britain and Ireland*, Vol. 25. London: Kegan Paul, Trench, Trübner, 1896.

Anthropological Society of Bombay. *The Journal of the Anthropological Society of Bombay*, Vol. 15. Bombay: Anthropological Society of Bombay, 1932.

Applegate, Melissa Littlefield. *The Egyptian Book of Life: Symbolism of Ancient Egyptian Temple and Tomb Art*. Deerfield Beach: HCI, 2001.

Aquino, María Pilar, Daisy L. Machado, and Jeanette Rodríguez. *A Reader in Latina Feminist Theology: Religion and Justice*. Austin: University of Texas Press, 2002.

Ara, Mitra. *Eschatology in the Indo-Iranian Traditions: The Genesis and Transformation of a Doctrine*. New York: Peter Lang, 2008.

Arnold, Clinton E. *Powers of Darkness: Principalities and Powers in Paul's Letters*. Downers Grove: InterVarsity Press, 1992.

Arnscheidt, Julia. *'Debating' Nature Conservation: Policy,*

Law and Practice in Indonesia: A Discourse Analysis of History and Present. Leiden: Amsterdam University Press, 2009.

Ashe, Steven. *Qabalah: The Complete Golden Dawn Initiate.* Raleigh: Lulu, 2007.

_____. *Qabalah: The Testament of Solomon; The Wisdom of Solomon.* Raleigh: Lulu, 2008.

Asher, Jerimiah. *Charting the Supernatural Judgments of Planet Earth: Journal to the End of Days.* Bloomington: AuthorHouse, 2010.

Ashkenazi, Michael. *Handbook of Japanese Mythology.* Santa Barbara: ABC-CLIO, 2003.

Ashley, Leonard R.N. *The Amazing World of Superstition, Prophecy, Luck, Magic and Witchcraft.* New York: Random House Value, 1988.

_____. *The Complete Book of Devils and Demons.* Fort Lee: Barricade, 1996.

_____. *What's in a Name? Everything You Wanted to Know.* Baltimore: Genealogical Publishing, 1989.

Ashton, John. *The Devil in Britain and America.* Adelphi: Ward and Downey, 1896.

Asiatic Society of Bengal. *Bibliotheca Indica,* Vol. 86, Issue 1. Calcutta: Baptist Mission Press, 1880.

Asiatic Society of Japan. *Transactions of the Asiatic Society of Japan,* Vols. 10–11. Yokohama: R. Meiklejohn, 1882.

Athenaeum, Part 1. London: John Edward Francis Athenaeum Press, 1897.

Atlantic Monthly, Vol. 54. Boston: Atlantic Monthly Company, 1884.

Atmosumarto, Sutanto. *A Learner's Comprehensive Dictionary of Indonesian.* Middlesex: Atma Stanton, 2004.

Aulestia, Gorka, and Linda White. *Basque-English, English-Basque Dictionary.* Reno: University of Nevada Press, 1992.

Awn, Peter J. *Satan's Tragedy and Redemption: Iblis in Sufi Psychology.* Leiden: Brill, 1983.

Ayers, Jerry. *Yahweh's Breath Bible, Vol. 1: Literal Strong's Version with Sacred Name Added.* Bloomington: AuthorHouse, 2010.

Aylesworth, Thomas G. *Servants of the Devil.* Reading: Addison-Wesley, 1970.

_____. *The Story of Vampires.* New York: McGraw-Hill, 1977.

Bacon, Benjamin Wisner, William H. Cobb, and James A. Montgomery. *Journal of Biblical Literature,* Vols. 31–32. Boston: Society of Biblical Literature and Exegesis, 1912.

Baddeley, John Frederick. *The Rugged Flanks of Caucasus,* Vol. 2. London: Oxford University Press, H. Milford, 1940.

Baerg, Gerhard. *The Supernatural in the Modern German Drama.* New York: G. P. Putnam's Sons, 1923.

Baglio, Matt. *The Rite: The Making of a Modern Exorcist.* New York: Random House, 2010.

Bailey, Michael David. *Historical Dictionary of Witchcraft.* Lanham: Scarecrow Press, 2003.

Bailey, Preston T., Jr. *Spiritual Warfare.* Longwood: Xulon Press, 2008.

Bakshi, Dwijendra Nath. *Hindu Divinities in Japanese Buddhist Pantheon: A Comparative Study.* Calcutta: Benten, 1979.

Balfour, Edward. *The Cyclopædia of India and of Eastern and Southern Asia, Commercial Industrial, and Scientific: Products of the Mineral, Vegetable, and Animal Kingdoms, Useful Arts and Manufactures,* Vol. 3. London: Bernard Quaritch, 1885.

Balfour, Walter, and Otis Ainsworth Skinner. *Three Inquiries on the Following Scriptural Subjects: I. The Person-* ality of the Devil; II. The Duration of the Punishment Expressed by the Words Ever, Everlasting, Eternal, etc.; III. Demoniacal Possessions. Boston: A. Tompkins, 1854.

Balkan Folklore: Bulgarian Folklore, Ala, Baba Yaga, Varkolak, German, Rusalka, Kukeri, Zmeu, Samodiva, Hitar Petar, Dodola, Veda Slovena. New York: General Books LLC, 2010.

Ballard, Frank R. *The Beasts of Eschatology and Related Subjects.* Canton: Xulon Press, 2002.

Bamberger, Bernard Jacob. *Fallen Angels.* Philadelphia: Jewish Publication Society of America, 1952.

_____. *Fallen Angels: Soldiers of Satan's Realm.* Philadelphia: Jewish Publication Society, 2006.

Bancroft, Hubert Howe. *The Works of Hubert Howe Bancroft.* San Francisco: History Company, 1886.

Banis, V.J. *Charms, Spells, and Curses for the Millions.* Holicong: Wildside Press, 2007.

Barber, Richard, and Anne Richer. *A Dictionary of Fabulous Beasts.* New York: Macmillan, 1971.

Bare, Charles W. *Do You Still Believe in the Devil?* Nashville: Turner Publishing, 2001.

Baretti, Giuseppe Marco Antonio, John Davenport, and Guglielmo Comelati. *A New Dictionary of the Italian and English Languages: Based Upon that of Baretti, and Containing, Among Other Additions and Improvements, Numerous Neologisms and a Copious List of Geographical and Proper Names.* London: John Bumpas, 1827.

Barford, Paul M. *The Early Slavs: Culture and Society in Early Medieval Eastern Europe.* Ithaca: Cornell University Press, 2001.

Baring-Gould, Sabine. *The Book of Were-Wolves: Being an Account of a Terrible Superstition.* London: Smith, Elder, 1865.

Barnes, Charles Randall. *The People's Bible Encyclopedia: Biographical, Geographical, Historical, and Doctrinal: Illustrated by Nearly Four Hundred Engravings, Maps, Chats, Etc.,* Vol. 2. Chicago: People's Publication Society, 1912.

Barnhart, Clarence Lewis. *The New Century Handbook of English Literature.* New York: Appleton-Century-Crofts, 1967.

Barnstone, Willis, and Marvin W. Meyer. *The Gnostic Bible.* Boston: Shambhala, 2006.

Baroja, Julio Caro. *The World of Witches.* Chicago: University of Chicago Press, 1965.

Baron, Salo Wittmayer. *Social and Religious History of the Jews, Vol. 5: High Middle Ages: Religious Controls and Dissensions.* New York: Columbia University Press, 1957.

Barrett, Francis. *The Magus.* London: Lackington, Allen, 1801.

Barton, George A. *Journal of the American Oriental Society,* Vol. 15. New Haven: American Oriental Society, 1893.

Barton, George A. and the Society of Biblical Literature, and the Society of Biblical Literature and Exegesis (U.S.). "The Origin of the Names of Angels and Demons in the Extra-Canonical Apocalyptic Literature," *Journal of Biblical Literature,* Vols. 30–31. New York: G.E. Stechert, 1911.

Barton, John. *The Oxford Bible Commentary.* New York: Oxford University Press, 2001.

Baskin, Wade. *Dictionary of Satanism.* New York: Philosophical Library, 1971.

_____. *Satanism: A Guide to the Awesome Power of Satan.* Secaucus: Citadel, 1972.

_____. *The Sorcerer's Handbook.* New York: Philosophical Library, 1974.

Bassett, Fletcher Stewart. *Legends and Superstitions of the Sea and of Sailors in All Lands and at All Times*. Chicago: Belford, Clark, 1885.

Bathgate, Michael. *The Fox's Craft in Japanese Religion and Folklore: Shapeshifters, Transformations, and Duplicities*. New York: Psychology Press, 2004.

Baty, John. *The Book of Enoch the Prophet*. Charleston: BiblioBazaar, 2008.

Bayle, Pierre. *An Historical and Critical Dictionary, Selected and Abridged*, Vol. 3. London: Hunt and Clarke, 1826.

Baynes, Thomas Spencer. *The Encyclopedia Britannica: A Dictionary of Arts, Sciences and General Literature*, Vol. 17. New York: Henry G. Allen, 1890.

Bear, H. "Asmodai," *The Quarterly Review of the Methodist Episcopal Church, South*, Vol. 7. October 1853, 500–12. Richmond: Methodist Episcopal Church, South, 1853.

Beard, John Relly. *The Autobiography of Satan*. London: Williams and Norgate, 1872.

Beattie, John, and John Middleton. *Spirit Mediumship and Society in Africa*. New York: Psychology Press, 2004.

Becker, Alton L. *Beyond Translation: Essays Toward a Modern Philology*. Ann Arbor: University of Michigan Press, 2000.

_____, and Aram A. Yengoyan. *The Imagination of Reality: Essays in Southeast Asian Coherence Systems*. Norwood: Ablex, 1979.

Beckwith, Martha Warren, Vassar College, and the Lucy Maynard Salmon Fund for Research. *Hawaiian Mythology*, Vol. 1940, Part 1. Charleston: Forgotten Books, 1940.

Bedi, Rahul Kuldip, and Subramanian Swamy. *Kailas and Manasarovar After 22 Years in Shiva's Domain*. New Delhi: Allied Publishers, 1984.

Beér, Robert. *The Encyclopedia of Tibetan Symbols and Motifs*. Chicago: Serindia, 2004.

Beeton, Samuel Orchart. *Beeton's Classical Dictionary: A Cyclopaedia of Greek and Roman Biography, Geography, Mythology, and Antiquities*. Charleston: Forgotten Books.

Behrens, Richard. *The Lost Scrolls of King Solomon*. Woodbury: Llewellyn, 1998.

Belanger, Michelle. *Dictionary of Demons: Names of the Damned*. St. Paul: Llewellyn, 2010.

Bell, John. *Bell's New Pantheon; or, Historical Dictionary of the Gods, Demi-Gods, Heroes, and Fabulous Personages of Antiquity: Also, of the Images and Idols Adored in the Pagan World; Together with Their Temples, Priests, Altars, Oracles, Fasts, Festivals, Games as Well as Descriptions of Their Figures, Representations, and Symbols, Collected from Statues, Pictures, Coins, and Other Remains of the Ancients: The Whole Designed to Facilitate the Study of Mythology, History, Poetry, Painting, Statuary, Medals, &c. &c. and Compiled from the Best Authorities: Richly Embellished with Characteristic Prints*. London: J. Bell, 1790.

Bell, Richard H. *Deliver Us from Evil: Interpreting the Redemption from the Power of Satan in New Testament Theology*, Vol. 216. Tuebingen: Mohr Siebeck, 2007.

Bellamy, Hans Schindler. *Moons, Myths and Man: A Reinterpretation*. London: Faber and Faber, 1949.

Bellamy, John. *The History of All Religions: Comprehending a Series of Researches Explanatory of the Opinions, Customs, and Representative Worship in the Churches, Which Have Been Established from the Beginning of Time to the Commencement of the Christian Dispensation; The Accomplishment of the Prophecies*. London: Longman, Hurst, Rees, Orme, and Brown, 1813.

Bellingham, David, Peter Casterton, Catherine Headlam, and Cynthia O'Neill. *Goddesses, Heroes, and Shamans: The Young People's Guide to World Mythology*. New York: Kingfisher, 1997.

Benardete, Seth. *The Rhetoric of Morality and Philosophy: Plato's Gorgias and Phaedrus*. Chicago: University of Chicago Press, 2009.

Benfey, Theodor. *A Sanskrit-English Dictionary: With References to the Best Editions of Sanskrit Authors and Etymologies and Comparisons of Cognate Words Chiefly in Greek, Latin, Gothic and Anglo-Saxon*. London: Longmans, 1866.

Bernstein, Jay H. *Spirits Captured in Stone: Shamanism and Traditional Medicine Among the Taman of Borneo*. Boulder: Lynne Rienner, 1997.

Berry, Brewton. *You and Your Superstitions*. Whitefish: Kessinger, 2006.

Best, Elsdon. *The Maori*, Vol. 1. Auckland: Polynesian Society, 1942.

Betz, Hans Dieter. *The Greek Magical Papyri in Translation, Including the Demotic Spells*, Vol. 1. Chicago: University of Chicago Press, 1997.

Bharati, Agehananda. *The Realm of the Extra-Human: Agents and Audiences*. The Hague: Mouton, 1976.

Bhāravi. *The Kiratarjuniye*, Vol. 1. Kathmandu: Ratna Pustak Bhandar, 1972.

Bhattacharji, Sukumari. *Fatalism in Ancient India*. Calcutta: Baulmon Prakashan, 1995.

Bias, Danny. *Freedom from the World of Satanism and the Power of Satan*. Raleigh: Lulu, 2006.

Bienkowski, Piotr, and Alan Ralph Millard. *Dictionary of the Ancient Near East*. Philadelphia: University of Pennsylvania Press, 2000.

Bildhauer, Bettina, and Robert Mills. *The Monstrous Middle Ages*. Toronto: University of Toronto Press, 2003.

Bizarre Notes and Queries in History, Folk-Lore, Mathematics, Mysticism, Art, Science, Etc., Vols. 3–4. Manchester: S.C. and L.M. Gould, 1886.

Bjerregaard, Carl Henrik Andreas, Eugénie R. Eliscu, William Frank Fraetas, and Grace Gallatin Seton. *The Great Mother, a Gospel of the Eternally Feminine: Occult and Scientific Studies and Experiences in the Sacred and Secret Life*. New York: Innerlife, 1913.

Black, Adam, and Charles Black. *The Edinburgh Review*, Vol. 107. Edinburgh: Adam and Charles Black, 1858.

Black, Jeremy A. *A Concise Dictionary of Akkadian*. Wiesbaden: Otto Harrassowitz, 2000.

_____, Anthony Green, and Tessa Rickards. *Gods, Demons, and Symbols of Ancient Mesopotamia: an Illustrated Dictionary*. Leiden: Brill, 1985.

_____, _____, and _____. *Gods, Demons, and Symbols of Ancient Mesopotamia: An Illustrated Dictionary*. Austin: University of Texas Press, 1992.

Black, Matthew, James C. Vander Kam, and Otto Neugebauer. *The Book of Enoch, or, I Enoch: A New English Edition; With Commentary and Textual Notes*. Leiden: E.J. Brill, 1985.

Blair, Judit M. *De-Demonising the Old Testament: An Investigation of Azazel, Lilith, Deber, Qeteb and Reshef in the Hebrew Bible*. Tubingen: Mohr Siebeck, 2009.

Blavatsky, Helena Petrovna. *Isis Unveiled: Science, Vol. 1 of Isis Unveiled: A Master-key to the Mysteries of Ancient and Modern Science and Theology*. New York: J.W. Bouton, 1877.

_____. *The Secret Doctrine: Anthropogenesis*. Point Loma: Aryan Theosophical Press, 1888.

_____. *The Secret Doctrine: The Synthesis of Science, Religion, and Philosophy*, Vol. 1. New York: The Path Office, 1893.

_____. *The Secret Doctrine: The Synthesis of Science, Religion, and Philosophy*, Vol. 2. Charleston: Forgotten Books, 1893.

_____. *The Secret Doctrine*, Vol. 3. Wheaton: Quest Books, 1993.

_____. *The Theosophical Glossary*. London: Theosophical Publishing Society, 1892.

_____. *The Theosophist 1884 to 1885*. Whitefish: Kessinger, 2004.

_____, and George Robert Stow Mead. *The Theosophical Glossary*. London: Theosophical Publishing Society, 1892.

Boccaccini, Gabriele. *Enoch and Qumran Origins: New Light on a Forgotten Connection*. Grand Rapids: William. B. Eerdmans, 2005.

Bodde, Derk. *Festivals in Classical China: New Year and other Annual Observances During the Han Dynasty, 206 B.C.–A.D. 220, Part 220*. Princeton: Princeton University Press, 1975.

Bodin, Jean. *Le Fleau des Demons et Sorciers*. Anyort: D. du Terroir, 1616.

Boehm, Roger J. *It's a Dark World*. Raleigh: Lulu, 2007.

Boguet, Henry. *An Examen of Witches: Drawn from Various Trials of Many of this Sect in the District of Saint Oyan de Joux, Commonly Known as Saint Claude, in the County of Burgundy, Including the Procedure Necessary to a Judge in Trials for Witchcraft*. London: J. Rodker, 1929.

Bohak, Gideon. *Ancient Jewish Magic: A History*. Cambridge: Cambridge University Press, 2008.

Bolton, Kingsley. *Western Accounts of the History, Sociology and Linguistics of Chinese Secret Societies*. London: Taylor and Francis, 2000.

Bonfante, Giuliano, and Larissa Bonfante. *The Etruscan Language: An Introduction*. Manchester: Manchester University Press, 2002.

Bonfante, Larissa, and Judith Swaddling. *Etruscan Myths*. Austin: University of Texas Press, 2006.

Bonnefoy, Yves. *Asian Mythologies*. Chicago: University of Chicago Press, 1993.

_____, and Wendy Doniger. *Asian Mythologies*. Chicago: University of Chicago Press, 1993.

_____, and _____. *Roman and European Mythologies*. Chicago: University of Chicago Press, 1992.

Book of Enoch the Prophet. London: Kegan Paul, Trench, 1883.

The Book of the Sacred Magic of Abramelin the Mage. Charleston: Forgotten Books, 2008.

Booth, Sally Smith. *The Witches of Early America*. New York: Hastings House, 1975.

Borges, Jorge Luis. *The Book of Imaginary Beings*. New York: E.P. Dutton, 1969.

Bossieu. "The Ocean of the Chaldean Traditions," *The Academy*, Issue 14. London: Robert Scott Walker, 1878, page 14.

Bosworth, Clifford Edmund, and Ehsan Yarshater. *The Sasanids, the Byzantines, the Lakhmids, and Yemen*. Albany: SUNY Press, 1999.

Bosworth, Joseph, and Thomas Northcote Toller. *An Anglo-Saxon Dictionary: Based on the Manuscript Collections of the Late Joseph Bosworth*. Oxford: Clarendon, 1882.

Bottéro, Jean, Clarisse Herrenschmidt, and Jean Pierre Vernant. *Ancestor of the West: Writing, Reasoning, and Religion in Mesopotamia, Elam, and Greece*. Chicago: University of Chicago Press, 2000.

Botterweck, G. Johannes, Heinz-Josef Fabry, and Helmer Ringgren. *Theological Dictionary of the Old Testament*, Vol. 11. Grand Rapids: Wm. B. Eerdmans Publishing, 2000.

Boulay, R.A. *Flying Serpents and Dragons: The Story of Mankind's Reptilian Past*. Palo Alta: Book Tree, 1999.

Bourke, Ulick Joseph. *Pre–Christian Ireland*. Dublin: Brown and Nolan, 1887.

Bousset, Wilhelm. *The Antichrist Legend: A Chapter in Christian and Jewish Folklore, Englished from the German of W. Bousset, With a Prologue on the Babylonian Dragon Myth*. London: Hutchinson, 1896.

Bowyer, Mathew J. *Encyclopedia of Mystical Terminology*. New York: A.S. Barnes, 1979.

Boyce, Mary. *A History of Zoroastrianism: The Early Period*. Leiden: Brill, 1989.

Brann, Noel L. *Trithemius and Magical Theology: A Chapter in the Controversy Over Occult Studies in Early Modern Europe*. Albany: SUNY Press, 1999.

Bray, Frank Chapin. *The World of Myths: A Dictionary of Mythology*. New York: Thomas Y. Crowell, 1935.

Breck, John. *Spirit of Truth: The Origins of Johannine Pneumatology*. Crestwood: St. Vladimir's Seminary Press, 1991.

Bremmer, Jan N. *The Apocryphal Acts of Andrew*. Leuven: Peeters, 2000.

_____. *The Early Greek Concept of the Soul*. Princeton: Princeton University Press, 1987.

Brenk, Frederick E. *Relighting the Souls: Studies in Plutarch, in Greek Literature, Religion, and Philosophy, and in the New Testament Background*. Stuttgart: Franz Steiner, 1998.

Brennan, Martin. *The Hidden Maya*. Rochester: Inner Traditions/Bear, 1998.

Brett, William Henry. *Indian Missions in Guiana*. London: George Bell, 1851.

_____. *Legends and Myths of the Aboriginal Indians of British Guiana*. London: William, Wells, and Gardner, 1870.

Brewer, Ebenezer Cobham. *Dictionary of Phrase and Fable: Giving the Derivation, Source, or Origin of Common Phrases, Allusions, and Words that Have a Tale to Tell*. London: Cassell, 1900.

_____. *The Reader's Handbook of Famous Names in Fiction, Allusions, References, Proverbs, Plots, Stories, and Poems*, Vol. 1. Philadelphia: Lippincott, 1899.

_____, and Marion Harland. *Character Sketches of Romance, Fiction and the Drama*. New York: Selmar E. Hess, 1892.

Briggs, Katharine Mary. *A Dictionary of British Folk-Tales in the English Language: Folk Narratives*. London: Taylor and Francis, 1991.

_____. *A Dictionary of British Folk-Tales in the English Language: Folk Narratives Part B, Folk Legends*. London: Taylor and Francis, 1991.

_____. *An Encyclopedia of Fairies: Hobgoblins, Brownies, Bogies, and Other Supernatural Creatures*. New York: Pantheon Books, 1976.

Britannica, Dale Hoiberg, and Indu Ramchandani. *Students' Britannica India*, Vols. 1–5. Mumbai: Popular Prakashan, 2000.

Britten, Emma Harding. *Art Magic: Or Mundane, Sub Mundane, and Super Mundane Spiritism 1876*. Whitefish: Kessinger, 2003.

Brittle, Gerald. *The Demonologist: The Extraordinary Career of Ed and Lorraine Warren*. New York: Universe, 2002.

Broedel, Hans Peter. *The Malleus Maleficarum and the Construction of Witchcraft: Theology and Popular Belief*. Manchester: Manchester University Press, 2003.

Broome, Fiona. *Is Your House Haunted?* Portsmouth: New Forest, 2010.

Brown, Robert. *The Unicorn: A Mythological Investigation.* London: Longmans, 1881.

Brück, Moses. *Pharisäische Volkssitten und Ritualien in ihrer Entstehung und geschichtlichen Entwicklung.* Frankfurt: Joh. Chr. Hermann, 1840.

Brucker, Johann Jakob. *The History of Philosophy: From the Earliest Times to the Beginning of the Present Century; Drawn up from Brucker's Historia Critica Philosophiae.* London: J. Johnson, 1791.

Bryant, Clifton D. *Handbook of Death and Dying.* Thousand Oaks, Calif.: Sage, 2003.

Bryant, Jacob. *A New System: Or, An Analysis of Ancient Mythology: Wherein an Attempt is Made to Divest Tradition of Fable, and to Reduce the Truth to Its Original Purity,* Vol. 2. London: W.J. and J. Richardson; R. Faulder, 1807.

Bryce, Archibald Hamilton. *First Latin Book.* London: T. Nelson and Sons, 1892.

Buck, William, and B.A. van Nooten. *Ramayana.* Berkeley: University of California Press, 2000.

Buckingham, J.T. "The Wood-Demon," *The New-England Magazine,* Vol. 5, July 1833, page 7. Boston: J.T. Buckingham, 1833.

Buckland, Raymond. *The Weiser Field Guide to Ghosts: Apparitions, Spirits, Spectral Lights and Other Hauntings of History and Legend.* Boston: Weiser, 2009.

Budge, Ernest A. Wallis. *The Babylonian Legends of Creation: And the Fight Between Bel and the Dragon.* New York: Cosimo, 2010.

Budge, Ernest Alfred Thompson Wallis. *Amulets and Superstitions.* Whitefish, Mont.: Kessinger, 2003.

_____. *Babylonian Life and History.* New York: Barnes and Noble, 2005.

Budge, Ernest Alfred Wallis. *The Gods of the Egyptians: or, Studies in Egyptian Mythology.* London: Methuen, 1904.

Buitenen, Johannes, and Adrianus Bernardus. *The Mahābhārata,* Vol. 1. Chicago: University of Chicago Press, 1973.

Bullinger, Heinrich. *Decades of Henry Bullinger,* Vol. 4. Cambridge: Cambridge University Press, 1849.

Bullough, Vern L., and Bonnie Bullough. *Human Sexuality: An Encyclopedia.* Oxfordshire: Taylor and Francis, 1994.

Bumbly, Terence. *The Museum of Unnatural History.* New York: Figment, 2009.

Bunce, Fredrick W. *An Encyclopaedia of Buddhist Deities, Demigods, Godlings, Saints, and Demons with Special Focus on Iconographic Attributes,* Vol. 1. New Delhi: D.K. Printworld, 1994.

_____. *Hindu Deities, Demi-Gods, Godlings, Demons, and Heroes.* New Delhi: D.K. Printworld, 2000.

Bunson, Matthew. *The Vampire Encyclopedia.* New York: Gramercy, 2000.

Burgess, Anthony. *Malayan Trilogy: Time for a Tiger: The Enemy in the Blanket; Beds in the East.* New York: Penguin, 1959.

Burland, Cottie Arthur. *The Gods of Mexico,* Vol. 1967, Part 1. London: Eyre and Spottiswoode, 1967.

Burrell, David James. *The Religions of the World: An Outline of the Great Religious Systems.* Philadelphia: Presbyterian Board of Publication and Sabbath-School Work, 1902.

Burton, Dan, and David Grandy, *Magic, Mystery, and Science: The Occult in Western Civilization.* Bloomington: Indiana University Press, 2003.

Burton, Isabel, Justin Huntly McCarthy, and Sir Richard Francis Burton. *Lady Burton's Edition of Her Husband's Arabian Nights: Translated Literally from the Arabic.* London: Waterlow, 1886.

Burton, Richard F. *Arabian Nights, in 16 Volumes.* New York: Cosimo, 2008.

Bush, Laurence C. *Asian Horror Encyclopedia: Asian Horror Culture in Literature, Manga and Folklore.* Omaha: Writers Club Press, 2001.

Butler, Eliza Marian. *Ritual Magic.* University Park: Penn State Press, 1998.

Caciola, Nancy. *Discerning Spirits: Divine and Demonic Possession in the Middle Ages.* New York: Cornell University Press, 2003.

Caillois, Roger, and Meyer Barash. *Man, Play, and Games.* Champaign: University of Illinois Press, 2001.

Calisch, Edith Lindeman. *Fairy Tales from Grandfather's Big Book: Jewish Legends of Old Retold for Young People.* Springfield: Behrman's House, 1949.

Calmet, Augustin. *Dictionary of the Holy Bible.* Boston: Crocker and Brewster, 1832.

_____. *The Phantom World: Or, the Philosophy of Spirits, Apparitions, Etc.,* Vol. 2; Vol. 42; Vol. 67. London: R. Bentley, 1850.

_____, and Henry Christmas. *The Phantom World; Or, the Philosophy of Spirits, Apparitions, Etc.* London: Richard Bentley, 1850.

Cambridge University Press. *Cambridge Advanced Learner's Dictionary.* Cambridge: Cambridge University Press, 2008.

Cameron, Euan. *Enchanted Europe: Superstition, Reason, and Religion 1250–1750.* New York: Oxford University Press, 2010.

Campbell, John Francis. *Popular Tales of the West Highlands: Orally Collected,* Vol. 4. Paisley: Alexander Gardner, 1893.

Campion-Vincent, Véronique. *Organ Theft Legends.* Jackson: University Press of Mississippi, 2005.

Carey, Bertram Sausmarez, and Henry Newman Tuck. *The Chin Hills: A History of Our People,* Vol. 1. Burma: Superintendent, Government Printing, 1896.

Carlyle, Thomas. "Gods of the Earth: Mythology of Finland," *Fraser's Magazine for Town and Country,* Vol. 55. London: James W. Parker and Sons, 1857.

Carlyon, Richard. *A Guide to the Gods.* London: Heinemann/Quixote, 1981.

Carroll, Peter. *Liber Kaos.* Boston: Weiser, 1992.

Carta, Dalida. *Djinn Summoning.* Raleigh: Lulu, 2008.

Carter, Sheila. *Myth and Superstition in Spanish-Caribbean Literature.* Mona: Department of Spanish, University of the West Indies, 1982.

Carus, Paul. *The History of the Devil and the Idea of Evil: From the Earliest Times to the Present Day.* Chicago: Open Court, 1899.

_____. *The Open Court,* Vol. 35. Chicago: Open Court Publishing, 1921.

_____. *The Open Court,* Vol. 43. Chicago: Open Court Publishing, 1929.

_____. *The Open Court,* Vol. 44. Chicago: Open Court Publishing, 1930.

Cary, Henry, and Herodotus. *Herodotus: A New and Literal Version from the Text of Bache with a Geographical and General Index.* London: Henry G. Bohn, 1848.

Castellani, Aldo, and Albert John Chalmers. *Manual of Tropical Medicine.* N.p., 1913.

Catholic University of America. *The Catholic University Bulletin,* Vol. 3, No. 1. Washington D.C.: Catholic University of America, 1897.

Cavendish, Richard. *The Black Arts.* New York: Perigee, 1983.

_____. *Man, Myth and Magic: An Illustrated Encyclopedia*

of the Supernatural, Vol. 1, Vol. 5, Vol. 7. New York: Marshall Cavendish, 1970.

_____. *The Powers of Evil in Western Religion, Magic and Folk Belief*. London: Routledge, 1975.

Cawthorne, Nigel. *Witches: History of a Persecution*. London: Arcturus, 2005.

Central Conference of American Rabbis, *CCAR Journal*, Vol. 10. New York: Central Conference of American Rabbis, 1962.

Chajes, Jeffrey Howard. *Between Worlds: Dybbuks, Exorcists, and Early Modern Judaism*. Philadelphia: University of Pennsylvania Press, 2003.

Chakravarti, Mahadev. *The Concept of Rudra-Siva Through the Ages*. Delhi: Motilal Banarsidass, 1995.

Chambers, Robert. *The Book of Days: A Miscellany of Popular Antiquities in Connection with the Calendar, Including Anecdote, Biography, and History, Curiosities of Literature and Oddities of Human Life and Character*, Vol. 2. Edinburgh: W. and R. Chambers, 1864.

Chambers, W. and R. *Chambers's Encyclopædia*. London: W. and R. Chambers, 1874.

The Chambers Dictionary. New Delhi: Allied Publishers, 2006.

Chambers's Encyclopaedia: A Dictionary of Universal Knowledge, Vol. 3. London: William and Robert Chambers, Ltd., 1901.

Chamchian, Michael, and John Avtaliantz. *History of Armenia, by Father Michael Chamich: From B.C. 2247 to the Year of Christ 1780, or 1229 of the Armenian Era, Tr. from the Original Armenian, by Johannes Avdall*. Calcutta: Bishop's College Press, 1827.

Chandra, Suresh. *Encyclopaedia of Hindu Gods and Goddesses*. New Delhi: Sarup and Sons, 1998.

Chang, H. C. *Chinese Literature: Popular Fiction and Drama*. Chicago: Aldine, 1973.

Chaplin, James Patrick. *Dictionary of the Occult and Paranormal*. New York: Dell Publishing, 1976.

Chapone, Hester, John Gregory, Hannah More, Edward Moore, M. Peddle, and Jonathan Swift. *The Lady's Pocket Library*. Philadelphia: Mathew Carey, 1809.

Charles, Robert Henry. *The Apocrypha and Pseudepigrapha of the Old Testament*. Oxford: Clarendon, 1893.

_____. *The Book of Enoch*. Palo Alta: Book Tree, 1999.

_____. *The Book of Enoch: One Enoch*. Pomeroy: Health Research Books, 1961.

_____. *Book of Enoch: Together with a Reprint of the Greek Fragments*. Whitefish: Kessinger, 1995.

_____. *The Book of Enoch: Translated from Professor August Dillmann's Ethiopic Text*. Oxford: Clarendon, 1893.

_____. *The Book of the Secrets of Enoch*. London: Clarendon, 1896.

_____. *A Critical and Exegetical Commentary on the Revelation of St. John: With Introduction, Notes, and Indices, Also the Greek Text and English Translation*, Part 1. New York: Charles Scribner and Sons, 1920.

Charlesworth, James H. *The Good and Evil Serpent: How a Universal Symbol Became Christianized*. New Haven: Yale University Press, 2009.

_____. *The Old Testament Pseudepigrapha*, Vol. 2. New York: Doubleday, 1985.

Cheo, Kim Ban, and Muriel Speeden. *Baba Folk Beliefs and Superstitions*. Landmark Books, 1988.

Cheyne, Thomas Kelly. *The Prophecies of Isaiah: A New Translation with Commentary and Appendices*, Vol. 2. London: Kegan, Paul, Trench, 1889.

_____, and John Sutherland Black. *Encyclopaedia Biblica: A Critical Dictionary of the Literary Political and Religious History, The Archaeology, Geography, and Natural History of the Bible*, Vol. 1. London: Adam and Charles Black, 1899.

Chihling, Wang Chen. *Traditional Chinese Tales*. New York: Read Books, 2006.

China Society of Science and Arts. *The China Journal*, Vol. 23. Shanghai: China Journal Publishing, 1935.

Chisholm, Hugh. *The Encyclopedia Britannica: A Dictionary of Arts, Sciences, Literature and General Information*, Vol. 3. New York: Encyclopedia Britannica, 1910.

_____. *The Encyclopædia Britannica: A Dictionary of Arts, Sciences, Literature and General Information*, Vol. 28. New York: Encyclopedia Britannica, 1911.

Choice, Eloise T. *The Secular and the Sacred Harmonized*. Bloomington: AuthorHouse, 2005.

Choksy, Jamsheed Kairshasp. *Evil, Good and Gender: Facets of the Feminine in Zoroastrian Religious History*. New York: Peter Lang, 2002.

Chong-Gossard, James Harvey Kim On. *Gender and Communication in Euripides' Plays: Between Song and Silence*. Leiden: Brill, 2008.

Chopra, Ramesh. *Academic Dictionary of Mythology*. Delhi: Gyan Books, 2005.

The Christian Examiner, Vols. 66–67. Boston: Crosby, Nichols, 1859.

Christiansen, Reidar Thoralf, and Pat Shaw Iversen. *Folktales of Norway*. Chicago: University of Chicago Press, 1964.

Christianson, Eric S. *Ecclesiastes Through the Centuries*. London: Wiley-Blackwell, 2007.

Churchill, Lida A., and Paul Christian. *The History and Practice of Magic*. Whitefish, Kessinger, 1994.

Cirlot, Juan Eduardo. *A Dictionary of Symbols*. North Chemsford: Courier Dover, 2002.

Clark, I. Edward. *Royal Secret*. Whitefish: Kessinger, 1995.

Classical Manual: Being a Mythological, Historical, and Geographical Commentary on Pope's Homer and Dryden's Aeneid of Virgil. London: John Murray, 1833.

Clemen, Carl. *Primitive Christianity and its Non-Jewish Sources*. Edinburgh: T. and T. Clark, 1912.

Clifford, Hugh Charles, and Frank Athelstane Swettenham. *A Dictionary of the Malay Language*. Taiping: Government Printing Office, 1894.

Clifford, Sather. *The Malevolent Koklir: Iban Concepts of Sexual Peril and the Dangers of Childbirth*. Leiden: Bijdragen tot de Taal-Land-en Volkenkunde, 1978.

Clough, B. *Sinhalese English Dictionary*. New Delhi: Asian Educational Services, 1997.

Clough, Benjamin Crocker. *The American Imagination at Work: Tall Tales and Folk Tales*. New York: A.A. Knopf, 1947.

Cobb, William Frederick. *Origines Judaicae: An Inquiry into Heathen Faiths as Affecting the Birth and Growth of Judaism*. London: A.D. Innes, 1895.

Codrington, Robert Henry. *The Melanesians: Studies in Their Anthropology and Folk-Lore*. Oxford: Clarendon Press, 1891.

Cohn, Norman. *Cosmos, Chaos, and the World to Come: The Ancient Roots of Apocalyptic Faith*. New Haven: Yale University Press, 2001.

Cole, Fay-Cooper. *Traditions of the Tinguian: A Study in Philippine Folk-Lore*. New York: Read Books, 2010.

Coleman, Christopher. *Ghosts and Haunts of Tennessee*. Winston-Salem: John F. Blair, 2011.

Coleman, J.A. *The Dictionary of Mythology: An A-Z of Themes, Legends and Heroes*. London: Capella, 2007.

Collin de Plancy, Jacques-Albin-Simon. *Dictionary of Witchcraft*. New York: Philosophical Library, 1965.
_____. *Dictionnaire Infernal*. Paris: Slatkine, 1993.

Colum, Padraic. *Myths of the World*. New York: Grosset and Dunlap, 1978.

Conner, Randy P., Gloria Anzaldúa, David Hatfield Sparks, and Mariya Sparks. *Cassell's Encyclopedia of Queer Myth, Symbol, and Spirit: Gay, Lesbian, Bisexual, and Transgender Lore*. London: Cassell, 1997.

Conway, D.J. *Guides, Guardians and Angels: Enhance Relationships with Your Spiritual Companions*. St. Paul: Llewellyn, 2009.
_____. *Magickal Mystical Creatures: Invite Their Powers Into Your Life*. Saint Paul: Llewellyn, 2001.

Conway, Moncure Daniel. *Demonology and Devil-Lore*, Vol. 1. New York: Henry Holt, 1881.
_____. *Demonology and Devil-Lore*, Vol. 2. New York: Henry Holt, 1879.

Conybeare, Frederick C. "The Testament of Solomon," *The Jewish Quarterly Review*, Vol. 11, October 1889, page 1–45. New York: Macmillan, 1899.

Cook, Albert Stanburrough. *Exercises in Old English: Based Upon the Prose Texts of the Author's "First Book in Old English."* Boston: Ginn, 1895.

Cooley, Arnold James. *Dictionary of English Language Exhibiting Orthography, Pronunciation and Definition of Words*. London: W. and R. Chambers, 1861.

Coomaraswamy, Ananda K., and Sister Nivedita. *Myths of the Hindus and Buddhists*. Whitefish: Kessinger, 2003.

Cooper, J.C. *Fairy Tales: Allegories of the Inner Life*. Wellingborough: Aquarian Press, 1983.

Cooper, Jean C., and Ebenezer Cobham Brewer. *Brewer's Book of Myth and Legend*. London: Helicon, 1995.

Cor de Vaan, Michiel Arnoud. *The Avestan Vowels*, Vol. 12. New York: Rodopi, 2003.

Corbey, Raymond, and Joep Leerssen. *Alterity, Identity, Image: Selves and Others in Society and Scholarship*. New York: Rodopi, 1991.

Cornelius, Izak. *The Many Faces of the Goddess: The Iconography of the Syro-Palestinian Goddesses Anat, Astarte, Qedeshet, and Asherah c. 1500–1000 BCE*. Fribourg: Academic Press, 2004.

Cotterell, Arthur. *A Dictionary of World Mythology*. New York: Perigee Books, 1982.

Coumont, Jean-Pierre. *Demonology and Witchcraft: An Annotated Bibliography: With Related Works on Magic, Medicine, Superstition, Etc.* Houten: Hes and de Graaf, 2004.

Couperus, Louis, E.M. Beekman, and Alexander Teixeira De Mattos. *The Hidden Force*. Amherst: University of Massachusetts Press, 1990.

Cowan, Frank. *Curious Facts in the History of Insects: Including Spiders and Scorpions. A Complete Collection of the Legends, Superstitions, Beliefs, and Ominous Signs Connected with Insects; Together with Their Uses in Medicine, Art, and as Food; And a Summary of their Remarkable Injuries and Appearances*. Philadelphia: J.B. Lippincott, 1865.

Cowan, James. "The Patu-Paiarehe: Notes on Maori Folktales of the Fairy People," *The Journal of the Polynesian Society*, Vol. 30. New Plymouth: Polynesian Society, 1921.

Cox, George William. *The Mythology of the Aryan Nations*. London: Kegan Paul, Trench, Trübner, 1887.

Cox, Simon. *Decoding the Lost Symbol: The Unauthorized Expert Guide to the Facts Behind the Fiction*. New York: Simon and Schuster, 2009.

Coxwell, Charles Fillingham. *Siberian and Other Folktales: Primitive Literature of the Empire of the Tsars*. London: C. W. Daniel, 1925.

Craig, Edward. *Routledge Encyclopedia of Philosophy: Index*, Vol. 10. London: Taylor and Francis, 1998.

Craig, R.D. *Dictionary of Polynesian Mythology*. Westport: Greenwood, 1989.

Cramer, Marc. *The Devil Within*. London: W.H. Allen, 1979.

Crane, Arthur. *The Great Exorcism*. San Francisco: Arthur Crane, 1915.

Crawford, John Martin. *The Kalevala: The Epic Poem of Finland*, Vol. 2. New York: John B. Alden, 1888.

Crisafulli, Chuck, and Kyra Thompson. *Go to Hell: A Heated History of the Underworld*. New York: Simon and Schuster, 2005.

Crone, Anna Lisa, Nicole Boudreau, Sarah Krive, and Catherine O'Neil. *Poetics, Self, Place: Essays in Honor of Anna Lisa Crone*. Bloomington: Slavica, 2007.

Crooke, William. *The Popular Religion and Folk-lore of Northern India*, Vol. 1 and Vol. 2. Westminster: Archibald Constable, 1896.
_____, and Reginald Edward Enthoven. *Religion and Folklore of Northern India*. London: Oxford University Press, H. Milford, 1926.

Crowley, Aleister. *The Book of the Goetia of Solomon the King*. New York: Equinox, 1976.
_____. *The Confessions of Aleister Crowley: An Autohagiography*. New York: Penguin, 1989.
_____. *777 Revised: Vel, Prolegomena Symbolica Ad Systemam Sceptico–Mysticae Viae Explicandae, Fundamentum Hieroglyphicum Sanctissimorum Scientiae Summae*. York Beach: S. Weiser, 1970.
_____, Mary Desti, and Leila Waddell. *Magick: Liber ABA, Book Four*, Parts 1–4. Boston: Weiser, 1998.
_____, Lon Milo DuQuette, and Christopher S. Hyatt. *Aleister Crowley's Illustrated Goetia: Sexual Evocation*. Las Vegas: New Falcon, 1992.
_____, and Samuel Liddell MacGregor Mathers. *The Goetia: the Lesser Key of Solomon the King: Lemegeton-Clavicula Salomonis Regis, book one*. Boston: Weiser, 1995.
_____, and Israel Regardie. *777 And Other Qabalistic Writings of Aleister Crowley*. Boston: Weiser, 1986.

Csonka-Takács, Eszter. *Witchcraft Mythologies and Persecutions*. Budapest: Central European University Press, 2008.

Cuevas, Bryan J. *Travels in the Netherworld: Buddhist Popular Narratives of Death and the Afterlife in Tibet*. New York: Oxford University Press, 2008.

Cuhulain, Kerr. *Witch Hunts: Out of the Broom Closet*. Darlington: Spiral, 2005.

Culianu, Ioan P. *Eros and Magic in the Renaissance*. Chicago: University of Chicago Press, 1987.

Cumont, Franz Valery Marie. *Afterlife in Roman Paganism*. New Haven: Yale University Press, 1922.

Cunningham, Graham. *Deliver Me from Evil: Mesopotamian Incantations, 2500–1500 BC*. Rome: Biblical Institute, 1997, 1997.

Curley, Richard T. *Elders, Shades, and Women: Ceremonial Change in Lango, Uganda*. Berkeley: University of California Press, 1973.

Curran, Bob. *Encyclopedia of the Undead: A Field Guide to Creatures that Cannot Rest in Peace*. Pompton Plains: Career Press, 2006.
_____. *Vampires: A Field Guide to the Creatures that Stalk the Night*. Pompton Plains: Career Press, 2005.

Curry, William, Jun. and Co. *The Dublin University Mag-*

azine, Vol. 66, July to December 1865. Dublin: Alexander Thom, 1865.

Curtis, Vesta Sarkhosh. *Persian Myths*. Austin: University of Texas Press, 1993.

Czigány, Lóránt. *The Oxford History of Hungarian Literature from the Earliest Times to the Present*. New York: Clarendon Press, 1984.

Daigaku, Nanzan, Jinruigaku Kenkyūjo, and Nanzan Shūkyō Bunka Kenkyūjo. *Asian Folklore Studies*, Vol. 56. Madras: Asian Folklore Institute, 1997.

Dalley S. *Myths of Mesopotamia*. New York: Oxford University Press, 1998.

Dalton, Bill. *Indonesia Handbook*. Chico: Moon Publications, 1985.

Daly, Kathleen N., and Marian Rengel. *Greek and Roman Mythology A to Z*. New York: Infobase, 2003.

Dan, Joseph. *Jewish Mysticism: The Middle Ages*. Northvale: Jason Aronson, 1998.

_____, and Ronald C. Kiener. *The Early Kabbalah*. New York: Paulist Press, 1986.

Dange, Sadashiv Ambadas. *Myths from the Mahābhārata: Quest for Immortality*. New Delhi: Aryan Books, 1997.

Dange, Sindhu S. *The Bhāgavata Purāṇa: Mytho-Social Study*. Delhi: Ajanta, 1984.

Daniélou, Alain. *The Myths and Gods of India: The Classic Work on Hindu Polytheism from the Princeton Bollingen Series*. Rochester: Inner Traditions/Bear, 1991.

Daniels, Cora Linn Morrison, and Charles McClellan Stevens. *Encyclopaedia of Superstitions, Folklore, and the Occult Sciences of the World: A Comprehensive Library of Human Belief and Practice in the Mysteries of Life*, Vol. 3. Milwaukee: J.H. Yewdale and Sons, 1903.

Darmesteter, James. *Avesta Khorda Avesta: Book of Common Prayer*. Whitefish: Kessinger, 2004.

_____. *Vol. 3 of Sacred Books of the East: The Zend-Avesta*. New York: Christian Literature, 1898.

Das, Abinas Chandra. *Rgvedic India*. Delhi: Motilal Banarsidass, 1971.

Das, Sarat Chandra. *Tibetan-English Dictionary*. Delhi: Motilal Banarsidass, 2004.

Davenport, Richard Alfred. *The Koran: Commonly Called the Alcoran of Mohammed*. London: W. Tegg, 1867.

_____. *Sketches of Imposture, Deception, and Credulity*. London: T. Tegg and Son, 1837.

Davids, Thomas William Rhys, and William Stede. *The Pali-English Dictionary*. New Delhi: Asian Educational Services, 2004.

Davidson, Gustav. *A Dictionary of Angels: Including the Fallen Angels*. New York: Free Press, 1971.

Davies, Owen. *Grimoires: A History of Magic Books*. London: Oxford University Press, 2009.

_____. *Witchcraft, Magic and Culture, 1736–1951*. Manchester: Manchester University Press, 1999.

Davies, Stevan L. *The Secret Book of John: The Gnostic Gospel Annotated and Explained*. Woodstock: SkyLight Paths, 2005.

Davies, Thomas Lewis Owen, and James Orchard Halliwell-Phillipps. *A Supplementary English Glossary*. London: George Bell and Sons, 1881.

Davies, Thomas Witton. *Magic, Divination, and Demonology Among the Hebrews and Their Neighbours: Including an Examination of Biblical References and of the Biblical Terms*. London: J. Clarke, 1898.

Davies, William David, and Louis Finkelstein. *The Cambridge History of Judaism: Introduction; The Persian Period*. Cambridge: Cambridge University Press, 1984.

Davis, Frederick Hadland. *Myths and Legends of Japan*. North Chemsford: Courier Dover, 1992.

Davis, John D. *Genesis and Semitic Tradition*. New York: Charles Scribner's Sons, 1894.

Davis, Stephan K. *The Antithesis of the Ages: Paul's Reconfiguration of Torah*. Washington, DC: Catholic Biblical Association of America, 2002.

Daw, Margery. "100 Questions," *McBrides Monthly Magazine*, Vol. 43. Philadelphia: J.B. Lippincott, 1889.

Dawes, Elizabeth Anna Sophia. *The Pronunciation of the Greek Aspirates*. London: D. Nutt, 1895.

de Barandiarán, José Miguel, and Jesús Altuna. *Selected Writings of José Miguel de Barandiarán: Basque Prehistory and Ethnography*. Reno: University of Nevada Press, 2009.

De Claremont, Lewis. *The Ancient's Book of Magic: Containing Secret Records of the Procedure and Practice of the Ancient Masters and Adepts 1940*. Whitefish: Kessinger, 2004.

De Colange, Leo. *The Standard Encyclopedia: a Complete Library and Universal Reference Book with Illustrations and Pronunciation*. New York: The Christian herald, 1896.

De Givry, Grillot. *A Pictorial Anthology of Witchcraft, Magic and Alchemy with 376 Illustrations*. Whitefish: Kessinger, 2006.

_____. *Witchcraft, Magic and Alchemy*. North Chemsford: Courier Dover, 1971.

De Grummond, Nancy Thomson. *Etruscan Myth, Sacred History, and Legend*. Philadelphia: University of Pennsylvania Museum of Archaeology, 2006.

_____. *A Guide to Etruscan Mirrors*. Tallahassee: Archaeological News, 1982.

_____, and Erika Simon. *The Religion of the Etruscans*. Austin: University of Texas Press, 2006.

De Gubernatis, Angelo. *Zoological Mythology: Or, The Legends of Animals*. London: Trübner, 1872.

De Jésus-Marie, Bruno. *Satan*. New York: Sheed and Ward, 1952.

De Laurence, Lauron William. *Ars Goetia, the First Book of the Lemegeton, the Lesser Key of Solomon, Goetia: The Book of Evil Spirits Contains Two Hundred Diagrams and Seals for Invocation Translated from Ancient Manuscripts in the British Museum, London, Only Authorized Edition Extant*. Chicago: De Laurence, 1916.

_____. *The Lesser Key of Solomon, Goetia: The Book of evil Spirits Contains Two Hundred Diagrams and Seals for Invocation, Translated from Ancient Manuscripts in the British Museum, London, the Only Authorized Edition Extant*. Chicago: De Laurence, Scott, 1916.

_____. *Occult Secrets: Hypnotism, Magnetism, Crystal Gazing, Spiritual Clairvoyance, and Emotional Control*. Whitefish: Kessinger, 2005.

De Puy, William Harrison. *The Encyclopædia Britannica: A Dictionary of Arts, Sciences, and General Literature; the R. S. Peale Reprint, with New Maps and Original American Articles*, Vol. 7. Chicago: Werner, 1893.

De Quincey, Thomas. *The Works of Thomas De Quincey: Suspiria De Profundis, Being a Sequel to the Confessions; Memorial Chronology*, Vol. 16. Whitefish: Kessinger, 2006.

De Sahagún, Bernardino, H.B. Nicholson and Thelma D. Sullivan. *Primeros Memoriales*. Norman: University of Oklahoma Press, 1997.

De Spina, Alphonsus. *Fortalitium Fidei*. Norimbergae: Antonius Koberger, 1494.

de Voragine, Jacobus. *The Golden Legend: Or, Lives of the Saints, as Englished by William Caxton*, Vol. 7. London: J.M. Dent, 1900.

Debus, Allen G. *Alchemy and Early Modern Chemistry: Papers from Ambix.* Huddersfield: Jeremy Mills, 2004.

Deck-Partyka, Alicja. *Poland, a Unique Country and Its People.* Bloomington: AuthorHouse, 2006.

Demetrio, Francisco R. *Encyclopedia of Philippine Folk Beliefs and Customs.* Cincinnati: Xavier University, 1991.

Dendle, Peter. *Satan Unbound: The Devil in Old English Narrative Literature.* Toronto: University of Toronto Press, 2001.

Dennis, Geoffrey W. *The Encyclopedia of Jewish Myth, Magic and Mysticism.* St. Paul: Llewellyne, 2007.

Dennys, Nicholas Belfield. *A Descriptive Dictionary of British Malaya.* London: London and China Telegraph Office, 1894.

Dennys, Rodney. *The Heraldic Imagination.* Barrie and Jenkins, 1975.

DePorte, Anton W. *Lithuanaia in the Last 30 Years.* New Haven: Human Relations Area Files, 1955.

Dequeker, Luc, and Werner Verbeke. *The Expulsion of the Jews and their Emigration to the Southern Low Countries: 15th–16th Century.* Leuven: Leuven University Press, 1998.

Dhalla, Maneckji Nusservanji. *History of Zoroastrianism.* New York: AMS Press, 1977.

_____. *Zoroastrian Theology from the Earliest Times to the Present Day.* New York: AMS Press, 1972.

_____. *Zoroastrian Theology: From the Earliest Times to the Present Day.* Whitefish: Kessinger, 2006.

Diagram Group. *The Dictionary of Unfamiliar Words: Over 10,000 Common and Confusing Words Explained.* New York: Skyhorse, 2008.

_____. *Little Giant Encyclopedia: Spells and Magic.* New York: Sterling, 2007.

Dickens, Charles. *All the Year Round: A Weekly Journal*, Vol. 75. London: The Office, 1894.

Dimmitt, Cornelia, and Johannes Adrianus Bernardus Buitene. "Putana: The Child Killer." *Classical Hindu Mythology: A Reader in the Sanskrit Purāṇas.* Philadelphia: Temple University Press, 1978.

Dingwall, Eric John. *Some Human Oddities: Studies in the Queer, the Uncanny.* New York: University Books, 1962.

D'Iseaeli, E. "The Midland Ocean," *The New World*, Vol. 6. January 7, 1843, page 72. New York: J. Winchester, 1843.

Dix, Tennille. *The Black Baron: The Strange Life of Gilles De Rais.* Whitefish: Kessinger, 2005.

Dixon-Kennedy, Mike. *Encyclopedia of Russian and Slavic Myth and Legend.* Santa Barbara: ABC-CLIO, 1998.

Djiwandono, Mun Cheong Yong Po Soedjati. *Journal of the Polynesian Society*, Vol. 15. Charleston: BiblioBazaar, 2009.

Dobbins, Frank S. *False Gods or the Idol Worship of the World.* Whitefish: Kessinger, 2006.

Dodson, Stephen, and Robert Vanderplank. *Uglier Than a Monkey's Armpit: Untranslatable Insults, Put-Downs, and Curses from Around the World.* New York: Penguin, 2009.

Dogra, R.C. *Thought Provoking Hindu Names.* Delhi: Star, 1999.

Doirievich, Tihomir R. "Doghead in Our People's Beliefs," *Srpski etnografski zbornik 66*: 106–107, 1959.

Doniger, Wendy. *Britannica Encyclopedia of World Religions.* Chicago: Encyclopædia Britannica, 2006.

_____. *Hindu Myths: A Sourcebook.* New York: Penguin Classics, 1975.

_____. *Merriam-Webster's Encyclopedia of World Religions.* Springfield: Merriam-Webster, 1999.

Donovan, Frank Robert. *Never on a Broomstick.* Harrisburg: Stackpole Books, 1971.

Dooling, D.M., and James R. Walker. *The Sons of the Wind: The Sacred Stories of the Lakota.* New York: Parabola Books, 1984.

Dooling, Richard. *White Man's Grave.* New York: Macmillan, 1995.

Doresse, Jean. *The Secret Books of the Egyptian Gnostics: An Introduction to the Gnostic Coptic Manuscripts Discovered at Chenoboskion.* New York: Viking Press, 1960.

Douglas, Mary, Cyril Daryll Forde, and Phyllis Mary Kaberry. *Man in Africa.* New York: Anchor Books, 1971.

Dowley, Tim. *Introduction to the History of Christianity.* Minneapolis: Fortress Press, 2006.

Dowman, Keith. *The Power-Places of Central Tibet: The Pilgrim's Guide.* Kathmandu: Vajra, 2008.

Downer, McNeil. *Ghastly Ghost Stories.* New York: Wings Books, 1993.

Downie, Robert Angus. *Anthologia Anthropologica: The Native Races of Asia and Europe.* London: P. Lund, Humphries, 1939.

Downs, James F. *The Two Worlds of the Washo: An Indian Tribe of California and Nevada.* New York: Holt, Rinehart and Winston, 1966.

Dowson, John. *A Classical Dictionary of Hindu Mythology and Religion, Geography, History, and Literature.* London: Trübner, 1870.

Drew, A.J.A *Wiccan Bible: Exploring the Mysteries of the Craft from Birth to Summerland.* Pompton Plains: Career Press, 2003.

Drogin, Marc. *Medieval Calligraphy: Its History and Technique.* Montclair: Abner Schram, 1980.

Drower, E.S. *The Mandaeans of Iraq and Iran.* Oxford: Clarendon, 1937.

Drury, Nevill. *The Dictionary of the Esoteric: 3000 Entries on the Mystical and Occult Traditions.* Delhi: Motilal Banarsidass, 2004.

Du Chaillu, Paul Belloni. *The Viking Age: The Early History, Manners, and Customs of the Ancestors of the English Speaking Nations.* New York: Charles Scribner's Sons, 1889.

Dublin University Magazine, Vol. 70. Dublin: George Herbert, 1867.

DuBose, Hampden C. *The Dragon, Image, and Demon or The Three Religions of China, Confucianism, Buddhism and Taoism: Giving an Account of the Mythology, Idolatry, and Demonolatry of the Chinese.* New York: A.C. Armstrong and Son, 1887.

Dumas, Alexandre. *The Crimes of Urbain Grandier, and Others.* London: Macmillan, 1907.

Dumas, François Ribadeau. *Histoire de la Magie.* Paris: P. Belfond, 1973.

Dunderberg, Ismo. *Beyond Gnosticism: Myth, Lifestyle, and Society in the School of Valentinus.* New York: Columbia University Press, 2008.

Dunglison, Robley. *Medical Lexicon: A Dictionary of Medical Science: Containing a Concise Explanation of the Various Subjects and Terms of Anatomy, Physiology, Pathology, Hygiene, Therapeutics With the Accentuation and Etymology of the Terms, and the French and Other Synonyms.* Philadelphia: H.C. Lea, 1868.

Dunlap, Samuel Fales. "The Origin of Ancient Names of Countries, Cities, Gods, Etc.," *The Christian Examiner and Religious Miscellany*, July 1865, pages 75–98. Boston: Crosby, Nichols, 1856.

_____. *Sod: The Son of The Man.* London: Williams and Norgate, 1861.

Dunwich, Gerina. *The Wicca Garden: A Modern Witch's Book of Magickal and Enchanted Herbs and Plants*. New York: Citadel Press, 1996.

_____. *A Witch's Guide to Ghosts and the Supernatural*. Pompton Plains: Career Press, 2002.

DuQuette, Lon Milo. *Angels, Demons and Gods of the New Millennium*. Boston: Weiser, 1997.

_____. *The Key to Solomon's Key: Secrets of Magic and Masonry*. San Francisco: CCC Publishing, 2006.

Duston, Allen, and the Art Services International. *The Invisible Made Visible: Angels from the Vatican*. Alexandria: Art Services International, 1998.

Dwyer, Graham. *The Divine and the Demonic: Supernatural Affliction and its Treatment in North India*. New York: Psychology Press, 2003.

Dyson, Verne. *Forgotten Tales of Ancient China*. Shanghai: Commercial Press, 1927.

Eberhart, George M. *Mysterious Creatures: A Guide to Cryptozoology*. Santa Barbara: ABC-CLIO, 2002.

Eckley, Grace. *Children's Lore in Finnegans Wake*. Syracuse: Syracuse University Press, 1985.

Eco, Umberto. *The Infinity of Lists: An Illustrated Essay*. New York: Rizzoli, 2009.

Edgar, Frank, et al. *Hausa Readings: Selections from Edgar's Tatsuniyoyi*. Madison: University of Wisconsin Press, 1968.

Editors of Thelema Press. *Gnostic Kabbalah 1: The World of Klipoth*. Brooklyn: Glorian, 2006.

Edwardes, Allen, and D.A. Kinsley. *The Jewel in the Lotus: A Historical Survey of the Sexual Culture of the East*. New York: Julian Press, 1959.

Edwards, J.C.W. "The Demoniacal Possessions of the New Testament Considered in the Light of the Hebrew Demonology," *The Melbourne Review*, Vol. 7, No. 27, July 1882. Melbourne: Walker, Mav, 1882.

Eliade, Mircea, and Charles J. Adams. *The Encyclopedia of Religion*, Vol. 1 and Vol. 2. New York: Macmillan, 1987.

Ellwood, Robert S. *Words of the World's Religions: An Anthology*. Englewood Cliffs: Prentice-Hall, 1977.

Elmer, Peter. *Challenges to Authority*. London: Yale University Press, 2000.

Elsie, Robert. *A Dictionary of Albanian Religion, Mythology, and Folk Culture*. New York: NYU Press, 2001.

Ember, Carol R., and Melvin Ember. *Encyclopedia of Medical Anthropology*. Berlin: Springer, 2004.

Encausse, Dr. Gerard (Papus). *The Qabalah: Secret Tradition of the West*. Boston: Weiser, 2000.

Encyclopædia Britannica, Vol. 1. Chicago: Encyclopædia Britannica, 1973.

_____. 11th edition, Vol. 19. (*A Dictionary of Arts, Sciences, Literature and General Information*). New York: Encyclopædia Britannica, 1911.

_____. *Encyclopedia of World Religions*. Chicago: Encyclopædia Britannica, 2009.

Encyclopædia Metropolitana; or, System of Universal Knowledge. Glasgow: Richard Griffin, 1855.

Encyclopædia Metropolitana; or, Universal Dictionary of Knowledge, ed. by E. Smedley, Hugh J. Rose and Henry J. Rose. London: B. Fellows, 1845.

Endicott, Kirk Michael. *An Analysis of Malay Magic*. London: Clarendon, 1970.

Ennemoser, Joseph. *The History of Magic*, Vol. 2. London: Henry G. Bohn, 1854.

Erdoes, Richard, and Alfonso Ortíz. *American Indian Myths and Legends*. New York: Random House, 1984.

Eubank, John W. *Secrets of the Bible "Unlocked."* Victoria: Trafford, 2005.

Euripides, and Michael R. Halleran. *The Heracles of Euripides*. Cambridge: Focus Information Group, 1988.

Evans, Roderick L. *Prophetic Ministry, Misery, and Mishaps: Rediscovering the Purpose of the Prophetic Gifts; Understanding the Pitfalls of Prophetic Ministry*. Camden: Kingdom Builders, 2005.

Evans, William A. *The Mayaad*. New York: Manyland, 1983.

Evans-Wentz, Walter Yeeling. *The Fairy-faith in Celtic Countries*. London: H. Frowde, 1911.

Eve, Eric. *The Jewish Context of Jesus' Miracles*. London: Continuum International, 2002.

Ewert, Alfred. *French Studies*, Vols. 7–8. Oxford: B. Blackwell, 1953.

Faber, George Stanley. *The Many Mansions of the House of the Father, Scripturally Discussed and Practically Considered*. London: 1854.

_____. *The Origin of Pagan Idolatry Ascertained from Historical Testimony and Circumstantial Evidence*, Vol. 2. London: F. and C. Rivingtons, 1816.

Facaros, Dana, and Michael Pauls. *Bilbao and the Basque Lands*. London: New Holland, 2008.

"Facts Relative to the State of the Heathen," *The Missionary Magazine*, June 21, 1802, pages 235–9, Edinburgh: J. Ritchie.

Fahlbusch, Erwin. *The Encyclopedia of Christianity*, Vol. 5. Grand Rapids: Wm. B. Eerdmans, 2008.

Fansler, Dean Spouill. *Filipino Popular Tale*. Charleston: BiblioBazaar, 2009.

Farmer, Hugh. *A Dissertation on Miracles: Designed to Show That They are Arguments of a Divine Interposition and Absolute Proofs of the Mission and Doctrine of a Prophet*. London: T. Cadell, 1810.

Faron, Louis C. *The Mapuche Indians of Chile*. New York: Holt, Rinehart and Winston, 1968.

Fauth, Wolfgang. "Ssm bn Pdrsa." *Zeitschrift der Deutschen Morgenlandischen Gesellschaft*, Vol. CXX, p. 229f, Wiesbaden: Germany, 1971.

Fear, A.T. *Rome and Baetica: Urbanization in Southern Spain c. 50 BC–AD 150*. New York: Oxford University Press, 1996.

Featherman, Americus. *Social History of the Races of Mankind*. London: Trübner, 1890.

Feller, Danielle. *The Sanskrit Epics' Representation of Vedic Myths*. Delhi: Motilal Banarsidass, 2004.

Fernández-Armesto, Felipe. *World of Myths*. Austin: University of Texas Press, 2004.

Ficowski, Jerzy. *The Gypsies in Poland: History and Customs*. Warsaw: Interpress, 1989.

Field, Henry. *Contributions to the Anthropology of the Caucasus*. Cambridge: Peabody Museum, 1953.

Findlen, Paula. *Athanasius Kircher: The Last Man who Knew Everything*. London: Psychology Press, 2004.

Finkel, Irving L., and Markham J. Geller. *Disease in Babylonia*. Leiden: Brill, 2007.

_____, and _____. *Sumerian Gods and Their Representations*. Groningen: Styx, 1997.

Finnegan, Robert Emmett. *Christ and Satan: A Critical Edition*. Waterloo: Wilfrid Laurier University Press, 1977.

Fishbane, Michael. *The Great Dragon Battle and the Talmudic Redaction*. Cambridge: Harvard University Press, 1998.

Fisher, James F. *Himalayan Anthropology: The Indo-Tibetan Interface*. New York: Walter de Gruyter, 1978.

Fisher, William Bayne, and Ilya Gershevitch. *The Cambridge History of Iran*. Cambridge: Cambridge University Press, 1985.

Fitzhugh, William W., Aron Crowell, and the National Museum of Natural History. *Crossroads of Continents: Cultures of Siberia and Alaska.* Washington, DC: Smithsonian Institution Press, 1988.

Flamel, Nicholas. *Nicholas Flamel and the Philosopher's Stone.* Whitefish: Kessinger, 2005.

Flaubert, Gustave. *Works,* Vol. 9. Akron: St. Dunstan Society, 1904.

Fleay, F.G. "On the Motive of Shakespeare's Sonnets: A Defense of his Morality," *Macmillan's Magazine, Vol. 31.* London: Macmillan, 1875, page 433–45

Fleg, Edmond. *The Life of Solomon.* New York: E.P. Dutton, 1930.

Fletcher, Roland S. *Hausa Sayings and Folklore.* Whitefish: Kessinger, 2003.

Fogelson, Raymond D., and Richard Newbold Adams. *The Anthropology of Power: Ethnographic Studies from Asia, Oceania, and the New World.* New York: Academic Press, 1977.

Foley, John Miles. *A Companion to Ancient Epic.* London: Wiley-Blackwell, 2005.

"Folk Books of France," *The Dublin University Magazine,* Vol. 66, November 1865, pages 516–32. Dublin: George Herbert, 1865.

Folkard, Richard. *Plant Lore, Legends and Lyrics: Embracing the Myths, Traditions, Superstitions, and Folk-Lore of the Plant Kingdom.* London: Sampson Low, Marston, Searle, and Rivington, 1884.

Folklore Society (Great Britain). *County Folk-lore,* Vol. 49. London: David Nutt, 1903.

_____. *Folklore: A Quarterly Review of Myth, Tradition, Institution and Custom,* Vol. 3. London: David Nutt, 1892.

_____. *Folk-lore Journal,* Vol. 7. London: Elliot Stock, 1889.

_____. *Folk-lore Journal,* Vol. 9. London: Elliot Stock, 1898.

_____. *Folk-lore,* Vol. 11. London: Folklore Society, 1900.

Fontenrose, Joseph Eddy. *Python: A Study of Delphic Myth and its Origins.* Berkeley: University of California Press, 1980.

Forbes, Duncan. *Dictionary, Hindustani and English: Accompanied by a Reversed Dictionary, English and Hindustani.* London: William H. Allen, 1858.

Ford, Michael. *The Bible of the Adversary.* Raleigh: Lulu, 2008.

_____. *Book of the Witch Moon,* Choronzon edition. Raleigh: Lulu, 2006.

_____. *The First Book of Luciferian Tarot.* Raleigh: Lulu, 2008.

_____. *Gates of Dozak.* Raleigh: Lulu, 2008.

_____. *Liber Hvhi.* Raleigh: Lulu, 2005.

_____. *Luciferian Witchcraft.* Raleigh: Lulu, 2005.

Forde, Cyril Daryll, Wendy James, and the International African Institute. *African Worlds: Studies in the Cosmological Ideas and Social Values of African Peoples; Classics in African Anthropology.* Hamburg: LIT Verlag Berlin-Hamburg-Münster, 1999.

Fordham, Michael, and Gerhard Adler. *Collected Works: Psychology and Religion, West and East.* New York: Pantheon, 1966.

Foreign Quarterly Review, Vols. 24–25. New York: Jemima M. Manson, 1840.

Fornander, Abraham. *An Account of the Polynesian Race: Its Origins and Migrations, and the Ancient History of the Hawaiian People to the Times of Kamehameha I.* Rutland: Charles E. Tuttle, 1969.

Forrest, M. Isidora. *Isis Magic: Cultivating a Relationship with the Goddess of 10,000 Names.* Saint Paul: Llewellyn, 2001.

Forsyth, J.S. *Demonologia.* London: John Bumpas, 1827.

Forsyth, Neil. *The Old Enemy: Satan and the Combat Myth.* Princeton: Princeton University Press, 1989.

Fossum, Jarl Egil. *The Name of God and the Angel of the Lord: The Origins of the Idea of Intermediation in Gnosticism.* Utrecht: Drukkerij Elinkwijk, 1982.

Fowler, Henry Watson, and Francis George Fowler. *The King's English.* Oxford: Clarendon Press, 1906.

Fox, Susan Leading, and Lisa J. Lefler. *Under the Rattlesnake: Cherokee Health and Resiliency.* Tuscaloosa: University of Alabama Press, 2009.

France, Anatole. *On Life and Letters: Works, in an English Translation,* Vol. 25. London: John Lane the Bodley Head, 1922.

Frankfurter, David. *Evil Incarnate: Rumors of Demonic Conspiracy and Ritual Abuse in History.* Princeton: Princeton University Press, 2006.

Franklyn, Julian. *A Survey of the Occult.* Whitefish: Kessinger, 2003.

Fraser, Thomas M. *Rusembilan: A Malay Fishing Village in Southern Thailand.* Ithaca: Cornell University Press, 1962.

Frazer, James George. *The Golden Bough: A Study in Magic and Religion,* Vol. 6. New York: Macmillan, 1919.

_____. *The Golden Bough: A Study in Magic and Religion,* Vol. 9. New York: Macmillan, 1913.

Frede, Dorothea, and Burkhard Reis. *Body and Soul in Ancient Philosophy.* New York: Walter de Gruyter, 2009.

Frédéric, Louis. *Japan Encyclopedia.* Cambridge: Harvard University Press, 2005.

Freeman, James M., and Harold J. Chadwick. *The New Manners and Customs of the Bible.* Alachua: Bridge Logos Foundation, 1998.

Frey, Joseph Samuel C.F. *A Hebrew, Latin, and English Dictionary.* London: Gale and Fenner, 1815.

Fröhlich, Ida. *Time and Times and Half a Time: Historical Consciousness in the Jewish Literature of the Persian and Hellenistic Eras: Issue 19 of Journal for the Study of the Pseudepigrapha.* London: Continuum, 1996.

Froissart, Jean. *Stories from Froissart.* New York: Macmillan, 1899.

Fukuoka, Yasunori, and Tom Gill. *Lives of Young Koreans in Japan.* Melbourne: Trans Pacific Press, 2000.

Fusco, S. *Insegnamenti Magici Della Golden Dawn: Rituali, Documenti Segreti, Testi Dottrinali.* Rome: Edizioni Mediterranee, 2007.

Gager, John G. *Curse Tablets and Binding Spells from the Ancient World.* New York: Oxford University Press, 1999.

Garg, Gaṅga-macron] R[a-macron]m. *Encyclopaedia of the Hindu World.* Delhi: Concept, 1992.

_____. *Encyclopaedia of the Hindu World,* Vol. 2. Delhi: Concept, 1992.

Garnier, John. *The Worship of the Dead; Or, the Origin and Nature of Pagan Idolatry and its Bearing Upon the Early History of Egypt and Babylonia.* London: Chapman and Hall, 1904.

Garnsey, Peter. *Famine and Food Supply in the Graeco-Roman World: Responses to Risk and Crisis.* Cambridge: Cambridge University Press, 1989.

Gaskell, G.A. *Dictionary of the Sacred Languages of All Scriptures and Myths,* Part 1. Whitefish: Kessinger, 2003.

Gasparin, Agénor. *Science vs. Modern Spiritualism: A Treatise on Turning Tables, the Supernatural in General, and Spirits,* Vol. 1. New York: Kiggins and Kellogg, 1857.

Gaspey, Thomas. *The Witch-Finder; or, The Wisdom of our*

Ancestors: A Romance, Vol. 2. London: Longman, Hurst, Rees, Orme, Brown, and Green, 1824.

Gaster, Moses. *Ma'aseh Book: Book of Jewish Tales and Legends*. Philadelphia: Jewish Publication Society of America, 1934.

_____. *Studies and Texts in Folklore, Magic, Mediaeval Romance, Hebrew Apocrypha, and Samaritan Archaeology*, Vol. 2. Hoboken: KTAV, 1971.

_____. *Sword of Moses, An Ancient Book of Magic*. Whitefish: Kessinger, 2003.

Gaster, Theodor Herzl, and Sir James George Frazer. *Myth, Legend, and Custom in the Old Testament: A Comparative Study with Chapters from Sir James G. Frazer's Folklore in the Old Testament*. New York: Harper and Row, 1969.

Gatan, Mariano, F. Landa Jocano, and Paz Policarpio Mendez. *Ibanag Indigenous Religious Beliefs: A Study in Culture and Education*. Manila: Centro Escolar University Research and Development Center, 1981.

Gebhardt, Magistra Artium Nadine. *Female Mythologies in Contemporary Chicana Literature*. Berlin: Grin Verlag, 2007.

Geertz, Clifford. *The Religion of Java*. Chicago: University of Chicago Press, 1976.

Geikie, John Cunningham, and Jesus Christ. *The Life and Words of Christ*. London: Henry S. King, 1877.

Georgieva, Ivanichka. *Bulgarian Mythology*. Sofia: Svyat, 1985.

Gerhardt, Mia Irene. *Old Men of the Sea: From Neptunus to Old French Luiton: Ancestry and Character of a Water-Spirit*. Amsterdam: Polak and Van Gennep, 1967.

Gettings, Fred. *Dictionary of Demons: A Guide to Demons and Demonologists in Occult Lore*. North Pomfret: Trafalgar Square, 1988.

Gibb, Hamilton Alexander Rosskeen, Johannes Hendrik Kramers, and Koninklijke Nederlandse Akademie van Wetenschappen. *Shorter Encyclopaedia of Islam*. Leiden: E.J. Brill, 1961.

Gijswijt-Hofstra, Marijke, Brian P. Levack, and Roy Porter. *Witchcraft and Magic in Europe: The Eighteenth and Nineteenth Centuries*. London: Continuum International, 1999.

Gilbert, R.A., J.W. Brodie-Innes, and Samuel Liddell MacGregor Mathers. *The Sorcerer and His Apprentice: Unknown Hermetic Writings of S.L. Macgregor Mathers and J.W. Brodie-Innes*. Wellingborough: Aquarian, 1983.

Gilchrist, Cherry. *Russian Magic: Living Folk Traditions of an Enchanted Landscape*. Wheaton: Quest Books, 2009.

Gill, William Wyatt, and Friedrich Max Müller. *Myths and Songs from the South Pacific*. London: Henry S. King, 1876.

Gilman, Daniel Coit. *The New International Encyclopaedia*, Vol. 3. New York: Dodd, Mead, 1906.

_____, Frank Moore Colby, and Harry Thurston Peck. *The New International Encyclopaedia*, Vol. 1. New York: Dodd, Mead, 1906.

Gilmore, David D. *Monsters: Evil Beings, Mythical Beasts, and All Manner of Imaginary Terrors*. Philadelphia: University of Pennsylvania Press, 2003.

Ginzberg, Louis. *The Legends of the Jews*, Vol. 3. Philadelphia: Jewish Publication Society of America, 1911.

_____. *The Legends of the Jews*, Vols. 3, 4 and 5. Charleston: Forgotten Books, 2008.

_____, and Boaz Cohen. *The Legends of the Jews: Bible Times and Characters from the Creation to Jacob*. Philadelphia: Jewish Publication Society of America, 1913.

_____, Paul Radin, and Henrietta Szold. *The Legends of the Jews Vol. 4: From Joshua to Esther*. Philadelphia: Jewish Publication Society of America, 1913.

_____, _____, and _____. *The Legends of the Jews: Notes to Vols. 1 and 2; From the Creation to the Exodus*. Baltimore: Johns Hopkins University Press, 1998.

Gittins, Anthony J. *Mende Religion: Aspects of Belief and Thought in Sierra Leone, Vol. 41 of Studia Instituti Anthropos*. Nettetal: Steyler Verlag/Wort und Werk, 1987.

Giversen, Søren, and Peder Borgen. *The New Testament and Hellenistic Judaism*. Aarhus: Aarhus University Press, 1995.

Glassé, Cyril. *The New Encyclopedia of Islam*. Lanham: Rowman and Littlefield, 2008.

Godfrey, Linda S., and Rosemary Ellen Guiley. *Lake and Sea Monsters*. New York: Infobase, 2008.

Godwin, David. *Godwin's Cabalistic Encyclopedia: A Complete Guide to Cabalistic Magick*. St. Paul: Llewellyn, 1999.

Godwin, William. *Lives of the Necromancers: Or, An Account of the Most Eminent Persons in Successive Ages, Who have Claimed for Themselves, or to Whom has been Imputed by Others, the Exercise of Magical Power*. London: F.J. Mason, 1834.

Goeje, C.H. *Philosophy, Initiation and Myths of the Indians of Guiana and Adjacent Countries*. Leiden: Brill, 1943.

Goethe, Johann Wolfgang von. *Goethes Faust: Erster teil*. New York: Henry Holt, 1907.

_____, and Carl Friedrich Zelter. *Goethe's Letters to Zelter: With Extracts from Those of Zelter to Goethe*. London: George Bell and Sons, 1892.

Golan, Ariel. *Prehistoric Religion: Mythology, Symbolism*. Jerusalem: Ariel Golan, 2003.

Goldwag, Arthur. *The Beliefnet Guide to the Kabbalah*. New York: Random House, 2005.

Gonda, Jan. *Sanskrit in Indonesia*. New Delhi: International Academy of Indian Culture, 1973.

González-Wippler, Migene. *The Complete Book of Spells, Ceremonies, and Magic*. St. Paul: Llewellyn, 1988.

Good, John Mason. *The Study of Medicine*. London: Baldwin, Cradock, and Joy, 1825.

Goodhugh, William, and William Cooke Taylor. *The Bible Cyclopædia: Or, Illustrations of the Civil and Natural History of the Sacred Writings*. London: John W. Parker, 1841.

Goodrich, Samuel Griswold. *Illustrated Natural History of the Animal Kingdom: Being a Systematic and Popular Description of the Habits, Structure, and Classification of Animals from the Highest to the Lowest Forms, with their Relation to Agriculture, Commerce, Manufactures, and the Arts*. New York: Derby and Jackson, 1859.

Goonatilleka, M.H. *Masks and Mask Systems of Sri Lanka*. Greensboro: Tamarind, 1978.

Gooneratne, Dandris de Silva. *On Demonology and Witchcraft in Ceylon*. New Delhi: Asian Educational Services, 1998.

Gordon, Cyrus Herzl. *Adventures in the Nearest East*. Fair Lawn: Essential Books, 1957.

Gore, J. Ellard. "The 'Demon' Star," *The Gentleman's Magazine*, Vol. 275, pages 345–350. London: Bradbury, Evans, 1893.

Gottschalk, Herbert: *Lexicon Der Mythologie*. Berlin: Safari, 1973.

Gould, S.C. *The Bizarre Notes and Queries in History, Folklore, Mathematics, Mysticism, Art, Science, Etc.*, Vols. 3–4. Manchester: S.C. and L.M. Gould, 1886.

Gow, Peter. *Amazonian Myth and Its History*. New York: Oxford University Press, 2001.

_____. *Of Mixed Blood: Kinship and History in Peruvian Amazonia*. New York: Oxford University Press, 1991.

Grace, Alfred Augustus. *Folk-Tales of the Maori*. Wellington, AZ: Gordon and Gotch, 1907.

Graf, Arturo. *The Story of the Devil*. Whitefish: Kessinger, 2005.

Grafton, Anthony, April Shelford, and Nancy G. Siraisi. *New Worlds, Ancient Texts: The Power of Tradition and the Shock of Discovery*. Cambridge: Harvard University Press, 1995.

Graham, Andrew Jackson. *The Standard-Phonographic Dictionary*. New York: Andrew J. Graham, 1890.

Graham, David Crockett. *The Customs and Religion of the Ch'iang*, Vol. 135. Washington, DC: Smithsonian Institution, 1958.

Grambs, David. *The Endangered English Dictionary: Bodacious Words Your Dictionary Forgot*. New York: W.W. Norton, 1997.

Grant, Robert J. *Edgar Cayce on Angels, Archangels, and the Unseen Forces*. Newark: A.R.E. Press, 2005.

Gras, Henk. *Studies in Elizabethan Audience Response to the Theater*, Part 1. New York: P. Lang, 1993.

Gray, Louis Herbert, and John Arnott MacCulloch. *The Mythology of All Races*, Vols. 1 and 4. New York: Cooper Square, 1964.

_____, and _____. *The Mythology of All Races*, Vol. 11. Boston: Marshall Jones, 1920.

Gray, Louis Herbert, George Foot Moore, and John Arnott MacCulloch. *The Mythology of All Races*. Boston: Marshall Jones, 1931.

_____, _____, _____, and Alice Werner. *The Mythology of All Races*, Vol. 6. Boston: Marshall Jones, 1917.

Greek Mythology. London: Paul Hamlyn, 1967.

Green, Thomas A. *Folklore: An Encyclopedia of Beliefs, Customs, Tales, Music, and Art*. Santa Barbara: ABC-CLIO, 1997.

Greenburg, William Henry. *The Haggadah According to the Rite of Yemen: Together with the Arabic-Hebrew Commentary*. London: D. Nutt, 1896.

Greer, John Michael. *Monsters: An Investigator's Guide to Magical Beings*. St Paul: Llewellyn, 2001.

_____. *The New Encyclopedia of the Occult*. St. Paul: Llewellyn, 2003.

Griffiths, Percival Joseph. *Modern India*. New York: F.A. Praeger, 1965.

Grimal, Pierre. *Larousse World Mythology*. New York: Gallery, 1989.

Grimassi, Raven. *Encyclopedia of Wicca and Witchcraft*. St. Paul: Llewellyn, 2000.

_____. *Italian Witchcraft: The Old Religion of Southern Europe*. St. Paul: Llewellyn, 2000.

Grimm, Jacob. *Teutonic Mythology*, Vol. 3. London: George Bell and Sons, 1883.

_____, and James Steven Stallybrass. *Teutonic Mythology*, Vol. 4. London: George Bell and Sons, 1888.

Grimm, Jacob Ludwig C. *Teutonic Mythology*, translated by J.S. Stallybrass. London: George Bell and Sons, 1882.

Griswold, Hervey De Witt. *The Religion of the Rigveda*. New York: H. Milford, Oxford University Press, 1923.

Grünwedel, Albert. *Buddhist Art in India*. London: B. Quaritch, 1901.

Guazzo, Francesco Maria. *Compendium Maleficarum*, Part 2. Whitefish: Kessinger, 2003.

_____. *Compendium Maleficarum: The Montague Summers Edition*. New York: Courier Dover, 1988.

Guénon, René, and S.D. Fohr. *The King of the World*. Hillsdale: Sophia Perennis, 2004.

"Guernsay Superstitions as Compared with those of Other Places," *The Guernsey Magazine: A Monthly Illustrated Journal of Useful Information, Instruction, and Entertainment*, Vol. 10, January, 1882, n.p. Guernsey: F. Clarke.

Guernsey, Julia. *Ritual and Power in Stone: The Performance of Rulership in Mesoamerican Izapa Style Art*. Austin: University of Texas Press, 2006.

Guggenheimer, Heinrich Walter, and Eva H. Guggenheimer. *Jewish Family Names and Their Origins: An Etymological Dictionary*. Hoboken: KTAV, 1992.

Guiley, Rosemary. *The Encyclopedia of Angels*. New York: Infobase, 2004.

_____. *The Encyclopedia of Magic and Alchemy*. New York: Infobase, 2006.

_____. *The Encyclopedia of Vampires, Werewolves, and Other Monsters*. New York: Infobase, 2004.

_____. *The Encyclopedia of Witches and Witchcraft*. New York: Facts on File, 1989.

_____, and John Zaffis. *The Encyclopedia of Demons and Demonology*. New York: Infobase, 2009.

Guirand, Félix. *New Larousse Encyclopedia of Mythology*. London: Hamlyn, 1968.

Gunkel, Hermann, and Heinrich Zimmern. *Creation and Chaos in the Primeval Era and the Eschaton: A Religio-Historical Study of Genesis 1 and Revelation 12*. Grand Rapids: William B. Eerdmans, 2006.

Gupta, Madan Gopal. *Indian Mysticism: Rigveda to Radhasoami Faith*. Agra: M.G. Publishers, 1993.

Gupta, Shakti M. *From Daityas to Devatas in Hindu Mythology*. Bombay: Somaiya, 1973.

Guthrie, Kenneth Sylvan. *The Hymns of Zoroaster, Usually Called the Gathas*. London: George Bell and Sons, 1914.

Gyarmathi, Sámuel, and Indiana University. *Uralic and Altaic Series*, Vol. 95. Bloomington: Indiana University, 1799.

Gypsy Lore Society. *Journal of the Gypsy Lore Society*. Edinburgh: The Society, 1941.

Hackin, J. *Asiatic Mythology: A Detailed Description and Explanation of the Mythologies of All the Great Nations of Asia*. New Delhi: Asian Educational Services, 1994.

Hackin, J. Paul Louis Couchoud. *Asiatic Mythology, 1932*. Whitefish: Kessinger, 2005.

Hadley, Judith M. *The Cult of Asherah in Ancient Israel and Judah: Evidence for a Hebrew Goddess*. Cambridge: Cambridge University Press, 2000.

Hageneder, Fred. *The Living Wisdom of Trees: Natural History, Folklore, Symbolism, Healing*. London: Duncan Baird, 2005.

Haldar, Alfred Ossian, and Henry Stanley Harvey. *Associations of Cult Prophets Among the Ancient Semites*. Uppsala: Almqvist and Wiksells, 1945.

Hall, Alaric. *Elves in Anglo-Saxon England: Matters of Belief, Health, Gender and Identity*. Woodbridge: Boydell Press, 2007.

Hall, Manly Palmer. *The Secret Teachings of All Ages: An Encyclopedic Outline of Masonic, Hermetic, Qabbalistic, and Rosicrucian Symbolical Philosophy*. Charleston: Forgotten Books, 2008.

Hamilton, Virginia. *In the Beginning: Creation Stories from Around the World*. Boston: Houghton Mifflin Harcourt, 1991.

Hammer, Jill. *The Jewish Book of Days: A Companion for All Seasons*. Philadelphia: Jewish Publication Society, 2006.

Hanauer, James Edward. *Folk-lore of the Holy Land: Moslem, Christian and Jewish*. London: Duckworth, 1907.

Handy, Edward Smith Craighill. *Polynesian Religion*. Honolulu: The Museum, 1927.

Haney, Jack V. *Russian Wondertales: Tales of Heroes and Villains*. Armonk: M.E. Sharpe, 1999.

Hansen, William F. *Classical Mythology: A Guide to the Mythical World of the Greeks and Romans*. New York: Oxford University Press, 2005.

Hanson, A., and L. Hanson. *Counterpoint in Maori Culture*. London: Routledge and Kegan Paul, 1983.

Hardiman, John Percy. *Gazetteer of Upper Burma and the Shan States*, Vol. 2, Part 1. Rangoon: Government Printing, 1900.

Hargreaves, J. *Hargreaves New Illustrated Beastiary*. Glastonbury: Gothic Image, 1990.

Harkness, Deborah E. *John Dee's Conversations with Angels: Cabala, Alchemy, and the End of Nature*. Cambridge: Cambridge University Press, 1999.

Harper, Katherine Anne, and Robert L. Brown. *The Roots of Tantra*. Albany: SUNY Press, 2002.

Harper, William Rainey, Ernest De Witt Burton, and Shailer Mathews. *The Biblical World*, Vol. 3. Chicago: University Press of Chicago, 1894.

_____, Ernest De Witt Burton, and Shailer Mathews. *The Biblical World*, Vol. 41. Chicago: University Press of Chicago, 1913.

Harris, Robert Laird. *Theological Wordbook of the Old Testament*, Vol. 2. Chicago: Moody Press, 1980.

Harrison, Charles. *Ancient Warriors of the North Pacific: The Haidas, their Laws, Customs and Legends, with some Historical Account of the Queen Charlotte Islands*. London: H.F. and G. Witherby, 1925.

Hart, George. *The Routledge Dictionary of Egyptian Gods and Goddesses*. New York: Psychology Press, 2005.

Hartnup, Karen. *On the Beliefs of the Greeks: Leo Allatios and Popular Orthodoxy*. Boston: Brill, 2004.

Hastings, James, Andrew Bruce Davidson, John Alexander Selbie, Samuel Rolles Driver, Henry Barclay Swete. *A Dictionary of the Bible: Kir-Pleiades*. New York: Charles Scribner's Sons, 1900.

_____, John Alexander Selbie, and Louis Herbert Gray. *Encyclopædia of Religion and Ethics*. Edinburg: T. and T. Clark, 1916.

_____, Louis Herbert Gray, and John Alexander Selbie. *Encyclopaedia of Religion and Ethics*, Vol. 3. New York: Scribner, 1961.

_____, John Alexander Selbie, and Louis Herbert Gray. *Encyclopædia of Religion and Ethics*, Vol. 4. Edinburgh: T. and T. Clark, 1916.

_____, and John A. Selbie. *Encyclopedia of Religion and Ethics*, Vol. 5. Whitefish: Kessinger, 2003.

_____, John Alexander Selbie, and Louis Herbert Gray. *Encyclopædia of Religion and Ethics*, Vol. 8. Edinburgh: T. and T. Clark, 1916.

_____, John Alexander Selbie, and Louis Herbert Gray. *Encyclopædia of Religion and Ethics*, Vol. 9. New York: T. and T. Clark, 1917.

_____, Louis Herbert Gray and John Alexander Selbie. *Encyclopedia of Religion and Ethics*, Vol. 11. New York: Charles Scribner's Sons, 1932.

_____. *Encyclopedia of Religion and Ethics*, Part 10. Whitefish: Kessinger, 2003.

_____. *Encyclopedia of Religion and Ethics*, Part 12. Whitefish: Kessinger, 2003.

_____. *Encyclopedia of Religion and Ethics*, Part 18. Whitefish: Kessinger, 2003.

_____. *Encyclopedia of Religion and Ethics*, Part 24. Whitefish: Kessinger, 2003.

Hastings, John, and John A. Selbie. *Encyclopedia of Religion and Ethics*, Part 2. Whitefish: Kessinger, 2003.

_____, and John A. Selbie. *Encyclopedia of Religion and Ethics*, Part 5. Whitefish: Kessinger, 2003.

_____, Louis Herbert Gray, and John Alexander Selbie. *Encyclopædia of Religion and Ethics*, Vol. 4. New York: Charles Scribner's Sons, 1932.

Havens, Norman, and Nobutaka Inoue. *An Encyclopedia of Shinto (Shinto Jiten): Kami*. Tokyo: Institute for Japanese Culture and Classics, Kokugakuin University, 2006.

Hawkins, Robb. *Getting Started In Paranormal Investigation*. Raleigh: Lulu, 2008.

Hayward, Robert. *Interpretations of the Name Israel in Ancient Judaism and Some Early Christian Writings: From Victorious Athlete to Heavenly Champion*. New York: Oxford University Press, 2005.

Hazlitt, W. Carew. *Tales and Legends of National Origin or Widely Current in England from Early Times*. Whitefish: Kessinger, 2003.

Headley, Stephen Cavana, and Institute of Southeast Asian Studies. *Durga's Mosque: Cosmology, Conversion and Community in Central Javanese Islam*. Singapore: Institute of Southeast Asian Studies, 2004.

Hearn, Lafcadio. *Glimpses of Unfamiliar Japan*. Charleston: BiblioBazaar, 2007.

_____. *Kwaidan: Stories and Studies of Strange Things*. Charleston: Forgotten Books, 1930.

_____. *Oriental Ghost Stories*. Leipzig: Bernhard Tauchnitz, 1910.

_____. *The Romance of the Milky Way and Other Stories*. Teddington: Echo Library, 2006.

Heckethorn, Charles William. *The Secret Societies of All Ages and Countries*, Vol. 1. London: R. Bentley and Son, 1875.

Heldreth, Leonard G. *The Blood is the Life: Vampires in Literature*. Popular Press, 1999.

Henderson, George. *The Norse Influence on Celtic Scotland*. Sine Nomine: Glasgow, 1901.

Henderson, Lizanne, and Edward J. Cowan. *Scottish Fairy Belief: A History*. Dundurn Press, 2001.

Henry, T. *Ancient Tahiti*. Honolulu: Bernice P. Bishop Museum, 1928.

Hensman, Bertha. *More Hong Kong Tale-spinners*. Hong Kong: Chinese University Press, 1971.

Hepburn, J.C. *A Japanese-English and English-Japanese Dictionary*. Tokyo: Z.P. Maruya, 1897.

Heraud, James Abraham. *The Judgement of the Flood* (Verse). London: James Fraser, 1834.

Herbermann, Charles C., the Knights of Columbus, and the Catholic Truth Committee. *The Catholic Encyclopedia: An International Work of Reference on the Constitution, Doctrine, Discipline, and History of the Catholic Church*, Vol. 1. New York: Encyclopedia Press, 1907.

Herbert, Algernon. *Nimrod: A Discourse on Certain Passages of History and Fable*, Vol. 2. London: Richard Priestley, 1828.

Herbert, J. "Sakata and Putana," *Encyclopaedia Indica*. New Delhi: Anmol Publications, 1996.

Herbert, Patricia, and Anthony Crothers Milner. *South-East Asia: Languages and Literatures; A Select Guide*. Honolulu: University of Hawaii Press, 1989.

Herczegh, Mihály, and Hungary Courts. *Magyar Családi És Öröklési Jog A Vonatkozó Újabb Törvények-, Felsobb Rendeletek- És Egy Döntvényfüggelékkel, Mely A M. Kir. Curiának, Úgyis Mint Hétszemélyes, Úgyis Mint Legfobb Itéloszéknek Elvi Határozatait Tartalmazza*. Budapest: Eggenberger-féle könyvkereskedés (Hoffmann és Molnár), 1885.

Herdt, Gilbert H. *Ritualized Homosexuality in Melanesia.* Berkeley: University of California Press, 1993.

Heremann-Pfandt, Adelheid. "The Good Woman's Shadow: Some Aspects of the Dark Nature of Dakinis and Sakinis in Hinduism," *Wild Goddesses in India and Nepal.* Bern: Peter Lang, 1996.

Herzog, Johann Jakob, Philip Schaff, and Samuel Macauley Jackson. *The New Schaff-Herzog Encyclopedia of Religious Knowledge: Embracing Biblical, Historical, Doctrinal, and Practical Theology and Biblical, Theological, and Ecclesiastical Biography from the Earliest Times to the Present Day,* Vol. 3. New York: Funk and Wagnalls, 1909.

Hibbard, George Richard, and Thomas Dekker. *Three Elizabethan Pamphlets.* London: Harrap, 1951.

Hibbert, Samuel. *Sketches of the Philosophy of Apparitions: Or, An Attempt to Trace Such Illusions to Their Physical Causes.* Edinburgh: Oliver and Boyd, 1825.

Higley, Sarah Lynn, and Saint Hildegard. *Hildegard of Bingen's Unknown Language: An Edition, Translation, and Discussion.* New York: Macmillan, 2007.

Hikosaka, Shu, and G. John Samuel. *Encyclopaedia of Tamil Literature: Introductory Articles.* Madras, India: Institute of Asian Studies, 1990.

Hill, Polly. *Rural Hausa: A Village and a Setting.* Cambridge: Cambridge University Press, 1972.

Hillman, James, and Wilhelm Heinrich Roscher. *Pan and the Nightmare.* Dallas: Spring Publications, 2000.

Hillmann, Michael C. *Unity in the Ghazals of Hafez.* Minneapolis: Bibliotheca Islamica, 1976.

Hirsch, Edward. *The Demon and the Angel: Searching for the Source of Artistic Inspiration.* Boston: Houghton Mifflin Harcourt, 2003.

Hlobil, Karel. *Before You.* Ontario: Insomniac Press, 2009.

Hoffman, Joel M. *And God Said: How Translations Conceal the Bible's Original Meaning.* New York: Macmillan, 2010.

Hoffmann, Matthias Reinhard. *The Destroyer and the Lamb: The Relationship Between Angelomorphic and Lamb Christology in the Book of Revelation.* Tübingen: Mohr Siebeck, 2005.

Hogbin, Herbert Ian, Lester Richard Hiatt, and Chandra Jayawardena. *Anthropology in Oceania: Essays Presented to Ian Hogbin.* Sydney: Angus and Robertson, 1971.

Home, Gordon. *France.* London: A. and C. Black, 1914.

Hooton, Earnest Albert. *The Ancient Inhabitants of the Canary Islands,* Vol. 7. Cambridge: Peabody Museum of Harvard University, 1925.

Hopkins, Edward Washburn. *Epic Mythology with Additions and Corrections.* New York: Biblo and Tannen, 1968.

_____. *The History of Religions.* New York: Macmillan, 1918.

Hoppál, Mihály. *Studies on Mythology and Uralic Shamanism.* Budapest: Akadémiai Kiadó, 2000.

Horne, Charles Francis. *Sacred Books and Early Literature of the East: The Great Rejected Books of the Biblical Apocrypha.* New York: Parke, Austin, and Lipscomb, 1917.

_____. *Sacred Books and Early Literature of the East: With Historical Surveys of the Chief Writings of Each Nation.* New York: Parke, Austin, and Lipscomb, 1917.

Houtsma, Martijn Theodoor. *E.J. Brill's First Encyclopaedia of Islam, 1913–1936,* Vol. 3. Leiden: E.J. Brill, 1993.

_____. *E.J. Brill's First Encyclopaedia of Islam, 1913–1936,* Vol. 2. Leiden: E.J. Brill, 1987.

Howe, Leo. *The Changing World of Bali: Religion, Society and Tourism.* New York: Psychology Press, 2005.

Howey, M. Oldfield. *The Cat in Magic and Myth.* North Chemsford: Courier Dover Publications, 2003.

_____. *The Encircled Serpent a Study of Serpent Symbolism in All Countries and Ages.* Whitefish: Kessinger, 2005.

Hsia, R. Po-chia. *The World of Catholic Renewal, 1540–1770.* Cambridge: Cambridge University Press, 1998.

Hughes, Thomas Patrick. *A Dictionary of Islam: Being a Cyclopaedia of the Doctrines, Rites, Ceremonies, and Customs, Together With the Technical and Theological Terms, of the Muhammadan Religion.* London: W.H. Allen, 1885.

Hugo, Victor. *The Toilers of the Sea,* Vol. 1. London: George Routledge and Sons, 1896.

Humphreys, David. *The Lost Book of Enoch.* London: Janus, 2005.

Hunt, Robert. *Popular Romances of the West of England, Or, the Drolls, Traditions, and Superstitions of Old Cornwall.* Bronx: Benjamin Blom, 1916.

Hunter, Henry. *Sacred Biography, or, The History of the Patriarchs: To Which is Added, the History of Deborah, Ruth and Hannah, and also the History of Jesus Christ: Being a Course of Lectures, Delivered at the Scots Church, London Wall,* Vols. 3–4. Walpole: Thomas and Thomas, by D. Newhall, 1803.

Hunter, Jennifer. *Magickal Judaism: Connecting Pagan and Jewish Practice.* New York: Citadel Press, 2006.

Hunter, Robert. *The Encyclopaedic Dictionary: A New Original Work of Reference to All the Words in the English Language, with a Full Account of Their Origin, Meaning, Pronunciation, and Use.* London: Cassell, Petter, Galpi, 1883.

Huntingford, George Wynn Brereton. *The Circle of Bliss: Buddhist Meditational Art.* London: Serindia, 2003.

_____. *The Nandi of Kenya: Tribal Control in a Pastoral Society.* London: Routledge, 2004.

Hurwitz, Siegmund. *Lilith: The First Eve; Historical and Psychological Aspects of the Dark Feminine.* Zurich: Daimon, 2007.

Husain, Shahrukh. *Demons, Gods, and Holy Men from Indian Myths and Legends.* New York: P. Bedrick Books, 1995.

Hyatt, Victoria, and Joseph W. Charles. *The Book of Demons.* New York: Simon and Schuster, 1974.

"Hystero-Demonopathy in Savoy," *The Intellectual Observer,* Vol. 7, February 1865, pages 354–77. London: Groombridge and Sons.

Icke, David. *The Biggest Secret: The Book That Will Change the World.* Scottsdale: Bridge of Love Publications, 1999.

Iliowizi, Henry. *The Weird Orient: Nine Mystic Tales.* Philadelphia: Henry T. Coates, 1900.

Illes, Judika. *Encyclopedia of Spirits: The Ultimate Guide to the Magic of Fairies, Genies, Demons, Ghosts, Gods and Goddesses.* New York: HarperCollins, 2009.

Indira Gandhi National Center for the Arts. *Iconography of the Buddhist Sculpture of Orissa: Text.* New Delhi: Abhinav, 2001.

Inman, Thomas. *Ancient Faiths Embodied in Ancient Names,* Part 3. London: Sine Nomine, 1868.

Isaac, Abram S. "The Faust of the Talmud," *The Contributor: Representing the Young Men's and Young Ladies' Mutual Improvement Associations of the Latter-Day Saints,* Vol. 10. 1889, pages 270–3. Salt Lake City: Contributor, 1889.

Isaacs, Darek. *Dragons or Dinosaurs? Creation or Evolution?* Alachua: Bridge Logos Foundation, 2010.

Isaacs, Ronald H. *Animals in Jewish Thought and Tradition.* Northvale: Jason Aronson, 2000.

_____. *Divination, Magic, and Healing: The Book of Jewish Folklore*. Lanham: Rowman and Littlefield, 1998.

_____. *Why Hebrew Goes from Right to Left: 201 Things You Never Knew About Judaism*. Hoboken: KTAV, 2008.

Jackson, A.V. Williams. *Zoroaster: The Prophet of Ancient Iran*. Whitefish: Kessinger, 2006.

_____. *Zoroastrian Studies: The Iranian Religion and Various Monographs, 1928*. Whitefish: Kessinger, 2003.

Jackson, Abraham Valentine Williams. *Researches in Manichaeism: With Special Reference to the Turfan Fragments*, Vol. 13. New York: Columbia University Press, 1932.

Jackson, David R. *Enochic Judaism: Three Defining Paradigm Exemplars*. New York: Continuum, 2004.

Jackson, Robert. *Mysteries of Witchcraft and the Occult*. London: Greenwich Editions, 2002.

Jacobsen, Thorkild. *The Treasures of Darkness: A History of Mesopotamian Religion*. London: Yale University Press, 1978.

Jahn, Johann. *Jahn's Biblical Archaeology*. Andover: Flagg and Gould, 1823.

Jahoda, Gustav. *The Psychology of Superstition*. New York: Penguin, 1970.

James, Montague Rhodes. *Old Testament Legends: Being Stories Out of Some of the Less-known Apocryphal Books of the Old Testament*. New York: Longmans, Green, 1913.

Jamieson, Robert, David Brown, and Andrew Robert Fausset. *A Commentary, Critical and Explanatory, on the Old and New Testaments*, Vol. 2. Philadelphia: S.S. Scranton, 1875.

Japan Society of London. *Transactions and Proceedings of the Japan Society, London*, Vol. 9. London: Kegan Paul, Trench, Trübner, 1912.

Jäschke, H.A. *A Tibetan-English Dictionary: With Special Reference to the Prevailing Dialects, to Which is Added an English-Tibetan Vocabulary*. London: Routledge, 1881.

Jastrow, Morris. *The Civilization of Babylonia and Assyria: Its Remains, Language, History, Religion, Commerce, Law, Art, and Literature*. Philadelphia: J.B. Lippincott, 1915.

_____. *The Religion of Babylonia and Assyria*. Boston: Ginn, 1898.

Jeffrey, David L. *A Dictionary of Biblical Tradition in English Literature*. Grand Rapids: Wm. B. Eerdmans, 1992.

Jehlen, Myra, and Michael Warner. *The English Literatures of America, 1500–1800*. London: Routledge, 1997.

Jennings, Hargrave. *Ophiolatreia: An Account of the Rites and Mysteries Connected with the Origin, Rise, and Development of Serpent Worship in Various Parts of the World: Enriched with Interesting Traditions and a Full Description of the Celebrated Serpent Mounds and Temples: The Whole Forming an Exposition of One*. London: J. G. and F. Rivington, 1889.

Jeremias, Alfred, and Claude Hermann Walter Johns. *The Old Testament in the Light of the Ancient East*, Vol. 1. London: Williams and Norgate, 1911.

Jinruigaku Kenkyujo, Nanzan Daigaku, and Nanzan Shukyo Bunka Kenkyujo. *Asian Folklore Studies*, Vol. 56. Madras: Asian Folklore Institute, 1997.

Jobes, Gertrude. *Dictionary of Mythology, Folklore and Symbols*, Vol. 1. New York: Scarecrow Press, 1962.

_____, and James Jobes. *Outer Space: Myths, Name Meanings, Calendars from the Emergence of History to the Present Day*. New York: Scarecrow Press, 1964.

Jocano, F. Landa. *Folk Medicine in a Philippine Municipality*. Manila: National Museum Publication, 1973.

Johnson, Kenneth. *Slavic Sorcery: Shamanic Journey of Initiation*. Woodbury: Llewellyn, 1998.

Johnson, Leslie M., and Eugene S. Hunn. *Landscape Ethnoecology: Concepts of Biotic and Physical Space*. New York: Berghahn Books, 2010.

Johnson, Severance. *The Dictator and the Devil*. New York: Ecnareves Press, 1943.

Johnston, Sarah Iles. *Religions of the Ancient World: A Guide*. Cambridge: Harvard University Press, 2004.

Jones, Alfred. *Jones' Dictionary of Old Testament Proper Names*. Grand Rapids: Kregel, 1990.

Jones, David E. *Evil in Our Midst: A Chilling Glimpse of Our Most Feared and Frightening Demons*. Garden City Park: Square One, 2001.

Jones, Ernest. *On the Nightmare*. London: Hogarth Press, 1949.

Jones, Lindsay. *Encyclopedia of Religion*, Vol. 4. New York: Macmillan Reference, 2005.

Jones, Roger Miller. *The Platonism of Plutarch*. Menasha: George Banta, 1916.

Jones, Sonia D. *Angels and Magic*. Raleigh: Lulu, 2007.

Jordan, A.C. *Tales from Southern Africa*. Berkeley: University of California Press, 1978.

Jordan, Michael. *Dictionary of Gods and Goddesses*. New York: Infobase, 2004.

_____. *Encyclopedia of Gods*, New York: Facts on File, 1993.

Jortin, John. *Discourses Concerning the Truth of the Christian Religion and Remarks on Ecclesiastical History*, Vol. 2. London: J. White by R. Taylor, 1805.

Journal of Theological Studies, Vol. 8. Oxford: Clarion Press, 1907.

Jung, Leo. *Fallen Angels in Jewish, Christian and Mohammedan Literature*. Whitefish: Kessinger, 2003.

Justi, Ferdinand, Morris Jastrow, and Sara Yorke Stevenson. *A History of All Nations*, Vol. 1. Philadelphia: Lea Brothers, 1905.

Kaegi, Adolf, and Robert Arrowsmith. *The Rigveda: The Oldest Literature of the Indians*. Boston: Ginn, 1886.

Kanellos, Nicolás, Claudio Esteva Fabregat, Alfredo Jiménez, Francisco A. Lomelí, Alfredo Jiménez Núñez, Félix Padilla, and Thomas Weaver. *Handbook of Hispanic Cultures in the United States: Literature and Art*. Houston: Arte Publico, 1993.

Kapferer, Bruce. *A Celebration of Demons: Exorcism and the Aesthetics of Healing in Sri Lanka*. Oxford: Berg, 1991.

_____. *A Celebration of Demons: Exorcism and the Aesthetics of Healing in Sri Lanka*. Bloomington: Indiana University Press, 1983.

Kaplan, Steven L. *Understanding Popular Culture: Europe from the Middle Ages to the Nineteenth Century*. New York: Walter de Gruyter, 1984.

Kasimin, Amran. *Religion and Social Change Among the Indigenous People of the Malay Peninsula*. Kuala Lumpur: Dewan Bahasa dan Pustaka, Kementerian Pendidikan Malaysia, 1991.

Kaye, Marvin. *Devils and Demons*. Rockleigh: Marboro Books, 1991.

Keay, S.J. *Roman Spain*. Berkeley: University of California Press, 1988.

Keeler, Clyde E. *Secrets of the Cuna Earthmother: A Comparative Study of Ancient Religions*. Whitefish: Kessinger, 2006.

Keightley, Thomas. *The Fairy Mythology, Illustrative of the Romance and Superstition of Various Countries*. London: G. Bell and Sons, 1900.

_____. *The Fairy Mythology: Illustrative of the Romance and*

Superstition of Various Countries, Vol. 1. London: Whittaker, Treacher, 1833.

———. *The Mythology of Ancient Greece and Italy*. London: Whittaker, 1854.

Keith, Aruthur Berriedale. *Religion and Philosophy of the Veda and Upanishads*. Cambridge: Harvard University Press, 1925.

Kelley, William V. *The Methodist Review*, Vol. 83. New York: Eaton and Mains, 1901.

Kelly, Henry Ansgar. *Satan: A Biography*. Cambridge: Cambridge University Press, 2006.

Kelly, Sean, and Rosemary Rogers. *Who in Hell: A Guide to the Whole Damned Bunch*. New York: Villard, 1996.

Kendra, Vivekananda. *Imprints of Indian Thought and Culture Abroad*. Madras: Vivekananda Kendra Prakashan, 1980.

Kensky, Tikva Simone Frymer. *Studies in Bible and Feminist Criticism*. Philadelphia: Jewish Publication Society of America, 2006.

Khanam, R. *Demonology: Socio-Religious Belief of Witchcraft*. New Deli: Global Vision, 2003.

Kieckhefer, Richard. *Forbidden Rites: A Necromancer's Manual of the Fifteenth Century*. University Park: Penn State Press, 1998.

Kiely, David, and Christina Mckenna. *The Dark Sacrament: True Stories of Modern-Day Demon Possession and Exorcism*. New York: HarperCollins, 2008.

Kilpatrick, Alan. *The Night Has a Naked Soul: Witchcraft and Sorcery Among the Western Cherokee*. Syracuse: Syracuse University Press, 1998.

Kindersley, Nathaniel Edward. *Specimens of Hindoo Literature: Consisting of Translations, from the Tamoul Language, of Some Hindoo Works of Morality and Imagination, with Explanatory Notes*. London: Bulmer, 1794.

King, John H. *The Supernatural: Its Origin, Nature and Evolution*, Vol. 1. London: Williams and Norgate, 1892.

King, Leonard W. *Babylonian Magic and Sorcery—Being the Prayers for the Lifting of the Hand—The Cuneiform Texts of a Group of Babylonian and Assyrian Incantations and Magical Formulae*. London: Luzac, 1896.

———. *Babylonian Religion and Mythology*. Whitefish: Kessinger, 2004.

Kipfer, Barbara Ann. *The Order of Things*. New York: Workman, 2008.

Kirchmayer, Georg Kasper, Hermann Grube, and Martinus Schoock. *Un-natural History: Or Myths of Ancient Science; Being a Collection of Curious Tracts on the Basilisk, Unicorn, Phoenix, Behemoth or Leviathan, Dragon, Giant Spider, Tarantula, Chameleons, Satyrs, Homines Caudati, Etc.*, Vol. 1. Edinburgh: Private Printing, 1886.

Kirk, G.S. *Myth: Its Meaning and Functions in Ancient and Other Cultures*. Cambridge: CUP Archive, 1970.

Kitto, John. *Daily Bible Illustrations: Being Original Readings for a Year on Subjects from Sacred History, Biography, Geography, Antiquities, and Theology: Especially Designed for the Family Circle*, Vol. 4. New York: Robert Carter and Brothers, 1881.

———, and William Lindsay Alexander. *A Cyclopædia of Biblical Literature*, Vol. 1. Edinburgh: Black, 1876.

Klaits, Joseph. *Servants of Satan: The Age of the Witch Hunts*. Bloomington: Indiana University Press, 1985.

Klaniczay, Gábor, Éva Pócs, and Eszter Csonka-Takács. *Christian Demonology and Popular Mythology*. Budapest: Central European University Press, 2006.

Kleivan, Inge, and Birgitte Sonne. *Eskimos, Greenland and Canada*. Leiden: Brill, 1985.

Kloppenborg, Ria, and Wouter J. Hanegraaff. *Female Stereotypes in Religious Traditions*. Leiden: Brill, 1995.

Kmietowicz, Frank A. *Slavic Mythical Beliefs*. Windsor: F. Kmietowicz, 1982.

Knapp, Bettina Liebowitz. *Machine, Metaphor, and the Writer: A Jungian View*. University Park: Penn State Press, 1989.

Knappert, Jan. *African Mythology: An Encyclopedia of Myth and Legend*. Berkeley: Diamond Books, 1995.

———. *The Aquarian Guide to African Mythology*. Wellingborough: Aquarian, 1990.

———. *Bantu Myths and Other Tales*. Leiden: Brill Archive, 1977.

———. *The Encyclopaedia of Middle Eastern Mythology and Religion*. Rockport: Element, 1993.

———. *Indian Mythology: An Encyclopedia of Myth and Legend*. Wellingborough: Aquarian Press, 1991.

———. *Islamic Legends: Histories of the Heroes, Saints, and Prophets of Islam*, Vol. 1. Leiden: Brill Archive, 1985.

———. *Pacific Mythology: An Encyclopedia of Myth and Legend*. Wellingborough: Aquarian/Thorsons, 1992.

———. *Swahili Culture*, Vol. 2. Lewiston: Edwin Mellen Press, 2005.

Knibb, Michael A. *The Ethiopic Book of Enoch*. Oxford: Clarendon Press, 1978.

Knight, Charles. *The Penny Magazine of the Society for the Diffusion of Useful Knowledge*, Vol. 11. London: Charles Knight, 1842.

Knowles, James. *The Nineteenth Century*, Vol. 31. London: Henry S. King, 1892.

Knox, Hubert Thomas. *The History of the County of Mayo to the Close of the Sixteenth Century*. Dublin: Hodges, Figgis, 1908.

Koén-Sarano, Matilda, and Reginetta Haboucha. *King Solomon and the Golden Fish: Tales from the Sephardic Tradition*. Detroit: Wayne State University Press, 2004.

Kõiva, Mare, and Kai Vassiljeva. *Folk Belief Today*. Tallinn: Estonian Academy of Sciences, Institute of the Estonian Language and Estonian Museum of Literature, 1995.

Koizumi, Fumio. *Dance and Music in South Asian Drama: Chhau, Mahākālī pyākhan and Yakshagāna*, Vol. 1981. Tokyo: Academia Music, 1983.

Koltuv, Barbara Black. *The Book of Lilith*. York Beach: Nicolas-Hays, 1986.

Kondos, Vivienne. *On the Ethos of Hindu Women: Issues, Taboos, and Forms of Expression*. San Rafael: Mandala Publications, 2004.

Konstantinos. *Summoning Spirits: The Art of Magical Evocation*. St. Paul: Llewellyn, 2004.

Koppedrayer, K.I., and Amir Harrak. *Contacts Between Cultures: South Asia*. New York: E. Mellen Press, 1992.

Korban, Ray. *Anastasis Dunamis*. Canton: Xulon Press, 2006.

Korpela, Jukka. *The World of Ladoga: Society, Trade, Transformation and State Building in the Eastern Fennoscandian Boreal Forest Zone c. 1000–1555*. Berlin: LIT Verlag Münster, 2008.

Kr Singh, Nagendra, David Bolland, and Vālmīki. *The Ramayana in Kathakali Dance Drama*. New Delhi: Global Vision, 2006.

Kraft, Charles H. *Defeating Dark Angels: Breaking Demonic Oppression in the Believer's Life*. Ventura: Gospel Light, 1992.

Kramer, Samuel Noah. *Sumerian Mythology: A Study of Spiritual and Literary Achievement in the Third Millennium B.C.* Charleston: Forgotten Books, 2007.

Kramrisch, Stella. *The Presence of Siva*. Princeton: Princeton University Press, 1994.

Krickeberg, Walter. *Pre–Columbian American Religions.* New York: Holt, Rinehart and Winston, 1969

Krill, Richard M. *Greek and Latin in English Today.* Wauconda: Bolchazy-Carducci, 1990.

Krummacher, Gottfried Daniel. *Israel's Wanderings in the Wilderness, From the German, by the Translator of Elijah the Tishbite.* London: James Nisbeth, 1837.

Kulik, Alexander. *3 Baruch: Greek-Slavonic Apocalypse of Baruch.* New York: Walter de Gruyter, 2010.

Kuriakos. *The Grimoire Verum Ritual Book.* Raleigh: Lulu, 2008.

Kurup, C.G.R., and B.G. Varma. *The Ramayana.* Nehru House: Children's Book Trust, 2002.

Labdrön, Machig, and Sarah Harding. *Machik's Complete Explanation: Clarifying the Meaning of Chöd: A Complete Explanation of Casting Out the Body as Food.* Ithaca: Snow Lion, 2003.

Lacks, Roslyn. *Women and Judaism: Myth, History, and Struggle.* New York: Doubleday, 1980.

Ladd, John D. *Commentary on the Book of Enoch.* Longwood: Xulon Press, 2008.

Laderman, Carol. *Wives and Midwives: Childbirth and Nutrition in Rural Malaysia.* Berkeley: University of California Press, 1987.

Lamb, Geoffrey. *Magic, Witchcraft and the Occult.* New York: Hippocrene Books, 1983.

Lambton, Ann K.S. *Persian Grammar.* Cambridge: Cambridge University Press, 1984.

Lane, Edward William. *The Thousand and One Nights.* London: Bell, 1906.

_____, and Stanley Lane-Poole. *Arab Society in the Time of the Thousand and One Nights.* North Chemsford: Courier Dover, 2004.

Lang, Andrew. *The Making of Religion.* New York: Longmans, Green, 1909.

Langond, Stephen, H. "Lilith," *Semitic Mythology of All Races,* Vol. V, June 1932. New York: Cooper Square, 1932.

Langton, Edward. *Essentials of Demonology: A Study of Jewish and Christian Doctrine, its Origin and Development.* London: Epworth, 1949.

Larkin, Clarence. *The Book of Revelation: A Study of the Last Prophetic Book of Holy Scripture.* Whitefish: Kessinger, 2004.

Larrington, Carolyne. *The Feminist Companion to Mythology.* London: Pandora, 1992.

Larson, Gerald James, C. Scott Littleton, and Jaan Puhvel. *Myth in Indo-European Antiquity.* Berkeley: University of California Press, 1974.

Larson, Jennifer Lynn. *Greek Nymphs: Myth, Cult, Lore.* New York: Oxford University Press, 2001.

Latham, Robert Gordon. *Descriptive Ethnology,* Vol. 1. London: J. van Voorst, 1859.

Latourette, Kenneth Scott. *The Chinese.* New York: Macmillan, 1934.

Laufer, Berthold. *Sino-Iranica: Chinese Contributions to the History of Civilization in Ancient Iran, with Special Reference to the History of Cultivated Plants and Product.* Chicago: Field Museum of Natural History, 1919.

Laurence, Richard. "Books of Isaiah and Enoch, The Ethiopians Apocryphal," *The Foreign Quarterly Review,* Vol. 24, No. 48, pages 351–386. London: Black and Armstrong, 1840.

_____. *The Book of Enoch, the Prophet: An Apocryphal Production, Supposed for Ages to Have Been Lost; But Discovered at the Close of the Last Century in Abyssinia; Now First Translated from an Ethiopic Manuscript in the Bodleian Library.* Oxford: Oxford University Press, 1821.

Laurent, Emile, and Paul Nagour. *Magica Sexualis 1934.* Whitefish: Kessinger, 2004.

Lawson, John Cuthbert. *Modern Greek Folklore and Ancient Greek Religion: A Study in Survivals.* Whitefish: Kessinger, 2003.

Layard, Austen-Henry. *Nineveh and its Remains with an Account of a Visit to the Chaldaean Christians of Kurdistan and the Yezidis or Devil-worshippers and an Enquiry into the Manners and Arts of the Ancient Assyrians,* Vol. 2. London: John Murray, 1849.

Layard, John. *Stone Men of Malekula,* Vol. 1. London: Chatto and Windus, 1942.

Laycock, Donald C., John Dee, and Edward Kelly. *The Complete Enochian Dictionary: A Dictionary of the Angelic Language as Revealed to Dr. John Dee and Edward Kelley.* Boston: Weiser, 2001.

Lazarus, William P., and Mark Sullivan. *Comparative Religion for Dummies.* Hoboken: For Dummies, 2008.

Le Plongeon, Augustus. "The Origins of the Egyptians," *The Word: Monthly Magazine Devoted to Philosophy, Science, Religion; Eastern Thought, Occultism, Theosophy and the Brotherhood of Humanity,* Vol. 17, April–September 1913. New York: The Word, 1913.

Le Strange, Guy. *Palestine Under the Moslems: A Description of Syria and the Holy Land from A.D. 650 to 1500.* London: Alexander P. Watt for the Committee of the Palestine Exploration Fund, 1890.

Lea, Henry Charles. *A History of the Inquisition of the Middle Ages,* Vol. 3. New York: Harper and Brothers, 1887.

_____. *Materials Toward a History of Witchcraft,* Vol. 2. Whitefish: Kessinger, 2004.

Leach, Maria. *The Beginning: Creation Myths from Around the World.* New York: Funk and Wagnalls, 1956.

_____. *Funk and Wagnall's Standard Dictionary of Folklore, Mythology, and Legend.* New York: Harper Collins, 1984.

Lederer, Wolfgang. *The Fear of Women.* New York: Harcourt Brace Jovanovich, 1968.

Leeming, David Adams. *A Dictionary of Asian Mythology.* New York: Oxford University Press, 2001.

_____. *The Oxford Companion to World Mythology.* New York: Oxford University Press, 2005.

_____, and Jake Page. *Goddess: Myths of the Female Divine.* New York: Oxford University Press, 1996.

Leger, Louis. *A History of Austro-Hungary from the Earliest Time to the Year 1889.* London: Rivingtons, 1889.

Lehrich, Christopher I. *The Language of Demons and Angels: Cornelius Agrippa's Occult Philosophy.* Leiden: Brill, 2003.

Leick, Gwendolyn. *A Dictionary of Ancient Near Eastern Mythology.* New York: Psychology Press, 1998.

_____. *Sex and Eroticism in Mesopotamian Literature.* London: Routledge, 2003.

Leland, Charles Godfrey. *Gypsy Sorcery and Fortune Telling: Illustrated by Incantations, Specimens of Medical Magic, Anecdotes, and Tales.* New York: Charles Scribner and Sons, 1891.

Lemaire, André, and Benedikt Otzen. *History and Traditions of Early Israel: Studies Presented to Eduard Nielsen, May 8th 1933.* Leiden: Brill, 1993.

Lenormant, François. *The Beginnings of History According to the Bible and the Traditions of Oriental Peoples: From the Creation of Man to the Deluge.* New York: C. Scribner's Sons, 1886.

_____. *Chaldean Magic: Its Origin and Development.* Whitefish: Kessinger, 1994.

Leslau, Wolf. *Arabic Loanwords in Ethiopian Semitic.* Wiesbaden: Harrassowitz, 1990.

Lessa, William Armand. *More Tales from Ulithi Atoll: A Content Analysis.* Berkeley: University of California Press, 1980.

_____. *Tales from Ulithi Atoll: A Comparative Study in Oceanic Folklore.* Berkeley: University of California Press, 1961.

Levack, Brian P. *New Perspectives on Witchcraft, Magic, and Demonology: Demonology, Religion, and Witchcraft.* London: Taylor and Francis, 2001.

Leven, Jeremy. *Satan, His Psychotherapy and Cure by the Unfortunate Dr. Kassler, J.S.P.S.* New York: Knopf, 1982.

Levertoff, Paul Philip. *The Zohar,* Vol. 1. London: Soncino, 1934.

LeVey, Anton Szandor. *The Satanic Bible.* New York: Avon Books, 1969.

Lévi, Éliphas. *History of Magic: Including a Clear and Precise Exposition of Its Procedure, Rites and Mysteries.* Whitefish: Kessinger, 1993.

_____. *Transcendental Magic, its Doctrine and Ritual.* Boston: Weiser, 1968.

_____, and Arthur Edward Waite. *The Mysteries of Magic: A Digest of the Writings of Eliphas Lévi.* London: G. Redway, 1886.

Lewis, D. Geraint. *Gomer's Dictionary for Young People.* Llandysul: Gwasg Gomer, 1994.

Lewis, James R. *The Astrology Book: The Encyclopedia of Heavenly Influences.* Detroit: Visible Ink Press, 2003.

_____. *Satanism Today: An Encyclopedia of Religion, Folklore, and Popular Culture.* Santa Barbara: ABC-CLIO, 2001.

Lewis, Maureen Warner. *Guinea's Other Suns: The African Dynamic in Trinidad Culture.* Dover: Majority Press, 1991.

Lewis, Thomas. *Origines Hebrææ: the Antiquities of the Hebrew Republic.* Oxford: Oxford University Press, 1835.

Li, Anzhai. *History of Tibetan Religion: A Study in the Field.* Beijing: New World Press, 1994.

Li, Michelle Ilene Osterfeld. *Ambiguous Bodies: Reading the Grotesque in Japanese Setsuwa Tales.* Stanford: Stanford University Press, 2009.

Liberman, Anatoly. *An Analytic Dictionary of English Etymology: An Introduction.* Minneapolis: University of Minnesota Press, 2008.

_____. *Word Origins and How We Know Them: Etymology for Everyone.* New York: Oxford University Press, 2009.

Lieban, Richard Warren. *Cebuano Sorcery: Malign Magic in the Philippines.* Berkeley: University of California Press, 1977.

Lieber, Francis, Edward Wigglesworth, and Thomas Gamaliel Bradford. *Encyclopædia Americana: A Popular Dictionary of Arts, Sciences, Literature, History, Politics and Biography, Brought Down to the Present Time; Including a Copious Collection of Original Articles in American Biography; on the Basis of the Seventh Edition of the German Conversations,* Vol. 5. Philadelphia: Carey, Lea and Carey, 1831.

Lincoln, Bruce. *Religion, Empire, and Torture: The Case of Achaemenian Persia, with a Postscript on Abu Ghraib.* Chicago: University of Chicago Press, 2007.

Linrothe, Robert N., Marylin M. Rhie, and Jeff Watt. *Demonic Divine: Himalayan Art and Beyond.* London: Serindia, 2004.

Littell, Eliakim, and Robert S. Littell. *Littell's Living Age,* Vol. 143. Boston: T.H. Carter, 1879.

Littleton, C. Scott. *Gods, Goddesses, and Mythology,* Vol. 1. Tarrytown: Marshall Cavendish, 2005.

_____. *Gods, Goddesses, and Mythology,* Vol. 6. Tarrytown: Marshall Cavendish, 2005.

The Living Age, Vol. 4. Boston: Littell, Son, 1845.

Lizot, Jacques. *Tales of the Yanomami: Daily Life in the Venezuelan Forest.* Cambridge: Cambridge University Press, 1991.

Loewenthal, Kate Miriam. *Religion, Culture and Mental Health.* Cambridge: Cambridge University Press, 2007.

Lommel, Andreas. *Masks: Their Meaning and Function.* New York: McGraw-Hill, 1972.

Lopez, Mellie Leandicho. *A Handbook of Philippine Festivals.* Honolulu: University of Hawaii Press, 2003.

Lowe, J.E. *Magic in Greek and Latin Literature.* Whitefish: Kessinger, 2003.

Lowell, James Russell. *The Writings of James Russell Lowell in Prose and Poetry: Literary Essays.* Boston: Houghton, Mifflin, 1898.

Lowry, Malcolm. *Under the Volcano.* New York: Harper-Collins, 2000.

Lumpkin, Joseph B. *Fallen Angels, the Watchers, and the Origins of Evil.* Blounstville: Fifth Estate, 2006.

_____. *The Lost Book of Enoch: Comprehensive Transliteration of the Forgotten Book of the Bible.* Blountsville: Fifth Estate, 2004.

Lunge-Larsen, Lise, and Beth Krommes. *The Hidden Folk: Stories of Fairies, Dwarves, Selkies, and other Secret Beings.* Boston: Houghton Mifflin Harcourt, 2004.

Lurker, Manfred. *Dictionary of Gods and Goddesses, Devils and Demons.* London: Routledge, 1987, 2004.

Lyon, William S. *Encyclopedia of Native American Healing.* New York: W.W. Norton, 1996.

Maberry, Jonathan. *Vampire Universe: The Dark World of the Supernatural Beings that Haunt Us, Hunt Us, and Hunger for Us.* Secaucus: Citadel Press, 1996.

_____. *Zombie CSU.* Secaucus: Citadel Press, 2008.

_____, and David F. Kramer. *The Cryptopedia: A Dictionary of the Weird, Strange, and Downright Bizarre.* Secaucus: Citadel Press, 2007.

_____, and _____. *They Bite: Endless Cravings of Supernatural Predators.* Secaucus: Citadel Press, 2009.

MacCulloch, John Arnott, Jan Máchal, and Louis Herbert Gray. *Celtic Mythology.* Boston: Marshall Jones, 1918.

MacDermott, Mercia. *Bulgarian Folk Customs.* London: Jessica Kingsley, 1998.

Macdonald, Frederika, and Vālmīki. *The Iliad of the East: A Selection of Legends Drawn from Vālmīki's Sanskrit Poem, the Rāmāyana.* London: Macmillan, 1870.

MacDonnell, Arthur Anthony. *Vedic Reader for Students.* Charleston: Forgotten Books, 1970.

Mack, Carol K., and Dinah Mack. *A Field Guide to Demons, Fairies, Fallen Angels, and other Subversive Spirits.* New York: Henry Holt, 1998.

Mackay, Charles. *The Gaelic Etymology of the Languages of Western Europe: And More Especially of the English and Lowland Scotch, and Their Slang, Cant, and Colloquial Dialects.* London: Trübner, 1877.

Mackenzie, Donald A. *Myths of Babylonia and Assyria.* Charleston: Forgotten Books, 2007.

_____. *Scottish Folk-lore and Folk Life: Studies in Race, Culture and Tradition.* New York: Read Books, 2010. Chicago: University of Chicago Press, 2008.

Mackenzie, Donald Alexander. *Myths from Melanesia and Indonesia.* London: Gresham, 1930.

MacKillop, James. *A Dictionary of Celtic Mythology.* London: Oxford University Press, 2004.

Maggi, Armando. *In the Company of Demons: Unnatural Beings, Love, and Identity in the Italian Renaissance.*

Mahadevan, T.M.P. and Śaṅkarācārya. *The Hymns of Śaṅkara.* Delhi: Motilal Banarsidass, 1997.

Malik, Subhash Chandra. *Mind, Man, and Mask.* New Delhi: Indira Gandhi National Center for the Arts, 2001.

Manual, Ronald, Christine A. Adamec, and Ada P. Kahn. *The Encyclopedia of Phobias, Fears, and Anxieties.* New York: Infobase, 2008.

Manuscripts and Books on Medicine, Alchemy, Astrology and Natural Sciences Arranged in Chronological Order. Whitefish: Kessinger, 2004.

Mao Zedong. *The Writings of Mao Zedong, 1949–1976: January 1956–December 1957.* Ed. Michael Y.M. Kau, and John K. Leung, Armonk: M.E. Sharpe, 1992.

Marcus, Jacob Rader. *The Jew in the Medieval World: A Source Book, 315–1791.* Cincinnati: Sinai Press, 1938.

Mark, Lisbeth. *The Book of Hierarchies: A Compendium of Steps, Ranks, Orders, Levels, Classes, Grades, Tiers, Arrays, Degrees, Lines, Divisions, Categories, Precedents, Priorities, and Other Distinctions.* New York: W. Morrow, 1984.

Marlowe, Christopher. *Tragical History of Dr. Faustus: Greene, Honourable History of Friar Bacon and Friar Bungay.* Oxford: Clarendon Press, 1887.

Marple, Eric. *The Domain of Devils.* London: Robert Hale, 1966.

Martin, John Stanley. *Ragnarok: An Investigation into Old Norse Concepts of the Fate of the Gods.* Assen: Van Gorcum, 1972.

Martínez, Florentino García, and W.G.E. Watson. *The Dead Sea Scrolls Translated: The Qumran Texts in English.* Leiden: Brill, 1996.

Masello, Robert. *Fallen Angels and Spirits of the Dark.* New York: Berkeley, 1994.

_____. *Raising Hell: A Concise History of the Black Arts— And Those Who Dared to Practice Them.* New York: Berkely, 1996.

Mason, Asenath. *Necronomicon Gnosis: A Practical Introduction.* Gesamtherstellung: Edition Roter Drache, 2007.

Maspero, Gaston, and Hasan M. El-Shamy. *Popular Stories of Ancient Egypt.* Oxford: Oxford University Press, 2004.

Maspero, Henri. *China in Antiquity.* Amherst: University of Massachusetts Press, 1978.

_____. *Taoism and Chinese Religion.* Amherst: University of Massachusetts Press, 1981.

Masters, Anthony. *Devil's Dominion: The Complete Story of Hell and Satanism in the Modern World.* Edison: Castle Books, 1978.

Masters, Robert E.L. *Eros and Evil: The Sexual Psychopathology of Witchcraft; Contains the Complete Text of Sinistrari's Demoniality.* New York: Viking Press, 1974.

Mather, George A., Larry A. Nichols, Alvin J. Schmidt, and Kurt Van Gorden. *Encyclopedic Dictionary of Cults, Sects, and World Religions.* Grand Rapids: Zondervan, 2006.

Mathers, S.L. *The Kabbalah Unveiled.* Pomeroy: Health Research Books, 2003.

Mathers, S.L. McGregor. *Magia Della Cabala*, Vol. 2. Rome: Edizioni Studio Tesi, 1981.

Mathers, Samuel Liddell MacGregor. *Book of the Sacred Magic of Abra-Melin.* Whitefish: Kessinger, 1998.

_____. *The Book of the Sacred Magic of Abramelin the Mage.* New York: Cosimo, 2007.

_____. *The Sacred Magic of Abramelin the Mage.* 1898.

_____. *Selected Occult Writings of S.L. MacGregor Mathers.* Whitefish: Kessinger, 2005.

Mathers, S.L. MacGregor, and J.W. Brodie-Innes. *The Sorcerer and His Apprentice: Unknown Hermetic Writings of S.L. Macgregor Mathers and J.W. Brodie-Innes.* Wellingborough: Aquarian, 1983.

_____, and William Keith. *The Grimoire of Armadel.* Boston: Weiser, 2001.

_____, and Aleister Crowley. *The Goetia: The Lesser Key of Solomon the King.* (1904) 1995.

_____, and R.A. Gilbert. *The Key of Solomon the King: Clavicula Salomonis.* Boston: Weiser, 2000.

_____, J.W. Brodie-Innes, and R.A. Gilbert. *The Sorcerer and His Apprentice: Unknown Hermetic Writings of S.L. Macgregor Mathers and J.W. Brodie-Innes, Roots of the Golden Dawn Series.* Wellingborough: Aquarian, 1983.

Matthews, Caitlin. *Sophia: Goddess of Wisdom, Bride of God.* Wheaton: Quest Books, 2001.

Matthews, Warren. *World Religions.* Stamford: Cengage Learning, 2008.

Maxwell, William George. *In Malay Forests.* Edinburgh: Blackwood, 1907.

Mayo, Margaret, and Jane Ray. *Mythical Birds and Beasts from Many Lands.* New York: Dutton Children's Books, 1997.

Mays, Ron. *Hell and Destruction.* New York: Vantage Press, 2005.

McClelland, Bruce. *Slayers and their Vampires: A Cultural History of Killing the Dead.* Ann Arbor: University of Michigan Press, 2006.

McClintock, John. *Cyclopaedia of Biblical, Theological, and Ecclesiastical Literature*, Vol. 11. New York: Harper, 1889.

_____, and James Strong. *Cyclopaedia of Biblical, Theological, and Ecclesiastical Literature*, Vol. 2. New York: Harper, 1868.

_____, and _____. *Cyclopaedia of Biblical, Theological, and Ecclesiastical Literature*, Vol. 4. New York: Harper, 1872.

_____, and _____. *Cyclopaedia of Biblical, Theological, and Ecclesiastical Literature*, Vol. 5. New York: Harper, 1873.

McCown, Chester Charlton. *The Testament of Solomon: Edited from Manuscripts at Mount Athos, Bologna, Holkham Hall, Jerusalem, London, Milan, Paris and Vienna.* Leipzig: J.C. Hinrichs, 1922.

McCoy, Edain. *Celtic Myth and Magick: Harness the Power of the Gods and Goddesses.* St. Paul: Llewellyn, 1995.

McDonough, Christopher Michael. "Carna, Proca and the Strix on the Kalends of June," *Transactions of the American Philological Association*, Vol. 127. 1997.

McGinn, Bernard. *Antichrist: Two Thousand Years of the Human Fascination with Evil.* New York: Columbia University Press, 2000.

McHugh, James Noel. *Hantu Hantu: An Account of Ghost Belief in Modern Malaya.* Singapore: Donald Moore for Eastern Universities Press, 1959.

McIntosh, Christopher. *Eliphas Lévi and the French Occult Revival.* York Beach: S. Weiser, 1974.

McKean, Erin. *Verbatim: From the Bawdy to the Sublime, the Best Writing on Language for Word Lovers, Grammar Mavens, and Armchair Linguists.* Boston: Houghton Mifflin Harcourt, 2001.

McKinnell, John, David Ashurst, and Donata Kick. *The Fantastic in Old Norse/Icelandic Literature.* London: Center for Medieval and Early Renaissance Studies, 2006.

McLean, Adam. *The Magical Calendar: A Synthesis of Magical Symbolism from the Seventeenth Century Renaissance of Medieval Occultism.* Boston: Red Wheel/Weiser, 1979.

_____. *Treatise on Angel Magic: Being a Complete Tran-*

scription of Ms. Harley 6482 in the British Library. Grand Rapids: Phanes Press, 1990.

_____. *A Treatise on Angel Magic: Maghum Opus Hermetic Sourceworks.* Boston: Weiser, 2006.

Mead, G.R.S. *Fragments of a Faith Forgotten: The Gnostics; A Contribution to the Study of the Origins of Christianity.* New York: Cosimo, 2007.

Mednick, Sara, and Mark Ehrman. *Take a Nap! Change Your Life.* New York: Workman, 2006.

Meier, John P. *A Marginal Jew: Rethinking the Historical Jesus.* New Haven: Yale University Press, 2009.

Meletinskii, Eleazar Moiseevich, Guy Lanoue, and Alexandre Sadetsky. *The Poetics of Myth.* London: Routledge, 2000.

Melton, J. Gordon. *Encyclopedia of Occultism.* Detroit: Gale Research, 1996.

Mercatante, Anthony S. *Good and Evil: Mythology and Folklore.* New York: Harper and Row, 1978.

Merriam-Webster, Inc. *Merriam-Webster's Collegiate Dictionary,* Edition 11. Springfield: Merriam-Webster, 2003.

Merriam-Webster, Inc. *Merriam-Webster's Encyclopedia of World Religions.* Springfield: Merriam-Webster, 1999.

Messadié, Gérald. *A History of the Devil.* New York: Kodansha Globe, 1997.

Methodist Book Concern. *The Methodist Review,* Vol. 35. New York: Methodist Book Concern, 1883.

Meurger, Michel, and Claude Gagnon. *Lake Monster Traditions: A Cross-Cultural Analysis.* London: Fortean Tomes, 1988.

Mew, James. "The Hebrew Hell," *The Eclectic Magazine of Foreign Literature, Science, and Art,* Vol. 115, September 1890, pages 404–14. New York: Leavitt, Trow, 1890.

Meyer, Johann Jakob. *Sexual Life in Ancient India: A Study in the Comparative History of Indian Culture.* New Delhi, India: Motilal Banarsidass, 1989.

Meyer, Marvin W. *The Ancient Mysteries, A Sourcebook: Sacred Texts of the Mystery Religions of the Ancient Mediterranean World.* Philadelphia: University of Pennsylvania Press, 1999.

_____. *The Gnostic Gospels of Jesus: The Definitive Collection of Mystical Gospels and Secret Books about Jesus of Nazareth.* New York: HarperCollins, 2005.

_____, and Richard Smith. *Ancient Christian Magic: Coptic Texts of Ritual Power.* Princeton: Princeton University Press, 1999.

Michelet, Jules. *La Sorcière: The Witch of the Middle Ages.* London: Simpkin, Marshall, 1863.

Middelkoop, Pieter. *Curse, Retribution, Enmity as Data in Natural Religion, Especially in Timor, Confronted with the Scripture.* Amsterdam: Jacob van Kampen, 1960.

Middleton, John, and E.H. Winter. *Witchcraft and Sorcery in East Africa.* London: Psychology Press, 2004.

Miguel de Barandiarán, José, and Jesús Altuna. *Selected Writings of José Miguel de Barandiarán: Basque Prehistory and Ethnography.* Reno: University of Nevada Press, 2009.

Mills, Hayworth Lawrence. "God and His Immortals: Their Counterparts," *Open Court,* Vol. 21. Chicago: Open Court, 1900.

_____. *Zarathustra, Philo, the Achaemenids and Israel: Being a Treatise Upon the Antiquity and Influence of the Avesta.* Cambridge: Andover Harvard Thelogical Library, 1906.

Minchero, Juan Ruiz. *The Voice from the Jordan.* Victoria: Trafford, 2003.

Mitchell, James. *Significant Etymology: Or, Roots, Stems, and Branches of the English Language.* London: William Blackwood and Sons, 1908.

Mittal, J.P. *History of Ancient India: From 7300 BC to 4250 BC.* New Delhi: Atlantic, 2006.

Mitter, Partha. *Much Maligned Monsters: A History of European Reactions to Indian Art.* Chicago: University of Chicago Press, 1992.

Monaghan, Patricia. *The Encyclopedia of Celtic Mythology and Folklore.* New York: Infobase, 2004.

_____. *Encyclopedia of Goddesses and Heroines.* Santa Barbara: ABC-CLIO, 2009.

_____. *Women in Myth and Legend.* London: Junction Books, 1981.

Monier-Williams, Monier. *Brāhmanism and Hindūism: Or, Religious Thought and Life in India, as Based on the Veda and Other Sacred Books of the Hindūs.* New York: Macmillan, 1891.

_____. *Buddhism in its Connexion with Brāhmanism and Hindūism, and in its Contrast with Christianity.* London: John Murray, 1890.

_____. *A Sanskrit-English Dictionary: Etymologically and Philologically Arranged with Special Reference to Cognate Indo-European Languages.* Delhi: Motilal Banarsidass, 2005.

Montgomery, James, Benjamin Wisener Bacon and William H. Cobb. *Journal of Biblical Literature,* Vols. 31–32. Boston: Society of Biblical Literature and Exegesis, 1912.

Moore, George F. *Journal of the American Oriental Society,* Vol. 21. New Haven: American Oriental Society, 1902.

Moore, Virginia. *The Unicorn: William Butler Yeats' Search for Reality.* New York: Macmillan, 1954.

Morgan, Genevieve, and Tom Morgan. *The Devil: A Visual Guide to the Demonic, Evil, Scurrilous, and Bad.* San Francisco: Chronicle Books, 1996.

Morley, Henry. *Cornelius Agrippa: The Life of Henry Cornelius Agrippa von Nettesheim, Doctor and Knight, Commonly Known as a Magician,* Vol. 1. London: Chapman and Hall, 1856.

Morrison, Robert. *Dictionary of the Chinese Language: In Three Parts,* Vol. 1. Macao: Honorable East India Company's Press, 1815.

Morrison, Simon Alexander. *Russian Opera and the Symbolist Movement.* Berkeley: University of California Press, 2002.

Mortenson, Terry, and Thane Hutcherson Ury. *Coming to Grips with Genesis: Biblical Authority and the Age of the Earth.* Green Forest: New Leaf, 2008.

Morvan, F. *Legends of the Sea.* London: Minerva, 1980.

Moss, Peter. *Distant Archipelagos.* Bloomington: iUniverse, 2004.

Mould, Elmer Wallace King. *Essentials of Bible History.* New York: Ronald Press, 1951.

Moura, Ann. *Mansions of the Moon for the Green Witch: A Complete Book of Lunar Magic.* St. Paul: Llewellyn, 2010.

Muchembled, Robert. *A History of the Devil: From the Middle Ages to the Present.* Malden: Wiley-Blackwell, 2003.

Müller, Friedrich Max. *Rig-Veda-Sanhita: The Sacred Hymns of the Brahmans,* Vol. 1. London: Trübner, 1869.

_____. *The Sacred Books of the East,* Vol. 23. London: Clarendon Press, 1883.

Mumford, Stan. *Himalayan Dialogue: Tibetan Lamas and Gurung Shamans in Nepal.* Madison: University of Wisconsin Press, 1989.

Munan, Heidi. *Culture Shock! Borneo: A Survival Guide to Customs and Etiquette.* Tarrytown: Marshall Cavendish, 2006.

Murray, Margaret Alice. *The Witch-cult in Western Europe.* Plain Label Books, 1962.

Muss-Arnolt, William. *A Concise Dictionary of the Assyrian Language,* Vol. 1. Berlin: Reuther and Reichard, 1905.

Myer, Isaac. *Qabbalah: The Philosophical Writings of Solomon ben Yehudah Ibn Gebirol, or Avicebron, and their Connection with the Hebrew Qabbalah and Sepher ha-Zohar, with Remarks upon the Antiquity and Content of the Latter and Translations of Selected Passages from the Same.* Philadelphia: Isaac Myer, 1888.

Mysticalgod. *Magical Advice, Part 5, from Mysticalgod.* Worcester: Mysticalgod, 2010.

Najovits, Simson R. *Egypt, Trunk of the Tree: A Modern Survey of an Ancient Land.* New York: Algora, 2004.

Nan Nü. Men, Women, and Gender in Early and Imperial China. Boston: Brill, 1999.

Narayan, R.K. *Gods, Demons, and Others.* Chicago: University of Chicago Press, 1993.

Nash, Thomas. *The Works of Thomas Nashe: The anatomie of absvrditie. A covntercvffe given to Martin Ivnior. The retvrne of Pasqvill. The first parte of Pasqvils apologie. Pierce Penilesse his svpplication to the divell. Strange newes of the intercepting certaine letters. The terrors of the night.* London: A.H. Bullen, 1904.

Nassau, Robert Hamill. *Fetishism in West Africa: Forty Years' Observation of Native Customs and Superstitions.* Whitefish: Kessinger, 2003.

National Psychological Association for Psychoanalysis. *The Psychoanalytic Review,* Vol. 20. New York: W.A. White and S.E. Jelliffe, 1933.

Neale, John Mason. *Notes Ecclesiological and Picturesque, on Dalmatia, Croatia, Istria, Styria: With a Visit to Montenegro.* London: J.T. Hayes, 1861.

Nettleship, Henry. *Contributions to Latin Lexicography.* New York: Clarendon Press, 1889.

Netzley, Patricia D. *Angels.* San Diego: Lucent Books, 2000.

Neusner, Jacob. *Christianity, Judaism and Other Greco-Roman Cults: Studies for Morton Smith at Sixty,* Vol. 2. Leiden: Brill, 1975.

_____. *A History of the Jews in Babylonia: Later Sasanian Times.* Leiden: E.J. Brill, 1970.

Newman, Paul. *A Hausa-English Dictionary.* London: Yale University Press, 2007.

NicMhacha, Sharynne MacLeod. *Queen of the Night: Rediscovering the Celtic Moon Goddess.* Boston: Weiser, 2005.

Nicoll, Allardyce. *Masks, Mimes and Miracles: Studies in the Popular Theater.* New York: Cooper Square, 1963.

Nigg, Joe. *Wonder Beasts: Tales and Lore of the Phoenix, the Griffin, the Unicorn, and the Dragon.* Englewood: Libraries Unlimited, 1995.

Norberg, Matthias. *Codex Nasaraeus: Liber Adami Appellatus, Syriace Transscriptus, Loco Vocalium, Ubi Vicem Literarum Gutturalium Præstiterint, His Substitutis,* Vols. 1–2. London: Literis Berlingianis, 1815.

Norbu, Namkhai, Adriano Clemente, Andrew Lukianowicz, and the Library of Tibetan Works and Archives. *Drung, Deu, and Bön: Narrations, Symbolic Languages, and the Bön Traditions in Ancient Tibet.* Dharamsala: Library of Tibetan Works and Archives, 1995.

Norwegian-American Studies and Records, Vol. 12. Northfield: Norwegian-American Historical Association, 1941.

Notestein, Wallace. *A History of Witchcraft in England from 1558 to 1718.* Washington, DC: American Historical Association, 1911.

Obeyesekere, Gananath. *The Cult of the Goddess Pattini.* Chicago: University of Chicago Press, 1984.

Oeconomides, D.B. "Yello danes les Traditions des peoples Hellenique et Roumain." *International Congress for Folk Narrative Research in Athens* (Athens, 1965): 328–34.

Oesterle, Joe, Tim Cridland, and Mark Moran. *Weird Las Vegas and Nevada: Your Alternative Travel Guide to Sin City and the Silver State.* New York: Sterling, 2007.

Oesterley, W.O.E. *Immortality and the Unseen World: A Study in Old Testament Religion 1921.* Whitefish: Kessinger, 2004.

Oesterreich, Traugott Konstantin. *Possession, Demoniacal and Other, Among Primitive Races, in Antiquity, the Middle Ages and Modern Times.* London: Routledge, 1999.

O'Flaherty, Wendy Doniger. *The Origins of Evil in Hindu Mythology.* Delhi: Motilal Banarsidass, 1988.

Ogilvie, John. *The Imperial Dictionary of the English Language: A Complete Encyclopedic Lexicon, Literary, Scientific, and Technological.* London: Blackie and Son, 1882.

O'Grady, Standish. *History of Ireland: Cuculain and His Contemporaries.* London: Sampson, Low, Searle, Marston, and Rivington, 1880.

O'Hanlon, John. *Irish Folk Lore: Traditions and Superstitions of the Country, with Humorous Tales.* Glasgow: Cameron and Ferguson, 1870.

Oinas, Felix J. *Essays on Russian Folklore and Mythology.* Bloomington: Slavica, 1985.

Olcott, Henry Steel. *People from the Other World.* Hartford: American, 1875.

Oldenberg, Hermann. *The Religion of the Veda.* Delhi: Motilal Banarsidass, 1988.

Oliphant, Laurence, Rosamond Dale Owen, and Haskett Smith. *Scientific Religion: Or, Higher Possibilities of Life and Practice Through the Operation of Natural Forces.* Edinburgh: William Blackwood and Sons, 1888.

Oliphant, Samuel Grant. "The Story of the Strix: Ancient," *Transactions and Proceedings of the American Philological Association,* Vol. 44, 1913.

Olsen, Dale Alan. *Music of the Warao of Venezuela: Song People of the Rain Forest.* Gainesville: University Press of Florida, 1996.

Olyan, Saul M. *A Thousand Thousands Served Him: Exegesis and the Naming of Angels in Ancient Judaism.* Tubingen: Mohr Siebeck, 1993.

Oort, Henricus, and Reinhart Pieter Anne Dozy. *The Worship of Baalim in Israel.* London: Longmans, Green, 1865.

Oppenheim, A. Leo. *Ancient Mesopotamia: Portrait of a Dead Civilization.* Chicago: University of Chicago Press, 1964.

Orbell, Margaret Rose. *The Illustrated Encyclopedia of Māori Myth and Legend.* Sydney: University of New South Wales Press, 1996.

Orellana, Sandra Lee. *Indian Medicine in Highland Guatemala: The Pre–Hispanic and Colonial Periods.* Albuquerque: University of New Mexico Press, 1987.

Országh, László, Ilona Lukácsné Láng, and Tamás Magay. *Magyar: Angol Szótár.* Budapest: Akadémiai Kiadó, 1963.

Osborne, Harold. "Library of the World's Myths and Legends," *South American Mythology.* New York: Peter Bedrick Books, 1968.

Osburn, William. *The Monumental History of Egypt.* London: Trübner, 1854.

Osman, Mohd Taib. *Indigenous, Hindu, and Islamic Elements in Malay Folk Beliefs.* Bloomington: Indiana University, 1967.

_____. *Malay Folk Beliefs: An Integration of Disparate Elements*. Kuala Lumpur: Kementerian Pendidikan, Dewan Bahasa dan Pustaka, 1989.

_____. *Malaysian World-View*. Singapore: Institute of Southeast Asian Studies, 1985.

Ouspensky, P.D. *Talks with a Devil*. Toronto: Penguin Group, 1989.

Owen, Robert. *Sanctorale Catholicum, or, Book of Saints: With Notes Critical, Exegetical, and Historical*. London: C. Kegan Paul, 1880.

Oxford Journals (Firm). *Notes and Queries*. Oxford: Oxford University Press, 1874.

Oxford University Press. *Catholic Comparative New Testament*. New York: Oxford University Press, 2006.

Oxford University Press. *The Periodical*, Vol. 8, Issue 113. New York: Oxford University Press, 1921.

Pacheco, Allan. *Ghosts-Murder-Mayhem: A Chronicle of Santa Fe; Lies, Legends, Facts, Tall Tales, and Useless Information*. Santa Fe: Sunstone Press, 2004.

Padfield, Joseph Edwin. *The Hindu at Home: Being Sketches of Hindu Daily Life*. Madras: Society for Promoting Christian Knowledge, 1896.

Paine, Lauran. *The Hierarchy of Hell*. New York: Hippocrene Books, 1972.

Parent, Michael, and Julien Olivier. *Of Kings and Fools: Stories of the French Tradition in North America*. Little Rock: August House, 1996.

Parker, Arthur Caswell. *The Code of Handsome Lake: The Seneca Prophet*. Albany: State University of New York, 1912.

Parker, Janet, Alice Mills and Julie Stanton. *Mythology: Myths, Legends and Fantasies*. Johannesburg: Struik, 2007.

_____, _____, and _____. *Mythology: Myths, Legends and Fantasies*. Capetown: Struik, 2007.

Parker, Richard Green. *Outlines of General History, in the Form of Question and Answer: Designed as the Foundation and the Review of a Course of Historical Reading*. New York: Harper and Brothers, 1848.

Parmeshwaranand, *Encyclopaedic Dictionary of Pura[amacron]as*, Vol. 1 and 3. New Delhi: Sarup and Sons, 2001.

Partridge, Eric. *Origins: A Short Etymological Dictionary of Modern English*. New York: Macmillan, 1966.

Paswan, Sanjay. *Encyclopaedia of Dalits in India: Women*. New Delhi: Gyan, 2002.

Patai, Raphael. *Gates to the Old City: A Book of Jewish Legends*. Detroit: Wayne State University Press, 1981.

_____. *The Hebrew Goddess*. New York: KTAV, 1978.

_____, and Francis Lee Utley, Dov Noy, Indiana University. *Indiana University Publications, Folklore Series, Issue 13*. Bloomington: Indiana University Press, 1960.

Patrich, Joseph. *The Sabaite Heritage in the Orthodox Church from the Fifth Century to the Present*. New Plymouth: Peters, 2001.

Paul, Robert A. *The Sherpas of Nepal in the Tibetan Cultural Context: The Tibetan Symbolic World, A Psychoanalytic Exploration*. Delhi: Motilal Banarsidass, 1989.

Pauley, Daniel C. *Pauley's Guide: A Dictionary of Japanese Martial Arts and Culture*. Delores: Anaguma Seizan, 2009.

Pearson, Birger A. *Gnosticism, Judaism, and Egyptian Christianity*. Minneapolis: Fortress Press, 2006.

Peck, Harry Thurston, Selim Hobart Peabody, and Charles Francis Richardson. *The International Cyclopaedia: A Compendium of Human Knowledge*, Vol. 11. New York: Dodd, Mead, 1900.

Peletz, Michael G. *Reason and Passion: Representations of Gender in a Malay Society*. Berkeley: University of California Press, 1996.

Penas, Beatriz. *The Intertextual Dimension of Discourse: Pragmalinguistic-Cognitive-Hermeneutic Approaches*. Zaragoza: Universidad de Zaragoza, 1996.

Pentikäinen, Juha. "The Nordic Dead-Child Tradition: Nordic Dead-Child Beings," *FF Communications*, No. 202. Helsinki: Suomalainen Tiedeakatemia, 1968.

Penwyche, Gosamer. *The World of Angels*. Minneapolis: Fair Winds, 2003.

Pepin, Ronald E. *The Vatican Mythographers*. New York: Fordham University Press, 2008.

Percy, Reuben. *The Mirror of Literature, Amusement, and Instruction*, Vol. 21. London: J. Limbird, 1833.

_____, and John Timbs. *The Mirror of Literature, Amusement, and Instruction*, Vol. 39. London: Hugh Cunningham, 1842.

Pereira, Filomena Maria. *Lilith: The Edge of Forever*. Las Colinas: Ide House, 1998.

Perry, E.D. "Indra in the Rig-Veda," *Journal of the American Oriental Society*, Vol. 11, page 199. New York: American Oriental Society, 1882.

Peschke, Michael. *International Encyclopedia of Pseudonyms: Part I, Real Names*. New York: Walter de Gruyter, 2006.

Peterson, Amy T., and David J. Dunworth. *Mythology in Our Midst: A Guide to Cultural References*. Westport: Greenwood, 2004.

Peterson, Joseph H. *The Lesser Key of Solomon: Lemegeton Clavicula Salomonis*. Boston: Weiser, 2001.

Petrie, F.W.H., and the Victoria Institute. *Journal of the Transactions of the Victoria Institute, or Philosophical Society of Great Britain*, Vol. 14. London: Victoria Institute, 1881.

Phillips, Charles, and Michael Kerrigan. *Forests of the Vampire*. Amsterdam: Time-Life Books, 1999.

Philological Society of Great Britain. *Transactions of the Philological Society*. London: George Bell, 1856.

Philpott, Don. *Trinidad and Tobago*. Madison: Hunter Publishing, 2002.

Pick, Daniel, and Lyndal Roper. *Dreams and History: the Interpretation of Dreams from Ancient Greece to Modern Psychoanalysis*. New York: Psychology Press, 2004.

Pietersma, Albert. *The Apocryphon of Jannes and Jambres the Magicians*. Leiden: E.J. Brill, 1994.

Pilch, John J. *The Cultural Dictionary of the Bible*. Collegeville: Liturgical Press, 1999.

Pinch, Geraldine. *Egyptian Mythology: A Guide to the Gods, Goddesses, and Traditions of Ancient Egypt*. New York: Oxford University Press, 2004.

_____. *Magic in Ancient Egypt*. Austin: University of Texas Press, 1995.

Pinches, Theophilus Goldridge. *The Religion of Babylonia and Assyria*, Vol. 8. London: Archibald Constable, 1906.

Pitrat, John Claudius. *Pagan Origin of Partialist Doctrines*. Cincinnati: Willliamson and Cantwell, 1871.

Placzek, B. "Arthropod Mythology," *Popular Science*, September 1882, Vol. 21, No. 37. New York: Bonnier, 1882.

Platts, John T. *A Dictionary of Urdu Classical Hindi and English*. Whitefish: Kessinger, 2004.

Plumptre, Edward Hayes. *The Bible Educator*. London: Cassell, Petter and Galpin, 1875.

Pócs, Éva. *Fairies and Witches at the Boundary of South-Eastern and Central Europe*. Helsinki: Suomalainen Tiedeakatemia, 1989.

Poignant, Roslyn. *Oceanic Mythology: The Myths of Polynesia, Micronesia, Melanesia, Australia*. New York: Hamlyn, 1975.

Poinsot, M.C. *Complete Book of the Occult and Fortune Telling*. Whitefish: Kessinger, 2003.

Poinsot, Mafféo Charles. *The Encyclopedia of Occult Sciences*. New York: R.M. McBride, 1939.

Pomfret, John. *Chinese Lessons: Five Classmates and the Story of the New China*. New York: Macmillan, 2006.

Poole, Edward Stanley. *The Thousand and One Nights: Commonly Called In England, the Arabian Nights' Entertainments; A New Translation From the Arabic, with Copious Notes*, Vol. 1. London: Routledge, Warne, and Routledge, 1865.

Popular Science Monthly, Vol. 21, May to October. New York: D. Appleton, 1882.

Porteous, Alexander. *Forest Folklore: Mythology and Romance*. Whitefish: Kessinger, 2006.

Porter, Joshua Roy. *The Lost Bible: Forgotten Scriptures Revealed*. Totowa: Humana Press, 2001.

Porterfield, Jason, and Corona Brezina. *Chile: A Primary Source Cultural Guide*. New York: Rosen, 2003.

Pospisil, Leopold J. *Kapauku Papuans and their Law*. New Haven: Human Relations Area Files Press, 1964.

_____. *The Kapauku Papuans of West New Guinea*. New York: Holt, Rinehart and Winston, 1963.

Powell, Barry B. *Classical Myth*. Upper Saddle River: Pearson/Prentice Hall, 2004.

Powell, Kathryn, and D.G. Scragg. *Apocryphal Texts and Traditions in Anglo-Saxon England*. Cambridge: D.S. Brewer, 2003.

Powers, William K. *Oglala Religion*. Lincoln: University of Nebraska Press, 1982.

Prabhupāda, A.C. Bhaktivedanta, and the International Society for Krishna Consciousness. *Srimad Bhagavatam: First Canto*, Vol. 1, Part 2. Los Angeles: Bhaktivedanta Book Trust, 1972.

Prasad, Sundari. *The Lilitu: The Best of Sundari Prasad*. Raleigh: Lulu, 2005.

Presutta, David. *The Biblical Cosmos versus Modern Cosmology: Why the Bible is Not the Word of God*. Coral Springs: Llumina Press, 2007.

Price, Charles Edwin. *Demon in the Woods: Tall Tales and True from East Tennessee*. Johnson City: Overmountain, 1992.

Price, David A. *Love and Hate in Jamestown: John Smith, Pocahontas, and the Start of a New Nation*. New York: Vintage Books, 2005.

Price, Robert M. *The Pre-Nicene New Testament: Fifty-Four Formative Texts*. Salt Lake City: Signature, 2006.

Prichard, James Cowles, and Edwin Norris. *The Natural History of Man*, Vol. 1. London: H. Bailliers, 1855.

Priest, Josiah. *The Anti-Universalist or, History of the Fallen Angels of the Scriptures: Proofs of the Being of Satan and of Evil Spirits, and Many other Curious Matters Connected Therewith*, Part 1. Albany: J. Munsell, 1839.

Prigent, Pierre. *Commentary on the Apocalypse of St. John*. Tubingen: Mohr Siebeck, 2004.

Prime, Ranchor, and B.G. Sharma. *Ramayana: A Tale of Gods and Demons*. New York: Springer Science and Business, 2004.

Prince, J. Dyneley. *Journal of the American Oriental Society*, Vol. 28. New Haven: American Oriental Society, 1907.

Princeton Theological Seminary. *The Princeton Theological Review*, Vol. 21. Philadelphia: MacCalla, 1923.

Prioreschi, Plinio. *Roman Medicine*. Omaha: Horatius Press, 1998.

Prophet, Elizabeth Clare. *Fallen Angels and the Origins of Evil: Why Church Fathers Suppressed the Book of Enoch and Its Startling Revelations*. Corwin Springs: Summit University Press, 2000.

Pu, Muzhou. *Rethinking Ghosts in World Religions*. Leiden: Brill, 2009.

Pullen-Burry, Henry B. *Qabalism*. Whitefish: Kessinger, 2003.

Pulszky, Ferencz Aurelius, and Terézia Pulszky. *Tales and Traditions of Hungary*. London: Henry Colburn, 1851.

Putney, Christopher. *Russian Devils and Diabolic Conditionality in Nikolai Gogol's Evenings on a Farm Near Dikanka*. New York: P. Lang, 1999.

Qu, Yuan, and Stephen Field. *Tian Wen: A Chinese Book of Origins*. New York: New Directions, 1986.

Quarterly Oriental Magazine, Review and Register, Vol. 6. Calcutta: Thacker, 1826.

Quispel, Gilles, R. van den Broek, and Maarten Jozef Vermaseren. *Studies in Gnosticism and Hellenistic Religions: Presented to Gilles Quispel on the Occasion of his 65th Birthday*. Leiden: Brill Archive, 1981.

Rachleff, Owen S., and Isaac Bashevis Singer. *The Occult in Art*. Warwick: Cromwell, 1993.

Raghavan, M.D., and R.C. de Sy Manukulasooriya. *Sinhala Natum: Dances of the Sinhalese*. Colombo: M.D. Gunasena, 1967.

Ramos, Maximo D. *The Creatures of Midnight: Faded Deities of Luzon, the Visayas and Mindanao*. Philippines: Island Publishers, 1967.

_____. *Creatures of Philippine Lower Mythology*. Philippines: University of the Philippines Press, 1971.

Ramsay, William M. *The Layman's Guide to the New Testament*. Louisville: Westminster John Knox Press, 1981.

_____, and William Ramsay. *Westminster Guide to the Books of the Bible*. Louisville: Westminster John Knox Press, 1994.

Randi, James. *An Encyclopedia of Claims, Frauds, and Hoaxes of the Occult and Supernatural: James Randi's Decidedly Skeptical Definitions of Alternate Realities*. New York: St. Martin's Press, 1995.

Rappoport, Angelo S. *Myth and Legend of Ancient Israel*, Vol. 1. Whitefish: Kessinger, 2005.

_____. *Superstitions of Sailors*. Ann Arbor: Gryphon Books, 1971.

Ras, J.J. *The Shadow of the Ivory Tree: Language, Literature and History in Nusantara*. Leiden: Talen en Culturen van Zuidoost-Azië en Oceanië, Rijksuniversiteit te Leiden, 1992.

Rasula, Jed, and Steve McCaffery. *Imagining Language: An Anthology*. Cambridge: MIT Press, 2001.

Rattray, Robert Sutherland, and Johann Gottlieb Christaller. *Ashanti Proverbs: The Primitive Ethics of a Savage People*. Ventnor, Isle of Wight: Clarendon Press, 1916.

Redfield, Bessie Gordon. *Gods: A Dictionary of the Deities of All Lands*. New York: G.P. Putnam's sons, 1931.

Redgrove, H. Stanley. *Bygone Beliefs Being a Series of Excursions in the Byways of Thought*. Whitefish: Kessinger, 1998.

Reed, Alexander Wyclif. *Treasury of Maori Folklore*. Wellington: A.H. and A.W. Reed, 1963.

Reed, Annette Yoshiko. *Fallen Angels and the History of Judaism and Christianity: The Reception of Enochic Literature*. Cambridge: Cambridge University Press, 2005.

Regardie, Israel. *The Tree of Life: A Study in Magic*. Boston: Weiser, 1972.

Reichel-Dolmatoff, Gerardo. *The Shaman and the Jaguar: A Study of Narcotic Drugs Among the Indians of Colombia*. Philadelphia: Temple University Press, 1975.

Reicke, Bo. *The Disobedient Spirits and Christian Baptism: A Study of 1 Pet. III. 19 and its Context.* Copenhagen: E. Munksgaard, 1946.

Reiling, J., and J.L. Swellengrebel. *A Translator's Handbook on the Gospel of Luke.* Leiden: Brill Archive, 1971.

Reiterer, Friedrich Vinzenz, Tobias Nicklas, and Karin Schöpflin. *Angels: The Concept of Celestial Beings—Origins, Development and Reception.* New York: Walter de Gruyter, 2007.

Religious and Cosmic Beliefs of Central Polynesia. Cambridge: Cambridge University Press Archive, 1933.

Remler, Pat. *Egyptian Mythology A to Z.* New York: Infobase, 2010.

Réville, Albert. *The Native Religions of Mexico and Peru.* New York: Charles Scribner's Sons, 1884.

Riasanovsky, Nicholas Valentine, Thomas Eekman, and Gleb Struve. *California Slavic Studies,* Vol. 11. Berkeley: University of California Press, 1980.

Riccardo, Martin V. *Liquid Dreams of Vampires.* Woodbury: Llewellyn, 1996.

Richards, Sue Poorman, and Larry Richards. *Every Woman in the Bible.* Nashville: T. Nelson, 1999.

Riesenfeld, Alphonse. *The Megalithic Culture of Melanesia.* Leiden: Brill, 1950.

Ringdal, Nils Johan, and Richard Daly. *Love for Sale: A World History of Prostitution.* New York: Grove Press, 2005.

Riordan, James. *The Sun Maiden and the Crescent Moon: Siberian Folk Tales.* Northampton: Interlink Books, 1991.

Ripley, George, and Charles Anderson Dana. *The American Cyclopaedia: A Popular Dictionary of General Knowledge,* Vol. 5. New York: D. Appleton, 1883.

_____, and _____. *The New American Cyclopaedia: A Popular Dictionary of General Knowledge,* Vol. 6. New York: Appleton, 1867.

Ritson, Joseph. *Fairy Tales, Now First Collected: To Which are Prefixed Two Dissertations.* London: Payne and Foss, 1831.

Rivers, William Halse. *Medicine, Magic, and Religion: The Fitzpatrick Lectures Delivered Before the Royal College of Physicians of London in 1915 and 1916.* London: Psychology Press, 2001.

Robbins, Richard Howard. *Global Problems and the Culture of Capitalism.* Boston: Allyn and Bacon, 1998.

Robbins, Rossell Hope. *The Encyclopedia of Witchcraft and Demonology.* New York: Crown, 1959.

Roberts, Jane, Christian Kay, and Lynne Grundy. *A Thesaurus of Old English: Index.* Atlanta: Rodopi, 2000.

Roberts, Jeremy. *Japanese Mythology A to Z.* New York: Infobase, 2009.

Roberts, Susan. *The Magician of the Golden Dawn: The Story of Aleister Crowley.* Chicago: Contemporary Books, 1978.

Roberts, William. *Memoirs of the Life and Correspondence of Mrs. Hannah More,* Vol. 2. New York: Harper and Brothers, 1834.

Robinson, Charles Henry, and the Hausa Association, London. *Dictionary of the Hausa Language,* Vol. 1. London: University Press, 1913.

Robinson, James M. *The Facsimile Edition of the Nag Hammadi Codices,* Vol. 12. Leiden: Brill, 1984.

Roff, William R. *Kelantan; Religion, Society, and Politics in a Malay State.* Oxford: Oxford University Press, 1974.

Rogers, Robert William. *The Religion of Babylonia and Assyria, Especially in its Relations to Israel: Five Lectures Delivered at Harvard University.* New York: Eaton and Mains, 1908.

Róheim, Géza. *The Eternal Ones of the Dream: A Psychoanalytic Interpretation of Australian Myth and Ritual 1945.* Whitefish: Kessinger, 2004.

Roper, Lyndal. *Witch Craze: Terror and Fantasy in Baroque Germany.* New Haven: Yale University Press, 2006.

Rose, Carol. *Giants, Monsters, and Dragons: An Encyclopedia of Folklore, Legend, and Myth.* New York: W.W. Norton, 2001.

_____. *Spirits, Fairies, Leprechauns, and Goblins: An Encyclopedia.* New York: W.W. Norton, 1996.

Rosen, Brenda. *The Mythical Creatures Bible: The Definitive Guide to Legendary Beings.* New York: Sterling, 2009.

Rosen, Steven. *Essential Hinduism.* Westport: Greenwood, 2006.

Rosenfield, John M., and Elizabeth Ten Grotenhuis. *Journey of the Three Jewels: Japanese Buddhist Paintings from Western Collections.* New York: Asia Society, 1979.

Roth, John E. *American Elves: An Encyclopedia of Little People from the Lore of 380 Ethnic Groups of the Western Hemisphere.* Jefferson: McFarland, 1997.

Roucek, Joseph Slabey. *Slavonic Encyclopaedia.* New York: Philosophical Library, 1949.

Roveda, Vittorio. *Images of the Gods: Khmer Mythology in Cambodia, Thailand and Laos.* Bangkok: River Books, 2005.

_____, and Jaroslav Poncar. *Sacred Angkor: The Carved Reliefs of Angkor Wat.* Bangkok: River Books, 2002.

Royal Institute of International Affairs. *International Affairs,* Vol. 32. London: The Royal Institute of International Affairs, 1956.

Rsheim, Giza. *Animism, Magic, and the Divine King.* New York: Cosimo, 2005.

Rubino, Carl R. Galvez. *Ilocano: Ilocano-English, English-Ilocano Dictionary and Phrasebook.* New York: Hippocrene Books, 1998.

Rudwin, Maximilian Josef. *The Devil in Legend and Literature.* New York: AMS Press, 1970.

Ruíz, Vicki, and Virginia Sánchez Korrol. *Latinas in the United States: A Historical Encyclopedia,* Vol. 1. Bloomington: Indiana University Press, 2006.

Russell, James R. *Zoroastrianism in Armenia.* Cambridge: Harvard University, Dept. of Near Eastern Languages and Civilizations, 1987.

Russell, Jeffrey Burton. *The Devil: Perceptions of Evil from Antiquity to Primitive Christianity.* Ithaca: Cornell University Press, 1987.

_____. *Lucifer, the Devil in the Middle Ages.* Ithaca: Cornell University Press, 1986.

_____. *The Prince of Darkness: Radical Evil and the Power of Good in History.* New York: Cornell University Press, 1992.

_____. *Witchcraft in the Middle Ages.* New York: Cornell University Press, 1984.

Russell, Michael. *A Connection of Sacred and Profane History, From the Death of Joshua to the Decline of the Kingdoms of Israel and Judah.* London: William Tegg, 1865.

Ryan, William Francis. *The Bathhouse at Midnight: An Historical Survey of Magic and Divination in Russia.* University Park: Penn State Press, 1999.

Ryken, Leland, Colin Duriez, Douglas Penney, Daniel G. Reid, Tremper Longman, and Jim Wilhoit. *Dictionary of Biblical Imagery.* Westmont: Inter Varsity Press, 1998.

Sabellicus, Jorg. *Magia Pratica,* Vol. 1 and 2. Rome: Edizioni Studio Tesi, 1992.

Sagan, Carl. *The Demon-Haunted World: Science as a Candle in the Dark.* New York: Random House, 1997.

Saini, Herman. *Satan vs. God: A Brief History*. Canton: Xulon Press, 2008.

Saletore, Rajaram Narayan. *Indian Witchcraft*. New Delhi: Abhinav, 1981.

Salmonson, Jessica Amanda. *The Encyclopedia of Amazons: Women Warriors from Antiquity to the Modern Era*. New York: Paragon House, 1991.

Samuelson, David N. *Visions of Tomorrow: Six Journeys From Outer to Inner Space*. New York: Arno Press, 1975.

Sands, Kathleen R. *Demon Possession in Elizabethan England*. Westport: Greenwood, 2004.

Sapir, Edward, Regna Darnell and Judith T. Irvine. *Ethnology*, Vol. 4. New York: Walter de Gruyter, 1994.

Sarachchandra, Ediriweera R. *The Folk Drama of Ceylon*. Colombo: Dept. of Cultural Affairs, 1966.

Saunders, John, and Westland Marston. *The National Magazine*, Vols. 5–6. London: W. Kent, 1859.

Savill, Sheila, Geoffrey Parrinder, Chris Cook, and Lilian Mary Barker. *Pears Encyclopaedia of Myths and Legends: Oceania and Australia, the Americas, Book 4*. London: Pelham, 1978.

Sayce, Archibald Henry. *Lectures on the Origin and Growth of Religion as Illustrated by the Religion of the Ancient Babylonians*. London: Williams and Norgate, 1888.

"Scenes in Tenerife, Some Accounts of the Guanches." *The Month, Magazine and Review*, Vol. 6. London: Simpkin, Marshall, 1867.

Scheiber, Sándor, and Róbert Dán. *Occident and Orient: A Tribute to the Memory of Alexander Scheiber*. Leiden: Brill Archive, 1988.

Scheible, Johann, and Moses. *The Sixth and Seventh Books of Moses: Or, Moses' Magical Spirit-Art, Known as the Wonderful Arts of the Old Wise Hebrews, Taken from the Mosaic Books of the Cabala and the Talmud, for the Good of Mankind*. Translated From the German, Word for Word, According to Old Writings. New York: Sine Nomine, 1880.

Schimmel, Annemarie. *Islamic Names*. Edinburgh: Edinburgh University Press, 1989.

Schlagintweit, Emil. *Buddhism in Tibet: Illustrated by Literary Documents and Objects of Religious Worship, With an Account of the Buddhist Systems Preceding it in India*. Leipzig: F.A. Brockhaus, 1863.

Schmidt, Alexander Gregor Sarrazin. *Shakespeare–Lexicon: A Complete Dictionary of All the English Words, Phrases and Constructions in the Works of the Poet*, Vol. 2. Berlin: G. Reimer, 1902.

Schneck, Jerome Mortimer. *A History of Psychiatry*. Springfield: Charles C. Thomas, 1960.

Schodde, George Henry. *The Book of Enoch: Translated from the Ethiopic, with Introduction and Notes*. Andover, Warren F. Draper, 1882.

Scholem, Gershom Gerhard. *Kabbalah*. Jerusalem: Keter Publishing House Jerusalem, 1978.

_____, Allan Arkushe Raphael, and Jehudah Zwi Werblowsky. *Origins of the Kabbalah*. Princeton: Princeton University Press, 1991.

Schön, James Frederick. *Dictionary of the Hausa Language, With Appendices of Hausa Literature*. London: Church Missionary House, 1876.

_____. *Vocabulary of the Mende Language*. London: Society for Promoting Christian Knowledge, 1884.

Schrader, Friedrich Otto. *Introduction to the Pāñcarātra and the Ahirbudhnya Saṃhit[a-macron]*. Adyar: Adyar Library, 1916.

Schwartz, Howard. *Lilith's Cave: Jewish Tales of the Supernatural*. New York: Oxford University Press, 1991.

_____. *Reimagining the Bible: The Storytelling of the Rabbis*. New York: Oxford University Press, 1998.

_____. *Tree of Souls: the Mythology of Judaism*. New York: Oxford University Press, 2004.

Schwarzbaum, Haim. *Jewish Folklore Between East and West: Collected Papers*. Beersheva: Ben-Gurion University of the Negev Press, 1989.

Scobie, Charles H.H. *The Ways of our God: An Approach to Biblical Theology*. Grand Rapids: William B. Eerdmans, 2003.

Scot, Reginald. *The Discoverie of Witchcraft*. North Chemsford: Courier Dover, 1989.

Scott, David. *Formations of Ritual: Colonial and Anthropological Discourses on the Sinhala Yaktovil*. Minneapolis: University of Minnesota Press, 1994.

Scott, James George. *Burma: A Handbook of Practical Information*. London: D. O'Connor, 1921.

_____. *The Burman: His Life and Notions*, Vol. 1. London: Macmillan, 1882.

_____, and Shway Yoe. *The Burman, His Life and Notions*. London: Macmillan, 1896.

Scott, John, and John Taylor. "The Imputed Attributes of Witches with the Ceremonies of Initiation," *The London Magazine*, Vol. 5. April 1822, pages 276–387. London: Baldwin, Cradock, and Joy, 1822.

Scott, Thomas. *The Holy Bible, Containing the Old and New Testaments, According to the Authorized Version*, Vol. 6. Boston: Crocker and Brewster, 1851.

Scott-Moncrieff, Philip David, and Norman McLean. *Paganism and Christianity in Egypt*. Cambridge: Cambridge University Press, 1913.

Scudder, Vida D. "Promethus Unbound of Shelley," *The Atlantic Monthly*, Vol. 70, August 1892, pages 261–72. Boston: Atlantic Monthly Company, 1892.

Scull, Sarah Amelia. *Greek Mythology Systematized*. Philadelphia: Porter and Coates, 1880.

Scurlock, Jo Ann, and Burton R. Andersen. *Diagnoses in Assyrian and Babylonian Medicine: Ancient Sources, Translations, and Modern Medical Analyses*. Champaign: University of Illinois Press, 2005.

Segal, Alan F. *Life after Death: A History of the Afterlife in the Religions of the West*. New York: Random House, 2004.

Sehgal, Sunil. *Encyclopaedia of Hinduism: (H–Q)*, Vol. 3. New Delhi: Sarup and Sons, 1999.

Seisenberger, Michael. *Practical Handbook for the Study of the Bible and of Bible Literature: Including Biblical Geography, Antiquities, Introduction to the Old and the New Testament, and Hermeneutics*. New York: J.F. Wagner, 1911.

Selby, Martha Ann, and Inndira Viswanathan Peterson. *Tamil Geographies: Cultural Constructions of Space and Place in South India*. Albany: SUNY Press, 2008.

Seligmann, Kurt. *Magic, Supernaturalism, and Religion*. New York: Pantheon Books, 1971.

Senior, Michael. *The Illustrated Who's Who in Mythology*. London: Orbis, 1985.

Sepharial. *The Book of Charms and Talismans with Numerous Diagrams of Talismans, Sigils and Seals*. Whitefish: Kessinger, 2004.

Severus (of Antioch), Athanasius (of Nisibis), Ernest Walter Brooks (editor and translator). *The Sixth Book of the Select Letters of Severus, Patriarch of Antioch, in the Syriac Version of Athansius of Nisibis: Parts 1–2*. London: Williams and Norgate, 1904.

Seymour, John D. *Tales of King Solomon*. Whitefish: Kessinger, 2003.

Shadduck, Gayle. *England's Amorous Angels, 1813–1823*. Lanham: University Press of America, 1990.

Shah, Idries. *Oriental Magic*. New York: Philosophical Library, 1957.

Shah, Sirdar Ikbal Ali. *Black and White Magic: Its Theory and Practice*. London: Octagon Press, 1975.

_____. *Occultism: Its Theory and Practice*. Whitefish: Kessinger, 2003.

Shailer Mathews, Shailer, and Gerald Birney Smith. *A Dictionary of Religion and Ethics*. London: Macmillan, 1921.

Sharf, Robert H. *Coming to Terms with Chinese Buddhism: A Reading of the Treasure Store Treatise*. Honolulu: University of Hawaii Press, 2002.

Shashi, Shyam Singh. *Encyclopedia Indica*. New Delhi, India: Anmol, 1996.

Shastri, Jagdish Lal, and Arnold Kunst. *Ancient Indian Tradition and Mythology*, Vol. 4. Delhi: Motilal Banarsidass, 1970.

Shendge, Malati J. *The Civilized Demons: The Harappans in Rgveda*. New Delhi: Abhinav, 2003.

Shepard, Leslie, Lewis Spence, and Nandor Fodor. *Encyclopedia of Occultism and Parapsychology*. Detroit: Gale Research, 1991.

Sherekh, Íuriĭ. *A Prehistory of Slavic: The Historical Phonology of Common Slavic*. Heidelberg: C. Winter, 1965.

Sherman, Josepha. *Storytelling: An Encyclopedia of Mythology and Folklore*. Armonk: Sharpe Reference, 2008.

_____, and David Boston. *Trickster Tales: Forty Folk Stories from Around the World*. Little Rock: August House, 1996.

Shoolbraid, G.M.H. *The Oral Epic of Siberia and Central Asia*, Vols. 111–112. London: Taylor and Francis, 1975.

Shuckford, Samuel. *The Sacred and Profane History of the World Connected, With the Treatise on the Creation and Fall of Man*. Oxford: Claredon Press, 1810.

Shuker, Karl. *The Beasts That Hide from Man: Seeking the World's Last Undiscovered Animals*. New York: Cosimo, 2003.

_____. *Mysteries of Planet Earth*. London: Carlton, 1999.

Shumaker, Wayne. *Natural Magic and Modern Science: Four Treatises, 1590–1657*. Binghamton: Center for Medieval and Early Renaissance Studies, 1989.

_____. *The Occult Sciences in the Renaissance: A Study in Intellectual Patterns*. Berkeley: University of California Press, 1972.

Simmons, Leo William. *The Role of the Aged in Primitive Society*. London: Yale University Press, 1945.

Simon. *Papal Magic: Occult Practices Within the Catholic Church*. New York: HarperCollins, 2007.

Simons, Geoffrey Leslie. *The Witchcraft World*. London: Abelard-Schuman, 1974.

Simons, Ronald C., and Charles Campbell Hughes. *The Culture–Bound Syndromes: Folk Illnesses of Psychiatric and Anthropological Interest*. Berlin: Springer, 1985.

Singer, Isidore, and Cyrus Adler. *The Jewish Encyclopedia: A Descriptive Record of the History, Religion, Literature, and Customs of the Jewish People from the Earliest Times*, Vol. 4. Jersey City: KTAV, 1894.

Singer, Isidore, and Cyrus Adler. *The Jewish Encyclopedia: A Descriptive Record of the History, Religion, Literature, and Customs of the Jewish People from the Earliest Times to the Present Day*, Vol. 1. New York: Funk and Wagnalls, 1912.

_____. *The Jewish Encyclopedia: A Descriptive Record of the History, Religion, Literature, and Customs of the Jewish People from the Earliest Times to the Present Day*, Vol. 4. New York: Funk and Wagnalls, 1912.

Singh, Har Gopal. *Psychotherapy in India: From Vedic to Modern Times*. Agra: National Psychological Corp., 1977.

Singh, Nagendra. *Encyclopaedia of Hinduism*. New Delhi: Anmol, 1999.

Singh, Nagendra Kr. *Vedic Mythology*. Delhi: APH Publishing, 1997.

Singh, Upinder. *A History of Ancient and Early Medieval India: From the Stone Age to the 12th Century*. Delhi: Pearson Education India, 2008.

Sinistrari, Ludovico Maria. *Demoniality; or, Incubi and Succubi: A Treatise Wherein is Shown That There are in Existence on Earth Rational Creatures Besides Man, Endowed like Him with a Body and a Soul, That are Born and Die Like Him, Redeemed by Our Lord Jesus-Christ, and Capable of Receiving Salvation or Damnation*. Paris: I. Liseux, 1879.

Sinor, Denis. *Inner Asia: History-Civilization-Languages: A Syllabus*. London: Routledge, 1997.

_____. *The Uralic and Altaic Series*, Vols. 1–150. New York: Psychology Press, 1996.

Skeat, Walter William, and Charles Otto Blagden. *Malay Magic: Being an Introduction to the Folklore and Popular Religion of the Malay Peninsula*. London: Macmillan, 1900.

_____. *Pagan Races of the Malay Peninsula: Part 3. Religion. Part 4. Language. Appendix. Comparative Vocabulary of Aboriginal Dialects. Index of Subjects. Index of Proper Names. Index of Native Words*. London: Macmillan, 1906.

Slavic and East European Folklore Association Journal, Vol. 3, Issue 2. Charlottesville: Slavic and East European Folklore Association, 1998.

Slavic Legendary Creatures: Vampire, Vampire Folklore by Region, Baba Yaga, Slavic Fairies, Drekavac, Domovoi, Leshy, Slavic Dragon, German. New York: General Books LLC, 2010.

Slifkin, Natan. *Sacred Monsters: Mysterious and Mythical Creatures of Scripture, Talmud and Midrash*. Southfield: Zoo Torah, 2007.

Sluhovsky, Moshe. *Believe Not Every Spirit: Possession, Mysticism, and Discernment in Early Modern Catholicism*. Chicago: University of Chicago Press, 2007.

Smedal, Olaf H. *Lom-Indonesian-English and English-Lom Wordlists Accompanied by Four Lom Texts*, Vol. 1, Vol. 3, Vol. 10. Jakarta: Badan Penyelenggaraan Seri Nusa, Universitas Katolik Indonesia Atma Jaya, 1987.

_____. *Order and Difference: An Ethnographic Study of Orang Lom of Bangka, West Indonesia, Issue 19 of Occasional Papers*. Oslo: University of Oslo, 1989.

Smedley, Edward, editor. *Encyclopaedia Metropolitana; Or, Universal Dictionary of Knowledge, on an Original Plan: Comprising the Twofold Advantage of a Philosophical and an Alphabetical Arrangement*, Vol. 18. London: B. Fellowes, Rivington, Ducan, Malcolm, Suttaby, Hodgson, 1845.

_____, and W. Cooke Taylor. *The Occult Sciences: Sketches of the Traditions and Superstitions of Past Times and the Marvels of the Present Day*. Whitefish: Kessinger, 2004.

_____, Elihu Rich, W. Cooke Taylor, and Henry Thompson. *The Occult Sciences: Sketches of the Traditions and Superstitions of Past Times and the Marvels of the Present Day*. London: Richard Griffin, 1855.

Smith, Andrew Phillip. *A Dictionary of Gnosticism*. Wheaton: Quest Books, 2009.

Smith, Evans Lansing, and Nathan Robert Brown. *The Complete Idiot's Guide to World Mythology*. New York: Penguin, 2008.

Smith, George, and William Makepeace Thackeray. *Cornhill Magazine*, Vol. 32. London: Smith, Elder, 1875.

Smith, George Adam. *The Book of Deuteronomy: In the Revised Version*. Cambridge: Cambridge University Press, 1918.

Smith, Jane I., and Yvonne Yazbeck Haddad. *The Islamic Understanding of Death and Resurrection*. New York: Oxford University Press, 2002.

Smith, Sydney. *Edinburgh Review, Or Critical Journal*, Vols. 106–107. London: A. and C. Black, 1857.

Smith, Uriah. *The Prophecies of Daniel and the Revelation*. Whitefish: Kessinger, 2004.

Smith, William. *Comprehensive Dictionary of the Bible*. New York: Appleton, 1888

Smithsonian Institution. *Thirteenth Annual Report of the Bureau of American Ethnology to the Secretary of the Smithsonian Institution*. Washington, D.C.: Government Printing Office, 1915.

Society for Jewish Study. *The Journal of Jewish Studies*, Vols. 34–35. Oxford: Oxford Centre for Hebrew and Jewish Studies, 1983.

Society of Biblical Archaeology. *Proceedings of the Society of Biblical Archaeology*, Vol. 9. London: Society of Biblical Archaeology, 1887.

Soothill, William Edward, and Lewis Hodous. *A Dictionary of Chinese Buddhist Terms: With Sanskrit and English Equivalents and a Sanskrit-Pali Index*. London: Routledge, 2004.

Sorensen, Eric. *Possession and Exorcism in the New Testament and Early Christianity*. Tubingen: Mohr Siebeck, 2002.

Sosnoski, Daniel. Introduction to Japanese Culture. Boston: Charles E. Tuttle, 1966.

Soucková, Milada. *The Czech Romantics*. The Hague: Mouton, 1958.

Sparks, Hedley Frederick Davis. *The Apocryphal Old Testament*. Oxford: Oxford University Press, 1984.

Spence, Lewis. *An Encyclopædia of Occultism: A Compendium of Information on the Occult Sciences, Occult Personalities, Psychic Science, Magic, Demonology, Spiritism and Mysticism*. New York: Dodd, Mead, 1920.

_____. *Encyclopedia of Occultism and Parapsychology*. New York: Dodd, Mead, 1920.

_____. *The Magic Arts in Celtic Britain*. North Chemsford: Courier Dover, 1998.

Sperling, Harry, and Maurice Simon. *The Zohar*, Vol. 5. London: Soncino Press, 1956.

Spivey, Thomas Sawyer. *Ecclesiastical Vocabulary and Apocryphal Code*. Whitefish: Kessinger, 2003.

Spradley, James P., and David W. McCurdy. *Conformity and Conflict: Readings in Cultural Anthropology*. Boston: Little, Brown, 1977.

Spradlin, Wilford W., and Patricia B. Porterfield. *The Search for Certainty*. Berlin: Springer-Verlag, 1984.

Sproul, Barbara C. *Primal Myths: Creation Myths Around the World*. San Francisco: Harper Collins, 1979.

Squire, Charles. *Celtic Myth and Legend: Poetry and Romance*. Charleston: Forgotten Books, 2003.

Sri Ram, N. "A Study in Shamanism," *Theosophist Magazine*, January 1962–August 1962, pages 42–9, May 1962. Whitefish: Kessinger, 2003.

Srivastava, Balram, and Krishnaraia Wodeyar III. *Iconography of Sakti: A Study Based on Sritattvanidhi*. New Delhi: Chaukhambha Orientalia, 1978.

Stafford, Leroy Hahn. *The Function of Divine Manifestations in New Testament Times*. Menasha: George Banta, 1919.

Stallings, Douglas, and Fodor's Travel Publications. *Fodor's Poland*. New York: Random House, 2007.

Stallybrass, James Steven. *Teutonic Mythology*, Vol. 4. London: W. Swan Sonnenschein and Allen, 1880.

Stearman, Allyn MacLean. *Yuquí: Forest Nomads in a Changing World*. New York: Holt, Rinehart, and Winston, 1989.

Steinberg, Paul. *Celebrating the Jewish Year*, Vol. 1. Philadelphia: Jewish Publication Society, 2007.

Steiner, Rudolf. *Apocalypse of St. John*. Great Barrington: Steiner Books, 1985.

Stephens, Walter. *Demon Lovers: Witchcraft, Sex, and the Crisis of Belief*. Chicago: University of Chicago Press, 2003.

_____. *Giants in Those Days: Folklore, Ancient History, and Nationalism*. Lincoln: University of Nebraska Press, 1989.

Sterckx, Roel. *The Animal and the Daemon in Early China*. Albany: SUNY Press, 2002.

Steward, Julian Haynes. *Handbook of South American Indians*, Vol. 1. Washington, D.C.: U.S. Government Printing Office, 1959.

_____. *Handbook of South American Indians: The Tropical Forest Tribes*. Washington, D.C.: U.S. Government Printing Office, 1959.

Stol, Marten, and F.A.M. Wiggermann. *Birth in Babylonia and the Bible: Its Mediterranean Setting*. Leiden: Brill, 2000.

_____. *Epilepsy in Babylonia*. Leiden: Brill, 1993.

Stone, Doris. *The Talamancan Tribes of Costa Rica*. Kraus Reprint Company, 1973.

Stone, Merlin. *When God Was a Woman*. New York: Barnes and Noble, 1990.

Stookey, Lorena Laura. *Thematic Guide to World Mythology*. Westport: Greenwood, 2004.

Stormonth, James. *Etymological and Pronouncing Dictionary of the English Language*. Edinburgh: William Blackwood and Sons, 1879.

Stratmann, Francis Henry. *A Middle-English Dictionary: Containing Words Used by English Writers from the Twelfth to the Fifteenth Century*. Oxford: Clarendon Press, 1891.

Streete, Gail Corrington. *The Strange Woman: Power and Sex in the Bible*. Louisville: Westminster John Knox Press, 1997.

Strickmann, Michel, and Bernard Faure. *Chinese Magical Medicine*. Palo Alto, Calif.: Stanford University Press, 2002.

Strong, James. *The New Strong's Complete Dictionary of Bible Words*. New York: Thomas Nelson, 1996.

Studies in the History of Religions, Vol. 26. Leiden: E.J. Brill, 1973.

Sturtevant, Edgar Howard. *A Comparative Grammar of the Hittite Language*. Philadelphia: Linguistic Society of America, University of Pennsylvania, 1933.

Sue, Jack Wong. *Blood on Borneo*. Perth: L. Smith, 2001.

"Sumerian Mythology: A Review Article." *Journal of Near Eastern Studies* 5, 1946. Chicago.

Summers, Montague. *A Popular History of Witchcraft*. London: K. Paul, Trench, Truber, 1937.

_____. *Vampire: His Kith and Kin*. Whitefish, Mont.: Kessinger, 2003.

_____. *The Vampire in Lore and Legend*. North Chemsford: Courier Dover, 2001.

_____. *Witchcraft and Black Magic*. North Chemsford: Courier Dover, 2000.

Susej, Tsirk. *The Demonic Bible*. Raleigh: Lulu, 2006.

Sutherland, Gail Hinich. *The Disguises of the Demon: The Development of the Yaksa in Hinduism and Buddhism*. Albany: SUNY Press, 1991.

Sutherland, Robert. *Putting God on Trial: The Biblical Book of Job*. New Bern: Trafford, 2004.

Swedenborg, Emanuel, and Robert Hindmarsh. *The Apocalypse Explained, According to the Spiritual Sense: In Which are Revealed the Arcana Which are Predicted and Have Been Hitherto Deeply Concealed*, Vol. 4. London: W. Newbery, 1871.

Swettenham, Frank Athelstane. *Malay Sketches*. London: John Lane, 1895.

_____. *A Vocabulary of the English and Malay Languages*, Vol. 2. London: W.B. Whittingham, 1887.

Sykes, Egerton, and Alan Kendall. *Who's Who in Nonclassical Mythology*. London: Routledge, 2001.

Symonds, John. *The Magic of Aleister Crowley*. London: F. Muller, 1958.

Szabad, Imre. *Hungary, Past and Present: Embracing its History from the Magyar Conquest to the Present Time: With a Sketch of Hungarian Literature*. Edinburg: Black, 1854.

Szabó, Éva. *Hungarian Practical Dictionary: Hungarian-English, English-Hungarian*. New York: Hippocrene Books, 2005.

Tait, John Robinson. *European Life, Legend, and Landscape*. Philadelphia: James Challen, 1859.

Tate, Peter. *Flights of Fancy: Birds in Myth, Legend and Superstition*. New York: Random House, 2008.

Taube, Karl A. *Aztec and Maya Myths*. Austin: University of Texas Press, 1997.

Taylor, George Floyd. *The Second Coming of Jesus*. Falcon: Press of the Falcon, 1916.

Tedlock, Dennis. *Popol Vuh*. New York: Simon and Schuster, 1996.

Thakur, Upendra. *India and Japan: A Study in Interaction During 5th Century–14th Century. A.D.* New Delhi: Abhinav, 1992.

Theal, George McCall. *History and Ethnography of Africa South of the Zambesi: From the Settlement of the Portuguese at Sofala in September 1505 to the Conquest of the Cape Colony by the British in September 1795*, Vol. 1. London: Swan Sonnenschein, 1907.

Thomas, David Winton, and W.D. McHardy. *Hebrew and Semitic Studies: Presented to Godfrey Rolles Driver in Celebration of his Seventieth Birthday, 20 August 1962*. Oxford: Claredon Press, 1963.

Thompson, Ashley. *Calling the Souls: A Cambodian Ritual Text*. Cambodia: Reyum, 2005.

Thompson, C.J.S. *Mysteries and Secrets of Magic*. Whitefish: Kessinger, 2003.

Thompson, R. Campbell. *Semitic Magic: Its Origins and Development*. Whitefish: Kessinger, 2003.

Thompson, Reginald Campbell. *The Devils and Evil Spirits of Babylonia: Being Babylonian and Assyrian Incantations Against the Demons, Ghouls, Vampires, Hobgoblins, Ghosts, and Kindred Evil Spirits, Which Attack Mankind*, Vol. 1. London: Luzac, 1903–1904.

_____. *Semitic Magic, Its Origins and Development*. London: Luzac, 1908.

Thorndike, Lynn. *History of Magic and Experimental Science*, Part 10 and Part 12. Whitefish: Kessinger, 2003.

Thurn, Everard Ferdinand Im. *Among the Indians of Guiana: Being Sketches Chiefly Anthropologic from the Interior of British Guiana*. Whitefish: Kessinger, 2006.

Tierney, Emiko Ohnuki. *Illness and Healing Among the Sakhalin Ainu: A Symbolic Interpretation*. Cambridge: CUP Archive, 1981.

Tigelaar, Jaap. *Karolus Rex: Studies Over De Middeleeuwse Verhaaltraditie Rond Karel de Grote*. Hilversum: Uitgeverij Verloren, 2005.

Tilakaratna, Minivan Pi. *Manners, Customs, and Ceremonies of Sri Lanka*. Delhi: Sri Satguru, 1986.

Timmons, W. Milton. *Everything About the Bible That You Never Had Time to Look Up*. Philadelphia: Xlibris, 2003.

Toki, Zemmaro D. *Japanese Nō Plays*. Japan Travel Bureau: Tokyo, 1954.

Torchia, Christopher. *Indonesian Idioms and Expressions: Colloquial Indonesian at Work*. North Claredon: Tuttle, 2007.

Torelli, Mario. *The Etruscans*. New York: Rizzoli, 2001.

Toynbee, Paget Jackson. *Concise Dictionary of Proper Names and Notable Matters in the Works of Dante*. London: Clarendon, 1914.

Trachtenberg, Joshua. *Jewish Magic and Superstition: A Study in Folk Religion*. Charleston: Forgotten Books, 2008.

Tregear, Edward R. *The Maori-Polynesian Comparative Dictionary*. Wellington: Lyon and Blair, 1891.

Tremearne, A.J.N. *Ban of the Bori: Demons and Demon Dancing in West and North Africa*. Whitefish: Kessinger, 2003.

Tresidder, Jack. *The Complete Dictionary of Symbols*. San Francisco: Chronicle Books, 2005.

Trithemius, Johannes, and Juan Caramuel Lobkowitz. *Steganographia nec non Claviculae Salomonis germane*. N.p.: Egmondanis, sumptibus auctoris, 1635.

Turner, Johnny. *The Sacred Art: Growing Faithful Disciples in the 21st Century*. London: Tate, 2007.

Turner, Patricia, and Charles Russell Coulter. *Dictionary of Ancient Deities*. New York: Oxford University Press, 2001.

Tyson, Donald. *Enochian Magic for Beginners: The Original System of Angel Magic*. St. Paul: Llewellyn, 1997.

_____. *The Power of the Word: The Secret Code of Creation*. St. Paul: Llewellyn, 2004.

_____. *Ritual Magic: What It Is and How to Do It*. St. Paul: Llewellyn, 1992.

_____. *Sexual Alchemy: Magical Intercourse with Spirits*. Woodbury: Llewellyn, 2000.

Ugresic, Dubravka, and Ellen Elias-Bursac. *Baba Yaga Laid an Egg*. New York: Grove Press, 2011.

Unger, Merrill F. *Biblical Demonology: A Study of Spiritual Forces at Work Today*. Grand Rapids: Kregel, 1994.

Universität Bonn, and Seminar für Sprach-und Kulturwissenschaft Zentralasiens. *Zentralasiatische Studien*. Wiesbaden: O. Harrassowitz, 1980.

University of Pennsylvania, University Museum. *The Museum Journal*, Vols. 3–4. Philadelphia: The Museum, 1912.

_____. *Publications of the Babylonian Section*, Vol. 3. Philadelphia: The Museum, 1913.

University of the Philippines. *Asian Studies*, Vol. 8–9. Quezon City: Philippine Center for Advanced Studies, 1970.

Ury, Marian. *Tales of Times Now Past: Sixty-Two Stories from a Medieval Japanese Collection*. Berkeley: University of California Press, 1979.

Van der Toorn, K., Bob Becking, and Pieter Willem van der Horst. *Dictionary of Deities and Demons in the Bible*. Grand Rapids: William. B. Eerdmans, 1999.

Van Doren, Mark. *Spring Birth, and Other Poems*. New York: Holt, 1953.

Van Loopik, Marcus. *The Ways of the Sages and the Way of*

the World: The Minor Tractates of the Babylonian Talmud: Derekh 'eretz rabbah, Derekh 'eretz zuta, Pereq ha-shalom: Translated on the Basis of the Manuscripts and Provided with a Commentary. Tuebingen: Mohr Siebeck, 1991.

Van Scott, Miriam. *The Encyclopedia of Hell*. New York: Macmillan, 1999.

Vargas Llosa, Mario, and Edith Grossman. *Death in the Andes*. New York: Macmillan, 2007.

Varner, Gary R. *Creatures in the Mist: Little People, Wild Men and Spirit Beings Around the World: a Study in Comparative Mythology*. New York: Algora, 2007.

_____. *The Mythic Forest, the Green Man and the Spirit of Nature: The Re-Emergence of the Spirit of Nature from Ancient Times into Modern Society*. New York: Algora, 2006.

Vasilakē, Maria. *Images of the Mother of God: Perceptions of the Theotokos in Byzantium*. Aldershot: Ashgate, 2005.

Vaughan, Robert. *British Quarterly Review*, Vol. 7. London: Hodder and Stoughton, 1848.

Vergati, Anne. *Gods and Masks of the Kāthmāṇḍu Valley*. New Delhi: D.K. Printworld, 2000.

Vermès, Géza. *Discovery in the Judean Desert*. New York: Desclee, 1956.

Victoria Institute. *Journal of the Transactions of the Victoria Institute, or Philosophical Society of Great Britain*, Vol. 28. London: Victoria Institute, 1896.

Vigil, Angel. *The Eagle on the Cactus: Traditional Stories from Mexico*. Englewood: Libraries Unlimited, 2000.

Vinycomb, John. *Fictitious and Symbolic Creatures in Art with Special Reference to Their Use in British Heraldry*. London: Chapman and Hall, 1906.

Volney, Constantin-François. *The Ruins: Or a Survey on the Revolutions of Empires, with Notes Historical, Geographical, and Explanatory, to Which is Annexed the Law of Nature*. London: T. Davison, 1819.

Voltaire. *Essays and Criticisms: Containing Letters on the Christian Religion; The philosophy of History; The Ignorant Philosopher; and The Chinese Cathechism*. New York: Peter Eckler, 1920.

_____. *A Philosophical Dictionary: From the French*, Vol. 3, Issues 1–2. London: W. Dugdale, 1843.

_____. *The Philosophy of History: Or a Philosophical and Historical Dissertation, on the Origin, Manners, Customs, and Religion of the Different Nations, and People of Antiquity; with a Clear and Concise Exposition, of the Usages, and Opinions Common Amongst Them; And, in Particular, of their Religious Rites, Ceremonies, and Superstitions*. London: Thomas North, 1829.

_____, and John G. Gorton. *A Philosophical Dictionary*, Vol. 1. London: J. and H.L. Hunt, 1824.

_____, Tobias George Smollett, and Thomas Francklin. *The Works of M. de Voltaire: The Ancient and Modern History*. London: J. Newbery, R. Baldwin, W. Johnston, S. Crowder, T. Davies, J. Coote, G. Kearsley, and B. Collins, at Salisbury, 1761.

Von Franz, Marie-Luise. *Alchemy: An Introduction to the Symbolism and the Psychology*. Toronto: Inner City Books, 1980.

Von Glahn, Richard. *The Sinister Way: The Divine and the Demonic in Chinese Religious Culture*. Berkeley: University of California Press, 2004.

Von Nettesheim, Heinrich Cornelius Agrippa, James Freake, and Donald Tyson. *Three Books of Occult Philosophy*. St. Paul: Llewellyn, 1993.

von Stietencron, Heinrich. *Hindu Myth, Hindu History, Religion, Art, and Politics*. Delhi: Orient Blackswan, 2005.

Von Worms, Abraham. *Book of Abramelin: A New Translation*. Boston: Red Wheel/Weiser, 2006.

Waardenburg, Jean Jacques. *Islam: Historical, Social, and Political Perspectives*. New York: Walter de Gruyter, 2002.

Wace, Henry. *The Holy Bible, According to the Authorized Version (A.D. 1611), With an Explanatory and Critical Commentary and a Revision of the Translation: Apocrypha*, Vol. 1. London: J. Murray, 1888.

Waddell, L. Austine. *A Sumer Aryan Dictionary*. Whitefish: Kessinger, 2004.

_____. *Tibetan Buddhism: With Its Mystic Cults, Symbolism and Mythology, and in Its Relation to Indian Buddhism*. Whitefish: Kessinger, 2004.

Waddell, Laurence Austine. *The Buddhism of Tibet, or Lamaism: With its Mystic Cults, Symbolism and Mythology, and in its Relation to Indian Buddhism*. London: W.H. Allen, 1895.

Waghorne, Joanne Punzo, Norman Cutler, and Vasudha Narayanan. *Gods of Flesh, Gods of Stone: The Embodiment of Divinity in India*. New York: Columbia University Press, 1996.

Waines, David. *An Introduction to Islam*. Cambridge: Cambridge University Press, 2004.

Waite, Arthur Edward. *The Book of Black Magic and Ceremonial Magic*. Palo Alta: Book Tree, 2006.

_____. *The Book of Black Magic and of Pacts: Including the Rites and Mysteries of Goëtic Theurgy, Sorcery, and Infernal Necromancy*. Chicago: de Laurence, 1910.

_____. *The Book of Ceremonial Magic*. New York: Cosimo, 2007.

_____. *The Book of Destiny*. Whitefish: Kessinger, 1994.

_____. *The Doctrine and Literature of the Kabalah*. London: Theosophical Publishing Society, 1902.

_____. *The Holy Kabbalah*. New York: Cosimo, 2007.

_____. *Manual of Cartomancy and Occult Divination*. Whitefish: Kessinger, 1994.

_____. *Unknown World 1894–1895*. Whitefish: Kessinger, 2003.

_____. "Waite's Occult Sciences," *The Literary World*, Vol. 45, January to June 1892, page 170.

Waite, Gary K. *Eradicating the Devil's Minions: Anabaptists and Witches in Reformation Europe, 1525–1600*. Toronto: University of Toronto Press, 2007.

Wakabayashi, Haruko Nishioka. *Tengu: Images of the Buddhist Concepts of Evil in Medieval Japan*, Vol. 1995, Part 1. Princeton: Princeton University Press, 1995.

Wakeman, Mary K. *God's Battle With the Monster: A Study in Biblical Imagery*. Leiden: Brill Archive, 1973.

Walker, Barbara. *The Woman's Encyclopedia of Myths and Secrets*. Cambridge: HarperCollins, 1983.

Walker, Benjamin. *The Hindu World: An Encyclopedic Survey of Hinduism*, Vol. 2. Westport: Praeger, 1968.

Walker, Deward E. *Witchcraft and Sorcery of the American Native Peoples*. Moscow: University of Idaho Press, 1989.

Walker, J.R. *Anthropological Papers of the American Museum of Natural History*, Vol. 16, Part 2. New York: Published by Order of the Trustees, 1917.

Wall, James Charles. *Devils*. London: Methuen, 1904.

Walsh, William Shepard. *Heroes and Heroines of Fiction: Famous Characters and Famous Names in Novels, Romances, Poems and Dramas, Classified, Analyzed and Criticised, with Supplementary Citations from the Best Authorities*. Philadelphia: J.B. Lippincott, 1914.

Wangu, Madhu Bazaz. *Images of Indian Goddesses: Myths, Meanings, and Models*. New Delhi: Abhinav, 2003.

Warner, Elizabeth. *Russian Myths.* Austin: University of Texas Press, 2002.

Watkins, Carl S. *History and the Supernatural in Medieval England.* Cambridge: Cambridge University Press, 2007.

Watson, Richard. *A Biblical and Theological Dictionary.* London: John Mason, 1842.

Watts, Gerry. *Ancient Prophecies Unveiled: The Times of the Nations.* Bloomington: iUniverse, 2003.

Waugh, Scott L., and Peter Diehl. *Christendom and Its Discontents: Exclusion, Persecution, and Rebellion, 1000–1500.* Cambridge: Cambridge University Press, 2002.

Webster, Richard. *Encyclopedia of Angels.* St. Paul: Llewellyn, 2009.

Wedeck, Harry Ezekiel. *Treasury of Witchcraft.* New York: Philosophical Library, 1961.

_____, and Wade Baskin. *Dictionary of Pagan Religions.* Secaucus: Citadel Press, 1973.

Weigel, John A. *Lawrence Durrell.* Boston: Twayne, 1989.

Weiss, Jerome. *Folk Psychology of the Javanese of Ponorogo,* Vol. 2. London: Yale University, 1977.

Wells, Jan. *The Sermon on the Mount.* Canton: Xulon Press, 2003.

Werne, Edward Theodore Chalmers. *China of the Chinese.* London: Sir Issaic Pitman and Sons, 1920.

Werner, E.T.C. *Myths and Legends of China.* Rockville: Wildside, 2005.

Werner, Roland. *Bomoh-Poyang: Traditional Medicine and Ceremonial Art of the Aborigines of Malaysia.* Kuala Lumpur: University of Malaya, 1986.

Wesleyan-Methodist Magazine, Vol. 63. London: Sine nomine, 1874.

West, E.W. *Sacred Books of the East,* Vol. 5. New York: Oxford University Press, 1897.

West, Robert Hunter. *The Invisible World: A Study in Pneumatology in Elizabethan Drama.* Athens: University of Georgia Press, 1939.

Westermarck, Edward Alexander. *Ritual and Belief in Morocco,* Vol. 1. New York: University Books, 1968.

Weyer, Johann, Benjamin G. Kohl and George Mora. *Witches, Devils, and Doctors in the Renaissance: Johann Weyer, De praestigiis daemonum.* Binghamton: Medieval and Renaissance Texts and Studies, 1991.

Wheeler, James Talboys. *The History of India from the Earliest Ages: The Vedic Period and the Mahá Bhárata.* London: N. Trübner, 1867.

Wheeler, William Adolphus. *A Dictionary of the Noted Names of Fiction: Including Also Familiar Pseudonyms, Surnames Bestowed on Eminent Men, and Analogous Popular Appellations Often Referred to in Literature and Conversation.* London: George Bell and Sons, 1889.

White, David Gordon. *Kiss of the Yogini: Tantric Sex in its South Asian Contexts.* Chicago: University of Chicago Press, 2003.

White, John. *The Ancient History of the Maori: His Mythology and Traditions,* Vol. 1. Wellington: George Didsbury, 1887.

_____. *The Ancient History of the Maori: His Mythology and Traditions,* Vol. 3. London: Sampson Low, Marston, Searle, and Rivington, 1889.

_____. *The Ancient History of the Maori: His Mythology and Traditions,* Vol. 7. London: Sampson Low, Marston, Searle, and Rivington, 1889.

Whitmore, Ben. *Trials of the Moon: Reopening the Case for Historical Witchcraft; A Critique of Ronald Hutton's The Triumph of the Moon, A History of Modern Pagan Witchcraft.* Auckland: Briar Books, 2010.

Whitney, William Dwight. *The Century Dictionary and Cyclopedia: A Work of Universal Reference in All Departments of Knowledge with a New Atlas of the World.* New York: Century, 1906.

Wicker, Nancy L., and Bettina Arnold. *From the Ground Up: Beyond Gender Theory in Archaeology—Proceedings of the Fifth Gender and Archaeology Conference, University of Wisconsin–Milwaukee, October 1998.* Oxford: Archaeopress, 1999.

Widengren, George. *The Accadian and Hebrew Psalms of Lamentation as Religious Documents: A Comparative Study.* Uppsala: Thule, 1936.

Wieczynski, Joseph L. *The Modern Encyclopedia of Russian and Soviet History,* Vol. 26. Gulf Breeze: Academic International Press, 1994.

Wiener, Margaret J. *Visible and Invisible Realms: Power, Magic, and Colonial Conquest in Bali.* Chicago: University of Chicago Press, 1995.

Wier, Johannes. *Johannis Wieri De Praestigiis Daemonum, Et Incantationibus ac veneficiis: Libri sex, aucti recogniti.* N.p.: Oporinus, 1568.

Wiggermann, F.A.M. *Mesopotamian Protective Spirits: The Ritual Texts.* Leiden: Brill, 1992.

Wijesekera, Nandadeva. *Deities and Demons, Magic and Masks, Part 2.* Colombo: M.D. Gunasena, 1987.

Wilbert, Johannes. *Folk Literature of the Warao Indians: Narrative Material and Motif Content.* Los Angeles: Latin American Center, University of California, 1970.

_____. *Yupa Folktales.* Los Angeles: Latin American Center, University of California, 1974.

_____, Karin Simoneau, and Horace Banner. *Folk Literature of the Gê Indians.* Los Angeles: UCLA Latin American Center Publications, 1984.

_____, Karin Simoneau, and Riena Louise Weidman Kondo. *Folk Literature of the Sikuani Indians.* Los Angeles: UCLA Latin American Center Publications, 1992.

Wilby, Emma. *Cunning Folk and Familiar Spirits: Shamanistic Visionary Traditions in Early Modern British Witchcraft and Magic.* Brighton: Sussex Academic Press, 2005.

Wilhelm, Richard. *The Chinese Fairy Book.* New York: Frederick A. Stokes, 1921.

Wilkins, William Joseph. *Hindu Gods and Goddesses.* Chemsford: Courier Dover, 2003.

_____. *Hindu Mythology, Vedic and Puránic.* Bombay: Thacker, Spink, 1882.

Wilkinson, Richard James. *An Abridged Malay-English Dictionary (Romanised).* Kuala Lumpur: F.M.S. Government Press, 1908.

_____. *Malay Beliefs.* London: Luzac, 1906.

Williams, George Mason. *Handbook of Hindu Mythology.* Santa Barbara: ABC-CLIO, 2003.

Williams, Joseph J. *Psychic Phenomena of Jamaica.* New York: Dial Press, 1934.

Williams, Thomas Rhys. *The Dusun: A North Borneo Society.* New York: Holt, Rinehart and Winston, 1965.

Willis, Roy G. *World Mythology.* New York: Macmillan, 1993.

Wilson, John. *The Pársí Religion as Contained in the Zand-Avastá.* Bombay: American Mission Press, 1843.

Winkler, Amanda Eubanks. *O Let Us Howle Some Heavy Note: Music for Witches, the Melancholic, and the Mad on the Seventeenth-Century English Stage.* Bloomington: Indiana University Press, 2006.

Winstedt, Richard Olof. *The Malay Magician: Being Shaman, Saiva, and Sufi.* London: Routledge and Kegan Paul, 1951.

Wippler, Migene González. *The Complete Book of Spells, Ceremonies, and Magic*. St. Paul: Llewellyn, 1988.

Wirz, Paul. *Exorcism and the Art of Healing in Ceylon*. Leiden: Brill Archive, 1954.

Wise, Isaac Mayer. *The Origin of Christianity and a Commentary to the Acts of the Apostles*. Cincinnati: Bloch, 1868.

Witches' Almanac. *Magic Charms from A to Z*. Newport: Witches' Almanac, 1999.

Wood, John George. *The Natural History of Man*. London: George Routledge and Sons, 1870.

Woodard, Roger D. *The Cambridge Companion to Greek Mythology*. Cambridge: Cambridge University Press, 2007.

Woods, William Howard. *History of the Devil*. New York: Putnam, 1974.

Woolley, Benjamin. *The Queen's Conjurer: The Science and Magic of Dr. John Dee, Adviser to Queen Elizabeth I*. New York: Macmillan, 2002.

Word Histories and Mysteries: From Abracadabra to Zeus. Boston: Houghton Mifflin Harcourt, 2004.

Word Monthly Magazine, Vol. 3. "A Devil, God, Man and the Dream." New York: Theosophical, 1906.

A Working Glossary for the Use of Students of Theosophical Literature, with an Appendix. New York: The Path, 1892.

Wray, T.J., and Gregory Mobley. *The Birth of Satan: Tracing the Devil's Biblical Roots*. New York: Macmillan, 2005.

Wright, Archie T. *The Origin of Evil Spirits: The Reception of Genesis 6.1–4 in Early Jewish Literature*. Tuebingen: Mohr Siebeck, 2005.

Wright, Dudley. *The Book of Vampires*. Detroit: Omnigraphics, 1989.

Wright, Robin M. *Cosmos, Self, and History in Baniwa Religion*. Austin: University of Texas Press, 1998.

Wright, Thomas. *Narratives of Sorcery and Magic: From the Most Authentic Sources*, Vol. 2. London: Richard Bentley, 1851.

Yadav, Rama Sankar, and B.N. Mandal. *Global Encyclopaedia of Education*. New Delhi: Global Vision Publishing House, 2007.

Yamamoto, Kumiko. *The Oral Background of Persian Epics: Storytelling and Poetry*. Leiden: Brill, 2003.

Yearsley, MacLeod. *The Folklore of Fairytale*. Whitefish: Kessinger, 2005.

Yolen, Jane, Paul Hoffman, and Shulamith Levey Oppenheim. *The Fish Prince and Other Stories: Mermen Folk Tales*. New York: Interlink Books, 2001.

Yolland, Arthur Battishill. *A Dictionary of the Hungarian and English Languages: English-Hungarian*. Budapest: Franklin-Társulat, 1908.

Yonge, Charlotte Mary. *The Lances of Lynwood*. New York: Macmillan, 1868.

Zabara, Joseph ben Meir Ibn, Moses Hadas, and Merriam Sherwood. *The Book of Delight*. New York: Columbia University Press, 1932.

Zaehner, Robert Charles. *Zurvan: a Zoroastrian Dilemma*. New York: Biblo and Tannen, 1972.

Zenos, Andrew Constantinides. *The Popular and Critical Bible Encyclopædia and Scriptural Dictionary: Fully Defining and Explaining All Religious Terms, Including Biographical, Geographical, Historical, Archæological and Doctrinal Themes*. Chicago: Howard-Severance, 1920.

Zepp, Raymond A. *A Field Guide to Cambodian Pagodas*. Phnom Penh: Bert's Books, 1997.

Zimmerer, Neil. *The Chronology of Genesis: A Complete History of the Nefilim*. Kempton: Adventures Unlimited Press, 2003.

Zwemer, Samuel Marinus. *Childhood in the Moslem World*. New York: Fleming H. Revell, 1915.

_____. *The Influence of Animism on Islam: an Account of Popular Superstitions*. New York: Macmillan, 1920.

Index